CONCISE
BIBLE
CHARACTERS

OTHER TITLES IN THE AMG CONCISE SERIES

Concise Bible Commentary

By Don Fleming ... ISBN: 978-0-89957-672-5

This commentary bridges the wide gap in times and culture that separate the reader from the original biblical events by providing the sort of information that ordinary readers are looking for in their search for a clearer understanding of the Bible.

Concise Bible Dictionary

By Don Fleming ... ISBN: 978-0-89957-675-6

With over 1,000 entries, the *Concise Bible Dictionary* covers all the major areas of biblical knowledge. It presents the material in an easy-to-read, non-technical style, and serves as an accurate, readable, and helpful source of information on the content of the Bible.

Concise Bible Doctrines

By Elmer Towns ... ISBN: 978-0-89957-695-4

Doctrines such as the trinity are discussed, as are current issues such as the work of angels, Satan, and demons, as well as the signs of the times. This is an engaging read for anyone interested in what the Bible has to say about what truly affects our lives.

Concise Church History

By John Hunt ... ISBN: 978-0-89957-769-6

Filled with the records of those vital events and key individuals that shaped the history of the Christian Church, with extracts from the writings of each period, this book will encourage and challenge the reader to live in this present day by learning from the past.

Concise Introduction to the Bible

By Dr. Howard Vos ... ISBN: 978-0-89957-447-9

Dr. Vos brings the Bible to life as he recounts the events of biblical history. This book is for everyone who wants to get a firm grasp of Bible history and meaning and answers to the big questions of life, but didn't have a clue how to do it or where to begin.

Concise Life of Christ

By James Stalker ... ISBN: 978-0-89957-699-2

James Stalker helps the reader grasp the meaning of the life of Christ. He explains how Christ lived at home and in the world, and challenges the reader to distinguish between what they have heard about Christ and what Christ Himself said was true.

Concise Names of Christ

By James Large ... ISBN: 978-0-89957-641-1

An understanding of who Jesus is lies at the very root of the Christian religion. James Large has compiled more than 280 titles of and symbols for Christ. His study will open the eyes of the reader to the glory and wonder of Jesus Christ and His redeeming work.

Concise Works of the Holy Spirit

By Abraham Kuyper ... ISBN: 978-0-89957-698-5

Kuyper combined in one volume a magnificent overview of all the works of the Holy Spirit, beginning with the works within the Church as a whole. Kuyper then declares the inward works of the Holy Spirit—salvation and the works after salvation.

✹ **AMG** *Publishers*

CONCISE
BIBLE
CHARACTERS

ALEXANDER **WHYTE**

Concise Bible Characters
Published by AMG Publishers
6815 Shallowford Road
Chattanooga, TN 37421

Originally published in seven volumes under the title *Bible Characters*.

ISBN-13: 978-0-89957-649-7
ISBN-10: 0-89957-649-4

Cover Design by Daryle Beam of Bright Boy Design

Interior Design and Typesetting by Scribe, Inc. (www.scribenet.com)

Made in Canada

15 14 13 12 11 10 –T– 8 7 6 5 4 3 2 1

Contents

Contents

OUR LORD'S CHARACTERS

Foreword

IN AMG's *Concise Bible Characters*, Whyte uses his storytelling skills to interact with the greatest content of all time, the Holy Bible. What results is a collection of more than 150 stories on the characters of the Bible. Whyte's writings, originally published in seven volumes, continue to inspire preachers, Sunday school teachers, and lay people more than 160 years after they were published.

Readers of these Bible character stories will feel like they are right there while things are happening. Whyte uses these stories to challenge each of us to consider our own character, to challenge us to be better than we have been, to reach for something beyond what we think we can attain. He challenges us to keep striving when life is tough, but more than that, he reveals how the characters of the Bible were able to do these things, and how we can accomplish them in our own lives.

In producing *Concise Bible Characters*, we at AMG Publishers have made some minor changes to the original work to help make its content more clear to modern readers: We have updated some archaic terms, and we have updated spelling in accordance with how our language has changed over the years; in some cases, unusual forms of punctuation have been simplified to eliminate confusion. Apart from these minor modifications, however, we have remained true to Whyte's original work in every way.

Additionally, readers should note that the points of current history mentioned by Whyte are from the nineteenth century.

1
Adam

IN the wise and good providence of Almighty God a new and an entrancing light has been cast in our day on the origin of the earth and on the early ages of mankind. A noble succession of ministers and interpreters of nature has been raised up in these later generations who, by the labors they have undertaken, and by the methods they have followed, have been enabled to make discoveries that had not entered the mind of man to imagine in former ages. Up till our day far more was known about the way and process of our redemption than about the way and process of our creation. But it will be in the complete and harmonious combination of these two kinds of knowledge, divine revelation and human science, that we shall come to a perfect man, in which the whole body of knowledge and faith and love shall be fitly joined together and compacted by that which every joint supplieth.

Magnificent as have been the services of such men as Herschel, and Faraday, and Lyell, and Darwin, and Spencer, at the same time their magnificent services have lain far more in the regions of matter and motion than in the mind and the heart of man. It is enough for any man, or for any school of men, to be enabled to take us back to the first beginnings of this present system of things, when as yet our earth was without form and void, and to lead us up step after step, age after age, till we open our eyes on this wonderful world as it now is. To one of His servants God gives the talents of revelation and inspiration, and to another the talents of observation, and experiment, and discovery, and the exposition of discovery—to each one of His servants separately as He will. And to each several steward and servant of His, according to his faithfulness to the talents committed to him, his Master at His coming will say, "Well done!" And it is surely a kind of forecast and foretaste of that "Well done!"—the warm exclamation of wonder and of worship that rises out of our enlarged minds and exalted hearts as we lay down *The Outlines of Astronomy, The Principles of Geology, The Origin of Species, The First Principles*, and such-like books. At the same time, at their best, those ministers and interpreters of nature do not satisfy their readers. Even in their own rich and well-worked fields they do not satisfy all their readers. Even after they have led us so far up on the shining path of scientific truth, we feel sure that there are still sources and paths and fields of light, as well as shadows and belts and whole worlds of darkness, over which we have been hurried, and into which we have not been led or let look. We feel not unlike that famous philosopher of our day who divined that there must surely be a serious disturbance somewhere in the order and stability of the solar system that no astronomy had as yet discovered, acknowledged, or attempted to account for. As we are carried away by the spell of the great writers on evolution, we feel all the time that, after all has been told, there is still something unrecognized and undescribed from which we suffer the most

1

disturbing and injurious influences. All the time we feel in ourselves a backward, sideward, downward, perverse pull under which we reel and stagger continually; it is an experience that makes us wiser than all our teachers in some of the most obscure, but at the same time some of the most certain matters of mankind and their spiritual history. Speaking for myself, as I read the great books of our modern scientific men with a delight and an advantage I cannot put enough words upon, I always miss in them—in them all, and in the best of them all—a matter of more importance to me than all else that they tell me. For, all the time I am reading their fascinating discoveries and speculations, I still feel in myself a disturbance, a disorder, a disharmony, and a positive dislocation from the moral, and even from the material, order of the universe around me and above me: a disorder and a dislocation that my scientific teachers neither acknowledge nor leave room for its acknowledgment or redress. That is magnificent! That is noble! That is divine! I exclaim as I read. But when I come to the end of my reading—Is that all? I ask. I am compelled by all my experience and all my observation to ask, Is that all? Is that your very last word to me? Then, if that is all, I must still go in search of a philosophy of nature and of man that understands me, and accounts for me, and has, if so be, a more comprehensive, a more scientific, a more profound, and a more consoling message to me. In one word, and to speak out the whole of my disappointment and complaint in one word, What about SIN? What is SIN? When and where did SIN enter in the evolution of the human race and seize in this deadly way on the human heart? Why do you all so avoid and shut your eyes to SIN? And, still more, what about JESUS CHRIST? Why do I find nothing in your best text-books about HIM who was WITHOUT SIN? About Him who is more to me, and to so many more of your best readers, than all Nature, and all her suns, and systems, and laws, and processes put together? Far more. For He has carried both our understanding and our imagination and our heart so absolutely captive that we cannot read with our whole heart the best book you have written because His name is not in it. WHO and WHAT is HE, we insist, who has leapt at a bound above all law and all order of matter and of mind, and of cosmic and ethic evolution, and has taken His stand of holiness at the head of the human race? Schools of science, schools of morals, schools of philosophy, ministers and interpreters of nature and of man, what is SIN? and what think ye of CHRIST?

Bishop Butler has taught us, and that with an impressiveness we can never forget, that knowledge at its best is not our proper happiness. With all his immense weight Butler has impressed upon us that our proper province is virtue and religion, life and manners; the science of improving the temper and making the heart better. This is the field assigned us to cultivate, he exclaims, and how much it has lain neglected is indeed astonishing! And thus it is that Moses, so to call him, with two or three splendid strokes, passes over all that which so fascinates and absorbs our modern men of science, and takes up mankind at that point when they have the image and likeness of God completely and perfectly stamped upon them. Nor does Moses delay long, even upon that, but, after one great and fruitful word upon that, he passes on to take up at more length, in his own wonderful way, and in answerable style, the temptation and the fall of Adam and of all Adam's offspring.

"The Scripture begins," says Butler, "with an account of God's creation of the world, in order to ascertain who He is concerning whose providences, commands, promises, and threatenings this sacred book all along treats, the Maker and Proprietor of the world, He whose creatures we are—the God of Nature. Revelation, indeed, considers the common affairs of this world, and what is going on in it, as a mere scene of distraction, and cannot be supposed to give any account of this wild scene for its own sake. This earth, our habitation, has everywhere the appearance of being a ruin, and revelation comes in on the supposition that this world is in a ruined state." Thus Butler. And Moses begins his priceless contribution to that revelation by telling us what, without him, would have remained a dreadful mystery to us—that is to say, he tells us how man was made upright, and how he fell from that estate wherein he was created by sinning against God. It is a fashion with the prevailing philosophy of our day to decry and condemn the old, orthodox, and fruitful argument from final causes; but I shall continue, in this matter also, to follow Bishop Butler, to me by far the deepest and the wisest philosopher the world has ever seen. Now Moses, long before Butler, is clear and sure as to the final cause of our creation. In his opening pages, Moses, after his royal manner, lets us hear the Maker of all things taking counsel with Himself concerning His end and object in the creation of man. "Let us make man in our image, after our likeness." And then, from this and from many other Scriptures, we learn that the image and likeness of God is love: love, knowledge, righteousness, and true holiness, with dominion over the creatures.

Now, the multiplication and the increase of the image of God is an altogether worthy reason, adequate explanation, and final cause for the creation of this world, and for all the processes, preparations, and providences through which this world has passed. Love amply accounts for and explains and justifies it all—God's love to man, and then man's love to God and to his neighbor. All of God's wisdom and power that was expended on this world, and on Adam its possessor and its priest, was all to find its reward and its return in a world replenished with a race of creatures who were to be such partakers of the divine nature that they would live for ever and grow for ever in the love, in the holy fellowship, in the blessed service, and in the full enjoyment of God. That was why God made man. That was why God prepared such a home for man as this world in Adam's day was, and still in our day is. The Garden of Eden in Moses, delightful as it is, is but a dim, a faded, and a colorless picture of what God had prepared for them that were to walk with Him in that garden, and were to tell Him, as they walked with Him, how much they loved Him who had planted it. But all the time, as Thomas Goodwin says, the true Garden of Eden was in the gardener's own heart. And his blessed task was set to Adam in his own heart. And what more blessed task could have been set by God to man than to till, and water, and dress, and keep, and reap his own heart for God? And that the serpent came in all his malignity and subtlety and sowed tares in that mystical garden—that should only have given God's son and servant an embraced opportunity and an occasion of all joy to show to God and to the serpent, to heaven and to hell, how much he loved and feared God for all that God had done for him. But, how it went with Adam and with Eve, and with the Garden of Eden, and with Cain and Abel their children, Moses tells us in his sad history. And then, by the time he takes his pen in hand to tell us all this, Moses himself has been banished out of Canaan for his sin, and is waiting for death in the wilderness. And thus it is that he dips his pen in such an inkhorn of tears, and describes to us with such sympathy, and in such sad words, that aboriginal mystery of iniquity—the temptation, the fall, and the expulsion of Adam from Eden. And then Moses adds in a psalm which he indites more immediately concerning himself the well-known words: "Thou turnest man to destruction; and sayest, Return, ye children of men. For we are consumed by Thine anger, and by Thy wrath are we troubled. Thou hast set our iniquities before Thee, our secret sins in the light of Thy countenance. Who knoweth the power of Thine anger? Even according to Thy fear, so is Thy wrath. Return, O Lord, how long? And let it repent Thee concerning Thy servants. Make us glad according to the days wherein Thou hast afflicted us, and the years wherein we have seen evil."

In one of William Law's finest dialogues Theophilus asks his pupil Humanus how he would set about convincing a man of his fallen estate. And Humanus answers to this effect: Man is a poor, miserable, weak, vain, distressed, corrupt, depraved, selfish, self-tormenting, perishing creature. And this world is a sad mixture of false good and real evil; a widespread scene of all sorts of trials, vexations, and miseries, all arising from the frame and nature and condition both of man and the world. This is the sure and infallible proof of the fall of man. The fall of man is not a thing to be learnt from any history whatsoever, but shows itself everywhere and every day and in every man with as much clearness as we see the sun. My first attempt, therefore, upon any man, to convince him of Adam's fall as the ground of Christ's redemption, should be an attempt to do that for him which affliction, disappointment, sickness, pain, and the approach of death have a natural tendency to do; that is, to convince him of the vanity, poverty, and misery of his life and condition in this world. I would appeal at first to nothing but his own nature and condition in this world to demonstrate this capital truth of Holy Scripture that all mankind lie in a fallen state. Humanus says that the mere approach of death is enough to bring any man to his senses. And so it is. Death is the great debater. Death does not bandy words. Death comes to us with overwhelming proofs of our fall in his hands. There is no brow-beating or perplexing of Death. Your smart replies and unanswerable arguments will not stagger Death. All your shafts are quenched like tow before the bosses of his buckler. Now, Death made his first approach to this world in that hour of Adam and Eve's first temptation. God's own fatherly and forewarning words first uttered the dreadful name of Death. O, if Adam had only believed God about sin and death! O, if he had only stopped his ears against the father of lies! O, if he could only have foretasted guilt and remorse and agony of conscience as he was led up to the tree! O, if he could only at that fatal moment have foreseen that coming garden where the Son of God Himself lay among the dark olive-trees recoiling from sin and death in a sweat of blood! O, if he could only have seen spread out before him all the death-beds of all his children on the earth, and all the beds of their second death in hell! O Adam and Eve in Eden, and still under the tree of temptation, look before it is too late;

look on through the endless ages at the unutterable woes that you are working! "Ye shall not eat of it, neither shall ye touch it, lest ye die."

An Egyptian Father has said somewhere that while the four evangelists supply the wool, yet it is Paul who weaves the web. And what Paul does in this respect for Matthew, and Mark, and Luke, and John, he does at the same time for Moses, and David, and Isaiah. Moses, indeed, supplies the history, but it is Paul, that prince of the apostles, who takes us down into the philosophy, as we say, of that history. As we go on speaking about this and that man of science, and this and that book of science and of the philosophy of science, the unlettered people who hear us are tempted to envy us our time and our talents and our books. But they need not. Really, if they knew it, they need not. For, as long as they have Moses and Paul, the Book of Genesis and the Epistle to the Romans, they need envy no man. Thomas à Kempis used to say that his idea of perfect rest and perfect happiness was "to sit with a little book in a little nook." Now, with these two little books of Moses and of Paul, and with another little epistle or two of Paul's added, those who are otherwise quite unlettered men will soon become wiser men than many of their teachers. The most unlearned and ignorant man among us has sin in himself; and he has Christ, if not yet in himself also, then in his Bible, and thus in his offer; and with both sin and Christ in his heart, and with Paul on sin and on Christ in his hand, the most unlettered man is already a man of the truest and the deepest science, and a philosopher of the first water. For it is just those two men, Adam and Christ, with their sin and their righteousness, that so stumble and so throw out our evolutionists; and it is in his handling of those two men, and of that which we have of those two men alone, that Paul shows his matchless philosophic power. Those two stumbling-stones on which so many false philosophies have been ground to powder are the very foundation-stones, corner-stones, and cope-stones of Paul's immortal school and far-shining temple of truth.

In every epistle of his the apostle's immediate, supreme, and alone subject is Jesus Christ. Paul has not a moment of his time, nor a corner of his mind, nor a beat of his heart, nor a stroke of his pen for any other person, great or small, but Jesus Christ. And Paul is in the very heat and at the very heart of one of his greatest chapters on Jesus Christ, and on the atonement that we sinners of mankind have received through Jesus Christ, when, if I may say so, the very sweep and grasp of Paul's mind, the very philosophical necessity of Paul's great intellect, all compel him to go back and take up Adam into his great argument and great gospel. The passage is one of the most profound and magnificent even in his profound and magnificent epistles. It runs thus: "Wherefore, as by one man sin entered into the world, and death by sin, therefore, as by the offence of one judgment came upon all men to condemnation, even so by the righteousness of one the free gift came upon all men unto justification of life. For as by one man's disobedience many were made sinners, so by the obedience of one shall many be made righteous." To Paul's so comprehensive mind, so far-sweeping imagination, and so righteousness-hungry heart, Adam and Christ are the two poles upon whom this whole world of human life revolves. As the best expositor of Paul I know of anywhere says, Adam and Jesus Christ, to Paul's heaven-soaring eye, stand out before God with all other men "hanging at their girdles." And it is in his evolution, illustration, and enforcement of this great truth that Paul brings in, and makes so familiar to us those peculiarly Pauline and polar terms—law and grace, faith and works, condemnation and justification, enmity and peace, alienation and reconciliation, imputation and sanctification, sin and holiness, the flesh and the Spirit, eternal life and eternal death, and such-like. On all these Scripture subjects the Westminster Catechisms supply us with Paul's doctrines in a nutshell; as will again be seen and acknowledged when theology shall have recovered herself from her temporary lapse into mere Bibliography, and when Bible history shall have again become Bible doctrine and a Bible life.

And then, just as the full truth about the atonement led the apostle back from Christ to Adam, so in another epistle of his, the resurrection of Christ, and the resurrection of all those who have fallen asleep in Christ, leads Paul back again to Adam in this way. "For since by man came death, by man came also the resurrection of the dead. For as in Adam all die, even so in Christ shall all be made alive. And so it is written, The first man Adam was made a living soul; the last Adam was made a quickening spirit. The first man is of the earth, earthy; the second man is the Lord from heaven." The "second man" and the "last Adam" are most happy names and most illustrious titles of Paul's bold invention for his Master, our Lord and Savior Jesus Christ. Which glorious Man is called the Second Adam, says Theophilus, as having in His regeneration that very perfection which the first Adam had in his creation. And because He is to do all that for us by a birth of grace, which we should have had by a birth of nature from Adam, had he kept his first estate of sinless perfection.

> Praise to the Holiest in the height,
>   And in the depth be praise;
> In all His words most wonderful,
>   Most sure in all His ways.
> O loving wisdom of our God!
>   When all was sin and shame,
> A second Adam to the fight
>   And to the rescue came.

Now, what say you, Academicus, to all that?

2
Eve

ACCORDING to Moses, and taking Moses as he has come down to us, Eve, the mother of mankind, was, so to speak, an afterthought of her Maker. And it is surely something remarkable that four of the devoutest, boldest, and most original writers that have ever lived have taken and have gone out upon the same view. The creation of this world was the work of love, for God is Love. God so loved the very thought of this world that He created it and made it the exquisitely lovely world that we read of in Moses. But love is full of afterthoughts, of new ideas, and of still better intentions and performances. And thus it is that Moses is very bold to write as if God in His growing love for this world had found out a still better way of peopling this world than the way He had at first intended—had finished, indeed, and had pronounced very good. A new kind of love; a love such as even heaven itself had never seen nor tasted anything like it; a love sweet, warm, tender, wistful, helpful, fruitful; a love full of a "nice and subtle happiness";—the mutual love of man and woman—took our Maker's heart completely captive as a still better way of replenishing earth with its children than even that noble and wonderful way by which heaven had been replenished with its angels. And thus it is that Moses, in his second chapter, lets us see our Maker coming back to earth; lets us hear Him finding fault with His first work in Adam, very good as it was; and lets us watch Him re-touching His work, till He takes Eve out of Adam and gives her back to Adam a woman to be his married wife, to be an help meet for him, and to be the mother of his children. So Moses in Genesis. And then, Plato in his *Symposium* teaches his Greeks the same thing: that man cannot live alone, that love is the true and only good of man, and that the best love of earth is but a foretaste and an assurance of the love of heaven. And then, Jacob Behmen has a doctrine all his own of the origin of woman; of the sphere and the functions of sex in this life, as well as of its absence from the life to come: a doctrine to enter on which would lead us too far away from our proper work tonight. Suffice it to say that for philosophical depth, for speculative power, for imaginative suggestiveness, and for spiritual beauty there is nothing better in Moses the Hebrew Plato, or in Plato the Attic Moses, than Behmen's doctrine of Adam and Eve. Behmen's reading of Moses leads him to believe that there must have been something of the nature of a stumble, if not an actual fall, in Adam while yet he was alone in Eden. Adam, at his own and alone creation, was pronounced to be "very good." There must therefore, Behmen holds, have been some sort of slip or lapse from his original righteousness and obedience and blessedness before his Maker would have said of Adam that he was now in a condition that was "not good." And thus it was that Eve was created to "help" Adam to recover himself, and to establish himself in paradise, and in the favor and fellowship and service of his Maker. "It is not good that man should be left alone. This shows us," says Jacob Behmen's best English interpreter, "that Adam had somehow altered his first state and had brought some beginnings of evil into it, and had made that not to be good which God at one time had seen to be very good. And, therefore, as a less evil, and to prevent a greater, God divided—ii. 21—the first perfect human nature into two parts, into a male and a female creature; and this, as you will see by-and-by, was a wonderful instance of the love and the care of God toward our new humanity. Adam was at first the total humanity in one creature, who should, in that state of perfection, have brought forth his own likeness out of himself in such purity of love and in such divine power as he himself had been brought forth by God. But Adam stood no longer in the perfection of his first estate as the image and the likeness of God. The first step, therefore, towards the redemption and recovery of Adam beginning to fall was to take Eve out of him, that he might have a second trial and probation in paradise; in which, if he failed, an effectual Redeemer might then arise out of the seed of the woman. Oh! my friends, what a wonderful procedure is there to be seen in the Divine Providence, always turning all evil, as soon as it appears, into a further display and an opening of new wonders of the wisdom and the love of God!" But you will start up as if you had been stung by the old serpent himself, and will angrily demand of me—Do I believe all that? My confident and overbearing friend, I neither believe it nor disbelieve it; for I do not know. But I believe about the first Adam, as I believe about the Second, that had it all been written even the world itself could not have contained the books. And the longer I live and listen and learn, the more slow I become of saying that I disbelieve anything that men like Moses hint at, and that men like Plato and Behmen and Law speak out: all three, all four, men whose shoe latchet neither you nor I are worthy to unloose. But, as Bishop Martensen quotes: "The time has not yet come, and our language has not yet acquired the requisite purity, clearness, and depth to permit us to speak freely, and without, in some respect or other, provoking misunderstanding, upon a subject in which the deepest enigma of human existence is concentrated."

But listen, and without interrupting him, to Moses on Eve, the mother of mankind. "And the Lord God said, It is not good that the man should be alone; I will make him an help meet for him. And the Lord God made a woman, and brought her unto the man. Now the serpent was more subtle than any beast of the field which the Lord God had made. And the serpent said to the woman, Ye shall not surely die. And when the woman saw that the tree was good for food, and that it was pleasant to the eyes, and a tree to be desired to make one wise, she took of the fruit thereof, and did eat, and gave to her husband with her, and he did eat. And the eyes of them both were opened." Eve gave to Adam that day, and Adam took at Eve's hand, what was not hers to give nor his to take. And any woman who gives to any man what is not hers to give nor his to take, their eyes, too, will be opened!

> Out of my sight, thou serpent! That name best.
> Befits thee with him leagued, thyself as false
> And hateful; nothing wants, but that thy shape,
> Like his, and color serpentine may show

Thy inward fraud, to warn all creatures from thee
Henceforth . . . Hate hard by lust.

O Eve, Eve! fatal mother of so many fatal daughters since! Would God thou
hadst resisted the devil for thyself, for thy husband, and for us thy hapless children! O Eve, Eve, mother of all flesh! "And the Lord God called unto Adam and
said unto him, Where art thou? And he said, I heard Thy voice in the garden, and
I was afraid, and I hid myself because I was naked. Who told thee that thou wast
naked? And the man said, The woman Thou gavest me to be with me, she gave me
of the tree, and I did eat. I was alone, and Thou broughtest this woman to me. I
rejoiced over her with singing. I blessed Thee for her. I took her to my heart. I said,
This is now bone of my bone and flesh of my flesh. And the Lord God said to the
woman, Woman what is this that thou hast done? So He drove out the man; and
He placed at the east of the garden of Eden cherubim and a flaming sword which
turned every way, to keep the way of the tree of life."

After the mystics, Milton is by far the best commentator on Moses. Masculine,
massive, majestic, magnificent, melodious Milton! Hear Moses, then, on Eve, our
much deceived, much failing, hapless mother, and then hear Milton.

MOSES

And the Lord God said, It is not good that the man should be alone: I will make
him an help meet for him.

MILTON

—I, ere thou spak'st,
Knew it not good for Man to be alone. . .
What next I bring shall please thee, be assured
Thy likeness, thy fit help, thy other self,
Thy wish exactly to thy heart's desire.

MOSES

And the Lord God made a woman, and brought her to the man. And Adam said,
Therefore shall a man leave his father and his mother, and shall cleave unto his wife.

MILTON

Under His forming hands a creature grew,
Manlike, but different sex, so lovely fair,
That what seem'd fair in all the world, seem'd now
Mean, or in her summ'd up, in her contain'd

And in her looks, which from that time infused
Sweetness into my heart, unfelt before,

And into all things from her air inspired
The spirit of love and amorous delight.
          On she came,
Led by her Heavenly Maker, though unseen,
And guided by His voice; nor uninform'd
Of nuptial sanctity, and marriage rites:
Grace was in all her steps, heaven in her eye,
In every gesture dignity and love.

Hail wedded love, mysterious law, true source
Of human offspring. By thee,
Founded in reason, loyal, just, and pure,
Relations dear, and all the charities
Of father, son, and brother first were known.
Perpetual fountain of domestic sweets.
Here Love his golden shaft employs, here lights
His constant lamp, and waves his purple wings.
Sleep on, blest pair!

MOSES

Now the serpent was more subtle than any beast which the Lord God had made.

MILTON

          —I now must change
These notes to tragic; foul distrust, and breach
Disloyal on the part of man, revolt,
And disobedience: on the part of Heav'n
Now alienated, distance and distaste,
Anger and just rebuke: sad task, yet argument
Not less but more heroic than the wrath
Of stern Achilles.

MOSES

And she took of the fruit thereof and did eat, and gave also to her husband with her, and he did eat.

MILTON

Earth felt the wound, and Nature from her seat
Sighing through all her work gave signs of woe,
That all was lost.
Earth trembled from her entrails, as again
In pangs, and Nature gave a second groan;

Sky lower'd, and muttering thunder, some sad drops
Wept at completing of the mortal sin
Original.

MOSES

And the man said, The woman whom Thou gavest to be with me, she gave me of the tree, and I did eat.

MILTON

To whom the Sovran Presence thus replied,
Was she thy God, that her thou didst obey
Before His voice, or was she made thy guide
Superior, or but equal, that to her
Thou didst resign thy manhood, and the place
Wherein God set thee? Adorn'd
She was indeed, and lovely to attract
Thy love, not thy subjection.

MOSES

And unto Adam He said, In the sweat of thy face shalt thou eat thy bread.

MILTON

Idleness had been worse;
My labor will sustain me.
So spoke our father penitent.
To whom thus also th' angel last replied:
—Only add
Deeds to thy knowledge answerable, and faith,
Add virtue, patience, temperance, add love,

By name to come called charity, the soul
Of all the rest; then thou wilt not be loath
To leave this Paradise, but shalt possess
A Paradise within thee happier far.
He ended, and they both descend the hill;
The world was all before them, where to choose
Their place of rest, and Providence their guide;
They hand in hand, with wand'ring steps and slow,
Through Eden took their solitary way.

Great-minded Milton! "The great number of books and papers of amusement, which, of one kind or another, daily come in one's way have in part occasioned, and most perfectly fall in with, and humor, our idle way of reading and considering things. By this means, time even in solitude is happily got rid of without the pain of attention; neither is any part of it more put to the account of idleness, one can scarce forbear saying, or spent with less thought, than great part of that which is spent in reading." Thus Butler. Let Moses and Milton and Butler be more read.

But it is high time to turn to Paul, who is a far greater authority and commentator on Moses than Plato, or Behmen, or Milton, or Law. Now, Paul does not say very much about Eve, but what he does say has in it all his characteristic strength, straightforwardness, and evangelical consolation. Adam was the protoplast, says Paul to Timothy, quoting the expression from the Wisdom of Solomon. Adam was first formed, then Eve. And Adam was not deceived, but the woman being deceived was in the transgression. "Of the woman," says the son of Sirach in his tremendous attack on women, "came the beginning of sin, and through her we all die." How it might have been with us today if the serpent had tried his flattery and his lies on Adam we do not know, and we need not ask. Only, let the truth be told. The devil, as a matter of fact, never spake to Adam at all. He approached Eve with his glozing words. He succeeded with Eve, and then Eve succeeded with Adam. Flattery led the woman astray. And then love led the man astray. The man could not refuse what the woman offered. "The woman was deceived," says Bengel, "the man was persuaded." And, because Eve was first in the transgression, Moses put certain special punishments upon her in his day, and Paul put certain other humiliations, repressions, and submissions in his day. God, in Moses, laid on Eve that day

> The pleasing punishment that women bear;

as, also, that her desire should be to her husband, and that he should rule over her. O husbands of women! O young men, to whom is their desire! God help all such women! And, if their desire must so be, let us pray and labor at our tempers and at our characters, at our appetites and at our inclinations, lest their desire be their everlasting loss. "With my soul have I desired Thee, O God, in the night. Delight thyself also in the Lord, and He will give thee the desires of thine heart. Because he hath set his love upon Me, therefore will I deliver him; I will set him on high, because he hath known My name. With long life will I satisfy him, and I will show him My salvation. As for me, I will behold Thy face in righteousness: I shall be satisfied, when I awake, with Thy likeness."

That emancipation of women which they owe to Jesus Christ had not had time to work itself fully out in Paul's day. And thus it is that we read in Paul's first Epistle to Timothy that the women are to learn in silence with all subjection, and that they are not to usurp authority, but are always to be in silence.

> To whom thus Eve with sad demeanor meek:
> Ill worthy I such title should belong
> To me transgressor, who for thee ordain'd
> A help, become thy snare; to me reproach
> Rather belongs, distrust and all dispraise.
> So spake, so wished, much humbled Eve.

"Let the women learn in silence," and, "I suffer not a woman to teach her husband, but to be in silence." Yes; truth and beauty, Apostle Paul. But who is to be her husband? Who is to fill up the silence? All women would be proud to sit in silence if their husbands were like the husbands in Timothy's diocese; that is to say, if they would but speak out in the silence, and would speak out wisely, and advisedly, and lovingly, and always well. And, once in every woman's life she does sit as silent and as teachable as Paul himself would have her sit. When God takes her by the hand and brings her to the man for whom He has made her, then she for a season puts on the ornament of a meek and a quiet spirit. "Even as Sara obeyed Abraham, calling him lord: whose daughters ye are, as long as ye do well, and are not afraid with any amazement. Likewise, ye husbands, dwell with them according to knowledge, giving honor unto the wife, as unto the weaker vessel, and as being heirs together of the grace of life, that your prayers be not hindered."

"Notwithstanding, she shall be saved in The Child-bearing, if they continue in faith and charity and holiness with sobriety." I am glad to see that the Revised Version leans to the mystical and evangelical interpretation of Paul's "childbearing." For, as Bishop Ellicott says, nothing could be more cold and jejune than the usual interpretation. And Paul is the last man to be cold and jejune on such a subject. Yes, I will believe with the learned revisers, and with some of our deepest interpreters, that Paul has the Seed of the Woman in the eye of his mind in this passage, and that he looks back with deep pity and love on his hapless mother Eve; and then, after her, on all women and on all mothers, and sees them all saved, with Eve and with Mary, by the Man that Mary got from the Lord, if they abide and continue in faith, in love, in holiness, and in sober-mindedness.

3
Cain

CAIN'S mother mistook Cain for Christ. As soon as Eve saw her first-born son she no longer remembered the anguish. What a joyful woman Eve was that day! For, what a new thing in the earth was that first child in the arms of that first mother! Just look at the divine gift. Look at his eyes. Look at his hands. Look at his sweet little feet. Count his fingers. Count too, his toes. See the lovely dimple in the little man's right hand. What a child! And all out of his own mother's bosom. And all his father's son. Adam's son. A second Adam. A new man all to themselves to keep for their own. Look at him taking his first step. Hear him essaying his first syllable; the first time he says, Mother! and the first time he tries to say, Father! The Garden of Eden, with all its flowers and fruits, was forgotten and forgiven from the day that heaven came down to earth; from the day on which Eve got her first-born son from the Lord God. Nor, if you think of it, is it at all to be wondered at that little Cain's happy mother mistook him for Jesus Christ. Put yourself back into her place. Eve had brought banishment from Eden on her husband and on herself by listening to the father of lies. But the Lord God had come down to Eve in her terrible distress, and, beginning His book of promises with His best promise, had promised to her that the seed of the woman should bruise the serpent's head, and should thus redeem and undo all the evil that she had brought on herself and on her husband. And here, already, blessed be God, is the promised seed! And that, too, sent in such a sweet, heart-satisfying, and heavenly way! A man from God in her own arms! Why, Eve would have been a cold-blooded, hard-hearted atheist if she had not so hailed the birth of her first-born son. She would have made God a liar unless she had said, This is our God: for we have waited upon Him and we have gotten a man from Him. And yet, with all that, it was not so to be. As we know now, Cain was not to be the Christ. No. The angel Gabriel was not sent to Adam and Eve. The Angel of the Annunciation who stands in the presence of God passed by Eve, and Sarah, and Rachel, and Hannah, and Elizabeth, and all the other mothers in Israel, and came to a virgin espoused to a man whose name was Joseph. And the angel came in unto her, and said, Hail, thou that art highly favored, the Lord is with thee: blessed art thou among women. And Mary said, My soul doth magnify the Lord.

And then, Cain and Abel as children together— till their mother's cup ran over. With what motherly love that first mother watched the two little brothers as they played together. Look at them planting a garden in their sport, and putting men and women of clay in the garden and calling the man a father and the woman a mother. Till, tired of their garden and its ever-falling fathers and mothers, the two little angels went off hand in hand to go and meet their own returning father. And then, with a child in each hand, Adam came home to Eve, saying, Surely these same shall comfort us concerning our work and toil of our hands, because of the ground which the Lord hath cursed.

"And in process of time Abel became a keeper of sheep, but Cain, like his father, became a tiller of the ground. And Cain brought of the fruits of the ground an offering unto the Lord. And Abel, he also brought of the firstlings of his flock and of the fat thereof. And the Lord had respect to Abel and to his offering; but unto Cain and to his offering the Lord had not respect. And Cain was very wroth and his countenance fell. And the Lord said to Cain, Why art thou wroth, and why is thy countenance fallen? If thou doest well, shalt thou not be accepted? and if thou doest not well, sin lieth at the door." Look at the seventh verse of the fourth chapter of Genesis, and you will see in that verse, and for the first time in the Bible, that terrible word SIN. That word, the most awful word ever uttered in heaven or earth or hell—SIN! John Milton is our best commentator on Moses. But Milton's description of SIN is far too dreadful for me to repeat it here. Read it yourselves. Read the second book of *Paradise Lost*, and you will see SIN with her father and her son both standing beside her. And read, and read, and read over and over again Moses and Milton and yourself till you both see and feel both SIN and her father and her son all in yourself. Moses and Milton write for grownup men, and not for babes who are still on their unskillful milk, as most men and women are.

Envy came to its full maturity all at once in Cain. Some sinful passions have taken time and environment to spring up and to mature to their full fruit in the human heart and in human life. But envy, the wickedest, the deadliest, and the most detestable of all our sinful passions, came to a perfect man all at once. Eve's first-born son envied his brother Abel. Cain envied Abel because of his goodness, and because his goodness had found him acceptance and praise of God. And in his envy and hate of his brother's goodness and acceptance Cain rose up and slew his brother. Envy, surely, even in the end of the world, can no further go than that. I defy the wickedest heart in this house tonight to improve upon the way of Cain. And yet let us not be too sure. Let us look yet closer at Cain; and, all the time, let us keep our eye upon ourselves and see.

Cain envied Abel. He envied his brother, his only brother, his trustful, confiding, affectionate brother, his brother who worshipped him, and who would have given him his altar, and his lamb, and his fire from heaven, and all that he had if Cain would but have laid aside his gloom and taken it all. But no; Cain will not be beholden to his younger brother. Nothing will satisfy Cain now but one thing. A coal from hell has by this time so kindled hell in Cain's heart that all the rebukes and commands of Adam, and all the tears and embraces of Eve, and all the soft answers and submissions of Abel could not quench the wrath in Cain's evil eye, or take the fall out of his sunken countenance. Let the holy man here who has never had this same hell-fire in his heart at his brother, at his dearest and best and only friend on earth, at his old playfellow, at his present fellow-worshipper, let that happy man cast stones at that miserable wretch with murder in his heart at Abel his unsuspecting brother.

"Some sins in themselves, and by reason of several aggravations, are more heinous in the sight of God than others." The offence was aggravated by the motive, says Bacon in one place. And so it was with Cain's offence. For his motive was envy of his brother's goodness, and of the acceptance and the praise that his brother's growing goodness was every day bringing him from the Lord. "The Lord had respect unto Abel, and to his offering." That was all. But that was quite enough to kindle all hell in Cain's evil heart. And let our brother worship God alongside of our altar also, and let him find more acceptance with God and with man than we find; let him be better gifted of God and better placed by God; more approved of God and of God's people than we are, and you will soon see Cain. Praise the talents, the industry, the achievements of our very best and dearest friend, and it is gall and wormwood to us. But blame him, belittle him, detract from him, pooh-pooh and sneer at him, and we will embrace you, for you have put marrow into our dead bones, you have given wine to him that was of a heavy heart. Praise a neighboring minister's prayer, or his preaching, or his pastoral activity at another minister's table, and you will upset both him and his listening house for days and for years to come. Of the six sins that are said to forerun the sin against the Holy Ghost, the fourth in the fatal order is "envy at another's grace." Take care, then, how you gad about with a tongue in your head that no man can tame, and tempt good men and women toward that sin which shall never be forgiven them.

"And Cain talked with Abel his brother; and it came to pass, when they were in the field, that Cain rose up against Abel his brother, and slew him." Abel might have escaped his end, and might have saved his brother, if he had not been so easy, so innocent, and so unsuspecting. If he had even attended to his dog at his heel he would have seen that there was something wrong somewhere that morning. For Cain had not shut his eyes all last night. Cain could not sleep all last night. He had been up and out and all about all night like a ghost. His face was fallen in. His eyes were green and black. Abel's dog growled and barked at Cain as if he had been a vagabond already. Abel had never seen a corpse, else Cain's face that day was like nothing in the world so much as the face of one of our corpses in its coffin. Nor did Cain talk like his usual self that morning. He stammered as he talked. He talked about things he had never, that Abel remembered, talked about before. Were it not that perfect innocence is so blind and so deaf, Abel would have found opportunity and would have turned home again that fatal morning. And even had Abel asked what Cain had against him that morning, Cain might have admitted fierce anger, or some other evil feeling at something or other, but he would never have admitted envy. No man from that day to this has ever admitted envy. To every other wickedness confession has often been made; but did you ever confess envy? or did you ever have envy confessed to you? No, never. I wonder, do the confessors in the confessional get at envy? If they do in the darkness and through the bitter brass, then there is something to be said for that heart-racking and sin-extorting system. No. Only by the stone, only by the dagger, only by the pistol, only by the cup, only by the bitten back and the slandered name is envy ever found out. In his noble answer to Tilken's abominable libel Jacob Behmen says, "We, poor children of Eve, no longer walk together in the love of God; but, full of passion, we envy, vilify, dishonor, and denounce one another, wishing to one another death and all kinds of evil; we enjoy, as we enjoy nothing else, each other's loss and pain and misery."

"And the Lord said unto Cain, Where is Abel thy brother?" The Lord asked at Cain what He knew quite well, in order that Cain might know that the Lord knew. But, instead of telling the Lord and Adam and Eve where Abel was buried, and instead of crying all his days ever after to the Lord, Deliver me from blood-guiltiness, Cain gave to the Lord the brazen-faced answer, Am I my brother's keeper? "And the Lord said, What is this that thou hast done? A fugitive and a vagabond shalt thou be in the earth." And not Cain, and all unarrested murderers only. We are all fugitives and vagabonds in the earth. We all are, or we ought to be. For the voice of our brother's blood cries to God against us. And, one day, we shall all be arrested and arraigned on that very same charge before the judgment-seat of Christ; unless, indeed, we surrender ourselves before that seat is set. "For this is the message that we have heard of Him, that we should love one another. Not as Cain, who was of that wicked one, and slew his brother. He that loveth not his brother abideth in death. Whosoever hateth his brother is a murderer; and ye know that no murderer hath eternal life abiding in him." It was an old superstition that a murdered man's body began to run warm blood again as soon and as often as its murderer was brought near it. And in this way they used to discover who the real murderer was. Now, just suppose that that was indeed a natural or a supernatural law in the age of the world and in the land in which we live—how many men still living would begin to be all over with blood in your presence? The man sitting next you at this moment would be like a murdered corpse. The preacher now standing before you; your mother's son; the very wife of your bosom, when she does not flatter and fawn upon you; your own son; your dearest friend. Yes; you would then be what Cain all his days was, and all men finding you would slay you. They would not know, they would be horrified at what it meant, when their throats began to run blood as they passed you on the street, or as you talked with them in the field, or as you sat eating and drinking with them at your table, or at their table, or at the Lord's table. But you know. And you know their names. Let their names, then, be heard of God in your closet every day and every night, lest they be proclaimed from the housetops to your everlasting confusion and condemnation at the last day.

And Cain went out from the presence of the Lord, and Cain wandered up and down a fugitive and a vagabond, thinking every bush an officer, till a child was born to him in his banishment. Dr. Delitzsch, that old evangelical exegete who is so much at home among all those Old Testament men, tells us that Cain called his child by a name such as the rich man in hell might have called his child by if an heir had been born to him in his place of torment. For Cain said, Let his name be called Enoch, for God hath sent His angel to dip the tip of his finger in water to cool my tongue. And little Enoch and his mother somewhat lifted the curse off Cain, and somewhat quieted and rested Cain's vagabond heart. And Cain built a city and called it Enoch, after his son, for he said, Here will I rest and dwell and hide myself, for God hath refreshed me and hath revived me with my wife and children. And, with that, Cain the murderer of Abel passes out of our knowledge.

But let us hope and believe that the presence of the Lord came and dwelt in that city of Cain and his wife and children, according to the splendid psalm—"O Lord, Thou hast searched me and known me. Whither shall I go from Thy Spirit? or whither shall I flee from Thy presence? If I make my bed in hell, behold, Thou art there. If I take the wings of the morning and dwell in the uttermost parts of the sea, even there shall Thy hand lead me and Thy right hand shall hold me."

Now, since all this was written for our warning, and for our learning—come, all envious-minded men and women, come with me, and let us offer to God the envious-minded man's prayer. We have never confessed envy to man, but God knows our hearts. "O dear God, never suffer the devil to rub his vilest leprosy of envy upon me. Never let me have the affections of the desperate and the damned. Let it not be ill with me when it is well with others. Let me have Thy Holy Spirit to promote my brother's good, and to give Thee thanks for all his prosperity and praise. Never censuring his actions curstly, nor detracting from his praises spitefully, nor upbraiding his infelicities maliciously, but pleased with all things that Thou doest or givest. That we may all join together in the communion of saints, both here and hereafter, in grace and in glory, through Jesus Christ our Lord. Amen."

4
Abel

RIGHTEOUS Abel would have silenced his own accusing blood if he only could. When Cain suddenly struck him down, dying Abel took all the blame on himself. As long as he could speak Abel excused his brother, and sought to be reconciled to his brother. He put himself in the wrong and his brother in the right. He saw, now, when it was too late, how he had grieved and vexed and offended his brother. He had not thought about his brother. He had not put himself into his brother's place. He had not looked at things with his brother's eyes. He had been glad, and he had let his gladness too much appear, when his own offerings were respected and his brother's despised. Forgive me, O my God! Forgive me, O my brother! was Abel's last prayer. Whatever dead Abel's blood may have cried, I feel sure what dying Abel himself cried. Lord, lay not this blow to my brother's charge, he cried. And when Abel had said that again and again he fell asleep.

If Cain had only done the exact opposite of what he immediately did as soon as he had buried Abel—if he had only determined in spite of it all still to abide in the land of Eden; if he had only kept himself in the presence of the Lord, and had not allowed himself to go out from the presence of the Lord; if he had only laid the foundations of his city beside Abel's grave, then Abel's prayer for his brother would have been heard, and Abel's blood from that day would have begun to speak almost like the blood of Christ itself. Had Cain all his after days prevented the dawning of the morning that he might offer unceasing sacrifices beside his brother's grave; had he risen from his bed at midnight till, being in an agony, his sweat was as it were great drops of blood falling to the ground on Abel's grave; then Cain would have been a pattern that in him God might first show forth all long-suffering to those who should after Cain believe to life everlasting. And if you would but determine to learn tonight of Cain and Abel; if you would but keep at home and dwell in the presence of your past sin, and in the presence of the Lord; if you would but build your house, and if God would but prepare your table, in the presence of your enemies; now that Christ's atoning blood has taken the place of Abel's accusing blood; now that Christ's peace-speaking blood is every day and every night being sprinkled from heaven upon His and other men's murderers— you would even yet escape being a fugitive and a vagabond on the earth, and would be made a fellow-citizen with the saints, and of the household of God.

Where, then, is Abel thy brother? Answer that on the spot. Where hast thou hid him? Say on the spot, Lord, come with me and I will show Thee. Go back often to Abel's grave. Go back continually to your past life. Go back to your school days. Go back to your college days. Go back to your first office, your first shop, your first workshop. Recall your first friend. Pass before your eyes the first young man, the first young woman, you were intimate with. Call up the long-moldered corpse of your first affection, your first passion, your first love, your first lust. Give instances.

Give names; and ask if God has another case like yours in all His Book. Face full in the face that monstrous folly; that word, that act, that makes you blush scarlet and turn in your seat to think of it. They are turning on their beds in hell at this moment for far less. Go back to that farmhouse in the country, to that hamlet up among the hills, out of which you were so glad to escape from the presence of the Lord, and from the place of your sin, and get away to hide yourself in the great city. See how one ghost awakens another ghost till they come up an army of the ghosts of dead men and dead women against you. Men and women now dead, and in their own places. Men and women also still alive, but dead to you—would God they were! Men and women who, when they, or their children, or only their spoken or written names pass before you, make you wish they were dead—they or you. Go back, I say. In God's name, in God's strength, go back! Take time, and go back. Take trouble, and go back. Take pains, and go back. Do not grudge time and trouble and pains. You will be well paid for all your time and trouble in humiliation, in remorse, and in godly sorrow. Even if you took, what Cain, it is to be feared, did not take—even if you took one whole hour every night alone with your past life, it would not be misspent time. Redeem the time. Redeem it, and you will be justified for so doing long before the great white throne is set. No; one whole hour every twenty-four hours of your present life would not be too much time to give to go over your past life. I undertake that if you will go home, and shut your door, and begin with such an hour tonight, you will not fall asleep in your chair. Why are you so pushed for time to repent? Why is retrospection the only thing that you have no time for, and always push it into a corner? Is it because you are not your brother's keeper? Is it because you never struck a foul blow in the field? Is it because no gray head has ever gone down to a grave that your hands dug? Is it because no young man's faith, and no young woman's trust, and no unsuspecting friend's good name has ever been shaken, or deceived, or pulled down and murdered by you? Have your hands been always so washed in innocency? Are there no tears against you in God's bottle, and no names in His book? God takes care and account not of murdered lives only, but also of murdered names and reputations. How many men and women have we all struck at with that sharp razor, an envious, malicious, murderous tongue? Work at your consciences, you children of God, till they are as quick to detect, to record, and to recollect an unkind, unjust, unhandsome, slighting, detracting, belittling, sneering word, or look, or shrug, as they are to keep you in mind of a foul blow in a field, and a far-back grave in a wood. It would lay some high heads here low enough this night if the graves of all the good names and reputations they have had a hand in murdering were to suddenly open around them. All good men, all men of God, keep a whole churchyard of such graves ever open before them. And, if you do not, whatever you may think you are, and whatever other men may think you are, Christ, your angry Judge, knows what you are.

There are no ministers here, but there are a good many divinity students who will too soon be ministers. Will they listen and let me speak a word or two to them on the blood of Abel? One word which I have purchased a right to speak. Alas! alas! We are called and ordained to be our brother's keeper long before any one has taken us and shown us the way to keep ourselves. And with what result? With what result let our communion-rolls and our visiting-books answer. If any minister would be shut up and determined to preach nothing else and nothing ever but the peace-speaking blood of Christ, let him read every night in his communion-roll, in his young communicants' class list, and in his pastoral visitation-book. *That* name, *that* name, *that* name, that *family* of names! Where are the owners of all these names? What account can I give of them? If they are not here tonight, where are they? Why are they not here, and why are they where they are? What a preacher Paul must have been, and what a pastor, and supported and seconded by what a staff of elders, since he was able to say to his assembled kirk-session in Ephesus that he was clear of the blood of all his people! What mornings to his tent-making, and to his sermons, and to his epistles; and what afternoons and evenings to humility, and to tears, and to temptations, both publicly and from house to house! Like Samuel Rutherford, and long before his day, always at his books, always among his people, always at their sick-beds, always catechizing their children, always preaching and always praying. No, I know no reading so humbling, so condemning, so killing to us ministers as our communion-roll. We ministers must always appear before our people, and before God, clothed from head to foot with humility, with a rope upon our heads, and with nothing in our hands or in our mouths but the cross of Christ and the blood of Christ, that speaketh better things than that of Abel.

The blood of Christ! O my brethren, what blood the blood of Christ must be! What wonderful, what wonder-working blood! What amazing blood! How can even the blood of Christ atone for, and make amends to God and man for, all our envy, and malice, and murder of men's bodies, souls, and reputations? The more I think of that—I do not know, I cannot tell, I cannot imagine. And then, not atonement and amends only, not bare pardon for all the past only, but eternal life, and all that leads up to eternal life, and all that eternal life is and contains. For the Holy Ghost also is the purchase of Christ's blood, a new heart also, and a whole lifetime of the means of grace. The Bible also, the Sabbath day, the Lord's table, a minister after God's own heart, deep, divine, unsearchable providences, a peaceful death-bed, a happy resurrection morning, a place at the right hand of the Judge, an open acknowledgment and acquittal on the day of judgment, "Come, ye blessed of My Father," and then a mansion with our own name in blood upon its door-post and its lintel to all eternity! Yes; precious blood indeed! What blood that must be that can so outcry and drown silent in its depths all the accusing cries that are even now going up to God all behind me and all around me! I feel that I would need a whole Redeemer and all His redeeming blood to myself. But, then, after that fountain filled with blood has drowned in the depths of the sea all the accusations that my sinful life has raised against me, that same blood will still flow for you and will do the same service for you. And the blood of Christ is the same blood yesterday, today, and for ever. For after it has spoken better things than that of Abel to you and to me, it will still abide and will still do the same service to our children and to their children, till a multitude that no man can number have washed their robes and made them white in the blood of the Lamb. No wonder that Paul called that blood not the blood of Christ only, but the blood of God.

5
Enoch

WHEN a reader of the Bible first steps across the borders of the Bible, and, for love of the Bible, begins to read the ancient books that lie around and beneath the Bible, he comes sometimes upon a real treasure, but more often upon a heap of rubbish. When a reader of the Bible first hears of The Book of Enoch, taking Coleridge's excellent advice, he sells his bed to buy that book. Enoch walked with God, he says to himself. I have the whole Bible in my hands, all written, he says to himself, by men all of whom so walked, but let me get all the books of all such men, before I have either time or money for any other manner of man or any other kind of book. But when, after long looking for it, he at last holds The Book of Enoch in his hand, it is with what a disappointment! For one thing, he soon sees that he has been deceived and imposed upon. Enoch! He has not read the first chapter of the book till it is as clear as day to him that Enoch never saw the book that goes under his ancient name; and besides, it is simply impossible that any man who had ever walked with God as Enoch walked could have written a single chapter of such an inflated and fantastic book. In four verses of his own Bible—in two verses in the Old Testament, and in two verses in the New Testament—there is more truth and more beauty and more guidance how he is to walk with God, than there is in all the hundred and eight chapters of the so-called Book of Enoch taken together. Still, our Bible scholars must work on in rubbish-heaps like The Book of Enoch, if only for the sake of the chips and the filings of the Bible that are sometimes to be found there. But unless you are a Bible scholar, and are able to get good out of a book that returns but a far-off echo of your Bible, you will spend your time and your money far better than by spending either on The Book of Enoch. "And Enoch walked with God; and he was not, for God took him." There is substance there for him who knows what substance is, and there is style there for him who knows what style is. And that is but one single verse out of a whole Bible full of such substance and such style.

This, then, is the book of the generations of Adam. "Adam begat a son in his likeness, after his image, and called his name Seth. And Adam lived after he had begotten Seth, he begat sons and daughters, and he died. And Seth lived, and died. And Enos lived, and died. And Cainan lived, and died. And Mahalaleel lived, and died. And Jared lived, and begat Enoch. And Jared lived after he begat Enoch, and begat sons and daughters, and he died. And Enoch begat Methuselah. And Enoch walked with God after he begat Methuselah, and begat sons and daughters. And Enoch walked with God; and he was not, for God took him." What is that? Let us go back upon that. Let us ponder all that passage over again. Adam and all his sons, after they had begotten sons and daughters, died. But of Enoch, the seventh from Adam, we read very differently. Adam, and Seth, and Enos, and Cainan, and Mahalaleel, and Jared all lived, they simply lived on, after they had had children

22

born to them, and then died. But Enoch walked with God after his first child was born. As much surely as to say—could anything be said with more plainness?—that it was only after his first child was born to him that Enoch really and truly began to walk with God. Fathers and mothers, young fathers and young mothers, fathers and mothers whose first child has just been born, and no more—seize your opportunity. Let not another day pass. Begin today. Begin tonight. It is late, if not yet too late, with the most of us; but it is not yet too late with you. Take Enoch for your father. Take him for your patron patriarch. Take him for your example. Follow him in his blessed footsteps in his family life. It was his first son that made Enoch a saint. As soon as he saw his first child in his image, and in his arms, Enoch became from that day a new man. All men begin to walk for a short season with God when their first child is born; only Enoch, alone almost of all men, held on as he had begun. Enoch's heart ran over to God when his first child was born; and his tender, noble, princely heart never went back from that day from God, never grew cold again, never grew hard again, and never again forgot or neglected God. And as child followed child, Enoch, their father, grew more and more in grace with the growth of his house, till at the last he was not, for God took him. What an inheritance of blessed memories Enoch's children must have had! We all have fathers and mothers with God, for God has taken them; but, unless it was Elijah's children, no man's children ever looked up to heaven with such wondering and worshipping eyes as Enoch's children looked. My father! my father! The chariot of Israel, and the horsemen thereof!

Enoch, the wisest and the happiest of men, began his religious life where most men have not yet come to at the end of their religious life. He began by believing that God IS. With us, with all that we can do, we but attain to occasional hopes and confused convictions that perhaps God IS. We do not, indeed, even at our worst, in as many words deny that God IS. But scarce one in a thousand of our actions is performed, scarce one in a thousand of our words is spoken, on the pure and clear and sure ground that God IS. At our best we believe in a languor and in a dream that God is away out somewhere in the universe. We call Him "infinite" in our catechisms and in our creeds, in our psalms and in our prayers, not thinking what we are saying, and then we go away and live as if He were infinitely far away from us and from this whole world. Only, after death, when at last death comes, we fear that, somewhere and somehow, we shall see God. But Enoch never saw death, because he ever saw God. Enoch never died. Enoch did not need to die. Death could do nothing for Enoch. Death was neither friend nor enemy, first nor last, to Enoch. Death was not appointed for men like Enoch. As Dr. Herrick has it in his *Heretics of Yesterday*, Enoch was the first recorded mystic. "The first mystic of whom we have any record was Enoch, and the four words which furnish us with his whole biography is the best definition we have of true spiritual mysticism—Enoch walked with God." You are an orthodox theologian when you take pen and ink and subscribe with your hand that God IS. But you become a mystical theologian and a spiritual man when you begin to believe with your whole heart that God is beside you, and within you, and is nowhere else for you but in your own heart. Commonplace men see now and then a skirt of God, and catch now and then a broken ray, a scintilla, as a mystic would say, of God's glory; but Enoch walked with God up and down the land of Eden, as a man walketh with his friend. God was in Enoch's heart. "He looked within and saw God mirrored there." Enoch, from the day that his little child was born, felt God shed abroad in his heart. He entered every new morning into his own heart to walk there with God. He walked abroad every morning with his child in his arms, and with his God in his heart. Enoch so entered and so dwelt with God in his own heart, that God could not endure to loan him to this world any longer. When I first heard tell that there was a Book of Enoch, did I not promise myself a great treat! What an autobiography that must be! I wonder, will Enoch enter into particulars, I said to myself, and will he give instances, and tell in plain pedestrian words, giving chapter and verse, and step after step, just as I can understand it and imitate it, how he, Enoch, walked with God: really, and on his own solid feet, and on this solid earth, how he walked with God? But when I made an effort and got the book, what was I in every chapter introduced to and made to walk with, but cherubim and seraphim, principalities and powers, angels and devils, seven holy ones, and four holy ones, and three holy ones; behemoth and leviathan; wild camels, wild boars, wild dogs; eagles and elephants and foxes; giant men and siren women—till I rose up and put Enoch in my shelf and took down William Law. Took William Law to my heart and read in him for the thousandth time his two golden chapters showing, How all orders and all ranks of men and women of all ages are obliged to devote themselves to God; as, also, How great devotion to God fills our lives with the greatest peace and happiness that can be enjoyed in this world. Till, like everybody who takes up William Law, I could not lay him down till I had come to his concluding chapter, "Of the excellency and greatness of a devout spirit." And then, when I turned the last page, and came to the printer's name, I felt like that member of my young men's class who told me that he read Law slowly and grudgingly, counting the pages every now and then, lest he should come too soon to the end. Yes, Dr. Herrick, you are right; Enoch was the first mystic, and his biography is written in as few words as would have pleased the arch-mystics themselves. Enoch, the true and genuine Enoch, never wrote a book, far less The Book of Enoch. But he did for us what very few books know anything about, he walked with God, and so sets us on thinking what walking with God might mean. My brethren, I am not making play with solemn words, nor am I practicing upon you when I say it—walking with God is both the most difficult thing and the most easy thing in all the world. It is so difficult as to be found positively an impossibility by most men; while to one man here and there among men it is as easy to him as breathing is, as easy as eating is when he is hungry, and as drinking is when he is thirsty. Suppose you had exhorted Cain to begin to walk with God from the day that he murdered Abel—it would have taken nothing short of a miracle to make the murderer do it. A miracle could have made him do it, but it would have been a miracle. But suppose, on the other hand, that Enoch had for any cause fallen out of step with God for a single day, what a weary and heavy-laden man you would have had in Enoch that night! But, not to wander so far from home, how few of us ourselves ever enter into our own hearts, where alone God walks with men. God dwelleth not in temples made with hands, nor walketh on the pavement that leads up to such temples. Your first step in the direction of God is not taken when you put on your Sabbath clothes and walk demurely into your pew. No; but it is taken when you put on humility upon your proud heart, and fill your hot heart full of meekness, and resignation, and quietness, and contrition, and a broken, heavenly, holy heart. To hold your peace when you are reproved is a direct and sure step toward God. To be silent when you suffer wrong—God takes at that great moment a great step of His toward you. To let a slight, an insult, a blow, a scoff, a sneer fall on your head like an excellent oil, and on your heart like your true desert—with that man will I dwell, says the God of Israel in His prophet. Every step you take out of an angry heart and into a meek heart; out of envy and into admiration and honor; out of ill-will and into good-will;—on the spot your heavenly Father seeth you and loveth you, and sayeth to His angels, Hast thou considered My new servant? Enoch, on the day his first child was born, just began to lay aside all malice, and all guile, and hypocrisies, and envies, and all evil-speakings, and as a new-born babe desired the sincere milk of the word that he might grow thereby. He just began to live in the Spirit before the dispensation of the Spirit, and walked in the Spirit even before the Spirit was as yet given. And though his family, and his friends, and his enemies did not know so much as the very name of the fruit of the Spirit, they all ate and drank that fruit in Enoch's walk and conversation; for the fruit of the Spirit is love, joy, peace, long-suffering, gentleness, goodness, faith, meekness, temperance, and such like.

Are any of you, my brethren, in your secret heart, in continual fear of death? Are you, though no one knows it, all your lifetime subject to that terrible bondage? Well, Enoch of all the Bible characters is the best of them all for you. For Enoch was translated that he should not see death. Begin then tonight, and as long as you are left on the earth a living man walk with Enoch. Walk with God. Walk with Him into whose presence death never comes, and in whose whole kingdom no grave is ever dug. You have neglected God until tonight. But you are not yet dead. Your body is still warm and free and your own. Your soul is still in this church this Sabbath night. You are not yet in hell. God has not yet in anger said, Cut that cumberer down! Instead of that, He is still waiting to be gracious to you. Begin, then, to walk all the rest of your life on earth with God. And, if you are not to have your name added to the names of Enoch and Elijah; if you are not to be translated; if you are not to remain and to be alive when Christ comes; even so, your death, if it must be, will only be a circumstance in your walk with God. It will only be a striking and a never-to-be-forgotten incident and experience to you. It will only be a new departure, the opening up of a new prospect, and your first entrance on that which God hath prepared for them that love Him. If you will only walk close enough with Enoch and with Enoch's God you will never really taste death. You will not know where you are. Is it past? you will ask in astonishment. Am I really gone over Jordan? And it will all be because you importuned so often on earth, and said, and would not be kept quiet from saying, O wretched man that I am! who shall deliver me from the body of this death? Behold, now, thy Deliverer for whom thou didst so often cry; behold, He has come at thy cry, and has come for thee out of Zion. O death, where is thy sting? O grave, where is thy victory? The sting of death is sin; and the strength of sin is the law. But thanks be to God which giveth us the victory through our Lord Jesus Christ.

6
Jubal

THE Bible has a way of its own of setting the solitary in families. Over and above, and sometimes entirely superseding the original and natural order of father and son, the Bible sets up an intellectual, a moral, and a spiritual order of fatherhood and sonship. As, for instance, thus: In the natural order, according to the flesh, as the Bible would say, Adam was the father of Cain, and Cain was Adam's first-born son. But, in the moral order, Cain was Satan's first-born son. Cain was of his father the devil. The devil was a murderer from the beginning, and Cain took, at his deepest, of his father in hell, for he hated his brother in his heart till he fell upon his brother at an unawares in the field and slew him. Cain was of that wicked one and slew his brother. And that deep and quick principle of family life runs through the whole of the Bible till it comes to a head, and to its fullest and clearest and most commanding expression in the other direction, in that house in Israel when the Son of God stretches forth His hand toward His disciples, and says, Behold My mother and My brethren!

Now, Jubal would seem to have been a solitary man so far as sons and daughters were concerned. Jubal had a brother, Jabal: he was the father of such as dwell in tents, and of such as have cattle. But the Bible is silent as to any children begotten of his own body that Jubal had. The only children that Jubal had in his image and after his likeness were his harp and his organ. For children's shouts and laughter all up and down his solitary house Jubal had only now the sound of his harp and now the sound of his organ. Jubal took to inventing and perfecting his harp and his organ because he had no other children with whom to play and to whom to sing. Or, perhaps, it was that the melodious soul of Jubal was so hurt within him at the way that

> disproportion'd sin
> Jarr'd against nature's chime, and with harsh din
> Broke the fair music that all creatures made
> To their great Lord,

that at last he rose up and said, Go to, I will make melody to God with a stringed instrument and with a praise-breathing pipe if men and women will so forget God. And it was so. And Jubal did so. As for me and my house, Jubal said, we shall make melody in our hearts to God. And he made that melody along with those two children of his, till his harp and his organ were more to him than sons and daughters; far more than Cain and Abel were to Adam, and far more than Shem and Ham and Japheth were to Noah. These same, he said, as he knit a new string into his harp, and hollowed out a new pipe for pipe for his organ—these same shall comfort me concerning my work and the toil of my hands, because of the ground which the Lord hath cursed. And Jubal walked with God after he begat

26

his harp and his organ. And Jubal lived and added string to string in his harp, and pipe to pipe in his organ, till God's angels came and took Jubal home to his harp of gold.

By the time of Moses and Aaron Jubal had a whole tribe to himself of sons and daughters in those melodious men and women who rose up and called him their very and true father, and blessed his honored name. Do you suppose that Jubal's great name was ungratefully forgotten on the shore of the Red Sea that morning? Do not think it. Then Miriam, the prophetess, the sister of Aaron, took a timbrel in her hand, and all the women went out after her with timbrels and with dances. "Who is like unto Thee, O Lord, who is like unto Thee, glorious in holiness, fearful in praises, doing wonders?" And after the schools of the prophets arose in Israel, Jubal's name would be written in letters of gold upon the lintels and the door-posts of those ancient homes of religion and learning and art. "And Samuel kissed the Lord's anointed, and he said to the Lord's anointed, After that thou hast come to the hill of God it shall come to pass that thou shalt meet a company of prophets coming down from the high place, with a psaltery, and a tabret, and a pipe, and a harp before them, and they shall prophesy. And the Spirit of the Lord shall come upon thee, and thou shalt prophesy with them, and thou shalt be turned into another man." And still if you would hear sacred music at its best, and see sacred spectacle at its best, do not go either to the Sistine chapel in Rome, or to the Bayreuth theater in Bavaria, but come to the temple of Solomon, the house of the Lord at Jerusalem. If you would see Jubal's children in their multitudes and at their highest honors, come up to Jerusalem at one of the great feasts. And if you would never be ungenerous again in your contributions to the worship of God, read over and over again the two Books of The Chronicles in your so musical Bible. "So when David was old and full of days, he made Solomon his son king over Israel. And he gathered all the princes of Israel, with the priests and the Levites. Now, the number of the Levites, man by man, was thirty and eight thousand. Of which, four thousand praised the Lord with the instruments which I made (said David) to praise therewith." And again, "He set the Levites in the house of the Lord with cymbals, with psalteries, and with harps, according to the commandment of David, and of Gad the king's seer, and Nathan the prophet, for so was the commandment of the Lord by His prophets. And the Levites stood with instruments of David, and the priests with the trumpets. Moreover, the king and the princes commanded the Levites to sing praises unto the Lord with the words of David, and of Asaph the seer; and they sang praises with gladness, and they bowed their heads and worshipped." The temple in Jerusalem was the earthly palace of Israel's heavenly King; and for riches, and for beauty, and for melody of voices, and for instruments of music God gave commandment that His earthly temple should be made as near to the pattern of His heavenly temple as the hands of His people Israel could make it. "Behold, bless ye the Lord, all ye servants of the Lord, which day and night stand before God in the house of the Lord. Lift up your hands in His sanctuary and bless the Lord. The Lord that made heaven and earth, bless thee out of Zion."

The experts in that kind of history tell us that all the evidence that is forthcoming goes to prove that the apostolic and post-apostolic churches did not make much use of musical instruments in public worship. And the reasons they give for that state of things—a state of things so unlike the Church in Israel in ancient times, and the Church Catholic in modern times—are such as these: The poverty of the people; their persecuted and unsettled condition; and the fact that all the musical instruments then attainable had become incurably tainted with the theatrical and other immoral associations of that dissolute day. But it is pointed out that, as time went on, and when the Christian faith and the Christian worship became the faith and the worship of the empire, then Jubal came back again; till, as we know, in some parts of Christendom today he takes up the whole time and performs the whole service. In the Life of St. Philip Neri, Dr. Newman's patron saint, there is a beautiful chapter on Music. It was written in dear old Philip's rule for his spiritual children that they should all study to rouse themselves to the contemplation of heavenly things by means of musical harmony. And we are told that the sweet old saint was profoundly convinced that there is in music and in song a mysterious and a mighty power to stir the heart with high and noble emotions; as also an especial fitness to raise the heart above time and sense to the love and pursuit of heavenly things. And it was his own exquisite sensitiveness to all harmony that gave him that extraordinary sweetness of expression, of speech, and of gesture which made him so dear to all.

As to the Reformers, we find Luther in his *Table Talk* full of his best heart-eloquence about music. "The fairest and most glorious gift of God," he exclaims, "is music. Kings and princes and great lords should give their support to music. Music is a discipline; it is an instructress; it makes people milder and gentler, more moral, and more reasonable." "Music," he says in another place, "is a fair and glorious gift of God, and takes its place next to theology. I would not part with my small skill in music for much." And yet again: "Music is a fair and sweet gift of God. Music has often given me new life, and inspired me with a desire to preach. Saint Augustine had a conscientious scruple about music. He was, however, a noble and a pious man. And if he lived now he would be on our side." As to the use of instrumental music in the services of the Church of England, it is most interesting and most instructive to find Taylor, with his resounding style, leaning, if anything, against it; while Hooker, with his magnificent sober-mindedness, stands up stoutly for it. Hooker, as his contention with the Puritans goes on, becomes all for instrumental music. That is to say, if Hooker can ever be said to be all for anything but height, and depth, and a superb sober-mindedness.

Those who, like St. Augustine, are noble and pious men, and who like him have a conscientious scruple about instrumental music, if they are determined to fight for their scruple, they will find an all-but-unanswerable arsenal of fighting materials in Jeremy Taylor. Yes, in Jeremy Taylor, of all men in the world. And lest they should not possess the incomparable preacher and debater, I will, in fairness to the truth, supply them with a stone or two for their sling out of that great genius. "The use of musical instruments," says Taylor in his *Ductor Dubitantium*, "may also add some little advantage to singing; but such instruments are more apt to change religion into airs and fancies, and to take off some of its simplicity. Organs are not so fitted as sermons and psalms are for edification. The music of instruments of itself does not make a man wiser; it does not instruct him in anything. At the same time, I cannot condemn it if it be employed as an aid to true psalmody. And yet, at its best, music must not be called so much as a circumstance of divine service, for that is the best that can be said even of the voice itself." And then the omnivorously bookish bishop goes on to fortify his cautious position out of all the apostolic fathers, as his way is. And his way is a right learned, able, and eloquent way, as you will see if you will buy or borrow his *Ductor Dubitantium*, and will redeem enough time to read it. Which you must all do before you root your mind and your heart and your will irrevocably either for or against instrumental music. Read the best that has been written both for and against every subject whatsoever, before you root your temper either for or against the subject in question. And if you are still deep in your reading when the debate is hot, and the votes are being canvassed for, just say to the canvasser that you are not yet half through your reading, and that he must go and enlist those whose reading is finished, and whose enlightened and enfranchised minds are ready for him. And if your too much reading holds you in from making a speech or even from recording a silent vote, you will have lost nothing. You know, and we all know, how you lost your temper, your self-command, and the respect and love of some of your fellow-worshippers, by the way you spoke so often and so long, and voted so ostentatiously, before you had begun to read, or to listen to those who had read, on a former occasion.

And then, reading, and listening to those who have read, and all—before we either open our mouth on this question of music, or cast our vote, a little imagination rightly directed, a very little imagination, will save us from making fools of ourselves, and it will keep us back from offering to God the sacrifice of a fool. Just imagine Almighty God, with this universe of angels and men in His heart and on His hands, and engaged day and night in steering it into an everlasting harbor of harmony and peace, and truth, and wisdom, and love. Take in something of the magnificence and the wisdom and the love of God. And then imagine Him looking down and listening to one of our debates with all our passions in a flame as to whether we are to worship our Maker with a psalm or with a hymn or with a sentence; with an American organ, or with a real, home-built, and high-priced English organ; and, in another place, whether the line is to be given out by the precentor, or the whole psalm read once for all by the minister—and so on to an adjourned meeting on the question. Imagine Gabriel who stands before God, with twain of his burning wings covering his face, and with twain covering his feet, and with twain wherewith to fly—imagine that seraph, full to a flame of the majesty and the glory of God, looking down on the church of God on earth and seeing a minister of Jesus Christ sewing up the paraphrases with needle and thread on a Sabbath morning in terror and in anger lest a neighbor minister should come and give out, "O God of Bethel" to be sung to the God of Bethel; or "'Twas on that night"; or, "How bright these glorious spirits shine." You have heard about the angels weeping, have you not? If you were where Jubal now is you would see their head waters over the way that we quarrel, fall out, and hate one another about our worship of God. Why, very Baal himself would be ashamed of such worshippers with such ideas and with such passions as we have. The fly-god himself would cast us and our vain oblations out of his presence. "God is a Spirit, and they that worship Him must worship Him in spirit and in truth; for the Father seeketh such to worship Him." Only be at peace among yourselves, He says to us. Only give place to one another. Only be of one mind. Only please one another to edification and you will best please Me. Only agree about it among yourselves first, and then come into My house with a psalm, or with a hymn, or with a spiritual song, or with a harp, or with an organ, or with what you will. Call in Jubal, My servant, to assist you, if you feel you need his assistance, and if you are unanimous in your call. Or, sit still as you are till you are unanimous, and let your neighbors call him in who are already unanimous. Only, My little children, have peace among yourselves, and love one another, and so shall ye be Mine accepted worshippers. "The sacrifices of God are a broken spirit: a broken and a contrite heart, O God, Thou wilt not despise. Whoso offereth praise glorifieth Me: and to him that ordereth his conversation aright will I show the salvation of God."

7
Noah

EVEN after the four full chapters that Moses gives to Noah, Peter in the New Testament makes a very important addition to our knowledge of Noah. "Noah the eighth person was a preacher of righteousness," adds the apostle. We have it in as many words from Moses himself, and he gives almost the half of one of his chapters to it, that Noah became a planter of vineyards and an owner of vineyards and a dealer with wine in his old age. But with only eight souls saved, and some of them scarcely saved, there was no evidence at all in Moses that the divine ordinance of preaching had been as yet set up on the earth, and much less that Noah was ordained to that office. Now, as a preacher myself I have a deep professional interest, as well as some other deep interests, in asking myself why it was that Noah was so signally unsuccessful as a preacher. Was it because it was righteousness that he preached? That may very well have been it; for so far as my own experience goes, righteousness is the one thing that our hearers will not have at our hands. All other kinds of preaching—polemical preaching, apologetical preaching, historical and biographical preaching, sacramental preaching, evangelical preaching—some of our people will welcome, and will indeed demand; but they will all agree in refusing and resenting the preaching of righteousness; the preaching of repentance and reformation; the preaching of conversation and conduct and character. No; they would not have it. Josephus supplements Moses and Second Peter, and tells us that Noah preached and pleaded with them to change their dispositions and their actions till he was afraid they would kill him. Of one thing we are sure, Noah did not discredit his preaching by his life, as so many of our preachers do. For Noah had this testimony as long as he was a preacher, that he walked with God. Thee, said the Lord to Noah in giving him his instructions about the ark—Thee only have I seen righteous before Me. My father's tutor, says the author of *The Decline and Fall of the Roman Empire*, believed all that he professed, and practiced all that he enjoined. Could it have been that the preacher's sons and daughters undid all their father's preaching as soon as he had preached it? Physician, heal thyself, did his congregations call out to the preacher of righteousness as he came down from his pulpit and went home to his house? Yes, that would be it. I am almost sure that would be it. For one sinner still destroyeth much good. And we know that Noah had one son—he was his second son, Ham—who helped to bring down his father's gray hairs with sorrow to the grave. What way could a preacher of righteousness be expected to make with a son like his second son among his sons at home? No way at all. It was impossible. That, I feel almost certain, would be it.

I am not to ask you to enter with me into the theophanies of the flood, nor into the naval architecture of Noah and Moses, nor into the geology that emerged after the flood was over, nor into the longevity of Noah and the distribution of his sons. My one and sole aim with you is a practical aim. My one and sole remaining ambition in life is to preach righteousness. To preach righteousness—the nature of it, the means to attain it, the terrible difficulty of attaining it, and the splendid reward it will be to him who at last attains it. To preach righteousness, and all matters connected with righteousness, first to myself, then to my sons, and then to my people. This one thing I do. And in this one light shall I ask you to look at Noah, and at his ark, and at his vineyards, and at his wine, and at Ham, his reprobate son.

Not only did Noah preach his best and his most earnest as the end drew near; not only Noah himself, but every tree that fell in the forest, and every plank that was laid in the ark; every axe-stroke and the echo of every hammer was a louder and ever louder call to the men of that corrupt and violent day to flee from the wrath to come. But, sad to say, the very men without whose help the ark would never have been built; the very men who felled the trees, and planed and laid the planks, and careened and caulked the seams of the finished ship—those very men failed to take a passage in that ship for themselves, for their wives and for their children. Many a skilled and high-paid carpenter, many a strong-limbed and grimy-faced blacksmith, and many a finisher and decorator in woodwork and in iron, must have gnashed their teeth and cursed one another when they saw their children drowning all around them, and the ark shut, and borne up, and lifted up above the earth. But those carpenters and blacksmiths and finishers were wise men and their loss was salvation compared with many of those architects and builders and ornamenters of churches who compete with one another and undersell one another in our day. As also compared with all those publishers and printers and booksellers of Bibles, and all those precentors and choirs and organists, and all those elders and deacons and door-keepers, who are absolutely indispensable to the kingdom of God, but who are all the time themselves outside of it. The Gibeonites in Israel were hewers of wood and drawers of water to Israel; they dwelt in Israel, and had their victuals there, but they were all the time aliens from the commonwealth of Israel. And all Noah's own excellent sermons, all his pulpit appeals about righteousness, and all his crowds of congregations would not have kept his gray head above the rising waters that he had so often described in his sermons, had he not himself gone and done what the Lord commanded him to do. That is to say, had he not, not only prepared the ark, but had he not gone up into the ark, and asked the Lord to shut him in. We ministers may preach the very best of gospels to you, and yet at the end of our ministry be castaways ourselves. "What if I," wrote Rutherford to Lady Kenmure—"What if I, who can have a subscribed testimonial of many who shall stand at the right hand of the Judge, shall myself miss Christ's approval, and be set upon the left hand? There is such a beguile, and it befalleth many. What if it befall me, who have but too much art to cover my own soul and others with the flourish of ministerial, country holiness!" The next Sabbath after that on which Noah preached his last sermon on righteousness, sea monsters were already whelping and stabling in his pulpit.

There had never been such dry seasons since the memory of man. It seemed as if the whole earth would surely die of famine. All the time the ark was a-building the heavens were as brass and the earth as iron. Had Noah preached and prophesied that this terrible drought of rain would last till this generation repented of their corruptions and their violence, there would have been a perfect pentecost among them. Thousands would have turned to the Lord that very day. As it was, many was the day that the worst scoffers at the preachings were of the preacher's own household. Many was the Sabbath-day when Noah disappeared into the forest and fell on his face and prayed that he might have a sign from heaven. But still the branches broke into dust and ashes under him as he wrestled with God for even one little cloud in the sky. And all the chapt and blasted earth around him mocked at him and at his sermons and at his threatenings of a flood of water. But all he ever got for answer to his prayer in the wood was what he already knew, and, indeed, every hour of every day called to mind: "My Spirit shall not always strive with man. Make thee an ark of gopher wood!" Till Noah, moved with fear, returned to his place and worked with all his might for another six days preparing an ark to the saving of his house. The Lord is slow to wrath; slow to a proverb and to a jest. But we have His own warning for it that His Spirit will not always strive with man. Not so much as a man's hand of cloud had been seen for weeks and for months in the west. But no sooner was the ark finished and Noah was shut in, than God arose and gave the signal. And the stormy wind that fulfills His pleasure struck the ark that moment like a park of artillery. And not the ark only, but the whole creation shook, and shuddered, and groaned, and travailed with the wrath of God. The firmament fell in sunder in the twinkling of an eye, and the waters which were below the firmament leaped up to meet the waters which were above the firmament. And the waters prevailed exceedingly upon the earth, and all the high hills that were under the whole heaven were covered. And Noah only remained alive, and they that were with him in the ark.

There has never been anything again on the face of this earth like that ark for the next hundred and fifty days. And there will never be anything like it again till the day of judgment. Such was the wrath of God, and such was the horror and the suspense, the roaring of the storm without, the roaring of the brute beasts within, and the overwhelming fear. There is only one thing that outdoes that ark on this earth, and that is the heart of every regenerate man. No; that is too much to say; not of every regenerate man, but only of that man among the regenerate who has been taken deep down into the noble and saving knowledge of his own heart. With God's judgments against him and against his sin all around him; with his past sin and his present sinfulness finding him out a thousand times every day, knocking at his door, calling in at his window, dogging his steps; with his soul reeling and staggering within him like a drunken man, and with earth and hell let loose within him—that rocking, reeling, midnight ark is a predestinated picture of the soul of every deeply true and deeply exercised saint. Not of sham saints, and not of saints on the surface, but of every son and daughter of fallen Adam who is truly being made in their heart of hearts, and in the divine nature, the sons and daughters of the Lord Almighty, the Lord All-Holy. And most of all are the hearts of God's great saints like that ark in the wild beasts that made that ark hideous to sit in, to eat and drink in, and to sleep and worship in for the next hundred and fifty days and nights. All the evil beasts that ever roared and ravened for their prey were in that ark; each one after his kind. Apes and peacocks were there also, and sparrows and magpies; snakes also, and vipers, and adders. Dogs with their vomit, and sows with their mire. As the blessed Behmen has it about himself: A man's soul is sometimes like a wolf, sometimes like a dog, sometimes like a lion, sometimes like a serpent—subtle, venomous, and slanderous; sometimes like a toad—poisonous, and so on; till my soul, says that singularly subtle and singularly saintly man, is a cage of cruel and unclean birds. And not Behmen's soul only, but yours and mine, if we really know anything at all about the matter in hand. Those wild beasts are all there till God in His great pity opens the windows of heaven over us and says to us: O thou afflicted, tossed with tempests, and not comforted. This is as the waters of Noah unto Me. The mountains shall depart and the hills be removed, but My kindness shall not depart from thee, neither shall the covenant of My peace be removed, saith the Lord that hath mercy on thee. This is the heritage of the Lord; and their righteousness is of Me, saith the Lord.

How did Noah and his household occupy themselves during the whole of that long and dreary voyage? They had no chess and no cards; no old newspapers and no sensational novels. I have no idea how the rest of the family occupied themselves; but I can tell you to a certainty what Noah did. I have no books, said Jacob Behmen, but I have myself. And Noah had himself all those hundred and fifty days and nights. Himself, and Ham, and the woman who had gone down at his door with Ham's name on her drowning lips. He had Shem also, and Japheth, and their wives, and their mother. And if all the romances that ever were written had been on board, and all the games with which men and women have murdered time since time began, do you think that Noah would have had either time or taste for them? What do you think? Do you think he would? There is no way of killing time like prayer. If you would be at the end of your longest voyage before you know where you are, walk with God on the deck of the vessel. Tell Him every day about your children. Tell Him their names. Describe their opening characters to Him. Confide to Him your fears about them. And if one of them has gone astray, or is beginning to go astray, you will have enough in him alone to keep you alone with God for, say, one hour every day. I warrant you the wettest ground under the ark was as dry as tinder before Noah's eyes were dry. They all feared to ask their father why he wept as he walked with God, for they all knew quite well that it was for them that he so walked and so wept.

"And the sons of Noah that went forth of the ark were Shem, Ham, and Japheth." There will be plenty of men that will go forth of earth and into heaven with all Ham's evil memories, and more. But from the north pole to the south pole, and from the rising to the setting of the sun in the new heavens and the new earth, there will not be so much as one man found there with Ham's still lewd, still hard, and still impenitent heart.

8
Ham

THERE was an old vagabond, to vice industrious, among the builders of the ark. He had for long been far too withered for anything to be called work; and he got his weekly wages just for sitting over the pots of pitch and keeping the fires burning beneath them. That old man's heart was as black as his hands. It was of him that God had said that it grieved and humbled Him at His heart that He had ever made man. The black asphalt itself was whiteness itself beside that old reprobate's heart and life. Now Ham, Noah's second son, was never away from that deep hollow out of which the preparing pitch boiled and smoked. All day down among the slime-pits, and all night out among the sultry woods—whereever you heard Ham's loud laugh, be sure that lewd old man was either singing a song there or telling a story. All the time the ark was a-building, and for long before that, Ham had been making himself vile under the old pitch-boiler's instructions and examples. Ham's old instructor and exemplar had gone down quick to hell as soon as the ark was finished and shut in. But, by that time, Ham could walk alone. Dante came upon his old schoolmaster in hell when he was being led through hell on his way to heaven; and so did Ham when he went to his own place. But that was not yet. Ham was not vile enough yet. His day of grace had not come to an end yet. His bed in hell was not all made yet. He had more gray heads to bring down to the grave first. He had to break his old father's heart first. As he will soon now do, if you will wait a moment. Ham had been born out of due time. Ham had not been born and brought up in his true and proper place. Ham should have been born and bred in Sodom and Gomorrah. Not the ark, lifted up above the waters of the flood, but the midnight streets of the cities of the plain were Ham's proper place. The pairs of the unclean beasts that Ham attended to with his brothers were clean and chaste creatures of God compared with Ham. For Ham could neither feed those brute beasts, nor bed them, nor look at them, nor think about them without sin. More than one of those abused beasts will be brought forward at the day of judgment to bear testimony against one of their former masters. From a little boy Noah's second son had been a filthy dreamer. The best and the holiest words his father could speak had an unclean sense to his son. Every vessel in the ark and every instrument held an unclean association for Ham. Within all those steaming walls the only truly brute beast was Noah's second son. Sensuality takes a most tremendous revenge on the sensual sinner. What an inexpiable curse is a defiled mind! Well might Bishop Andrewes pray every night of the week for all his life, and that too, with sweat and tears, that his transgressions might not be retained upon him as his punishment. It would be ill to imagine a worse punishment than an imagination steeped in sin. "O!" cries Dr. Newman, "the inconceivable evil of sensuality!" "If you once begin to think about forbidden things," says Cicero, "you will never be able to think about anything else."

It is not in as many words in Moses, but I have read it elsewhere, that there was a woman who clung to the door of the ark which was in the side thereof; and the woman cried and prayed. Ham! she cried. Ham, my husband! she cried. Ham, my destroyer! Preacher of righteousness! she cried, open thy door! Where is thy God? Open thy door and I will believe. Throw out thy son Ham to me, and I will take him to hell in my arms! Is there a woman within these walls, or are they all she-wolves? and she dashed her head against the shut door. Mother of Ham! Wife of Ham! Sisters of Ham! she cried. My mother's blood is on his skirts. My own blood is on his hands! Cursed be Ham! And the ark shook under her words and her blows. And Ham, Noah's second son, listened in the darkness and through the seams of pitch. And then he kneeled in prayer and in thanksgiving, and he blessed the God of his fathers that she had gone down, and that the waters still prevailed.

Why do the sons of our preachers of righteousness so often go wrong? you will often hear it asked. I do not know that they do. But, even if they did, I would not wonder. Familiarity, and near neighborhood, to some orders of mind, naturally breed contempt. And then, our preachers are so busy. Composing so many sermons; holding together, by hook or by crook, so many straggling congregations; fighting, now this battle and now that in church and in state; and worst of all, with all that, sitting down to write a book. As good almost kill a man as kill a good book, said a great man, who was much better at making a good book than he was at bringing up a good child. But what a bitter mockery it must be, especially to a minister, to hear his books called good on every hand and bought by the thousand, and then, soon after, to see his sons and his daughters neglected, grown up, and gone astray! To me there is one specially awful word in Bishop Andrewes' *Devotions*. Words like that word always make me hide my Andrewes out of sight. "What a strange person Keble is! There is Law's *Serious Call*—instead of leaving it about to do people good, I see he reads it, and puts it out of the way, hiding it in a drawer." The word I refer to may not make you hide your Andrewes out of sight. Words differ and grow awful or otherwise as the people differ who employ them. "I have neglected Thee, O God!" That, to me, is the awful word. We speak of parents neglecting their children. But we, your ministers, above all other men, neglect God, and that in nothing more than in the way we neglect our children. After the clean beasts and the beasts that are not clean shall have witnessed against Ham, and before Ham is taken away, he will be taken and questioned and made to tell how busy his father was, day and night, all these years, preaching righteousness and building the ark. Everybody all around knew what went on among the slime-pits by day and among the warm woods by night—everybody but the preacher of righteousness. Ham will tell—you will all hear him telling—how his father worked, in season and out of season, at the work of God. Concerning Noah standing on His right hand the angry Judge will interrogate Ham standing on His left hand. Did My servant here, thy father, ever restrain thee from making thyself vile? Did he, or did he not? Speak to Me the truth. And Ham will swear to it, and will say before the great white throne this: My father is innocent of me, Ham will say. My father never knew me. My vileness is all my own. No man ever had a father like my father. O Noah, my father, my father! Ham will cry.

All this time, as Ham will witness, Noah knew nothing of all that we know now. Noah was as innocent of the knowledge of his second son's past life as he still is of what will come to light at the last day. And thus it was that, as soon as the preacher of righteousness stepped out of the ark, he did exactly what we could have told you he would do. Noah went forth, and his sons and his wife, and his sons' wives with him. And Noah built an altar unto the Lord, and the Lord smelled a sweet savor, and said, While the earth remaineth, seedtime and harvest, and cold and heat, and summer and winter, and day and night shall not cease. And now, with all that has passed, what a Noah you will surely see! Come, all you fathers who have come through trouble, and you will see here how you are to walk with a perfect heart before your house at home. What a father Noah will be, and what a husband, and what a husbandman! If we had come through a hundredth part of Noah's terrible experience; and then had found a hundredth part of Noah's grace at God's hand; we, too, would have said, As for me and my house, we shall walk with a perfect heart and shall serve the Lord. And God spake unto Noah, and to his sons with him, saying, And I, behold, I establish My covenant with you, and with your seed after you. And the bow shall be in the cloud, and I will look upon it that I may remember My everlasting covenant. And the sons of Noah that went forth of the ark were Shem, Ham, and Japheth; and Ham is the father of Canaan.

In his beautiful sermon on "The World's Benefactors," Dr Newman asks, "Who, for example, was the first cultivator of corn? Who first tamed and domesticated the animals whose strength we use and whom we make our food? Or who first discovered the medicinal herbs which, from the earliest times, have been our resource against disease? If it was mortal man who first looked through the animal and vegetable worlds, and discriminated between the useful and the worthless, his name is unknown to the millions whom he has benefited." Only, Noah's name is quite well known to the millions he has benefited; as, also, to the millions he has cursed and destroyed. Corn and wine, the Bible always says. The first farmer who sowed, and reaped, and threshed, and ground, and baked corn, we do not know his name. But we have Noah's name now open before us; it was he who first planted a vineyard and manufactured its grapes into intoxicating drink. Millions every day bless the day he did it, and pledge his name for doing it; while other millions curse the day. And which of these cries goes up best before God another day will declare. Only, if you would read and remember your Bible before you eat and drink, you would know better how to eat and how to drink so as to do all to the glory of God, and against that day. And it is surely significant, with an immense and an eloquent significance, that the Bible tells us that the first vine-dresser at his first vintage was found in a state such as Ham and Shem and Japheth found their father. It would be at the time of harvest and ingathering. Or, perhaps, it was a birthday feast—the birthday feast of his first son, or it might be of his second son. Or, to make another guess where we do not know, perhaps it was the anniversary of the laying of the keel of the ark; or of the shutting-to of the door of the ark; or of the day when the tops of the mountains were seen; or of the day when the dove came into the window of the ark with an olive-leaf in her mouth plucked off. It was certainly some such glad and exalted day as one of these. Come, my sons, said the old saint over his wine;

come, let us eat and drink today and be merry. The fathers are full of far-fetched explanations and apologies for Noah. One will have it that, admitting the drunkenness, still Noah was all the time innocent; it was the unusually strong wine that did it. It was the too-heady wine that was alone to blame. Another will have it that Noah did not know this new drink he had stumbled on from milk. And yet another, that the whole history is a mysticism, and that the preacher of righteousness was only drunk in a figure. But the Bible does not mince matters; nor does it waste words even on Noah. In the Bible the "saints are lowered that the world may rise."

Now, who of all Noah's household should happen to come in at that evil moment but Ham; and he, too, flown with insolence and with his father's wine. But, blessed be the Lord God of Shem; and God from that hour shall surely enlarge Japheth. How, still, it humbles and chastens such sons as Noah's first and third sons to see their parents' imperfections—their father's faults at table, and their mother's follies everywhere. Shem's and Japheth's respect and reverence all remained. Their love for their father and their honor for him were not any less, but were much more, after the noble and beautiful service they did him that day. Only, ever after that terrible day, with what watchfulness did those two brothers go out and come in! With what wistfulness did they look at their father as he ate and drank! With what solicitude, and with what prayer, and not for their father only, did Shem and Japheth lie down at night and rise up in the morning! It brought Noah, and Shem, and Ham, and Japheth back again to Moses' mind when he received and read and transcribed the Fifth Commandment on Mount Sinai: Honor thy father and thy mother, that thy days may be long upon the land which the Lord thy God giveth thee.

It is easy for those who are standing on the shore to shout their counsels to those who are sinking in the sea. It is easy for those who are in cold blood to tell a man in hot blood how he should behave himself. And it is easy for us sitting here, with all our passions at our heel for the moment, to moralize over the preacher of righteousness when he awoke from his wine. At the same time, it is only by laying such sudden and ungovernable outbursts as his was to heart that we shall ever learn how to hold ourselves in when we are mad with anger at our children. I have more understanding, says the psalmist, than all my teachers; for Thy testimonies are my meditation. I understand more than the ancients, because I keep Thy precepts. Now, if David's hot anger against Absalom or Solomon had come upon him when he was in that mind, and had he remembered ancient Noah and his wakening from his wine, what would David have done? With the Holy Spirit not taken away from him, David would have recollected his former falls, and he would have retreated back upon his own fifty-first psalm. He would have taken Absalom, whom he so much loved, and the angry father and the exasperating son would have kneeled down together, and then David would have said, with weeping, Who can bring a clean thing out of an unclean? Wash me thoroughly from mine iniquity. Purge me with hyssop. Then will I teach transgressors Thy way! And Ham himself would have fallen on his father's neck, and would have said, I am not worthy to be called thy son! Fathers and mothers, when our children are overtaken again in a fault, instead of cursing them and striking at them, and casting them out of doors as Noah did, let us say to ourselves that we have only begotten our children in our own image. Let us then, for that is the best time to do it—let us take them, and go with them, and beseech God to melt them, and change them, and alter them, and make them not our sons and daughters any more, but His own. And see if He will not do it. See if He will not deliver them over again to us with these words, Take them and bring them up for Me, and I will give thee thy wages. "If a father is intemperate," says William Law, "if he swears and converses foolishly with his friends, let him not wonder that his children cannot be made virtuous. For there is nothing that teaches to any purpose but our ordinary temper, our common life and conversation; and almost all people will be such as those amongst whom they were born and bred. If a father would pray every day to God to inspire his children with true piety, great humility, and strict temperance, what could be more likely to make the father himself become exemplary in these virtues? How naturally would he grow ashamed of wanting such virtues as he thought necessary for his children."

Now, all we here are the sons and daughters of one or other of Noah's three sons. By those three men were all the nations of the earth divided after the flood. And we are the sons of Ham, if we are his sons, by this—When every imagination of our heart is defiled. When we are in lewd company. When we have enjoyment over an unclean song, an unclean story, or an unclean newspaper report. When we steal a lewd book and take it to our room with us at night. When we hide away an impure picture in our drawer, where Keble hid the *Serious Call*. When we report our neighbor's shame. When we tell our companion not to repeat it; but when we would burst if we did not repeat it. When we rush to pen and ink to advertise abroad some fall or some fault of our brother. When we feel that we have lost something when his fault is explained, or palliated, or covered and forgotten, and when he is set on his feet again. Ham's sons and daughters have not all black hands and black faces. Many of them have their hands and their faces as white as a life of cosmetics and idleness can whiten them. While, all the time, Ham holds their black hearts. My brethren, let us henceforth begin to be the sons and daughters of Shem and Japheth. Let us refuse to look at, or to be told about, anything that exposes, not our own father or son or brother only, but all other men's fathers, and mothers, and sons, and brothers. Let us keep our eyes shut to the sight of it, and our ears shut to the sound of it. Let us insist on looking on the best, the most blameless, and the most serviceable side of our neighbor. Let us think of Noah as a preacher of righteousness; as the builder of the ark; as elected, protected, and delivered by God; and as, with all his falls, all the time in God's sure covenant of peace, and under God's rainbow and God's oath. And when he is overtaken in a fault, ye that are spiritual restore such an one in the spirit of meekness, lest thou also be tempted. Some one has called the Apostle Paul the first perfect Christian gentleman. I shall always after this think of Shem and Japheth as Paul's Old Testament forerunners in that excellent, beautiful, and noble character.

9
Nimrod

NIMROD was Noah's great-grandson through Ham; and he was a mighty hunter. He was the father, as William Law has it, of all those English gentlemen who take their delight in running foxes and hares out of breath. With one drop of his ink, and with one stroke of his pen, Moses tells us a great deal about Nimrod; and, the masterly writer that he is, Moses leaves still more to our imagination. "And Cush begat Nimrod; he began to be a mighty one in the earth. He was a mighty hunter before the Lord; wherefore it is said, Even as Nimrod the mighty hunter before the Lord." Nimrod's name, you will see, was a proverb in Israel down even to the day that Moses composed this book. Dante, also, Moses' equal in condensation and in force, lets us see that vast, vague, looming, swelling, gibbering giant in his thirty-first Inferno. His shoulders, his breast, his arms, his ribs—Dante is amazed at the cloudy glimpse he gets of Ham's grandson down among the gloomy pits. O senseless spirit! shouts Virgil at the giant. And then to his charge:

> Nimrod is this,
> Through whose ill-counsel in the world no more
> One tongue prevails. But pass we on, nor waste
> Our words; for so each language is to him,
> And his to others, understood by none.

Matthew Henry, still the prince of commentators for the common people, says that Nimrod, no doubt, did great good by his hunting instinct at the beginning of his career. He would put his people under deep obligation by ridding them of the wild beasts that infested those early lands. But then, as time went on, and as Nimrod's ambition grew, he would seem to have taken to hunting men instead of beasts. Great conquerors, after all, are but great hunters before the Lord. Alexander himself, the Great, as we call him, is to Daniel but a great pushing he-goat. And from that Nimrod was led on to build cities with walls, and towers, and barracks, and fortresses. Note of Nimrod's ambition, says our sagacious commentator, that it was boundless, expensive, restless, over-bold, and blasphemous.

Archbishop Whately thinks that the whole story of the building of the Tower of Babel, the confounding of the speech of the builders, and their consequent disruption and dispersion, north, south, east, and west, is a veiled history of a great outbreak of religious controversy in that early and eastern day. The archbishop does not pretend to have discovered just what the great controversy was all about; probably the whole thing would be unintelligible to us. But, on the whole, he thinks it must have been some dispute connected with the worship of God. In 1849 there was much less freedom allowed in the Church of England for such speculations than there is in our day; and thus it was that Dr. Whately had to come out about the Tower of Babel in one of the foreign tongues of Babel, and behind the veil of anonymity. A living writer in the same church looks on the Tower of Babel as a "sublime emblem"; and Landor makes Isaac Barrow and Isaac Newton talk together in his noble English about that Tower as if it had been, at the top at least, the first astronomical observatory of those Babylonian fathers of that queen of the sciences. But we come back from all these, not uninstructive speculations in their way, to the powerfully written passage before us, in which so much is told us in such small space. "Go to, let us go down, and there confound their language, that they may not understand one another's speech."

Philo Judaeus, the father of allegorical interpretation, has a beautiful tract entitled *The Confusion of Languages.* But Jacob Behmen, Philo's Teutonic son, far outstrips his Hebrew father in the depth, pungency, directness, and boldness of his interpretations and his applications. Babel, to Philo, is the soul of man; the confounded, confused, and scattered-abroad soul of man; and in his confused and scattered treatise we stumble on not a few things that are both wise and deep and beautiful. To Behmen, Babel is all that it is to Philo, with this characteristic addition, that Behmen's books are full of contemporaneous examples and illustrations of the Babel-like confusion that had come already to the Reformed Church of his day. Babel, to Behmen, is full of the controversies, verbal orthodoxies and heterodoxies, misunderstandings, misconstructions, and heart hatreds of the mighty hunters of his day. Babel, "philosophically taken," was to Philo the sum total of the passions of the soul let loose on the individual; evangelically taken, to Behmen, Babel was all those passions let loose also on the body of Christ. It is not easy and plain for any one of us to put our finger on our own Babel, says Behmen. For we are all working at the building of that Tower: we are all too much given over to words and to names, to sects and to parties, to men and to churches. Words rule us, and things lose all power over us. Names master us and tyrannize over us. Let every man enter into himself, and he will be sure to find a whole Tower of Babel, with all its consequences, standing in his own mind and in his own heart continually. The only possible escape from that Tower and its confoundings and confusions is to get clean away from the letter which killeth, and to go down into the spirit which giveth liberty and life. Leave off all disputations and all divisive words and names, and begin thy life again with God and with love alone. As Paul was not to be absolutely ignorant of everything but Christ and Him crucified all the time that he was to know nothing else, so Behmen is not to deny, or forswear, or for ever forget the Lutheran catechisms and confessions of his day; only, he is to go beneath them all to the ground out of which they all spring, and above them all to the light and the air in which they all live and grow. And then he hopes to return to them with a love and a light and a life and a freedom that verbal Babel knows nothing of. Arguments, controversies, debates, disputes, even when they are true and needful, have always something of Babel in them; and they who must engage in them will have need of another and a better life outside of them, beneath them, and above them, as Jacob Behmen had.

And thus to come home, and to take current controversy among ourselves: political, religious, and, indeed, all kinds of controversy; if you will look well to it you will soon see why the name of it all is to be called Babel. All true moralists, all true logicians, all true teachers of rhetoric, unite to tell us and to testify to us that we all deceive and damage both ourselves and our neighbors and the truth every day by our words; by our misuse and our abuse of words. Words, indeed, are both the instrument and the vehicle of all thought and all intercourse. We cannot think, any more than we can speak or write, without words. But, unless we are early and well-taught, and unless we continually watch and teach ourselves, we shall become the complete slaves of our own instruments, and our carriages shall run away with us continually. "Words are wise men's counters; wise men do but reckon by them; but they are the money of fools." To prove that and to illustrate that, I had collected and arranged a table of wise men's counters and fools' moneys, and had intended to take in that table here. But I have departed from that intention. I have departed from that intention lest some of you should go off upon a word, and leave the proper and full lesson unlearned. It will be far better that each man who is intent on his own deliverance and improvement, should make up such a table of political, theological, scientific, and social controversialisms for himself, and out of his own conversation, and should, as Socrates would have taught him, ask himself, cross-question himself even, as to what he means by them when he uses them. Let us get into the truly intellectual, truly moral, and truly religious habit of asking ourselves, and insisting on an answer from ourselves, What is that name, nickname, by-word, that I am casting abroad about my brother so loudly and so loosely? What is the original root of it in language, and in me? What does it connote, as the schools say, first in my own mind, and then in its true content, and then in my hearer's or reader's capacity? Is it fair to use such a name and nick-name? Is it just? Is it true? Would I like such and such names and nicknames to be attached to me by those who are opposed to me? It is very annoying, and, indeed, exasperating, to be pulled up in that way when our eloquence and our indignation and our denunciation are in full flood. But truth, love, goodness, godliness, are to be achieved by no man on any easier terms. As Behmen would say, Babel is to be escaped in no other way. And, since Behmen is so full and so good, as I think, on Babel, and since he himself has been so much the victim of Babel—more almost than any man I know—let me show you once more the kind of thing that has made me love him: and, almost to say of him, as Dr. Newman says of Thomas Scott, that he owes him his own soul. I do not owe my soul to Behmen, or to any of his school; but I owe some lessons in my soul's deliverance and purification that I would be a cold-hearted creature if I did not on all hands acknowledge and share with you. A true Christian, says Teutonicus in his *Regeneration*, a Christian who is born anew into the Spirit of Christ, has less and less mind to contend and strive about matters of religion. He has enough to do within himself. A true Christian is really of no church. He can dwell surrounded by all the churches. He can even enter them all, and take part in all their services, without being bound up with any one of them. He has but one creed, which is, Christ in him. If men would but as fervently seek after love and righteousness as they do after disputatious matters, we should soon all be the children of one Father; and there would be no matters left to dispute about. If we did not know half so many contrary doctrines, and were more like little children; if we only had more good-will to those who hold the contrary doctrine, the contrariness would soon give way, and we would all be of one mind. Ungodly ministers go about sowing abroad contentions, reproaches, misconstructions; and, then, ungodly people catch all these up and make an ungodly religion out of them, and bring forth fruit accordingly. They despise, revile, slander, and misrepresent one another, till Babel, and all its sins and miseries, is again falling on us and burying us. What, asks Freher at himself and at the Spirit of his Master—what is an honest, simple Christian to do amidst such a variety of sects and contentions? He is to keep out of them; and he is to thank God that he has neither the call, nor the talent, nor the temptation to enter into them. He is to keep his heart clean and sweet to all men, and hot and bitter only at himself. No man's persuasion justifies me in hating him. And if I hate his persuasion too much, if I give up too much of my passion to hating any man's persuasion, I will soon end in hating himself. I must hate that only which hinders me myself from being a new creature in Christ Jesus. Therefore is the name of all controversy called Babel by the great mystics, the great masters of the life of love in the soul.

10
Terah

THE first Jew was a Gentile. The first Hebrew was a heathen. The father of the faithful himself was, to begin with, a child of wrath even as others. To no man on the face of the earth had it been said as yet that to him and to his seed pertained the adoption, and the glory, and the covenants, and the giving of the law, and the service of God, and the promises. Why, we may well wonder, why was the covenant of life so long in coming in, and in taking effect? Why—since God will have all men to be saved, and to come unto the knowledge of the truth—why were all the families of the earth not embraced in the covenant of life at once? Why was that new covenant not made with Adam, the father of us all? There would surely have been a fine fitness had Adam been our father in the covenant of grace as well as in the covenant of works. Now, why was he not? It may have been because he had made such a fatal breakdown in his first covenant. Or, it may have been because he had never taken that tremendous breakdown sufficiently home to heart. Neither the greatest sanctity nor the greatest service is forfeited by the truly and sufficiently penitent man. And it must surely have been that Adam lost the fatherhood of all penitent, believing, and holy men by the lack of depth and intensity and endurance in his repentance. Abel, Adam's second son, would have made a most excellent covenant-head. And, almost to a certainty, we, today, would have been called the children of faithful and acceptable Abel but for his brother's envy, and but for that foul and fatal blow in the field. Enoch, in the lack of Abel, would have made a model Abraham. How Enoch would have walked with God in Ur of the Chaldees, and in Haran, and in Canaan, and in Egypt, and back again in Canaan, confessing, all the time, that he was a stranger and a pilgrim with God on the earth! How Enoch would have told and would have taught his children after him that without faith it is impossible to please God! How he would have gone before them and shown them the way to come to God, believing that He is, and that He is a rewarder of them that diligently seek Him! But the divine will was in a strait betwixt two in Enoch's case. Enoch was sorely needed on earth, indeed; but his own desire to depart, taken together with God's desire to have Enoch with Him, carried the day; which carriage, for Enoch, at any rate, was far better. Noah, we would have boldly said, was expressly made for the faithful place, and the place for him. For by faith Noah, being warned of God of things not seen as yet, moved with fear, prepared an ark to the saving of his house; by the which he condemned the world, and became heir of the righteousness which is by faith. And then, Noah was a preacher of righteousness to boot. But, instead of the faithful, Noah lived to become the father of all those who drown all their covenants of faith and of works alike, both with God and with man, in the wine-fat. All this time, then, all this disappointed and postponed time, the angel of the covenant had been passing unceasingly from land to land, and from nation to nation, and from tongue to tongue seeking for some of Adam's sons who should be found worthy to take up the calling and election of God; till, at last, the star came and stood over the house of Terah, on the other side of the flood. Now, this Terah, in his inherited and invincible ignorance, served other gods, and he had brought up Abram, his so devout son, to the same service. But those two Gentile men, father and son, served their Gentile gods with such truly Jewish service that God was constrained to wink at their unwilling ignorance. The God of all grace graciously accepted Terah and Abram for their love and for their obedience to the light that lighteth every man that cometh into the world. And thus it was that the true God raised up Abram the son of Terah, that righteous man from the east, and called him to his foot, gave the nations before him, and made him rule over kings. And thus it was also that Abram's second greatest son put Abram his father into his great catholic sermon on Mars hill, and said this about Abram: God, he said, that made the world, hath made of one blood all nations of men, that they should seek the Lord, if haply they might feel after Him and find Him, though He be not far from every one of us. For in Him we live and move and have our being; for we also are His offspring. To Him that hath shall be given, is an absolute and a universal law and rule with the God of righteousness. And thus it was that He said to Abram, the son of Terah, in Ur of the Chaldees: Well done, good and faithful servant. Because thou hast been faithful over a few things, I will make thee ruler over many things. Get thee out of thy country, and from thy kindred, and from thy father's house, into a land that I will show thee.

It would have been entirely true to nature, and it would have been a most beautiful and a very fine lesson to all the families of the earth, had the divine call come to Terah, the father, and had Terah taken Abram, and had the son set out with the father to go together to the land of promise. But it is above and beyond nature, and it is a still nobler and a still more sublime sight, to see the call coming to the son, and then to see the father submitting himself to that call; entirely and immediately accepting it; and setting out under his chosen son to act upon that call and to follow it out. I can easily imagine a thousand suspicions, and rebukes, and remonstrances, and threatenings that Terah might have addressed to his son Abram when he first communicated the vision and the voice to his Chaldean father. It would be no imagination to repeat to you some of Terah's refusals, and remonstrances, and indictments, and protestations, and punishments. We have heard them, or the like of them, a thousand times. We have heard them as often as the same heaven opened and the same voice spoke to the young intellectual and spiritual emigrants of our New Testament day. But not one word of such stagnation, stubborn, unbelieving speeches came out of the mouth of Abram's noble father. Far from that. Nay, I know not that we would ever have had Abram, or would ever have heard his name, unless his humble-hearted, youthful-hearted, brave-hearted and believing-hearted old father had taken his chosen son by the hand, and his chosen son's wife, and had said, Yes, my son Abram, and my daughter Sarai, yes, let us set out at once for the land of Canaan. Why Terah himself was not taken, and himself made the father of the faithful, we do not know; unless it was that he was to stand at the head of human history in a still nobler fatherhood and a still more honorable office. That is to say, to be the patron patriarch and first father of all humble-minded, open-minded, free-minded, and hospitable-minded old men all the world over. Yes, that was it. Terah was taken in Ur of the Chaldees, and was there made the type and the teacher of all those wise men of the east, and of the west, and of the north, and of the south: all the elect within the election, and without: all those men old in years, but whose eye is not dim, nor their intellectual nor their spiritual strength one iota abated. Terah is the Magian father of all those sweet, wise, beautiful souls who stand rooted in a green and genial old age: all those in whom, though their outward man may perish, yet their inward man is renewed day by day. Terah, the father of Abram, is at the same time the father of all those statesmen, and churchmen, and theologians, and philosophers, as well as of all those many plain men among us, who to old age are still open to all divine visions and to all divine voices; to all new truth and to all new light; to all new departures in divine providence and in divine progress, and then to all new opportunities and all new duties. They are all Abram's brethren, and they all take of Terah, his father. All they whose living faith in the ever-living God is such that they see and feel His heavenly life still quickening all existence, and His heavenly light still lighting all men in His living word, in His living church, in His living providences, and in the living souls of all His children. A teachable, tractable, pliable son is a fine sight to see, and such a son is the best blessing that any good father can have of God. But a still teachable, tractable, pliable-minded, genial-minded, hopeful-minded father is a still finer sight to see; a still rarer, nobler, and even more delightful sight to see. A father who reads his reading son's best books, and who sits at the feet of his student son's best teachers, and who walks arm in arm with his elect son away out of the worn-out past and away up into the land of promise—that is a father to descend from, and to be proud of above peers and princes. A father who unites a large and a sage experience to a free spirit of expectation, and enterprise, and hope, and steadfast faith, and full assurance. And, thank God, at every new vision and at every new voice of His we ever find such sons of Terah in the church and in the state, in the congregation and in the family, and a right honorable place they fill, and a right fruitful. Get thee out of thy country, and from thy kindred, and from thy father's house, into a land that I will show thee. And Terah took Abram his son and Sarai his daughter-in-law, his son Abram's wife, and he went forth with them from Ur of the Chaldees, to go into the land of Canaan. Let all our old and venerable men continue to take Terah for their first father till their flesh is given back to them like the flesh of a little child, and till their youth is renewed like the eagle's.

As it turned out, then, it was neither Adam, nor Abel, nor Enoch, nor Noah, nor Terah, but it was Abram, Terah's choicest son, who was installed of God into the fatherhood of all foreknown, predestinated, called, justified, and glorified men. But, with all his excellent natural qualities and abilities, and with all that Terah could teach his son—and then, to crown all, when he took his staff in his hand and walked out of Ur not knowing whither he went—with all that parental instruction and example, Abram still had, himself, great things both to undergo and to perform before he was ready to be made the father of a faithful seed. A great bereavement,

a great disappointment, a great temptation, a great transgression, a great humiliation, and a great surrender of his rights—all these great experiences, and more
than all these, had to be passed through, and their full fruits had to be reaped up
into Abram's heart and life and character, before Abram could be trusted, could be
counted on, as the foundation stone of the Old Testament Church; and before the
patriarchs, and prophets, and psalmists, and kings of Israel could be built up upon
him. I am the Almighty God; walk before Me and be thou perfect. But, like his
far-off Son, Abram had first to be made perfect through suffering. And Abram's
first baptism of suffering was not so much the leaving of his fatherland; it was
much more the death of Terah his father and his fellow-traveller. Plato says that
there is always a little child hidden away deep down in the very oldest man's heart.
And Abram's heart was just the heart to have hidden away deep down in it Terah's
little child. And that little child awoke in Abram's heart, and filled the tent and
the camp with its cries and with its tears when Terah too soon gave up the ghost
in Haran. As long as Abram had his father beside him and before him, faith, and
love, and hope, and obedience were all easy to Abram. With a father like Terah to
talk to, to pray and to praise with, and to walk arm in arm with at the head of the
emigrant household, Abram's face shone like the sun as he turned his back on the
land of his nativity. All that Abram really cared for came out of Chaldea with him.
Terah, his venerable father; Sarai, his beautiful sister-wife; and Lot, his managing
nephew; and under Lot's charge all his flocks and herds; and, above all, with this
new, amazing, divine hope and secret in his heart—with all that with him Abram
walked with God, and was already perfect. But the sudden death of Terah made
that happy Chaldean company to come to a standstill in Haran. It made Abram
stand still. It changed the whole world to Abram. Abram's believing heart was
absolutely buried in his believing father's grave in Haran. But such was the depth,
and the sincerity, and the true piety of Abram's mourning for his father, that, by
the time that the days of his mourning were accomplished, Abram's first faith in
God had come back again to his dead heart. The call of God sounded more and
more commanding in his mourning heart; till the promise became, even more
than at the beginning, both a staff of God in his hand and a cordial of God in his
heart. As a great psalmist-son of his sang of himself in after days in Israel—when
Abram's father and mother forsook him, then the Lord took him up. All the same,
the whole after way from Haran to Shechem was often a solitary and a steep way to
Abram: a dim, a headless, and a leaderless way to Terah's pious and childlike son.
At the same time, when Terah died in Haran, and when Abram took the old man's
death to heart with such grief, with such resignation, with such an assured reliance
upon the divine promise, and with such full assurance of God's grace, and truth,
and power, and faithfulness, a great step was taken both to the land of promise,
and to Abram's predestination as the father of all faithful men.

Abram's great bereavement was immediately followed by a great disappointment. The Lord thy God, so sang the call and the promise in Abram's hopeful
heart—The Lord thy God bringeth thee into a good land, a land of brooks of
water, of fountains and depths that spring out of valleys and hills; a land of wheat,
and barley, and vines, and fig trees, and pomegranates; a land of oil olive and

honey; a land wherein thou shalt eat bread without scarceness, thou shalt not lack anything in it; a land whose stones are iron, and out of whose hills thou mayest dig brass. But no sooner had Abram begun to build an altar at Bethel; no sooner had he begun to lengthen his cords and to strengthen his stakes, than a terrible famine of all these things fell on the whole land. Till Lot only put words upon the terrible darkness that fell on Abram's overwhelmed heart when he upbraided Abram, and said, Would God we also had died in Haran! Would God we had listened to our kinsmen in Chaldea when they dissuaded us from this folly and from this wilderness! The hands of the pitiful women have sodden their own children; they that did feed delicately are desolate in the streets; they that were brought up in scarlet embrace the dung-hill. We have drunken our water for money; our wood is sold to us. We have given the hand to Egypt, and to Assyria that we may have bread. No wonder that after such a sudden collapse of hope as that, Abram's faith completely gave way for a season. Sarai was all that Abram now had. She was the wife of his youth. She had come with him and she had stood beside him in all his losses and disappointments; and if he should lose Sarai in Egypt everything was lost. Say, I pray thee, that thou art my sister, that it may be well with me for thy sake, and my soul shall live because of thee. And Sarai was as weak as her husband was, and she fell into the same snare of unbelieving fear. Till the end of that sad business was that the Lord plagued Pharaoh and his house with great plagues because of Sarai, Abram's wife. And till Pharaoh called Abram and bitterly rebuked him. Were you ever bitterly rebuked for your sin by some one far beneath you in age, in knowledge, in experience, and in the calling and the grace of God? Did you ever taste that bitterest of all galls of seeing innocent men and women plagued for your sin? Then you will understand better than even Moses could tell you, what Abram felt as he saw the unoffending king of Egypt struck with plagues for Abram's falsehood and for Abram's deceit. It is not told in Moses, but I can well believe it, that nothing that ever happened to Abram so hastened forward his humility, his detachment from this world, and his heavenly-mindedness, as his fall in Egypt, and all its consequences to Pharaoh and to Pharaoh's household. What is this that thou hast done to me? Those who have these accusing words sounding in their ears from the reproaches of innocent and injured people, they will be shut up like their father Abram to that grace of which God so timeously and so fitly spake to Abram when He said to him: Fear not, Abram, for I am thy shield and thy salvation.

Jonathan Edwards, one of the purest and princeliest souls that ever were made perfect through suffering, has told all that fear God what God did for his soul. In intellect Edwards was one of the very greatest of the sons of men, and in holiness he was a seraph rather than a man. And to have from such a saint, and in his own words, what God from time to time did for his so exercised soul is a great gift to us out of the unsearchable riches of Christ. Well, Edwards testifies to the grace of God that immediately after every new season of great distress, great mortification, great humiliation, great self-discovery, and great contrition, there was always given him a corresponding period of great liberty, great enlargement, great detachment, great sweetness, great beauty, and great and ineffable delight. Till he testifies to all who fear God, and challenges us out of Hosea, saying to us: Come, let us return to the Lord our God: for He hath torn, and He will heal us; He hath smitten, and He will bind us up. His going forth is prepared as the morning; and He shall come to us as the rain, as the latter and former rain unto the earth. And so was it with Edwards's first father in his re-migration out of Egypt back to Canaan. But if Pharaoh was sore plagued because of Abram's transgressions, then Lot, at any rate, had his advantage out of all that. As our magnificent New Testament commentary on the Old Testament has it, Abram came out of his trespass in Egypt more than ever a stranger and a pilgrim with God on the earth. He came back to Canaan very rich in cattle, in silver, and in gold. But, like all his mortified sons, his heart was no more in his riches. God makes men rich who do not care for riches, and He brings to poverty those who like Lot sell their souls for sheep and oxen. He hath filled, sang Mary, the hungry with good things, and the rich He hath sent empty away. Abram was filled with good things as he came back to Canaan, which had now recovered from her famine. As full as he could hold, and more. But Abram's heart was less and less in his cattle pens and in his money bags; and more and more his heart was in those promises that are never received in this life, but are kept for us in that city which hath foundations, whose builder and maker is God. In former days, in the days before Haran and Bethel, and especially in the days before Egypt, if the land had not been able to bear both Abram and Lot, Abram would have said to Lot, I will journey east to Jordan, where it is well watered like the garden of the Lord, and the rest of the land thou canst take after I have left it. But after Egypt, and all the other times and places that Abram has come through, he has no heart left for any such choice or any such contention about cattle and sheep, and corn and wine. Let there be no strife, I pray thee, between me and thee, for we be brethren. In Edwards's experience, Abram's mortifications and humiliations in Egypt and elsewhere had resulted in an amazing elevation, detachment, supremeness, and sweetness of soul. Till, without knowing it, on the heights above Bethel, Abram was made the father of Him who sat on those same heights long afterwards, and, remembering Abram, opened His mouth and taught His disciples, saying: Where your treasure is, there will your heart be also. Blessed are they which do hunger and thirst after righteousness, for they shall be filled. Seek ye first the kingdom of God, and His righteousness, and all these things shall be added unto you.

And now, as Terah and Abram were in all that, so are all their true children. We also are continually being called to go out, not knowing whither we go. We also are sojourners in a strange land. We also die in faith, not having received the promises. We also desire a better country, that is, an heavenly. And, O! how well it is with us if God is not ashamed to be called our God, and if He has prepared for us a city! Like Abram in Ur, we are the sons of a father who hears our call, and who takes us by the hand and leads us on the way. Or it is otherwise, just as God in His deep wisdom and love wills it to be. But, fatherful or fatherless; with Terah for our father, or with God alone; still His call comes to us all to arise and come out with Him to a land that He will show us. Arise, He says to us, and go forward in faith, in obedience, in trust, and in a sure hope. The very progress of the years, were it nothing else, would be a continually renewed call to go forward, and to walk henceforth with God. From childhood, ere ever we are aware, we have migrated into youth. From youth we are soon ushered into manhood, and from one stage of manhood on into another; till, if we have God's blessing on us, we become old like Terah, with our eye not dim, nor our strength abated. Youth, man, married man, father, master, citizen, and so on. Maid, wife, mother, mistress, widow indeed, and so on. Migrating from one field of human life into another, and never leaving one field till we have reaped in its full harvest, and never entering upon a new field till we are prepared to plow it, and sow it, and reap it—what a noble life we are called to lead on this earth, and all the time the pilgrims of God, and preparing ourselves for His city! What a noble education did divine providence pass Terah's son through, and with what profit to his mind, and heart, and temper, and whole moral character. His childhood spent in ancient Chaldea; his very crossing of the flood Euphrates on such an errand; the snows of Lebanon; the oaks of Bashan; Damascus; Salem; the Nile; the pyramids; the great temples; the famous schools and schoolmasters of Egypt, at whose feet Moses was to sit in after days—all that, and much more that we neither know nor can imagine. What a noble education Terah's son was passed through of God. But not half so noble, not half so wonderful, not half so fruitful as our own. What were Babylon, and Nineveh, and Damascus, and Salem, and all Egypt, to this western world and to this nineteenth century after Christ! What were all the science of Chaldea, and all the lore of Egypt, but the merest rudiments and first elements of that splendid sunshine of all manner of truth and opportunity which floods around us from our youth up! And as we are led on from school to school; and from author to author; and from preacher to preacher; and from one stage of intellectual and spiritual migration and growth to another; to what a stature, to what a breadth, and to what a height of faith, and knowledge, and love, and all manner of grace and truth may we not attain. Let us be up and doing. Let us open our eyes. Let us open our ears. Let us open our hearts. For thou, Israel, art My servant, Jacob whom I have chosen, the seed of Abraham my friend.

11
Abraham

I DID not know before that God had ever needed a friend. I did not know, I could not have believed, that any mortal man could possibly have befriended Almighty God. I need a friend. I need companionship. I need advice and counsel and correction. I need to be cheered and comforted. I often feel lonely. I often despond. I often miss my way in life. I often commit myself to rash, ill-considered, and irretrievable steps. I often hurt both myself and other men with me. And, therefore, I need near me a faithful friend. A friend to speak to me in time, and with wisdom, and with both sympathy and encouragement. A friend loveth at all times, and a brother is born for adversity. And there is a friend that sticketh closer than a brother. Faithful are the wounds of such a friend. Ointment and perfume rejoice the heart: so doth the sweetness of a man's friend by hearty counsel. Iron sharpeneth iron: and so doth a man sharpen the countenance of his friend. Bacon needed a friend. The principal fruit of friendship is the ease and discharge of the fullness of the heart. You may take sarza to open the liver, steel to open the spleen, flower of sulphur for the lungs, castoreum for the brain; but no receipt openeth the heart but a true friend—a true friend to whom you may impart griefs, joys, fears, hopes, suspicions, counsels, and whatsoever lieth upon the heart to oppress it. And our own Edward Irving, a great student of Bacon, often sorely needed a wise friend, as we see in his sad life and read in his superb sermons. The great office of a friend is to try our thoughts by the measure of his judgments; to task the wholesomeness of our designs and purposes by the feelings of his heart; to protect us from the solitary and selfish part of our nature; to speak to and to call out those finer and better parts of our nature which the customs of this world stifle; and to open up to us a career worthy of our powers. "Now," adds the most eloquent of all our Presbyterian preachers, "as every man hath these four attributes—infirmity of judgment, selfishness of disposition, inactivity and inertness of nature, and adversity of fortune—so every man needeth the help of a friend, and should do his endeavor to get one." For all these four attributes Solomon needed a friend, and Bacon, and Irving, and you, and I—but, surely, not God. And yet it stands written out in more scriptures than one that Almighty God endeavored to get a true friend in Abraham, and got one.

Now, of no mortal man but of Abraham alone does Almighty God ever speak and say, He was My friend. God employs many gracious, beautiful, and endearing names in speaking of the patriarchs, and prophets, and psalmists, and other saints of His in Israel; but it is of Abraham alone that God testifies to Israel and says, Thou art the seed of Abraham, My friend. Now, I wonder if we can get at what was in the Divine Mind, and at what He put into the prophet's mind in that so remarkable and unparalleled expression. Can we put our finger on anything in Abraham's life and say, Here, and here, and here, that wonderful man proved himself to be the friend of God? We have only a few short chapters to cover the long life of Abraham. I wonder shall we find enough in those chapters to satisfy us why Isaiah, and James, and then why both Jew and Mussulman and Christian, all unite in calling Abraham what they call no other man—the friend of God? Let us try.

Well then, we see this, to begin with, that God appeared and asked of Abram a service; a kind of service, and an amount and a degree of service, that He has never needed to ask the like of it again of any other man, if we except the Man Christ Jesus. God had for long—from the fall—been looking out for some man with mind enough and with heart enough to be made the father and the founder of a family into which He could send His Son. God promised His Son to Adam and Eve; but generations and generations had to pass before the fullness of time came. And all those successive generations had to be filled with all that with which our Bible is filled from Genesis to the Gospels. And the foundations of all that had first to be laid in some elect, called, believing, obedient, godly-minded, heavenly-minded man. Only, where was the man to be found who had all the qualifications needful for this supreme post? The long-looked-for man was found at last in Abram, Terah's choice son, in Ur of the Chaldees. To Terah's son, first of all good men on the face of the earth, was God able to say, Get thee out of thy kindred; walk before Me, and be thou perfect. And Abram believed God. Abram believed God with such a depth, and with such a strength, and with such a promptitude, and with such a perseverance that by Abram's faith the foundations of the whole Church of God on earth and in heaven were laid in him. No doubt, the beginning and the middle and the end of that friendship was all in God. No doubt, Abram would have protested against, and would have repudiated the name of friend of God with fear and with shame. But that does not alter the fact. It is still God's way to impute to us what He does for us: and to reward us for what we let Him do in us. God works in us both to will and to do; but, at the same time, He holds that we work out our own salvation. And so it was in the beginning of His ways with Abraham. God chose Abraham, and called him, and blessed him. But at the same time, God always has made much of the fact that Abraham had the mind and the heart to do what he did both for God and for all the families of the earth. And that immense venture of faith and of love on the part of Abraham, to call it a venture, was so original, so unheard of, and so full of all the great qualities of a godly heart and a heavenly life, that Abraham has ever since been called, not only the father of the faithful, but also the foremost and topmost friend of God. You understand, then, and will take home the lesson. Abraham had the heart to choose, and to prefer, and to venture for God, and for the will and the call of God, before everything else in this world. Abraham immediately, unquestioningly, cheerfully, joyfully arose and went out to do and to be all that God had asked him to do and had promised him to be. Till, as Butler has it, God justified Abraham's taste, and supported his cause, and acknowledged and claimed him as His friend: him, and his seed after him.

Edward Irving says that it is part of the office and service of a true friend to call out, and to prepare a scope for those finer feelings of the heart which are chilled and driven back upon the heart in this cold, distrustful, selfish world. Now, if that is true, and if God's heart and our hearts are in the same image in that also; if His heart also is chilled and shut up within itself in this same selfish world; then Abraham's so pressing intercession for Sodom was the part of a true friend to God. Humanly speaking, Sodom and Gomorrah would have been destroyed, and God's heart which was so full of answer to intercessory prayer would never have been discovered, had it not been for Abraham's so friendly part performed that day both to God and to the doomed cities of the plain. And while Abraham was seeking first his own ends and the ends of the two cities in his persevering prayer, he was at the same time without knowing it serving God's greatest ends still more. For God's greatest ends always are that His great Name may be known; His great grace helped down and experienced; and His great heart drawn out to all its depth; and that, too, by persevering and importunate prayer. You are a good man's best friend when you provide him with, and press upon him, opportunity upon opportunity of doing good. And Abraham was the opportune and importunate friend of the Hearer of Prayer when he said, Peradventure, and peradventure, and peradventure, and peradventure, and again, peradventure, and when God in friendly answer reduced the price of Sodom from fifty righteous men to ten. And the Lord went His way as soon as He had left communing with Abraham; and Abraham returned to his place.

Honest Joseph Hall counts up ten trials of Abraham's faith and friendship through which God saw good to pass His friend. And the last of the ten was more terrible to Abraham than all the rest taken together. If any of you is a father, and has a son of your old age; a son of much faith and of much prayer on your part, and of much pure miracle on God's part; then add to that, that your only son is the one and only instrument and chosen vessel of all God's remaining promises to you: and then, that he lies at the point of death. I do not add that he is to die under your hand like Isaac; I only add that he is to die with your consent and surrender and approval. If any of you that is a father or a mother has, or has had, a child like that, then you are the seed of Abraham, the friend of God. For, how you lay all night on the earth before God. How you would neither eat bread nor drink water. How you pleaded and promised and protested; how you vowed and swore and despaired. Then you will know something of how God did tempt Abraham. I do not understand this dark dispensation of God—all the seed of Abraham are often compelled to say. All is dark as midnight to me. Why should my dear, pure, inoffensive, so indispensable, and so promising son be taken away from me in the bloom of his beautiful youth? But God knows. God gave him, and it is God's place to take him when He pleases. I do not understand it. But God's understanding is infinite and unfathomable, and He does nothing of caprice, or of arrogance, or of hard-heartedness, or of oversight, or of neglect. And, when I come to myself, and think of it, if I had ten sons, and all of them were Isaacs, I would build the ten altars with my own hand. In His will is my tranquillity of mind, and my strength of heart, and my submission, and my obedience—so all Abraham's seed are called on and are enabled to say.

Abraham withheld not Isaac from his Friend on one of the mountains of Moriah; and in the same country, two thousand years after, God was not to be outdone by Abraham in the seal of His friendship to Abraham and to his seed for ever. And the bare mention of that brings God, and His friendship to us and our friendship to Him, two thousand miles nearer us and two thousand miles more possible to us than Abraham's too splendid faith and too wonderful love. With all that has been said I have difficulty in believing what has been said. No; not exactly in believing it, but in what we call realizing it. For all that we have read and heard in Abraham's history—that any mortal man should be able to befriend Almighty God, still remains a very startling thing to say about Almighty God. But not about Jesus Christ. We could have befriended Him ourselves. And I think, nay, I feel sure, we would have done it too. Multitudes of men and women who were as weak and as evil and as unbelieving as we are, will be led out at the last day to receive the thanks of the Father because they befriended His friendless Son. The women of Galilee who ministered to Him of their substance will be brought forward; Martha will be brought forward, and the woman at the well; the owner of the ass's colt, and the owner of the upper room, and the owner of Gethsemane; Simon the Cyrenian also, who helped Him to carry His cross; the soldier also who gave Him some of his vinegar to drink; and Joseph of Arimathea, and Nicodemus, and the women with their spices, and the angel who rolled away the stone. O!—you start up and exclaim: O! if my lot had only been cast in Galilee, or in Samaria, or in Judea, or in Jerusalem! O! you cry, how you envy the men and the women to whom the Father will say, Inasmuch as ye did it to Him, ye did it to Me! But, as you still cry that, this scripture comes up into my mind. You will remember it when I repeat it: "Ye are My friends if ye do whatsoever I command you." And again: "Greater love hath no man than this, that a man lay down his life for his friends." And again, in the same kind: "Henceforth I call you not servants, but I have called you friends." And then, to His Father, this: "Neither pray I for these alone, but for them also which shall believe on Me through their word." Well then, we do not need, we have no temptation now, to challenge the wisdom and the love that cast our lot two thousand years after Christ; as the same wisdom and love cast Abraham's lot two thousand years before Christ. Abraham believed the word of the Lord in his day; and if we believe in our day through the word of the disciples, then are we Abraham's seed, and need envy neither Abraham our father nor any of our brethren. Abraham laid down his life and the life of Isaac at the call of God. And Jesus Christ, Son of God, and Son of Abraham, laid down His life at the same call. But our call, our first call, is not yet to lay down our life, but to take Him as our Friend who has laid down His life for ours. Now, what do you all say to that? Are you His friends on that footing? A friend gives full scope to his friend's love and goodness. Have you given Jesus Christ full scope to His life and death for you? Has this Man laid down His life for you? He has, if you have ever asked Him to do it. He has, if you have ever come up to His cross and said over Him, He gave Himself here for me. He has, if you have ever said, I lay my sin and my death on Jesus Christ. Did it ever come to this terrible pass with you, your life or His? And how did that terrible pass end? When was it? Where was it? How long ago was it? When did it take place last? Has it taken place today? Is it taking place every day? Then you need envy neither Abraham nor any other man. Your day is the best of days for you. Your call is the best of calls for you. And you will be brought forward among the very first and the very best as that sinner who has adorned the doctrines of the death of Christ, and of the heart of God to sinners, as no other sinner has done from Abraham's day to the day of judgment. Does that amazing Man still stand offering me His death for me, and His living and everlasting friendship to boot? Then, this moment; then, in this house, and on the spot, I am His friend, and He is my friend.

All that is most commendable to speak, and most consoling to hear. It is very blessed to speak and to hear about Christ and His friendship to death in the sanctuary tonight; but it will all die out of our hearts in the shop, in the office, in the kitchen, in the drawing-room, and in the dining-room tomorrow. So it will. But, then, that is not all that our Lord says about how we are to make friends with Him, and to keep up that friendship. He is very practical and matter-of-fact in His friendship. "Ye are My friends," he goes on to say, "if ye do whatsoever I command you." Well then, take the thing by that handle. Try that door. Strike up, and keep up, the friendship on that plain, pedestrian footing. You cannot attain to His cross, you complain. His blood is too remote, too transcendental, too, somehow, spiritual, and too altogether heavenly for you. I wonder at you. But let that pass. Try this commonplace way. Do this and that which He commands you to do, and you will be as much—ay, and more, His friend than if you preached and prayed and praised His blood and righteousness day and night, and did nothing else. Do this for one thing that He so pointedly commands. Shut your door tonight. And if you have no door to call your own, yet you have a heart with doors. Enter your heart, then, and pray to your Father, whose true temple is the praying man's heart. And see if He does not one day tell all the world who took His Son in earnest, and who did not. O, how easy on that footing is the friendship of God! O, how impossible it is to get past it! And then, do this tomorrow—tomorrow when the lights shall all be out in the church, and when the preacher's voice shall be silent, and when the Chaldeas and the Sodoms and the Egypts of this world shall have all men's choices and friendships—do this. God has the day prepared, and has filled it full for this purpose. All tomorrow love your enemies, and your rivals—that is to say, try to do it. Work at it. Enter into the strait gate of it. Bless them that curse you. Do good to them, and to their wives and children, who hate you, with, or without cause. Ye are My friends, says the Son of God, if ye do that. Then, again, if you are a father with a sick son, or a son in a sudden accident; or a son who has not succeeded at school, or at college, or in life; or a son who has brought gray hairs here and there upon you, till all men mark it. How you deal with that son of yours will prove, or will disprove, you a friend of God as much and as surely as if your name had been Abraham, and your son's name Isaac. Or, if God needs you or your son to go abroad on any mission of His, as He needed Abraham, then go. Be like noble old Terah, go half the way with your elect and expatriated son, till God arises out of His place and comes to meet you, and says to you—As sure as I live, all the land on which thou standest will I give to thee and to thy seed with thee, because thou hast not withheld thyself or thy son from Me. Or, if it is this. If there is a famine of bread and water where corn and wine had been promised and expected; or if the laughters and the shouts of baptized children are silent where they would have been as the voices of God's angels to you—what then? Then thy God will descend into thine heart, and He will ask: Am I not more to thee than sons and daughters? Is My love not better to thee than corn and wine? Am I, and My salvation, and that city of Mine which hath foundations, not more to be desired by thee than all else that I could give thee? Till you will find it in your bereaved and broken heart to say to Him henceforth and continually, Whom have I in heaven but Thee? And there is none upon earth that I desire beside Thee. My flesh and my heart faileth; but God is the strength of my heart, and my portion for ever.

12
Lot

WE are still away up among the fathers and the founders of the great families of mankind. Terah was the father of all those old men among us whose day is not done, nor their eye dim, nor their natural force abated. Abraham was the father of the faithful. And Lot, his nephew, was the father of all such as are scarcely saved. Lot began his religious life very early in life, and he began it very well. Lot was singularly happy in having a grandfather like Terah, and an uncle like Abraham. And Lot himself must have had something very good about him to begin with, when he left all his youthful associates, both young men and young women, and set out he knew not whither. Only, the two best men on earth—they knew. They were going out of Chaldea; and if they would let him Lot would go with them. Now that same is all the religion that many of our own young men have still. And, in a way, and for some men, it is quite enough to begin with. All men are not gifted as Abraham was gifted. All men are not called as Abraham was called. All men are not made to lead. All men are not fitted to be explorers and pioneers in morals or in religion, any more than in science, or in art, or in business, or in public life. There are great, and powerful, and original, and epoch-making men; and then there are men who follow those great men, and who fill up what they find out and set agoing. And the most part of our young men cannot do a wiser or a better thing for a long time to come than just to follow their fathers and their other forerunners like Terah and Abraham. Had Lot just held on as he began; had he kept close to Abraham, and had he been content to share Abraham's prospects and prosperity and peace, Lot would have lived a pure and a happy life; he would have escaped many sorrows, and, instead of being scarcely saved; saved indeed, but saved with the fire and brimstone of Sodom and Gomorrah smoldering in his skirts; he would have gone down to a truly patriarchal grave, an elder of a good report and a father of a blameless name. All went well enough with Lot as long as he had the good sense, and the good feeling, and the good manners to know his proper place and to keep it. He left Chaldea and came to Haran with the Abrahamic emigration. He held a grandson's cord at Terah's grave, and he received his share of Terah's testament. When Abraham rose up and left Haran and entered the land of promise Lot went all the way with him. Wherever Abraham went, Lot went. Where Abraham built an altar, Lot either offered at that altar or he built another like it for himself. When the Lord spoke to Abraham, the uncle never hid from the nephew any word of the Lord that could either guide him in his behavior or confirm him in his pilgrimage. When the terrible famine fell on Canaan, Abraham took Lot down to Egypt with him; and after the famine passed off, Lot returned to the land of promise with his chastened uncle.

I am not sure that Egypt had not been a sore temptation to Lot as well as to Abraham. Nay, I am quite sure, when I think of it, that it must have been.

Mean-minded men, sordid-minded men, self-seeking men have constant temptations wherever they go. Wherever they go they carry their temptations with them. They manufacture temptations to themselves in every place and out of every thing. And Lot was not a high-minded man. With all his early opportunities, and with all his early promises, Lot was not, and never became, a high-minded man. We are never told all his life one large-hearted, or one noble-minded, or one single self-forgetful thing about Lot. Low-minded men see their opportunity in everything. Your stumble, your fall, your misfortune, your approaching age, your illness, your death—all is grist to the mill of the mean-minded man. And Abraham's fall in Egypt, and, especially, Abraham's fast-growing indifference to his fast-growing wealth, would be a secret delight to Lot. And then, that Abraham and Sarah with all their wealth had no son! Why, let Lot just wait on a few years and the whole of the immense family inheritance will be his. He will be the undisputed heir of Terah, and Abraham, and Sarah, and all. Lot is the father of all of you who are waiting for dead men's shoes. You all take of Lot who marry, and build, and borrow money on the strength of this rich man's old age, and that ageing woman's childlessness. True, there was that Eliezer of Damascus, and some other men who were deep in Abraham's confidence, and much trusted by him—but blood is thicker than water, and Lot will live in hope.

It was Lot's highest interest to behave himself well before Abraham, and to do nothing that would lead Abraham to suspect his nephew's false and sordid heart. But sordid-heartedness like Lot's will not always hide. Lot struck what might well have been a fatal blow at his own dearest hopes with his own hand. And had Abraham not been a weak, old, unworldly soul; had Abraham not borne all things, and believed all things, and hoped all things, and endured all things, Lot would soon have reaped as he had sown. But Abraham was what he was, and Lot had his profit out of that. Abraham had come up out of Egypt overwhelmed with shame and broken in his heart; and one result of all that was that he was overwhelmed with shame at his increasing prosperity also. Abraham, after Egypt, was the first father of all those who since his day have every day said, He hath not dealt with us after our sins, nor rewarded us according to our iniquities. Every new acre of pasture land, and every new well of water for his cattle, and every new time of stocktaking, only made Abraham confess himself more and more a stranger and a pilgrim with God on the earth. But not his nephew. Not Lot. Lot was fast becoming the father of all hard-faced, hard-hearted, close-fisted, money-loving men. And Lot's herdmen knew their master, took of him, and studied how to please him. They removed the landmarks; they drew off the water; they picked constant quarrels with Abraham's patient herdmen, till the strife between the two camps was the scandal of the whole country round. But blessed are the peacemakers. Hear, then, what the first peacemaker in the Bible said, and go and say and do likewise, "And Abraham took Lot and said to him, Let there be no strife, I pray thee, between me and thee, and between my herdmen and thy herdmen; for we be brethren. Is not the whole land before thee? Separate thyself, I pray thee, from me. If thou wilt take the left hand, then I will go to the right; or, if thou depart to the right hand, then I will go to the left." And then hear this, and resolve never, all your days, under any offer, or opportunity, or temptation of any kind to do what miserable, mean-spirited Lot did. Just hear what he did. You would not believe it. "And Lot lifted up his eyes and beheld all the plain of Jordan, that it was well watered everywhere, before the Lord destroyed Sodom and Gomorrah, even as the garden of the Lord, like the land of Egypt as thou comest into Zoar. And Lot chose all the plain of Jordan, and Lot journeyed east, and Lot dwelled in the cities of the plain, and pitched his tents toward Sodom." O my friends, labor to have a heart created within you that will make it simply impossible for you ever to do to anybody what Lot did that day to Abraham. What a man chooses, and how a man chooses, when opportunities and alternatives and choices are put before him—nothing more surely discovers a man than that. Abraham chose household peace; while Lot chose good pasture ground at the cost of disgrace, and shamelessness, and all unhandsomeness and ingratitude, and got Sodom to the boot of the bargain. Abraham, though the older man, and the man, moreover, with all the title-deeds to all the land of Canaan in his hands, put all that wholly aside and placed himself on an equality with his dependent nephew; placed himself under Lot, indeed, and gave him his choice. One would have thought that if anything would have melted Lot's brazen face and made him blush and become a man, it would have been the nobility, the munificence, and the fine high-mindedness of his uncle. But Lot's heart was turned to stone. Till with his hard eyes Lot stood up and looked out the best land and the best water in all the country round, and drove his flocks down into it without a moment's hesitation, or a touch of remorse, or so much as a Thank you. Lot knew quite well both the name and the character of that city lying in the rain and sunshine below. He had often heard his uncle praying and plotting with God with all his might for Sodom. But Lot had no fear. Lot did not care. His cattle were already up to their bellies in the grass around Sodom, and that was heaven upon earth to Lot.

It is a time of most tremendous import when a young man is still choosing toward what city he is to pitch his tent for life. And how often our young men make their choice as if the history of Lot had never been written. Think, fathers; oh, think, mothers; think, young men, also, with so much at stake—think what the temptations and the dangers and the almost sure issues of this and that choice in life must be. All our trades, professions, occupations in life have, each one, its own perils and temptations and snares to the soul; as well as its own opportunities of gain, and honor, and praise, and service. The ministry, teaching, law, medicine, the army, political life, newspaper life, trade of all kinds, the money-market of all kinds, and so on. Open your eyes. Count the cost. Are you able? Will you venture? Take that line of life which you are just about to choose. Take time over it. Look all round it. Imagine yourself done with it. Look at this man and that man who are done with it. Would you like to be like them? Study well the successes and the failures in that line of life. Read the thirteenth and the nineteenth chapters of Genesis, and then take those two chapters with you to your knees, and so make your choice. Look at your motives in making your choice. Look at its dangers, its temptations, and especially at its companionships. Look at the people you will have to part company with, and at the people among whom you will henceforth dwell, and then let the die be cast. Lot chose all the plain of Jordan, and pitched his tent toward Sodom.

Just when Lot is beginning to make the acquaintance of the men of Sodom, and is finding them, as he was sure he would find them, not so bad as they were reported; just as he was opening accounts for his tent and his camp with the merchants of Sodom, the Lord is hastening down to redress the wrong and to recognize and recompense Abraham. You put God in your debt as often as you do any handsome and unselfish thing; and, especially, anything in the pure interests of righteousness and peace. And it is wise and politic to put God in your debt now and then. For He always pays His debts sooner or later. And He always pays you with His gold for your paper, and with His usury to your uttermost farthing. And thus it is that we go on to read that the Lord said to Abraham, after that Lot was departed from him, "Lift up now thine eyes, and look from the place where thou art, northward, and southward, and eastward, and westward. For all the land which thou seest, to thee will I give it, and to thy seed for ever. Arise, walk through the land, in the length of it and in the breadth of it, for to thee will I give it. Then Abraham removed his tent, and came and dwelt in the land of Mamre, and built there an altar to the Lord." With all that, then, which is it to be with you? The plain of Jordan with Lot, or the plain of Mamre with Abraham? A family altar with the father of the faithful, or a seat at sunset in the gate of Sodom with Lot?

Lot was not long in getting a lesson that would have brought a less besotted sinner to his senses. The first war in the Bible broke out in the valley of the Jordan not very long after Lot had settled in Sodom. The war is known in ancient history as that of the four kings against five. Moses would have had no interest in that dim old dispute but for Lot. Lot, with all his great faults, nay, rather, because of his great faults, gets chapter after chapter of Moses' precious space. Well, the upshot of that war was that the kings of Sodom and Gomorrah were defeated and fled, and Lot was taken prisoner with all his possessions, and was marched off in great haste up the Jordan and away to the mountains. But as Lot's guardian angel would have it, one of Lot's herdmen escaped; and how his heart would sink as he came near Abraham's encampment at Hebron! But to whom else could he go? His own conscience of the past bitterly upbraided him as he told Abraham the disaster; but Abraham had something else to do than to trample on a fallen man. In three crowded verses Moses tells his readers the result. Abraham fell upon the sleeping camp, and Lot was a free man next morning with all his goods. Now, you know yourselves how you return back again to your former life as soon as the strain of the tribulation is over. As the cruel kings hurried Lot up the Jordan with a rope round his neck, how that chastised saint vomited up Sodom and all her works, and how he cursed himself as the greatest fool in all the land of Canaan. You can all cast your stones of anger and scorn and astonishment at Lot; I cannot. Till you try to break loose from an old evil way, you will never believe me how impossible it is for you to do it.

All this time there must have been something far better in Lot than anything that Moses lets us see. To read Second Peter on Lot is far more comforting than to read Moses. For Peter tells us in his Second Epistle that, when God turned the cities of Sodom and Gomorrah into ashes, He delivered just Lot, vexed with the filthy conversation of the wicked. But, then, to read that only makes us stop and say and ask, Why did a man with a beginning like Lot, and with past experiences like Lot, why did he not rise up and leave a life, and a neighborhood, and an occupation, and a companionship out of all which so much danger and so much vexation of soul continually sprang? The reason was that he had invested in Sodom, as our merchants would say. He had invested money, and he had embarked himself and his household in the land round Sodom, in the produce of Sodom, and in her splendid profits. And with all the vexations that wrung his heart Lot could never make up his mind to be done with Sodom and Gomorrah for ever. I suppose there must be just men among ourselves who have chosen early in life, or who have inherited, or who have themselves built up a business, the partners in which, the questionable righteousness of which, nay, the not questionable unrighteousness of which, often vexes their hearts far more than we know or would believe. But to come out of that manufacture, that import, that export; to refund with usury those moneys; to rise up at the loss of thousands and thousands, nay, possibly at the loss of every penny a man possesses; to leave a splendidly paying business merely at the twinge of a secretly tortured conscience—no man ever does it. Lot therefore is the father of all those men whose righteous souls are vexed with the life they are leading, but who keep on enduring the vexation. And Peter's New Testament point is this—that righteous men will go on enduring vexation like that of Lot till the Lord Himself rises up and comes down to deliver them. Lot's deliverance came through a catastrophe the sound of which and the smoke of which blows like opening hell into our eyes to this day. Just what God will have to do to deliver your soul and mine from the things that so endanger our souls and so vex them His time will tell. Only, this we may rely upon, that the Lord knoweth how to deliver the godly out of their temptations, and He will do it too, if He has to burn up all we possess with fire and brimstone from heaven. In that terrible day may His angels be near to lay hold of us!

13
Sarah

"WHICH things are an allegory," says the Apostle when he brings in Sarah and Hagar her handmaid into the fourth chapter of his Epistle to the Galatians. And no doubt, his first readers must have understood the Apostle's mystical argument and must have got the good they needed in their day out of his spiritual exposition. But if Paul had only been led to take up our text of tonight, and to treat Sarah and her childlessness as an allegory, what an evangelical argument, and what a fruitful and far-reaching application both the Galatian Church and all the churches ever after would have got! For, out of this little, parenthetical, hidden-away verse the whole of the succeeding eleven epoch-making chapters of Genesis immediately spring. Chaldea, and Canaan, and Egypt; Hagar and Ishmael; the promise of Isaac, and then the birth, the circumcision, the sacrifice, and the deliverance of Isaac; all the trials and all the triumphs of his father's and his mother's faith; all their falls; all their victories; all God's promises, and all His wonderful and adorable providences in their so exercised lives; all their attainments in truth and in obedience; and then, to crown all, the complete fulfillment of God's so long delayed promise—all that, and much more that has not been told—it all arose out of this, that Sarah had no child. "It is an allegory," says Bengel, "when anything is said and another thing more excellent is signified." And I cannot get it out of my heart that my text tonight, biographical reality, real historicity, and all, is somehow an allegory also. It will persist in my heart that Abraham is my faith in God's promise to me of the fruit of the Spirit in me; while childless Sarah, Abraham's married wife, is my still unfruitful heart. For I have some faith, but I have no love. I have not enough faith to make my love fruitful. My heart is as much without a spiritual seed as was Sarah's silent tent. I laugh at the idea, like Sarah behind her tent door. I say to myself, half in faith, half in fear, half in mockery at myself, Shall I ever have pleasure? Shall Christ ever be formed in me? Till I am sometimes, like poor Sarah in her sterile tent, driven desperate. Driven desperate, and reckless, and wild. Like Sarah, I fall into sore temptations between the Divine promise on the one hand, and my own evil heart on the other hand. Like her, also, I am driven to dangerous, and, sometimes, I fear, to positively sinful expedients, in my desolation and desperation. And, like Sarah, I involve and fatally injure other people also in my desperation. But still the great promise holds on its course, and is repeated, and enlarged, and enriched, and sealed; and still it is with me as it has been from the beginning. Till, as I believe, and am determined to go on believing—God help my unbelief!—God's promise to me also shall, in God's way and at God's time, be all fulfilled. And my heart also, like Abraham and Sarah, shall see of her travail and shall be satisfied. Yes. Had Paul, or even Philo; had Behmen, or Bunyan but taken up this text, and said, "Which things are an allegory," we would have had doctrine, and depth, and beauty, and assurance, and comfort to our heart's content.

But to come back to solid ground, and to speak no more about parables. As time went on, and as the hope of any possibility of her ever becoming a mother died out of Sarah's heart, she became absolutely desperate. Had meekness, and humility, and resignation, and the blotting-out of herself, but grown apace with her disappointment, that would have hid Sarah from all her temptations, and it would at the same time have hastened the lifting off of her cross. But her terrible cross had but inflamed and intensified her pride; it had but determined her to find some wild and willful way for herself out of God's way and God's will. It was intolerable to Sarah to live on any longer such an embarrassment to her husband, such an evident obstacle to the prosperity of his house, and such an eye-sore and jest to all the camp and to all the country around. And in the wildness of her pride Sarah determined to as good as slay herself, and to make it impossible for Abraham in his heart of hearts any longer to despise her. And thus it was that what looked like a perfect miracle of humility in Sarah, was really an act of exasperated pride. Sarah sacrificed herself on the cruellest altar on which any woman ever laid herself down; but the cords of the sacrifice were all the time the cords of a suicidal pride; till the sacrifice was both a great sin in the sight of God, a fatal injury to herself, to her husband, and to innocent generations yet unborn. What looks to all men's eyes like a martyr's devotion may all the time be but impatience, and petulance, and pride, and revenge. The outward act may sound heroic, while all the time cowardice and selfishness and exasperated pride may be at the bottom of it. To sacrifice yourself, therefore, is not enough. Your mind, your motive, your spirit, and your temper in making the sacrifice, that is everything. Sarah sacrificed herself to the last drop of a woman's blood; but all the time her heart was as high as heaven and as hot as hell both against God and against her husband also. "Behold, now, the Lord hath restrained me; but there is my maid!"

You are a truly humble man when you are truly despised in your own eyes. But your humility has not stood its very last test till you are despised in our eyes also every day. The truest humility is attained; the truest humility is ascertained, and certified, and sealed only by humiliations being heaped upon it from without; from above, from beneath, and from all around. And, had Sarah's humility been a true and a genuine humility; had her ostentatious sacrifice of herself not had its secret roots in a deep and a cruel pride; she would have opened her heart to all Hagar's contempt. Hagar's scorn would have been an excellent oil to Sarah's head, and she would thus have secured and hastened her own fruitfulness and motherhood. But Sarah of herself had run herself into a temptation too terrible for her to bear. Her humiliating childlessness was honor, and rest, and peace, and love compared with her uttermost and incessant misery now. "My wrong be upon thee," she assailed her husband, "for I am despised in the eyes of my own maid!" My brethren, you must make up your mind to bear with what has sprung upon you out of your own past misdeeds. It is the least you can do to hold your peace, and to bear with meekness the hand of God. Your life all your days may henceforth be made bitter to you because of your past. But what would you have? Would you have a peaceful, a free, an untrammelled, and a happy after-life out of a past life like yours? You cannot have it. Life is not built on that plan. God does not live in heaven and rule on earth on that principle. Or, if He does, the worse it will be for you in the long-run. Put it in words and look at it. Would you run yourself and other people into sin and guilt as suits you, and then would you wipe your mouth and walk off as a guileless and an innocent man? You cannot do it. And you need not try. Kiss the rod rather. Kiss the rod, and the hand that holds it. Say, It is the Lord. Say that though He should slay you, yet you will not complain. Say this; say it with Micah when he was in some such distress, say, "I will bear the indignation of the Lord, because I have sinned against Him, until He plead my cause and execute judgment for me." Cast out the bondwoman and her son! No, Sarah, you cannot do it. You may try to do it, but the angel of the Lord will bring Hagar and Ishmael back again upon you. You surely know Hagar, Sarah! She is your own handmaiden. But for you, you must remember, Hagar would have still been a pure, modest, obedient child. And if she and her unlawful son are thorns in your eyes, they are both thorns of your own planting. You bought Hagar in Egypt. You bribed her to leave her mother's house. You engaged to be a mother to her. You took her, and made her your tool; you debauched her, and then you would cast her out. And you did, and would do all this, in spite both of God and man. And now you would like to get back to where you were before your terrible trespass. You would fain have Hagar and her fatherless boy back in Egypt, and your tent in Canaan the abode of peace and love and honor it was at the beginning. No, Sarah, mother of so much mischief, you cannot have it. It cannot be. Shall not the Judge of all the earth do right?

Hagar had not come from Ur of the Chaldees with the immigration, neither had she been bought by Abraham in Canaan. Hagar, originally, was an Egyptian child. When Sarah was down in Egypt with her husband Abraham, young Hagar had been recommended to Sarah for a lady's maid. And Sarah had made trial of the girl in the place, and had been glad to find that she had all the talent and all the character she had been certificated to have. And though it looked a wild proposal that Hagar should leave her mother's house, and all the religion and civilization of Egypt, to go to the savage land of the Philistines, yet, what a princess like Sarah had once set her heart upon, poor people like Hagar's parents could not oppose. Sarah was rich, and she had the imperious temper of riches. And, besides, Sarah, the sister of Abraham, was a favorite in Pharaoh's palace. Hagar's expatriation and banishment so far from home made her all the better a maid to Sarah. Hagar had no choice. She must please her mistress. She had no temptation or opportunity to do anything else. She was so far from home now that Sarah became both mistress and mother to the poor Egyptian girl. All went well, only too well, indeed, with Sarah and Hagar till Sarah's sin began to find her out. And when Sarah dealt hardly with Hagar she fled from the face of her mistress. Poor Hagar! Mother of so many miserable women in all lands and in all ages ever since. Hundreds of miles, weeks of wilderness, and of tears, and of bleeding feet, and of a bleeding heart from her mother's door. Afraid to face her mother. Terrified at the thought of her father. Spat upon and cast out of doors by her sisters and their husbands. Shall she kill her child? Shall she kill herself? Oh, why was I born? Oh, why did I ever come to this cursed land? Why did I ever take the wages of that wicked woman? Let the night perish on which she took me and led me up into her bed! Let darkness and the shadow of death stain it; let a cloud dwell upon it; let the gross darkness terrify it! Till she awakened and found herself with a well of water close beside her. "Return to thy mistress. Submit thyself to thy mistress. Not only to the good and gentle, but also to the froward," said the angel at the well. And as she drank of the well she said, Beer-lahai-roi. Thou God seest me! Behold, that well still springs up in the wilderness of Shur; it is to be found on the road between Kadesh and Bered.

BEER-LAHAI-ROI. THOU GOD SEEST ME! Hagar, by reason of the extremity of her sorrow; by reason of the utter desolateness and brokenness of her heart; and by reason of the sovereign grace and abounding mercy of God—Hagar, I say, stands out before us in the very foremost rank of faith, and trust, and experience, and assurance. Hagar, to me, stands out among God's very electest saints. Hagar has only one or two who can stand beside her in her discovery of God, in her near-ness to God, in her face-to-face fellowship with God, in the instructiveness, in the comfort, and in the hopefulness of her so close communion with God. Not Adam before his fall; not Enoch, who so pleased God; not Abraham at his call, or after offering his son; not Jacob at Bethel, nor Israel at the Jabbok; not Moses on the mount and in the cleft rock; not Isaiah in the temple, and not John in the spirit—not the best and the most blessed of them all was more blessed or better blessed than was Hagar the polluted outcast on her weeping way to Shur. The pure in heart shall see God. And, what impurity Hagar had contracted of Sarah and Abra-ham she had washed away, her head waters and her eyes a fountain of tears, all the way from Abraham's tent door to that well in the wilderness. She had washed her polluted body and her scornful and revengeful heart with her penitential tears, till, by the time she came to the well, she was counted clean enough to see God. And she saw God at that wilderness-well with a clearness, and with an assurance, and with a rapture, and with a submission, and with an immediate obedience that all combine to lift up Hagar and to set Hagar beside, and even before, both her master and her mistress in the favor and in the fellowship of God. For, from that day on the way to Shur, all the days of Hagar's pilgrimage on earth, we still see Sarah and Abraham entreating Hagar with hardness till she drinks again and again of the well of God, and again and again has Almighty God given to her and to him as the heavenly Father of her fatherless son. In Thee, O God, the fatherless have always found mercy.

Now, in God's mercy, is there any Hagar here? Is there any outcast here? Is there any soul of man or woman ready to perish here? Who can tell who is here? Where would such be found if not here? Is not this the house of God? Does this house not stand on the wayside to Shur? Has this house not been Beer-lahai-roi to many who were in far greater straits, and under far greater guilt, than ever Hagar was? Many have said of this house, Thou God seest me! Many have come up to this house with a secret burden. Many have gone home from this house to take up their cast-off cross, and to endure to the end. Is there a motherless woman-child here? Is there a deceived, injured, cast-out sinner here? My sister, thy God is here. Thou hast been led of His angel in coming here. His well is here. He has dug that well for thee. Spring up, O well! And that is He Himself, His true and very Self, Who is now laying His hand on thy dishonored and downcast head. That is His Holy Spirit who is now bringing these tears to thine eyes. That is His voice in thy heart, saying "Hagar, Sarah's maid, whence comest thou, and whither wilt thou go?" Stoop down, Hagar, and drink and be refreshed and revived. Fall down and weep. Lift up thy heart and pray. Behold, Hagar, He is lifting thee up. He is washing thy feet. He is washing thy hands. He is washing with water and with blood thy heart. Think, Hagar, think. Believe, Hagar, believe. Admire, Hagar, and praise. For He is the same wonderful, wonderful, most wonderful God who met the first Hagar on her way back to her mother's disgraced and angry door. Wonderful is His name. He was in Egypt, He was in Canaan, He was in Mamre, and He appeared at Shur. He was there when thou wert born in thy mother's house in Scotland also. He swaddled thee, He girded thee, He called thee by thy name. The foolishness of thy youth was not hid from Him. He bore with thee, and still bore with thee. And when thy lovers had hold of thy deceived heart, He pitied thee, and had thoughts of love toward thee. And when thy lovers wearied of thee, and had served themselves of thee, then His time of love began with thee. When thou didst fall His hand held thee up. When thou hadst destroyed thyself He redeemed thee. He made thy sin bitter to thee. He made thy life a wilderness around thee. He made thy heart a wilderness within thee. He made this whole world flint to thy feet, and dust to thy mouth, and a very hell to thy cast-off heart. And when He had humbled thee, and tried thee, and utterly broken and silenced thee, He came near at the well of Shur to thee, and these, to His everlasting praise, were His words to thee, "Fear not, for thou shalt not be confounded. For thy Maker is thy husband. For the Lord hath called thee as a woman forsaken and grieved in spirit. For a small moment have I forsaken thee, but with everlasting kindness will I have mercy upon thee, saith the Lord, thy Redeemer. O thou afflicted, tossed with tempest, and not comforted; no weapon that is formed against thee shall prosper, and every tongue that shall rise in judgment against thee shalt thou condemn. This is the heritage of the servants of the Lord, and their righteousness is of Me, saith the Lord."

"Doubtless Thou art our Father, though Abraham be ignorant of us, and Israel acknowledge us not. Thou, O Lord, art our Father, our Redeemer. Thy name is from everlasting."

14
Isaac

THE patriarch Isaac presents but a pale appearance as he stands planted between two so stately and so impressive personages as his father Abraham on the one hand, and his son Jacob on the other hand. Isaac, notwithstanding our familiarity with his name, has hitherto made very little impression on our minds. Were we suddenly asked what we remember about Isaac, the chances are that we would get very little further than that memorable day when Abraham took his only son, and bound him, and laid him on the altar, upon the wood. And, indeed, as we follow out the sad declension of Isaac's character to the end, it is forced upon us that it would have been well for Isaac, and for all connected with Isaac, that Abraham's uplifted hand had not been arrested by the angel of the Lord. Had Isaac died on his father's altar, an immense impression for good would have been made on all who ever heard of his submission and devotion; and, besides, the whole after-history of Israel, and of the nations around Israel, would have been far purer, far more peaceful, and every way far more happy. But all that is in the far future.

Isaac, like Noah and Lot before him, those two other shipwrecks of the best early promise, made a splendid start. In his early start in faith and in obedience, Isaac by a single bound at once out-distanced all who had gone before him. We are so taken up with Abraham's faith and surrender in the matter of Moriah, that we forget the splendid part that Isaac must have performed in that terrible trial; that magnificent triumph of faith and submission. I do not wonder that the Church of Christ has all along persisted in seeing in Isaac an outstanding type of our Lord, and in making Mount Moriah a clear forecast of Gethsemane and of Calvary. For, when it came to the last agony beside the altar on that terrible hill-top—"Not my will, but thine be done," was wrung from Isaac's broken heart, just as long afterwards, and not far from the same spot, this same surrendering cry was wrung from the broken heart of our Lord. Josephus reports a remarkable dialogue that passed between Abraham and Isaac that day, in addition to the dialogue that Moses reports. As soon as the altar was prepared, and all things were entirely ready, Abraham said to Isaac his son: "O my son! I poured out a vast number of prayers that I might have thee for my son. And since it was God's will that I should become thy father, it is now His will that I shall relinquish thee. Let us bear this consecration to God with a ready mind. Accordingly, thou, my son, wilt now die, not in any common way of going out of the world, but sent to God, the Father of all men, beforehand, in the nature of a sacrifice. I suppose He thinks thee worthy to get clear of this world neither by disease, neither by war, nor by any other severe way, but so that He will receive thy soul with prayers and holy offices of religion, and will place thee near to Himself, and thou wilt there be to me a succourer and supporter in my old age; and thou wilt there procure me God for my Comforter instead of thyself." Now, Isaac was of such a generous disposition that he at once answered that he was not worthy to be born at first, if he should now reject the determination of God and his father, and should not resign himself up readily to both their pleasures. So he went up immediately to the altar to be sacrificed. The rest we know from Moses. To which Josephus only adds that Abraham and Isaac, having sacrificed the ram, embraced one another and returned home to Sarah, and lived happily together, God affording them His assistance in everything.

"And Isaac dwelt by the well Lahai-roi." That arrests us. That must have been intended to arrest us. And to make sure that it shall arrest us and shall not escape us, the sacred writer is not content with having told us that once; he tells us that again, and still more emphatically the second time. At the same time, having with such repeated point told us that, Moses leaves it to his readers to make of it what they are able to make, and what they like to make. Make anything of it, or not, there stands the fact—that, in broad Canaan, as soon as Isaac had a tent of his own to pitch, he pitched his tent toward Hagar's well. Hagar, you must remember, had been Isaac's mother's maid. Not only that, but Hagar had been Isaac's own first nurse. Isaac and Ishmael, the two innocent half-brothers, had learned their lessons together, and had played together, till the two mothers fell out, and till Hagar and her unlawful son had to flee to the wilderness. But, little children never forget their first nurse, especially when she has such stories to tell as Hagar had to tell little Isaac about the palaces, and the pyramids, and the temples, and the Nile, and the crocodiles of Egypt. And then, as her charge grew up, in seasons of trouble and sorrow and mutual confidence, Hagar would be led into telling the devout little lad her wonderful story of Beer-lahai-roi. And that heavenly story took such a hold of young Isaac that to the end of his life he never found himself within a day's journey of Hagar's well without turning aside to drink of its waters and to meditate and to pray and to praise beside its streams. Where, then, when he was choosing a site for his future tent, where should he choose that site after Moriah, but on a spot scarcely less solemn to Hagar's pious little nursling than Jehovah-jireh itself. Lahai-roi was one of the two most sacred spots on earth to Hagar's two boys; and, as sometimes happens, the boy of the two who was not her own, best remembered all she had told him, and shaped his course accordingly. It is no superstition to seek out the spots where God has come down to visit His people. It is not that God is any more there, or is any more likely to return there; but we are better prepared to meet with Him there. And God comes to those who are ready to meet with Him wherever they are. There is no respect of places with God. And nothing draws God down to any place like a heart like His own. As often, therefore, as He saw Isaac's tears dropping into the water he was drinking, God again visited Isaac also. And Isaac could never walk round that well, or sit down beside it, or drink out of it, but his tears would come fast for poor ill-used Hagar, and for poor outcast Ishmael, till he wished again that he had never been born rather than that they should both be outcast from their proper home on his account. I, for one, thank Moses warmly for writing it, and then for underscoring it, that, as soon as Isaac had a tent of his own to pitch, he pitched that tent toward Hagar's holy well.

It is now the late afternoon before the day of Isaac's marriage. Abraham's servant has performed his errand to perfection, and he is now nearing his young master's tent with Isaac's bride under his charge. "And Isaac went out to meditate in the field in the even-tide; and he lifted up his eyes, and saw, and behold, the camels were drawing near." All that day Isaac had spent in prayer and in meditation. Isaac was greatly given to solitude and to solitary thoughts, and he had much that day to think upon. The day it was made him think. He thought of his father Abraham and his mother Sarah; and then he thought of his own wonderful birth as of one born out of due time. From that, he went on to think of Hagar his Egyptian nurse, and of Ishmael his half-brother, and of all the evil fate that had befallen both Hagar and Ishmael because of him. And then this well, whose sacred waters were now shining in the setting sun. And all that took place at this well; and that which Hagar exclaimed over this well, and which was never a day, scarcely ever an hour, out of Isaac's thoughts. And then Moriah, Mount Moriah, the mount of the Lord, had been so burned into Isaac's heart, that, for years and years, he felt its cords knotted round his arms, and saw its knife gleaming over his head. Till his heart gave a great bound as he suddenly looked up and saw the distant thread of Chaldean camels drawing slowly near with their precious burdens. And till they came near, and till Isaac met the rich procession, Isaac still prayed, and praised, and vowed to God, the God of Abraham, his godly father. It is a beautiful scene in the setting sun. "And Isaac went out to meditate in the field at the even-tide; and he lifted up his eyes, and saw, and behold, the camels were coming. And Rebekah lifted up her eyes, and when she saw Isaac she lighted off her camel. For she had said to the servant, What man is this that walketh in the field to meet us? And the servant had said, It is my master. Therefore she took a veil and covered herself. And Isaac brought Rebekah into his mother Sarah's tent, and she became his wife; and he loved her; and Isaac was comforted after his mother's death."

The prophetic travail of Rebekah in giving birth to the twin-brothers Esau and Jacob, and then Esau's sale of his birthright, fill one graphic chapter, and then after another chapter we are all at once introduced to Isaac's deathbed. And then, the space given to the deathbed scenes; the dramatic situations; the eloquence and the pathos; and at the same time the suppression and the severity of the composition—all that of itself would kindle an intense interest in the story of Isaac's last hours. And then both the writer's pains, and the reader's strained interest and attention, are all amply rewarded as we stand by and look on, and lay to heart all that goes on around that distressing deathbed. "And it came to pass that when Isaac was old, and his eyes were dim, so that he could not see, he called Esau his eldest son, and said unto him, My son; and he said to him, Behold, here I am. And he said, Behold, now, I am old. I know not the day of my death. Now, therefore, I pray thee, take thy weapons, thy quiver and thy bow, and go out to the field, and take me some venison. And make me savory meat, such as I love, and bring it to me, that I may eat; that my soul may bless thee before I die." The inspired writer had already been compelled to set it down, on the sad occasion of the barter of Esau's birthright, that Isaac loved Esau and despised Jacob, because he did eat of Esau's venison. And, altogether, the place that "venison" holds on this page of the patriarchal history, and the part it plays in the tragedy now on the stage, compel us to consider and to think what it all means to us, and what it all warns us of.

When I read Isaac's whole history over again, with my eye upon the object, it becomes as clear as a sunbeam to me that what envy was to Cain, and what wine was to Noah, and what lewdness was to Ham, and what wealth was to Lot, and what pride and impatience were to Sarah—all that, venison and savory meat were to Isaac. I cannot get past it. I have tried hard to get past it. Out of respect for the aged patriarch, and out of gratitude for the mount of the Lord and Hagar's well, I have tried to get past it; but I cannot. "Take me some venison. Make me savory meat such as I love, and bring it to me, that I may eat, and that my soul may bless thee before I die. And Esau went out to hunt for venison. And Rebekah said to Jacob, I will make savory meat for thy father, such as he loveth. And she made savory meat such as Isaac loved. And Jacob said, Sit up, and eat of my venison. And he said, Bring it near to me, and I will eat of my son's venison. And he brought it near to him and he did eat; and he brought him wine and he drank. And Esau he also made savory meat, and said, Let my father arise and eat of his son's venison," and so on till Isaac's deathbed reeks with venison. The steam of the savory meat with which his two sons bid for his blessing chokes us till we cannot breathe beside Isaac's deathbed. But Isaac's ruling passion is still strong in death, so strong, that the very smell of Esau's venison-stained coat is sweet to the old patriarch's nostrils. My brethren, there is no respect of persons in the Bible. The Bible puts the simple, naked truth before everything else. Before the consistency, before the honor, and before the good name of the saints. Before propriety, before partiality, before what is seemly to be told, before what is consoling, before what is edifying even.

The inordinate and unseemly love of good eating has an undue hold of many otherwise blameless men, of many able men also, and even of many old men. Neither the grace of God, nor some true love of the things of the mind, nor the decays of nature, would seem to be able to root out or at all to weaken this degrading vice; so deeply is it seated in some men's habits of life and character. It would not be so much to be wondered at that out-of-door men like Esau should eat and drink with a passionate delight; but that a quiet, home-keeping, devout old saint like Isaac should let his table become such a snare to his soul—that does startle and alarm us. And we see the same thing still. Sedentary men, bookish men, and men who are never out of their study, are sometimes as fond of savory soup and venison as ever Isaac or Esau was. That they take too little exercise seems sometimes to make them seek their relaxation and refreshment in their table even more than other men. The greatest glutton I ever knew never crossed his doorstep. His only walk all the day was from his desk to his dinner-table, and then from his dinner-table back to his desk. Now, Isaac in his old age was the father of all such men. Isaac's very love for his sons depended on their skill and success in hunting. If a son of his could not hunt, could not run down and entrap venison, he might be a saint, but old Isaac had no blessing for him. Isaac was only happy, and full of good-humor and benediction, when he had just had another full meal. But he was sulky and peevish and fretful if his soup was short or out of season. If you would enjoy Isaac's benediction, you must get him after his dinner, and it must be of the best, and at the moment. Old Isaac, with his eyes so dim that he could not see, is the father of all those men who make their god their belly, who think too much and too often of what they shall eat and what they shall drink, who value their friends by the table they keep, and who are never so happy as when they are sitting over their venison and their wine. Isaac was the father of Ciacco in the *Inferno* and of Succus in the *Serious Call*. Of him also "who makes every day a day of full and cheerful meals, and who by degrees comes to make the happiness of every day to depend upon that, and to consider everything with regard to that. He will go to church, or stay at home, as it suits with his dinner, and he will not scruple to tell you that he generally eats too heartily to go to the afternoon service." And, lastly, Isaac in his infirm years, and in his increasing appetite, is the father of "all those people, with whom the world abounds, who are weakly and tender merely by their indulgences. They have bad nerves, low spirits, and frequent indispositions, through irregularity, idleness, and indulgence." Such to this day are some of Isaac's sons and daughters. Four rules for such.

1. Never accept a second helping at table.

2. Never rise from table without an appetite, and you will never sit down without one.

3. Never sit down at table till you have said this for a grace—What! Know ye not that your bodies are the members of Christ? Shall I, then, take the members of Christ and make them the members of a glutton? God forbid!

4. Only love God enough, and then eat anything you like, and eat as much as you like, said St. John of the Cross to his over-ascetical disciples.

15
Esau

ESAU lost his birthright with all its blessings largely through his lack of imagination. The things that are unseen and eternal had neither substance nor evidence to Esau compared with the things that are seen and temporal. Jacob, his brother, had many faults, but Jacob inherited the blessing because after all is said he had eyes and a heart for the unseen and the spiritual. But Esau had no such speculation in his eyes. The covenant promises made to his fathers had no interest, they had no existence even, to Esau. They can take the promises who care for them; as for Esau, a bird in the hand is worth two in the bush. At the same time, Esau had many not wholly ignoble things about him. Esau was full of the manliest interests and occupations and pursuits. He was a very proverb of courage and endurance and success in the chase. He was the ruggedest, the brawniest, and the shaggiest of all the rugged, brawny, and shaggy creatures of the field and of the forest, among whom he lived and died. Esau had an eye like an eagle. His ear never slept. His foot took the firmest hold of the ground. And his hand was always full both of skill, and strength, and success. Esau's arrow never missed its mark. He was the pride of all the encampment as he came home at night with his traps, and his snares, and his bows, and his arrows, and laden to the earth with venison for his father's supper. Burned black with the sun; beaten hard and dry with the wind; a prince of men; a prime favorite both with men, and women, and children, and with a good word and a good gift from the field for them all. But, all the time, a heathen. All the time, an animal more than a man. All the time, all body and no soul. All the time a profane person, who failed of the grace of God.

In that extraordinary solidity of style, in which Moses sometimes surpasses Dante himself, we have Isaac and Esau and Jacob set before us to the life in six or seven verses. "And Jacob sod pottage; and Esau came from the field, and he was faint. And Esau said to Jacob, Feed me, I pray thee, with that same red pottage; for I am faint. And Jacob said, Sell me this day thy birthright. And Esau said, Behold, I am at the point to die; and what profit shall this birthright do to me? And Jacob said, Swear to me this day; and he sware unto him; and he sold his birthright unto Jacob. Then Jacob gave Esau bread and pottage of lentils, and he did eat and drink, and rose up, and went his way. Thus Esau despised his birthright." This was not the first time that Esau and Jacob had exchanged words about that birthright. No man sells his birthright on the spot. He who sells his birthright, sells it many times in his heart before he takes it so openly as that to the market. He belittles it, and despises it, and cheapens it, at any rate to himself, long before he sells it so cheaply to another. No man, and no woman, falls in that fatal way without having prepared their fall for themselves in their hearts. Esau had showed his contempt for his birthright a thousand times, and in a thousand ways, before now. Everybody knew that Esau's birthright was for sale, if anybody cared to bid for it. Isaac knew, Rebekah knew, and Jacob knew; and Jacob had for long been eyeing his brother for a fit opportunity. It had for a long time back been marrow to Jacob's bones to hear Esau jesting so openly about his birthright over his venison and his wine; jesting and being jested about the covenant blessing. "As much as you are able to eat, Esau! and anything else you like to name, to boot; only, say that you toss me today your worthless birthright," said Jacob. "Take it, and welcome!" said Esau. "And much good may it do you! It has never been worth a haunch of good venison to me. You may have it, and my oath on it on the spot, for a good dish at once, and be quick, of your smoking pottage. Take it, and let me be done with it. Take it, and let me hear no more about it." And Esau did eat and drink, and rose up, and went his way.

Esau's roving habits of life; his increasing distaste for the life and the religion of his father's house; and, now that he had cut himself so completely adrift by openly selling his birthright, with all its privileges, and obligations, and responsibilities— all that combined to throw Esau more and more into the company of the old Canaanite communities that lay all around the patriarchal settlements. Esau, alas! was all the time himself a true Canaanite at heart. Son of Isaac and Rebekah, and grandson of Abraham and Sarah, as he was, Esau had nothing of his forefathers or his foremothers in him, unless it was some of the dregs of their remaining vices; and, as the apostle has it, some of their springing up roots of bitterness. All that Abraham and Sarah, and Isaac and Rebekah, had passed through; all their trials, and all their triumphs, and all their attainments of faith and of obedience, had left no mark at all on Esau, their so profane descendant. And everything that Esau did, every step that he took in life, every choice that he made in life, and every bargain that he struck, only made that more and more manifest. A man's choice in his marriage, more than anything else in this life, makes it manifest what that man is, and where his heart is. Now, Esau's marriage, fatal step as it also was, was not the passionate impulse of a moment, any more than his sale of his birthright had been. Esau had hunted for years with the brothers of Judith and Bashemath. He had eaten and drunken and danced with the Hittite inhabitants of the land. He had sacrificed and sworn and vowed to their false gods of the fields, and of the streams, and of the unclean groves. Like every reprobate from a better life, Esau had far outdone the sons of Beeri and Elon in their impieties and debaucheries. Till, at last, and in open defiance of all decency and religion, he brought home two Canaanite wives to his father's covenanted camp. "Now, all these things happened unto them for examples, and they are written for our admonition, upon whom the ends of the world are come." And thus it is that we see the same things in the end of the world that has come upon ourselves. A child is born and baptized in a God-fearing house; and yet, by some fatality, or what shall we call it, he grows up as much outside the best life of his father's house as Esau all his days was outside the best life of Isaac's house. He is a little heathen among his brothers and sisters and school-fellows. His birthright is the Sabbath-day, and the Lord's table, and the society of the best people in the city, and, first a youthhood, and then a manhood, of purity and piety and the service of Christ in His church. But his first act of free and independent life is to sell all that, sometimes for a better salary; sometimes for the smile and the patronage of the open enemies of his father's faith; and some-times for a coarser mess than even that. Years pass on till Esau sets up an openly heathen household in defiance of father and mother and all, which is ever after a grief of mind to Isaac and Rebekah. The tragedy is not so patent to us because we do not have Moses to write out our household histories, and Paul to comment on the writing, as in Esau's case; but to those who train themselves and accustom themselves to look on the world around them in this one single view as God's world, there is plenty of such profanity and self-reprobation going on among us every day.

What with the purpose of God according to election, and that purpose com-municated to Rebekah when she went to inquire of the Lord; what with Isaac's love for Esau because he did eat of his venison; what with Rebekah's retaliatory love for Jacob; what with Esau's increasing levity and profanity, and Jacob's increas-ing subtlety; what with Esau's defiant Canaanite marriage; and now, to crown all, Isaac's old age, blindness, and fast-approaching end—what with all that, that was as unhappy a house as was at that moment on the face of this unhappy earth. So full is that house, covenant promises and all, of guilty secrets, guilty memories, guilty wrongs, guilty remorses, guilty intentions, and guilty hopes and fears. It has often been pointed out what a mercy it is that God keeps our own future, and the future of our families, to Himself; and does not burden, and entangle, and tempt us with a knowledge that we are not able to bear. Rebekah would have children; and then she would know the secret things that belonged to Him who was form-ing her children in her womb; and, then, not able to wade into, and to keep her feet in the deep places of God, she fell into a life-long snare and sea of trouble, and labored all her days under a life-long cross. It would take a Shakespeare, as deep in grace as in nature, to put upon the stage that hell upon earth that opened its mouth day and night in Isaac's covenant tent. A more powerful and a more fruitful chapter for the sacred ends of tragedy was never written than the tragical chapter of Isaac's deathbed. The decayed life, and the still more decayed faith, of Abraham's only son Isaac; the cunning and treachery of Rebekah, the bride he had brought into his mother Sarah's tent in love; Jacob, the too willing tool of his cunning mother's chicanery and lies; the pitiful imposition perpetrated upon the blind old epicure; and, then, reprobate Esau's unavailing cry of remorse and revenge. Yes, verily. The ways of transgressors are hard! The wages of sin is death!

On the principle, then, that all these things about Esau are written for our admonition, how shall we be best admonished against Esau's profane and disas-trous mind? To know the truth about him, and about ourselves, is the first thing for us all to set about tonight. Well, to begin with, we are all more or less like Esau in our birth, and in our birthright, and in our profane and brutish mind about our birthright. Like Esau, we have all been born inside the covenant. We have all been sealed with the seal of the covenant. We have all been baptized for a future far greater, and far more full of blessing, than that future which fell either to Esau or to Jacob. But we have all Esau's profane mind and hard heart in us also. And, if any one would but teach us; if any great writer or great preacher, if any wise father or loving mother could and would but take us early in hand, and tell us, and let us see, that all this life is not to make what is called money, or to attain what is called success, or to fill our belly with what is called pleasure, but that God Himself has set us here so to live, and so to choose, and so to act as to put off every day this profane mind, and to put on a sacred, a spiritual, a divine, a heavenly mind—if any one with authority and with influence would but tell and teach us that! For, like Esau, to begin with, we have no imagination. We have no eyes, neither of body nor of mind, for God, or for Jesus Christ, or for heaven, or for hell, or for holiness, or for eternal life. Before we are out of our boyhood we are become vain in our imaginations, and our foolish hearts are darkened, and we worship and serve the creature more than the Creator. And for this cause God gives us over to vile affections, and to a reprobate mind. That was Esau's early history; and that is the early and life-long history of multitudes among ourselves. There is an intellectual, and with it a spiritual stupidity—there is no other name for it—that has already taken possession of one out of every two children that are born in our most covenanted households. They soon declare and show themselves to be utterly insensible to everything intellectual, spiritual, moral, noble, and above the world that knows not God. If they are rich and idle, they spend their days, like Esau, hunting down creatures of God that have more of God's image in them than their hunters have. They eat, and drink, and dress, and dance like Esau, with any Canaanite household which has sons and daughters like themselves. But they never read a good book. They never attend a good teacher. They have neither time nor taste for anything that pertains to the mind or the heart. Philo calls Esau a "wooden" man; and the number of wooden men and women who sit at our dinner tables eating venison and drinking wine, and who are then driven all the noisy night after to our city assemblies, far outnumber those people who are made of any finer or more spiritual material. Put off the wood and the earth, put off the insensibility and the profanity that are still in you all, my brethren. And put on mind, and heart, and understanding, and consideration, and imagination. Choose your reading. Choose your company. Choose your husband and your wife. Choose your birthright. Choose life, and not death; blessing, and not cursing; heaven, and not hell. You can, if you choose. You can, if you like. Only, lay this to heart with all holy fear, that there is insensibility, and stupidity, and profanity enough in you by nature, and up to this day, to make you, amid all your covenant surroundings, a reprobate of a far worse kind than ever Esau was, unless, with tears, you seek a place of repentance. And it will take all your tears, and all your time, and all the repentance, and all the remission of sins, that Christ can give you out of His place of exaltation, to enable you to escape his end at last who ate and drank, and despised his birthright.

Young men! come, come, and I will tell you! All of you who have not up to this night quite sold the whole of your birthright. Oh! never, never do it. Die, and we shall bury you with honor, and with assurance; but, oh! my son, my brother, never, never, till the day of your death, sell to man or woman or devil your divine birthright. Your birthright of truth, and honesty, and honor, and, especially, of chastity. Sell everything but that! There must be some men here tonight just at the crisis, and just in the temper, in which Esau came home so hungry from the hunt.

There are men in this house who are saying this to themselves: "I am alone. I have nobody to care for me. If I had, it would be different, and I would be a better man. But in all this big city, in all broad Scotland, there is no one for whose sake I need keep my head above water. Though I go out of this house, and sell myself to hell tonight, no one will lament me. What profit shall it do to me to make any more stand against the gambling-table, or the dram-shop, or anything else!" My own son! ring my bell tonight, and I will talk with you and will tell you the rest. I have not lived to gray hairs in a city, and been a minister of city families, and city young men, without learning things about birthrights and their sale and their redemption too—things that cannot be told on the housetop. No minister in Edinburgh knows more or can speak better about these things than I can do. If you have no minister who can and will tell you about Esau, and about himself, and about yourself, and about Jesus Christ, ring my bell! It will be late that I do not open the door! I will be busy that we do not have another hour over Esau—you and I.

But what is to be said to those who are long past all that? What is to be said to those whose birthright has been sold past all redemption long ago? To those who have sold, not their birthright only, but their very selves, soul and body, so long ago, and so often since then? All this about Esau is agony to them. They are beside themselves with remorse and with misery. They are tired to death seeking for a place of repentance. They are beginning to seek for a field of blood, and some Sabbath night, unless God himself prevent them, they will go out like Judas. But God will prevent. He will come, and He will prevent all that from this time henceforth. "Save from going down to the pit, I have found a ransom. O Esau, thou hast destroyed thyself; but in Me is thine help. Ye have sold yourselves for naught, but ye shall be redeemed without money. What fruit had ye then in those things of which ye are now ashamed? For the end of those things is death. For the wages of sin is death; but the gift of God is eternal life. Who is a God like unto Thee, that pardoneth iniquity, and passeth by the transgression of the remnant of His heritage? He retaineth not His anger for ever, because He delighteth in mercy. He will turn again, He will have compassion upon us, He will subdue our iniquities; and Thou wilt cast all our sins into the depths of the sea. Blessed be the God and Father of our Lord Jesus Christ, who, according to His abundant mercy, hath begotten us again to a lively hope by the resurrection of Jesus Christ from the dead; to an inheritance incorruptible, undefiled, and that fadeth not away, reserved in heaven for you, who are kept by the power of God through faith unto salvation, ready to be revealed in the last time."

16
Rebekah

A SWEETER chapter was never written than the twenty-fourth of Genesis, nor a sadder than the twenty-seventh, and all the bridge that spans the gulf between them is the twenty-eighth verse of the twenty-fifth chapter. The picture of aged Abraham swearing his most trusty servant about a bride for his son Isaac; that servant's journey to Padan-aram in the far east; Rebekah, first at the well, and then in her mother's house; and then her first sight of her future husband—that long chapter is a perfect gem of ancient authorship. But, the sweetness of the picture, and the perfection of the writing, only go to deepen and darken the terrible tragedy of Isaac's deathbed. That the ship was launched on such a golden morning only the more darkens the surrounding gloom when she goes to the bottom.

"And they said, We will call the damsel, and inquire at her own mouth. And they called Rebekah, and said unto her: Wilt thou go with this man? And she said, I will go." Though no one knew it, and though she did not know it herself, Rebekah's heart had been Isaac's all the time. The story of Abraham her old kinsman's call; the aged Terah's enterprise and pilgrimage; Isaac's fair and princely youth, and then his offering on the altar—all that had been a household word in Rebekah's mother's house, and all that had for long fired Rebekah's so easily fired heart. And thus it was that, every day for long, as she went out to the well for water, she had looked away west over the vast sands of Mesopotamia, and had wished to heaven that she had been born a man-child, so that she, too, might have been called of God to go out to His land of promise, and there to have her part in the founding of a family of saints, and princes, and great men of God. And, now, what has God wrought for Rebekah! Is she beside herself? Is she awake, and is this broad daylight, and not a dream? Her heart bounds up to God and blesses Him, as she goes down to the well and waters camel after camel, the camels that are Abraham's and Sarah's and Isaac's camels. And never did woman's heart so go forth of her as Rebekah's heart did when Abraham's servant put an earring of gold upon her face, and bracelets of gold upon her hands. Had Rebekah had to walk barefoot over all the burning sands that separated Padan-aram from the land of promise, nothing would have kept Rebekah back from an election and a call so divine, so sweet to her heart, and so welcome as was that warm argument of the aged Eliezer of Damascus. Hearken, O daughter, and consider, and incline thine ear; forget also thine own people, and thy father's house. Or ever I was aware, says the bride in the Song, my heart had made me like the chariots of Amminadib. And Rebekah said, Yes, I will go.

The single plank that spans the terrible gulf between Isaac's marriage-bed and his death-bed is laid for us in this single sentence: "Isaac loved Esau because he did eat of his venison; but Rebekah loved Jacob." And, standing on that plank, he that hath ears will hear that bottomless pit of married sorrow that Isaac and Rebekah had dug and filled for themselves and for their two sons, boiling up and roaring all around him. It sickens us to stand there and to think of such life-long sorrow after such a sweet start. There are years and years and years of secret alienation, and distaste, and dislike in that little verse. There are heart-burnings and heart-breaks; hidden hatreds and open quarrels; deceits and duplicities, and discoveries of deceits and duplicities, enough to make Isaac old and blind and dead before the time. When the two twin-brothers were brought up day after day and hour after hour in an atmosphere of favoritism, and partiality, and indulgence, and injustice, no father, no mother, can surely need to have it pointed out to them what present misery, and what future wages of such sin, is all to be seen and to be expected in that evil house. Eloquent with wickedness as the words are—Isaac loved Esau, but Rebekah loved Jacob—yet they make little impression on us till we have read on and on through chapter after chapter, full of the fruit of that wicked little verse. But, then, after we are glutted with the woes of that long and sorely chastised house, if we have any heart, and conscience, and imagination, we come back and stand on that reeling plank till the smoke of the torment of Isaac's and Rebekah's sin comes up like Sodom itself into our blinded eyes.

> Not in their brightness, but their earthly stains,
> Are the true seed vouchsafed to earthly eyes,
> And saints are lowered that the world may rise.

One of the very first fruits of that devil's garden that Isaac and Rebekah had sowed for themselves was the two heathen marriages that Esau went out and made and brought home, and which were such a grief to Isaac and to Rebekah. That great grief would seem to have been almost the only thing the two old people were at one about by that time. It was a bitter pill to Rebekah, those two marriages of Esau. And it was bitter only. She got no after-sweet out of it, as she might so well have got. For the old disorder and disgrace still went on; only, henceforth to be increased and aggravated by the introduction of those two new sources of disorder and disgrace, Judith and Bashemath, into that already sufficiently disordered and disgraced house-hold. Esau is greatly blamed by some preachers for his heathen marriages; but, surely, quite unfairly. We talk to Esau about the covenant, and what not. But Esau answers us that, for his part, he saw little covenant in his father's house beyond the name. And Esau might very well think that he could surely get a mother for his children from nearer home than Padan-aram, who would be as fair, and wise, and kind, and good to them as his covenant mother had been to him. Poor Esau could not say what Santa Teresa says about herself in her happy *Life of Herself*. "It helped me, too," she tells us, "that I never saw my father and my mother respect anything but goodness." And again: "My mother was a woman of great goodness, and had great sense." Poor, mishandled Esau could not say that to his children. The disrespect and utter lack of reverence that his mother showed to his father made Judith's respect and reverence to Beeri, and Bashemath's respect and reverence to Elon, an attraction and a refuge and a rest to Esau's restless heart. And I do not believe that the two Hittite women, whom Esau made his two wives, ever played him such a trick in his old age as Rebekah played his old father Isaac.

My brethren, let our children not hear any less in our houses about calls, and covenants, and covenant promises, and covenant hopes; but let them see far more covenant fruit in family love, family fair-play, family reverence, and family oneness of mind.

As to Rebekah's treatment of her quiet, silent, retiring, fast-aging husband, there is this to be said for her, that there is some reason to believe that she had not had a very good example set her in this respect in her old home. She had seen her old father Bethuel overlooked, slighted, often forgotten, and often pushed aside in his own house. Had Bethuel's daughter been made of the finest and most womanly-hearted stuff, that humiliating sight at home would have secured to her future husband all the more reverence and honor, deference and love. That Bethuel seldom spoke at his own table would have made a daughter of the finest kind to say to herself that, if ever she had a husband—let her tongue be cut out before her husband was ever talked down in his own house. Only, Rebekah, with all her beauty, and with all her courage, and with all her ambition to be in the covenant line, lacked the best thing in a woman, covenant line or no—womanly sensibility, tenderness, quietness, humility, and self-submission. And, though that speck on her heart was so small as to be wholly invisible as long as she was still a maid, and a bride, and a young wife, yet it was there. And by the time that Rebekah became no longer a bride or a young wife, this speck had spread till both her heart and her character had wholly lost all wholesomeness, and sweetness, and strength. "The one thing certain about a wife is that the result is different from the expectation—that is, if there were ever any particular and defined expectations at all. Age, illness, an increasing family, no family at all, household cares, want of means, isolation, incompatible prejudices, quarrels, social difficulties, all tell on the wife more than on the husband, and make her change more rapidly into that which she was not. Be she strong or weak, she is apt to revert to her own ways, if she has them, and if she has what is called a will of her own." And, after a rest and some refreshment Isaac still went on: "There will not be real union without much self-sacrifice; each chiefly bent on pleasing the other. To most men and women this is not easy; for, what with self-confidence, self-will, self-esteem, and selfishness pure and simple, they enter the marriage state with a foregone conclusion on all the points upon which difference is possible. And there are many. And they will remain stumbling-blocks and rocks of offence, unless one will give way to the other, or both are softened by higher influences."

"And the wife see that she reverence her husband," says Paul, with his eye on Rebekah. Yes; but what if she cannot? What if there is so little left that is to be reverenced about her husband? "It is one of the best bonds in a wife," says Bacon, "if she think her husband wise." No doubt. But what if he is not wise? What if he is a fool? What if a wife wakens up to see that she has yoked herself till death to a churl, or to a boor, or to an ignoramus, or to a coxcomb, or to a lazy, idle log, or to a shape of a man whose God is his belly, or his purse, or just his own small, miserable self? What is a woman, so ensnared, to do? Well, she will need to be both a true woman and a true saint, if she is to do right: if she is to do the best now possible in a life of such exquisite and incessant misery. But it can be done.

It has been done. And it is being done all around her by thousands of her sisters in the strength of their womanhood, and by the help of God. Let her say: I would have him. I would not see what everybody else saw, and what some of my people were so bold and so cruel as to tell me they saw. I walked into it with my eyes shut. I thought that just to be married would be heaven upon earth. I was sure he would improve. I said that if ever woman helped a man to improve I would be that woman. And he said with such warmth that I was that woman to him, and that there was not another woman like me in the whole earth. I made this bitter bed with my own hands; and no one shall ever know, and last of all my poor husband, what a bitter bed it is to his weak and evil wife! That is the true line to take when a woman is told to reverence a husband for whom no one else has any reverence or affection. Let her determine to be a New Testament wife to him. Let her believe that Jesus Christ said, and still says, Take up thy cross daily! And let her rise up to believe and to see this, that a salvation for her immortal soul of a far deeper, a far more inward, a far more perfect, and a far more everlasting kind, lies for her in her unhappy marriage, than if she had been the proudest and most puffed-up wife in the city. These are they which came out of great tribulation, it is said in heaven over multitudes of such wives. Let her say to herself, then, every day, that this is her great tribulation. Let her put her finger on it and say, This is that through which I must go up, if I am to go up at all. And, at the worst, he is my husband. And if he is not all I would fain believe him to be, yet let me go on trying to believe it. And, perhaps, that will help him. I have not helped him as I promised and intended to do. I have dwelt on my own disappointment and shipwreck, and not enough on his. There are two sides to our married life. There is my husband's side as well as mine; and there is his mother's side as well as my mother's. Perhaps it will help him to overcome if I behave as if he had overcome. Perhaps, if I act as if I were happy, it may help to make him happy. Let me behave myself as if he were wise, and true, and noble, and every way good, and it will greatly help to make him all that. Is there not a Scripture somewhere which says that husbands are sometimes to be won by the conversation of their wives? And, that a wife's best ornament is a meek and quiet spirit? Let me be such a wife as I have never yet been. She who so bends her back to the burden will soon find that the load is not so heavy as she thought it was. What a pity it was that Rebekah did not go to Hagar's well for water every morning, and there talk to herself in that way till she went home to reverence and to love Isaac her husband, saying all the way, Thou God seest me! What a pity it was that Rebekah did not do that!

17
Jacob

THERE was no Old Testament saint of them all who, first and last, saw more of the favor and forgiveness of God than Jacob. And yet, with all that, the great sins of Jacob's youth and the great sinfulness of Jacob's heart both found him out every day he lived down to the day of his death. Of Jacob, and of Rebekah his mother, it may truly be said, Thou, O Lord, wast a God that forgavest them, though Thou tookest vengeance on their inventions. It is part of Moses' subtlety, as Philo calls it, to tell us how much more Rebekah loved Jacob than she loved Esau, whom Isaac loved; and then, to go on to give us two examples, and two examples only, of that love. The first example of Rebekah's motherly love is seen when she dresses up Jacob in Esau's clothes, and drills him into the very tones of Esau's voice, as also into all Esau's hearty huntsman's ways in the house, till she has rehearsed her favorite son Jacob into a finished and perfect supplanter. And then, her second love is seen in the terror and in the haste with which she ships off Jacob to Haran lest Esau in his revenge should send one of his shafts through the supplanter's heart. All that stands in Moses, and much more like that, both in and after Moses; and yet here are we, down in the days of the New Testament, still dressing up our daughters, and emigrating our sons, as if we had been the first fathers and mothers in all the world to whom God had said, I will give thee thy wages.

Esau had been all up and down the whole country round about a hundred times. That bold and cunning hunter would be days and weeks away from home when the season came round for the venison to be on the hills. But Jacob had never been out of sight of his mother's tent-pole till now. The fugitive spent his first night in a herdman's hut, and his second night in the hut of a friendly native of the land; but after that all his nights were spent in the open air. And the first of Jacob's open-air nights is a night to be remembered, as we say. Poor Jacob! This is the beginning of the visitation of the iniquity of the fathers upon the children to the third and fourth generation. A Syrian ready to perish, were it not that man's extremity is God's opportunity. And were it not that Jacob, and all his true seed, are known to themselves and to us by the hundred and sixteenth psalm: "The sorrows of death compassed me, and the pains of hell gat hold upon me; I found trouble and sorrow. I was brought low, and He helped me." And he took of the stones of that place and put them for his pillows, and lay down in that place to sleep. And he dreamed. God spake in divers manners in those early days. Jacob dreamed that night because Rebekah had neither a Bible nor a *Pilgrim's Progress*, nor a hymn-book, to put into his scrip beside his bread and his dates and his oil. No; nor, worst of all, a good example. Still, she may forget her sucking child that she should not have compassion on the son of her womb, yet will God not forget him. And thus it was that Jacob dreamed as he did dream his first night away from home. How dreadful is this place! Jacob had been taught to feel and to say how dreadful was that place where his father's altar was built; and those places where God had come down to talk with Adam, and Abel, and Noah, and Abraham, and Hagar. But Jacob had no idea that God was at Luz, or would ever come down to talk with him there. And, then, more than that, there was this. God's presence, God's holiness, but above all God's great grace, will always make the place dreadful to a great sinner. Dreadful, with a solemnizing, awful, overwhelming dread that there is no other word for. How dreadful did all Jacob's life of sin look at Luz! He had had his own thoughts about himself, and about his mother, and about his father, and about his brother all these last three days across the wilderness. But it was not till that morning at Luz that Jacob learned to say: Against Thee, Thee only, have I sinned! How dreadful did his past life look now, as it lay naked and open under that gate of heaven and that shining ladder! The lasting lesson of that best of all mornings to Jacob is memorably preserved to us and to our children in our Second Paraphrase; and as often as we sing or say to God that noble piece we still reap into our own hearts the first sheaf out of the rich harvest of Jacob's life. We always read that chapter and sing that paraphrase on the Sabbath night before we emigrate another of the sons of Jacob; but, alas! too late; for by that time our family worship, like Isaac's that night, is but locking the stable door after the steed is stolen.

What a down-come it was from the covenant-heights of Bethel to the cattle-troughs of Haran! What a cruel fall from the company of ascending and descending angels into the clutches of a finished rogue like Laban! Jacob had been all but carried up of angels from Bethel and taken into an inheritance incorruptible and undefiled; but, instead of that, he is taken down to Padan-aram, where he is cheated out of his wages, and cheated out of his wife, and cheated, and cheated, and cheated again, ten times cheated, and that too by his own mother's brother, till cheating came out of Jacob's nostrils, and stank in his eyes, and became hateful as hell to Jacob's heart. We say that Greek sometimes meets Greek. We say that diamond sometimes cuts diamond. We calculate the length of handle his spoon would need to have who sups with the devil. We speak about the seller being sold. And we quote David to the effect that to the froward God will show Himself froward; and Paul to the same effect, that as a man soweth so shall he reap. Yes. Other people had been cheating their fathers and their brothers all these years as well as Rebekah and Jacob. Other little boys had been taking prizes in the devil's sly school besides Rebekah's favorite son. Laban, Rebekah's brother, and bone of her bone, had been making as pious speeches at Bethuel's blind bedside as ever Jacob made at Isaac's. And now that the actors are all ready, and the stage is all built, and the scenery is all hung up, all the world is invited in to see the serio-comedy of the Syrian biter bit, or Rebekah's poor lost sheep shorn to the bone by the steely shears of Shylock her brother. "What is this that thou hast done unto me? Wherefore hast thou so beguiled me?"—Jacob appealed and remonstrated in his sweet, injured, salad innocence. Jacob had never seen or heard the like of it in his country. It shocked terribly and irrecoverably Jacob's inborn sense of right and wrong; it almost shook down Jacob's whole faith in the God of Bethel. And so still. We never see what wickedness there is in lies, and treachery, and cheatery, and injury of all kinds till we are cheated and lied against and injured ourselves. We will sit all our days and speak against our brother till some one comes and reports to us what they say who sit and speak against us. And then the whole blackness and utter abominableness of detraction and calumny and slander breaks out upon us, till we cut out our tongue rather than ever again so employ it. It was Jacob's salvation that he fell into the hands of that cruel land-shark, his uncle Laban. Jacob's salvation is somewhat nearer now than when he believed at Bethel; but, all the same, what is bred in the bone is not got clean rid of in a day. It were laughable to a degree, if it were not so sad, to see Jacob, after all his smart, still peeling the stakes of poplar, and chestnut, and hazel where the cattle came to drink, till it came about that all the feebler births in the cattle-pens were Laban's and all the stronger were Jacob's. And till Laban had to give it up and to confess himself completely out-witted; and till he piously and affectionately proposed a covenant at Mizpah, saying, This pillar be witness that I will not pass over it to harm thee, nor thou to harm me.

Before we leave Laban and his enfeebled cattle, we take some excellent lessons away with us. And one of those excellent lessons is a lesson in the most perfect English style. The whole Laban episode is rich in gems of composition and expression. The Master of expression himself falls far below Moses more than once in these chapters. The prince in the *Tempest* is wine and water compared with Jacob. Even Burns has it better than Shakespeare:

The man that lo'es his mistress weel
Nae travel makes him weary.

But this is still better than either: "Jacob served seven years for Rachel, and they seemed to him but a few days, for the love he had to her." And there are other gems of the pen scattered lavishly about this same passage quite as good as that. Only, we are in quest tonight of better gems than gems of English, beautiful and rare and precious as they are.

We may emigrate our sons to the gold-fields of South Africa, or to the cattle-ranches of America or Australia, and they may make such a fortune there as to be able to come home after we are no more, and build in the West-end, and educate their children in this capital of learning. But as long as Esau lives, as long as that man or that woman lives whom our son supplanted so long ago, he will build his house over a volcano, and will travel home to it with a trembling heart. And Jacob's heart often trembled and often stood still all the way of the wilderness from Haran to the Jabbok. Your son will send home secret instructions to some old class-fellow who is now at the top of the law to effect a peace, if not forgiveness and reconciliation, at any price. And so did Jacob. Jacob took a great herd of Laban's whitest cattle: goats, and camels, and kine, and everything he could think of, and sent herd after herd on beforehand so as to quench the embers of his brother's wrath. We have a like instance in that Highlander who, on hearing Robert Bruce inveighing in the High Kirk against those sins of which he knew himself to have been guilty, came up to the great preacher and said, "I'se gie thee twenty cows to gree God and me." But, to Jacob's consternation, Esau never looked at those lowing, snow-white herds, but put on his armor in silence, and came posting north at the head of four

hundred men. When Jacob's scouts returned and told him all that, he was in absolute desperation. Had he been alone it would have been easy. But, with all these
women and children, and with all these cattle and other encumbrances, was there
ever a man taken in such a cruel trap! But he had still one whole night to count
on before Esau could be at the Jabbok. And here is his prayer that night, preserved
word for word to us his sons; his instant prayer after the scouts came back: "I am
not worthy of the least of all the mercies, and of all the truth, which Thou hast
showed to Thy servant: for with my staff I passed over this Jordan; and now I am
become these two bands. Deliver me, I pray Thee, from the hand of my brother
Esau, lest he smite me, and the women with the children." That is a fine sentence
about the staff. It is points like that in a prayer and in a psalm that touch and take
captive both God and man. That staff at the first had been a birthday gift from his
twin-brother Esau. The cunning hunter had cut it out of the wood one day, and
had carried home his snares and his venison slung over it on his shoulder. When
he saw that Jacob envied it, Esau smoothed the stout branch better, and straight-
ened it out, and carved E. and J. into a true lover's knot under the handle of it,
and laid it beside Jacob's lentil dish on the morning of their double birthday. That
staff felt like so much lead when Jacob took it into his hand to run from home; but
he would need it, and, though it sometimes burned his hand to a red-hot cinder,
somehow he never could throw it away. That staff stood sentinel over its dreaming
master at Bethel, and with its help he waded the Jordan, and sprang the Jabbok, till
he laid it down to water Rachel's sheep in Padan-aram. Jacob and his staff were a
perfect proverb in Padan-aram. They were never found separated. Jacob never felt
alone when he had his staff in his hand; and many a time he was overheard talking to it, and it to him. And now, at the return to Jabbok, with that staff he made
his prayer and praise to God, as if it had been some sacred instrument of a priest
which had power with God. And, no doubt, we all have a staff, or a pen, or a ring,
or book, or a Bible, or something or other that has gone with us through all our
banishments, migrations, ups and downs in life, and when our hearts are soft and
our prayers come upon us we again take that old companion by the hand. You will
have a blue old cloak, like Newman's, or a brown old plaid that you bought while
yet you were in your mother's house—I have one—and you feel sure that you
could pit that old plaid with a story hanging at every single thrum and tassel of it,
against Jacob's so-travelled staff any day. You will give orders that that old wrap is
to be your winding-sheet; and you will wear it, with all its memories of judgment
and of mercy, under your wedding garment in heaven. "With my staff I passed
over this Jordan, and now I am become these two bands."

   And he took them and sent them over the brook, and sent over all that he had.
And when the night fell upon him Jacob was left alone. But now, who can tell how
near Esau may be by this time! That cunning, cruel, revengeful man! Till, as the
darkness fell so obscure, every plunge of the Jabbok, and every roar of the storm,
made Jacob feel the smell of Esau's coat and the blow of his hairy hand. Whether
in the body, Jacob to the day of his death could never tell; or whether out of the
body, Jacob could never tell; but such a night of terror and of battle no other man
ever spent. It was Esau, and it was not Esau. It was God, and it was not God. It

was both God and Esau; till Jacob to the day of his death could never tell Who the terrible Wrestler really was. Just before the morning broke, with one last wrench Jacob was left halt and lame for life. When, as if from the open heaven, he was baptized of the gracious Wrestler into a new name. For as He departed and the morning broke, the mysterious Man said to Jacob as he lay prostrate at His feet, Thou art henceforth no longer Jacob, but Israel, for as a prince thou hast power with God and with men, and hast prevailed.

Jacob's new name is a great surprise to us. We would never have called Jacob a prince. There are many other names and titles and epithets we would have given to this overtaken son of Isaac and Rebekah; this broken brother of Esau, whose sins have so found him out. But God proclaims Jacob ever after the Jabbok none of our names, but a prince. And for this reason. Prayer, such prayer as Jacob prayed that night, is the princeliest act any man can possibly perform. The noblest, the grandest, the boldest, the most magnificent act a human being can perform on this earth is to pray; to pray, that is, as Jacob prayed at Peniel. No man is a prince with God all at once; no, nor after many years. Few men—one here and another there—ever come to any princeliness at all, either in their prayers or in anything else. Jacob had twenty years, and more, of sin and of sorrow, of remorse and of repentance, of gratitude for such a miraculous past, and of beaten-back effort after a better life, and then, to crown all, he had that unparalleled night of fear and prayer at the Jabbok; a night's work such that even the Bible has nothing else like it till our Lord's night in Gethsemane—and it is only after all that, and far more than Moses with all his honesty and all his subtlety has told us—it is only then that Jacob is proclaimed of God a prince with God. You must understand that prayer, to be called prayer, is not what you hear people all about you calling prayer. That is not prayer. Jacob's thigh was out of joint, and our Lord's sweat was as it were great drops of blood falling to the ground. Prayer is colossal work. There were giants in those days. Prayer takes all our heart, and all our soul, and all our strength, and all our mind, and all our life, sleeping and waking. Prayer is the princeliest, the noblest, the most unearthly act on this side heaven. Only pray, then; only pray aright, and enough, and it will change your whole nature as it changed Jacob's. Till, from the meanest, the falsest, the most treacherous, the most deceitful, the most found-out, and the most miserable of men, it will make you also a very prince with God and with men. Happy is he that hath the God of Jacob for his help!

18
Joseph

JOSEPH, the future ruler of Egypt, was the late-born and the greatly-beloved son of Jacob and Rachel. Joseph inherited all his mother's proverbial gracefulness and sweetness and attractive beauty. And then Joseph's intellectual gifts were such that, taken along with the purity and the nobility of his character, they lifted him up out of a pit, and out of a prison, and set him in a seat of power and of honor scarcely second to the seat of Pharaoh himself. At the same time Joseph climbed up to that high seat through many great risks and out of many great sufferings; and he ran some of the greatest of those risks at the hand of his too-doting father. Were it not that our own hearts so continually condemn us, we would turn on Jacob with indignation for his mischievous treatment of Joseph. Can Jacob have forgotten the sea of trouble into which his father's favoritism, and his mother's indulgence, cast both themselves and their children? The woeful harvest of all that long past folly is still making both Jacob's life and many other lives as bitter as death to this day; and yet here is Jacob poisoning the whole of his family life also, and spoiling Joseph, just as Isaac and Rebekah had spoiled and poisoned their own and their children's lives when Jacob and Esau were still their children. We would denounce Jacob for his insane treatment of Joseph were it not that we are all ourselves repeating sins and follies every day from which we and our families have suffered for generations.

Joseph's coat of many colors was like to have been his winding-sheet, such was the envy and the hatred of his half-brothers at Rachel's well-favored, richly-talented, and over-ornamented son. "Our coats be of one color; so should his," grumbled Dan, and all Dan's brothers agreed with his spiteful and angry words. The patriarchs, moved with envy, says Stephen in the Acts, sold Joseph into Egypt. And Jacob, on his death-bed, when he was blessing Joseph, said of him that the archers had hated him, and had shot their arrows at him, and had sorely wounded him. It is usual for mankind, says Josephus on the text, to envy their nearest relatives and their best friends for their eminence and for their prosperity. And yet, if Dan would but wait a little, and would but command himself a little, the brightness will soon begin to fade out of his brother's many-colored coat. Let a short season run and there will be nothing to pain Dan's eye and to wring and heat his heart. Some other fond father will soon begin to clothe his spoiled son in a coat full of more and more brilliant colors than Joseph's coat; till Joseph's coat will be so eclipsed that he also will join the archers' ranks, and will shoot at his rival with their envious arrows. Another author will soon rise and will take the public taste. His new books will soon be on every table, and his new name in every mouth, till that success which so galls you today will be completely forgotten by you and forgiven. His crowded pews will before long begin to thin out, and new orators will spring up and will attract and draw off that preacher's painful crowd. And if none of these considerations will quiet Dan's evil eye, and if he really feels his eye to be an evil and a wicked and a murderous eye, let him take his evil eye to God. To whom else can such an eye as that be taken? Let him lift his so sorely stung eye up to Joseph's God. Ask the God of love to consider you and to pity you. Ask Him not to spurn and spit on you. Ask Him to be merciful to your secret and incessant misery. Shut your door on God and yourself, and on your knees ask Him still to add to your brother's goodliness, and to his talents, and to his honor, and to his happiness, and to his usefulness; if only He will anoint your eyes with enough love, and if only He will take out of your eyes that same evil light that glanced so murderously in the patriarchs' eyes as often as they again saw Joseph in his shining coat. Importune Him to enable you to love Joseph, till you enjoy, as if they were your own, those so many and so shining colors of his coat. If ever Almighty God has wrought that salvation in Dan, or in any of Dan's brothers on this side the new Jerusalem, ask Him, for Christ's sake, to do it a little to you.

Joseph was only seventeen years old when his two so intoxicating dreams came to him. You must always recall Joseph's unripe age, and his complete inexperience, before you blame him too much for the way he talked about his prerogatives and prospects of greatness. The time will come when all Joseph's splendid achievements, and all his matchless honor and glory, will not make Joseph open a lip about himself. But he was only seventeen as yet, and he had never been for an hour out of his father's flattering sight. And thus it was that Joseph's future modesty, and humility, and self-command, and knowledge of other men's hearts, and thoughtfulness for other men's feelings and temptations, had not yet begun to come to him. Had Joseph been but a little older, and had he been but once or twice at Dothan, he would have hidden his dreams in his heart like so many guilty secrets. But, innocent child that he was, he must up and out of his bed, and tell all his dreams to all the house. And so intent was he in what so much interested himself that he did not see the ugly looks on the faces of his brothers. And, like Joseph, till we are well past seventeen, and have been for some time away from home, we talk about nothing else but our own dreams also. Other men dreamed last night as well as we, but they never get their mouths open where we are. We talk the whole table down. We have just come home from the pulpit, or from the platform, or from the desk, or from the instrument, or from a visit, or from an entertainment, or from what not, and our vain hearts are full. We never think that all the other people at table are as full of themselves as we are. We never see that they also are bursting to get at the only topic that interests them, which is not at all the same topic that so interests us. We mistake that silence and that suspense. We think that all that silence and all that suspense means that all our audience are as full of our interests as we are ourselves, and are waiting to hear us. While all the time, they can scarcely command themselves with weariness and disgust. Be sure your company is as full of you as you are of yourself before you again give the reins to your galloping tongue. Be sure that they all worship you. Be sure that you are their god. Be sure that they are all your wife and children. Be sure that they have no interests, or occupations, or vanities of their own. Be sure of all their love and devotion and patience. In short, be sure that you are in heaven before you keep the whole house waiting to break their fast till you have told out to the end all your dreams of last night. And it came to pass that they stripped Joseph of his coat, his coat of many colors, that was upon him. And they took him and cast him into a pit, and then they sat down to eat bread. Is that another subtlety of Moses? Does Moses insinuate that Joseph's brothers had never till now sat down to eat bread in entire peace since the day that Joseph began to dream? With all their faults, Joseph would have been eating bread at that moment with the patriarchs but for his spotted coat and his irrepressible dreams. I overheard a conversation something like this not long ago: "Shall we ask him to dinner, and invite So-and-so to meet him?" "No, I think not." "Why?" "Why? Because the last time he was with us he talked two mortal hours about himself, till everybody but himself must have seen contempt and disgust written as plain as day on every face. No. But if only he were not so full of himself, what a welcome guest he would be! And with such talents, and with such a position, what might he not do!"

There are some men, on the other hand, whom you can never waylay into once opening their lips about themselves. Two such men stand out enviably and honorably to me in my acquaintance. And they are just the two men in all my acquaintance I would most like to hear on themselves. But, no. Never they. Whether it is pride—I sometimes think it is; or whether it is scorn of their company—as it may well be; or whether it is absence of mind, or age, or experience, or knowledge of the hearts of men, till they will not commit themselves to men, I am sometimes divided; but, be it what it may, I never yet saw either of them take up a single moment of Joseph's time. There is such a thing as having too much of a good thing. And there is a golden mean in this matter also, if Joseph from the one side, and my two friends from the other side, could only strike it.

That dreadful pit in Dothan was the beginning of Joseph's salvation. The first night he spent in that pit recalled to Joseph's mind what his father had often told him of his first night from home, as also of that other night at the Jabbok. And as Joseph lay in that horrible pit, and dreamed and prayed, behold, the very same ladder of Bethel is let down into the bottom of the pit. "I am the Lord God of Abraham, and of Isaac, and of Jacob thy father. And behold, I am with thee, and will keep thee in all places whither thou goest. For I will not leave thee till I have done all that which I have spoken to thee of." And, all that night after, Joseph could think of nothing else but the sins of his youth; his vanity, his proud superiority and superciliousness to his brothers, his evil reports concerning his brothers, his talkativeness about himself, and all the temptations and provocations into which he had led his brothers. That deep pit was brimful of such remorseful thoughts and prayers, when Judah appeared at its mouth with cords and grappling irons to draw Joseph up to the daylight. But it was only to kill him with a far worse death; for that morning Joseph was sold to the Midianite slave-dealers of Egypt for twenty pieces of silver. Twenty pieces of silver was Joseph's whole price that day in Dothan. Those who know Joseph's after-history will flash forward their minds, and will contrast the Prime Minister of Pharaoh with that slave lad sold for that paltry price at the mouth of that pit that day. And, tomorrow, when you buy an apprentice, or a message boy, of his widowed mother for five shillings a week, think of Joseph for a moment, and say to yourself, Who knows what the future may have in store for my message boy and for me? Who knows how I may go down, while he goes up? Who knows the talents of God that may lie hidden in that friendless boy? Who knows what place he may be predestined to fill in the church and in the world? And even if he comes to nothing of all that; if he never becomes a great man, yet, even so, such thoughts, such imaginations, such forecasts will help you to treat him well, and will help to make you a good man and a good master, whatever your slave-boy may come, or may not come, to be.

The good work that the pit in Dothan began in Joseph, those still more terrible days and nights on the way down to Egypt carried on. Lashed to the loaded side of a huge cane-waggon, and himself loaded with the baggage of Gilead for the Egyptian market, Joseph toiled on under the midday sun, thankful to be left alone of his churlish masters in the red-hot air. Put yourself in Joseph's place. The favorite of his father; a child on whom no wind was ever let blow, and no sun was ever let strike; with servants to wait on his every wish, and to dress and anoint him for every meal; with loving looks and fond words falling continually upon him from the day he was born; and now, lashed to the side of a slave caravan, and with the whistling whip of his Ishmaelite owner laid on his shoulder till he sank in the sand. But you must add this to the picture, else you will not have the picture complete: "The Lord was with Joseph, and Joseph found grace in the sight of the Lord." Yes, the Lord was more with Joseph, more and better far, than ever He had been as long as Joseph was the spoiled child of his father, and the continual snare of his brothers. And there are young men in this city suffering hardships and persecutions in workshops and in offices as sore to bear as was Joseph's load of labor and ill-usage of the Ishmaelites. And the Lord is with them also as He never was so long as they were spoilt sons at home, getting all things their own way. And as they silently and prayerfully take up their cross daily, and wait out the will of God, they are thereby putting off a past that would have been their sure destruction— and had almost been—and are preparing themselves for a future as sure, and as full of the providence of God, as ever was Joseph's future. It is good for a man that he bear the yoke in his youth. He sitteth alone and keepeth silence, because he hath borne it upon him. He putteth his mouth in the dust, if so be there may be hope. He giveth his cheek to him that smiteth him; he is filled full with reproach. For the Lord will not cast off for ever; but, though He cause grief, yet will He have compassion according to the multitude of His mercies. "How many saints," William Law rejoices, "has adversity sent to heaven! And how many poor sinners has prosperity plunged into everlasting misery! This man had never been debauched, but for his fortune and advancement; that had never been pious, but through his poverty and disgrace. She that is envied for her beauty may perchance owe all her misery to it; and another may be for ever happy for having no admirers of her person. One man succeeds in everything, and so loses all; another meets with nothing but crosses and disappointments, and thereby gains more than all the world is worth."

Even if Potiphar paid thirty or even forty pieces of silver for his Hebrew slave, we know now what a good bargain he got that day. For that handful of silver the captain of Pharaoh's guard came into possession of all the splendid talents that lay hid in Joseph's greatly gifted mind, and all the magnificent moral character the first foundations of which had been laid in the pit in Dothan, and had been built up in God every step of the long wilderness journey. All Joseph's deep repentance also, and all his bitter remorse; all his self-discovery, and all his self-condemnation; with all his reticence and all his continence—Potiphar took all that home from the slave-market that day in exchange for his handful of Egyptian silver. Joseph was now to be plunged into the most corrupt society that rotted in that age on the face of the earth. And had he not come into that pollution straight out of a sevenfold furnace of sanctifying sorrow, Joseph would no more have been heard of. The sensuality of Egypt would have soon swallowed him up. But his father's God was with Joseph. The Lord was with Joseph to protect him, to guide him, and to give him the victory. The Lord was with him to more imprisonment, and then to more promotion; to more and more honor, and place, and power, till this world had no more to bestow upon Joseph. And, through it all, Joseph became a better and an ever better man all his days. A nobler and an ever nobler man. A more and more trustworthy, and a more and more trusted and consulted man. More and more loyal to truth and to duty. More and more chaste, temperate, patient, enduring, forgiving; full of mind and full of heart; and full, no man ever fuller, of a simple and a sincere piety and praise of God, till he became a very proverb both in the splendor of his services, and in the splendor of his rewards.

19
Aaron

WHAT a gifted house! What an honor to that man of the house of Levi who took to wife a daughter of Levi! What a rich slave-hut was that with Miriam and Aaron and Moses all born of God into it! What splendid wages to have three such children given to that son and daughter of Levi to nurse up for the Lord, and for Israel, and for all the world; three such goodly children as Miriam the prophetess, and Aaron the high priest, and Moses the deliverer and leader and lawgiver of Israel. Has there ever been another house gifted like that house in Goshen on the face of the earth? I have not heard or read of another house in all the world like the house of Amram of the house of Levi, and his wife God-my-glory. And, then, the sovereign distribution and allotment of their gifts and their graces and their offices, the dividing-out of the family genius, was no less wonderful than the immense amount of it. For, by that sovereign division and distribution Moses was made the first and the greatest of all the prophets of Israel. Aaron, again, must have been the most eloquent of all eloquent men, since the fame of his eloquence had reached up to heaven itself till it was acknowledged and talked of and boasted about there. What oratory must Aaron's oratory have been when God Himself both felt and confessed its power. I know, said the Divine Voice, that he can speak well. And, then, Miriam, in sacred drama, in sacred dance, in sacred song, and in sacred instruments of music, was quite worthy to stand out beside her two unapproachable brothers. While, all the time, each several one of the three was all the more dependent on the other two just because of the greatness of his own and her own special gift. The very magnitude of their own gifts made the others' gifts more necessary to them, till the whole house of Amram was a complete and a rounded and a perfect gift of God to all Israel. And till all that Israel could ever need as a nation and as a church, as fathers and as mothers, as masters and as servants, as slaves and as redeemed from slavery, as sinners and as the chosen people of God—all Israel was complete in Moses and Aaron and Miriam, even as they also were complete in God and in one another. Yes, indeed, what a highly honored house was the house of that son and daughter of Levi, Amram and God-her-glory.

And Moses said unto the Lord, O my Lord, I am not eloquent. Neither heretofore nor since Thou hast spoken to Thy servant; but I am slow of speech and of a slow tongue. It was the depth and the weight and the fullness of Moses' mind that made him a man of such slow speech and of such a slow tongue. Moses had lived so long alone in Horeb that he had well-nigh forgotten the everyday language of everyday men. He had been so much alone with God that he felt like a man away from home when he met again with any man of many words. He had taken the shoes off his feet so often before God that he never could put them on again or walk in them with any ease or any freedom before men. I AM! was all that God had said to Moses, year after year, as Moses fed the flock of his father-in-law in the mount of God. And, who am I? was all that Moses answered God for forty years. Moses was a great philosopher, says Matthew Henry, and a great statesman, and a great divine, and yet he was no orator. And one great statesman of England speaking of another great statesman, says of him, He was without any power to be called oratory, and yet I never heard a man speak in the House of Commons who had so much power over the House. He had those great qualities that govern men, and that has far more influence in the House of Commons than the most brilliant flights of fancy, or the keenest wits. But, better than all his great philosophy and great statesmanship, Moses was a great divine, the greatest of Old Testament divines; the greatest because the first of all divines. And yet he was no preacher, as we say. In this Moses was somewhat like certain of our own great divines. They have such a depth and weight of matter that they also are slow of speech and of a slow style. Butler for one, and Foster for another. Whereas certain others of our great divines are like Aaron in this, that they can speak well. And yet we have sometimes heard of great divines and great preachers too who shrank back from the pulpit as much as Moses himself shrank. The call of Isaiah, and the call of Jeremiah, and the call of Calvin, and the call of Knox, and the call of Bruce all remind us of Moses' noble modesty, his fear of his office, his fear of himself, and of his fellow-men. And the Lord said to Moses, "Who hath made man's voice? Is not Aaron the Levite thy brother? And he shall be thy spokesman unto the people; he shall be to thee instead of a mouth, and thou shalt be to him instead of God."

Cato the Censor defined a great orator to be nothing else than a good man well skilled in speaking. And Quintilian, in his *Institutes of Oratory*, has a noble passage on the great Roman's great text. Let all our young orators, and, especially, let all our sacred and Aaronic orators, study the delightful *Institutes*, that perfect treasure-house of ancient letters, ancient wisdom, and ancient truth and beauty. Now, Aaron was one of Cato's good men skilled in speaking. We are sure of that, because for Aaron's goodness as a man we have not only his long lifetime in the most sacred of all services, but also the psalmist's testimony that Aaron, with all his great trespass, was a great saint of God. And, besides, for his great skillfulness in speaking we have the great certificate of the Divine Voice itself. The sword had entered Aaron's soul also. The iron furnace of Egypt had been burning for long in Aaron's covenant heart also. But when Aaron looked at the tremendous and impossible task of delivering Israel out of Egypt, he felt that he was helpless and hopeless. At the same time, he felt sure that if there was a man on the face of the earth made of God on special purpose for such a service, it was just his own banished brother Moses. And thus it was that Aaron set out to Horeb to seek for Moses just at the moment when the bush began to burn on Horeb, and when the Lord began to speak to Moses out of the bush. "Behold, Aaron thy brother cometh forth to meet thee, and when he seeth thee he will be glad in his heart. And thou shalt speak to him, and put words in his mouth; and I will be with his mouth and with thy mouth, and will teach you both what you shall both do. And he shall be, even he shall be to thee instead of a mouth, and thou shalt be to him instead of God." And Aaron went and met Moses in the mount of God. And Aaron kissed Moses, and Moses told Aaron all that the Lord had said concerning him, till Aaron answered, and shrank back, and said: Surely it is not so. Surely the Lord did not so speak concerning me. I speak well! I speak for thee, my brother! I am not worthy to unloose thy shoe-latchet. I am not worthy to be of the same name with thee. I should always sit silent. I should never speak. My tongue will not tame. I need thee, my brother. I need thy wisdom. I need thy patience. I need thy counsel. I need thy command. Thou art the wisest and the best of men. Thou art a king in Israel. Moses, my dear brother! While all the time Moses felt more than ever before how all this must be of God. For even as Aaron so spake, Moses saw to his delight that Aaron had always the right word ready. No man could resist Aaron. No man could refuse Aaron. Pharaoh himself would not be able to resist and refuse Aaron. Moses felt beside Aaron that he would never open his mouth again. The right word always went away, somehow, when Moses opened his mouth to speak. Whereas Aaron had but to open his mouth and the right word always came out of his mouth. Till, with Aaron beside him, Moses felt that he could face without fear of failure both all Israel and Pharaoh with all his priests and all his magicians.

Now, as we have already seen, we have always had men among ourselves more or less like Moses, and other men more or less like Aaron. Men like Moses—that is, men of great originality, and of great depth and grasp and strength of mind. And yet men who have been of a stammering tongue. Carlyle has made Cromwell's "mute veracity" noble and venerable to us to all time, and Lord Acton has told us that Dr. Döllinger knew too much to write much. On the other hand, what are those men to do, who, like Aaron, have no such depth, and grasp, and originality, and productivity of mind as Moses and the great thinkers and great scholars of our race have had? A common man and a man of no gifts may be set in a place, and may have a calling of God that he cannot escape—a place and a calling which demand constant speaking and constant teaching at his hands. A minister, for instance. He may not be a great scholar or a great thinker himself, but he is set over those who are still less scholars, and who think still less. Now, what is such a man to do? What, but just to take Moses instead of God. What, but just to find out those great divines and other great authors who have been so immediately and so richly gifted of God, and to live with them, and work with them, and make them his own, just as if God had given him all the great gifts He has given them. If I am a man of no learning and no originality, then I know men, both living and dead, who are; and they are all that, of God, and under God, for me. And, if I had to travel barefoot to Horeb for them; if I had to sell my bed for them, at any cost I would have them. I would take no rest till I had found them, and then, as God said of Aaron, I would be glad when I saw them, and I would kiss them, and claim them as my own. We are not all the men of Moses-like genius and originality we might like to be. We are not all epoch-making, history-making, nation-making men. But we are what we are. We are what God has made us to be; and Moses himself is no more. And Moses may be as glad to meet me in my teachableness and in my love and in my reverence as I am to meet him in his magnificent supremacy and high solitariness of gift and of office. Yes; and who knows what our Master may graciously say to us after He has rewarded Moses for his magnificent talents and for his magnificent services? One thing is sure: we shall be satisfied with what He shall say to us, and we shall have no room left in our hearts wherewith any more to envy Moses for his god-like gifts and for his god-like services.

All went well with Aaron as long as he had Moses beside him to inspire him, and to support him, and to be to him instead of God. Aaron faced the elders of Israel, and scattered all their objections and all their fears as a rushing mighty wind scatters chaff; and the long struggle with Pharaoh and with his magicians has surely been preserved to us by Aaron's eloquent pen. The crossing of the Red Sea also, Mount Sinai, and the giving of the tabernacle and the law—it has certainly been by some one who could both speak well and write well also that all that wonderful piece has been put into our hands. And, whatever part Aaron and Aaron's great gifts may have had in all that, at any rate, all went well with Aaron through all that. Aaron did splendid service through all that, and both his great name and his great service would have gone on growing in love and in honor to the end if only he had never let Moses out of his sight. But always when Moses was for any length of time out of sight, Aaron was a reed shaken with the wind; he was as weak and as evil as any other man. Those forty days that Moses was away on the Mount brought out, among other things, both Moses' strength and greatness and Aaron's littleness and weakness in a way that nothing else could have done. "Up, make us gods, which shall go before us; for, as for this Moses, we wot not what is become of him." And Aaron went down like a broken reed before the idolatrous and licentious clamor of the revolted people. A man may be able to speak well when all men's ears are open to him, and when all men's hands are clapping to what he says, who is yet a very weak man, and a very helpless man, and a very mischievous man in a time of storm and strain and shipwreck. A man may be, if not one of Cato's orators, yet a great favorite with the multitude, who has no real root in himself. He may speak well under sufficient applause who has no nobility of character, and no strength of will, and no backbone or brow of courage, and no living and abiding faith in God and in the truth of God. It has often been seen, both in sacred, and in profane, and in contemporary history, how soon the man of a merely emotional, impulsive, oratorical temperament goes to the wall in the hour of real trial. It is popular clamor, and the dividing and receding wave of popular support, that tries a true statesman's strength. The loud demands and the angry threats of the excited people soon serve to discover whether the wonted leader is really able and really worthy to lead or no. And men of the oratorical order have so often flinched and failed in the hour of action and of suffering that our eloquent men are apt to be too lightly esteemed. The love of popularity, and the absolute necessity to have the multitude with him, is a terrible temptation to that leader of men and of movements in the church and in the state who has the gift of popular speech, and who loves to employ it. What would the people like me to say to them on that subject? Will they crowd to hear it? How will they take it? And what will be said about what I have said after I have said it and cannot unsay it? And, in my heart of hearts, can I let them go? Shall I not tune my pulpit just a touch or two, so as to attract this man, and so as to keep that other man from going away? Moses had his own temptations and snares that even he did not always escape and overcome; but it was the good speaker's temptation, it was the popular preacher's temptation, that led Aaron into the terrible trespass of the golden calf.

There is a fine sermon by the finest of English preachers under this fine title—"Saintliness not forfeited by the penitent." And though that unique preacher, after his provoking manner, gives with the one hand and takes away with the other all through that fine sermon, at the same time the sermon is full of subtle truth and exquisite beauty. No; by the true penitent neither saintliness nor service is ever forfeited. Blessed be God, both saintliness and service too are, in such a case, only the better secured and the more fruitfully employed. But then, in order to either saintliness or service being preserved and maintained in a penitent, his penitence must be of the very best kind. It must be penitence indeed. It must be a breaking, burning, consuming, and ever-deepening life of penitence, and that, too, both before God and man. And it was because Aaron's penitence was at once so saintly, and so laid out in service, that we hear so little, and in as many words, about it. We would be nearer the truth about Aaron if we put him at the very head of all Old Testament penitents, both for his own sins and for the sins of all other men. Luther speaks with Isaiah-like boldness when he says that Jesus Christ, by reason of the law of imputation, was the greatest sinner that ever was. Now, Aaron had to be Jesus Christ till Jesus Christ came. And while Aaron was Jesus Christ in type and by imputation, at the same time, and to give the uttermost reality and the uttermost intensity to that, he was himself Aaron all the time, Aaron of the golden calf and of many other untold transgressions besides. And you may be quite sure that Aaron never slew a sacrifice for sin that he did not lay the golden calf, and the nakedness, and the dancing, and the shame, and all the never-to-be-forgotten sin upon its bleeding head. You may be quite sure that Aaron never went into the holy place any day for the sin of others till he had gone first for his own sin. You may rely upon it that many an Israelite whose sin had found him out had a prayer offered for him and for his case at the altar such that the penitent never knew where all the compassion, and all the sympathy, and all the humility, and all the holiness, and all the harmlessness of his high priest came from. Little did the penitents in Israel think how much of his high priesthood Aaron had put on under Sinai and on the scene of that idolatrous and licentious revelry. Moses in his anger had ground the golden calf to ashes, and had sprinkled the ashes on the waters of the brook that ran down out of the Mount of God, till all the people drank of the sin-laden water. And to this day the children of Israel have a saying to this effect—that when any terrible judgment of God or any great remorse, or any great repentance comes upon them there is always an ounce of the ashes of the golden calf in it. And Aaron kept in the holy place, and beside the pot of manna and the rod that budded, a silver chest full of that same accursed ashes, and out of which chest he always sprinkled, and with many tears, all that he ate and all that he drank on every returning day of atonement. By these things priests pray, by these things prophets preach, by these things psalmists sing, and by things like these there comes to all sinful men the best life of their souls. John Foxe used to declare that both he and his people had got much more good out of his sins than ever either he or they had got out of his good works. And, though they did not know it, and would not have believed it, the penitents in Israel got far more good out of their high priest's trespass in the matter of the golden calf, than ever they got out of his broidered garments, and his silver bells, and his fair miter upon his head.

20
Miriam

WATCH well, Miriam, and never let thine eyes off that ark of bulrushes. Watch that little ark with all thy wit, for no other maiden shall ever have such another watch till the fullness of time, when another Miriam shall watch over another child still more fair to God. Of those born of women only One shall ever be greater than thy little brother away down there among the flags by the river's brink. Watch well, Miriam, the brink of the river, and that ark among its waters, and thou shalt not want thy wages. For far greater riches are hidden in that little ark than all the treasures of Egypt. The civilization and the sanctification of the whole earth is in thy keeping; the law and the prophets to come; the very Lion of the tribe of Judah Himself and all His kingdom, are all under thine eye today. O highly favored Miriam, the sister of Moses. Only perform thy part well, and wherever this gospel shall be preached in the whole world, there shall this also that thou art doing be told for a memorial of thee!

What a witty little woman did Moses' sister prove herself to be that day! If it was all out of her own head, what a quick-witted little prophetess she was already! "Shall I go and call to thee a nurse of the Hebrew women, that she may nurse the child for thee?" And then, ye mothers among us, what amazing self-control that was in God-my-glory, the mother of Miriam and Moses. Just the proper proportion, and just the perfect mean, between a nurse's paid love for a foundling, and a mother's love for her own restored child. Could you have so hardened your heart till you got him home? And could you have always been on your guard to hold him at arm's length when an Egyptian neighbor came near as Moses' Hebrew nurse did? A mother worthy of prophets, and priests, and prophetesses; and, best of all, God-her-glory!

By the next time we see Miriam, Moses and Aaron and Miriam are at the head of the children of Israel. All Israel under their leadership have escaped out of the land of Egypt, and are standing on the shore of the Red Sea singing the praises of the Lord like the sound of many waters. By this time Miriam herself is a prophetess, and is able to take the foremost place in the women's sacred songs and sacred dances. Some sharp-eyed scholars who are able to read between the lines assure us that they see tokens of Aaron and of his eloquence in the triumphant song that Miriam took down from Aaron's lips and taught to the devout and talented women, till Aaron and Miriam, with Moses so proudly looking on, made that day a day to be remembered for its songs and for its dances, as well as for its great deliverance, in the house of Israel. And we have the promise that if we flee from Egypt, and do not return to it, we ourselves also shall one day join Moses and Aaron and Miriam on the sea of glass, where, with the harps of God in our hands, we shall all sing together the song of Moses and the Lamb, saying, Great and marvellous are Thy works, Lord God Almighty; just and true are Thy ways, Thou King of saints. For Thou hast brought them in, Thou hast planted them in the mountain of Thine inheritance, in the place, O Lord, which Thou hast made for Thee to dwell in; in the sanctuary, O Lord, which Thy hands have established.

But for her brother's marriage, Miriam would have been the sovereign woman in all Israel for all her days. But Moses' marriage was more than Miriam could bear. Miriam had been Moses' sister, and his mother, and his closest companion, and his most confidential friend now for forty years. Miriam had sat at the council-table with Moses and Aaron and the assembled elders of Israel. What Moses and Aaron were to the one half of the people, Miriam the sister of Moses was to the other half. Miriam was the first famous woman in Israel who had borne the honorable and universal name of a mother in Israel. And, but for Moses' marriage Miriam would have shone beside Moses till her eye also was not dim, nor her natural strength abated. But Moses' marriage made Miriam as weak and as evil and as wicked as any weak and evil and wicked woman in all the camp. Set me as a seal upon thine heart! Miriam cried to Moses, in a storm of tears, when she saw the Ethiopian woman coming to take her place. Set me as a seal upon thine arm! For love is strong as death. Jealousy is cruel as the grave. The coals thereof are coals of fire, which hath a most vehement flame. What a life of torment did Miriam live in those days because of Moses' marriage! Her heart was full of hell-fire at Moses' innocent wife and innocent children, and even at her meek and innocent brother himself. Till her wild jealousy kindled her wild pride, and her wild pride her wild, insane, and impious envy, and then her insane and impious envy soon led her into her fatal trespass against Moses and against God.

Aaron had great gifts of the intellectual kind, and he performed great services both of that and of the spiritual kind; but Aaron had little or no strength of character. Aaron could speak well when some stronger man inspired him and held him up, but that was all. Aaron never had much mind of his own. He was always weak in his will. He was easily caught up, easily tossed about, and easily swept away. His two great trespasses were at bottom not his own trespasses at all. In the one case it was the idolatrous and rebellious people, and in this case it was his envious and rebellious sister. We have not a thousandth part of what Miriam said to Aaron. There are days, and nights, and weeks, and years of insinuation, and suspicion, and wounded pride, and gnawing envy all gathered up into a few words, as the manner of Scripture is. "Hath the Lord spoken only by Moses?" Miriam demanded of Aaron. "Hath He not also spoken by us?" And Aaron had pride enough and ambition enough and envy enough smoldering in his own heart, that when Miriam blew long enough upon it, Aaron's heart also burned up into an answering flame. And all the time Moses was not blind. Moses was not deaf. And Moses' wife was not a stock nor a stone, though she was not a prophetess. And no little shame and pain—great distress and great and sore sorrow—was seen of the Lord in Moses' tent because of Miriam's abominable injustice and cruelty. But, all the time, Moses her brother was as if he were a deaf man who heard not, and a dumb man who openeth not his mouth. My lovers, said David, and my friends stand aloof from me, and my kinsmen stand afar off. They also that seek after my life lay snares for me; and they that seek my hurt speak mischievous things, and imagine deceits all the day long. Hear me, lest otherwise they should rejoice over me; when my foot slippeth they magnify themselves against me. For yet my prayer also shall be for them in their infirmities. And the Lord heard it. And the Lord spake suddenly unto Moses, and unto Aaron, and unto Miriam—Come out, ye three, unto the tabernacle of the congregation. And they three came out. Look at them. Pity them. Pray for them. Moses the leader and lawgiver of Israel, and Aaron the high priest, and Miriam the prophetess, and all Israel looking after them in terror, and the anger of the Lord kindling round about them. That is the wages of Miriam's sin begun. That is the fruit of all her envy, and insinuation, and detraction, and slander against her brother and her brother's wife. And that in Aaron is what comes of weakness and softness and easiness under temptation. Aaron feels now the full shame of letting Miriam come to his tent and sit and whisper and backbite, when he should have turned her to the door, prophetess and all. How they both wish now that he had! And the Lord called Aaron and Miriam, and they both came forth. What was it that ye two so sat and spake against your brother? In what had he hurt you? In what had he taken any word of Mine out of your mouth? In what had he failed in all his duty to Me? My servant Moses is not so, who is faithful in all Mine house. And the cloud departed from off the tabernacle; and, behold, Miriam became leprous, white as snow. And Aaron looked upon Miriam, and behold, she was leprous. And for seven days and seven nights Miriam was shut out of the camp of Israel, and the people journeyed not till Miriam was brought in again.

Look well at Miriam, all you envious and evil-spoken women. Look back at Miriam's beginning. Look at her watching the ark of bulrushes. Look at her nursing her little brother in the house of her godly mother. Look at her in her rapture, like one out of the body with the joy of the Lord, at the Red Sea. And now see to what her wicked heart and her wicked tongue have brought her. Look at her with her hand upon her throat, and with a linen cloth upon her lip, and with her hoarse, sepulchral, noisome voice wandering far from the camp, and compelled to cry Unclean! Unclean! when any one came in sight. Look at all men fleeing from her. Look at her hiding her shame all day behind the sandhills of the wilderness, and coming out at night to look at the lights in Moses' tent and in Aaron's tabernacle. Look, O envy-filled men and women, look at your mother with her flesh half consumed upon her as if she had been seven days dead. Go out and walk all night with her. Go out and hide all day with her. Go out and cry her cry, all you who cannot endure to see or to hear the honors, and the successes, and the services, and the calling, and the gifts of God in your brother. Go out; your true place is not here. Your true place is outside the gates of all good and honest men. Your heart is hard and dry, and like a leper's dead body. You very voice is hoarse as with the asthma of hell.

What a week that was in the camp of Israel! How many thoughts of how many hearts were that week revealed! Miriam's thoughts of her heart were that week revealed. For seven days and seven nights she dwelt alone among the multitude of her own miserable, remorseful, despairing thoughts. What all her thoughts were that week let him tell us who is the chief of sinners, and whose sin has found him out to public exposure and public outcasting. What Aaron's thoughts were as he exercised his office on his sister, and pronounced it leprosy, and passed sentence upon her, and hurried her out of the camp, and shut the gate upon her—what Aaron's thoughts all that week were let him tell us who has had to bear witness against, and to sentence, and to execute judgment on some one in whose sin he himself had been a partaker. I tell you the lepers in Israel had extra-tender treatment at Aaron's hands ever after that awful week. I would like much to know what Moses' wife's thoughts were all that week. Her thoughts, I mean, about her banished sister-in-law. If I knew her thoughts that week on that subject, I would know then to a certainty whether Moses had married well or no. I would know then whether Miriam had any good reason and justification for resisting her brother's marriage. I would know then whether the Lord God had made that Ethiopian woman an help meet for Moses. I would know then whether she was black, but comely, and whether she was a good minister's wife or no. Was she glad in her heart when she heard of Miriam's leprosy? Did she laugh behind the door like Sarah? Did she say, Let her rot in the wilderness, for she deserves it? Was she sad all the eighth day and night after Miriam had been healed? Or, did she go up to the court of the Ethiopians, and there importune her brother Aaron to importune his God on behalf of his sister? Did she look out at the gate many times every day all that week, but could never see or hear Miriam for weeping? Did she buy the two birds for the cleansing of a leper with her own money, and did she have them all ready with her own hands for days before Aaron could as yet take Miriam back? I do not know. I do not read. Only, I know that the thoughts of no woman's heart in all Israel were more revealed all that week than the thoughts of that Ethiopian woman, Moses' much-injured wife. I can well believe that was the best week for the whole house of Israel till that week came when a Greater than Moses and Aaron and Miriam all put together suffered without the gate for their envy and for all their other trespasses. I can believe that that week's halt did more to secure and to hasten their subsequent march through the wilderness than a year of their best roads and their best weather. I can well believe that we have many psalms and the seeds of many psalms out of that fruitful week. I can easily believe that many future judges and prophets and priests in Israel were inquiring and thinking children for the first time that stand-still week. Why are we standing still? they would ask. Where is Miriam all this week? Why is Aaron always so sad? Why is Moses always walking alone? Why is my mother always weeping so? And why, when the seventh day came to a close, was there such gladness again? Imagine for yourselves the questions and the answers in every tent in Israel that week. Imagine the wise answers, and the foolish answers, and the silences, and the embraced and the lost opportunities. Imagine the young minds that would open that week, and the young hearts that would break for the first time, and begin to bleed for sin for the first time, that week. It was that week!—they would often say after they were home in the promised land—it was that week in the wilderness!

Miriam did not live long after that week. It was not her age, and was not the dregs of the leprosy. Miriam died of a broken heart. All the sprinklings, and all the bathings, and all the thanksgivings, and all the benedictions of Aaron her brother; and all the love, and honor, and trust, and confidence of Moses her other brother; and all the sisterly tenderness of Moses' wife; and all the sports, and plays, and leaps, and laughters of Moses' children—all could not heal Miriam's broken heart. Miriam's name is never heard of again in Israel. From that week Miriam blotted herself out of all her brother's books. Miriam died to Israel and to all the world in the lazar-house of Hazeroth. Miriam's songs and dances were all past. Not even on the Sabbath-day would Miriam leave her weeping tent. Unclean! Unclean! If you would ever see or hear Miriam now you must venture and go out of the gate to where the lepers sit solitary, and where they follow the camp afar off. That is Miriam the prophetess, the sister of Moses and Aaron, who is taking out meat and medicine and linen for the lips of the lepers. She is sitting down with them. She is talking to them. She is telling them all about herself. She is pledging herself to speak to Aaron her brother for them. She will buy the two birds on her way home after dark. No. It was not years. And it was not sickness. But Miriam soon died. And Miriam sleeps at Kadesh in the wilderness of Zin till they shall awaken her with the song of Moses and the Lamb, saying, and she answering them with a timbrel, Just and true are Thy ways, Thou King of saints. Who shall not fear Thee, O Lord, and glorify Thy name? for Thou only art holy.

21
Moses

WERE I to let myself once expatiate on the whole of Moses' life I would not know where to begin or where to end. But my method and my endeavor in these expositions is the study of those Bible men and women in their moral character alone. My intention and my aim is to try to find out how the foundations of their moral character were laid in those Bible men and women; how their respective lives and characters were built up, what the instruments were, and what the occasions and opportunities by means of which those men and women made themselves what they were and are; as, also, to search out and ponder the wonderful ways in which God worked in and around those men and women to make them His workmanship also, created under His hand unto good works. And my present text is the very best text in all the Five Books of Moses for this purpose in the case of Moses himself. For the text is the copestone and the crown and the perfect finish of Moses' moral character and spiritual life. And our chief interest in all that Moses came through from the beginning to the end of his wonderful history is just to find out how it all contributed to and told upon his incomparable meekness and humility; that is to say, upon the perfection and the finish of his matchless moral character.

By all accounts Moses did not begin by being a meek man. The truth is, no truly meek man ever does so begin. It is not true meekness if it is found in any man at the beginning of his life. It may be sloth, it may be softness, it may be easiness, it may be indifference, it may be policy and calculation, it may be insensibility of heart, it may be sluggishness of blood, but true meekness it is not. True meekness it is not till it has been planted, and watered, and pruned, and purified, and beaten upon by every wind of God, and cut to pieces by every knife of God, and all the time engrafted and seated deep in the meekness and in the gentleness and in the humility of the Spirit of God and the Son of God. It would be far nearer the truth to say that Moses, to begin with, was the hastiest and the hottest and the least meek and the least longsuffering of men. It was but a word and a blow with young Moses. And it was a word and a blow that laid you on the spot in your grave in the sand. No; the meekness of Moses was not a case of complexion, nor a matter of temperament, any more than it was the grace of a new beginner in godliness and virtue. Moses would by that time be well on to threescore and ten of our years, as we count our years, before it was written of him what stands written of him in our noble text.

I for one will all but exonerate and absolve that grave in the sand. The Egyptian slave-driver, as I take it, deserved all that he got. But if you still protest in your distance and security and indifference against the lynch-law of Moses, then you have Augustine on your side to support you. "I affirm," says that great father, "that the man, though criminal, and really the offender, ought not to have been put to death by one who had no legal authority to do so. But minds that are capable of virtues often produce vices also." Yes: and as I read this ancient narrative, and look human nature in the face, unless that young Hebrew had had this vice in his blood that day, he would never have had the virtue in after days that made him Moses. Unless he had had it in him, vice or virtue, to strike that bold blow at that insolent Egyptian, he would never have had it in him to strike off Israel's fetters. If he had hesitated and calculated and looked this way and that way that day, we would not have had his perfected meekness before us for our text tonight. I like to think of the son of Pharaoh's daughter out for a drive toward the land of Goshen that tempting sunset. I like to see the old nursling of God-her-glory still showing to all men what he had been suckled on. I rejoice to see that all the learning, and all the art, and all the luxury, and all the licentiousness, and all the dazzling prospects of Egypt have not emasculated Moses, nor made him ashamed of his oppressed kinsmen. You and I would have taken up discretional ground. We would have said that it would be eminently unwise to meddle between a master and his servant. We would have said that we had not time to go into the case. We would have told Pharaoh's second charioteer to drive on. We would have gained Augustine's approval. We would have been law-abiding Britons that day. Unfortunately for Moses, it was not our calm Christian blood that was running in his veins that day; and thus it was that he had to pay with forty years' banishment for his sudden spring upon that Egyptian taskmaster, and for the life-long thanks of that delivered slave.

John Cairns refusing at forty to be called the Principal of Edinburgh University, and choosing rather to be the pastor of a despised dissenting congregation of his evangelical fellow-countrymen than to be a philosopher of European reputation, is the nearest thing I know to Moses at forty. Cairns and Keble. Having carried off as a mere boy the highest honors of the University, says Newman in his *Apologia*, Keble turned from the admiration which haunted his steps, and sought for a better and a holier satisfaction in pastoral work in the country. This, also, which is continually happening in Scotland, is not unlike the son of Pharaoh's daughter. The son of a shepherd, or of a stone-breaker, will take a bursary at school. He will thus get his foot on the lowest spar of the ladder. He has talents, and industry, and character, and religion. He takes his degree with classical or philosophical or mathematical honors at Glasgow or Aberdeen His scholarship carries him up to Oxford or Cambridge. He becomes learned in all the wisdom of the Egyptians; as Philo has it, "making himself master of all their disputes without encouraging any disputatious disposition in himself." The news soon comes that he has taken the highest honors. The University takes him up and nourishes him for her own son. His way is open. There is nothing to which he may not aspire. The Scottish crofter's son may yet wear an English miter. But, like Moses, it comes into his heart to visit his brethren in Argyll or Inverness, till he esteems a Gaelic congregation in his father's church and in his father's land a greater honor to him than all the honor and glory of England, as seeing Him who is invisible. Ouranius is a holy priest, full of the spirit of the Gospel, watching, laboring, and praying for a poor country village. When Ouranius was still a young man he had an ambition in his heart, a haughtiness in his temper, and a great contempt and disregard of all foolish and unreasonable people. But he has prayed away that spirit, and has now the greatest tenderness for the most obstinate sinners. The rudeness, ill-nature, or perverse behavior of any of his flock used at first to betray him into impatience, but now it raises no other passion in him than a desire of being upon his knees in prayer to God for them. Thus have his prayers for others altered and amended the whole state of his own heart. This devotion softens his heart, enlightens his mind, sweetens his temper, and makes everything that comes to him instructive, amiable, and affecting. He now thinks the poorest creatures in his parish good enough and great enough to deserve the humblest attendances, the kindest friendships, the tenderest offices he can possibly show them. He is so far from wanting great or learned or courtly people that he thinks there is no better conversation in the world than to be talking to mean and poor people about the Kingdom of Heaven. All this makes Ouranius more and more careful of every temper of his heart according to the strictest rules of temperance, meekness, and humility, that he may in some degree be like Abraham and Moses and Job in his parish ministry.

Some of you will know what forty years in the wilderness, and at the back of the Mount of God, have done for yourselves. You know how those years have reduced and subdued your too-high temper, and weaned you off from the shams and the sweetnesses of this world, and given you some eyes and some heart to suffer the loss of all things for the recompense of your reward in heaven—in heaven, where the least and the lowest reward is greater riches than all the gain and all the glory of the present world. And if forty years have wrought such a change in such a slow-hearted scholar of God as you are, you will not wonder at the man Moses as he came back from the land of Midian. Any use you are, or are ever likely to be, or have now any hope or any ambition to be—it all has its roots in the great grace of God to you, and in any little humility and meekness that has come out of all that to you. And when you multiply all that, and yourself as the result of all that, by ten thousand, then you will have Moses in Midian, the herdman and the son-in-law of Jethro, the priest of Midian. Forgotten John Foster has a fine lecture on Jethro and Moses, in which that great preacher's philosophical and imaginative and spiritual power all come out. And all John Foster's power is needed to construct and to let us see Moses' life in Jethro's household, and out among his sheep, for those forty exiled years. Moses' magnificent powers of mind: his possession with him in his exile of all the learning and religion of Egypt; all Egypt's power and glory and cruelty and pollution, were before Moses as he wandered and pondered over Horeb; the past of his own people, and their future; his own wonderful youth and early manhood; that taskmaster's blood still upon his hands, and God coming nearer and nearer, and becoming clearer and clearer, more awful, but at the same time more good and more gracious every day—forty years of that to such a man as Moses already was, that was God's way He took to make Moses the meekest man and the greatest prophet till Christ came. Nothing so occupies a man like Moses as solitude. Nothing so humbles a man like Moses as great gifts and great providences. And nothing so meekens a man like Moses as the sins of his youth; added to the corruption and the dregs of corruption that he still sees and feels in his own heart. And all that, and far more than we are told, or can ourselves divine—all that went from forty years and onwards to make Moses the meekest of men and the most prepared for his magnificent work.

There is another thing that God sometimes overrules and employs to break and humble and make more and more meek the hearts of His best servants, and that is family misunderstandings, family disputes, and family quarrels, and, especially, misunderstandings and disputes and explosions between husband and wife. And there are three most obscure and most mysterious verses in Moses' history that mean, if they mean anything at all to us, just such an explosion of ill-temper as must have left its mark till death on the heart of Moses and Zipporah. The best of wives; his help meet given him of God; the most self-effacing of women; the wife who holds her husband in her heart as the wisest and the best of men—under sufficient trial and provocation and exasperation, even she will turn and will strike with just one word; just once in her whole married lifetime, as in that wayside inn on the way to Egypt, and as in Henrik Ibsen's latest and ripest tragedy. She does it only once; but when she does it, she does it as only the wife of a good man can do it. Till Moses lies done to death between his two best friends, who have both united to kill him that terrible day in that terrible inn. Zipporah may, or may not forget that day, and forgive it; but Moses never forgot it. And though he covers up that wayside scene as much as he may, no husband and no wife ever read that covert, and to all other readers enigmatical passage, without their hearts bleeding for Moses, and for Moses' wife, and for themselves. Moses' heart went to pieces that day between God and Zipporah, till he took his staff in his hand next morning, the solitariest, the meekest, and the most surrendered of men, and the most meet to be the best prophet of God and the best redeemer of Israel till the Man of all Sorrows came to leave Moses, and all his meekness and all his services to God and man, far behind.

It was on the occasion of the disgraceful attack of Miriam and Aaron on Moses at Hazeroth that this testimony was borne to Moses, that he was by that time the meekest man on the face of the earth. It was when Miriam and Aaron determined to pull down Moses from the supreme place that God had gifted him for and had put him into—it was then that God set on Moses His open and His lasting seal to the greatness of Moses' office as a prophet, and the greatness of Moses' meekness as a man. "That incident," says Ewald, the great philosophical historian of Israel, "furnishes a grand exemplification of the universal truth, that the best and the most capable man in a community is often the most misunderstood and the best persecuted." And it was just this persecution that drew out the divine vindication and valuation that is here put of God upon Moses. Luther's translation of the Hebrew text is a fine stroke both of exegetical license and of exegetical genius. Moses was very much plagued, Luther renders; he was plagued, indeed, above all the men which were upon the face of the earth. Yes; "plagued" exactly describes the life that Moses had led ever since he was called of God to take Israel in hand: and all Moses' plagues came to a head in the matter of Miriam and Aaron and their envy and evil-speaking. But just then, or not long after then, the copestone and the full finish was put on Moses' meekness. God is fast putting His last touch to His servant's meekness and humility of heart when He shows him what a terrible temptation his great gifts and his great services are to his brother and his sister.

For a man like Moses to see how his high place as God's prophet to Israel, and, especially, his sovereign superiority to all other prophets, was a constant source of sin and misery to Miriam and Aaron, his own sister and brother, plunging them into such envy and ill-will—what a last blow to all Moses' remaining pride and ambition and self-exalting was that! And when we have eyes and a heart to take it to heart ourselves, how our very best things also are made a continual occasion to our brother of his worst things—our good his evil, our lifting up his casting down, our health his sickness, our life his death—when we lay that aright to heart, then there will be more men than Moses who will be meek above all the men that are on the face of the earth.

The perseverance of the saints, says an excellent old adage, is made up of ever new beginnings. So it is. And Moses' perseverance in meekness was exactly of that ever-beginning kind. For Holy Scripture exhibits and exposes Moses as back again at the very beginning of his meekness when he is on the very borders of the promised land. Moses, with humility and with fear let it be seen and said, was as hasty, and as hot, and as violent away on at the rock of Meribah as ever he was among the sands of Goshen. Moses struck the rock that late day with the very same stroke of angry passion with which he had killed the Egyptian in that early day. And all the rest of his days on earth, all the way from Meribah to Pisgah, Moses went mourning, praying, and importuning for his sin against meekness in his old age, as much and more than he had done from Goshen to Midian in the days of his youth. The perseverance of the saints is indeed made up of ever new beginnings. Put on therefore, as the elect of God, holy and beloved, bowels of mercies, kindness, humbleness of mind, meekness, long-suffering, forbearing one another and forgiving one another. If any man have a quarrel against any, even as Christ forgave you, so also do ye. And, again, a still meeker than Moses says to us every day, Take My yoke upon you, and learn of Me; for I am meek and lowly in heart; and ye shall find rest unto your souls.

> Moses, the patriot fierce, became
>   The meekest man on earth,
> To show us how love's quick'ning flame
>   Can give our souls new birth.
>
> Moses, the man of meekest heart,
>   Lost Canaan by self-will,
> To show where grace has done its part,
>   How sin defiles us still.
>
> Thou, who hast taught me in Thy fear
>   Yet seest me frail at best,
> O grant me loss with Moses here,
>   To gain his future rest.

22
Moses the Type of Christ

I WISH that Moses had either told me less or had told me more about his mother. It is very tantalizing to be told her remarkable name and to be told no more. Was "God-thy-glory" the remarkable name that Moses gave to his mother as often as he looked back at all that he owed to her, and as often as he rose up and called her blessed? Or was her very remarkable name her own invention? Was her striking name her own seal that she had set to her own vow which she made to her own God after some great grace and goodness of her own God? Or, again, did the angel of the Lord visit that daughter of the house of Levi on some Jabbok-like or Annunciation-night, and so name her as the sun rose upon her prayer? I call to remembrance the unfeigned faith that is in thee, wrote Paul to young Timothy, and which faith dwelt first in thy grandmother Lois, and in thy mother Eunice. And I call to remembrance also how God-her-glory dwelt in her husband's hut among the brick-fields of Egypt, and was nothing daunted, or dazzled, or seduced by all the state, and wealth, and power, and pollution of Egypt. She stayed her great heart on the God of Abraham, and Isaac, and Jacob, and Joseph, till she saw in her sleep a bush burning but not consumed, and till she, too, sang her own Magnificat. And then, one after another, she bore and suckled three such children as Miriam, and Aaron, and then the son of Pharaoh's daughter—bore and suckled all three on the same strong milk, till she weaned them from milk and put them on the marrow of lions. The oak has its roots round the rock, and men like Moses have their roots round their mother.

Neither do we know much about the mother of that Prophet like unto Moses. All that we know about the Virgin Mary might have been excellently gathered up of the angel into the remarkable name of Moses' mother. Mary said as much herself when she was with Elizabeth in the hill-country. My soul doth magnify the Lord, she said, and my spirit hath rejoiced in God my Savior. How both those young mothers nursed their sons for God, and how they are now getting their wages from God, as they look upon their sons in their glory together, every mother among us must think continually. And no mother can think of Moses' mother, and of the mother of that Prophet like unto Moses, without asking of God, night and day, that their sons also may all in their measure be like Moses, and like that Prophet like unto Moses. And He went down, and came to Nazareth, and was subject unto them; but His mother kept all these things in her heart. And Jesus increased in wisdom and stature, and in favor with God and man. By faith Moses, when he was come to years, refused to be called the son of Pharaoh's daughter. By faith he forsook Egypt, not fearing the wrath of the king; for he endured as seeing Him who is invisible. In the old Hebrew, says Albert Bengel, the whole is ascribed to the mother.

Glancing at the Alexandrians among his accusers, Stephen, the witnessing deacon, said to them that Pharaoh's daughter took Moses up and nourished him for her son. And Moses, he added, was learned in all the wisdom of the Egyptians, and was mighty in words and in deeds. Now, the very opposite upbringing was appointed to our Lord. For his detractors never ceased to cast it up to Him that He had never learned letters like Moses: which was quite true. But the fact was, the letters of that day had nothing really to teach the child Jesus, else He would have diligently learned them. He did learn them as far as they were worthy to be called letters, and to be learned. You may be sure there were no children in all Israel at that day whose fathers and mothers taught them more diligently both when they sat in the house, and when they walked in the way, and when they lay down, and when they rose up, than Joseph and Mary taught both the letter and the spirit of Moses to Jesus and to His brothers and to His sisters. And then, as He grew up He had nature to observe and to study and to learn, and man, and, best of all, Himself. He had the carpenter's shop, and the carpenters—an excellent school for a future preacher; and He had the sky and the sea and the mountains. The foxes in their holes, the birds in their nests, the lilies of the field outstripping Solomon in all his glory, the hen and her chickens, the mustard seed in Joseph's garden, the wheat seed in the fields around, and spring-time, and summer, and harvest, and winter—that He was at school of His Father in all that, every sermon of His in after years is the abundant proof. But, best of all, He had Himself. If "Know thyself" was ever said with any fitness to any man, it was surely said with supreme fitness to the Man Christ Jesus. For He was the Mystery of Godliness Itself. He was God manifest to Himself first in the flesh. He was The Word of God. In Him were hid all the treasures of wisdom and of knowledge. Now, all our young preachers are to be as like Moses as they possibly can, and as like their Divine Master as they possibly can. They are all to be classical scholars, like Moses, if we can help it. But, above all, they are to be Christian men. Pascal went to hear a great preacher in Paris, and found a man in the pulpit. And that made all the difference to a man like Pascal. And we want to rear up true and genuine men for all our pulpits, men who shall set themselves resolutely to all learning, but who shall on that account be all the more men, and all the better men. It is not what the preacher has learned in the schools—it is not the preacher's literature—that impresses Pascal; it is the preacher himself. And what our examiners are bent upon is not conic sections, or even Chaldee, in our candidates for the ministry; it is habits of work, and discipline of mind, and seriousness of purpose, and the ability, and the determination, and the perseverance to go on to old age, bringing out every Sabbath day to their people things new and old. Paracelsus denounced those doctors of medicine and those ministers of religion in his day who roasted pears all day.

Very much what the burning bush was to Moses—that His baptism at the Jordan must have been to our Lord. He that dwelt in the bush called Moses to the work of his life that eventful day on Horeb; and, so far as we can gather, our Lord received and accepted His full and final call also at the Jordan. So far as we can see, our Lord had the great seal of His Messiahship set upon His heart that day. And with that there came that unparalleled outpouring and indwelling of the Holy

Ghost which made Him without measure equal to all His high call. Never did mortal man set out to such a task as that which was set to Moses at the bush. But what a far greater call was that which came to our Lord at Bethabara for our salvation! Look into your own heart and you will see there what Jesus Christ was called, and baptized, and anointed, and sworn in that day to do. You will never wonder and stand amazed and aghast at His awful task by studying it in any book—not even in the New Testament. But you will so stand, and so fall down, every day and all your days, if you only begin to study all the call and all the offices of Christ in yourself. As He so studied His call; as He saw more and more what was in the heart of man, and what came out of the heart of man, He sometimes seemed inclined to repent of and to resign His awful call, and to despair of His terrible office. And you will not wonder at that; you will expect that, when you look into yourself as He looks into you. But He went through with His call. He did not throw it up. He finished it. And He is finishing it still tonight in you and in me. And the Lord said, I have surely seen the affliction of my people which are in Egypt, and have heard their cry by reason of their taskmasters; for I know their sorrows. And the people believed; and when they heard that the Lord had visited the children of Israel, and that He had looked upon their affliction, then they bowed their heads and worshipped.

And Moses was in the mount with God forty days and forty nights; he did neither eat bread nor drink water. And it came to pass, when Moses came down from the mount, that Moses wist not that the skin of his face shone. And when Aaron and all the children of Israel saw Moses, behold the skin of his face shone, and they were afraid to come nigh him. On reading that we instinctively pass on and remember this. And He was transfigured before them. And His raiment became shining, exceeding white as snow; so as no fuller on earth can white them. There are some things there that go far down beyond our utmost depth. At the same time, there are some things there that speak very plainly to us, and speak no parable. Did you ever happen to pass a looking-glass as you rose off your knees after an unusually long or unusually close season alone with God? Then you must have been startled and delighted to see that your plain, dull, old, haggard face was for the moment positively youthful and beautiful. Well, that was a ray or two of the identical same light that shone through Moses' skin of his face, and through our Lord's very raiment. Another thing. Moses neither ate bread nor drank water on the mount. And every meal you miss when you are in the Mount with God gives a new fineness, transparence, translucence, and fore-glow of glory to the skin of your face also. Then, again, you must often have seen two young lovers just parting, and as one of them passed you, you turned and looked after him for his face so shone out upon you. It was the light of heaven that filled his heart coming out at his face. All our lovers are so transfigured when they are still young. And it is only when they become old and cease to love that they become gross, and sodden, and stupid, and full of earth in their faces, and void of heaven. In paradise, Dante tells us, the more they love the more they shine. In heaven you will recognize and discover the great lovers of God and of man by the greater splendor and by the more exquisite beauty of their faces, and of their raiment, and even of the very street of gold they walk upon. What Moses said to Jesus on the New Testament mount about his ancient exodus from Egypt, and about the far greater exodus which should so soon be accomplished at Jerusalem—what would we not have given had Peter, James, and John but told us! But Peter was asleep as usual; and thus it is that we are left without a conversation we would have given—what would we not have given?—to have overheard.

Another thing in which Moses was a type of Christ was in the way he was envied and hated and detracted; and that, too, of his brother and sister, and of those he was serving with all his might, in season and out of season. For this is the diabolical distinction and supremacy of envy, that it boils up not in the hearts of enemies but of friends; in the secret hearts of brothers and sisters and bosom friends. The Athenians put it on Plato's tombstone—"Here lies a man much too great for envy." Well, Moses was a much greater prophet than Plato, and yet he was not too great to Miriam and Aaron for envy. And Jesus Christ was a far greater prophet than Moses and Plato put together, and yet Pilate saw it in their evil faces, and heard it in their evil voices, that it was for envy His own had delivered Him. Some of you will be thankful from the bottom of your heart that you read so much about such envy in the Bible. It makes you feel somewhat less lonely. But all that does not satisfy you. You sometimes wish that such envy had been far more in the Bible than it is. In your absolute agony, in your absolute madness, in your absolute despair, you will sometimes have the blasphemous wish that another Bible Character than either Aaron or Miriam or the elders of Israel—that He, with all His humiliation, and with all His agony, and with all His abandonment and darkness, had just had one of your days and nights of such envy. You feel as if you could then have had more hope in drawing near Him and of opening up your hell to His heart.

Another thing in which Moses and Christ are type and anti-type to one another is their consummate meekness under all envy and all detraction and all other ill-usage. It is a translation that is also an exposition and an illustration when Luther renders the Hebrew for meekness into the German for plagued; plagued and trampled on. For never were two servants of God so plagued, and so trampled on, and so ill-used in every way as Moses and Christ; and hence their never-equalled meekness. The divine use of envy, and detraction, and insolence, and ingratitude, like all that through which first Moses and then Christ were passed, was to give meekness her perfect work in them both. And as they were, so are we in this world. All that cruelty, and injustice, and impudence, and insolence, and unthankfulness that fill some men's and some ministers' lives so full—it is all because God has it in His plan for them to make them meek like Moses and meek like Christ. Learn of Me, our Savior says to all such men, and ye shall have My peace of mind, and My inward rest and repose in yourselves also. Aaron and Miriam and all the people of Israel were to Moses what Jeremy Taylor calls "the instruments of his virtue." And so were all the bad men around our Lord. And so are all such men that are ordained and permitted to be round about us. May we all make as good a use of our instruments of virtue as Moses and Jesus made of theirs!

Those forty years of Moses in the land of Midian were great and fruitful years for Israel and for us. But those thirty-three years of Jesus Christ in Galilee and

Jewry were far away and out of sight the greatest and the most fruitful years this world has ever seen, or ever again will see. All eternity itself—past, present, and to come—holds no such years for us as those thirty-three years of Jesus Christ. For during those thirty-three years God became man. God entered into man, and man entered into God, till God and man became for ever One. All through those supreme years the soul and the body of the Man Christ Jesus were being built up into an everlasting temple of God. All down those splendid years the soul and the body, the mind and the heart of Jesus Christ were being refined and transfigured, and made transparent and transpicuous, till he who saw and handled the Man Christ Jesus saw and handled The Very Word of Life. He in those happy days who saw and handled the Man Christ Jesus saw and handled Almighty God Himself. Hence at His baptism, His Father said: This is My Beloved Son, in whom I am well pleased. And, again, at His transfiguration—Hear ye Him. And thus it was that henceforth and as often as He opened His mouth and said, Verily, verily, I say unto you—all the ancient oracles fell dumb, Urim and Thummim themselves ceased to shine and seal, and Moses answered again and said, Send, O Lord, by the hand of Him whom Thou wilt send. As Peter, now for ever awakened out of sleep, had it in his great address—Moses said truly to the fathers, A prophet shall the Lord your God raise up unto you like unto me; Him shall ye hear in all things whatsoever He shall say unto you. For unto you first God, having raised up His Son Jesus, sent Him to bless you, in turning away every one of you from his iniquities.

And, to crown all, and to come to his nearest and his best to Christ, Moses in Israel's terrible extremity fell down before God and said, Blot me, I pray Thee, out of Thy book which Thou hast written, if Thou wilt not otherwise forgive Israel their sins. And, both for their sin and for his own sin, God took Moses at his word, and for a season and to some extent He did blot Moses out of the book which He had written. What a sad end was Moses' end, after such a great and such a noble life! And what a sad end was that of a far greater than Moses after a far greater and a far nobler life! And it was sin that did it to them both: actual sin to Moses, and imputed sin to Christ. But what is sin, do you ask? Well, sin passeth, like salvation, all understanding. Only look for yourselves at Moses shut out of Canaan, and look for yourselves at Christ shut up to Gethsemane and to Calvary, and you will see something of what sin deserves. And then stop and consider what you owe to Him who blotted Himself out of God's book for you and for all your sins. Let this cup pass from Me. But if not, then blot Me out of Thy book. Receive, O sinner, on the spot where thou sittest, receive and ever after keep fast hold of Him and of His salvation.

23
Pharaoh

WHEN King Ahasuerus could not sleep at night he used to have his chamberlains called in to read the books of the chronicles of the kingdom at his bedside. And as the reading went on King Ahasuerus would stop them and would ask them, What honor and what reward have been done to Mordecai for all this? And then when the king's ministers answered him that nothing had been done, the first orders that the king gave in the morning were that Mordecai and all his descendants should be set straightway among the men whom the king delighted to honor. Now it was just because Pharaoh the father did not have the history of Egypt read to him in that way that he and his son came to such a terrible end. Poor, misguided crown-prince, when he was still the crown-prince! His tutors and his governors had destroyed their royal charge for lack of knowledge. They had amused him, and flattered him, and let him run wild, and let him have his own way in everything, when they should have been bringing him up as David brought up Solomon, and as the wise men in the east brought up Cyrus. The only claim any man has to reign over other men is that he is wiser and better than they are. The divine right, as it used to be called, of every true king is grounded in his wisdom, and in his good-ness, and in his truth, and in his justice; he is the best born, the best brought up, the best read, the best experienced, the largest-minded and the noblest-hearted man in all the land. But the times are changed since Pharaoh's day. We are all kings, in a manner, in our day. We all have a crown on our head, and a sword and a scepter in our hand. And, in our measure, we should all be instructed statesmen, like the royal patron of Mordecai and Esther; and it will go ill with us, and with those who come after us, if we are like Pharaoh, who had never heard of Joseph, and what Joseph had done for the land of Egypt. That will be the best election-time Scot-land has ever seen, not when this or that party comes into power, but when every enfranchised man has already read about Wallace and Bruce, and about Cromwell and Milton, and about Hampden and Pym, and about Knox and Melville, and about Henderson and Rutherford and Chalmers. When all who have votes prepare themselves for the polling-booth in that way, then we shall see a House of Com-mons composed of the best and ablest men the land can produce; the most loyal, the most fair and just, the most God-fearing, and the least self-seeking of men. Then Ireland, and India, and China, and Africa, and Armenia, and Macedonia shall hold out their hands to England; and all lands shall both love and fear England and her Queen because of that knowledge and that righteousness which alone exalteth a nation, and which alone enthroneth and establisheth a sovereign.

Come on, let us deal wisely with them, said the ill-read and ignorant sovereign who sat on the throne of Egypt at the time when the children of Israel were fast becoming more and mightier than their masters. Come on, was his insane edict, let us deal wisely with them, lest they multiply and it come to pass that, when there falleth out any war, they join themselves to our enemies and fight against us. Therefore, they did set taskmasters over them to afflict them with their burdens. But the more they afflicted them the more they multiplied and grew. Till in a policy of despair this demented king charged all his people, saying, Every son of the Hebrews that is born ye shall cast into the river, and every daughter ye shall save alive. This is all that remains on the statute-book of Egypt to testify to the statesmanship of that king of Egypt who had never heard of Joseph the son of Jacob, the servant of Potiphar, and the counsellor and deliverer of the kingdom. That was the statute-book, and that was the sword and the scepter, that this Pharaoh handed down to his son who succeeded him, and who was that new Pharaoh whom God raised up to show in him His power, and that through him His name might be declared throughout all the earth. A Pharaoh, says Philo, whose whole soul from his cradle had been filled full of the arrogance of his ancestors. And indeed, he was no sooner sat down on his throne, we no sooner begin to hear his royal voice, than he at once exhibits all the ignorance and all the arrogance of his ancestors in the answer he gives to Moses and Aaron: Who is the Lord that I should obey Him? I know not the Lord, neither will I let Israel go. Get you to your burdens. It is because you are idle that you say, Let us go and do sacrifice to the Lord. Go, therefore, for there shall no straw be given you, and yet you shall deliver your tale of bricks! The father had not known Joseph, and the son knew neither Joseph, nor Moses, nor Aaron, nor God. Moses! Moses is my slave, he shouted. Moses should be baking his tale of bricks all this time. What! Moses! of all men in the world, to come into my presence with a demand like that! Had Moses been some great ambassador who had come in a ship from some far country; had Moses and Aaron come with great gifts and in a great name to negotiate a royal league with Egypt, Pharaoh would have done them honor. A banquet would have been spread for Moses and Aaron, and the great council of the kingdom would have been called together to receive them, and to hear what they had to say. But Moses and Aaron! Why, they should have been at their tasks! Who are they, to come like ambassadors to me? No; to your bricks and to your burdens, you Moses and Aaron! And if only your minister were some great one, it would go so much better with him and with you. If he only came from some far-off city, and from some famous pulpit. If you only heard him preach once or twice in a lifetime, then you would attend to what he says; and you might, who knows, be prevailed on to do it. If your minister were only Dr. Chalmers, or Dr. Candlish, or Mr. Spurgeon. But he is nobody. And, besides, he has offended you, and has not always pleased you. And he is full of faults. And, besides, you know all about him. Moses had blood upon his hands in his youth, as Pharaoh's counselors kept him well in mind. Yes, you stick to it like that royal spirit. It would be weak, it would be an impossible humiliation in you, to make any alteration in your heart or in your life for what your present minister says. Talk on after every sermon. Show your children after every sermon and every prayer of his how much better their father could preach and pray. Tell them about Disruption times. Laugh at their weak impressions and at their foolish praises, and tell them that they have never heard preaching to be called preaching. And if it turns out with you like Pharaoh, and if Pharaoh rises up in the day of judgment

to condemn you, then stand up on the left hand and tell the Judge to His face that
He never gave you and your children a chance. With such a minister, you never
had fair play and a proper chance. Moses! Who, I would like to know, is Moses?
Pharaoh was still shouting out that to his captains when the Red Sea rolled in and
cut short his scorn.

What sign showest Thou, said the unbelieving Jews to our Lord, that we may
see, and believe Thee? What dost Thou work? Let me see a miracle, said Pharaoh
to Moses and Aaron, and then I will let Israel go. And to satisfy Pharaoh, and to
soften his heart, Aaron cast down his rod before Pharaoh, and before his servants,
and it became a serpent. But instead of saying, This is the Lord, and proclaiming
an edict that the people should go free, Pharaoh called in his sorcerers and his
magicians, and they did in like manner with their enchantments. And miracle succeeded miracle; miracles of judgment were wrought and miracles of mercy; but
they all ended in the same way—Pharaoh's heart was only the more hardened. It
looked a very innocent request. We would have said that it was a very promising
and a very hopeful state of mind in Pharaoh to ask for some proof of the divine
embassy of Moses and Aaron, and then he would obey. But, all the time, the evil
seed of all Pharaoh's after life and death of sin lay at the heart of that innocent-
looking, hopeful-sounding demand. For, innocent as it looked, and hopeful as
it sounded, Pharaoh's demand put upon God, and upon Moses and Aaron, the
first step of Pharaoh's repentance and obedience. If no miracle had followed his
request, then Pharaoh would have felt fully justified in holding to his refusal. And,
as it was, when his magicians did something sufficiently like Aaron's rod, then
Pharaoh fell back and took his stand upon that, till the miracle upon which he
had suspended his obedience was wrought in vain. No. Pharaoh's first step to his
salvation, had he but taken it, was not to see a miracle, but to do what he knew to
be right. Had Pharaoh said to his servants—Come, let us read in the book of the
kingdom. Come, let us see what manner of life the people of Israel live in Goshen.
What are their sorrows? What are their complaints? What are their requests? Then
he would have soon after said, Yes, let them sacrifice to their God without molesta-
tion; and then let them come back again to their work. That was all that was asked
of Pharaoh for the time; and, had he not been filled full from his cradle with the
ignorance and arrogance of his ancestors, Moses and he would soon have come
to terms, and Egypt and Israel would have been friends and allies to this day. But
Pharaoh took a wrong turn and a false step when he still asked for evidence where
he should have offered obedience; and that wrong turn and that false step laid him
at last in the bottom of the Red Sea.

No. It is not more evidence you need. Or, if it is evidence, then it is the evidence
of obedience and experience. It is not a course of Lectures on Apologetics you
need. All the Bridgewater and Bampton treatises together would only mislead you
and harden your heart. Neither is it a special providence, nor an extraordinary
interposition on the part of Almighty God that you need. No. Be not self-deceived.
For this cause, among others, God raised up Pharaoh that he might speak to you
out of the Red Sea, saying, Learn of me. Burn your books about miracles. If I had
not bargained for miracles I would not have been here. Read books of obedience.

Read books of prayer and repentance and obedience. Cease from debate and betake yourselves to be alone with God. Yes. A voice comes from the depth below, as well as from the height above, saying to us all, He among you that doeth the will of God, even he shall know of the doctrine, and shall not need to seek after a miracle. Do the will of God in the thing that lies nearest you, and in the thing that God has been so long asking of you; do it; resolve to do it; begin to do it tonight and before tomorrow; and then all past miracles in Egypt and in Israel, and all present providences and all coming experiences, will all work together to soften your heart and thus to strengthen and assure your faith. But turn away tonight from your first duty; make post-ponements; seek more convenient seasons; raise obstacles; make conditions; seek for signs, and put it off yourself, and put it upon God and upon His servants, to wait for you and to make terms with you, and from this night your heart will harden like Pharaoh's heart till your end is like his. Two young men are sitting in one seat, and, to look at them, you would say that they are not far from the kingdom of God. Their hearts are in the balance. They are almost persuaded. The intimation is made to them of the approaching celebration of the Lord's Supper. The time and the place are told them when their names may be entered for the Table. They both listen to the intimation. They both think about it; both in their own way. Yes, the one says, I have put it off too long. And I am no better. I think I will take what looks like God's word to me tonight. I will offer myself just as I am. And he does it. And his name is enrolled for the coming communion. He begins tonight and he goes on from tonight. The church is henceforth his church. The minister is henceforth his minister. He comes up to the church Sabbath after Sabbath now with a new interest in everything, and a stake of his own in everything. His heart softens and softens. And his faith clears up, and strengthens, and strikes root, and brings forth fruit; till, after years and years and years spent among us, he passes over into the promised land. His neighbor looks at the communion invitation also, and almost accepts it. No. I will wait, he says. I have some difficulties not yet resolved. I have not seen the unbelieving argument of that new book sufficiently answered. I must first read what is to be said on the other side. No, not tonight. No, not this communion yet. And he goes home. And, you could not detect it, it is so little, but his heart is just the smallest degree hardened tonight. He was at the sharp turning of the way, and he took, if anything, the wrong turn. He took Pharaoh's turn. May he turn again! Turn him, O Lord, before he goes on to Pharaoh's end.

The magicians led on Pharaoh so far, but a time came when their enchantments could carry them no farther. This is the finger of God, the outdone magicians had the insight and the honesty to say. This is the finger of God, and there is no use, and it would be death to us, to go on fighting with our enchantments against God's finger any further. Do, they advised Pharaoh—do what is asked of thee, and let the people go. But those magicians had done their evil work better than they knew. For, by that time, Pharaoh's heart was so hardened by their enchantments that he would not hearken to the too late advice of his old enchanters. Just so. We have seen it ourselves a thousand times. We have seen magicians who could begin a work of deception and delusion, but who could not stop the deception and undo the delusion when they fain would. We have seen philosophers putting nature in the place of God till their scholars went against both God and nature too. We have seen fathers and mothers indulging their sons, and letting them take their own way in religion and in life till they could not stop them. We have seen infidels, and scoffers, and gamblers, and drunkards, and all manner of profligates made by the score, as the magicians made Pharaoh; made, that is, little by little, till the work was finished, and till those who began it and carried it so far on were laughed at when they said, This, I fear, is the finger of God. The very sorcerers themselves at last believed, but Pharaoh still held out. They could set a bad work a-going; but, with all their advice, and with all their authority, they could not stop their evil work, nor in one iota undo it.

But stroke after stroke, plague after plague, fell upon Pharaoh till even he was brought at last to his knees. Then Pharaoh called for Moses and Aaron, and said, Entreat the Lord and I will let the people go. And Moses cried unto the Lord, and the Lord did according to the word of Moses. But when Pharaoh saw that there was to be respite, he hardened his heart and hearkened not unto them. Fatal Pharaoh! Everything that came to Pharaoh hardened his hard heart. God was fairly baffled with Pharaoh. God was completely defeated by Pharaoh. Good and evil, grace and judgment, plague and respite from plague—it was all one. Pharaoh's heart was hardened. Pharaoh was his name. What is your name? Well, when we substitute your name for Pharaoh's name in the terrible passage about the respite, we have in that passage the last chapter, the latest written-out chapter, of your evil life. Your present respite is fast running out, and up to this holy day you are still hardening your heart. You have gone on doing the things you swore to God and to man you would never do again. Because judgment against your evil work was not executed out, when it began to be executed, you have lifted up your heel to this very day in the face of God. There are men here tonight who were in that same seat on the New Year's day before last. And they have often remembered, sometimes with tears, but more often with a hard remorse as of hell, the text of that New Year's day address. The text that day was out of à Kempis, and it was to this effect. That spiritual writer said to us that, if we would root out but one of our vices every new year, we should soon become perfect men. And, as I know, there were some men present here that New Year's day who were so touched and so taken with that striking counsel of à Kempis that they asked for a respite for that year. Now, that is a year and a half ago. They have had a whole half-year to the bargain, till their vice is all the deeper in their bodies and in their souls to this day. Stop tonight before you sleep. Stay up alone and set yourself to think what conceivable end God can have had in raising you up, and in filling your life so full of so many accumulated and aggravated sentences and respites of sentences? God tells us Himself for what purpose He raised up Pharaoh. And, read what God says about His purpose with Pharaoh in what light you like, and offer what explanations of it you like, still it remains a terrible story and a terrible sentence. What do you think, what do you suppose, God has raised you up for? Are you, do you think, would you believe, being sentenced and respited, sentenced and respited, and sentenced and respited again in order to show how far grace can go—your sin and God's grace? Who can tell, but that as Pharaoh stands to the end of time the proof of God's power, so you are to stand at the opposite pole as the proof of His long-suffering and super-abounding grace? Yes, that must be it in you. After so many respites, and so much sin after so many respites, if you die under respite, that must be it. Yes, this must be the key to your so often respited life—this: that, where sin abounded, grace did much more abound. And that, as sin hath reigned unto death in you, even so might grace reign through righteousness unto eternal life in you by Jesus Christ your Lord. May it be so!

24
Balaam

I SHALL take it for granted that you all have the Balaam chapters in the Book of Numbers by heart. You certainly ought to have those chapters by heart; for, taken together, they make up a narrative which Ewald pronounces to be unparalleled in effectiveness and unsurpassable in artistic finish. I shall assume, then, that you all have that artistic and effective narrative by heart, and I shall enter at once on some of the lessons I have been enabled to gather out of Balaam's awful history.

In the first place, then, that True Light which lighteth every man that cometh into the world kindled up in Balaam to an extraordinary brilliance and beauty. Balaam stands out in the selectest rank of those patriarchs and princes, those prophets and priests, who were raised up outside of the house of Israel in order that men might nowhere be left to live without a divine witness. To keep to the Old Testament—Melchizedek, and Jethro, and Balaam, and Job were all such divine witnesses to the profane lands in which they lived. Balaam, then, in his place, and to begin with, was a true and a greatly gifted prophet of Almighty God. Just listen to some passages out of Balaam's prayers and prophecies and exhortations, and judge for yourselves whether he was a man of divine gifts or no. "And Balaam answered and said unto the servants of Balak, If Balak would give me his house full of silver and gold, I cannot go beyond the word of the Lord my God, to do less or more. And he took up his parable and said, Balak hath brought me out of Aram, saying, Come, curse me Jacob, and come defy Israel. But how shall I curse, whom God hath not cursed? Or how shall I defy, whom God hath not defied? Who can count the dust of Jacob, and the number of the fourth part of Israel? Let me die the death of the righteous, and let my last end be like his!" And, again, on the top of Pisgah, he takes up his parable in a way not unworthy of the place of Moses' grave: "God is not a man, that He should lie; neither the son of man, that He should repent. Hath He said, and shall He not do it? Or, hath He spoken, and shall He not make it good? He hath not beheld iniquity in Jacob, neither hath He seen perverseness in Israel. Surely there is no enchantment against Jacob, neither is there any divination against Israel; according to this time it shall be said of Jacob and of Israel, What hath God wrought!" And on the top of Peor, that looketh toward Jeshimon, Balaam positively saw the day of Christ Himself afar off. "I shall see Him, but not now; I shall behold Him, but not nigh. There shall come a star out of Jacob, and a Scepter shall rise out of Israel, and out of Jacob shall come He that shall have the dominion." And, to crown all, when Balak consulted Balaam, "Wherewith shall I come unto the Lord, and bow down myself before the High God? Shall I come before Him with burnt offerings, with calves of a year old? Will the Lord be pleased," inquired Balak, "with thousands of rams, or with ten thousands of rivers of oil? Shall I give my first-born for my transgression, the fruit of my body for the sin of my soul?" "He," answered Balaam—"He hath showed thee,

O man, what is good; and what doth the Lord require of thee, but to do justly, and to love mercy, and to walk humbly with thy God." Could Moses, could Isaiah, could Paul himself have answered Balak better? No. The Great Prophet Himself never answered Balak better than that. Calvin is the prince of commentators, and Calvin has this on this passage: "Certain it is that though Balaam was an impostor and full of deceits, yet he was endued with the gift of prophecy. This was the case, no doubt. God has often so distributed the gifts of His Spirit that He has honored with the prophetic power even the ungodly and the unbelieving. The prophetic office was at that time a special gift, quite distinct from the grace of regeneration. Balaam, then, was a prophet." A thing terrible to any man to think about; but terrible to a minister above all men to read, and to think, and to take home to his heart. For the gift of preaching, too, is a special and an official gift, altogether distinct from the gift of a new heart or a holy life. A man may be an impostor, as Calvin says; he may be full of deceit, and yet may be an eloquent preacher. Moses, as we have seen, could not preach at all, as our fault-finding people would have said. And even Aaron, who was Moses' mouth, never came within sight of the sacred eloquence of Balaam. In fact, I have a remorseful feeling within myself that Balaam's pulpit eloquence, and the dust that his pulpit eloquence cast in his own and other men's eyes, largely helped him to his ruin. Some eloquent preachers put all their religion into their eloquence. Some impressive preachers put all their tears into their pulpit voice, and all their repentance and reformation into those powerful appeals they periodically make to their own and to other flocks. That burning passage in the Book of Numbers should be appointed to all divinity students to make an exegesis and a homily upon it before they receive license. They should have to bring out and exhibit from Balaam, and from other instances in church history, how fine natural gifts, and great learning, and great eloquence in the pulpit may all lie like so much far-shining whitening on the surface of a sepulchre. One of their points should be that official excellence often consists in a preacher with much secret corruption, and that a minister may have a great name, and may make a great income, who has no name at all, and no reward at all with God. Many will say to Me in that day, Lord, have we not prophesied in Thy name, and in Thy name have cast out devils, and in Thy name have done many wonderful works? And then will I profess unto them, I never knew you. What we ministers are in our closets, says John Owen, and not in our pulpits, just that we are in the scales of God: just that, and no more. Let us, then, who are ministers, or who are looking to be ministers, so live, lest, by any means, when we have preached to others, we ourselves should be cast away as reprobate Balaam was cast away.

Balaam's importunity in prayer: Balaam on his knees all night to know God's will, when he knew it all the time—a great deal of our own anxiety, and perplexity, and prayer, and importunity in prayer is made up out of the same self-deceit. "I am afraid I cannot go; but tarry over the night till I see." And Balaam actually went all night to God again about going to Balak. He was up a great while before day about going to Balak. Had God been a man, as Balaam in a fine sermon warned Balak He was not, then we would have said that Balaam was imposing upon God, and was laughing at Him behind His back. Had Balaam been a sincere and an honest man, he would have refused so much as to see Balak's second deputation of princes. He would have said to his servants that he was engaged and could not come down. He would have said to his servants to see that the princes of Moab and their companions and their camels had proper supper and lodging, as became a king's embassy; but that Balak had his last answer from him already. Had Balaam not been given over to making a great name for himself and a great fortune; had this prophet been working out his own salvation with fear and trembling, instead of making beautiful pictures of salvation, and astonishing people with his eloquence on salvation, then Balaam would have put on strength when he saw that long string of camels on their way to his house. Now is my time! Balaam would have said to himself—Now is my accepted time! Now is the day of my salvation! A thorough honest man, as Butler says in his celebrated sermon on Balaam—a thorough honest man would have known how set upon the praises of men and the wages of unrighteousness his own heart was, and had all along been; and he would have acted that day accordingly. But Balaam, with all his talents and with all his opportunities, was a thorough dishonest man.

With all his fine sermons Balaam has his price, said Balak to himself when his first princes came back without Balaam. And Balak sent again princes, more, and more honorable than they. And with a profanity and an impudence that might well have made Balaam blush and become a new man, Balak said to Balaam, Let nothing, I pray thee, hinder thee from coming to me. Neither thy God nor anything else. For I will promote thee to very great honor, and I will do for thee whatsoever thou askest of me. Come, therefore, I pray thee, curse me this people. The salmon is the king of fish; but, all the time, he is ridiculously easily taken. Ridiculously. Two or three inches of a sufficiently red rag drawn over a sufficiently sharp hook, and, with half an hour of a sufficiently strong and supple wrist, the fool is in your basket. In that self-same, bare-faced, and rag-hooked way did Balak angle for Balaam, ay, and took him too. And in that self-same, bare-faced, and rag-hooked way are men and women being angled for and taken every day. A ribbon, a tassel, a shoulder-knot, a rosette, a garter, a feather, two or three empty letters before or after an equally empty name, and the fish is yours.

Yes, surely; go, if you would so much like to go, God said to Balaam as the day broke. At any rate, you may go so far. As you would have Me go against you, if you go all the way, take care what you say and do when you go. Beholding Balaam's insincerity, and being angry at it, says Philo, God said, By all means go. And Balaam's God is our God. And thus it is that as often as Balaam's insincerity, hesitation, sleepless anxiety about duty, prayer, and importunity in prayer are seen in us, He who gave way to Balaam gives way to us also, and says, Yes, surely. Our Maker does not place us under lock and key. He does not tie up our hands. He does not strike us lame or blind to make us obedient. He made us in His own image. He endowed us with free will. He did not intend us to be so many stocks and stones in His hands. Yes, certainly, He says; choose for yourself. What would you like best? Where is your treasure? Well, you are your own master. You are in this matter entirely in your own hands. There it stands in Holy Writ for all you who are in hesitation—If the men come to call thee, rise up, and go with them.

But the angel of the Lord stood in a path in the vineyard, a wall being on this side and a wall on that side. And when the ass saw the angel of the Lord she thrust herself into the wall, and crushed Balaam's foot against the wall. The dumb ass was doing her best to arrest and to save her eloquent master. And, had he not preached himself long past all hope of salvation, he would have divined the accident and interpreted the providence. Had he not been bereft of all sense and honesty, he would have turned his ass's head in that narrow lane, and would have carried his crushed foot home to rest it and to heal it, and to begin a new life after it. And ever after he would have caparisoned that ass with gold and silver, and would all but have made her his household god. And she would have deserved it all; for she did all she could do to save her devoted master, who had ridden her without a single swerve or stumble of hers to that day. But Balaam was too far gone for a bruised foot to bring him back. And, besides, the prevaricating angel practiced upon the prophet, and perplexed the prophet's intellect and judgment, till he did not know what to do. We would never have taken that angel for an angel of the Lord had he not been so named of the sacred writer. For it is surely not usual with such angels at once to oppose a man and to push him on. I pity Balaam—what with his ass; what with that angel of the Lord; what with his crushed foot; and then with all his other bones out of joint, since his ass fell down under him. If it displease thee, said the so pious and so perplexed prophet to the two-faced angel—if it displease thee for me to go on, then I will turn and get me back again. By no means, said the angel. By no means. Having come so far, you are not to lose all your travel and go back. No; go with the men. They are waiting till you mount. Come, and I will help you to your seat. And Balaam mounted his ass with the help of the angel and came to Balak. Have any of you a crushed foot tonight? I have. I can scarcely stand before you to finish for pain and for loss of blood. And, as the Lord liveth, all His angels, with all their irony and all their evil help, shall not sophisticate me out of my soul tonight. I, for one, am to turn tonight in the path between the vineyards. I shall not ask any angel, from heaven or from hell, whether it displeases him or no. I am determined to turn tonight. I have gone far too far already. I bless God for my crushed foot. Indeed I do. I know what I am saying, if you do not know. But, if you do, then come with me. Come, let us return to the Lord our God; for He hath torn, but He will heal us; He hath smitten, but He will bind us up. Only, Balaam went with the princes of Balak.

And then, look and learn how Balak, once he had got a hold of Balaam, cadged the prophet about from one hill-top to another to get the proper place from which to curse Israel. The first point of view to which Balak took Balaam was to one of the high places of Baal. But, when Balaam saw Israel shining in her tents below, his curses all stuck in his throat. He could not do it. Come, then, said Balak, to a better place. I will take thee this time to a hill where thou shalt not see all their tents, and thou shalt curse them from thence. And Balak, not knowing what he was doing, brought Balaam to the top of Pisgah, till Moses' mantle fell on Balaam, and till Balaam was carried on in the Spirit to prophesy good things, and better things than ever, concerning Israel. Let us try the top of Peor this time, suggested Balak in his discomfiture. Build me then three altars there, said Balaam, and I will see what I can do. But, no. The sight of Israel lying below made the spirit of blessing to come upon Balaam again, till Balak smote his hands together, and in his anger dismissed Balaam to his home without his wages, since he had not done his work. Yes, truly, this narrative is unparalleled in its effectiveness. For, with what sure effect it discovers Balaam's seed to this day. Do you know Balaam's seed when you see them, or when you are yourself one of them? That is one of Balaam's seed in the ministry, that preacher who does his best to tune his pulpit to please the king. He cannot do it; but, as Davison says of Balaam, the will is not wanting. Do you remember how James Stuart dragged Robert Bruce about, seeking a place and a point of view from which that great preacher and great patriot might be got to preach and to pray to the king's dictation? If our young ministers would have a life-long lesson and illustration in fearlessness, in fidelity, and in a good conscience to the end of a life of bribes on the one hand, and of persecution and banishment on the other, let them read themselves deeply into those two narratives so unsurpassable in effectiveness for a minister, the Life of Balaam in the history of Israel, and the Life of Bruce in the history of Scotland and of England. That church member also who changes his minister in the interests of his business, he is of the offspring of Balaam. And that other who changes his minister for the peace of his conscience, he also is Balak and Balaam seeking a spot where they can get at their sin without that restraint. You can live a life of uttermost selfishness, and worldliness, and wicked tempers, and idleness, and vanity, and vice, and total and absolute neglect of prayer in one church, and under one minister, that you could not long live under another. We cannot shut our eyes to men and women choosing their hill-tops and building and kindling their altars all around us every day, exactly as Balak and Balaam chose their hilltops and built and kindled their altars in their day. And some of you may be strongly tempted sometimes to try a change of church or a change of minister for liberty of action and for peace of mind. But you cannot do it. Like Balaam, you know too much, and you have seen too many of the tents of Israel. You may try to shut your eyes, and you may let Balak lead you about promising you your wages, but you shall never see the place where you can give your whole heart to evil, or where you can sin on without an inward rebuke.

But, Balaam—ass, and angel, and crushed foot, and Almighty God Himself notwithstanding, he would have the wages of unrighteousness. He would have Balak's gold. After his foot was whole again—Balaam was a very clever man—and he somehow got expectation and hope kindled again in Balak that Balaam might have changed his mind by this time. And, after some underground management, they met once again, Balak and Balaam, in the dark. You who know your Milton have there the identical advice that Balaam gave to Balak. It was the very same advice, to the letter, that Belial, the dissolutest spirit that fell, gave to the old serpent. Set women in their eye, counselled the old reprobate. And for his so late but so successful counsel Balaam got his house filled with Balak's silver and gold when Israel sinned and fell in the wilderness.

Let me die the death of the righteous! That was Balaam's noble peroration on the high place of Baal. But as we pass on from the Book of Numbers, with its unparalleled effectiveness, to the end of the history in the Book of Joshua, we find in that book this: Balaam also, the son of Beor, the soothsayer, did the children of Israel slay with the sword among them that were slain by them. And then, the apostle Jude, in denouncing certain evil men who had crept into the ministry and into the membership of the church of his day, says, Woe unto them! For they have run greedily after the error of Balaam. They are spots in your feasts of charity, feeding themselves without fear; clouds they are without water; trees without fruit; wandering stars, to whom is reserved the blackness of darkness for ever. Such are some of the lessons of Balaam's lost life.

25
Joshua

WHERE were Gershom and Eliezer all this time? Were they both dead? Or, if living, had they no heart for their father's God till it had been better for them and for their father that they had never been born? Can it be possible that even Moses had come so far short as this, in the supreme duty and fast-passing opportunity of bringing up his own sons? Had her husband been so cumbered with the exodus, and with the law, and with all the cares and labors of the leadership in Israel, that he had no leisure so much as to eat his meals beside Zipporah and her two sons? Had Moses been far too long in accepting a staff of elders to assist him in ruling and judging Israel? And were Gershom and Eliezer grown up and gone clean out of hand before their father had wakened up to that and was aware of it? But, when all is said, it is far less the father than the mother in this matter. Had Moses' house, then, been so divided against itself that it fell upon his two sons? And had Miriam and Aaron been right after all in their hot opposition to their brother's marriage with the Ethiopian woman? We ask these questions at the text, but we get no answer. We are left to look for the answers to all these questions in our own house, among our own sons and daughters, and in our own heart and conscience. At the same time, though Moses had wholly lost hold of his own sons, there is this to be said for the father of Gershom and Eliezer: that he had an immense attraction for some other men's sons. There was nothing more remarkable about Moses than the openness of his heart and the freshness of his mind to double the age of ordinary men; as Isaac Walton says, God had blessed Moses with perfect intellectuals and a cheerful heart to old age; and the young men who were always about him had had a great deal to do with that. You will sometimes see stranger young men crowding around a minister in his classes and in his congregational work, and saving their own souls by so doing, while those young men that have been born in the family are never so much as seen or heard of. And that was always the case with Moses. There was quite a circle of young men continually around Moses, and Joshua, the son of Nun, was the choicest and the most capable of them all. We know nothing as yet about Joshua—nothing but this, that he was not the son of Moses and Zipporah, but of a certain unknown man named Nun, of the tribe of Ephraim. Joshua had no such start in life as Gershom and Eliezer had, but by his high character and his great services he not only took their crowns from them, but at the same time he won a crown and scepter and a great name in Israel all his own.

It is stated again and again in the sacred history that Joshua stood before Moses and was his minister. Stood ready, that is, to run the great man's errands, and to set out with him on his hallowed expeditions, and, in short, to be more than a son to Moses in the absence of his own sons. "He departed not out of the tabernacle" is another very remarkable testimony for that time concerning the son of Nun. Now, in that Joshua was exactly like his Great Namesake in the New Testament whose

124

wont it was to go up to the synagogue of Nazareth every Sabbath day, and who said to His father and mother when they sought Him all through Jerusalem sorrowing: "How is it that ye seek Me? Wist ye not that I must be about My Father's business?" Joseph and Mary had sought the child Jesus in all those places where other sorrowing fathers and mothers were seeking their lost sons also—among the theaters, and the circuses, and the shows, and the races, and the wrestling arenas, and the inns, and shops, and streets of Jerusalem; but He departed not out of the temple. We, too, have boys sometimes among ourselves not unlike that. They love and choose and are always to be found among good things, in good places, and reading good books while yet they are still mere children. They take to the Sabbath-school, and to the church, and to the Bible-class, and to the missionary meeting as other boys take, and no blame to them, to cricket, and football, and fishing, and shooting. Wordsworth has two such boys:

> Never did worthier lads break English bread:
> The finest Sunday that the autumn saw,
> With all its mealy cluster of ripe nuts,
> Could never keep those boys away from church,
> Or tempt them to one hour of Sabbath breach,
> Leonard and James!

And as such boys rise to be young men they are already promising pillars in the house of their fathers' God. They are our Sabbath-school teachers, our elders and our deacons, our best preachers and pastors, and the heads of our seminaries and colleges. And Joshua, the son of Nun, was the first figure and far-off forerunner of all such young men as he stood before Moses, and was his minister, and went up with him to the mount, and never departed out of the tabernacle.

There is no finer grace to be found in any young man's heart than his admiration and reverence for great and good men. We really are already what we love and admire and honor. And when a young man has eyes to see and a heart to love and honor those good and gifted men he reads and hears about; or, still better, those who live near him, nothing could be a sounder sign or a surer promise of his own future character than that.

> We live by admiration, hope, and love;
> And even as these are well and wisely fixed,
> In dignity of being we ascend.

The mother of Gershom and Eliezer, from the very little that we see of her, would seem to have been a froward, forward woman, and a rude and disrespectful wife; and a worse up-bringing than that what child could ever have? But Joshua's nameless mother—judging her from her son, she must have been a true mother in Israel. And she had already her full wages paid her when she saw her son Joshua standing of his own accord before Moses and serving him as his minister. And if she lived to see him at the head of the tribes of Israel, and leading them on from victory to victory, she would feel herself to have been far more than overpaid for all the watchfulness, and all the care, and all the nights of prayer she had laid out on her noble boy. And thus it came about that through her, and through some other nameless mothers like her, what Moses missed so much at home he found so thankfully as often as he went abroad, when Joshua and his companions gathered round Moses to drink in his counsels and to execute his commands. But it was Joshua alone in all the camp who was all to Moses that John was to Jesus. Moses loved and trusted Joshua, and Joshua lay at Moses' feet. At the same time, the defect of Joshua's finest quality, as we are wont to call it, came out on an occasion, and was warmly and nobly rebuked by Moses, as we read in a very beautiful passage in the Book of Numbers. There was a day of Pentecost in Israel as Moses grew old, when the Spirit of the Lord fell on seventy of the elders of Israel in order to fit them to be Moses' assessors and assistants in ruling and in teaching the refractory people. And, as God would have it, over and above the selected seventy, there were two exceptional men on whom the Spirit fell also, till Joshua grudged and fretted at the way the people's eyes were drawn off his master and turned to Eldad and Medad as they prophesied in the camp. "Forbid them, my lord!" said Joshua, in his jealousy for Moses. To which speech of Joshua Moses made the golden answer: "Enviest thou for my sake? Would God that all the Lord's people were prophets, and that the Lord would put His Spirit upon them!" See John iii. 26, the margin steps in and says. And when we turn to John's gospel we find this fine parallel passage: "A man can receive nothing," said the Baptist, "except it be given from heaven. Ye yourselves bear me witness that I said, I am not the Christ. The Christ must increase, but I must decrease." It is beautiful to see Moses' best disciple so jealous of other gifted men, and all out of pure honor and love to his great master; and it is beautiful to see the same mistaken loyalty in John's disciples. But both Moses and John shine splendidly to all time in their rebukes to their disciples, and show themselves to be the true masters of such deserving disciples in their never-to-be-forgotten answers and lessons and reproofs. Moses, and John, and Paedaritus of Sparta, Moses' contemporary, who, when he was passed over and left out in the election of the Three Hundred, went home to his house beaming with happiness, it did him so much good to see that there were so many men in Sparta who were better men than himself.

For years and years, and all the time wholly unknown to anybody but himself, Moses had been schooling his own heart till the case of Eldad and Medad only called out into words what had for long been in his thoughts. Joshua had but put in rude and angry words the bitter jealousy that Moses had for years and years been battling with in secret. And Moses' magnificent answer to Joshua was but another proof of the incomparable meekness and sweetness of Moses' so subdued heart. And then, when long afterwards we find Moses suing for a successor who should take up his work and finish it, he does it in a way that proclaims Moses to have been a man after God's own heart long before David was born. "Let the Lord, the God of the spirits of all flesh, set a man over the congregation, which may go out before them, and which may lead them out, and which may bring them in; that the congregation of the Lord be not as sheep which have no shepherd." Noble soul! Great servant and great saint of God! Though his eye was not dim, nor his natural strength abated, yet because it was made clear to him that it was the will of God, and that the time had now come when he was to stand aside and give up his place to another man, he put off his harness and his honor without one murmur. The cross would, no doubt, have been somewhat less sharp had Gershom or Eliezer stood ready to take up the laid-down leadership, and it may well have been the last pang of that painful time to Moses that he had no son of his own to take his place, to finish his work, and to transmit his name. Aaron, the high priest, under a like bereavement, held his peace. And so did his desolate brother, the great law-giver and leader of Israel. And the Lord said unto Moses, Take thee Joshua, the son of Nun, a man in whom is the Spirit, and lay thine hand upon him. And thou shalt put some of thine honor upon him, that all the congregation of Israel may be obedient. And Moses did as the Lord commanded him. "A man in whom is the Spirit," said the Lord, who gave to Joshua that great gift. The Spirit of the Lord had begun in Joshua from a child, from his mother's milk, indeed; and to him that hath shall be given, till by the time that Moses died we are reassured and rewarded as we read that Joshua, the son of Nun, was full of the spirit of wisdom, and the children of Israel hearkened unto him, and did as the Lord commanded Moses.

It is a great epoch to a nation and to a church, as well as a great testing time to all concerned, when an old leader has to put off his harness, and when a new and an untried man is summoned up to put on his harness for all the toils and crosses that await him. I was present once at such an impressive moment, and I often remember it. An old servant of God who had been a very Moses to multitudes in our land was about to die when he sent for the man who had been a very Joshua, a son and a servant to him, and from his death-bed addressed him in words of love and trust and prophetic assurance that must often come back to his heart, as they often come back to mine. And then the old leader put his arms round his successor's neck and kissed him, and lay down and died. Men like Moses and Joshua, and all who serve God and man, pass through extreme and painful experiences. The time had been when Caleb and Joshua stood absolutely alone with their life in their hand as all Israel bade stone them with stones. But never, all his days, was Joshua more or better the servant of God, and the best and the most far-seeing friend of the people of Israel, than he was just at that solitary, slanderous, murderous moment.

Just when Joshua was in the act of putting on his armor to attempt his first battle, he looked up, and, behold! a man stood over-against him with his sword drawn in his hand. "Art thou for us?" demanded Joshua of the armed man; "or art thou for our adversaries?" "Nay," answered the mysterious soldier, "but as Captain of the Lord's host am I come." And Joshua fell on his face, and said, "What saith my Lord unto His servant?" And on the seventh day Jericho fell into Joshua's hands without sword or spear of Joshua.

Fell flat every stone wall of it before a blast of rams' horns only blown over Jericho in the name of the Lord. And Joshua from that day learned how to enter on the wars of the Lord in a way he never forgot. David, also, while yet a ruddy youth, had read the Book of Joshua in the intervals of feeding his father's flock. For we hear him as he puts off Saul's helmet of brass and coat of mail and takes five smooth stones out of the brook. Turning to Goliath, David said, "Thou comest to me with a sword, and with a spear, and with a shield, but I come to thee in the name of the Lord of hosts. For today all this assembly shall know that the Lord saveth not with sword and spear, for the battle is the Lord's, and He will give you into our hands." And all down sacred history, through Israel, and not less through England and Scotland, there have never failed prophets to preach how to war a good warfare, nor has the Lord's hosts lacked leaders like Joshua, who fell at that Divine Captain's feet and worshipped. Theodor Keim, in his volume of genius on our Lord's early life on earth, says that in His choice of a trade, which He was bound to choose, though He chose to be a carpenter, Jesus of Nazareth might have chosen anything else, anything but to be a soldier. But, surely, He was a soldier before Jericho, when He said to Joshua that He had come to him as Captain of the Lord's host. And we see Him in the thick and at the head of many a bloody battle all down the ages, till at last we are let see Him clothed with a vesture dipped in blood, and on His vesture and on His thigh a name written, King of kings, and Lord of lords. But we are not all soldiers, and we civilians have this same Divine Man as our forerunner and example as well as soldiers. For, in the manifold wisdom and abounding grace of God, the Son of God appears to each one of us as we enter life, and summons us to put the shoes off our feet as we stand on that holy ground. To the young soldier He appears in vision as a captain, to the young preacher He appears as a preacher, to the young pastor He is the chief shepherd, to the young merchant He is an example of successful buying and selling, to a master He appears as a master, and to a servant as a servant; sometimes He is a lover, sometimes He is a husband, sometimes a son, and sometimes a brother, and so on, till He never leaves any man at his entrance on life without a divine vision, and an ideal example, and a sacred summons to take his shoes off his feet. And all young men who, like Joshua, make their start on this holy ground—they shall surely finish their course and keep the faith till the Captain of their salvation shall not be ashamed to call them His brethren. Loose thy shoes from off thy feet. And Joshua did so.

With all his clearness of head and with all his honesty of heart, Joshua made one great mistake in the opening of his military and diplomatic life. That great mistake arose out of his youth and inexperience, and he is not much to be blamed—by us, at any rate—for making that mistake. All the same, that mistake, once made, was disastrous and irretrievable. The Gibeonites were terrified to death at the approach of Joshua and his army. And they made as if they were come to him from a far country, a country that he would never have commission or interest to conquer, but with whose people it would be to his advantage in many ways to be good friends and in a league of peace. And their old shoes, and old bottles, and old bread, and their wily speeches, and other fine fetches completely circumvented Joshua, till he made a covenant of peace with a cruel, corrupt, and accursed people that he had been armed and ordained and commanded to sweep off the face of the earth. And for this, and for other like mistakes of ignorance, and simplicity, and over-leniency, both Joshua and all Israel suffered long and bitterly. The mystical interpretation here tells us that pride was the sin of the Amorite, and envy the sin of the Hittite, and wrath of the Perizzite, and gluttony and lechery of the Girgashite and the Hivite, while covetousness and sloth were the corruptions of the Canaanite and the Jebusite. And then that same method of interpretation passes on to this, that many young men when they first enter on their inexperience of sanctification are cheated into sparing some of their pride under this disguise, and some of their envy under that. Gluttony and lust also come to them each under its own cloak of deceit, and covetousness and sloth also each under its own mask, till all their days many men are tempted and led into this and that besetting sin through early ignorance and simplicity and self-will. Still, just as Joshua put the Gibeonites to hew wood and draw water for the altar of the Lord when he could not root them out, so we may turn the remnants of our pride, and envy, and ill-will, and gluttony, and sloth to this same good use. These things will try us and will prove us, as the Scripture says, to see what is in our hearts, and whether we will serve God in spite of them or not. It was the thorn that was in the apostle's flesh that brought down this word to him: "My grace is sufficient for thee, and My strength is made perfect in weakness." And the children of the Gibeonites, while thorns in their eyes and scourges in their sides, and snares and traps to them, were at the same time hewers of wood and drawers of water for the congregation, and for the altar of the Lord to this day, in the place which the Lord shall choose.

Joshua never ceased all his life long to mourn over the great mistake he had made at Gilgal. He could not shut his eyes a single day to the disastrous results of that great mistake to himself and to all Israel. And when he was on his death-bed it all came back to him, till he summoned the heads of Israel around him to hear his dying apology and protest; "Choose you out this day among all the gods of the Gibeonites and the other Canaanites the god that you and your children will serve; but know this, that as for me and my house we will serve THE LORD." You all know, I suppose, what that meant on Joshua's dying lips that day. Joshua had never forgotten that day of days in the great days of his youth, when Moses took his young servant up with him to the top of the mount, ay, and even into the cleft rock itself.

From that awful day never a day, never a night, never an hour of a day or a night, had passed over Joshua that he had not heard the Lord passing by and proclaiming, THE LORD, the LORD God, merciful and gracious, long-suffering, and abundant in goodness and truth, keeping mercy for thousands, forgiving iniquity, and transgression, and sin. Ever since that day on the mount and in the cleft rock the LORD, and no heathen god of them all, had been Joshua's God. Happy man who had such a revelation made to him in the days of his youth! Happy man, who could call all Israel to come and see that he was leaving a house behind him of the same experience, of the same fixed mind, and of the same assured and inherited happiness. Young men, still choosing whom and what you will serve; young fathers and young mothers, still choosing a God for yourselves and for your household—Joshua speaks to you out of his noble life, so nobly begun and now so nobly ended. Choose and say. Are you yourselves to be, and are you to bring up your children after you to be, Amorites, and Hittites, and Hivites, and Canaanites, and Jebusites in the land? Are you to let ambition, and envy, and pride, and anger, and self-will rule in your hearts and be your household gods? No! Never, never! Not so long as you have still this day in your choice for yourselves and for your households the LORD, the LORD God, merciful and gracious, and abundant in goodness and truth. And Moses and Joshua made haste in the cleft rock, and they bowed their heads to the earth, and they said, If now we have found grace in Thy sight, pardon our iniquity and our sin, and take us for Thine inheritance. And from that day it was so.

26
Achan

JERICHO was one of the largest and richest cities in all ancient Canaan. But for the terrible ban pronounced by Joshua, Jericho might have taken the place of Jerusalem itself as the chief city of ancient Israel. Jericho was an excellently situated and a strongly fenced city. Broad and lofty walls ran all round the city, and the only way in and out of the city was by great gates which were scrupulously shut every night at sundown. There were great foundries of brass and iron in Jericho, with workshops also in silver and in gold. The looms of Babylonia were already famous over all the eastern world, and their rich and beautiful textures went far and near, and were warmly welcomed wherever the commercial caravans of that day carried them. Balak's gold had long before now brought Balaam the soothsayer across the plains of Mesopotamia, and the gold and silver of Jericho had also drawn toward that city the travelling dealers in the woven work of the Babylonian looms. A goodly Babylonish garment plays a prominent part in the tragical history that now opens before us.

The rich and licentious city of Jericho was doomed of God to swift overthrow and absolute extermination, but no part of the spoil, neither thread nor shoe-latchet, was to be so much as touched by Joshua or any of his armed men. Nothing demoralizes an army like sacking a fallen city. To spring like a tiger at a wall that reaches up to heaven, and then to extinguish all a tiger's thirst for blood and plunder, that is the high ideal of a true soldier's duty. And it is a splendid certificate to Joshua's discipline, and to the morality of his army, that only one of his men gave way in the time of temptation. And the swift and heavy fall of Joshua's hand on that one man must have still more consolidated Joshua's authority, and transformed his wilderness hosts into true soldiers, where other soldiers would have been thieves and robbers. The army of Israel crossed the Jordan, entered the devoted land, besieged its cities, and marched from victory to victory under the banners of their respective tribes; very much as a modern army is made up of companies of men compacted together under the colors and the denominations of their respective clans and nationalities. Each of the twelve tribes of Israel had its own regiment, as we would say, marching and camping and entering battle under its own ensign; and thus it was that when the armies of Israel marched round Jericho on the way to their miraculous conquest of that city the standard of the tribe of Judah led the sacred host. Every single soldier in all Israel had heard Joshua's proclamation about Jericho; both what his men were to do till the walls fell, and how they were to demean themselves after the city had been given of God into their hands. But war is war; and the best of commanders cannot make war a silken work, nor can he hold down the devil in the hearts of all his men. In the hearts of many of them he may, if he first does that in his own heart; but scarcely in the hearts of them all. Night fell on the prostrate city, and the hour of

131

temptation struck for Joshua and all his men. Blessed is the man that endureth temptation; for when he is tried he shall receive the crown of life. And Joshua and all his men received the crown of life that night—all his men but one. Who is that stealing about among the smoking ruins? Is that some soldier of Jericho who has saved himself from the devouring sword? When the night wind wakens the embers again these are the accoutrements and the movements of one of Joshua's men. Has he lost his way? Has he been half dead, and has he not heard the rally of the trumpet? He hides, he listens, he looks through the darkness, he disappears into the darkness. No one has slept for joy in all the camp of Israel that night. And no one has slept for sorrow in one of Judah's tents that night. For, what is the fall of Jericho to them in that tent when it has cost them the life of their husband, their father, and their master? When the door of that tent is suddenly lifted, and the face of a corpse comes in, takes a spade, and buries a strange burden in the earth in the midst of the astounded tent. God giveth His beloved sleep. But—

> Methought I heard a voice cry, Sleep no more!
> Macbeth doth murder sleep, the innocent sleep!
> And still it cried, Macbeth doth murder sleep!

So the Lord was with Joshua; and his fame was noised throughout the whole country. But the men of Israel fled before the men of Ai, wherefore the hearts of the people melted and became as water. And the Lord said to Joshua, Get thee up; wherefore liest thou upon thy face? Up, sanctify the people, for there is an accursed thing in the midst of them. And Joshua rose up early in the morning, and brought Israel by their tribes, and the tribe of Judah was taken; and he brought the family of Judah, and he took the family of Zarhites; and he brought the family of the Zarhites, man by man, and Zabdi was taken; and he brought his household, man by man, and Achan of the tribe of Judah was taken. My son, said Joshua, give, I pray thee, glory to the Lord God of Israel, and make confession to Him; and tell me what thou hast done; hide it not from me. And Achan answered Joshua, and said, Indeed, I have sinned against the LORD God of Israel, and thus and thus have I done: When I saw among the spoil a goodly Babylonish garment, and two hundred shekels of silver, and a wedge of gold of fifty shekels weight, then I coveted them, and took them; and, behold, they are hid in the earth in the midst of my tent, and the silver under it. And all Israel raised over him a great heap of stones to this day. So the Lord turned from the fierceness of His anger. Wherefore the name of that place was called The Valley of Achor unto this day.

Everybody who reads the best books will have long had by heart Thomas à Kempis's famous description of the successive steps of a successful temptation. There is first the bare thought of the sin. Then, upon that, there is a picture of the sin formed and hung up on the secret screen of the imagination. A strange sweetness from that picture is then let down drop by drop into the heart; and then that secret sweetness soon secures the consent of the whole soul, and the thing is done. That is true, and it is powerful enough. But Achan's confession to Joshua is much simpler, and much closer to the truth. "I saw the goodly Babylonish garment, I coveted it, I took it, and I hid it in my tent." Had Joshua happened to post the ensign of Judah opposite the poor men's part of the city, this sad story would never have been told. But even as it was, had Achan only happened to stand a little to the one side, or a little to the other side of where he did stand, in that case he would not have seen that beautiful piece, and not seeing it he would not have coveted it, and would have gone home to his tent that night a good soldier and an honest man. But when once Achan's eyes lighted on that rich garment he never could get his eyes off it again. As à Kempis says, the seductive thing got into Achan's imagination, and the devil's work was done. Achan was in a fever now lest he should lose that goodly garment. He was terrified lest any of his companions should have seen that glittering piece. He was sure some of them had seen it and were making off with it. He stood in between it and the searchers. He turned their attention to something else. And then when their backs were about he wrapped it up in a hurry, and the gold and the silver inside of it, and thrust it down into a hiding-place. His eyes were Achan's fatal snare. It was his eyes that stoned Achan and burned him and his household to dust and ashes in the Valley of Achor. Had God seen it to be good to make men and women in some way without eyes, the fall itself would have been escaped. It was at Adam and Eve's eyes that the devil came into man's heart at first. In his despair to get the devil out of his heart Job swore a solemn oath and made a holy covenant with his eyes. But our Savior, as He always does, goes far deeper than Job. He knows quite well that no oath that Job ever swore, and no covenant that Job ever sealed, will hold any man's eyes from sin; and therefore He demands of all His disciples that their eyes shall be plucked out. He pulls down His own best handiwork at its finest part so that He may get the devil's handiwork destroyed and rooted out of it; and then He will let us have all our eyes back again when and where we are fit to be trusted with eyes. It is better to go to heaven like a blind man led by a dog, says our Lord; ten times better than to dance all your days down to hell with Babylonian bangles on and all ornaments. Miss Rossetti is writing to young ladies, it is true; but what she says to them it will do us all good to hear. "True," says that fine writer, "all our lives long we shall be bound to refrain our soul, and to keep it low; but what then? For the books we now forbear to read, we shall one day be endued with wisdom and knowledge. For the music we will not listen to we shall join in the song of the redeemed. For the pictures from which we turn we shall gaze unabashed on the Beatific Vision. For the companionships we shun, we shall be welcomed into angelic society and the communion of triumphant saints. For all the amusements we avoid, we shall keep the supreme jubilee." Yes, it is as certain as God's truth and righteousness are certain, that the mortified man who goes about with his eyes out; the man who steals along the street seeing neither smile nor frown; he who keeps his eyes down wherever men and women congregate—in the church, in the market-place, at a railway-station, on a ship's deck, at an inn table—where you will; that man escapes multitudes of temptations that more open and more full-eyed men and women continually fall before. You huff and toss your head at that. But these things are not spoken for you, but for those who have sold and cut off both eye and ear and hand and foot and life itself, if all that will only carry them one single step nearer to their salvation.

So Joshua rose early in the morning—Joshua, like every good soldier, was an early riser—and he brought all Israel by their tribes, and their families, and their households, that the Lord Himself might make inquisition, and might put His finger upon the marked man. Look at the camp of Israel that awful morning! It is the day of judgment, and the great white throne is set in the Valley of Achor before its proper time. Look how the hearts of those fathers and mothers who have sons in the army beat as if it were the last trump! Did you ever spend a night like that in Achan's tent? A friend of mine once slept in a room in a hotel in Glasgow through the wall from a man who made him think sometimes that a madman had got into the house. Sometimes he thought it must be a suicide, and sometimes a damned soul come back for a visit to the city of its sins. But he understood the mysterious noises of the night next morning when the officers came in and beckoned to a gentleman who sat surrounded by the luxuries of the breakfast table, and drove him off to a penal settlement. Groanings that cannot be uttered to you were heard by all Achan's neighbors all that night. Till one bold man rose and lifted a loop of Achan's tent in the darkness, and saw Achan still burying deeper and deeper his sin. O sons and daughters of discovered Achan! O guilty and dissembling sinners! It is all in vain. It is all utterly and absolutely in vain. Be sure as God is in heaven, that He has His eyes upon you, and that your sin will find you out. You think that the darkness will cover you. Wait till you see! Go on sowing as you have begun, and come and tell us when the harvest is reaped how it threshes out and how it tastes.

The eagle that stole a piece of sacred flesh from the altar brought home a smoldering coal with it that kindled up afterwards and burned up both her whole nest and all her young ones. It was very sore upon Achan's sons, and his daughters, and his oxen, and his asses, and his sheep, and his tent, and all that he had. But things are as they are. God gathers the solitary into families for good, and the family tie still continues to hold even when all the members of the family have done evil. Once a father, always a father: the relationship stands. Once a son, always a son, even when a prodigal son. Every son has his father's gray hairs and his mother's anxious heart in his hands, and no possible power can alter that. Drop that stolen flesh! There is a coal in it that shall never be quenched.

Achan, after all, as is sometimes the case, had all the time the root of the matter in him. Achan made a clean breast of it, and gave himself up to Joshua before all Israel, and walked out to the Valley of Achor without a murmur. But Joshua had no choice. Joshua could not help himself. Joshua was a man under authority. And Achan had to die. But the point and the proper end of the whole story to us is this: that a greater than Joshua is here. Joshua bore a Name greater than his own, but that only brings out all the better the blessed contrast between Achan and you. Make a clean breast of it, then. Go home to your tent tonight, take up the accursed thing out of its hiding-place, and lay it out before Joshua, if not before all Israel. Lay it out and say—Indeed I have sinned against the Lord God of Israel, and thus and thus have I done. And if you do not know what more to say, if you are speechless beside that accursed thing, try this; say this. Ask and say, Is thy Name indeed Jesus? Dost thou indeed save found-out men from their sins? Art thou still set forth to be a propitiation? Art thou truly able to save to the uttermost? For I am the chief of sinners, say. Lie down on the floor of your room—you need not think it too much for you to do that, or that it is an act unworthy of your manhood to do it; the Son of God did it for you on the floor of Gethsemane. Yes, lie down on the floor of your room, lay your head in the dust of it, and say this about yourself: Say that you, naming yourself, are the offscouring of all men. For thus and thus, naming it, have I done. And then say this—

> The dying thief rejoiced to see
> That Fountain in his day—

and see what the true Joshua will stand over you and will say to you.

Therefore the name of that place is called The Valley of Achor to this day. Achor, that is, as it is interpreted on the margin, trouble; the Valley of Trouble. Why hast thou troubled us? demanded Joshua of Achan. The Lord shall trouble thee this day. The Lord troubled Achan in judgment that day, but He is troubling you in mercy in your day. Yes; be sure, in mercy. If I were suddenly to open your door tonight, and find you on your face, I would clap my hands with gladness. I would lie down on the spot beside you, and would share your trouble, and you would share mine, and I would lift you up and share your joy. It is not possible, you say. Look at your Bible again, and see. "And Sharon shall be a fold of flocks, and the Valley of Achor a place for the herds to lie down in, for the people that have sought Me." And, again—"And I will give her her vineyards from thence, and the Valley of Achor for a door of hope; and she shall sing there, as in the day of her youth, and as in the day when she came up out of the land of Egypt." Your soul, that is. Your soul shall sing there. There, in that Valley of Achor. There in that room. There where your sin found you out. There where I found you on your face. Yes; already your trouble is a door of hope. You will sing yet as you never sang in the days of your youth. You never sang songs like these in the days of your youth, or before your trouble came—songs like these: The Lord will be a refuge for the overwhelmed: a refuge in the time of trouble. Thou art my hiding-place; Thou shalt preserve me from trouble; Thou shalt compass me about with songs of deliverance. He shall call upon Me, and I will answer him; I will be with him in trouble; I will deliver him and honor him. The sorrows of death compassed me, and the pains of hell gat hold upon me; I found trouble and sorrow. Though I walk in the midst of trouble Thou wilt revive me, and Thy right hand shall save me. O the Hope of Israel, the Savior thereof in the time of trouble! You will sing that song in your Valley of Achor till this song shall be taken up over you by saints and angels—These are they which came out of great tribulation, and have washed their robes, and made them white in the blood of the Lamb.

27
Gideon

WE are not told to whom we are indebted for the Book of The Judges, but whoever he was, he was a master of the pen, and the story of Gideon is his masterpiece. A powerfully built, middle-aged man of Manasseh is busy beating out a few blasted ears of corn in a secret winepress. He beats the sheaves softly lest the sound of his staff should tell the Midianites where the wheat is. He stops his work to dry his face and to wet his lips, but all the water in the well would not put out the fire that is in his eye, for the fire that is in his eye is his hot heart rising to heaven against the oppressors of his people. "The Lord is with thee," the angel of the Lord appeared at that moment and said to Gideon, "for thou art a mighty man of valor." Gideon thought that the angel of the Lord was mocking at him in so speaking. The Lord with me! and I have not meal enough to make my children's supper! I a mighty man of valor, when I am afraid to thrash out my few stalks of wheat on the thrashing-floor, but must hide myself in this hidden winepress! Call me not a mighty man of valor. Call me a God-forsaken coward! But the angel of the Lord only the more went on, "Go in this thy might and thou shalt save Israel."

No sooner had the angel of the Lord taken his departure than Gideon threw down his staff and went into the house where his mother sat mourning day and night for the loss of her sons slain at Tabor, each one resembling the son of a king. And Gideon said to his weeping mother, "Awake, my mother, and sing to me the song of Deborah." And while she only the more sat and wept, her son took out and whetted his sword and sharpened his axe. "Sing to me," he said, "how Deborah and Barak arose and delivered Israel. Sing to me, ye daughters of Joash, of how the stars in their courses fought against Sisera." Night fell; and at midnight, behold ten men, and each man with a pitcher and a lamp in it in his left hand, and with his axe in his right hand, stole out of his house and met Gideon. Their meeting was beside the altar of Baal and in the grove of Baal, which was built and planted in Joash's high place. For, how could Joash's son think to cast out a single Midianite as long as that unclean altar and those unclean trees stood beside his father's house? He could not. But at every blow of Gideon's swift axe new strength came into his arm. At every tree that fell before his axe his courage rose. And the light of God's countenance returned already to Israel in every star that shone down through the opening spaces in the grove of Baal. Why is *your* life in such bondage and fear and famine tonight? Why have you not been fed today and every day with the finest of the wheat? Why are you not satisfied every day with honey out of the rock? Arise in this thy might, and the Lord will make of thee also a mighty man of valor. Be sure of this, that thy sure way to deliverance and peace and plenty lies for thee also through that levelled grove and over that prostrate altar.

The dearest idol I have known,
Whate'er that idol be,
Help me to tear it from Thy throne,
And worship only Thee.

The worshippers of Baal never neglected their morning devotions. "Early will I seek thee," they could say to their god with truth and a good conscience. And thus it was that before Joash was up that morning the men of the city were gathered already round his door, shouting and demanding, and saying—"Bring out thy son Gideon that he may die: because he hath cast down the altar of Baal, and because he hath cut down the grove of Baal." Many men who have not the courage to do a righteous deed themselves have the sense and the grace to be glad when other men do it. And sometimes you will see a father who is entangled in some evil or doubtful business, but has not the courage or the strength to cut himself and his house clear of it, a proud enough father when his son rises up and sets the whole household free. A vein of true humor ran in the Joash blood; for that morning the old man met the men of the city with a jest that scattered them all home, just as Gideon his son has enriched our literature to this day with more than one witty word and ready and racy answer. "For shame!" said Joash, "for shame, sirs! Stand back, and go home. Let Baal redress his own wrongs. Baal is a god: and you are only my everyday neighbors. Let Baal arise, but go you home." And Joash brought out Gideon and baptized him Jerubbaal before them all, saying, "Let Baal settle his own scores with my sacrilegious son." "Let her ladyship now save herself," said John Knox, as he cast the wooden idol overboard. "She is light enough; let her learn to swim." After that, we read, was no Scottish man ever urged with that idolatry.

Gideon was a great favorite with Pascal. Gideon's fleece had taken a great hold of Pascal's imagination. You all know the fine story of Gideon's fleece. Gideon was a humble-minded man. Not Moses himself was a more humble-minded man than Gideon was, or more unwilling to come out and be a great man before Israel. "Oh, my Lord, wherewith shall I save Israel? Behold, my family is poor in Manasseh, and I am the least in my father's house." But, had Gideon not been poor in Manasseh, and the least in his father's house, God would have gone elsewhere for a leader to deliver Israel. And this is always the way of the Lord with men who are to do a great work for Him and for His people—"to that man will I look, saith the Lord, even to him that is poor and of a contrite spirit, and who trembleth at My word." And God said to Gideon, What sign shall I show thee to assure and to confirm thee that thou art he who shall deliver Israel? And the quaint fancy of Gideon fell on a sheep's fleece now wet and now dry when all around it was now dry and now wet. A strange, indeed a fantastic, request to make of God. But, all the same, Gideon made it and got it. "Is there humor in the divine mind?" asked one of his congenial students at Dr. Duncan, instancing, at the same time, what looked to him like some examples of something not unlike humor both in creation and in providence. "It's true and it's no true," was the old doctor's answer. And God did so that night; for it was dry upon the fleece only, and there was dew on all the ground. You have the whole story from "a pen that ennobles and idealizes all that it touches." But you may not have read this addition from another pen, that Gideon's mother took that so versatile fleece of his, and cut it out, and sewed it up with her own hands into a soldier's mantle for her elect son: a mantle which he wore under his armor and next his heart in all his after-battles; and his men always witnessed that Gideon with his fleece on was full of hope when they were full of despair; and again, that he was full of a good captain's caution and forethought when they would have gone headlong to their own destruction. How often I wish with all the world that Pascal had been spared to develop his Thoughts and finish his Apology. What lessons I could then have read you out of Gideon's wonderful fleece! Pascal must have had something great in his mind about Gideon, for we see him taking down Gideon's name in his notebook again and again. But, as we know, Pascal did not live to digest his rich notebook into the great book of his life.

But it is time to come to Gideon's three hundred Ironsides, so to call them. Not a man of Colonel Cromwell's soldiers swears but he pays his twelve-pence. No drinking, no disorders, no plundering, no impiety permitted. They were men that had the fear of God in them, and that made them put away all other fear. "Truly they were never beaten at all," boasted their colonel. "My troops increase," he wrote to his friend, Oliver St. John. "I have a lovely company; you would respect them did you know them. They are no anabaptists. They are honest, sober, Christian men; and they expect to be used like men. The result was I raised such men as had the fear of God before them; such men as made conscience of what they did; and from that day forward they were never beaten, but wherever they were engaged against the enemy they beat continually. And truly this is matter of praise to God, and it hath some instruction in it." You see, then, what an Ironside was. An Ironside was a soldier whose whole soul was ribbed and plated all round with sound morals and true religion. Colonel Cromwell's Ironsides were that, and so were Judge Gideon's. And Gideon's three hundred has still some instruction in it, as Cromwell says. And one of these instructions is this, that three hundred good and true men are far better for a great campaign of truth and righteousness than ten thousand men swept together by chance conscription, or picked up for a shilling a head in a public-house. The men are too many, said the Lord to Gideon. And the Lord took one of Gideon's own original and characteristic ways of weeding out that army of deliverance. The day was hot, and the ten thousand came to a river on their march. Their fathers in leaving Egypt had eaten their last supper without taking off their hats or their shoes. They ate that memorable supper standing, with a piece of the Passover lamb in one hand and with their staff in the other. And three hundred of Gideon's men out of the ten thousand remembered that supper that day, and they swore to themselves and to one another that they would not sit down to eat bread at a table, nor so much as lie down to drink water out of a river, so long as there was a single Midianite left alive in the land. And thus it was that without even taking off their helmets, the three hundred wet their lips out of the hollow of their hand, and were back again that moment in their unbroken ranks. As for Gideon, the dew glistening on his mother's mantle was water enough for him that day. "Alexander, being parched with thirst in the desert, took the helmet full of water, but perceiving that the men of arms that were about him did thrust out their necks to look upon this water, he gave it back again unto them that had given it unto him, and thanked them, but drank none of it. For, said he, if I drink alone all these men here will faint. And what wonder if his men began to spur their horses, saying that they were not weary nor athirst, nor did think themselves mortal as long as they had such a king." And all the best work and all the best warfare of the world is done still as it was done in Manasseh and in Macedonia; it is done by those men who are more intent on their work than on their wages: who think more about their armor than about their rations: who eat less that they may work more: and who lap up a mouthful and lose not a moment as they dash on to meet the enemy away past every running water.

But time would fail me to tell you all about Gideon: all about his battles, and all about his victories: about how he behaved himself in battle, and how he bore himself in victory. Like the Ironsides of England, the Ironsides of Israel said to their captain, "Rule thou over us, for thou hast delivered us from the hand of Midian." But Gideon said, "I will not rule over you, neither shall my son rule over you: the Lord only shall rule over you." And had Gideon only stopped there, what a noble name, and what a blameless name Gideon's name would have been to us to this day! But:

> The gray-hair'd saint may fail at last,
> The surest guide a wanderer prove;
> Death only binds us fast
> To the bright shore of love.

> I have seen
> The thorn frown rudely all the winter long,
> And after bear the rose upon its top;
> And bark, that all the way across the sea
> Ran straight and speedy, perish at the last,
> E'en in the haven's mouth.

And Gideon was that gray-haired saint; that sure guide; he was that straight and speedy bark.

"Rule thou over us," said all the soldiers and all the people. And Gideon said unto them, "I will not rule over you. But," he went on—and as he went on the devil entered into Gideon and he went on—"I would desire a request of you that you would give me every man the earrings of his prey." And Gideon made an ephod of the earrings and put it in his city, even in Ophra; and all Israel went a-whoring after it, which thing became a snare to Gideon, and to all his house. It must have been the very devil himself. There is no other way of accounting for this terrible catastrophe. The devil has seldom since his first success had such another success over God and God's servants as he had in Gideon's awful fall. For Gideon, when he died, and long before he died, left Israel very much where he had found her when he cut down his father's unclean grove and overthrew his father's lewd altar. Gideon left Israel under the heel of her oppressors; or if not that just yet, then fast and sure on the way to that. Gideon's great mistake, Gideon's great crime, Gideon's great sin, and Satan's great triumph over Gideon all arose out of this, that all through his magnificent life of service, in Paul's words, the law of Moses, the law of God, had never entered Gideon's heart. In Paul's words, again, Gideon did not know what sin was. He knew suffering in plenty; but, shallow old soldier as he was, he did not know the secret of all suffering. Gideon was as ignorant as the mass of you are what God's law really is, what sin really is, and what the only cure of sin really is. At bottom, and in New Testament words, that was Gideon's fall. And accordingly Gideon made a mock ephod at Ophra, while all the time God had made a true and sure ephod both for Himself and for Gideon and for all Israel at Shiloh. And God's ephod had an altar connected with it, and a sacrifice for sin, and the blood of sprinkling, and the pardon of sin, and a clean heart, and a new life; all of which Israel so much needed, but all of which Gideon, with all his high services, knew nothing about. Sin was the cause of all the evil that Gideon in his bravery had all his life been battling with; but, instead of going himself, and taking all his Ironsides and all his people up with him to God's house against sin, Gideon set up a sham house of God of his own, and a sham service of God of his own, with the result to himself and to Israel that the sacred writer puts in such plain words. Think of Gideon, of all men in Israel, leading all Israel a-whoring away from God! The pleasure-loving people came up to Gideon's pleasure-giving ephod, when both he and they should have gone to God's penitential ephod. They forgot all about the Midianites as they came up to Ophra to eat and to drink and to dance. Whereas, had they been well and wisely led, they would have gone to Shiloh with the Midianites "ever before them," till the God of Israel would have kept the Midianites and all their other enemies for ever away from them. Gideon was a splendid soldier, but he was a very short-sighted priest. He put on a costly ephod indeed, but it takes a great deal more than a costly ephod to make a prevailing priest. Gideon could hew down the enemies of Israel by the thousand; but all the time, he was doing absolutely nothing to heal the real hurt of the daughter of his people. Gideon could not possibly heal that hurt as long as he did not know what it was nor where it lay.

Your time would not wait for me to make all the application. But, surely, there can be no need; if you have half an eye in your head you must long before now have made the application for yourself. I see, and you must see, men every day who are as brave and as bold as Gideon, and as full of anger and revenge against all the wrongs and all the miseries of their fellow-men; men and women who take their lives in their hands to do battle with ignorance and vice and all the other evils that the land lies under: and, all the time, they go on repeating Gideon's fatal mistake; till, at the end of their life, they leave all these wrongs and miseries very much as they found them: nothing better, but rather worse. And all because they set up an ephod of their own devising in the place of the ephod and the altar and the sacrifice and the intercession that God has set up for these and all other evils. They say, and in their goodness of heart they do far more than merely say—What shall the poor eat, and what shall they drink, and how shall they be housed? At great cost to themselves they put better houses for the working classes, and places of refreshment and amusement, and reading-rooms, and libraries, and baths, and open spaces, and secular schools and still more secular churches in the room of the cross and the church and the gospel of Jesus Christ; and they complain that the Midianites do not remove but come back faster than they can chase them out. But, as Joash or Gideon might have said in one of their humorous moments, all these things are so many apothecary's pills to protect a man from the earthquake. Only, there is much more fitness and sense and likelihood in the mountebank's prescription than there is in all your costly but unchristian ephods. Either the cross of Christ was an excess and a superfluity, or your expensive but maladroit nostrums for sin are an insult to Him and to His cross. . . . It only remains to say that from that day on which Gideon put on his ephod of earrings, his mantle which his mother made ceased to move on his bosom and to speak to his heart. From that day his mantle was no longer the miraculous fleece of his great days of victory; from that day and thenceforth it was only the dead skin of a dead sheep.

28

Jephthah and His Daughter

"PROSPERITY," says Bacon, "is the blessing of the Old Testament, but adversity is the blessing of the New." "How many saints," exclaims Law, "has adversity sent to heaven! And how many poor sinners has prosperity plunged into everlasting misery! This man had never been debauched, but for his fortune and advancement; that had never been pious, but through his poverty and disgrace. She that is envied for her beauty may perchance owe all her misery to it, and another may be for ever happy for having no admirers of her person. One man succeeds in everything, and so loses all; another meets with nothing but crosses and disappointments, and thereby gains more than all the world is worth." "Adversity," says Albert Bengel, "transfers our affections to Christ." "Caius Martius," says Plutarch, "being left an orphan of his father, was brought up under his mother, a widow, and he has taught us by his experience that orphanage brings many disadvantages to a child, but does not hinder him from becoming an honest man, or from excelling in virtues above the common sort."

Jephthah the Gileadite was the most ill-used man in all the Old Testament, and he continues to be the most completely misunderstood, misrepresented, and ill-used man down to this day. Jephthah's ill-usage began before he was born, and it has continued down to the last Old Testament Commentary and the last Bible Dictionary that treats of Jephthah's name. The iron had entered Jephthah's soul while yet he lay in his mother's womb; and both his father and his brothers and the elders of Israel helped forward Jephthah's affliction, till the Lord rose up for Jephthah and said, It is enough; took the iron out of His servant's soul, and poured oil and wine into the lifelong wound. Born, like his great Antitype, under a cloud, Jephthah, like his great Antitype also, was made perfect through suffering. Buffeted about from his birth by his brothers; trampled upon by all men, but most of all by the men of his father's house; called all manner of odious and exasperating names; his mother glad to get the servants' leavings for herself and her son; when a prophet came to dine, sent away to the fields to be out of sight; My son, his mother said, as she died on her bed of straw among Gilead's oxen—My son, shall not the Judge of all the earth do right? And from that day, if earth had been hell to Jephthah before, the one drop of water that had hitherto cooled his tormented heart was now spilt to him for ever, never to be gathered up again. For his mother was dead.

If at the death of his father Jephthah had got his proper portion of his father's goods, then Jephthah might have become as great a prodigal as his brothers became. But the loss of an earthly inheritance was to Jephthah, as it has been to so many men since his day, the gaining of an inheritance incorruptible and undefiled, eternal in the heavens.

And Gilead's wife bore him sons; and his wife's sons grew up, and they thrust out Jephthah, and said unto him, "Thou shalt not inherit in our father's house, for thou art the son of a strange woman." Then Jephthah fled from his brethren and dwelt in the land of Tob; and there were gathered vain men to Jephthah, who went out with him. "Vain men"; yes; no doubt. But, then, we must remember that misery has always acquainted even the best of men with strange bedfellows. David's misery acquainted him with every one that was in debt, and with every one that was in distress, and with every one that was discontented, and he became a captain over them, as did Jephthah long before David's day. You must not sit in your soft chair and shake your head over Jephthah and David. They were not all highwaymen; they were not all unmitigated freebooters either in Adullam or in Tob. They were not unlike those Armenians or Greeks who have taken to the hills in our day against the Turks. Still, we must stand to the text; and it is to Jephthah's advantage that we do so stand. Yes; fill the mountain-fastnesses of Tob as full as they can hold of vain men, and their captain's true character will only all that the better come out. Debtors, broken men, injured and outcast men, orphan and illegitimate sons, prodigal sons, and sons with whom their fathers were wearied out; with, no doubt, a sprinkling of salt here and there, as there always is among the most corrupt characters and the most abandoned men. But, bad as they were, Jephthah turned none of them away, but took them all the more into his own hand. I told you Whose type Jephthah was, and Who was his Antitype. And thus it was that he took that great rabble of refuse and of offscourings, and year after year gradually chastised them into an army of obedient and capable men. He took them to his own cave man by man, to sup with himself and to talk with himself. He listened to their story, and they listened to his. He told them what he would give them to do, and what he would give them for doing it. He made them captains over tens and over fifties and over hundreds. He trusted them, he praised them, he promoted them. And then he hurled them like a stone cut out of the mountain against the enemies of the King of Tob; till the elders of Israel in their absolute despair were compelled to approach and to beseech Jephthah to come down from his fastness and rid them of their enemies also.

It was a bitter pill to those elders of Israel. Some of the prouder stomachs among them would have died rather than swallow it The stone which the builders had refused was become the head stone of the corner; and it broke every bone in their body to lift that stone up into its place. You know how you hate and fear and shrink back from meeting, not to speak of being beholden for your life to, the man or woman you once greatly injured. You will know, then, what it was to be an elder in Israel in that day and among the hills of Tob. Their hearts were as black as hell with remorse and with terror as they approached Jephthah's dreadful den and saw his naked savages glowering at them through their spears. Look at that poor elder of Israel of eighty. His old face is as white as his old hair. An old man like that should not be out on an errand like this. He drinks at every stream. He falls down with fear at every breath of wind. Who, you ask, is that so venerable figure they have placed at the head of the sacred deputation? Oh, that, you must know, is the ruling elder, to whose door Jephthah went in his despair when his mother was dying in Gilead's stable. That is the hand, so helpless today, that shut the door so sternly in Jephthah's face that day. That is the mouth, so dry today, that was so full of such evil names at Jephthah that day. And he would never have got through his mission to Tob that day unless Jephthah had made his daughter spread out some venison on a shelf of a rock and pour out some of the old wine of their mountains. That old elder's sin found him out that day, when the sweetest woman-child he had ever seen washed his feet, and anointed his head, and kissed his outstretched and deprecating hand. Jephthah's daughter shall never wash my feet! the old man had said; but she both washed his feet and kissed them too, in her beautiful honor to old age. Jephthah would have been more than a mere man, as, indeed, he some-times was, if he had not reminded those elders of the old days. Only, if the depu-tation had had any sense; if they had not been so many idiots; if all their tongues had not been cleaving to the roofs of their mouths over Jephthah's hospitality and his daughter's devotion, they would surely have taken the upbraiding words out of his mouth. What a pity it is that Jephthah did not hold himself in to the end of the interview! What a lesson he would then have been to us in the New Testa-ment art of taming an injured tongue! But let him who has always tamed his own tongue in Jephthah's opportunity cast the first stone at Gilead's disinherited and cast-out son. At the same time, Jephthah soon put a bridle on his mouth, and that lest his old wrongs should set sudden fire to what he knew was only waiting the match in the hearts of his men. And he was very glad when he got all those elders of Israel safely out of Tob and back again within the borders of their own land. He was angry with himself all down the long hill-road that he had ever told those wild men one word about the days of his youth. But by quick marchings and by strict orders Jephthah got his bodyguard held in till all danger was past.

THE LORD dwelt in those days at Mizpeh; THE LORD had a house and an altar at Mizpeh; and Jephthah opened all that was in his heart; past injury, present oppor-tunity, and future surrender and service before THE LORD at Mizpeh. This is what we mean by masterly writing, sacred or profane. This: "Jephthah uttered all his words before THE LORD in Mizpah." The truly masterly part was in Jephthah him-self. But it is not every masterly part that gets such a masterly reporter. "Before THE LORD," I am much afraid, is only so much pen and ink to you even when it stands in these reader-arresting capitals. But, to Jephthah, Mizpeh was all that the Mount was to Moses when THE LORD descended there with His great Name. Tob, and Mizpeh, and all, were full of THE LORD and all His Attributes to Jephthah. I expect to read in *The Athenaeum* or *The Academy* some Saturday night soon that the land of Tob has been discovered and identified, and Jephthah's headquarters in it, with Exodus thirty-fourth and sixth and seventh still legible on its doorpost. Perhaps Dryasdust will then begin to open his eyes over his ordered article on Jephthah. Only, if they had been made to open they would surely have opened long ago at the last clause of the eleventh verse of the eleventh chapter of Jephthah's history. Time has failed me to make an exhaustive induction over the whole of the Old Testament, but I have a conviction that The Name of THE LORD occurs oftener in Jephthah's history than it does in the history of any other Old Testament saint, at any rate between the days of Moses and those of David. If the Name and Presence of THE LORD is the supreme distinction in any man's life and history, Old Testament or New, prosperity or adversity, then he that runs might surely have read in that Jephthah's character and Jephthah's standing in the true Israel. How I wish this fine narrator had taken time to tell us down to every jot and tittle all that Jephthah said and did when he uttered all his words before THE LORD at Mizpeh! Were this sacred writer on the earth in our day, and were he recasting his Judges in the light of the New Testament, I feel sure he would give us all Jephthah's words before THE LORD at Mizpeh, and that verbatim too, even if he had to leave out the Levite and his concubine. But this sacred writer knew his own business, and I can well believe it of him that he buried Jephthah's words before THE LORD at Mizpeh out of sight in order that we might have to dig for those words as for hid treasure—the hid treasure of the kingdom of heaven, as Jephthah had been taught by his mother about that kingdom, and had already taken, and will soon still more take, that kingdom by force.

Along with Jephthah we have Jephthah's father, and his mother, and his brothers, and the elders of Israel, and the King of Ammon, and Jephthah's daughter, and the daughters of Israel—but we have not one word about Jephthah's wife. Richard Owen, the great anatomist, from a few inches of fossil bone constructed a complete creature of a long past and forgotten world, and made it live and go about again before us. And from a few words of her daughter I can see and understand that nameless princess of the land of Tob better than I can see and understand some men and women who live next door to me. I conclude the long-dead mother from a single glimpse of her noble daughter. I see the mother of Jephthah's daughter the light of Jephthah's eyes in the dark cave of Tob. Those terrified elders owed their life that day to her. It was her love and her life and her death that so softened and so reconciled her husband. "Yes," she said to her father, after Jephthah had delivered her father's city—"Yes, I will go with this man." And when her daughter was born in Adullam that finished her work on her husband's savage soldiers. Always lions in war, they were now lambs in peace. "My father," said her daughter, long after her mother was dead and buried among her father's hills— "My father, if thou hast opened thy mouth unto THE LORD, do to me according to that which hath proceeded out of thy mouth." No, there can be no doubt at all about the mother of Jephthah's daughter. Moses had laid down a law that Jephthah was never to get a wife out of any family in Israel, nor was he ever to be let worship God in the same house with the virtuous elders of Israel. But men like Jephthah are above all such laws, and they break through them all as a lion breaks through a hedge. For Jephthah got of THE LORD in Tob a better wife and a better daughter too, than were to be seen in all Israel from Dan to Beersheba. And as for their tabernacle, he took it by storm, or, if not it, then that temple not made with hands, eternal in the heavens. Pericles' mother dreamed one night that she was brought to bed of a lion. And Jephthah's mother again and again had the same dream.

After all that, it does not at all upset me to read that Jephthah built an altar and offered up his daughter. That was their terrible way sometimes in those twilight, uncivilized, and unevangelical ages. What God bade Abraham and Isaac do on

Moriah, that Jephthah and his daughter actually did at Mizpeh. No doubt, had God sent an angel and provided a ram, Jephthah and his daughter would have returned home together willingly enough. But God did better for Jephthah and his daughter than He did for Abraham and Isaac, and both Abraham and Isaac in their old age would have been the first to admit it. The finished work of this earthly life of fathers, and mothers, and sons, and daughters, is to hold them all as not ours but God's. It is really of little consequence in what age of the world, or in what dispensation of providence, patriarchal, Mosaic, pagan, or Christian, or just in what way, and just among what things, the mind and the heart and the will of Jephthah and Jesus Christ are worked out within us—If only they are worked out within us.

The one question is, Am I or am I not my own? Am I bought with a price or am I not? In all that do I not sin, nor charge God foolishly? In all that do I say, Lo, I come, in the volume of the book it is written of me? You take a right step. You take up a holy calling. You enter a holy covenant. You open your mouth to the Lord, and you put your hand to His holy plow. And, come what may, you never go back. You only all the more say, I will pay my vow. Thy will be done. My times are in Thy hand. The cup, shall I not drink it? All I have is Thine, said Jephthah. I had nothing. I had not even a name to be known by. No man would let me sit at his table. No mother would let me look at her daughter. No elder in Israel but spat in my face. It is all Thine. I am Thy servant, and the son of Thine handmaid; Thou hast loosed my bonds. Take it all back again if Thou seest good; only let me redeem Thy people Israel. And God took Jephthah at his word, till wherever the Book of the Judges of Israel is read this that Jephthah and his daughter did shall be told for a memorial of them. And it was a custom in Israel that the daughters of Israel went to that altar once every year to lament the daughter of Jephthah the Gileadite four days in a year. And they came back from that altar to be far better daughters than they went out. They came back softened, and purified, and sobered at heart. They came back ready to die for their fathers, and for their brothers, and for their husbands, and for their God. Weep not for me, Jephthah's daughter said to them from off her altar and from out of heaven. Weep for yourselves and for your children.

And that the very fragments of such a history may be gathered up, and may not be lost, we are let read this on the margin—That though Jephthah had neither wife, nor son, nor daughter of his own any more, yet his palace at Mizpeh was only all that the more replenished and full of people. Old soldiers from the fastnesses of Tob were pensioned in that palace; prodigal sons worked in its fields; illegitimate sons sat at its table; foundling children played upon its doorsteps; nephews of its owner, the debauched sons of the rich brothers of his youth, became honest men—what between their uncle's house and the house of the Lord beside it. Long ago, when Jephthah first uttered his words before the Lord at Mizpeh, he read these words on the wall of that altar. These words: The Lord your God regardeth not persons, nor taketh rewards. He doth execute the judgment of the fatherless and the widow; He loveth the stranger, and giveth him food and raiment. Love ye, therefore, the stranger, for ye were strangers in the land of Egypt. And many of the sons of the elders of Israel ate the fat and drank the sweet at Jephthah's orphaned table, because of what Jephthah had read long ago on the Lord's wall at Mizpeh. For six years this life for others went on with Jephthah. He buried his grief as much as he might in warfare for Israel and in labors in her seat of judgment and among her outcasts, till he died in Mizpeh in midtime of his days. For he said, They shall not return to me, but I shall go to them, and so died.

29
Samson

SAMSON'S tragical story has been treated in three ways. Some commentators on the Book of Judges have treated the story of Samson as an excellent piece of Hebrew folklore. They have collected out of all the ancient books of the world wonderful tales of giants, and heroes, and demigods, with their astonishing feats of strength in war, and in love, and in jealousy, and in revenge; feats more or less like the feats of strength and of revenge we have in Samson. They have produced remarkable parallels to Samson's exploits out of Atlas and Cyclops, Hercules and Odin, and many suchlike mythological characters. And then their work on Samson has been done when they have illustrated his history with romances and legends of sufficient likeness and richness. Some evangelical preachers, again, have gone out to the opposite extreme, and have displayed Samson to us solely as a type and pattern of Jesus Christ. They have selected texts out of Samson's extraordinary history, and they have suspended excellent New Testament sermons on these adapted texts; hanging great weights on small wires. The former is the mythical way of dealing with Samson's history; the latter is the mystical way. But there is a third way. And the third way is the way that Paul takes, not only with Samson, but with all the patriarchs, and judges, and kings, and great men of Old Testament times. We have this apostle's way with all those Old Testament men and women set before us again and again in his own conclusive words: "For whatsoever things were written aforetime were written for our learning, that we through patience and comfort of the Scriptures might have hope." And again, "All Scripture is given by inspiration of God, and is profitable for doctrine, for reproof, for correction, for instruction in righteousness." And again, "Now, all these things happened unto them for ensamples, and they are written for our admonition, upon whom the ends of the world are come. Wherefore let him that thinketh he standeth take heed lest he fall." And yet again, "Therefore, seeing we are compassed about with so great a cloud of witnesses, let us lay aside every weight, and the sin which doth so easily beset us, and let us run with patience the race that is set before us." Now, neither the mythical nor the mystical method shall be followed upon Samson tonight. All my leanings and all my drawings, all my reading and all my experience—all combine to make me to sit at Paul's feet, and to pursue, so far as I am able, Paul's expository and homiletical methods. While listening attentively, then, to all that the mythologists and the mystics have to say on Samson; having done so, I feel all the more safe and sure in asking you to look at Samson as John Milton looked at Samson when he treated him with such "verisimilitude and decorum." For "Tragedy, as it was anciently composed, hath been ever held the gravest, moralest, and most profitable of all other poems: therefore said by Aristotle to be of power by raising pity and fear, or terror, to purge the mind of those and suchlike passions; that is, to temper and reduce the passions to their just measure."

What more could God, or man, or angel of God have done for Samson that was not done? Every man must work out his own salvation with his own hands, or not at all; but, short of doing for Samson what neither God nor man could do, what more could God or man have done that was not done? From his birth, and for long before his birth, the gifts of God were simply showered on Samson. He had a father and a mother of the very best. Over and above what the Bible tells us about Samson's father and mother, Josephus, in supplement of the Bible, tells us that there was "one Manoah, a person of such virtue that he had few men his equals, and without dispute he was the principal person in his country. And Manoah had a wife celebrated for her beauty, and excelling her contemporaries." Now, Manoah and his wife had been prepared to be the father and mother of a great deliverer of Israel. And they had been prepared in the same way that God had often taken to prepare the parents of those children who were predestinated to be great and famous men. Like Abraham and Sarah, like Isaac and Rebekah, like Jacob and Rachel, like Hannah, like Zacharias and Elizabeth, and like many more, it was as it were by a special and immediate act of creative power that Manoah and his wife got Samson their son at the hand of God.

And not only was Samson to be separated to God's service from his mother's womb; but, in order to make his separation and dedication both sure and easy and natural to him, his mother was separated and dedicated to God long before her child was born. "Of all that I said to the woman let her beware. She may not eat of anything that cometh of the vine, neither let her drink wine nor strong drink, nor eat any unclean thing: all that I commanded her let her observe," said the angel of the Lord a second time to Manoah. "Not," says Joseph Hall, "that there is more uncleanness in the grape than in the fountain; but that wine finds more uncleanness in us than water finds; and that the high feed is not so fit for devotion as abstinence."

> Desire of wine and all delicious drinks,
> Which many a famous warrior overturns,
> Thou couldst repress; nor did the dancing ruby,
> Sparkling, outpour'd, the flavor, or the smell
> Or taste that cheers the heart of gods and men,
> Allure thee from the clear crystalline stream:
> .... Nor envied them the grape,
> Whose heads that turbulent liquor fills with fumes.
> But what avail'd this temperance not complete
> Against another object more enticing?
> What boots it at one gate to make defence,
> And at another to let in the foe,
> Effeminately vanquished?....

"I am weary of my life!" said Rebekah to Isaac over the marriage of Esau, and in terror of a like marriage of Jacob. And both Manoah and his wife said the same thing over Samson's marriage. How twice happy are those parents who get a child born in the Lord, and then live to see their child married in the Lord! What a crown of blessing it is to a godly mother to get a second daughter in her son's wife; and what a happy father he is who gets a second son in his daughter's husband! But, then, all the more, what a gnawing sorrow it is when a son or a daughter marries away outside of all sympathy with their father's house! Better, cries many a mother's broken heart—better they had never been born than to be so mis-married. Samson's father and mother never saw another happy day after that day when their son—miraculous birth, Nazarite vow and all—went down to Timnath and saw a woman, a daughter of the Philistines, and said, Get her for me to wife! Then his father and his mother said to Samson, Is there never a woman of the daughters of thy brethren, that thou goest to take a wife of the uncircumcised Philistines? Was it for this day they had sanctified their unborn child? In his misery Manoah declared that he would never all his days pray for anything after this, lest it should turn to his bane, as his prayer for a son had so turned. For how is a child who brings such shame on his father and mother ever to fulfill the promise of his birth? How shall the son-in-law of an uncircumcised Philistine ever deliver Israel? Nor did all Samson's riddles, and jests, and sports, and revenges against the Philistines scatter or relieve the cloud that his first fatal step had brought down on his father's and his mother's heart.

Though we look with fear for it, and almost expect it, and though Josephus actually says it, yet we are not told it in the Bible, and we simply cannot believe Josephus, that Samson broke his Nazarite vow. Could we believe Josephus in what he writes, what a treasure-house for Bible readers he would be! But wherever Josephus stands without corroboration and confirmation, we simply cannot believe a word he says. We shall, therefore, set it down to Samson's credit that, with all his license and with all his riot, he never became a drunkard. But, then, as it always comes into my heart when I read of Samson's total abstinence—

> What boots it at one gate to make defence,
> And at another to let in the foe?

You are making a gallant defence at one gate, but what about all the other gates; and, especially, what about the gates on the other side of the city? You keep, with all diligence, this and that gate of the body, but what about the more deadly gates of the soul? Plutarch tells us of a great Roman who was very brave; but, then, he was very envious of other brave men, and his envy did himself and them and the state more mischief than if he had been a coward. You work hard for God at your books and your visiting as a minister or as a Sabbath-school teacher, but you restrain prayer. You stand up for use and wont in public worship, and in pulpit and in published doctrine; but, then, you hate and hunt down the men who innovate upon you in these things. You go out, like Samson, against the enemies of God and His Church, but all the time you make your campaign an occasion for your own passions, piques, retaliations, and revenges. You do not touch wine, but how do you stand to all Samson's other sins? Death and hell will come still more surely into your hearts through the gates of envy, and ill-will, and hatred, and pride, and revenge, and malice, and unbelief, and neglect of God in prayer, than at those more yawning gates that all decently living men make a defence at. What avails this "temperance not complete"?

Young men are not raised up among us nowadays with Samson's size and strength. The age of the Judges was a rude age, and God condescended to its rudeness, and raised up rude instruments to shape it. Samsons in body are not born among us in our day, but Samsons in mind are sometimes given us in room of them. And it is not seldom seen that our greatly gifted youths work as little deliverance for themselves and for us as Samson did for Israel. You hear of some young man's Samson-like feats of strength at the University or at the Divinity Hall. He rose from his shoulders upwards above all the men of his time. What was toil and defeat to them was but child's-play to him. Samson rent a lion that roared against him, as if it had been a kid. In the quickness and versatility of their minds our young Samsons set us riddles to which we Philistines cannot supply an answer. They make sport of our slow wits. They tie firebrands to foxes' tails, and turn the foxes in among our standing corn. But we endure it all, looking on it all as but the rough sport of young giants, and we wait with hope for the day when they shall be found working painfully among those very cornfields and vineyards over which they are now making their too destructive sport.

But it often happens with our promised deliverers also that they fall far short of far weaker men in the after-work they do for themselves and for us. A common man, over whose birth no angel did wondrously, will often at the end of the day far outstrip his brilliant neighbor who started with all heaven and all earth looking on with applause and expectation. Genius is genius; but the oil-fed lamp of an honest mind and a humble heart will, not seldom, light its owner better home. Weak men must husband their strength. They have neither time nor strength to spare on those Samson-feats that end in a day's amazement, but work no deliverance in the land. And, moreover, the very diligence and assiduity that their few talents compel them to, keep them from those idle and ruinous dalliances with the Delilahs of the flesh and of the mind that more affluent men are more easily led into.

But, still, in spite of it all, Samson actually judged Israel for full twenty years. At the same time, for some reason or other, a reason we can only guess at, the sacred writer tells us not one single word about what we would give a great deal tonight to know. Not one word are we told, neither about what kind of cases came up before Samson, nor how he managed his court, nor about the wisdom, or otherwise, of his judgments, nor about the manner of life that Israel lived for that whole generation under her gigantic judge. We sometimes hear it complained in our day that all the romance of the world is used up; that there is little or nothing left to the ambitious man of genius of these latter days but the most barren and most trampled spots of sacred and profane history. And, as a sad consequence to them and to us, that our dramatists and tragedians can never again give us such masterpieces as their forerunners have left behind them. Well, were I a sacred dramatist, I would ask for no better scope for my craft tonight than just the twenty years of Samson's judgeship. The whole magnificent drama of *Samson Agonistes* begins and ends, according to ancient rule and best example, within the space of twenty-four hours. Well, here are twenty untouched and absolutely silent years, during which the plot was laying deep and thickening fast toward the terrible catastrophe of Milton's masterpiece. Those twenty loaded years stand beckoning for a Milton or a Wells or a Browning to enter them, and to give us out of them a companion and a key to the *Agonistes*—a poem grave enough, moral enough, and profitable enough to satisfy the master of all these matters himself. Such an artist would let us see Samson repenting of having broken his mother's heart, and repenting with the passion of a hundred penitents poured into one. He would let us see the Lord turning again to give Samson another chance. He would let us hear evil men in Israel mocking at Samson and his seat of judgment because of Timnath and Gaza. He would raise pity and anger wherewith to purge our hearts as we saw Samson striving to do only what was right, with men of Belial all about him waiting for his halting, and dwelling on all his past wrong-doing. And his chorus would purge our breasts with fear and with terror as they lifted the veil and let us see the passions of lust, and jealousy, and hatred, and revenge that were all the time tearing at the great heart of Manoah's miserable son. Till one of those passions, even after he had judged Israel twenty years, again broke out, and laid Samson low, never to rise again in this world.

> Myself my sepulchre, a moving grave.
>   Prison within prison,
>   Inseparably dark!
> Nothing of all these evils hath befall'n me
> But justly; I myself have brought them on,
> Sole author I, sole cause. If aught seem vile,
> As vile hath been my folly.

But man's extremity is God's opportunity. And in such words as were possible to Samson's Old Testament biographer, that sacred writer tells us that in Samson also, where sin abounded, grace did much more abound, and that God's strength was made perfect in the day of Samson's weakness. That dark cell in Gaza—in Gaza, the scene of some of Samson's greatest sins—that shameful cell was a house of God, and a place of prayer and repentance to Manoah's overtaken and overwhelmed son. What a past Samson looked back upon as he sat at the mill! What he might have been! What he might have done! How he might have departed to his fathers and left Israel! Three thousand years dissolve, and *this* is Gaza. *This* is the mill with slaves. *This* man, and *that* man there, is Samson over again. Only, over again against light and truth that Samson never saw. "What profit is there in my blood," our Samson cries, "when I go down to the pit? Shall the dust praise Thee? Shall it declare Thy truth? Hear, O Lord, and have mercy upon me. Lord, be Thou my helper. Turn my mourning into dancing, my dreaming into earnestness, my falls into clearings of myself, my guilt into indignation, my sin into fear, my transgression into vehement desire, and my pollution into revenge. Rejoice not against me, O mine enemy; when I fall, I shall arise; when I sit in darkness, the Lord shall be a light unto me. I will bear the indignation of the Lord, because I have sinned against Him, until He plead my cause, and execute judgment for me; He will bring me forth to the light, and I shall behold His righteousness. Who is a God like unto Thee, that pardoneth iniquity, and passeth by the transgression of the remnant of His heritage? He retaineth not His anger for ever, because He delighteth in mercy. He will turn again, He will have compassion on us; He will subdue our iniquities, and Thou shalt cast all their sins into the depths of the sea."

30
Ruth

BOTH the Bible, and all the books that take after the Bible, are full of fine stories of love. The love of the mother for her child. The love of the lover for her he loves. The love of the brother for the sister. The love of Jonathan for David, and of David for Jonathan. The love of Paul for his people Israel. The love of Christ for His own and for all men, and so on. But neither in the Bible, nor anywhere else that I know of, is there another such story of love told as the love of Ruth for Naomi; the love of this Moabite daughter-in-law for her Hebrew mother-in-law. Ruth's love for her dead husband's decayed mother is as pure as gold and as strong as death. Many waters cannot quench Ruth's love. And her confession of her love, when she is constrained to confess it, is the most beautiful confession of love in all the world. The world has nothing after Ruth's confession of her love like it. And Naomi said unto her two daughters-in-law, Go, return each to her mother's house; the Lord deal kindly with you, as ye have dealt with the dead, and with me. And Ruth said, Intreat me not to leave thee, or to return from following after thee; for whither thou goest, I will go, and where thou lodgest, I will lodge; thy people shall be my people, and thy God my God; where thou diest, will I die, and there will I be buried. The Lord do so to me, and more also, if aught but death part thee and me. No. There is nothing again like it "The same is my mother."

"She clave to her mother-in-law," says the Scriptures. Ruth's heart was so full of the cords of love to Naomi that those strong cords drew her out of the land of Moab and knit her deep into the lineage of Israel, and into the ancestry of Jesus Christ. And thus it is that our great seer discovers Ruth seated on her glorious seat in the rose of the seventh heaven, beside the glorious seats of the greatest dames of Scripture story—Mary, and Eve, and Rachel, and Beatrice, and Rebecca. Before Ruth had given Naomi the full proof of her love, that desolate woman had bestowed her highest praise on Ruth's past love, not only as a wife, but still more as a daughter-in-law. The Lord deal kindly with thee, as thou hast dealt with the dead, and with me. And the women of Bethlehem at once caught up this quite singular feature of Ruth's affection when they came to congratulate Naomi on the birth of Obed. "Thy daughter-in-law," they said to Naomi, "which loveth thee, and which is better to thee than seven sons, hath borne him." And in this salutation of theirs the women of Bethlehem are in entire harmony with the whole world about Ruth's so pure, and so noble, and so unparalleled love. Every language spoken among men has its own stock of cruel proverbs and satires and lampoons at the expense of their mothers-in-law. But Ruth and Naomi go far to redeem that relationship from all that obloquy. No only daughter of her own body could have been so devoted to Naomi as her son's young Moabite widow was. All the relationships of human life demand faith, and love, and patience, and forbearance, and good temper, and good sense, and good taste, and good feeling; but, perhaps, above all the other relationships of life that of a mother-in-law and a daughter-in-law demands all those gifts and graces. But, then, the relationship that offers scope and operation and reward for all those gifts of heart and graces of character is just that relationship that should be entered on by all men and women with much watchfulness, solicitousness, prayer, tenderness, sympathy, and loyalty; in short, with the mind and the heart of Ruth, that Moabitess maiden, and Naomi, that mother in Israel; that widow indeed.

Moses was as much opposed to Ruth's marriage as he had been to Jephthah's. A Moabite woman shall never be married by an Israelite man if I can help it, said that inexorable old law-giver; not to ten generations shall any of their offspring enter the congregation of the Lord. Yes, said Naomi, who had made up her mind to the interdicted marriage—Yes, she said to her more conservative and scrupulous husband, as she milked her kine under the top of Pisgah—Yes, she said, but marriage laws are made for men and women, and not men and women for marriage laws. And had Moses been here, she went on; had Moses been famished out of Bethlehem-Judah, as we have been; and had he been received and entertained of Ruth's and Orpah's fathers and mothers, as we have been, he would to a certainty have torn that revengeful leaf out of his law. Depend upon it, she said, as she saw her husband beginning to give way, depend upon it, Moses had altogether other Moabites in his mind's eye than Ruth and Orpah, and their so hospitable fathers, when he set down his retaliatory marriage laws. And Elimelech at last gave way. Nehemiah also, as well as Moses, visited the iniquity of the Moabite fathers upon the Moabite children to too many generations. For that merciless reformer and iconoclast contended with, and smote with his fists, and forcibly divorced the men of Jerusalem who had married Moabite women in his day. But, there again, this is to be said for Nehemiah, that the lawbreakers of his day had not married such dear, sweet, generous-hearted women as Ruth and Orpah were. "Because their fathers met not the children of Israel with bread and with water," said Nehemiah. But, then, that was just what Ruth and Orpah and their fathers had done. They had met Elimelech, and Naomi, and Mahlon, and Chilion, not with bread and water only, but with wine, and milk, and honey, and spices, and all manner of Moabite fruits, till the land of Moab became to that famished-out family of Bethlehem-Judah a land of Moab indeed, a most delectable mountain, a place to dwell in, and to see their sons and their sons' sons settled in. And thus it came about that those two Israelite youths, Mahlon and Chilion, were married to those two Moabite maidens, Orpah and Ruth. And thus, through all that, it came about in God's providence that a rich stream of Moabite blood ran first in King David's veins, and then through David's veins into the veins of a far greater King than David.

After the death of Elimelech, Naomi was a widow after Paul's own heart. Naomi was a widow indeed. She was desolate, but she trusted God, and continued in supplication and prayer night and day. She was in behavior likewise as becometh holiness. She taught the Moabite young women about her to be sober, to love their husbands, to love their children, to be discreet, chaste, and keepers at home. In short, she taught them to be wives and mothers in Moab like the wives and mothers in Israel. I feel sure we shall not be far wrong to trace up a great part of Ruth's courage, devotion, extraordinary loyalty, and exquisite love, not so much to Naomi's schooling as to her example. She, no doubt, had something to get over, as well as her husband, when the two marriages first began to dawn upon her. At the beginning she, too, had her own struggle with her Hebrew pride when she saw that her two Hebrew-born sons were not to be married into some of the oldest and best of the families of Bethlehem-Judah. But when she saw that was not to be, she bore no grudge against the two Moabite maidens, but went over to their side, and stood up for them against both Moses and Elimelech. And then; now among the joys of marriages, and now among the sorrows of deathbeds, Naomi showed to those two Moabite women what a widowed wife and mother had to rest on in Israel; and one, at least, of her daughters-in-law laid the lesson and the example well to heart. Yes; behind all the nobleness, steadfastness, beauty, and tenderness of Ruth, I see inspiring and sustaining and maturing it all, the wise, chastened, weaned mind of one who was a mother in Israel and a widow indeed.

But you must not think of Naomi as a broken reed. You must not picture Naomi to yourself as a woman whose spirit was utterly and irrecoverably crushed. Widowhood with Naomi, and childlessness added to it, was not the dregs of life. It was not a few years of bitterness, and fretfulness, and listlessness, and ostentatious sorrow. No! Naomi is full of experience and full of resource. She knows the world. She knows the hearts of all the men and women about her. She knows the right way to act, and the right time to speak, widowhood, childlessness, and poverty, and all. With a rare and a delicate divination of how matters stood between Boaz and Ruth; knowing her kinsman and her kinswoman better than they knew themselves; Naomi struck the red-hot iron with the right stroke and at the right moment. Age and experience have their privileges and their opportunities, and Naomi possessed both age and experience, and employed them to purpose in the matter of Boaz and Ruth. "Sit still, my daughter," Naomi said to Ruth, while, all the time, her own heart was in a hidden flutter of love and of hope.

> Not obvious, not obtrusive, but retired,
> The more desirable.

What a blessing it is to a young man at Boaz's state of mind, and to a young woman at Ruth's stage of things, to have a mother in Israel, or a widow indeed, to whom to open their hearts! Or, still better, to have such an one to love them so that their hearts are divined and read before they are opened. One would think at first sight that a girl's own mother, or a young man's own father, was the natural adviser and bosom friend of their children. And that a parent should be the first to be confessed to, consulted, trusted in, and followed. And, again, that they should be the first to see and to take to heart all that is going on in their child's heart. But, as a matter of fact and experience, wherever the blame or the inability may lie, it is never, it is not once in a thousand, that a young man takes his father, or a young woman her mother, into their confidence and into their whole heart. And still less seldom does a father or a mother make it natural and easy and sweet for their child to do so. All the better, therefore, when our young people find a second father or a second mother in some friend older, wiser, more tried, and more skilled in the providences of God and in the passions of man than they are as yet themselves. Some one just to say, Sit still, my daughter. Some one just to say, with an anecdote to illustrate it, My times are in Thy hand. Some one just to say, I once knew a case exactly like yours. Or, better still, some one to tell them his own case, and to send them away with an *à Kempis* or an *Andrewes*, and this upon the fly-leaf, "Your Father knoweth what things you have need of before you ask Him." Then said Naomi to Ruth, "Sit still, my daughter, until thou know how the matter will fall; for the man will not be at rest until he have finished the thing this day."

The women are so delightful in this delightful little book that there is no room left for the men. The men fall into the background of the Book of Ruth, and are clean forgotten. But this must not be. One, at any rate, of the men of the Book of Ruth deserves a better fate. One of them was certainly written for our learning. And more especially for the learning of all landlords and farmers and employers of labor. "Then Naomi arose with Ruth, for she had heard in the country of Moab how that the Lord had visited His people in giving them bread, and they came to Bethlehem in the beginning of barley harvest. And Ruth the Moabitess said to Naomi, Let me now go to the field, and glean ears of corn after him in whose sight I shall find grace. And she said unto her, Go, my daughter. And she went, and came, and gleaned in his field after the reapers; and her hap was to light on a part of a field belonging to Boaz, who was of the kindred of Elimelech. And, behold, Boaz came from Bethlehem, and said unto the reapers, The Lord be with you. And they answered him, The Lord bless thee. Then said Boaz unto his servant that was set over the reapers, Whose damsel is this? And the servant that was set over the reapers answered and said, It is the Moabitish damsel that came back with Naomi out of the country of Moab." Both Boaz's heart and his conscience were sorely struck within him at his servant's answer. For Naomi was a kinswoman of his own. He had known Naomi in better days. And he had heard of her widowhood, and of her return to Bethlehem; but he had not yet gone to see her, nor had he asked her to come to see him. He had made no inquiry of how she managed to live without husband or son. But here is a Gentile girl, a Moabite maiden, who has left her own proverbially abundant land to glean and to beg for the widow of his old friend Elimelech! And Boaz felt himself to be a beast on his own harvest field, while that gleaning Moabitess shone out like a princess in his eyes. "Then said Boaz unto Ruth, Hearest thou not, my daughter? Go not to glean in another field, neither go from hence, but abide here fast by my maidens. The Lord recompense thy work, and a full reward be given thee of the Lord God of Israel, under whose wings thou art come to trust. So Ruth kept fast by the maidens of Boaz to glean unto the end of the barley harvest and of wheat harvest, and Ruth dwelt with her mother-in-law." Time would fail me to tell all the story of Boaz and Naomi and Ruth. Suffice it here to say that after two more chapters Boaz took Ruth, and she was his wife, and she bore a son. And the women her neighbors gave him a name, saying, There is a son born to Naomi, and they called his name Obed; he is the father of Jesse, the father of David.

Yes, Boaz is a splendid pattern to be set before all landowners, and farmers, and masters, and employers of labor. Courteous, solicitous, affectionate, devout, bountiful; Boaz greets his reapers in the harvest field as if they had been his sons and daughters. He meets them in the morning with a benediction, as if he had been a priest, and they with a salutation answer him, The Lord bless our master. We hear him, indeed, in his jealousy for the reapers and the gleaners, issuing the strictest of orders to his young men; but Boaz's own character and example are his young men's best law. Just, honorable, and upright in the market and in the gate, he is kind, generous, and hospitable at home. He eats and drinks with a merry heart in the happy harvest season; but with it all he is at all times and in all places both temperate and chaste. A master to make his servants worship him. A mighty man of wealth, but forgetting and despising all that he possesses before beauty, and piety, and goodness, and truth. Altogether a husband worthy of Naomi's dear daughter Ruth, and after that what more can be said? From gleaning in his fields, and from falling at his feet, on till she sat at his table and lay in his bosom—Ruth from first to last had nothing in her heart but pride, and respect, and love for Boaz. And he had neither act, nor word, nor look, nor wish to repent of, though Ruth had been found at his feet when his heart was merry. A happy pair, with a romantic history behind them, and with a future before them that it had not entered into their sweetest dreams to dream.

With all that, it is not at all to be wondered at that the Church of Christ, with such a dash of romance and mysticism in her heart, should have seen in Ruth's husband, Boaz, a far-off figure of her own Husband, Jesus Christ. For she, like Naomi and Ruth, was disinherited, disconsolate, despised, forgotten, and without kinsman-redeemer in her famine and all her deep distress, when His eye and His heart fell on her in the field. And how well He has performed a kinsman's part all the world has read in a Book that for truth and beauty far outstrips the Book of Ruth. How He has not only redeemed her, but has given her rest in His own house, in His Father's house, and in His own heart—what written book can ever fully tell? Boaz the Bethlehemite and Ruth the Moabitess made a noble marriage, and a noble race sprang out of that marriage. Obed, and Jesse, and David, and Solomon, and Joseph, and Mary, and Jesus Christ—my Kinsman-Redeemer, and yours.

31
Hannah

ABRAHAM and Sarah had no children. Isaac and Rebekah had no children. Jacob and Rachel had no children. Manoah had no children. Hannah had no children. The Shunamite had no children. Zacharias and Elizabeth had no children. Till it came to be nothing short of the mark of a special election, and a high calling, and a great coming service of God in Israel to have no children. Time after time, time after time, till it became nothing short of a special providence, those husbands and wives whose future children were predestinated to be patriarchs, and prophets, and judges, and forerunners of Jesus Christ in the house of Israel, began their married life with having no children. Now, why was that? Well, we may make guesses, and we may propose reasons for that perplexing dispensation, but they are only guesses and proposed reasons. We do not know. We cannot guess; for it is only those who are intimately and eminently godly, and who are at the same time childless, who can have any experience and assurance of what God's motives are in that matter. And I do not know that any of that inner circle have anywhere come out and broken the divine silence. All the more—Why is it? Is it to spare and shield them from the preoccupation and the dispersion of affection, and from the coldness and the rudeness and the neglect of one another that so many of their neighbors suffer from? And is it to teach them a far finer tenderness, and a far rarer honor, and a far sweeter solicitude for one another? Or, on the other hand, is it out of pure jealousy on God's part? Is it that He may be able to say to them, Am I not better to thee than ten sons? Or, again, is it in order to make them meet, long before His other sons and daughters around them are made meet, for that life in which they shall neither marry nor be given in marriage? Which of all these reasons, or what other reason, has their God for what He does with so many of His best saints? But all this time we have been intruding into those things of which he says to us—What is that to thee?

Elkanah of Mount Ephraim, Hannah's husband, was, as we say, a true gentleman. He would have been a perfect and a spotless gentleman but for one hard spot in his heart; a hard and a dark spot in his heart that came out in a hard and a dark spot on his life. It was because of that hard spot in Elkanah's heart that Moses had consented to let Elkanah take two wives. But Elkanah's shameful license which he had taken in that matter had by this time sufficiently revenged itself on Elkanah and on his whole house; for by the time we are introduced to Elkanah and to his house, his transgression has been made so terribly his punishment, that his heart is as soft now, and as full of tears, as Hannah's heart itself is soft and a fountain of tears. And Elkanah's heart, far more than even Hannah's, was such a fountain. For to a man like Elkanah, to have done any one a great wrong, is, for all his after-days, to suffer far more than they can possibly suffer who only endure the wrong. I find a law, said Elkanah, as he went up out of his city yearly to worship and to sacrifice unto the Lord of hosts in Shiloh, that the greater the wrong done, and the greater the sorrow caused, the more all that comes back on him who did the wrong and caused the sorrow. But, Elkanah, sorrow upon sorrow at home, and yearly worship and sacrifice at Shiloh and all, never could undo the wrong he had done to Hannah and to all his house. He could only take every opportunity to sweeten a little, if possible, Hannah's great and bitter sorrow. But such was the cruel snare that Elkanah lay in, that every effort he made to lighten a little his own and Hannah's load, that effort only locked the teeth of the snare deeper than before into his soul. Elkanah could not move a finger to comfort Hannah's stricken heart without that instant provoking her adversary to fresh insults and fresh injuries. What Elkanah might have been driven to do had it not been for the worship and the sacrifices at Shiloh, we tremble to think of.

Of Peninnah, Elkanah's wife with children, we know nothing—nothing but what we hear from her own cruel and scurrilous tongue. Those of you who are living in the same house with a woman like Peninnah, you could best picture to us poor Hannah's life. The servants who most slighted and insulted Hannah, were Peninnah's prime favorites; and her children were sharp to find out how to please their mother and get their own way. The sacred writer does not keep us long in Peninnah's company: he hastens past Peninnah to tell us about Hannah, that sorely-fretted and sequestered woman, who waters her couch with her tears. But, unless God was mocked on Mount Ephraim as He has never been mocked anywhere else, it does not need a prophet to tell us, if not Peninnah's past as a maiden and a young wife, then her future as an old mother and a widow. There were more sons and daughters of Belial being born and brought up in the house of Israel in these days, than Hophni and Phinehas. Take this child also, Belial had said to Peninnah over her successive child-beds, bring this one also up for me. And she did it. And you may take it for Holy Writ, though it is not written in as many words, that her children, when she was old, did not depart from the way in which she had brought them up.

I am filled with shame for myself and for my order as I see Eli sitting upon a seat by a post of the temple, and as I see Hannah's lips moving in prayer, and then hear Eli's rebuke of Hannah. "Put away thy wine," said Eli to Hannah. If he had said that to Hophni and Phinehas twenty years before, and had, at the same time, put away his own, Eli would have had another grandson than Ichabod to bear and to transmit his name. "How long wilt thou be drunken?" said Eli to Hannah. I do not wonder that Hophni and Phinehas became prodigals. What else could they become with such a father? When the blind lead the blind, what can you look for? That temple post, and that doited old priest sitting idle in the sun, and Hannah drunk with sorrow, and the way that Eli looks at her, and the things he says to her—Rock of Ages, let me hide myself in Thee! Only to Thy cross I cling—as I see Eli, and myself in Eli, and my children in Hophni and in Phinehas and in Ichabod. I see in Eli my idleness, my blindness to my own vices, and to my children's vices, my blindness also to my people's trials and temptations—one provoking and another being provoked, one drunk with pride and insolence, and another drunk with ill-usage and sorrow. I see in Eli my brutish ignorance while all that is going on round about me; as also my headlong and unjust judgments, and the way I preach at my people when I should be away out of sight and deep in God's holy place in prayer for them and for myself and for my children. O my God, when Thou sayest that Thou wilt do a thing at which both the ears of every one that heareth it shall tingle, I understand what Thou sayest and concerning whom Thou speakest. And I know, and I acknowledge, that had it not been for Thy long, long suffering, Thou wouldest have done all that to me and mine long before now. But, O my God, let Thy mercy endure for ever. Say to me that in Thy mercy I am to have this year also in which to rise off my seat and to acquaint myself with my people's sorrows, and to go out and in among them spending and being spent. Let me have the grace to preach to them out of Hannah's song, as I have never yet done. To preach to them, and to tell them that there is none holy as the Lord: neither is there any Rock like our God: that the Lord God is a God of knowledge, and that by Him actions are weighed: that He raiseth the poor out of the dust, and lifteth the beggar from the dunghill, and that He will keep the feet of His saints. But, all the time—

> Could my zeal no respite know,
> Could my tears for ever flow,
> All for sin could not atone,
> Thou must save, and Thou alone.

If Hannah was Elkanah's first wife, then there is nothing to be said but severe blame of Elkanah and deep sympathy with Hannah. But if Hannah was hood-winked with her own wish to enter Elkanah's household as a second wife in those indecent days, then Hannah's bitter sorrow is just another harvest reaped according to the seed sown. How Hannah must often have envied, not the mothers of children so much, as those bright and merry maidens of Ephraim and Shiloh, whose souls were still their own. And how, as she went up to the temple and came home from it, she must have filled up the time with recalling the way the Lord had led her till she so let herself be misled by Elkanah. Had Elkanah been a bad man, Hannah would not have been misled by him. In that case, Hannah would not have been in this snare. But when it was too late, Hannah learned that evil in a good man is just as deadly as the same evil in a bad man; as deadly, and far more dangerous. Hannah would never have crossed the threshold of any but a good man. You would never, all her days, have seen Hannah the wife of a son of Belial. But when Hannah crossed good Elkanah's threshold, she had still to learn that a sin against purity, a sin against human nature and the human heart, will bring down just as heavy a punishment on a patriarch's tent as on a profligate's. Punishments of that kind are no respecters of persons. And even when some might think your person respected, it may be to this extent, to the great and gracious extent of forgiveness; while, all the time, a sharp vengeance is taken on your inventions. Elkanah and Hannah invented a sin against married life on Mount Ephraim, and, while they were forgiven for it, all the time the vengeance that was taken on it, and on them on account of it broke every bone in their body and every hard spot in their heart.

"Her adversary provoked Hannah sore to make her fret." Little did her adversary think—only, people like Hannah's adversary never think—little, I was going to say, did Peninnah think what a life of sin she had plunged Hannah into. And little do we think—only one here and there has the power and the will, the mind and the heart so to think—how we plunge this man and that woman into a lifetime of deadly sin just by the way we provoke them to anger at us. Little do we think the sins that we are the true cause of, and of which we shall one day have to share the guilt. If you could see into this man's and that woman's heart, it would frighten you for once. We speak in a hyperbole about hell upon earth; but all the time there is one of the mouths of very hell in that heart that you have hurt till it so hates you. Exercise, I implore you, all your powers of imagination to put yourself in the place of that man or woman you so fret and provoke. Strive with all your might to put yourself inside his heart, so as to see and feel and sin and suffer as he does. Labor to see your self as others see you. Be sure that Butler is right. Be sure that you differ from other people as much as they differ from you; and that you are as offensive to other people, and that they are as full of wicked passions at you as you are at them. And, then, this is terrible. This, that the most obscure of us, the most innocent of us, nay, the very best of us, and the most blameless—we all have many hearts burning like hell underground against us. There are men we have never seen, and men who have never seen us, who are yet provoked and fretted out of all their composure and all their grace and truth at the bare hearing or reading of our names. We never saw them or they us; and if we had the opportunity we would forgive them and do them a service; yet such are the blind and furious passions of their hearts that our very names are a madness to them. Surely the thought of that should make us all walk softly and speak seldom and seek solitude and circumspection. Surely we should seek obscurity, and wish with all our heart that our so offensive name should never be spoken in this world again, or written or read. Nay, your very virtues are a provocation and a constant fury to men it would astonish you to be told about. Your very services, even to themselves; your very talents of which you are so innocent, and of which your Maker must bear the blame—what is there?—there is absolutely nothing in us, or about us, that does not provoke and exasperate somebody. Let God hide us all in the secret of His presence from the pride of men! Let Him keep us secretly in His pavilion from the strife of tongues!

Well, it was all that: it was Hannah's diabolical ill-usage at her adversary's hands, and it was still more, her own wicked and revengeful heart at her ill-usage: it was all that that made that saintly woman absolutely drunk sometimes with her sorrow. She staggered with her sorrow; she fell against the altar; she did not know what she was saying or where she was going; she actually forgot her own name, and did not answer when her name was spoken. Aaron himself would have been provoked to say to Hannah to put away her wine. Hannah was a saint; but she was a woman-saint; and hence her reeling heart. Hannah was able to command herself sometimes for weeks and months after she had been again at Shiloh. But something would happen in the household that would soon show that even Shiloh had made Hannah nothing better but rather worse; for her chastised and well-bridled tongue would all of a sudden break out again till, had it been in Greece or in Rome, she would have been called a fury rather than a woman and a saint. The milk of human kindness, not to say of womanhood, would suddenly turn to burning brimstone in Hannah's bosom. For days and weeks she would be able in the strength of the Shiloh meat to teach them their letters and to play with Peninnah's children better than if they had been Elkanah's and her own. She would toss them up in the air and make them light on their father's knee, till he clean forgot his sin and his shame and his pain. But the very next moment Hannah was within an inch of dashing them against the stones. Elkanah's happiness through any other wife but herself, and his rapture over her adversary's child's delightful ways, made Hannah sometimes go away to her bed like a she-tiger to her den. You will charge me with mocking you, and with an abuse of sacred words, when I call such a woman a saint. "Among all the saints I have never found one," said Santa Teresa, "out of whose case I could take any comfort." Well, speaking for myself, I can take comfort out of two saints. And one of them is Hannah of Mount Ephraim, and the other is Teresa of Mount Carmel. And out of another. "Begone!" shouted the aged Philip, "Begone! you do not know me. I am a devil if you knew me!"

"Whom do men say that I, the Son of man, am? Some say that thou art Jeremias." Our Lord makes no remark upon that. But I do not think that He was greatly offended to be so taken. Had He said anything about the men of Caesarea Philippi who took Him to be Jeremias, I am mistaken if He would not have said that they were not far from the kingdom of heaven. For they had been drawn to Him just as we have been drawn to Hannah. They had seen Him in the Temple with His lips moving. No, they held, He is neither Moses nor Elias: He is the Man whose sorrow was like no other sorrow that has ever been seen. Pascal is continually preaching to us that the more spiritual light we have, the more spiritual sorrow we have. No wonder, then, that the Spiritual Light Himself was the Man of supreme spiritual sorrow. Who would not have been sad who had eyes to see what went on in Elkanah's house at Shiloh? No man but a blind and a hopeless fool would have been other than sad over houses like the house of Elkanah and Peninnah, and Eli and Hophni and Phinehas. And the land was full of such houses in the days of our Lord, and thus it was that He was what the observing men of Caesarea Philippi saw that He was. There are multitudes of men and women amongst us who are drunk and dazed with many kinds of sorrow. But it is only now and then that you will come—now in life and now in literature—on a man who is drunk and dazed with sorrow for sin. "Pascal was greedy of happiness," says Sainte-Beuve in a fine essay, "but of a noble and an infinite happiness. He had that profound inquietude which attests a moral nature of a high order, and a mental nature stamped with the seal of the archangel! Pascal is of this leading and glorious race: he has more than one sign of it in his heart and on his brow: he is one of the noblest of mortal men, but he is sick, and he would be cured. Pascal sweats blood. Pascal clings to the Cross as to a mast in shipwreck." His sister tells us that the noblest and most self-denying of brothers was sometimes so stupefied by reason of his own sinful nature that his very family affections were withered up in the terrific fires that burned his heart to ashes. And an intellectual and a moral nature like Pascal's; a spiritual sensibility like Pascal's; will always bring along with it Pascal's exquisite and awful sorrow. But let not your hearts be troubled, for it is a noble sorrow. It is a supernatural sorrow. It is the sorrow of the great saints; it is the sorrow of the Son of God. And as He was so are we in this world. Our present sorrow for sin is the exact measure and the sure seal of our future joy.

32
Eli

"SEEST thou a man that is hasty in his words? There is more hope of a fool than of him." Yes; but we have hope of Eli in spite of his hasty words. For Eli never forgave himself for his hasty words to Hannah. Eli had many bitter memories as he sat by the wayside watching for the ark of God. And one of the bitterest of those memories was the lasting memory of his insulting language to Hannah. No sooner was that hasty word gone out of Eli's mouth than he would have given all the world to have had that hasty word back again. "Go in peace," Eli said, "and the God of Israel grant thee thy petition which thou hast asked of Him." And all his days, in his sore remorse for what he had said to Samuel's mother before Samuel was born, Eli tried to make up for that insult to Samuel her son. Eli's extraordinary care over young Samuel; his extraordinary tenderness toward the child; and, as Samuel grew up, the old priest's secret fear at Samuel; and his growing reverence for him—all that was all that Eli could do to undo the insult and the injury he had done to Samuel's mother.

Samuel was predestinated soon to succeed to all Eli's forfeited offices. All Eli's high positions were soon to descend to Samuel. And Eli saw all that preparing to come about, and preparing to come about soon. But all that did not alter or abate by one iota Eli's notable goodness to Samuel. Eli could not have treated Hophni or Phinehas better than he treated Samuel, his immediate successor. Frederick Robertson, in his able apology for Eli, makes a great deal of the total absence of envy in Eli. But surely not with that great preacher's wonted insight. My tongue may be cleaving to the roof of my mouth with envy; I may be as blind with envy as Eli was blind with old age; the hair may have fallen off my head till I am bald with envy—and yet no man about me may so much as guess it. What Eli is to be praised for is this—not that he felt no envy of Samuel; but that, feeling envy every day, as he could not fail to feel it, he kept his envy down, and did not let it come out in his treatment of Samuel. Of course Eli had envy of Samuel; all men have envy in their hearts who are placed by God in Eli's circumstances, and it is misleading and mischievous in the last degree in any preacher to say anything else. God alone could say whether Eli had envy or not. And he never says that about Eli or any other man. He says about Eli and all men the very opposite. The point with God is not whether I have envy or not; but it is this, how I deal with the envy that He knows I have. All that my fellow-men can see in me is not the envy of my heart, but that of my life. They can see and hear whether or no I backbite, and belittle, and detract, and depreciate; as also whether I consent and take part and pleasure with them who do. And while that is much to see and to judge, it is far from being all. If the Baptist had no envy and no jealousy of his fast-rising Cousin, then he has all that the less praise for his noble reply to his envious and jealous disciples. But if the Forerunner had to fast from his locusts to help him to subdue his pride; if it was only after many unwitnessed days and nights of sweat and prayer and blood that he was enabled to hand over John and Andrew to Jesus whom he had baptized but yesterday beyond Jordan; then John the Baptist is of some use to you and to me. But if John had no such envy and no such jealousy himself as his disciples had on his account, then he was not a man of like passions as we are. If John did not sometimes find himself hating Jesus in his heart till, in his agony, he threw himself over the bleeding rocks of the wilderness, then all I can say is, that Elizabeth's sanctified son was not made of the same rotten stuff with you and me.

Not only had Eli, with all his envy, a very real and a very deep love for little Samuel; but along with that, and kept alive by that, he had a real, a living, and a deep faith in God, and in God's voices and visions and answers to men. Eli's fine benediction spoken over Hannah the next moment after he had mistaken her for a daughter of Belial; his open-hearted adoption of little Samuel to be his assistant and successor in the temple service; his rich and recompensing benediction pronounced on Samuel's mother because she had lent little Samuel to the Lord; his midnight lesson to his little elect companion; his solemn demand next morning to be told what the Lord had said to the prophetic child during the night; and his instant acceptance of the terrible message that little Samuel was compelled to deliver—all that shows us that Eli, with all his shipwreck of life and opportunity and privilege, had the root of the matter all the time in him. There had been no "open vision" for many a day in Israel. But Eli's mind had been open all the time. You will see men with great faults, and even with completely lost and wasted lives, who yet all through, and to the end, have a certain openness of mind to divine truth, and a certain sure and spontaneous sympathy with divine truth to whomsoever it comes, and through whomsoever it speaks. And poor old Eli was one of those open-minded and truth-loving men. If his own sins and his sons' sins had shut silent the divine vision, then Eli was all the more prepared to believe that the divine vision would hereafter speak to better men than he had been. And when the divine vision did begin to break its long silence, and to speak again—for Eli to accept that vision, even when it came in the shape of a sentence of capital punishment on himself and on his house—well, if ever faith had her perfect work in an open mind, it was surely in castaway Eli's open mind. What a lesson is here, and what a noble example to all old castaways among ourselves! The Spirit and the providences of God in His Church have stood still in our day. There has been nothing to call an open vision. We have sinned away the open vision. We have quenched the speaking Spirit. But, all the time, the Spirit of God is only waiting till we are out of His way, and then He will return and will not tarry. As soon as we are dead and gone, and obstruct the Spirit of God no more, Samuel will come, and the Lord will be with Samuel, and will let none of his words fall to the ground. But God's mercies always come mingled up with God's judgments, and if you have Eli's loving heart for the rising generation of God's ministers; and if with that you have a still living, if hitherto a too-barren faith in the ever-living God; in alleviation of your punishment, and in reward of your faith and your love, He will send the beginning of the returning vision before the end of your lost life. And even if that vision comes to condemn your whole life, and to pass sentence on you, and on your evil house; yet, even so, better that than to live and die in the long absence and the total silence of an angry God. Let us expect, then, for our successors what we have sinned away from ourselves. Let us believe and be sure that the coming generation will see visions and hear voices that we have not been counted worthy to see or to hear, because of our great unfaithfulness and unfruitfulness, and because of our great blindness and disobedience.

And then, look at old Eli's splendid resignation and Gethsemane-like submission. "It is the Lord: let Him do what seemeth Him good." I shall never believe that Eli is lost. Broken neck; dead sons and daughters lying strewed all around him; the ark taken; the temple in ruins, and the glory departed, and all—Eli is not lost. No man is wholly lost who lies lost before God like that. "Though He slay me," said Job. But He did not slay Job as He slew Eli. Job's patience, and meekness, and submission, and resignation were terribly enough tried; but they were not tried down to death as Eli was. And He who so rewarded Job, and who so supported and rewarded His own Son—no, I shall not believe it till I see it that Eli is among the reprobate. "It is the Lord." If anything will cover a multitude of sins; if anything will draw down the mercy of God, surely that cry of Eli's will do it.

Away back, at the beginning of his life, Eli had taken far too much in hand. Eli was not a great man like Moses or Aaron, but he took both the office of Moses and the office of Aaron upon his single self. Eli was both the chief judge and the high priest in himself for the whole house of Israel. The ablest, the most laborious, the most devoted, the most tireless and sleepless of men could not have done what Eli undertook to do. They called Origen "Brazen-bowels," he was such a sleepless student. But Eli would have needed both bowels of brass, and a head and a heart of gold, to have done the half of what he undertook to do.

And, taking up what was beyond mortal power to perform, the certain result was that he did nothing well, but did everything ill. Both his high priesthood at the altar, and his chief judgeship at the gate, and his sole fatherhood in his own house; both God's house and his own house, and the whole house of Israel, went to wreck and ruin under overladen Eli. It is startling and terrible to think that the unparalleled catastrophe of Eli's awful end had its first and far-back roots in what is as much a virtue, surely, as a vice: his determination to do two men's work with his own hands. But, whatever Eli's motives were for loading himself with all this plurality of offices and emoluments, the terrible catastrophe of his own end and his sons' end and the end of Shiloh—all this had its earliest roots in Eli's vaulting ambition and consequent incapacity and neglect. The mischief was widespread. But it was at home that the widespread mischief rose to a height that went beyond human remedy and beyond divine forgiveness. And may something of that same kind not be the explanation of some of those sad cases where the houses of able and good and devoted ministers come to such ruin? What with the pulpit of our land and our day—more than enough of itself; and what with the resulting and accompanying pastorate—more than enough of itself also for one man working at it in season and out of season; with so many public demands and claims, and with such incessant calls and encroachments at all hours of the day and night, there is neither time nor strength to do any part of a minister's work as it ought to be done. And one worried week follows another worried week till his children grow up and grow out of his knowledge. "A bishop must be vigilant." Yes; but a bishop in our day would need to have a hundred eyes and a hundred hands and a hundred feet. "He must rule well the house of God." Yes; but the apostle tells Timothy that he must know how to rule his own house first. It is a fine picture: "One that ruleth well his own house, having his children in subjection with all gravity." It would almost seem that Paul had had the ruins of Eli's house before his mind when he wrote that fine instruction. All other men have the grave sweet Sabbath-day to spend with their children, ruling and teaching them: all but ministers, and police-men, and some other slaves. But ministers have neither Saturday, nor Sabbath, nor Monday. And I never hear them complaining of that, unless it is when they think of their children. We call Eli old, and blind, and idle, and inefficient, and ignorant, and neglectful of his own children and of God's people; and so he was. But all that was not because he did nothing, but because he did too much to do anything well. Till, at last, broken in life and broken in heart, with his nation and his church and his household lying all in ruins round about him, we see Eli sitting by the wayside waiting for death. A terrible end to such a bold and ambitious beginning.

"Now the sons of Eli were sons of Belial; they knew not the Lord." Impossible! you would protest, if it were not in the Bible. But just because it is in the Bible, we are compelled to ask ourselves how it could possibly come about that the sons of such a sacred man as Eli was could ever become sons of Belial. What! not know the Lord, and they born and brought up within the very precincts of the Lord's house! Were not the first sounds they heard the praises of God in His sanctuary? Were not the first sights they saw their father in his robes beside the altar with all the tables, and the bread, and the sacrifices, and the incense round about him? And yet, there it is in black and white; there it is in blood and tears—"The sons of Eli were sons of Belial; they knew not the Lord." Let me think. Let me consider well how, conceivably, it could come about that Hophni and Phinehas could be born and brought up at Shiloh and not know the Lord? Well, for one thing, their father was never at home. What with judging all Israel, and what with sacrificing and interceding for all Israel, Eli never saw his children till they were in their beds. "What mean ye by this ordinance?" all the other children in Israel asked at their fathers as they came up to the temple. And all the way up and all the way down again those fathers took their inquiring children by the hand and told them all about Abraham, and Isaac, and Jacob, and Joseph, and Moses, and Aaron, and the exodus, and the wilderness, and the conquest, and the yearly passover. Hophni and Phinehas were the only children in all Israel who saw the temple every day and paid no attention to it. And, then, every father and mother knows this, how the years run away, and how their children grow up, till all of a sudden they are as tall as themselves. And very much faster than our tallest children did Eli's children grow up. All things, indeed, were banded against Eli; the very early ripeness of his sons was against Eli. He thought he would one day have time; but it was his lifelong regret that he had never had time. And, what with one thing, and what with another; what with their father's preoccupation and their own evil hearts; the two young men were already sons of Belial when they should still have been little children. "Why do ye do such things? For I hear of all your evil dealings by all this people. Nay, my sons, this is no good report that I hear." Like our own proverb, Eli is seen shutting the stable-door with many tears and sobs years and years after the steeds have been stolen. I have spoken of Job. Well, I always think that Job was the very best father in all the Old Testament, while Eli was surely the very worst. Job—let this passage be repeated to himself by every father every day from the first day he is a father, this golden passage—"Job was one that pleased God and eschewed evil. And it was so, when the days of their feasting were gone about, that Job sent and sanctified them, and rose up early in the morning and offered burnt-offerings according to the number of them all; for Job said, It may be that my sons have sinned and cursed God in their hearts. Thus did Job continually." Our old ministers when they had a father at the pulpit-foot were used to make him swear that he would pray "both with and for" his children. Now, it was just here that Eli went wrong. And it is just here that so many of ourselves go wrong, and our children. We scold and scowl at them, and we beat and bruise and lock them up, when we should pray both with them and for them. If, when they tell a lie, or steal, or speak bad language, or strike one another, or defiantly disobey us, we would neither lift a hand nor a tongue at them, but would take them to our place of prayer, and there pray both with and for them—as sure as I stand here and you sit there—there would be fewer sons and daughters of Belial in our houses. Let us do it. Let us, after Eli tonight, go home and do it. And if our children are grown up and gone away, let us all the more go after them, like Job, with that sacrifice and that importunity which have the promise and the power to apprehend them and to bring them back. Thus did Job continually. You will all have it well in your mind how this all ended. How the ark of God was taken, and the two sons of Eli, Hophni and Phinehas, were slain. And how Eli, when he heard the evil tidings, fell from off his seat backward, and his neck brake, and he died. And how his daughter-in-law, her pains came upon her, but she answered not, neither regarded it; and how she named her son Ichabod, and so died.

"The Psalm of Ichabod, the son of Phinehas, the son of Eli, which he sang after that the Lord had repented Him of the evil, and had restored the priesthood to the house of Eli: I will confess my iniquity and the iniquity of my fathers. The fathers have eaten sour grapes, and the children's teeth are set on edge. But pardon the iniquity of Thy servant, according to Thy great mercy, and as Thou hast been a father to the fatherless, so hast Thou been to Thy servant. I was a reproach among all mine enemies, but especially among my neighbors, and a fear to mine acquaintances. I was like a broken vessel. But I trusted in Thee, and Thou didst deliver me. I was cast upon thee from my mother's knees, and Thou didst hide me in the secret of Thy presence from the pride of men. Thou didst show me Thy loving-kindness in a fenced city. I am a wonder to many, but my boast is in God. Thou hast restored to me what the locust had eaten. Thou hast anointed my head with oil and made my cup to run over. Thou hast taken off my sackcloth and hast girded me with gladness. Come, all ye that fear God, and I will declare what He hath done for my soul. The sorrows of death compassed me, and the pains of hell gat hold on me; but Thou hast brought up my life from the pit that I might show forth Thy praise. O Lord, I am Thy servant: I am Thy servant, and the son of Thine handmaid. I will pay Thee my vows which my mouth spake when I was in trouble. Bless the Lord, O my soul, and forget not all His benefits." Thus sang Ichabod, the son of Phinehas, after that the Lord had repented Him of the evil.

33
Samuel

SIR JOSHUA REYNOLDS has made all our children familiar with little Samuel. In the beautiful picture that sanctifies the walls of all our nurseries our children see and hear little Samuel kneeling and saying, Speak, Lord, for Thy servant heareth. And many a mother has taken the opportunity from that sweet picture to teach her child the same lesson that Eli taught the child Samuel. "Sometimes when you are alone, my child, and both while you are yet a child, and after you are a big man, the same God of little children and of big men who spoke to little Samuel will come and speak to you. He will call you by name. If your name is Samuel, He will call and say, Samuel, Samuel, or whatever else your name is. And, be sure, my child, to answer at once. Be sure you say that moment, Speak, Lord, for Thy little servant heareth. And God will speak to you just as sure as He spoke to Samuel. Be sure He will. For He is about your path, and about your bed. Yea, the darkness hideth not from Him; but the night shineth as the day; the darkness and the light are both alike to God." Good Sir Joshua has helped multitudes of good mothers to teach their children to pray.

Hannah lent little Samuel to the Lord according to her promise. That is to say, she lent Samuel to Eli the Lord's servant, and to the temple at Shiloh, which was the Lord's house. As soon as he was able to put on his own clothes and run about, his mother kept her promise. Hannah took Samuel up to Shiloh, and the child was young. And she said to Eli: O my lord, as thy soul liveth, I am the woman that stood by thee here, praying unto the Lord. For this child I prayed: therefore also I have lent him to the Lord: as long as he liveth he shall be lent to the Lord. And Samuel ministered before the Lord, being a child, and he was girded with a linen ephod. Little Samuel was the little doorkeeper of God's house in Shiloh. He ran messages also for Eli. He opened the doors of the tabernacle in the morning, and he shut them at night. He lighted the seven-branched candlestick at sunset, and he put it out at sunrise, and did everything his quick little hands and quick little feet could do to keep the house of God in order and beauty, serving the Lord. Once every year his mother came up to Shiloh to see her son, and to bring him a little coat that she made a little bigger and a little bigger every year till he grew to be a man. And after his mother was taken home to heaven and came no more to Shiloh, when Samuel the prophet needed another coat he had it always made of the same substance and of the same shape that his mother wove for him on her loom in Ephraim. It was her favorite substance and her favorite pattern, and the old prophet would never wear anything else. All his days the people knew Samuel by his "mantle," which was just his little coat made larger for a man. And he wears it to this day as he serves God beside his mother in heaven. When he came back from heaven to rebuke Saul for his sins, and to announce to that bad king his fast-approaching end, Samuel had still the very same mantle on. Only it was made

171

now of finer linen, and it was cleaner and whiter than any weaver or fuller in Israel could weave it or whiten it. All the same, it was the very same mantle—the very same little coat his mother had made him when he was her little son, only of a substance now and a beauty fit for the heavenly Shiloh.

If Samuel's mother was still in this world when the ark was taken, and when Shiloh was laid waste, then the likelihood is that he went back to live with his mother till he should see what the Lord had for him to do. Wherever Samuel lived I am sure he lived a good life, and was never idle. Only, for the next twenty years, or thereabouts, Samuel is quite lost to us in that wild and lawless world. From about his twelfth to his thirtieth year, like Another, Samuel was ripening in secret for his future work as a great prophet. Ripening; because he had already been planted in the house of God in his early youth. In after-years Samuel's best-known name in Israel was "The Seer." "Tell me," said Saul on one occasion to a stranger he met, "where the Seer's house is." "I am the Seer," said Samuel; "come with me, and tomorrow I will tell thee all that is in thine heart." And if you will weigh that name of Samuel well, and will carry that name deep enough into the things of God and man, you could not have anything told about Samuel that would better help you to understand him. "I am the Seer, and I will tell thee all that is in thine heart." And, not only in Saul's heart, but in God's heart also. For God opened His mind and heart to Samuel, and when the people discovered that, all Israel from Dan to Beersheba knew that Samuel was established to be a prophet of the Lord. "The Seer," they said. "Samuel, the Seer. The man amongst us who sees God, and who tells us what is in our hearts."

When he was yet a child, Samuel was made a seer before he knew. He saw enough of God and man that terrible night to make him an old man and a seer before the morning. As he lay awake till the morning he saw what was the wages of all that wickedness that had so horrified him to see and to hear in Eli's sons. He saw, while yet a child, that the wages of such sin is death. And he saw what would be the end of all that to Eli also, his father in the Lord. Till it was no wonder that he hesitated to tell to Eli all that he had seen and heard that terrible night. And all that must have worked powerfully together to make young Samuel the pure, prayerful, holy child before God and man that he early was and continued to be. His purity of heart and his love for holy things prepared Samuel early to be a seer; and the sights he saw both in heaven and in earth; both in God and in man, only perfected all his days what had been so early and so well begun.

And all happy children who have mothers like Hannah, and who all their days keep themselves pure in heart and pray like Samuel, they see God clearer and clearer all their days. They are still the seers in Israel. Every Scripture testifies to that, and every great saint and servant of God is a fresh proof of that. The impure in heart never see God. Hophni and Phinehas never saw God. The darkness shall cover us, they said, and it did. It did, till a Hand out of the darkness struck them down in their sin. They had no mother, and therefore they never saw God till they came to their awful end. Had Hannah been their mother; had Hannah adopted the two sacred orphans; and had she adopted them in time: then they, as well as Samuel, would have seen God; and all the awful overthrow of Eli's house, and

God's house, and the whole house of Israel would have been averted and escaped. Such blessedness is there in a good mother; in an early plantation in the house of God; and in a pure heart; for, then, with Hophni and Phinehas for Israel's high priests, and with Samuel for her prophet from Dan to Beersheba—"I should soon have subdued their enemies, and turned My hand against their adversaries. He should have fed them also with the finest of the wheat; and with honey out of the rock should I have satisfied thee." Mothers in Israel, would you have your sons to be seers and life-long servants of God? Now is your opportunity. Teach them early, as Eli taught Samuel. Teach them under the picture of Samuel hanging over their bed. And never lie down in your own bed without prayer for them till you are sure that they see God. And then you can take your well-earned rest. "Lord, now lettest Thou Thy servant depart in peace, according to Thy word; for mine eyes have seen Thy salvation." And, would any young man here see God? Would he see God in his own heart and mind and imagination, where God is best seen? Then let him keep God's temple clean. And then he will not only see God in his own mind and heart and imagination, but in Holy Scripture also, in Jesus Christ, in creation, in providence, in the means of grace, and eventually where Samuel now sees Him. The promise is plain, and the thing is true. "Blessed are the pure in heart." And again, "If any man will do His will, he shall know of the doctrine." And again, "And holiness, without which no man shall see God." The true doctrine of seeing God is written in Scripture with a thousand sunbeams, and every man's own life is to him the seal of it. Every pure man's life is to him the seal of it. And every impure man's life is no less to him the seal of the other side of it. Hophni and Phinehas's lives were the seals of it to them. And Samuel's life was the seal of it to him. And your life is the seal of it to you. And my life is the seal of it to me.

> Blest are the pure in heart,
>   For they shall see their God:
> The secret of the Lord is theirs;
>   Their soul is Christ's abode.

Without being prophets we could predict what kind of a judge Samuel would make when he sat down on the seat of justice. Seeing God; remembering what Abraham said to God on one occasion about the Judge of all the earth; able to tell men all that was in their hearts; Israel never had a judge like Hannah's son. Josephus says that Samuel had an "inborn love of justice." And so he had. Some men still, both in public and in private life, have that same love of justice born in them. And they are happy men, and all men are happy who have to do with them. Some other men, again, most men indeed, have an inborn love of injustice that they have to fight against all their days. The golden rule is written, as if with nature's own finger, on some men's hearts; while other men are never able all their days to learn that rule. Samuel was still "The Seer" as he sat on the judgment-seat; but there was nothing enthusiastic, carried-away, or impracticable about Samuel. He was a clear-eyed, firm-handed, sure-footed, resolute-minded, righteous man, with an inborn sense of truth and righteousness: and all his opinions, and decisions, and sentences carried all men's consent and conscience with them. In ancient Rome they used to put on a white robe when they went out to ask for the votes of the voters, and it was for this that they were called "candidates" in the language of Rome: spotless men, that is, in our language. But it was only one famous name here and another famous name there that came out of office as clean as they entered it. Look at Samuel laying down his office, and putting on his snow-white mantle. "Behold, now, I am old and gray-headed: and I have walked before you from my childhood unto this day. Behold, here I am. Witness against me before the Lord. Whose ox have I taken? or whose ass have I taken? or whom have I defrauded? Whom have I oppressed? or of whose hand have I received any bribe to blind mine eyes therewith? And I will restore it to you. And they said, Thou hast not defrauded us, nor oppressed us, neither hast thou taken aught of any man's hand. And he said to them, The Lord is witness. And they answered, He is witness."

Samuel was removed from his mother's side while still a child. No sooner was he at home in Shiloh than Shiloh fell, and he had again to change his home. In his office of judge he was continually on circuit dispensing justice and judgment up and down the land. And then when Saul became king, Samuel was compelled to retire into obscurity, and become of no reputation. Samuel was emptied from vessel to vessel till there was no lees left in the wine. The noblest thing, in some respects, in all Samuel's noble life was the way he took the providence of God in the establishment of the monarchy. The monarchy was a great innovation. It was a great revolution. And even more than that, it was a severe condemnation, if not of Samuel's own life, yet of his office and his order, which are sometimes dearer to a man than life itself. And, in addition to that, it was the deposition and dismissal of his two sons from the office and the rank to which he had raised them. Everything was against Samuel taking kindly to the thought of the new monarchy. All Samuel's past life had been spent in animating and purifying, and restoring the republic; but when he saw that a kingdom was coming in, instead of meeting it with resistance and obstinacy and lifelong hostility, the great man bowed to the will of God and the will of Israel, and cast in his lot with the new dispensation. Samuel had a great struggle with himself to do it; and he did not hide that struggle from Israel. But, that struggle over, Saul had no such loyal and faithful friend as Samuel the deposed judge. The State and Church of Israel shall have Samuel's service to the end. What there is out of the great past that is worth preserving he will do his best to preserve. What of the old order can safely be carried over into the new order he will do his best to carry that over. As far as Samuel is concerned Saul and his kingdom shall not only have fair play; but they shall have all Samuel's influence with God and with man. It is only a great man and a noble who can act in that way. And the more individuality of character, and the more independence of mind, and the more strength of will such men have, the nobler is the thing they do. It takes the very finest natures to pass over from one generation to another, and to work in the new generation as they worked in the old. It was splendidly done by Samuel. And it has been splendidly done, now and again, since Samuel's day. And, best of all, it has been splendidly done in our own day. And it is one of the finest sights to be seen among men when men have eyes and hearts to see it. It is only the old, and the ripe, and the much-experienced, and the men fullest of past service, who can do Samuel's service to our generation and the generation which is coming up after us. No amount of talent; no amount of loyalty; no amount of humility, even, can make up in the young—in young statesmen and in young churchmen—for the wisdom, and the experience, and the standing, and the influence of the aged. If the past time is to hand over its proper heritage to the present time, it is the old who can best do it. And I do not know that history, either sacred or profane, holds out a better example of this large-hearted, public-spirited wisdom than Samuel the deposed judge, and now the chief counsellor of Saul.

But Samuel, deposed and superseded as he was, was full of new and still more fruitful ideas and intentions for Israel. And what did Samuel do to occupy his talents in his ripe age, and still to serve God and God's people? Never mortal man did a better, or a more fruitful thing than Samuel now did. Samuel planned and set up an institution, so to call it, that has made far more mark on the world than anything else that survives to us out of Israel or Greece or Rome. In his ripe and farseeing years Samuel devised and founded and presided over a great prophetical school in his old age. That school of the prophets to which we owe so much of Samuel himself; to which we owe David, and Gad, and Nathan, and all their still greater successors; that great school was the creation and the care of Samuel's leisure from office. How much of the Old Testament itself we owe to the prophets, and the preachers, and the psalmists, and the sacred writers, and other trained students of Samuel's great school, we have not yet fully found out. The day may come when all the Old Testament, as we now have it, will be traced back to that great institution that God honored Samuel to plan and to set up as his reward for his pure heart, and his holy, studious, self-sacrificing life. And it is admitted—it is no fancy to say it—that our modern universities, divinity halls, and great public schools, have all their far-down roots in Mount Ephraim, and in Samuel's great college which he founded there. True, divine prophecy does not come by the will of man in prophetical schools, or anywhere else. School or no school, holy men of God will always speak as they are moved by the Holy Ghost. No man knew that better than Samuel; but at the same time, no man ever struck out a more fruitful line of action in the things of God than when Samuel laid the foundation of the sacred school of Ramah. Israel had already a divine deposit of religion and worship and morality and civilization, all of which they had but to accept and assimilate in order to be the strongest, the safest, and the happiest nation on the face of the earth. But the divine law was too high and too good for Israel. Their hearts were hard, and they were not upright in God's covenant. And the new monarchy was already threatening to become a very stronghold of that hard, worldly, rebellious spirit. Saul, in spite of all that Samuel could do, was soon to become a complete shipwreck. But the throne was destined to stand long after Saul was cast out of it; and Samuel is determined to do his very best to secure it that Saul's successors shall have around them and over their people a class of men who, if not indeed prophets—Samuel cannot secure that—the wind bloweth where it listeth—yet Samuel can and will secure that there shall be an estate of learned and earnest-minded men, who shall watch over the religion and the morals of the people, in the prophetical spirit and in the prophetical name. And thus it came about that at Naioth in Ramah the first school of the prophets was set up. Ramah was Elkanah's old property; it had now come into Samuel's hands; and at Naioth, the quietest and sweetest spot of all his patrimonial estate, Samuel set up the first divinity hall; the first school for prophets and psalmists in Israel.

But, crowning all and sanctifying all was Samuel's life of prayer. Samuel was a proverb of prayer. The tradition of Hannah's psalm and prayer was well known to every young prophet in Samuel's school, and her best memories were perpetuated and transmitted in the devotional life and labors of her son. "Moses and Aaron among His priests, and Samuel among them that call on His name." As much as to say that Samuel stands at the head of all the men of prayer in Israel, just as Moses and Aaron stand at the head of all the prophets and priests in Israel. The successors of Moses and Aaron were a glorious enough succession; but all that fades and vanishes away before the far greater glory of pure and unceasing prayer, and especially of unceasing intercessory and undeserved prayer. "As for me," said Samuel, "God forbid that I should sin against the Lord in ceasing to pray for you." Samuel said that as his answer to his sentence of deposition and banishment from being their head and their king in all but the name. Samuel, then, among them that pray for their enemies and for them that despitefully use them. Samuel among them that are cast off and forgotten after a lifetime of self-forgetful service. Samuel among them that cease not to pray for the prosperity of those who have taken their place in the world and in the Church, and in the hearts and the mouths of men. Samuel among them who have such a pure heart that nothing will ever turn their heart to gloom, or bitterness, or discontent, or retaliation, or to anything else, but to still more prayer.

Such, then, was some of the interest that the Lord paid to Hannah for the early loan of Samuel her son. And the Lord is the same yesterday, today, and for ever.

34
Saul

DR. NEWMAN, after attempting three times to preach on Saul, is compelled to confess that Saul's character continues to be obscure to him, and he warns us that we must be exceedingly cautious while considering Saul's so obscure character. Now, if Saul's character was still so obscure to the subtlest and the acutest of all our preachers, I cannot expect to be able to say much to purpose upon it. At the same time, with so much told us about Saul; and told us in such a plain, open, and straightforward style; and told us, as it must have been, for our instruction, we may surely hope to be able, amid all his acknowledged obscurity, to gather sufficient instruction out of Saul to justify us in taking him up for our subject this evening.

But, unhappily, the obscurity begins further back than Saul. The obscurity begins with Saul's father and mother. We never hear of Saul's mother; but what kind of a father can Kish have been? We know all about Samuel. There is no obscurity about Samuel. All Israel, from Dan even to Beersheba, knew that Samuel was established to be a prophet of the Lord; all Israel but Kish and his son Saul. Hannah, and Samuel, and Eli, and Hophni and Phinehas, and Ichabod were all household words, as we say, in every household in Israel. Only, there was a man of Benjamin whose name was Kish, and he had a son whose name was Saul, a choice young man, and a goodly, but neither father nor son, neither Kish nor Saul, had ever heard of Samuel. Kish the father, and Saul the son, were so busy breeding asses that they made light of Samuel, and would not come. Samuel was an old man by this time. Samuel had grown gray in a service that made all Israel acknowledge and know God from the one end of the land to the other; but Saul, all the time, did not know Samuel when he saw him. "Tell me, I pray thee," said Saul to a stranger he met on his way when he was in despair about his father's lost asses, "where is the Seer's house." "I am the Seer myself," said Samuel. "Come with me, and I will tell thee all that is in thine heart." Yes, there is some quite inexplicable obscurity about Kish as well as about Saul; an obscurity that perplexes us, and throws us out at the very opening of his son's sad history. And yet, when we turn back and begin to read Saul's whole history over again with our eye on the object; when we stop and look round about us as we read, the ancient obscurity begins to pass off, but only to let alarm and apprehension for ourselves and for our own sons take its place. The prophet Samuel had been a public man, as we say, long before Saul was born. And, but for Saul, we would have said that there could not possibly be a child, or a youth, or a grown-up man in all Israel who had not often sat at Samuel's feet and drunk in his divine words. But the most public men, after all, have only their own public. Saul staggers us and throws us out till we look at ourselves and at the men round about us, and then we soon see, what had before been obscure to us, that our inborn and indulged tastes, likings, dispositions, inclinations, and pursuits rule us also, shape us, occupy us, and decide for us the men we know and the life we lead. Josephus says that Samuel had an inborn love of justice. But Saul had inherited from Kish an inborn and an absorbing love of cattle and sheep; and, till they were lost, Saul had no errand to Samuel's city. Why hold up our hands at Saul's obscurity, and at Saul's ignorance of Samuel? We have it in ourselves. We also see what we bring eyes to see, and ears to hear, and hearts to love. To go no further; take just yesterday's journals. They were full of good books. They were full of public meetings, lectures, classes, sermons, speeches, till reading men, and thinking men, and men set on their own self-improvement and their own salvation from sin, do not know where to turn or what to do next, the doors of life are so many and so wide open. Let him who passed all that before him yesterday, and then laid out all this week, redeeming all the time, that he might read the best and hear the best—let that man, and let no other man, cast the first stone at stupid Saul and his stupid father. For Saul was not more stupid among the pastures of Benjamin than we are among the churches, and the classes, and the libraries, and the reading-rooms, and the booksellers' shops of Edinburgh. "Behold now," said Saul's servant when the asses were hopelessly lost, "there is in this city a man of God, and he is an honorable man: all that he saith cometh surely to pass; now, let us go thither." If you have no more sense of religion and life than Saul and his father had, at least, like them, see that you have a religious servant. Saul's servant knew Samuel. Saul's servant had sat at Samuel's feet as often as he had a holiday. He had bargained with Kish for a day now and then to see Samuel when he was on circuit, and to hear the prophet when he preached. And your servant who stipulates to get out to church, and takes less wages in order to do so, he will be able to tell you where the Seer lives when you have lost all, and yourself to the bargain. Insignificant people—the sacred writer does not even know that servant's name—have sometimes most important information. Saul was led up to the door of his earthly kingdom by the piety of his father's servant; and you may be led up some day to the door of the heavenly kingdom by one of your servants who has interests and acquaintances and experiences that up to tonight you know nothing about.

After Samuel had anointed Saul to the kingdom, we come upon this very obscure Scripture: "And it was so that when Saul had turned his back to go from Samuel, God gave Saul another heart, and the Spirit of God came upon Saul, and he prophesied." Saul, you exclaim, a prophet! Saul with "another heart"! Saul with the Spirit of God upon him! You cannot understand. No. But words must be read in the light of facts; and Bible words in the light of Bible facts. Profession must be judged by practice, and faith shown by works. And "another heart" judged what it is by what comes out of it. Nay, prophecy itself is only a sounding brass or a tinkling cymbal if the prophet has not charity. "Another heart" has more meanings than one in Holy Scripture; and so has the Spirit of God; and so has prophecy. Isaiah prophesied of the atoning death of Christ, but so did Caiaphas. The Spirit of God came upon Jesus at the Jordan, but He came also upon Samson at the camp of Dan, and upon Balaam beside the altar of Baal. Matthew Henry in two or three words makes clear to us all the obscurity of Saul's "other heart." "Saul," says the most sensible of commentators, "has no longer the heart of a husbandman, concerned only with corn and cattle; he has now the heart of a statesman, a general, a prince. When God calls to service He will make fit for it. If He advances to another station, He will give another heart; and will preserve that heart to those who sincerely desire to serve Him." So He will. But that is just what Saul, another heart and all, did not sincerely desire to do. And here hangs the true key to the whole of Saul's sad history. He was elected and crowned king over Israel, but he was as ignorant all the time of the God of Israel as he was of Samuel, the great prophet of the God of Israel. The Spirit of God came upon Saul for outward and earthly acts, but never for an inward change of heart. Saul prophesied, whatever that may mean; what he said has not been thought worthy of preservation; but after he had so prophesied he relapsed and remained the same man he had been before. Saul was like ninety-nine out of a hundred of us preachers. The truth is, another heart, prophetical spirit and all, Saul all along was little better than a heathen at heart. And hence it is that what has often been called the profanity of Saul's character scarcely rises to the dignity of profanity. Saul's most presumptuous sins scarcely attain to profaneness. You must have some sense of what is sacred before you can be really profane. But Saul has no such sense. In his youth he had not one spark of insight or interest in the religious life and worship of Israel. He had never heard of Samuel. What he could not but hear he immediately forgot. When his sin found him out, and when salvation was at his very door, the poor graceless castaway had no higher request to make of Samuel than this: "Honor me, I pray thee, before the people." All sure marks of a man who has not learned the very first principles of the divine life. No. Saul the anointed king of Israel had all the time neither part nor lot in the true kingdom of God. At the same time, in giving Saul another heart, the God of Israel gave Saul the greatest opportunity of his life to make himself a new heart. God suddenly made a break in the ungodly and heathenish life of the son of Kish. So much so that Saul for the moment was almost persuaded to become an Israelite indeed. Saul all his days was never so near the kingdom of heaven as when he said to Samuel, "Am not I a Benjamite, of the smallest of the tribes of Israel, and my family the least of all the families of Benjamin? Wherefore, then, speakest thou so to me?" That is the language of a man whose heart is really touched for the time with divine grace. That is real humility; and humility is the root of all the graces, both natural and supernatural. And had Saul only dwelt on that thought; had he returned all his days to that thought; that thought dwelt upon and added to at every new occasion and fresh proof of God's goodness and his own ill deserts— that would soon have made Saul's heart a new heart; that would soon have made Saul another man. But it was not so to be with Saul. As time went on, and as trials and temptations beset Saul, a hard and stony heart, a spirit of rebellion, and pride, and envy, and jealousy, and despair took possession of Saul, and held possession of Saul to his terrible end.

No; there is no such obscurity about Saul getting another heart and yet that heart coming to nothing. We have all had the same thing in ourselves. We ourselves have gone out on an errand of duty or of pleasure, and have come back with another heart. We were for the time like new creatures. Very little more at that time would have made us new creatures altogether. Such surprises of providence, such opportunities of making ourselves a new heart, are occurring continually.

Sometimes it has been at a time of sorrow, and sometimes at a time of joy and gladness. At the death of a father or a mother; at the time of leaving home to take our place in a lonely world; or, again, at that happy time when our loneliness was so graciously dealt with by God. God, I feel sure, lets no man become a married man, for instance, without giving him the great opportunity and the new start in religion He gave to Saul when He made him king of Israel. In the kingly heart that God gives to every bridegroom we are not far for the time from the kingdom of heaven. No man, the most heathen of men, ever became a bridegroom and a married man without having opportunities and intentions and commencements of a new heart and a better life. We have all had times when our hearts were too big for our bosoms. And at such times we were almost persuaded to become Christian men. Yes; at one time or other, and more than once, you have all had Saul's great opportunity. Did you or did you not embrace it? The bare remembrance of those times of another heart all but brings them back again. Bring them back. You can. You still can, if you choose. And though their first impression must be somewhat faded and spent, let your resolution in God be all the greater that even yet you are determined to make yourself a new heart out of them. Determine to do it, and God will see it done. Say it, and see if He will not.

Had Saul's change of heart only held, had his conversion only become complete, Saul would have been one of the greatest of all the Old Testament men. Saul was not a common man. He was a choice young man, and a goodly; there was not among the children of Israel a goodlier person than he; from his shoulders upward he was higher than any of the people. He had a splendid body and a stately gait, and the very sins of his soul had a certain lurid grandeur about them also. After God gave Saul another heart his life was full for a time of the finest promise. What could have promised better than his strict silence to his inquiring uncle about his anointing by Samuel? Where a weaker man would have had his head turned and his tongue loosed, Saul told his uncle that the stray asses were at last found; but of the matter of the kingdom he was strictly silent. We are bound to put a good construction on Saul's silence in that matter. It is but fair and just to set Saul's silence that day down to humility and modesty. As also when he hid himself among the stuff on the day of his election. As also when he held his peace at the men of Belial mocking at his election. As also after his first great victory. Bring the men who say, Shall Saul rule over us, said the people, and put them to death this day. But Saul said, There shall not a man be put to death this day, for today the Lord hath wrought salvation in Israel. If all that is not to be set down to Saul's humility, self-command, and magnanimity, not to say piety, then Saul's character is obscure indeed. We would have had no hesitation in setting all that down to the best motives had it not been that all his future so terribly belied all such modesty, humility, self-command, magnanimity, and piety. The great preacher did not say it till he had felt it to be quite impossible to draw out Saul's obscure life into a consistent and open piece. And the more we work on Saul under that great preacher and after him, the more we feel the obscurity and the mystery of Saul's dark character. It would take a Shakespeare to put himself into Saul's place and let us see the obscure working of Saul's heart under all his temptations. But he has gone away and left us to deal with such characters as Esau, and Balaam, and Saul, and Judas for ourselves. Only, there is one dark passage toward the end of Saul's insane life that we need neither Shakespeare nor Newman to open up to us. Saul's mad and murderous envy of David is as clear as day to every man who puts its proper name on what goes on every day in his own evil heart.

Who is your Saul, my brethren? Who is the man that stands in the way of your promotion? Who sits in the seat that should by this time have been yours? Who is the man that casts the javelin of slander and detraction at your good name? Who has cost you home and friends by his spite, and malice, and jealousy? Mark that man. Never let your eye off that man. God will bring that man to your feet one day. He will lie under your sword some day soon. But touch not a hair of his head. Touch not the skirt of his robe, neither the spear at his bolster, nor the cruse at his side. Remember who and what you are. Remember what Name you bear, and walk worthy that day of that Name. Love your enemies, bless them that curse you, do good to them that hate you, and pray for them that despitefully use you and persecute you. Therefore, if thine enemy hunger, feed him; if he thirst, give him drink. Be not overcome of evil, but overcome evil with good.

Oh! exclaims Thomas Shepard, the grievous shipwrecks of some great ships! We see some boards and planks lying in the mud at low water, but that is all!

35
David — In His Virtues

JESSE the Bethlehemite, the father of David, and the far-off father of Jesus Christ, was the son of Obed, who, again, was the son of Boaz and Ruth. Jesse had an illustrious past to look back to. He was the tenth in direct descent from his father Jacob, and more than one shining name stood in his illustrious ancestry. But it is not his so illustrious past, it is the surpassing splendor of his future that makes us look with so much interest on David's father. We are not told as much about Jesse as we might like. He is already an old man when we first see him. And it is somewhat remarkable that we are told nothing at all about David's mother. The more so, that there would seem to have been nothing about Jesse to lead us on to think of him as either transmitting the extraordinary ability of his youngest son, or as discovering or fostering his youngest son's extraordinary gifts and character. Jesse's sole interest to us is in this, that he had David among his sons. We bow before the old Bethlehemite because of the branch that grew out of his roots.

> Latest born of Jesse's race,
> Wonder lights thy bashful face,
> While the Prophet's gifted oil
> Seals thee for a path of toil.
>
> Twofold praise thou shalt attain,
> In royal court and battle-plain,
> Then comes heartache, care, distress,
> Blighted hope, and loneliness;
> Wounds from friend and gifts from foe,
> Dizzied faith, and guilt, and woe;
> Loftiest aims by earth defiled,
> Gleams of wisdom sin-beguiled,
> Sated power's tyrannic mood,
> Counsels shared by men of blood,
> Sad success, parental tears,
> And a dreary gift of years.

For the Lord had said to Samuel, Fill thine horn with oil, and go, I will send thee to Jesse the Bethlehemite; for I have provided Me a king among his sons. God sees not as man sees, and God works not as man works. In providing Him a king, God worked in a way strange and unlikely to our eyes. We would not have committed our coming king to Jesse to bring up. It was a strange school for a future king—the lonely sheepfolds of Bethlehem. So we think who look at the outward appearance. David was forgotten and neglected by his father; he was scoffed at and trampled upon by his brothers; but you cannot sour, or starve, or poison, or pervert a nature like David's. There is a well-spring of piety and of poetry in David that makes David independent of adverse circumstances. Nay, he takes prosperity out of adversity. That ruddy stripling has his harp and his sling and his father's sheep, and what more does he need to make him happy? He has the glorious traditions of his far-off father Israel to dream about. Isaac, and Jacob, and Joseph, and Moses, and Joshua, and Jephthah, and Samuel: his poet's eye doth glance from the one to the other till they are all with him as he folds his flock under the stars of Bethlehem. "Now, as they were going along and talking, they espied a boy feeding his father's sheep. The boy was in very mean clothes, but of very fresh and well-favored countenance, and as he sat by himself he sang. Then said their guide, Do you know him? I will dare to say that this boy lives a merrier life, and wears more of that herb called heart's-ease in his bosom than he that is clad in silk and velvet. So they hearkened, and he sang:—

> The Lord's my Shepherd, I'll not want,
>> He makes me down to lie
> In pastures green; He leadeth me
>> The quiet waters by."

And, again, "When I consider the heavens, the work of Thy fingers, the moon, and the stars, which Thou hast ordained; what is man, that Thou art mindful of him? and the son of man, that Thou visitest him?" And, again, this: "Day unto day uttereth speech, and night unto night showeth knowledge. There is no speech nor language where their voice is not heard." No; that was not an erroneous school for David. All his days the remembrance of those days was dear to him. A draught of the water of the well of Bethlehem, even to old age, would make King David pure, and free, and young, and himself again.

"And Saul's servants said to him, Behold now, an evil spirit from God troubleth thee. Let our lord seek out a man who is a cunning player on an harp: and it shall come to pass, when the evil spirit is upon thee, that he shall play with his hand, and thou shalt be well. Behold, answered one of Saul's servants, I have seen a son of Jesse the Bethlehemite that is cunning in playing, and a mighty valiant man, and a man of war, and prudent in matters, and a comely person, and the Lord is with him. Wherefore Saul sent messengers to Jesse, and said, Send me David thy son, which is with the sheep. And it came to pass, when the evil spirit was upon Saul, that David took an harp, and played with his hand. So Saul was refreshed and was well, and the evil spirit departed from him." Browning's *Saul* is a wonderful piece of writing. The color, the movement, the insight, the passion of that piece are astonishing. What a gift is poetic genius! And how well laid out by Robert Browning. Let all young men be readers of Robert Browning, and imitators of David in *Saul* in this, that what David puts his hand to, you may depend upon it, he will carry that through. There is an inborn temper of masterfulness in David. David never does anything by halves. Energy, decision, resolution, devotion, finish, scorn of idleness, scorn of ease, love of labor, love of danger—you will always find virtues like these in young David. Saul's servants had all heard of David. David's harp had sounded farther than David ever dreamed. Plenty of shepherd-boys had a harp, but there was no man in all Israel who could make his harp play and work cures of the mind like David. David was a man of strong passions, good and bad: but no passion in David's heart was stronger than the noble passion to do with all his might whatsoever his hand found to do. Harp, or sling, or sword, or scepter, or psalmist's pen—it was all the same. David was a cunning man, and the Lord was with David. It would soon change the face of the world if all our young men would but determine to put on David's masterful mind. How much power is wasted; how many talents are let rot; how many opportunities are lost for ever for want of David's eager, onward, hopeful, masterful mind. How few men come to anything eminent, or distinguished, or praiseworthy. Jesse's son was not the only son in Israel who had an ear for music. But he was the only owner of an ear for music who did his very best by his ear. All the men in Saul's camp had the best-made slings hung at their belts, but it was the homeliest piece of skin and cord in all Israel that delivered the smooth stone into Goliath's forehead. How much half-finished work is gathering dust in all our houses! How many books, bought or borrowed, and let fall out of sight unread! How many costly instruments of music that nobody can play! How many languages smattered over! What heaps of sluggard's litter lying all around us! How few of our children can translate a page to perfection, or polish a sentence, or play a tune, or patch a garment, or prepare or eat a meal so that you can say, The Lord is with them! In His name, what your hand finds to do, do it with all your might to Him who slumbers not nor sleeps. Whether it is learning a language, or preparing a speech, or singing a song, or composing a sermon or a prayer, or visiting a stair, or teaching and training up a class, or plowing a furrow, or sweeping a house, lay it not down till you can say, It is finished.

The eighteenth chapter of First Samuel contains some of the most difficult and dangerous passages in David's whole life, and four times in that single chapter David's wisdom is remarked on. David, we read, went out whithersoever Saul sent him, and behaved himself wisely. And after the foolish women had aroused Saul's envy and endangered David's life with their thoughtless songs and silly dances, we read again that David behaved himself wisely in all his ways. Wherefore, when Saul saw that David behaved himself very wisely, Saul was afraid of David. And then, summing up David's residence at Saul's difficult and dangerous court, the sacred writer says that David behaved himself more wisely than all the servants of Saul; so that his name was much set by. I feel certain that the extravagant and ill-considered songs of the excited women pained David far more deeply than they pained Saul. Their coarse chants must have grated painfully on David's finely-strung heart. Their singing and dancing drove Saul mad. But all that—the women's folly and the king's jealousy—only made David a wiser and a wiser man every new day. If David could have shut the mouths of these mischief-making women, how willingly would he have done it. They could not understand what was the matter with the usually so open David, the victorious captain who rode past them in silence, and with a dark cloud on his countenance. It says much for David, and it says no little for the sound public opinion of Israel in that day, that David's name was so celebrated for his wisdom. Men of a cold, cautious, reserved character far sooner gain and far easier keep the name of wise men than their fellows do who are of warmer feelings and more generous impulses. The fullness and the openness of some men's hearts obscure to the multitude the lucidity and the solidity of their minds. We are ready to think the man wise and able who is silent, and reserved, and proud, and whose temper and tongue are edged in all he says and does with slight and scorn of other men. The warm-hearted man is a far wiser man than the cold-hearted man ever can be, but it takes a warm heart and a wise to see that. David must have had great strength of character and great solidity of judgment, and he must have had good and honest hearts round about him, fully appreciating him, and guiding public opinion concerning him, when, with so much openness, friendliness, geniality, and humility, he gained such a name for prudence and wisdom. The voice of the people is sometimes, after all, the voice of God.

David's fine humility is beautifully brought out in the matter of his marriage. Saul's diabolical design was to get David murdered in connection with his marriage. But, without having discovered that, David's humility of heart and delicacy of mind became, unknown to himself, a shield to save his life. A less humble, a less noble man, might very well, in David's place, have given loose reins to his imagination and his ambition, and let himself dream about the king's daughter. The more so, that, after the coarse custom of the time, Saul had promised his daughter to the man who should rid him of Goliath. And David had done that. But it had never entered David's fondest dreams that King Saul should fulfill his proclamation to an obscure man like him. Nay; even when Saul thought he saw a way of getting David killed in connection with his marriage, David scorned the proposal of the plotters. They might think as meanly of Saul and Saul's house as they chose; but let them not so speak to the king's armor-bearer. "Seemeth it to you a light thing to be a king's son-in-law, seeing that I am but a poor man, and lightly esteemed!" David has not forgotten his father's house. David has more place and honor already than he knows how to bear. He would lay it all down and return to the sheepfolds of his youth if he only could. Whatever he may be to those foolish women, David is no hero to himself. To himself he is still the youngest son of Jesse the Bethlehemite. Well may Solomon say, looking back with a son's pride to his father's character and career, By humility and the fear of the Lord are riches, and honor, and life.

It is to David's lasting honor also that the land of Israel was not plunged into all the horrors of civil war. His men were increasing in numbers every day, and their extraordinary devotion to David, added to the rankling of their own wrongs, made them ready for anything. David's self-restraint was the one thing that stood between Saul and the loss of his throne and the loss of his life. It happened one day about that time that David and his outlawed men were hiding in a cave among the rocks of the wild goats, when, as Providence would have it, Saul, who was pursuing David, came up to that very cave to sleep. Now is David's opportunity. The Lord, said David's men, hath today delivered your enemy into your hand. David drew his sword and stepped down to where the sleeping king lay, and cut off the skirt of Saul's garment, and withdrew again into the darkness. His men wondered why he had not brought the king's head in his hand instead of the lappet of his robe. When Saul rose from his sleep and left the cave, David went to the mouth of the cave and called out, My lord, the king! Think of Saul's feelings when he looked up and saw David, whom he was hunting to death, standing on the spot where he had just risen from sleep, and standing with his sword in one hand and the skirt of Saul's robe in the other. When Saul looked up, David stooped with his face to the earth, and bowed himself. And David said to Saul, Wherefore hearest thou men's words against me? See the skirt of thy robe in my hand, and know that though some bade me kill thee, mine eye spared thee; for I said, I will not put forth mine hand against my lord, for he is the Lord's anointed. Is this thy voice, David? exclaimed Saul. My son David, thou art more righteous than I; for thou hast rewarded me good, whereas I have rewarded thee evil!

In the court, in the camp, in the caves of Engedi and Adullam, on the throne, in the sanctuary—all hearts, good and bad, fly open in David's presence. Like his New Testament Son, David's life, in its way, was the light of men. We see all the men and women of David's day in the light of David. All who come near David, ever after their hearts are naked and open to us. Saul, Jonathan, Merab, Michal, Nabal, Abigail, Abner, Joab, Uriah, Nathan, Shimei, Absalom, Solomon—we see them all in the light of David's blazing presence among them. There are some men who shut up every heart that comes near them. They chill, and cramp, and shut up every heart. But David warmed, and enlarged, and enriched, and lighted up, for good or for evil, every heart that came into his generation. Even Saul is no longer obscure after David enters Saul's court. It was David's heart. It was his talents; it was his character; it was his virtues; sometimes it was his vices; but it was always his heart. It was his heart; it was his love; it was his magnificent and unparalleled power of sympathy. It was the divine nature in David: it was Jesus Christ in David long before Jesus Christ came. Bring my soul out of prison, sang David in one of his most solitary and forsaken psalms. Bring my soul out of prison, that I may praise Thy name. The righteous shall compass me about; for Thou shalt deal bountifully with me. How well that prayer and hope was fulfilled in Israel: and how well it is fulfilled still among ourselves let David's psalms testify. Look how the righteous everywhere compass about David the sweet psalmist of Israel. Arise, anoint him: for this is he.

36

David — In His Vices

BUTLER has a sermon on self-deceit which you should all read till you have it by heart. If you will listen to him, Butler will prove to you and will convince you that self-deceit, or internal hypocrisy, as he sometimes calls it, is the greatest of all your guilt, and is, in addition, the corruption of your whole moral character. He will show you also, in a way that will startle you, that David was guilty of this worst of all sins beyond any other saint or sinner in all the Bible. In Butler's sober, but most convincing and most solemnizing words, David's is the most prodigious instance of the very wickedest and the very deadliest of all the vices of the vicious heart of man. All David's other vices were but skin wounds and surface sores that might soon have been bound up; at their worst, to borrow David's own words about them, they were but so many broken bones. But David's self-deceit was deep-seated, and it would have been deadly to David but for Nathan, or, rather, but for the LORD. As for David's fall, let it not be once named among you, as becometh saints. But, past speaking about as David's fall was, it was what followed his fall that so displeased the Lord. In the words of Butler's latest editor, "it is safer to be wicked in the ordinary way than from this corruption lying at the root." As Thomas Goodwin points out in his great treatise on the *Aggravation of Sin*, it was the "matter of Uriah," even more than the matter of Bathsheba, that awakened the anger of the Lord against David. That is to say, it was David's sin of deliberation and determination, rather than his sin of sudden and intoxicating passion. It was both matters; it was both sins; but it cannot be overlooked that it was after a twelve-month of self-deceit, internal hypocrisy, and self-forgiving silence on David's part that Nathan was sent to David in such divine indignation. How a man like David could have lived all that time soaked to the eyes in adultery and murder and not go mad is simply inconceivable. That is to say, it would be inconceivable if we had not ourselves out of which to parallel and illustrate David, and thus to make David both possible and natural to us. Before you begin to read and think; as long as you confine your reading and thinking to the reading and thinking of children and fools, you will think it impossible that all the self-deceit-fullness and internal hypocrisy that could possibly be in David and in the devil taken together, could have so blinded David to the blackness of his sin, and to the absolute certainty of God's dreadful judgments. But when you become a man in the books you read, and in the matters of your own heart; and especially in the superlative deceitful-ness and desperate wickedness of your own heart, you will stop all your childish exclamations over David, and will say to yourself, I myself am David; I myself am that self-deceiving man. "What the particular circumstances were with which David extenuated his crimes, and quieted and deceived himself, is not related." No. They are not related; but we may guess at some of them to our own self-discovery and self-advantage. David would say to himself such things as these: "I am the

king, and Uriah and his wife are both my servants. All that he has is mine. She is
not for such as he. She should be a queen, and she shall be. And I can make it up to
him, and I will." And then, after that, there was Uriah's disobedience and insolence
to his king; his open disloyalty and his boasted indifference to his king's discovery
and disgrace. "Yes, the sword devoureth one as well as another," David would say.
"And it might have devoured Uriah even if I had not written that letter." And then,
to repay, and repair, and cover it all up, David fetched the woman to his house,
and she became his wife, and bare him a son. And, besides all that, it was all past:
and why go back upon the past? David, you may be sure, had all these, and many
more than all these, "distinctions to fence with." And then, what was wanting in all
that, himself came in to complete and carry off the case; self, "the most disingenu-
ous and abominable principle that ever was." Self, that utterly ungodly, diabolical,
inhuman, inconceivably wicked, and detestable thing that was so strong in David
and is so strong in you and in me. He who watches the workings of self in his own
mind and heart he will not be forward to throw a stone at David: he will not be
surprised at anything he reads about David or any other man. He will not wonder
either at David's fall or at his subsequent self-deceit. I can fully, and down to the
bottom, study the curse and shame and pain of self in no other heart but in my
own; not even in David's heart. And I am warned of God that, with all my study
and all my watchfulness and all my prayerfulness, the deceitfulness and the internal hypocrisy of my own heart will still deceive me. Well, all I shall say in answer to
that is this, that if my heart is worse than I know it to be, then the God of all grace,
with all the blood of His Son, and with all the patience and power of His Spirit,
help me! Me, and all men like me; if there is another man like me in this matter on
earth or in hell. My brethren, beware how you shield yourself from yourself, and
use "distinctions" when you are conversing with your conscience about yourself.
To be pointed at, and told to his face that he was unclean, and cruel, and cowardly,
and guilty of blood, was David's salvation. And to have some one injured enough
and angry enough; or friendly and honest and kind enough, to call you to your
face false, or cruel, or envious, or malicious, or hard-hearted, or ignorant and
narrow-minded and full of prejudice and party-spirit, or sycophantic to the great,
and supercilious and harsh to the poor, or all that together, might be the beginning of your salvation. And would he then be your enemy who first told you that
saving truth? Surely you will not think it. Let the righteous smite me, and it shall
be a kindness. Let him reprove me, and it shall be an excellent oil that shall not
break my head. But, far best of all, let my conscience smite me, and about my self-
love and my self-deceit in me.

Butler points out at the same time that, portentous as David's internal hypocrisy and self-deceit was, it was all the time local and limited in David. That is to
say, his self-deceit had not as yet spread over and corrupted his whole life and
character. There was real honesty in David all this self-deceiving time. David gave
scope, in Butler's words, to his affections of compassion and goodwill, as well as to
his passions of another kind. And, while this is some comfort to us to hear, there
is a great danger to us in this direction also. The whited sepulchres fasted twice in
the week, and they gave tithes of all that they possessed. They made broad their

phylacteries, and made long prayers, and were always to be seen in the synagogues, with their mint and anise and cumin. They made clean, no men made so clean, the outside of the cup and platter. Many of them had begun, like David, with only one thing wrong in their life; but it was a thing that they hushed up in their own consciences, till by that time the self-deceit was spreading and was well-nigh covering with death and damnation their whole life and character. David was rescued from that appalling end; but he was fast on the way to that end when the Lord arrested him. David all the time was administering justice and judgment as boldly, and with as much anger at evil-doers, as if there had never been a man of the name of Uriah on the face of the earth. And just because he was making men who had no pity restore the lamb fourfold; just because of that he was more and more confirmed in his own self-deceit. We would need Nathan and his parable at this point. Only, your self-deceit would make you miss his point, till he drove it home into your deceitful heart. You are the man. You are all the more severe with one class of sinners that you sin yourself so much with another and opposite class. You are terrible to see and hear on the sins of the flesh, because you are up to the eyes in the far more fatal sins of the mind. You despise and detest publicans and sinners, while you dine and sup and plot against Christ with Pharisees and internal hypocrites. We all turn away our eyes and our ears from parables like that. Yes, but Butler warns us that it is as easy to close the eyes of the mind as those of the body, as, also, that though a man has the best eyes in the world, he cannot see in any direction but in that to which he turns his eyes. Let the man, then, who would discover his own self-deceit, if there is one such here, let him turn his eyes in upon his own heart, and especially let him turn his eyes in the opposite direction in his own heart to that in which his easy and untempted virtue displays itself.

But so bold, and towering, and self-deceived is our self-deceit, that it invades and entrenches itself, not in the matters of morals only; it comes to its fullness and to a positive grandeur in our devotions; in our daily dealings with God Himself. Nothing can be more open and notorious than the self-deceit and utter hypocrisy of our psalms and our prayers. David says, and he says it, no doubt, from his own devotional experience, that if he regards iniquity in his heart, the Lord will not hear him. How much less would the Lord have heard him if he had carried out his iniquity openly, and had put all the deepest deceit of his heart into his psalms and his prayers, as we do. I do not read that David composed any penitential psalms during those self-deceiving twelve months. And yet there is no saying. There is no limit to the sacrilege and profanity of an internal hypocrisy. Be that as it may, if David did not, we do. What could be more self-deceitful than our public worship in this house? Stop and think over the next psalm that is given out, and say if you have forehead enough to sing it after you understand it. And, whether you do that or no, let any man venture to accept your psalm as sincere, and attempt to deal with you accordingly, and you will open his eyes. Let him venture with a counsel, or a correction, or a warning, or a reproof, and he will not take you at your word in the church or in the prayer-meeting again. Woe to the man who believes that you are in earnest as you prostrate yourself before God and man in your psalms and prayers. You will soon undeceive him if he thinks that you are broken and contrite in heart, or meek and lowly in heart, or that you lack wisdom, love the cross, wait for light, and are the little children of the kingdom of heaven. "Julius goes to prayers, he confesses himself to be a miserable sinner, he accuses himself to God with all the aggravations that can be, as having no health in him; yet Julius cannot bear to be informed of any imperfection, or suspected to be wanting in any degree of virtue. Now, can there be stronger proof that Julius is wanting in the sincerity of his devotions? Is not this a plain sign that his confessions to God are only words of course, an humble civility of speech to his Maker, in which his heart has no share? If a man was to confess that his eyes were bad, his hands weak, his feet feeble, and his body helpless, he would not be angry with those that supposed he was not in perfect strength, or that he might stand in need of some assistance. Yet Julius confesses himself to be in great weakness, corruption, disorder, and infirmity, and yet is angry at any one that does but suppose his defection in any virtue. Is it not the same thing as if he had said, You must not imagine that I am in earnest in my devotion?"

He was a happy preacher whose pulpit awakened David and brought David back to God. Nathan took his life in his hand that day. But he had his reward. And what a reward it was! Think of having David's soul set down to your account at the great day! What shall we ourselves owe to Nathan at that day for that sermon? We would never have had David's psalms but for Nathan's sermon. And what should we have done, I cannot conceive, without David's psalms. Preaching is magnificent work if only we could get preachers like Nathan. If our preachers had only something of Nathan's courage, skill, serpent-like wisdom, and evangelical instancy. But even Nathan himself would be helpless with some of you. You would have turned upon Nathan; you would have taken his good name and his life; you would have written a letter about him to Joab at Rabbah. Brutus never read a book but to make himself a better man. When will that be said about your coming to church? Happy the preacher who has so much as one Brutus a Sabbath day among his hearers! Happy the preacher who has a David among his hearers from time to time, so that he can pass on and say to him, The Lord also hath put away thy sin! We ministers must far more study Nathan's method; especially when we are sent to preach awakening sermons. Too much skill cannot be expended in laying down our approaches to the consciences of our people. Nathan's sword was within an inch of David's conscience before David knew that Nathan had a sword. One sudden thrust, and the king was at Nathan's feet. What a rebuke of our slovenly, unskillful, blundering work! When we go back to Nathan and David, we forget and forgive everything that had been evil in David. The only thing wanting to make that day in David's life perfect was that Nathan should have had to come to David. Now, what will make this the most perfect day in all your life will be this, if you will save the Lord and His prophet all that trouble, so to speak, and be both the Lord and His prophet to yourself. Read Nathan's parable to yourself till you say, I am the man! And so ever after with every parable, and with every psalm, and with every prayer, and with everything of that kind. When we preach anything of that kind, all the time we are preaching, be you fast kindling your own anger against yourself. And as soon as we are done preaching, speak you out in yourself and at yourself, and say, As the Lord liveth, the man that hath done this thing shall surely die. And he shall restore the lamb fourfold, because he did this thing, and because he had no pity. And, always, when the thirty-second psalm is announced to be sung, and when innocent men and women and children are getting their instruments of music ready, be you getting yourself ready till you cannot wait for them. Blessed is the man!—lead the congregation, and sing. And, when, by a happy inspiration the fifty-first psalm is again given out, do you ejaculate up to David's God your daily thankfulness that there is such a psalm in existence. For it is new to you every morning and every night. Just hear a verse of it, and say if it is not. "Behold, Thou desirest truth in the inward parts; and in the hidden part Thou shalt make me to know wisdom. Create in me a clean heart, O God, and renew a right spirit within me. Cast me not away from Thy presence, and take not Thy Holy Spirit from me." "I conceal nothing," sobbed out Bishop Lancelot Andrewes every Lord's Day morning before he could face his congregation and his clergy. "I make no excuses. I denounce against myself my sins. Indeed, I have sinned against the Lord, and thus and thus have I done. O Lord, I have destroyed myself. And Thou art just in all that has come upon me. I acknowledge my transgressions, and my sin is ever before me. I abhor and bruise myself that my penitence, Lord, O Lord, is not deeper. Help Thou mine impenitence, and more, and still more, pierce Thou, rend, and crush my heart. Magnify Thy mercies toward the chief of sinners, and say to me, Thy sins are forgiven thee. Say, O God, unto my soul, I am thy salvation!"

And, then, David's "way of lying." Did any of you ever suppress and keep silent about your principles, say, at an election time? Did you ever hedge and double in your public life in order to get a post, or in order to stand well with those who have posts and pieces of bread to give away? Did you ever tune a speech or a sermon or a prayer to turn away the anger of a man whose anger you feared, or with an eye to a man you wished to stand well with? Or, did you ever "tell a vain lie upon yourself," ascribing something falsely or exaggeratingly to yourself through vanity or other self-interest? And, alongside of that, when and where did you last put forward, or allow another to put forward, a detracting word about your friend or about your rival, and hold back what you felt would be for his advantage? Then, the story of David and the priest of Nob is, in that case, written for your learning. You will see in that chapter how David obtained hallowed bread of Ahimelech, and what that bread cost Ahimelech and his house. "Remove from me the way of lying, and grant me Thy law graciously. He points to the sore of his guileful heart," says Goodwin, "wherein his grief lay. David, among other corruptions, had a lying spirit sometimes."

Or, again, were you ever driven to simulate sickness, or even madness, in order to get out of some dreadful crime or scrape you had fallen into? See, then, God's compassion for you at David's cost, in His having had that so humiliating chapter put into your Bible. What a state of mind must David have been in that day when the servants of King Achish led David like a madman or a wild beast to the borders of their land, and then let him loose, as you would let loose and hound out a madman or a wild beast you were terrified at! O what a bottomless mystery and misery and agony of sin and shame the heart of man is, and most of all the heart of a man after God's own heart! From the same fountain will spring forth, on sufficient temptation and opportunity, the noblest deeds, and the most debasing and despicable. Had it not been in the Bible, we would have denounced that chapter as the cruelest, the most blasphemous, and the most utterly impossible slander. And, then, to have two splendid psalms as the immediate outcome of that sickening chapter! Truly they would need to be men in understanding, and not children, who read the Bible. For,

> Not in their brightness, but their earthly stains,
> Are the true seed vouchsafed to earthly eyes,
> And saints are lowered that the world may rise.

37
David — In His Graces

DR. THOMAS GOODWIN says that David's youthful virtues differed from his old-age graces somewhat as wild marjoram differs from sweet. Now, the wild marjoram is little better to begin with than a useless wandering weed; whereas the sweet is a planted, a protected, and a most precious herb. Your meekness, and your humility, and your industry, and so on, proceeds the incomparable Puritan preacher, must spring up, not only out of your constitution and your temperament; it must spring up out of your heart, as your heart is more and more softened, and tamed, and humbled, and sweetened by the grace of God and by the indwelling Spirit of Christ. Many a man, the sometime President of Magdalene is continually warning us, may live and die a model and a praise of "civil virtues," who never all his days comes within sight of the first principles of gospel holiness. At the same time, marjoram is marjoram, whether it is found running wild on the sides of the hills, or is watched over, and weeded, and watered, and gathered till it makes our whole house full of sweetness and health with its odorous fragrance. And teachableness, and meekness, and gentleness, and submissiveness, and thankfulness, and suchlike, are what they are, even before they are engrafted on Him who is the true and original root both of our wild and fast-fading flowers, as well as of our most fragrant and most fruitful herbs.

I would fain begin David's shining graces by saying that faith in God is the true and real and living root of them all. I would fain begin with David's faith, were it not that there is no word in all our tongue that carries less meaning and less vision to most people's minds and hearts than just this so frequent sound—faith. As Pascal says, We all believe in that dead word God; but there is only one here and another there who really and truly believes in the living, ever-present, and all-present God. But this is David's shining distinction above all God's saints— unless there are two or three in the New Testament who equal and excel David. In his pure, courageous, noble youth; all through his hunted-down days; fallen and broken and full of the pains of hell; filling up his dreary gift of years—David is always the same unconquered miracle of faith in God. Take and read and hear what David says to the Philistine giant about God, and you will see somewhat of his youthful faith in God. Then pass on to far on in his life, and open the hundred and thirty-ninth psalm; and I am safe to say that David, the author of that psalm, and Jesus of Nazareth, whom I may call the finisher of it, have been the only two saints and sons of God on the face of this earth who have ever taken up, understood, and imaginatively and unceasingly employed in their prayers that great believing psalm. And therefore it has been that they are the only two, father and son, to whom a voice came from heaven saying, Thou art a man after Mine own heart, and, This is My beloved Son, in whom I am well pleased. Jesus Christ was out of sight the greatest and the best believer this earth has ever seen. But the

best of it is that He was beholden to David's psalms of faith, and trust, and resignation, and assurance to support and to give utterance to His faith in His Father.
The psalms of David, says Isaac Williams, were our Lord's constant prayer-book.
When, therefore, you begin to ask after and to enter on the life of faith, open and
read David's life and David's psalms, comparing them together; and then pass
on to Jesus Christ, and then to the Apostle Paul. "Faith is the modestest of all the
graces," says the princely preacher I began with, "and, at the same time, it is the
most masterful. Wherever true faith is, it frameth the heart to the most childlike
and friendlike dispositions towards God. Faith, my brethren, is a passion; it is a
strong and a commanding instinct of our hearts after Christ, and after mystical
union with Christ, so that we cannot be at peace and satisfied without Him."

But, who is that roaring all the day long on the murderous wheel? Who is that
stretched and stretched again on the rack all night till all his bones are out of
joint—out of joint and broken in pieces with the hammer and the anger of God?
The voice of whose roaring is that—According to the multitude of Thy tender
mercies blot out my transgressions? And that—For I acknowledge my transgressions, and my sin is ever before me? Do you ask who that is? Do you not know?
That is the prodigal son of the Old Testament. That is the same man who sometime
went out against the giant, and against the bear, and against the lion in the name and
in the strength of God. That is the anointed of the Lord. That is the King of Israel.
That is the man after God's own heart. And he lies roaring on the rack—

> Thus on us to impress
> The portent of a blood-stained holiness.

For, holiness it still is; a true, a great, and an ever-growing holiness, though a holiness ever after to be stained with blood; but, also, to the end to be washed whiter
than the snow in better blood. And a holiness, too, with a height, and a depth, and
a fire, and an inwardness, and a solemnity, and a farsounding psalmody in it, all
of which would seem scarcely to be attainable in this life unless under the stain of
blood, or of something that stains still worse than blood. Dreadful sin! that can
only be propitiated by blood, and then washed off heart and life by blood upon
blood! Dreadful holiness! that can only be attained through tears and blood! But,
blessed holiness that is still attainable by us all at that, or at any other price possible
to be paid by God or man! As David's holiness was, and as all their holiness is, to
whom David is set forth as a portent, and at the same time as an encouragement.

I was always exceedingly pleased with that saying of Chrysostom, says Calvin,
"The foundation of our philosophy is humility." And yet more pleased with that
of Augustine: "As," says he, "the rhetorician being asked what was the first thing
in the rules of eloquence, he answered, Delivery. What was the second? Delivery.
What was the third? still he answered, Delivery. So if you ask me concerning the
graces of the Christian character, I would answer firstly, secondly, and thirdly, and
for ever, Humility." And thus it is that God sets open His school for teaching us
humility every day. Humility is the grace of graces for us sinners to learn. There
is nothing again like it, and we must have a continual training and exercise in it.
You learn to pronounce by your patrons complaining that they cannot hear you,

and that they must carry their cases to another advocate unless you learn to speak better. And, as you must either please your patrons or die of starvation, you put pebbles in your mouth and you go out to recite to yourself by the river-side till your rhetoric is fit for a Greek judge and jury to sit and hear. And so with humility, which is harder to learn than the best Greek accent. You must go to all the schools, and put yourself under all the disciplines that the great experts practice, if you would put on true humility. And the schools of God to which He puts His great saints are such as these. You will be set second to other men every day. Other men will be put over your head every day. Rude men will ride roughshod over your head every day. God will set his rudest men, of whom He has whole armies, upon you every day to judge you, and to find fault with you, and to correct you, and to blame you, and to take their business away from you to a better—to a better than you can ever be with the best pebbles that ever river rolled. Ay, He will take you in hand Himself, and He will set you and will keep you in a low place. He will set your sins in battle-array before your face. He will exact silence, and your mouth in the dust, and a rope on your head, and your heart a pool of tears, long after you had thought that you were to be set in a wealthy place. But let me say David at once. For it is David who rises before me as I speak of injuries, and insults, and detractions, and depreciations, and threats, and yet sorer, and yet severer and more immediate handlings by God Himself. David might have put Joab, and Shimei, and all the rest of his tutors and governors, in the front of the battle as he put Uriah; but he could not cast a piece of a millstone on his Maker from the walls of Rabbah, and he would not now if he could. And no more will he seek to silence a single one of his many reminders and accusers; no, not the most malignant, insolent, and unceasing of them all.

Once let David, or any other man, begin to taste the heavenly sweetness of true humility over against pride, and over against rebellion, and over against retaliation, and he will become positively enamored and intoxicated with his humiliations. What once was death and hell to him will now be life and peace and salvation to him. What at one time he had almost committed murder to cover up, he will now hearken for from every housetop. When I was a child I used every Sabbath-day to read David's challenge to the giant, and I thought I was sanctifying the Sabbath over that Scripture. But for many years now, and more and more of late years, my Bible opens of itself to me at the place where Shimei casts stones and dirt at David, till David says, So let him curse, because the Lord hath said to him, Curse David. My children still read Goliath on Sabbath evenings, but I am on the watch to see how soon I can safely introduce them to Shimei. Shimei is the man for me and mine! Only, may I endure my schoolmaster to the bitter end better than even David did. Let me take insults, and injuries, and slights, and slings from men, and God's hand itself, as David that day took Shimei's curses. Nay, things that would seem to you to have nothing in the world to do either with my past sins or with my present sinfulness—let me have David's holy instinct, let me lay down David's holy rule, to look at everything of that kind that comes to me as so many divine calls and divinely opened doors to a deeper humility. Graces also grow by what they feed on; and humility grows by deliberately dieting itself on such humiliations as these, both human and divine. And evangelical humility grows by being fed, and by feeding itself on evangelical humiliations. If any one has the steadiness of eye and the strength of head, and the spiritual ambition and enterprise, to penetrate into this region of things, he will find a field rich in these and in many suchlike spiritual blessings in Jonathan Edwards's *Religious Affections*. I shall close up this grace of David by this specimen of mighty Edwards: "Evangelical humiliation is the sense that a Christian man has of his own utter despicableness and odiousness, with an always answerable frame of heart. This humiliation is peculiar to true saints, for it is always accompanied with a sight of the transcendent beauty of divine things. And then, God's true saints all see, more or less, their own odiousness on account of sin, and the exceedingly hateful nature of all sin. Evangelical humiliation consists in a mean esteem of ourselves, as in ourselves nothing, and altogether contemptible and odious. This, indeed," Edwards goes so far as to say, "is the greatest and the most essential thing in all true religion."

"The gray-haired saint may fail at last"; and the last sight we see of David is his deathbed shipwreck on that very same sunken rock he had steered past so often in the stormy voyage of his life. On his deathbed, David failed in that very grace which had been such a strength and such an ornament to his character on till now, and such a pride and such a boast to us. But the truth is, the only saint whose path has ever been as the shining light was not David, but David's far-off Son. And it was exactly where David so sadly struck and sank that his divine Son touched and attained to the top of His obedience, and gave to Himself the finishing touch of His full sanctification. Father, forgive them, He said, and gave up the ghost. I do not know that of all the bad blood of which all our hearts are full there is any that lasts longer than anger, and resentment, and ill-will at our enemies, at our detractors, and at those who despise and deride us. It is only the cold, firm fingers of death that will squeeze the last dregs of that worst of all bad blood out of our hearts. We would draw the curtains of David's deathbed if we dared. But we dare not, and we would not if we could. For, after all, David is not our surety. David is not our righteousness. David did not die the just for the unjust. Nor at his very youngest and best is David set forward as an example to the disciples of Jesus Christ. David at his best, as at his worst, is one of ourselves. David is a man of like passions with ourselves. David was cut out of the same web, and he was shaped out of the same substance as ourselves. He was a man of like passions with us, and, like our passions, his were sometimes at his heel, but more often at his throat. David held back his bad passions at Saul, and at Shimei, and at Joab, occasion after occasion, till we were almost worshipping David. But, all the time, and all unknown to us, they were there. Till, of all times and of all places in the world, David's banked-up passions burst out on his deathbed, that no flesh might glory in God's presence. But that, according as it is written, He that glorieth, let him glory in the Lord. And, like David, we sometimes master somewhat and smother down our passions of resentment and retaliation and ill-will. But with us as with David, at our best it is only a semblance and a surface of self-mastery. The bad blood is there still. And if it is not roaring in every vein as it used to do, the thick pestiferous dregs of it are all the more settled deep down in our hearts. Jeremiah is entirely right about us.

He is divinely and entirely right about us. He is divinely and entirely right about the resentment, and the hatred, and the ill-will of our hearts at all who have ever hindered us, or injured us, or detracted from us, or rebuked us, or refused to flatter us. Yes, we will put our mouth in the dust, and a rope upon our head; and, as at the day of judgment, we will tell the truth, and will say it in words which the Holy Ghost teacheth: Yes, we will say, my injured and resentful heart is desperately and deceivingly wicked. Desperately, and deceivingly, and down to death wicked. But no longer than that. No longer after death. After death we shall be done both with death and hell; and after death we shall awake in His likeness who died, not cursing Judas, and Annas, and Caiaphas, and Herod, and the soldier with the spear, but saying over them all with His last breath, Father, forgive them, for they know not what they do. For even hereunto were we called.

There is one thing, so far as I remember, that David never failed or came short in. "My honest scholar," says Isaac Walton, when he is giving his companion a lesson in making a line and in coloring a rod, "all this is told you to incline you to thankfulness; and, to incline you the more, let me tell you that though the prophet David was guilty of murder and adultery, and many others of the most deadly sins, yet he was said to be a man after God's own heart, because he abounded more and more with thankfulness than any other that is mentioned in Holy Scripture. As may appear in his book of Psalms, where there is such a commixture of his confessing of his sins and unworthiness, and such thankfulness for God's pardon and mercies as did make him to be accounted, and that by God Himself, to be a man after His own heart. And let us, in that, labor to be as like David as we can. Let us not forget to praise Him for the innocent mirth and pleasure we have met with since we met together." Would you know? asks William Law in his beautiful chapter on singing psalms—would you know who is the greatest saint in the world? Well, it is not he who prays most or fasts most; it is not he who gives most alms, or is most eminent for temperance, chastity, or justice; but it is he who is always thankful to God, who wills everything that God wills, and who receives everything as an instance of God's goodness, and has a heart always ready to praise God for His goodness. And then Law winds up with this, and I wish it would send you all to the golden works of that holiness-laden writer—Sometimes, he adds, imagine to yourselves that you saw holy David with his hands upon his harp, and his eyes fixed upon heaven, calling in transport upon all creation, sun and moon, light and darkness, day and night, men and angels, to join with his rapturous soul in praising the Lord of heaven. Dwell upon this imagination till you think you are singing with this divine musician; and let such a companion teach you to exalt your heart unto God every new morning in his thanksgiving psalms. Or make a morning psalm suitable to your own circumstance out of David's great thanksgiving psalms. You should take the finest and the selectest parts of David's finest and selectest psalms, and adding them together make them every morning more and more fit to express your own thankful hearts. And, till you have had time to compose a psalm exactly suitable to your own standing in grace, you might meantime sing this psalm of David every morning with a spiritual mind and a thankful heart:

Bless, O my soul, the Lord thy God,
   And not forgetful be
Of all His gracious benefits
   He hath bestow'd on thee.

For Thou art God that dost
   To me salvation send,
And I upon Thee all the day
   Expecting do attend.

38
David — In His Services

GOD is the only master with servants who accepts the intention for the action. God alone of all paymasters pays as good wages for the good intentions of His servants as He pays for their best performances. One of David's greatest and best services to God and man never went further than the good intention. But David was as much praised and as much paid for his good intention to build the temple as if he had lived to see the golden towers of God's house shining in the Sabbath sun. It will help on your salvation to lay it to heart that hell is paved with good intentions; and it will, at the same time, comfort every good and honest heart to be told that good intentions form some of the surest of stepping-stones to heaven. Think much about intentions. Give, and it shall be given you; good measure, pressed down, and shaken together, and running over, shall men give into your bosom. For with the same measure that you mete withal it shall be measured to you again. After which Bengel acutely annotates that it is by our hearts that we both mete out to others and have it meted out to ourselves. It would have gone hard with the poor widow if she had only had a farthing meted out to her in her Lord's judgment on her. But her Lord looked on her heart. And thus it is that she sits in heaven today among the queens who sit there on their thrones of gold, because she had such a queenly heart that day in the temple porch. Both from David's intended temple; from the poor widow's actual collection at the door of David's temple; and from Bengel's spiritual annotation let us learn this spiritual lesson, that our hearts are the measure both of our work and of our wages in the sight of God. You cannot build and repair all the churches and mission-houses and manses at home and abroad you would like to build and repair. You cannot endow all the chairs of sacred learning you would like. You cannot contribute to the sustentation and spread of the Christian ministry as you would like. You cannot visit and relieve all the fatherless and widows in their affliction as you would like. You cannot stop all the sources of sin and misery in this world as you would like. You cannot make the reading, or the religion, or the devotional life of your people what your heart is full of. You wish you could. So did David. David had magnificent dreams about the temple. He built the temple every night in his sleep. And had he been permitted he would not have slept with his fathers till he had dedicated a most magnifical house to the name of the Lord. But it stands in God's true and faithful word that it was all in David's heart.

And He who looks not so much on the action as on the intention, He saw in this also a man after His own heart. May all David's good intentions, and generous preparations be found in all our rich people; and may all the widow's love and goodwill be found in all our poor people. For the heart is the measure. And as we measure out good words, and good wishes, and good purposes, and good preparations, and good performances in our heart, so will it be measured back to us by Him who sees and weighs and measures the heart and nothing but the heart.

"Thou hast shed blood abundantly, and hast made great wars; thou shalt not build an house to My name, because thou hast shed much blood upon the earth in My sight. But, behold, a son shall be born to thee, and his name shall be Solomon, and he shall build an house for My name." When I first read that sentence of such terrible disappointment to David, I looked to see David all that night on his face on the earth. But I did not know David; I had not yet got into all the depths of David's deep heart. For, instead of refusing to rise up and eat bread with the elders of his house, David was never in a happier frame of mind than he was all that night. David not only said, "It is the Lord," but his heart broke forth in a psalm such that there is nothing nobler in his whole book of Psalms. David not only consented that it was both good, and right, and seemly, that hands like his should not touch a stone of the house of God; but, that his son should be chosen of God to build Him an house—that set David's heart on fire as never Old Testament heart was set on fire like David's heart. As we read the psalm that poured out of David's heart that chastised and disappointed day, David is a man after our own heart. A psalm of resignation, and self-sacrifice, and thanksgiving, and many other virtues and graces like that psalm, covers a multitude of David's sins. Then went David in, and sat before the Lord; and he said, Who am I, O Lord God, and what is my house, that Thou hast brought me hitherto? And this was yet a small thing in Thy sight, O Lord God; but Thou hast spoken also of Thy servant's house for a great while to come. And is this the manner of man, O Lord God? Would God we all had a heart like that! I have found David, my servant.

It makes it possible, and, more than possible, pleasant to a father to lie down and leave his work unfinished when he sees his son standing at his bedside ready to take up his father's unfinished work to finish it. Nay, I suppose a father who loved his son aright and enough would almost rather leave all his work and all his hope unfinished if he saw his son able and willing and chosen and called to take it up. This, no doubt, greatly helped David to resign his great hope of being spared to build the temple, that Solomon, his greatly-gifted, wise-hearted, pure, and noble-minded son was standing ready to take up and to carry out his father's long-intended task. Judging David that day by myself, David must have been a happy father and a thankful, as, indeed, the fine psalm he sang that day lets us see that he was. I myself would willingly lie down tonight and leave all my mismanaged and mangled life; all the mistakes and misfortunes and mishaps of my ministry; all the obstacles and offences I have been to so many of my people; all my wrong dividing of the word of truth; and all else that you know so well and sorrow so much over. I declare to you that I would lie down with a good will tonight and wrap my head out of sight in my winding-sheet, if I saw my son standing ready to take up and repair and redeem my lost life. I would say, Lord, now lettest Thou Thy unfaithful and unfruitful and offensive and injurious servant depart in pardon, since mine eyes have seen Thy salvation begun in my son. And if I saw all my sons preparing for the ministry of Christ in the Church of Christ I would die in a far greater triumph than David's death-bed could possibly be. Well, why not?

Come, my soul, thy suit prepare.—
Thou art coming to a king;
Large petitions with thee bring;
For His grace and power are such,
None can ever ask too much.

David did many other services, both intended and executed, both in the field, and on the throne, and in the house of God; but by far and away David's greatest service was his Psalms. The temple was built, and built again, and built again; but for two thousand years now not one stone of that so sacred and so stately structure has stood upon another. The very foundations of the temple have been razed out, sown with salt, and for ever lost. But the Psalms of David shine to this day with a greater splendor than on the day they were first sung. And long after the foundations of this whole earth shall have been plowed up and removed out of their place, David's Psalms will be sounding out for ever beside the song of Moses and the Lamb. "I have reared a monument of myself more lasting than brass." And time, which has ground to powder so many temples of marble and of brass, has only set a more shining seal to the poet's proud boast. But how poor was his boast, and how short-lived will be his best work beside David's immortal Psalms! What a service has David done, not knowing that he was doing it; and not to his own nation only, but to the whole Israel of God. And not to Israel only, but to the God of Israel, and to the Redeemer of Israel. "I have found David My servant, with My holy oil have I anointed him. I have exalted one chosen out of the people."

I have said that David did a great service to the Redeemer of Israel, and I intended to say it. When I think of that service, all the other services that David has done by his Psalms shine out in a far diviner glory. I bless David's name for the blessing my own soul gets out of his Psalms every day I live. But when I trace that blessing up to its true source, I find that true and grace-gushing source in Jesus of Nazareth, whom I see growing in grace every day as He goes about in Galilee with David's Psalms never out of His hands. Think, people of God, of the honor to David, higher far than all the thrones on earth and in heaven—the unparalleled and immortal honor of being able to teach Jesus Christ to sing and to pray. For, when the Holy Child said to Mary, Mother, teach Me to sing and to pray, what did Mary do, hiding all that in her heart, but put into her Child's hands David's golden Psalm beginning thus: The Lord is my Shepherd, I shall not want. And then, think of Him as He grew in wisdom, and in stature, and in strength of spirit beginning to discover Himself in this Psalm of David and in that. Think of the sweet start, the overpowering surprise, the solemnity, the rejoicing with trembling, the resignation, the triumph with which the growing Savior was led of the Spirit from Psalm to Psalm till He had searched out all David's Psalms in which David had prophesied and sung concerning his Messiah Son. See Jesus of Nazareth on His knees in the Sabbath synagogue with this place open before Him for the first time—Lo, I come; in the volume of the book it is written of Me, I delight to do Thy will, O My God; yea, Thy law is within my heart. And, having once begun to read and to think in that way you will go on till you come to the cross, where you will see and hear your dying Redeemer with one of David's Psalms on His lips when He can no longer hold it in His hands. And He said unto them, These are the words which I spake unto you while I was yet with you, that all things must be fulfilled which were written in the law of Moses, and in the prophets, and in the Psalms, concerning Me. And they said one to another, Did not our heart burn within us while He talked with us by the way, and while He opened to us the Scriptures?

O two disciples, on your way that same day to Emmaus, how I envy you your travelling Companion that day! My heart burns to think of your Divine Companion opening up to you David's Messianic Psalms that memorable day. And when I think also of the multitudes that no man can number to whom David's Psalms have been their constant song in the house of their pilgrimage; in the tabernacle as they fell for the first time hot from David's heart and harp; in the temple of Solomon his son with all the companies of singers and all their instruments of music; in the synagogues of the captivity; in the wilderness as the captives returned to the New Jerusalem; in the New Jerusalem every Sabbath-day and every feast-day; in the upper room, both before and after supper; in Paul's prison at Philippi; in the catacombs; in Christian churches past number; in religious houses all over Christendom at all hours of the day and the night; in deserts, in mountains, in dens and caves of the earth; in our churches; in our Sabbath-schools; in our families morning and evening; in our sickrooms; on our death-beds; and in the night-watches when the disciples of Christ watch and pray lest they enter into temptation. A service like all that is surely too much honor for any mortal man! Then David went in and sat before the Lord; and he said, Who am I, O Lord God? and what is my house? And is this the manner of man, O Lord God? And what can David say more unto thee! for Thou, Lord God, knowest thy servant.

Then, take David's knowledge of God, and his communion with God. There is nothing like it in the whole world again. There are many mysteries of godliness not yet revealed to us; but, to me, the mystery of David's knowledge of God and his communion with God is one of the most mysterious. Had Paul sung David's Psalms, and sent, now the twenty-third Psalm to the Philippians, and now the thirty-second and the hundred and thirtieth to the Romans, and now the forty-fifth and the seventy-second to the Colossians, and so on, I would not have wondered. I would wonder at nothing after the coming of Christ, and after His death and His ascension. But it baffles me to silence to see such Psalms as David's before the day of Christ. And I have never, with all my search, seen an intelligent attempt made to face that mystery.

No; David is scarcely second to the Man Jesus Christ Himself in this mystery of mysteries, the mystical communion of the soul of man with the Living God. Such knowledge is too wonderful for us; it is so high that we cannot attain to it. "O God, Thou art my God. Early will I seek Thee. My soul thirsteth for Thee; my flesh longeth for Thee in a dry and thirsty land where no water is; to see Thy power and Thy glory, so as I have seen Thee in the sanctuary. Because Thy loving-kindness is better than life, my lips shall praise Thee. My soul shall be satisfied as with marrow and fatness, and my mouth shall praise Thee with joyful lips when I remember Thee upon my bed, and meditate on Thee in the night watches. My soul followeth hard after Thee." That would not have stumbled me had I come on it in the heart of the seventeenth of John itself. To David in the sixty-second, and in its sister Psalms, there is only I AM and David himself, in all heaven and earth. Against Thee, Thee only, have I sinned, David says in another Psalm. And, "Thee, Thee only," is the sum and the substance, the marrow and the fatness, the beauty and the sweetness of all David's communion Psalms. To know God, and to be in constant communion with God, this is life to David; this is better than life; this is love; this is blessedness. Then, again, it is told of Luther in his "Table Talk," that being asked one day which were his favorite Psalms—Why, to be sure, he answered, Paul's four Psalms—"Blessed is the man whose transgressions are forgiven, whose sin is covered," "Have mercy upon me, O God," "Out of the depths," and "Enter not into judgment with Thy servant." Do you not see, he demanded, that all these Psalms tell us that forgiveness comes without the law and without works? Forgiveness and peace come to him that believeth. "That Thou mayest be feared." That dusts away all merit; that teaches us to uncover our heads before God and to confess that forgiveness is of His grace and not of our desert at all. "Even as David describeth the righteousness of the man unto whom God imputeth righteousness without works, saying, Blessed is that man." David knew it experimentally. It was Paul's privilege to know it both historically and experimentally, as we say, and then to set it forth doctrinally, as we say also. And it is our privilege to have it in all these three ways, if we love and value such things above all other love and value. Even David without Paul was not made perfect. Nor will we be without them both. "I have found David, My servant. And My mercy will I keep for him for evermore, and My covenant shall stand fast with him. My covenant will I not break, nor alter the thing that is gone out of My lips. Once have I sworn by My holiness that I will not lie unto David."

But, with all that, the half, and the best half for you, has not yet been told you. After all that, listen to this. He that hath ears to hear, let him give ear to this. "In that day he that is feeble in Jerusalem shall be as David, and the house of David shall be as God." Does Feeble-mind hear that? Then let him receive and rest on that. Let him wake up psaltery and harp at the hearing of that. And let all that is within him sing and play like David. Let him sing and play, and that with the mind and the heart and the spirit like David. Let him sing and play to God, and to God only, like David. Let him who is feeble in faith, and in repentance, and in holiness, and in communion with God, be much in the Psalms. Let the Psalms dwell richly in the feeblest among us, and the feeblest among us will yet be a man of more spiritual strength than David. Sing a heart-strengthening Psalm every morning, and a heart-cleansing and a heart-quieting Psalm every night. Seven times every remaining day of your earthly pilgrimage sing a Psalm. Let no place, and no conversation, and no occupation delude you out of your heart-refreshing Psalm. Fill the house of your pilgrimage with the sound of Psalms. Let the prisoners hear you. Let the angels hear you. Let God hear you. Let Him bow down His ear and hear you. And let Him say to His Son, and to His angels, and to His saints, over you and over your house, I have found a man after Mine own heart; with My holy oil have I anointed him.

39

Jonathan

JONATHAN was the eldest son of Saul, and he was thus the heir-apparent to the throne of Israel. The crown prince was a young man of great mental gifts, and he was endowed also with many most impressive moral qualities. Handsome and high-mettled, full of nerve and full of heart, Jonathan was the pride of the army and the darling of the common people. His comrades, for his beauty of person and for his swiftness of foot, were wont to call him The Gazelle. In all that, the heir-presumptive was the son of his royal father's early and best days. But the piety, the humility, the generosity, the absolutely Christ-like loyalty, tenderness, self-forgetfulness, and self-sacrifice of Jonathan—all that the son had drawn from some far higher source than from his fast-falling father Saul. But for his father's great and disastrous transgressions, Jonathan would soon have been the second king of Israel; second in succession to Saul, but second to no king that ever sat on a throne in those great qualities of mind and heart and character that give stability to a throne and add luster to a crown.

The first time that Jonathan and David ever saw one another was on the day when Goliath fell under David's sling. Jonathan had stood beside his father Saul, and had been a spectator of the never-to-be-forgotten scene. Brave and bold and practiced in war as Jonathan by that time was, with all that he had not been bold enough to face the gigantic braggart. But, with all the army, with both armies, he had been astounded to see a Bethlehemite stripling, fresh from his father's sheep, step out into the open space to face the champion of the opposing host. And when the five thousand shekels of brass rang on the open plain no voice shouted over David so soon or so long as the voice of Jonathan, the king's son. And when Saul sent for David and talked with him, Jonathan's heart went out to David, and the soul of Jonathan was knit to the soul of David, and Jonathan loved David as his own soul. And from that day on till the day when David sang his splendid elegy over Saul and over Jonathan his son, the mutual love of Jonathan and David is described all along in words of such warmth and such beauty that there is nothing like them in literature again, if we leave out the love of Christ.

"And it came to pass that the soul of Jonathan was knit to the soul of David." You knit things together that are of the same kind; things that are of the same substance, and fiber, and texture, and strength, and endurance. You knit a thread to a kindred thread. You knit a cord to a kindred cord. You knit a three-fold cord to a three-fold cord. You knit a chain of iron to a chain of iron; a chain of brass to a chain of brass; a chain of gold to a chain of gold; and a chain of gold of the same size, and strength, and purity, and beauty to a chain of gold of the same size, and strength, and purity, and beauty. Now Jonathan's soul was a chain of gold, of the same size, and strength, and purity, and beauty as David's soul. Jonathan, as being the elder man, had for long been looking and longing for a soul like

David's soul to which his own soul might be knit; and before the sun set that day the son of Saul had found in the son of Jesse a soul after his own soul, and he was at rest. Jonathan's soul was that day knit to another soul, if possible, still more tender, and pure, and pious, and noble, and loyal than his own; till Jonathan was the happiest man in all Israel that day. And that pattern of friendship, knit that day between Jonathan and David, has been the ensample and the seal of all true friendships among men ever since. It was a sweet fancy of Plato that at the great aboriginal creation of human souls they all came from the hand of the God of power, and wisdom, and love, and holiness twain in one. All human souls came into existence already knit together like the souls of Adam and Eve, like the souls of David and Jonathan, like the souls of Jesus and John, like the souls of Christ and His church. But Sin, the great sunderer and separater and scatterer of souls, came in and cleft asunder soul-consort from soul-consort till all our souls since the fall start this lonely life alone. And all the longings, and cravings, and yearnings, and hungerings, and thirstings, and faintings, and failings that fill the souls of men and women—it is all in search of that brother-soul, that sister-soul, that spousal-soul that we have all loved long since and lost a while. And every true comradeship, every true courtship, every true espousalship, every true married life is the divine recovery and reunion of twin-soul to twin-soul, as all human souls were in the great beginning, and will for ever be in God and in God's house of love and rest and satisfaction. And had Plato read Hebrew, how he would have hailed Jonathan and David as another example of two long-lost and disconsolate souls, finding rest in their primogenial, spousal, re-knit, and never-again-to-be-separated soul.

"And Jonathan loved David as his own soul." Had I read this for this once only, I would have passed over it as a permissible hyperbole in the sacred writer. But when I read again and again and again that Jonathan loved David as his own soul, till I come down to David's splendid hyperbolical elegy over the slaughter of Saul and Jonathan; and then, when I go back and read Jonathan's whole dealing with David in the light of that golden chain of hyperboles, I stop, and think, and say to myself that there must be much more here than stands on the surface. Till I find myself saying to this sacred writer, Lo, in all this speakest thou plainly, and speakest no hyperbole. Yes; happy, happy Jonathan! For it was not of thee that David spake in that bitter psalm. "Yea, mine own familiar friend," David said, but not of thee, "in whom I trusted, which did eat of my bread, hath lifted up his heel against me." Nor was it of thee in another still more bitter psalm, "But it was thou, a man mine equal, my guide, mine acquaintance. We took sweet counsel together, and walked unto the house of God in company. The words of his mouth were sweeter than butter, but war was in his heart; his words were softer than oil, yet were they drawn swords." No, happy Jonathan, it was not of thee. Nor was this of thee, "Thou didst speak peace to thy neighbor, while mischief was in thy heart." Nor this, "Thou didst bless with thy mouth, whilst thou didst curse inwardly." Thy tongue, saintly man, did not frame deceit. Thou didst not sit and speak against thy brother. Jeremiah never said of thee in the bitterness of his heart that he heard the defaming of many. Thou never saidest concerning the friendless prophet, Report, and I will report it. He excepted thee when he upbraided them all round, and said, All my familiars watch for my halting. Nor did David's Son after thou hadst kissed Him say to thee, Friend, wherefore art thou come? Nor did Hamlet ever say to thee, "O villain, villain, smiling, damned villain! My tables—meet it is I set it down, that one may smile, and smile, and be a villain." Thy sin never found thee out. Thou never knewest the plague of a villain's heart. Thou never criedst, Create in me a clean heart, O Lord! Isaiah said, but thou never needest to say, I am a man of unclean lips. Great Jonathan! Dear Jonathan! We kiss thy feet. Till thy great Antitype comes we shall see no man born of woman again like thee!

"Then Jonathan and David made a covenant because he loved him as his own soul." Jonathan's love was like the love of women in this, that it led Jonathan to leave his father's house behind him and to give his hand and his heart in a covenant to David. A woman cannot find rest but in the house of her husband. Knit as her heart is, and will for ever be, to her father and to her mother, yet there is a soul somewhere in God's hand to whom she was knit before she was born, and when God opens His hand twin-soul leaps out to meet twin-soul, and she is married in the Lord. Now, it was something like that. David, in the warmth of his heart and in the sharpness of his sorrow, said that the love of Jonathan to him was still more wonderful than that. No love can be more wonderful than the love of a woman when she loves in God; when the warmth, and the tenderness, and the faithfulness, and the endurance, and the self-sacrifice of nature is all deepened, and strengthened, and ennobled, and made everlasting in the transforming and transcending love of God. And it was because Jonathan's love had so much of a woman's love in it; and, added to that, so much of God's love, that David's rapture rose to such a sublime height over it. There was something in Jonathan's love that David had never met with in any of the women whose love he had ever been blessed with, Abigail's, or Michal's, or Solomon's mother's love, or any love his fathers had told him of in their days. And the surpassing love of Jonathan stood so alone because it stood so in God. Jonathan's heart had for long been full of God, and God is love. Under Samuel's ministry, Jonathan's heart had early been knit to God, and thus it was that his heart so knit itself round David's heart, in whom he found a man after God's own heart. And thus it was that father, and mother, and crown of Israel, and all, were counted loss to Jonathan as soon as he found David who had been so found of God. You will see the same thing to some extent in your own house every day. True religion, the knowledge and the love of God in your child's heart, will compel him to seek friends outside of your door if you are without the knowledge and the love of your son's God. How happy is that son who can love and honor and open all his heart to his father and mother in the Lord! But how unhappy if not! Jonathan loved Saul his father with a noble, devoted, loyal, and truly filial love. He followed his father's falling fortunes till father and son and all fell at last in the field. But all the time Saul had a son at his side whose deep and pure and holy heart he could neither understand, nor value, nor satisfy. Saul had begotten a son in Jonathan who was as much greater and better than himself as heaven is greater and better than earth; I might almost say than hell. Jonathan made a covenant with David, and with the house of David; and in making that covenant, and in the very terms of it, Jonathan, as we see in the Scriptures of it, spake less to David than he spake to David's God, the Lord God of Israel.

"And Jonathan stripped himself of the robe that was upon him, and gave it to David, and his garments, even to his sword, and to his bow, and to his girdle." A wife's marriage ring is the seal of her husband's covenant with her, and her covenant with him. The rainbow in heaven is the seal of God's covenant with Noah, and with the earth. The water is the seal of God's covenant in baptism; and the bread and the wine in the supper. And, in like manner, Jonathan's robe, and his garments, and his sword, and his bow, and his girdle, were the signs and the seals of Jonathan's covenant that he made that day with David. In the bread and in the wine, Christ and all the benefits of the new covenant are represented, sealed, and applied to believers. And in Jonathan's robe, and raiment, and sword, and bow, and girdle, the kingdom of Israel, and all its honor and power and glory, were represented and sealed to David by this extraordinary action of Jonathan. The son and heir of Saul stripped himself naked for the sake of his sworn friend. Jonathan was such a miraculous and sacramental friend to David, that he stripped himself bare in order to clothe, and adorn, and seal David to the throne of Israel. In his measure, and so far as was in his power, Jonathan did that day all that Jesus Christ did in the fullness of time. Jonathan was only the sinful son of a sinful father, whereas Jesus Christ was the Son of God. But nothing more is said even of the Son of God Himself in this respect, than that He stripped Himself bare for His enemies, and clothed them with His robe and with His diadem. Well, all that Jonathan does to David. Jonathan is a disciple of Jesus Christ, born out of due time. Jonathan is all but Jesus Christ Himself come already in the Old Testament. As Jonathan strips himself to the bone, you look at him doing it and you exclaim, How could he ever do it! My brethren, your amazed exclamation betrays you. It is natural to you, and it shows to all who hear you that you have not yet begun to strip yourself for friend or enemy. If you had, if you had once even begun so to strip yourself, you would not cry out in such astonishment how Jonathan could do it. If you knew it, how could he help doing it? How could he do anything else? How could he stop doing it, till it was all done? He could not. And neither can you when once you have begun to do it. For the first time you will taste what true life is when you strip yourself bare of your best robe to put it upon your rival: upon him who is coming up so fast to supplant you. And you will drink deeper and deeper of the fountain of life as you go on to strip off your sword, and your bow, and your girdle to put them upon him. Of such is the kingdom of heaven. To such, and to such only, will it be said, Come up hither. Such, and such only, are highly exalted at the last. Such, and such only as make themselves of no reputation now. If you do it as they did it, you will yet sit down beside Jesus Christ and Jonathan, but not otherwise. At no less price to you than to them. But at the same price to you as to them. And it is for this cause that you have a robe given you, and garments, and a sword, and a bow, and a girdle, and a rival, and a supplanter.

"And it was told Saul. And Saul sought David every day. And David saw that Saul was come out to seek his life. And David was in the wilderness of Ziph in a wood. And Jonathan, Saul's son, arose and went to David into the wood, and strengthened David's hand in God." There is a two-edged sword in the French tongue to this effect, that there is something in the misfortunes of our best friends that is not wholly displeasing to our secret hearts. But not to Jonathan's secret heart. Let every man defend himself from that sword of God as he is best able. Here is Jonathan's defence and shield, this: "And Saul's son arose and went to David in the wood, and strengthened his hand in God." That is Jonathan's shield against that sharp sword, and the hand of God in His own word holds it up over Jonathan. Be sure you see the full truth and the full beauty of that visit of Jonathan to the wood of Ziph. David was in danger of losing his faith in God. Which, if he had lost, he would have been the coming king of Israel, and Jonathan's rival, no longer. And Jonathan seeing that, came to the wood of Ziph to strengthen David in God lest his faith should fail. Was there ever a nobler deed done on the face of the earth till the Son of God came to do such deeds, and to show us all the way? If I had been Jonathan, I would have looked to David to strengthen me. I would have insisted that I needed the sympathy and the strength. It would have been a long time before I would have left my palace in Gibeah to go down to the wood of Ziph to strengthen the hand of my best friend, if that strength was to carry him over my head and put me under his feet. And Jonathan said to David, "Fear not, for thou shalt be king over Israel, and I shall be next unto thee."

Are any of you being sent at this moment to that school to which God sent Jonathan? Are humiliations, and disappointments, and losses, and defeats your tutors and governors? Then, take Jonathan's history home with you tonight to imitate it. Grudge not your neighbor his divinely ordained promotion or praise. But, rather, as you have opportunity, strengthen his hand in God. As many as I love, I rebuke and chasten, and humble, and put down, and make second. But to him that overcometh will I grant to sit with Me in My throne, even as I also overcame.

> He always wins who sides with God,
>   To him no chance is lost;
> God's will is sweetest to him when
>   It triumphs at his cost.

The cross of Christ was made of a tree that had grown in the wood of Ziph, and yours will be made of the same shining timber.

40
Nabal

WE see Nabal on two occasions only. On the occasion of the sheep-shearing ten days before his marriage, and then on the occasion of the sheep-shearing ten days before his death. Had David been in the wilderness of Paran at that sunny sheep-shearing immediately before Nabal's marriage, and had he asked for the crumbs that fell from the bridegroom's table, David would have been set in the place of honor at the smiling sheep-master's right hand. All that happy time when their master went out to the sheep-folds, he said to the sheep-shearers, The Lord be with you. And they answered him, The Lord bless thee. The-Joy-of-her-father—for that was the name of the sheep-master's beautiful bride—was also the joy of her bridegroom, till he sent two hundred loaves of bread, and two bottles of wine, and five sheep ready dressed, and five measures of parched corn, and an hundred clusters of raisins, and two hundred cakes of figs to Adullam, so that every one that was in distress, and every one that was in debt, and every one that was dis-contented, ate and drank and said, Let the God of Abraham and Sarah, and Isaac and Rebekah, and Jacob and Rachel be the God of that great man in Maon and Abigail his bride. "The Lord make the woman that is come into his house like Rachel, and like Leah, which two did build the house of Israel." And because of the blessing of all the poor and needy round about, and because of the beauty and the good understanding of Abigail, her husband was the happiest and the most open-handed man that day among all the men in Maon. And the man was very great, and he had three thousand sheep and a thousand goats, and he was shearing his sheep in Carmel.

The Bible has a way of its own of taking great leaps sometimes over long spaces of some men's lives. And thus it is that the next time we see Abigail's bridegroom we would not know him. And we are left of the sacred writer to compose the whole married life of Nabal and Abigail out of our own married lives. And the Bible, with great safety and great assurance, leaves us to do that. Because it knows that as face answers to face in water, so do betrothed, and married, and churlish lives in ancient Israel, answer to married and churlish lives among ourselves.

The second sheep-shearing scene is set before us in a chapter of great pictorial power. With quite extraordinary concentration and strength, Nabal and Abigail are made to stand out before us in their great pictorial chapter. Abigail is still a woman of a good understanding. But Matthew Henry says that her understanding was all little enough for her exercises in it, for the man was churlish and evil in his doings. Abigail to all appearances is the same woman she was at the first sheep-shearing, but her husband has sadly gone down. It was the season of the year when the most churlish of men were wont to melt for the moment into hospitality and self-enjoyment, and even Nabal held a feast in his house. David and his six hundred men were lying in exile in the adjoining wilderness. Persecuted and cast out as David and his men were, they never forgot that they were men of Israel; and up among the mountains, and out on the borders, they were a kind of volunteer protectors and patrolling police over the flocks and herds of men like Nabal. As a matter of fact, David had interposed again and again, and been a wall, as Nabal's shepherds themselves said, round them and their sheep against the sheep-stealing tribes. The starving exiles had looked for some reward for their work; but Nabal was Nabal. Till sheer famine made David send to Nabal's feast and ask a share of his hospitality to "thy son David," as he called himself in his courteous but bold message. But Nabal's softness of heart over his sheep-shearing was only skin-deep. "Who is David," Nabal snapped out, "that I should share my feast with him and his vagabonds?" And no sooner did David hear Nabal's churlish and insulting answer than he said, and it was all he said, "Gird ye on every man his sword." But, as good providence would have it, Abigail had heard both of David's embassy and of her husband's churlish answer, and she lost not a moment. Sending on before her a present of meat and drink, she hastened after it, and met David and his four hundred men just in time. How Abigail behaved herself before the insulted and revengeful soldiers; with what tact and understanding she spake to David; and how she melted David and turned away his hot anger—all that we read in the matter and the manner of this sacred writer. And, then, in two verses of crowning strength of style we have Nabal's drunken debauch all night, and his sudden death of fear and hate and hardness of heart in the morning.

"Nabal was of the house of Caleb." But there is a Latin proverb to this effect, that to be the son of a good father is the shame of a bad son. Now, Caleb was a good father. Caleb was a large-hearted, hopeful, God-serving man. And Caleb and his house held their large estates in the land of Israel on that tenure. The family property was a witness to their father's great services in a dark day in Israel. Caleb lived to a green old age, crowned with all the love and honor that Nabal had by this time wholly lost. By his birth Nabal had come into great possessions in Carmel; and, as if to make him a man like his father—as if to keep his heart soft and full of love to God and man—God had added to all that a wife who shines high up among the household saints of the house of Israel. But, all the time, Caleb and Abigail, great inheritance and great dowry, happy home, and all, there was a "stone of obstination" in Nabal's heart that nothing could melt or remove, till his whole heart was turned to stone and he died.

"Our master flew at David's messengers," reported the young man to Abigail. "He railed on them," as we excellently read it in the text. He snarled and snapped at them, as Josephus so graphically has it. You see the man. You know the man. Your young men know the man. Your wife knows the man. Your children know the man. "Who is David? And who is the son of Jesse? There be many servants nowadays that break away every man from his master." It is a glass, this chapter, in which we all see our churlish selves to the life. Who is he? we demand, with all the contempt and scorn we can call up out of our contemptuous and scornful hearts. Who is he to speak to me and to treat me in that way? And we go on to put the worst construction upon him, and upon his family, and upon his friends. A parcel of vagabonds! snarled out Nabal. And how much of our own speaking and writing about people we do not like is exactly like that churlish outbreak of Nabal. And what mischief Nabal's tongue and pen work among us also! Nothing roots our wicked hearts deeper into our whole life and character than a snarling tongue or a railing pen let loose. And nothing puts David and his men into a more wicked and murderous temper than to be railed at as Nabal railed. Do not do it. Do not listen to it. Do not read it. It is the death of your heart to speak it and to hear it. When you speak it your conversation is in hell; and when you write or read it, it is the literature of hell. It kindles hell in him who is railed at, and it spreads, and it feeds hell in him who writes it, or reads it, or speaks it. Nabal's railing tongue kindled such an outburst of murderous hate in David and in his men that, another half hour and it would have been put out in Nabal's blood.

"The man was churlish," says this shorthand writer, giving us Nabal's whole character in a single word. That is to say, Nabal had allowed and indulged himself in his snarling, snappish ways till he was known in his own house, among his shepherds, and all round about, as Nabal the churl. "A devil at home" is one of the sure marks of Thomas Shepard's "evangelical hypocrite. He shines like an angel in the church. Christ and mercy are never out of his mouth. He is much to be heard on closing with Christ. He is raised up to heaven with liberty and joy on Sabbath, and especially on communion days. But he is a devil at home." Whereas we find that "hyperbole of sin," Lancelot Andrewes, on his knees night and day, "to be kind to mine own." And you will remember that other portrait of the same family in John Bunyan. Obstinate also gave a great sheep-shearing feast before his marriage. And his bride also led her bridegroom to church and market in a silken bridle—for a time. But time passes, and there passes away with time all the hospitality, humility, pliability, and sweetness of the churlish and obstinate man. It is not that he has ceased to love his wife and his children. It is not that. But there is this in all genuine and inbred churlishness and obstinacy, that, after a time, it comes out worst beside those we love best. A man will be affable, accessible, entertaining, the best of company, and the very soul of it abroad, and, then, the instant he turns the latch-key in his own door, Nabal himself was not worse, he sinks back into such an utter boorishness, and mulishness, and doggedness. He swallows his meal in silence, and then he sits all night with a cloud on his brow. He is silent to no children but his own; he is a bear to nobody but his own wife. Nothing pleases him; nothing in his own house is to his mind. And all the time it is not that he does not pray to love his own, like Andrewes; but there is a law of obstinacy in his heart that still makes him a devil at home. And then hear Christiana: "That which troubleth me most is my churlish carriages to my husband when he was in his distress. I am that woman that was so hard-hearted. And so guilt took hold of my mind, and would have drawn me to the pond." Yes, constant fault-finding; constant correction, and that before strangers; gloomy looks; rough words and manners; all blame and no praise—with these things we are all driving one another to the brink of the pond every day.

"And it came to pass in the morning, when the wine was gone out of Nabal, and his wife had told him all these things, that his heart died within him, and he became as a stone." Nabal died of a stone in his heart. Nabal died of pride and rage. Nabal died of a strange disease—indebtedness to his wife. Nabal would rather have died of David's sword than have been saved from David's sword by the understanding and the interposition and the intercession of his wife. Nabal died rather than admit that he had played the fool through all that sheep-shearing time. Had Nabal kissed Abigail that morning; had he kissed her hand; had he kissed her feet; he would have been living to this day; and when he died like a shock of corn fully ripe, all Israel would have mourned that they had lost him, and David would have sung a psalm over him that we would have put upon the tombstones of all our magnanimous and much-lamented men. As it was, it became a proverb in Israel to ask when a madman, or a man possessed with a devil, or a man who took his own life, died, Died he as Nabal died? Take care, O churlish husband! Take care, O man with a heart of stone beginning in thy bosom. For Satan is fast entering into thee. Take care.

But, now, can such churlishness be cured? Can it really be cured? some of you who have that cruel stone for long spreading in your hearts will ask me. Yes, it can, if it is taken in time, and if it is treated in the right way. And the first thing in the cure is to admit and accept the disease. It is to say, I am Nabal. Had Nabal taken it to heart how it would end, as soon as he felt the tenderness, and the honorableness, and the nobleness, and the manliness of his betrothal and bridegroom days beginning to wear off his heart and his life; had he been man enough, and man of God enough, and husband enough to watch and know the stopping of his heart and the creeping-on coldness of his heart to God and man, and especially to Abigail; and had he confessed to himself his fears how all that would end, it would all have ended the entire opposite of how it did end. Had he been thankful also. Had he practiced himself in going back upon Caleb and the inheritance he had got because of Caleb; had he taken his flocks and his herds, and all that he had, every sheep-shearing time, again from the hand of God; had he every night and every morning taken Abigail in all her understanding and all her beauty again from the hand of God; and had he prevented David's petition and sent him a share of the sheep-shearing feast before he asked for it—by all that, Nabal would have made himself a new heart, and he would have come down to us in as good a report as any of the elders of Israel. Kick, then, the dog out of your heart. Hammer the stone out of your heart, and you will get back the days of your first sheep-shearing; you will get back your bride, and your own tender, hopeful, noble, manful heart. But the one, the only real and sure cure for all our New Testament Nabals is that supreme antidote and counter-poison to all churlishness, the cross of Christ. Whatever we start with, we always end with the cross of Christ. Try it, for it cures everything, and especially churlishness and all its bad effects. It cures churlishness in Nabal; and impatience, and weariness, and despair of life in Abigail; and anger and revenge in David. Come near to the cross, both Nabal, and David, and Abigail, and look and hear. Hear those churlish men as they pass by and wag their heads, and rail at David's Son cast out upon the cross from among men, while, all the time, He dies to save and bless them. Great Example! Great Refuge and Great Strength to us all! The Butt, the Jest, the Scoff, the Flout of all who pass by! We come to Thee. We need Thee. We have no cure for our hearts, and no pardon for our hearts but

Thee. Churls, and churls' victims, we come to Thee. Railing and railed at, we come to Thee. Nabal, and David, and Abigail, and the shepherds, and the soldiers, we all come to Thee. We hang by our hands and our feet and our hearts beside Thee. We forgive all those who revile us, and buffet us, and despitefully use us beside Thee. We die, and are buried, and rise again, and sit beside Thee. Finally, be ye all of one mind, having compassion one of another, love as brethren, be pitiful, be courteous. Not rendering evil for evil, or railing for railing, but contrariwise blessing; knowing that ye are thereunto called, that ye should inherit a blessing.

41
Michal, Saul's Daughter

NEVER, surely, were man and wife more unequally yoked together than was David, the man after God's own heart, with Michal, Saul's daughter. What was David's meat was Michal's poison. What was sweeter than honey to David was gall and wormwood to Michal. The things that had become dearer and dearer to David's heart every day, those were the very things that drove Michal absolutely mad; furiously and ungovernably mad that day on which the ark of God was brought up to the city of David.

It was the greatest day of David's life. And, sad to say, it was the very greatness of the day to David that made it such a day of death to Michal, Saul's daughter. Michal, Saul's daughter, died that day of a strange disease—a deep distaste at the things that were her husband's greatest delight. A deep distaste that had grown to be a deep dislike at David, till that deep distaste and settled dislike burst out that day into downright hatred and deliberate insult. You must understand all that the ark of God was to David, and the home-bringing of the ark, before you can fully understand the whole catastrophe of that day. It would take me till midnight to tell you all that was in David's heart as he sacrificed oxen and fatlings at six paces, and leaped and danced before the ark of God all the way up to the city of David. And, even then, you would need to be a kind of David yourself before you would look with right reverence and love at David that day. For David was beside himself that day. David never did anything by halves, and least of all his worship of God. It was like that day long afterwards in that same city when we read that His disciples remembered that it was written, The zeal of Thine house hath eaten Me up. With all his might, then—and you know something of what all David's might in such matters was—with all his might David leaped and danced before the Lord till Michal despised him in her heart.

Those who are deaf always despise those who dance. The deaf do not hear the music. And, on the other hand, those who do hear the music, they cannot understand those who can sit still. David could not understand how Michal could sit still that day. But Michal's ear had never been opened to the music of the ark. She had not been brought up to it, and it was not her custom to go up to the house of the Lord to sing and play like David. Had Michal been married in the Lord; had Michal reverenced her husband; had she cared to please her husband; had she played on the psaltery and harp sometimes, if only for his sake—what a happy wife Michal would have been, and David what a happy husband! Had her heart been right with her husband's heart when he blessed his household every night; had she been wont with all her heart to unite with her husband when he blessed them every night and sang psalms with them; had she sung with him and said, We will not go up into our bed till we have found out a place for the Lord, an habitation for the mighty God of Jacob: how well it would have been. Lo! sang

214

David alone with the handmaids of his servants, Lo! we heard of it at Ephratah; we found it in the fields of the wood. Arise, O Lord, into Thy rest; Thou and the ark of Thy strength. Had David not been so unequally yoked, Michal would have put on David's shoulder that day an ephod that she had worked for that day with her own hands; and as she put it on him she would have sung and said, I will clothe her priests with salvation, and her saints shall shout aloud for joy. And then all that day in Jerusalem it would have been as it was at the Red Sea when Miriam the prophetess took a timbrel in her hand, and all the women went after her with timbrels and with dances. But it was not so to be. For Michal sat at home that great day in Israel, and forsook her own mercy. Michal was not in the spirit of that day. And thus it was that she despised David in her heart when the very gates of brass and iron were lifting up their heads at David's psalm to let the King of Glory come in.

Not to speak of the past, had Michal done that day what any woman with any sense of decency left in her would have done—had she put on her royal garments and set out with David to the house of Obed-Edom, how differently for her and for David that day would have ended! For, once on the ground; once surrounded with the assembled people, the magnificent scene would have carried Michal away. The fast-dying ashes of her first love for David would have been blown up into all their former flame as she shared in the splendid salutation that David received from the assembled land. No ambitious woman, and least of all Saul's royal-hearted daughter, could have seen assembled Israel that day without being swept into sympathy with the scene. But Michal lost her last opportunity that morning. Michal did not overcome herself that morning. Her proud and unsympathetic temper got the better of her that morning, till David had to set out on the royal duties of that day alone. And as the day went on, Michal was left alone with a heart the most miserable in all Israel that day. And Michal's heart became harder and darker and fiercer as the day went on. Harder and darker and fiercer at David, and at all the ordinances and delights of that day. And then, when all Jerusalem rang with the ark just at her door, Michal stole to her shut window and saw nothing but David dancing before the Lord. At the despicable sight she spat at him, and sank back in her seat with all hell in her heart. You have had Michal's heart in yourselves, in your measure, on some Sabbath-day when you remained at home for some wrong reason, and when your husband came home with his face shining. And on other days, when you should have been at his side, but some distaste, some dislike, some pique, some catishness kept you at home to eat your heart all the time. And then the very high spirits of the party when they came home made your day end sufficiently like Michal's day. What a pity that David did not better prevail with Michal to accompany him to the fields of the wood that day!

The wife see that she reverence her husband, says the apostle. Yes; but even Paul himself would have allowed that it was impossible for Michal to reverence David all at once that day. Paul would have needed to have got Michal's ear early that morning when she tarried at home in the palace. Nay, he would have needed to have got her heart while she was yet Saul's daughter in Saul's palace. It is to tell a waterfall to flow uphill to tell Michal at this time of day to reverence David. Reverence does not come even at a divine command. Reverence does not spring up in a day. Reverence is the result of long teaching and long training. Reverence has its roots in the heart and in the character; and the heart and the character only come and bring forth reverence as life goes on. That may be all true, but the apostle does not say that. He does not say that any of the wives to whom he wrote were too late now to reverence their husbands. He speaks it to all wives, and he expects that all wives who hear it shall lay it to heart, and shall do it. And yet their husbands, their very best husbands, are in so many things so difficult, so impossible, to reverence. They fall so far short of their young wife's dreams and visions. They are so full of faults, and follies, and tempers, and habits to which no wife can possibly be blind. Most husbands are at so little trouble, after they have been for some time husbands, to make it easy, or indeed possible, for their wives to continue to love, and respect, and reverence them. All our wives have dreary, lonely, sorely disappointed days at home—partly our fault and partly theirs, but mostly ours—that we know nothing about. Now, what are they to do between Paul on the one hand demanding in the name of God that they shall love and reverence us, and us on the other hand with all our might making both love and reverence impossible? Well, with God all things are possible. Let our wives, then, take us, with all our faults and infirmities, and let them think that with all our faults and infirmities we are still their husbands.

And let them take this to heart also, that though we fall ever so far below ourselves, that is all the more reason why they should rise all the more above themselves. It does not divorce a wife from her affection and respect for her husband that he causes her much pain and shame: many a blush in public, and many a tear in private. His sins against good taste, his clownish or churlish habits, his tempers, his prejudices, his ignorance, his rude, insolent, overbearing ways, not to speak of still grosser vices—all that will not absolve a wife from a wife's solicitude and goodwill to her husband. All that will not discharge her from her command over herself. She must often see and feel all that like a wolf under her gown as she sits at the top of the table and her husband sits at the foot. But she must all the more learn to say her own grace to herself before she sits down to her temptation, till she is able to return thanks as she rises to go upstairs. All the time they are talking and eating and drinking at the other end of the table, she must set a watch on her ears and on her eyes and on the blood in her cheeks. She must be as full of guile as her husband is of meat and drink and himself. The keenest and cruelest eye must not find her out. Its deceived owner must be sent home saying, What a fool of a wife that brute, that bore, that goose has! I declare the blind thing is still in love with him! The wife see that she is hypocrite enough to throw dust into the eyes of her oldest, closest, and most familiar friend. Dante describes Michal as a woman who stood scornful and afflicted at her royal window. But let not even Dante's terrible eyes see either your scorn of your husband or your affliction on account of his exposure of himself. Throw dust even into Dante's blazing eyes. We are poor creatures, the best of us husbands; and, at our best, we are still full of appetites and egotisms and all the other dregs of our indwelling sin. But if Almighty God bears with us, and does not despise us and spurn us and refuse us His love, neither will you. And you will be well paid for it all, and well acknowledged. For when we praise God at last, and say, To Him who loved us! we will not forget you. The wife see, then, that she prays for and puts up with her husband. The wife see that she makes his self-improvement easy for her husband. And if, after all is done, there is an irreducible residuum of distaste, and almost dislike left, well, all the more let her see to it that she work out his and her own salvation under that secret, life-long, household cross. To your thorn, as to the apostle's, Christ will come and will say, My grace is sufficient for it. My strength is made perfect even in such weakness as yours.

Being the woman she was, and having the husband she had, Michal could not but feel both scorn and affliction that day. But, when all is said for her, and all allowance made, she should not have spoken to David as it is recorded she did speak. She could not command her proud heart when she saw David dancing, but by the time he came home she should have had her tongue tamed and under a bridle. David was, no doubt, a great provocation and a constant cross to Michal. They were never made for one another. It was impossible they could ever be happy as man and wife, short of a miracle. David was all emotion, especially in divine things; whereas Michal was as proud and cold as if she had been a daughter of Lucifer, as indeed she was. David that day was like one of our own ministers coming home from the communion table. It takes a night and a day and more than that till the agitation and the emotion of a communion day subsides and settles in a minister's heart. And if he were met with a blow in the face about his sermon or his prayer or his table service as he opened his own door, that was exactly the reception that poor David met with at Michal's hands that day. The wife see, at any rate, that she holds her tongue. I do not now speak of communion time. There is no fear of any minister's wife speaking on that day as Michal spoke. But there are other times with ministers and with all men. Times when husband and wife do not see eye to eye. Times when their two hearts do not beat as one heart. Times of distaste, and disapproval, and difference of opinion, and positive dislike; when Michal, who is written for our learning, must be called to every wife's mind. Michal with her heart full of war, and her mouth full of wicked words, and her whole after-life full of remorse and misery for that evil day in her house in Jerusalem—Michal is a divine looking-glass for all angry and outspoken wives.

"It was before the Lord," was David's noble answer to Michal's taunting and insulting words. That was the whole explanation of David's emotion and the sufficient justification of it. David's overflowing joy that day had its deep and full spring in that far-off but never-to-be-forgotten day when Samuel came to Bethlehem with his horn of oil. To understand David and to sing David's psalms, you must have come through David's experiences. You must have had David's birth and upbringing; David's election and anointing and call; David's sins and David's salvation; David's falls and David's restorations; David's offices and David's services in the church of God. No wonder, then, that so many of David's psalms are as much beyond your depth today as his dancing was beyond Michal's depth that day. Michal thought of her royal father Saul that day, and despised David. David thought of his poor father Jesse that day, and danced before the Lord. And, as he says, he would have danced all the same, and still more, had earth and hell both been all let loose to scoff and scout at him. "Both less and more than king," is Dante's whole remark on David's dance. As we shall be on that day when we look down at the hole of the pit from whence we were digged, and cast our crowns at His feet who took us from the dung-hill and set us beside David.

And then, the truly noble, the truly humble, and the terribly lonely man that he was, David took up the taunt of his godless and heartless wife, and wore it as a badge of honor before the Lord that day. Yes, he said, it will be as you say. I will seek and I will find among the poorest and the most despised of God's people that which my own married wife denies me at home. And who can tell how many husbands here are in David's desolate case? Who can tell how many have to go out of their own homes to find the finest sympathy, and the fullest utterance, and the completest rest for their hearts? The wife see that her husband has not to go abroad to find his best friend, his most sympathetic and fellow-feeling friend, and, above all, in his religion. A minister once told me that he preached best and prayed best when his wife was at home. What a gulf there was between David and Michal; between Jesus and His brethren, not to say His mother; and between my desolate friend and his wife! My brethren, the Holy Ghost knew what He was doing, and for whom He was doing it, when He moved the sacred writer to put that day in David's life into our Bible. And this—"Husbands, love your wives, even as Christ loved the church, and gave Himself for it." And this—"And the wife see that she reverence her husband."

42
Solomon

THE shipwreck of Solomon is surely the most terrible tragedy in all the world. For if ever there was a shining type of Christ in the Old Testament church, it was Solomon. If ever any one was once enlightened, and had tasted the heavenly gift, and was made a partaker of the Holy Ghost, and had tasted the good word of God, and the powers of the world to come, it was Solomon. If ever any young saint sought first the kingdom of God and His righteousness, and had all these things added unto him, it was Solomon. If the kingdom of heaven was ever like a lord's servant with five talents, who went and traded with the same and made them other five talents, it was Solomon. If ever there was any one of whom it could be said that he had attained, and was already perfect, it was Solomon. If ever ship set sail on a sunny morning, but all that was left of her was a board or two on the shore that night, that ship was Solomon. A board or two of rare and precious wood, indeed; and some of them richly worked and overlaid with silver and gold—it was Solomon with his sermons, and his prayers, and his proverbs, and his songs, and his temple. If ever a blazing lighthouse was set up in the sea of life to warn every man and to teach every man, it was Solomon.

Solomon was born of a father and a mother, the knowledge of which was enough to sanctify and dedicate both him and them from his mother's womb. If ever it was said over any child's birth, Where sin abounded, grace did much more abound, it was surely over the birth, and the birth-gifts and graces of Solomon. If ever a father's and a mother's son said when he was come to years, And is this the manner of man, O Lord God? that son come to years was surely Solomon. And, then, with a tutor and governor like Nathan—Judge, I pray you, betwixt me and my vineyard. What more could have been done to my vineyard that I have not done in it? And then his father's deathbed, and all those terrible tragedies on the back of that; all ending in Solomon sitting down on the throne of Israel amid such a blaze of glory. Solomon would have been made of stone not to have been moved to make those vows, and promises, and choices of wisdom and truth and righteousness, which we read so beautifully that he did make at the beginning of his reign in Jerusalem.

The Holy Child Himself never dreamed a better dream than that dream was which Solomon dreamed after that day of a thousand burnt-offerings on the altar of Gibeon. And a nobler choice was never made by any elect man in his most waking and most enlightened hours, than was the choice that Solomon made that midnight in his sleep. As soon as Lord Melbourne had announced to the young Princess Victoria that she was now Queen of England, he opened the Bible and read to the young sovereign the story of Solomon's dream at Gibeon. It was a stroke of genius. It was an inspiration. It was a prophetic Scripture in her case and in ours. Would God it had come half as true in his case who dreamed the dream!

"And the speech pleased the Lord that Solomon had asked this thing. And God said unto him, Because thou hast asked this thing, and hast not asked for thyself long life; neither hast asked riches for thyself, nor hast asked the life of thine enemies; but hast asked for thyself understanding to discern judgment. Behold, I have done according to thy words; lo, I have given thee a wise and an understanding heart; so that there was none like thee before thee, neither after thee shall any one arise like unto thee. And I have also given thee that which thou hast not asked, both riches and honor; so that there shall not be any among the kings like unto thee all thy days." And both the riches and the honor promised at Gibeon were all fulfilled in Jerusalem, till the half had not been told to Solomon.

Magnifical, a mountain of cedar and wrought gold, as Solomon's temple was, it is all gone to dust and ashes millenniums ago. As the Lord warned Solomon, the temple soon became an astonishment and a hissing. But the dedication prayer that Solomon offered on the opening day before the altar is a far better prayer to us today than it was that day on which it first fell from Solomon's lips. Stone and timber, gold and silver, crumble to dust and are forgotten. But once a piece like that is composed, and spoken, and taken down, and read, it lasts for ever. No doubt it may be said in suspicion and in depreciation of Solomon that kings are wont to get their speeches and their prayers written for them by their ministers, secular and sacred; and that what falls from a king's lips before his people need not have come from his heart. But in the case of a king of Solomon's birth and upbringing and great gifts, such a libel would never have been let light had it not been that it is a real relief to hear it. If Solomon actually, and all of himself, made and offered that wonderful prayer, then when we think of it, he is more a mystery of perdition to us than ever. That wonderful discovery and operation of our day which is called Biblical Criticism has let in a most piercing and searching and edifying light, not only upon Bible books, but also upon Bible men. And upon no man more than upon both Solomon and his books. "The prayer of Solomon," says a scholar of no less grace and genius than of scholarship, "so fully reproduced, and so evidently precomposed, may well have been written under Nathan's guidance." He does not say positively that it was so precomposed and written. But he evidently believes, for his part, that it was; and he says what he does say in this matter for the sake of those who will let him say it, and not for those who will not. Had Solomon lived up to that prayer; no, I must not say that, for no man could do that, not Nathan himself; but if Solomon in all his unspeakable sensualities and idolatries had ever given the least sign or symptom that he felt shame for his life, or remorse when he remembered his prayer: had it not been for that, I, for one, could never have let it light on my mind that any one but Solomon himself composed what is here called Solomon's prayer. But I must say it is both a relief and an edification to my mind that the greatest castaway in the Bible may not have been the original and real and only author of one of the greatest and best prayers in the Bible. I can hold up my head better when I am opening a church and am reading and expounding this prayer, when I think of Nathan's pure and noble soul rather than of Solomon, who is so soon to be such a scandal and reprobation. I do not know how you feel about a matter like that. But I shall always return to that splendid prayer with the author of the parable of the one little ewe lamb before my mind, rather than the reprobate lover of no end of strange women, and the fatal father of Rehoboam. I can imagine many open-minded young men here, and many open-minded old men like Jonathan Edwards, who will go back to the prophetic precomposition and the prophetic reproduction of this great prayer with thankfulness to God for the splendid service that Christian scholarship is doing to Holy Scriptures, and not least to Solomon's psalms and songs and prayers and proverbs in our open-eyed, believing, and truly reverential day.

Our own Lord Bacon always comes to my mind when I think about Solomon. For Bacon also took all wisdom and all knowledge, past, present, and yet to be discovered, for his province. Bacon also spake of trees, from the cedar tree that is in Lebanon, even to the hyssop that springeth out of the wall. He spake also of beasts, and of fowls, and of creeping things, and of fishes. Bacon, like Solomon, put tongues into trees and made them speak proverbs. The streams round Verulam and Gorham-bury ran excellent books to Bacon, till he extracted wisdom absolutely out of everything. Solomon's House in *The New Atlantis* is the best commentary that will ever be written on the wisdom of Solomon. Bacon's Essays are our English Book of Proverbs, and an English Ecclesiastes could easily be collected out of Bacon's Letters and Speeches. For he, too—

> he felt from time to time
> The littleness that clings to what is human,
> And suffered from the shame of having felt it.

And then, with it all, Bacon's superb genius followed by his awful fall, makes us almost believe that Solomon has come back to this earth again in the lord chancellor of England. Only, how happy it would have made us had Nathan found among Solomon's parchments, and in Solomon's own handwriting, a psalm or prayer like that which Bacon's executors found in his dead desk. Will you join me in the following petitions out of Bacon's prostrate prayer: "Most gracious Lord God, my merciful Father from my youth up, my Creator, my Redeemer, my Comforter. Thou, O Lord, soundest and searchest the depths and secrets of all hearts. Thou acknowledgest the upright in heart, Thou judgest the hypocrite, Thou ponderest men's thoughts and doings as in a balance, Thou measurest their intentions as with a line, vanity and crooked ways cannot be hidden from Thee. Lord, I have loved Thy assemblies. I have mourned for the divisions of Thy church. I have delighted in the brightness of Thy sanctuary. Thy creatures have been my books, but Thy Scriptures much more. I have sought Thee in the courts, in the fields, and in the gardens, but I have found Thee in Thy temples. Thousands have been my sins, and ten thousand my transgressions; but Thy sanctifications have remained with me, and my heart, through Thy grace, hath been an unquenched coal upon Thy altar. As Thy favors have increased upon me, so have Thy corrections; so as Thou hast been always near me, O Lord, and ever as my worldly blessings were exalted, so secret darts from Thee have pierced me; and when I have ascended before men, I have descended in humiliation before Thee. Besides my innumerable sins, I confess before Thee that I am debtor to Thee for the gracious talent of Thy gifts and graces, which I have neither put into a napkin nor put it as I ought to exchangers, but have misspent it in things for which I was least fit, so as I may truly say my soul hath been a stranger in the house of my pilgrimage. Be merciful unto me, O Lord, and guide me in Thy ways, and afterwards receive me to glory." No. That is not Solomon come back again. Would God it were! Solomon has nothing like that to come back with. That is Solomon's father come back to fallen Bacon. That is the man after God's own heart.

What malice there must be in our hearts when God's very best gifts to us, and our very best blessings, are turned by us to be our temptation and our snare! David's terrible fall took place not among the cruel rocks of his exile, but on the roof of the king's palace in Jerusalem. And it was Solomon's very wisdom and wide understanding; it was his great riches; it was his wide dominion; it was his large-ness of heart and his long and peaceful life that all worked together to make his path so slippery and so deadly. It is not to be wiser than what is written to say that it was not a vulgar and an everyday sensuality that made Solomon in the end such a castaway. There was that in it. But there were more things, and more seductive and dangerous things in it than that. There was this: There was what the inspired text calls largeness of heart—very much what we would call in our day open-ness and breadth of mind, hospitality and catholicity of mind, even to sympathy and symbolism with beliefs, with ways of worship, and with ways of no worship, against which it had been the divine call and whole ministry of Moses, and Aaron, and Joshua, and David to warn and to protect the children of Israel. That Solo-mon should go down to Egypt, of all places on the face of the earth, for his queen; that Pharaoh's daughter should sit on the throne of David, that must have given a shock to the more conservative, and sober, and thoughtful, and religious, and far-seeing minds in Israel—a shock that we wonder we do not hear more about it while Solomon is yet young and yet alive. We shall hear plenty about it when he is dead, and when Rehoboam's teeth are set on edge. No doubt, largeness of heart, even as the sand that is on the seashore, and breadth and openness of mind, and a catholic and a hospitable temper, and the charity that believeth all things and hopeth all things, is all of God, and is all to be seen in Jesus Christ and in His church. At the same time, such is the malignity of our hearts, that even charity itself has its temptations and its snares when it becomes our charity. Even grace itself, says Shepard, is flesh in respect of God. And Solomon's largeness of heart soon ended in sheer flesh itself. His wisdom as his life went on descended not from above. The wisdom that is from above is first pure, then peaceable. We see it every day. We see men absolutely revolting against all smallness of heart. They loath all your bigotry, and narrowness, and hardness, and suspicion, and superstitition. They see a soul of good especially in things evil. They fraternize with men and with movements that their fathers abominated. They pare down and prune away the decalogue, and the creed, and the catechism, and the books of discipline of their godly upbringing. They rehabilitate and reinvest names and reputations that were a shame and a reproach in their father's house. They go down to Egypt for a wife, and they bring up her false gods with her. "And it came to pass that, when Solomon was old, his wives turned away his heart after other gods; and his

heart was not perfect with the Lord his God, as was the heart of David his father."
And, if not in them, then in their children, all that Moses, and Aaron, and Joshua,
and David had won for them and for their children at a great price is surrendered
up and sold for naught, till the old great price has to be paid for it again in their
children's sin, and suffering, and defeat, and captivity. Every generation has its
own sword sent to it: its own peculiar trial of faith and holiness and severe obedience. And there is no shipwreck of faith and holiness and severe obedience in all
the world that is written more for the men of our generation than just the terrible
shipwreck of Solomon amid his wealth, and his wisdom, and his largeness of hori-
zon and hospitality of heart, even to strange women and to their strange gods, till
that end came which always comes.

The books of Solomon so-called—the Proverbs, the Ecclesiastes, and the
Song—had a great struggle to get a footing inside the Old Testament. Each one
of Solomon's books had its own difficulty to those who sifted out and sealed up
the Hebrew Bible. There was something in all the books that were in any way
associated with Solomon's name that made the Hebrew Fathers doubt their fitness for a place in Holy Scripture. There is one fatal want in them all. There is no
repentance anywhere in Solomon. There is no paschal lamb, or young pigeon, or
bitter herb among all the beasts, and birds, and hyssop-plants of which Solomon
spoke and sang so much. There is no day of atonement, or so much as one of the
many ordained sacrifices for sin, in any of Solomon's real or imputed writings.
Both the sense of truth and the instinct of verisimilitude kept back all those who
ever assumed Solomon's name from ever putting a penitential psalm, or a proverb
of true repentance, in Solomon's mouth. The historical sense, as we call it, was
already too strong for that even in the deathbed moralizings and soliloquizings
that have come down to us under Solomon's name. There is no thirty-second, or
fifty-first, or hundred and thirtieth Psalm of David in all the volume of "Psalms
of Solomon" that were composed in the century before Christ. No; there is no real
repentance, real or assumed, anywhere in Solomon. There is remorse in plenty,
and weariness of life, and discontent, and disgust, and self-contempt, bitterer to
drink than blood. There is plenty of the sorrow that worketh death; but there is
not one syllable of the repentance to salvation not to be repented of. "All taste
for pleasure is extinguished in the king's heart," wrote Madame de Maintenon
from the deathbed of Louis the Fourteenth. "Old age and disappointment have
taught him to make serious reflections on the vanity of everything he was for-
merly fond of." Bathsheba might have written that letter from her dying son's
bedside. Vanity of vanities, groaned out Solomon, with his heart full of the ashes
of a lost life. All is vanity and vexation of spirit. Dreams at Gibeon, building of
temples and kings' houses, largeness of heart, gifts of prophecy, a tongue of men
and angels, proverbs and songs and Songs of songs—all is vanity if there is not
along with it all constant repentance, daily self-denial, and a heart more and
more perfect with God. The wise men of the east, wiser than Solomon, have a
proverb upon the secret worm that was gnawing all the time in the royal staff
upon which Solomon leaned. What, to end with, is the secret worm that is gnawing in your staff on which you lean?

43

Solomon, and a Greater Than Solomon

WE have, as I believe, a suddenly passing, but a true and a deep glimpse into the working of our Lord's mind when He says, "Behold, a greater than Solomon is here." And there is nothing in heaven or in earth, in God or in man, so interesting to us as the working of our Lord's mind; especially when His mind is working upon Himself. Well, as it appears to me, we have here an example of how our Lord read, and thought, and saw, and felt about Himself, till He had fully discovered Himself, and had fully and for ever taken possession of Himself. The apostle says that it is not wise in us too much to measure ourselves by ourselves, or to compare ourselves with ourselves. But He who is the Wisdom of God itself here measures and compares Himself with Solomon, and that, to us, in a most intensely interesting and instructive way. As the Holy Child read the story of Solomon, as that so beautiful and so tragical story is still told in the First Book of the Kings—as He read and saw how Solomon was born of David and Bathsheba; how he was named first the Divine Darling, and then the Son of Peace: how the young king chose wisdom and understanding as his royal portion; how wise he already was, and how wise he became, above all the wise men of the East; what a great kingdom he had, and what untold wealth, and what far and near renown he had; what a service he did in building and furnishing the House of the Lord; how the Queen of Sheba came to Jerusalem to hear his wisdom; and then, after all that, Solomon's songs and sermons and proverbs—as the Child Jesus read all that, and asked questions about all that; and then, when He became a man, and saw Himself as in a glass in all that—ere ever He was aware, the Holy Ghost had witnessed it and had sealed it on His mind and on His heart, that, in all that He, the Son of Mary, was made of God a far greater than Solomon. The same thing must have come to Him as He read, and prayed, and pondered about David, and Moses, and Abraham, and Adam, till our Lord stood alone among all men, and above all men, and till of the people there was none with Him. And this went on, and increased in all clearness and in all assurance, till He was enabled and constrained to say, I and My Father are One. In some such way as that, as I believe, our Lord was led up of the Spirit from strength to strength, till He stood before God and Man the Messiah of Israel, the Son of God, and the Savior of all them that believe.

Let us, then, if so be it may be given to us, follow out some of the steps that our Lord took in His own mind till He was able to say to the Scribes and Pharisees who would see a sign from Him, "Behold, a greater than Solomon is here." They were all at one as to Solomon's extraordinary greatness in the matter of his birth. Now, though our Lord was not born at once in David's house, He was born none the less in David's line; so much so, that there was no name by which He was oftener named, and no name He was more ready to answer to, than just the name, Son of David. The Syrophoenician woman came out of the same coasts, and cried unto

Him, saying, Have mercy on me, O Lord, thou Son of David. And her daughter was made whole from that very hour. Have mercy on us, O Lord, thou Son of David, the two blind men sitting by the wayside cried, and immediately their eyes received sight, and they followed him. Blind Bartimaeus also: Jesus, thou Son of David, have mercy on me. And after a short conversation he also received his sight and followed Jesus in the way. Hosanna to the Son of David, Hosanna in the highest, the multitude cried, singing at His last entry into Jerusalem. Now, Solomon in all his glory never went beyond that. Israel had no nobler salutation for any of her kings than to call him the Son of David. But our Lord was both Son of David and Son of God. It is on those two strong foundation-stones that Paul builds his Epistle to the Romans. "Jesus Christ our Lord, which was made of the seed of David according to the flesh, and declared to be the Son of God with power." No wonder that Isaiah, who foresaw His glory, said that His name would be called Wonderful! To be at once begotten of God from everlasting, and to be born of Mary in the fullness of time; and to be, and to continue to be, God and man in two distinct natures, and one person, for ever, how wonderful is that! Yes; truly, it is far less than the truth to say that a far greater than Solomon is born here.

The exquisitely-told story of Solomon's choice leads us to think of the many untold dreams and visions that must have come to the Holy Child Jesus, and of the many sleeping and waking choices He must have made both before and after His first visit to Solomon's temple. It was after Solomon had offered sacrifices on the altar at Gibeon that the Lord appeared to him and said, Ask what I shall give thee. And we may well believe, that after Jesus at twelve years old saw Jerusalem and the temple and the passover for the first time, a dream would come to Him that night through the multitude of that day's business; a dream, and a voice, and a choice, and a benediction that would all send Him home to Joseph and Mary saying, Wist ye not that I must be about My Father's business? And then, what with dreams, and visions, and temptations, and trials, and right choices, and victories day and night untold, our Lord came forth to begin His Messianic life in Israel, as much greater than Solomon as heaven is greater than earth, and as the Son of God is greater than the Son of David. What we know not now about the Mystery of godliness during those eighteen, during those thirty-three years—the most wonderful years this wonderful world has ever seen—it will be our discovery and delight to know when Wisdom shall have builded her house, and hewn out her seven pillars, and mingled her wine, and furnished her table. "I have yet many things to say unto you, but ye cannot bear them now."

The second Psalm, the forty-fifth Psalm, the seventy-second Psalm, and the hundred and twenty-sixth Psalm, all have Solomon's name associated with them in one way or other. But no New Testament man can read those Psalms without this coming up on his mind, that a far greater than Solomon is here also. How completely Solomon has passed out of the second Psalm, and how entirely Jesus Christ has taken possession of it till His enemies be made His footstool. "Yet have I set my king upon my holy hill of Zion. I will declare the decree: the Lord hath said to me, Thou art My Son; this day have I begotten thee. Ask of Me, and I shall give thee the heathen for thine inheritance, and the uttermost parts of the earth for thy possession." And the forty-fifth Psalm has been made into action-sermons, into table-services, and into prayers and praises at communion-seasons, till, not once in a thousand, do we ever think for a moment of Solomon and Pharaoh's daughter. It is blasphemy to speak to us about "Solomon in all his glory" when we see and sing Jesus Christ. "Thou art fairer than the children of men; grace is poured into thy lips; therefore God hath blessed thee for ever. Thou lovest righteousness, and hatest wickedness: therefore God, thy God, hath anointed thee with the oil of gladness above thy fellows. Hearken, O daughter, and consider, and incline thine ear; forget also thine own people, and thy father's house; for He is thy Lord, and worship thou Him." And then The Song. Whatever may be the last word to be said about The Song, the Church of Christ has taken such possession of The Song of Songs for her Husband and for herself that it will be His and hers for ever. The Song of Solomon will be sung like the voice of many waters at the marriage-supper of the Lamb. "I sat down under His shadow with great delight, and His fruit was sweet to my taste. He brought me to the banqueting-house, and His banner over me was love."

The Proverbs, also, of Solomon, the son of David, king of Israel. "A wise man will hear, and will increase learning; . . . to understand a proverb, and the interpretation; the words of the wise, and their dark sayings. . . . Go to the ant, thou sluggard; consider her ways and be wise; which, having no guide, overseer, or ruler, provideth her meat in the summer, and gathereth her food in the harvest. . . . I went by the field of the slothful, and by the vineyard of the man void of understanding. And, lo, it was all grown over with thorns, and nettles had covered the face thereof, and the stone wall thereof was broken down. . . . So shall thy poverty come as one that travelleth; and thy want as an armed man. . . . If the tree fall toward the south, or toward the north, in the place where the tree falleth, there shall it be." . . . And again, When the almond tree shall flourish, and the grasshopper shall be a burden; or ever the silver cord be loosed, or the golden bowl be broken, or the pitcher be broken at the fountain, or the wheel broken at the cistern. . . . All well worth coming from Sheba to Jerusalem to hear such parables as these, and much more as good as these. But those who went out among the vineyards, and the sheepfolds, and in the sowing time, and in the reaping time, and suchlike, in Galilee, and Samaria, and Judea with our Lord, they would be the first to exclaim to themselves, Behold, a greater than Solomon is here also. Solomon, at his best, was of the earth, earthy. Jesus Christ is always the Lord from heaven; and, carrying the kingdom of heaven always in His heart, He saw that kingdom everywhere and in everything—in land and sea and sky. What if earth, said the angel to Adam—

> Be but the shadow of heaven, and things therein
> Each to other like, more than on earth is thought?

But that is just how it is when the Lord of angels takes His disciples out among the things of earth, and points out to them how the kingdom of heaven is like this beast, and that bird; this herb, and that tree; this sower with his seed-basket, and that reaper with his reaping-hook; this enemy sowing tares, and that husbandman sifting with his sieve and winnowing with his winnowing-fan; this woman leavening her meal, and that woman sweeping the house; this lost sheep, and that lost son; this marriage with its five wise and its five foolish virgins, and that great supper where they were compelled to come in. No; never man spake like this man. And all men felt it. "And it was at Jerusalem the feast of the dedication, and it was winter. And Jesus walked in the temple in Solomon's porch. Then came the Jews round about Him, and said unto Him, How long dost Thou make us to doubt? If Thou be the Christ, tell us plainly. Jesus answered them, My sheep hear my voice, and I know them, and they follow Me: and I give unto them eternal life; and they shall never perish, neither shall any man pluck them out of My hand. And many believed on Him there." Yes. An infinitely greater than Solomon stood and spake in parables in Solomon's porch that day.

But it was the wisdom of Solomon that brought the Queen of Sheba to Jerusalem, and it was her visit to Jerusalem to see Solomon, that gave us our present text. The Queen of the South, to her immortal honor, came from the uttermost parts of the earth, as our Lord so picturesquely has it, to see the wisdom of Solomon. Never king nor queen set out on a nobler errand than did she of the South; and, according to the beautiful history, she was not only wholly satisfied with what she saw and heard, but she testified to Solomon and said that the half of what she had seen and heard in Jerusalem had not been told her in Sheba. Now, there is no richer, finer, more beautiful, and more winning word in the whole of the Old Testament than just this same word "wisdom." And then, when we pass over into the New Testament, we find Wisdom exalted, and honored, and glorified, and made one of the many names of Him, than whom, and than whose name, there is none other name given among men whereby we must be saved. The Solomonic books have some incomparably splendid passages on wisdom; and if Solomon had fallen, and repented, and risen again, and begun again, till he ended in living up to his own sermons on wisdom, what a glory, both in sacred letters and in a holy life, Solomon's name would have been! "Wisdom," says Sir Henry Taylor, one of the wisest writers in the English language, "is not the same with understanding, talents, capacity, ability, sagacity, sense, or prudence—not the same with any one of these; neither will all these taken together make it up. Wisdom is that exercise of the reason into which the heart enters—a structure of the understanding rising out of the moral and spiritual nature. It is for this cause that a high order of wisdom, that is a highly intellectual wisdom, is still more rare than a high order of genius. When they reach the very highest order they are one; for each includes the other, and intellectual greatness is matched with moral strength." And then this fine essayist goes on to point out how Solomon's great intellectual gifts, coupled as they were in him with such an appetite for enjoyment, together became his shipwreck. And Bishop Butler, as I think, the very wisest of all our English writers, though he does not, like Sir Henry Taylor, name Solomon, he surely had him in his eye when he penned that memorable and alarming passage about those men who go over the theory of wisdom and virtue in their thoughts, talk well, and paint fine pictures of it, till their minds are hardened in a contrary course, and till they become more and more insensible to all moral considerations. I wish the great preacher had gone on in the Rolls Chapel to a sixteenth sermon on Solomon and his fine pictures of wisdom. But in lieu of Butler let Sir Henry Taylor's *Notes from Life* be read by all men who lack wisdom. Our Lord also made fine pictures of wisdom, and virtue, and the kingdom of heaven; but He was constantly correcting His pictures and counselling His hearers that the true wisdom, and the true kingdom of heaven, stands not in the head, but in the heart; not in light, however immediately it comes from heaven, but in both light and love; not in theories, however brilliant and beautiful, but in practices; and in practices, the humbler, the more obscure and despised, and the more full of crosses and crooks they are, the better they are for the purpose.

Our Lord did not absolutely shut great and gifted men like Solomon in all his glory out of the kingdom of heaven, but He did the next thing to it. For, while admitting that all things are possible with God, at the same time, both His own life and all His preaching went to proclaim that great intellect, with great station, and with great appetite for enjoyment, divine possibility and all, were, and would be, all but absolutely fatal to Solomon, and to all Solomon-like men. A far greater intellect than Solomon's was in our Lord; He was ordained and anointed to a far greater station and seat; and He had the capacity, if not the appetite, for far greater enjoyment. But all that was all balanced in our Lord, and built up into moral character, by great humility, great submissiveness, great labors, and great love. As I do the will of my Father; as I in everything submit Myself to the will of My Father; and as I thus learn more and more of the will of My Father, both to submit Myself to it and to do it; so do ye, He was constantly teaching. And ye also, like Me, shall both know the doctrine that it is of God, and shall come at last with Me to His heavenly kingdom. Here, then, is wisdom, as John says in the Revelation. And here is the mind which hath wisdom. A greater than Solomon in all his wisdom is indeed here.

And when the Queen of Sheba, so we read, had seen all Solomon's wisdom, and the house that he had built, and the meat of his table, and the sitting of his servants, and the attendance of his ministers, and their apparel, and his cupbearers, and his ascent by which he went up into the house of the Lord, there was no more spirit in her. Solomon had built two houses—one a house for the Lord and another a house for himself. And what the Queen of Sheba saw we also see to this day in the sixth and seventh chapters; and, at this distance of time and space, as we read them we feel like her about them. But, proud of his house of God as Solomon was, he had grace enough to say that the heaven of heavens could not contain the God of Israel, much less this house that he had built. And as time went on in Israel, it became more and more clear that Solomon's temple, from heaven as it was at that time, became more and more a hindrance, rather than a help, to God dwelling on the earth; till Christ came in the temple of His body, and till Paul built up beside that temple, and leaning upon it, the similar temple of the believer's body. And then John Howe comes to us in our own day, and in our own tongue, with his *Living Temple*, a piece that Paul would have given orders to read to all the churches. And I promise the student of these things, who will begin with Solomon and go on to John Howe, that he will write to me after he has read it all, and will say, that there is no spirit left in him as he lays down the Plato of the Puritans on *That Notion that a Good Man is a Temple of God.*

But my time has failed me. And all I shall attempt to say more at this time is this, that if the Queen of Sheba was so overpowered as she saw the meat of Solomon's table, and the sitting of his servants, and the attendance of his ministers, and their apparel, and his cupbearers, what would she have said had she ever sat down at the Lord's Table? I wonder what she would have said when she went south about the Lord's Table, and the meat upon it, and the sitting of His servants, and the attendance of His ministers, and their apparel, and His cupbearers. No, she would have said, the tenth of that had not been told me. Thy wisdom, O Thou Greater than Solomon, she would have broken forth, and Thy prosperity, far exceedeth all the fame that I had heard. Happy are Thy men, happy are those Thy servants, which stand continually before Thee, and hear Thy wisdom. And blessed be the Lord Thy God which delighted in Thee, to set Thee on the throne of Israel.

44
The Queen of Sheba

I SHALL take up somewhat high ground with you concerning the Queen of Sheba. For, so far as I have seen, that wonderful woman has never had adequate justice done to her. As I see her, the Queen of Sheba came to Jerusalem on the very highest of errands. She was moved to undertake her journey by the very strongest and the very loftiest of motives. And she saw and heard and took home in her heart far more than her very highest expectations. And while the sacred writer has told us her story in his very best manner, at the same time, it is our Lord's acknowledgment and confession of her in the judgment—it is this that lifts her up in my eyes till I see her among the foremost of those who shall come from the east, and the west, and the north, and the south, and who shall hear the wisdom, and taste the grace, and share the glory of a greater than Solomon in the Jerusalem which is above, and which is the mother of us all.

The first thing that is told us concerning the Queen of Sheba is this, that she had heard in Sheba concerning the Name of the Lord. It may very well be that this has bribed my eyes and perverted my judgment in the matter of the Queen of Sheba. The Name of the Lord so construes and so glorifies the whole of the Old Testament to me that the more I read the Old Testament the more I find nothing else in it worth its ink but the Name of the Lord. If I once find the Name of the Lord in the life of any Old Testament man or woman, I can never again forget that man or that woman. And, on the other hand, however great, and good, and wise, and famous any man is, if the Name of the Lord is not his strong tower, I fear I do not do that man full justice. If this sacred writer means nothing more by it but a sonorous and a stately turn of expression when he mentions the Name of the Lord as the motive of the Queen of Sheba's mission to Jerusalem; if he means as little by it as the run of the commentators say that he means, then, all I can say is that he has set a trap for my feet in the text. You all know the Name of the Lord, and I hope you all feel about that Name with me. You remember it, and never an hour of any day can you forget it. The Name of the Lord is written all over Moses and David and Isaiah in letters of gold, a finger deep. For the Name of the Lord is "The LORD God, merciful and gracious, long-suffering, and abundant in goodness and truth, keeping mercy for thousands, forgiving iniquity and transgression and sin."

Well, it had all come about under the good hand of God somewhat in this way. It simply must have all come about somewhat in this way. Some of those merchantmen who went down to the Red Sea in ships, and did business for Solomon all along its shores in gold, and silver, and ivory, and apes, and peacocks, and almug-trees, and what not, one of their ships on one occasion was driven in for want of fresh water near the summer palace of the Queen of Sheba. And as the seamen of Israel filled their water-pots, it was an ordinance that they should sing, saying, Spring up, O well; in the Name of the Lord, spring up! When, who should pass by but the Queen of Sheba herself with her maidens with her? Sing still another of the songs of Zion, she said to Solomon's sailors. At which they sang a psalm that a prophet who was in their ship had taught them to sing on the occasion of a great tempest they had just passed through. "These see," they sang, "the works of the Lord, and His wonders in the deep. For He commandeth, and raiseth the stormy wind, which lifteth up the waves thereof. They mount up to the heaven, they go down again to the depths; their soul is melted because of trouble. Then they cry unto the Lord in their trouble, and He bringeth them out of their distresses. Oh that men would praise the Lord for His goodness, and for His wonderful works to the children of men!" And, then, at the Name of the Lord, and without being told to do it, all the seamen standing on the shore lifted up their hands to heaven and proclaimed the Name of the Lord, and worshipped, saying, "The LORD, the LORD God, merciful and gracious." And ever after that day the Queen of Sheba watched at her window for the ships of Solomon, till, above all else, the Name of the Lord took entire hold of her heart. The Queen of Sheba had lords many and gods many of her own. She and her people had their gods of the sea and their gods of the land; their gods of war and their gods of wine; their gods of the night and their gods of the day, and many more. But there was no name of any god given in Sheba that took such hold of the Queen of Sheba's heart as did the Name of the God of Israel. Till she took a very great train, with camels that bare spices, and very much gold, and precious stones, there came no such abundance of spices as these which the Queen of Sheba brought to Jerusalem, because of the Name of the Lord.

Even Homer himself was sometimes seen to nod. And that is the explanation of Matthew Henry's unaccountable slander that some of the Queen of Sheba's questions that she put to Solomon, some were frivolous, some were captious, and some were over-curious. I do not see what business the best of commentators has to say that, unless it be to teach us always to read our Bible with our own eyes and with our own hearts for ourselves. And when I read with my own eyes all I can find about the Queen of Sheba, I see neither caption, nor frivolity, nor idle curiosity about her. And I cannot think there could have been, since our Lord sets His seal upon her, and takes her and her questions as His accusation and condemnation of the Pharisees of His day. The sacred writer knew far more about the Queen of Sheba than the minister of Chester did; and what he says about her questions is this, that they were hard to Solomon to answer; especially when she went deep down into her heart for her questions. "All that was in her heart." I suppose the sacred writer means all matters, or, at least, very many matters connected with the throne and the state of Sheba. Affairs of state, as we would say: her anxieties about her treaties of war and peace; her seat of judgment and justice over her own people; royal-family matters also, no doubt; and matters, maybe, still nearer her heart. The Queen of Sheba had heard in the south country all about Solomon's dream at Gibeon. She had it all read to her when her royal cares would not let her sleep. And, ever since, she had kept all these things in her heart against her long-intended visit to Jerusalem. But from the day when she first heard the Name of the Lord, from that day her heart had grown every day and every night deeper and fuller of hard questions; questions so hard that I doubt if she broke them all even to Solomon. At the same time, her heart in Sheba at its fullest of hard questions was not a New Testament heart, and could not in Sheba be. Of no New Testament heart does the New Testament ever say that its owner ever told to any man all that was in her heart; unless it was to our New Testament Solomon. And, then, He is such a Solomon that He does not need that communication to be made to Him. For He is wiser in men's hearts than all men; than Ethan the Ezrahite, and Heman and Chalcol and Darda, the sons of Mahol; and His fame is now in all the nations round about. Only, in His wisdom He will have it that we come, if it is from the uttermost part of the earth, and tell Him as if He did not already know all the hard questions of our hearts; and then there will not be anything hid from the King that He will not tell us. Oh no, sacred writer! you do not really mean us to understand that the Queen of Sheba told to any man all that was in her heart. We quite well understand what you mean. She told Solomon so much about herself and about her people, and got so much help and advice from Solomon, that "all that was in her heart" is just your hyperbolical and impressive way of putting her before us in your great regard for her, and in your great admiration of him.

Matthew Henry is more like himself when he goes on to say that we may be sure that Solomon gave the inquiring Queen a *rationale* of the temple and all its offices and all its services. That is a handsome retraction and apology for what he had said so rashly and so censoriously about the frivolity and the captiousness of the Queen's questions. You could not possibly give a *rationale* of the communion services of this house on a communion Sabbath-day to a frivolous and captious-minded man. Now, the temple was just the Lord's Supper already in type and prophecy. And when you try it, there is no subject in heaven or earth more impossible to rationalize to a frivolous or a captious mind than just what lies behind the Lord's Supper the substitution and the propitiation made for sinners by the blood of Christ. The Queen of Sheba was like one of those children in Israel who asked their fathers at every passover supper, What mean ye by this service? Only, she was not a child, but a woman of a strong understanding and a deep heart, and both Solomon and the high priest and the prophet, all three together, were at their wits' end; it took them all their might to open up all the parts of the temple and its sacrifices to her satisfaction: the reason of this, and the reason of that; the use of this, and the use of that; the antitype of this, and the antitype of that—she both hearing them and asking them questions. Till, when they had taken her through it all, there was no more spirit left in her to ask any more. I can believe it. For to this day nothing more completely subdues the spirit than the hard questions of the heart when they are honestly put and fully met and answered in the house of the Lord, and at His table. Nothing satisfies and silences the heart like the *rationale*, that is to say, the revelation of the truth and the grace of God to the heart that is hungry both for His truth as it is in Jesus, and for His grace as it is in Jesus also, and in Jesus alone.

No; there was neither captiousness nor frivolity in the Queen of Sheba when she came out of her own country, and neither was there detraction, nor depreciation, nor envy when she returned home. What say you? Had I been in her place, I do not feel guilty that I would have been either captious or frivolous in the house of God or in Solomon's own house. But I would have had things in my heart worse than captiousness or frivolousness; things that I would never have told to

Solomon, or to Nathan, or even to the high priest over the scapegoat. Had I been a king, and had I been shown through Solomon's temple, and through his palace, and through all that the Queen of Sheba saw in Jerusalem, I know only too well what would have been in my heart. Ay, even when I was being taken over the Lord's house and was being instructed in its sacrifices. Bishop Lancelot Andrewes has no more private devotion than that is where we come upon him praying to God to be delivered from his envy of another man's grace. Oh, where will that sin of sins, that so besetting sin, not intrude itself! If all this good queen's appreciation, and admiration, and congratulation was absolutely sincere and without offence in the sight of God who seeth the heart, well does she deserve all the honor that both the Old Testament and our Lord bestow upon her. Only, Blessed be His name, even if you are sick till you have no spirit left in you at the sight of other men's great houses, and great riches, and wise words, and fame, and great happiness—even so, Blessed be his name, He will not despise you nor spit upon you. He will only take you all that the more and all that the deeper into His temple, and will show you all that the more the riches of His grace, till He has given to you all you desire. And, Lord Jesus, all our desire in this matter is before Thee and is not hidden from Thee. It was a true report, she said, that I heard in mine own land, of thy acts and thy wisdom. Happy are thy men, happy are these thy servants, which stand continually before thee, and that hear thy wisdom. Only, had she known it, and seen the end of it, she was far more happy herself; as much more happy as it is to be faithful over a few things, and to admire rather than to be admired, and to bless than to be blessed, and to give than to receive.

Returning toward the same south a thousand years after the Queen of Sheba, the Ethiopian eunuch sat in his chariot and read Esaias the prophet. Esaias had not yet risen in the day of the Queen of Sheba; but she had the best reading of her day in her hand as she rode south. She had Solomon's prayer at the dedication of the temple in her hand. And the place in the prayer which she reads and prays all the way from Jerusalem to the south is this—"Moreover, concerning a stranger, that is not of Thy people Israel, but cometh out of a far country for Thy Name's sake. For they shall hear of Thy great Name, and of Thy strong hand, and of Thy stretched-out hand. When the stranger shall come and pray toward this house, hear Thou in heaven Thy dwelling-place, and do according to all that the stranger calleth to Thee for, that all people of the earth may know Thy Name, to fear Thee, as do Thy people Israel." All Ethiopia and all the south has not yet been explored. And who can tell but that the foundations of a long-lost temple may yet be laid bare in that ancient and honorable land; a temple, too, with no middle wall of partition with its excluding inscription engraven upon it; but in room of that an open door with this evangelical writing in gold of Ophir over it: "Doubtless Thou art our Father, though Abraham be ignorant of us, and though Israel acknowledge us not. Thou art our Father. Thou, O Lord, art our Redeemer. THY NAME is from everlasting." And then this beside it in the same gold from a Psalm for Solomon: "The kings of Tarshish and of the isles shall bring presents; the kings of Sheba and Seba shall offer gifts. And He shall live, and to Him shall be given of the gold of Sheba: and blessed be His glorious Name for ever; and let the whole earth be filled with His glory."

45
Shimei

SHIMEI was a reptile of the royal house of Saul. When Shimei saw David escaping for his life out of Jerusalem, Satan entered into Shimei, and he came forth and cursed at David as he passed by. And he cast stones at David, and cried, Thou bloody man, thou man of Belial, he cried. The Lord hath returned upon thee all the blood of the house of Saul. Behold, thou art taken in thy wickedness, because thou art a bloody man. Why should that dead dog curse the king in that way? said Abishai to David. Let me go over and take off his head. But the king answered to Abishai, So let him curse, because the Lord hath said unto him, Curse David. Let him alone, and let him curse, for the Lord hath bidden him. And still as David went on his way, Shimei also went along on the hillside over against David, and he cursed as he went, and he threw stones at David and cast dust. But David held his peace; for David had said to Abishai, It is the Lord.

Political and ecclesiastical party spirit turn us all, on occasion, into reptiles like Shimei. Shimei knew as well as you do that David had never shed a single drop of Saul's blood. So far from that, David's men were astonished and offended at David that he had let Saul go scot-free again and again when he had him in his power. And Shimei knew that quite well. But Shimei hated the truth that he knew. It was not Shimei's interest to admit the truth that he knew. He would not let the truth light on his mind for one moment, especially about David. Nothing was right that David did. Everything was wrong that David had any hand in. If you had a word to say for David, Shimei would follow you about also with curses and stones and dust. Shimei had everything to expect from Saul, and he knew that he had nothing to expect from David; and, therefore, David was a bloody man and a son of Belial. You know Shimei. At any rate, all who know you intimately know Shimei. Charity seeketh not her own, is not easily provoked, thinketh no evil; rejoiceth not in iniquity, but rejoiceth in the truth. But you never yet knew a fierce political or ecclesiastical partisan who had charity. When our political and ecclesiastical partisans begin to have charity we shall no longer need to offer the Lord's prayer every day, and say, Thy kingdom come.

Abishai looked up and saw a dead dog barking and biting out of his own kennel-door in Bahurim that day. But it was the Lord to David. David had nothing to do with the fall of Saul on Mount Gilboa; but the fall of Uriah in the front of the battle before Rabbah was ever before David, and never more so than it was that day as he crossed the Kedron, and passed through Gethsemane, and descended upon Bahurim. So let him curse, for the Lord hath said to him, Curse David. To such a divine use was Shimei put of God that greatest day of David's life. For Shimei that day perfected the good work on David that Absalom and Ahithophel had so well begun. Shimei was David's crowning means of grace that day. That day adorns and seals all David's psalms, and it was Shimei that did it. David had only to point with his finger to the hillside, and Shimei's insult and injury would have ceased for ever. But what profit would Shimei's blood have been to David? David had more sense. David had more grace. David knew himself better than that. And he knew God better than that. There is a Shimei that you wish he were dead. He is such a trial and torment to you. He so hampers and hinders you. He is such a rival to you. He is such a thorn in your pillow, and such a crook in your lot, and such a cross on which you are crucified, and are to be crucified, every day you live. You count up how old he is, and you promise yourself to have so many years of relief and enjoyment after he is in his grave. Oh no! Oh no! Let him live. Let his doctor lengthen his days. Let his bow long abide in its strength. Let him see all the days of his fathers. Let him close your eyes. Let him stand over your grave. Let him inherit your substance. Let him live long after you and rejoice in your portion. For it is the Lord. It is your salvation. And who, then, shall say to the Lord, Why hast Thou done this? Shall the thing formed say to Him that formed it, Why hast Thou made me thus? O the depth both of the wisdom and knowledge of God! How unsearchable are His judgments, and His ways past finding out! For who hath known the mind of the Lord? Or who hath been His counsellor?

Now, what is true of bad men is equally true of all our other bad surroundings, and all our other adverse circumstances, as we call them. For they also are all set of God, and kept of God, and made of God to operate on us for a good use. God sets to each one of us all the special surroundings, good and evil, of our several lives. It is too high for us to attain to and to understand. How He can do that to you, and to me, and to all other men, as much as to you and me, that surpasses us. But over-work and difficulty and impossibility are only true of men; they are not true of God. The Divine Nature is not like human nature; at least, not in things like that. God is everywhere, and He is wholly everywhere; and all His power, and all His wisdom, and all His grace, and all His truth, are with, and for, and around, and within every man. And thus it is that He sets every man's circumstances to him, good and bad, as much and as well as if He had no other man on His hand in earth or in heaven. When Almighty God creates another soul; when He elects to eternal life another new sinner; when He regenerates and begins to sanctify another new saint, He, from that moment, besets him behind and before, and lays His hand upon him. And when we awake to all that, we fall in with it all with unceasing wonder and with unceasing thanksgiving. O Lord, Thou hast searched me, and known me. Thou compassest my path and my lying down, and art acquainted with all my ways. Whither shall I flee from Thy Spirit? How precious, also, are Thy thoughts unto me, O God! How great is the sum of them! He believes nothing who does not believe that. He knows nothing who does not know that. He has not begun to live who lives not always under that. And he will soon come to see God in everything that befalls him; and not God only, but God his Sanctifier and his Savior. And then he will not let one atom of his most adverse circumstances be altered, lest he should thereby lose something of his full salvation. And when any of his friends, for his protection, or for his peace, or for his comfort would fain remove out of his life aught that tempts and tries him; aught that tramples on him and humbles him; aught that plagues him and vexes him and leads him into sin, like David to

Abishai at Bahurim he says to him, Let it alone, for it is the Lord. You say to me rare things about design, and adaptation, and environment, and means to ends, and final causes, and what not; and you both astonish and edify me. But if you fear God, and come, I will tell you how He environs my soul, and how He adapts you and all you say and do, to the good of my soul. If you could see and study my soul, even as I see it and study it, you would see something to make a science out of it. You would see a design and an end and a final cause, the greatest and the best—your soul under sanctification and mine—a final cause and an end next to God Himself. You would see all things in my world and in my generation, all working together upon me for my good. And all so secretly, so exquisitely, so intricately, so surely, and so infallibly working together of God. No. If you love my soul and its salvation, you must not alter by a single hair's breadth any single thing of all my circumstances; not, at least, till you are sure that I have got its divine end and design out of it. Especially not my trying, and tempting, and searching, and sifting, and sanctifying circumstances. And least of all Absalom and Ahithophel and Shimei. Every hour of every day; every man I meet; every word that enters my ear; every sight that enters my eye; all my thoughts within me that like a case of knives wounds my heart—it is all the Lord! If this life were all, then, I admit, it might be different. If you denied the resurrection of the body and the immortality of the soul, then I could understand you. But I cannot understand a man who believes in the sanctification and the eternal life of his own soul escaping the only and sure path of life like that. It is the Lord, and He is set upon my salvation. He is set upon my humility, my submissiveness, my meekness, my gentleness, my resignation, my contentment, my detachment, my self-denial, my cross, my death to sin, my death to myself, my unearthliness, my heavenly-mindedness, my conformity to Christ, and my acceptance of Him—and what a splendid use is all that to which to put all the things that otherwise would be so much against me! And David said to Abishai, and to all his servants, Let this Benjamite alone, and let him curse; for the Lord hath bidden him. It may be that the Lord will look upon mine affliction. And as David and his men went by the way, Shimei went on the hill's side over against David, and cursed David, and threw stones at him, and cast dust.

The magnificent use to which God puts the greatest of all His people's evils must not be attempted before a common congregation. Had we an elect-enough and a sympathetic-enough audience, this would make a splendid subject for the evening of the Lord's day. But we would need to have before us only the heavenly-minded, and the much-exercised, and the teachable, and the child-like; while all the frivolous and the captious, and all those given to disputes and debates about divine things should stay at home. There are plenty of materials for this great head of our subject lying scattered over the whole face of Holy Scripture. And the great masters have sometimes taken up this subject, after Holy Scripture. Samuel Rutherford, for example, comes often upon it in his Letters and in all his books. But after he has said all that it is possible to say upon it, he exclaims, Oh! what a deep is here, that created wit cannot take up! Jonathan Edwards takes it up with all his matchless wit in his fine letter to Thomas Gillespie of Carnock, and elsewhere in his golden works. And what do you say to Shakespeare himself?

O benefit of ill! now I find true
That better is by evil still made better!
And ruined love, when it is built anew,
Grows fairer than at first, more strong, far greater.
    So I return rebuked to my content,
    And gain by ill thrice more than I have spent.

And then, of death, the wages of sin. Can any good be said of death? Yes; by the proper man.

"Death," says Thomas Shepard, "is the very best of all our gospel ordinances. For in all His other ordinances Christ comes, on occasion, to us; but in a believer's death Christ takes us to be for ever with Him." A fair specimen of Shepard. And, to bind up this bold anthology with George Herbert:

Death, thou wert once an uncouth, hideous thing,
    Nothing but bones.
But since our Savior's death did put some blood
    Into thy face;
Thou art grown fair and full of grace,
Much in request, much sought for as a good.

This brings us to David's deathbed; and David's deathbed has never been without its own difficulties to thoughtful and reverential readers. For Shimei with all his good and all his bad uses comes back again to David's deathbed to tempt and to try David, and to discover what is in David's dying heart. The deathbed sayings of God's saints have a special interest and a delightful edification to us; but David's last words to Solomon about Shimei—we would pass them by if we could. Three or four several explanations of those terrible words of David have been offered to the distressed reader by able men and men of authority in such matters. I shall only mention some of those offered explanations, and leave you to judge for yourselves. Well, some students of the Old Testament are bold to take David's dreadful words about Shimei out of David's mouth altogether, and to put them into the mouth of the prophet who has preserved to us David's life and death. Those awful words, they say, are that righteous prophet's explanation and vindication of the too late execution of Shimei by Solomon after his reprieve had come to an end with the death of David. Others, again, and they, too, some of our most conservative and orthodox scholars, say to us that the text should run in English in this way: "Hold him not guiltless; at the same time bring *not* his hoar head down to the grave with blood." You will blame me for my too open ear to such bold scholarship; and you will think it very wrong in me to listen to such bad men. But the heart has its reasons, as Pascal says, and my heart would stretch a considerable point in textual criticism to get Shimei's blood wiped off David's deathbed. Another interpretation is to take the text as it stands, and to hear David judicially charging Solomon about a case of too long delayed justice against a blasphemer of God and the king. And then the last explanation is the most painful one of all, and it is this, that David had never really and truly, and at the bottom of his heart, forgiven Shimei for his brutality and malignity at Bahurim. And that all David's long-suppressed revenge rushed out of his heart against his old enemy when he lay on his bed and went back on the day on which he had fled from Jerusalem. You can choose your own way of looking at David's deathbed. But, in any case, it is Bahurim that we shall all carry home, and carry for ever henceforth, in our hearts. We shall have, God helping us, David's Bahurim-mind always in us henceforth amid all those who insult and injure us, and say all manner of evil against us falsely; and amid all manner of adverse and sore circumstances, so as to see the Lord in it all, and so as to work out our salvation amid it all. And the Lord will look upon our affliction also, and will requite us good for all this evil, if only we wisely and silently and adoringly submit ourselves to it.

46
Joab

JOAB, the son of David's sister, was a man of the very foremost ability. Had it not been for David, Joab would have climbed up into the throne of Israel. As it was, he stood on the steps of the throne and faced the king all his days. Notwithstanding their family relationship, David and Joab were much of an age, and that, no doubt, helps to account for a good deal that went on between the uncle and the nephew. Joab was a stern, haughty, imperious, revengeful man. His only virtue was a certain proud, patronizing loyalty to his king. Joab's ambition might surely have been satisfied, for he was in more respects than one the most privileged man in the land. Even the king himself was afraid of his commander-in-chief. The sovereign took his orders meekly from his subject. After his own contemptuous way, Joab was always true to David. That is to say, he made short work with any one else who was false to David. And he performed some splendid services both as a soldier and a statesman in the extension and consolidation of David's kingdom. In his own well-read and picturesque way, Dean Stanley describes Joab very aptly as the Marlborough of the empire of Israel.

Over-ambition, to put it all in one word, was Joab's besetting sin; over-vaulting ambition. But what more would Joab have had? you may well ask. Only, do not ask that any more about Joab, or about any other ambitious and self-seeking man. Look into your own heart and answer. If you look well into your own heart, you will see there that as long as any one else has anything at all of his own, it does not matter how much you have. Joab was king in all but the crown. King, and more. But as long as his weaker uncle wore the crown, Joab's heart raged like hell. Jonathan gave over to David all that he possessed, and all that he ever expected to possess, and died a king. Joab envied David and every one else all that they had, and died an outcast. Pride, jealousy, malignity, revenge, assassination, with now and then a gleam of satanic loyalty lighting up his terrible heart—such is the son of Zeruiah. The land trembles as Joab rises on the stepping-stones of murdered men to the shining top of power and honor, only to fall under the sword of a too-slow justice an outlaw from the love and the pity of all men.

David was all heart, and passion, and sensibility; while Joab was all self-will, and pride, and as hard as a stone. David's sudden and unparalleled exaltation was never forgiven him at home. His brothers and his sisters were sufficiently proud of David toward all their neighbors; at the same time they could never enough let him see how much they thought themselves as good as he was when they were alone together. But it was Joab who carried all that to a head. David and Joab were by far the ablest members of a very able household; but David was hampered with his heart, till Joab, having no heart, got the mastery. And thus it is that, already, and before David has well sat down on the throne, we hear him saying such things as these: "The sons of Zeruiah," David burst out, "be too hard for me. I am this day weak, though anointed king." And you may be sure that when that so unkingly speech was reported to the sons of Zeruiah, it did not make them any the less hard for David. Joab's temper was not any sweeter, nor his hand any lighter, after that and many suchlike deplorably foolish speeches of David. Already David lay and writhed in a net of ten thousand invisible threads and stings; and a chain of iron is soon to be forged for David by his own besotted hands. Men of much heart are always men of much mischief to themselves and to other men. To keep much of a heart with all diligence every moment—what a superhuman task is that! To keep much of a heart, to keep it in, to keep it down, to keep it open, but not too open— who is sufficient for these things? David yielded to Joab out of simple good-nature yesterday, and again today, and he will yield something far more important tomorrow, and so on. Each time he yields it is an act of rare courtesy, fine consideration, and most beautiful good-feeling and good-will—all touched, at the same time, with a certain tincture of fear. In any other world but this, and to any other man but Joab, David's heart would be an open heaven. But as it is, David wakens up too late to find out that he is king in nothing but in name. Neither his royal word, nor his personal liberty, nor his children, nor his tears over his dead children, are his own. Such is the mischief of too much heart and too little will in one member of a family, and too little heart and too much will in another. Let both look at David and Joab, and learn, and lay to heart. For we are all in this world, and in families, for this end, to learn how to rule our hearts; now to reduce and now to enlarge; now to harden and now to soften our hearts. The heart is the man. In this world, and in the world to come, the heart alone is the man. And we are in this world and in its families to make ourselves an everlasting heart.

"It is worse than a crime," says an astute politician, "it is a blunder." And though it was a clear enough crime in David to pass by Joab's murder of Abner, it came out afterwards to be a most terrible blunder. All David's after-life might well have been different but for that blunder. There might have been no "matter of Uriah," and no rebellion of Absalom, and none of the many other miseries that so desolated David's house, had he not committed this fatal blunder of letting Joab live. David knew his duty quite well. "The Lord shall reward the doer of evil according to his wickedness," David proclaimed over Abner's mangled body. Yes; but David held the sword for no other purpose than to be the Lord's right hand in rewarding all the evil that was done in Israel in his day. But, then, Joab was the most powerful and the most necessary man in Israel, and Abner had no friends, and David contented himself with pronouncing an eloquent requiem over Abner, and leaving his murderer to go free in all his offices and all his honors. Joab was deep enough to understand quite well why his life was spared. He knew quite well that it was fear and not love that had moved David to let him live. It was a diplomatic act of David to spare Joab, but David was playing with a far deeper diplomatist than himself. Very soon we shall see this respited assassin ordering David about and dictating to him, till we shall pity David as well as blame him. Joab's impunity speedily shot up into an increased contempt for David, till secret contempt became open insolence, and open insolence open and unavenged rebellion. Was it not a blunder?

In the corrupted currents of this world,
Offence's gilded hand may shove by justice,
And oft 'tis seen, the wicked prize itself
Buys out the law: but 'tis not so above;
There is no shuffling, there the action lies
In his true nature; and we ourselves compell'd,
Even to the teeth and forehead of our faults,
To give in evidence.

"And it came to pass in the morning that David wrote a letter to Joab, and sent it by the hand of Uriah. And he wrote in the letter saying: Thou shalt set Uriah in the forefront of the hottest battle, and retire from him, that he may be smitten and die." That dreadful letter shows us David's desperation, indeed; but it shows us also David's estimate of Joab. Had Jonathan been spared to be second to David this would never have happened. David would never have dared to send such a letter as that to Jonathan. But Jonathan was taken and Joab was left, and David had Joab for his tool to impress on our hearts the terrible portent of a bloodstained holiness. But how could Joab have the utter depravity and the cold blood to do it? you ask. How could he plan an attack, and sham a retreat, and risk a defeat, and all to murder a noble, spotless, unsuspecting comrade? It was not soldierly obedience. Joab did not care one straw for the king's letter. When it suited him, Joab could tear up the king's letters and throw them in his face. Unless you can tell us, we shall never in this world know why Joab murdered Uriah after that letter. Unless you are astute enough, and wicked enough, and then honest enough to tell us, we shall not know till the day of judgment what all passed through Joab's heart when he read that letter, and read it again with his glancing eyes. Joab had some sufficient motive for following out David's detestable orders. But unless you find out Joab's motive among your own motives, we shall have to leave him alone. It was like Pilate and the chief priests with our Lord between them. They also had their motives. Only, their motives are as plain as day, while Joab was a deep man— deeper, quite possibly, than any man here. And it came to pass that, when Joab observed the city, he assigned Uriah unto a place where he knew that valiant men were on the wall. And Uriah fell. And David said to Joab's messenger, Let not this thing displease thee. But the thing that David had done displeased the Lord. And the Lord had Joab in His hand henceforth as the rod of his displeasure, and Joab had David's letter in his hand till, if there is a man on the face of the earth to be pitied from that time forward, it is David.

Better a living dog than a dead lion. David was the first lion of the tribe of Judah, and it is sad to see how his teeth and his claws were broken, and his sinews cut, by his tormentors. You are but a dog beside David. Only, you have this, that you are still alive, and young, and free, and unsold as yet, whereas David is dead. You are too young to have written any letters yet worth any one keeping. "Destroy this letter as soon as you have read it," David wrote at the top of it. "Under the strictest seal of secrecy, and on the king's own business," Uriah read on the envelope, and handed it with all speed and respect to his chief. "Read and burn instantly," wrote

David in state cipher. But Joab was not the man to throw an autograph letter of the king into the fire. Joab recollected what prices such letters bring in the auction rooms, and, instead of burning David's letter, he folded it carefully, and buttoned it up in his breast-pocket. That letter was still deep down in Joab's breast-pocket when Benaiah at David's demand fell upon him and slew him in spite of the horns of the altar. You are still in your innocence, and have written no letters. And were you my only son, may I bury you first before you write your first letter to Joab.

Tool turned tyrant—that shortly sums up Joab and David for the next thirty years. Only an insult here and a humiliation there has been preserved to us out of the daily insults and humiliations that Joab heaped upon David. Joab had no more pity than a tiger, and the tiger's claws were never out of David's flesh from the matter of Uriah down to David's death. David had said unto Nathan, I have sinned against the Lord. And Nathan had said unto David, The Lord also hath put away thy sin, thou shalt not die. But David had far better have died and been buried beside his sin. Thou answeredst them, O Lord our God; Thou wast a God that forgavest them, but Thou tookest vengeance of their inventions. And Joab was just the instrument to glut himself in the divine vengeance. "Joab insolently falls foul of David," is one of Matthew Henry's plain-spoken remarks. And again, "He calls David a fool to his face." We have only one in a thousand of Joab's insolent speeches to David's face. But the sacred writer surely selects and preserves his very best instance of tool turned tyrant and his insolent speech, in the case of Absalom. Joab ran Absalom three times through the heart right in the teeth of David's command to spare and save Absalom alive. And then, when David broke out in that terrible sorrow which sounds in our hearts to this day, Joab would not have it. There has been enough weeping now for Absalom, said Joab to David. Let there be no more. And David dried his eyes on the spot like a cowed child, and turned to the business of the kingdom, cursing Joab all the time in his heart. It was David's sad case that made our Lord say in David's city a thousand years after, Verily, verily, I say unto you, whosoever committeth sin is the servant of sin. And all Scripture is full of the same warning. Know ye not that to whom ye yield yourselves servants to obey, his servants ye are whom ye obey? For of whom a man is overcome, of the same he is brought in bondage. All this of David and Joab is only the life of some of ourselves sold for naught, and written out with all plainness of speech, and put of God into our hands.

I have been sorely tempted to take up the mystical interpretation of Shimei and Joab. Those two Scripture characters so lend themselves to the mystical method. Those two thorns in David's flesh—and there are more like them—so suit into the secretest depths of our own spiritual experience. Those two bad men were, each in his own wicked way, of such rich and indispensable use to David, if David was to be searched out, hunted down, laid low, and saved at last. They so struck in, made of God and kept of God for the very purpose, to tempt, and to vex, and to humiliate, and to weaken, and to keep broken David's broken heart. They, Joab especially, were ever with David. Joab with his insolence, and his cruelty, and his family familiarity, and his equality in years, and all that eating in and growing, on to David's deathbed—I declare it is another parable of that cunning Nathan, and not a true and honest history at all! It is a subtle allegory all the time; and that, too, of our own life. Yes, that is it. It is my life and yours; if your life is at all like mine, or is going to be, you who are yet young. It is our own life under sin, as Paul says, and under grace. Under forgiveness, and then under vengeance, as David says, and had such a good right to say. Only, come, all ye who would learn beforehand the ways of God, and we will tell you as good as anything that ever was told even of David. As good. As sad. As painful. As awful. And still more amazing in its grace. Shimei cursing and throwing stones. Joab, first tool and then ever after tyrant. We will show you such a letter. A sackful of such letters. And the writer of them walking softly, and never ceasing from prayer and tears on account of them all his days. O sacred chronicler, look well to your laurels! If once we take pen in hand, where would you be—Shimei, and Joab, and Absalom, and Ahithophel and all! O Lord, open Thou my lips, and I will show forth Thy praise. Then will I teach transgressors Thy ways, and sinners shall be converted unto Thee. Thou art my hiding-place; Thou shalt compass me about with songs of deliverance. Thou shalt hide them in the secret of Thy presence from the pride of men. Thou shalt keep them secretly in a pavilion from the strife of tongues. Be of good courage, and He shall strengthen your heart, all ye that hope in the Lord.

47
Absalom

POLYGAMY is just Greek for a dunghill. David trampled down the first and the best law of nature in his palace in Jerusalem, and for his trouble he spent all his after-days in a hell upon earth. David's palace was a perfect pandemonium of suspicion, and intrigue, and jealousy, and hatred—all breaking out, now into incest and now into murder. And it was in such a household, if such a cesspool could be called a household, that Absalom, David's third son by his third living wife, was born and brought up. But be not deceived; God is not mocked: for whatsoever a patriarch, or a prophet, or a psalmist soweth, that shall he also reap. For he, saint or sinner, that soweth to his flesh shall of the flesh reap corruption.

Maachah, Absalom's mother, was the daughter of a king. And this, taken together with his distinguished appearance and his princely manners, gave Absalom the pre-eminence over all his brethren. Absalom inherited all the handsomeness, manly bearing, and beauty of his father's handsome and manly house. The sacred writer expatiates with evident relish upon Absalom's extraordinary beauty. In all Israel there was none to be so much praised as Absalom for his beauty. From the sole of his foot even to the crown of his head there was no blemish in him. And the hair of his head is a proverb to this day.

A little ring of jealous and scheming parasites, all hateful and hating one another, collected round each one of David's wives. And it was in one of the worst of those wicked little rings that Absalom grew up and got his education. Absalom had a sister, named Tamar, who was as beautiful as a woman as Absalom was as a man. And how her beauty became the occasion of her ruin in that horrible household the sacred historian tells us with sufficient plainness of speech. Suffice it here to say that Absalom determined, sooner or later, to wash off his sister's terrible wrongs in the blood of the wrongdoer. And, then, as the divine vengeance would have it to be, that wrongdoer to one of David's fairest daughters was one of David's favorite sons. The Septuagint frankly tells us that David loved the wrongdoer so much that he could not so much as rebuke him for his brutality. But, after giving his father two full years to avenge his sister's ruin, Absalom took the law into his own hand till Amnon fell, when his heart was merry with wine, under Absalom's revengeful sword. And, then, all the plots and counter-plots connected with Absalom's revenge, and flight, and restoration, and too-late reconciliation to his father; his deep-laid schemes to wrench the kingdom out of his father's hands; and then his defeat and murder by Joab—all that, if we have the courage to look at it, will give us a picture of the men and the times, humiliating beyond all words, and never to be forgotten. David and his wives and concubines and mixed-up children, Tamar and her half-brother Amnon, Absalom and Jonadab, Joab and the wise woman of Tekoa, Ittai and Shimei, Ahithophel and Hushai, and the righteousness and the grace of God reigning over them all. Truly, all Scripture is given by inspiration of

God, and is profitable for doctrine, for reproof, for correction, for instruction in righteousness; that the man of God may be perfect, thoroughly furnished unto all good works.

It is this so terrible plain-spokenness of the Bible that makes it so precious to all who are in earnest about themselves and their children. Had this sacred writer not been in earnest in his work, we should have had an altogether different David. And we make an altogether different David to ourselves in spite of the sacred writer, and in spite of all that David himself can say and do. The David that we set up for ourselves has always a halo round his head and a harp in his hand, and his eyes fixed on the heavens. We are willingly ignorant that David had ever any other wife but Solomon's mother, as also that she had ever any other son but Solomon. And, then, our Solomon is always dreaming his dream at Gibeon, and when he is not choosing wisdom for himself he is always writing inspired proverbs about wisdom for his son. While all the time David prevents the night-watches with psalms like this: I will behave myself wisely in a perfect way. O when wilt thou come unto me? I will walk within my house with a perfect heart. I will set no thing of Belial before mine eyes: I hate the work of them that turn aside; it shall not cleave to me, and so on. A David like that in our Bible would have delighted us, and would not have offended and shocked us. No. But then neither would he have been of any real use to us when we went to our Bible for real use. It is when we go to our Bible for real use, for the experiences of men of like passions with ourselves, it is then that we discover and see the pen of God in the Bible life of David. And it is from that pen that I gather these closing lessons out of the life of David and out of the death of Absalom.

"The inconceivable evil of sensuality" was surely never more awfully burned in upon any sinful house than it was upon David's house. David himself is a towering warning to all men, and especially to all godly men against this master abomination. And, all the more that he sinned so terribly against such singular grace. David, to use his own words, was as white as snow as long as he was young, and poor, and struggling up, and oppressed, and persecuted, and with Samuel's horn of oil still sanctifying all the thoughts and all the imaginations of his heart. But no sooner had David sat down on the throne of Israel than his life of sin and shame began. And all the woe upon woe of his after-life, almost every single deadly drop of it, came down out of that day when he first introduced open and unblushing sensuality into his palace in Jerusalem. There was military success, and extended empire, and great wealth, and great and far-sounding glory in David's day in Israel; but beneath it all the whole ground was mined and filled to the lip with gunpowder, and the divine tinder all the time was surely burning its way to the divine vengeance on David's house. Our doctors, our lawyers, our ministers, and many of ourselves, will all subscribe to Newman's strong words in one of his sermons—"The inconceivable evil of sensuality."

You sometimes hear speak about the historical imagination, and the right and the fruitful uses of the historical imagination. Well, here is the history of young Absalom, and you must bring your imagination to bear upon it. You must read all the chapters about David's manner of life in Jerusalem, and all the chapters in which Absalom's name comes up, and then you must imagine yourself to be Absalom, and to be in his place. I dare not put in words what you will see when you read Second Samuel with your eye upon the object. For one thing, Absalom did not see his father David at all as we see him. He saw him as his enemies then saw him, and as infidels and scoffers see him now. It was impossible that Absalom could look on his father with our admiring eyes. "It helped me, too," says Santa Teresa in her happy "Life of Herself"; "It helped me much that I never saw my father and my mother respect anything but goodness." "It poisoned me at my father," said Absalom to Ahithophel; "the life we all led in our several stews." Yes, polygamy is indeed a dunghill. Only, it is a dunghill with hell at the heart of it. We have nothing like the city of David on this side the Dardanelles. And no real lesson for our day and our household can be got out of Absalom's early life. Unless it is that far-fetched lesson to that fatal house where there is a father who is no father. And to that house where the father and the mother are full of divided lives, divided interests, divided counsels, divided tastes, and divided desires for themselves and their children. The sons and the daughters of such divided fathers and mothers will need neither history nor imagination to see and to feel with poor Absalom. Only, this lesson to such fathers and mothers is all but too late and irrecoverable.

The Hebrew Bible for some unaccountable reason is silent where the Greek Bible speaks out boldly about David, and delivers a great lesson to all of us who are fathers. The law of Moses was plain. It is to be read in the Book of Leviticus to this day. "It is a wicked thing. And he that does it shall be cut off in the sight of all the people. He shall bear his iniquity." Well, Amnon did it. Amnon was worse than if he had been the actual murderer of his own sister. But what do we read on this matter in the Septuagint? We literally read this: "Notwithstanding Amnon's sin David did not trouble the spirit of Amnon his son, because he loved him, and because he was his first-born." But, not to trouble the spirit of your son for his sin is to trouble other people's spirit all his days, ay, and your own spirit and his too, to the bargain. The Greek Bible has recovered for us one of the lost links in David's downward career, and in the downward career of Absalom his son. For it was David's unwillingness to trouble Amnon that made Absalom in the cause of his sister first a murderer, and then a conspirator, and then, after a life of terrible trouble, himself a mangled corpse under the revengeful and murderous hands of Joab, that other arch-troubler of Israel. "Praise them openly, reprehend them secretly," is the second of Lord Burleigh's ten precepts to his son concerning his children. But David did the very opposite of that with Absalom. All Jerusalem heard David for two years reprehending his half-pardoned son Absalom openly, till Absalom was exasperated out of all endurance, and till the last link of sonship was broken for ever between David and Absalom.

But, with all that, it is the terrible cry that comes out of the chamber over the gate of Mahanaim that makes the name of Absalom so well known and so full of the most terrible lessons to us. "O my son Absalom, my son, my son Absalom! Would God I had died for thee, O Absalom, my son, my son!" Yes, that is love, no doubt. That is the love of a broken-hearted father, no doubt. But the pang of the cry, the innermost agony of the cry, the poisoned point of the dagger in that cry is remorse. I have slain my son! I have murdered my son with my own hands! I neglected my son Absalom from a child! With my own lusts I laid his very worst temptation right in his way. It had been better Absalom had never been born! If he rebelled, who shall blame him? I, David, drove Absalom to rebellion. It was his father's hand that stabbed Absalom through the heart. O Absalom, my murdered son! Would God thy murderer had been in thy place this day. And the king covered his face, and the king cried with a loud voice, O my son Absalom, O Absalom, my son, my son!

Come all you who are fathers and mothers, come to the chamber over the gate of Mahanaim, and let us take counsel together as to how we are to bring up our children to virtue and godliness and everlasting life. Let us read all Holy Writ on this subject together; and after Holy Writ, all other good and true books that in any way bear upon this supreme subject. Let us set ourselves to gather together all our experience and all our observation, and let us counsel and correct and comfort one another concerning this one thing that we do, our children. Let us take time to it, and pains, and pursue it until we succeed in it. Let us search the Scriptures up to the top and down to the bottom for this pearl of great price. Let us set on one side all the fathers and mothers in Israel to whom God hath ever said, I know him that he will command his children and his household after him, and they shall keep the way of the Lord, to do justice and judgment, that the Lord may bring upon Abraham that which He hath spoken of him. And then let us set on the other side David and all those fathers and mothers on whom God took vengeance, and said, Now, therefore, the sword shall never depart from thine house. I will raise up evil against thee out of thine own house. Let us collect into a secret and solemn book all such instances; and let us, husband and wife, minister and people, and one anxious parent with another, let us meet together, and confer together, and pray together, saying, This one thing will we do. Why do men and women combine and consult together about everything else but the thing in which so many are so ignorant, so stupid, and so full of fatal mistakes? If we asked our happy neighbors, they would surely tell us the secret of their success in their children. How did they come so well and so soon to understand their children? How early did they discover what manner of heart was already in their children? And at what age did they begin to deal with the hearts of their children? What amount of time did they set aside and keep sacred for reflection and for prayer to God for their child; naming their child and describing him; and how did God's answer begin to show itself first in the parents and then in the child? When did your child first begin to show some sure signs of saving grace? And how did that grace show itself to your satisfaction and thanksgiving; first in one child and then in another? Tell us about the Sabbath—how it was observed, occupied, and sanctified as your children grew up? About the church also and the Sabbath-school? About the books that were read on Sabbath-days and week days; both by your children alone and of their own accord, as also with you all reading together; one reading and all the rest listening? Things like that. All that you can tell us about such children as yours will be eagerly listened to and attended to. What priceless stores of experience, and observation, and success and defeat are lost all around us just because we do not speak more to one another about our ways with our children; our hopes and our fears; our neglects and our recoveries of neglects; the things that one household is so happy in, and the same things that cause such unavailing remorse in another household. Yes, this whole matter must surely be collected together and made into a science soon, and taught in every true church to every young father and young mother as their very life.

48
Ahithophel

I AM not going to whitewash and rehabilitate Ahithophel. I am neither to extenuate nor am I to denounce Ahithophel. I shall put myself back into Ahithophel's place, and I shall speak of Ahithophel as I see and feel Ahithophel to have been. I shall do my best to put myself first into Ahithophel's place, and then into David's place, and then I shall tell you exactly and honestly what I see and what I feel, first as to Ahithophel, and then as to David. But, to begin with, who was Ahithophel, and what were the facts?

Well, Ahithophel was far and away the ablest and the most famous politician, as we would say, in that day. The counsel of Ahithophel was a proverb in Israel in David's day. There was no one fit to hold the candle to Ahithophel in that day, unless it was Hushai the Archite, another of David's astutest counselors. "For the counsel of Ahithophel," says the sacred writer, "which he counselled in those days, was as if a man had inquired at the oracle of God: so was all the counsel of Ahithophel both with David and with Absalom."

> Of those the false Ahithophel was first:
> For close designs and crooked counsels fit,
> Sagacious, bold, and turbulent of wit,
> Restless, unfixed in principles and place,
> In power unpleased, impatient of disgrace;
> A fiery soul, which, working out its way,
> Fretted the pigmy body to decay,
> And o'er-informed the tenement of clay.

So Dryden describes Lord Chancellor Shaftesbury in his *Absalom and Ahithophel*, that very able but still more truculent and time-serving piece. Matthew Henry is always worth consulting. "Ahithophel was a politic, thinking man, and one that had a clear head, and a great compass of thought," and so on. If the traditional interpretation of the fifty-fifth and some other Ahithophel psalms is true and is to be taken, David and Ahithophel had been bosom friends from their boyhood up. Ahithophel may not have been exactly a Jonathan, and yet he may have been a very dear and well-deserving friend for all that. David and Ahithophel were such close companions, indeed, that had it not been for Jonathan, the proverb might have run thus—David and Ahithophel: so was the soul of David knit to the soul of Ahithophel. Jonathan strengthened David's hand in God, it is true; but this out of David and about Ahithophel is almost as good. "A man, mine equal, my guide, and mine acquaintance. We took sweet counsel together, and walked unto the house of God in company." Till, when David's time came to be lifted up of God into the throne of Israel, Ahithophel was proud to lay all his magnificent gifts of sound advice and incomparable counsel at David's feet. And Ahithophel continued to do that for all the best and most shining years of David's kingdom. David never made a law nor gave a judgment, nor proclaimed a war, nor negotiated a truce, nor signed a peace, till Ahithophel had been heard, and till his advice had been taken. But the sacred writer has already given you all that, and far more than all that, in one of his incomparably strong and satisfying sentences; it was, he says, as if a man had inquired at the oracle of God.

All that Ahithophel was to David in the councilchamber, all that Eliam, Ahithophel's only son, was in the army. The father's splendid talents for counsel came out in the shape of soldierly service in the son; and the son was as devoted to David in the field as his father was in the chamber. Now, Eliam had a daughter at home, a beautiful woman-child, who was the one ewe-lamb of her father Eliam and her grandfather Ahithophel. And it so happened that Eliam had a very trusty under-officer among the captains of the mighty men, whose famous name was Uriah. This Uriah was not an Israelite—he was a Hittite; but he was as brave and as loyal to David as if he had been an Hebrew of the Hebrews. And his high talents and his great services had carried him to the very top of the six hundred, where he stood clothed with worth and with honor beside Eliam the son of Ahithophel. With his whole soul Uriah loved Eliam's daughter, and both Eliam and Ahithophel gave to young Uriah the desire of his heart. David's devoted bodyguard had their quarters built for them in the city of David, and just under the walls of David's palace; and when Uriah came home on furlough, he was the happiest man in all Jerusalem with such a wife, and with Eliam and with Ahithophel. As time went on, and as Ahithophel counselled for David, and as Eliam and Uriah fought for David, David's power increased till the King of Israel denied himself nothing on which he had once set his heart. And in an evil hour he set his heart on Uriah's wife, who was also Ahithophel's one grandchild. And it does not need an oracle of God to tell us how Ahithophel took the ruin of his grandchild and the murder of her husband. Ahithophel would have been Jesus Christ Himself to have continued after all that to take sweet counsel with David, and to walk with David unto the house of God in company. I do not like to listen to all the names you would have called Ahithophel and Eliam had they still remained in David's service, and had they still eaten David's bread, with Bathsheba in David's bed and with her husband in his grave. I do not know what all you would have called Eliam and Ahithophel had they winked in that way at David's adultery and blood-guiltiness.

It was all that Ahithophel could do: he shook the dust off his feet, and Ahithophel returned home out of the city of David to his own city of Giloh. And no sooner had Ahithophel left David than the Lord sent Nathan to David. And Nathan said to David, Thus saith the Lord God of Israel, I anointed thee king over Israel, and I delivered thee out of the hand of Saul. And I gave thee thy master's house, and gave thee the house of Israel and of Judah; and if that had been too little, I would moreover have given unto thee such and such things. Wherefore hast thou despised the commandment of the Lord, to do evil in His sight? Thou hast killed Uriah the Hittite with the edge of the sword, and hast taken his wife, Ahithophel's granddaughter, to be thy wife, and hast slain Uriah with the sword of the children of Ammon. Now, therefore, the sword shall never depart from thy house. For thus saith the Lord, I will raise up evil against thee out of thine own house. For thou didst it secretly, but I will do this thing before all Israel and before the sun. And, after that, our hearts stand still as we watch how the vengeance of God came down on David's head, and how the vengeance of God travelled, as it always does, on stepping-stones which David laid for it with his own hands. As thus: And Amnon loved Absalom's sister. . . . But David did not trouble the spirit of Amnon, because he was his first-born. . . . And Absalom's servants did to Amnon as Absalom had commanded. And Absalom fled and went to Geshur, and was there three years. . . . And David said, Let him return to Jerusalem, but let him not see my face. . . . And Absalom stole the hearts of the men of Israel. . . . And Absalom sent for Ahithophel the Gilonite, David's counsellor, from his city, even from Giloh. And the conspiracy was strong, and the people increased continually with Absalom. For the counsel of Ahithophel, which he counselled in those days, was as if a man inquired at the oracle of God; so was all the counsel of Ahithophel with Absalom as it had been wont to be with David.

Absalom had no head of his own. But he had what was better than ten heads of his own, for he had a head to know those who had heads and to send to their cities for them. And with Ahithophel's head like the oracle of God, and with his heart rankling against David like hell, the conspiracy was strong, and the people increased continually with Absalom. Ahithophel was worth ten thousand men to Absalom, and no one knew that better than David. And one told David, saying, Ahithophel is among the conspirators with Absalom. And David said, O Lord, I pray thee, turn the counsel of Ahithophel into foolishness. And then David took Hushai, his next astutest counsellor to Ahithophel, and filled him with guile and sent him back to deceive Absalom and to counteract all the counsels of Ahithophel. Which he did. For at the end of all their cross-counsels we read this report and this reflection of the sacred writer on it all: And Absalom said, The counsel of Hushai the Archite is better than the counsel of Ahithophel. For the Lord had appointed to defeat the good counsel of Ahithophel, to the intent that He might bring evil upon Absalom. Ahithophel gave two of his deepest counsels to Absalom. Ahithophel has been called Judas, and all manner of evil names, for his first counsel that he gave to Absalom. And, no doubt, Ahithophel's first counsel sounds in our ears at this time of day abominable enough. But you will believe all things, and will hope all things even about Ahithophel. You will judge neither Ahithophel nor any other man, "without necessity, nor without knowledge, nor without love." For Absalom had said to Ahithophel, Give counsel among you what we shall do. And Ahithophel gave Absalom a counsel that you know already, or if you do not know it you will read it at home. Nothing, certainly, could sound worse. But, when I put myself in Ahithophel's place, for anything I know, the so subtle and so sorely injured Ahithophel may honestly enough have said something like this to himself. Something, possibly, like this: "Has not David cast himself completely out of the throne? Has he not destroyed himself? Has he not thrown down the scepter? Has not the Lord turned against him? And did not the Lord's righteous servant say that the Lord would do this same thing to David that David had done before all Israel and before the sun? I am only counselling Absalom to fulfill as the hand of the Lord what the Lord swore that He would do Himself to David." Ahithophel's extraordinary and superhuman subtlety may honestly enough have led him to think that he saw in his counsel both prophecy, and policy, and payment back again into David's own bosom of all that David had done to other men, and to no man more than to Ahithophel himself. But whatever may be said about Ahithophel's first counsel, his second counsel to Absalom is pronounced to be good by the sacred writer; but, then, what of that, when the Lord had appointed to defeat it that the Lord might bring evil upon Absalom? When we are working upon Ahithophel in this way, and when our minds and our hearts are full of Ahithophel, we cannot but wish that we had been told some more about him, and especially about his latter end. But the sacred writer has to hasten on. He has David and Absalom so much on his mind and on his heart that he draws a black border round Ahithophel's deathbed in these terrible words, and then leaves him: And when Ahithophel saw that his counsel was not followed, he saddled his ass, and arose, and gat him home to his own house, to his city, and put his household in order, and hanged himself, and died, and was buried in the sepulchre of his father.

Now, as you know, Ahithophel, from that day to this, has been stoned in his grave at Giloh, and all manner of names called at him as he lies there: Deserter, traitor, apostate, Judas Iscariot, suicide, and all manner of evil names, because he left David and joined Absalom. And, no doubt, had Ahithophel seen to the end, as he should have seen; had Ahithophel known all that we know—and if he had been a better man he would have known more than even he was let know—had he known the half of what we know, Ahithophel would have held fast to David, let David do what he liked. But Ahithophel lived in the day of David and not yet in the day of Christ; and he suffered at the hand of David what neither you nor I have ever suffered at any man's hand. And if he did not live and die in David's service, and if you will never forgive him for that; then, if it will do you any good, you can go home casting stones all the way at Bathsheba's broken-hearted grandfather. My business tonight is neither to whitewash Ahithophel nor blacken David, even were that possible, but to let you see yourselves in them both as in a glass. How, then, have you always acted toward those of your former friends who have injured you and yours? Did you shut your door this morning and pray in secret, saying, Forgive me my trespasses against God and man, as I forgive him—naming him— who has so trespassed against me? When you stood here praying tonight, did you forgive some enemy? Ahithophel should have conquered himself. Ahithophel was not a Hittite. Ahithophel was well read in all the law of Moses, if not yet in the law of Christ. Ahithophel should have gone on with his work in the city of David. He should have said—what, indeed, had he got his great head and his deep heart for but to say it with them?—Vengeance is not mine. I have eaten David's bread when he had plenty, Ahithophel should have said, and he shall come to Giloh now and eat my bread. Yes, Ahithophel, like the oracle of God he was, should have called to mind this psalm of David, and said: It shall be an excellent oil, which shall not break my head; for yet my prayer shall be for David in all his calamities.

And, then, on the other hand, though it is not written out, I for one shall continue to believe it, that David in his best moments took it all home to himself that Ahithophel was gone over to Absalom. David knew quite well all the time whose grandchild Uriah's wife was. As soon as David came to himself he must have foreseen all this. David was not so quick in the uptake as Ahithophel, but he was not a fool—when he came to himself. David knew as well as all Jerusalem did what it was that had thrown Ahithophel over to Absalom's side. We see it every day in our own parties in the state, in our parties in the church, in our parties in the city, in our parties in our families. We have the gall and wormwood in ourselves that it was we ourselves that did it. It was our bad temper, our bad tongue, our want of thought, our want of love, our want of patience, our want of humility that threw this old ally and that old adviser, this able man and that rich man, into the opposite camp. We all know men who have, to all appearance, gone over for ever from truth and goodness, and from the winning to the losing side, because of us. Every time we meet them on the street, every time we hear their name spoken, every time we call them in any way to mind, something says within us—You did it. We ministers especially have our own very heavy hearts on this account. Our neglect of duty, our laziness and procrastination at a moment that went in a moment, and that we shall look back to with remorse all our days; our hot-headedness, our domineeringness, our indiscretions of speech, and our follies in conduct. Where is that family? Where is that former friend? Where is he who was once to us as the oracle of God? Where is that man, mine equal, my guide, and mine acquaintance? We took sweet counsel together, and walked unto the house of God in company. Why is he no longer here? Why is he where he now is?

And, then, what did David think when Ahithophel's terrible end was told him? And what did Bathsheba think? Did she curse David to his face when it was told her what her grandfather had done to himself? Did Uriah's wife fling David's psalms in his face in her agony of horror and self-disgust? Did she scream in her sleep till all Jerusalem heard her as she saw in her sleep her grandfather's gallows at Giloh? Or was this prophecy fulfilled before it was spoken: In that day there shall be a great mourning in Jerusalem, the house of David apart, and their wives apart, till there shall be a fountain opened to the house of David for sin and for uncleanness? And then did David go out to Giloh, and over the sepulchre of the suicide did David fall down and cry, past all consolation, O Ahithophel, the friend of my youth and my best counsellor, Ahithophel! Would God I had died for thee! O Ahithophel, mine equal, my guide, and mine acquaintance! If he did—then this would come in, The sacrifices of God are a broken heart. What did David think, and what did Bathsheba think? True. But what would you think if the first thing you saw tomorrow morning was the suicide of some one who has been the victim of your lust or your lies? Pray, man, pray. In God's name, pray. And though the poison may be bought, and the rope put up, God can do it. God can deliver you. With God all things are possible. Pray, you great sinner; pray, you great fool, pray. Pray, lest the newspaper run blood on your hands some morning, as the letters from Giloh ran Ahithophel's blood on David's hands. Pray for your Ahithophel without ceasing, and for all your Ahithophel's house. Give God no rest till He has remitted to you Ahithophel and all his injuries, and till He has repented of the evil He has reserved out of Ahithophel and out of his house against you. Every day you live, and till the day of your death, beseech the living God to make it all up to your Ahithophel and to set it all down to your account.

49
Mephibosheth

MEPHIBOSHETH has been an enigma of motive and a study in self-interest from David's day down to our own day. Wherever the heart of man comes in you have always an enigma of motive and a study in self-interest. Wherever the heart of man plays a part you are soon out of your depth. There are many devices in a man's heart, and counsel in a man's heart is like deep water. The sacred writer sets us the enigma of Mephibosheth and his servant Ziba; but he gives us no hint at all as to how we are to decipher that enigma. He tells us Mephibosheth's story from the outside and on the surface, and so leaves us to make of the inside of it what we can. By that time both Mephibosheth and Ziba and David had long passed away; and already their motives and their mainsprings may well have become a sacred riddle in Israel. Given the story of Mephibosheth, and the story of Ziba, first at the flight of David and then at his victorious return, and then—was Mephibosheth a heartless, selfish, contemptible time-server, while Ziba, his servant, was a prince beside him? Or, was Ziba a lying scoundrel, and Mephibosheth a poor, innocent, ill-used, lameter saint? Let us see the surface of the story.

Mephibosheth was the son and heir of Jonathan, David's oldest and best friend. Mephibosheth, the future king of Israel, was only five years old when Jonathan his father, and Saul his grandfather, both fell in the same battle on Mount Gilboa, and with their fall their family fell from the throne. In the terror that took possession of Jonathan's household that terrible day, Mephibosheth's nurse caught up the child and fled with him in her arms. But in her haste she let the little prince fall, and from that fall Mephibosheth was lame in his feet all his days. Years pass on. David sits in the throne of Saul and Jonathan and Mephibosheth, and his enemies are all subdued round about David. In his remembrance of God's great mercies, and in the magnanimity of his heart, David often called Saul and Jonathan to mind. And David said, Is there yet any that is left of the house of Saul, that I may show him kindness for Jonathan's sake? And there was of the house of Saul a servant whose name was Ziba. And when they had called him unto David, the king said unto him, Art thou Ziba? And he said, Thy servant is he. And the king said, Is there not yet any of the house of Saul, that I may show the kindness of God to him? And Ziba said unto the king, Jonathan hath yet a son, which is lame on his feet. And the king said unto him, Where is he? And Ziba said unto the king, Behold, he is in the house of Machir, the son of Ammiel, from Lo-debar. Then King David sent and fetched Mephibosheth out of the house of Machir, the son of Ammiel, from Lo-debar. And David said unto him, Fear not, for I will surely show thee kindness for Jonathan, thy father's sake, and will restore thee all the lands of Saul thy father, and thou shalt eat bread at my table continually. So Mephibosheth dwelt in Jerusalem, for he did eat continually at the king's table, and was lame on both his feet.

Years passed on again, till Absalom by fair speeches and skillful courtesies had stolen the hearts of all Israel, of all of which Mephibosheth was a silent student, eating at David's table continually. And Absalom sent for Ahithophel the Gilonite, David's old counsellor, from his city, even from Giloh. And the conspiracy was strong, for the people increased continually with Absalom, but Mephibosheth still ate at the king's table. And there came a messenger to David, saying, The hearts of the men of Israel are gone after Absalom. And David said unto his servants, and to them that sat at his table, Arise, let us flee. And the king went forth, and all his household after him. But Mephibosheth was lame on both his feet. And when David was a little past the top of the hill, behold, Ziba, the servant of Mephibosheth, met David with a couple of asses saddled, and upon them two hundred loaves of bread, and an hundred bunches of raisins, and an hundred of summer fruits, and a bottle of wine. And the king said to Ziba, What meanest thou by these? And Ziba said, The asses be for the king's household to ride on, and the bread and the summer fruits for the young men to eat, and the wine that such as be faint in the wilderness may drink. And the king said, Where is thy master's son? And Ziba said to the king, Behold, he abideth in Jerusalem; for he said, Today shall the house of Israel restore to me the kingdom of my father. Then the king said to Ziba, Behold, thine are all that pertained to Mephibosheth. A few days after that the great battle was set in the wood of Ephraim, and of Absalom's side there was a great slaughter of twenty thousand men. And it was on that day that David went up to the chamber over the gate of Mahanaim, and wept; and as he went there he said, O my son Absalom; my son, my son Absalom! would God I had died for thee, O Absalom, my son, my son!

So the king returned and came to Jordan. And Shimei, who had cursed and stoned David on the day of his flight from Jerusalem, hasted first and came down to meet King David. And Shimei fell down before the king and said, Let not my lord impute iniquity unto me, neither do thou remember that which thy servant did perversely the day that my lord the king went out of Jerusalem, that the king should take it to his heart. For, behold, I am come the first this day to go down to meet my lord the king. And the king said to Shimei, Thou shalt not die. And the king sware unto him. And Mephibosheth also, the son of Saul, came down to meet the king. Our too otiose English is unjust to Mephibosheth; or else it has taken Mephibosheth's infirmity in his feet much too seriously. Mephibosheth was not so crippled in his intellects, at any rate, as to stay in Jerusalem till the king came home. He was too eager for that to congratulate the king on his victory. We all know how the mind overmasters the body, and makes us forget all about its lameness, on occasions. And Mephibosheth was at the Jordan all the way from Jerusalem almost as soon as Shimei himself. Four hundred years before, just at the same place, when the inhabitants of Gibeon heard what Joshua had done to Jericho and to Ai, they did work wilily, and went and made as if they had been ambassadors, and took old sacks upon their asses, and wine bottles old and rent and bound up, and old shoes and clouted upon their feet, and old garments upon them, and all the bread of their provisions was dry and moldy. And Joshua said, Who are ye, and whence come ye? And they said, From a very far country thy servants are

come, because of the name of the Lord thy God. And Joshua made a league with
them, to let them live; and the princes of the congregation sware unto them. And
all that about Joshua and the Gibeonites came back to David's mind when he saw
Mephibosheth lifted down from off his ass. For Mephibosheth had not dressed his
wooden feet, nor trimmed his beard, nor washed his clothes for grief, so he said,
from the day that the king departed. Nor had he taken time today to make himself
decent for such a journey, such was his joy that the king was coming back again to
Jerusalem. Yes, but what came of thee that morning, Mephibosheth? asked David.
I looked for thee. I was afraid that in the overthrow some evil had befallen thee.
Thou art not able to bear arms for me; but thy father so strengthened my hands
in God, that to have seen the face of his son that morning, and to have heard the
voice of Jonathan's son would have done for me and for my cause what thy father
did. My lord, said Mephibosheth—but "the tale was as lame as the tale-bearer."
Ziba had stolen his ass just as he was mounting him to come with the king—
and so on. David did not stoop to ask whose ass this was that Mephibosheth had
got saddled so soon this morning. Say no more, Mephibosheth, said David, as
he saw Jonathan's son crawling so abjectly before him. Dr. Kitto complains of
David's tart answer to Mephibosheth. But if David was too tart, then with what
extraordinary and saintly sweetness Mephibosheth received the over-tartness of
the king. "Let Ziba take all my estates today, forasmuch as my lord the king is come
again in peace to his own house." No, there was nothing cripple in Mephibosheth's
intellects. "Mephibosheth was a philosopher," says Dr. Parker. "I find no defect of
his wits in Mephibosheth," says honest Joseph Hall. And the king spared Mephibosheth, the son of Jonathan, the son of Saul, because of the Lord's oath that was
between them, between David and Jonathan the son of Saul.

   Now, the first thing that goes to our hearts out of this miserable story is this,
that Mephibosheth was the son of Jonathan. But Solomon, as he moralizes in one
place on fathers and sons with Jonathan and Mephibosheth before him, tells us
to rejoice with trembling when our sons are born to us for who knoweth whether
they shall be wise men or fools?

> Rarely into the branches of the tree
> Doth human worth mount up: and so ordains
> He who bestows it, that as His free gift
> It may be called.

   The poor child's accident while he was yet a child may well have been at the
bottom of it all. Diminutive and dwarfed persons, deformed persons, and greatly
crippled persons are sometimes so thrown in upon themselves as to make them
melancholy, morbid, and misanthropic. If their hearts are bad, their bodily dis-
abilities will sometimes work in their hearts to a deep and a malignant wickedness.
Both true history and truthful fiction have taken firm hold of this frequent fact in
human life. I do not know that the other side has been so often brought out—that
great bodily infirmity and disability, alongside of a renewed and a humble heart,
will sometimes result in a sweetness and a saintliness of a most uncommon kind.
In poor Mephibosheth's case, it would seem as if his early and life-long infirmity,
taken along with the hopeless loss of his brilliant prospects, had all eaten into his

heart till he became the false, selfish, scheming creature that David found him out
to be.

Hephaestion loved Alexander, while Craterus loved the king. And Jonathan
was like Hephaestion in this, that he loved David at all times whereas his son
Mephibosheth resembled Craterus in this, that he preferred David on the throne
to David off the throne. Jonathan strengthened David's hand in God in the wood
of Ziph; but Mephibosheth, like another classical character, fled the empty cask.
How Mephibosheth's heart had overflowed with gratitude to David when the
royal command came that he was to leave Machir's house in Lo-debar, and was
henceforth to take up his quarters in the king's house in Jerusalem! All Mephibosheth's morosity and misanthropy melted off his heart that day. But such was
Mephibosheth at the bottom of his heart that, as he continued to eat at David's
table, Satan entered into Mephibosheth and said to him in his heart that all this
was his own by original and divine right. All this wealth, and power, and honor,
and glory. But for the bad fortune of his father's royal house on Mount Gilboa,
all this would today have been his own. "Ingratitude," says Mozley, "is not only
a species of injustice, it is the highest species of injustice." And the ingratitude
of Mephibosheth grew at David's table to this high injustice, that, he waited for
both David and Absalom to be chased out of Jerusalem, that he might take their
place. There is no baser heart than an ungrateful heart. And it was Mephibosheth's
ungrateful heart that prepared him for the baseness that he was found out in both
at the flight of David and at his victorious return.

> The virtues were invited once
>   To banquet with the Lord of All:
> They came—the great ones rather grim,
>   And not so pleasant as the small.
>
> They talked and chatted o'er the meal,
>   They even laughed with temp'rate glee;
> And each one knew the other well,
>   And all were good as good could be.
>
> Benevolence and Gratitude
>   Alone of all seemed strangers yet;
> They stared when they were introduced—
>   On earth they never once had met.

Dean Milman says that the writings both of Tacitus and Dante are full of
remorse. And it is, as I believe, in our own remorse that we shall find the true key
to Mephibosheth's heart and character. When a government goes out of power,
when a church is under a cloud, when religion has lost her silver slippers, and
when she walks in the shadow of the street, and when any friend of ours has lost
his silver slippers—then we discover Mephibosheth in ourselves, and hate both
him and ourselves like hell. And commentators have taken sides over the case of
Mephibosheth very much as they have found that contemptible creature skulking
in themselves, and have had bitter remorse on account of him. "I am full of self-
love, fear to confess Thee, or to hazard myself, or my estate, or my peace. . . . My

perplexity continues as to whether I shall move now or not, stay or return, hold by Lauderdale, or make use of the Bishop. I went to Sir George Mushet's funeral, where I was looked at, as I thought, like a speckled bird. . . . I find great averseness in myself to suffering. I am afraid to lose life or estate. Shall I forbear to hear that honest minister, James Urquhart, for a time, seeing the stone is like to fall on me if I do so?" And then our modern Mephibosheth has the grace to add in his diary, "A grain of sound faith would easily answer all these questions. I have before me Mr. Rutherford's letter desiring me to deny myself." And though you will not easily believe it, the author of that letter himself has enough of Jonathan's crippled and disinherited son still in himself to give a tang of remorse to some of his very best letters. "Oh," agonizes Samuel Rutherford, "if I were only free of myself! Myself is another devil, and as evil as the prince of devils. Myself! Myself! Every man blames the devil for his sins, but the house and heart devil of every man is himself. I think I shall die still but minting and aiming to be a Christian man!"

This, then, is the prize for finding out that enigma of motive, Mephibosheth's hidden heart. This is the first prize, to receive of God the inward eye to discover Mephibosheth ever deeper down in ourselves. And the eye never to let Mephibosheth for a moment out of our sight as he sits at David's table feeding his ingratitude, and his duplicity, and his calculation of his chances. To see him also as he waits on providence in Jerusalem to hear how the battle is to go. And then to see him in his hurry to get to Jordan, where he arrives by a sport of providence just at the same moment with Shimei. If all that is the riddle of the sacred writer, and if all that is the right answer, then the reward of our skill is that we shall be made both able and willing to see Mephibosheth in everything in ourselves. For are we not told that all these Old Testament men are there as our examples? And that the wheel of providence is still turning in our day as it turned in their day? One man goes up on that wheel of God and another man goes down. One cause prospers and another cause decays. And in the manifold wisdom of God it is all ordered and overruled, as if both the wheel, and He whose wheel it is, and all the men, and movements, and governments, and churches, and everything else that is tied to that wheel were all tied to it and lifted, now up and now down, in order to discover us to ourselves, and to send us to His feet, who will not cast away even Mephibosheth himself if he comes to His feet in time. Our own good name and fame also, all our possessions, and all our expectations are all tied on to that wheel, for our hearts to be discovered and denounced, and for deliverance to be wrought in us from the dominion of such a heart. Every day, by the sovereign and electing grace of God, we are surely making some way in this knowledge of the wickedness past finding out of our own hearts, and some progress in the clearing out and conquest of that wickedness. Every day we are surely putting ourselves more and more in the place of our neighbor, and are doing more and more to him as we would he did to us. Till at last—O blessed hope!—every tang and taint of Mephibosheth's heart shall be taken out of us, and till truth, and righteousness, and fidelity, and gratitude, and courage, and love shall for ever reign in us and around us and over us. Even so, come quickly, Lord Jesus!

50
Barzillai

BARZILLAI, to put it all into one word, was an aged, venerable, hospitable Highland chief. Barzillai, by this time, was eighty years of age, and he was as full of truth, and courage, and goodwill, and generosity as he was full of years. From within the walls of his lofty keep in far-off Gilead, Barzillai had watched the ways of God with His people Israel in the south country all through the days of Eli, and Samuel, and Saul, and David, and Joab, and Jonathan, and Mephibosheth, and Absalom, and his humble heart and his hospitable house had always been open to the oppressed, and to the persecuted, and to the poor. And thus it was that when David fled from Jerusalem to escape from Absalom, and when David made his final stand at Mahanaim, Barzillai lost no time in coming down to David's assistance. The sacred writer is at particular pains to tell us the whole of that truly Highland hospitality with which Barzillai replenished the king's camp at Mahanaim. Beds, we read, and basons, and earthen vessels, and wheat, and barley, and flour, and parched corn, and beans, and lentils, and parched pulse, and honey, and butter, and sheep, and cheese of kine for David, and for his people that were with him. For Barzillai said, The people is hungry, and weary, and thirsty in the wilderness. Then come the two chapters about the successful battle; after which, when David sets out to return to Jerusalem, the sacred writer takes up the noble name of Barzillai again in this fine passage: "And Barzillai the Gileadite came down from Rogelim, and went over Jordan with the king, to conduct him over Jordan. And the king said to Barzillai, Come thou over with me, and I will feed thee with me in Jerusalem. And Barzillai said unto the king, How long have I to live that I should go up with the king to Jerusalem? I am this day fourscore years old, and can I discern between good and evil? Can thy servant taste what I eat or what I drink? Can I hear any more the voice of singing men and singing women? Wherefore, then, should thy servant be yet a burden to my lord the king? Thy servant will go a little way over the Jordan with the king; and why should the king recompense it me with such a reward? Let thy servant, I pray thee, turn back again, that I may die in mine own city, and be buried by the grave of my father and my mother. And when the king was come over the king kissed Barzillai and blessed him; and Barzillai returned to his own place." A beautiful old man, and a beautiful incident in a far from beautiful time.

Now, to begin with, Barzillai was a true Highlander in his splendid loyalty to David in his distress. Many men who had sat at David's royal table, and who had held their lands at David's royal liberality; many such men hedged and held back till they should see whether David's sun was to set, never to rise again, or not. Where is thy master? said David to Ziba, the servant of Mephibosheth. But Barzillai was not Mephibosheth. There was no lameness in Barzillai's allegiance to David. Barzillai did not wait to see how the wind would blow. The old hero took his ancient tower, and his great estate, and his own future, and the future of his family all in his hand that day. And, had Absalom succeeded, Barzillai would have been an outlawed and a sequestered man; and all the omens, to those who went by omens, looked that way that day. But Barzillai had steered all his eighty years by the fixed stars of truth, and righteousness, and duty, and loyalty, and he would steer by the same sure stars to the end. Even had David's cause been as bad as it was good, Barzillai's loyalty would have been noble to contemplate. Wrong-headed and short-sighted as was our own Highland loyalty to the Stuart House, there was not a little that was noble and brave and beautiful in it. It was a mad project to think to solder the crown of Charles Stuart to the crown of Jesus Christ; at the same time, there was a pathos and a poetry in it that still touch our hearts to this day. But Barzillai's loyalty to David was as sane-headed as it was warm-hearted. It was as far-seeing and as sure-footed as it was warmhearted and open-handed. David, on the throne or off the throne; David, in Jerusalem or in Mahanaim, is our divine king, said Barzillai to his household. The God of battles will do as seemeth Him good in this business, but our duty is clear, and it is pressing. Make haste and make up a present for David, and let it be the best. And say to the king that Barzillai, his servant, follows after the present as fast as his fourscore years will let him. Had Barzillai been tempted to hedge at dangers, and to calculate chances, and to weigh likelihoods, and to find excuses, he would not have wanted materials. No doubt David had done not a little to bring this terrible overthrow upon himself. And a cautious man would have considered all that. There are always sufficient reasons why a deliberating and a considering man should stand aloof for a time from a fallen man. But Barzillai had no head for such reserves and calculations. David was David to Barzillai, and as long as Barzillai has a roof over his head and a morsel of meat on his table, David shall not want. David's adversity was only all the more Barzillai's duty and opportunity.

And, every day, we all have Barzillai's duty and opportunity too, if only we have Barzillai's mind and heart. Not that kings and princes lie in want in our neighborhood every day; but good causes do, and needy and deserving men, and old and distressed friends. There is not a day passes but our boldness, and our courage, and our loyalty, and our fidelity are put to the test. There is not a day that we do not hear some censuring, fault-finding, detracting, and injuring word spoken against an absent friend. And what do we do? Do we let it pass? Do we in our heart of hearts like to hear it? Do we silently, or with a half-uttered consent fall in with it? How seldom do we stand up as we would be stood up for! How seldom do we pluck out the false and spiteful tongue! Let us be men the next time. Let us be Barzillai the next time, if Absalom, and Ahithophel, and Mephibosheth, and all the miserable house of Israel are all arrayed against David. Let them know from Jerusalem to Mahanaim that there is one man in Israel who is a man and is not a dog.

Barzillai's truly Highland courtesy, also, is abundantly conspicuous in the too-short glimpse we get of the lord of Rogelim. For, how he anticipated all David's possible wants! How he put himself into all David's distressed place! How he did to David as David would have done to him! How he came down from his high seat, with all his years on his head, in order with his own hand to conduct the king over Jordan! And, then, with what sweetness of manner and music of speech he excused himself out of all the royal rewards and honors and promotions David had designed and decreed to put upon him!

> The service and the loyalty I owe,
> In doing, pays itself. Your Highness' part
> Is to receive our duties; and our duties
> Are to your throne and state children and servants,
> Which do but what they should, by doing everything
> Safe towards your love and honor.
> The rest is labor which is not used for you.

The humility, also, of that Old Testament hero is already our New Testament humility in its depth and sweetness and beauty. A perfect and a finished courtesy has always its roots struck deep down into humility; which humility, again, has its roots struck deep down into the grace of God. In lowliness of mind let each esteem others better than themselves. Be kindly affectioned one to another with brotherly love; in honor preferring one another; submitting yourselves one to another in the fear of God. Yea, all of you be clothed with humility, for God resisteth the proud and giveth grace to the humble. Humility and courtesy are the court manners of the kingdom of heaven. A true, a finished, and an unconscious courtesy is the perfected etiquette of the palace and the presence of the great King.

And, then, there can be no doubt about Barzillai's Highland hospitality. Highland hospitality is a proverb of honor among us; and Barzillai's hospitality was the same proverb in the whole after history of Israel. As hospitable as Barzillai of Rogelim, they used to say. A bishop must be like Barzillai of Rogelim, wrote Paul to both Timothy and Titus. One would think that the two asses that stood so laden and waiting for David on the top of the hill had marched straight out of Barzillai's butler's pantry. As, indeed, so they had. For Ziba, who had saddled and so loaded them, had first learned how to saddle and how to load an ass when he lived at Lodebar. He had found out how much charity a strong ass could carry when he and his master lived on charity at Rogelim and Lodebar. A couple of asses saddled as they used to saddle them at Rogelim and Lodebar could carry two hundred loaves of bread, and a hundred bunches of raisins, and a hundred of summer fruits and a bottle of wine. But it is not great lords only like Barzillai of Rogelim and Machir of Lodebar and Shobi of Rabbah who are summoned to show hospitality. No class of men could be poorer than were the bishops of Paul's day, and yet the apostle enjoins Titus and Timothy to ordain no man who is not given to hospitality. And the same apostle reminds the poor Hebrew laity that some men in old times have entertained angels unawares. But the truth is, true Highland hospitality is in the mind and in the heart of the host and hostess. A poor widow's hut will show you Highland hospitality in the way she comes out and offers you a drink of milk or even of water. You cannot tie up the hands of a hospitable heart. Does not Aristotle himself tell us that a munificently-minded man is seen as well in his present of a ball or a top or a picture to a little child as in a temple or a sacrifice or a banquet to a God? And has not a Greater than Aristotle told us that the widow's mite will be extolled for its splendid munificence wherever His munificent gospel is preached? Hospitality and munificence and magnanimity are in the mind and in the heart, and it is the mind and the heart that are accepted and acknowledged of God. "With what measure you mete, it shall be measured to you"; so our Lord lays down His last-day law. And then Bengel annotates our Lord's law thus: *Mensura est cor.* The measure is the heart, with its capabilities, desires, anxiety to impart blessings to others, and loving obedience. And thus it is that hospitality, with its present blessedness and its everlasting rewards, is not a matter of wealth or poverty, any more than it is of race or region.

Barzillai's passionate love of his Highland hills and valleys is another fine feature in this ripe old saint. As also his brooding, emotional, melting, Gaelic-like eloquence when he opens his whole heavenly-minded heart to David. Like Moses also in his old age, Barzillai has numbered his days, and has applied his heart to wisdom. Like Paul also, if his outward man must perish, then Barzillai will see to it that his inward man shall not be squandered abroad and lost. No! "Let the king pardon and discharge his servant," Barzillai said. "The king, I fear, forgets how old I am. This is my birthday, and I am fourscore years old today. No; it is not for an old man like me to go up to Jerusalem. My time is past to be eating and drinking as they will eat and drink in Jerusalem when God sends back their king to his people. I would be a burden to myself and to the king's servants. But take my son, if it please thee, and let him see Jerusalem. But as for me, the king will let me return home to die and to be buried beside my father and my mother. I shall need all my time; for I am fourscore years old this day, and how shall I go up with the king to Jerusalem?" Who can help loving the octogenarian Barzillai, with his "courtesy in conversation," and when, like Pompey in Plutarch, he "gave without disdain, and took with great honor"? And the king kissed Barzillai and blessed him, and Barzillai returned to his place at Rogelim.

And in this also the wise and good Barzillai is surely a beautiful lesson to all old men. Barzillai shows us how to take our advancing years. He shows us how to apply our hearts to wisdom as we number our days. He shows us also how, with all willingness, and sweetness, and courtesy, and divine wisdom to leave cities, and feasts, and crowds, and trumpets, and honors, and promotions to younger men, and to apply our whole remaining strength, and our whole remaining time, to end our days as our days should be ended. Barzillai having showed us how to live, shows us also how to die. Barzillai dies the same devout and noble and magnanimous man he has all his days lived. We have not as yet learned to live; and how, then, can we know how to die? We die like a man run down in a race. We die like a man who has not lived half his days. We die while yet this word is in our mouth, Today or tomorrow I will go to such a city, and will buy and sell, and get gain. We die like a fox taken in a trap. We die like a rat poisoned in a hole. But Barzillai died like the heavenly-minded man he had always lived. Barzillai died like our own Highland laird, Fraser of Brea. For Fraser of Brea died still "laying his pipe" ever closer and closer up and up to the fountain, till the Lamb which is in the midst of the throne led him to the living Fountain itself, and till God wiped all tears from his eyes.

51

Heman

HEMAN was "David's seer in the matters of God." Now a seer is just a man who sees. He is just a man who has eyes in his head. Other men also have eyes indeed, but, then, they do not see with their eyes as a seer sees. A seer stands out among all other men in this, that he sees with all his eyes. Heman, then, was a seer. And he was a seer in this. Heman saw constantly a sight that to most men even in Israel was absolutely invisible. Heman saw, and saw nothing else, but his own soul. From his youth up Heman had as good as seen nothing in the whole world but his own soul. And, after he was well on in life, Heman was moved of God to set down the sight of his own soul in the eighty-eighth Psalm. David, on occasion, was a wonderful seer himself. But David had not given himself up from his youth up to the things of his own soul as Heman had done. David was a man of affairs, and he had many other matters to see to besides the matters of God and of his own soul; but Heman saw nothing else. Separate me Heman and Heman's soul, the Holy Ghost had said. And it was so. And David, discovering that, made Heman the king's seer. Saul also in his day had sought out a seer. Only, the seer that Saul sought out was a seer who could see stolen sheep on the mountains a hundred miles away. Whereas David sought in Heman a seer who could see both David's soul and his own; and who could see sin in David's soul and in his own when no other eye in all Israel could see it. My sin is ever before me, said David, when his eyes were once opened. And it was to Heman, under God, even more than to Nathan or Gad, that David owed that ever-present sight. "In the matters of God Heman was the King's seer," says the sacred writer. God had many matters, first and last, with David; but God's first matter with David, as with all men, was David's sin and David's soul. And Heman from his youth up had been kept so close at God's school for seers in the matters of sin and the soul, that David sought out Heman and established him in Mount Zion as the King's most private, most trusted, and most highly-honored seer. This, then, was Heman, the seer of David in the matters of God.

"My soul is full of troubles," says this great seer, speaking about himself in the eighty-eighth Psalm. What led Heman to speak about himself in that way to a people who could not understand what he said, we do not know. What led Heman to speak and to publish abroad this most melancholy of all the Psalms we are not told. He speaks in this Psalm as he was moved to speak by the Holy Ghost: but more than that we do not know. It may have been to console David in some of his many inconsolable seasons. It may have been to rebuke David by letting him see that a saint of God who had never sinned as David had sinned, had, nevertheless, been cast of God into depths that even David had never known. Or it may have been that there might be a Psalm grievous enough for our Lord to recall it and to repeat it during His three hours darkness on the cross. Or it may have been because God, in His far foreknowledge, saw some one in this house this night that

263

no other Psalm would suit but this saddest of all the Psalms. Who can tell? Now, Heman's soul so full of troubles, you must understand, was not on account of Heman's outward estate. It was not Heman's actual sin like David's. Neither was there any terrible trouble, like David's, among his large family of sons and daughters. Heman had brought up his sons and daughters far more successfully than David had done. For all Heman's sons and daughters assisted their father in sacred song in the house of the Lord. Some of the worst troubles we see and hear men's souls to be full of all around us come to them through their children. But that was not Heman's case. At the same time Heman cannot take a happy father's full joy out of his talented and dutiful children because of the overwhelming trouble of his own soul. He cannot sing and play with his gifted and gracious children with all his heart as other happy fathers sing and play. And that is another trouble to Heman's soul already so full of troubles. It is a terrible price to pay for his post as David's seer to have a soul like that. It is a terrible baptism into the matters of God to have a soul from his youth up so full of inconsolable troubles.

"My soul is full of troubles," says Heman, "till I am driven distracted." Every day we hear of men and women being driven distracted through love, and through fear, and through poverty, and through pain, and sometimes through over-joy, and sometimes, it is said, through religion. It was thought by some that the Apostle Paul was quite distracted in his day through his too much thought and occupation about divine things. And our Lord Himself was again and again said to be beside Himself. And no wonder. For if love, and fear, and pain of mind and heart, and sometimes over-joy have ever driven men distracted: who ever had all these things, and more, on his mind and on his heart like our Lord? To see what was in man, and what comes out of the heart of man: and to see all that with such holy eyes and with such a holy heart as His, and then to see and understand how all that so concerned Himself—had the very Godhead not held Him up, no mortal mind and heart could have endured under the sight. No wonder that Jesus of Nazareth was often, even to His mother and His brethren, like a man that should be kept close watch over at home. The Second Evangelist was a remarkable seer in all the matters of our Lord. He saw things in our Lord that no other Evangelist had the eyes to see: and he writes about our Lord in words that no other Evangelist can command. And one word he writes in goes so near describing absolute distraction that we shrink back from truly and fully translating it. We water it down till we say that our Lord was sore amazed and very heavy. To be made sin sore amazed our Lord. It almost drove Him beside Himself. A terror at sin, and a horror: a terror and a horror at Himself, took possession of our Lord's soul in the garden till He was full of a trouble beyond all experience and imagination of mortal men. It was not death. Death is nothing. Death is nothing to sin. Death and all its terrors did not much move our Lord. He went up to meet death with a serenity and with a stateliness of soul that confounded and almost converted those who saw it. No; it was not death. It was sin. It was that in which our mothers conceived us. It was that which we drink up like water. It was that which we are all full of from the sole of the foot even unto the head. It was sin. It was hell-fire in His soul. It was the coals, and the rosin, and the juniper, and the turpentine of the fire that is not quenched.

The pains of hell gat hold upon Him, He found trouble and sorrow till He was well-nigh distracted. Now there was no Old Testament saint so like our Lord in all that as was Heman. And in the measure that we have our Lord's eyes and Heman's eyes wherewith to see sin, in that exact measure will we each one of us fill up what is behind of these tremendous distractions. As it is, our brain sometimes reels in its distracted globe. We know that we sometimes talk distractedly. We know that we terrify and torment other men. We terrify and are a torment to ourselves when no one knows it. We tremble sometimes at the thought of what this may yet grow to if it goes on, as it will go on, all our days. But be not too much cast down. Comfort my people. Say to them that for all their present shame they shall yet have double. Say to them that this is wisdom. Say to them that this is the only mind that hath the true wisdom. Say to them, and assure them, that this is the beginning in them of the wisdom, and the truth, and the love, and the salvation of their God and Savior Jesus Christ.

Now, with all that, this is not to be wondered at that Heman says next. Anything else but this is not to be expected from Heman. Heman makes it an additional complaint, but it is a simple and a necessary consequence of his own troubled and distracted soul. "Thou hast put mine acquaintance far from me. Lover and friend hast thou put far from me, and mine acquaintance into darkness." Job, Heman's spiritual equal almost, has the very same complaint again and again. "He hath put my brethren far from me, and mine acquaintance are verily estranged from me. My kinsfolk have failed me, and my familiar friends have forgotten me. All my inward friends have abhorred me; and they whom I loved are all turned against me." And no wonder. Who that could help it would live in the same house with Heman? With such a morose and melancholy man? Friends and lovers, the oldest, and the warmest, and the best—they all have their several limits. Most men are made with little heart themselves, and they are not at home where there is much heart, and much exercise of heart. They flee in a fright from the heights and the depths of the high and deep heart. It needs a friend that sticketh closer than a brother to keep true to a man who has much heart, and who sees and feels with all his heart. Heman had wife and child: he had David, and Asaph, and Jeduthun also; and a whole choir-seat full of smiling acquaintances; but all that only made him feel the more alone. Asaph, also, in the same seat, felt the same loneliness. "Whom have I in heaven but Thee? And there is none upon earth that I desire beside Thee." Much as Heman and Asaph had in common, they were all the time such strangers to one another when their distractions were upon them that they felt, as we say, as far as the poles asunder. When thou prayest, said our Lord, enter thy closet. That is to say, enter thine own distracted heart. And there is One, and only One, with thee in thy lockfast heart. David and Asaph and all—there is nothing that sifts out lover and friend like prayer; the prayer that is, that takes up the troubles and the distractions of the soul. When our Lord took His distracted soul to His Father, the most that His best lovers and friends could do for Him was to fall asleep three times outside the door. Heman, besides being the king's seer, was also an eminent type of Christ, both in the distracting troubles of his soul, and in the fewness and in the infidelity of his friends.

Down to Gehenna, and up to the Throne,
He travels the fastest who travels alone.

Now all that, bad as it was, would have been easily borne had it been a sudden stroke and then for ever over. Had it been a great temptation, a great fall, a great repentance, a great forgiveness, and then the light of God's countenance brighter than ever all Heman's after-days. Had it been with Heman as it was with David: "For His anger endureth but a moment; in His favor is life; weeping may endure for a night, but joy cometh in the morning." Or had it been with Heman as it was with Isaiah: "For a small moment have I forsaken thee; but with great mercies will I gather thee. In a little wrath I hid my face from thee for a moment; but with everlasting kindness will I have mercy upon thee, saith the Lord thy Redeemer." Josiah and Jeremiah bore their yoke also all their youth; but Heman bore his yoke all his days. Heman is now an old man; but like the woman in the gospel he is nothing better but rather worse. There are troubles and distractions in a man's youth sometimes that turn his hair gray before its proper time. But in most cases, by God's goodness, a life like that either comes to an early end altogether, or some great relief and great recovery comes in His grace from God. For the Lord will not cast off for ever. He doth not afflict willingly, nor grieve the children of men. But Heman's yoke from his youth up has been of that terrible kind that it has eaten into his soul deeper and deeper with every advancing year. Had Heman lived after Paul's day he would have described himself in Paul's way. He would have said that the two-edged sword had become every year more and more spiritual, till it entered more and more deep every year into his soul. And since souls like Heman's are absolutely bottomless and shoreless; and since the law of God is infinitely and increasingly holy and just and good; how could a man like Heman escape being every day of his life more and more sold under sin? He could not. All that Heman had hitherto come through was like child's-play at trouble and distraction compared with this. For his troubles have now taken on an inwardness and an incessancy such as an old saint of God once said would surely some day drive her into the pond.

God forbid, when God is a little displeased with any of His saints, that I should by a single hairbreadth help forward their affliction. God forbid that I should in anything make the heart of any righteous man more sad and should take away from him any of his true refuges. Before I do that may my tongue cleave to the roof of my mouth. At the same time, I will risk it lest they be refuges of lies. I will risk it so that some one here present may perchance be discovered to himself and so saved. Heman's sad case has sometimes been set down to God's sovereignty. And so may all your sadness, possibly. But I would not have you believe that too easily. The chances with you lie all the other way. Are you quite sure that this deep darkness of yours is quite unaccountable to you short of God's sovereignty—short of His deep, hidden, divine will? I doubt it, and I would have you doubt it. I would have you make sure that there is no other possible explanation of this darkness of His face. All the chances are that it is not God's ways that are so distractingly dark, but your own. Look yet closer and yet deeper into yourself for the bottom of this dark mystery. If I were you I would let no man, not even an angel of light, cheat me out of my soul with any of his antinomianisms about the divine sovereignty. Is it not rather a divine controversy? Lean to that explanation. Look as you have never yet looked, and see if there is not some sinful way in you that is the cause of all this darkness on God's part, and all this distraction on your part. The only thing you can think of is such a little thing, that, if it is a sin, it is not worth God's pains to take so much notice of it, and to punish you so persistently for it. It is not a thing for God to stand upon; it is such a small affair. Well, if it is so small, all the more put it away. Put it away for a time at any rate, and, if light does not come, then return to it, if you cannot live without it. Only, there is a sermon of authority which says, Be ye therefore perfect; and it is through terrible distractions, and darknesses, and severities, and sanctifications that this perfect salvation comes to some men: and it looks to me as if you were one of them.

And to close with, there is a singular use in Heman for ministers. When God is to make a very sinful man into a very able, and skillful, and experimental minister, He sends that man to the same school to which He sent Heman. This was God's way, on the side of His sovereignty, with the Servant of the Lord also in the 50th of Isaiah. "Who comforteth us in all our tribulations," says Paul also, "that we may be able to comfort them which are in any trouble." His own troubles and distractions give a minister "a lady's hand," as an old writer has it, in dealing with troubled and distracted souls. Now, who can tell what God has laid up for you to do for Him and for men's souls when you are out of your probationership of trouble and distraction, and are promoted to be a comforter of God's troubled and distracted saints? He may have a second David, and far more, to comfort and to sanctify in the generation to come; and you may be ordained to be the King's seer in the matters of God. Who can tell? Only, be you ready, for the stone that is fit for the wall is not left to lie in the ditch.

52
Jeroboam

GOD may have that in his heart for you, which you must not once let enter your heart for yourself. Your name may be written in the divine decree for something, the bare thought of which you must cast out of your heart like poison. And all Jeroboam's great talents, and all his great services, and all his great prospects, and all his great temptations, and all his great sins—all happened to him for ensamples; and they are all written for our admonition, upon whom the ends of the world are come.

But we must go back to the first beginning of Jeroboam's great temptations and great transgressions. It was King Solomon's many and terrible falls from godliness and from virtue that first set such a fatal snare before Jeroboam's feet. Solomon by this time was rushing insensate to his own ruin, and to the ruin of his royal house. If it were not written all over the Bible we would not believe it. Solomon's beautiful dream at Gibeon, his splendid prayer at the dedication of the temple, his wisdom, and his understanding, and his largeness of heart—it is all clean forgotten now. It is all become now like the morning cloud and the early dew. Can this be the same Solomon? Can this be that Solomon to whom the Lord appeared twice? For Solomon went after Ashtoreth, the goddess of the Zidonians, and after Molech, the abomination of the Ammonites. Then did Solomon build an high place for Chemosh, the abomination of Moab, in the hill of God that is before Jerusalem, and for Molech, the abomination of Ammon. In his old age, and when he should have been by this time a rare and a ripe saint of God, Solomon added this also to his other transgressions, an insane passion for building palaces both for himself and for his heathen queens, and temples and altars for their cruel and unclean gods, and great fortifications, and all manner of proud and costly and reckless public works. And, with it all, there was this also: Every stone of all Solomon's temples and palaces and heathen altars was laid wet with the blood of an oppressed and exasperated people. The prophet Samuel had foretold all this to the elders of Israel, and had got little thanks from them for so foretelling it. But every jot and tittle of God's great prophet had by this time been long proved true; and every warning word of his was now like a fire in the bones of Solomon's miserable subjects. As they bled to death under the whip of the tax-gatherer and the taskmaster, the people gnashed their teeth at their fathers and at themselves. For had not Samuel told it thus to their face? "He will take your sons and appoint them for himself, for his chariots, and for his horsemen; and he will set them to ear his ground, and to reap his harvest, and to make his instruments of war. And he will take your fields, and your vineyards, and your olive-yards, even the best of them, and will give them to his servants. And he will take your menservants and your maidservants, and your goodliest young men, and will put them to his work, and ye shall be his servants. And ye shall cry out in that day, and the Lord will not hear you in that day." Well, that day was now fully come. And it was amid all the terrible oppression and suffering of that day that Jeroboam rose so fast and so high in Solomon's service. Jeroboam's outstanding talents in public affairs, his skillful management of men, his great industry, and his great loyalty, as was thought, all combined to bring the son of Nebat under Solomon's royal eye, till there was no trust too important, and no promotion too high for young Jeroboam. And then, to crown it all, as time went on Satan more and more entered into Jeroboam's heart. And Jeroboam allowed Satan in his heart, and listened to Satan speaking in his heart. "You are a greatly talented man. There is no other man in all the land fit to be your equal. Solomon is old, and his son is a fool. And who is to be king after Solomon dies? Thinkest thou ever who is fit to be king? Saul was but the son of Kish. David himself was but the son of Jesse. There has never been, and there never will be, respect of persons with the God of Israel. Jeroboam, you love your widowed mother. Play the man, then, but a little longer, and your mother will live to hear the cry of the people before she dies, this so sweet cry to her ears, Long live King Jeroboam!" And Jeroboam kept all these things and pondered them in his heart.

All this time, Ahijah the prophet, with those terrible eyes of his, was sleeplessly watching both the fast-coming fall of Solomon, as well as the immense industry and steady rise of Jeroboam. Ahijah's eyes, like a flame of fire, saw, naked and open, all that was hidden so deep in Jeroboam's heart; and he heard, as with God's own ears, all that Satan said to Jeroboam in his heart. Ahijah watched Jeroboam at his work, and he saw, till he could not be silent, that Jeroboam was fast undermining the walls of Jerusalem in his heart, all the time that he was receiving praise and promotion for building those walls up with his hands. "Lay down thy plummet," said Ahijah in hot anger to Jeroboam one day—"lay down thy measuring line, and come out to the potter's field with me." And Jeroboam laid down his building and came out after Ahijah. Then Ahijah suddenly turned and stripped off his new garment that was upon Jeroboam, and tore it up into twelve pieces, and said, "Thus and thus hast thou torn up the kingdom of Solomon in thine heart. And it shall be so. Take thee ten of these torn-up pieces and hide them with thee till all that is in thine heart shall come true." And then the prophet, softening somewhat, went on to tell the trembling builder that if he would but cast Satan and all his counsels and all his hopes out of his heart from that day, then the God of Israel would make him a sure house, so that he and his seed should sit on the throne of Israel for ever. And Ahijah thrust the ten torn pieces upon Jeroboam and departed. And Jeroboam returned to his work on the wall of Jerusalem with his heart all in a flame. And it came to pass that when Solomon heard of all that, Solomon turned to be against Jeroboam. And Solomon eyed Jeroboam as Saul had eyed David, and as we all eye those gifted men who are fast rising to push us out of our seat. And just as David fled to Ramah from the javelin of Saul, so Jeroboam fled to Egypt from the same weapon of Solomon. And not Joseph, and not Moses himself, rose so fast and so high in Egypt as Jeroboam rose. In a short space of time the fugitive overseer of Solomon's works had actually become the son-in-law of Pharaoh himself. Jeroboam was a born king and statesman; and both Israel and Egypt, both heaven and earth, confessed it to be so. And if only Jeroboam had tarried the Lord's leisure, and had kept his heart clean and humble, Jeroboam would soon have been king over all Israel, he and his sons, till the Messiah came Himself to sit down on David's undivided throne.

All this time, matters went on from bad to worse in Jerusalem, till Solomon died and Rehoboam his son reigned in his stead. But with all that God's prophets and God's providences could do, neither Solomon nor his son altered their insane and suicidal ways one iota. In their utter exasperation and despair the oppressed people at last took the strong and desperate step of sending a secret embassy to Egypt to beseech Jeroboam to return and deliver them from their miseries. And Jeroboam left Egypt at once, and came back with the Hebrew ambassadors. And, whatever may have been in Jeroboam's heart, no fault at all can be found with the words of his ultimatum to Rehoboam. "Thy father made our yoke grievous; now, therefore, make thou the grievous service of thy father and his heavy yoke lighter, and we will serve thee." But Rehoboam was demented enough to answer Jeroboam and the people with this insolence: "My father chastised you with whips, but I will chastise you with scorpions." At that, "To your tents, O Israel," rose the cry of rebellion till it rent the air. "Now see to thine own house, O David." So Israel rebelled against the house of David that day. And Jeroboam was made king over the ten tribes that day. There was none that followed the house of David but the tribe of Judah only.

Now, here is our first admonition. Had Jeroboam on the day of his coronation, and henceforth, but taken Ahijah home to be his counsellor, Jeroboam had ability enough, and divine right enough, to have built up Israel into a great kingdom for God and for himself. But Jeroboam never loved Ahijah. He both feared and hated Ahijah. He was never at home, as we say, with Ahijah. He was never happy when he was alone with Ahijah. His heart, neither on the wall nor on the throne, was ever single enough for Ahijah's all-searching eyes. And thus it was that Satan still kept his place in Jeroboam's heart, and was still Jeroboam's counsellor in all the affairs of the state, and in all the affairs of the family, till Jeroboam's great fall, from which he and his people never recovered, came about in this way. The ten tribes continued to go up to Jerusalem to Solomon's temple to worship God. And as they did so Jeroboam began to fear lest, in their worship together, Judah and Israel should both so return to the Lord together, that the breach in the kingdom would be healed, and he and his son cast out of his rebellious throne. The fact is, we have here before us in black and white, to this day, the very identical words that Jeroboam at that time spake in his heart. He said this in his heart: "If my people go up to do service in this way in the house of the Lord at Jerusalem, then shall the hearts of this people turn back to Rehoboam, and they will kill me and my son with me." Whereupon Jeroboam took counsel, and made two unclean idols of gold, and said, It is too much for you to go up to Jerusalem; behold thy gods, O Israel, which brought thee up out of the land of Egypt. You are not to suppose that Jeroboam was so stupid as to believe what he said and did that day. No. But he knew how stupid, and, indeed, how brutish at bottom his people were, as well as how superstitious. He knew well, also, how party spirit and ill-will had all along prevailed between Samaria and Jerusalem; and, the bad man that he was, Jeroboam deliberately set himself to traffic, and to establish his throne, in the sensuality, in the stupidity, and in the ill-will of his hoodwinked subjects.

But, happily for us all, there is nothing in God's name to usward that is more sure and more true than is His long suffering, and His immense patience, and the many calls to repentance that He sends us before He finally casts us off. And, lest Jeroboam should lose himself through his fear and hate at Ahijah, God actually condescended to set the old and faithful prophet aside and to send a new prophet to Jeroboam: a prophet whose eyes had not yet read Jeroboam's heart, and against whom Jeroboam could have taken up no umbrage. Unless we both know ourselves and hate ourselves, we shall be certain both to hate and put away from us the preacher who tells us to our faces what is in our heart, as Jeroboam hated and put away Ahijah; which hatred of Jeroboam at him was all the time one of Ahijah's surest seals, both to himself and to Jeroboam, that he was a true prophet of the heart-searching God.

With all that, Jeroboam was not a common man. And Jeroboam's sins were not the sins of a common man. It is only kings, and kings' counselors, and popes, and bishops, and ministers, and elders, and such like, who can sin and make nations and churches and congregations to sin. But they can do it. And they are doing it every day. All who divide, and keep divided, nations, and churches, and families, and friends in order to make a name, or a living, or a party, or just a despite for themselves out of such divisions, they are the true seed of Jeroboam. All who inflame and perpetuate such divisions lest they should lose their stake of money, or of influence, or of occupation, or of pure ill-will; all able men who prostitute their talents to write or speak about men on the other side, as they would not like themselves to be spoken or written about—let them lay it to heart in whose lot they shall surely stand when every man shall give an account of himself to God. But common and mean men are not incapacitated and shut out by their commonness and meanness from sharing in Jeroboam's royal sin. The commonest and meanest man among us has more than enough of this terrible power of both sinning himself and making other men to sin. Every man among us has, in countless ways and on countless occasions, first sinned himself and then made other men to sin. Go back honestly into your past life and see. Take time; take a true light back with you, and look around, and see. Come up, as you shall one day be compelled to come up through your past life whether you will or no, and see. Some of them are dead and gone to judgment with the lesson in sin you gave them laid up before God against you. Some of them are still sinning here, and are prolonging your days in teaching a new generation to sin your sin. Sin yourself, if you will sin. But, as you would have a drop of water to cool your tongue in that torment, do not make other men to sin. Break the Sabbath law, neglect God's house, do despite to His means of grace, drink, bet, pollute yourself, scoff, blaspheme: your soul is your own. Make your bed in hell, if you will have it so; but, as God will smite you for it, let alone the young, and the innocent, and the pure, and the unsuspecting. So Jeroboam, who sinned and who made Israel to sin, though dead, yet speaketh.

53

The Disobedient Prophet

IT was an high day of idolatry at Bethel. And, all the time, Bethel, of all the cities of Israel, was one of the most ancient and the most sacred. Bethel, as its name bears, was none other but the house of God, and it was the very gate of heaven. Bethel was built on that very spot on which their father Jacob had slept and dreamed when he was on his lonely way to Padan-aram; and it is that very heaven out of which the ladder was let down on Jacob's pillow that is today to be darkened by the unclean incense of Jeroboam's altar-fires. It was a brave step in Jeroboam to set up his false gods at Bethel, of all places in the land. And he needed a stout heart and a profane to support him as he stood up to kindle with his own hands the heathen fires of idolatry and impurity at Bethel.

> Where angels down the lucid stair
>> Came hovering to our sainted sires,
> Now, in the twilight glare
>> The heathen's wizard fires.

And, behold, there came a man of God out of Judah by the word of the Lord unto Bethel: and Jeroboam stood by the altar to burn incense. And the man of God cried against the altar of the Lord, and said, O altar, altar! And then he foretold the fall of the altar, and with it the fall of him who stood in his royal robes that day ministering to his unclean gods at that altar. And how Jeroboam's hand was withered that moment; how it was healed immediately at the intercession of the man of God; how Jeroboam invited the prophet to come home with him to eat and to drink and to get a reward; and how the prophet answered the king that he had the command of the Lord neither to eat bread nor to drink water in that polluted land, but to return home to Judah as soon as he had delivered his prophetic burden—all that is to be read in the thirteenth chapter of First Kings. At the same time, we are not told so much as this great prophet's name. He was wholly worthy thus far to have his name held up aloft along with the names of Samuel and Elijah themselves, for he stood up alone against Jeroboam and against all Israel and nailed the curse of God to Jeroboam's altar under the king's own eyes. We would hold his name in more than royal honor if we knew it. But for some reason or other of her own the Bible holds his great name back. This great man of God comes out of a cloud, he shines for a splendid moment before all men's eyes, and then he dies under a cloud. Alas, my brother!

As the man of God from Judah so nobly refuses Jeroboam's royal hospitality, I am reminded of Lord Napier. On one occasion his lordship was sent down to Scotland by the Queen on a royal errand of review and arbitration between a great duke and his poor crofters. The duke, the administration of whose estate was to be inquired into, was good enough to offer his lordship his ducal hospitality for as long as the royal session of review lasted. But her Majesty's Deputy felt that neither his Royal Mistress nor himself could afford to be for one moment compromised, or even suspected, by her poorest subject; and therefore it was that his lordship excused himself from the duke's table, and took up his quarters in the little way-side inn. "At any rate, you will come to the manse," said the minister, who was on the crofters' side. "Thank you," said Napier. "But in your college days you must have read Plutarch about Caesar's wife. No, thank you." And his lordship lodged all his time in the little hotel, and went back to his Royal Mistress when his work was done, not only with clean hands, but without even a suspicion attaching to her or to him. "Come home with me and refresh thyself." But the man of God said to the king, "If thou wilt give me half thine house, I will not go in with thee, neither will I eat bread nor drink water with thee." So he went another way, and returned not by the way that he came to Bethel.

Just as the man of God is setting out to go back to Judah with a hungry belly indeed, but with a good conscience, we are taken by the hand and are led into the house of an old prophet who dwells at Bethel. Yes. There are prophets and prophets' sons all this time at Bethel. Only, they had their domiciles and their doles from Jeroboam's bounty on the strict condition that they kept at home and kept silence. Well, this old Bethelite prophet was keeping at home and was keeping silence when his sons burst in upon him with the great news of the day. Father, you should have come with us! We asked you to come. What a day it has been! And what a man of God we have seen! Till they told him all that we are told about Jeroboam, and his altar, and the man of God from Judah, and his cry that shook down the altar, and the king's withered hand, and the prayer of the man of God, and the king's hospitality, and the man of God's refusal of the king's hospitality. "What way went he home?" demanded the old prophet of his excited sons. "Saddle me the ass," he instantly ordered. "Art thou the man of God from Judah?" he asked, as he overtook the man of God sitting under an oak. "Come home with me and eat bread." "I may not eat bread, nor drink water by the word of the Lord," said the man of God. "But I am a prophet also as thou art," said the old Bethelite; "and an angel bade me bring thee back." But it was a lie, adds the sacred writer. So the man of God rose and went back and did eat bread and drink water. And so on; till a lion met him in the way home that night, and slew him because he had gone back. And when the old Bethelite prophet, who had deceived him, heard of it, he mourned over him, and said, "Alas, my brother!" And he said to his sons, "Bury me beside this man of God. Lay my bones beside his bones."

What is it that makes the decrepit old prophet of Bethel post at such a pace after the man of God who is on his way home to Judah? Has his conscience at last been awakened? Have the tidings of his delighted sons filled the poor old time-server with bitter remorse for his fat table and for his dumb pulpit? Or, is it deadly envy and revenge at the man who has so stolen his sons' hearts that day till they are about to set off to Judah to go to school to this man of God? It is too late now for him to command his sons' reverence and love. And how can he ever forgive the man who has so taken from him his crown as a prophet and as a father? "Saddle me the ass," he shouted. And the decayed old creature rode down the Judean road at a pace he had not ridden since he used, as a godly youth, to be sent out on errands of life and death and mercy from Samuel's School of Mount Ephraim. If lies will do it; if flattery, flesh, and wine will do it; if there is man or woman in Bethel that will do it—that Judean prophet's pride shall be brought down today! "Saddle me the ass!" he thundered. So they saddled him the ass, and he rode after the man of God. "I am a prophet as thou art!" But he lied unto him.

Let us all take care of the swift and sure collapse that always comes on us after every great excitement. As sure as we are made of flesh, and blood, and brains, and nerves, and feelings, a great reaction always takes place in body and mind after any unusually great effort of body and mind. And especially after any great preaching effort. After you have faced for hours a surging congregation, and have worked yourself and them up to heaven—to see them scatter, and to be left worn out and alone—then comes the hour of temptation: a temptation that has been fatal in more ways than one to some temperaments of men. Some temperaments are tempted at such times to eat and drink and smoke and talk all night to any listener if they have done well; and the same temperaments are just as much tempted to silence, and gloom, and bad temper if they have not done well: if they have not come up to themselves, and have not got the praise they worked for and expected. We are not told why this great man of God stopped short so soon on his way home from Bethel, and sat down so soon under one of the oaks of Bethel. He had done a splendid day's work. Never prophet of God did a more splendid day's work. But our hearts sink as we see him stop short, and then take his seat under that tempting tree. What was the matter? We are not told. He may have been very hungry by this time, and he may have begun to repent that he had not accepted the penitent king's hospitality. Who knows what good might have come of it had he, God's acknowledged prophet, been seen sitting in the place of honor at the royal table? Had he not been somewhat short, and sharp, and churlish after his great battle with Jeroboam's altar? Stern men have often been known to soften and secretly repent of their too-ascetical self-denial. They have felt it hard to have to pay the whole self-denying vow which they made when some great exaltation was upon them. Some men have gone so far, indeed, as to call back in imagination the hour or temptation, and wish that they had not let it slip so soon. Well, then, if that was the case with the man of God from Judah—here is the forbidden fruit of Bethel back and at his open mouth this moment: "I am a prophet as thou art, and an angel spake unto me by the word of the Lord, saying: Bring him back to eat and to drink." So he went back with him to his house.

As a rule let ministers sup at home on Sabbath nights; and let them sup alone. As a rule. It cannot always be acted on, but it is a good rule, nevertheless. Many a good sermon has been drowned dead in the supper, and in the supper-talk that followed it. Your people will not care one straw what you say to them from the pulpit if you sup heartily with them immediately after it. All the great awe of the morning went off the Bethelite prophet's sons and servants, as the man of God sat and ate and drank and laughed and talked over his supper that night. And the old Bethelite himself was quite at home, hail-fellow-well-met, with the terrible preacher of that awakening morning.

I was once spending a Sabbath in a well-known farm-house in Glenisla, and after church the old laird and I began to talk about John Duncan and his great sermons when he was a probationer in a chapel of ease in the neighborhood. After supper and worship I was anxious to hear more about Dr. Duncan, and to hear more of his old sermons read. "No," said the old patriarch to me; "No: no more tonight; we always take our candles immediately after family worship." How often has that rebuke come back to me as another Sabbath night closed with all kinds of talk after public and family worship; talk that but too plainly had blotted out for ever all that had been said and heard that day. It is not possible that we should all spend the last hours of the Sabbath alone; but, most certainly, many a deep impression has been obliterated as the preacher ate and drank and talked and laughed after his solemn sermon.

And then this—follow your conscience to the end, let men and angels say what they will. A man is but a man: an angel is but an angel: and false prophets have come out into the world. But conscience is more than conscience. Conscience is God. Conscience is Immanuel, God in us. My conscience, accordingly, is more to me than all prophets and apostles and preachers, and very angels themselves. If that had been Paul sitting under that oak, and had the old Bethelite deceiver come riding on his ass, with his certificate of office, and with his story about an angel to Paul, we have Paul's answer to him in the Galatians: "If an angel from heaven bids me go against God in my conscience, let him be accursed." And the old deceiver would have fallen down and would have reported at home that God was in the man of God from Judah of a truth. So would the secrets of his heart have been made manifest. "Conscience," says Sanderson, "is a fast friend, and a fierce foe." "I take my ears," said King Charles, "to other preachers; but I take my conscience to Mr. Sanderson." And go you to the preacher who speaks closest to your conscience, whatever denomination he preaches in, and then hold fast by your enlightened and awakened conscience against men and devils.

At the same time, to be slain by a lion on the way home was surely much too sharp a punishment for taking one's supper with a prophet and an angel; uneasy conscience and all. But then, "some sins," says that noble piece, the Westminster Larger Catechism, "receive their aggravation from the persons offending; if they be of riper age, greater experience in grace, eminent for profession, gifts, place, office, and as such are guides to others, and whose example is likely to be followed by others." The very case, to the letter, of the man of God out of Judah. The sublimity of his public services that morning had henceforth set up a corresponding standard for his private life. And this is one of our best compensations for preaching the grace of God and the law of Christ. Our office quickens our conscience; it makes the law cut deeper and deeper into our hearts every day; and it compels us to a public and private life we would otherwise have escaped. Preaching recoils with terrible strokes on the preacher. It curtails his liberty in a most tyrannical way; it tracks him through all his life in a most remorseless manner. Think it out well, and count the cost, before you become a minister. For, it was surely a little sin, if ever there was a little sin, to sup that Sabbath night at an old prophet's table, and that, too, on the invitation of an angel. But the lion that met the disobedient prophet that night did not reason that way.

"Bury me," said the remorseful old man to his sons standing in tears round his miserable deathbed, "bury me in the same grave with the bones of the man of God out of Judah." And the old prophet's sons so buried their father. And an awful grave that was in Bethel, with an awful epitaph upon it. Now, suppose this. Suppose that you were buried on the same awful principle—in whose grave would your bones lie waiting together with his till the last trump to stand forth before God and man together? And what would your epitaph and his be? Would it be this: "Here lie the liar and his victim"? Or would it be this: "Here lie the seducer and the seduced"? Or would it be this: "Here lie the hater and him he hated down to death"? Or would it be this: "Here lie the tempting host and his too willing to be tempted guest"? Or, if you are a minister, would it be this: "Here lies a dumb dog, and beside him one who was a crowded preacher in the morning of his days, but a castaway before night"? Alas, my brother!

54
Rehoboam

JUST by one insolent and swaggering word King Rehoboam lost for ever the ten tribes of Israel. And all Rehoboam's insane and suicidal history is written in our Bibles for the admonition and instruction of all hot-blooded, ill-natured, and insolent-spoken men among ourselves.

The beginning of it all was the domestic disorders and the cancerous immoralities of David's house. And then it was the heathen idolatry and the heathen immorality and the reckless and exasperating extravagance of Solomon's declining years. Prophet after prophet had been sent of God to Solomon because of his shameful apostasies, but it was all in vain. Solomon's old advisers besought his son Rehoboam, as soon as he had sat down on the throne of his father Solomon, to attend to the complaints of the people, and to lighten their terrible burdens. But Rehoboam shut his ears to the wisdom of the elders of Israel, and answered the oppressed people in the insolent and insulting words that the young men about him had put in his mouth. "My father made your yoke heavy, and I will add to your yoke; my father also chastised you with whips, but I will chastise you with scorpions." At that the long-suppressed shout rose and rang through the angry land, "To your tents, O Israel! Now see to thine own house, David!" So Israel rebelled, says the sacred writer, against the house of David to this day.

One might well be tempted to think that the sacred writer had told Rehoboam's history wholly in vain, so often has his insane folly been repeated east and west since his fatal day. And in no land has his folly been oftener repeated or better written about than just in our own England.

> I am solicited [says Queen Katherine], not by a few,
> And those of true condition, that your subjects
> Are in great grievance; there have been commissions
> Sent down among 'em, which have flaw'd the heart
> Of all their loyalties; wherein, although,
> My good lord cardinal, they vent reproaches
> Most bitterly on you, as putter on
> Of these exactions, yet the king our master—
> Whose honor heaven shield from soil!—even he escapes not
> Language unmannerly, yea, such which breaks
> The sides of loyalty, and almost appears
> In loud rebellion.—I would your highness
> Would give it quick consideration, for
> There is no primer business.

Our own Henrys, and Jameses, and Charleses, and Georges—the books of the kings of Israel were eminently written for their learning. But preaching like Bishop

Hall's *Contemplation* on Rehoboam—if the light that is at our kings' courts be darkness, how great is that darkness. And such servile preaching as Joseph Hall's too often was, went on till the kings of England lost, not their kingdoms only, but their own heads to the bargain. Take Joseph Hall away from court, and there is not a racier or a more sagacious preacher in England; but put James's lawn sleeves on Bishop Hall, and there are few in their hour of temptation who are more contemptible. How much more true and just and wise is Dean Stanley: "The demands of the nation were just. The old counselors gave such advice as might have been found in the Book of Proverbs. Only the insolence of the younger courtiers imagined the possibility of coercing a great people. It was a doomed revolution."

Every morning, all the last wet summer, my children and I read an hour in the best story-book in the world. And having Rehoboam in my mind, we came upon this about Coriolanus: "But on the other side, for lack of education, he was so choleric, and so impatient, that he would yield to no living creature: which made him churlish, uncivil, and altogether unfit for any man's conversation. They could not be acquainted with him as one citizen careth to be with another in the city. His behavior was so unpleasant to them by reason of a certain insolent and stern manner he had, which, because it was too lordly, was disliked. And, to say truly, the greatest benefit that learning bringeth men unto is this: that it teacheth them that be rude and rough of nature, by compass and rule of reason, to be civil and courteous, and to like better the mean state than the higher. But Martius was a man too full of passion and choler, and too much given over to self-will and opinion, and lacked the gravity and affability that is gotten with judgment of learning and reason. He remembered not how willfulness is the thing of all the world which the governor of a state should shun. For a man that wishes to live in this world must needs have patience which lusty bloods [like Rehoboam's young counselors] make but a mock at." Reading the same charming book another wet morning we came on this: "Now, Caesar immediately won many men's goodwill at Rome through his eloquence in pleading their causes, and the people loved him marvellously also because of the courteous manner he had to speak with every man, and to use them gently, being more ceremonious therein than was looked for in one of his years. How little account Caesar made of his diet, this example doth prove it. Supping one night in Milan with his friend Valerius Leo, there was served asparagus to his board and oil of perfume put into it instead of salad oil. Caesar simply ate it and found no fault, but reproved his friends who were offended: and told them that it had been enough to have abstained to eat of that they misliked, and not to shame their friend, and how much he lacked good manners who found fault with his friend." The whole chapter, indeed, is one of Plutarch's masterpieces. Though the great republican does not like Caesar, yet his instinct as an author and his nobility as a man compel Plutarch to extol continually Caesar's exquisite courtesy, his noble urbanity, and his unfailing good manners.

True, there are neither kings, nor kings' sons, nor kings' counselors, nor kings' chaplains here, but there are plenty of hot-blooded, hectoring, insolent, and ill-natured men. There are husbands, and fathers, and masters, and many other kinds and classes of men to whom this Scripture comes direct from God. Husbands especially. You husbands, never, all your days, speak an impatient or an angry or an insolent word to your wife. And if you have already lost your fireside, which it is worse to lose than a kingdom; if you have spoken not one angry and cruel word, but many, which cannot now be unspoken, it is not too late even yet. Even if things have been said between you and your wife that neither of you can ever forget, your whole life is not lost. At the worst, if you both like, if you are both able, meat may yet come to you both out of the eater; that is to say, out of your angry, insolent, heart-cutting words to one another. You may gather quietness, and self-command, and a bridle for your mouth, and a balm for two sore hearts out of the carcass of your all-but-dead tenderness to one another. When the next debatable matter comes up between you, let it not come up. Put your foot upon it. Keep your foot firm down upon it.

> Prune thou thy words, the thoughts control
>   That o'er thee swell and throng;
> They will condense within thy soul,
>   And change to purpose strong.

All Scriptures are not written for all men alike. Some men are already strong men and wise masters of themselves. There are men from whom you will never hear one angry, sulky, insolent word all their days. But there are other men whose lips simply spit hell-fire as often as they open them upon your heart.

One would think that if there was any one of the near relationships of human life more than another that would of itself absolutely secure kindness, and tenderness, and affability, and love, it would be that of a father. But, as a matter of fact, it is often the very opposite. You never see more impatience, and harshness, and sullenness, and sourness than you see in some fathers. Why is that so, I wonder? It is very difficult to explain and account for it. Let every silent, sulky, churlish father watch and examine the working of his own heart till he understands and overcomes this monstrosity in himself. It is against nature. But it cannot be denied that it is very common. It is not for nothing, you may be very sure, that Paul gives to fathers this, at first reading, somewhat startling counsel, not to provoke their children to wrath. The apostle must often have seen it done. He must often have suffered from seeing it done. He must often have felt sore in his heart for such unhappy children, else he would never have said what he says in his Epistle to the Ephesians. He must often have sat at tables where the children were incessantly corrected and rebuked and exasperated. He must often have seen all-but-innocent children nagged and worried into answers and actions the whole blame of which he laid on their fathers and their mothers. Treat your children, he says to us, as your Father treats you. For His name is merciful, and gracious, and long-suffering, and slow to wrath. Study your children. Command your temper towards your children. Do not worry, and vex, and insult, and exasperate your children. "When they do right, make a point of praising them openly," says Cecil. "And when they do wrong, reprehend them secretly." A word of encouragement, a touch of the hand, a smile even; how easy to a wise and loving father it is to bring up his children in the nurture and admonition of the Lord, and how happy it makes him and them. But how hard and impossible all that is to a churl and a curmudgeon.

And King Rehoboam consulted with the old men that had stood before Solomon his father while he yet lived, and said, How do ye advise that I should answer this people? And they advised the king, saying, If thou wilt answer them, and speak good words unto them, then they will be thy servants for ever. But he forsook the counsel of the old men. The best sermon I know on that scene is to be read in a letter of Mr. Ruskin's to the editor of the *Daily Telegraph*. The editor had said in a leading article that it is the hardest thing in the world in these days to find a good servant. And that called out Mr. Ruskin the same day. I will not spoil his English. "Sir," he wrote, "you so seldom write nonsense that you will, I am sure, pardon your friends for telling you when you do so. Your article on servants today is sheer nonsense. It is just as easy and just as difficult now to get good servants as ever it was. You may have them, as you may have pines and peaches, for the growing; or you may even buy them good, if you can persuade the good growers to spare them off their walls; but you cannot get them by political economy and the law of supply and demand. Sir, there is only one way to have good servants, and that is to be worthy of being well served. All nature and all humanity will serve a good master, and will rebel against an ignoble one. There is no surer test of the quality of a nation than the quality of its servants. A wise nation will have philosophers in its servants' hall, a knavish nation will have knaves there, and a kindly nation will have friends there. Only let it be remembered that 'kindness' means, as with your child, so with your servant, not indulgence, but rare." And then Mr. Ruskin winds up the whole correspondence with an apt and beautiful reference to Xenophon's *Economics*, and an advice to all his lady readers to get the old Greek book by heart, as the most perfect ideal of kingly character and kingly government ever given in literature, as also the ideal of domestic life.

No; there can be no manner of doubt that Mr. Ruskin is wholly right. Our servants would never leave us if we were sufficiently kind to them. Unless, indeed, it were to go to serve those who had sworn to be still kinder to them. And we would get two men's, two women's work out of each one of them while they are with us if we were only twice more kind to them. A word of recognition and appreciation; a word of trust and confidence and real respect now and then; a nod, a smile as you meet them in the passage or on the stair; once in a while to eat a meal or a part of a meal with them; to give them now and then the gift or the loan of a book that has done yourself real good to read, and to say so. O yes! the hearts and minds of men and women are neither better nor worse than ever they were. They live upon love, and esteem, and respect, and praise, just as much as ever they did. Just try them and see.

55
Josiah

JOSIAH was born with a tender heart, says Huldah the prophetess. Josiah's father and grandfather were the two worst kings that had ever sold Israel into slavery. And Josiah inherited from his father and from his grandfather a name of shame, an undermined throne, a divided and a distracted kingdom, a national religion and a public worship debased, and, indeed, bestialized; and, over all, a fearful looking for of judgment. And all that broke and made tender Josiah's heart from the day of his birth. We are told nothing of Josiah's unhappy mother. But may we not be allowed to believe that her heart also was made tender within her by all that she had come through, till she bore and brought up her son Josiah to be the most tender-hearted man in all Israel, till Mary bore and brought up her child to be the most tender-hearted man in all the world?

If a boy has a good mother and a good minister he is all but independent of his father. And with Jedidah for his mother, and with Jeremiah for his minister, both Manasseh his grandfather and Amon his father taken together did not succeed in corrupting and destroying young Josiah. The tender heart of the young prince took all the good out of his so terribly untoward circumstances, and escaped all the evil, till Jeremiah was able to pronounce this noble panegyric over the too early grave of Josiah—"That it is good for a man to bear the yoke in his youth; and that it is also good for such a man quietly to hope and to wait for the salvation of the Lord." With Jeremiah every Sabbath-day among the ruins of the temple, and with Jedidah every week-day at home, notwithstanding all Josiah's drawbacks and heart-breaks—or, rather, because of them—I do not wonder that Josiah soon became the very best sovereign that had ever sat on the throne of David.

Early in the days of his youth Josiah began to seek after the God of David his father. That is to say—however well a boy may have been brought up; however good a mother he may have had, and however efficient and faithful a minister, the time soon comes when every young man must seek his own God for himself. Neither David's God, nor Jedidah's God, nor Jeremiah's God will suffice for Josiah. Josiah is an orphan and a prince with a terrible heritage of woe. And a second-hand and a merely educational and hereditary knowledge of God will not suffice for Josiah's singular and extraordinary case. Josiah cannot rest till he is able to say for himself—"Thou art my God. Early will I seek thee. O Lord, truly I am Thy servant, the son of Thine handmaid; Thou hast loosed my bonds." And, all the time, while Josiah still sought the Lord, and till he found Him, the tenderness of Josiah's heart kept him safe and unspotted from all the corruptions of the world. A boy will be at a school where all kinds of evil are rampant. He will then enter a workshop or an office where so many young men go astray. But there has always been something about that boy that has kept him through it all both pure and pious. And it has been his tender heart that has done it. Augustine has his finest passage in point. Monica's son, like Jedidah's son, had drunk in the name of Jesus Christ with his mother's milk; and all the folly of philosophy, and all the sweetness of sensuality could never seduce nor satisfy Augustine's heart. God had made Augustine's great heart for Himself; and neither true nor false, neither sweet nor bitter, neither good nor bad, could solace or satiate that deep, predestinated heart. Nothing, and no one, but God Himself. So it was with Josiah. And so it was with ourselves. And so it has been, and so it will be, with thousands of the sons of mothers like Jedidah, and with thousands of the scholars and young communicants of ministers like Jeremiah and Zephaniah.

Josiah was only twenty years of age when he set about a national reformation of religion as radical and as complete as anything that Martin Luther or John Calvin or John Knox themselves ever undertook. But with this immense difference. Both Luther and Calvin and Knox had the whole Word of God in their hands both to inspire them and to guide them and to support them in their tremendous task. But Josiah had not one single book or chapter or verse even of the Word of God in his heathen day. The Five Books of Moses were as completely lost out of the whole land long before Josiah's day as much so as if Moses had never lifted a pen. And thus it was that Josiah's reformation had a creativeness, an originality, an enterprise, and a boldness about it, such that in all these respects it has completely eclipsed all subsequent reformations and revivals, the greatest and the best. The truth is, the whole of that immense movement that resulted in the religious regeneration of Jerusalem and Judah in Josiah's day—it all sprang originally and immediately out of nothing else but Josiah's extraordinary tenderness of heart. The Light that lighteth every man that cometh into the world shone with extraordinary clearness in Josiah's tender heart and open mind. And Josiah walked in that Light and obeyed it, till it became within him an overmastering sense of divine duty and an irresistible direction and drawing of the Divine Hand; and till he performed a work for God and for Israel second to no work that has ever been performed under the greatest and the best of the prophets and kings of Israel combined. It is a very noble spectacle. This royal youth of but about twenty years old, and the son and heir of Manasseh and Amon, having the intellectual boldness and the spiritual originality to take all his statesmanship, and all his churchmanship, and all his international politics, and all his righteous wars, as well as all his personal and household religion, all out of his own tender heart. There never was a nobler proof of our Lord's great New Testament principle that he that doeth the will of God shall know the doctrine. For it was in the progress of that reformation and revival of religion which his own tender heart had alone dictated to him that the long-lost law of Moses was recovered. And recovered in as many divine and commanding and rewarding words, so as to sanction and seal, as if from heaven itself, all the bold and believing task that Josiah had wholly of himself undertaken. We all profess to believe in special providences and in divine interpositions; but, surely, the extraordinary providence that brought to the light of day and put into Josiah's hands the long-lost law of Moses concerning the worship and morals of Israel was an incomparable miracle of the Divine grace and goodness. Josiah was worthy; and God's recognition and reward of Josiah's worth came to Josiah at the very best moment, and in the very best way; for it came to him as the very law of the living God; and that, too, as good as if it had been written on the spot by God's own living hand. Humanly speaking, we should never have heard of the Five Books of Moses, as we have heard of them, but for Josiah's tender heart. Humanly speaking, and popularly speaking, our Old Testament would have begun with the Book of Joshua but for Josiah's tender heart. Had Josiah's heart not been tender toward the house of God, the temple would have been let lie in its utter ruin, till the buried Books of Moses would have been to this day the possession and the prey of the moles and the bats. Moses, says Matthew Henry, had a narrow turn for his life in Josiah's day. You do well to tremble at the thought of how near you were to the total loss of Moses and his law. And you are almost angry at Matthew Henry for telling you what you did not know before. But try your own hand on Moses and Josiah, and explain to me how you think you could have had Moses in your Bible but for Josiah; and, again, but for Josiah's tender heart. I defy you to do it. At any rate—this is far more to your purpose—be sure of this, that both Moses, and David, and Paul, and John, and Jesus Christ Himself, are all as good as never written; they are as good as completely lost to you; till you take to them a tender heart, and out of that, a reformed and a repaired life. It will only be after your heart is tender and your life repaired that Hilkiah and Shaphan and Huldah the prophetess will be able to discover and to read to you either the law of Moses, or the grace and truth that has come by Jesus Christ. Till then, your Bible also is as good as buried under the ruin and rubbish of your fallen life. But when your heart is made tender by your father's sins and by your own; as also, by all God's providences towards you, and by all His grace in you; and when, in addition, your life has been made believing and obedient; then God's Word will more and more flash out continually upon you, a lamp to your feet and a light to your path.

When the law of the Lord, as it was written in the newly disinterred Books of Moses, was read for the first time to Josiah, and while Shaphan the scribe was still reading it, Josiah rose up and rent to pieces his royal robe. After having looked for it, I do not read that Shaphan the scribe rent his robe, nor Ahikam the son of Shaphan, nor Hilkiah the priest, nor Achbor, nor Asahiah the servant of Josiah, nor Huldah the prophetess. Josiah alone rent his robe as the law was read. Their hearts were not so tender as was Josiah's heart. They had not come through so much from their youth up. The iron of God had not entered their hearts, and the law of God after it. The finding of the law was, no doubt, a great event in sacred archaeology, as well as in sacred letters, to Shaphan and Hilkiah; but it did not come home to their hearts as it all came home to Josiah's heart. It was Moses speaking to them: but it was God Himself speaking to Josiah. It was an old book to them: but it was the Word of the Living God to him. He felt—such was his tender heart—that all he had attained to, and all he had reformed and done, was just nothing at all while so much remained to be and to do. He felt, as Isaiah felt, that all his righteousnesses were but so much filthy rags. If you have any real interest in these things; if you care to go to the sources and are not indolently content with my poor paraphrase of these intensely interesting Scriptures: if you are a true student, a true sinner, and a true reformer of yourself and of the ruins that lie all around you—you will read 2 Kings and 2 Chronicles to yourselves, if only to see what a reformer both of himself and of his whole land Josiah was: and all that out of his own tender heart. And, best of all, how unsatisfied, and how tender-hearted he was with all he had done. All which, you must know, was the Holy Ghost in Josiah's tender heart before the Holy Ghost had yet been given. Has He even yet been given in that way to you? Do you rend your heart every day as you hear and read the Word of God? Or, are your clothes as whole, and your hearts, as were Hilkiah's and Shaphan's, and all the rest of the merely official and salaried servants of the palace and the temple? On the other hand, if all you have done only adds itself on to what you have not done: if your best works break your heart even more than your worst: if it is no rhetoric that all your righteousnesses are so much filthy rags: then, I wish much to assure you, that so it always is when the Holy Spirit accompanies the Word of God, either read or heard. Jeremiah—you all know the proverbial penitent, and the contrite heart, that Jeremiah was—but Jeremiah did not think that. He did not feel that. Oh that mine head were waters, and mine eyes a fountain of tears! wept that hard-hearted and dry-eyed prophet. "I can sin much," cries holy Lancelot Andrewes to God every night, "but I cannot repent much. Woe is me for my hard and dry heart. Give me, O God, a molten heart. Give tears. Give the grace of tears. Give me, O Lord, this great grace. None were so welcome to me. Not all the good things of this life are to be coveted by me in comparison with tears. Tears such as Thou didst give to David, and to Jeremiah, and to Josiah, and to Peter, and to her out of whom were cast seven devils. O God, give the chief of sinners some tears for his great sin, and for Thy great salvation." And the Word of God has never yet been aright read to you, or aright heard and believed by you, unless you feel like Josiah, and Jeremiah, and Peter, and Andrewes every day. Your religion is not worth one straw, as true religion, unless it is every day breaking and making more tender your hard heart. Woe unto you that laugh now, for ye shall mourn and weep. But blessed are ye that weep now, for ye shall laugh for it all when all tears shall have been wiped from your eyes.

Only, if you will have Josiah's tender heart in this hard-hearted world, you will have to pay a heavy price for it. Josiah paid a heavy price at the last for his tender heart. Josiah's tender heart, after it had done him all the good that we have seen, and more, at last it did him this terrible evil, that it lost him his life for this life. Josiah's tender heart was the cause of his too early death. The narrative is obscure and perplexed, and it lends itself to be read in more ways than one. But as I read Josiah's end it is something like this—The king's tender heart led him out to do battle against the hereditary enemy of Israel and the oppressor and persecutor of the weak; in short, he went out against the Sultan of Turkey of that day. And the Judge of all the earth and the God of battles, for His own deep ends, let that battle go against Josiah, till Josiah said, Have me away, for I am wounded. Being unsuccessful, as we say, Josiah is almost universally blamed for letting his tender heart take up the sword. But I, for one, am quite content to leave Josiah's tender-hearted statesmanship to the arbitrament of the last day. I, for one, will applaud Josiah till my applause is reversed by Him whose tender heart took Him also to His death. And till Jesus Christ from the great white throne condemns and sentences Josiah for his too tender heart, I shall continue to read this to myself on his tombstone in the valley of Megiddo:—This,

THE REMEMBRANCE OF JOSIAH IS LIKE THE PERFUME OF THE APOTHECARY, AND HIS NAME IS LIKE MUSIC AT A BANQUET OF WINE. FOR HIS PURE AND HOLY YOUTH JEHOVAH WAS HIS SHIELD IN THE HOUR OF TEMPTATION, TILL HE BEHAVED HIMSELF RIGHTLY IN THE CONVERSION OF HIS PEOPLE, AND TILL HE TOOK AWAY ALL THEIR ABOMINATIONS OF INIQUITY. HE DIRECTED HIS HEART TO THE LORD, AND HE ESTABLISHED THE WORSHIP OF GOD: AND ALL BECAUSE HIS HEART WAS SO TENDER. THE REMEMBRANCE OF JOSIAH IN JUDAH AND IN JERUSALEM IS LIKE THE PERFUME OF THE APOTHECARY, AND LIKE MUSIC AT A BANQUET OF WINE.

56
Elijah

THE prophet Elijah towers up like a mountain in Gilead above all the other prophets. There is a solitary grandeur about Elijah that is all his own. There is a mystery and an unearthliness about Elijah that is all his own. There is a volcanic suddenness, and a volcanic violence, indeed, about all Elijah's descents upon us and all his disappearances from us. We call him Elijah the Tishbite, but we are no wiser of that. We do not even know where Tishbe is. Elijah has neither father nor mother. As Elijah never died, so he was never born, as we are born. Elijah came from God, and he went to God. Elijah stood before God till God could dispense with and spare Elijah out of His presence no longer. Elijah's very name will tell you all that, and more than all that, concerning both Elijah and his father and his mother, Elijah—my God is Jehovah. You may know the hearts of fathers and mothers to some extent, even among ourselves, by the names they give to their children. And I leave you to judge what kind of a father and mother they must have been who so boldly coined out of Moses, and out of their own hearts, this magnificent name for their circumcised child. Elijah had a heavenly name, but he had, to begin with, but an earthly nature. Elijah was a man, to begin with, subject to like passions as we are. Elijah was a man, indeed, of passions all compact. We never see Elijah that he is not subject to some passion or other. A passion of scorn and contempt; a passion of anger and revenge; a passion of sadness and dejection and despair; a passion of preaching; a passion of prayer. Elijah was a great man. There was a great mass of manhood in Elijah. He was a Mount-Sinai of a man, with a heart like a thunderstorm. That man among ourselves who has the most human nature in him and the most heart; the most heart and the most passion in his heart; the most love and the most hate; the most anger and the most meekness; the most scorn and the most sympathy; the most sunshine and the most melancholy; the most agony in prayer, and the most victorious assurance that, all the time, his prayer is already answered—that man is the likest of us all to the prophet Elijah; that man has Elijah's own mantle fallen upon him. Only, alas! there is no such man among us. There is no man among us fit, for one moment, to stand like Elijah before God.

Now, whatever is the matter with us that God has not an Elijah among us, or anything like an Elijah, it is not that we are wanting in passions. We have all plenty of passions; and too much, since we are all so subject to our passions. What an ocean of all kinds of passions all our hearts are; and lashed with what winds without rest. What dark depths of self-love are in all our hearts. And what a master-passion is that same self-love. Self-love is a serpent; and, like the famous serpent in Scripture, it swallows up and swells out on all the other serpents of which our hearts are full. Yes; we all have passions enough to make us not Elijahs and Ahabs only, but angels in heaven, or devils in hell. And our passions are every day doing that within us. All the difference between Elijah and Ahab was in the subjection of their passions. Elijah was a man of immensely stronger passions than poor Ahab ever was; only Elijah's powerful passions all swept him up to heaven, whereas all Ahab's contemptible passions shouldered and shovelled and sucked him down to hell. Queen Jezebel, also, Ahab's wife, when she was still a woman-child, her passions were as sweet and pure and good and subject as were the passions of the Virgin Mary herself. The whole difference between Elijah and Ahab, and between Jezebel and the mother of our Lord was in their hearts' desires, till their hearts' desires grew up into all-consuming passions.

> On life's vast ocean diversely we sail,
> Reason the card, but passion is the gale.

> May I govern my passions with absolute sway,
> And grow wiser and better as my strength wears away.

And what a passionate preacher Elijah was. You know the story of the play-actor who scouted the minister because he dawdled over his prayers and his sermons as if he was ashamed of his message. "We act our parts in dead earnest," he said; "and that is the reason that you have to sell your empty churches to us to make our theaters out of them."

>   Yea,
> This man's brow, like to a title-page,
> Foretells the nature of a tragic volume.
> Thou tremblest, and the whiteness of thy cheek
> Is apter than thy tongue to tell thy errand.

"Hear, O Lord, and have mercy upon me in this matter of preaching. Lord, be Thou my helper. Turn my dreamings," implores the passionate Andrewes, "into earnestness, my follies into cleansings of myself, my guilt into indignation, my past sin into all the greater fear for the future, my sloth into passionate desire, and my pollution into revenge. And enable me, O my God, to bend all my passions of faith, and love, and hate, and fear, revenge, and remorse, and what not, in upon my own salvation, and the salvation of my people!"

And then in prayer. The translators of the New Testament tell us that they have preserved the Apostle James's passionate idiom in the margin of the text, "Elias with all his passions prayed in his prayer." And I, for one, am for ever deep in their debt for their so doing, for the prophetic and apostolic idiom in the margin takes possession of my imagination. It touches my heart; it speaks to my conscience and that because, after all these years of prayer, how seldom it is that we really "pray in our prayers," as the apostle tells us that the prophet prayed. We repeat choice passages of scripture in our prayers. We recite with studied pathos classical paragraphs out of Isaiah and Ezekiel. We praise one man and we blame another man in our prayers. We pronounce appreciations and we pass judgments in our prayers. We do everything in our prayers but truly pray. The Bible naturally shows a preference for men of like passions with itself; and the more of his passions any man puts into his prayer, the more space and the more praise the Bible gives to that man. Jacob was a prince in the passionateness of his prayer all that night at the Jabbok. What a tempest of passion broke upon the throne of God all that night. What a tempest of fear, and despair, and remorse, and self-accusation, of all indeed that was within Jacob's passionate heart. Jacob's raging passions really tore him to pieces that terrible night in his prayer. His very thighbones were twisted and torn out of their sockets, and his strongest sinews snapped like so many silly threads. There was not on the face of the earth another night of passion in prayer like that for the next two thousand years. Esau, also, often halted upon his thigh. But that was with hunting too hard; that was with running down venison, and leaping hedges and ditches after his quarry. Esau wrestled with wild beasts with all his passions, but Jacob wrestled with the angel. Now, let any man among ourselves henceforth pray in his prayers like Jacob and Elijah: let any man among ourselves determine to put his passions into his prayers like Jacob and Elijah, and it will make him a new man. His heart, and all the passions of his heart, will, in that way, more and more be drawn off the things of this life, and will be directed in upon the great world that is within him, and above him, and before him. The heat of his heart will begin to burn after heavenly things. His passions, that have made him so impossible for men to live with, will now all become subdued, and softened, and sweetened till he will be like a little child in your hands. He was at one time so hard, so harsh, so impossible to please, so full of his own opinions and prejudices, so loud, and so forward, and so willful. But you never hear him now, he so despises himself, and so honors, and respects, and yields up to you. Nothing in the world so renews a man as putting his passions into his prayers. This, in time, will make a saint of the very chief of sinners. This, in time, will turn a heart of stone into a heart of flesh. O why do we ministers not preach more about prayer, and about the employment of our own and our people's passions in prayer! But if your ministers do not so preach, and do not know the way—you are independent of them. There is a great literature of prayer, and it would splendidly and immediately repay and reward you and your households to have it in your hands every day.

But Elijah would not be the great lesson to us that he is if he were always Elijah, with all his passions at all times at a flame in his prayers. That no man may glory before God, after all that Elijah has done, we see him before he dies just as weak, and as downcast, and as embittered, and as unhappy as if he had never known how to subdue and subject and sanctify his passions. No. It is no strange thing that is happening to us when we sit under our juniper-bush and say, "It is enough. Now, O Lord, take away my life, for I am no better than my fathers." Elijah was getting old. He was feeling lonely. His work seemed to him to have all come to nothing. Till death was now his only desire, and the grave his true resting-place. All men have their own dejections, and defeats, and despairs. But ministers far more than all other men. Partly from themselves; partly from the peculiar nature of their work; and partly from the deadly opposition to it in the world, and in the hearts of their people. What have I been spending all my life for? an old minister asks himself. Who is any better of all my work? Who is any holier or any happier, or whose house? Who is any less selfish, any less proud, any less worldly-minded, any less envious, any less ill-natured, any less faultfinding, any less evil-spoken?

So we despond. So we repine. So we despair. So we sit and say after the triumphs, and the praises, and the hopes of our youth are all past, and our early successes are all over. It is enough. And now, O Lord, take away my life. But it is our pride. It is our self-will. It is our passions coming out of our prayers and coming in between us and our despisers, opposers, and persecutors. How much better did Samuel behave himself when he was deprived and dismissed and his work all forgotten. Samuel's wisdom and sweetness and absolute heavenly-mindedness never came out more than in his solitary and superseded old age, when he counselled and comforted the people, and said, God forbid that I should sin against the Lord in ceasing to pray for you; but I will still teach you the good and the right way. In this way Samuel showed Elijah the way to keep his old heart young to the end, and his spirit quiet, and good, and sweet, and beautiful. And it was prayer that did it; and it was putting all his remaining passions still into his prayers to his very end; and it was in that way that Samuel did it, and that Elijah at last learned to do it also.

For Elijah's passions all came back to all their first obedience, and to all their former splendid service, as he stood by Jordan and waited for his signal from the Lord. For, what was the chariot of Israel to Elijah that day, but Elijah's heart already in heaven? And what were those horses of fire that day, but all Elijah's passions all harnessed, in all their heaven-bounding strength, to that heavenly chariot? His faith, his fearlessness, his scorn of evil, his prayerfulness, his devotion to Israel and to God. Those horses of heavenly fire all spurned the earth as they stood and champed by the Jordan. And when the Lord would take up Elijah to Himself, all those horses of fire sprang with one leap up to heaven. And when Elisha saw it he cried, My father, my father, the chariot of Israel, and the horsemen thereof! And he saw him no more.

57
Elisha

ELISHA, the servant and the successor of Elijah, was the son of a prosperous farmer in Israel. Shaphat, the father of Elisha, was a man of substance, but, like all true Israelites, rich and poor, he had brought up his son Elisha to a life of hard work. And thus it is that we come upon Elisha standing in the office of superior over his father's plowmen, while he is, at the same time, one of those same plowmen himself. One spring day, when all Shaphat's plows were at work in the spring-time meadow, and Elisha's plow the foremost among them, Elijah, the old prophet, came up suddenly behind Elisha and cast his rough mantle over Elisha's shoulder. In a moment the young plowman saw and understood what it was that had happened to him. Elijah had not spoken a single word to Elisha. But Elijah's solemn silent act was sufficiently clear and eloquent to Elisha. "When a great teacher dies," says Sir John Malcolm in his *History of Persia*, "he bequeaths his patched mantle to the disciple that he most esteems. And the moment the elect disciple puts on the holy mantle he is vested with the whole power and sanctity of his predecessor. The mantles which were used by ascetics and saints have always been the objects of religious veneration in the East. The holy man's power is founded upon his sacred character, and that rests upon his poverty and contempt of worldly goods. His mantle is his all, and its transfer marks out his heir. Some of these sacred mantles can be traced for several centuries, and their value increases with their age." This is an old and superstitious tradition now; but in the plowed field of Abel-Meholah we are back at its very beginning and first performance, when Elijah comes up behind Elisha and casts his cloak of camel's hair over the shoulders of Shaphat's son. And, as if to make it impossible for himself ever to turn back from following Elijah, Elisha made a fire of the wood of his familiar plow, and slew his favorite oxen and made a feast of the flesh, and thereby proclaimed openly to all men that he had put his hand to another plow than that plow of wood, from which he would never draw back. Elisha burned his ships that day, as the Romans would have said. Shaphat, Elisha's father, was growing old, and Elisha would soon have inherited the rich meadow he was then working in; but, in a moment, all that was for ever changed; and Shaphat may now cast his husbandman's mantle over what young farmer he will; his son Elisha is henceforth dead to all that Abel-Meholah has to hold out to him. For the next fifty years Elisha is to be a spiritual plowman in the Lord's meadows, which are the hearts and lives of the men of Israel.

Elijah's mantle is one of our most expressive proverbs, and so is Elisha's request for a double portion of his departing master's spirit. "Ask what I shall do for thee," said Elijah, "before I be taken away from thee." And Elisha said, "I pray thee, let a double portion of thy spirit be upon me." Not the double of all the gifts and all the graces that Elijah had possessed and had so well employed. That is an impossible explanation of Elisha's petition. I can easily imagine Elijah feeling now that life was over with him, that he had been an unprofitable servant. All true men so feel.

290

I can easily imagine Elijah seeking of God in prayer that his successor should be twofold, should be tenfold, more gifted and more successful than he had been. But I cannot imagine a humble and loyal soul like Elisha so insulting his master on his deathbed as to say to him: "I hope to have double thy success to show when I come to die." No; the thing is inconceivable. What Elisha really asked for was simply the fulfillment of what had been already promised him when Elijah's mantle fell on his shoulders. That act of Elijah was the sign and the seal of Elisha's adoption. And the adopted son had always allotted to him the double portion that belonged to the first-born. Not the double of what the adopting father possessed himself; for no man can put into his testament the double of what he has of his own. But he can double the portion that would properly have belonged to one of his younger children. And thus it is that, when it is put to him, Elisha simply, and dutifully, and humbly asks that the divine law of adoption and primogeniture may immediately begin to hold and to take effect in his spiritual sonship to the departing prophet.

The world and the church live and thrive and grow from generation to generation under the guiding and upholding hand of God. All the time that Elijah was repining and meditating death under the juniper tree, God was preparing the young plowman of Abel-Meholah to wear Elijah's mantle, and to carry forward Elijah's work. And when we are prognosticating the headlessness and the collapse of the church when this man and that man shall have fallen asleep, all the time God has His hidden servants, quite well known to Him, and quite ready to take up this man's and that man's great office when they shall demit it. There may be to be seen following the spring plow in Strathmore or in the Lothians at this moment, some young man who shall be as well known and as great in a few years in Scotland as Elisha was in Israel. There are certainly at school, at college, in the shop, in the office, on the hills, in the mine, young men who, five-and-twenty years after this, shall be as great preachers, as great writers, as great statesmen, as great administrators, and as great discoverers as any of those who are now in such fame, and far better suited for the time to come. Elisha was not Elijah. But he was the gift of the living God to the living Israel of his day. And I would have you all keep your dejected hearts in perfect peace, sure of this, that God will look after both the church and the world far better than the most anxious-minded and censorious-minded of His people.

And let all our prophets, and all the sons of our prophets, go to school in manners and in morals to those fifty sons of the prophets in that day in Israel. Look at them as they hail and bow down before a better man than themselves, though he is as young as themselves, and withal, has not had their schooling for his office. There is blessing in store for Israel, from such young ministers. Elisha had been a plowman till he became Elijah's servant. And, yet, in a moment, and without a murmur, the fifty sons of the prophets at once accept Elisha as the true successor of Elijah, and as their young master. The old men who had not had great success themselves did not cast up Elisha's youth to him when his success began, nor did the sons of the prophets keep up against him his humble origin, or his lack of letters. There must have been good Divinity Halls in those days when there were fifty probationers just come out of them of such humility, and admiration, and belief in better men than themselves. These prophetical graces are beautiful to us to read about at a distance, but they are far more beautiful to God when they are seen in everyday men like ourselves. Those fifty students must have had good tutors and governors in ministerial morals and in pastoral theology.

About dead men's mantles. Elisha's first instinct was to bury and blot himself out under Elijah's coat of camel's hair and his leathern girdle. And he did actually begin his public life wearing those ancient coverings and austere accoutrements. But Elisha was far too simple and far too sincere a man to continue long wound up in such cerements. He set out, and I do not wonder at it, in Elijah's mantle, and he did his first prophetical work in it; but he wore it awkwardly, and he soon laid it aside. Elisha was an altogether smaller and more homely man than Elijah, and he wisely preferred before long to put on much less startling and outstanding clothes. Elisha was a gentle, homely, kindly lowland minister; as unlike Elijah as the green meadows of Abel-Meholah were unlike the savage solitudes of mountainous Gilead. And we must not demand of our young preachers that they shall all stride out with the same step, and pronounce just with the same accent as the Elijah of our youth. We had Elijah, and he fulfilled his day, and did his work. And no men among us need more to be men of today, and not of yesterday, than they who preach the Word of God to us and to our children. Even the Elijah you so often go back upon, were he here again, he would not be exactly the same man, with exactly the same mantle, the hem and the hair of which you were so wont to kiss.

Every ill-brought-up boy who calls names at old people and at odd people must be reminded of those miserable boys and girls of Bethel who called bad names at Elisha till two she-bears came out of the wood, and tore forty and two children of them. The Areopagus on one occasion sentenced a Greek boy to death only for plucking out a quail's eyes, because, they said, if that boy was let live, he would do widespread cruelty and mischief when he grew up, and he had better die at once; and so they sent him to the executioner. On December the 21st, 1719, Thomas Boston writes this in his journal: A poor boy came into the house begging, having such a defect in his speech that he pronounced the words father and mother *fao* and *moa*, at which my wife and others smiling, desired him to speak over again what he had said. In the meantime my little daughter stood looking on with tears in her eyes and in great distress, and at length she came up to her mother, and said, "Mother, did God make that laddie?" "Yes, my dear, He did." "Will He not then be angry at us all for laughing at the laddie, for my lesson says, 'He that mocketh at the poor, reproacheth his Maker'?" She was in mighty concern also to let the boy have some old clothes.

With all that the sacred writer has given us about Elisha, I am not satisfied. I would have liked some more about Elisha's father and mother. I always regret hearing Elisha calling Elijah his father, and no more word of honest Shaphat. Fathers, come with me, and let no man run away with our best name from us! Let no man, no, not Elijah himself, take our crown. Let us determine to be the fathers of our children in the spirit also. Let us be specially jealous of our best ministers, lest our children pass us by, and claim any other man whatsoever as their spiritual father. Let our children be able all their days to say—it was my father; it was my mother. We feed them, we clothe them, we send them to school, and we work and lay up for them. O let no other man, the very best, cast the mantle of the Christian calling and the Christian spirit on the shoulders of our children. Let us do that ourselves; let us do it early; let us do it now. Here am I and the children which Thou hast given me!

58
Naaman

THE instructive story of Naaman is known to all. His valiantness in battle, his greatness with his master, and the high honor in which he was held among his own people; and, with all that, his incurable leprosy—in two or three of his most eloquent strokes the sacred writer sets Naaman most impressively and most memorably before our eyes. The little captive maid also who whispered to Naaman's wife, "Would God my lord were with the prophet that is in Samaria, for he would recover him of his leprosy." And, then, how Naaman came to Samaria with his horses and his chariot; how Elisha sent out and told him to go and wash seven times in Jordan; how Naaman was wroth and would not wash in Jordan, but went away home in a rage: how his excellent servants reasoned with their angry master and how he repented and went and washed in Jordan till his flesh came again like the flesh of a little child—all that is told in fourteen as solid and as eloquent verses as ever were written. They have a miraculous talent of style, those Old Testament authors. Our very best authors cannot hold the candle to them. And those who are counted worthy to stand second to those Old Testament artists have come to their skill by reading nothing else but their Bible day and night. But we have opened our Bible this night—not to study the excellent art of writing, excellent art as it is; but to seek in our Bible the salvation of our souls; without which salvation, all our writing, and all our reading, and every other art and science of human life, is but whitewashing a sepulchre, which all the time is full within of dead men's bones and all uncleanness.

With all his valiantness, and with all his honors, Naaman was nothing better all the while than a dead man. For Naaman was a leper. Naaman had all that heart of man could wish; but, what of that, when he was what he was? Leprosy was feared and fled from in Israel as the stroke of God. Leprosy was the most fearful and the most hateful disease known to man. Leprosy was so loathsome, and so utterly incurable and deadly, that it was not looked on as an ordinary disease at all: but, rather, as a special creation in His anger, and a direct curse of God, both to punish sin, and, at the same time, to teach His people something of what an accursed thing sin really is; till the whole nature of leprosy and all the laws laid down for its treatment, and the miraculous nature of its so seldom cure, all combined to work into the imagination, and into the conscience, and into the heart, and into the ritual, and into the literature of Israel, some of her deepest lessons about the terrible nature and the only proper treatment of sin.

For sin is like leprosy in this, that it is the most mysterious, stroke-like, malignant, loathsome, and mockingly incurable of all our incurable ills. Sin is like Naaman's leprosy in this also, that a man is great with men, and honorable, and a mighty deliverer—but all the time he is a sinner. And all a sinner's life, and all his greatness, and all his honor, and all his praise is but dressing a dead body with

rich ornaments, and sprinkling a sepulchre with sweet smells. It needed no divine
grace in Naaman to teach him that he was a leper. Day and night; in the council-
chamber and in the field; eating and drinking; waking and sleeping, Naaman was
a leper. But it needs a wisdom, and a truth, and an experience, and a stage of
salvation that few men have attained to, before a sinner knows that he is a sinner;
really and truly knows it, as Naaman knew his leprosy. Some men do: one here
and another there. If you have made the discovery that you are a leprous sinner:
if you have found no figure that so well describes you as Naaman's leprosy—then
you have made the greatest discovery a man can make in this world. "What was
your greatest discovery, Sir James?" asked an interviewer of the discoverer of chlo-
roform. "That I am a sinner," answered the saintly man, "and that Jesus Christ
is my Savior." Yes, that was out of all sight Sir James's greatest and most fruitful
discovery, for that made him a great man with his Master; and it made him full of
love and honor among all the best people in the land. You will not yet believe it,
but you also begin to belong to the race of the greatest men that have ever lived
when you begin to make the deadly discovery that you are a leper at heart. Nay;
not only is that the beginning of all your true greatness; but your knowledge of
sin all along to the end of life—that is the best measure of your true greatness. All
our true greatness has been lost to us through sin; and it is in sin, and through sin,
and by escaping out of sin, that we shall not only recover all our lost greatness but
shall attain to a far greater greatness than that we had lost. I do not care a straw
to go to see the greatest scholar, or the greatest author, or the greatest preacher, or
the greatest soldier, or the greatest statesman. But I would go a long way to see the
greatest sinner; to see and to converse with that man still on this earth who has
the deepest knowledge of his own heart. The man who has made that discovery,
and who is daily and hourly making that discovery, and who is every hour of every
day acting before God and man on that discovery—that is the man of all men to
me. The fifty-first Psalm is David's masterpiece to me. Isaiah's greatest chapters to
me are his fifth and his fifty-third. Paul's greatest passage is his immortal morsel
of autobiography in the seventh of the Romans. Augustine's best book is his *Confessions* and John Bunyan's his *Grace Abounding*, and Jacob Behmen's his *Way to
Christ.* "Sin?" exclaims even our own Carlyle in indignation; "the deadliest sin of
all is to be conscious of no sin." And so it is.

But, leprosy and all, Naaman was still a very proud man; for all the leprosy in
the world will not make a proud man meek and lowly in heart. When Naaman was
told how he could be made clean, because the prophet's counsel did not fit in with
Naaman's prejudices and his sense of his own importance, he was wroth at Elisha,
and went home, leprosy and all, in a rage. "Behold, I thought, he will surely come
out, and stand, and will call on the name of the Lord his God, and strike his hand
over the place, and recover the leper." And there are men among ourselves who go
home in the same rage as often as they are told their deadly disease and the only
way of recovery from it. With all your prepossessions and prejudices, many of you
must know that you are not one step nearer anything that could be called salvation than ever you were. There is as much leprosy in your heart tonight as ever
there was. And in your best moments you would give ten talents of silver, and six

thousand pieces of gold, and ten changes of raiment to be for ever rid of it. What do you say just to give a trial to the things that hitherto have most angered you to hear them spoken about? The real spiritual nature of salvation has always been an unwelcome subject to you. Preaching you greatly enjoy, and you are a great judge of it. Naaman went to the prophet's house to tell him how to preach, and because the prophet did not take his lesson from Naaman, Naaman went home in a rage. My brethren, salvation is not cut to your pattern. Leprosy is not cured on your prescription; its true and only cure has laws, and rules, and obediences, and submissions, and sacrifices of its own that may all anger you to be told them, but it can be had in no other way. What do you say to humble yourself for once, and to try the thing that has hitherto most exasperated you to be tied down to it? All the chances are that your salvation lies out in the direction of far more secret prayer, far more self-denial, far less eating and drinking, far less talking, and far more submission of your opinions and habits of life to other men. It may lie in putting away all your present reading, and giving up much more of your time and attention to books that treat of the soul, its diseases, its discipline, and its salvation. I advise you to get over your temper, and to try that very way that you have up till now been so hot and so loud against. It will humble you to do it, and you are not a humble man; but if you ever come back from Jordan with your flesh like the flesh of a little child, you will be the foremost to confess that you had almost been lost through your pride, and your prejudice, and your ill-nature.

What a fool that man Naaman must have been! everybody has exclaimed over his history ever since his day. He did not deserve to be healed! Surely he was not so ill after all! Either he had not much leprosy upon him, or else he was a perfect madman to do as he did. Yes; but madman with pride, and self-importance, and self-will as he was, Naaman will stand up in the day of judgment and will condemn some of us who have his history before us; for, like him at one time, we do not even yet feel the full curse and deadliness of our sin, else we would do very differently with it. Other men who see what the things are that stand between us and the salvation of our souls are astounded at us. Naaman's very heathen servants were astounded at him, till they broke through all their fear of him and told him so. We sell our souls every day for such contemptible things; such a small outlay would buy us eternal life. Jacob bought his birthright by denying himself just a single mess of pottage. And all that stood between Naaman and perfect health and long life was just to ascend his chariot, and let himself be driven to Jordan, when his servants would have undressed him and dipped him seven times; and, ere ever he was aware, he would have come up out of the water as sweet as a child. O son of Naaman, the suicidal leper! Day after day, year after year, you go on selling the health, the strength, the sweetness, and the whole salvation of your soul for a thing that I may not name; it is so impossible to be believed. It is so mad in you, so self-murderous. The devil, who so deceives you, laughs before God at the price you put upon the blood of His Son, and upon the grace of His Spirit, and upon your own soul. "My father," his servant came near and said to Naaman, "if the prophet had bid thee do some great thing, wouldest thou not have done it? How much rather, then, when he saith to thee: Wash, and be clean?"

But, to speak still more face to face. To put away all types, and figures, and metaphors, however true and terrible. You all know, surely, what the true leprosy is. You all know what the leprosy of your own soul is. It is sin; yes, it is sin. Or, rather, to speak still more true and plain to you, it is yourself. Sin is self. Your true leprosy is yourself. There is no leprosy, there is no sin, but yourself. Get yourself killed in your heart; and God, and love, and heaven, and holiness, and eternal life are all, from that moment, in you. Self is an evil mother big with children tenfold more the children of hell than herself. And her firstborn is your pride, and your anger, and your envy, and your ill-will, and your hatred of so many men around you. O leper! leper! go out with thy loathsome and deadly heart from among living men. Go to thy charnel-house at once; or else, for thou art still a man, and not yet fully and finally a devil, go wash in Jordan.

Go in God's name. Go in God's strength. Go in God's pity, and patience, and mercy. Go on the spot. Go this moment, and go every day, and every hour of every day, and, blessed be God, every moment, as often as thy self-filled heart again stirs and sins in thee. There is a fountain filled with blood. Filled, that is, with the humiliation, and the obedience, and the submission, and the whole life and death of the Son of God. O son of sin and Satan, O child of wrath, wilt thou not submit thyself to be saved? Wilt thou not so much as wash thyself? Wilt thou not say there is a fountain opened for sin and for uncleanness like mine? And wilt thou not go down into it continually, saying without ceasing: O Holy God. O pure, and clean, and sweet, and blessed Son of God. Pity a man made of sin. Pity this leper of all lepers. Pity, if Thou hast such pity, the most miserable man on the face of the earth. A man who, as Thou seest, does nothing before Thee but sin. O pity and spare me, my God, for my sin is ever before me. Oh, able to save to the uttermost, wash me, Savior, or I die! "How," asks the disciple in Jacob Behmen's *Supersensual Life*, "How shall I be able to subsist in all this anxiety and tribulation so as not to lose the eternal peace?" And the Master answers: "If thou dost once every hour throw thyself by faith beyond all creatures into the abysmal mercy of God, into the sufferings of our Lord, and into the fellowship of His intercession, and yieldest thyself fully and absolutely thereunto, then thou shalt receive grace from above to rule over death and the devil, and to subdue hell and the world under thee. And, then, thou mayest not only endure in all manner of temptation, but be actually the better and the brighter because of all thy temptations." Then went he down and dipped himself seven times in Jordan, according to the saying of the man of God, and his flesh came again like the flesh of a little child, and he was clean.

59
Job

THE greatest of all the men of the East, as Job afterwards became, he began his life with having nothing. In his own lowly-minded words, Job was at one time poor even to nakedness. When he was at the top of his shining prosperity, and when he suddenly lost it all in one day, his utter desolation threw his mind back on his absolutely destitute youth. The Lord gave, he said, with splendid thankfulness and with splendid submission, and the Lord hath taken away; blessed be the name of the Lord. But, far worse than all his early poverty, and far more difficult to escape and to surmount, were the long-lived sins of his youth. I have been in the same great trespass, says old Bishop Andrewes, from my youth up, and even to this day. Perfect and upright, and one that feared God and eschewed evil, as Job had now for such a long time been, at the same time he tells us that the heels of his feet still left an accusing and an arresting mark behind him, whatever he did, and wherever he dwelt. Job had been freely and fully forgiven of God, but vengeance was still being taken of God on all Job's inventions, as God's way has always been with His best saints, and always will be. My sins are ever before me, was Job's continual confession made toward God; while, all the time, he held fast his integrity toward all men, and in the face of all men. To his three friends, who so cruelly accused him of hypocrisy, and who kept insisting that there must be some cloaked-up sin in Job's present life that was the cause of all his terrible troubles, he replied with a magnificent and a conclusive vindication of his absolute innocence and perfect integrity. But, all the time, we see Job turning from all men to God and confessing, with the most poignant shame and sorrow, both his past sins and his present sinfulness. "How many are mine iniquities and my sins! For Thou writest bitter things against me, and makest me to possess the iniquities of my youth. Thou puttest my feet also into the stocks, and lookest narrowly to all my paths. Thou settest a print on the heels of my feet. If I wash myself with snow water, and make my hands never so clean, yet Thou wilt plunge me into the ditch, and mine own clothes shall abhor me." The truth is: Job is both guilty and not guilty. Job is both unclean and vile. Job is absolutely innocent of all that Eliphaz and his fellows insinuate and impute to him. The Philistines understand me not, says John Bunyan in his *Grace Abounding*. But Job is not without much sin in his past life, and much sinfulness in his present heart. And it is this—with his unparalleled sufferings, and with the incessant insinuations and insults of his three friends—it is all this that so racks and tortures Job's tender conscience, and so darkens and crushes his pious heart, and so embitters and exasperates, sometimes almost to rank blasphemy, his far too many defences of himself.

"How long have I to live?" said Barzillai to David, when, at his restoration to the throne, David invited the loyal, hospitable, Highland chieftain to a thanksgiving feast in Jerusalem. "I am this day fourscore years old. Can thy servant taste what

I eat or what I drink? Can I hear any more the voice of singing men and singing women?" And in like manner, when Job's sons and daughters said to their old father, "Come to our feasts with us!" Job answered them thus: "No, my children. There is a time for everything. I am no longer young as you are. Rejoice," said the genial old man, "in the days of your youth. Go your way; eat the fat and drink the sweet, and send portions unto them for whom nothing is prepared." Only, all the time, Job had not forgotten his own early days. He knew to his lasting cost that folly is bound up in a young man's heart, and that eating and drinking and dancing, more than anything else, lets all that folly out. And thus it was that Job's sons and daughters had no sooner set out to the days of their feasting and the nights of their dancing, than their father set himself to his days and nights of prayer on behalf of his children. And every morning and every evening till the days of their feasting were all gone about Job never ceased his sacrifices and intercessions in his children's behalf. For each one of his sons and daughters their old father offered a special sacrifice, and set apart for each a special diet of intercession. So much so, that there is not a father or a mother among us to this day to whom God has not often said, Hast thou, in this matter of thy children, considered my servant Job? No. We confess with pain and shame and guilt concerning our children, that Job here condemns us to our face. But we feel tonight greatly drawn, if it is not too late, to imitate Job henceforth in behalf of our children. We have not wholly neglected them, nor the Great Sacrifice in their behalf. But we have not remembered it and them together at all with that regularity, and point, and perseverance, and watchfulness, that all combined to make Job such a good father to his children, and such a good servant to his God. But if our children are still about us, and if it is not yet too late, we shall vow before God tonight that whilst they are still with us we shall not again so forget them. When they set out to school we shall look out of our windows after them, and we shall imagine and picture to ourselves the life into which they must all enter and cannot escape. We shall remember the streets and the playgrounds of our own schooldays, and the older boys and their conversations. And we shall reflect that the games, and sports, and talks of the playground will bring things out of our children's hearts that we never see nor hear at home. And, then, when they come the length of taking walking and cycling tours, and fishing and shooting expeditions; and, still more, when they are invited out to eat and to drink and to dance, till they must now have a latch-key of their own—by that time it is more than time we had done with all our own late hours, and had taken ourselves to almost nothing in this world but intercessory prayer. We shall not go with them, but we shall not sleep till they have all come home and shut the door to our hearing behind them. And we shall every such night, and in as many words, plead before God the sacrifice of Jesus Christ, for each several one of our own and our neighbors' children. We shall go over their names, one after another. We shall spread out our fears and our hopes before God. We shall go over their ages, their temperaments, their inherited virtues and vices. We shall call up and remember where we were living, and what we were doing at their age; and that will make us fall on our face and plead with God that the heels of our son's feet shall leave no such marks behind them as our feet have left. It had been better they had never been born; it were better they died even now than that they should live to possess the iniquities of their youth, and to be put into those terrible stocks that God still keeps for young sinners. And, then, when they come home late at night, and see his candle still burning in their father's room, without any one pointing it out to them, or casting it up to them, they will understand their father's wistful ways, and that will bring them to their own knees also for the day past, and for the night past, and for their own souls, and for the souls of their companions. Thus did Job and his sons and his daughters continually.

The curse that always waits in this world on controversy and contradiction has never been clearer seen than it is seen in Job's case. For never was so much shrewd truth, and so many truly pious positions, and so much divine and human eloquence heard on both sides, and from any other five debating men, as was heard all round Job's ash-heap. The authorities on these things tell us that the debating in the Book of Job is the most wonderful piece of genius that has ever been heard or read since debating genius was. And, yet, such is the malignant and incurable curse of all controversy, even at its best, that Job and all his four friends seem sometimes as if they are to be consumed one of another—out of the same mouth so much blessing and so much cursing both proceed. If Job could have but endured to the end the near neighborhood, and the suspicious looks, and the significant gestures, and the open broadsides of his four friends, "that daily furnace of men's tongues," as Augustine has it, Job would have been far too patient and far too perfect for an Old Testament saint. For, till Christ came, no soul was ever made such a battle-ground between heaven and hell, as Job's soul was made. Job's sorrows came not in single spies, but in battalions. Like the Captain of Salvation Himself, Job, His forerunner, took up successful arms against a whole sea of sorrows, and he would have won every battle of them all had he only been able to bear up under the suspicious looks and the reproving speeches of his four friends. But what Satan could not do with all his Sabeans, and all his Chaldeans, and all his winds from the wilderness to help him, that he soon did with the help of the debating approaches and the controversial assaults of Eliphaz, and Zophar, and Bildad, and Elihu. Oh, the unmitigable curse of controversy! Oh, the detestable passions that corrections and contradictions kindle up to fury in the proud heart of man! Eschew controversy, my brethren, as you would eschew the entrance to hell itself. Let them have it their own way. Let them talk. Let them write. Let them correct you. Let them traduce you. Let them judge and condemn you. Let them slay you. Rather let the truth of God itself suffer, than that love suffer. You have not enough of the divine nature in you to be a controversialist. He was oppressed, and He was afflicted, yet He opened not His mouth; He is brought as a lamb to the slaughter, and as a sheep before her shearers is dumb, so He opened not His mouth. Who, when He was reviled, reviled not again; when He suffered, He threatened not: by whose stripes ye were healed. Heal me, prays Augustine again and again, of this lust of mine of always vindicating myself. Read Santa Teresa's advice about self-excusing.

But, splendid, and, to this day, unapproached composition as the Book of Job is; and, magnificent victory of faith and patience as Job at last achieved; at the same time, the whole tragedy, down to its completion and coronation, is all displayed on an immensely lower stage of things than are a thousand far greater tragedies at present in progress among ourselves. For, after all, both Job's trials, and his triumphs of faith and patience also, savor somewhat too much of this present world. Job suffers first the loss of his oxen, and his asses, and his sheep, and his camels, and his servants; and then, with that, the loss of his sons and daughters; after which the patriarch is smitten in his own body with such a dreadful disease that he is more like a rotten carcass than a living man. All of which was surely tribulation enough for that day and that dispensation. But the fatal loss and the absolute despair of ever attaining to any true holiness of heart; to any true and spiritual love either to God or man; that is a trial of faith and patience to some men in our day that Job with all his battalions of trials knew nothing about. The Lord chastens some men among us with a heart so full of the blains, and boils, and elephantiasis of spiritual sin that a single day of it would have driven Job downright mad. Under it, in his day, Job would have cursed God, and died. But let those among us who are God's elect to the sanctification of the Spirit take comfort. And let them have patience; ay, and far more patience than all the patience of Job, even as they are called to endure far more than all the accumulated losses and all the intolerable diseases of Job. Let them be absolutely sure that when God has sufficiently tried them, they, too, shall come forth as gold. Behold, we count them happy which endure. Ye have heard of the patience of Job, and have seen the end of the Lord; that the Lord is very pitiful, and of tender mercy. The time is long; but the thing is true. Behold, I am vile; what shall I answer Thee? I shall lay my hand upon my mouth. I have heard of Thee by the hearing of the ear; but now mine eye seeth Thee. Therefore, I abhor myself, and repent in dust and ashes. It was when Job had been taught of God to see and to say all that, as never before; it was then that the Lord took pity and turned the captivity of Job. And it will just be when you both see and feel all that; and that a thousand times clearer and a thousand times keener than Job could either see it or feel it; it will just be then that the Lord will turn your captivity also till you will be like men that dream. For I know that my Redeemer liveth, and that He shall stand at the latter day upon the earth. And though after my skin worms destroy this body, yet in my flesh shall I see God. Whom I shall see for myself, and mine eyes shall behold, and not another; though my reins be consumed within me. For the which cause I also suffer these things; for I know in whom I have believed, and am persuaded that He is able to keep that which I have committed unto Him against that day. For I reckon that the sufferings of this present time are not worthy to be compared with the glory which shall be revealed in us. Be ye also patient, and stablish your hearts, for the coming of the Lord draweth nigh.

60
Jonah

THE Prophet Jonah was both the elder son and the unmerciful servant of the Old Testament. He was the elder son. For, as he came nigh to the house, he heard music and dancing. And he called one of the servants, and asked him what these things meant. And he said to him, Thy brother is come; and thy father hath killed the fatted calf, because he hath received him safe and sound. And he was angry, and would not go in; therefore, his father came out and entreated him. And the Lord entreated Jonah to leave his withered gourd and his sunbeaten booth, and to come in and share the joy of the spared city. Jonah was the unmerciful servant of that other New Testament parable also. O thou wicked servant, I forgave thee all that debt, because thou desiredst me: shouldest not thou also have had compassion on thy fellow-servant, even as I had pity on thee?

Everybody has the Book of Jonah by heart. How the word of the Lord came to Jonah, Arise, go to Nineveh, that great city, and cry against it, for their wickedness is come up before me. And how Jonah fled to Tarshish, and would not go to Nineveh; and how, on going down to Joppa, he found a ship going to Tarshish; so he paid the fare thereof, to go down to Tarshish from the presence of the Lord. The runaway prophet parted with far more than his proper passage-money that day. He paid the advertised fare in the current Joppa coin, with the image and superscription of Jeroboam II stamped upon it. But no booking-clerk in Joppa could have counted up to Jonah all it would cost him all his future life on earth to have fled to Tarshish from his duty to Nineveh, and from the presence of the Lord his God.

Dr. Pusey tells us that the ships of Tarshish corresponded very much to the great East Indiamen of the days of his youth. And that to "break the ships of Tarshish with an east wind" was a sailors' proverb for a terrible storm among the seafaring folk of those ancient days. But she would need to be a far more skillfully constructed, and a far more solidly built, and a far more scientifically navigated vessel than even an English East Indiaman that would engage to carry a disobedient prophet away from his post, and to land a guilty sinner in a harbor where God's hand would not hold him. As it was, the ship of Tarshish now in question soon began to give forth signs that she was not chartered to carry to Tarshish such a contraband cargo as that prophet of God was who now lay in her sides fast asleep. For no sooner was she well away to sea than the Lord sent out a mighty wind against that guilty ship, till every moment it seemed to all on board that she would go to the bottom. You may think the mariners to have been too superstitious, but you must judge gently of a crew of heathen men taken so suddenly between the jaws of death. Come, they said, this is no common storm. Come, therefore, and let us cast lots, that we may know for whose cause this evil is come upon us. Did you ever hold your breath while God and man were casting the discovering lots of life or death over you? What is thine occupation? And whence comest thou? What is thy country, and of what people art thou? I am an Hebrew; and I fear the Lord, the God of Heaven, which hath made the sea and the dry land. Why hast thou done this? And what shall we do unto thee? And he said unto them, Take me up, and cast me into the sea; so shall the sea be calm unto you; for I know that it is for my sake that this great tempest is come upon you. So they took up Jonah, and cast him forth into the sea; and the sea ceased from her raging.

Before we leave this remarkably-written chapter of this every way remarkable little book, let me again call your attention to the power and the piety of the Bible style. "The Lord hurled out," as old Coverdale excellently translates it, "a great wind into the sea." And Jonah himself says, speaking of that sea long after, "Thou didst cast me into the deep; and all Thy waves and all Thy billows passed over me." The science of storms was still in its first infancy in Jonah's day; but even if it had already attained a greater maturity and sure-footedness than it has come to down even to our own day, that would not have debased, or in any way undeified, this sacred writer's so strong and so splendid style. The advance of science does not involve the retreat of religion. Nor does the uniformity and harmony of Nature enable her to dispense with the sleepless oversight of her Creator. The heavens may become still more astronomical than they yet are, without that making them any the less conspicuously the immediate movement of the Divine Hand. And the sea herself will yet be found to ebb and flow, and toss and storm, according to fixed and foreseen laws, without thereby blotting out God's footprints in the deep, or causing any less praise to arise to Him from a smooth sea or any less prayer from a storm. Our meteorology has still a multitude of confused and restless phenomena to register, and a great mass of carefully-taken inductions to reduce to a rule: but, all the time, our Bible keeps impressing upon us that bad weather overtook Jonah for his bad behavior; and that his disobedience before God had disturbed an equilibrium that was far too delicately poised for any earthly instrument of heat or cold, or dry or moist, to take account of.

That terrible storm arose because of quite open and quite easily ascertainable disturbances in the surrounding and overhanging atmosphere. Yes; most certainly and most indisputably it did. But it also arose—the less reason does not deny the greater, nor does the proximate cause supersede the ultimate—it also, and much more, arose, says the word of God, because there was a controversy being carried on that day between God and His vagabond servant. Saints and sinners, prophets and mariners, are not made for the sake of the sea and the sky, but the sea and the sky are made for the sake of saints and sinners. Seas and skies and storms and fair weather all work together under the most complex and the most majestic laws for our good. Every disobedient sinner suddenly startled out of his sleep at midnight is wiser than all his teachers when he repents, and prays, and vows, and refuses to be comforted by the most correct barometric calculations. There is the making of a rare man of science in that young transgressor who wakens with a start, and cannot sleep for fear as the Great White Throne flashes into his prayerless room, and the last trump makes his sinful bed to shake.

After the terrible tempest, and the still more terrible outcome of the sin-discovering lots, and after his being taken up and cast out by the mariners into the raging sea, and by God into the belly of hell, and after his life was brought up from corruption, and his prayer came into God's holy temple; after all that you would have said that Jonah, so purified in such a furnace, would now be the best prophet that God had ever had. He will be the very best ambassador that could possibly be sent to the king of Nineveh. With a great joy in God Jonah will be an ambassador to beseech the king of Nineveh and all his nobles and all his people to be reconciled to the righteous God of Israel. He had so tasted the bitterness of death in his own soul; and, then, after that, he had so tasted that the Lord is gracious—Jonah will preach repentance with a will. Yes. He who had been three days and three nights in such remorse was surely the very preacher to be sent to a people who were, every man ᴜᶜ them, within forty days of destruction. Come and see a man who has just come up out of hell, whispered the trembling people of Ravenna to one another, as Dante staggered through their streets. Come, said the men of Nineveh, and hear what the prophet from Israel has to say to our city, for he has just been vomited out of the fish's belly to preach repentance to us, and to our city.

Till the people of Nineveh believed God, and proclaimed a fast, and put on sackcloth, and turned every one from his evil way, and from the violence that was in their hands. And till God saw their works, that they turned from their evil way: and God repented of the evil that He had said He would do unto them: and He did it not.

But it displeased Jonah exceedingly, and he was very angry. And he said, Therefore now, O Lord, take, I beseech Thee, my life from me; for it is better for me to die than to live. I do well to be angry, even unto death. What ails Jonah? Why is God's prophet in such a passion? Why is it better for Jonah to die than to live? Even Calvin confesses that he suspects some of his own explanations and apologies for Jonah to be but specious pretences, as they are. Jonah would thank no man for his specious apologies for him. Jonah did not write his noble book in an apologetic interest. He wrote his book in sackcloth and ashes. And, as it was written, so it must be read, if it is not to be read in vain: if it is not to be wholly misread, and its lessons wholly lost.

> Biting my truant pen,
>> Beating myself for spite,
> Fool, said my muse to me.
>> Look in thy heart and write.

Jonah was exceedingly displeased, and he was very angry at the repentance and deliverance of Nineveh, because, like all his people in the house of Israel, he both feared and hated Nineveh with his whole soul. Nineveh, as Jonah knew, was predestinated and prepared, and prophesied of God to be the fast-coming scourge and the cruel prison-house of the conquered and captive Israel. And, such was the power and the policy of Nineveh, and such was the sin and the weakness of Israel, that Jonah could look for not one atom of hope for his country unless it was in the great and insufferable wickedness of Nineveh, and in the swift and sure judgment of God against Nineveh. And thus it was that every report that came across the wilderness of the increasing wickedness of Nineveh, Jonah rejoiced in that, and took comfort out of that both for himself and for his people. It was the best thing that could happen to Jonah when the word of the Lord came to him and said, Arise, go to Nineveh, that great city, and cry against it, for their wickedness is come up before me. Jonah's heart beat high with hope that Nineveh was now so near her destruction. And if only all possibility of her repentance and reformation could be kept back from Nineveh for forty days, then all might yet be well with Jonah and with his foredoomed people. But, with such a God as his God was, Jonah had no security. With a God so given to mercy at the first sign of repentance in a sinner, Jonah felt that Israel was not safe till Nineveh was completely destroyed, and for ever blotted out. If I go and preach that preaching to them; if I go and warn and alarm them; and if they repent and turn them to God; then it were better I were dead. Perish my prophet's place: perish the presence of God and all, rather than that I should take a single step to preach repentance to Nineveh! And Jonah rose up to flee to Tarshish from the presence of the Lord, with the result that all the world knows. And, then, when he was shut up to choose between preaching in Nineveh, or making his bed in the belly of hell; and, then, when his compulsory preaching ended as he felt sure it would end—it displeased Jonah exceedingly, and he was very angry. "Were it known to us," says Dr. Pusey, "that some European or Asiatic people were to carry our own people captive out of our land, more than would be willing to confess it of themselves, would still inwardly rejoice that such a calamity as the earthquake of Lisbon befell the capital of that people." Ay, and far short of our captivity, let any Continental people, by the education and the indus- try of their workmen, threaten to take away some of our foreign markets from us, and what an outburst of scorn and indignation will immediately sweep over our land. What is that upstart Germany that she should make better merchandise and sell it cheaper than England! What is that volatile France that she should with such insistence demand what we intend to do in Egypt! And what is our secular rival Russia that she should seek an outlet to any ocean east or west! Does Britannia not rule the waves by Divine right and by her ironclad fleet! Let England expand and increase, and let all the other nations of the earth keep silence. It displeased Jonah exceedingly that the Lord had not destroyed Nineveh, and he was very angry. And not only between contending and competing nations, but much more so between contending and competing churches. With what Jonah-like displeasure do we Free Churchmen and Dissenters hear that an Established Church is prospering, and with what a like uneasiness do State Churchmen read that our Sustentation Funds stand firm. We hear much worse news than that a certain church is likely to have to withdraw from some of her mission-fields because her people will not support her work. We are not overwhelmed with sadness when we read of a morning how her greatest orators drew but a thin house on that subject last night. Better the heathen perish than that such prosperity should attend the labors of our rival. Better that the whole city lapsed than that her communion-roll should so run over. How angry Jonah is still made—he never forgives you—if you have any good to say of any other church than his own, or of any party in his own church than his own party. Till you come down to this—if you have any good to say of any man but himself. Poor Jonah! who had to make his choice between the belly of hell and the possible repentance, and preservation, and prosperity of Nineveh. But far poorer, and far more to be both blamed and pitied, you and I who have to make our choice between that same arrest and imprisonment and a life of service and of continual prayer and good-will for all our enemies. Behold, I will move them to jealousy with those which are not a people. I will provoke them to anger with a foolish nation!

John Calvin is certainly correct when he says that Jonah had far more respect to his own reputation as a prophet of the divine judgment to Nineveh than he had either to the good of Nineveh or to the glory of God. And we are all like Jonah in that respect. Our reputation is our first and our chief regard in all that we do. At any rate, when I watch the working of my own heart in this matter, and then write honestly out of my own heart, this is what I am compelled to write: I am Jonah. In the matter of my own reputation as a preacher, that is. For I used to say, Let me die first before I am eclipsed by another in my pulpit, and among my people. I fought with a Jonah-like fierceness against the remotest thought of my reputation ever passing over, in my day at any rate, to another. I kept my eyes shut to the decay going on around my pulpit till I could shut my eyes to it no longer. And then, when the proper cure came for that decay, how unwelcome at heart all the time that cure was to me. Jonah was exceedingly displeased at the success of his mission to Nineveh, and I myself have taken a part in missions in my ministry also, the success of which sometimes makes me sick at heart. "I beseech Thee now, O God"—they are Augustine's words—"to reveal me to myself still more than Thou hast yet done; so that I may confess myself to my brethren, who have promised to pray for me." "And those things, my brethren"—they are Paul's words—"I have in a figure transferred to myself for your sakes, that ye might learn in me not to think of men above that which is written. We are fools for Christ's sake, but ye are wise in Christ; we are weak, but ye are strong; ye are honorable, but we are despised"— and deserve to be.

But Jonah came to himself again during those five-and-twenty days or so, from the east gate of Nineveh back to Gath-hepher, his father's house. "He travels the fastest who travels alone." Week after week, Sabbath day after Sabbath day, alone with God and his own thoughts in that sacred wilderness made Jonah another man. So much so, that by the time that Jonah crossed the Jabbok, and spent the night at Peniel, Jonah was prepared not only to go to whatever work God sent him, but far more than that, and far better than that, Jonah was now prepared to pay his vow, and to write his book, and to say in every humiliating chapter of it—Come and hear, all ye that fear God; I will declare what He hath done for my soul. And, long before the first day of atonement after his flight to Tarshish came round, Jonah had his autobiography ready to bind it with cords to the horns of the altar. And thus it is that we have now lying open before us to this day the very identical psalm that Jonah sang every new morning on his way home from Nineveh to the land of Israel. And a splendid and a fruitful psalm it is for the use of all redeemed and restored sinners, and especially for the use of all redeemed and restored ministers of such sinners. I cried by reason of mine affliction to the Lord, and He heard me. Out of the belly of hell cried I, and Thou heardest me. I am cast out of Thy sight, yet will I look again toward Thy holy temple. I went down to the bottoms of the mountains; the earth with her bars was about me for ever; yet hast Thou brought up my life from corruption, O Lord my God. They that observe lying vanities—their own reputation, that is—forsake their own mercy. But I will pay that that I have vowed. Salvation is of the Lord.

61
Isaiah

IT was the day of atonement in the Temple. And a sadder day of atonement had never dawned on Jerusalem. For King Uzziah, one of the best kings Jerusalem had ever seen, had been struck of the Lord with leprosy but yesterday. For fifty years Uzziah had reigned in Jerusalem, and had done judgment and justice till he was accepted of his people as almost the promised Messiah Himself. But his great services, and his great successes, and his great honors had all exalted and intoxicated Uzziah's heart till he fell in his old age into what was the unpardonable sin of the Old Testament. And thus it was that on that atonement day he lay in a lazar-house waiting for his death and burial, a castaway from before both God and man. And thus it was that all Judah and Jerusalem were afflicting their souls that day because of the fall of their aged king, and because of his hopeless leprosy. And thus it was that Isaiah also, the son of Amoz, came up to the Temple that day clothed with sackcloth, and with ashes upon his head, and with the leper's rag upon his upper lip. You speak of your preachers, and you praise their power of imagination, and their eloquence, and their dramatic passion, and the way they sink and lose themselves in their work. But if you had lived in Israel in those days you would have seen imagination, and eloquence, and dramatic passion, and all else to astonish you. You would have seen Elijah running with girded-up loins before Ahab's chariot from Mount Carmel to the entrance of Jezreel, while the little cloud like a man's hand made the heavens black with wind and with a great rain. And then you would have seen the same prophet in his old age casting his mantle in silence on the shoulders of Elisha the son of Shaphat, as he plowed in his father's field with the twelfth yoke of oxen. At another time, you would have seen the prophet Jeremiah hiding his girdle in the hole of a rock of Euphrates till it was marred so that it was profitable for nothing. Again, you would have seen the same sad prophet preparing a prophecy as he stood in the potter's house while the potter wrought a work on the wheels. Again, the same prophet at another time took a potter's earthen bottle, and taking with him of the ancients of the people, and of the ancients of the priests, he brake the bottle in the valley of Hinnom and said, This will I do to Jerusalem, saith the Lord. At another time Jeremiah made him bonds and yokes upon his neck, and even went up into his pulpit with the bonds and the yokes upon his neck. At another time he buys a field in Anathoth and weighs the money, and subscribes the evidence, and takes witnesses, and seals the purchase according to law and custom, and then takes that field in Anathoth for his text. And, then, toward the end of his ministry, this same prophet wrote in a book all he had ever said about Babylon, and bound a stone to the book, and cast it into the river Euphrates, and said, Thus shall Babylon sink, and shall not rise again from the evil that the Lord shall bring upon her. And you would have seen Ezekiel actually lying on his right side for three hundred and ninety days, while he

307

ate his bread off the dunghill, and thus preached the hardness of the famine that the Lord would send upon his people for their sin. And again we read in Ezekiel: I did so as I was commanded; I brought forth my stuff by day, as stuff for captivity, and in the even I digged through the wall with my hands; I brought it forth in the twilight, and I bore it upon my shoulder in their sight. And, in like manner, with all the passion and sin and shame of the future foremost prophet of God, Isaiah, the son of Amoz, put the leper's filthy rag upon his lip, and took up all Uzziah's sin and misery upon his heart, and went and stood beside the altar that day of atonement in the Temple. Then said I, Woe is me! for I am undone; because I am a man of unclean lips, and I dwell in the midst of a people of unclean lips; for mine eyes have seen the King, the LORD of hosts. Then flew one of the seraphims unto me, having a live coal in his hand, which he had taken with the tongs from off the altar: and he laid it upon my mouth, and said, Lo, this hath touched thy lips; and thine iniquity is taken away, and thy sin purged. Also I heard the voice of the Lord saying, Whom shall I send, and who will go for us? Then said I, Here am I: send me. And thus it was that that day of atonement for King Uzziah's leprosy was the day of Isaiah's call to be the prophet of the Lord to the leprous people of Jerusalem. The son of Amoz "offered himself to great inspiration by means of great humiliation," as Pascal so often repeats it, and so delights to repeat it.

"Whom shall I send? And who will go for us?" Why does the Lord ask that question with such anxiety when He has all these shining seraphs standing at His side, and each one of them with six wings? Why was Isaiah, the son of Amoz, a man of such unclean lips, and a man so woeful and undone, so accepted, and so sent? Seraphs, not sinners, should surely be the preachers of such holiness as that of the God of Israel, and the heralds of such a Savior—that is what we would have expected. But God's thoughts in these things are not as our thoughts. It was not a seraph burning with heavenly love that was sent to preach to Jerusalem in Uzziah's day, but a young man who but a moment before had been full of leprosy to his lips, and laden to the earth with his own and his people's sin. It was Isaiah, the son of Amoz, who took boldness to say, Here am I, send me. And it was to that same Isaiah that the Lord said, Go and tell this people. And this has always been God's way in choosing and in ordaining and in sending both prophets, and psalmists, and priests, and preachers for His Church on earth. Only once did God choose a completely sinless preacher. Always, but that once, God has chosen sinful men; and, not seldom, the most sinful of men He could get to speak to their fellow-men about sin and salvation.

Gabriel might come with his six wings to announce to Mary that the fullness of time had come and that the Word was to be made flesh, but it was John, who was less than the least in the kingdom of heaven, who was sent to preach repentance to the vipers of his day, and to urge them to flee from the wrath to come. And, just as for the awakening and the warning of sinners, so for the edification and the comfort of saints. "For every high priest is taken from among men, who can have compassion on the ignorant, and on them that are out of the way; for that he himself also is compassed with infirmity." Isaiah, accordingly, of all men on the face of the earth at that moment, and of all angels in heaven, was the man chosen of God to preach repentance to Jerusalem, and to prophesy to her, as never before, the coming of her Messiah. And he preached on all these matters as no angel in all heaven could have preached. He preached as only a leper could preach to his brother lepers, and as only one undone man could preach to other undone men. Just hear him in his first sermon. "The ox knoweth his owner, and the ass his master's crib. Ah! sinful nation, a people laden with iniquity, a seed of evil-doers. Why should ye be stricken any more? The whole head is sick, and the whole heart faint. From the sole of the foot even unto the head there is no soundness in it; but wounds and bruises and putrefying sores." All God's seraphs taken together could not preach like that. It takes a great sinner to preach as well as to hear like that. You must call, and ordain, and inspire a leper if you would have passion in your pulpits like that. And you must be lepers yourselves to put up with passion in your pulpits like that. You cannot have preaching like that from your commonplace men, and from your commonplace sinners. You must have a man of men to see, and to feel, and to say things like that. And then, on the other hand, no seraph of them all, with all his eyes and with all his wings, had seen down so deep, and had come up so close to the holiness of God as Isaiah had seen and had come close. The seraphs cry Holy, Holy, Holy, to one another, but they do not know what they are saying. The seraphs are innocent children. And He whom they so innocently praise charges His seraphs with folly. But, "Woe is me! for I am undone!" The Lord likes to hear that. He takes great pleasure in that. He bows down from His high throne at the sound of that. He sees what pleases Him in every syllable of that. With that young man will I dwell, He says to Himself, as He sees and hears Isaiah on that day of atonement. This young preacher, then, having seen both sin and holiness as no seraph ever saw these terrible things, proceeds in his sermon in this way: "Wash you, make you clean; cease to do evil, learn to do well; judge the fatherless, plead for the widow. Come now, let us reason together, saith the Lord: though your sins be as scarlet, they shall be as white as snow: though they be red like crimson, they shall be as wool." Every syllable of all that is out of Isaiah's own experience. Preaching like that never yet came out of the schools of the prophets, any more than it ever came out of the mouth of an angel. Isaiah had done it all to himself, and had had it all done to him of God. From unclean, he had washed him and made himself clean. From doing evil, he had put away the evil of his doings from before God's eyes. He had judged the fatherless, and he had pleaded for the widow. We hear him doing all that in tremendous words in this very sermon. And then the Lord had commanded His most evangelical seraph to take a live coal with the tongs from off the altar till Isaiah's iniquity was taken away and his sins purged, and till all Jerusalem knew that a prophet of the Lord had arisen among them.

Saint Jerome called Isaiah the evangelical prophet, and it was a very happy hit of the great translator. But we are entangled with a whole net-work of questions about the evangelical prophet that had not yet arisen in men's minds in Jerome's day. Are there *two* Isaiahs bound up together in this great evangelical book? Or is it the same son of Amoz we have here from the first chapter to the last? I do not know. I am like Mr. Spurgeon: my heart leans to one Isaiah, but the facts must be heard. And I shall resist to the death every attempt to keep the facts from being heard by those who are able to hear them. But I shall also claim for them and for myself that the common people shall be allowed to come to church to worship God without being teased and tormented about the age and authorship of this and that chapter of Holy Scripture. I shall take it for granted tonight, therefore, that the name of the son of Amoz may, with the utmost confidence and the very best propriety, be used here of the whole of his sixty-six bold and eloquent chapters. I shall always say "Isaiah" here, just as the New Testament, and Jerome, and the universal Church of Christ has said "Isaiah" about this book from the beginning down to our own day.

The now well-known name that Jerome first gave to Isaiah out of his cave at Bethlehem is a great name. There is no greater name that Old Testament prophet or New Testament preacher can bear. You will all think that you know quite well already how great a name Jerome's name to Isaiah was. But there is nothing that we know less than just those things that we think we know so well that we do not need to know any more about them. Feeling very sure that I did not know all that Jerome meant in his great name that he gave to Isaiah, I took down Dr. Murray's New English Dictionary, and turned to the part containing the word "evangelical." All who are able should order Dr. Murray's magnificent dictionary. It is a patriotic act to order it. It is to support the best scholarship of our land and our day to order it. And it is nothing less than a liberal education to have it delivered every three months at your door. You can have no idea what an ancient, what a noble, what a deeply-rooted, and what a far branching name that was that Jerome gave to Isaiah till you have read through the seven quarto columns that Dr. Murray, with such exact scholarship, and with such exquisite carefulness, gives to it. Beginning with Isaiah, the greatest preachers have all along been evangelical preachers. There is everything in the Evangel of the grace of God and of the work of Christ to make every man who preaches it a great preacher: and, besides the Evangel, there is nothing to inspire, or to uplift, or to empower and embolden any preacher. From Isaiah to Spurgeon the evangelical succession has run on through Paul, and Augustine, and Luther, and Calvin, and Knox, and Rutherford, and Baxter, and Bunyan, and Edwards, and Wesley, and Chalmers. And the great doctrines that have made all those great men such great preachers are all what we call the doctrines of grace. They are very bold doctrines; but then, they were all given by divine inspiration to Isaiah and to Paul, and they are all backed up in the preacher of our day by the authority of the Word of God, and by the testimony of the Spirit of God, and by the deepest and best and surest experiences of nineteen centuries both of the best preaching and the holiest life. They are such doctrines as—the image of God in the soul of man; the dreadful depravity and loathsome corruption of the soul of man by reason of original and indwelling sin; the spotless heart and life, and the sin-atoning death, of Jesus Christ; the mission and work of the Holy Ghost in the spiritual enlightenment of the soul, and its new birth to God and holiness; and the gradual but sure sanctification of the renewed soul to the fullness of eternal life for ever. Isaiah did not preach explicitly, and in as many words, all these evangelical doctrines, but they are all latent and involved in his preaching; and had he lived in our day he would have preached them all as boldly and as unceasingly as Wesley or Spurgeon preached them. The great evangelical books you all know, by name at least; the great evangelical hymns we sing in our families and in our own hearts every day; and the great evangelical hopes form great part of our evangelical preaching to you every Sabbath-day.

John Foster has one of his masterly Essays entitled, "The Aversion of men of Taste to Evangelical Religion." It is a piece of such great intellectual power on some of the besetting sins of evangelical preachers that all we who are evangelical preachers, and all you who are evangelical people, should read it till we have all laid it up in our hearts, as our evangelical catechism has it, and have practiced it in our lives. John Foster was a preacher himself of such intellectual strength, and depth, and suggestiveness that I should have included his name in my too rapid enumeration of the great names of the evangelical succession. But many great names belong to that shining succession who would not by everybody be included in it: Law for one; Newman, one of Law's spiritual children, for another. I am bold to include Newman, for there is not a bolder sermon on substitution in the English language than Dr. Newman's post-Anglican sermon on "The Mental Sufferings of our Lord in His Passion." I was proceeding to say that Isaiah's style, so to call it, is one of the secrets of his so splendid and so abiding power. The Evangel of Salvation was his one goodly pearl, to buy which he had sold all; and then he always set that so goodly pearl in the shining casket of his superb style. "In every kind of discourse," says Dante in *The Banquet*, "the speaker ought to think of what will be sure to charm his hearers"—a rhetorical rule that the eloquent author of the *Divine Comedy* never neglected to observe and obey. "Because," he says, "if a hearer is not well disposed to us our best teaching will be but badly received." Now, that is what the evangelical prophet always does. He always charms us with the music, and the melody, and the march of his style. Even when his message is the most accusing and condemning; even when there is no beauty in his doctrine that we should desire it, even then we are spellbound and held to the end in the great preacher's splendid hands. You will not have read or thought much about Isaiah's style. You have other things of more importance, and more worth your time and trouble to read in that prophet and to think about continually. But, for once, you will not grudge to hear a few words on that not irrelevant matter out of one who has given a long and a laborious lifetime to such subjects. "Isaiah," says Ewald, "is not the especially lyrical prophet, or the especially elegiacal prophet, or the especially oratorical or the hortatory prophet—as we should describe a Joel, a Hosea, a Micah, with whom there is a greater prevalence of some particular color. But just as the subject requires it, Isaiah has immediately at command every several kind and quality of style, and every several change and variety of delineation. And it is precisely this that, in point of language, establishes the prophet's personal greatness, as well as forms one of his most towering points of intellectual excellence. His discourse varies into every possible complexion: it is tender and stern, it is didactic and threatening; it is mourning and again exulting in divine joy; it is mocking and it is in earnest; but, ever, at the right time, Isaiah's style returns back to its original elevation and repose, and never loses the clear ground-color of its divine seriousness."

Yes; Esaias is very bold—

With mouth of gold, and morning in his eyes.

62
Jeremiah

THE most exquisite sensibility of soul was Jeremiah's singular and sovereign distinction above all the other Hebrew prophets. It was Jeremiah's life-long complaint to his mother that she had borne him, a man with such an unearthly sensibility of soul, into a world so out of joint for such souls. Such another child for sensibility of soul was not born of woman until the Virgin Mary brought forth the Man of Sorrows Himself. Those men of Caesarea Philippi showed their own sensibility of soul when some said John the Baptist; some, Elias; but they would have it that Jesus of Nazareth was none other than Hilkiah's son, come back again with his broken heart. Woe is me, my mother, that thou hast borne me the man that I am! Is it nothing to you, all ye that pass by? Behold, and see if there be any sorrow like unto my sorrow.

Jeremiah was far and away the most spiritually-minded of all the prophets. Howbeit that was not first which is spiritual, but that which is natural; and afterward that which is spiritual. That is to say, it was the inborn, original, and unparalleled sensibility of Jeremiah's mind and heart that the Lord took up and turned to His own service both in the preaching of this prophet and in the production of this book, which stands to this day second only to the Psalms as the most spiritual book in the Old Testament. Some other prophets stand in time and in place nearer to the New Testament; but it is only in time and in place. No prophet of them all stands in reality so near to Jesus Christ. Jeremiah is the true forerunner of our Lord. Even Isaiah himself, evangelical as he is, still retains some of the shadowy and unspiritual elements of that imperfect economy in his prophecy. The restored kingdom of David and Solomon still haunts Isaiah's heart, and it still shapes and colors some of the finest pictures of his imperial imagination. But Jeremiah has nothing of that decayed economy either in himself or in his book. Jeremiah's extraordinary inwardness, and depth, and absolutely pure spirituality, have all combined to deliver both himself and his book from all those apocalyptic, secular, and unspiritual interpretations which have so infested the other prophets. Neither Peter nor the mother of Zebedee's children, could accuse Jeremiah of having misled them in one word of his, in any chapter of his, concerning the coming Kingdom of the Messiah. And more and more as his ministry went on, Jeremiah strove with all his might to draw both the hearts and the imaginations of his people not only off all alliance with the kingdoms that were around them, but also off the too pictorial Kingdom of the Messiah that had been hung up before them. And, for his pains, Jeremiah was cast into prison again and again, and was maltreated as only the offscourings of the city were maltreated. But his consolation and his hope always lay in that noble doctrine of the Kingdom of God, which he had been honored to have revealed to him, and which he had preached for forty years at such a price. The depth, the purity, the beauty, the absolute heavenliness of his doctrine were the reward and the joy of his heart, let his fellow-citizens and his fellow-prophets and priests do to him what they pleased. Jeremiah was of all the prophets of the Old Testament the supreme prophet of the human heart. "The heart is my haunt," says Wordsworth. And again, "My theme is no other than the heart of man." But in an infinitely deeper sense than that, Jeremiah was the prophet of God to the human heart. Jeremiah would have nothing from his hearers and readers but their heart. Let other prophets negotiate and send embassies as they pleased; Jeremiah, in season and out of season, for a long lifetime, laid siege to the hearts of his hearers. The cure of all your famines, he cried, and all your plagues, and all your defeats, and all your captivities—the cause and the cure of them all is in your own heart: in the heart of each inhabitant of Jerusalem and each captive in Babylon. And your prophets who say Peace, peace!—like Law, he called all such preachers so many dancing-masters; and, like Leighton, he called them so many mountebanks, till they smote him, and imprisoned him in the dungeon, and put his feet in the stocks.

And this is the true way still to preach, even at the same price; if only we had been born of our mothers to preach like Jeremiah. If only we had something of his sensibility, and spirituality, and knowledge of the heart. The salvation of our hearers must always begin with our own salvation: and it must go on to perfection with our perfection. And we cannot be the salvation to any perfection either of ourselves or of our people unless we have a pervading, and prevailing, and increasing sensibility of what salvation is, and what the want of it is. He who has—I will not say a full sensibility of the evil of sin, for he would go mad if he had—but a true beginning of such sensibility, he has the making of a true minister of Jesus Christ in him; otherwise he has not, and should at once go to make his bread in some more lawful calling. "They will be thankful for your telling them the particular times when the gospels were writ: for explaining the word Euroclydon, or anathema maranatha; they will be glad of such useless instruction; but if you touch upon such subjects as really concern them in a high degree, such subjects as try the state and way of their lives, these religious people cannot bear to be thus instructed." Yes, morning lectures on Euroclydon: evidences of Christianity; defences and debates round and round the subject: whole cartloads of Bampton, and all like lectures: they are all so much lost time and strength in the pulpit. They have their place elsewhere, and among those who get any good from them, but they would get all that good, and would not need it any more, if we had taught them some real sensibility for spiritual things. It is Jeremiah's sensibility and spirituality that both preachers and hearers need, and then we would both have the evidence in ourselves. Speak to your hearer's heart and you will soon undermine his head. All his lofty imaginations, with all his high thoughts, will lie all around him as soon as he lies in the dust himself; but not till then, with all your artillery. Young preachers, with your great life still before you, study your own heart day and night. Watch every beat, and flutter, and creep of your own heart day and night. Seek sensibility of heart above all Latin, and Greek, and Hebrew: above all logic, and style, and delivery. Add all these things, and everything else, to sensibility of heart: but one thing is needful if you would not be a castaway in the end. Were you spiritually-sensible preachers you would soon get inside your people's hearts, and you would hold your people's hearts to the end. Deep answers to deep. And if one here and another there should smite you as Pashur smote Jeremiah, say to him, "The Lord hath not called thy name Pashur, but Magor-missabib," and go on with your heart-searching and heart-sanctifying preaching to other people. And your sensibility of heart and mind once well begun will grow till your name is as famous as you could wish it to be where fame and name is alone worth working for. With ever-increasing sensibility preach every day to them the meekness, and the humility, and the spirituality, and the obedience, and the whole mind of Christ and you will surely see Christ formed in your people before you are compelled to bequeath your pulpit to your successor. And oh, believe me, the shame and the remorse of having to hand over your pulpit, and you only beginning to preach! And it all lies in a true and a timely sensibility, and in saying, The heart is my haunt, till you know the heart, and can preach to it to some purpose. Return, thou backsliding Israel, saith the Lord, and I will give you pastors after mine own heart, which shall feed you with knowledge and understanding.

Nazianzen says somewhere that Jeremiah was both by nature and by grace the most inclined to pity of all the prophets. Which is just to say over again that he was the most sensitive and the most spiritual. Take natural sensibility and supernatural spirituality together, and you will have the most exquisite sympathy and the most perfect pity possible. There is nothing like the Lamentations of Jeremiah in the whole world again. There has been plenty of sorrow in every age, and in every land; but such another preacher and author as Jeremiah, with such a heart for sorrow, has never again been born. Dante comes next to Jeremiah, and we know that Jeremiah was that great exile's favorite prophet. Both prophet and poet were full to all the height and depth of their great hearts of the most thrilling sensibility; while, at the same time, they were both high towers, and brazen walls, and iron pillars against all unrighteousness of men. And they were alike in this also, that, just because of their combined strength, and sternness, and sensibility, no man in their day sympathized with them. They made all men's causes of suffering and sorrow their own, till all men hated them, and put a price on their heads. "There is nothing in all Scripture," says Isaac Williams, "so eloquent of love and sorrow and consolation as the 31st and 33rd chapters of Jeremiah. No words can be found in any language of such touching beauty as all that strain." So surely does natural sensibility, when it is steeped in the Spirit of God, become the most perfect pity and the most exquisite sympathy.

In an unaccountably silly passage in his *Life of Erasmus*, Froude actually prints it that "Erasmus, like all men of real genius, had a light and elastic nature." That senseless and impossible passage came back to my mind as I read this melancholy book of this man of real genius. And this also came to my mind out of North's *Plutarch*: "Aristotle has a place where he says that the wisest men be ever melancholy, as Socrates, Plato, and Hercules were." And I have read somewhere also on this matter that "merely to say man is to say melancholy." I wish it were. At any rate, to say "man endued by nature with sufficient sensibility, and then by grace with sufficient spiritual sympathy," is to say the most profoundly melancholy of men. "O hear me," says the profoundly intellectual and equally spiritual Jacob Behmen in a comforting passage. "Hear me, for I know well myself what melancholy is! I also have lodged all my days in the melancholy inn!" As Jeremiah lodged also. And how could it have been done otherwise? In such a land: in such a city: among such a people with such a past and with such a present, and doing their best to make their future as bad as their past and their present—it was enough to make the glorified on their thrones melancholy. Jeremiah's inconsolable melancholy was the mark and the measure of his greatness both as a man and as a prophet. It was a divine melancholy that made his head waters and his eyes a fountain of tears. "Tears gain everything," says Santa Teresa in her autobiography. No: not everything—much; but not everything. Tears, when bitter enough, and in secret enough, always gain forgiveness indeed, which is almost everything, and is on the way to everything. But while such tears will always avail under grace to blot out the past, they have no power to bring back the past. Nor do they bring in the sure future so much as one day before its time. All Jeremiah's tears did not keep back the Chaldeans for a single day's march. But his tears softened his heart and bowed his head till he was able to go out to meet the Chaldeans, and almost to welcome them to Jerusalem in the name of God. Neither his tears, nor his prayers, nor his resignations, nor his submissions, shortened by a single hour the seventy years' captivity. But his tears did far better for himself at least. They softened his heart to the very core. They perfected what both nature and grace had so well begun. For they made him not only an evangelical prophet, but an all but New Testament apostle. Jeremiah's tears were such that they gained the Holy Ghost for him before the Holy Ghost was given, and before Christ was glorified. Till Santa Teresa is amply justified when she says that tears gain everything. And till I am justified in saying that Jeremiah at any rate was not a man of a light and elastic nature.

"Oh that I had in the wilderness a lodging-place of wayfaring men; that I might leave my people, and go from them!" The loneliness of a man's heart among his own people is one of the heaviest crosses that any man has to take up. Jeremiah, to borrow one of his own bitter words, had plenty of "familiars" among his own people, but he had very few friends. And his familiars watched for his halting and rejoiced over it, and said, Report, said they, and we will report it. Had Jeremiah had a friend among all his familiars, that solitary friend would have proved himself such by refusing to report it. "He has fallen away to the Chaldeans," was the report made among his familiars. But Jeremiah had no friend who would take the risk to understand and to defend his friend. And it was among such familiars, and in the lack of such friends, that Jeremiah sighed the sigh that has been taken up and sighed so often since that day: "O that I might leave my people!" Jeremiah never was a married man. And it was as well that he was not. Men, and especially ministers, of much sensibility, and spirituality, and sympathy, and melancholy are not made to be married. A helpmeet for Jeremiah was not to be found in all the house of Israel. If his Master had seen it good for His servant to have a wife and children, He would have made Jeremiah's second self, and would have brought her to him till Jeremiah's melancholy would for the time have been somewhat abated. But whether it was that the Lord saw that His servant's sensibility was too exquisite, and his melancholy too extreme, or whatever it was, the Lord said to His servant,

"Thou shalt not take thee a wife, neither shalt thou have sons and daughters in this place." And thus it was that what a sensitive and melancholy minister takes home and tells only to his wife, when he has a wife who is his friend, and not merely his familiar, all that Jeremiah took and told to God. Till his whole book before us is one long confidence, and conversation, and debate, and remonstrance; and, again, one long submission, and silence, and surrender, and service of God. And till he is home now where all men are friends, and where the familiars of Jerusalem, with their watching and their reporting, do not enter.

And, then, all that made Jeremiah the red-hot preacher that we still feel him to this day to have been. We see with what a fiery sensibility he both prepares and delivers his sermons. At one time we hear him groaning over his text as he stands beside the potter at his wheel, while the potter mars his vessel and casts it away. At another time he does not preach for many weeks. He is away at the Euphrates learning how to illustrate and enforce his next sermon, and he preaches it over and over to himself as he sees in the sand the footprints of his captive people. Another Sabbath morning he takes his elders out to the valley beyond the city, and dashes an earthen vessel to pieces before their amazed and angry eyes, and that is all the sermon they get that morning. A preacher—like a great preacher of our own land—to "terrify even the godly." A preacher for his familiars to take him and speak to him. And so they did, and almost succeeded. Pashur, the chief governor, was deputed on one occasion to tame, as we say, Jeremiah's pulpit. And of such sensibility and melancholy was the prophet at the visit of Pashur that the thing was almost done. Till the prophet appeared all of a sudden with a yoke of wood on his neck in his former pulpit next Sabbath, and with this apology to Pashur, and with this autobiographic introduction to his sermon that day: "Then I said, I will not make mention of Him, or speak any more in His name. But His word was in my heart as a burning fire shut up in my bones, and I was weary with forbearing, and I could not stay." I suppose every preacher with any fire in his bones has a Pashur or two among his governors. A familiar or two who say among themselves, Report, and we will report it. But I do not read that Jeremiah spake as he was moved by Pashur, the governor. Let Pashur preach himself if Jeremiah has too much sensibility, and spirituality, and sympathy, and melancholy for him. And let Jeremiah go on and preach out all the fire that God has kindled in his prophet's bones. "I could have used a more adorned style," says John Bunyan, in his *Grace Abounding*, "but I dared not. God did not play in tempting me; neither did I play when the pangs of hell gat hold on me. Wherefore I may not play in relating those pangs, but be plain and simple, and lay down the thing just as it was."

> Lo! this man's brow, like to a title-page,
> Foretells the nature of a tragic volume.
> Thou tremblest, and the whiteness in thy cheek
> Is apter than thy tongue to tell thine errand.

When Jesus came into the coasts of Caesarea Philippi, He asked His disciples, saying, Whom do men say that I the Son of Man am? And they said, Some say that thou art John the Baptist; some, Elias; and others, Jeremias.

63
Daniel

THERE is always a singular luster, and nobility, and stately distinction about Daniel. There is a note of birth, and breeding, and aristocracy about Daniel's whole name and character. There is never at any time anything common or conventional in anything that Daniel says or does. Munro has gathered it all up in these three eloquent words: "His refinement, his reserve, and the high sculpture of his character."

The first thing in which Daniel's great qualities all come out is his so wise and so noble self-control and self-denial at the king's table. The narrative is a noble one. "And the king appointed them a daily provision of the king's meat, and of the wines which he drank, so nourishing them three years, that at the end thereof they might stand before the king. But Daniel proposed not to defile himself with the portion of the king's meat, nor with the wine which he drank: therefore he requested of the prince of the eunuchs that he might not defile himself. Prove thy servants, I beseech thee, ten days; and let them give us pulse to eat and water to drink. Then let our countenances be looked upon before thee, and as thou then seest deal with thy servants. And at the end of the ten days their countenances appeared fairer and fatter in flesh than all the children that did eat of the king's meat." "I have remarked," says an Eastern traveller, "that their faces are in fact more rosy and smooth than those of others, and that those who fast much, I mean the Armenians and the Greeks, are very beautiful, sparkling with health, and of a clear and lively countenance." At the same time, Daniel did not at all times and in all places live on bare pulse and water. Calvin says that when Daniel and his three companions got far enough away from the royal table they would both eat flesh with pleasant bread, and would drink wine also in the wayside inns of Babylon, just as they had done when they were at home in Jerusalem. It was the company at the king's table; it was the idolatry, and the self-indulgence, and the indecency, and the riot among the young men of the palace that made Daniel determine that it would be both far easier and far safer to abstain altogether and from the beginning. When he was far enough away at any time from those snares and temptations and associations, and when he was alone with his three virtuous and temperate companions, Daniel did not make a voluntary and an ostentatious virtue of pulse and water.

> A neat repast shall feast us, light and choice,
>> Of Canaan's taste, with wine, whence we shall rise.
> He who of those delights can judge, and spare
>> To interpose them oft, is not unwise—

Belteshazzar would say on occasion to Shadrach, Meshach, and Abed-nego, just as our English Daniel said in his fine sonnet to

Lawrence, of virtuous father virtuous son.

At the same time, there was nothing morose or melancholy in Daniel's total abstinence. Daniel was not of a sad countenance over his pulse and water. Daniel did not disfigure his face at the royal feasts. Because of his abstinence Daniel all the more anointed his head and washed his face; till, unless you had watched him well, you would have thought that all that affability, and good humor, and merriment of his must come of the abundance of the king's wine that he drank. Unless you had been in the secret you would never have supposed that Daniel was not eating and drinking with the same self-indulgence as all the rest. In nothing was Daniel's fine character finer seen, not even when his window was set open towards Jerusalem, not even when he stepped down into the den of lions, than it was when he was the last to rise from the royal feasts, with such sweetness, and geniality, and simplicity did he converse with the men of Babylon. Daniel did not expect the young men of Chaldea to deny themselves like captive Hebrews. They had not either his Hebrew sorrow or his Hebrew hope in their hearts, and he did not look for those things in them. Now it is just here that so many of ourselves both injure ourselves and injure other people by our abstinence. We enter on our abstinence out of some constraint and compulsion. We are abstainers, many of us against our own hearts; or, if our hearts are in our abstinence, then it is our hard and self-righteous hearts. We abstain with self-importance, and with self-righteousness, and with sourness and soreness at those who still preserve their liberty. And this makes one man peevish and melancholy in his abstinence, and another man fierce and intolerant. And thus our latter end is worse than our beginning; and our self-denial than our self-indulgence. We must not only abstain, but we must make our abstinence genial and full of liberty and delight. "Furthermore," says Plutarch, "Alexander was far less given to wine than men would have judged. He was thought to be a far greater bibber than he was because he sat long at the board, but it was rather to talk than to eat and drink. For even when he ate and drank he would propound some new and interesting subject, and yet but when he was at leisure. For, having matters to do, there was neither feast, nor banquet, nor marriage, nor any pastime that could stay him, as they had done other captains. He would ever sup late, and after his long day's work was done, and he was very curious to see that every man at his board was alike served, and would sit long at the table, because he ever loved to talk, as we have told you before. And in all other ways he was as gracious a prince and as noble to wait upon, and as pleasant as ever was." One of Lord Ardmillan's daughters used to say of my dear old friend her father, that "he breakfasted on the newspapers and dined on conversation." And so he did; and thus it was that his step was the lightest, and his laugh the merriest, and his heart the most childlike of all the Parliament House men of his day. And in all other ways, like Plutarch's Alexander, Ardmillan was, I think, the most gracious and gentlemanly man I ever knew.

The Chaldean Schools: their literature, their true science and their pseudo-science, their architecture, their music, their political and military methods, their religion and the sacred arts connected with their religion—nothing of all that was at all foreign, or alien, or despicable to Daniel. The captive prince entered into all that with all the zest and with all the labor of what we would call a true student. Daniel foresaw that his whole life would have to be spent in Babylon, and he determined that his exile there should not be so much lost time either to his mind or to his heart. The Chaldean astrology has long since given way before the modern science of astronomy, and with it the so-called Magi, the star-gazers, and the soothsayers, and the sorcerers. But the truly philosophic temper that Daniel exhibited among the wise men of Babylon is still the true and wise temper for us all among the studies and the speculations and the scepticisms of our more learned, more scientific, and more speculative day. Daniel, by God's mercy, possessed the truth that the Chaldeans sought after in sun and moon and stars: in dreams and in incantations. And when he was cast among the speculations and superstitions of Chaldea he was able to study all he saw and all he heard with an interest, with an intelligence, and with a sympathy that are only to be found in a truly religious and a truly cultivated mind. In his birth, in his upbringing, in his breeding, and in his books, Daniel possessed a knowledge of God and of man that no sage of Chaldea could possibly approach: but, at the same time, Daniel was student enough to see that Chaldea had attained to a learning and to a religion of her own that well deserved his best attention. Till Daniel at last came to be acknowledged as more than the equal of the king's most learned and most consulted men. It was the largeness, and the expansiveness, and the hospitality of Daniel's fine mind, all combined with his extraordinary nobility and beauty of character, that gave Daniel such an unparalleled position in the court of Chaldea, and which has gained for Daniel such a famous and such a proverbial name in all subsequent literature. Ezekiel, a contemporary prophet, has heard so much of the wisdom of Daniel, that, to a proud enemy of Israel, he exclaims in irony: Thou art wiser than Daniel! We see the popular belief about Daniel strikingly illustrated also in the Apocryphal addition that was made to the Book of Daniel by its Greek translator and editor, and which was called the story of Susannah and the judgment of Daniel. And we are gratified to read in our own tongue a tribute to the same noble tradition in Shylock's exclamation:—

A Daniel come to judgment! yea, a Daniel!
O wise young judge, how I do honor thee!

The prophet Daniel became a great proficient both in penitential and in intercessory prayer also as the years went on. And he came to that great proficiency just as a great proficiency is come to in any other science or art: that is to say, by constant, and unremitting, and enterprising practice. Lord, teach us to pray, said a disciple on one occasion to our Lord. But not even our Lord with all His willingness, and with all His ability, can teach any of us off-hand to pray. Every man must teach himself, every day he lives, this most personal, most secret, and most experimental of all the arts. Every man must find out the best ways of prayer for himself. There is no royal road; there is no short or easy road to proficiency in prayer. It is like all the other arts that you have ever mastered; it must be early begun and assiduously practiced, else you will be but a bungler at it all your days. You must also have special and extraordinary seasons of prayer, as Daniel had, over and above his daily habit of prayer. Special and extraordinary, original and unparalleled seasons of prayer, when you literally do nothing else day nor night but pray. You must pray in your very dreams. Till you will come at last to live, and move, and have your whole being in prayer. Now, it is plain that you cannot teach a lifetime of experiment and attainment like that to any chance man: and, especially, you cannot teach it to a man who still detests the very thought of such prayer. It was his yoke in his youth that first taught Daniel to pray. And Babylon taught Daniel and his three friends all to pray, and to pray together in their chambers, as we read. To be arrested in their fathers' houses by Nebuchadnezzar's soldiers; to have Babylonian chains put on their hands and their feet: to see the towers of Zion for the last time: to be asked to sing some of the songs of Zion to amuse their masters as they toiled over the Assyrian sands—you would have become experts yourselves in a school of prayer like that. You would have held little prayer-meetings yourselves with your class-fellows and your companions, if you had come through the half that Daniel and his three companions came through. It is because you are not being emptied from vessel to vessel all the week that we never see you at the prayer-meeting. Jeremiah, a great authority on why some men pray, and why other men never pray, has this about you in his book: "Moab hath been at his ease from his youth up: he hath settled on his lees: he hath not been emptied from vessel to vessel: neither hath he gone into captivity; and, therefore, his taste remaineth in him, and his scent is not changed."

"Why," asks Pascal, "has God established prayer?" And the first answer out of the three that Pascal gives to himself is this—"To communicate to His creatures the dignity of causality." And Daniel was of Pascal's deep and original mind. For Daniel, just because he read in Jeremiah that deliverance was at the door, all the more set himself to pray as if his prayer was to be the alone and predestinated cause of the coming deliverance. Daniel put on sackcloth, and fasted, and prayed, and went back upon all his own and all his people's sins in a way that confounds us to our face. We cannot understand Daniel. We are not deep enough. He prayed, and fasted, and returned to an agony of prayer, as if he had never heard of the near deliverance: he prayed in its very presence as if he despaired of ever seeing it. He fasted and prayed as he had not done all those seventy fasting and praying years. Read, all you experts in prayer, with all your mind, and with all your heart, and with all your experience, and with all your imagination this great causality chapter. It is written by a proficient for proficients. It is written by a great saint of God for all such. Read it and think about it. Read it with your Pascal open before you. Read it and sink down into the deep things of God and the soul. Read it and practice it till you know by experiment and by experience that decree, and covenant, and prophecy, and promise, and all, however sure, and however near, are only fulfilled in immediate and dependent answer to penitential and importunate prayer. Read it and pray as never before after the answer has actually begun. See the answer out to the last syllable before you begin to restrain penitence and prayer. And after the answer is all fulfilled, still read it and the still deeper chapters that follow it, till you learn new fastings, and new sackcloth, and new ashes, and new repentance, away out to your saintliest old age. Read Daniel's greatest prayer and

Know thy dread power—a creature, yet a cause.

64
Nebuchadnezzar

I FRANKLY confess myself a convert to Nebuchadnezzar. I frankly acknowledge my great debt to Nebuchadnezzar. I frankly confess that I had wholly misunderstood Nebuchadnezzar, and both the design and the end of God's ways with Nebuchadnezzar. And I would like to share with you tonight the great lesson in humility and in obedience that I have been led to learn out of Nebuchadnezzar.

Nebuchadnezzar was by far the most famous of all the kings of the East. In his early years, and before he came to his great throne, Nebuchadnezzar had won victory after victory over all the surrounding nations. Jerusalem fell before his army after eighteen months' siege, and Tyre, the proudest of ancient cities, succumbed to him after an investiture of thirteen years. The proud position of the king of Babylon among all the kings of that day will best be seen from the words of Daniel who assuredly was no flatterer of great men. "Thou, O king, art a king of kings, for the God of heaven hath given thee a kingdom, and strength, and glory. The tree which thou sawest, which grew, and was strong, whose height reached to heaven, and the sight thereof to all the earth: whose leaves were fair and the fruit thereof much, and in it was meat for all: under which the beasts of the field dwelt, and upon whose branches the fowls of the heavens had their habitation: It is thou, O king, that art grown, and become strong: for thy greatness is grown, and reached unto heaven, and thy dominion to the end of the earth." It could have been no ordinary greatness that drew from a man like Daniel an estimate and an eulogium like that.

But the fame of this magnificent monarch has rested even more on his unparalleled works of peace than on his great successes in war. Great as Nebuchadnezzar was as a warrior, he was still greater as a statesman and an administrator. The vast public works that he planned and executed for his capital and his kingdom in walls and in water-works: in parks and in gardens: in palaces and in temples—all these things, in their vastness, in their usefulness, in their beauty, and in their immense cost make Nebuchadnezzar to stand out absolutely unapproached among the great builder-kings of the ancient East. After we have read all that the historians and the travellers have to tell us about ancient Babylon, no wonder, we say to ourselves, that Nebuchadnezzar's dreams were the dreams of a magnificent imagination. No wonder that his heart swelled within him with pride: and no wonder that it took a stroke such as God has seldom struck before or since to humble and to abase Nebuchadnezzar, this great king of Babylon. "This is the interpretation, O king, and this is the decree of the Most High: that they shall drive thee from men, and thy dwelling shall be with the beasts of the field, and they shall make thee to eat grass like an ox, and they shall wet thee with the dew of heaven, and seven times shall pass over thee, till thou know that the Most High ruleth in the kingdom of men, and giveth it to whomsoever He will." All this came to Nebuchadnezzar the

king, till at the end of it all he said—"I thought it good to show the signs and wonders the high God hath wrought toward me. Those that walk in pride the King of
heaven is able to abase." Though long dead, King Nebuchadnezzar still speaks in
the Book of Daniel, and on a thousand cylinders in the British Museum; and, as
on every page of Daniel, so on every brick of Babylon, he that runs may read this
evening's text:—"Those that walk in pride the King of heaven is able to abase."

But Nebuchadnezzar's pride, after all is said, was but the petty pride of a puffed-
up and self-important child. If you have eyes in your hearts you will see all Nebuchadnezzar's pride in your own nursery every day. Nebuchadnezzar's bricks were
made of clay; whereas the bricks of your nursery-Nebuchadnezzar are made of
wood. That, and their ages, is all the difference. Look! your little Nebuchadnezzar cries after you as he pulls your gown, and will not give you peace till you lift
up your hands in wonder over his great Babylon with its wonderful doors, and
windows, and bridges and portcullises. Is not this a great house that I have built?
he demands of you. Is my house not far bigger, and far better every way, than my
brother's house that he has built? Look, father! Look mother! Look, nurse! Look,
visitor! All wise-hearted mothers see and hear all that with tears behind their eyes,
till they are at their wits' end how to deal with their so boastful and so imperious little emperor. The ancient Areopagus sentenced an Athenian boy to death
because he had plucked out the eyes of a captive quail. For, said the wise and pre-
scient judges, if that little savage does that to a tame bird when he is still young,
what will he not do to the men who are in his power when he is hardened in vice?
And they put him to death, and paid no attention to the prayers of his mother. Let
all fathers and mothers give their best heed to their little Nebuchadnezzar and to
his little Babylon which he has built for the honor of his majesty. This is the beginning. And you know what a great fire sometimes a little spark, if it is let fall and
let burn, kindleth. You know the prophetic proverb also about the letting out of
water. Let every father, and mother, and nurse, and tutor, and school-master read
and lay to heart, as they shall answer for it, William Law's eighteenth chapter, in
which he shows "How the education which men receive in their youth makes the
doctrine of humility so difficult to be practiced all their after-days."

But, with all that, I see in my own children every day a far worse kind of pride
than any that the big child Nebuchadnezzar shows either in the Book of Daniel,
or on the bricks of Babylon. Nebuchadnezzar never, that I have read of, got one
single lesson from God or man that he did not instantly lay it to heart. As I read
of Nebuchadnezzar's humility, and makeableness, and teachableness in Daniel's
hands I am amazed at the boldness of the young Belteshazzar, and still more at the
behavior of his mighty master. When I put myself into Nebuchadnezzar's place,
when I recall my own temper and my own conduct, I honor Nebuchadnezzar, and
I cannot cease from wondering that the king of Babylon has not been far more
made of as a pattern of humility and meekness both under the dispensations of
God and under the doctrines of Daniel. After his orders had been disobeyed—in
his own palace, remember, and at his own table—in the matter of the meat that
Daniel and his three companions were to eat, and the wine they were to drink:
and after he was compelled publicly to admit that the prince of the eunuchs had

acted on far better advice than the king's commandment—instead of Melzar's head being endangered to the king, Nebuchadnezzar communed with Daniel, and Daniel stood before the king. Then, again, after his great dream, and its interpretation to the destruction of his kingdom, "King Nebuchadnezzar fell upon his face, and worshipped Daniel, and commanded that they should offer an oblation and sweet odors unto Daniel." And, then, after his abominably despotic edict about the image of gold in the plain of Dura, and the furnace seven times heated, when the intoxicated king came to himself he said, Lo! I see four men loose, walking in the midst of the fire, and they have no hurt; and the form of the fourth is like the Son of God. Then Nebuchadnezzar spake and said, Blessed be the God of Shadrach, Meshach, and Abed-nego, who hath sent His angels, and delivered His servants that trusted in Him, and have changed the king's word and yielded their bodies that they might not serve nor worship any god except their own God. And, then, at the end of his life, the king not only let Daniel say this to him, "Wherefore, O king, break off thy sins by righteousness, and thine iniquities by showing mercy to the poor, if it may be a lengthening of thy tranquillity," but he bowed his head and did it. A nobler state paper was never sent out even by the most Christian of kings than is that great document that we have in the fourth chapter of the Book of Daniel. Nebuchadnezzar is another illustration how we go on traditionally calling good men by bad names without looking at what is written out plain before our eyes. I cannot conceive where I got my bad opinion about Nebuchadnezzar. At any rate, I cannot entertain it any longer after I have read that magnificent chapter. I have read nothing nobler about the best kings of Judah, or Israel, or Scotland, or England. I do not know where among them all to look for its equal. But it was not great and ancient kings, but our own little children I was speaking about; and about our proud-blooded little children inevitably growing up into proud-blooded and bad men. And the hopeless unteachableness of the proud child and the proud man was the all-important point in hand. The proud man holds you henceforth to be his mortal enemy if you tell him the truth as Daniel told Nebuchadnezzar, and as Daniel was honored and rewarded for telling it. Try to teach, try to correct a proud man, and you will not readily do it a second time. It may now be many years since some one found a true and notorious fault with some of us; but we cannot hide from ourselves the state of our heart after all these years at the mere mention of that insolent man's name. But Daniel's counsel was acceptable to Nebuchadnezzar, till that king broke off all the sins and all the iniquities that Daniel so boldly named to him. Can it be said about any of our living preachers of righteousness that his counsels have been acceptable to us, and that we have forgiven and obeyed him to the tranquillity of our conscience to this day?

> Rather than bear the pain of truth, fools stray;
> The proud will rather lose than ask their way.

It is true Nebuchadnezzar got a tremendous lesson. It was a lesson, as we would have thought, away out of all proportion to the king's transgression. It was one of those tremendous lessons that God only gives to His own sons whom He loves, and whom He is to chasten till they are made partakers of His holiness. To any man who is not a chastened son and a true saint of God it must look a small sin, if it is a sin at all, for a great king to walk in his own palace and to say to himself the simple truth. For Babylon was undoubtedly great. No greater city has ever been seen on the face of the earth than Babylon. And if Nebuchadnezzar had not built every single street of it, this, at any rate, he could say, that he had found Babylon a city of brick and had made it a city of marble. We hear of baptized kings every day walking in their palaces in Christendom at the end of the nineteenth century, and speaking far more proudly than heathen Nebuchadnezzar spake, and no Daniel dares to stand up and tell them that their feet are partly iron mixed with miry clay. It is as if God had predestinated Nebuchadnezzar to come out of that heathen dispensation, and to sit down in the kingdom of heaven, while the emperors of our modern Christendom are to be cast out. It would look like that; God took such unheard-of vengeance on Nebuchadnezzar's inventions. Did you ever read the fourth chapter of the Book of Daniel?—that splendid autobiographic chapter which king Nebuchadnezzar wrote out of his own inkhorn, and gave the document to Daniel to embody in his book? "Come, all ye that fear God," Nebuchadnezzar begins, "and I will tell you what He did for my soul. I have thought it good to show the signs and wonders that the high God had wrought towards me. For how great are His signs, and how mighty are His wonders! I was walking proudly in my palace in the kingdom of Babylon, and I said, Is not this great Babylon, that I have built for the house of the kingdom by the might of my power, and for the honor of my majesty? And while the word was yet in my mouth, there fell a Voice from heaven, saying, O King Nebuchadnezzar, to thee it is spoken; The kingdom is departed from thee. And they shall drive thee from among men, and thy dwelling shall be with the beasts of the field; they shall make thee to eat grass as oxen, and seven times shall pass over thee until thou know that the Most High ruleth in the kingdom of men, and giveth it to whomsoever He will. The same hour was the thing fulfilled upon Nebuchadnezzar, and he was driven from men, and did eat grass as oxen, and his body was wet with the dew of heaven, till his hairs were grown as eagles' feathers, and his nails like birds' claws. And at the end of the days I, Nebuchadnezzar, lifted up mine eyes to heaven, and mine understanding returned to me, and I blessed the Most High, and I praised and honored Him who liveth for ever, whose dominion is an everlasting dominion, and His kingdom is from generation to generation: and all the inhabitants of the earth are reputed as nothing: and He doeth according to His will in the army of heaven, and among the inhabitants of the earth: and none can stay His hand, or say to Him, What doest Thou? Now I, Nebuchadnezzar, praise and extol and honor the King of heaven, all whose works are truth, and His ways judgment; and those that walk in pride He is able to abase." Has our own Christendom another royal edict anywhere to show like that chapter? If it has, I do not know where to find it.

To be driven out among the oxen made Nebuchadnezzar a new man. Asaph in Israel also, for his humiliation and his sanctification, was as a beast before God. The blessed Behmen, as his disciples all call him, teaches his disciples the same doctrine. "Listen to my own process," says that great spiritual genius. "My soul will sometimes be all of a sudden turned into a wolf within me. Again, I am a dog at home; churlish, snappish, malicious, envious; my heart hides its bone that it cannot eat, lest another dog should get it. Then there is a lion within me; not in his nobility, but in his strong and proud cruelty. At another time, and at the proper provocation, I am a viper, as John preached to his hearers from Jerusalem, venomous, poisonous, and with a stealthy sting. At another time I am loathsome as a toad: at another time timorous as a hare." Yes; our souls are now this beast within us, and now that—when the law enters. Only, the law has not entered one in a hundred of us to that depth: and thus it is that we are all still so proud and so disputatious at the hearing of all these things. But when we see and feel ourselves to be oxen in our stupidity, and dogs in our selfishness, and swine in our miryness, and vipers in our poisonousness—then we have got the key within ourselves to God's great dispensation of humiliation with Nebuchadnezzar. Then we say to Belteshazzar, and to Behmen, Thou art able: and the spirit of the God of holiness is in thee. And then we leave it like Nebuchadnezzar to be read on our tombstone by all that pass by—

Those that walk in pride He is able to abase.

But Nebuchadnezzar would not have needed to be made to eat grass as an ox if he had early enough and often enough asked Daniel to teach him to pray. Prayer would have done it to Nebuchadnezzar also. Daniel himself was mightily tempted to pride—far more than Nebuchadnezzar ever was with all his wars and with all his palaces. For, was not Nebuchadnezzar, with all his power and with all his pride, prostrate again and again at Daniel's feet? Did not king Nebuchadnezzar fall upon his face, and worship Daniel, and command that they should offer an oblation and sweet odors to Daniel? What could it have been, then, that kept Daniel's heart so sweetly humble through all that, till Daniel was a man greatly beloved of Him who resisteth the proud and giveth grace to the humble? It was prayer that did it. It was secret prayer that did it. It was his place of secret prayer three times a day every day he lived that did it. Look in at that window in Babylon that stands open toward Jerusalem, and you will see Daniel on his knees and on the palms of his hands till all his comeliness is turned to corruption. It was that that did it. Seneca says somewhere that nothing is bought so dear as that which is bought with prayer— that is to say, you must sell all if you would truly pray. You must begin with selling all your pride, and everything else as you proceed in prayer, down to your whole soul. I am dust and ashes, said Abraham, not at the beginning, but as he went on in prayer. We are dust and ashes, and far worse than that, says Hooker also, as he went on in prayer. Count the cost, then, before you propose to be a man of prayer. But, then, on the other hand, if any man has come to this, that he would fain, if it were possible, put on humility before both God and man, then let that man pray without ceasing. Enough prayer will work all possible humility into the proudest heart. Prayer every day, and many times every day, and all the day, would bring down and would abase into the very dust very Lucifer himself.

65
Belshazzar

NEVER did a military commander attempt a more impossible task than Cyrus attempted when he sat down before Babylon to blockade it. For Babylon was indeed "Babylon the Great." Babylon was great in size, in fortified strength, in wide dominion, in wealth, in every kind of resource, and in her proud defiance of all her enemies. But then, to set over against all that, Cyrus was a soldier of the foremost military genius: and, besides that, Almighty God was with Cyrus, and was against Belshazzar.

That was an high day in all the temples and palaces of Babylon. It was the day that Bel had made, and all Babylon was in public worship before Bel their god. And as an evening sacrifice to Bel, a great feast was to be held in Belshazzar's palace that night. But before the sunset, and to prepare his proud heart for his great banquet, Belshazzar rode out in his royal chariot that afternoon on that splendid chariot-drive that his famous father, Nebuchadnezzar, had built round about Babylon. The wall of Babylon was the wonder of the world. The wall of Babylon reached unto heaven; and such a mighty rampart was that wall round the city, that no less than four royal chariots were driven abreast on the top of the wall that afternoon, and all in the sight of Cyrus lying below. And as Belshazzar saw Cyrus and his thin red line lying round the mighty fortress, he mocked at Cyrus, and all Belshazzar's princes laughed with him at that spider's thread laid round a sleeping lion. It was a dazzling spectacle at Belshazzar's supper-table that night. All the grandeur, all the wealth, all the princely blood, and all the beauty of Babylon, drank wine at the king's table, and praised the gods of Babylon. When, just as Belshazzar lifted to his lips that cup of the Lord, which had been carried captive out of the temple of Jerusalem, a man's hand suddenly came out and wrote a writing on the wall over against the king's candlestick. But what is that writing on the wall? Neither the king nor any of his Chaldeans can either read the writing or understand the interpretation thereof. Till Daniel is brought in—"Let thy gifts be to thyself, and give thy rewards to another; yet will I read the writing to the king, and make known to him the interpretation. Mene, Mene, Tekel, Upharsin. God hath numbered thy kingdom. Thou art weighed in the balances. And thy kingdom is given to the Medes and Persians." And while Daniel was yet speaking to Belshazzar, Jehovah was at that same moment saying to Cyrus, "Thou art Mine anointed, and I will loose the loins of kings, and will open before thee the two-leaved gates. I will break in pieces the gates of brass, and cut in sunder the bars of iron. I will say to the deep, Be dry, and I will dry up the rivers. I am the Lord, and there is none else." And Cyrus arose, and lifted up the great sluices that he had made in secret, and the Euphrates flowed away into the new bed that Cyrus had dug for it, till the former bed of the river became the broad and open way by which Cyrus led his men into the revelling city. And that night was Belshazzar, the king of Babylon, slain.

Belshazzar's grave is made,
   His kingdom's passed away,
He, in his balance laid,
   Is light and worthless clay.
The shroud his robe of state,
   His canopy the stone;
The Mede is at his gate,
   The Persian on his throne!

But come back and look at this. Did you ever think of this? How do you account for this? If King Belshazzar does not know what the words are that are written on the wall, why do his knees smite so, the one against the other, and why is his countenance so changed? Is this not a banquet to Bel tonight? And are not all these princes and lords and queens and concubines all Bel's worshippers tonight? Why, then, is Belshazzar in such a terror? Why does he not salute with joy and assurance that divine hand? That must be Bel's hand. Rise up, Belshazzar, and kiss the great hand of thy god. Rise up and command more wine. Rise up and call for music and dancing. For that must be the mighty arm of thy god denouncing destruction to Cyrus, and sealing down thy victory to thee. What a cold welcome to give to thy god! O unbelieving and unthankful king Belshazzar! But Belshazzar knew better. Belshazzar's conscience had already interpreted the words before they were all written. You can all sympathize with Beshazzar's state of mind as that hand went on with its awful writing over against the candlestick. You have all come through the same thing yourselves. When something shot in upon you without warning. Something when you were at your ungodly feast with your ungodly companions, or when you had just said, Surely the darkness shall cover me. Something sudden and unaccountable. When your heart suddenly stood still, and did not beat again for a moment. When you were in some sudden accident so that your hair has been white ever since. THAT IS GOD! your conscience whispered to you. That is God come in anger at last. No wonder your knees shook. No wonder you were as cold as a corpse. If a hand came out on the plaster of the wall opposite the pulpit lamp at this moment you would all swoon in your seats. You would know that that hand had come to write your sentence on that wall. Sitting there in your own soft seats you would all, in a moment, be Belshazzar over again.

Belshazzar was as good as dead and at the judgment-seat already. And this was the sentence of the last day upon Belshazzar: "Thou art weighed in the balances, and art found wanting." What balances! What tremendous balances! Balances with all Belshazzar's power, and riches, and opportunities, and responsibilities in the one scale, and then Belshazzar himself, naked and open, in the other scale. Belshazzar was weighed that night with weights of the most absolute truth and justice. Belshazzar was not weighed with King Saul's weights, nor with King David's weights, nor with King Solomon's. Belshazzar was weighed with weights of his own, that no man, before nor since, has ever been weighed with but Belshazzar himself. And you will be weighed, you are being weighed at this moment, with your own proper weights also. God Almighty has a special pair of balances beside Him, waiting and filling up till your life also is numbered and finished. Look up, sinner, at the awful instrument. Forecast the awful scene. All that God has done for you in your birth, in your godly upbringing, in your means of grace, in providences, in all privileges, in divine calls to a better life; all such warnings and all such instructions are collecting into one scale, and your soul—your naked and shivering soul—into the other scale with the whole universe looking on. Well may your knees knock! Well may your thoughts trouble you! How wilt thou do in the swelling of Jordan?

"The Lord is a God of knowledge," says a solemn Scripture, "and by Him actions are weighed." That is to say, you will be weighed in those scales of God by means of which He gets at the very heart's blood of all your actions. Till He has got at the very heart's blood, till He has got at the thoughts and intents of an action, at its most secret motive, He is not yet a God of knowledge. But after that He is. You deceive us, you and your actions both pass with us for what at your heart you are not. But God is not mocked. He knows your exact weight and worth; and the exact weight and worth of all your words and all your deeds. He knows down to the bottom why you did this; and down to the bottom why you did not do that. He has known it all the time, only He has numbered your kingdom, and He lets you go on, deceiving and being deceived, till the Persian is at your gate.

> For I am 'ware it is the seed of act
> God holds appraising in His hollow palm,
> Not act grown great thence in the world below—
> Leafage and branchage vulgar eyes admire.

O my soul, what a day that will be for thee when the God of truth, and not any more of lies, brings forth His great balances! His balances, so awful in their burning truth and holiness! What a reversal of reputations! What a stain and overthrow of great names! What a dreadful trumpet-blowing upon the house-tops! What nakedness! What shame! What everlasting contempt! Rocks, fall on us and hide us. O ministers! O people! But O ministers, above all, on that day! your people will gnash their teeth at you on that day unless you preach to them now the terrible balances of that day. Be sure you preach for one whole sermon every Sabbath the terrors of the Lord. To have even one of your people saved as by fire on that terrible day will be your salvation. For your God is a God of knowledge, and by Him every minister's motives and aims and ends will be weighed before the whole assembled world that day. Rock of Ages, cleft for me!

As you go about in this city you will see great scales sometimes at the street corner, sometimes in a shop for loungers, sometimes at a railway station, strong scales, in which, for a penny, you will see people amusing themselves by weighing themselves and one another, some for pure sport and just to kill time, and some in fear and anxiety lest they should turn out lighter and less in health than they were yesterday. Seek out the places where the scales of the soul are kept open, and seat thy soul in them every day. And, especially, never pass a Sabbath day without comparing your light soul with last Sabbath. God hangs out His scales in the heavens every Sabbath morning. And, above all, He weighs ministers, and their pulpits, and their people on that day. Choose your church, then, above all your choices, choose well your church. The city is before you. Choose a church with God's scales in it at any price. Call a minister who, when he is a probationer, and preaches two trial sermons, at one of the diets hangs God's great balances out of his pulpit and over your pew. And if there is no such probationer in all the poor leet, and no such preacher in all the besotted parish then, all the more, and better for you, learn how to weigh yourself without a minister. Weigh and weigh, and weigh yourself till, in all you think, and all you say, and all you do, you find yourself wanting. Be sure there is something wrong with the balances; all the weights are not in, or there is some hidden rust in the hinges, or you have not read the index right, or something, if you do not find yourself wanting. If you are satisfied with yourself any one day, be sure there is a fatal mistake somewhere. Be sure that a dreadful awakening awaits you if you think that all things are fairly well with you. Never go up into your bed till you have been back in the balance; you and your past day. Never sleep till you know how you weigh, well or ill tonight. Weigh, and weigh, and weigh yourself every day, every night—till there is no more left for the last day to do. Weigh yourself till you have relieved that terrible day of some of its pressure of business on God's hand. He will be pleased, amid much displeasure, on that day, to be lightened of His strange work even in one sinner. When the book comes to your name, He will say: "Pass by that man, I know all about him; he is weighed and settled up with Me already." It will be in that case as the Catechism, which is in your other scale, has it; you will be "openly acknowledged and acquitted in the day of judgment." Weigh yourself, and find yourself ever more and more wanting, till, in pure pity, God will put away His balance behind His back, and will bring forward His touchstone. I got that out of Thomas Goodwin's fine book, *A Child of Light Walking in Darkness.* "For God brings not a pair of scales to weigh your graces with, and if they be too light refuseth them. No: but He brings a touchstone to try your graces. And, if they be true gold, though never so little of it, that gold will pass current with Him. Though it be but smoke, and not yet flame; though it be but as a wick in the socket, Matt. xii. 20 (as it is there in the original), likelier to die and to go out than to continue, and which we use to throw away; yet He will not quench it, but will accept it. These things you are to recall and to consider in times of distress." That is to say, as often as you every day and every hour weigh yourselves, and find yourselves wanting, after the balance make use of the touchstone. And then, as King Brennus, in the old history book, cast his heavy sword into the too-light scale when the gold was being weighed; so will Christ cast in His cross into your too-light scale where His gold is being weighed on that day in you.

66
Esther

THE Ahasuerus of the Book of Esther was the same sovereign as the Xerxes of Herodotus and Plutarch and Thirlwall and Grote. The Ahasuerus of Holy Scripture was the Xerxes who, after he had subdued Egypt, set out to invade Greece with an army and a navy of absolutely fabulous size and strength. He was the madman who beheaded his chief military engineers, and bastinadoed the Hellespont, and laid fetters of iron upon its waves, because a terrible storm had risen on its waters and had destroyed his great bridge of pontoon boats. He was that incubus of carnage who seated himself on a throne of gold on a hill-top of Greece to see his vast fleet of ships sweep off the sea the sea-forces of Athens.

> A king sat on a rocky brow,
>   Which looks o'er sea-born Salamis:
> And ships by thousands lay below,
>   And men in nations all were his.
> He counted them at break of day,
> But when the sun set, where were they?

"That Ahasuerus," says an old Hebrew treatise called the Second Targum on Esther, "whose counsels were perverse, and whose orders were not right: who commanded Queen Vashti to appear unveiled before him, but she would not appear. That Ahasuerus in whose time the house of Israel was sold for naught, and in whose time Israel's face became black like the side of a pot. That Ahasuerus in whose days was fulfilled the threatening that in the morning thou shalt say, Would God it were evening! and in the evening, Would God it were morning!"

The sacred writer makes us respect Queen Vashti amid all her disgusting surroundings. Whether or no the drunken despot actually sent to her the whole cruel order that the Targumist reports, the sacred writer does not in as many words say. But, whatever the royal order that came to her out of the banqueting-hall exactly was, the brave queen refused to obey it. Her beauty was her own and her husband's: it was not for open show among hundreds of half-drunk men. And in the long-run, the result of that night's evil work was that Vashti was dismissed into disgrace and banishment, and Esther, the Hebrew orphan, was promoted into her place. The whole story of Vashti's fall and Esther's rise would take us into too many miry places for us tonight to wade through. I shall leave this part of the unsavory story veiled up in all the restrained and dignified language of the sacred writer. Only, let us take heed to note that the sacred writer's whole point is this, that the Divine Hand was, all the time, overruling Ahasuerus's brutality, and Vashti's brave womanliness, and Esther's beauty, and her elevation into Vashti's vacant seat, all this, and more than all this, to work together for the deliverance and the well-being of the remnant of Israel that still lay dispersed in the vast empire of Persia.

330

Mordecai was the uncle and the foster-father of the orphaned Esther. He had brought Esther up, and his one love in his whole life, after his love for Israel and for the God of Israel, was his love for his little adopted daughter. You may be sure that the devout old man had many thoughts in his heart that he could not get to the bottom of, as he stood by and watched his sister's child lifted up in a moment from her exile and poverty, and actually made the queen of the greatest empire then standing on the face of the earth; and, what was to him still more full of faith, and hope, and love, the favorite queen of the absolute earthly master of all Mordecai's brethren of the house of Israel both at home in Jerusalem, and still scattered abroad over the whole of the Persian empire. I leave you to imagine what were the prayers and psalms that Mordecai offered up with his window open towards Jerusalem, as he saw all Esther's election, and promotion, and coronation, and all her splendor and all her power. And Mordecai walked every day before the court of the women's house, to know how Esther did, and what should become of her.

You would need to transport yourselves away east to the Constantinople of our day at all to understand Haman, and all his diabolical plots against Esther, and against Mordecai, and against all the people of Israel. Diabolically wicked as our own hearts often are with jealousy and with revenge, at the same time, our hearts are so held down and covered over by religion and civilization that we do not know ourselves. There is no difference, says Paul. All vices are in us all, says Seneca; only, all vices are not equally extant in us all. But you will see all but all the vices extant in Haman, the favorite, for the time, of Ahasuerus. How Haman rose, and how he fell: how his seat was set above all the other princes of the empire at the beginning, and how his face was covered at the end; how he and Ahasuerus arranged it between themselves that Israel should be exterminated on a set day by a universal slaughter: how Haman had a gallows of fifty cubits high built for Mordecai yesterday, only to be hanged himself on that same gallows today: how Israel was sold to Haman by the seal of Ahasuerus, and was delivered by the perilous but successful interposition of Esther, all that is told as only a sacred writer could tell it. He that diggeth a pit shall fall into it. And he that rolleth a stone, it shall return upon his own head.

Such, then, was Esther's circle, so to call it. But what, exactly, was her opportunity? What was Esther's great opportunity that put her watchful uncle Mordecai into such sleepless anxiety lest she should either miss it, or betray it? Esther's splendid opportunity rose out of that extraordinary combination and concentration of circumstances in the very heart of which she had been so providentially placed. Haman, as we have seen, was the very devil himself. Haman, the son of Hammedatha the Agagite, was seven devils rolled into one. He was a very devil of pride, and of jealousy, and of revenge, and of an insatiable thirst for Hebrew blood. How almighty God should have let so many devils loose in one devil-possessed man is another mystery of His power, and wisdom, and judgment, and love. But there it is, as plain as inspired words can write it. Only, when the end comes, we see that all the time the God of righteousness had His rope round Haman's neck. And when Haman got to the end of his rope, God said over Haman also: Hitherto thou shalt go in thy diabolical wickedness, but no farther. And, then, as another stepping-stone up to Esther's incomparable opportunity, Ahasuerus,

Haman's master, was a fit master, as we have seen, for such a servant of Satan as Haman was. Till, between them, the children of Israel of that day were on the very point of being exterminated all over the land by a universal and prearranged assassination. But, as God's providence would have it, step after step, Esther was on the throne, and was in all the fullness of her first influence with Ahasuerus just at that critical moment for the Church of God in the empire of Persia. The great war with Greece; the great national feast consequent on that great war; the absolute intoxication of the king's mind with pride, and with ambition, and with wine; the brutal summons to Vashti; her brave refusal of her master's brutal demand; her fall and her banishment; the election and elevation of Esther, and her immense influence with the despot; all these things were so many stepping-stones on which Esther had so providentially risen to her splendid opportunity. And, then, to complete and finish it all, there was added to it all, Mordecai's so watchful solicitude over the wickedness of Haman, and over the caprice of Ahasuerus, and over the safety of Israel, and over the miraculous opportunity of Esther. What a long, and complex, and shining chain, link after link, till Mordecai fashioned its last link and bound it with his strong but tender hands upon both the imagination, and the conscience, and the heart of Esther in these noble words: "Think not with thyself that thou shalt escape in the king's house, more than all the Jews. For if thou altogether holdest thy peace at this time, then shall there enlargement and deliverance arise to the Jews from another place; but both thou and thy father's house shall be destroyed; and who knoweth whether thou art come to the kingdom for such a time as this?" Then Esther bade them return to Mordecai this answer: "I will go in unto the king, and if I perish, I perish." But she did not perish. For she obtained favor in the sight of the king; and the king held out to her the golden scepter that was in his hand, and said to her, "What wilt thou, Queen Esther? And what is thy request? For it shall be given thee to the half of the kingdom." And the end was that Haman and all his murderous plots fell, and Mordecai was promoted to sit in Haman's seat, and Israel was saved. And all because, under God, Esther had her opportunity pointed out to her till she saw it and seized it.

The Book of Esther is surely a very clear prophecy and a very impressive parable of the plots, and the persecutions, and the politics of our own day. Armenia under the Sultan is Israel over again under Haman and Ahasuerus. Western Christendom, and England especially, is Esther with her opportunity and her responsibility over again, and the voice of warning by whomsoever spoken is the summons of Mordecai to Esther over again. It is three hundred years of God's long-suffering since Bacon wrote his *Holy War*. "There cannot but ensue a dissolution of the State of the Turk," said Bacon, "whereof the time seemeth to approach. The events of the times do seem to invite Christian kings to a war in respect of the great corruption and relaxation of discipline in the empire of the enemy of Christendom." So wrote Bacon in 1622. But our Christian kings, if not our Christian people, are still, at the end of the nineteenth century, keeping Haman in his seat, and holding up his hands. In a very fine sermon on my present text, Mr. Spurgeon, in the very spirit and power of Mordecai, has warned England that the God of all the earth has raised her up to her supreme position among the nations of the earth, not for her own aggrandizement, and power, and glory—but for the glory of God, and for the good of mankind. And, that there is no respect or immunity of nations, any more than of men, with the Judge of all the earth. And that if England, for fear, or for favor, or for ease, or for herself only, flinches and fails God and man in the hour of her opportunity, deliverance will come somehow to the cause of God and man; and—one holds back his tongue from saying it, and his pen from writing it—"Thou and thy father's house shall be destroyed." As I read Captain Mahan's masterly and noble *Life of Nelson* the other day with Esther in my mind, I could not but mark such things as these in that great sea-captain who had such a hand in setting England up on her high opportunity. "Opportunity," says the excellent biographer, "flitted by, but Nelson was always ready and grasped it." Again, and again, and again the same thing is said of Nelson. Till it shines out above all his other great gifts, and becomes the best description of his great genius. Opportunity, opportunity, opportunity! And, again, "duty, not ease; honor, not gain; the ideal, not the material—such, not indeed without frailty and blemish, were ever Nelson's motives." This new *Nelson* is a noble book for sailors and for all men to read. It is a noble book to be written and read at any time, but especially at this present time of gain with dishonor, and of ease at the sacrifice of duty.

But we are not great queens like Esther, with the deliverance of Israel in our hands; nor are we great sea-captains like Lord Nelson, with the making of modern England in our hands. No. But we are what we are; and what God has made us to be and to do. We all have our own circle set round us of God, and out of our own circle our own opportunities continually arise. Our opportunities may not be so far-reaching or so high-sounding as some other men's are; but they are our opportunities, and they are far-reaching enough for us. Our opportunities are life or death to us and to others; they are salvation or condemnation to our immortal souls; and is that not circle and opportunity enough? We are all tempted every day to say: If I only were Esther! If I only had a great opportunity, would I not rise to it! Would I not speak out at any risk! Would I not do a work, and win a name, and deliver Israel, and glorify God! Did you ever read of Clemens, and Fervidus, and Eugenia, and their imaginary piety? Clemens had his head full of all manner of hypothetical liberalities. He kept proposing to himself continually what he would do if he only had a great estate. Come to thy senses, Clemens. Do not talk what thou wouldst be sure to do if thou wast an angel, but think what thou canst do as a man. Remember what the poor widow did with her two mites, and go and do likewise. Fervidus, again, is only sorry he is not a minister. What a reformation he would have worked in his own life by this time, and in his whole parish, if only God had made him a minister! He would have saved his own soul, and the souls of his people, in season and out of season. Do not believe yourself, Fervidus. You are deceiving yourself. You hire a cabman to drive you to church, and he sits in the wet street waiting for you, and you never ask him how he manages to live with no Sabbath. It is not asked of you, Fervidus, to live and die a martyr; but just to visit your cabman's wife and children, and have family worship with them on a Sabbath night as you would have done if you had been a minister. Eugenia, again, is a young lady full of the most devout dispositions. If she ever has a family she will let you see family religion. She is more scandalized than she can tell you at the way that some of her school-fellows have married heathens, and at the life they lead without God's worship in their newly-married houses. But, Eugenia, you may never be married so as to show married people how to live. At the same time, you have a maid already, all to yourself. She dresses you for church, and then you leave her to have as little religion as a Hottentot. You turn her away when she displeases you, and you hire another, and so on, till you will die unmarried, and without a godly household, and your circle will be dissolved and your opportunity for ever lost. Your maid, and her sister, and her widowed mother, and her ill-doing brother, and her lover, all are your circle at present, and your opportunity is fast flitting by; and, because it is so near you every day, you do not discover it. Oh, Eugenia, full to the eyes of so many vain imaginations!

You never heard of Eugenia, and Fervidus, and Clemens before, and do not know where to find them. But, no matter. You and I are Fervidus and Eugenia ourselves. You and I are Mordecai and Esther ourselves. We are in that circle, and we are amid those opportunities, the very best that all the power, and all the wisdom, and all the love of God can provide for us. If it had been better for you and me that we had been born in Jerusalem, and had been exiles in Shushan, and subjects of King Ahasuerus, instead of the free-men of Queen Victoria, Almighty God could as easily have ordered it so when He was ordering all such matters. But, according to His best judgment, you are in the very best place for you in all the world. He could as easily have made you rich as poor. He could have made you successful in life, and married, and at the head of a house of your own, as easily as He has made you what you are. He could have made you a captain as easily as a common sailor. A queen, also, is as easy to God as a kitchen-maid. But we are all talented of God, each according to our several ability. And the servant-maid has as good an opportunity, in the long-run, as her mistress. And the cabin-boy as the captain. A cabin-boy saved Nelson's life at Teneriffe, and thus won the Nile, and Copenhagen, and Trafalgar, for England. And he who with love and prayer and sweet civility keeps a door in God's house, has a far easier and a far safer life of it; he has his salvation at far less risk than he who has to work out his own salvation, and the salvation of so many others, on the slippery floor of a popular pulpit. All God's very best wisdom, and all His very deepest counsel, and all His very greatest love, have all been laid out in collecting and concentrating our circle round us, and in evoking our opportunities out of our surroundings, and we pay Him back with grumblings, and with neglect, and with the loss of our own souls and the souls of all who have anything to do with us.

Only open your eyes, and you will see all around you your circle set of God, and all dazzling you with its endless and splendid opportunities. Your most common-place, most monotonous, most uninteresting, and most everyday circle so shines, if you only saw it aright. What a magnificent and unparalleled opportunity—you dare not deny it—is yours, for your self-control, for the reducing of your pride, for the extermination of your temper, for your humility and your patience, for the forgiving of your injuries, and for hiding your hungry, broken, bleeding heart with God! And what more would you have? Yours is a circle with opportunities in it that an elect angel might well envy. Look, O my soul! how many, and what manner of people, are in thy very family and all around thee, and every one in his evil, even more than in his good, a divine stepping-stone laid there of God for thee whereon to climb up to the place that He has prepared for thee in His heavenly kingdom. What an antipathy you feel, and cannot get over, at that pestilential man. What an ever-gnawing envy at that other man. What an everlasting resentment and retaliation at such and such a man. What a genius has that fourth man for finding out for you the most corrupt places in your so corrupt and so deceitful heart. And so on, till there is nobody on earth, or in hell, like you. What a circle for a soul like your soul to be set in! What a sin-discovering and sin-exasperating circle! What a seven-fold furnace you walk in every day! There is nobody like you. There never was. O, man, what a chance you have! They know nothing about it sitting there in their soft seats. But what is the chaff to the wheat, if only you will let God cleanse you? These are they—the elders in heaven look down and say over you—who come up hither out of great tribulation! The chaff think that I am describing a monstrosity and an impossibility in my poor description of you. Never mind them. They and their thoughts are nothing to you. You know that the half of your temptations, and exasperations, and mortifications, and humiliations, and harassments of God, and men, and devils, has not been told. There is no tongue to tell it in, and no ear on earth to hear it with. Never mind them. All the deeper, then, is God's so deep plot for thee. All the more secret and unfathomable are His judgments for thee. All the richer set about thee is thy circle. All the more a miracle of grace are thy endless opportunities. All the more incomparable will be thy salvation, and all the more lustrous and weighty thy crown. Let neither man nor devil take it. Have it on thy head, all shining with pearls out of thy seas of sorrow, to cast at thy Savior's feet on that day.

There is just one circle in the whole universe better than yours for a sinful man's most superb sanctification and salvation, and that is the pulpit, and the pastorate round about the pulpit. I do not wonder that Fervidus never forgave his father for not having made him a minister. For the divine subtlety has surpassed itself in the circle and in the opportunity it has set round every pulpit. O, all you who are our very best young men, all you, our ablest, foremost at college, most gifted, most many-sided, most original, most speculative, most intellectually pioneering and enterprising young men, I beseech you with all my might, do not miss the magnificent opportunity that the pulpit offers to him who can fill it as you could. Even we who will never now fill it—unless it is with tears and prayers night and day—we see, when it is too late, the incomparable life it at one time held out to us, and now holds out to you. There is no circle anywhere under heaven for individual interest; for all kinds of influence, the most immediate and the most lasting; and for the ever-deepening discipline of your own mind, and heart, and life, like the evangelical pulpit. O young men of Scotland, our choicest and our best young men, why stand ye so long hesitating? Open your eyes. Look around. Look within. Look at the church. Look at the world. Look forward to death and to the last day. And then look at the everlasting reward. They that be wise shall shine as the brightness of the firmament; and they that turn many to righteousness as the stars for ever and ever. Then Esther bade them return to Mordecai this answer: Fast ye, and pray for me, and so will I go in unto the king.

EZRA was a great student, he was a great statesman, he was a great reformer, and he was a great preacher. Ezra was born in Babylon. Ezra was a child of the Captivity. But all that only made his heart break all the more for the longing he had to see the land of his fathers, and to do what in him lay fully to turn back again the captivity of Judah and completely to rebuild and restore Jerusalem. Ezra was as near as possible Daniel over again, only in other circumstances. For Ezra also was a youth in whom was no blemish, but well-favored, and skillful in all wisdom, and cunning in knowledge, and understanding science. But Ezra was all the time essentially himself. He was the slavish copy of no man over again—no, not even of Daniel. Ezra was what no man had ever been before him. He was the first scribe in Israel, whatever that was, and he was the first Scriptural preacher, as we say, and his original principle in preaching lasts on to this day, as it will last on and will grow in power and in fruitfulness till the last day. Ezra was full of originality and of distinction of mind, and his originality and his distinction of mind had their roots deep down in a heart and in a character of the very foremost and the very rarest order. For he was "a ready scribe in the law of Moses, which the Lord God of Israel had given. Because Ezra had prepared his heart to seek the law of the Lord, and to do it, and to teach in Israel the divine statutes and the divine judgments"— a noble introduction, truly, to a noble life.

We are not told why it was that Ezra had not gone up out of Babylon along with the first body of returning exiles. "The chaff came out of Babylon, but the wheat remained behind," is a pungent saying of the Jews to this day about the first return of their forefathers from the Babylonian captivity. But, just as our own forefathers had a reformation in Scotland, and then a second reformation, so there was a return and a second return of the children of Judah from their captivity in Babylon. For when the new Jerusalem was in the very greatest straits from her enemies round about, and still more from the slackened faith and the corrupt life of her first return, Ezra rose up and came from Babylon, and was the salvation of Jerusalem. Happily for us, Ezra has embodied in his autobiography the remarkable letter that King Artaxerxes gave to him, and by which the Chaldean scribe was made nothing less than the king's viceroy in Jerusalem. Here are some sentences out of that royal edict: "Artaxerxes, king of kings, unto Ezra the priest, a scribe of the law of the God of heaven, perfect peace, and at such a time. I make a decree, that all they of the people of Israel, and of the priests and Levites, in my realm, which are minded of their own free will to go up to Jerusalem, go with thee. And I, even I, Artaxerxes the king, do make a decree to all the treasurers that are beyond the river, that whatever Ezra the priest, the scribe of the law of the God of heaven, shall require of you, it be done speedily. And thou, Ezra, after the wisdom of thy God that is in thine hand, set magistrates and judges, which may judge all the people that are beyond the river, all such as know the law of thy God; and teach ye them that know them not." And so on. A remarkable glimpse into the mind and heart of Artaxerxes, and a remarkable tribute, from a remarkable quarter, to the ability, and to the worth, and to the immense influence of Ezra.

Before Ezra had time to rest himself from the fatigue of his long journey, he was plunged into a perfect sea of trouble in Jerusalem. Ever since the death of the two great leaders of the first return, the social and the religious life of the new Jerusalem had been fast going down to moral corruption and death. And had Ezra not come to her deliverance, Jerusalem would soon have become again what she had so often been before—as Sodom, and like unto Gomorrah. The complete and even scrupulous separation of Israel from the absolute brutishness of the nations round about her—this was the first law of Israel's life as a nation and as a church. There was no reason why Jehovah, at such a cost, so to speak, should continue to preserve Israel alive on the earth, unless she was to be a people pure and holy, and separated to the Lord, till the time should come when she would be able to be the salt of the whole earth and the light of the whole world. How Jerusalem could have fallen so suddenly and so low the history does not tell us; it leaves us to read all that in our own hearts. But, to his absolute consternation, Ezra found that already every wall of separation had been broken down between Israel and the Canaanites round about, till both the domestic life and the public life of Jerusalem was in nothing but in name to be distinguished from the abominations of the nations that their fathers had been brought out of Egypt to avenge and to root out. It was only then that Ezra saw how good the providence of God had been to him in having provided him with an instrument of such absolute authority as the king's letter was. For it needed all the authority of this autograph letter, and all the courage and resolution of Erza to boot, in order to deal with the terrible disorders that everywhere faced him as he went about in Jerusalem. Those who are well enough read to remember how John Calvin ruled Geneva, and how John Knox and his colleagues did their best to rule Edinburgh—they will best understand and appreciate the rule of Ezra in Jerusalem. So far as those great men could do it, Jerusalem and Geneva and Edinburgh were for the time true theocracies: cities of God, that is; governed as Artaxerxes decreed that Jerusalem should be governed, by the law of the God of heaven. Not perfectly; not without many mistakes and infirmities of temper, and even crimes. But withal, both Ezra and Calvin and Knox made most able and most fearless efforts to set up the Kingdom of God in those three famous cities. So like, indeed, were those three statesmen and churchmen to one another that the modern historians of Israel are fain to come to Edinburgh for their best parallels and illustrations when they are engaged in writing about the Jerusalem of Ezra's day. Our Reformation, our Congregation, our First and Second Books of Discipline, our Solemn League and Covenant, and our Edinburgh pulpit—without those illustrations, taken from our own city, some of the most brilliant pages of Ewald, and Milman, and Stanley, and Plumptre, and our own Robertson Smith, would never have been written.

Ezra, while yet a young man in Babylon, had become "a ready scribe in the law of Moses; in that law which the Lord God of Israel had given." In the words of the 45th Psalm, Ezra's was already the "pen of a ready writer." By his high birth Ezra was by office a priest; when he cared to do it he could trace his unbroken and unblemished descent back to Aaron himself. But what of that, when there was neither temple, nor altar, nor mercy-seat, nor anything else of all the temple apparatus in Babylon? And had Ezra not discovered other and better work for himself: had Ezra not adapted himself to his new circumstances, and fitted himself into his new world, his would have been an idle and a lost and an embittered life in Babylon. But Ezra had the humilty and the insight, the genius and the grace, to see that the future seat of spiritual worship, and the true source of spiritual life on earth was not to be a building any more, but a book. Ages and ages before books became what they now are, Ezra was a believer in books, and in the Book of books. You who make a truly evangelical use of your Bible, and thus have a truly evangelical and a truly intelligent love for your Bible, must not forget what you owe to Ezra; for it was in Babylon, and it was under Ezra's so scholarly and so spiritual hands, that your Bible first began to take on its shape and solidity. When all the other priests and Levites were moping about, not knowing what to do with themselves because they had no traditional altar at which to minister, Ezra struck out a new kind of priesthood and ministry in Israel which has outlasted all the temples and priesthoods in Israel, and which will last till the end of time. We can easily see what a splendid time the young priest-scribe must have spent in Babylon when we imaginatively construct to ourselves those eloquent and epoch-making words: "Ezra prepared his heart to seek the law of the Lord, and to do it; and to teach in Israel statutes and judgments." Ezra's true successors among ourselves; and, especially, those who, like Ezra, are still in their opportune youth and with their life in Jerusalem all before them—they will not fail to take note that Ezra's studies began and were carried on in his own heart. Having no temple precincts made with hands in which to dwell with God, Ezra dwelt all the more with God in the New Testament temple of his own heart. All other studies may more or less prosper independently of the state of the student's heart— language, law, medicine, science, philosophy even—but not divinity. Divinity, and the great Ezrahite text-book of divinity, absolutely demand a devout, a humble, a penitent and a clean heart. And Ezra, the father of all our expository and experimental preachers, has this testimony, that he prepared his heart to seek the law of the Lord, and to do it. Ezra was of Luther's mind, so long before Luther's day, that it is the clean heart even more than the clear head that makes the theologian. Let all our intending preachers examine themselves, and so let them enter on their ever venerable, ever fresh, and ever vacant office.

A distinguished critic has claimed for Jonathan Edwards that his favorite and most frequently recurring word is "sweetness." At the same time, I see that a truly Catholic and Episcopal Professor holds that the word "light," even more than sweetness, is Edwards's characteristic word. Had I been suddenly asked that about Edwards, I would have said "beauty." You are safe to take all the three. John's favorite utterance is "love," as all the world knows; while Paul's peculiar mark and sure token in every epistle of his is "grace." Now, what is Ezra's most frequent and most often-recurring utterance in his autobiography? Well, it is not taxes nor tithes, though he was a great civil and ecclesiastical administrator. It is nothing technical to masons or carpenters, though he has armies of such workmen engaged in the temple and on the walls of Jerusalem. It is not even the words that we would look for in a ready writer. Ezra's peculiar and characteristic expression is "The hand of the Lord," "The hand of the Lord," "The hand of the Lord." The hand of the Lord is constantly upon Ezra. When anything prospers with Ezra it is again, not Artaxerxes, nor himself, but "The hand of the Lord." He introduces himself to his readers as a man in all things under the hand of the Lord. The king granted him all his requests according to the hand of the Lord his God upon him. And upon the first day of the first month began he to go up out of Babylon, and on the first day of the fifth month came he to Jerusalem according to the good hand of his God upon him. And I was strengthened as the hand of the Lord my God was upon me, and I gathered together out of Israel chief men to go with me. And as soon as he secured a suitable colleague to assist him in his immense work, "by the good hand of God upon us, they brought me a man of understanding." Just as he had refused an armed convoy with these same words, The hand of our God is upon all them that seek Him. "And from the river Ahava to Jerusalem the hand of our God was upon us to deliver us out of the hand of the enemy." Our learned men are able to trace and detect the authorship and the authenticity of anonymous and pseudonymous books and manuscripts by the peculiar words and phrases and constructions that occur in them. I think we might almost let the higher critics assert that if there is any page of personal narrative, and no acknowledgment of the hand of God in it, whoever may have written that self-sufficient page it cannot have been Ezra.

Have you discovered and appropriated to yourself Ezra's great prayer? Bishop Andrewes discovered and appropriated it bodily. For that, as you know, was Andrewes's famous and fruitful way with himself. Whenever he came in his reading on any prayer, or psalm, or verse, or even a single word that first spoke to his heart from God, and then uttered his heart to God, he straightway took it down till his *Private Devotions* became the extraordinary treasure-house that it is. I do not remember another such intercession and suretyship prayer in all the Bible as Ezra's prayer was in the temple of the new, but already backsliding, Jerusalem. How this true priest makes himself one with the great transgressors for whom he prays! As you listen you would think that Ezra had been a very ringleader in all those utter abominations that he blushes to have to name. Ezra confesses Jerusalem's sin with an agony such as if all that sin had all been his own. Ezra's spirit in public prayer, his attitude, and his utterances are enough to scandalize all hard and dry and meager-hearted men. But Ezra's prayer, whether in his own book, or borrowed into another book, or assimilated into another praying heart, will always carry captive all tender, and generous, and deep, and holy hearts around it. And thus it was that day that a kindred spirit in that congregation named Shechaniah broke in upon Ezra's prayer and declared that he and his fellow-elders could stand such praying no longer. If Ezra would only stop they would do anything he was pleased to command them. It is always so. If you would move me with your preaching, or with your praying, or with your singing, first be moved yourself. Only, where have we the chance of such commanding and contagious prayer as that was which made all Jerusalem take such sudden fire that day? There had been a long-laid and a daily-built-up altar-fire in Ezra's own heart ever since that early day in Babylon when he first began to prepare his heart to seek the law of the Lord.

A life like Ezra's life, first in Babylon and then in Jerusalem—that is the real secret of every sudden and all-prevailing out-burst of prayer both with God and with man.

But, with all that, such is my immense and ever-growing appreciation of the pulpit that I look on all that—Ezra's birth in Babylon, his suspension from his priesthood, his great and original work upon the law of Moses, his summons to Jerusalem, his hourly and unceasing experience under the hand of the Lord, his extraordinary exercises both in personal and in intercessory prayer—as but so much providential preparation for Ezra's expository and experimental pulpit. It is a grand picture—who will worthily paint it?—and it is only the first of a multitude of such grand pictures. Ezra, standing in his pulpit of wood, with his thirteen elders standing supporting him, six on his right hand and seven on his left. And Ezra opened the book in the sight of all the people, and he and his colleagues caused the people to understand the law and the people stood in their place. So Ezra read in the book in the law of God distinctly, and gave the sense, and caused the people to understand the reading. That is delightfully described, is it not? And that is the very first original and most ancient type and pattern of our best pulpit work to this day. And that type and that pattern has been kept up with splendid success down to this day. To name some of the very masters of pulpit exposition—we have Chrysostom, and Augustine, and Calvin, and Matthew Henry, and, the richest of them all to me, that masterly exegete of the Puritan pulpit, an interpreter, one of a thousand, Thomas Goodwin. And, because he is still alive, and not two hundred years dead, is that a right reason why I should not here name Goodwin's direct successor in his incomparable pulpit—Dr. Joseph Parker? An expositor and a commentator quite worthy to be written in that shining roll. If you have not enough brotherly love to believe that, just borrow, if you will not buy, say the tenth volume of the People's Bible, and read what Dr. Parker says about Ezra, and then be honest enough to agree with me and to thank me. All those men laid out their pulpit life on Ezra's exact plan. That is to say, not so much preaching trite and hackneyed sermons, on trite and hackneyed texts; but reading in the law of God consecutively, giving the sense, and causing the people to understand the reading. That exactly describes our own Scottish habit of "lecturing," as we call it. And it was to that pulpit practice, in no small degree, that our forefathers owed it that they came to know their Bible so well, till they were, and are, so ill to please with the pulpit work of their preachers. It is a noble tradition and a perfect method; only, to do it well demands very hard labor, and very wide reading, and very deep thinking, as well as an early and a life-long preparation of the preacher's heart. But he who sets to himself this noblest of all possible tasks, and perseveres to the end in it, ever learning in it, ever improving in it, ever adding to his treasures of exposition and illustration, ever putting himself into his lecture, and ever keeping himself out of it, he will never grow old, he will never become worked out, he will never weary out his people, but he will to old age bring forth his fruit in his season, and his leaf will not wither. And, then, both to him and to his happy people, will be fulfilled every new Sabbath morning some of the most blessed promises in all the Word of God. "For I will bring you to Zion, saith the Lord, and I will give you pastors after mine own heart, which shall feed you with knowledge and understanding, till we all come in the unity of the faith, and of the knowledge of the Son of God, unto a perfect man, unto the measure of the stature of the fullness of Christ."

YOU must clearly understand, to begin with, that Samaria was already, even in that early day, the deadly enemy of Jerusalem, and also that Sanballat was the governor of Samaria. And Sanballat was a man of this kind, that he was not content with doing his very best to make Samaria both prosperous and powerful, but he must also do his very best to keep Jerusalem downtrodden and destroyed. And thus it was that, when Sanballat heard that Nehemiah had come from Shushan with a commission from Artaxerxes to rebuild the walls of Jerusalem, the exasperating news drove Sanballat absolutely beside himself. And thus it is that such a large part of Nehemiah's autobiography is taken up with Sanballat's diabolical plots and conspiracies both to murder Nehemiah and to destroy the new Jerusalem.

The Book of Nehemiah, you must know, is the last written of all the historical books of the Old Testament. We have nothing in our Bible between Nehemiah and Matthew. Nehemiah, among the historical books of the Old Testament, is just what Malachi is among the prophetical books. Nehemiah is not much read, but his book is full of information and instruction and impression of the most inter-esting and fruitful kind. And as we work our way through Nehemiah's memoirs of himself, we see in Sanballat an outstanding instance of the sleepless malice and the diabolical wickedness of all unprincipled party spirit and besotted partisanship.

Now, in the first place, diabolically wicked as party spirit too often becomes, this must be clearly understood about party spirit, that, after all, it is but the excess, and the perversion, and the depravity of an originally natural, and a perfectly proper principle in our hearts. It was of God, and it was of human nature as God had made it, that Sanballat should love and serve Samaria best, and that Nehe-miah should love and serve Jerusalem best. And all party spirit among ourselves also, at its beginning, is but our natural and dutiful love for our own land, and for our own city, and for our own Church, and for those who think with us, and work with us, and love us. And as long as this world lasts, and as long as human nature remains what it is, there will always be predilections, and preferences, and parties both in the family, and in the city, and in the State, and in the very Church of Christ itself. As long as there is such a rich variety and diversity of talents, and capacities, and dispositions, and tastes, and interests among men, there will always be bodies of men thinking together, and working together, and living together, and loving one another, more than they can live with, and work with, and love other men who see their duties and pursue their interests in another light. Now, this natural principle of mutual attraction is not planted in human nature for no reason. But all the discoverable final causes of this principle are too many for me to enter on now; to enter on them at all would lead me far away from far more important and urgent work tonight. Suffice it to say then, that party spirit, at its very worst, is but another case and illustration of the corruption and the depravity of the very best.

But, then, when it comes to its worst, as it too often does come, party spirit is the complete destruction both of truth and of love. The truth is hateful to the out-and-out and thoroughgoing partisan. We all know that in ourselves. When we have, at any time, become abandoned partisans in anything, then, farewell the truth. We will not have it. As many lies as you like, but not the truth. We hate and detest both you and your truth. It exasperates us to hear it. You are henceforth our enemy if you will insist on speaking it. We cast it, and all its organs, out of our doors. We shut our eyes to the truth, and we stop our ears. It is not truth that divides us up into such opposed parties as we see all around us in Church and State; it is far more lies. It is not principle once in ten times. Nine times out of ten it is pure party spirit. And I cling to that bad spirit, and to all its works, as if it were my life. I feel unhappy when you tell me the truth, if it is good truth, about my rival. I feel the sore pain of concession. I feel as if all my foundations were being taken away from under me. How fierce you always make me when you so rejoice in the truth and go about spreading it! I am a Jew, and I want no dealings with the Samaritans. All I want is to hear that fire has fallen from heaven to consume them. I am a Protestant, and a Presbyterian, and a Free Churchman, and I want to stand aloof all my life from all who differ from me. I do not want to hear what they have to say for their fathers and for themselves. I hate like poison all your proposed fraternizings and unions. I hope that the old walls of separation will hold together all my time.

And where truth is hated in that way love can have no possible home. Truth is love in the mind, just as love is truth in the heart. Trample on the one, and you crush the other to death. Cherish and be tender with the one, and you will eat the fruits and drink the sweets of the other. Now the full-blown party spirit is utter poison to the spirit of love as well as to the spirit of truth. "Love suffereth long, and is kind: love rejoiceth not in iniquity, but rejoiceth in the truth; beareth all things, believeth all things, endureth all things." But party spirit is the clean contradiction of all that. "No assurances," says Thucydides, "no pledges of either party could gain credit with the other. The most reasonable proposals, coming from an opponent, were received not with candor, but with suspicion. No artifice was reckoned dishonorable by which a point could be carried. Every recommendation of moderate measures was reckoned either a mark of cowardice, or of insincerity. He only was considered a completely safe man whose violence was blind and boundless; and those who endeavored to steer a middle course were spared by neither side." That might have been written yesterday, so true to our own public life also is every syllable of it. Archbishop Whately's Bampton Lecture, for the year 1822, has for its subject, "The Use and the Abuse of Party Spirit in matters of Religion," and a very able piece of work it is. Whately was one of the ablest men in a very able day in the Church of England. His strong Saxon sense, supported by wide reading, and by clear and disciplined habits of thought, rose almost to the level of genius. Could Whately and Newman have been mixed together we should have had a perfect English theologian. Whately's third lecture is entitled "A Carnal Mind the

Cause of Divisions," and at the foot of a page in which he shows "how self-interest may chance to be the first mover of discord," this footnote stands, which I repeat to you with both pain, and shame, and indignation: "It happens but too often, it is to be feared," so the note runs, "that a dissenting chapel is regarded as a profitable speculation by persons of corrupt minds, and destitute of the truth, looking upon religion as a gainful occupation." Why, I wonder, should it be so much feared that a dissenting chapel is a profitable speculation to persons of corrupt minds, more than a cathedral stall or an Episcopal palace? What an indecent blot is that on such an able book! And what an illustration it supplies of that very vice the Archbishop is so ably exposing—the blinding and perverting influences of party positions and of a party spirit! Those five lines of prejudice and partisanship made far more impression on me than all the rest of the Archbishop's so masterly and so impressive volume. With my own ears I once heard the late Canon Liddon, when preaching in St. Paul's Cathedral, class Oliver Cromwell with Alexander the Sixth and Richard the Third! To such lengths will a malevolent party spirit go even in the Christian pulpit!

By the just and righteous ordination of Almighty God all our sins carry their own punishment immediately and inseparably with them. And party spirit, being such a wicked spirit, infallibly inflicts a very swift and a very severe punishment on the man who entertains it. You know yourselves how party spirit hardens your heart, and narrows and imprisons and impoverishes your mind. You must all know how party spirit poisons your feelings, and fills you with antipathy to men you never saw, as well as to men all around you who have never hurt a hair of your head, and would not if they could. We read in the *Apologia* how Newman's imagination was stained by his prejudices and his passions. And every man who labors to keep his imagination and his heart open and clean and unstained, will have to confess what a tremendous task he has undertaken. You must either be a great saint, or a great fool, if your imagination and your heart are not stained to absolute wickedness against men, and against churches, and against this and that party in the Church and in the State. It humiliates my head to the dust of death, and it breaks my heart before God and before myself every day I live, to discover such stains in my heart against men who have hurt me in nothing but in this—that they have given their great talents and their shining services to another church than my church, and to another party than my party. I cannot meet such men on the streets but they scowl at me, and I at them back again. Or if we must stop and speak for a moment, we put on Sanballat's face to one another, and take hold of Sanballat's hand, while all the time our hearts are as full as they can hold of Sanballat's mischief that he thought to do to Nehemiah. What a terrible punishment all that is, let him tell us who, before God, is keeping his heart clean of all that. Unless it is casting pearls before swine to attempt to tell such things to us. No! Do not attempt to tell such things to us lest we turn again and rend you.

Another divine punishment of party spirit is seen in the way that it provokes retaliation, and thus reproduces and perpetuates itself till the iniquity of the fathers is visited upon the children to the third and fourth generation of them that hate the truth and murder love. Sanballat hated Nehemiah and plotted against him;

and Nehemiah, not yet being Jesus Christ, nor one of His disciples, retaliated on Sanballat and on Samaria in a way that sadly stains the otherwise spotless pages of his noble book. And between them, Sanballat and Nehemiah kindled that intense and unnatural hatred that is still burning in every heart in Jerusalem and Samaria, when the woman at the well refuses a cup of cold water to our Lord, and when the Samaritans will not make ready for Him nor receive Him, because His face is as though He would go to Jerusalem; and till He pays the woman back with a well of water springing up to everlasting life, and the men of Samaria with the parable of the Good Samaritan. As you know, it takes two to make a complete and a lasting quarrel; so it takes many more than two to make party spirit perfect. And if Nehemiah, and the other builders of Jerusalem, had but had our New Testament truth and love, long centuries of ill-will, and insult, and injury, would have been escaped, and a welcome given to the Lord of truth and love that He did not get. And, inheriting no little good from our contending forefathers, we have inherited too many of their injuries, and retaliations, and antipathies, and alienations also. And the worst of it is, that we look on it as true patriotism, and the perfection of religious principle, to keep up and perpetuate all those ancient misunderstandings, and injuries, and recriminations, and alienations. "Ye know not what spirit ye are of," said our Lord to His disciples when they wished Him to consume the Samaritans off the face of the earth, "for the Son of Man is not come to destroy men's lives, but to save them." To save them, that is, from all their inherited hurts, and hatreds, and antipathies, and animosities, and suspicions. Who, then, is a wise man, and endued with knowledge among you? Let him show, out of a good conversation, his works with meekness of wisdom. But if ye have bitter envyings and strife in your hearts, glory not, and lie not against the truth. This wisdom descendeth not from above, but is earthly, sensual, devilish; for where envying and strife is, there is confusion and every evil work.

Who, then, is a wise man, and endued with wisdom among you? Who would fain be such a man? Who would fain at once and for ever extinguish out of his heart this fire from hell? Who would behave to his rivals and enemies, not as Nehemiah, good man though he was, behaved to the Samaritans, but as Jesus Christ behaved to them? Who, in one word, would escape the sin, and the misery, and the long-lasting mischief of party spirit? Butler has an inimitable way of saying some of his very best and very deepest things. Our master-moralist seems to be saying nothing at all, when all the time what he is saying is everything. And here is one of his great sayings that has helped me more in this matter than I can tell you. "Let us remember," he says, "that we differ as much from other men as they differ from us." What a lamp to our feet is that sentence as we go through this world! As we travel from home and go abroad; as we see other nations with their own habits and their own manners; as we see other churches at their worship; as we read other men's books, and speeches, and newspapers, and they ours; as we encounter other men's principles, and prejudices, and habits of mind, and life and heart—what a light to our path are Butler's wise words! And till we come, in God's spirit of truth, and humility, and love, to take every other man's place and point of view, till we look at all things, and especially at ourselves, with all other men's eyes, and ears, and hearts.

But why multiply many words about this plain matter? It is all contained long ago in the two old Commandments—to love our neighbor as ourselves, and to love God with all our mind, and heart, and strength, and will.

And, then, when at any time, and towards any party, or towards any person whatsoever, you find in yourself that you are growing in love, and in peace, and in patience, and in toleration, and in goodwill, and in good wishes, acknowledge it to yourself; see it, understand it, and confess it. Do not be afraid to admit it, for that is God within your heart. That is the Divine Nature, that is the Holy Ghost. Just go on in that Spirit, and ere ever you are aware you will be caught up and taken home to that Holy Land where there is neither Jerusalem nor Samaria. There will be no party spirit there. There will be no controversy there. There will be no corruption of motive there, and no imputation of it. No ignorance will be found there, and no prejudice, no partiality, no antipathy, no malignity, and no delight in doing mischief. The envy also of Ephraim shall depart, and the adversaries of Judah shall be cut off. Ephraim shall not envy Judah, and Judah shall not vex Ephraim. Violence shall no more be heard in thy land, wasting nor destruction within thy borders; but thou shalt call thy walls Salvation, and thy gates Praise. Thy sun shall no more go down, neither shall thy moon withdraw itself; for the Lord shall be thine everlasting light, and the days of thy mourning shall be ended.

69

Nehemiah

FOR a long time I was not much drawn to Nehemiah. I did not aright understand Nehemiah, and I did not love him. He was not my kind, as we say: the kind, that is, that I like best to read about, and to think about, and to imitate and to preach. I thought him, if a patriotic, at the same time, an outside, a surface, a hard, and an austere man. And, worst of all, a man who was always well pleased with himself; the first of Pharisees, in short, as Ezra was the first of Scribes. I should have remembered what Canon Gore puts so well in *Lux Mundi*: "At starting, each of us, according to our disposition, is conscious of liking some books of Scripture better than others. This, however, should lead us to recognize that, in some way, we specially need the teaching that is less attractive to us. We should set ourselves to study what we less like, till that, too, has had its proper effect in molding our conscience and shaping our character." "If I met a man from New England," said Dr. Duncan, "I would say to him, 'Read the Marrow Men.' If I met a Marrow Man, I would say, 'Read the New-Englanders.'"

Like Daniel and his three companions, and like Ezra his own colleague, Nehemiah was a child of the Captivity. They had all been born and brought up in the furnace of affliction. And they were all children in whom was no blemish, but well favored, and skillful in all wisdom, and cunning in knowledge, and understanding science, and such as had ability in them to stand in the king's palace. Like Ezra also, Nehemiah has written his own biography, and like Ezra also, he both begins and ends his autobiography with great abruptness. We have neither Nehemiah's youth nor his old age in his autobiography. His whole memoir of himself is taken up with his leave of absence from Shushan the palace, and with what he was able to do for Jerusalem during his furlough from Shushan. By the time that Nehemiah's fragment of autobiography opens, the first return from the captivity has for some time taken place. Jerusalem, in a way, has been largely rebuilt. The temple also, after a fashion, has been restored, and the daily services of the temple are in full operation. But the walls and the gates and the towers and the battlements of the new Jerusalem still lie in ruins all round the city; and while that is the case, the whole city stands open to the inroads and the ravages of their enemies round about. Nor is all that the worst. It is a weariness and a despair to read it—but the returned captives themselves were living in far greater poverty and bondage in Jerusalem than in all their seventy years in Babylon itself. Those of you who have ever read and at all understood the two sad little books of Ezra and Nehemiah, and the still more sad little book of Malachi—that saddened and despairing reader will have seen in those three books what a hopeless people God had to do with. And, with still more self-disgust and self-despair, he will have seen what an Old Testament type and example the Jews always are of ourselves.

The schoolboys who have read the *Cyropaedia* can best picture Nehemiah to themselves when he says that he was the King of Persia's cupbearer. The amusing episode of Cyrus and his grandfather's cupbearer is the best commentary we possess on the position of Nehemiah in Shushan the palace. The Persian cupbearer was far more than a cupbearer. He was a kind of prime minister, and master of the ceremonies, both in one. He was the royal favorite above all the rest of the palace, till his privileges and his powers and his wealth were all a proverb. He was able to keep a table and set up an equipage at his own expense like a prince. Daniel's youthful beauty, his graces of character and manner, his shining talents, and his high state-services may all be borrowed and set down as the opening pages of Nehemiah's memoirs of himself. Where Josephus got it he does not tell us, but he gives us a most picturesque and pathetic account of the way in which the terrible state of Jerusalem came to the cupbearer's ears. Nehemiah was taking the air one evening outside the walls of Persepolis when some travel-stained men passed him on their way into the gate of the city. As they passed him he over-heard them conversing together in the Hebrew tongue. You know how your mother-tongue would go to your heart if you were an exile in a far country, however prosperous outwardly you were. And Nehemiah forgot all about Artaxerxes' supper as he talked with the travellers, till he said to them as he bade them farewell, "If I forget thee, O Jerusalem, let my right hand forget her cunning; if I do not remember thee, let my tongue cleave to the roof of my mouth; if I prefer not Jerusalem above my chief joy!" Young John Milton, you will remember, could not enjoy the skies, or the art, or the letters of Italy, while England at home was as she was. And it came to pass in the month Nisan, in the twentieth year of Artaxerxes the king, that wine was before him: and I took the wine and gave it to the king. Now I had not been sad in his presence heretofore. Wherefore the king said unto me, Why is thy countenance sad, seeing thou art not sick? This is nothing else but sorrow of heart. Then I was very sore afraid, and said unto the king, Let the king live for ever! Why should not my countenance be sad, when the city, the place of my fathers' sepulchres, lieth waste, and the gates thereof are consumed with fire? Then the king said to me, For what dost thou make request? So I prayed to the God of heaven, says the cupbearer. How he was heard, and how the king's heart was moved, and how Nehemiah got leave of absence to go and build the walls of Jerusalem, and the letters that he carried to the king's foresters, and to those that kept the royal quarries, and how he set out to the city of his fathers to finish it—all that is to be read in Nehemiah's own memoirs written out for us to this day by his own graphic hand.

If the style is the man in the Scriptures also, then we see Nehemiah to the very life in the whole of his book; but, especially, in his second and third chapters. We see him as well as if we had carried the candle before him all those three nights in which he went round the ruins of Jerusalem. So I came to Jerusalem, and was there three days. And I arose in the night, I and some few men with me: neither told I any man what my God had put in my heart to do at Jerusalem: neither was there any beast with me, save the beast that I rode upon. And I went out by night by the gate of the valley, even before the dragon well, and to the dungport, and viewed the walls of Jerusalem, which were broken down, and the gates thereof were consumed with fire. Then went I up in the night by the brook, and viewed the wall, and turned back, and entered by the gate of the valley, and so returned. And the rulers knew not whither I went, or what I did: neither had I as yet told it to the Jews, nor to the priests, nor to the nobles, nor to the rulers, nor to the rest that did the work. A self-contained man. A man of his own counsel. A man with the counsel of God alone in his mind and in his heart. A reserved and a resolute man. A man to take the command of other men. A man who will see things with his own eyes, and that without all eyes seeing him. A man in no haste or hurry. He will not begin till he has counted the cost. And then he will not stop till he has finished his work. The way that Nehemiah took to build and complete the whole wall round about Jerusalem was this: Every trade, and profession, and corporation, and outstanding city family took a portion, and undertook either to build that portion with their own hands or to see it built. And, to begin with, as was but natural and seemly, Eliashib the high priest began first to build; and, as was to be expected, he held a special sacrifice and spiritual service both at the beginning and at the end of his portion of the wall. A volunteer party from the neighboring city of Jericho took up the portion of the wall adjoining Eliashib; and next to them a man whose name we do not know. "I will take the fish gate," said Hassenaah. "I and my sons will lay the beams thereof, and set up the doors thereof, the locks thereof, and the bars thereof." Then came three men—but we have never heard their strange names before nor since: their names are only written in heaven, and in the third chapter of Nehemiah. And next unto them the Tekoites repaired; "but their nobles," Nehemiah takes this note on his tablets, "put not their necks to the work of the Lord." "Let me have the old gate to repair," said Jehoiada, the son of Paseah. "My heart warms to the old gate." And he and Meshullam divided the old gate between them. Then the guild of the goldsmiths did a large piece, and next to them the apothecaries. These last fortified a strong and a broad portion of the wall, as I have known apothecaries do among ourselves. And, then, after some unknown but noble men: look here at the ruler of the half of Jerusalem and his daughters. I opened Matthew Henry in a hurry here, so sure was I that he would have something specially shrewd on the daughters of Shallum. But even Homer sometimes nods. To my great disappointment I found nothing in the unfailing annotator worth repeating to you. But he wakens up when he comes to the thirtieth verse. Meshullam Matthew Henry holds to have been a lodger who undertook a piece of the wall the size of his own rented room. So that you see our adherents here, and our seat-holders, and those not yet full members, may take their part in all our work till the time comes when they shall have sons and daughters to help them. Thus, at any rate, did Berechiah's lodger, if he was not also his son. That is not the half of Nehemiah's roll of noble names; but you can go round the whole wall for yourselves, and see the rest of the builders at their work for yourselves, till you come to the goldsmith's son at the going up of the corner.

And let it not be overlooked, to their praise, that all the builders builded every man with his sword by his side because of the deadly envy and ill-will of their enemies round about. The enemies of Jerusalem "took it heinously," says Josephus, that the wall of Jerusalem was in the way to be rebuilt. They so labored, Nehemiah proudly writes it about them, from the rising of the morning till the stars appeared. And all the time Artaxerxes' cupbearer had his eye on everything. He was everywhere, and he was the power and the success of everything. The young cupbearer has now become a great statesman and an experienced administrator, till he has left his mark on Jerusalem as long as one stone shall stand upon another. But you must really take time and read the whole of this inimitable little book for yourselves at a downsitting. And that, if only to see how Ezra and Nehemiah worked together, the old scribe and the young cupbearer. How the priests' pulpit of wood was set up, how the support of the altar and the pulpit was seen to, how the public sanctification of the Sabbath was secured, and other reforms instituted with a firmness of hand that there was no resisting. Altogether, this little book is full of Nehemiah's absolute mastery in Jerusalem, and his determination that Jerusalem shall be both a safe, a happy, and a holy city to dwell in. Speaking of the preachers of Jerusalem and their support, just as we get our Presbytery, and our Kirk-Session, and our Expository Pulpit, and our Puritan Sabbath from the new Jerusalem of that day, so we get our Deacons' Court and our Sustentation Fund from Ezra and Nehemiah. Ezra was an old preacher, full of years, full of learning, and full of an experienced piety, giving himself continually to prayer and to the ministry of the Word, while young Nehemiah, like Stephen in the Acts, served tables in the new Jerusalem. That is to say, he looked after the walls of Jerusalem, and the whole temple furniture, and the support of the temple ministry. If our pulpit of wood and its method of work on the Word of God is ancient and honorable, so also is our Deacons' Court. And neither in the new Jerusalem of Nehemiah's day, nor in the same Jerusalem in Peter's day, was the prophetic and apostolic and diaconate compact better observed, on the deacons' side at any rate, than it is in our own congregations at the present moment. And because of all this, says Nehemiah, we make a sure covenant and write it out, and our princes, Levites, and priests all seal unto it, that we will not forsake nor forget the house of our God.

Nehemiah was such a worker in and around the house of God that he would have satisfied James the Just himself. James, the brother of the Lord, was always insisting on work in all the twelve tribes scattered abroad. "Even faith, if it hath not works, is dead, being alone. Wilt thou know, O vain man, that faith without works is dead? For as the body without the spirit is dead, so faith without works is dead also." But for his love of work, Nehemiah again and again would have been a dead man. Again and again Sanballat would have had Nehemiah in his clutches, but that Nehemiah would not come down. "Come out to a conference in the plains of Ono, at any rate," said Sanballat. "No," answered Nehemiah, "I have no time for conferences. I am doing such a great work on the wall up here that I cannot for one moment leave it." Yes, it was the cupbearer's quenchless love of work that both saved his life on several occasions, as well as built and finished the wall of Jerusalem. Cupid, in the old fable, complained bitterly to Jupiter that he could never debauch the Muses, because he never could come on them sitting idle. If work is not worship, then it is surely the next thing to it, so much so that, just bring up your son in idleness, and your gray hairs are as good as in their grave already. Whereas, give your son something to do, from making tables to serving

them, and you have as good as saved his soul. He has no time so much as to speak
to Sanballat. Let every young man then begin early to do something. Let him be
a student and a lover of good books. Let him teach a class. Let him be honored,
and trusted, and elected like Stephen to be a deacon. Let him do his noble duties
with the understanding and the heart. Let him know what he is doing every time
he does it, and he will thus purchase for himself a good degree; that is to say, good
work, and a real love for the good work, and step after step, he will escape all the
Sanballats of the city, and will go on from work to work, through a youth and a
manhood of interest and usefulness, occupation and protection, to an old age of
the best love among us and the highest honors.

And if any young minister should be ordained, like Nehemiah, over such a
congregation as Jerusalem was in that day; if he finds the gates thereof burned
with fire, and the walls laid waste, and the whole house of God in reproach round
about; let him read the Book of Nehemiah till he has it by heart. Let him view the
wreck and ruin on his arrival as the young cupbearer did. Let him say nothing to
any man. Only let him rise up in the King's name and build. Let him come to the
King's quarries for stone, and to the King's forests for timber. The good hand of
his God being upon him. Let him preach his very best to his long-starved people
every Sabbath morning; and better and better every year he lives. Let him visit
his long-neglected people night and day. Let him be like Samuel Rutherford in as
small a church as was in Scotland in that day, and now and for ever as famous. Let
him be his people's boast. Let him be always in his study, always at their sickbeds,
always preaching, always praying. So neither I, nor my brethren, nor my servants,
nor the men of the guard that followed me, none of us put off our clothes, saving that every one put them off for the washing. And at the dedication of the wall
there was great gladness, both with thanksgivings and with singing, with cymbals,
with psalteries, and with harps. For God had made them to rejoice with great joy;
the wives also and the children rejoiced. So that the joy of Jerusalem was heard
even afar off. And it was Nehemiah's faith in God, his love of Jerusalem, and his
hard work for Jerusalem that did it.

70
Joseph and Mary

SAINT MATTHEW and Saint Luke, the first and the third Evangelists, tell us all that we are told of Mary. They tell us that she was the espoused wife of Joseph a carpenter of Nazareth, and that the Divine Call came to her after her espousal to Joseph and before her marriage. What a call it was, and what a prospect it opened up! No sooner was Mary left alone of the angel than she began to realize something of what had been appointed her, and what she must now prepare herself to pass through. The sharp sword that the aged Simeon afterwards spoke of with such passion was already whetted, and was fast approaching her devoted and exposed heart. On a thousand sacred canvases throughout Christendom we are shown the angel of the annunciation presenting Mary with a branch of lily as an emblem of her beauty and as a seal of her purity. But why has no spiritual artist stained the whiteness of the lily with the red blood of a broken heart? For no sooner had the transfiguring light of the angel's presence faded from her sight than a deep and awful darkness began to fall upon Joseph's espoused wife. Surely if ever a suffering soul had to seek all its righteousness and all its strength in God alone, it was the soul of the Virgin Mary in those terrible days that followed the annunciation. Blessed among women as all the time she was; unblemished in soul and in body like the paschal lamb as she was; like the paschal lamb also she was set apart to be a divine sacrifice, and to have a sword thrust through her heart. Mary must have passed through many dark and dreadful days when all she had given her to lean upon would seem like a broken reed. Hail, thou that art highly favored of the Lord, the angel had said to her. But all that would seem but so many mocking words to her as she saw nothing before her but an open shame, and, it might well be, an outcast's death. And, so fearfully and wonderfully are we made, and so fearful and wonderful was the way in which the Word was made flesh, that who can tell how all this may have borne on Him who was bone of her bone, and flesh of her flesh; to whom Mary was in all things a mother, as He was in all things to her a son. For,

Hers was the face that unto Christ had most resemblance.

Great is the mystery of godliness: God manifest in the flesh. A man of sorrows, and acquainted with grief. These are the beginnings of sorrows.

Joseph's part in all this is told us by Saint Matthew alone. And as we read that Evangelist's particular account of that time, we see how sharp that sword was which pierced Joseph's soul also. His heart was broken with this terrible trial, but there was only one course left open to him. Conclude the marriage he could not, but neither could he consent to make Mary a public example, and there was only left to him the sad step of revoking the contract and putting her away privately. Joseph's heart must have been torn in two. For Mary had been the woman of all women to him. She had been in his eyes the lily among thorns. And now to have to treat her like a poisonous weed—the thought of it drove him mad. Oh, why is it that whosoever comes at all near Jesus Christ has always to drink such a cup of sorrow? Truly they who are brother or sister or mother to Him must take up their cross daily. These are they who go up through great tribulation.

What a journey that must have been of Mary from Nazareth to Hebron, and occupied with what thoughts. Mary's way would lead her through Jerusalem. She may have crossed Olivet as the sun was setting. She may have knelt at even in Gethsemane. She may have turned aside to look on the city from Calvary. What a heavy heart she must have carried through all these scenes as she went into the hill country with haste. Only two, out of God, knew the truth about Mary; an angel in heaven, and her own heart on earth. And thus it was that she fled to the mountains of Judah, hoping to find there an aged kinswoman of hers who would receive her word and would somewhat understand her case. As she stumbled on drunk with sorrow Mary must have recalled and repeated many blessed scriptures, well known to her indeed, but till then little understood. "Commit thy way unto the Lord; trust also in Him, and He will bring it to pass; and He shall bring forth thy righteousness as the light, and thy judgment as the noonday. Thou shalt keep them in the secret of thy presence from the pride of men; thou shalt keep them in a pavilion from the strife of tongues." Such a pavilion Mary sought and for a season found in the remote and retired household of Zacharias and Elizabeth.

It is to the meeting of Mary and Elizabeth that we owe the Magnificat, the last Old Testament psalm, and the first New Testament hymn, "My soul doth magnify the Lord, and my spirit hath rejoiced in God my Savior." We cannot enter into all Mary's thoughts as she sang that spiritual song, any more than she could in her day enter into all our thoughts as we sing it. For, noble melody as her Magnificat is, it draws its deepest tones from a time that was still to come. The spirit of Christian prophecy moved her to utter it, but the noblest and fullest prophecy concerning Christ fell far short of the evangelical fulfillment.

She is a happy maiden who has a mother or a motherly friend much experienced in the ways of the human heart to whom she can tell all her anxieties; a wise, tender, much-experienced counsellor, such as Naomi was to Ruth, and Elizabeth to Mary. Was the Virgin an orphan, or was Mary's mother such a woman that Mary could have opened her heart to any stranger rather than to her? Be that as it may, Mary found a true mother in Elizabeth of Hebron. Many a holy hour the two women spent together sitting under the terebinths that overhung the dumb Zacharias's secluded house. And, if at any time their faith wavered and the thing seemed impossible, was not Zacharias beside them with his sealed lips and his writing table, a living witness to the goodness and severity of God? How Mary and Elizabeth would stagger and reason and rebuke and comfort one another, now laughing like Sarah, now singing like Hannah, let loving and confiding and pious women tell.

Sweet as it is to linger in Hebron beside Mary and Elizabeth, our hearts are always drawn back to Joseph in his unspeakable agony. The absent are dear, just as the dead are perfect. And Mary's dear image became to Joseph dearer still when he could no longer see her face or hear her voice. Nazareth was empty to Joseph; it was worse than empty, it was a city of sepulchres in which he sought for death and could not find it. Day after day, week after week, Joseph's misery increased, and when, as his wont was, he went up to the synagogue on the Sabbath day, that only made him feel his loneliness and his misery all the more. Mary's sweet presence had often made the holy place still more holy to him, and her voice in the Psalms had been to him as when an angel sings. On one of those Sabbaths which the exiled Virgin was spending at Hebron Joseph went up again to the sanctuary in Nazareth seeking to hide his great grief with God. And this, I feel sure, was the Scripture appointed to be read in the synagogue that day: "Ask thee a sign of the Lord thy God; ask it either in the depth, or in the height above. Therefore the Lord Himself shall give you a sign: Behold, a virgin shall conceive, and bear a son, and shall call his name Immanuel." Joseph's heart was absolutely overwhelmed within him as he listened to that astounding Scripture. Never had ear or heart of man heard these amazing words as Joseph heard them that day. And then, when he laid himself down to sleep that night, his pillow became like a stone under his head. Not that he was cast out; but he had cast out another, and she the best of God's creatures. Ay, and she perhaps—how shall he whisper it even to himself at midnight—the virgin-mother of Immanuel! A better mother he could not have. So speaking to himself till he was terrified at his own thoughts, weary with another week's lonely labor, and aged with many weeks' agony and despair, Joseph fell asleep. Then a thing was secretly brought to him, and his ear received a little thereof. There was silence, and he heard a voice saying to him, "Joseph, thou son of David, fear not to take unto thee Mary thy wife, for that which is conceived in her is of the Holy Ghost." Gabriel was sent to reassure Joseph's despairing heart, to demand the consummation of the broken-off marriage, and to announce the Incarnation of the Son of God. Did Joseph arise before daybreak and set out for Hebron to bring his outcast home? There is room to believe that he did. If he did, the two angel-chastened men must have had their own thoughts and counsels together even as the two chosen women had. And as Joseph talked with Zacharias through his writing table, he must have felt that dumbness, and even death itself, would be but a light punishment for such unbelief and such cruelty as his. But all this, and all that they had passed through since the angel came to Zacharias at the altar, only made the re-betrothal of Joseph and Mary the sweeter and the holier, with the aged priest acting more than the part of a father, and Elizabeth acting more than the part of a mother.

For my own part, I do not know the gift or the grace or the virtue any woman ever had that I could safely deny to Mary. The divine congruity compels me to believe that all that could be received or attained or exercised by any woman would be granted beforehand, and all but without measure, to her who was so miraculously to bear, and so intimately and influentially to nurture and instruct, the Holy Child. We must give Mary her promised due. We must not allow ourselves to entertain a grudge against the mother of our Lord because some enthusiasts for her have given her more than her due. There is no fear of our thinking too much either of Mary's maidenly virtues, or of her motherly duties and experiences. The

Holy Ghost in guiding the researches of Luke, and in superintending the composition of the Third Gospel, especially signalizes the depth and the piety and the peace of Mary's mind. At the angel's salutation she did not swoon nor cry out. She did not rush either into terror on the one hand or into transport on the other. But like the heavenly-minded maiden she was, she cast in her mind what manner of salutation this should be. And later on, when all who heard it were wondering at the testimony of the shepherds, it is instructively added that Mary kept all these things and pondered them in her heart. And yet again, when another twelve years have passed by, we find the same Evangelist still pointing out the same distinguishing feature of Mary's saintly character, "They understood not the saying which Jesus spake unto them; but His mother kept all these sayings in her heart."

And, again, if we are to apply this sure principle to Mary's case, "according to your faith so be it unto you," then Mary must surely wear the crown as the mother of all them who believe on her Son. If Abraham's faith has made him the father of all them who believe, surely Mary's faith entitles her to be called their mother. If the converse of our Lord's words holds true, that no mighty work is done where there is unbelief: if we may safely reason that where there has been a mighty work done there must have been a corresponding and a cooperating faith; then I do not think we can easily overestimate the measure of Mary's faith. If this was the greatest work ever wrought by the power and the grace of Almighty God among the children of men, and if Mary's faith entered into it at all, then how great her faith must have been! Elizabeth saw with wonder and with worship how great it was. She saw the unparalleled grace that had come to Mary, and she had humility and magnanimity enough to acknowledge it. "Blessed art thou among women: Blessed is she that believeth, for there shall be a performance of those things which were told her from the Lord." "Blessed is she that believeth," said Elizabeth, no doubt with some sad thoughts about herself and about her dumb husband sitting beside her. "Blessed is the womb that bare Thee," cried on another occasion a nameless but a true woman, as her speech bewrayeth her, "and Blessed be the paps that Thou hast sucked." But our Lord answered her, and said, "Yea, rather, blessed are they that hear the word of God and keep it." And again, "Whosoever shall do the will of My Father in heaven, the same is My brother, and sister, and mother."

SIMEON was one of the Seventy. Simeon sat in the Jerusalem Chamber of that day. And it fell to the lot of the Old Testament company on which Simeon sat to render the prophet Isaiah out of the Hebrew tongue and into the Greek tongue. All went well for the first six chapters of the evangelical prophet. But when they came to the seventh chapter, and to this verse in that chapter, "Behold, a virgin shall conceive, and bear a son, and shall call his name Immanuel," Simeon at that impossible prophecy threw down his pen and would write no more. "How shall this be?" demanded Simeon. And with all they could do, the offended scholar would not subscribe his name to the *parthenos* passage that so satisfied and so delighted all the rest. Till in anger he threw down his pen and went home to his own house. But at midnight an angel appeared to Simeon, and said to him: "Simeon, I am Gabriel that stand in the presence of God. And, behold, thou shalt remain in this thy captivity till thou shalt see with thine own eyes the Lord's Christ, made of a woman, and till the virgin's son shall put his little hand into thine aged bosom, and shall there loose thy silver cord." And it was so. And the same Simeon was just and devout, waiting for the consolation of Israel. And he was still waiting in the temple when his parents brought in the child Jesus, to do for him after the custom of the law. Then he took him up in his arms, and blessed God, and said: "Lord, now lettest Thou Thy servant depart in peace, according to Thy word: for mine eyes have seen Thy salvation."

I can only guess at Simeon's real meaning and whole intention when he said in the temple that day that his waiting eyes had now seen God's salvation. For salvation in that day, as in this day, had as many meanings as there were men's minds. Salvation had the very heavenliest of meanings to one man, and the very earthliest of meanings to another man. To one man in the temple that day the salvation of God meant salvation from Caesar; while to another man it meant his salvation from himself. To one man it was the tax-gatherer, and to another his own evil heart. And, with all that we are so instructively told about Simeon, still it is not possible to satisfy ourselves as to what, exactly, that aged saint and scripture scholar had in his mind when he said that his eyes had now seen God's salvation. But it is not Simeon and his salvation who is our errand up into this temple tonight. It is ourselves. What, then, is our salvation—yours and mine? When we speak, or hear, or read, or sing about salvation, what exactly do we mean?—if, indeed, we have any meaning at all, or intend to have any. "My son"—one of Simeon's sacred colleagues used to say to his scholars—"My son, the first thing that you will be examined upon at the day of judgment will be this: What was the salvation that you pursued after? What salvation did you study, and teach, and preach, and yourself seek after when you were still in time and upon the earth?" How happy will it be with old Simeon on that terrible day when he hears this read out over him before men and angels: "The same man was just and devout, waiting for the consolation of Israel, and the Holy Ghost was upon him." "Mine eyes," said Simeon, "have seen Thy salvation." And Joseph and His mother marvelled at those things which were spoken of Him.

And, being full of the Holy Ghost, Simeon went on to say: "Behold, this child is set for the fall and rising again of many in Israel." So He was in Israel, and so He is still. There are schools and systems of interpretation of Scripture; there are schools and systems of philosophy; and of this and that, in which this prophecy uttered by Simeon that day, is still being fulfilled. They rise, and they stand, and they fall, just as they receive or reject Immanuel. But our question with this Scripture before us is not about schools and systems of theology and philosophy, but about our own souls. Has Mary's Son, then; has God's Son, been a stumbling stone to me? Or, has He been the one foundation laid in Zion for me? Has He, to my everlasting salvation, and to His everlasting praise, lifted me up from all my falls and made me to stand upon His righteousness as upon a rock? Simeon himself had at one time stumbled and been broken on this child, and on His too great name. But the steps of a good man are ordered of the Lord, and He delighteth in his way. Though he fall he shall not be utterly cast down, for the Lord upholdeth him with His hand. Now, unto Him that is able to keep you from falling, and to present you faultless before the presence of His glory with exceeding joy: to the only wise God, our Savior.

"And for a sign that shall be spoken against." We wonder to hear that. We are shocked to hear that. We say in amazement at that: What did He ever say or do that He should be spoken against by any man? He did the very opposite. He went about doing and speaking only good. But that made no difference to those men in that day who spake so spitefully against Him. Some spake against Him out of sheer ignorance of Him. They had never even seen Him. But they spake against Him in their distant villages as if He had come and done them and theirs some great injury. And many who saw Him every day spake against Him every day, just because they did not understand Him, and would not take the pains and pay the price to understand Him and to love Him. Some, again, were poisoned against Him by what other people, and people of power, said against Him; some through envy, and some just because they had once begun to speak against Him, and could never give over what they had once begun to do. And they went on so speaking till they were swept on to cry, Crucify Him! not knowing what they were saying, or why. Take good care how you begin to speak against any man, good or bad. The chances are that, once you begin it, you will never be able to give it over. When you have once begun the devil's work of evil-speaking, he will hold his hook in your jaws, and will drag you on, and will give you a stake and an interest in lies and slander, till it will enrage and exasperate you to hear a single word of good spoken about your innocent victim. "Judge not," said our Lord, feeling bitterly how He was misjudged Himself. And Albert Bengel annotates that in this characteristic way: *sine scientia amore, necessitate.* "I spoke not ill of any creature," said Teresa, "how little soever it might be. I scrupulously avoided all approaches to detraction. I had this rule ever present with me, that I was not to wish, nor assent to, nor say such things of any person whatsoever that I would not have them say of me. Still, for all that, I have a sufficiently strict account to give to God for the bad example I am to all about me in some other respects. For one thing, the very devil himself sometimes fills me with such a harsh and cruel temper—such a wicked spirit of anger and hostility at some people—that I could eat them up and annihilate them." That was the exact case with the detractors of Jesus Christ. They had no peace in their hearts, or in their tongues at Him, till they had eaten Him up and annihilated Him. This is such a horrible pit of a world that not even the Son of God Himself could come down into it, and do the work of God in it, without being hunted to death by evil tongues. And with that awful warning, and after nineteen centuries of His grace and truth, no man of any individuality, and talent, and initiative for good, can, to this day, do his proper work without straightway becoming a sign to be spoken against. To this day some of the most Christlike of men among us have been the most written against and spoken against, till such speech and such writing may almost be taken as the seal of God set upon His best servants and upon their best work. "And for a sign that shall be spoken against," said Simeon, as he returned the Holy Child to His mother.

72
Zacharias and Elizabeth

HIGH up in the hill-country of Judea there dwelt a certain priest named Zacharias with his wife Elizabeth. They were no longer young; they had lived a long and a happy lifetime together. The single shadow that had ever lain upon their serene and saintly life had been this that their house was childless. But all that was now long past—long past and quite forgotten. "For thus saith the Lord to them that choose the things that please me, and take hold of my covenant, even unto them will I give in mine house and within my walls a place and a name better than of sons and of daughters: I will give them an everlasting name, that shall not be cut off." And while the Lord spake thus to them both, Zacharias in his holy office spake thus to Elizabeth: "Why weepest thou, and why is thy heart grieved? Am not I better to thee than ten sons?" Thus the God of Israel spake to them both, and thus they spake to one another, till Luke is able to record this of them both, that they were both righteous before God, walking in all the commandments and ordinances of the Lord blameless.

It is the fullness of time at last. It is at last the great day on which the New Testament has been predestinated to open. Zacharias has gone up to Jerusalem according to his course. The priestly lot has again been cast and has fallen this time on Zacharias. He is chosen of God and called upon to enter the Holy Place, to minister at the altar, and to make morning and evening intercession for the sinful people. Never before, in all his long lifetime, has Zacharias had this awful privilege; only once in a priest's whole lifetime was this great office put upon any son of Aaron. Clothed in his spotless robes, with his head covered and with his shoes off, this holy man and elect priest disappears within the golden doors of the Holy Place. As he enters he sees the golden candlestick, and the table of showbread, and the altar of incense. From that altar there rises the sacred flame that had been lighted at the pillar of fire in the wilderness, and which has burned on unconsumed ever since. Taking his censer full of incense into his hand Zacharias pours it on the perpetual altar-fire, and says: Lord, let my prayer come before thee like this incense; and the lifting up of my hands like the evening sacrifice! And the whole multitude of the people were praying without at the time of incense. And there appeared unto Zacharias an angel of the Lord standing on the right side of the altar of incense. And when Zacharias saw him he was troubled and fear fell upon him. But the angel said unto him: Fear not, Zacharias; for thy prayer is heard, and thy wife Elizabeth shall bear thee a son, and thou shalt call his name John. And thou shalt have joy and gladness, and many shall rejoice at his birth. And many of the children of Israel shall he turn to the Lord their God: to make ready a people prepared for the Lord. Then follows Zacharias's fear, and doubt, and disbelief; and then his deafness and dumbness; and then the visit of Mary to the hill-country of Judah, where Zacharias and Elizabeth had hid themselves; and then the Magnificat, as we call it: and then the birth and the circumcision of Elizabeth's son; and then the opening of Zacharias's mouth and the loosening of his tongue, all wound up with his magnificent Benedictus. A splendid preface to a splendid book!

"They were both righteous before the Lord, and blameless." This is an excellent instance of the frank and fearless, if confessedly condescending, style of Holy Scripture. Holy Scripture has no hesitation lest it should contradict or stultify itself. Holy Scripture speaks out its whole heart on each occasion boldly, and leaves the reconciling and the harmonizing of its strong and sometimes startling statements to those of its readers who feel a need and have a liking for such reconciling and harmonizing. As a matter of fact that was the widespread good name and spotless character of Zacharias and Elizabeth. Zacharias among his brethren in the priesthood, and Elizabeth among her kinsfolk and neighbors in Hebron, were both blameless. Holy Scripture in saying this simply classifies Zacharias and Elizabeth with Abraham, and with Samuel, and with Job, and with all such Old Testament saints. And if such generous judgments are not so often passed on men and women in New Testament times, that is so for reasons that are very well known to every New Testament mind and heart. And if those noble tributes to Zacharias and Elizabeth stagger and condemn us; if we read of their righteousness and their blamelessness with envy and with despair; what is that envy and what is that despair but two of our finest New Testament graces through which we are being led on to a righteousness and a blamelessness that shall not be economical and of condescension, but shall be true and perfect and everlasting. That righteousness, in short, and that blamelessness of which a New Testament apostle prophesies in these so comforting words: "Nevertheless we, according to His promise, look for new heavens and a new earth, wherein dwelleth righteousness. Wherefore, beloved, seeing that we look for such things, be diligent that ye be found of Him in peace, without spot, and blameless." Blessed are they which do hunger and thirst after righteousness, for they shall be filled.

And the angel said unto him: Fear not, Zacharias: for thy prayer is heard. Had the angel come with that answer forty years before he would have been welcomed and well entertained both by Zacharias and Elizabeth. But he has come too late. "No," said Zacharias; "no. It is far too late. The time is past—long past. The thing is impossible—quite impossible. And, indeed—and let not my lord be angry—it is no longer desirable." Zacharias had long outlived his prayer for a son. He had long retracted his prayer. He had a thousand times justified the Hearer of prayer for not hearing and not answering his too impatient prayer. He had long ere now seen some very good and sufficient reasons why he and Elizabeth should end their days together. And, even if it were still possible, Zacharias was not willing to be plunged back at this time of day into all the anxieties, and uncertainties, and responsibilities, and dangers he had now for so long left for ever behind him. "My prayer is not to be heard," Zacharias had long ago said to himself. "Let me direct my prayer and look up for far better, and far more sure, and far more steadfast, and far more satisfying things. The will of the Lord be done," he had said long ago. But behold, to Zacharias's confusion, his prayer has been heard all the time! All these long past years of prayer, and waiting, and ceasing from prayer and turning to other things—all that time Zacharias's answer has been ready before God, and has only been waiting till the best time for the answer to be sent down. Pray on, then, all you postponed and disappointed and impoverished people of God; pray on and faint not. Pray on: for the prayer is far better than the answer. And, besides, your answer may all the time be ready, as Zacharias's answer was. But other people's prayers and other people's providences may be so mixed up with yours that you will have to wait till their prayers, and their preparations, and their providences are all as ripe and as ready as yours. The fastest ship in the British fleet has to wait for the slowest, and that explains why that fine vessel is not led into battle and let home to harbor with its full and proper spoil. Zacharias and Elizabeth were ready long ago. But Joseph and Mary were not ready; they were still but new beginners in faith and in prayer, in righteousness and in blamelessness. And thus it was that, without knowing why, Zacharias and Elizabeth and John the Baptist had to wait in the hill-country of Hebron till Joseph and Mary were made ready for the Divine predestination and for their prayer away north in Nazareth.

And Zacharias and Elizabeth hid themselves up in the hill-country for the next five months. Look at them. Look at Zacharias with his writing table, and Elizabeth with her needle. And never one word spoken between them all that time, only smiles and tears. What, do you suppose, was Zacharias doing all that time with no altar to minister at, and no neighbors to talk to, and no tongue, indeed, to talk with? "I have no books," said Jacob Behmen, "but I have myself." And Zacharias had himself. Zacharias had himself, and the wife of his youth, who was also the light of his eyes: he had himself and all those past years of prayer, and waiting, and resignation, and peace of mind. And then he had these past overwhelming weeks also. Do you still ask what Zacharias was doing all that time? Has your New Testament a margin with readings? Your so instructive margin, if you will attend to it, will tell you the very Scriptures over which Zacharias spent his days and nights all that silent time in Hebron. All you have got to do some day, when you are in the mind, is to consult the margin over against Zacharias's prophetical song, and you are in that as good as looking over his shoulder at his writing table. You are as good as walking out alone with him when he goes abroad among the sunsetting rocks of Judea to wonder, and to praise, and to pray over Elizabeth and himself and their unborn son.

Zacharias and Elizabeth were sitting alone with their own thoughts one day when who should knock at their door but the Virgin Mary herself all the way from Nazareth. Luke takes up his very best pen as Elizabeth and Mary embrace one another. He had it all long afterwards from an eye and ear witness, so that we might know the certainty of all that took place that day in Zacharias's house up in the hill-country. With the embrace and with the authority of a prophetess Elizabeth saluted Mary, and said: "Blessed art thou among women, and blessed is the fruit of thy womb. And whence is this to me, that the mother of my Lord should come to me?" What a day! What a dispensation! What a meeting! What a household! What a predestination descended on that roof! What unsearchable riches! What great and precious promises! What prayers! What psalms! What laughter! What tears! And Mary said: "My soul doth magnify the Lord, and my spirit hath rejoiced in God my Savior." And Mary abode with Elizabeth about three months, and then returned to her own house.

And it came to pass, that on the eighth day Elizabeth's neighbors and her cousins came to the circumcision of the child; and they called him Zacharias, after the name of his father. But his mother answered and said: "Not so; but he shall be called John," that is to say, The-Grace-of-God. And they said unto her: "But there is none of thy kindred that is called by that name." And they made signs to his father what he would have the child called, and he asked for his writing table and wrote, saying; "His name is The-Grace-of-God." And they marvelled all. They marvelled all because it was a new name to them, and it offended them to hear it. It was to them an outlandish and an unintelligible name. They had never prayed for a son, or for anything else. They had never been visited of an angel. They had never hid themselves five months. Their husbands had never been struck deaf and dumb for their doubt. No babe had ever leaped in their womb because they were filled with the Holy Ghost. No. None of all their kindred had ever been called by this so stumbling name. Fathers and mothers of new-born children, be like Elizabeth and Zacharias in the naming of your children. Be very bold, if need be, in the naming of your children. Be original and independent in the naming of your children. Be truthful. Be thankful. Be believing. Be hopeful, and be assured. Be not afraid to write an altogether new name in your Family Bible. Go back to your true ancestors for a name sometimes, and not to those of flesh and blood only. Fish no more for testaments in the waters of baptism. Or if for a testament at all, then secure, as far as your naming of him lies, that your son shall be an heir of God, and a joint-heir with the Son of God. Name the name of God over your son. Name over your son what God has done for your soul. Name over him some secret of the Lord with you. Name him something that God has showed you out of His holy covenant. Elizabeth was very bold. She named her little son after no man on earth, but, actually, after Almighty God Himself in heaven. And her husband Zacharias was of one mind with her in that, as soon as he got his writing table into his hands. The God-of-all-Grace was thus made Sponsor and Name-Father to Elizabeth's only son, who was born of her so out of all ordinary time. Elizabeth and Mary had spent three months together since Gabriel's visit to them both. And all those three months—morning, noon, and night—when they talked together, it was about nothing else but about the angel, and his visits, and his messages. And among other things that they less talked about to one another than whispered to themselves, was the naming of their unborn sons. "Immanuel!" and "Jesus Christ!" Mary would whisper to herself, with an ever-increasing wonder and awe at the awful words. While "The-Grace-of-God" was Elizabeth's holy secret. And, then, how the two children were born, and how they were brought up, and how they both justified, and fulfilled, and adorned their new and unheard-of names, let Luke and his fellow-evangelists say. And they will tell you, to begin with, how John—The-Grace-of-God—grew and waxed strong in spirit, and was in the deserts till the day of his showing unto Israel.

73

John the Baptist

"WHAT manner of child shall this be!" was the universal exclamation of the whole hill-country of Judea over the birth of John. The old age of Zacharias and Elizabeth; the errand from heaven of Gabriel; the dumbness in judgment of Zacharias; and the strange things that he wrote on his writing table; all that made all who heard of it to exclaim, "What manner of child, we wonder, shall John, the son of Zacharias and Elizabeth, turn out to be!" And the whole manner and character and service of John's childhood and youth and manhood, down to the day of his death, turned out to be wonderful enough to satisfy the most wonder-loving of Elizabeth's neighbors, both in Jerusalem and in all Judea.

John was in the deserts till the day of his showing unto Israel, so Luke tells us. And from Luke, and from some other trustworthy sources, we can see John for the first thirty years of his sequestered life as well almost as if we ourselves had lived in the very next desert to his deserts. For you must always remember this about John that he was in the deserts, and was with the wild beasts, till he began to be about thirty years of age. He was in those terrible deserts that lay all around the Dead Sea. Up and down John wandered, and fasted, and prayed, where Sodom and Gomorrah had once stood till the Lord rained fire and brimstone upon all the inhabitants of those cities, and upon all that grew upon the ground. And John was clothed with camel's hair, and with a leathern girdle about his loins; and he did eat locusts and wild honey. A terrible man. A man not to come near. The very bitumen-miners, whom everybody feared, were afraid of John. It made them sober and civil to one another when John came down to visit them in their squalid settlements. It was not that John was a misanthrope. John was the right opposite of a misanthrope. It was because all other men were misanthropes; were hateful, and were hating one another, that John could not any longer dwell among them, either in Judea or in Jerusalem, either in Sodom or Gomorrah. You totally misread and misunderstand John if you think that it was either misanthropy or moroseness that made John what he was. It was simply John's extraordinarily deep insight into the holy law of God that made him such a monastic of fasting and self-flagellation and prayer.

Before his father Zacharias died, and as long as Elizabeth lived, John had heard things like this at their lips in family worship every day: "The Lord shall lay on Him the iniquity of us all. He shall be stricken, smitten of God, and afflicted. His soul shall be made an offering for sin." It was on such things as these that Elizabeth suckled her heavensent son till it sometimes seemed to him in his loneliness of soul and in his agony of heart that he himself had been made sin, and nothing but sin. And, indeed, in some ways, John came as near being made sin as any mortal man ever came to that unparalleled experience. John was the man of sorrows till the true Man of Sorrows Himself should come. All the appetites of John's body,

and all the affections of John's mind and heart, were drunk up and drained dry by
the all-consuming fires of his unquenchable conscience. If all sight and sense and
conscience of sin had utterly died out of Israel in that day, it had only died out of
all other men's hearts to rage like the bottomless pit itself in the great broken heart
of Elizabeth's substituted son. And thus it was that the very robbers ran and hid
themselves among the rocks of the hill-country when they saw that terrible man
standing again over against the city, and crying out, "Oh Jerusalem! Jerusalem!
how shalt thou abide the day of His coming? For, behold! that day shall burn
as an oven. That great and terrible day, when all that do wickedly shall be as the
stubble!" A man alone. A man apart. A great man. "A greater man has never been
born of woman," said He who knew all men. "What went ye out into the wilderness to see? A reed shaken with the wind!" He who said that never smiled, say
some. I see Him smiling for once as He says that. "A man clothed in soft raiment!
No; anything but that. And anything but a reed; and with anything on but the soft
clothing that they put on in kings' houses!"

And, now, from such a divinity-student as that, and after thirty years of such
a curriculum and probationership as that, what kind of preaching would you go
to church to look for? A dumb dog that cannot bark? A trencher-chaplain? A soft
thing of gown and bands and lawn sleeves? A candidate for a manse and a stipend?
"O generation of vipers, who hath warned you to flee from the wrath to come?
Bring forth, therefore, fruits meet for repentance. And now the axe is laid at the
root of the trees. Therefore every tree that bringeth not forth good fruit is hewn
down and cast into the fire. He that hath two coats let him impart to him that hath
none; and he that hath meat, let him do likewise. Do violence to no man. Neither
accuse any man falsely, and be content with your wages. He shall baptize you with
the Holy Ghost, and with fire. Whose fan is in His hand, and He will gather the
wheat into His garner, but the chaff will He burn up with fire unquenchable."
The greatest preacher of the past generation when preaching to a congregation
of young preachers said this to them. "He who has before his mental eye the four
last things will have the true earnestness. He will have the horror and the rapture
of one who witnesses a conflagration, or discerns some rich and sublime prospect
above and beyond this world. His countenance, his manner, his voice will all speak
for him in proportion as his view has been vivid and minute.

> Yea, this man's brow, like to a title-leaf,
> Foretells the nature of a tragic volume.
> Thou tremblest, and the whiteness in thy cheek
> Is apter than thy tongue to tell thine errand.

It is this earnestness, in the supernatural order, which is the eloquence of saints;
and not of saints only, but of all Christian preachers, according to the measure of
their faith and love."

But why, I wonder, was the forerunner able to content himself all his days with
being no more than the forerunner? Why did John not leave off his ministry of
accusation and condemnation? Why did he not wait upon, and himself take up, the
ministry of reconciliation? When he said to his disciples, Behold the Lamb of God!

why did the Baptist not go himself with Andrew and the others and become, first, a disciple, and then in due time an apostle, of Jesus Christ? Zacharias's son would have made a better son of thunder than both of Zebedee's sons taken together. Why, then, did John not leave the desert, and the Jordan, and follow Christ? Well, to begin with, he could not help himself. Jesus did not call John any more than He called His own brother James. "Go you," John said to Andrew, and to Peter, and to James and John, the sons of Zebedee. "Go you: I am not worthy to enter under the same roof with Him. I will remain where I am. I will work at the Jordan. I will preach repentance, and He will teach you to preach pardon. The Kingdom of Heaven is soon coming, but I shall not live to see it. I shall not live to see Tabor, and Calvary, and Olivet, and Pentecost, like you. He and you, His disciples, must increase, but I must decrease." John was a great man and a great preacher, but, as we are wont to say, he never quite escaped out of the seventh of the Romans.

John the Baptist, like some much more evangelical men, was well-nigh smothered out of life in the slough of despond. "Art thou He that should come, or do we look for another? Why dost thou eat and drink with Scribes and Pharisees, and leave me lying here in this prison-house of Herod and his harlots? Why dost thou eat and drink and make wine out of water for weddings? Rather, surely, should all God's true servants put on sackcloth and ashes and mourn apart, every family apart, and their wives apart. Art thou He that should come, or do we look for another?" Yes; this is Elias come back again. "I have been very zealous for the Lord," complained Elias in his cave in Horeb. "I only am left, and they seek my life. It is enough. Let me die, O Lord, for I am no better than my fathers." The God of all comfort be thanked for Elias, and for John, and for the slough of despond! They are all written for our rebuke, and for our learning, and for our sure consolation. Had these things not been written we would have turned away from our Bible in despair, saying: "These men are giants and saints. These are not men of like passions as we are. Why," we are often tempted to complain, "Why is God's Kingdom so long in coming? What hinders it, if indeed Christ is on His throne and has all things in His hand? Why does He not burst open my prison-house and redress my cause? Why is my sanctification so postponed? Art thou He that should come, or do we look for another?" "Go and show John again those things that ye do see, and hear. The blind receive their sight, the lame walk, the lepers are cleansed, the deaf hear, the dead are raised up, and the poor have the Gospel preached to them. And blessed is he, whosoever shall not be offended in Me. He that believeth, and hopeth against hope, and endureth to the end, he alone shall be saved."

But by far the very best thing that the Baptist ever said or did was what he said to his jealous disciples. "A man can receive nothing," he said, "except it be given him from Heaven. He that hath the bride is the bridegroom. He must increase, but I must decrease." I would rather have had the grace from God to say that than have been the greatest man ever born of woman. For he who thinks, and says, and does a thing like that is born, not of blood, nor of the will of the flesh, nor of the will of man, but of God. And yet, when I come up close to it and look it in the face, this great utterance of the Baptist is not by any means so unapproachable as I took it to be at my first sight of it. I myself could have said and done all that John said and did that day. That is to say, had I been in his exact circumstances? For what were his exact circumstances? They were these, and much more than these. John had drunk in the Sonship and the Messiahship of Jesus of Nazareth with his mother's milk. And he had been brought up all his days on that same marrow of lions. His mother Elizabeth, you may be very sure, did not die, nor did Zacharias depart in peace, till they had both told over and over again to their forerunner-son every syllable they had to tell. And thus it was that for full thirty years John did nothing else but wait for the Messiah. John thought about no one else, and spake about no one else, for all these endless years, but the Lamb of God. And thus it was that when Jesus of Nazareth came south to the Jordan to be baptized of John, the Baptist remonstrated and refused, and said: "I have need to be baptized of Thee." No, there was nothing at all so great or so good in John's self-effacing speech to his disciples. The most envious-minded man in all the world does not envy a lion, or an eagle, or an angel. A beggar does not envy a king. He only envies his neighbor-beggar whose pockets are so full of coppers and crumbs at night. "Potter envies potter." And the more theology there was in John's first great utterance, "Behold the Lamb of God," the less morality there was in his second great utterance, "He must increase, but I must decrease." No thanks to John not to be jealous of the Son of God! But had Jesus been simply a carpenter of Nazareth, and John's cousin to boot, turned suddenly such a popular preacher with all men, and with all John's baptized disciples going after him; and had John, in that case, said all this about his own decreasing, then I would down on the spot and kiss his feet.

"I was to preach in Clackmannan, where the most of the people were already for me to be their minister, but some that had the greatest power were against me, as it ordinarily fared with me in the places where I used to preach. On the Saturday afternoon there came a letter to my hand, desiring me to give the one-half of the day to another probationer, whom those who were against me had their eye upon. In these circumstances, seeing what hazard I was in of an evil eye, I committed the keeping of my heart to the Lord that I might be helped to carry evenly. He got the forenoon, for so it was desired by his friends. I was, as I expected, terribly assaulted by the tempter. When I came home from church my heart was in a manner enraged against itself on that account, and I confessed it before the Lord, abhorring myself, and appealing to God's omniscience, that I would fain have had it otherwise. As I was complaining that Satan had winnowed me, and had brought up much filthy stuff out of my heart, it came to my mind: 'But I have prayed for thee that thy faith fail not.' And then, in the evening, after service, while I sat musing over the day, I proposed this question to myself: Wouldest thou be satisfied with Christ as thy portion, though there was no hell to be saved from? And my soul answered, Yes! Supposing, further, wouldst thou be content with Christ, though likewise thou shouldest lose credit and reputation, and see other men before thee, and meet with much trouble and trial for His sake? And my soul answered, Yes! This was the last sermon I preached in Clackmannan, for I was going out of the country; and neither of us two preachers of that Sabbath was the person that God had designed for that pulpit."

He that hath the bride is the bridegroom.

74
Nicodemus

THIS, I feel sure, is not the first time that Jesus of Nazareth and Nicodemus of Jerusalem have met. The sudden and trenchant way in which our Lord receives the cautious old ruler's diplomatic certificates and civilities, and every single word of the whole subsequent conversation, all point unmistakably, as I feel sure, to some previous meeting. The meeting took place in this wise; it must have taken place in some such wise as this:

Nicodemus was one of the oldest and most honored heads of that overawing deputation which was sent out to Bethabara by the Temple authorities to examine into the Baptist's preaching, and to report to the Temple on that whole movement. "Who art thou?" Nicodemus demanded. "I am not the Christ," the Baptist answered. "Why baptizest thou then?" "I indeed baptize thee with water unto repentance, but, Behold the Lamb of God which taketh away the sin of the world, He will baptize thee, when thou comest to Him, with the Holy Ghost." And, had Nicodemus only been alone that day, there is no saying what he might not have said and done on the spot. Nicodemus was mightily impressed with all that he had seen and heard at the Jordan. But he was not free; he did not feel free and able to act as his conscience told him he ought immediately to act. He was at the head of that Temple embassy of inquisition, and he simply could not extricate himself from the duties, and the responsibilities, and the entanglements of his office. He and his colleagues had, by this time, seen and heard more than they well knew what to say to the Temple about it all. And, accordingly, glad to get away from Bethabara, they took up their carriages and set out for Jerusalem, compiling all the way home their perplexing and unsatisfactory report upon John and, especially upon Jesus of Nazareth.

The third chapter of the Fourth Gospel is in many things an absolutely classical chapter. In his third chapter the fourth Evangelist introduces us into an inquiry-room, as we would call it, in which our Lord is the director and the counsellor of souls, and in which Nicodemus is the inquirer and the convert. Nicodemus had not slept soundly one single night, nor spent one single day without remorse and fear, ever since that scene when he saw Jesus of Nazareth baptized by John, and coming up out of the water. And thus it was that he stole out of the city that night, and determined to see in secret this mysterious man. I cannot put you back into Nicodemus's state of mind as he stumbled out to Bethany in the dark that night. To you, Jesus of Nazareth is the Son of God, and your Savior, and Lord, and Master. But to Nicodemus that night Jesus of Nazareth was—Nicodemus staggered and stood still—he was afraid to let himself think Who and What Jesus of Nazareth was, and might turn out to be. "Rabbi, we know that thou art a teacher come from God." But it took the old ruler's breath away when it was answered him in such a sudden and sword-like way: "Except a man be born of water and of the Spirit he cannot enter into the Kingdom of God." To me it is a most extraordinary and impossible

366

hallucination. My whole mind and imagination and heart and conscience would have to be taken down and built up again upon an absolutely other pattern; my whole experience, observation, and study of all these divine things would have to be turned upside down before I could possibly believe in what is called "baptismal regeneration." No! there is no such thing. Believe me, whoever says it, and however long and learnedly and solemnly they have been saying it, there is no such thing. There could not be. And, certainly, there is no such materialistic, mechanical, immoral, and unspiritual doctrine and precept here. But there is in place of it a divine doctrine and a divine precept that goes at one stroke down into Nicodemus's self-deceiving heart, and cuts his self-deceiving heart open to the daylight. If our masters of Israel do not know what our Lord pointed at when he said "water" with such emphasis, Nicodemus could have told them. And had Nicodemus only been brave enough; had he only had brow enough for a good cause; had he only gone down into the waters of Jordan beside Jesus of Nazareth, we would have been counting up today Peter, and James, and John, and Nicodemus, as all apostles of Christ. And we would have had an Epistle of Nicodemus to the Pharisees, and in it such a key to this whole conversation as would have made it impossible for any man to preach regeneration by water out of it. But Nicodemus missed his great opportunity, and both he and the whole Church of Christ have been terrible losers thereby down to this disunited and distracted day. Nicodemus, ruler of Israel just because he was, he was not equal to face such a loss of reputation and of other things as would immediately have descended upon him on the day he was publicly baptized. And as he lay and tossed on his bed every night after Bethabara, he thought he had at last devised a compromise so as to get into sufficient step with this teacher come from God, or whatever else He was, and yet not needlessly break with the Temple and its honors and emoluments. But there is no deceiving of Jesus Christ. For, have we not been told just before Nicodemus knocked at Martha's door, that Jesus knew all men, and knew what was in all men? And thus it was that Nicodemus had scarcely got his lips opened to pay his prepared compliments to our Lord when he was met again with that dreadful "water," which had haunted him like an accusing spirit ever since he had not gone down into it at Bethabara. Nicodemus stood ripe and ready for his regeneration, and for his first entrance into the kingdom of heaven, and he was within one short step of its gate at the Jordan, but that step was far too strait and sore for Nicodemus to take. Nicodemus saw the pearl, and knew something of the value of it, but he could not make up his mind to sell all he possessed so as to pay the price. In our Lord's words, which He was always repeating, Nicodemus had not the strength of mind and heart to take up his cross and be born again. He was not able to be baptized—not into regeneration, there is no such baptism—but into evangelical repentance and the open loss of all things. And thus it was that our Lord, with all His affability, would not enter on any closer intimacy or confidence with Nicodemus till he had gone out to John at the Jordan. There were a thousand things that held Nicodemus back from John's baptism at his age and in his office, and our Lord saw and sympathized with every one of them. But, King of the kingdom of heaven as He was that night in Bethany, even He could not make the door of the kingdom one inch wider, or one atom easier, than it was out at Bethabara. "No!" our Lord said to Nicodemus, as he lay struggling in the net of his old heart and life all that night—"No! We do not need to talk any more about my mighty works or your new birth. You know your first duty in this whole matter as well as I can tell you. John told you, and you would not do it. And I cannot relieve you of your first duty any more than I can do it for you. And you may go away tonight, again leaving your immediate duty undone, but mark my words, till the day of your death and judgment there will be no other way to a new heart and a new life for you but to go out to the waters of Jordan and be baptized of John before all Judea and Jerusalem, and then come after Me and be My disciple." Nicodemus, that blind leader of the blind, had always taken it for granted that when the kingdom of God should come to Israel he would be taken up to sit in one of the highest seats of it. It had never once entered his snow-white head to doubt for one moment but that he would sit on a throne up at the right hand of the Messiah. Imagine, then, what a sudden blow in the face it was to Nicodemus to be told, and that by the very Messiah Himself, that he had neither part nor lot in that kingdom, and could not have, until he had been baptized in Jordan confessing his sins beside the offscourings of the city.

At the same time, Nicodemus that night was in Martha's house beside Jesus Christ, and not out at the Jordan beside John the Baptist. And Jesus Christ did not open the door and dismiss Nicodemus as John the Baptist would certainly have done. The very opposite. Our Lord, with His utmost tenderness for the ensnared and struggling old man, took patience to put all John's best preaching over again to Nicodemus, and added some of His own best preaching to it, and, all the time, in His most attractive and most winning way. John had scoffed at Nicodemus's boasted birth from Abraham; but Jesus contented Himself with simply saying that Nicodemus must be born of water and of the Spirit. John had assailed the Temple representatives as a generation of vipers; and, while Jesus did not withdraw or apologize for one single syllable of His so-outspoken forerunner, He veiled His forerunner's strong language somewhat under the sacramental and evangelical typology of the serpent in the wilderness. And, then, from that He went on to honor and to win Nicodemus with that golden passage that "Even so must the Son of Man be lifted up." And that golden passage was, I feel sure, Nicodemus's salvation that very night, as it has been the salvation of so many sinners ever since. And then, as He shook hands with Nicodemus just as the cock was crowing in Martha's garden, Jesus said to Nicodemus, with a look and with a manner that the old ruler never forgot, "But he that doeth good cometh to the light, that his deeds may be made manifest that they are wrought in God." John, our evangelist, was present all that night, and he has written this chapter also of his book so that we might believe that Jesus is the Christ, the Son of God, and that believing we might have life through His name. And this evangelist, after that ever-memorable day at Bethabara, and that equally memorable midnight and morning at Bethany, never lets Nicodemus out of his sight. And thus it is that we read this in John's seventh chapter: "Then Nicodemus said to the chief priests and to the Pharisees, Doth our law judge any man before it hear him, and know what he doeth?" And then as we read John's nineteenth chapter, we come on this. "And there came also Nicodemus, which at the first came to Jesus by night, and he brought a mixture of myrrh and aloes, about a hundred pounds weight."

"Now I saw that there would be no answer to me till I had entire purity of conscience, and no longer regarded any iniquity whatsoever in my heart. I saw that there were some secret affections still left in me, which, though they were not very bad in themselves perhaps, yet in a life of prayer, such as I was then attempting, these remanent affections certainly spoiled all." Just so. Just so in Teresa, and in Nicodemus, and in you, and in me. It was surely not so very bad in itself for Nicodemus to let himself be put at the head of that Temple embassy of inquisition upon the Baptist. It was surely not so very bad in itself for Nicodemus, once having set out, to keep true to his colleagues, even if that was done somewhat at the expense and the injury of John. It was not such a great crime, surely, for Nicodemus to yield to such strong pressure so far as to put his name to the somewhat unfriendly report that his less scrupulous colleagues wrote out for the Temple. And it could only be good, surely, and to Nicodemus's credit, that he went out to Bethany at an hour most convenient for a ruler of the Jews. And it is not so very bad surely in itself in you—everybody does it—to take up a distaste at some man or some movement that you know quite well you have absolutely nothing against. It is surely not enough to cost you in the end the loss of your soul for you to think first of your prospects in life, and how you will continue to stand with this great man and with that, according as you cast in your lot with this party in the state, or with that denomination in the church. Everybody does it. And who but John would denounce so fiercely and so contemptuously such secret affections as these are in you? But then, if John and then Jesus denounce, and despise, and deny you, what will it profit you if you gain the whole of this world? But, happily, there is a second lesson out of Nicodemus, and out of his subsequent history, and it is this: Though you have been a coward and a dark friend to truth and to duty up to this night, if God in His great goodness should give you yet another offer and opportunity, seize it on the spot. Jesus Christ is still among His enemies in many ways. Recognize and acknowledge Jesus Christ, and stand up for Him in your Sanhedrim like Nicodemus. Do you know Him? ask them. Have you ever gone to where He lodges and seen and heard Him for yourselves? Have you read the book you speak against? ask them. Do you love the writer, and do you wish him well? ask them. Do you rejoice in an evil report? demand boldly of them. Or do you rejoice, to your own loss, in the truth? The whole Seventy will turn on you, and will rend you. But what of that? For unless you are rent here for His name's sake, the Son of Man will be ashamed of you when He is suddenly revealed and suddenly descends on you in all His glory.

But for Nicodemus, and another timid friend to truth, the dead body of our Lord might have been taken out of the city and cast into the flames of Tophet, that type of Hell, along with the carcases of the two thieves. All the disciples had forsaken their crucified Master and had fled. But Joseph of Arimathaea and Nicodemus went boldly to Pilate and besought him to let them bury the dead body that all other men hid their faces from that day. And Joseph and Nicodemus took the body of Jesus and wound it in linen clothes with the spices, as the manner of the Jews is to bury their dead. It was the same Joseph of Arimathaea who had been a disciple of Jesus, but secretly for fear of the Jews; and it was the same Nicodemus, which at the first came to Jesus by night.

75

Peter

THE Four Gospels are full of Peter. After the name of our Lord Himself, no name comes up so often in the Four Gospels as Peter's name. No disciple speaks so often and so much as Peter. Our Lord speaks oftener to Peter than to any other of His disciples; sometimes in blame and sometimes in praise. No disciple is so pointedly reproved by our Lord as Peter, and no disciple ever ventures to reprove his Master but Peter. No other disciple ever so boldly confessed and outspokenly acknowledged and encouraged our Lord as Peter repeatedly did; and no one ever intruded, and interfered, and tempted Him as Peter repeatedly did also. His Master spoke words of approval, and praise, and even blessing to Peter the like of which He never spoke to any other man. And at the same time, and almost in the same breath, He said harder things to Peter than He ever said to any other of His twelve disciples, unless it was to Judas.

No disciple speaks so often as Peter. "Depart from me, for I am a sinful man, O Lord. Lo, we have left all and followed Thee; what shall we have therefore? Be it far from Thee, Lord; this shall never be to Thee. Lord, if it be Thou, bid me come unto Thee on the water. Lord, save me. The crowd press Thee, and how sayest Thou, Who touched me? Thou art the Christ, the Son of the living God. To whom can we go but unto Thee? Thou hast the words of eternal life. Lord, it is good for us to be here; let us make three tabernacles: one for Thee, and one for Moses, and one for Elias. How oft shall my brother sin against me, and I forgive him? Though all men deny Thee, yet will not I. Thou shalt never wash my feet. Lord, not my feet only, but also my hands and my head. I know not the man. Lord, Thou knowest all things: thou knowest that I love Thee." And, to crown all his impertinent and indecent speeches, "Not so, Lord, for I have never eaten anything that is common or unclean." And then, in that charity which shall cover the multitude of sins, "Forasmuch then as God gave them the like gift as he did unto us; what was I that I could withstand God?" These are Peter's unmistakable footprints. Hasty, headlong, speaking impertinently and unadvisedly, ready to repent, ever wading into waters too deep for him, and ever turning to his Master again like a little child. Peter was grieved because He said unto him the third time, Lovest thou me? And he said unto Him, Lord, thou knowest all things: Thou knowest that I love Thee.

The evangelical Churches of Christendom have no duty and no interest to dispute with the Church of Rome either as to Peter's primacy among the twelve disciples, or as to his visits to Rome, or as to his death by martyrdom in that city. If the Church of Rome is satisfied about the historical truth of Peter's missionary work in the west, we are satisfied. All that can be truthfully told us about Peter we shall welcome. We cannot be told too much about Peter. And as to his primacy that Rome makes so much of, we cannot read our New Testament without coming on proofs on every page that Peter held a foremost place among the twelve disciples.

In that also we agree with our friends. Four times the list of elected men is given in the Gospels; and, while the order of the twelve names varies in all other respects, Peter's name is invariably the first in all the lists, as Judas's name is as invariably the last. The difference is this: The New Testament recognizes a certain precedency in Peter, whereas the Church of Rome claims for him an absolute supremacy. The truth is this. The precedency and the supremacy that Peter holds in the Four Gospels was not so much appointed him by his Master; what supremacy he held was conferred upon him by nature herself. Peter was born a supreme man. Nature herself, as we call her, had, with her ever-bountiful and original hands, stamped his supremacy upon Peter before he was born. And when he came to be a disciple of Jesus Christ he entered on, and continued to hold, that natural and aboriginal supremacy over all inferior men, till a still more superior and supreme man arose and took Peter's supremacy away from him. We all have the same supremacy that Peter had when we are placed alongside of men who are less gifted in intellect, and in will, and in character, than we are gifted. Peter's gifts of mind, and force of character, and warmth of heart, and generosity of utterance—all these things gave Peter the foremost place in the Apostolic Church till Paul arose. But Peter, remarkable and outstanding man as he was, had neither the natural ability nor the educational advantages of Saul of Tarsus. His mind was neither so deep nor so strong nor so many-sided nor at all so fine and so fruitful as was Paul's incomparable mind. And as a consequence he was never able to come within sight of the work that Paul alone could do. But, at the same time, and till Paul arose and all but totally eclipsed all the disciples who had been in Christ before him, Peter stood at the head of the apostolate, and so leaves a deeper footprint on the pages of the Four Gospels at any rate, than any of the other eleven disciples.

John was intuitive, meditative, mystical. Philip was phlegmatic, perhaps. Thomas would appear to have been melancholy and morose. While Peter was sanguine and enthusiastic and extreme both for good and for evil, beyond them all. Peter was naturally and constitutionally of the enthusiastic temperament, and his conversion and call to the discipleship did not decompose or at all suppress his true nature; the primal elements of his character remained, and the original balance and the proportion of those elements remained. The son of Jonas was, to begin with, a man of the strongest, the most willful, and the most wayward impulses; impulses that, but for the watchfulness and the prayerfulness of his Master, might easily have become the most headlong and destructive passions. "Christ gives him a little touch," says Thomas Goodwin, "of some wildness and youthfulness that had been in Peter's spirit before Christ had to do with him. When thou wast young thou girdedst thyself and walkedst whither thou wouldest. But when thou art old, thou shalt stretch forth thy hands, and another shall gird thee, and carry thee whither thou wouldest not. Peter had had his vagaries, and had lived as he liked, and, Peter, says Christ to him, when thou art hung up by the heels upon a cross, there to be bound to thy good behavior, see that thou, remembering what thou wast when young, show them thy valor and thy resolution when thou comest to that conflict; and Peter remembered it, and was moved by it.—2 Peter i. 14." Such, then, was Peter's so perilous temperament, which he had inherited from his father

Jonas. But by degrees, and under the teaching, the example, and the training of his Master, Peter's too-hot heart was gradually brought under control till it became the seat in Peter's bosom of a deep, pure, deathless love and adoration for Jesus Christ. Amid all Peter's stumbles and falls this always brought him right again and set him on his feet again—his absolutely enthusiastic love and adoration for his Master. This, indeed, after his Master's singular grace to Peter, was always the redeeming and restraining principle in Peter's wayward and willful life. To the very end of his three years with his Master, Peter was full of a most immature character and an unreduced and unbridled mind and heart. He had the making of a very noble man in him, but he was not easily made, and his making cost both him and his Master dear. At the same time, blame Peter as much as you like; dwell upon the faults of his temperament, and the defects of his character, and the scandals of his conduct, as much as you like; I defy you to deny that, with it all, he was not a very attractive and a very lovable man. "The worst disease of the human heart is cold." Well, with all his faults, and he was full of them, a cold heart was not one of them. All Peter's faults, indeed, lay in the heat of his heart. He was too hot-hearted, too impulsive, too enthusiastic. His hot heart was always in his mouth, and he spoke it all out many a time when he should have held his peace. So many faults had Peter, and so patent and on the surface did they lie, that you might very easily take a too hasty and a too superficial estimate of Peter's real depth and strength and value. And if Peter was for too long like the sand rather than like the rock his Master had so nobly named him, the sand will one day settle into rock, and into rock of a quality and a quantity to build a temple with. If Peter is now too forward to speak, he will in the end be as forward to suffer. The time will come when Peter will act up to all his outspoken ardors and high enthusiasms. In so early designating the son of Jonas a rock, his Master was but antedating some of Simon's coming and most characteristic graces. His Divine Master saw in Simon latent qualities of courage, and fidelity, and endurance, and evangelical humility that never as yet had fully unfolded themselves amid the untoward influences round about his life. In any case, an absolute master may surely name his own servant by any name that pleases him; especially a Royal Master; for the Sovereign in every kingdom is the true fountain of honor. Whatever, then, may be the true and full explanation, suffice it to us to know that our Lord thus saluted Simon, and said to him, Simon, son of Jonas, thou shalt be called Cephas, which is, by interpretation, a rock.

Of the four outstanding temperaments then, Peter's temperament was of the ardent and enthusiastic order. And, indeed, a deep-springing, strong-flowing, divinely-purified, and divinely-directed enthusiasm is always the best temperament for the foundation and the support of the truly prophetic, apostolic, and evangelic character. For what is enthusiasm? What is it but the heart, and the imagination, and the whole man, body and soul, set on fire? And the election, the call, the experience, and the promised reward of the true prophet, apostle, and evangelist, are surely enough to set on fire and keep on fire a heart of stone. It was one of the prophetic notes of the coming Messiah's own temperament that the zeal of God's house would eat Him up. And there is no surer sign that the same mind that was found in Jesus Christ is taking possession of one of His disciples than that he more and more manifests a keen, kindling, enthusiastic temper toward whatsoever persons and causes are honest, and just, and pure, and lovely, and of good report; just as there is nothing more unlike the mind and heart of Jesus Christ than the mind and heart of a man who cares for none of these things. Let us take Peter, come to perfection, for our pattern and our prelate; and, especially, let us watch, and work, and pray against a cold heart, a chilling temper, a distant, selfish, indifferent mind.

Closely connected with Peter's peculiar temperament, and, indeed, a kind of compensation for being so possessed by it, was his exquisite sense of sin. We see Peter's singular sensitiveness and tenderness of spirit in this respect coming out in a most impressive and memorable way on the occasion of his call to the discipleship. Andrew was not an impenitent man. John was not a hard-hearted man. But though they both saw and shared in the miraculous draught of fishes on the sea of Galilee, Peter alone remembered his sins, and broke down under them, in the presence of the power and grace of Christ. "Depart from me, O Lord, for I am a sinful man." "No; fear not," said his Master to Peter, "for from henceforth thou shalt so catch men." Peter's prostrating penitence at such a moment marked Peter out as the true captain of that fishing fleet that was so soon to set sail under the colors of the Cross to catch the souls of men for salvation. That sudden and complete prostration before Christ at that moment seated Peter in a supremacy and in a prelacy that has never been taken from him. And there is no surer sign of an evangelically penitent and a truly spiritual man than this—that his prosperity in life always calls back to him his past sins and his abiding ill-desert. He is not a novice in the spiritual life to whom prosperity is as much a means of grace as adversity. They are wise merchantmen who make gain in every gale; who are enriched in their souls not only in times of trial and loss, but are still more softened and sanctified amid all their gains and all their comforts both of outward and inward estate. Well may those mariners praise the Lord for His goodness whose ships come home sinking with the merchandise they have made in the deep waters. But still more when, with all their prosperity, they have the broken heart to say, He hath not dealt with us after our sins, nor rewarded us according to our iniquities.

It was Peter's deep and rich temperament, all but completely sanctified, that made Peter so forgetful of himself as a preacher, and so superior to all men's judgments, and so happy, to use his own noble words, to be reproached for the name of Christ. Can you imagine, have you come through any experience that enables you to imagine, what Peter's thoughts would be as he mounted the pulpit stairs to preach Judas's funeral sermon? Judas had betrayed his Master. Yes. But Peter himself; Peter the preacher; had denied his Master with oaths and curses. And yet, there is Peter in the pulpit, while Judas lies a cast-out suicide in Aceldama! "O the depths of the Divine mercy to me! That I who sinned with Judas; that I who had made my bed in hell beside Judas; should be held in this honor, and should be ministering to the holy brethren! O to grace how great a debtor!" And again, just think what all must have been in Peter's mind as he stood up in Solomon's porch to preach the Pentecost sermon. That terrible sermon in which he charged the rulers and the people of Jerusalem with the dreadful crime of denying the Holy One and the Just in the presence of Pilate. While he, the preacher, had done the very same thing before a few serving men and serving women. You may be sure that it was as much to himself as to the murderers of the Prince of Life that Peter went on that day to preach and say, "Repent, therefore, that your sins may be blotted out; since God hath sent His Son to bless you, in turning away every one of you from his iniquities." The truth is, by this time, the unspeakably awful sinfulness of Peter's own sin had completely drunk up all the human shame of it. If they who know about Peter's sin choose to reproach him for it, let them do it. It is now a small matter to Peter to be judged of men's judgment. They sang David's Psalms in Solomon's porch; and that day Peter and the penitent people must surely have sung and said, "Wash me thoroughly from mine iniquity, and cleanse me from my sin. For I acknowledge my transgression, and my sin is ever before me. Restore to me the joy of thy salvation, and uphold me with thy free spirit. Then will I teach transgressors thy ways, and sinners shall be converted unto thee." And if preachers pronounced benedictions after their sermons in those days, then we surely have Peter's Solomon's-porch benediction preserved to us in these apostolic words of his: "Ye therefore, beloved, seeing ye know all these things, beware lest ye also fall from your steadfastness. But grow in grace, and in the knowledge of our Lord and Savior Jesus Christ, to whom be glory both now and for ever. Amen."

76
John

JOHN, fisherman's son and all, was born with one of the finest minds that have ever been bestowed by God's goodness upon any of the sons of men. We sometimes call John the Christian Plato. Now when we say that our meaning is that John had by nature an extraordinarily rich and deep and lofty and beautiful mind. John had a profoundly intuitive mind. An inward, meditating, brooding, imaginative, mystical, spiritual mind. Plato had all that, even more perhaps than John. But, then, Plato had not John's privileges and opportunities. Plato had not been brought up on the Old Testament, and he had only had Socrates for his master. And thus it is that he has only been able to leave to us the *Symposium*, and the *Apology*, and the *Phaedo*. Whereas John has left to us his Gospel, and his Epistles, and his Apocalypse. John has the immortal honor of having conceived and meditated and indited the most magnificent passage that has ever been written with pen and ink. The first fourteen verses of John's Gospel stand alone and supreme over all other literature, sacred and profane. THE WORD WAS GOD, AND THE WORD WAS MADE FLESH. These two sentences out of John contain far more philosophy; far more grace, and truth, and beauty, and love; than all the rest that has ever been written by pen of man, or spoken by tongue of man or angel. Philo also has whole volumes about the Logos. But the Logos in Philo, in Newman's words, is but a "notion": a noble notion, indeed, but still a cold, a bare, and an inoperative notion. Whereas the WORD of John is a Divine Person; and, moreover, a Divine Person in human nature: a revelation, an experience, and a possession, of which John himself is the living witness and the infallible proof. I have heard of him by the hearing of the ear, said Philo. But mine eyes have seen and mine hands have handled the Word of Life, declares John. And, with the WORD MADE FLESH, and set before such eyes as John's eyes were, no wonder that we have such books from his hands as the Fourth Gospel, the First Epistle, and the Apocalypse.

How did John sink so deep into the unsearchable things of his Master, while all the other disciples stood all their discipleship days on the surface? What was it in John that lifted him so high above Peter, and Thomas, and Philip, and made him first such a disciple, and then such an apostle, of wisdom and of love? For one thing it was his gift and grace of meditation. John listened as none of them listened to all that his Master said, both in conversation, and in debate, and in discourse. John thought and thought continually on what he saw and heard. The seed fell into good ground. John was one of those happy men, and a prince among them, who have a deep root in themselves. And the good seed sprung up in him an hundredfold. The first Psalm was all fulfilled in John. For he meditated day and night on his Master, and on his Master's words, till he was like David's tree that was planted by the rivers of water so that its leaf never withered, nor was its fruit ever wanting in its season. Meditate on Divine things, my brethren. Be men of mind, and be sure you be men of meditation. Mind is the highest thing, and meditation is the highest use of mind; it is the true root, and sap, and fatness of all faith and prayer and spiritual obedience. Why are our minds so blighted and so barren in the things of God? Why have we so little faith? Why have we so little hold of the reality and nobility of Divine things? The reason is plain—we seldom or never meditate. We read our New Testament, on occasion, and we hear it read, but we do not take time to meditate. We pray sometimes, or we pretend to pray; but do we ever set ourselves to prepare our hearts for the mercy-seat by strenuous meditation on who and what we are; on who and what He is to whom we pretend to pray; and on what it is we are to say, and do, and ask, and receive? We may never have heard of Philo, but we all belong to his barren school. The Lord Jesus Christ is but a name and a notion to us; a sacred name and notion, it may be, but still only a name and a notion. The thought of Jesus Christ seldom or never quickens, or overawes, or gladdens our heart. Whereas, when we once become men of meditation, Jesus Christ, and the whole New Testament concerning Him, and the whole New Jerusalem where He is preparing a place for us, will become more to us than our nearest friend: more to us than this city with all its most pressing affairs. Our conventional morning chapter about what Jesus Christ did and said, and is at this moment doing and saying, will then be far more real to us than all our morning papers and all our business letters. Nor is this the peculiar opportunity and privilege of men of learning only. John was not a man of learning. John was described as an ignorant and an unlearned man, though all the time he was carrying about in his mind the whole of the Fourth Gospel. My brethren, meditate on John's Gospel. Meditate on that which was not made without long, and deep, and divinely-assisted meditation. You may be the most unlearned man in this learned city tonight, and yet such is John's Gospel, and such is the power and the blessedness of meditation on it, that John will look down on you after your house is asleep tonight, and will say over you, as you now sit, and now stand, and now kneel with his Gospel in your hands—"That which we have seen and heard declare we unto you, that you may have fellowship with us; and truly our fellowship is with the Father and with His Son Jesus Christ."

Meditation with imagination. All that John writes is touched and informed and exalted with this divinest of all the talents. The Apocalypse, with all its splendors, was in God's mind toward us when He said, Let us make Zebedee's son, and let us make him full of eyes within. Do not be afraid at the word "imagination," my brethren. It has been sadly ill-used, both name and thing. But it is a noble name and a noble thing. There is nothing so noble in all that is within us. Our outward eye is the noblest of all our outward organs, and our inward eye is the noblest of all our inward organs. And its noblest use is to be filled full of Jesus Christ, as John's inward eye was. John did not write his Apocalypse without that great gift in its fullest exercise. And we cannot read aright what he has written without that same exercise. We cannot pray aright without it. We cannot have either faith or love aright without it. And just in the measure we have imagination, and know how to use it, we shall have one of the noblest instruments in our own hand for the enriching and perfecting of our whole intellectual and spiritual life. I do not say that the Book of Revelation is the noblest product of John's noble imagination. For, all that was within John, imagination and meditation and love, was all moved of the Holy Ghost up to its highest and its best in the production of the great Prologue to the Fourth Gospel. At the same time, it is in the Revelation that John's glorified imagination spreads out its most golden wings and waves them in the light of heaven. Only it will take both meditation and imagination to see that. But to see that will be one of our best lessons from this greatly-gifted and greatly-blessed apostle tonight.

And, then, as was sure to come to pass, the disciple of meditation and imagination becomes at last the apostle of love. At the Last Supper, and as soon as Judas had gone out, Jesus said to the eleven, "A new commandment I give unto you, that ye love one another. As I have loved you, that ye also love one another. By this shall all men know that ye are my disciples, if ye have love one to another." Eleven thoughtful and loving hearts heard that new commandment and the comfort that accompanied it. But in no other heart did that Divine seed fall into such good ground as in his heart who at that moment lay on Jesus' bosom. "Little children, love one another," was the aged apostle's whole benediction as the young men carried him into the church of Ephesus every Lord's Day. And when he was asked why he always said that, and never said any more than that, he always replied, "Because this is our Lord's sole commandment, and if we all fulfill this, nothing more is needed. For love is the fulfilling of the law."

77
Matthew

MATTHEW loved money. Matthew, like Judas, must have money. With clean hands if he could; but, clean hands or unclean, Matthew must have money. Now, the surest way and the shortest way for Matthew to make money in the Galilee of that day was to take sides with Caesar and to become one of Caesar's tax-gatherers. This, to be sure, would be for Matthew to sell himself to the service of the oppressors of his people; but Matthew made up his mind and determined to do it. Matthew will set his face like a flint for a few years and then he will retire from his toll-booth to spend his rich old age in peace and quietness. He will furnish a country-house for himself up among the hills of Galilee, and he will devote his last days to deeds of devotion and charity. And thus it was that Matthew, a son of Abraham, was found in the unpatriotic and ostracized position of a publican in Capernaum. The publicans were hard-hearted, extortionate, and utterly demoralized men. Their peculiar employment either already found them all that, or else it soon made them all that. "Publicans and sinners"; "publicans and harlots"—we continually come on language like that in the pages of the four Gospels. Well, Matthew had now for a long time been a publican in Capernaum, and he was fast becoming a rich man. But, over against that, he had to content himself with a publican's companionships, and with a publican's inevitable evil conscience. Matthew could not help grinding the faces of the poor. He could not help squeezing the last drop of blood out of this and that helpless debtor. His business would not let Matthew stop to think who was a widow, and who was an orphan, and who was being cruelly treated. The debt was due, it was too long overdue, and it must be paid, if both the debtor and his children have to be sold in the slave-market to pay the debt.

Jesus of Nazareth, the carpenter's son, knew Matthew the publican quite well. Perhaps, only too well. Jesus and His mother had by this time migrated from Nazareth to Capernaum. He had often been in Matthew's toll-booth with His mother's taxes, and with other poor people's taxes. Even if not for Himself and for his widowed mother, the carpenter would often leave His bench to go to Matthew's toll-booth to expostulate with him, and to negotiate with him, and to become surety to him for this and that poor neighbor of His who had fallen into sickness, and into a debt that he was not able to pay. The sweat of Jesus' own brow had oftener than once gone to settle Matthew's extortionate charges. "If he hath wronged thee, or oweth thee aught, put that to mine account. I, Jesus, the son of Joseph, have written it with mine own hand, I will repay it"—that would stand in Matthew's books over and over again, till Matthew was almost ready to sell the surety Himself. But by this time Jesus, first of Nazareth and now of Capernaum, who had been every poor widow's cautioner for her rent and for her taxes, had left His father's inherited workshop, and had been baptized by John into a still larger

378

Suretyship. And thus it is that He is back again in Capernaum, no longer a hard-working carpenter, mortgaging all His week's wages and more for all His poor neighbors. But he is now the Messiah Himself! And Matthew in his toll-booth has a thousand thoughts about all that, till he cannot get his columns to come right all he can count. And till one day, just as He was passing Matthew's well-worn doorstep, a widow woman of the city, with her child in her arms, rushed up against our Lord, and exclaimed to Him: "Avenge me of mine adversary!" till she could not tell Him her heart-breaking tale for sobs and tears. And then, with that never-to-be-forgotten look and accent of mingled anger and mercy, our Lord went immediately into the publican's office and said to him: "Matthew, thou must leave all this life of thine and come and follow Me." Matthew had always tried to stand well out of eyeshot of our Lord when He was preaching. He felt sure that the Preacher was not well disposed toward him, and his conscience would continually say to his face, How could He be? But at that so commanding gesture, and at those so commanding words, the chains of a lifetime of cruelty and extortion fell on the floor of the receipt of custom; till, scarcely taking time to clasp up his books and to lock up his presses, Matthew the publican of Capernaum rose up and followed our Lord.

Matthew does not say so himself, but Luke is careful to tell us that Matthew made a great feast that very night, and gathered into it a supper-party of his former friends and acquaintances that they might see with their own eyes the Master that he is henceforth to confess, and to follow, and to obey. What a sight to our eyes, far more than to theirs, is Matthew's supper-table tonight! There sits the publican himself at the head of the table, and the erewhile carpenter of Capernaum in the seat of honor beside him. And then the whole house is full of what we may quite correctly describe as a company of social and religious outcasts. An outcast with us usually means some one who has impoverished, and demoralized, and debauched himself with indolence and with vice till he is both penniless in purse and reprobate in character. We have few, if any, rich outcasts in our city and society. But the outcast publicans of that night were well-to-do, if not absolutely wealthy men. They were men who had made themselves rich, and had at the same time made themselves outcasts, by siding with the oppressors of their people and by exacting of the people more than was their due. And they were, as a consequence, excommunicated from the Church, and ostracized from all patriotic and social and family life. What, then, must the more thoughtful of them have felt as they entered Matthew's supper-room that night and sat down at the same table with a very prophet, and some said—Matthew himself had said it in his letter of invitation—more than a prophet. And, then, all through the supper, if He was a prophet He was so unlike a prophet; and, especially, so unlike the last of the prophets. He was so affable, so humble, so kind, so gentle, with absolutely nothing at all in His words or in His manner to upbraid any of them, or in any way to make any of them in anything uneasy. They had all supped with Matthew before, but that was the first night for many years that any man with any good name to lose had broken bread at the publican's table. He had given suppers on occasion before, but Jesus had never been invited, nor Peter, nor James, nor John. And it was the presence of Jesus and His disciples that night that led to the scene which so shines on this page of the New Testament. For there were Pharisees in Capernaum in those days, just as there were publicans and sinners. And just as the publicans were ever on the outlook for more money; and just as the sinners were ever on the outlook for another supper and another dance; so the Pharisees were ever on the outlook for a fresh scandal, and for something to find fault with in their neighbors. "Why eateth your Master with publicans and sinners?" the Pharisees of Capernaum demanded of Jesus' disciples. And the disciples were still too much Pharisees themselves to be able to give a very easy answer to that question. But Jesus had his answer ready. Grace was poured into His lips at that opportune moment till He replied: "They that be whole need not a physician, but they that are sick. I came not to call the righteous, but sinners to repentance." Long years afterwards, when Matthew was writing this autobiographic passage in his Gospel, the whole scene of that supper-party rose up before him like yesternight. "Jesus, now in glory," he said to himself, "was sitting here, as it were. James and John there. Myself at the door, divided between welcoming my old companions and warning them off. Some Pharisees from the synagogue are coming up with their lamps. Then their loud and angry voices; and then His voice with more pity in it than anger, calling sinners to repentance." It was a night to be remembered by Matthew.

When Matthew rose up and left all and followed our Lord, the only thing he took with him out of his old occupation was his pen and ink. And it is well for us that he did take that pen and ink with him, since he took it with him to such good purpose. For, never once did our Lord sit down on a mountain side or on a sea-shore to teach His disciples; never once did He enter a synagogue and take up the Prophets or the Psalmists to preach; never once did He talk at any length by the way, that Matthew was not instantly at His side. Till Matthew came to be known not so much as Matthew the disciple, or as the former publican of Capernaum, but rather as that silent man with the sleepless pen and ink-horn. It needed a practiced, and an assiduous, and an understanding pen to take down the Sermon on the Mount, and to report and arrange the parables, and to seize with such correctness and with such insight the terrible sermons of his Master's last week of preaching. But Matthew did all that, and we have all that to this day in his Gospel. The bag would have been safe, and it would have been kept well filled, in Matthew's money-managing hands, but Matthew had far more important matters than the most sacred money matters to attend to. What a service, above all price, were Matthew's hands ordained to do as soon as his hands were washed from sin and uncleanness in the Fountain opened in that day! What a service it was to build that golden bridge by which so many of his kinsmen according to the flesh at once passed over into the better covenant, the Surety of which covenant is Christ! "The Gospel according to St. Matthew: the Book of the generation of Jesus Christ, the son of David, the son of Abraham." "Saintliness not forfeited by the penitent," is the title of one of our finest English sermons, and, it may here be added, neither is service.

"And Matthew the *publican*." Now, we would never have known that but for Matthew himself. Neither Mark, nor Luke, nor John, nor Paul ever calls Matthew by that bad name. It is Matthew himself alone who in as many words says to us, "Come, all ye that fear God, and I will tell what He has done for my soul." It is Matthew himself alone who publishes and perpetuates to all time his own infamy. Ashamed of himself, both as a publican and an apostle, till he cannot look up, the text is the only footprint of himself that St. Matthew leaves behind him on the sands of Scripture. Our first Gospel is his holy workmanship, and this text, so deeply embedded into it, is the sure seal of its author's Christian temper and Apostolic character. "Position and epithet are indicative both of natural humility and modesty, as well as of evangelical self-abasement."

"They that be whole need not a physician, but they that are sick." Happy intrusion, and fortunate fault-finding of the Pharisees which ended in these ever-blessed words of our Savior! And then, these words also: "I am not come to call the righteous, but sinners to repentance." Sick and sinful men, do you hear that? Are you truly and sincerely sick with sin? Then He who has made you sick will keep you sick till you come to Him to heal you. Are you a sinner with an evil life holding you like a chain in a cruel, an unclean, a hopeless bondage? Then—

> He comes! the prisoners to relieve,
>   In Satan's bondage held;
> The gates of brass before Him burst,
>   The iron fetters yield.
>
> He comes! from darkening scales of vice
>   To clear the inward sight;
> And on the eyeballs of the blind
>   To pour celestial light.
>
> He comes! the broken hearts to bind,
>   The bleeding souls to cure:
> And with the treasures of His grace
>   T' enrich the humble poor.

Are you that prisoner? Are you held in Satan's bondage? Is your inward sight clogged up with the scales of vice? Is your heart broken? And is your very soul within you bleeding? Are you a publican? Are you a sinner? Are you a harlot? Look at Matthew with his Gospel in his hand! Look at Zacchaeus restoring fourfold! Look at Mary Magdalene, first at the sepulchre. Look unto Me, their Savior says to thee also: Look unto Me, and be thou saved also. And so I will!

> Thy promise is my only plea,
>   With this I venture nigh:
> Thou callest burden'd souls to Thee,
>   And such, O Lord, am I.

78
Zacchaeus

THERE was a soft spot still left in Zacchaeus's heart, and that soft spot was this: Zacchaeus was as eager as any schoolboy in all Jericho to see Jesus who He was. And like any schoolboy he ran before and climbed up into a sycamore tree to see Jesus, for He was to pass that way. And simple things like that, childlike and schoolboy-like things like that, always touched our Lord's heart. Of such is the kingdom of Heaven, He was wont to say when He saw simplicity like that, and self-forgetfulness, and naturalness, and impulsiveness, or anything else that was truly childlike. We would not have done what Zacchaeus did. We are too stiff. We are too formal. We have too much starch in our souls. Our souls are made of starch, just as Bishop Andrewes's soul was made of sin. But starch is more deadly than sin. Your soul may be saved from sin, but scarcely from starch. "Curiosity and simplicity," says Calvin, "are a sort of preparation for faith. Nay, it was not without a certain inspiration from heaven that Zacchaeus climbed up into that sycamore tree. There was a certain seed of true piety in his heart when he so ran before the press, and so climbed up into that sycamore tree," so says on this subject the greatest of all the commentators upon it.

Had our Lord considered public opinion He would have looked straight before Him when He came to that sycamore tree, and would not have let His eyes lift till He was well past Zacchaeus's perch. But our Lord was as simple and as natural and as spontaneous that day as Zacchaeus was himself. Our Lord paid no attention to the prejudices or to the ill-will of the populace. The more ground there was for their prejudices and their ill-will the more reason there was to Him why He should stop under Zacchaeus's tree and call him to come down. The windows and the walls and the roofs of Jericho were all loaded with sightseers that day, but our Lord did not stop under any of them. It was at Zacchaeus's sycamore tree alone that our Lord stopped and looked up and said: "Zacchaeus, make haste and come down, for today I must abide at thy house." All Zacchaeus's past life, all his real blamefulness, all the people's just and unjust prejudices, and all the bad odor of Zacchaeus's class, it all did not for one moment turn our Lord away from Zacchaeus's house. Had our Lord asked Himself—What will the people think and say, He would not have imperilled His popularity in Jericho by sitting at the tax-gatherer's table. But one of our Lord's absolute rules of life and conduct was to make Himself at all times and in all places of no reputation. And thus it was that the thought of how Jericho would take it never for one moment entered our Lord's mind. Not for years had any man who wished to stand well with the people so much as crossed Zacchaeus's threshold. Zacchaeus, with all his riches, was a very lonely man. He was a well-hated and a universally-avoided man. And thus it was that our Lord's conduct that day towards him completely overcame Zacchaeus. He could not believe his own eyes and ears. That this great Prophet, whose

382

face he had been so breathless to see, should actually stop and call his name, and invite Himself to his house, and that He should actually be walking with him back to his house! Zaccheus was well-nigh beside himself with amazement and with delight. That halt under the sycamore tree, that summons of our Lord, that walk back together through the astonished and angry streets, and then the supper and the conversation over it and after it—all that entered into and at last completed Zaccheus's salvation. Are you a minister, or an elder, or a missionary, or a district visitor? Then, sometimes, invite yourself to the hospitality of the poor, and the outcast, and the sunken, and the forlorn. Knock civilly at their door. Ask the favor of a chair and a cup of cold water. Join them in their last crust. And see if salvation does not from that day begin to come to that house also.

I cannot get it out of my mind the deep share that Matthew the publican must have had in the conversion of Zaccheus. You remember all about Matthew. How he was sitting in his toll-booth one day when Jesus came up to him and said: "Follow me." And how Matthew left all and followed Him. And how Matthew made Him a great feast, and how the scribes and Pharisees found fault, and said to the disciples, Why do ye eat and drink with publicans and sinners? And especially, you can never forget our Lord's golden answer: "They that are whole need not a physician, but they that are sick." Well, do you not think that Matthew must have had an intense interest in Zaccheus that night? Even if the eleven supped and lodged elsewhere in the city that night, our Lord would be sure to take Matthew with Him in order to encourage and to advise Zaccheus. When two members of any craft come together you know how they draw to one another and forget the presence of all the rest, there is such a freemasonry and brotherhood between them. They have so many stories to tell, experiences to compare, confessions to make, and confidences to share, that those who are not of the same occupation know nothing about. It is now going on to three years that Matthew has been a disciple, but it is like yesterday to him to look back to his receipt of custom. And when Jesus suddenly stopped under the sycamore tree that day and said, Zaccheus, come down, and when Zaccheus dropped that moment at our Lord's feet, no one's heart in all the crowd went out to the trembling little tax-gatherer like Matthew's heart. And all that night the two publicans had scarcely broken ground on all they had to tell one another. "If He calls you to leave all and follow Him, you must do it at once. You will never repent it. You have no idea of Him. What a man He is, and what a master; and, how it is all to end, God only knows. But if He invites you to join us, I beseech you not to hesitate for one moment." "Tell me all about yourself," said Zaccheus. "What did He say to you? And how did you manage to cut off, and leave for ever behind you, the work and the wealth of your whole life so soon and so completely?" And Matthew told Zaccheus all we know, and far more that we need not listen to, for we would not understand it. Till, what Zaccheus stood forth and said next morning before our Lord, and before all Jericho, was fully as much at Matthew's instance and dictation as at Zaccheus's own repentance and resolution. "Behold, Lord, I have made up my mind overnight, and I wish you and all men to know it—the half of my goods I give to the poor; and if I have taken anything from any man by false accusation, I restore him fourfold." Brave little gentleman! By that noble speech of thine thou hast added more than many cubits to thy stature! Thy bodily presence, say they, is weak, and thy height contemptible; but all thine after life will be weighty and powerful!

"It is a determined rule in divinity," says a great divine, "that our sins can never be pardoned till we have restored that which we unjustly took away, or which we wrongfully detain. And this doctrine, besides its evident and apparent reasonableness, is derived from the express words of Scripture, which reckons restitution to be a part of repentance, and necessary to the remission of sins. For these are the determined words of Scripture—If the wicked restore the pledge, and give again that he hath robbed, and walk in the statutes of life, without committing inquity, he shall surely live; he shall not die. None of his sins that he hath committed shall be mentioned unto him; he hath done that which is lawful and right, he shall surely live."

79

Lazarus

LAZARUS of Bethany comes as near to Jesus of Nazareth, both in his character, and in his services, and in his unparalleled experiences, as mortal man can ever come. Lazarus's name is never to be read in the New Testament till the appointed time comes when he is to fall sick, and to die, and to be raised from the dead, for the glory of God. Nor is his voice ever heard. Lazarus loved silence. He sought obscurity. He liked to be overlooked. He revelled in neglect. You could have taken any liberty you pleased with Lazarus with the most perfect impunity. Our Lord and His twelve disciples often found where to lay their head in Martha's house, as it was called. But where Lazarus laid his head at such times no one ever asked. The very evangelists pass over Lazarus as if he were a worm and no man. They do not give him the place of a man in his own house. But Lazarus never takes offence at that. "He is a sheep," said the men and the women of Bethany. And so he was. For, when Jesus of Nazareth and His twelve disciples came to Martha's house, Lazarus hewed wood, fetched water, and washed the feet of the whole discipleship; and then, when they were all asleep, "though he was the staff and sustentation of the family," he supped out of sight on the fragments that remained. All Bethany was quite right, Lazarus was a perfect sheep. They laughed him to scorn, they shot out the lip at him, and he never saw it. At any rate, he never returned it. Let Martha sweat and scold; let Mary sit still and listen; and let Lazarus only be of some use to them, that he would never believe he was, and that was Lazarus's meat and drink. So much so, that the world would never have heard so much as Lazarus's name unless the glory of God had been bound up with Lazarus's sickness, and death, and resurrection.

Our Lord had this happiness, that He loved all men whether they loved Him or no. But there were some men that He loved with a quite special and peculiar love. And Lazarus was one of the most eminent of those men. But, even in our Lord's love to His friend, Lazarus is pushed back almost out of sight. Martha and Mary always come in before their brother in our Lord's love, as in everything else. This evangelist, that bare record according as he saw, had seen his Master's love to Martha and Mary many a time; but it was only now and then that he had the opportunity of seeing either Lazarus's love to his Lord, or his Lord's love to Lazarus. Lazarus loved his Lord far more than they all. But his love had this defect about it that it was a silent love. It was what we call a worshipping love. It was a wholly hidden love. Only, Lazarus's love could not elude His eyes Who knows what is in man without man testifying what is in him. And He so loved Lazarus back again, and so expected all His disciples to love Lazarus also, that He was wont to call Lazarus their universal friend. "Our friend Lazarus sleepeth," He said. For Lazarus by that time, for the glory of God, and for the glory of the Son of God, had fallen into a fatal sickness. And Martha had despatched a swift messenger to

Bethabara beyond Jordan to summon Him and to say, Lord, he whom Thou lovest is sick. "Trouble not the Master," Lazarus had said to his sister in his sickness. "The Jews of late sought to stone Him, and wouldest thou bring Him hither again?" And with a great shame and a great pain at himself for so troubling his sister and his Master, and with a great hunger in his heart for his Father's house in heaven, Lazarus turned his face to the wall and fell asleep.

Lazarus is altogether left out by us as we read this heavenly chapter. We leave out Lazarus in glory even more completely than he was left out by all men in this life. We leave out of this chapter heaven itself also as much as if we were all Sadducees. And not till we have our eyes opened to the ascended Lazarus, and to his throne in glory, will we ever read this magnificent chapter aright, or at all aright understand why in all the world Jesus should groan and weep all the way to where Lazarus's dead body lay and decayed in the grave. Our Lord did not leave Lazarus out. No, nor his glory either. Our Lord knew what He was on His way to do, and He took to heart what He was on His way to do, and it repented Him to a groaning that could not be uttered, to work His last miracle for the awakening of Jerusalem at such a cost to Lazarus. He knew all the time how it would all end. He knew what Caiaphas would say. And He knew what Judas and Pilate and Herod and the people would do. And He groaned in His spirit because He so clearly foresaw that His friend Lazarus, like Himself, was to be such a savor of death in them that perish, and at such a price to Lazarus.

> So o'er the bed where Lazarus slept,
> He to His Father groan'd and wept:
> What saw He mournful in that grave,
> Knowing Himself so strong to save?

> The deaf may hear the Savior's voice,
> The fetter'd tongue its chain may break:
> But the deaf heart, the dumb by choice,
> The laggard soul that will not wake,
> The guilt that scorns to be forgiven:—
> These baffle e'en the spells of Heaven:
> In thought of these, His brows benign,
> Not even in healing cloudless shine.

Jesus wept. Yes: and if you saw a friend of yours in glory, and then saw also that he was to be summoned to lay aside his glory and to return to be a savor of death to so many of your fellow-citizens, you could not but weep also. Even if you knew that it was the will of God, and for the glory of the Son of God, your friend was coming, you could not but weep. And our Lord wept because Lazarus, who had been but four days in glory, was to be summoned to lay aside his glory and to return to this world of sin and death, and that on such an errand; an errand, as it would issue, of exasperation and final hardness of heart to his enemies. Chrysologus, the Chrysostom of Ravenna, has it: "When our Lord was told of Lazarus's death He was glad; but when He came to raise him to life, He wept. For, though

His disciples gained by it, and though Martha and Mary gained by it, yet Lazarus himself lost by it, by being re-imprisoned, re-committed, and re-submitted to the manifold incommodities of this life."

"This last and greatest of His miracles was to raise our Lord much estimation," says the distinguished John Donne, "but (for they always accompany one another) it was to raise both Him and Lazarus much envy also." And I will always believe that the sight of Lazarus's share in this terrible tragedy mingled with the sight of His own share. Dante wept when he saw that he had to return to envious Florence from the charity of Paradise, even though it was to compose *The Commedia* for God and for the world. And Teresa has it that Lazarus entreated his Master not to summon him back to this life for any cause whatsoever. But it was to be to Lazarus as it was to be to his Master, and that is enough. "Now is my soul troubled: and what shall I say? Father, save me from this hour; but for this cause came I unto this hour. Father, glorify Thy name."

And thus it was that scarcely had Lazarus sat down in his Father's house: he had not got his harp of gold well into his hand: he had not got the Hallelujah that they were preparing against the Ascension of their Lord well into his mouth, when the angel Gabriel came up to where he sat, all rapture through and through, and said to him: "Hail! Lazarus: highly honored among the glorified from among men. Thy Master calls up for thee. He has some service for thee still to do for Him on the earth." And the sound of many waters fell silent for a season as they saw one of the most shining of their number rise up, and lay aside his glory, and hang his harp on the wall, and pass out of their sight, and descend to where their heavenly Prince still tarried with His work unfinished. And Lazarus's soul descended straightway into that grave, where for four days his former body had lain dead, and towards which our Lord was now on His way. And the first words that Lazarus heard were these, and the voice that spake was the voice of his former Friend—"Father, I thank Thee that Thou hast heard me. And I knew that Thou hearest me always. Lazarus, come forth." And he that was dead came forth bound hand and foot with grave clothes; and his face was bound about with a napkin. And Jesus wept at the contrast between heaven and earth, and said, "Loose him, and let him go." Just where did Lazarus go? Like himself, he no doubt hid himself till his Master would not eat till Lazarus was called. For they made our Lord a supper again in those days, and Martha served again, and Lazarus this time was one of them that sat at the table with Him. But the chief priests consulted that they might put Lazarus also to death: because that by reason of him many of the Jews went away and believed on Jesus.

Whether they carried out their counsel and put Lazarus to death the second time we are not told. The evangelist to whom we owe Lazarus had not room within his limits to tell us any more about Lazarus. But a post-canonical author has these entries in his Arabic diary, which I will faithfully copy out for your satisfaction about Lazarus. The entries are abrupt, and unfinished, and broken off, and sometimes quite unintelligible, as you will see. "The man had something strange and unearthly in the look of him." "He eyed the world like a child." "He was obedient as a sheep, and innocent as a lamb." "He let them talk." "A word, a gesture, a glance from a child at play, or in school, or even in its sleep, would startle him into an agony." "His heart and brain moved there, his feet stay here." "Often his soul springs up into his face." "The special marking of the man is prone submission to the will of God." "He merely looked with his large eyes on me." "He loves both old and young; able and weak; he affects the very brutes, and birds, and flowers of the field." "The man is harmless as a lamb, and only impatient at ignorance and sin." You can construct for yourselves out of these authentic fragments what Lazarus's second life was as long as the chief priests let him alone.

God's great demands that He sometimes makes on His great saints, is the great lesson that Lazarus teaches us. As, also, that great lowliness of mind, and great meekness, and great self-surrender, is our greatest saintliness. And, accordingly, that God made His greatest demands on His own lowly-minded Son, the meekest and the most self-emptied of all men. And, after Him, on Lazarus the friend of His Son. A demand on Lazarus that made his divine Friend mourn and weep for him, as he came down to earth to comply with the demand. Lazarus was the most lamb-like of men in all the New Testament, next to the Lamb Himself; and his services and his experiences were, if after a long interval, yet not at all unlike the services and the self-surrenders and the self-emptyings of his Master. For Lazarus also laid aside his glory.

Now, God's work in this world demands this very same meekness, and lowly-mindedness, and self-emptiness, and laying aside of our own glory, from some men among us every day. And God's work stands still in our hands, and all around us, just because He has no men like-minded with Jesus of Nazareth and Lazarus of Bethany. Who will offer themselves to take up the kenotic succession? Some humiliation, some self-emptying, some surrender, as of heaven itself in exchange for earth, may be demanded of you as your contribution to the glory of God, and to the glory of the Son of God. Something that will make your best friends groan and weep for you, as Lazarus's best friend groaned and wept for him. Yes; God may have as terrible a service to ask of you, when you are ready for it, as when He asked His own Son to go down to Bethlehem, and to Nazareth, and to Gethsemane, and to Calvary. Some self-emptying and self-sacrifice like that He asked of the glorified Lazarus also, when He sent him back to Bethany which was so nigh unto Jerusalem. Are you able? Are you ready? Are you willing to be made able and ready? Let your answer be the answer of Jesus of Nazareth, and of Lazarus of Bethany: "Lo, I come. In the volume of the book it is written of me, I delight to do Thy will, O my God; yea, Thy law is within my heart."

80
The Woman with the Issue of Blood

OUR Lord was on His way to raise the ruler's little daughter from the dead. Now, this woman who overtook Him on the way was not actually dead like the ruler's little daughter, but she often wished she was, for she was worse than dead. She had tried everything for her deadly disease. There was not a physician far nor near that she had not consulted as to whether he could cure her. She had spent all her living upon physicians, till, today, she is beside herself with downright despair. And so am I. I am not dead, but I often wish I were. For I, too, am all my life sick to death. And I have tried everything. Every preacher, every author, every discipline, every medicine of the soul. And I am worse tonight than ever I was. I am in a strait betwixt two. I love my work more than ever. I love my family more than ever. No man ever loved his family more than Martin Luther did, but all the time he told his hearers who had head enough and heart enough to understand him, that he had no real joy in his children because of his sin. And I, for one, am exactly like Luther in that.

But to return to the text. "And a certain woman, which had an issue of blood twelve years, and had suffered many things of many physicians, and had spent all that she had, and was nothing bettered but rather worse—when she heard of Jesus, came in the press behind, and touched the hem of His garment. For she said within herself, If I may but touch His clothes I shall be whole. And straightway the fountain of her blood was dried up, and she felt in her body that she was healed of her plague." Well, blood is blood; and blood is bad enough; but blood at its worst is not sin. Sin is SIN. Sin has no fellow. Sin has no second, unless it is death and hell. Sin tries Christ Himself to His utmost, as this woman's bloody issue tried and found wanting all the best physicians in all the cities round about. Christ could cure a twelve year old issue of blood incidentally, and just by the way, as we say; ere ever He was aware He had healed that woman of her blood, but not for all her remaining life of her sin. All her days, you may depend upon it, she was nothing better of her sin, but rather worse. None of the three evangelists tell it, but it is as true as if they had all told it in the same words. She followed Him about with her sin wherever He went. She went up to Jerusalem after Him with her sin. She was one of the women who were beholding afar off when He died on the tree for her sin. She often went out all her days to the Garden of Gethsemane, and lay all night on her face because of her sin. And sometimes at a passover season, and such like, she felt in herself as if she was going to be healed this time; but, before the sun set, she was worse with her secret sinfulness than ever. And till her innermost soul ran pure sin day and night, and would not be staunched of heaven or earth. And all that is our own very exact case to a scriptural parable. Long after we have sold all to win Christ; long after He has begun at times to shed abroad all that He has promised to shed abroad in our heart; long after that we will still be nothing

389

better, but infinitely far worse. One stolen touch was sufficient for an issue of blood; but a long and close lifetime of absolute clasp of Christ will not heal us of our sin. Oh, the malice of sin! Oh, the height, and the depth, and the hold, and the absolute incurableness, of sin! Only, with all that we must not despair. We must not go back. We must not give over. Even if it is incurable, let us not say so. It is; but let us not say it even within ourselves. Let us be like this bleeding woman. Tonight, put out your hand and touch Christ. Never mind the gaping crowd pressing behind and before on Him and on you. They are nothing to you, and you are nobody to them. Never mind what they do, or do not do. They are not bleeding to death like you, and they are no rule to you. They did not come up here tonight on your errand. You are as good as dead, and this may be your last chance of Christ. Make a grasp at Him. Make a great grasp, however unceremonious and desperate, at the hem of His garment. Actually stretch out your hand where you now sit, and the stretch of your hand will sacramentally help your heart. Never mind the people in the same seat staring at you, and thinking you are mad. So you are, and you need not sit and look as if you were not. Never mind that you have not all your days till tonight so much as once touched Christ by faith. This woman had suffered enough to drive her beside herself for twelve years before she ever thought of the hem of His garment, and she went home that night healed of her plague. Press through, and grasp tight, and hold fast till you hear Him say, "Somebody is detaining me." And till you go home laughing in your guilty heart at your new-found peace and strength and joy. What a power you have, O sinner, and what an opportunity! "Somebody hath touched Me; for I perceive that virtue has gone out of Me."

And then, if you succeed in touching Him tonight, you must not do that once for all, and never again. You must touch Him every day; and if you will not call me extravagant, and carried away, I will say—Do the same thing every hour and every moment of the week. One thing all the week is needful. And that is to keep that hem firm in your hand. Even when you feel completely disenchanted of this scripture and this night and this house; even when you feel shame as you look back at your intensity tonight; even when you feel that this woman, and Christ, and this church, and the present preacher are all a piece of the same entire dream—still grope after His garment. Believe in Him and in His garment. Keep believing and keep praying when no one knows. Lift up your heart to Him even in the press of business, and among the cumber of the house, and week-day and all. And He will let down into your hand the hem of His High Priestly garment, all tingling with bells, and all laden with pomegranates, and all shining with strength and with beauty. And when again your evil heart runs with envy, and anger, and pride, and ill-will, and unkindness, and all the rest of the bad blood of hell—all that the more grasp you at Him and at His garment. It is like the precious ointment upon the head, that ran down upon the beard, even Aaron's beard, that went down to the skirts of his garment: His grace and His salvation, that is. Here love runs down, and here joy in your neighbor's joy, and here sweetness of temper, and here humility of mind, and here goodwill, and here attraction to people, and here brotherly kindness, and all the rest of that holy oil.

The healing of His seamless dress
   Is by our beds of pain;
We touch Him in life's throng and press,
   And we are whole again.

Now, why was it, did you ever think, that when our Lord healed so thoroughly this woman's sick body, He did not in an equally immediate, and in an equally thorough way, heal her far more sick soul? Why did He stop short at her blood? Why did He not work a far better cure on her sin? Was it because she was not sick of sin? Was it because she had not come, with all those twelve years, to know the plague of her own heart? Or was it because He did not come the first time to this world with a full salvation? Or was it, and is it, because sin is such a mystery of iniquity that it takes not only both His first and His second comings to heal our souls of sin; but long time, and great labor, and great pain, and great faith, and great prayer on our part also, before even His Divine power can perform and pronounce a perfect cure? Yes, that is it. Be sure that it is. Even if this woman had come on a very much better errand than she did come; and with a far better kind of faith and love; even had she come as David and Paul and Luther came all their days; she would only have gone home to a more horrible pit in her own heart than ever, and to a more corrupt and abominable and burdensome body of death than ever, and to a loneliness that the happiest home in Canaan could not have comforted; to a lifelong death indeed, of which her twelve years' issue of blood was but a far off and feeble emblem. Did you ever read Richard Baxter's Reasons why the Rest that remains for the people of God is never entered on and enjoyed here? What a splendid debate that seraphic preacher holds with all those saints of God whose hearts are broken continually with an unallievable pain and with an insatiable hunger after holiness. What depths, both in God and man, Baxter sounds on that great subject, and what heights he scales! O my brethren, be pleaded with to read almost exclusively the books that are pertinent to your sinful and immortal souls—such as The Saint's Rest. Listen to the great saints as they come together to tell and to hear from one another what God has done for their souls. And O, as many of you as are torn to pieces every day with the torture of sin, as well as covered with inward shame at the degradation and pollution of sin, keep yourselves in life by hope. You are saved by hope. Keep every day numbering your days, and forecasting that Great Day on which Christ shall come to you and shall make you perfect as He and His Father are perfect. Give reins to your imagination and think—all sin for ever gone! Think of that! All sin gone clean out of your sinful heart for ever! I cannot believe it possible. All things are possible to me but that. I, for one, will not be the same man, if ever that crowning work of Omnipotence is wrought in me. I will not know myself, that it is myself. Now, nothing but sin and misery; and then, nothing but love, and holiness, and unspeakable blessedness. This horrible and loathsome incubus, myself, for ever cast off, and for ever cast down into the depths of hell, never to come up again. And I set free from myself for ever, and admitted to the New Jerusalem to walk with Christ and with His saints, in all the holiness and all the beauty of the Divine Nature! "Comfort ye, comfort ye my people, saith your God. Speak ye comfortably to Jerusalem, and cry to her that her warfare is accomplished, that her iniquity is pardoned. What are these which are arrayed in white robes? and whence came they? These are they which came out of great tribulation. And God shall wipe all tears from their eyes. And there shall be no more death, neither sorrow, nor crying, neither shall there be any more pain: for the former things are passed away. And He that sat upon the throne said to me: These things are true and faithful."

81

Mary Magdalene

THERE is a still unsettled dispute among New Testament scholars as to how many Marys there are in the Gospels, and then as to their identification. But our dispute will not be as to this Mary or that, but only as to ourselves. No, nor even as to who and what were the seven devils that at one time had made such a hell in Mary Magdalene's heart. Our whole dispute and debate shall be to let in some light from heaven on the bottomless pit of our own hearts, so as to scare out of our hearts some of the seven devils who still haunt and harbor there.

> Seven times
> The letter that denotes the inward stain,
> He on my forehead, with the truthful point
> Of his drawn sword inscribed. And, "Look," he cried,
> "When enter'd, that thou wash these scars away."

We do not know just what Mary Magdalene's seven scars were. But for our learning, Dante's own seven scars are written all over his superb autobiographical book. And Dante's identical scars are inscribed again every returning Fourth Day in Bishop Andrewes's *Private Devotions*. Solomon has the same scars also: "These six things doth the Lord hate. Yea, seven are an abomination unto Him." And, again: "When he speaketh fair, believe him not, for there are seven abominations in his heart." And John Bunyan has the very same number at the end of his *Grace Abounding*: "I find to this day these seven abominations in my heart." And then Bunyan is bold enough, and humble-minded enough, to actually name his scars for the comfort and encouragement of his spiritual children. Now, what are your seven scars? What are your seven abominations in your heart? What are the six things, yea seven, in your heart that the Lord hates? It is almost our whole salvation to ask and to answer that question. Because it is a law of devils; it is their diabolical nature, and it is a first principle of their existence and indwelling and possession of a man, that they never make their presence known in any man till he begins to name them and curse them and cast them out. He does not at all feel their full power, and the whole pain, and shame, and distress, and disgust of their presence till he is almost delivered from them. They rage and roar and tear and gnash our hearts to pieces when they begin to see that their time in us is to be short. But, till then, we are absolutely insensible to their very existence, either outside of us or inside. It was an old aphorism of the deep old divines, and they took it, if I mistake not, out of the deep old stoics: "All vices are in all men; but all vices are not all extant in all men." As much as to say: "All the seven devils are in every man's heart, but they do not all rage and rend equally in every man's heart: no, nor in the same man's heart at all times. The very devils have their times and their seasons like everything else." Now, though Mary Magdalene is my text, it is of little real interest or importance to me who and what her seven devils were, unless in so far as that would cast some light in upon my own possession; yours and mine. But, on the other hand, if I have come by any means to know something of the terrible plague of my own heart, then, in that measure, I am a real authority as to the Marys of the four Gospels; and especially as to Mary Magdalene. To have grappled long, even with one inward devil, and to have had him at my throat day and night for years, and I at his—that is true New Testament scholarship. That throws a flood of light on all the Marys who followed our Lord about, and that makes Mary Magdalene a minister's own and peculiar field, and his specialized department of pulpit work. And the same inward experience is making not a few of my hearers far better genealogists, and harmonists, and exegetes, and demonologists, than all their teachers.

Pride, envy, anger, intemperance, lasciviousness, covetousness, spiritual sloth— these were Dante's seven scars on his sanctified forehead. I had a great dispute on the subject of Dante's scars the other day with one of the best Dante scholars in this country. He contended against me with great learning and great eloquence that Dante's besetting sin was pride—a towering, satanic, scornful pride, to the contemptuous and complete exclusion of all possible envy. He had Dante on his side in one passage at any rate. I could not deny that. And I confess it seemed to me that Dante and he together had established the doctrine that any envy at all is absolutely, and in the nature of things, quite incompatible with such a lofty pride as that was which wholly possessed Dante's heart. Till, staggered, if not truly convinced, I gave in: so browbeaten was I between two such antagonists. But when I came to myself; when I left all books, the very best, about pride and envy, and when I was led again of God's Holy Spirit into the pandemonium that is in my own heart, I recovered courage, till, tonight, I have my harness on again to fight the battle of divine truth against any man, and all men, and even Dante himself. And the divine truth to me in this matter is this: That in my heart, if not in Dante's, both pride and envy have their full scope together; and that they never, in the very least, either exclude, or drink up, or narrow down, the dreadful dominion of one another. Now, what do you say to that? How is it with your heart? "I have no books," said Jacob Behmen. "I have neither Aristotle, nor Dante, nor Butler, nor Brea, nor Shepard, nor Edwards; I have only my own heart." You have none of these books either, but you surely have your own heart. Who, then, for the love of the truth, will so read his own heart as to take sides with me? Come away. Take courage. Speak out. Speak boldly out. You must surely know what pride is, and you must all know, still better perhaps, what envy is, and at whose payments and praises and successes and positions your heart cramps and strangles and excruciates itself. Do you not both know and confess all these things before yourself and before God every day? Do you not? O stone-dead soul! O sport and prey of Satan! O maker of God a liar, and the truth is not in you! I would not have your devilpossessed heart, and your conscience seared with a redhot iron, for the whole world. I would rather be myself yet, and myself at my worst, a thousand times, than be you at your best. Whether you are true enough and bold enough to be on my side or no, I shall not be so easily silenced in my next debate about these two devils. For a man is more to himself, on such inward matters, than the whole *Commedia* and the whole *Ethics* to boot, with all their splendid treasures of truth, and power, and experience, and eloquence. As I was saying, I have not the least notion as to who or what Mary Magdalene's seven devils were, and much less do I know how they could possibly be all cast out of her heart in this life. I do not know much, as you will see, about Mary Magdalene, but I would not give up the little knowledge I have of myself, no, not for the whole world. For what would it profit me if I gained the whole world of knowledge and everything else, and lost my fast-passing opportunity of having all this pandemonium that is within me for ever cast out of me?

I will confess it again: How the whole seven could possibly be cast out of her heart in this present life, I, for one, cannot imagine; and I do not believe it. Complete, or all but complete, deliverance from two, say, of the seven I could easily believe, but the remaining five are quite beyond me. Two of the seven scars are on the surface. They are but skin-deep. Two of Dante's seven devils have their holes in the sand; in the soft earth and on the exposed outside of our hearts. Properly speaking, they are rather mole-heaps and rabbit-burrows than the dens of devils. Properly speaking, they are not devils at all. Till any man who is in any earnest at all can easily dig them out with a spade, and wring their necks, and nail their dead carcases up on the church door and be for ever done with them. But if you do that with those two it will only the more terrify and exasperate the other five. When the outposts of hell are stormed and taken and put to the sword, that only drives the real hell, with its true and proper devils, deeper down into their bottomless entrenchments. There are some wild beasts so devilish in their bite; they make their cruel teeth so to meet and lock fast in a man's flesh; that the piece has to be cut out if he is to be saved from their deadly hold. And the fangs of these five genuine devils must be broken to pieces in their heads with the hammer of God, and the flesh and bone into which they have locked their cursed teeth must be cut out and sacrificed before the soul is set free. And in this case the surgeon with his hammer and his knife is Death, and the full science and success of his operations will not be all seen till the Resurrection morning. "Like as a lion that is greedy of his prey, and as it were a young lion lurking in secret places. Arise, O Lord! disappoint him, cast him down. As for me, I will behold Thy face in righteousness; I shall be satisfied, when I awake, with Thy likeness." It is better to enter into heaven with seven devils excavated out of our hearts as with a knife, than to have them gnawing in our hearts to all eternity.

Since ever there were women's hearts in this world, were there ever two women's hearts with such emotions in them as when Mary the mother of Jesus, and Mary Magdalene, stood together beside His Cross? Did you ever try to put yourself into His mother's heart that day, or into Mary Magdalene's heart? They stood and wept as never another two women have wept since women wept in this world, till John at Jesus' command took His mother away from Calvary and led her into the city. But Mary Magdalene still stood by the Cross. He dismissed His mother, but He kept Mary; she would not be dismissed, and she stood near to His crucified feet. All His disciples had forsaken Him and fled. And thus it was that there was no eye-witness left to tell us how Mary Magdalene stood close up to the Cross weeping, and how she did wash His feet with her tears, and did wipe them with the hairs of her head. And then, when He said, I thirst, how she took the sponge out of the soldier's hand and put it up to His lips. When He bowed His head she saw Him do it, and she heard Him say, It is finished! It was not a place for a woman. But Mary Magdalene was not a woman; she was an angel. She was the angel who strengthened Him. She was the whole Church of God and ransomed bride of Christ at that moment in herself: she and her twin-brother, the thief on the Cross. How the next three days and three nights passed with Mary Magdalene I cannot account for her to you. But on the first day of the new week cometh Mary Magdalene early, when it was yet dark, unto the sepulchre. And Jesus saith unto her, Mary! She turned herself, and saith unto Him, Rabboni! Jesus saith to her, "Touch me not with thy tears, nor with the hairs of thy head, nor with thy ointment." And, had He not said that, she would have been holding His feet there to this day. And now that He has ascended to His Father's house, He is saying to His saints and to His angels to this very day the very same words that He said in Simon's house—"This woman since I came in hath not ceased to kiss my feet."

But the supreme lesson to me out of all Mary Magdalene's marvellous history is just the text: "He appeared first to Mary Magdalene, out of whom He had cast seven devils." As much as to say—it was not to Peter, nor to James, nor to John, that He gave that signal favor and unparalleled honor. It was not even to His own mother. It was to Mary Magdalene. It was to her who loved Him best, and had the best reason to love Him best, of all the men and women then living in the world. While this world lasts, and as long as there are great sinners and great penitents to comfort in it, let Mary Magdalene be often preached upon, and let this lesson be always taught out of her, this lesson—that no depth of sin, and no possession of devils even, shall separate us from the love of Christ. That repentance and love will outlive and overcome everything; as also, that there is no honor too high, and no communion too close, for the love of Christ on His side, and for the soul's love on her side, between them to enjoy. Only repent deep enough and to tears enough; only love as Mary Magdalene loved Him who had cast her seven devils out of her heart; and He will appear to you also, and will call you by your name. And He will employ you in His service even more and even better than He honored and employed Mary Magdalene on the morning of His Resurrection.

Mary Magdalene! my sister, my forerunner into heaven till I come, and my representative there! But, remember, only till I come. Cease not to kiss His feet till I come, but give up thy place to me when I come. For to whom little is forgiven, the same loveth little. Give place then; give place to me before His feet!

82
The Mother of Zebedee's Children

WHY does the Evangelist write the text in that round-about way? Why does he not write the text in his own simple and straightforward style? Why does he not simply say: Salome, the mother of James and John? I do not know for certain why the Evangelist writes in that ambiguous and intentionally obscure way, but I will tell you what I think about it. By the time that Matthew sat down to compose his Gospel, James, the eldest son of Zebedee and Salome, had already been a long time in heaven with Christ; and John, his brother, was a high and an honored Apostle in the Church of Christ on earth. James had long ago drunk of Christ's cup and been baptized with Christ's baptism. While John was, by this time, as good as the author of the Fourth Gospel, and the three Epistles, and the Apocalypse. All the same, nay, all the more, John had not forgotten the sins and the faults and the follies of his youth; and, above all, he had not forgotten that for ever disgraceful day when he got his mother to beg the best throne for him and for his brother. That disgraceful day though now so long past was ever before John. And thus it was, as I think, that Matthew wrote in this roundabout way about it. "May my right hand forget its cunning," said Matthew, "before I bring back a single blush to that great saint of God! No enemy of Christ and of His Church shall ever blaspheme out of my book if I can help it." And thus it was that this Evangelist took a garment, and laid it on his shoulder, and went backward, till he had all but completely covered up the sin of Salome and James and John. "Blessed Antonomasiast!" exclaimed John, when he read this chapter of Matthew for the first time. "Yes," said John; "all Scripture is indeed given by inspiration of the Spirit of God: and God is love!" And it was so certainly with this special Scripture. For Matthew's heart of love and honor for John had taken his inspired pen out of his hand at the opening of this passage till this stroke of sheltering style was struck out before the writer knew what he is doing. Dante is full on every page of his of this same exquisite device. Dante, indeed, is the fullest of this exquisite device of any of the great writers, either sacred or profane. But the Bible had this exquisite device, as it had all Dante's exquisite devices, long before he was born. And still the Bible is by far our finest education in morals, and in manners, and in love, and in letters, as well as in our everlasting salvation.

"Leave it to me, my sons," said Salome; "leave it to me. Do not be in any doubt about it. It will all come right. I am not to be His mother's sister for nothing, and I have not followed Him about all this time, and ministered to Him out of my substance, for nothing. Blood is thicker than water," she said, "and you, my sons, will see that it is so. Leave it to me. Who is Andrew? And who is Peter? And who is their father? And who is their mother, I would like to know, that they should presume to be princes over my sons? It shall never be! Leave it to me, my sons; leave it to me." "Then came to Him the mother of Zebedee's children with her sons,

397

worshipping Him, and desiring a certain thing of Him. And He said to her, What wilt thou? She saith unto Him, Grant that my two sons may sit, the one on Thy right hand and the other on the left, in Thy Kingdom." Well done, Salome! Well done! As long as this Gospel is preached this splendid impudence of thine shall be told of thee! "Let the sons of all the other mothers in Israel sit, or stand, or lie as they like; only, let my two sons sit high above them all, and have their feet on the necks of all the ten." Had Salome's presumption been less magnificent, our Lord would have been very angry at her. But the absolute sublimity of her selfishness completely overcame Him. He had met with nothing like it. The splendid humility of the Syrophoenician woman completely overcame Him, and now He is equally overcome with the splendid shamelessness of Salome's request. Her cold-blooded cruelty to Himself also pierced His heart as with a spear. This is the Monday, and He is to be betrayed on the Thursday, and crucified on the Friday. All the same, Salome went on plotting and counter-plotting for a throne for her two sons that only existed in her own stupid and selfish heart. And it was the sight of all this that made our Lord's rising anger turn to an infinite pity, till He said to her two sons: "Are ye able to drink of My cup, and to be baptized with My baptism?" And what do you think the two insane men said? They actually said: "We are able!" In such sin had their mother Salome conceived them. In such stupidity of mind. In such hopeless selfishness, combined with such hard-hearted presumptuousness. And then, that it should be John! That it should be the disciple who had been chosen to such a coming sanctification and to such a coming service! That it should be John, who had been so loved, and so trusted, and so leaned upon, and so looked to! And at this time of day, that John should be so deep in this miserable plot. Our Lord often spoke about a daily cross. Well, that was His cross that Monday, and a very bitter cross it was. More bitter to His heart by far than all the thorns and nails and spears of next Friday. What a cup of red wine that miserable mother and her two sons like her, made our Lord to drink that day! "O Salome," He said, "and O James and John her sons, you little know the baptism you are all baptizing Me with. But your own baptism, also, will soon come. And mine is at the door."

A little imagination, with a little heart added to it, would have saved Salome and her two sons from making this shameful petition. Salome should have said to herself something like this. She should have said this, and should have dwelt on it, till it made her shameful petition to be impossible. She should have said: "But Andrew, and Peter, and all the ten, have mothers like me. All their mothers are just as ambitious for all their sons as I am for mine. And they will feel toward me and toward my sons just the same suspicion, and jealousy, and envy, and hatred, and ill-will, that I feel toward them. And what would I think of them if they took advantage of their friendship with Christ, as I am taking advantage of my friendship with Him, in order to get Him to favor them and their sons at our expense? And what would I think of Him if He was imposed upon, and prevailed upon, to overlook, and neglect, and injure my sons, at the shameful plot of some of their mothers?" Had Salome talked in that way to her own heart; and, especially, had she brought up her sons to look at themselves and at all their fellows in that light; she would then have been as wise a woman as she now was a fool, and as good a mother as she now was a bad. Where had Salome lived all her days? What kind of a mother had she herself had? In what synagogue in all Israel had she worshipped God? Who had been her teachers in the things of God? What had she been thinking about all the time our Lord had been teaching and preaching in her hearing, as He did every day, about seeing with other people's eyes, and feeling with other people's hearts, and doing to other mothers and to their sons as she would have them do to her and to her sons? How could she have lived in this world, and especially in the day and in the discipleship of Christ, and how could she have borne and brought up her sons to be His disciples, and still be capable of this disgraceful scheme? Had she possessed one atom of experience of the world, not to say of truth and wisdom and love, she could never have petitioned for a place of such offence and such danger for her two sons. Even if Christ had asked it of her, she would have shrunk from exposing her two sons to the envy and the anger and the detraction of all the ten, and of many more besides. "Employ my sons in Thy service," she would have petitioned; "but let it be in some secluded and obscure place. Make them Thy true disciples even to death; but, I do beseech Thee, if it be Thy will, hide them in the secret of Thy presence from the pride of men, and keep them secretly in Thy pavilion from the strife of tongues." She would have kneeled and worshipped and so spoken if she had had a mother's eye and a mother's heart in her bosom. But instead of that, this cruel woman to her own flesh and blood was for exposing her two sons to every possible shaft and spear of envy, and anger, and ill-will, and injury. "How great they will be, if I can help it," the heartless creature talked to herself and said: "What titles they will wear! What power they will exercise! And how all Galilee will hear of it, and how they will all envy Salome!" Till she said: "Leave it to me, my sons; leave it to me." And James and John left it to her, and they both knelt down beside her as she said: "Lord, I have a certain thing to ask of Thee."

It was our Lord's continual way to make Scriptures out of His disciples, and to have those Scriptures written and preserved for our edification. And He made this Scripture for us out of Salome and James and John and the ten; this solemn Scripture: "It must needs be that offences come, but woe to that man by whom the offence cometh!" Woe to Salome and to her two sons, that is, for she made herself a great offence to the ten that day. She would have been offence enough simply with her so-near relationship to Christ, and with her so-gifted and so-privileged sons. But not content with that, she must needs take and lay both her sons as sheer rocks of offence right in the way of the headlong ten. Just because she was His mother's sister; just because James and John were His cousins; she and they should have kept in the background of the discipleship, and should never have come out of that background but with tender and slow and softly-taken steps. But it will take all the tremendous disenchantment of the coming Thursday and Friday to bring James and John and the others to their sober senses. And oh! you who are not come to your sober senses yet, with all Salome's shame all written for that purpose—what, in the name of God, is to bring you to yourself? Oh, born fools and blind, not to see what stumbling-stones and what rocks of offence you are to other men, just as they are to you! Not to see the broken bones that other men take from you, just as surely as you take the same from them. Salome could not help it that she was His mother's sister. And James and John could not help it that they were their mother's sons. And you may be as blameless and as innocent as they were in that, and yet you may be a stone of stumbling down to death and hell to many men around you. At every talent that has been committed to you; at every added talent that you make for yourself and for the Church and for Christ; at every sweet word of praise that sounds around your honored name; at every step you are summoned to take up to higher service; there are men all around you eyeing you with an evil eye. It is the same evil eye, with the same javelin in it, that Saul threw at David. It is the same evil eye with which both Peter and Judas shot hatred that day at James and John. And all the time, and till the javelin sang past their heads and stuck fast in the wall just beyond them, the two besotted brothers were in uttermost ignorance of what they and their mother had done, and what they had led the ten into doing, and what shame and pain they had caused their clear-eyed and pure-hearted Master. And even had James and John got their two thrones, would they, do you think, have got one-thousandth part of the pleasure out of their thrones that Peter and the nine would have got pain? And your own cup of honor, and praise, and what not, is not half so sweet to you as it is bitter as blood to the Peters and the Judases who see it in your hand. There is nothing but the merest and the sourest dregs in your cup, but they who see it at your lips do not know that. "It is impossible but that offences will come; but woe unto him through whom they come!"

83
The Widow with the Two Mites

SHE was a widow. And she was surely the poorest widow in all the city that day. But she had this—that she was rich toward God, and that He was rich toward her. For she loved the house of God. She was another Anna. Only, Anna lodged in the precincts of the temple, and departed not from the temple night and day, whereas this poor widow somehow and somewhere had an impoverished house of her own. "O God, thou art my God," she kept saying to herself all the way up from her own impoverished house with the two mites in her hand; "my soul shall be satisfied as with marrow and fatness; and my mouth shall praise Thee with joyful lips, when I remember Thee upon my bed, and meditate on Thee in the night watches." When one after another of her neighbors and her kindred railed on her for going up to the Court of the Women in her deep poverty, she answered them not again. Only, she did not turn back, nor did she lose hold of her two mites. "Two mites," says Mark, "make a farthing." She had no great temptation to let her left hand know what her right hand intended to do. And thus it was that without once lifting her eyes off the temple steps she cast her contribution into the temple-chest, and passed on into the temple to offer her morning prayer, and then went down to her own house. She had seen nobody, she had spoken to nobody, and nobody had seen or spoken to her. And she does not know to this day what we know. Nor will she know till that day when everything shall be known and made manifest. What would she have thought if she had been told Who had watched her that day, and what He had said about her, and that we would be reading about her tonight in this far-off island of the sea? As also that her two mites would multiply, all down the ages, into millions upon millions of gold and silver, the same Eyes still watching the process all the time? And what will she think and what will she say when all that is told from the housetop on that day about her, and about her two mites, by the Judge of all? And still He sits over against the treasury in this temple tonight, and calls unto Him His disciples among us, and says to us, "Verily I say unto you also." And as He sits and speaks to us, and points us to this poor widow, we lay to heart from Him many lessons.

In every department of merely secular finance money is just money. The Chancellor of Her Majesty's Exchequer does not care one straw what our feelings toward him and toward his office are when he sends us in our income-tax schedule. He does not interrogate us as to our political principles, or even as to our loyalty to the throne. Only pay your taxes promptly and he will not trouble you again till next year. But it was very different from that in those communities where Paul was the collector of the contributions of the apostolic churches. "Brethren," he wrote, "we do you to wit of the grace of God bestowed on the churches of Macedonia, who first gave themselves to the Lord. For ye know the grace of our Lord Jesus Christ, that, though He was rich, yet for your sakes He became poor. Therefore, see that ye abound in this grace also." And, as our Lord sat over against the thirteen chests in the temple that day, and all thirteen for the temple upkeep in one way or another, it was not the money so much as the mind of the contributors that He watched and weighed. And thus it was that this poor widow's mind weighed out for her this never-to-be-forgotten approval and applause of our Lord, "Verily I say unto you, that this poor widow hath cast more in than all they which have cast into the treasury." Because, as Paul has it, she had first cast in herself. That, then, is our first and fundamental lesson in all church finance. It is ourselves first; and then, after ourselves, it is our time, and our money, and our work. Two mites of mind and intention outweigh out of sight a million of mere money in the balances of the sanctuary.

"For if there be first a willing mind, it is accepted according to that a man hath, and not according to that he hath not." And thus it comes about that such a noble and ennobling equality is established in the Church of Christ. Why, our very Lord Himself, though He was rich, yet for our sakes had become so poor that the poor widow was richer than He was that day. He had absolutely nothing; not so much as two mites, to call His own that day. He had literally and absolutely nothing but a willing mind. And thus it was that He sat so near the treasury enjoying the sight of the liberality of those who had both the willing mind and money also. He had no money. He had only Himself. And as they cast in their money, He again cast in Himself. All the time the poor widow was coming up the street singing to her own heart the sixty-third Psalm, our Lord was sitting in the treasury singing to His Father the fortieth Psalm. "Sacrifice and offering Thou didst not desire. Mine ears hast thou opened; burnt offering and sin offering hast Thou not required. Then said I, Lo, I come. In the volume of the book it is written of me, I delight to do Thy will, O my God; yea, Thy law is within my heart." I have an ancient friend in this congregation who, also, has God's law in this respect within her heart. Like Paul's Macedonian saints she has very little more than a willing mind. She puts on her old bonnet once a year and is announced into my study with five shillings in her hand. Where she gets it I cannot imagine, but this is what she does with it. I have another fellow-communicant who calls on me annually with a pound. But the five-shilling one touches me most. For her little room looks to me when I visit it as if she had far more need, not of five shillings, but of five pounds every year either from me or from the poor's box. But she has always a clean chair and a cup of tea for me when I call to see her. "A shilling," she said to me the other day when she came on her annual errand, "for Armenia. A shilling for the Jewish schools in Constantinople. A shilling for the miners' mission. A shilling for the Zenana ladies. And a shilling, over and above Dr. Chalmers's penny a week, for the Sustentation Fund." I would be a brute if I refused to take it. I would have yet to learn the first principles of the grace of God if I were tempted to say to her to take it away and to buy coals with it. For all the coals in the bowels of all the earth would not warm her heart and mine; and, shall I not say it, her Master's heart, as her love for these causes of His warms His heart, and hers, and her minister's heart. A well-to-do worshipper sent me the other day a hundred pounds as a special donation, over and above the hundred he gives in monthly instalments to his deacon. For more reasons than the coming dividend in May I was mightily delighted with his noble and timeous donation. But the five shillings melted my heart far more. He who sits over against His treasury here also, will Himself tell you in your hearing that day what He has to say about these two, and all such like princely minds. "That"—it was said by a great preacher in a land of vineyards and olive yards in illustration and in enforcement of this very same subject of a willing mind—"that which comes from His people at the gentle pressure of their Lord's simple bidding, comes as the fine and sweet and golden-colored olive oil which runs freely from the fruit, almost before the press has ever touched it. That, again, is as the dark and coarse dregs, which is wrung out by the force of a harsh constraint at the last." "When I was in France," says Bacon, "it was said of the Duke of Guise that he was the greatest usurer in all the land, because he had turned all his estates into obligations; meaning that he had left himself nothing, but only had bound great numbers of persons in life-long indebtedness to him." It is not for the lip of mortal man to say it, but it is true, that Almighty God holds Himself under obligations to us all, corresponding to all the estates, great or small, that we have spent upon Him and upon His house. And if it is only the inward estate of a more and more willing mind, what usurers we are, and what an obligation will He acknowledge and repay!

Mutatis mutandis, as the Latin lawyers said; making all allowance, that is, for the immense change of dispensation and of all other circumstances, the thirteen temple-chests of our Lord's day were just the Endowment Funds, and the Augmentation Funds, and the Sustentation Funds of our own land and day. There were special chests elsewhere in the temple for the poor, and for the education of the children of the poor, but the treasury chests over against which our Savior sat that day were just the Deacons' Courts of our own Free Church and other churches. It is doing no exegetical or homiletical violence to this exquisite scene to transfer every syllable of it to ourselves as a congregation and a court. Indeed it would take some blindness of mind and some pulpit ineptitude to lead us past the outstanding lessons and applications of this delightful Scripture. For our own Sustentation Fund is just that very same temple treasury over again exactly. By means of those chests the temple worshippers by their daily and weekly and monthly and yearly contributions supported the priests, the doctors, the readers of the law, and all the other office-bearers of the sanctuary. And, like our Sustentation Fund also, all classes contributed to the support of the sacred house; from the rich among the people down to this poor widow. Just as with ourselves where some give to this one fund hundreds of pounds a year and others a penny a week. And then out of our great central fund an equal dividend is made every May to every minister of the Free Church, from John O'Groats to Maidenkirk. So much so, that wherever you see a Free Church door open on a Sabbath morning, in town or country, and the people flocking up to it, you have had a hand in opening that door, and in sustaining that minister, and in preaching the unsearchable riches of Christ to that congregation. And if, under God's hand, you are such a widow that you have nothing to give to your deacon but a willing mind, and a word of God-speed, that is quite enough. You are a rich contributor and a true pillar of the Free Church. It is no irreverence, but only a becoming gratitude and love to say it, that as I sit at the head of the monthly table of our Deacons' Court I have something in my heart not unlike what was in His heart who sat that day in the treasury of the temple. As I see our deacons coming in and laying down on the table, one a few shillings, and another hundreds of pounds, like Him I rejoice at the sight, and a little like Him I hope, I give myself again to the service of God and to the service of His people. If you could all see, as I every first Monday of every month see, our splendidly-equipped and splendidly-managed Deacons' Court, the sight would both move, and inflame, and sanctify your heart also. Tens and twenties of the finest young fellows in the city; arts, law, medical, and divinity students; young merchants, young bankers, young advocates, young tradesmen—all tabling the income of their districts, and all received with the applause of the elders sitting around. And if you could hear the treasurer's monthly report, and then the censor's so stringent monthly scrutiny, and then the thanksgiving psalms and prayers, you would give far more to this so sustaining and so sanctifying Fund than you have yet given. And you would see, not by any means to perfection, but to a certain honest approximation, what a modern treasury-chest of the Lord's house ought to be, and what it will yet be in every congregation in the coming days of the Church of Christ in Scotland. For it is not by any means the enormous wealth of this congregation that has given to Free St. George's its honorable place at the head of this honorable Fund. It is, I shall say it in your presence, the exceptional intelligence in church matters and in personal religion that has all along, with all its drawbacks, characterized Dr. Andrew Thomson's and Dr. Candlish's congregation. And, taken along with all that, its absolutely unique and unapproached Deacons' Court.

84
Pontius Pilate

IT was Pontius Pilate who crucified our Lord. But for Pontius Pilate our Lord would not have been crucified. In spite of Pontius Pilate our Lord might have been stoned to death before the palace of the high priest that passover morning. Or, lest there should be an uproar among the people, He might have been fallen upon and murdered when He was on His knees in the garden of Gethsemane that passover night. The assassins of the city might have covenanted with Caiaphas that they would neither eat bread nor drink water till they had killed Jesus of Nazareth. The whole council of the scribes, and the elders, and the chief priests had finally determined that Jesus of Nazareth, one way or another, must be put to death; but, with all that, it was Pontius Pilate who put Him to the death of the cross.

Pontius Pilate was the Roman governor. He was the Roman procurator placed at that time over Judah and Jerusalem. He was Caesar's representative and viceroy. What Tiberius himself was in Rome, all that Pontius Pilate was in Jerusalem. The Emperor Tiberius had made a special selection of Pontius Pilate, and had sent him east with special instructions to govern, with his very best ability, the very difficult province of Judea. Pilate's was a much-coveted post among his rivals in Rome, but he had not found it to be a bed of roses. For, as the Jews had been the hardest to conquer, so had they continued to be the hardest to hold down, of all the races that ever writhed under Caesar's heel. The conquest of Jerusalem, and the military occupation and civil management of that city and the surrounding country, cost the Roman Empire far more men and far more administrative anxiety than all that Jewry was ever worth. But the Roman statesmanship was not to be baffled, nor were the Roman eagles to be chased out of Jerusalem, by that malignant remnant of the Hebrew race. And thus it was that a procurator of such sleepless vigilance and such relentless temper as Pontius Pilate was selected and sent out to mingle the blood of all Jewish insurrectionaries with their sacrifices. And it had demanded all Pilate's personal astuteness, and all his practiced statecraft, and it had called forth no little of his proverbial cruelty also, in order to stamp out one outbreak of the insurgent Jews after another. Till it would be hard to tell which of the two was by this time the more exasperated at the other: Pontius Pilate at the rulers of Jerusalem, or the rulers of Jerusalem at Pontius Pilate. The rage and the revenge of the rulers of Jerusalem against Pontius Pilate burn to this day like coals of juniper in the pages both of Philo and of Josephus.

But of all the problems and responsibilities that had arisen in his province during Pilate's procurator-ship, nothing had so much perplexed him, nothing had put him so completely out of his depth, as this widespread and mysterious movement originated by John of Jerusalem, and carried on by Jesus of Nazareth. Pilate had often wished that he could detect one single atom of danger to the Roman domination in John or in Jesus, or in any of their disciples, or in any of their doctrines

405

or practices. But, absolute wolf for Jewish blood as Pilate always was, he was not wicked enough nor wolf enough to murder an innocent man merely because he could not comprehend him.

"Divine and Most Illustrious Tiberius," so ran one of Pilate's procuratorial reports about this time,

> all is quiet here. I have had my troubles with this insufferable and ungov-
> ernable people, but neither watchfulness nor firmness has been wanting on
> my part. Only, the former matter of Jesus the son of David still perplexes
> me. I sometimes wish that a wiser man than I am were in my place, so that
> he might better report to you about this mysterious movement among this
> people. Had this Jesus been an ordinary Jewish zealot, or an insurrectionary
> of an everyday order, my duty to my master would soon have been fulfilled.
> But, as a matter of fact, Jesus the Christ, as he is called, is worth more to my
> administration than any legion of my armed men. He is the most peace-
> able and inoffensive of men. I know what I say, for I have had him and his
> discipleship watched and reported on in all places and at all times. Not only
> so, but it was only last week that I determined to be a spy upon him myself,
> so perplexed was I with all that I had heard about him. I accordingly most
> effectually disguised myself, a thing I had never done before, and went to
> where he dwelt and told him that I had for long been a secret disciple of
> his. I am come by night, I told him, for fear of his enemies and mine. But
> instead of his royal descent from David, or his Hebrew Messiahship, or any
> pretensions or expectations of his of any kind, he would speak to me about
> nothing and about no one—David nor Solomon, Caesar nor Caiaphas—but
> only about myself. Jew, or Roman, or whatever I was, I must be born again,
> he insisted. I must be baptized in Jordan, confessing my sins. Till I was so
> born again, I, like all men, loved the darkness rather than the light, because
> my deeds were evil. And, that the only way to know the truth, and to be sure
> of the truth, and not to be afraid or ashamed of the truth, was just to do
> my duty to the truth, and to do nothing else. And when I asked him why he
> did not leave this so untruthful and so unfriendly land, and go and open a
> philosopher's school about all these things in Rome or Athens or Alexandria,
> his only reply to me was that he was not sent but to the lost sheep of the
> house of Israel. And, then, his eyes and his hands as he dismissed me from
> his presence were absolutely the eyes and the hands of a king. I shall not lift
> a single finger against this "King of the Jews," as his disciples call him, till I
> am commanded by Caesar so to do.

Well, it was while Pontius Pilate's procuratorial despatch was still on its way to Rome that the case contained in it came to a head in Jerusalem. It was the morn-ing of the passover, and it was still early, when Jesus of Nazareth, with His hands bound behind His back, was led up by the whole Sanhedrim to Pilate's judgment-seat. As soon as he had sat down on his seat of judgment-Pilate demanded of the rulers of Jerusalem, "What accusation bring ye against this man?" They answered and said, "If he were not a malefactor, and indeed deserving of the death of the cross, we would not have brought him before thee. We found this fellow perverting the people and forbidding the people to give tribute to Caesar, saying that he himself is Christ a king, and the Son of God." When Pilate heard that, he took the prisoner apart, and asked Him, "Whence art Thou?" Pilate's heart was made of Roman iron, and his Roman heart had never failed him before. But, altogether; what with all he had heard and seen of our Lord already; and what with all he heard and saw of Him that morning; Pilate's heart absolutely stood still as he ventured to put to Him the staggered question: "Whence art Thou?" And Pilate's secret fear became downright terror when his prisoner looked up at him with such eyes, but answered him nothing. It was at that very moment that Pilate's wife exclaimed to her husband: "How dreadful is this Roman praetorium to me this pass-over morning! Let us arise and return to Caesarea! Have thou nothing to do with this just man, for I have suffered many things this whole past night in dreams and in visions because of him!" Just what shape her great sufferings had taken all that night we are not told. She, too, may have had reports brought to her about the preaching of John and Jesus. She, too, may have had her spies set upon Him. She, too, may have had told her some of His tremendous sermons that very passover week. For all Jerusalem—from top to bottom—was ringing with those terrible passover parables of His. And, out of all that she had seen and heard and apprehended—what sufferings may not have come to Pilate's wife in her divinely-ordered dream that so awful night? She may have seen the Son of Man coming in His glory, and all His holy angels with Him. And she may have seen the kings of the earth, and the great men, and the rich men, and the mighty men, and her husband among them, hiding themselves in the dens and in the rocks of the mountains: and saying to the mountains and the rocks, Fall on us, and hide us from the face of Him that sitteth on the throne. "Have thou nothing to do with that just man," she said, "for I have suffered some fearful sights this night because of Him!" "Wife," said the gaoler of Derby, with a doleful voice, "I have seen the day of judgment: and I saw George Fox there, and I was afraid of him, because I had done him so much wrong, and had spoken so much against him in the taverns and the alehouses."

With all his heart would Pilate have fallen in with his wife's warning, had it been possible for him to do so. He did not need her urgent message. He knew far better than she did that the prisoner at his bar was a just man, and something more than a just man, but that only tied up Pilate's hands all the tighter. "Have thou nothing to do with that just man!" Yes; but how is Pilate to get rid of that just man, hunted to death as both that just man and his judge both are by those inhuman hyenas who fill the palace court with their bloodthirsty cries? "Tell me," was Pilate's despairing reply to his trembling wife; "tell me how I am to wash my hands of this just man: tell me how I am to set him free, and at the same time to satisfy his enemies, who have both him and me in their power?" But as their clamor still went on Pilate caught at one of their cries and thought he saw in it a loop-hole for himself at any rate, if not for his prisoner. "He stirreth up the people from Galilee to this place!" they cried. Now, as Pilate's good planet would have it, who should

be in Jerusalem that passover morning but Herod Antipas, under whose jurisdiction all Galilee was, and Jesus therefore, as a Galilean. And the tetrarch was vastly
pleased with the unexpected recognition of his royal scepter, when this Galilean
prisoner was sent by Pilate to receive Herod's sentence on him. And all the more
so, that Pilate and Herod had had so many quarrels together about this very matter of Herod's jurisdiction. But here is the Roman governor, in his own city, and
at his own instance, recognizing in the most open and handsome way the too-oft
invaded rights and prerogatives of the king of Galilee. "And the same day," says
the Evangelist, "Pilate and Herod were made friends together again." And made
friends, as that poor fox little knew, at such a cheap price on Pilate's part! But
Pilate was not to get so easily rid of our Lord as all that. Herod Antipas was more
of a circus-master than a serious-minded monarch; and, instead of taking up the
case that had been referred to his jurisdiction, all that Herod aimed at was to get
some amusement out of the accused. "He is the King of the Jews, is he? He is a
candidate for my royal seat, is he? Then put the white coat of a candidate upon
him, and send him back to Pilate. The Governor will enjoy my jest: and it will
somewhat cement our recovered friendship!"

It is impossible for us to enter into all our Lord's thoughts as He was dragged
up and down the streets of Jerusalem that passover morning. Dragged in cords
from Gethsemane to Caiaphas, and from Caiaphas to Pilate, and from Pilate to
Herod, and from Herod back again to Pilate. And all the time with all the shame
and insult heaped upon Him that the evil hearts of His enemies could devise. Our
Lord's thoughts and feelings at all times are a great deep to us. But Pilate was a
man of like passions with ourselves, and we can quite well understand what his
thoughts and his feelings were when the chief priests were back again with their
prisoner at the praetorium. What is Pilate to do? With all his power and with all
his diplomacy what is Pilate to do next? You all know what he did next. He put
up Jesus to the vote of the people against Barabbas, trusting that the gratitude
and the pity and the sense of fair play among the common people would carry
the day. But, difficult as it is to explain, they all suddenly turned round and cried
out with one voice, "Away with Him! Away with Him, and release to us Barabbas!"
"Why?" demanded Pilate, with indignation and exasperation, "What evil has this
man ever done? Neither Herod nor I have found the shadow of a fault in Him."
You have seen the vote taken at an election-time in your own city. And you have
seen how ill-will, and envy, and personal spite are so much more active at such
times than justice, and gratitude, and goodness, and truth. Ignorance, and prejudice, and pure maliciousness, will come out to the polling-booth on their crutches
and will need neither your canvasser nor your carriage to come for them. "Not
this man, but Barabbas!" cried the rulers of the Jews; and to a man the rabble of
the people cried out with them, "Away with Him! Away with Him! Crucify Him!
Crucify Him!"

Whatever the wicked spirit may have been that took possession of the populace
of Jerusalem that awful passover morning, the Holy Ghost Himself witnesses to
us that it was the wickedest spirit in all hell that had come up and had taken possession of Caiaphas and his colleagues now for a long time. And we knew it before

it was told us. We have seen it coming all the time. And Pilate saw it that morning, and had seen it coming all the time, and had told Tiberius about it. Our Lord's life and teaching and wonderful works, and the multitudes that were attracted to Him by all that;—it would have been the New Jerusalem above, and Caiaphas would have been a sanctified saint in heaven, not to have had his heart burned up with envy within him at our Lord's popularity with the people. It is at this moment in the Passion Play at Ober-Ammergau that the chorus comes forward with this warning to us:

> 'Tis envy—which no mercy knows,
> In which hell's flame most fiercely glows—
> Lights this devouring fire.
> All's sacrificed unto its lust—
> Nothing too sacred, good, or just
> To fall to its desire.
> Oh! woe to those this passion sweeps
> Helpless and bound into the deeps!

Pilate had never heard of the Jerusalem that is above, but no man knew better than he did the Jerusalem that was yelling like all the furies all around him. Caiaphas had put on his holiest of masks that holiest of mornings, and he had demanded swift execution to be done on this traitor against Caesar and this blasphemer against God. But Pilate was not a child. Heathen as Pilate was, and hardened as a stone in his heart as he was, he both saw down into, and despised and detested every high priest, and scribe, and elder of them all. It was a noble hyperbole that was put upon Plato's tombstone: "Here lies a man too good and too great for envy." But that literally true epitaph, and no hyperbole, could not have been written even on Joseph's new tomb as long as Caiaphas remained alive in Jerusalem. Our Lord Himself was neither too good nor too great for Caiaphas's envy and ill-will, nor for Pilate's selfish cowardice and open sale of truth and justice. For, all this time, with all his power, and with all his pride, and with all his astuteness, and with all his resource, the chain of his terrible fate was fast closing around Pontius Pilate. And his rage, and his pain, and his pride drove him well-nigh demented. Never, surely, since mortal man was first taken and held fast in the snare of Satan, was any miserable man more completely seized and carried captive of his past sins and his present circumstances, than Pontius Pilate was that passover morning. And it all came to a head, and the fatal chain was all riveted round Pilate for the last time, when the savage threat was spat up at him: "If thou let this man go, thou art not Caesar's friend!" That was enough. For at that Pilate took water, in his defeat and despair, and washed his hands before the multitude, and said: "I, at any rate, am innocent of the blood of this just person: See ye, his murderers, to it." And they saw to it.

All that is not the half of the history of that awful morning to Pontius Pilate, and of all that he went through. But that is enough to set Pilate sufficiently before our eyes in the hour and power of his fatal temptation. And all that is told us in order that we may turn our eyes inward and ask ourselves what we would have done that passover morning had we been in Pilate's place; had we stood between the deadly anger of Caesar at us on the one hand, and with only a just man to be scourged and crucified on the other hand! We would have done just what Pilate did. To protect ourselves; to stand well with our masters, and to preserve our paying post; we would have washed our hands, and would have scourged Jesus, righteous man and all. Who here, and in this hour of truth, will dare to cast a stone at Pontius Pilate? What self-seeking, what self-sheltering, what truth-selling, what soul-selling man?

> O break, O break, hard heart of mine!
>   Thy weak self-love and guilty pride
> His Pilate and His Judas were:
>   Jesus, our Lord, is crucified!

I know all the old legends, sacred and profane, about Pontius Pilate, and about his miserable end. But I shall not believe any of them. I shall continue to hope against hope for poor Pontius Pilate. If my sale of my Savior, and of my own soul, has so often chased me up to the Cross of Christ, so I think Pilate's remorse must have chased him. And as he washed his hands in water that passover morning, so I shall hope he washed his hands and his heart ten thousand times in after days in that Fountain for sin which he had such an awful hand in opening. The world would not contain the books if all the names of all the chief priests, and scribes, and inhabitants of Jerusalem; and all the governors, and centurions, and soldiers of Rome, who came to believe on Christ crucified were to be written in them. "Ye men of Israel, hear these words: Jesus of Nazareth, a man approved of God, Him ye have taken, and by wicked hands have crucified and slain. And now, brethren, I wot that through ignorance ye did it, as did also your rulers. But unto you first, God, having raised up His Son Jesus, has sent Him to bless you, in turning away every one of you from his iniquities." Who can tell? With that glorious Gospel preached far and wide, and with the Redeemer's prayer offered with His own blood to back it on the Cross, Father, forgive them: who can tell? I, for one, shall continue to hope for Pontius Pilate, as for myself. For—

> O love of God! O sin of man!
>   In this dread act your strength is tried,
> And victory remains with love:
>   Jesus, our Lord, is crucified!

85
Pilate's Wife

OUR men of natural science are able sometimes to reconstruct the shape and the size of a completely extinct species from a single bone, or splinter of a bone, that has been quite accidentally dug out of the earth. And in something of the same way Pilate's wife rises up before us out of a single sentence in Matthew's Gospel. We see the governor's wife only for a moment. We hear her only for a moment. But in the space of that short moment of time she so impresses her sudden footprint on this page of this Gospel, that as long as this Gospel is read, this that Pilate's wife said and did that Passover morning shall be held in remembrance for a most honorable memorial of her.

Both Pilate and his wife, in Paul's words, were Gentiles in the flesh, being aliens from the common-wealth of Israel, and strangers from the covenants of promise, having no hope, and without God in the world. Both Pilate and his wife were perfect heathens, as we would say. They were still at what we would call the pre-patriarchal period of divine revelation. They were still very much what Abraham himself was when God chose him, and spake to him, and said to him, "Get thee out of thy country, and from thy kindred, and from thy father's house, unto a land that I will show thee." As regards many of the good things of this life; learning, civilization, refinement, and such like; the Roman governor and his gifted wife were very far advanced; but as regards what our Lord estimates to be the one thing needful for all men, they were not unlike Terah, and Nahor, and Abram, when they still dwelt in old time on the other side of the flood, and still served other gods. Both Pilate and his wife were still at that stage in which God was wont to speak to men at sundry times and in divers manners; and, among other manners, in the manner of a dream. For, till Holy Scripture came to some fullness and to some clearness, we find God revealing Himself in a dream, not only to Abraham, and Pharaoh, and Nebuchadnezzar; but even to Jacob, and Joseph, and Solomon, and down even to such New Testament men as Peter, and Paul, and John. Almighty God has complete control and continual command of all the avenues that lead into the soul of man, and He sends His message to this soul and to that at the very time and in the very way that seems wisest and best in His sight. And Elihu's remarkable description of the manner and the matter of one of his own divine dreams may be taken as a prophetic forecast of this passover dream of Pilate's wife: "In a dream, in a vision of the night, when deep sleep falleth upon men, in slumberings upon the bed: then He openeth the ears of men, and sealeth their instruction, that He may withdraw man from his purpose, and hide pride from man. He keepeth back his soul from the pit, and his life from perishing by the sword. He is chastened also with pain upon his bed, and the multitude of his bones with strong pain." A perfect picture of Pilate's wife's dream in the Praetorium that night, and

411

of its divinely-intended purpose toward Pilate himself, which was to withdraw Pilate from his purpose, and to keep back his soul from the pit.

Long before that passover morning Pilate's wife had made up her mind about Jesus of Nazareth. With all the wealth and all the rank of the city against Him; with all the temple learning and all the temple authority against Him; with, without exception, every responsible ruler and every influential man in all Jerusalem against Him; and with all her own and all her husband's original interests and natural instincts strongly prejudicing her against Him—she had overcome all that, and had deliberately and resolutely taken up His side. She had made up her mind that whatever else He was, or might turn out to be, at any rate up to the present moment, He had been a blameless man. He had gone about doing good. The procurator's palace was the center and the seat of everything. All the telegraph wires ran up and delivered themselves there. Everything that took place in the province was instantly reported at the Praetorium. Not a word of rebellion was whispered in closets, not a zealot stirred a foot in the greatest stealth, not a sword was sharpened at midnight in all the land, but it was all as well known to Pilate and to his wife as to the intending insurrectionary himself. And, though the Roman procurators were wont to leave their wives at home when they set out to their provinces, Pilate's wife was far too meet a help to him to be left behind him when he was wrestling for his life with those rebellious and treacherous Jews in Jerusalem. And it was so. The procurator's wife shared all her husband's anxieties, all his responsibilities, and all his apprehensions. She was with him in everything with her keen mind and her noble heart. And with all her swift divination she had come to the sure conclusion long ago that Jesus of Nazareth was all and more than He seemed to be. Her Hebrew maid could not assist her Roman mistress to dress, but, one way or other, the same subject of conversation continually came up—what He had last said, and what He had last done. She could not drive out through the gate of the city but there was His congregation covering the highway. She could not return home that He was not healing some sick man at the door of the temple. And, all that passover week—what with her husband's spies, and what with her own, she knew as well as Annas and Caiaphas themselves knew what they had determined to do. She had watched out of her window what we now know as the entry into Jerusalem. She had heard coming over the valley the voices of the children in the temple crying out and saying, "Hosanna to the Son of David!" till she wished that her children were among them. The last thing that absolutely carried her whole heart captive was Martha and Mary and their brother Lazarus. And it had needed all her own self-command, and all her husband's command over her as her husband, to keep her from going out to Bethany to see Lazarus with her own eyes. She had often read of such things in her own ancient books at home, but such a thing as this had never come so near her before. And then, when the report came to the Praetorium that Lazarus's friend had been betrayed and taken prisoner, and was all that night to be under trial before Caiaphas and the council; and then, that it would all roll in upon her husband the next morning—if a dream cometh through the multitude of business—no wonder that Pilate's wife dreamed about Jesus of Nazareth all that passover night!

Just what shape her dream took that passover night, I would give something for myself to know. And it is not mere and idle curiosity that makes me say that, for it would be to me a great lesson in the first principles of divine revelation to the Old Testament Church, as well as to this Roman matron's soul, and to my own soul. It would be as good as another disinterred manuscript of the Acts of Pilate, did we know something of the multitude of this business about Jesus that had gone that night to make up that so suffering and so opportune dream. With the books of the Hebrew prophets on her table, and with the echoes of John's preaching and Jesus' parables filling the air all around her, what may the governor's wife not have seen and heard in the visions and voices of that ominous night? She may have seen a hand coming out and writing it on the wall of the Praetorium, "Mene, Mene, Tekel, Upharsin." She may have seen the same sight that made Daniel himself to be troubled, and his countenance to change. She may have seen the Ancient of days, with His throne like the fiery flame, and His wheels as burning fire, and the judgment set, and the books opened. She may have seen one like the Son of Man come with the clouds of heaven, till His kingdom was an everlasting kingdom, and His dominion that shall not be destroyed. Till, "For God's sake," she said, "have thou nothing to do with that dreadful man?" Now, among all your dreams and visions on your bed do you ever dream about Jesus Christ? You dream every night about this man and that woman that you love or hate. Do you ever dream about your Savior? Do you love and fear Him to that extent? If He were actually engaged within you on the salvation of your soul, the multitudinous business connected with that inward work would surely make you think about Him all day till you would dream about Him all night. Do you ever do it? Will you be able to say to Him at the last day, "Lord, Thou knowest that I often thought about Thee all day and dreamed about Thee all night, and told my husband my dreams about Thee in the morning?" Will you have as much as Pilate's heathen wife will have to say for herself and for him? Will you; or will you not? What do you think? What do you say?

And then, this will be openly acknowledged and admitted in the day of judgment that Pilate's wife was fearlessly true and faithful to all her light. Her best light was as yet but candle-light. It was but as rush-light. But, even candle-light, even rush-light, even the faintest reflection of candle-light or rush-light is, all the time, the very same light as the light of the noonday sun. All light of all kinds comes, in one way or another, from one and the same source. And the lurid light of Pilate's wife's dream that night all came to her and to him from the Light of the world. The identical same Light that is lighting you and me with such brilliance and beauty in this house tonight, that very same Light struggled within that Roman lady's soul on her bed and in her dreams in Jerusalem that night. And nothing in divine things is more sure than this, that they who love the light—be it candle-light or be it sun-light—shall have more light sent to them, till they have all the light that they need. To them their path shall shine more and more to the perfect day. They who love the light, and walk in what light they have, they shall never lie down in darkness. You may absolutely depend upon it that the True Light Himself, who stood under such a cloud before Pilate's bar that daybreak, both overheard and laid up in His heart the noble message that came out to the procurator. You may rely on it that He who had already sent her so much of His own light, continued to send her more, till she became one of those princess-saints of Caesar's household, whom Paul so saluted in long after days. And may we not hope that Pilate himself was at last completely won with the holy walk of his wife, as he beheld her chaste conversation coupled with fear?

JACOB BEHMEN says that a man is sometimes like a wolf, cruel and merciless, and with an insatiable thirst for blood; sometimes like a dog, snappish, malicious, envious, grudging, as a dog is with a bone that he cannot himself eat; sometimes like a serpent, stinging and venomous, slanderous in his words, and treacherous in his actions; sometimes like a hare, timorous and starting off; sometimes like a toad, and sometimes like a fox, and so on. The Teutonic philosopher has a whole incomparable chapter on "The Bestial Manifestations in Man." "My dear children in Christ," he proceeds, "my sole purpose in writing in this way to you is not to revile you or to reproach you with your fallen and bestialized estate. What I here write to you is the simple and naked and open truth. I am as certain as I live that it is the truth of God, because I have the daily experience of it all in myself. Every day, and every hour of every day, I have the bondage of it all, and the shame of it all, and the degradation and the guilt of it all, in myself, and not in another. And, therefore, your embruted estate is here told you not to exclude any of you from the hope of salvation. The most wolf-like man among you, the most dog-like man among you, the most toad-like man among you, the most fox-like man among you—all such men are invited, and, indeed, commanded, to arise every moment and flee from themselves into the new birth in God. And, moreover, it was for this very purpose that the Son of God was mani-fested. It was to turn us all from being beasts and devils everlastingly, and to make us all with Himself, the new and born-from-above sons and daughters of the living God. Jesus Christ, the very Mouth of Truth Himself, called Herod a fox, not to sentence him, and to fix him for ever the fox that he was, but it was in order, if possible, to turn him from all his guiles, and all his lusts, and all his lies, and to make him even yet a child of God, and an heir of everlasting life." So writes "the illuminated Behmen" in his *Election of Grace*.

All the historians and all the biographers of that time, both sacred and profane, agree about Herod Antipas. They all agree that Antipas was his father's son in all that was worst in his father's character. Old Herod, with all his brutalities and with all his devilries, had at the same time some of the possibilities in him that go to the making of a great man. But by no possibility could his second son ever have been a great man. Antipas was a weak, cruel, sensual, ostentatious, shallow-hearted crea-ture. He is known to the readers of the New Testament first as the dupe of a bad woman, and then as the murderer of John the Baptist, and then as one of the judges of Jesus Christ. He was that fox who tried to frighten our Lord to flee from His work; and at last he was that puppet-king, and reprobate sinner, to whom our Lord would not answer one word. His licentious life, his family miseries, his political maneuvers, his sycophantic and extravagant expenditures, his ruinous defeats, both in war and in diplomacy, his fall from his throne, and his banishment from his kingdom, are all to be read in the books of Josephus, who is an author altogether worthy to chronicle the deeds, and to tell the exploits, of such a hero. Avoid giving of characters, says Butler in his noble sermon on "The Government of the Tongue." At the same time, as Bengel says, the truth must sometimes be spoken, and must sometimes be all spoken. Sometimes a dog must be branded to all men to be a dog, and a serpent advertised to be a serpent, and a swine to be a swine. "Go back," said our Lord, "to that fox which sent you, and tell him what I have said about him: tell him the name I have denounced upon him." And we understand and accept both what our Lord and His two servants have said on this subject of the giving of characters. It is a large part of our daily lesson and discipline and duty in this life, to be able to give the proper characters, and to apply the proper epithets, to men and to things; and to do that at the right time and in the right temper. It is a large and an important part of every preacher's office especially, to apply to all men and to all their actions their absolutely and fearlessly right and true names. To track out the wolf, and the serpent, and the toad, and the fox, in the men in whom these bestialities dwell, and to warn all men how and where all that will end; no minister may shrink from that. All the vices and all the crimes of the tetrarch's miserable life, and all the weakness and duplicity of his contemptible character, are all summed up and sealed down on Herod Antipas in that one divine word that day: "That fox."

But what makes Herod Antipas such a poignant lesson to us is not that he was a fox, it is this rather, that he began by being a fox, and ended by being a reprobate. You know what reprobation is, my brethren? This is reprobation. "As soon as Pilate knew that this prisoner belonged to Herod's jurisdiction, he sent Him to Herod, who was in Jerusalem at that time. And Herod questioned Jesus with many words, but He answered him nothing." That is reprobation. It is our reprobation begun when God answers us nothing. When, with all our praying, and with all our reading, and with all our inquiring, He still answers us nothing. Herod's day of grace had lasted long, but it is now at an end. Herod had had many opportunities, and at one time he was almost persuaded. At one time he was not very far from the Kingdom of Heaven. But all that is long past. Herod had smothered and silenced his conscience long ago, and now he is to be for ever let alone. Nay—and let all beginning reprobates attend to this—not only was Herod let alone, but when he put many eager questions to our Lord, He answered him nothing. It is here that the real horror and the awful fascination to me of all Herod's case comes in. It is in this: because we also go on exactly like Herod, cheating ourselves, and thinking, poor self-entrapped foxes that we are, that we are all the time mocking God also, till it is too late; for God is not to be mocked by any man. David has drawn out this solemnizing lesson, and has set it in a singularly impressive Psalm of his, and in never-to-be-forgotten words: "If I regard iniquity in my heart, the Lord will not hear me." Now, it was just because this lewd and cruel fox had so defiantly, and so flagrantly, and so criminally, and for so long, regarded the greatest iniquity in his heart and in his life, that now at last when he put so many questions to our Lord He answered him nothing. We all know the same thing ourselves. Fox-like, Antipas-like, Doth God see us? we say. Surely the darkness shall cover us, we say. Just this once more, we say. At a more convenient time I will reform myself, we say. We take our own way and our own time, and, fox-like, we have many tricks in our eye by which we will escape the trap. We have all gone on in that way, till these words of reprobation—"no answer"—describe to perfection many of us in this house tonight. In Herod it was murder and incest, never repented of and never forsaken, that so absolutely shut our Lord's mouth toward Herod and toward all his requests and all his questions. There are no controversies so dark and so terrible between God and our souls as the murder of John the Baptist. But God may be as silent and as angry at all our prayers and questions and casuistries as ever He was at Herod's. Nobody would believe, but those of us who have come through it, the little things, the trivial things, that will stop God's ear, and shut His mouth, and make Him our enemy. Somewhat too much money spent on ourselves, and somewhat too little spent on the Church of Christ and on His poor will do it. Too little time and strength spent in closet and intercessory prayer will do it. A secret ill-feeling entertained at somebody will do it. A debt not paid and with interest will do it. A prejudice nursed and not surrendered in time will do it. A grudge kept up will do it. An apology not made will do it. A too long and a too free tongue will do it. An impertinent book, and the time and money spent upon that book will do it. A second sleep in the morning more than is necessary will do it. A pipeful of doubtful tobacco will do it. A daily glass or two of inexpedient wine will do it. A knuckle of too-savory mutton will sometimes do it, as Dr. Jowett was wont to say. Nobody could tell, nobody who has not himself come through it all could imagine or could believe if it were told them, the triviality, and the absolute immateriality, of the things that will in some men's cases do it. God has kept up a life-long controversy with some of His saints about little things that they could not put words upon, so unlike Almighty God and so beneath Him, as one would say, is the whole dispute. The truth is, when Almighty God is bent upon the absolute sanctification of some elect sinner, no autobiography, no *Brea*, no *Reliquiae*, no *Grace Abounding*, no amount of imaginative genius and a corresponding style, could possibly convey to another man all the controversies, great and small, that all through his life go on between God and that elect sinner's soul. There are some terribly predestinated saints. There are some elections that almost consume those chosen souls to dust and ashes in the awful furnace of their sanctification. The apostle had this same terrible election, and sin-consuming ambition, for his Thessalonian converts. "And the very God of peace sanctify you wholly: and I pray God your whole spirit, and soul, and body be preserved blameless unto the coming of our Lord Jesus Christ." You have it all there. It is as much as to say, the very God of peace turn a deaf ear to your most importunate and agonizing prayers, as long as there is a single speck of sin secretly staining any part of your soul. The very God of peace crucify every remaining lust in your body, and every remaining affection in your spirit, and every remaining thought, and feeling, and passion, in your soul, till you are absolutely blameless in His consumingly holy sight. The very God of peace empty you from vessel to vessel, and prune you to the quivering quick, and keep you in a sevenfold-fire, till the coming of the Great Refiner in the glory of His Father. And, in like manner, the very God of peace demands of you also every moment of your time, and every mite of your money, and every word of your mouth, and every beat of your heart. And not till He gets all that from you will He answer you one word; no, not for all your prayers, and all your sweats, and all your tears. It is not lawful for a child of God to have it, He will say, till He will make your disobedient life a burden to you past bearing, a racking torture, and one long agony. No! He denies you, till you can hear nothing in all your conscience but these angry words with you. No! it is not lawful for you. It is not right. It is not safe. It is not seemly. It is not expedient. It may be for others, but it can never now be for you. And as long as God in your conscience says that to you about anything whatsoever, you may debate, and question, and pray, and seek for marks and evidences till your dying day, but the very God of peace will answer you nothing.

And then there is this complication also: there are things that it is not lawful for one man to do, that his very next-door neighbor may do every day, and walk with God and talk with God all the time. There are things that are unpardonable in the sight of God in one man, but which are not only entirely innocent and inoffensive, but are positively virtuous and praiseworthy in another man. There are things that will be the ruin of one man's soul, that may all the time be the very sweetness and strength of his neighbor's soul. I may have to deny myself, on the pain of reprobation, every day, what you may eat and drink every day and ask a blessing on it. I may have to spend all the rest of my redeemed life in this world in a daily battle and a nightly self-examination against habits of body and mind that you cannot so much as imagine. I may have to sit up at my salvation every night of the week, while you are sleeping like an innocent child. I may have to meditate on David's Psalms continually, and on nothing else any more, while you are doing nothing else all your time and thought but either telling or hearing some new thing. I may have, till the day of my death, to fight against a slavery that makes you, in your lush liberty, say that I am beside myself. I may have iniquities in my heart absolutely shipwrecking all my prayers: iniquities that even David in his very best Psalms knew nothing about: iniquities that did not even exist in David's day, because the Holy Ghost was not yet given. So beset behind and before are some New Testament men, and some men far on in the life of grace, that God scarcely ever answers them one word from one year's end to another. Then king Herod questioned with Jesus in many words; but He answered him nothing. But, sings David, verily God hath heard me. He hath attended to the voice of my prayer.

87
The Penitent Thief

THE two malefactors who were crucified with Christ had been ringleaders in Barabbas's robber band. And had Barabbas himself not been pardoned by Pilate that morning, he also would have carried his cross out to Calvary that day and would have been crucified upon it. But when Barabbas and his band are called thieves and robbers it is but due to them to give them the benefit of the doubt. In our noble British law and administration there is a deep and a fundamental distinction taken between ordinary criminals against all civilized society, and political criminals against this or that foreign government for the time. We give up swindlers and murderers when they flee to our shores, but we provide a safe and an honorable asylum for political refugees and state criminals, as we call them. Now all the chances are that Barabbas and his band had begun simply by being rebels against Rome, as, indeed, all the Jews were everywhere in their hearts. Though no doubt their repudiated, outlawed, exasperated, and hunted-down lives had by degrees made Barabbas and his band desperate and reckless, till they had become in many cases pure thieves and robbers. David in the cave of Adullam is not a bad picture of Barabbas at the beginning of his life of outlawry. For every one that was in distress came to David, and every one that was in debt, and every one that was discontented, and he became a captain over them; and there were with David about four hundred men. Only, no doubt, David was a far better captain than Barabbas ever was. David, no doubt, kept his men in far better hand, till he turned them out such splendid specimens of soldiers and mighty men of war, and the best law-abiding citizens in all Israel. But David had only Saul to overthrow, whereas Barabbas had Caesar.

The Evangelist Luke had perfect understanding of all things from the very first. And no doubt he knew all about the early life of Barabbas and his band. And especially, I feel sure, he would make every possible inquiry concerning the early days of this remarkable man who is discovered to us in this Gospel as the penitent thief. But it would have been out of place in Luke to have gone into this man's whole past life at the moment when he is fixing all our eyes on the crucifixion of our Lord. At the same time, it is as clear as daylight to me that this is not the first time that this crucified thief has seen our Lord. He knew both our Lord's life and teaching and character quite well, though he had cast it all behind his back all his days up till now. He knew that our Lord had done nothing amiss all the time that he and his companions were fast ripening for the due reward of their deeds. There was not a Sabbath synagogue, nor a passover journey, nor a carpenter's shop, nor a tax-gatherer's booth, nor a robber's cave in all Israel where the name, and the teaching, and the mighty works of Jesus of Nazareth were not constantly discussed, and debated, and divided on. And Barabbas and his band must have had many a deliberation in their banishment about Jesus of Nazareth. Is He indeed the promised Messiah? Is He really David's Son? Is this really He who is to overcome and cast out Caesar? If it is, we shall join His standard immediately, and He will remember us when He comes into His kingdom. Week after week, month after month, year after year, this went on till their hearts became sick and desperate within them. A hundred times Barabbas and this one and that one of his band had disguised themselves as fishermen and shepherds to come down to hear our Lord preach and to see the mighty works that He did. Nay, for anything we know, this man may at one time have been one of our Lord's disciples, quite as well as Simon Zelotes and Judas Iscariot. In his early, and enthusiastic, and patriotic days he may have been one of John's disciples. He may have seen Jesus of Nazareth baptized that day. He may have been baptized himself that day. He may have heard the Baptist say: "Behold the Lamb of God!" He may have been among the multitude who sat and heard the Sermon on the Mount. He may actually have closely companied with our Lord for a season. Till he was at last one of those who went back and walked no more with Him, because our Lord would not be taken by them and made a king. But, go back to Barabbas's band as he did, I defy him ever to forget what he had seen and heard down among the cities, and the villages, and the mountain-sides, and the supper-tables of Galilee and Jewry. This man, and many more like him, went back to their farm, and to their merchandise, and to their toll-booth, and to their robber-cave, but they took with them memories, and visions, and hearts, and consciences, they could never forget. As we see was the case conspicuously with this thief on the cross.

And all this went on: our Lord finishing the work His Father had given Him to do, while Barabbas and his band were fast ripening for their cross; till, as God would have it, our Lord and Barabbas, with these two of his band, were all taken and tried, and were sentenced to be crucified all four on the same passover morning. Now, when a man is on his way out to his own execution he would be more than a man if he paid much attention, to the circumstances attending the execution of his neighbors. At the same time, this thief was no ordinary man. "This is Jesus of Nazareth," he would say to himself. "This is the carpenter-prophet I used to steal into His presence to hear Him preach. I once thought to be one of His men myself to deliver Israel." And then as men among ourselves do on the morning of their execution, the psalms and hymns of his boyhood came back into his mind. Till he did not hear the mockery and the insults of the people who filled the streets as he went on and said to himself: "Remember not the sins of my youth, nor my transgressions. For thou writest bitter things against me, and makest me to possess the iniquities of my youth. Thou puttest my feet also in the stocks, and lookest narrowly unto all my paths; thou settest a print upon the heels of my feet. We lie down in our shame, and our confusion covereth us; for we have sinned against the Lord our God; we and our fathers, from our youth even unto this day, and have not obeyed the voice of the Lord our God." Till, by that time, the terrible procession had got to Golgotha. And all the way, as already in the high priest's palace, and in the Praetorium, and now at Golgotha, all hell was let loose as never before nor since. And Satan entered into the two thieves, and into this thief also. And no wonder that they both cursed and blasphemed and raved and gnashed their teeth and spat upon their crucifiers, as all crucified men always did, so insupportable to absolute insanity was the awful torture of crucifixion. And all the time God was laying on His Son the iniquity of us all, and all the time He was dumb, and opened not His mouth. "Save Thyself and us!" the two crucified and maddened men both cried to Him; the one in fiendish ribaldry, and the other out of a heart in which heaven and hell were fighting with their last stroke for his soul. Till this one of the two thieves at last came to himself. And the thing that made him come to himself was this: Our Lord had never opened His mouth. He had neither cursed, nor gnashed His teeth, nor spat at His crucifiers and revilers. But, at last, He also spoke. And it was the same voice—the thief had never heard another voice in all the world to compare with it! For, looking up into the fast-darkening heavens, our Lord exclaimed, "Father, forgive them; for they know not what they do." That benediction of our blessed Lord did more to benumb the agony of body and mind in this thief than all the wine mingled with myrrh the women of Jerusalem had made for him and for his fellows to drink that morning. "Father, forgive them!"— it absolutely broke the thief's hard heart to hear it. And as his hardened companion still reviled our Lord hanging beside him, the now penitent thief looked across and said to his old companion and fellow-malefactor the words that all the world knows.

John Donne, in a Lent sermon that he preached at Whitehall, dwells on what he calls "The despatch of the grace of God in the case of the penitent thief." The *per saltum* character of the thief's repentance and faith, and the full and immediate response of our Lord to his so-sudden repentance and faith, make a fine sermon. The kingdom of heaven suffered violence that day at this thief's so suddenly repentant and so believing hands. He took heaven, so to speak, at a leap that day. The swiftness of the thief's repentance, and faith, and confession, and pardon, and sanctification, and glorification, is something very blessed for us all to think about, and never to forget; and, especially, those of us who must make haste and lose no more time if we are to be for ever with him and with his Lord in Paradise. Let all old and fast-dying men have this written up, like Augustine, on the wall over against their bed—"There is life in a look at the crucified One." For we may not have time nor strength for more than just one such look of despatch.

And, then, if you would see the most wonderful believer this world has ever seen, come to the cross of Christ, and to that cross beside it, and look at the penitent thief. He was a greater believer than Abraham, the father of believers. Greater than David. Greater than Isaiah. While Peter, and James, and John, with all their privileges and opportunities, are not worthy to be named in the same day with this thief. For they had all forsaken their Savior that awful day and had fled from Him. It was of the thief, and of his alone and so transcendent faith, that our Lord spoke in such praise and in such reproof to Thomas eight days afterwards, and said, "Blessed is he in heaven with Me this day, who saw nothing but shame, and defeat, and death in Me, and yet so believed in Me, and so cheered Me that day." For our Lord never, all His life, got such a surprise and such a delight as He got on the cross that day—not from Peter, not from the Syrophoenician woman, not from the centurion, not from Mary Magdalene, as He got on His cross that morning from the thief who hung beside Him. There was nothing, after His Father's presence with Him, that held our Lord's heart up all His life on earth like faith on Him in any sinner's heart. And now that His Father also has forsaken Him; now that He is so absolutely deserted and so awfully alone; it is this thief's faith, and love, and hope that is such a cup of cold water to our Lord's fast-sinking heart. All faith and all hope on Christ were as dead as a stone in Peter's heart and in John's heart. Mary Magdalene herself, with all her love, had given Him up as for ever dead. But not the thief. It was at the very darkest hour this world has ever seen, or ever will see, that this thief's splendid faith flashed up brighter than the midday sun that day. Some say that Paul will sit next to Christ in Paradise. I cannot but think that Paul will insist on giving place to this very prince and leader of all New Testament believers. Anybody could have believed and labored all their days after being caught up into the third heaven, and after seeing Christ sitting there in all His glory. But Christ was still on His cross, and His glory was as black as midnight, when all the faith of the church of God found its last retreat and sure fastness and high tower in the thief's unconquerable and inextinguishable heart. Paul deserves a high seat in heaven, and he will get all that he deserves, and more. But the penitent thief could say, "I am crucified with Christ" in a sense that even Paul could not say that. And however high the thief's throne in heaven is, the whole church of angels and saints will acclaim that he is worthy. Well done! O greatest and bravest-hearted of all believers! Well done!

88
Thomas

THE character of Thomas is an anatomy of melancholy. If "to say man is to say melancholy," then to say Thomas, called Didymus, is to say religious melancholy. Peter was of such an ardent and enthusiastical temperament that he was always speaking, whereas Thomas was too great a melancholian to speak much, and when he ever did speak it was always out of the depths of his hypochondriacal heart.

It was already the last week of his Master's life before we have Thomas so much as once opening his mouth. And the occasion of his first melancholy utterance was this: Lazarus was sick unto death in Bethany. And when Jesus heard that His friend was so sick, He said to His disciples, "Let us go into Judea again." "Master," they answered, "the Jews of late have been seeking opportunity to stone Thee to death, and goest Thou thither again?" And it was when Thomas saw that his Master was walking straight into the jaws of certain destruction that he said, in sad abandonment of all his remaining hope, "Let us also go, that we may die with Him." Thomas felt sure in his foreboding heart that his Master would never leave Judea alive; Thomas loved his Master more than life, and therefore he determined to die with Him. And, indeed, that determination was not very difficult for Thomas to take. Life had not yielded much to Thomas. And its best promises, more and more delayed, and more and more deluding him, were taking less and less hold of Thomas's heart as the years went on. We see now that the disciples of Jesus of Nazareth had the very best cause for high hope and full assurance. But at that time, and especially that week, Thomas had only too good ground for all his anxiety, and despondency, and melancholy. And a whole lifetime of melancholy, constitutional and circumstantial, had by this time settled down on Thomas, and had taken absolute and tyrannical possession of him. The disciples were all sick at heart with hope deferred; as also with the terrible questionings that would sometimes arise in their hearts, and would not be silenced; all kinds of questionings about their more and more mysterious Master; and about His more and more mysterious, and more and more stumbling, sayings, both about Himself and about themselves. And then His certainly impending death, and the unaccountable delay and disappearance of His promised kingdom: all that doubt, and fear, and despondency, and despair, met in Thomas's melancholy heart till it all took absolute possession of him. And till he sometimes said to himself that it would be the best thing that could happen to him if he could but die at once and be done for ever with all these difficulties and delays and bitter and unbearable disappointments. The discipleship-life, at its very best, had never been very satisfying to Thomas's heart; and, of late, it had been becoming absolutely unbearable to this melancholy and morose man. "Let us go," he said, "that we may die with Him."

The next time that Thomas speaks is when Jesus and His disciples are still in the upper room where the last passover had just been celebrated and the Lord's

Supper instituted. "In My Father's house are many mansions: I go to prepare a place for you. And whither I go ye know, and the way ye know." The other disciples may know whither their Master is going, and they may know the way, but Thomas knows neither. The other disciples, as a matter of fact, know quite as little, and even less, about this whole matter than Thomas knows: only they think they know, when they do not: they have not knowledge enough to know that they know nothing. "His Father's house?" said Thomas to himself. "What does He mean? Why does He not speak plainly?" Thomas must understand his Master's meaning. Thomas is one of those unhappy men who cannot be put off with mere words. Thomas must see to the bottom before he can pretend to believe. Thomas was the first of those disciples, and a primate among them, in whose restless minds

>   doubt,
> Like a shoot, springs round the stock of truth.

At the same time, Thomas in his melancholy candor and saddened plainness of speech was but ministering an opportunity to his Master to utter one of His most golden oracles. Jesus saith unto Thomas, "I am the way, the truth, and the life: no man cometh unto the Father but by Me." We cannot much regret that restless and realistic melancholy of Thomas since it has procured for us such a satisfying and ennobling utterance as that. "All His disciples minister to Him," says Newman; "and as in other ways, so also in giving occasion for the words of grace which proceed from His mouth."

Ten days pass. But what days! The betrayal, the arrest, the trial, the crucifixion, the burial, and the resurrection of Thomas's Master. What days and nights of trial, and that not for faith and hope only, but for reason herself to keep her seat! All the faith and all the trust of the disciples have not only fallen into a deep doubt during those terrible days and nights: all their faith and all their trust have been actually crucified and laid dead and buried, and that without a spark of hope. For as yet the disciples knew not the Scripture, that their Master must rise again from the dead. "Then the same day at evening, being the first day of the week, came Jesus and stood in the midst, and saith unto them, Peace be unto you. And when He had so said, He showed them His hands and His side. Then were the disciples glad when they saw the Lord." But Thomas was not with them when Jesus came. Where was Thomas that glorious Sabbath evening? Why was he not with the rest? How shall we account for the absence of Thomas? It could not have been by accident. He must have been told that the ten astounded, overwhelmed, and enraptured disciples were to be all together that wonderful night; astounded, overwhelmed, and enraptured with the events of the morning. What conceivable cause, then, could have kept Thomas away? Whatever it was that kept Thomas away, he was terribly punished for his absence. For he thereby lost the first and best sight of his risen Master, and His first and best benediction of peace. He not only lost that benediction, but the joy of the other disciples who had received it filled the cup of Thomas's misery full. The first appearance of their risen Master, that had lifted all the other disciples up to heaven, was the last blow to cast Thomas down to hell. The darkness, the bitterness, the sullenness, the pride, that had its seat so deep down in

Thomas's heart, all burst out in the presence of his brethren's joy. Thomas would have none of their joy. Thomas would not believe it. They were dreaming. They were deluded. They were mad. And the pride, and jealousy, and bitterness of his heart, all drove Thomas into a deeper rage and a deeper rebellion. "Except I shall see in His hands the print of the nails, and put my finger into the print of the nails, and thrust my hand into His side, I will not believe." We all understand Thomas's misery. We have all been possessed by it. It is the jealousy and the rage of a guilty conscience. It is the jealousy and the rage of a disappointed and a revengeful heart. When any good comes to others that we should have been sharers in, when we are absent through our own fault, and when those who were present come to tell us about all that we have lost, we have all been like Thomas. We said, I do not believe it. It was not all that you say it was. You are exalting yourselves over me. You are boasting yourselves beyond the truth. And if the truth cannot be hid from us, or denied by us, we hate them, and the thing we have lost, all the more. Thomas is told us for our learning. We see ourselves in Thomas as in a glass. Thomas, in all his melancholy and resentment, is ourselves. Unbelief, and obstinacy, and loss of opportunity, and then increased unbelief, is no strange thing to ourselves.

And after eight days the disciples were again within, and this time Thomas was with them. It had taken the disciples all their might all these eight days to prevail with and to persuade Thomas. And all of us who know what it is to wage a war with our own wounded pride, and with nothing but our own sullenness, and stubbornness, and mulishness to oppose to the pleadings of truth and love, we know something of what Thomas came through before he consented to accompany the other disciples to the upper room at the end of those eight days. "Then came Jesus, the doors being shut, and stood in the midst, and said, Peace be unto you. Then saith He to Thomas, Reach hither thy finger, and behold My hands; and reach hither thy hand and thrust it into My side, and be not faithless but believing." How Thomas would hate himself when his own scornful, unbelieving, contemptuous words came back to him from his Master's gracious lips! How utterly odious his own words would sound as his Master repeated them. And worst of all when his risen Master humbled Himself to meet Thomas's unbelieving words and to satisfy them! Thomas would have killed himself with shame and self-condemnation, had it not been given him at that grandest moment of his whole life to say, "My Lord and my God!" Jesus saith unto him, "Thomas, because thou hast seen Me, thou hast believed; blessed are they that have not seen, and yet have believed!"

Now, my brethren, do you clearly understand and accept this peculiar blessedness of believing without seeing? Do you clearly see and fully accept the blessedness of a strong and an easy acting faith in the things of Christ? Faith is always easy where love and hope are strong. What we live for and hope to see, what we love with our whole heart, what we pray for night and day, what our whole future is anchored upon, that we easily believe, that we are ready to welcome. In that case our faith is to us nothing less than the substance of the thing hoped for; it is the evidence of the thing not seen as yet. What with Thomas's temperament of melancholy; what with his not having hid in his heart the things that our Lord had so often said about His coming death for sin and His resurrection for salvation;

and then his hot jealousy and ill-will at the joyful news of the disciples; with all that Thomas's heart was in a state most deadly to faith. Had Thomas's heart been tender, had he had seven devils cast out of his heart like Mary Magdalene, he also would have gone out to the sepulchre while it was yet dark, and would have been the first of all the disciples to see his risen Lord. But, as it was, he was the last to see Him, and ran a close risk of never seeing Him in this world. Now, how is it with you in this same matter? Are you hard to convince? Are you slow of faith? Is your heart so set upon this world that you have no eyes or ears for the world to come? Are you able to dispense with Jesus Christ day after day till He dies out of your heart, and imagination, and whole life, altogether? Unbelief grows by what it feeds upon, just like faith and love. To him who has no faith in God, in Christ, in the Holy Scriptures, in the unseen world, and in the world to come, from him is even taken away the little faith that he had, till he has none at all. You know men in whom that awful catastrophe has taken place. You know it, in measure, in yourself. Your faith is all but dead. You do not wait for Christ's coming, either to judge the world, or to take you to Himself, or to sanctify you, and comfort you, and answer your prayers. And then you are uneasy, and unhappy, and jealous, and angry, when you hear that He has been manifesting Himself in all these ways to them that believe. But you were not waiting for Him. You neither expected Him nor wished for Him: and He never comes to the like of you till He comes at last and too late. You will be horrified when it is told you what your whole life, and your whole heart, and all your desires and hopes say when words are put upon them. They all say, "I will not believe till the last trump awakens me, and the graves are opened, and the great white throne is set."

Now, from Thomas and his Lord that night let us learn this also, and take it away. Let us act upon the faith we have. Let us frequent the places where He is said to manifest Himself. Let us feed our faith on the strong meat of His word. And, since here also acts produce habits, and habits character; let us act faith continually on faith's great objects and operations. And, especially, on our glorified Redeemer. To Thomas He was crucified yesterday. But to us He is risen, and exalted, and is soon to come again. That the trial of your faith, being much more precious than of gold that perisheth, might be found unto praise, and honor, and glory at the appearing of Jesus Christ. Whom having not seen, ye love: in whom, though now ye see Him not, yet believing, ye rejoice with joy unspeakable and full of glory.

> For all thy rankling doubts so sore,
>   Love thou thy Savior still,
> Him for thy Lord and God adore,
>   And ever do His will.
> Though vexing thoughts may seem to last,
> Let not thy soul be quite o'ercast;
> Soon will He show thee all His wounds and say,
> Long have I known thy name: know thou My face alway.

89
Cleopas and His Companion

CLEOPAS and his companion were two men of Emmaus who had gone up the week before to Jerusalem to keep the passover. Cleopas and his companion were not exactly disciples of our Lord. That is to say, their names were not among the twelve; though the likelihood is that they were numbered and were well known among the seventy. And they had gone up to the feast in the hope that their Lord would be there, and that they would both see and hear Him as on former feast-days. It seemed to them like a year, like a lifetime, like another world, since last week they walked and talked together so full of hope and expectation, all the way up from Emmaus to Jerusalem. For Jesus had come up to the passover, as they had expected He would. And they had both seen Him, and had heard Him speak. They had followed Him about in the streets of Jerusalem as He preached His last sermons, so terrible to them to see and to hear. They were not among the twelve, and they had not been invited to the upper room, but they had done the next best thing to that, for they had eaten their passover supper out at Bethany with their friend Lazarus, and with Martha and Mary his sisters. The whole of Bethany was absolutely overwhelmed when the news came out at midnight that Jesus had been betrayed by one of His disciples, and was at that moment in the hands of His enemies. And with their loins girt, and with their passover-staff in their hands, Lazarus, and Cleopas, and his companion, were abroad in the streets of Jerusalem all that night, and till after the crucifixion was finished next morning. And now the third day of that tremendous overthrow and shipwreck had come, when, with a sickness of heart indescribable, Cleopas at last said to his companion, "Rise, and let us shake the dust off our feet against this accursed city, and let us escape to our own home." True; certain women of their company had rushed into the city that morning, saying that they had seen a vision of angels who told them that their crucified Master had risen and left His grave; but to Cleopas all that was so many idle tales. "No, no!" Cleopas said to his companion, "come away home. Believe me, we have seen the last of the redemption of Israel in our day, at any rate." Why, you will ask, was Cleopas in such a hurry to get home? Might he not have gone out to see the empty grave for himself? Might he not have waited in Jerusalem till the end of "the third day" that his Master so often foretold about Himself? As it was, Cleopas, like Pliable in the *Pilgrim's Progress*, was making a desperate plunge through the Slough of Despond so as to get out on the side next his own house, when a man whose name was Help came and held out His hand to him, and to his companion, in the midst of the Slough.

Yes: Cleopas and his companion, like Mr. Fearing, had a perfect Slough of Despond in their own hearts that sunset as they walked down to Emmaus and reasoned together and were sad. "Where did you see Him first? What was it that led you to think that He was the Christ? And, did you hear this sermon, and that?

And this parable and that?" And then the arrest, and the trial, and the crucifixion. No wonder they reeled to and fro, and staggered under their load of sorrow, till the workers in the fields said they were two drunken men on their way home from the feast. When a stranger overtook them as they halted, and reasoned, and debated together in their sadness. "Peace be with you both!" said the stranger with a pleasant voice as he joined himself to their company. But Cleopas was scarcely civil. Cleopas scarcely returned the salute of the stranger, so overwhelmed was he with his sadness. And they walked on in silence, Cleopas and his companion, and the stranger. Till the sympathizing stranger broke the sad silence with these confiding words: "What manner of communications are these that ye have one to another, as ye walk and are sad?" "Art thou such a stranger in Jerusalem," answered Cleopas, "as not to know the things which are come to pass there in these days? Where wert thou all last week? Where wert thou last Friday? Thou canst not have been in Jerusalem, surely, for all Jerusalem was out at Calvary that morning. And if thou hadst been out there thou wouldst not wonder at our sadness." The stranger did not say whether he had been out at Calvary last Friday morning or no. "What things?" He asked, bowing, at it were, to Cleopas's reproof and reproach at such unaccountable ignorance at such a time. And then we have Cleopas's reply in his own very identical words. For Luke, you must know, when he was preparing himself for his Gospel, and when he had read Mark's meager verses about the Emmaus meeting, said to himself, "I must be at the bottom of this! I must have a much fuller record of all this in my Gospel. I wonder if Cleopas is still alive?" And thus it is that we have before us, *verbatim et literatim*, the exact answer that Cleopas gave to the stranger when he asked, "What things?" "I remember, as if it were but yesterday," said Cleopas to Luke, "the whole scene, and every word that He said to us, and that we said to Him. How could I ever forget a single syllable of it? It was all so burned into my heart that I have told it a thousand times." And Cleopas took the Evangelist out of Emmaus and showed him the very spot just where the stranger joined them, and just where He said, "What things?" "And just where I said—these were my very words to Him—I said, Concerning Jesus of Nazareth, which was a prophet mighty in deed and in word before God and all the people. And how the chief priests and our rulers delivered Him to be condemned to death, and have crucified Him. But we trusted, I went on in my folly, that it had been He who should have redeemed Israel: and beside all this, today is the third day since these things were done. And from that hour to this, I have never for an hour or may say never for a moment, forgotten the look He gave us when He said to us, 'O fools, and slow of heart to believe!'" And then Cleopas continued to relate to Luke the rest of that never-to-be-forgotten conversation concerning the true Christ in Moses and the prophets. What an hour that was to Cleopas and to his companion! They did not know where they were. They forgot themselves. They were carried captive with the stranger's amazing knowledge, and with His supreme authority, and with His burning words. And no wonder. Many learned, and earnest, and eloquent men have expounded Moses, and David, and Isaiah since that Emmaus afternoon; but human ears and human hearts have never heard such another exposition of Holy Scripture as Cleopas and his companion heard at that stranger's lips. For, this was an Interpreter, one among a thousand! When this Interpreter gave His first interpretation of Scripture in Nazareth three years before, there was delivered to Him the book of the prophet Isaiah. But they had no book to deliver Him on the way to Emmaus. Nor did He need a book. This stranger, whoever He was, seemed to Cleopas to have the whole book unrolled within Himself. He seemed to have Moses, and David, and Isaiah, and Jeremiah, absolutely by heart. And the way He spake to them called to His two companions' remembrance all that they had ever heard or read in Moses, and the Prophets, and the Psalms. The seed of the woman; the brazen serpent; the paschal lamb; the scapegoat; the thirty pieces of silver. My God, my God, why hast thou forsaken me? They part my garments among them, and cast lots upon my vesture. Reproach hath broken mine heart: I looked for some to take pity, but there was none: and for comforters, but I found none. They gave me also gall for my meat, and in my thirst they gave me vinegar to drink. He was wounded for our transgressions, He was bruised for our iniquities; the chastisement of our peace was upon Him: and with His stripes we are healed. He is brought as a lamb to the slaughter, and as a sheep before her shearers is dumb, so He opened not His mouth. "O, fool that I was!" Cleopas cried out to Luke. "I had seen it all fulfilled the week before with mine own eyes. But, that evening, our eyes were somehow holden that we did not know Him again! At the same time how our hearts did burn as He spake these things to us. And then He said to us, appealing to us to reply: May not Jesus of Nazareth be the true Christ of God, and your own Redeemer after all? After all, may not Jesus of Nazareth be He who was to come? Do not all your own prophets tell you that the true Christ must be denied of His own, and delivered up to Pilate to crucify? Must not the Prince of Life, when He comes, be killed and raised from the dead on the third day? What think ye? What say ye? And have you not just told me yourselves that certain women of your own company were early this very morning at the sepulchre, and that the angels of heaven were descended there to testify that Jesus of Nazareth was alive again?" And so on, till their hearts burned within them like two coals of juniper.

O ye men still of Emmaus, now sitting and hearing all that in this house! I implore you to open your heart also to your Lord's burning words about Himself. To speak plainly, I implore you to seek out in this city that expounder, that one of a thousand preachers, who makes your heart to burn. If by chance, so to call it, you enter a church in this city of churches on a Sabbath day, with your heart sad, with your hopes ashamed, with your expectations a complete shipwreck, like Cleopas and his desponding companion, and the preacher so opens God's word to you, so sets forth the redemption of Israel and your own redemption, so sets forth a suffering Redeemer and His suffering people, that your heart is in a flame all that day, then, that is the preacher in all this world for you. That is my servant for you, says your God to you. I have made his mouth like a sharp sword for you. I have made him a polished shaft for you. I have hid him in my quiver for you. Hear him, said the Father, concerning his preacher-Son. And that preacher you have just heard may be as great a stranger to you as our Lord was to Cleopas on that highway that afternoon; but, if I were you, I would find out his name, and where God has given him his pulpit. If I were you I would have him for my minister, and for my children's minister, at any cost. I would sell my present house and buy another to be near that preacher. And if you never hear such a preacher; if no preacher has ever made your heart to burn; if there is not in all the city a single heart-kindling, heart-commanding, heart-capturing preacher for you, then, at any rate, there are not a few heart-kindling and heart-holding authors to be had. Authors, thanks be to God, that will make you all but independent of us lukewarm preachers. Do you know some of those authors' names? Do any of you almost owe your soul to some of them? Do you have a select shelf of them within reach of your chair and your bed? Could you say, if not of some spiritual preacher, then of some spiritual writer, what Crashaw says of Teresa: "The flame I took from reading thee." And what Cleopas said to Luke about this stranger's words, "Did not our heart burn within us?" I preached sin with great sense, says John Bunyan. And I warrant you that stranger preached the Messianic and the Atonement passages in David, and in Isaiah, and in Jeremiah, and in Zechariah, with great sense also, and for a very good reason.

> Yea, this man's brow, like to a title-leaf,
> Foretells the nature of a tragic volume:
> He trembles, and the whiteness in his cheek
> Is apter than his tongue to tell his errand.

Never did threescore furlongs seem so short since furlongs were laid out on the face of the earth. "Come and sup with us," said the entranced Cleopas to this mysterious stranger who had so over-mastered him, and so set his heart on fire. "Abide with us, for the day is far spent." And when they had sat down to supper, Cleopas naturally asked the stranger, as you would have done, to say grace. What grace did that stranger say in that supper-room in Emmaus, I wonder? John Livingstone tells us that John Smith of Maxtown in Teviot-dale had all the Psalms of David by heart, and that, instead of our curt and grudging grace before meat he always repeated to his attentive table a whole Psalm. Would it be at Emmaus the twenty-third Psalm? Would it be the twenty-seventh and the twenty-eighth verses of the hundred and fourth Psalm? Or, would it be Job's every Sabbath morning and every Sabbath evening grace and blessing? Or, would it be something that the stranger made up on the spot? Would it be this, at the hearing of which Cleopas's heart would kindle again? "Except ye eat the flesh of the Son of Man, and drink His blood, ye have no life in you. For My flesh is meat indeed, and My blood is drink indeed." Whatever the grace was that He said, you may be quite sure He did not say it as we say our graces. He did not mumble it over so that nobody could hear it. He did not say it as if He was ashamed of it. He did not say, Amen! with His hand down already in the dish. Neither did Cleopas and his companion sit down and begin to eat before the grace was finished. No! for the truth is, the three men got no further than the grace that night. That sacred supper, with such a grace said over it, stands on that table to this day. It is not eaten to this day. For as the stranger handed to Cleopas and to his companion the bread He had blessed and broken, they could not but see His Hands! And the moment they saw His Hands, He had vanished out of their sight.

90

Matthias the Successor to Judas Iscariot

IN the opening chapter of the Acts of the Apostles we are introduced into the first congregational meeting, so to call it, that ever was held in the Church of Christ. There are a hundred-and-twenty members present in the upper room, and the Presbytery of Jerusalem are met there with the congregation: moderator, clerk, and all. Peter presides; and he discharges the duties of the day with all that solemnity of mind and all that intensity of heart which we seldom miss in Peter. The solemnity of the meeting would solemnize any man. It would melt a far harder heart than the heart of the emotional son of Jonas ever was. For Judas Iscariot, a member of the Presbytery, so to call him, has turned out to have been the son of perdition all the time. For thirty pieces of silver he had become guide to them that took Jesus. Peter himself had wellnigh gone down into the same horrible pit with Judas: and he also would have been in his own place by this time, had it not been that his Master prayed for Peter that his faith might not fail. And thus it is that Peter is now sitting in that seat of honor and influence and authority, and is conducting the election of a successor to Judas, with all that holy fear and with all that firm faith which makes that upper room, under Peter's presidency, such a pattern to all vacant congregations to all time. Considering her age and her size, the Church of Jerusalem had a large number of men any one of whom could quite well have been put forward and proposed for the vacant office. But Peter and his colleagues, with a great sense of responsibility, had prepared a short leet of two quite outstanding and distinguished men; Joseph, who was surnamed Justus, and Matthias. And then one of the eleven led the congregation in prayer in these well-remembered words—"Lord, Thou knowest the hearts of all men: show whether of these two Thou hast chosen." And the lot fell upon Matthias, and he was numbered with the eleven apostles.

Now, somewhat remarkable to say, never before the day of his election, and never after it, is Matthias's name so much as once mentioned in all the New Testament. At the same time, we have Matthias's footprints, so to speak, oftener than once on the pages of the four Gospels. And a man's mere footprints, and the direction they point to, will sometimes tell us far more about the real character and capacity of the man than whole volumes of printed matter about him. The first time we see one of Matthias's footprints is on the sands of Bethabara beyond Jordan, where John was baptizing. Like Andrew and Simon the sons of Jonas, and like John the son of Zebedee, Matthias was a disciple of the Baptist at that time, confessing his sins. The next day John seeth Jesus coming to him, and saith to Matthias, Behold the Lamb of God. And Matthias heard him speak, and he followed Jesus, along with John and Andrew. And when Peter tabled Matthias's name on the day of the election, he certified all these things about Matthias to the ten, and to the women, and to Mary the mother of Jesus, and to His brethren, and to the whole

hundred-and-twenty. And more than that, Peter certified to the whole congregation that, when many who had been baptized, apostatized and went back and
walked no more with John and Jesus, Matthias, said Peter, has this to his praise,
that he has endured and has persevered up to this very present. Not only so, but
this also, that Matthias had been a witness with the eleven of the resurrection of
the Lord. And these, added Peter, are the two indispensable tests of fitness for this
vacant office; a three years' conversion and faithful discipleship, and this also, that
he had seen the risen Lord with his own eyes. And the lot fell upon Matthias.

Now, it is sometimes not very unlike that when you yourselves meet to call a
minister. Tremendous as the moment is: everlasting as the issues are that hang
upon that moment: you may never have heard so much as the name of that candidate for the pastorate of your immortal soul. You may never so much as have
heard him once open his mouth either to pray or to preach. Not one of the hundred-and-twenty had ever heard this stranger man Matthias once open his mouth.
But Peter has had his eye on Matthias all along. Peter knew far more about both
Joseph and Matthias than they could have believed. Peter was all ears and all eyes
where a future apostle and pastor was concerned. And so it is sometimes still. All
you really know about your future minister you have to take sometimes on the
best testimony you can get. As one of our own elders once said when we were calling our young minister: "I would rather trust to those two capable men who know
him and have heard him preach, than I would trust to my own ears." And he spake
with both wisdom and humility in so saying. Like the hundred-and-twenty, little
as you know about your future minister, you know this much, that when all the
other young men at school and college were choosing learning, and philosophy,
and medicine, and law, and the army, and the navy, and trade, and manufactures,
and so on; this youth now in your offer was led to choose the word of God, and
the pulpit, and the pastorate, for his life-work. And, with all that, you may with
some assurance, put your hand to his call, after you have made your importunate
and personal prayer about this whole momentous matter to Him who knows the
hearts of all men. For He knows your heart better than you know it yourself: and
He knows just what kind of a minister your heart needs: your own heart and your
children's hearts. And, then, He knows the hearts of all those probationers also,
and whether their hearts are properly in their Master's work or no. As also what
motive it was that made them ministers at first, and with what motive and with
what intention they are laying out their future work among you. How well it is,
both for congregations and candidates, that He knows all men's hearts, and that
all men's hearts are in His hands.

Three years ago Matthias had come through a very sharp trial of faith, and love,
and patience, and perseverance. At his conversion and baptism Matthias had prepared his heart to leave all and to follow Christ. But instead of being invited to do
what with all his heart he wished to do, Matthias was deliberately passed over by
our Lord in His election of the twelve. Matthias had been in Christ, as Paul says, a
long time before some of those men who were lifted over his head; and here was
he as good as set aside and clean forgotten. And, just suppose, what is more than
likely, that Matthias knew Judas's secret heart and real character quite well; what

a shock it was to Matthias's faith, and love, and whole religious life, to see such a deceiver as Iscariot was, deliberately chosen by Christ, when Matthias would have shed the last drop of his blood for the Master who had refused to employ him. But Matthias, for all that, did not let his heart sour. He accepted being set aside as his proper place. He found in himself only too many reasons why he was so set aside. He was like the defeated candidate in Plutarch who, departing home from the election to his house, said to them at home that it did him good to see that there were three hundred men in Athens who were better men than he was. And thus it was that when many men would have turned away and gone after another master, Matthias said to himself: "Office or no office, election or rejection, call or no call, to whom else can I go?" Nay, not only did Matthias keep true to his Master through all these humiliations and disappointments, but he continued to behave himself and to lay out his life just as if he had been elected and ordained. So much so, that without ordination he worked harder at the out-of-the-way work of the discipleship than some of those did who were elected, and ordained, and honored, and rewarded men. And thus it was that Peter was able to certify to the hundred-and-twenty that Matthias had been as true and as loyal to his Lord all those three years as the very best of the eleven had been. "And thus," said Peter, "if there were some who were numbered among us who were not at heart of us, there were others who were at heart and in life really of us, though they were not as yet written down among us." So have I myself seen heaven-born and highly-gifted ministers of Christ passed over in the day when this and that vacant charge met to cast their lots. And, like Matthias, I have seen such men left out at the beginning only to be the more promoted and employed in the end. But then, to be sure, they were like Matthias in this also, that all their days they were men of staunchest loyalty to their Master, and men of sleepless labor for His cause. When a door shall open, and where, is not the true servant's business, nor his anxiety. It is the true servant's part to be ready; which the truest of all servants never feels that he is. And disappointments and procrastinations to all such men are but extended opportunities to enable them to be somewhat less unready for their call when it comes. If Matthias had been a modern probationer you would not have found him going about complaining against this committee and that congregation. You would not have seen him going about idle all the week, and then turning up at each new vacancy with the same old and oft-fingered sermon. No. You may shut all your doors on some candidates, but you cannot shut them out from their books, and from the hidden and unstipended work that their hearts love. You cannot, with all your ill-cast lots, either embitter or alienate a truly elect, and humble-minded, and diligent disciple of Christ. And with all your ill-advised elections the stone that is fit for the wall will not always be let lie in the ditch.

But is there anything possible to our very best probationers that can at all be compared to this qualification of those days—to have companied with the Lord Jesus all the time He went out and in among His disciples? Yes; I think there is. Nay, not only so; but when we enter into all the inwardness and depth of this matter we come to see that our students of divinity and our probationers have actually some great advantages over the twelve disciples themselves. Our Lord's words are final, and full of instruction and comfort to us, on this matter. His words to Thomas, I mean. Jesus saith to him "Thomas, because thou hast seen, thou hast believed; blessed are they that have not seen, and yet have believed." And you will all recall Sir Thomas Browne's noble protestation: "Now, honestly, I bless myself that I never saw Christ nor His disciples. I would not have been one of Christ's patients on whom He wrought His wonders. For then had my faith been thrust upon me, nor should I enjoy that greater blessing pronounced to all that believe and saw not. I believe He was dead and buried, and rose again: and desire to see Him in His glory, rather than to contemplate Him in His cenotaph or sepulchre. They only had the advantage of a bold and noble faith who lived before His coming, and who upon obscure prophecies and mystical types could raise a belief and expect apparent impossibilities." To have seen and handled the Word of Life; to have had Him dwelling among them, full of grace and truth, as John says; to have had Him going in and out among them, as Peter says, was a privilege incomparable and unspeakable. At the same time, let any student in our day read his Greek Testament, with his eye on the Object: let him be like John Bunyan:—"Methought I was as if I had seen Him born, as if I had seen Him grow up, as if I had seen Him walk through this world, from the Cradle to the Cross: to which, when He came, I saw how gently He gave Himself up to be hanged and nailed on it for my sins and wicked doings. Also, as I was musing on this His progress, that dropped on my spirit, He was ordained for the slaughter," and so on. Let any of our students company with Christ all the time He went in and out in that manner, and he may depend upon it that the beautiful benediction which our Lord addressed in reproof to Thomas will be richly fulfilled to that wise-hearted student all his happy ministerial days, and through him to his happy people. Now, if there were a divinity student here I would ask and demand of him out of this Scripture for students—Are you so companying with Christ while you are still at college? Do you see with all your inward eyes what you read in your New Testament? Do you believe and believe and believe your way through the four Gospels? Is your faith the very substance itself of the things you hope for, and the absolute and conclusive evidence of the things you do not as yet see? Do you pray your way through the life of Christ? Do you put the lepers, and the sick, and the possessed with devils, and the dead in their graves, out of their places, as you read about them; and do you put yourself into their places, and say what they say, and hear and accept what is said to them? For, if so, then you will receive, all your preaching and pastoral days, the end of your faith, the salvation of your own soul, and the salvation of the souls of your people.

Then, again, could any of our probationers be put forward by his proposer as Matthias was still put forward by Peter? No. It could not possibly be said of any man living in these dregs of time of ours that he had been an actual witness of the resurrection of Christ. And yet I am not so sure of that. Strange things can be said when you come to speak about a true probationer. With man it is impossible; but not with God With God all things are possible. I myself know probationers who are witnesses of the very best authority that Christ is risen indeed. Let such a young preacher come to your vacant pulpit with Ephesians i. 19 to ii. 1 for his

Sabbath morning exposition; and let him set forth with Paul, that the spiritual quickening of a soul dead in trespasses and sins is done by the same mighty power that quickened and raised up Christ, and you will soon see if he knows what he is speaking about. And if he does: if he makes your hearts to burn with the noble doctrine of his and your oneness with the risen Christ, then you have in your offer a living witness of apostolic rank for Christ's resurrection. You might have the angel who rolled away the stone and sat on it for your other candidate, but he should have no vote of mine. Give me for my minister, not Gabriel himself, but a fellow-sinner who has been quickened together with Christ, and who can describe the process and the experience till my death-cold heart burns within me with the resurrection-life of Christ. Give me a minister whom God has raised from the dead, and you may have all the sounding brasses and tinkling cymbals in heaven and earth for me. And I am glad to say that there are not a few probationers abroad of that experience. Only, are you sure you will recognize them when they appear and preach in your pulpit? For—

> A jest's prosperity lies in the ear
> Of him that hears it, never in the tongue
> Of him that speaks it.

Let the hundred-and-twenty take heed how they hear.

91

Ananias and Sapphira

THEMISTOCLES tossed all night and could not sleep because of the laurels of Miltiades. And Ananias was like Themistocles because of the praises poured upon Barnabas by Peter, and by all the apostles, and by all the poor. Ananias and Sapphira could not take rest till they, like Barnabas, had sold their possession, and laid the price of it at Peter's feet. "Lay it at Peter's feet," said Sapphira to her hesitating husband, "and say that you are very sorry that the land did not sell for far more. And after I have made my purchases, I will come to the Lord's Supper with you. Keep a place for me at the Table, and I will join you there in good time in breaking of bread and in prayers." And Ananias did as Sapphira had instigated him to do. Only, Ananias was not at all happy in his approach to Peter's feet that day. Somehow or other, Ananias could not summon up that gladness and that singleness of heart with which all the other contributors came up that day. With all he could do there was a certain awkwardness and stumblingness of manner that Ananias, somehow or other, could not shake off all that day. You who are collectors for churches and charities are well accustomed to all Ananias's looks and ways of speaking that day. You often hear from us the very same explanations and apologies and self-defences. "There had been a great fall in the rent of land in Judea of late. And thus the old estate had not nearly yielded its upset and expected price. But what it had yielded, Peter was welcome to it."

Everything fell to Peter in those days. The offices and services of the early Church had not as yet been divided up and specialized into the apostleship, and the eldership, and the deaconship, and, till that was done, Peter had to be everything himself. Peter was premier apostle, ruling elder, leading deacon, and all. It was like those country congregations where the minister has to do everything himself, till he has neither time nor strength nor spirit left to give himself continually to prayer, and to the ministry of the word. But Peter was a perfect Samson in the Israel of that day. He was a minister of immense capacity, gigantic energy, endless resource, and overpowering authority. And thus it was that it had fallen to Peter to sit over against the treasury, and to enter the Pentecostal contributions that day. And it struck Ananias like a thunderbolt, when Peter, instead of smiling upon him and praising him, denounced and sentenced him so sternly. "Ananias, why hath Satan filled thine heart to lie to the Holy Ghost?" And the young men arose, and wound him up, and carried him out, and buried him. And then, three hours after, just as Peter was shutting up his books to go to dispense the Lord's Supper, at that moment Sapphira appeared. "You sold your farm for so much, your husband tells me?" "Yes, my lord, for so much." And the young men came in and found her dead, and they buried Ananias and Sapphira in Aceldama, next back-breadth to Judas Iscariot, the proprietor of the place. That the prophecy of Isaiah might be fulfilled: "They shall go forth, and look upon the carcases of the men that have transgressed against me; for their worm shall not die, neither shall their fire be quenched, and they shall be an abhorring unto all flesh." And that the prophecy of Daniel also might be fulfilled: "Many of them that sleep in the dust of the earth shall awake, some to everlasting life, and some to shame and everlasting contempt."

What a world this is we live in! What a red-hot furnace of sin and of sanctification is this world! How we all tempt and try and test and stumble one another in everything we say and do! Barnabas cannot sell his estate in Cyprus and lay the price of it at Peter's feet, but by doing so he must immediately become the sudden death of Ananias and Sapphira. But for the Pentecostal love, and but for Barnabas's baptism into that love, Ananias and Sapphira would have lived to see their children's children and peace upon Israel. They would have sat down together at the Lord's Table till Peter preached their funeral sermon and held them up as two pattern proprietors of houses and lands. But Barnabas and his renowned name became such a snare to Ananias and Sapphira that they were buried on the same day and in the same grave. *Ama nesciri* has been the motto of more than one of the great saints. Seek obscurity, that is. Subscribe anonymously, that is. Do not let your collectors and the advertising people print your name or your amount, that is. Say, A Friend. Say, A Well-wisher. Put a star, put a cross, put anything but your name, not even your initials. Or, if you are a popular author, say, and not a landowner in these days; publish your books without your name. Employ another name. You may miss something that is very sweet to you by doing that; but it will be made up to you afterwards when all your royalties come in, and all your last day reviews. Think of Ananias and Sapphira when all men praise your generosity, or your Shakesperian genius, or your enormous emoluments. Be sure of this, that all Peter's praises of Barnabas did not refresh Barnabas's heart half so much as they caused that sinful sleeplessness, and all its consequences, to Ananias and Sapphira.

"Satan hath filled thine heart, Ananias." That was a terrible salutation for a man to be met with who had just sold a possession and laid such a large part of the price at the apostle's feet. But Peter knew all Satan's processes. Peter knew by experience what he was speaking about. And that is the reason why Peter speaks with such assurance and severity and indignation and judgment. And had Ananias at that moment gone out and wept bitterly, we would have been drawing far other lessons tonight out of that terrible Communion morning. Do you know the premonition, the sensation, the smell, so to say, when Satan approaches you to fill your heart? And what do you say to him? What do you do to him? Do you set a chair for him? Do you lay a cover and set glasses for him? Do you share your pillow with him? "Ah! you are there again, my man!" So an old saint in the congregation salutes Satan as often as her practiced nostrils catch the beginning of his brimstone on her stairhead. "But you are too late this time. I am engaged today. There is Some One with me. And you had better flee at once. Come sooner next time!" Luther threw his ink-bottle. What do you throw? What do you do? Or is Satan in on you, and are you in his hands and at his service, in money matters, and what not, before you know where you are? "Ah, sir, you are there again, are you? But my heart is as full today as it can hold of Another," calls out my stairhead friend by reason of her exercised senses.

The stroke was sudden, and, as we say, severe. But even at this distance of time and place we can see some good and sufficient reasons for the severity of the stroke. *Poena duorum doctrina multorum*, is the epigrammatic comment of an old writer. On two hands that sore stroke would tell for long. On the one hand, on those who were tempted to join the Christian community in order to share in the Pentecostal charity. For, then as now, a crowd of impostors would dog the steps of the open-hearted and open-handed church. On the other hand, we all give very much as others have given before us. We measure our givings, not by our duty nor by our ability, but by what others have done, and by what is expected of us. We wish to impress you. We wish to have your approval. We say with Ananias: "This is all I can spare; indeed, this is all I possess." Our sin, and our danger of death in our giving, lie not so much in that we have given less than we could have given, but in that we have not told the truth. "Yea, for so much," we say, till the feet of the young men are almost at our door. The stroke was sudden and severe to the onlookers, but it was not at all so sudden or so severe to Ananias and Sapphira themselves. It was not so unexpected and without warning to them. There were many provocations and aggravations on their part of which we are quite ignorant. Ananias may at one time have been a poor man's son, and when he came up to Jerusalem in his youth to push his fortune, he may have knelt down on the side or Olivet and said, "Thy vows are upon me, O God. And if Thou wilt give me bread to eat, and raiment to put on, and a wife and children in Jerusalem, then the Lord shall be my God, and the God of my household." Or, again, in some time of adversity he may have said, "The pains of hell gat hold upon me; but I will pay that which my mouth spake when I was in trouble." Or, again, in those sweet but soul-deceiving days when they were bridegroom and bride together; in those Beulah days—"As for me and my house, we will serve the Lord. Like David, we will walk with a perfect heart in all our household affairs at home." Ah, yes; God was no doubt quite sufficiently justified to Ananias and Sapphira themselves, when He judged them so swiftly that day. At the same time, Jeremy Taylor, who has given immense learning and intellect to all such cases, says that God sometimes accepts a temporal death in room of an eternal. And that, to some persons, a sudden death stands instead of a long and an explicit repentance. While Augustine, I see, and some other great authorities, are bold to class the awful case of Ananias and Sapphira under that scripture of the apostle where he assures us that some church members are delivered unto Satan for the destruction of the flesh, so that the spirit may be saved in the day of the Lord Jesus. Let us join with Augustine and Taylor in their burial-service over Ananias and Sapphira in the trembling hope that they were struck down in a sanctifying discipline, rather than in an everlasting condemnation. And that they so died that we might learn of them so to live as not to die. Let us hope that both husband and wife had the root of the matter in them all the time; and that we shall see them also saved in that day, in spite of Satan and all his fatal entrances into their hearts. The Lord rebuke thee, O Satan, is not this a brand plucked out of the fire?

And now to come home to ourselves. As you all know, we have an institution in full operation in the Free Church of Scotland which is based and built up and worked out on exactly Pentecostal and Barnabas principles. Dr. Chalmers's conception of the Sustentation Fund was derived and developed from the spirit and the example of the Apostolic Church of Jerusalem. The same Pentecostal spirit was poured out at the Disruption of the Established and Endowed Church of Scotland, to support the Free Church of Scotland under her injuries and her impoverishments for Christ's sake, and for the sake of His people. And thus it was that the ministers and deacons' courts of the Free Church were then, and are still, all of one mind and spirit, and have all things in common. And that same Pentecostal spirit breathes and burns, and that same Apostolic institution still stands and extends and expands, to this day. And still the Prophetic and Apostolic benediction is pronounced over the Free Church and her liberal-hearted people—"Bring ye all the tithes into the storehouse, saith the Lord of Hosts, and prove Me now herewith, if I will not open the windows of heaven, and pour you out a blessing, that there shall not be room enough to receive it."

"Prove Me now herewith," said the Lord. And He has promised that when we prove Him with our tithes, all manner of prosperity will follow our practice of that Scriptural rule and pattern. And the rule is not a Scriptural one only. Somehow or other, the tithe, the tenth part, fills all classical literature, as well as the whole of Holy Scripture. And yet, with all that before our eyes, as plain as plain can be, here we are, at this time of day, blundering about and telling lies, many of us, like Ananias and Sapphira, without any method, or principle, or rule in our givings, any more than if Scripture had never spoken on this matter, or as if a rule of love and common-sense had never been laid down. Till we waken up, and take the Patriarchal, and Mosaic, and Prophetic, and Apostolic, and even Pagan way of taxing our income, and laying aside a definite and a liberal part of it for church and charity, we need never expect to inherit the promises, or to enter into that liberty of heart and hand which awaits us and our children. It is surely time that we had found out some better way than our present haphazard way of dealing with this great and pressing matter. For everything comes on us in this city. All Scotland, all Ireland, and many parts even of rich England; France, Switzerland, Italy; churches, manses, missions—everything comes on Edinburgh, and on a limited field of Edinburgh. When some great financial genius, say, like Dr. Chalmers, arises in the Church to expound and enforce this disastrously neglected law of God, a new day will dawn on our whole religious and charitable exchequer. Then the Christian child will be brought up to tithe his pocket-money of sixpence a week for Jesus his Savior's sake. And his father his pound a week, or his ten pounds, or his hundred, or his thousand. And, then, all we shall have to do, without straining our hearts or souring our tempers, will be calmly, and at our leisure, to exercise our best discretion as to the proportion and the destination of the stewardship-money we have had entrusted to us. And, when that Apostolic day dawns, our successors in the churches and charities of the land will look back with amazement at our poverty-stricken ways of collecting church money, leaning on State endowments, and all such like un-Pentecostal expedients. And all because our eyes had, somehow, not been opened to Scriptural wisdom, and to Scriptural love, and to Scriptural liberality, in this whole matter of our Lord's money.

92
Simon Magus

BUT who, to begin with, was Simon Magus? And how did it come about that he believed, and was actually baptized by Philip the evangelist; and then was detected, denounced and utterly reprobated by the Apostle Peter? How did all that come about?

Well, you must know that Samaria, where Simon Magus lived and carried on his astounding impositions, was a half-Hebrew, half-heathen country. Samaria had just enough of the Hebrew blood in its veins to make it full of the very worst qualities of that blood, mixed up with some of the very worst qualities of the heathen blood of that day also. And Simon Magus was at once the natural product, and the divine punishment, of that apostate land in which we find him living in such mountebank prosperity. Simon Magus was a very clever man, and he was at the same time a very bad man; till, by his tremendous pretensions, he had the whole of Samaria at his feet. There was something positively sublime about the impudence and charlatanry of Simon Magus, till he was actually feared and obeyed and worshipped as nothing short of some divinity who had condescended to come and take up his abode in Samaria. But the whole man and the whole situation is best set before us in the two or three strokes of the sacred writer. "There was a certain man called Simon, which beforetime in the same city used sorcery, and bewitched the people of Samaria, giving out that himself was some great one. To whom they all gave heed, from the least to the greatest, saying, This man is the great power of God. And to him they had regard, because that of long time he had bewitched them with sorceries. But when they believed Philip preaching the things concerning the kingdom of God, and the name of Jesus Christ, they were baptized, both men and women. Then Simon himself believed also; and when he was baptized, he continued with Philip and wondered, beholding the miracles and signs which were done."

Philip had extraordinary success in his evangelizing mission to Samaria. It was like New England, or Cambuslang, or 1859-60, or Moody and Sankey's first visit to Scotland. For the people with one accord gave heed unto those things that Philip spake, hearing and seeing the miracles which he did. And there was great joy in that city. "The very devil himself has been converted and has been baptized by me," Philip telegraphed to Jerusalem. "I actually have the name of Simon Magus on my communion-roll." At the hearing of that, the apostles sent two of their foremost men down to Samaria to superintend the great movement, and God sent the Holy Ghost with them, till the whole of Samaria seemed to have turned to God and to the name of Jesus Christ. Only, Simon Magus was all the time such an impostor that in his conversion and baptism he had completely deceived Philip. Nay, I think it but fair to Simon Magus to say that he had completely deceived himself as well as Philip. I think so. I am bound in charity to think so. When Simon Magus came

440

up out of the water, had a voice from heaven spoken at that moment, it would surely have been heard to say, "This is an arch-deceiver, deceiving, but, at the same time, being deceived." Some men have far more self-discernment than other men, and self-discernment is the highest and rarest science of all the sciences on the face of the earth. And, usually, there is united with great self-discernment, and as a reward and a premium put by God upon its exercise, the power of deeply discerning other men's spirits also. Now, though Philip was a prince of evangelistic preachers, and a good and an able man, at the same time he was far too easily satisfied with his converts. Philip was far better at preaching than he was at catechizing. And thus it was that it fell to Peter and John to purge Philip's communion-roll of Simon Magus immediately on their arrival in Samaria. At the same time, this must be said, that Simon Magus had never come out in his true colors till after Peter's arrival, and till after all the true converts had received the Holy Ghost.

The circumstances were these: It was part of the Pentecostal equipment of the apostles to possess for a time some of the miracle-working powers that their Divine Master had exercised in order to arrest attention to His advent, and to secure a hearing to His ministry. And thus it is that we find the apostles speaking with tongues, healing the sick, opening the eyes of the blind, casting out devils, and many suchlike miracles and signs. Now, Simon Magus, like everybody else in Samaria, was immensely impressed with all that he saw and heard. No man was more impressed than Simon Magus, or more convinced of the divine mission of the apostles. But, with all his wonder and with all his conviction, he was never truly converted. The love of money, and the still more intoxicating love of notoriety, had taken such absolute possession of Simon Magus that he simply could not live out of the eyes of men. He must be in men's mouths. He must have a crowd around him. Themistocles could not sleep because of the huzzas that filled the streets of Athens when Miltiades walked abroad; and the crowds that followed Peter and John were gall and wormwood to Simon Magus. For, still greater crowds used to take him up and carry him on their shoulders in the days of his great power before Philip came to Samaria. Now, Peter had never liked the look of Philip's great convert, and it completely justified Peter's incurable suspicions when Simon Magus came one night into Peter's lodgings, and, setting down a bag of money on the table, said, "What will you take for the Holy Ghost? If you will show me the secret of your apostleship so that I may work your miracles like you, I have plenty of money, and I know where there is plenty more." The sight of the bag, and the blasphemous proposal of the owner of the bag, nearly drove Peter beside himself. And the old fisherman so blazed out at the poor mountebank that the page burns red to this day with Peter's denunciation. "Thy money perish with thee, for I perceive thou art still in the gall of bitterness, and in the bond of iniquity!"

"Giving out that himself was some great one." That is our first lesson from this Holy Scripture about Simon Magus. Let those take the lesson to heart who specially need it, and who will humble themselves to receive it. It may be in sorcery and witchcraft like that of Simon Magus; it may be in the honors of the kingdom of Heaven like the sons of Zebedee; it may be in preaching sermons; it may be in making speeches or writing books; it may be in anything you like, down to your child's possessions and performances; but we all, to begin with, give ourselves out to be some great one. Simon Magus was but an exaggerated specimen of every popularity-hunter among us. There is an element and first principle of Simon Magus, the Samaritan mountebank, in all public men. There is still a certain residuum of Simon left in order to his last sanctification in every minister. But the most Simon Maguslike of all sanctified ministers I know is Thomas Shepard, and that just because he is the most self-discerning, the most honest, and the most outspoken about himself of us all. Popularity was the very breath of life to that charlatan of Samaria. He could not work, he could not live, he could not be converted and baptized, without popularity. And there is not one public man in a thousand, politician or preacher, who will go on living and working and praying out of sight, and all the time with sweetness, and contentment, and good-will, and a quiet heart. All Samaria must give heed to Simon Magus from the least to the greatest. And so still with his successors. A despairing missionary to the drunken navvies on a new railway, complained to me the other day that one of our great preachers, who was holidaying in the neighborhood, would not give an idle Sabbath afternoon hour to the men loitering about the bothy door. It was the dregs of Simon Magus in the city orator; he could not kindle but to a crowd. "Seek obscurity" was Fénelon's motto. Whether he lived up to his motto or no, the day will declare; if he did, there will not be many wearing the same crown with him on that day. But Richard Baxter will be one of them. "I am much less regardful of the approbation of men, and set much lighter by contempt or applause, than I did long ago. All worldly things appear most vain and unsatisfactory when we have tried them most. But though I feel that this hath some hand in the effect, yet the knowledge of man's nothingness, and of God's transcendent greatness, with whom it is that I have most to do, and the sense of the brevity of human things, and the nearness of eternity, are the principal causes of this effect, and not self-conceitedness and morosity, as some suppose." These things will help to do it, but above all these things a completely broken heart will alone cast Simon Magus out of us ministers. A heart broken beyond all mollification or binding up in this world; but not even a broken heart, unless it is daily broken. Nothing will root the mountebank out of us ministers but constant self-detection, constant self-contempt, constant self-denunciation, and constant self-destruction. Oh, my friends, you do not know, and you are not fit to be told, the tremendous price of a minister's salvation. It is this that makes our crucified Master say to us ministers continually, "Few of you there be that find it."

You will not know what a "law-work" is; but Simon Magus was simply lost for want of a law-work. You never nowadays hear the once universal pulpit word. The Romans and the Galatians are full of the law-work, and so have all our greatest preachers been. Those two great evangelical Epistles were not yet written, but there was enough of their contents in the Pentecostal air, if Simon Magus had had any taste for such soul-searching matters. I must not allow myself to say a single word as to Philip's mismanagement of his catechumens' and young communicants' classes. Only, the sorcerer must have sadly bewitched the evangelist before Philip put Simon Magus's name down on his communion-roll. Philip knew his business and his own heart. I dare not doubt that. Only, somehow or other, he let Simon Magus slip through his hands much too easily. Believing, baptism, communion table and all, Simon Magus had neither part nor lot in this matter of the work of the law. I would not keep either a young communicant or an old convert away from the table because he was not deeply learned in all the Pauline doctrines; but I could not undertake to recommend his name to the kirk-session unless he gave me some evidence of what the masters of our science call the law-work. He might never have heard the word, and I would never mention it to him unless, indeed, he was a man of some mind. But it is mocking God, and deluding men, to crowd the table with communicants like Simon Magus, who do not know the first principles either of sin or of salvation. The best law-work comes to us long after conversion and admission to the table; but neither before his so-called conversion, nor after it, did this arch-impostor know anything about it—"for thy heart," said Peter, tearing it open to its very core, "is not right in the sight of God."

"Fictus," that is to say, a living and breathing fiction, was the name given to such converts as Simon Magus in those early days. Ignorance, Temporary, Pliable, and Turnaway, were some of their names in later days. Now, you are not an impostor by profession like Simon Magus. You do not make your living by deluding other people. But there may very easily be an element of fiction, of self-delusion and self-imposition, in your supposed conversion, as there was in his. Calvin's moderation, saneness of judgment, and spiritual insight, carry me with him here also. "I am not of their mind," he says, "who think that Simon Magus made only a semblance of religion. There is a middle ground between saving faith and sheer dissimulation. Simon Magus saw that the apostles' doctrine was true, and he received the same so far; but the groundwork was all along wanting; that is to say, his denial of himself was all along wanting." Just so. I see and feel Calvin's point. Your religion is not all a sham on your part. You are not a pure and unmixed hypocrite. But neither is your religion of the right kind. It is not saving your soul. It is not making you every day a new and another man. Your heart is not right in the sight of God. It is not, and it never will be, till, as Calvin says, and as Christ says, you deny yourself daily. And that, every day, to your heart's blood, and in the matter of the sin that so easily besets you. With Simon Magus it was the praise of men, and their crowding round him, and their adulation of him. Now, what he should have done, and what Philip should have insisted on him to do, was to discover to himself and to confess to himself his besetting sin, and every day to drive another nail of self-crucifixion into it. Another new nail every day, till it gave up the ghost. Instead of that the poor impostor tried to get Peter to share his apostolic popularity with him for thirty pieces of silver! If you are a platform, or a pulpit, or any other kind of mountebank, seek obscurity, for your soul's salvation lies there. If you are a popular preacher, flee from crowded churches, and hold services in bothies, and in poorhouses, and in barns, and in kitchens. Never search the papers to see what they are saying about you. Starve the self-seeking quack that is still within you. Beat him black and blue, as Paul tells us he did, and as Thomas Shepard tells us he did, every time he shows his self-admiring face.

Simon Magus put the thought of his heart into the form of a money-proposal to Peter. But, bad as the proposal was, it was not so much the proposal that Peter so struck at as the heart of the proposer. "If perhaps the thought of thine heart may be forgiven thee." Now, answer this, as we shall all answer it one day—What about the thoughts of your heart? Are the self-seeking, self-exalting thoughts of your heart dwelt on and indulged, or are they the greatest shame to you, and the greatest torment to you, of your life? Do you hate your own heart as you would hate hell itself, if you were about to be cast down into it? Do you beat your breast and cry out, Oh, wretched man that I am! Has the law entered, and is the law-work deep enough, and spiritual enough, to make all the Simon Magus-like thoughts of your hearts to be an inward pain and shame to you past all knowledge, and past all belief about you, of mortal man? His thoughts, that is, of self-advertisement, self-exaltation, and self-congratulation? Does the praise of men puff you up, and make you very happy? And is their silence, or their absence, something you cannot get over? Is he a good man who follows you about, and believes in you, and applauds you: and is he an unpardonably bad man who prefers Philip, and Peter, and John to Simon Magus? Then, be not deceived, God is not mocked, and neither are the self-discerning men round about you. Both your happiness and your sadness: both your love and your hatred of men; are quite naked and open to those with whom you have to do. "For I perceive that thou art still in the gall of bitterness, and in the bond of iniquity." "We may conjecture," says Calvin, "that Simon Magus repented." Whereas Bengel leaves it to the last day to discover that and to declare that.

93
The Ethiopian Eunuch

OUR Lord gave the Pharisees of His day this praise, that they would compass sea and land to make one proselyte. Now, this Ethiopian eunuch was one of their proselytes. Like the Scotch and English of our own day, the Jews of our Lord's day compassed sea and land to make money; but, almost more, to make converts to Moses and Aaron. Bent as their hearts were on making a fortune, the Jews of that day were almost more bent on spreading the faith of Abraham, and the hope of their fathers. And it would be in his business relations with the heads of some of the trading and banking houses that the Jewish merchants had set up in Ethiopia, that Queen Candace's treasurer came into contact with the worshippers of Jehovah, till it all ended in his becoming a proselyte of the gate. Think, then, of this Ethiopian treasurer and his royal retinue coming up all the way from the far south to pay his vow, and to seek the face of the Lord in His holy temple. Think you see his conversion in Ethiopia, his sojourning for a season in Jerusalem, and then his returning home; and these pictures of him in your mind will greatly help you to understand and appreciate this remarkable man and his remarkable story.

Now, what the Ethiopian eunuch saw and heard in Jerusalem, and took home with him from Jerusalem, would almost entirely depend on the introductions he brought with him, and on the houses to which he took those introductions. If an eastern prince were to come, say at an Assembly time, to our own city, his impressions of the city and of the country would entirely depend on the hands into which he fell. We are so partitioned off into churches, and sects, and sub-sects; into professions, and political parties, and social castes; into likes and dislikes; into sympathies and into antipathies; that, if the Ethiopian eunuch had his first introduction into any of those hot-beds of ours, he would return home a total stranger, and almost an enemy, to many of the best men and to much of the best life of our city and our country. Unless indeed, he had brought from his bitter experience of controversy, and faction, and party spirit in Ethiopia, that open and liberal mind, and that humble and loving heart, which no designed introduction will mislead, and no invidious patronage or privilege will poison.

Had this been an ordinary Ethiopian eunuch he would have spent his holiday among the theaters, and circuses, and bazaars, and other Roman amusements, of Pilate's procuratorship. As it was, he may, for anything we know, have brought an introduction to the Roman Procurator, and may have been entertained by Pilate's wife herself in the Roman Praetorium. On the other hand, it is much more likely that he was directed and recommended to some of the heads of the Temple: to Annas, or to Caiaphas, or to some other ecclesiastical dignitary. You may make use of your own knowledge of the condition of Jerusalem, and of the rank of the eunuch, and of his religious errand, to choose for yourselves just where the Ethiopian eunuch was lodged, and just in what light he saw the life of Jerusalem. Only,

I fear, with all his ability, and with all his insight, and with all his seriousness of mind, the eunuch's furlough came to an end before he had well begun to see daylight on the Pharisees and the Sadducees, the Essenes and the Herodians, the Zealots and the Publicans, the devotees of Moses, and the disciples of Jesus Christ.

Was the Book of the prophet Isaiah the parting gift of his Jerusalem host to this eastern prince on the day of his departure home? And did the donor of the sacred book, with an earnest look and with delicate kindness, point out to his guest as he mounted his chariot steps, the fifty-third and fifty-sixth chapters of the evangelical and ecumenical prophet? Or was the sacred book this good eunuch's own selection? After he had purchased some of the rarest specimens of recent Roman art for his royal mistress, did he seek out the sacred scriptorium and price for himself the richest-set roll of the prophet Esaias that the scribes possessed? In whatever way he had come by the fascinating book, he was away out of the city, and well on to the border of the land, before he was able to take his eyes off his purchase. The Ethiopian eunuch will be summoned forward with his Isaiah in his hand at the last day to witness against us all for the books we buy and read, and for the way we murder time, both at home and on our holidays, as well as on our long journeys. Did you ever see any one reading his Bible in a railway carriage, or on the deck of a steamboat? Did you ever see Isaiah, or Paul, in text or in commentary, exposed for sale on a railway bookstall? Oh, no! the very thought is profanity. We load our bookstalls, and our newsboys' baskets, and our travelling-bags, with all the papers of the morning and the evening; and with piles of novels of all colors; and with our well-known Protestant reticence and reverence for divine things, we reserve our Bibles for home, and give up our Sabbath-days to Paul and Isaiah. One in a thousand will break through and will re-read on a railway journey his Homer or his Virgil; his Milton or his Shakespeare; his Bacon or his Hooker; his à Kempis or his Bunyan; while one in a hundred thousand will venture to take out his Psalms or his New Testament. "The great number of books and papers of amusement, which of one kind or another, daily come in one's way, have in part occasioned, and most perfectly fall in with, and humor, this idle way of reading and considering things. By this means time, even in solitude, is happily got rid of, without the pain of attention. Neither is any part of it more put to the account of idleness—one can scarce forbear saying is spent with less thought, than great part of that which is spent in reading." If that accusation was laid against the readers of 1792, how much more have we laid ourselves open to it in 1899?

But, all this time Philip is wandering up and down the wilderness, thinking that he must have mistaken his own imagination for the voice of the Lord. Caravans of pilgrims come and go: merchants of Egypt and of Arabia and cohorts of Roman soldiers. but all that only makes the evangelist the more lonely and the more idle. But, at last, a chariot of distinction comes in sight, and as it comes within earshot Philip hears with the utmost astonishment the swarthy master of the chariot reading aloud. Philip was not astonished at the distinguished man reading aloud, but his astonishment and admiration were unbounded when he began to make out at a distance what the dark-skinned stranger was reading. "He was led as a sheep to the slaughter; and like a lamb dumb before his shearer, so opened he not his

mouth." "Understandest thou what thou readest?" said Philip, as the chariot came
to a standstill. All this took place in the simple, unsophisticated, hospitable East;
and it must not be measured by our hard and unbending habits of intercourse in
the West; and, especially, in dour-faced Scotland. It would be taken as the height
of intrusion, and, indeed, impudence, among us if one man said to another sitting
over his book on a journey, "Are you understanding what you are reading?" But if
we sat beside a foreigner who was struggling with one of our complicated guide-
books, and was just about to start off in a wrong direction, it would be no intrusion if we leaned over and said to him, "I fear, sir, that our barbarous language
is not easily mastered by foreign scholars; but English is my native tongue, and I
belong to this country. Can I be of any use to you?" "How can I," said the eunuch,
"except some man should guide me?" And he desired Philip that he would come
up and sit with him. Had the eunuch come to Jerusalem last year at this passover
time, as he had been urged to come, and as he had at one time intended to come,
he might have had Philip's Master sitting beside him today and reading Isaiah with
him. But the eunuch had missed that opportunity by putting off paying his vow
for another year. He was a year too late for ever seeing Jesus Christ in the flesh,
and hearing Him open up Isaiah concerning Himself. But, better late than never.
Better meet the meanest of His servants, than miss the Master altogether.

Was it the eunuch's own serious instincts, I wonder, that led him to the fifty-
third of Isaiah? Or had he heard that profound and perplexing chapter disputed
over by Stephen and Saul in one of the synagogues of Jerusalem? I cannot tell.
Only, it strikes me, and it struck Philip, as a remarkable fact that out of the whole
Old Testament this utter stranger to the Old Testament was pondering over its
most central chapter, and its most profound prophecy, as he rode home in his
chariot. When Augustine was a catechumen in Milan, and was just at the eunuch's
stage in the truth, Ambrose directed his pupil to the study of Isaiah. "But I, not
understanding my first lesson in that prophet, laid it by to be resumed when I was
better practiced." Bunyan also tells us that when he was beginning to read his Bible
he much preferred the adventures of Joshua and Samson and Gideon to Isaiah or
Paul. But, explain it as we may, this Ethiopian neophyte was already far ahead of
Bunyan, and even of Augustine. For he held in his hands the most Pauline page in
all the Old Testament, and he would not lay it down till he got to the bottom of
it. "I pray thee, of whom speaketh the prophet this? of himself, or of some other
man?" What struck the imagination and the conscience of the eunuch was this:
the absolutely unearthly picture that the prophet draws of his own character and
conduct: if indeed it is of his own character and conduct the prophet speaks. "He
was led as a sheep to the slaughter," the eunuch read again, "and like a lamb dumb
before his shearer, so opened he not his mouth." The eunuch knew not a few good,
and humble, and patient, and silently-suffering, men in Ethiopia, but he knew no
one of whom the half of these things could be said. And, if this was the prophet
himself, no wonder then at the reverence in which both the name of the prophet,
and the name of his book, were held in Jerusalem. "Oh, no! "said Philip. "Oh, no,
no! the prophet did not speak of himself, nor of any other mortal man. Oh, no, no!
far from that! The prophet was a man of like passions with other men. He was a

man of unclean lips, like all other men. Oh, no! the prophet did not speak of himself, but of another manner of man altogether. Thou art a stranger in Jerusalem, but thou must have heard something of the things that have come to pass there in these last days. Thou must surely have heard the name of Jesus of Nazareth?" "I did hear that name," answered the eunuch. "I often heard it. Sometimes I heard that name blessed, and sometimes I heard it cursed. And I was warned that all the time I was in Jerusalem I must not once speak that name, nor listen to any one speaking it to me. But we are far from Jerusalem here; and of whom speaketh the prophet this?" "Should we make it our first aim in the pulpit to do full justice to the subject we have in hand; or should our immediate and sole endeavor be to do good to our hearers?" said one of my most thoughtful friends to me the other day. What do you do yourself? was my reply to him. But we had to part before we had time to argue it out. Philip, at any rate, set himself in the first place, and with all his might, to do full justice to his great subject. And it was in the progress of that full justice that the eunuch got all the good that the best hearer even in our day could get from the best preacher. Sometimes the one way is best, in some hands, and sometimes the other, according to the preacher, according to the hearer, and according to the subject. For the most part surely, first the subject thoroughly studied down, and handled with our utmost ability and finish, and then application made with our utmost skill and urgency and love. "Mix your exhortation with doctrine," said Goodwin to the divinity students of Oxford. Better still, in our day at any rate, begin your exhortation well with doctrine, and then end your doctrine with its proper exhortation springing out of it. Only, the eunuch did not wait for Philip's exhortation. He did not give Philip time to wind up and round off his doctrine. Philip's sermon on the fifty-third of Isaiah is not finished to this day. "See, here is water!" broke in the eunuch. "I see it!" broke in a young Forfarshire farmer in the middle of my prayer with him in the minister's study late that night after a fine revival meeting conducted by Mr. Low of Fountain-bridge, and Dr. Macphail of Liverpool. And my prayer lies there to this day, like Philip's sermon, never finished, and that is five-and-twenty years ago. "I see it!" and we both sprang to our feet; and, instead of the rest of my prayer to God I said to the farmer, "Never lose sight of it, then. Never lose sight of it all your days!" He did lose sight of it, and went back, to the breaking of his minister's heart. But the backslider returned, and, as I was told, died in raptures, exclaiming, "I see it! I see it!" "See, here is water!" exclaimed the eunuch, cutting short Philip's sermon. "I see it!" exclaimed the farmer, cutting short my prayer.

"And when they were come up out of the water, the Spirit of the Lord caught away Philip, that the eunuch saw him no more; and he went on his way rejoicing." Rejoicing that those Jewish merchants had ever opened their warehouse in Ethiopia. Regretting that he had not come up sooner to Jerusalem, when he might have seen his Savior's face, and heard His voice. But, all the more rejoicing that he had not put off coming to the passover altogether. Rejoicing also that he had not talked about the sights of Jerusalem all the way to Gaza, but had read all the way in the prophet Isaiah. And rejoicing, above all, that he had said it the moment it came into his heart to say it, "See, here is water!" And, still, as the chariot travelled its long stages toward far Ethiopia, the eunuch thought with a humble and a holy joy of all the way his God had led him, and of the singular grace that had at last apprehended him. And who can tell but that Queen Candace, and a great multitude of her black, but comely people, will yet be seen by us stretching out their hands and casting their crowns at His feet of whom Isaiah spake, and of whom Philip preached!

> Let it no longer be a forlorn hope
>   To wash an Ethiope;
> He's washed: his gloomy skin a peaceful shade
>   For his white soul is made.
> And now, I doubt not, the Eternal Dove,
>   A black-faced house will love.

94
Gamaliel

READ for the first time, and looked at on the surface, Gamaliel's speech in the council of Jerusalem was both an able and a successful performance. The argument of the speech carried the consent of the whole council—not an easy thing to do—for Peter had just cut the whole council to the heart. But Gamaliel calmed the whole council; he reassured the most hesitating; and he all but satisfied the most bloodthirsty; till the whole Sanhedrim broke up that day with loud and universal congratulations pronounced upon the ability and the sagacity of Gamaliel's speech. But, in order to see what was the real and ultimate value of Gamaliel's speech; and, still more, in order to a true and ultimate estimate of Gamaliel himself, let us look with some closeness at the whole situation with which Gamaliel was called upon to deal that day.

Well, then, this was the situation. Gamaliel had brought forward Theudas, who had boasted that he was somebody; and Judas of Galilee, who had drawn away much people after him; and Gamaliel had made some good points in his speech by his references to those two dispersed men. But Jesus Christ was not a Theudas, nor a Judas of Galilee, nor a dispersed man. Jesus Christ was Jesus Christ. He was Himself, and not another. Jesus Christ had been promised in every page of the law and the prophets and the psalms, all of which were the daily text-books in Gamaliel's school. And Jesus Christ had come, and had fulfilled, and that a thousand times told, every jot and tittle of all that had been prophesied and promised concerning Him. And Gamaliel had been set in his high seat by the God of Israel in order that he might watch for the coming Messiah, and might announce His advent to the people of Israel. But, for some reason or other, instead of recognizing and announcing the true Christ of God when He came, as, for instance, John the Baptist did; instead of casting in his lot with Jesus of Nazareth; instead of dissolving his school and sending Saul of Tarsus and all his other scholars to follow the Lamb of God, Gamaliel, for some reason or other, still kept his seat in the Sanhedrim all through the arrest, the trial, the crucifixion, the resurrection, and the ascension of Jesus Christ, and when Christ's disciples were on their trial for their lives this short speech contains all that Gamaliel has to say for them and for himself. We must, at all times, and to all men, do as we would be done by: and therefore it is that we seek again and again for some explanation, some excuse, some apology, for Gamaliel's remaining a member of the council that had tried and crucified Jesus Christ. But, with all our search, we can find nothing out of which to make a cloak for Gamaliel's case. Had Gamaliel been an ignorant and an unlearned man there might have been some excuse for him. But Gamaliel had not that cloak at any rate for his sin. So far as I can see it, the simple truth in Gamaliel's deplorable case was this. With all his learning, and with all his ability, and with all his address, Gamaliel had approached this whole case concerning Jesus Christ from the wrong side; he had taken hold of this whole business by the wrong handle. And we all make Gamaliel's tremendous and irreparable mistake when we approach Jesus Christ and His cause and His kingdom on the side of policy, and when we handle Him as a matter open to argument and debate. He is not a matter of argument and debate; He is an ambassador of reconciliation. We are simply not permitted to sit in judgment on Almighty God, and on His message of mercy to us. He who sends that message to us is our Maker and our Judge. And Gamaliel, with all his insight, and with all his lawyer-like ability, has turned all things completely upside down when he sits in judgment, and gives this carefully-balanced caution, concerning the Son of God.

Speaking philosophically and politically and ecclesiastically, Gamaliel was a liberal, and he has this to be said for him, that he was a liberal long before the time. He was all for toleration, and for a free church in a free state, in an intolerant and persecuting day. He was far in advance of his colleagues in observation, and in reading, and in breadth and openness of mind. He was tinctured with the Greek learning that so many of his class were now beginning innovatingly to taste. And we cannot but wonder whether, among all his stores of ancient instances, that of the Greek Socrates had come that day into his mind. "We ought to obey God rather than men," Peter had just said. "Whether it be right in the sight of God to hearken unto you rather than unto Him, judge ye," he had also said. "Athenians," said Socrates, "I hold you in the highest reverence and love; but I will obey God rather than you. I cannot hold my peace, because that would be to disobey God." And Socrates continued so to obey God till his self-examining voice was put to silence in the hemlock-cup. And much more must Peter summon all Jerusalem to repentance in spite of the prison and the scourge and the cross. The Athenians, in their philosophical and political liberality, would have let Socrates alone, if he would have let them alone; but not for his life could he do that. And Peter was under a far surer and a far stronger constraint than Socrates. The one was the apostle of truth as it is in the reason, and in the conscience, and in the self-examined heart; while the other was the apostle of the truth as it is in all that, and in Jesus over and above all that. The French, with their keen, quick, caustic wit, have coined a nickname for those politicians who neglect principles and study the skies only to see how the wind is to blow. They call all such public men by the biting name of "opportunists." Now, Gamaliel was the opportunist of the council of Jerusalem in that day. He was a politician, but he was not a true churchman or statesman. He was held in repute by the people; but the people were blind, and they loved to be led by blind leaders. And Gamaliel was one of them. For, at this supreme crisis of his nation's history, when there was not another moment to lose, this smooth-tongued opportunist came forward full of wise saws and modern instances. But the flood was out, and the time was past, if ever there was a time for such fatal counselors as Gamaliel. His own opportunity has of late been passing with lightning-speed: and, now, when God, in His long-suffering, has given Gamaliel his last opportunity, he deals with God and with his own soul as we here see.

Erasmus and the Reformation always rise before me when I read of Gamaliel and study his character. Erasmus, the fastidious, cautious, cool, almost cold scholar,

Always stepping lightly over thin ice, always calculating consequences, and always missing the mark. Convinced of the truth, but a timid friend to the truth. Clear-eyed enough to see the truth, but built without a brow for it. Lavater thus analyses Holbein's portrait of Erasmus, and as we read the remarkable analysis we see in it a replica of Gamaliel's portrait.—"The face is expressive of the man. There is a pose of feature indicative of timidity, hesitancy, circumspection. There is in the eye the calm serenity of the acute observer who sees and takes in all things. The half-closed eye, of such a depth and shape, is surely such as always belongs to the subtle and clever schemer. That nose, according to all my observation, is assuredly that of a man of keen intellect and delicate sensibility. The furrows on the brow are usually no favorable token: they are almost invariably the sign of some weakness, some carelessness, some supineness, some laxness of character. We learn, however, from this portrait that they are to be found in some great men." Altogether a man of maxims and not of morals; a man, as he said of himself, who had no inclination to die for the truth: a man, as Luther said of him, in whose estimation human things stood higher than divine things: a man, two men, Gamaliel and Erasmus, a large class of men. "Speak not of them," said the master, "but look at them and pass them by."

Young men! with your life still before you, Gamaliel, the fluent and applauded opportunist, is here written with a special eye to your learning. Make your choice. It is an awful thing to say, but it is the simple truth; God and His Son, His church and His gospel, His cause and His kingdom, all stand before your door at this moment, waiting for your choice and your decision. Gamaliel decided, and his day is past, and he is in his own place. And now is your day of decision. Everlasting and irremediable issues for you and for others depend on this day's decision. Make up your minds. Take the step. Take sides with Peter and John. Take sides with Jesus Christ. And, as time goes on, having taken that side, that step will solve for you a thousand perplexities, and will deliver you from a thousand snares. You will be the children of the light and of the day: and you will walk in the light when other men all around you are stumbling in darkness, and know not whither they are going. Suppose that you had been Gamaliel, and act now as you so clearly see how he should have acted then.

This is our sacrament evening, and we have come to Gamaliel, and to his choice, and to his speech, not inopportunely, as I think, for our ensample on such an evening. For, what is a sacrament, and a sacrament day, and a sacrament evening? Well, Gamaliel may very well have seen the sacramental oath taken by the young soldiers under the walls of Jerusalem. At any rate, if he had ever been at Rome on a deputation, he would to a certainty have seen and heard the Sacramentum sworn to on the field of Mars. For the Sacramentum was the well-known military oath that the young soldier took when he entered on his place in the world-conquering legions of Rome. It was his sacramental oath when he lifted up his hand to heaven and swore that he would follow the eagles of Caesar wherever they flew; to the swamps of Germany, to the snows of Caledonia, to the sands of Arabia, to the Jordan, to the Nile, to the Ganges, to the Thames, to the Clyde, to the Tay. And we, this day, old soldiers of the cross, and new recruits alike, have called upon God and man to see us that we will not flinch from the cross, but will follow it to heat and cold, to honor and shame, to gain and loss, to life and death. We have eagles to fight under, of which the angels desire to be the camp-followers. Only, let us all well understand, and without any possibility of mistake, just where our field of battle lies; just who and what is our enemy, just who is our Captain, just what is His whole armor, and just what hope He holds out to us of victory.

Well, then, lay this to heart, that your battlefield is not over the seas: it is at home. It is in the family, it is in the office, it is in the shop, it is in the workshop, it is at the breakfast and dinner-table, it is in the class-room, it is in the council-chamber. Your battlefield is just where you are. Your battle follows you about the world, and it is set just where you are set. And that is because your enemy, and the enemy of your Captain, is yourself. It is no paradox to say that; it is no hyperbole, no extravagance, no exaggeration. "The just understand it of their passions," says Pascal. That is to say, they understand that their only enemy is their own sensuality, their own bad temper, their own hot and hasty and unrecalled words, their own resentment of injuries, their own retaliation, their own revenge, their own implacable ill-will, their own envy of their dearest friend when he excels them in anything—and so on. What a sacramental oath that is, to swear to take no rest, and to give God no rest, till He has rooted all these, and all other enemies of His and ours, out of our heart! But, then, let us think of our Captain, and of our armor, and of our rations, as in this house this day, and of our battle-cry, and of our sure and certain victory. And, then, eye hath not seen, nor ear heard, the things that God hath prepared for him that overcometh. "To him that overcometh will I grant to sit with Me in My throne, even as I also overcame, and am set down with My Father in His throne."

95
Barnabas

BARNABAS, I am afraid, is little more than a bare name to the most of us. Paul so eclipses every one of his contemporaries, that it is with the utmost difficulty we can get a glimpse of any one but Paul. How much do you know about Barnabas? Who was Barnabas? Why was Joses called Barnabas? You would have some difficulty, I am afraid, in giving answers to all these questions. And I do not blame you for your ignorance of Barnabas. For, Paul is so great, that the very greatest and the very best men look but small when placed alongside of him. At the same time, there were great men before Agamemnon, and Barnabas was one of them.

"Barnabas, a Levite, of the country of Cyprus, having land, sold it, and brought the money, and laid it at the apostles' feet." Cyprus is a large and fertile island situated off the coast of Syria. In ancient times Cyprus was famous for its wines, its wheats, its oils, its figs, and its honey. To possess land in Cyprus was to be a rich and an influential man. Many men who possessed houses and lands sold them under the Pentecostal fervor, and laid their prices at the apostles' feet. But Barnabas stood at the head of them all; such was his great wealth, such was his great generosity, such was his high character, and such were his splendid services in this and in many other ways to the apostolic church.

As we read on in the Acts of the Apostles we come to the sad story of Ananias and Sapphira; then to the creation of the office of the deaconship; then to the great services and the triumphant translation of Stephen; and, then, the east begins to break in the conversion of Saul of Tarsus. And it is in the first rays of that fast-rising sun that we see for once, if not again, the full stature and the true nobility of Barnabas. It was but yesterday that Saul was seen setting out for Damascus, breathing out threatenings and slaughter against the disciples of the Lord. And, today, he has fled back to Jerusalem, the most hated, the most feared, and the most friendless man in all that city. And, with the blood of so many martyrs still on his hands, it was no wonder that the disciples in Jerusalem were all afraid of Saul, and would not believe that he really intended to be a disciple. Saul of Tarsus a disciple of Jesus Christ! Saul of Tarsus converted, and baptized, and preaching Jesus Christ! No! Depend upon it, this is but another deep-set snare for our feet! This is but another trap baited for us by our bitter enemies! So all the disciples said concerning Saul, and they all bore themselves to Saul accordingly.

Barnabas alone of all the disciples and apostles in Jerusalem opened his door to Saul. Barnabas alone held out his hand to Saul. Barnabas alone believed Saul's wonderful story of his conversion and baptism. Barnabas alone rejoiced in God's saving mercy to Saul's soul. "They were all afraid of Saul, and believed not that he was a disciple. But Barnabas took Saul, and brought him to the apostles, and declared unto them how he had seen the Lord in the way to Damascus, and that the Lord had spoken to him, and how he had preached boldly at Damascus in the name of Jesus Christ." If Barnabas had never done anything else but what he did in those days for Saul of Tarsus, he would deserve, and he would receive, our love and our honor for ever. Barnabas so firmly believed what Saul told him, and so nobly acted on it. He so stood up for Saul when all men were looking askance at him. He so trusted and befriended Saul when every one else suspected him, and cast his past life in his face. Barnabas staked all his good name in Jerusalem, and all his influence with the apostles, on the genuineness of Saul's conversion, and on the sincerity and integrity of his discipleship. Barnabas stood by Saul till he had so turned the tide in Saul's favor, that, timid as Peter was, he actually took Saul to lodge with him in his own house in Jerusalem. And Barnabas gave Saul up to Peter, only too glad to see Saul made so much of by such a pillar of the Apostolic Church as Peter was. With Saul staying fifteen days under Peter's roof, and with James treating Saul with his cautious confidence, Barnabas's battle for Saul was now completely won. Very soon, now, it will be the greatest honor to any house on the face of the earth to entertain the apostle Paul. But no proud householder of them all can ever steal this honor from Barnabas, that he was the first man of influence and responsibility who opened his heart and his house to Saul of Tarsus, when all Jerusalem was still casting stones at him. Barnabas was not predestinated to shine in the service of Christ and His Church like Paul; but Paul himself never did a more shining deed than Barnabas did when he took Saul to his heart at a time when every other heart in Jerusalem was hardened against him. Everlastingly well done, thou true son of consolation!

The scene now shifts to Antioch, which is soon to eclipse Jerusalem herself, and to become the true mother-church of evangelical Christianity. The apostolic preaching had an instantaneous and an immense success at Antioch, and it was its very success that raised there also, and with such acuteness, all those doctrinal and disciplinary disputes that fill with such distress the book of the Acts, and the earlier Epistles of Paul. Jerusalem still remained the Metropolitan Church, and the difficulties that had arisen in Antioch were accordingly sent up to Jerusalem for advice and adjudication. And, that the heads of the Church at Jerusalem chose Barnabas out of the whole college of the apostles to go down and examine into the affairs of Antioch, is just another illustration of the high standing that Barnabas had, both as a man of marked ability, and of high Christian character. "Who, when he came, and had seen the grace of God was glad, and exhorted them all, that with purpose of heart they would cleave unto the Lord. For he was a good man, and full of the Holy Ghost and faith; and much people was added unto the Lord." How full of the Holy Ghost Barnabas was we are made immediately to see. For Barnabas had not been long in Antioch till he became convinced that Antioch was very soon to hold the key of the whole Christian position. Already, indeed, so many questions of doctrine and administration were come to such a crisis in the Church of Antioch, that Barnabas felt himself quite unable to cope with them. And, worse than that, he could not think of any one in Jerusalem who was any better able to cope with those difficult questions than he was himself. In all Barnabas's knowledge of men, and it was not narrow, he knew only one man who was equal to the great emergency at Antioch, and that man was no other than Saul of Tarsus. But, then, Saul was comparatively young as yet; he was not much known, and he was not much trusted. And shall Barnabas take on himself the immense responsibility, and, indeed, immense risk, of sending for Saul of Tarsus, and bringing him to Antioch? And shall Barnabas take this great step without first submitting Saul's name to the authorities at Jerusalem? There were great risks in both of these alternatives, and Barnabas had to act on his own judgment and conscience and heart. There are supreme moments in the field when an officer of original genius, and of the requisite strength of character, will determine to stake all, and to do some bold deed, on his own single responsibility. He will take an immense and an irretrievable step without orders, and, sometimes, against orders. He will thus win the battle, and then he will not mind much either the praise or the blame that comes to him for his successful act of disobedience. Antioch must have Saul of Tarsus; and Barnabas, taking counsel with no one but himself, set out to Tarsus to seek for Saul. "Leaving France, I retired into Germany expressly for the purpose of being able to enjoy in some obscure corner the repose I had always desired, and which had so long been denied me. And I had resolved to continue in the same obscurity, till at length William Farel detained me at Geneva, and that not so much by counsel and exhortation, as by a dread imprecation, which I felt to be as if God from heaven laid His mighty hand upon me to arrest me. For after having learned that my heart was set upon devoting myself to my private studies, for which I wished to keep myself free from all other engagements, and finding that he could gain nothing by entreating me, he proceeded to utter an imprecation that God would curse my retirement, and would blast my selfish studies, if I should refuse to come to Geneva when the need was so great." John Calvin was Saul of Tarsus over again. William Farel was Barnabas over again. And the reformed city of Geneva was the evangelized city of Antioch over again. "Then departed Barnabas to Tarsus to seek for Saul. And when he had found him, he brought him to Antioch." To have the heart to discover a more talented man than yourself, and then to have the heart to go to Tarsus for him, and to make way for him in Antioch, is far better than to have all Saul's talents, and all the praise and all the rewards of those talents to yourself. Speaking for myself I would far rather have a little of Barnabas's grace than have all Saul's genius. Give me Barnabas's self-forgetful heart, and let who will undertake Saul's so extraordinary, but so perilous, endowments. Luther says that we cannot help being jealous of the men who are in our own circle and are more talented than ourselves. Perhaps not. But if Barnabas had to get over any jealousy in connection with Saul's coming to Antioch, that jealousy, at any rate, did not hinder him from setting out to Tarsus to seek for Saul. He must increase, but I must decrease, said Barnabas to himself and to his subordinates as he set his face steadfastly to go down to Tarsus. Barnabas had taken his own measure accurately, and he had taken Saul's measure accurately also, and he took action accordingly. Now, noble conduct like that of Barnabas is always its own best reward. Christ-like conduct like that instantly reacts on character, and character like Barnabas's character manifests itself in more and more of such Christ-like conduct. Barnabas had done Saul a good turn before now, and that only made him the more ready to do him this new good turn when the opportunity was afforded him. "Barnabas was a good man, and full of the Holy Ghost and faith." And three times he publicly proved that; first, when he sold his estate in Cyprus and brought the money, and laid it at the apostles' feet. And he proved that again when he took Saul in his friendlessness and brought him to the apostles in Jerusalem, and compelled them to believe in Saul, and to trust him, and to employ him. And still more conclusively did Barnabas prove his fullness of the Holy Ghost, when he set out to Tarsus to seek for Saul in order that Saul might come to Antioch, and there supersede and extinguish Barnabas himself.

But, as if to chasten our too great pride in Barnabas, even Barnabas, this so pentecostal and so apostolic man; even Barnabas, so full hitherto of the Holy Ghost and of faith—even he must fall at last, and that too all but fatally. For God speaketh once, yea twice, yet man perceiveth it not, that He may withdraw man from his purpose, and hide pride from man. We would have been too much lifted up tonight about Barnabas if we had not had his whole history written to us down to the end. For, what two chosen and fast friends in all the New Testament circle of friends, would you have wagered would be the last to fall out fiercely, and to turn their backs on one another for ever? Not Paul and Barnabas, at any rate, you would confidently and proudly have said. Whoever will quarrel, and fall out, and forget what they owe to one another, that can never, by any possibility, happen to Paul and his old patron Barnabas—so you would have said. But you would have lost your wager, and your confidence in the best of men to boot. "Let us go," said Paul to Barnabas, "and visit our brethren in every city where we have preached the word of the Lord and see how they do." And Barnabas determined to take with him John, whose surname was Mark. And Paul thought not good to take Mark with them. And the contention was so sharp between them that they departed asunder the one from the other. And Barnabas took Mark, and Paul chose Silas. Has Paul forgotten all that he once owed to Barnabas? And why does Barnabas's so sweet and so holy humility so fail him when he is so far on in the voyage of life? "Mariners near the shore," says Shepard, "should be on the outlook for rocks." And Barnabas was so near the shore by this time that it distresses us sorely to see his ship strike the rocks and stagger in the sea in this fashion. Barnabas's ship strikes the rocks till one of the noblest characters in the New Testament is shattered and all but sunk under our very eyes. Who was right and who was wrong in this sharp contention I have no heart to ask. Both were wrong. Paul, and Barnabas, and Mark too—all three were wrong. And multitudes in the Apostolic churches who heard of the scandal, and took contending sides in it, were wrong also. And this sad story is told us to this day, not that we may take sides in it, but that the like of it may never again happen amongst ourselves.

> The gray-haired saint may fail at last,
> The surest guide a wanderer prove;
>> Death only binds us fast
>> To the bright shore of love.

The last time we see Barnabas, sad to say, Paul and he are contending again. But I will not draw you into that contention. We have had instruction, and example, and warning, and rebuke, enough out of Barnabas already. Instruction and example in Barnabas's splendid liberality with his Cyprus possessions. Instruction and example in his openness and hospitality of mind and heart toward a suspected and a friendless man. And still more instruction and example in his noble absence of all envy and all jealousy of a man far more gifted, far more successful, and soon to be far more famous than himself. And, then, this warning and this rebuke also, that at the end of such a life, even Paul and Barnabas should contend so sharply with one another that they scandalized the whole Church of Christ, and departed asunder never to meet again, unless it was to dispute again in this world.

> Let not the people be too swift to judge,
> As one who reckons on the blades in field
> Or ere the crop be ripe. For I have seen
> The thorn frown rudely all the winter long
> And after bear the rose upon its top;
> And barque, that all the way across the sea,
> Ran straight and speedy, perish at the last,
> Even in the haven's mouth.

The evening praises the day, and the chief grace of the theater is the last scene. Be thou faithful unto death, and I will give thee a crown of life.

96

James the Lord's Brother

I OFTEN imagine myself to be James. I far oftener imagine myself to be in James's place and experience, than in the place and experience of any other man in the whole Bible, or in the whole world. The first thirty years of James's life fascinate me and enthrall me far more than all the rest of human life and human history taken together. And I feel sure that I am not alone in that fascination of mine. Who, indeed, would not be absolutely captivated, fascinated, and enthralled, both in imagination and in heart, at the thought of holding James's relationship to Jesus Christ! For thirty years eating every meal at the same table with Him; working six days of the week in the same workshop with Him; going up on the seventh day to the same synagogue with Him; and once every year going up to Jerusalem to the same passover with Him. For James was, actually, the Lord's brother. Not in a figure of speech. Not mystically and spiritually. But literally and actually—he was James the Lord's brother. Jesus was Mary's first-born son, and James was her second son. And the child James would be the daily delight of his elder Brother; he would be His continual charge and joy; just as you see two such brothers in your own family life at home. When Mary's first-born Son was twelve years old it was the law of Moses that He should be taken up to Jerusalem to His first passover. James was not old enough yet for his first passover, but you may be sure he missed nothing with his father and mother and Brother to tell him all about Jerusalem and the passover when they came home; James both hearing his elder Brother and asking Him questions. For the next eighteen years Joseph's door is hermetically shut to our holy curiosity. All we know is, that one, at any rate, of Joseph's household was filled with wisdom, and the grace of God was upon Him. Not another syllable more is told us about Joseph or Mary, or any of their household, till the preaching of the Baptist broke in on that house, as on all the houses of the land, like the coming of the kingdom of heaven. John and his baptism was the talk of week-day and Sabbath-day in Nazareth, as in all the land, till at last a company of young carpenters and fishermen went south to Bethabara beyond Jordan where John was baptizing. And Jesus of Nazareth, known as yet by that name only, was one of them. You have by heart all that immediately took place at the Jordan. "Behold the Lamb of God, which taketh away the sin of the world. We have found the Messiah. We have found Him, of whom Moses in the law, and the prophets, did write, Jesus of Nazareth, the son of Joseph. Rabbi, Thou art the Son of God, Thou art the King of Israel. And Jesus returned in the power of the Spirit into Galilee. And He came to Nazareth where He was brought up; and, as His custom was, He went into the synagogue on the Sabbath-day and stood up for to read. And there was delivered to Him the book of the prophet Esaias. And when He had opened the book He found the place where it was written, The Spirit of the Lord is upon Me, because He hath anointed Me to preach the gospel to the poor; He hath sent Me to heal the broken-hearted, to preach deliverance to the captive, and recovering of sight to the blind, to set at liberty them that are bound, to preach the acceptable year of the Lord. And all bear Him witness, and wondered at the gracious words which proceeded out of His mouth." But, all the time, James His brother did not believe on Him. No, nor did James believe down to the very end. I wish I had the learning and the genius to let you see and hear all that must have gone on in Joseph's house for the next three years. The family perplexities about Jesus; the family reasonings about Him; the family divisions and disputes about Him; their intoxicating hopes at one time over Him, and their fears and sinkings of heart because of Him at another time. Think out for yourselves those three years, the like of which never came to any other family on the face of the earth. And, then, think of the last week of all; the arrest, the trial, the crucifixion, the resurrection of Mary's first-born Son—whose imagination is sufficient to picture to itself Joseph and Mary and James and the other brothers and sisters of Jesus all that week! Where did they make ready to eat the passover? What were they doing at the hour when He was in Gethsemane? Were they standing with the crowd in the street when He was led about all night in His bonds? And where were they while He was being crucified? For, by that time, no one believed on Him but the thief on the cross alone. All the faith in Christ that survived the cross was bound up in that bundle of smoking flax, the penitent and praying thief. The next time we come on James is in these golden words of Paul written concerning him long afterwards, "and that Jesus Christ was buried, and that He rose the third day according to the scriptures. After that, He was seen of James; then of all the apostles." He was seen of James somewhere, and to somewhat of the same result, that He was seen of Saul at the gate of Damascus.

Three years pass on, during the progress of which James has risen to be one of the pillars of the Church of Jerusalem. James's high character, and his close relationship to Jesus Christ, taken together with his conservative tone of mind, all combined to give him his unique position of influence and authority in the Church of Jerusalem. We have a life-like portrait of James as he appeared to the men of his day which it will interest and impress you to look at for a moment. "Now, James was holy from his mother's womb. He drank no wine or strong drink. He ate no animal food. No razor ever went on his head. He anointed not himself with oil, and used not the indulgence of the bath. He wore no wool, but linen only, and he was such a man of prayer that when they came to coffin him his knees were as hard and as stiff to bend as the knees of a camel. On account of the sternness of his character he was called James the Just, and James the bulwark of the people." Now, in that contemporary account of James may we not have a clue to the obstinacy of his unbelief, and to his all but open hostility to our Lord? For James was a Nazarite of such strictness and scrupulosity that he could not fail to be greatly offended at his Brother's absolute and resolute freedom from all such unspiritual trammels. James's eldest Brother was no Nazarite. He was no Scribe. He was no Pharisee. And He must often have stumbled James, so far did He come short of a perfect righteousness, as James understood and demanded perfect righteousness. In His public preaching He was compelled to denounce what James scrupulously practiced as the law of Moses and the law of God. The Scribes and the Pharisees were continually finding fault with James's Brother for His laxity in the traditions of the elders, and no man would feel that laxity so acutely as James would feel it. So rooted was James in the old covenant that, even after his conversion, he still continued to cleave fast to his unevangelical habits of thought and practices of life, in a way and to an extent that caused the greatest trouble to the rest of the apostles, and to Paul especially. In our Lord's words, James, all his days, was one of those men, and a leader among them, who continued to pour the new wine of the gospel into the old bottles of the law, till the old bottles burst in their hands and the new wine was spilled. Converted as he undoubtedly was, James was half a Pharisee to the very end. And, if ever he was a bishop at all, he was the bishop of a half-enlightened Jewish ghetto rather than of a Christian church. Still, when all is said, we have an intense interest in James; not so much for his position or for his services in the apostolic church, as for this, that he was the brother, the born and brought-up brother, of our Lord.

James was the born and brought-up brother of our Lord, and, by that, he being dead, yet speaketh. And the one supreme lesson that James teaches us tonight is surely this, "Keep your eyes open at home, for I made this tremendous mistake. The unpardonable and irreparable mistake of my whole life was this, that my eyes were never opened at home till it was too late. I never once saw what was for thirty years, day and night, staring me in the face, if I had not been stone-blind. It never entered my mind all those years that He was any better than I was myself. Indeed, I often blamed Him that He was not nearly so good as myself. But I remember now: we all remember now, endless instances of His goodness, His meekness, His humility, His lowliness of mind and heart. We often recall to one another how we all took our own way with Him, and got our own way with Him in everything. How silent He was when we were all speaking, and would not hold our peace. How obliging He was, how gentle, how sweet. But, all the time, we saw it not till it was all over, and it was too late." The kingdom of heaven did not come with sufficient observation to James. Had his elder Brother been a Pharisee, had He been a Scribe, had He been a John the Baptist, had His raiment been of camel's hair, had His meat been locusts and wild honey, and had He had His dwelling among the rocks, James would have found it far easier to believe in his Brother. But the still small voice of a holy life at home made no impression on James. Yes: let us all acknowledge James's tremendous mistake, and let us all go home with our eyes opened lest the kingdom of heaven may have come to our own house also, and we may not see that till it is too late. A Christian character may be displayed before our eyes at home, and we may never discover it, just because it is at home. Ay, and let us beware of this, lest our hard ways, our proud ways, our selfish tempers and our want of love, may all be the daily cross and thorn of some child of God hidden from our eyes in our own homes, as James was to Jesus. Out of doors many began to believe in James's Brother, but no one indoors. In His own home, and among His own brothers and sisters, our Lord had no recognition and no honor.

And James is a warning to us all in this respect also, that he never, to the very end, became a true and complete New Testament believer. Whether it was that he had been too long an unbeliever, and never could make up for the opportunities he had lost; or whether it was that he yielded to his natural temper too much, and let it take too deep a hold of him; or whether it was that he was never able to suppress himself so as to submit to sit at Paul's feet; or whether it was that he could never shake off the hard and narrow men who hampered and hindered him; or whether it was his life-long chastisement and impoverishment for neglecting the incomparably glorious opportunity God had given him for thirty-three years—whatever was the true explanation of it, the fact is only too clear on too many pages of the New Testament, that James, all his days, was far more of a Jew than a genuine Christian. His canonical Epistle itself belongs more to the Old Testament than to the New. Luther felt afterwards that he had gone too far in what he had said in his haste about the Epistle of James. But every one who knows and loves and lives upon Paul's Gospel as Luther did, will sometimes feel something of Luther's mind about James and his Epistle. Though his risen Brother appeared to James as he appeared to Paul, at the same time, God could never be said to have manifested His Son in James as He had manifested Him in Paul. Account for it as we may: brother of our Lord, Bishop of Jerusalem, pillar of that Church as he was and all, James never came within sight of Paul as a New Testament saint of Christ and an evangelical apostle. James never entered himself, and he never led his people, into the glorious liberty of the sons of God. Surely a most solemn warning to us, that our natural tempers, our traditional prejudices, our early sympathies, the school of life and thought and worship in which we have been brought up, and our not ignoble loyalty to that form of doctrine into which we were in our youth delivered,—all that may stand in our way; all that may have to be fought against and conquered; if we are ever to come in the unity of the faith, and of the knowledge of the Son of God, unto a perfect man, unto the measure of the stature of the fullness of Christ.

97
Stephen

IN the stoning of Stephen there was lost to the Pentecostal Church another Apostle Paul. Stephen was a young man of such original genius and of such special grace, that there was nothing he might not have attained to had he been allowed to live. His wonderful openness of mind; his perfect freedom from all the prepossessions, prejudices, and superstitions of his day; his courage, his eloquence, his spotless character; with a certain sweet, and at the same time majestic, manner; all combined to set Stephen in the very front rank both of service and of risk. In all these things, and especially in the openness, receptiveness, and ripeness of his mind, Stephen far outstripped even such pillar apostles as Peter and James and John themselves. Stephen had anticipated also, and had forerun, and had all but carried off the apostolic palm from Paul himself. All these things made Stephen already all but the foremost man of his day, and, as a consequence, the first man to be struck at and struck down. Simple deacon and servant of tables as Stephen was, it was impossible that a man of such ability and such distinction should be confined and limited to that. His intellectual power, his spiritual insight and foresight, with the strength of his faith and the warmth of his devotion, were all such that he soon found himself deep in apostolic duty, as well as in the proper work of the deaconship. After his purely deaconship work was done, and springing immediately out of his way of doing it, Stephen felt himself constrained on many occasions to take a still more public part in the support and the defence and the edification of the infant Church of Jerusalem. But malice always follows eminence in this world, as Stephen soon found out to his cost. Ignorance, superstition, prejudice, ill-will, odium, all began to dog Stephen's footsteps and to raise their murderous misrepresentations against him in every synagogue into which he entered. And the better he spoke, and the more unanswerably, the more were the enemies that he raised both against himself and against the truth, till his enemies had their own way with him. "We have heard him speak blasphemous words against Moses, and against God." That was his indictment, as we say; and then we have his apology in the seventh chapter of the Acts, and a very remarkable piece of speaking it is in many ways.

As often as we hear of an Apology we always think of Socrates. On the other hand, our Lord, when on His trial, offered no Apology. He held His peace, insomuch that the governor marvelled greatly. What, I reverently wonder, would His Apology have been? You who are students of the New Testament might do worse, now that your college exereises are nearly over, than to continue your great studies and try to construct, with all your learning and ability and insight, the Apology that our Lord, had He seen fit, might have addressed to that same Council. An intelligent congregation would greatly delight in that supposed Apology for a Sabbath evening lecture, if you did it well. At any rate, if your sense of reverence will not let you put His Apology into your Master's mouth, you might do this:

you might sometime take the trouble to compare the Apology that Plato puts into his Master's mouth with this Apology of Stephen that you have here in Luke. The one, the first great defence of truth and righteousness in the Pagan Dispensation; and the other, the first great defence of Christ and His infant Church in the Apostolic and Evangelic Dispensation. "Men, brethren, and fathers, hearken!" Stephen commences. Always commence by conciliating your audience, says Dante. In his introduction, says Augustine, Stephen practices the Quintilianian art of capturing the goodwill of his hearers, however stoutly and sternly and plain-spokenly he may have to end.

It almost looks as if we had Stephen's Apology verbatim in the Book of the Acts. His speech reads as well to us as if we had sat in the Council that day and had heard it with our own ears. The beloved physician, when he turned Church historian, had a perfect understanding of all things from the very first; and, among other things, he supplies us with remarkably full reports of some of the great sermons and speeches and apologies of that all-important time. Sometimes a single word, sometimes an accent on a single word, sometimes the shaping and insertion of a single phrase, sometimes a quotation or a paraphrase of a quotation, sometimes what he does not say, as well as what he does say, sometimes what he manages to suggest without saying it at all: little things like these will discover and proclaim the true orator. And that is the case again and again in Stephen's Apology. Pericles, Plutarch tells us, never spoke that he did not leave a secret sting in the hearts of his hearers. And all Stephen's eloquent review of Old Testament history drew on and gathered itself up to drive this terrible sting through and through the hearts of the whole Council, "As your fathers did, so do ye! For ye have now been the betrayers and murderers of the Just One!"

Now, out of all that, quite a crowd of lessons and instructions and examples and warnings rise up before us, and press themselves upon us. Let us select two or three of those lessons, and leave the others for the present unspoken.

1. Up to this time the twelve had done everything with their own hands. They had been evangelists, preachers, apologists, pastors, ruling elders, session-clerks, servants of tables, and everything else, for the daily increasing congregations of Jerusalem and the whole country round about. But it was the money matters of the Pentecostal Church that completely broke the apostles down, and brought things to a perfect standstill. When thousands of people were contributing to a central sustentation fund, and were again, rich and poor, supported out of it; when the rich were selling their possessions and were laying the prices at the apostles' feet; and when the increasing crowds of poor members were receiving their daily dole directly from the apostles' hands; it is plain that all this would soon result in the serious encroachment of the secular side of their work, so to call it, on the purely spiritual side. Their public teaching and preaching, and certain still more important matters, would be seriously interfered with, till the twelve apostles took the wise step that is recorded in this chapter. It is not reason, they said, and we cannot go on with it, that we should leave the Word of God in order to serve tables to this extent. Wherefore, brethren, look out among yourselves seven men whom we may appoint over this business. And we will, all the more, give ourselves continually to prayer and to the ministry of the Word. And this proposal of the apostles commended itself to the common sense of the whole Church, and they chose seven

select men and set them before the apostles for ordination. And we inherit the wisdom and the benefit of that apostolic example to this day. The Church of our day also says to her members and to her office-bearers something like this:—"It is utterly unreasonable that our ministers should all alone be expected to perform all the multitudinous work that arises out of a great congregation. It is quite preposterous that any one man should be expected to preach two or three sermons a week, keep in close contact with a thousand people, baptize our children, marry our sons and daughters, console our sick, bury our dead, find work for our unemployed, negotiate loans of money and gather gifts for our embarrassed members, get our aged and our orphaned into asylums and hospitals, besides many other things that can neither be foreseen nor set aside by our ministers." And thus it comes about that a compact is entered into and a division of labor is made. The young men take the financing of the congregation off their minister's hands, while the more experienced men share with him in the teaching and the ruling and the visiting of the flock. Never more than just at the present day did the Church see the divine wisdom of the apostolic institution of the deaconship, or feel more the need of adhering to it and extending it. And, then, the minister who honestly performs his part of the compact in prayer and in preaching will not lack, any more than Peter and John lacked, the willing and capable help of Stephen and of Philip. As James Durham says: "In all this we see what a minister's great task is, and wherein he should be taken up—secret prayer, reading, and meditation, and then the public preaching of the Gospel. We see also that though all ministers are virtually both elders and deacons as the twelve were, yet ought they to regulate both of these offices with respect to the former two of secret prayer and public preaching. As also that elders and deacons ought to have respect to keep ministers from being overburdened and too much toiled, that they may have freedom to follow their main work. Yea, even to have frequent and lengthened access to aloneness and solitariness, which is both most necessary as well as well becoming in a minister." And so on at great depth and fullness in "The Dying Man's Testimony to the Church of Scotland."

2. *Nomina debita*, says John Donne; that is to say, "Every man owes to the world the signification of his name, and of all his name. Every new addition of honor or of office lays a new obligation upon him, and his Christian name above all." Now, when you name a man a deacon, as the apostles named Stephen, from the day you do so he begins to owe to the world and to the Church some new obligations. He is called and ordained and named because he is a man of honest report, and full of wisdom and devotedness; and all these graces grow in every new deacon as he goes on to exercise them. I do not know so well how it is with other Deacons' Courts, but I know to my continual delight and refreshment how it is with our own. I know how nobly our deacons fulfill the Pentecostal programme. And that is why our name as a congregation stands in such honor among the congregations of the land. It is our deacons who do it. It is the successors of Stephen and Philip who do it. Every penny of our Pentecostal thousands is collected personally by our deacons. And collected too with a spontaneity and a punctuality and a knowledge of what they are doing, and a love for what they are doing, that make our monthly meetings one of the greatest delights and refreshments of my whole ministerial life. It all depends on our clerk, and on our treasurer, and on our censor, and on our splendid

staff; all our ability to serve the tables of our poorer brethren depends absolutely on our deacons. Take away our deacons, or let them stand idle while other people do their work, and we would very soon drop down from the front rank to which they and they alone have raised us. "Bring ye all the tithes into the storehouse, that there may be meat in Mine house, and prove Me now herewith, saith the Lord of Hosts, if I will not open you the windows of heaven, and pour you out a blessing, that there shall not be room enough to receive it." It is because our Stephen-like staff hear their Master saying that to them every month, that they purchase to themselves such a good degree, and purchase for Free St. George's congregation such a good degree also. Wherefore, all my brethren, look ye out among you men of mind, and men of heart, and men of business habits, and they will purchase a good degree for you also when you appoint them over this business. I only wish that every deacon in Scotland could come and see how our deacons in Edinburgh do their work.

3. And now to pass on to the day when Stephen finished his course, kept the faith, and resigned the deaconship. "Behold!" he exclaimed with the stones crashing about his head, "I see the Son of Man standing on the right hand of God!" But the Son of Man does not now any more stand, surely. For when He had by Himself purged our sins He surely sat down for ever on the right hand of God. "Sit, said the LORD to my Lord, at My right hand until I make Thy foes Thy footstool." But, with all that, He could not sit still when He saw them stoning Stephen. And so it is with Him always. He sits, or He stands, or He comes down to earth again, just according to our need, and just according to our faith. I see Him standing up, says Stephen. What a power, what a possession, is faith! For faith can make the Son of Man do almost anything she likes. As William Guthrie says of her, "Faith sometimes acts in a very willful way upon her Lord." So she does. For look at what a willful way the Syrophoenician woman acted upon her Lord, till, to get rid of her, He said to her, Take anything you like. Only go home to your daughter. And so still. The faith of His people gives Him absolutely no rest. Their faith makes Him stand up long after He has sat down. Their faith makes Him do everything and be everything that they need and ask. He did everything on earth, and He still does everything in heaven, by which He can be useful to poor souls. As for example, Is the soul naked? Then Christ on the spot is fine raiment. Is the soul hungry and thirsty? Immediately Christ is its milk and its wine, its bread of life and its true manna. Is the avenger of blood at the heels of the sinner? Then just one step and the blood-guilty man is in the city of refuge. In one word, tell Him how He can help a poor sinner who has no other help, and all the high and honorable seats in heaven will not hold our Lord down. And, then, as He honors faith, so faith honors Him. Is He a bridegroom? Faith is in His arms. Is He a shepherd? Faith is at His feet. Is He a rock? Faith has already begun to build her house on Him for eternity. Is He the way? Faith runs with all her affections to the Father by Him. And they stoned Stephen, calling upon God, and saying, Behold, I see the Son of Man standing on the right hand of God. Lord Jesus, receive my spirit. And he kneeled down, and cried with a loud voice, Lord, lay not this sin to their charge. And when he had said this, he fell asleep. For they that have used the office of a deacon well purchase to themselves a good degree, and great boldness in the faith which is in Christ Jesus.

98

Philip: Deacon and Evangelist

"THE more we are mown down by you, the more we multiply among you," said Tertullian in his proud Apology. "Every single drop of our blood springs up, in some thirty, in some sixty, and in some an hundred-fold." And thus it was that the banishment of Philip from Jerusalem was the salvation of Samaria, and thus it was also that the martyrdom of Stephen was the conversion of Saul. *Semen est sanguis Christianorum.*

Stephen was the first martyr, and Philip was the first missionary. The deacon-ship adorned itself and did nobly in those early days. Stephen and Philip were not apostles to begin with; they were simply deacons. They were not ordained, like the apostles, to prayer and to the ministry of the Word. But you cannot limit, and narrow, and bind down to the serving of tables two powerful and original men like Stephen and Philip. Paul had Stephen and Philip in his mind when he said to Timothy long afterwards, that they who have used the office of a deacon well, purchase to themselves a good degree, and great boldness in the faith which is in Christ Jesus. All of which both Stephen and Philip had emphatically done.

"And," writes Luke to Theophilus, "at that time there was a great persecution against the Church which was at Jerusalem; so that they were all scattered abroad throughout the regions of Judea and Samaria. And Philip went down to the city of Samaria, and preached Christ unto them. And there was great joy in that city." Now, just suppose for a moment that you had been Philip. Suppose that you had been scattered abroad like Philip and his colleagues. And suppose that you had escaped with the Gospel in your hands, and were chased into some half-heathen city that had just been touched on the surface with the knowledge of Christ. You would be sure to seek out those who had been so touched, and you would throw yourself on their hospitality and protection. And thus it was that Philip would certainly seek out the woman of Samaria that all the world knows about now, and in whose heart, and in whose house, there was now a well of water springing up unto everlasting life. Peter and John would give Philip an introduction to her; and to reassure him about his reception, they would tell him, John especially, all about that oft-remembered day when their Master must needs go through Samaria, and when, being wearied with His journey, He sat thus on the well. And the woman would welcome Philip, and would say to him, Come in, thou blessed of the Lord, for when I was thirsty He gave me drink. And when Philip said to her, Sit down, woman, sit down and eat, she only served his table all the more hospitably, and said, I have meat to eat that thou knowest not of. Come to my house, she said also to all her neighbors, and see and hear a man who has come to my house from the very risen Christ Himself. And, taking his text from the woman's words, Philip preached the risen Christ in Sychar till there was great joy in that city. Luke is a scholar, and so is Theophilus. Luke is a student and an artist in his words, and

Theophilus attends to what Luke writes. And thus it is that when Luke tells Theophilus that Philip preached "Christ" to the Samaritans, and then that the same evangelist preached "Jesus" to the Ethiopian eunuch, it is not for nothing; it is not of no consequence what Luke says, or how he says it. It is not without good reason that such a scrupulous composer as Luke is selects his names and his titles in this exact way for our Lord. Bengel is the very commentator for such a composer as Luke. And Bengel writes with his needle-pointed pen and says that "from the Old Testament point of view, progress is made from the knowledge of Christ to the knowledge of Jesus; while from the New Testament point of view, the progress is made from the knowledge of Jesus to the knowledge of Christ." "Not a single syllable," says Basil, "of all that is written concerning Jesus Christ should be left uninvestigated. The men who trace the hidden meaning of every word and even of every letter in the New Testament are those who understand best the end and nature of our Scriptural calling." Let our theological students, then, study out the fact of Philip's preaching "Christ" in the city, and "Jesus" in the desert, and make an Ellicott-like thesis for themselves and for their people on this subject taking in Romans viii. 11.

Now, I must stop for a moment at this point to say how much I feel both impressed and rebuked by the noble conduct of Peter and John. Both Stephen and Philip were by far the subordinates of Peter and John. And there is no sin that so easily besets some of us ministers as just the sudden success of those who are by far our subordinates. There is nothing that more tries us and brings to the surface what we are made of at heart than just to be outstripped and extinguished by those who but yesterday were mere boys beside us. And it takes the strongest man among us and the holiest man all his might to behave himself with humility and with generosity to his late subordinates at such a time. But let us stop at this point and see how well both Peter and John came out of that furnace of theirs. They did not grudge, nor resent, nor suspect, nor despise the success of Stephen in Jerusalem, nor of Philip in Samaria. They did not say, The deacon has his proper place. They did not complain that he had so soon left the serving of tables. They did not say that Philip should attend to his proper work, and let preaching alone. They did not shake their heads and forecast that it would soon turn out to be all so much Samaritan excitement. They did not have it reported to them every word that Philip had at any time spoken that was out of joint. Far no. To their great honor be it told, they behaved themselves in all this temptation of theirs in a way altogether worthy of their apostolic office. They did not wait to see if the awakening was real and would last, as we would have done. But the twelve sent down Peter and John, their two best men, to assist Philip to gather in the results of his so suddenly successful mission. And Peter and John set to work with all their might to found a church out of Philip's converts, to be called the Church of the Evangelist, after the name of their deacon and subordinate. I, for one, must lay all that Samaria episode well to heart. I, for one, must not forget it.

Both Stephen and Philip have made this impression also upon me that they were born preachers, as we say. Born, not made. Born, not college-bred. Born, and not simply ordained. And if a man is a born preacher, you may set him to serve tables, or, for that matter, to make tables, but he will preach in spite of you. You may suborn men to bear him down. You may banish him away to Samaria, but I defy you to shut his mouth. Stephen and Philip were born with such a fire in their bones that no man could put it out. There is a divine tongue in their mouth that you cannot silence. The more you persecute them and cast them out, and the more tribulation you pass them through, they will only preach all that the better. Now, that there were two men of such rare genius among the first seven deacons is a remarkable proof of the insight of the congregation that elected them, as well as of the wealth of all kinds of talent in the Apostolic Church. I have often wished that I could have been one of the two Emmaus-men whose hearts burned within them as their risen Lord expounded unto them in all the Scriptures the things concerning Himself. And, then, after that I would fain have been the servant of the Ethiopian eunuch, so as to have sat beside him and heard him reading the prophet Esaias till Philip came up and said to him, Understandest thou what thou readest? How can I, except some man should guide me? And he desired Philip that he would come up and sit with him. And Philip opened his mouth, and began at the 53rd of Isaiah, and preached unto him Jesus. All this took place in the primitive, simple, unsophisticated east, and we must not measure any part of all this history by our western habits of intercourse. It would be resented as the height of intrusion and incivility among us if one man were to say to another over his book on the deck of a steamer or in a railway carriage, Are you understanding what you are reading? But look at it in this way. Suppose you sat beside a foreigner who was struggling with one of our English guide-books, and was evidently missing the sense, till he was starting off in a wrong direction; it would be no intrusion or impertinence if you made up to him and said to him something like this: "I fear our barbarous tongue is not easily mastered by foreign scholars, but it is my native language, and I may be able to be of some use to you in it." "How can I?" said the humble-minded eunuch, "except some man should guide me?" Now, we all think, because we know the letters of it, and are familiar with the sounds of it, that we understand the Bible: Isaiah, and John, and Paul. But we never made a more fatal mistake. There is no book in all the world that is so difficult to read, and to understand, and to love, as the Bible. Not having begun to understand it, some of you will turn upon me and will tell me that even a little child can understand it. And you are perfectly right. "A lamb can wade it," said a great Greek expositor of it. But he went on to add that "an elephant can swim in it." And thus it was that, over and above the apostles, all the deacons of intellect and experience were drawn on to expound the Scriptures, first to the learned Council of Jerusalem, then to the sceptical men of Samaria, and then to the Ethiopian neophyte in his royal chariot. And thus it is still that the Church collects into her colleges the very best minds she can lay hold of in all her families, and trains them up under her very best teachers, and then when they are ready says to them, Go join thyself to this and that vacant pulpit, and make the people to understand what they read. And you must often have both felt it and confessed it to be so. How different the most superficially familiar chapter looks to us ever after some great expounder, by tongue or by pen, has opened it up to us! A book of the Bible read in routine chapters in the pulpit or at family worship, how dull, and unmeaning, and immediately forgotten it is! Whereas, let an interpreter, one of a thousand, open it up to us, and we never forget either the chapter or him. "The Spirit of God maketh the reading, but especially the expounding of the Word, an effectual means of convincing and converting sinners, and of building them up in holiness and comfort, through faith, unto salvation." "It is mainly by the institution of expounding and preaching," says John Foster, "that religion is kept a conspicuous thing, a public acknowledged reality. If we are told that we should rather say that it is public worship that has this effect, we have to answer that public worship, apart from expounding and preaching, has a very small effect in favor of religion. It is quite certain that where the conductors of that worship have not knowledge and religion enough to expound and preach, that worship will be little more than a ceremonial routine of idle forms."

Years and years and years pass on. Philip has for long been a married man, and is now the father of four grown-up daughters. His wife is a good woman. She is a grave woman, as Paul exhorted her to be. And, between them, Philip and his grave and faithful wife both ruled themselves well, and thus their four extraordinarily-gifted daughters. And with such a father and such a mother, I do not wonder that when such things were abroad in those days as gifts of tongues, and gifts of healing, and gifts of prophecy, and many other operations of the Holy Ghost, a double portion of some of those miraculous things came to Philip's four daughters. Luke has a quick eye for everything of that kind, and thus it is that he interpolates this footnote in his history of Paul. "And the next day we came to Caesarea, and we entered the house of Philip the evangelist, which was one of the seven; and abode with him. And the same man had four daughters, virgins, which did prophesy. And as we tarried there many days, there came down from Judea a certain prophet, named Agabus. And when he was come to us, he took Paul's girdle, and bound his own hands and feet, and said, Thus saith the Holy Ghost, so shall the Jews at Jerusalem bind the man that owneth this girdle," and so on. And thus it was that this strange Agabus was the last sanctification of Philip and his wife and his four prophetical daughters. To begin with, his own children had been gifted and employed and honored far above Philip himself. And then Agabus arrived just at the moment to be gifted and employed and honored far above them all. In the rich grace and manifold wisdom of God, outwardly and ostensibly and on the surface, Agabus's errand was to foretell Paul about his future arrest at Jerusalem. But, far deeper than that, Agabus had a finishing work of the Holy Ghost to perform on Philip, and on his four daughters, and on their mother, that grave woman. A work of humility. A work of resignation. An evangelical work. A work far above the best prophecy. A work of lowly-mindedness. A work of esteeming others better than themselves. A work of saying, Agabus must increase, and I must decrease. And a work that, no doubt, began by reproaches and rebukes and charging God foolishly, like this. "Why were not my prophetical daughters employed to deliver this prophecy to Paul? Why was a stranger brought in over our heads in this way? We cannot ever again have the same standing and esteem in Caesarea after this so open slight. What a strength it would have been to us in our pulpit and pastoral work had my daughters been honored of the Holy Ghost to utter this prophecy concerning the Apostle. It would have established us and honored us in our work in Caesarea like nothing else." Agabus was an evil enough messenger to Paul; but he was such a staggering blow to Philip and to his whole household that it took all Paul's insight, and skill in souls, and authority with Philip, and power with God, to guide and direct Philip so as that he should get all God's intended good to himself and to all his house out of it.

Now, Agabus does not come to your house and mine in such open and such dramatic ways as he came to Philip's house; but he comes. Agabus of Jerusalem came to Jonathan Edwards's grave and godly wife in Northampton in the shape of a young preacher. "On Monday night, Mr. Edwards being gone that day to Leicester, I heard that Mr. Buell was coming to this town. At that moment I felt the eye of God on my heart to see if I was perfectly resigned with respect to Mr. Buell's expected success among our people. I was sensible what great cause I had to bless God for the use He had made of my husband hitherto, and I thought that if He now employed other ministers more I could entirely acquiesce in His will. On Tuesday night there seemed to be great tokens of God's presence at Mr. Buell's meeting; and when I heard of it, I sat still in entire willingness that God should bless his labors among us as much as He pleased, even though it were to the refreshing of every saint and the conversion of every sinner in the whole town. These feelings continued afterwards when I saw his great success. I never felt the least rising of heart against him, but my submission to God was even and uniform and without interruption or disturbance. I rejoiced when I saw the honor God had put upon him, and the respect paid to him by the people, and the greater success attending his preaching than had now for some time past attended my husband's preaching. I found rest and rejoicing in it, and the sweet language of my soul continually was, Amen, Lord Jesus. Amen, Lord Jesus. I had an overwhelming sense of the glory of God, and of the happiness of having my own will entirely subdued to His will. I knew that the foretaste of glory I then had in my soul came from God, and that in His time I shall be with Him, and be, as it were, swallowed up in Him." Agabus, and Mr. Buell, and another. But who is that other? And what is his name?

99

Cornelius

CORNELIUS had been sent out from Rome to Caesarea, very much as our English officers are sent out to India. The Romans both despised and hated the Jews, as we, with all our proverbial pride, neither despise nor hate any of our subject races; and, sharing both that despite and that hatred, Cornelius had come out to his centurionship in Caesarea. But Cornelius was no ordinary Roman centurion, and he soon discovered that the Jews of Caesarea were no ordinary tributary people. The wide and deep contrast between Italy and Israel soon began to make an immense impression on Cornelius's excellent and open mind. Israel's noble doctrine of Jehovah and His Messiah; the spotless purity of Israel's morality, with the sweetness and the sanctity of its home life; its magnificent and incomparable literature, even to a man fresh from Athens and Rome; and its majestic and overpowering worship;—all these things immensely impressed Cornelius, till, by the time we are introduced to him, Cornelius is already a devout man, and one that fears the God of Israel, and prays to the God of Israel always.

It was one of the conspicuous characteristics of Cornelius that all his servants, both domestic and professional, stood on such a friendly footing with their master. His family religion, as we would call it, was one of the most outstanding and attractive things about Cornelius. Long before Cornelius was a baptized man at all, this mind of Christ was already found in the centurion. "I call you not servants," said One whom Cornelius did not yet know. "For the servant knoweth not what his lord doeth; but I have called you friends: for all things that I have learned of my Father I have made known unto you." So did Cornelius. Cornelius was already one of those Christian gentlemen who hold their commissions in the army less for their own sake than for the sake of their soldiers; and their landed estates less for their own sake than for the sake of their farmers, and gardeners, and coachmen, and grooms; and their factories less for their own sake than for the sake of their factory-hands; and their offices less for their own sake than for the sake of their clerks; and their shops less for their own sake than for the sake of their shopmen and their shop women; and their houses at home less for their own sake than for the sake of their children, and their domestic servants, and their ever-welcome guests. Of all holy places in the Holy Land, few places, surely, were more the house of God and the gate of heaven in those days than just the Roman castle of Caesarea, where the centurion of the Italian legion lived in the fear of God with all his household, and with all his devout soldiers, who were daily learning more and more devoutness from the walk and conversation of their beloved and revered centurion.

Well, one day Cornelius was fasting and praying all that day till three o'clock in the afternoon. It must have been some special and outstanding day in his personal life, or in his family life, or in his life in the army. We are not told what anniversary-day it was; but it was a day he had never forgotten to commemorate in prayer: and he has never forgotten it in alms nor in thanks-offerings since: no, nor ever will. It had just struck three o'clock in the afternoon, when an angel descended and entered the barrack-room where Cornelius was on his knees. For are they not all ministering spirits sent forth to minister for them who shall be heirs of salvation? "What is it, Lord?" said Cornelius, looking up in holy fear. "Thy prayers and thine alms," said the angel, "are come up for a memorial before God." We have no Bible dictionary on earth that is able to explain to us the language of heaven, and thus we are left to compare Scripture with Scripture in this matter of a memorial. "This shall be told for a memorial of her," said the Master of angels, when the woman poured the alabaster box upon His head. And this remarkable and unique word stands in the text in order that we may exercise some under-standing, and imagination, and encouragement, in our alms and in our prayers in our day also. There was joy in heaven—this is part of what a memorial in heaven means—over every good deed that Cornelius did, and over every good word that Cornelius spake, both to God and to man. They had their eyes upon Cornelius, those angels of God, because he had been pointed out to them as one of the heirs of salvation. And, you may be sure, they did not keep Cornelius's alms and prayers to themselves; but, the holy talebearers that they are, they sought out the prophets and the psalmists who had prophesied concerning the salvation of the Gentiles, and told them that the great work had begun at last in the conversion of the Ethiopian eunuch and the Roman centurion. And it was not left to their winged visits up and down with the last news from Caesarea; but there were great books kept also, and one of them with Cornelius's name embossed on the back of it, with all his prayers, and all his alms, day and date, times and places, opportunities and people, with all their other circumstances and accompaniments. The memorial books are kept with such scrupulous care in heaven, because so much already turns there, and will afterwards turn there, on things that we might quite overlook down here. And those great volumes, kept with such insight and truth, lie open before the throne of God for a memorial, for the instruction of His angels, and for the joy of all the already saved. How it was decreed from all eternity that Cornelius should be a centurion; should be commissioned by Caesar to Caesarea; should be an open-minded man; should open his mind to the Old Testament and to the temple; should begin to pray, and should sometimes fast that he might the better pray; and should be always waiting to see what he ought to do;—all that was writ-ten in the book of his memorial concerning Cornelius. And, as time went on, Cornelius's memorial-volume grew till there was written in it how Peter came to him, and how he was baptized, and how he finished his course, and kept the faith, first at Caesarea, and then at Rome, till it was said to him, that, as he had been faithful over a few things in Caesarea, so let him come up to where his memorial was writ-ten, and he would be set over twelve legions of angels. "For," says John Calvin on Cornelius, "God keeps a careful memorial concerning all His servants, and by sure and certain steps He exalts them till they come to the top."

Now, the main point is, what about your memorial and mine? What about your alms and your prayers and mine? What about your fastings, and shut doors, and mine, in order that we may have a day now and then of undistracted, and concentrated, and self-chastening prayer? Has there ever been joy in heaven over your prayers and your alms and mine? Real joy in heaven among the angels and the saints of God? And do the faces and the wings of those messenger-spirits shine as they carry the latest memorial that has come up to heaven concerning us to tell the news of it to those in heaven who loved us on earth? Let us pray more, and give alms more, if only to add to the joy of God's angels and saints who remember us and wait for news about us in heaven.

But, a man of prayer, and a benevolent man, and a man with a memorial in heaven, as Cornelius was, he had still much to learn. He had still the best things to learn. He had still to learn CHRIST. And the difficulties that lay in the Roman centurion's way to learn Christ, you have simply no conception of. Till you read the Acts of the Apostles, as not one in a thousand reads that rare book; nay, till you have to teach that rare book to others, you will never at all realize what the centurion had to come through before he could be a complete Christian man. Ay, and what Christ's very best apostles themselves had to come through before they would have anything to do with such an unclean and four-footed beast as Cornelius was to them. It was twelve o'clock of the day at Joppa, and it was the very next day after the angel had made his visit to Cornelius about his memorial. And Peter, like the centurion, was deep that day in special prayer. Now, Peter must surely have been fasting far too long, as well as praying far too earnestly, for he fell into a faint as he continued to pray. And as he lay in his faint he dreamed, as we say; a vision was sent to him, as Scripture says. And in his vision Peter saw heaven opened above him, and a certain vessel descending unto him, as it had been a great sheet knit at the four corners and let down to the earth. Wherein were all manner of four-footed beasts of the earth, and wild beasts, and creeping things, and fowls of the air. And there came a voice to him, Rise, Peter, kill, and eat. But Peter said, Not so, Lord: for I have never eaten anything that is common or unclean. And the voice spake unto him again the second time, What God hath cleansed, that call not thou common. And scarcely had the sheet been drawn up to heaven, when three of Cornelius's servants knocked at the tanner's door, and asked if one Simon Peter lodged here. And when Peter saw the three men, and heard their message from Cornelius, he at once comprehended and fully understood the heavenly vision. And the vision was this. Cornelius and all his soldiers, devout and indevout, and all his domestic servants, and all the Roman people, good and bad, and all other nations of men on the face of the earth; all mankind, indeed, except Peter and a few of his friends, were bound up together in one abominable bundle. And Peter was standing above them, scouting at and spitting on them all. All so like ourselves. For, how we also bundle up whole nations of men and throw them into that same unclean sheet. Whole churches that we know nothing about but their bad names that we have given them, are in our sheet of excommunication also. All the other denominations of Christians in our land are common and unclean to us. Every party outside of our own party in the political state also. We have no language contemptuous enough wherewith to describe their wicked ways and their self-seeking schemes. They are four-footed beasts and creeping things.

Indeed, there are very few men alive, and especially those who live near us, who are not sometimes in the sheet of our scorn; unless it is one here and one there of our own family, or school, or party. And they also come under our scorn and our contempt the moment they have a mind of their own, and interests of their own, and affections and ambitions of their own. It would change your whole heart and life this very night if you would take Peter and Cornelius home with you and lay them both to heart. It would be for a memorial about you before God if you would but do this. If you would take a four-cornered napkin when you go home, and a Sabbath-night pen and ink, and write the names of the nations, and the churches, and the denominations, and the congregations, and the ministers, and the public men, and the private citizens, and the neighbors, and the fellow-worshippers—all the people you dislike, and despise, and do not, and cannot, and will not, love. Heap all their names into your unclean napkin, and then look up and say, "Not so, Lord. I neither can speak well, nor think well, nor hope well, of these people. I cannot do it, and I will not try." If you acted out and spake out all the evil things that are in your heart in some such way as that, you would thus get such a sight of yourselves that you would never forget it. And, for your reward, and there is no better reward, like Peter, you would one day come to be able to say, "Of a truth I perceive that God is no respecter of persons. But in every nation, and church, and denomination, and party of men, and among those I used to think of as four-footed beasts of the earth, and wild beasts, and creeping things, God has them that fear Him, and that work righteousness, and that are accepted of Him." And then it would go up for a memorial before God, the complete change and the noble alteration that had come to your mind and to your heart. For you would be completely taken captive before God by that charity which vaunteth not itself, is not puffed up, thinketh no evil, believeth all things, hopeth all things. And now abideth faith, hope, charity; but the greatest of these is charity.

Such are some of the lessons it is intended we should take to heart out of the story of Cornelius, the Roman centurion.

100
Eutychus

THIS Eutychus is the father of all such as fall asleep under sermons. And he well deserves all his fame, for he fell sound asleep under an action sermon of the Apostle Paul. We do not know how much there may have been to be said in exculpation or extenuation of Eutychus and his deep sleep during that sacrament service. Eutychus may have suppered his horses four-and-twenty hours before, and given a boy a shilling to look after them till his return home from the Communion Table at Troas. Like an old friend of mine who used to do that, and then to travel all night from Glenisla to Dundee in order to be present at Mr. M'Cheyne's Communion. After which he walked home and took his horses out to the plow in good time on Monday morning. Only, I feel quite sure that Mr. M'Cheyne never needed to go down and raise my old friend to life again, as Paul had to do to the dead Eutychus. For he never fell asleep, I feel quite sure, neither under Mr. M'Cheyne's action sermon, nor during the three afternoon tables, no, nor under the evening sermon of Daniel Cormick of Kirriemuir, who used to preach not short sermons on such occasions, but never one word too long for St. Peter's, Dundee, in those pre-disruption days.

The sacred writer does not in as many words take it upon himself to blame the Apostle for his long sermon that night. Though what he does say so emphatically and so repeatedly would be unpardonable blame to any other preacher. What blame, indeed, could be more unpardonable to any of your preachers than what the Apostle was guilty of that night? The like of it has never been seen again since that night. To keep his hearers from the time of lighting the candles till the sun rose next morning! Matthew Henry would like to have had the heads of Paul's sermon that night. But my idea is that Paul's sermon had no heads that night. My idea is that as soon as the candles were lighted Paul recited his warrant for the celebration of the Lord's Supper, as we now read that warrant from his pen in First Corinthians. After which he would enter on the nature and the ends of the Supper, which would take some time to explain and exhaust. He would then diverge to tell the Troas people the never-ending story of how he came to be a catechumen and a communicant himself at first. He would then go on to the mystical union that subsists between Jesus Christ and all true communicants, during the deep things of which Eutychus would fall fast asleep. I know nothing so like that richest part of Paul's sermon as our own Robert Bruce's not short Sermons on the Sacrament, which Dr. Laidlaw has put into such good English, and Mr. Ferrier into such good buckram, for us the other day. And then, even after the accident to Eutychus, Paul was still so full of matter and of spirit, that he actually went on with his post-communion address till the sun rose on the cups still standing on the table, and on the elders standing beside them, and Paul still pouring out his heart from the pulpit.

Now, notwithstanding Paul's example, all our preachers should, as a rule, be short in their sermons. In Luther's excellent portrait of a good preacher, one of such a preacher's nine virtues and qualities is this, that he should know when to stop. So he should. Only, you have no idea how fast the pulpit clock goes when a preacher has anything still on his mind that he wishes to say. At the same time, every sermon is not to be cut according to the sand-glass. John Howe first attracted Cromwell by preaching for two hours and then turning the sand-glass for a third hour. And Coleridge in his notes on Dr. Donne, and on an hour and a half sermon of his preached at Whitehall, says: "Compare this manhood of our Church divinity with our poor day. When I reflect on the crowded congregations, and on the thousands who with intense interest came to those hour and two-hour sermons, I cannot believe in any true progression, moral or intellectual, in the minds of the many." And since I have Coleridge open at any rate, I must not deny you what Hazlitt says about Coleridge's own preaching: "It was in January, 1798, that I rose one morning before daylight, to walk ten miles in the mud, to hear this celebrated person preach. When I got there, the organ was playing the hundredth Psalm, and when it was done Mr. Coleridge rose and gave out his text. And his text was this: 'He departed again into a mountain Himself alone.' As the preacher gave out his text his voice rose like a stream of distilled perfumes; and when he came to the last two words of the text, which he pronounced loud, deep, and distinct, it seemed to me, who was then young, as if the sounds had echoed from the depths of the human heart. The preacher then launched into his subject like an eagle dallying with the wind. For myself, I could not have been more delighted if I had heard the music of the spheres. Poetry and philosophy had met together, truth and genius had embraced each other, and that under the sanction of religion." Now, a preacher like Coleridge, and a hearer like Hazlitt, are not to be cut short by all the sandglasses and pulpit-clocks in the world. Sandglasses and pulpit-clocks are made for such preachers and hearers, and not such preachers and hearers for sand-glasses and pulpit-clocks.

But another thing. Paul did not have his manuscript before him that night, and that circumstance was partly to blame for the too-great length of his sermon. I will be bold to take an illustration of that night in Troas from myself. When I am in Paul's circumstances; that is to say, when I have only once the opportunity to preach in any place, I never on such an occasion read my sermon from a paper. I just give out the Scripture text that I am myself living upon at that time, and then I speak out of such a heart as is given to me at that moment. But the danger of such preaching is just that which Luther has pointed out—I never know when to stop. Just as Paul did not know when to stop that night. And just as Luther himself, not seldom exceeded all bounds. Without a paper, not one preacher in a hundred knows when to stop. He forgets to look at the clock till it is far too late. With a paper, and with nothing more to say than is down on the paper, you stop at the moment. But not restricted to a paper, and with your mind full of matter, and your heart full of feeling, you go on till midnight. At home you hearers know what your minister is going to say, and you are able to settle yourselves down to sleep as soon as he gives out his text. But he has much more honor when he goes outside of his own congregation. And thus it is that you hear of how he preached so long, and was so much enjoyed, when away from home. That was Paul's exact case. If this was not his first and his only sermon at Troas, it was certainly his last. The Apostle would never see those Troas people again till the day of judgment; and who shall blame him if he completely forgot the sand-glass, and poured out his heart all night upon that entranced congregation, At the same time, and after all is said, Luther is quite right. A good preacher should know when to stop. In other words, as a rule, and especially at home, he should be short.

But, then, there are two sides to all that also. And your side is this. I never see any of you fall asleep at an election time. No, not though the speaking goes on till midnight. And, yet, I do not know that the oratory of the political candidates and their friends is so much better than the oratory of the pulpit. But this is it. Your own passions are all on fire in politics, whereas you are all so many Laodiceans in religion. Yea, what carefulness your politics work in you; yea, what clearing of yourselves; yea, what indignation; yea, what fear; yea, what vehement desire; yea, what zeal; yea, what revenge. So much so, that the poorest speaker on the party-platform will have no difficulty in keeping your blood up all night to the boiling point. At the same time, I frankly admit, few preachers preach with the passion, and with the issues at stake, that the politicians, or even the playactors, speak. And thus, on the whole, the sum of the matter is this—that, what between too long sermons, and too cold, the blame lies largely at every preacher's door.

And, then, even more than our sermons, our prayers should be short; our public prayers, that is. You may be as long as you like in secret, but not in public, not in the family, not in the prayer-meeting, and not in the pulpit. Bishop Andrewes, the best composer of prayers in all the world of prayers, is not short. His prayer for the first day of the week occupies fifteen pages. His prayer for the second day of the week covers eight pages. His three prayers on awaking take up six pages. His Horology five pages. His four Acts of Deprecation eleven pages, and so on. But then these not short prayers are printed in his *Private Devotions*, which his trustees could scarcely read, so kneaded into a pulp were they with Andrewes's sweat and tears. And no wonder, if you knew his history. William Law, on the other hand, was short and exact in his private devotions. But, then, to make up for that, he was so incomparably methodical, so regular, so punctual, and so concentrated, in the matter of his prayers. He was like James Durham, of whom William Guthrie said that no man in all Scotland prayed so short in public as Durham did; but, then, "every word of Durham's would have filled a firlot." Look at Paul's short prayers also. Every word would fill a firlot. And so the hundred and nineteenth Psalm. Every single verse of that psalm is a separate prayer which might have been written by the laird of Pourie Castle. At any rate, we are saying that every night in our family worship at home at present. We take a different kind of Scripture in the morning when all the children are with us. But at night we just take one verse of that Old Testament James Durham, and every heart in the house is straightway filled like a firlot before God. The Lord's Prayer is short also, because it is not His prayer at all, but is composed for us and for our children. But His private devotions were not only far longer than Bishop Andrewes's, but are far more illegible to us with His tears and His blood.

And, then, if you ever rise to be an author, make your books short. You may be a great author and yet your books may all the time be very short among books. The Song is a short book. So is the Psalms. So is the Gospel of John. So is the Epistle to the Romans. So is the *Confessions*. So is the *Divine Comedy*. So is the *Imitation*. So is the *Pilgrim's Progress*, and so is the *Grace Abounding*. Brother Lawrence *On the Practice of the Presence of God* is so short that it will cost you only fourpence. I had occasion a moment ago to mention William Guthrie. Said John Owen, drawing a little gilt copy of Guthrie's *Saving Interest* out of his pocket, "That author I take to be one of the greatest divines that ever wrote. His book is my *vade mecum*. I carry it always with me. I have written several folios, but there is more divinity in this little book than in them all." "I am finishing Guthrie," said Chalmers, "which I think is the best book I ever read." And I myself read the whole of Guthrie in Melrose's beautiful new edition the other day between Edinburgh and London. All the greatest authors have been like Guthrie, and like Luther's best preachers, they have known when to stop. Let all young men who would be great authors, study and imitate all the short books I have just signalized. And though it is not a short book, and could not be, let them all read Professor Saintsbury's new book, out of which I borrow this last advice: "Phrynichus is redundant and garrulous; for when it was open to him to have got the matter completely finished off in not a fifth part of his actual length, by saying things out of season, he has stretched his matter out to an unmanageable bulk."

Now, after all that about preaching, and about prayer, and about great authorship, Eutychus did not fall out of the window for nothing, if we learn from his fall some of these valuable lessons.

OUR original authorities for the life of Felix are Luke in the Acts of the Apostles, Josephus in the *Antiquities* and in the *Wars of the Jews*, and Tacitus in the *Annals of the Romans*. Luke gives us one of his most graphic chapters about Felix; but he abstains, as the Bible manner is, from judging even Felix before the time. Josephus is graphic enough about Felix, but we are sure neither of Josephus's facts nor of his judgments. We cannot go very far either for or against any man on the word of such a witness as Josephus. But Tacitus scars Felix's forehead as only Tacitus's pen can scar. Tacitus, as his manner is, anticipates the very day of judgment itself in the way he writes about Felix. Felix began his life as a slave, and he ended his life as a king. But, as Tacitus says, there was a slave's heart all the time under Felix's royal robes. All what evil secrets lay hidden in Felix's conscience we do not know; but we have only too abundant testimony as to how savage, how treacherous, and how steeped in blood, Felix's whole life had been. Luke calls Drusilla the wife of Felix. Drusilla was a wife, but she was not the wife of Felix. Drusilla was still a young woman, but she had already come through wickedness enough to stamp her as one of the worst women in the whole of human history. Paul was lying in prison waiting for his trial at Felix's judgment-seat, when, most probably to satisfy Drusilla's guilty curiosity about Paul and about Paul's Master, Felix sent for Paul to hear what he had to say for himself and for his Master. How the interview opened, and how Paul conducted his discourse, we are not told. But this we are told, that as Paul continued to reason of righteousness, temperance, and judgment to come, Felix trembled, and answered, "Go thy way for this time; when I have a convenient season, I will call for thee."

"The ears of our audiences must first be propitiated," says Quintilian in his *Institutes of Oratory*. And Dante but borrows from that fine book when he tells all public speakers in his *Banquet* that they must always begin by taking captive the good will of their hearers. Now, just how Paul managed to propitiate Felix's unfriendly ears that day, and to take captive his hardened heart, we are not told. But that the great preacher did succeed in getting a hearing from Felix is certain. And it was neither a short hearing nor a hostile that Felix gave to Paul that day. Felix sat in transfixed silence while Paul stood up before him, and plunged the two-edged sword of God's holy law into his guilty conscience, till the hardened reprobate could not command himself. A greater seal was never set to the power of Paul's preaching than when Felix shook and could not sit still under the Apostle's words. And a greater encouragement could not possibly be given to all true preachers than that scene in the palace of Caesarea gives to them. What an ally, unseen but omnipotent, all true preachers have in the consciences of their hearers! "The conscience," says the prince of Puritan expository preachers, "is what the snout is in a bear, a tender part to tame him by. Conscience is acutely sensible to God's wrath. And hell-fire itself could not take hold of the soul but at this corner."

O conscience! who can stand against thy power!
Endure thy gripes and agonies one hour!
Stone, gout, strappado, racks, whatever is
Dreadful to sense are only toys to this.
No pleasures, riches, honors, friends can tell
How to give ease to thee, thou'rt like to hell.

If Felix had but sat still a little longer, Paul was just going on to tell him how to get ease to the hell that was beginning to burn in his bosom. But I suspect Drusilla at that moment. I cannot get over my suspicion that it was Drusilla who so suddenly cut short Paul's discourse, and sent him back to his prison. I do not read that Drusilla trembled. My belief about that royal pair is, that had Drusilla not sat beside Felix that day, Felix would have been baptized, and Paul would have been set free, before the sun had gone down. But Drusilla and her sisters have cast into their graves many wounded. Many strong men have been slain to death by them. Their house is the way to hell, and their steps go down to the chambers of death.

"Go thy way for this time," said Felix to Paul, "when I have a convenient season, I will call for thee." Felix never sat at a Communion Table. But many of us here tonight who sat at that table today have in effect said Felix's very words today to God and to our own consciences. Many of us trembled at the table today, but we recovered ourselves with this resolution—that we would repent and amend our ways at another time. More action-sermons and more table-addresses have been silenced and forgotten because of a postponed repentance than because of anything else. Felix did not really intend to shut Paul's mouth for ever. He did not intend to go before God's judgment-seat just as he was that day. And no more do we. We honestly intend to live righteously and temperately—after a time. When we are in other circumstances. When we have other companionships. When we have formed other and better relationships. After that happy alteration in our life to which we are looking forward, you will find us very different men. When I am old, says one. Not too old. But when I am somewhat older and much less occupied. I will then have time to give to secret prayer. I will then have on my table, and near my bedside, some of those books my minister has so often besought me to buy and to read at a Communion season. I will then attend to God and to my own soul. Poor self-deceived creature that you are! Cruelty and uncleanness have slain their thousands; but a life like yours, a life simply of putting off repentance and reformation, has slain its tens of thousands.

But Felix, after all, was as good as his word, so far. Felix did actually call for Paul again, and that not once nor twice, but often, and communed with him in the palace. Only, it had almost been better he had not done so, for he always did it with a bad motive in his mind. It was not to hear out Paul's interrupted discourse that Felix sent for Paul. The sacred writer is able to tell us what exactly Felix's secret motive was in so often giving the Apostle an audience. "He hoped also that money should have been given him of Paul, that he might loose him; wherefore he sent for him the oftener, and communed with him. But after two years Porcius Festus came into Felix's room; and Felix, willing to show the Jews a pleasure, left Paul bound." And it is because our motives in coming to church are so mixed that the years allowed us for our salvation pass on till some one else occupies our pew, and the preaching of salvation has for ever come to an end as far as we are concerned.

> Pulpits and Sundays; sorrow dogging sin;
> Afflictions sorted; anguish of all sizes;
> Without our shame; within our consciences;
> Yet all these fences, and their whole array,
> One cunning bosom sin blows quite away.

I have known a man come to a church for a slip of a girl; another as a stepping-stone to some great man's favor; another for the advantage of his shop; and another for the chance of a tippet and a chain and a hoped-for handle to his name, and so on. Felix sat under Paul's preaching because his household expenses in Caesarea were so great, and his resources so low, and his debts so heavy. And because he had been told that Paul had such rich friends, that they could and would pay any price for his release. And who can tell how Felix's calculations might have turned out, had it not been that Caesar so suddenly sent for Felix to come to Rome to give an account of his stewardship; and all that, most unfortunately, before Paul's rich friends had time to come forward. Many that sleep in the dust of the earth shall awake, some to everlasting life, and some to shame and everlasting contempt for the found-out reasons why they went to this church or to that.

It is like the fresh air of heaven itself to turn from Felix's church attendances in this matter of motive, and to turn to Paul. For, when the royal message summoning Paul to the palace was delivered to him in his prison, what was Paul's first thought, do you think? Paul was a great man. Paul was a noble-minded man. Paul was a true and a pure-hearted man. Paul never thought of himself at all. He never once said to himself how all this might tell upon his release and his liberty. Dear and sweet as release and liberty were to Paul, these things never once came into his mind that day. Felix and Drusilla alone came into his mind that day; Drusilla especially. For Drusilla was a Jewess; she was a daughter of Abraham; and Paul's heart's desire and prayer to God for long had been that Drusilla might be saved. And here, in this opportunity to him, was the answer to his prayer! And thus it was that all the way up from his prison to her palace Paul was thinking only of that wicked and miserable pair, with their fearful looking for of judgment. Till, with his heart full of all that, as Paul was led into the presence-chamber, Felix turned to Drusilla, and pointing to Paul, he as good as said to her—

> Lo! this man's brow like to a title-leaf,
> Foretells the nature of a tragic volume!
> He trembles, and the whiteness in his cheek
> Is apter than his tongue to tell his errand!
> > Even such a man
> Drew Priam's curtain in the dead of night.

It was the snow-white purity of Paul's motives that gave to his words, and to his whole look and manner, such last-day power as he stood and spoke before Felix. Paul's eye was so single at that moment that the whole palace was filled to Felix as with the light of the great white throne itself. No other man knows with a full certainty any or all of his neighbor's motives. At the same time, I have come to think that the purity of a preacher's motives has very much to do with his success. Not always, perhaps; but sufficiently often to make it a good rule for all of us who are, or are to be, preachers. For instance, to speak of two very successful preachers who have lately gone to give in their account and to reap their reward—Moody and Spurgeon. I have always attributed their immense and their lasting success to the singleness of their eye and the transparency of their motives. And therefore it is that I am always directing young probationers who are going to preach in a vacancy to read before they go Dr. Newman's sermon entitled, "The Salvation of the Hearer the Motive of the Preacher." I constantly tell them that this desired call, if it is to be a call to them from Christ, will largely lie in their motive that day. If the preacher makes the vacant congregation tremble like Felix till they forget themselves, that is the preacher for them, and that is the people for him. Let all probationers of the pulpit study that same great writer's noble lecture, entitled "University Preaching," and they will thank me for this instruction all their days.

And now to conclude. I can imagine no other night in all the year so convenient as just the night after a Communion day. I can imagine no night in all the year so acceptable to Christ, and so welcome to His Father. No day and no night in which our Redeemer so desires to see of the travail of His soul. No night in which He has so much joy in seeing either a sinner repenting, or a saint returning. It is a special night for new beginners, and it is famous for the restoring of backsliders' souls. This is the night, then, for us all to date from. It was that day, it was that night, when we had Felix, you will say all your days on earth. My Lord met me, you will say, in that house of His, and on that night of His. Come away then, and make a new start on the spot. Come away, and there will be a joy in heaven tonight that there will not be but for you. Oh! do come, and let this house have this honor in heaven henceforth, because this man and that man were born here. And, in saying that, it is not I that say it. Jesus Christ Himself singles you out of all the congregation and says to you, as if you were alone in this house, Come! Come, He says, and let us reason together. And if you are a very Felix and a very Drusilla; if your unrighteousness, and your intemperance, and your fearful looking for of judgment, are all as dreadful as were theirs; even were your sins as scarlet as were theirs, they shall be as white as snow. And though they be red like crimson, they shall be as wool. Who, then, this Communion evening, will come forward like the brave man in Bunyan, and will say to him who has the book and the pen and the ink-horn in his hand, Set down my name, sir! At which there was a most pleasant voice heard from those within, even of those who walked upon the top of the king's palace, saying—

Come in, come in,
Eternal glory thou shalt win.

So he went in, and was clothed with the same garments as they were clothed with. Then Christian smiled, and said, I think verily that I know the true meaning to me of this great sight, and the true intention to me of this great Scripture.

102
Festus

A SINGLE word will sometimes immortalize a man. Am I my brother's keeper? was all that Cain said. And, What will you give me? was all that Judas said. One of his own words will sometimes, all unintentionally, sum up a man's whole past life. A man will sometimes discover to us his deepest heart, and will seal down on himself his own everlasting destiny, just with one of his own spoken words. By thy words thou shalt be justified, and by thy words thou shalt be condemned. And as Paul thus spake for himself, Festus said with a loud voice, Paul, thou art beside thyself; much learning doth make thee mad. With that one word Festus ever after it is known to us quite as well as if Tacitus himself had written a whole chapter about Festus. This is enough: Festus was that Roman procurator who said with a loud voice that Paul was beside himself. That one word, with its loud intonation, sets Festus sufficiently before us.

Their ever-thoughtful ever-watchful Lord had taken care to prepare His apostles for this insult also. The disciple is not above his master, nor the servant above his Lord. It is enough for the disciple that he be as his master, and the servant as his Lord. If they have called the Master of the house Beelzebub, how much more shall they call them that are of His household. And the loud and unbecoming outbreak of Festus would have staggered Paul much more than it did, had he not recollected at that moment that this very same thing had been said about his Master also. And that not by heathens like Pilate and Festus, but by those whom the Gospels call His friends. "And when His friends heard of it they went out to lay hold on Him, for they said, He is beside Himself." And many of the Jews, as soon as they had heard His sermon on the Good Shepherd, of all His sermons, had nothing else to say about the Preacher but this, He hath a devil, and is mad; why hear ye Him?

First, then, as to our Master's own madness. It is plain, and beyond dispute, that either He was mad, or they were who so insulted Him. For He loved nothing that they loved. He hated nothing that they hated. He feared nothing that they feared. Birth, wealth, station, and such like things, without which other men cannot hold up their heads; of all that He emptied Himself, and made Himself of no reputation. And, to complete the contrast and the antipathy, the things that all other men despise and spurn and pity He pronounces to be alone blessed. Meekness under insults and injuries, patience amid persecutions, poverty of spirit, humbleness of mind, readiness to serve rather than to sit in honor and eat—these are the only things that have praise and reward of Paul's Master. The things, in short, we would almost as soon die as have them for our portion. And the things we would almost as soon not live at all as not possess, or expect one day to possess, Jesus Christ cared nothing at all for such things. Absolutely nothing. It was no wonder that her neighbors and kinsfolk condoled with His mother who had borne such a son. It was no wonder that they worked incessantly upon His brethren till they also said, Yes; He must be beside himself; let us go and lay hold on him.

Now, Paul came as near to his Master's madness as any man has ever come, or ever will come, in this world. For, what made Festus break out in that so indecent way was because Paul both spake and acted on the absolute and eternal truth of the things we speak about with bated breath, and only faintly and inoffensively affect to believe. Paul had been telling his royal auditors what he never wearied telling; his undeserved, unexpected, and unparalleled conversion. His manner of life before his conversion also, when he put this very same word into Festus's mouth. I was exceedingly "mad," he said, against the saints. And at midday, O king, he said, addressing himself with an orator's instinct to Agrippa, a light from heaven above the brightness of the sun, and a voice speaking to me in the Hebrew tongue—and so on, till Festus broke out upon him, as we read. Now, if you had come through the half of Paul's experience, we also would have charged you also with being beside yourself. To have had such bloody hands; to have been carried through such a conversion; to have had, time after time, such visions and revelations of the Lord; and, especially, to have had such experiences and such attainments in the divine life—certainly, to us you would have been beside yourself. To have seen you actually and in everything counting all things, your very best things, your very virtues and very graces, to be but dung, that you might win Christ; to have seen you continually crucified with Christ; what else could we have made of you? How else could we have defended ourselves against you, but by calling you mad?

But Paul had more than one experience that made him appear mad to other men. And another of those experiences was his unparalleled experience and insight into sin. Paul's sinfulness of his own heart, when he was for a moment left alone with it, always drove him again near to distraction. As the sight of the ghost drove Hamlet mad, so did the sight of sin and death drive Paul. And not Paul only, but no less than our Lord Himself. If ever our Lord was almost beside Himself, it was once at the sight, and at the approach, and at the contact, of sin. We water down the terrible words and say that He was sore amazed and very heavy. But it was far more than that. A terror at sin, a horror and a loathing at sin, took possession of our Lord's soul when He was about to be made sin, till it carried Him away beyond all experience and all imagination of mortal men. And the servant, in his measure, was as his Master in this also. For, as often as Paul's eyes were again opened to see the sinfulness of his own sin, there was only one other thing in heaven or earth that kept his brain from reeling in her distracted globe. And the sight of that other thing only made his brain reel the more. And so it has often been with far smaller men than Paul. When we ourselves see sin; even such a superficial sight of sin as God in His mercy sometimes gives us; both body and soul reel and stagger till He has to hold us up with His hand. And were it not that there is a fountain filled with something else than rose-water, there would be more people in the pond than the mother of Christian's children. What a mad-house because of the sinfulness of sin the church of God's saints would be were it not for His own blood! And this goes on with Paul till he has a doctrine of himself and of sin, such that he cannot preach it too often for great sinners like himself. No wonder, with his heart of such an exquisite texture and sensibility, and continually made such an awful battle-ground, no wonder Paul was sometimes nothing short of mad. And why should it be so difficult to believe that there may be men even in these dregs of time; one man here, and another there, who are still patterns to God, and to themselves, and to saints and angels, of the same thing? Beside themselves, that is, with the dominion and the pollution of sin. Was there not a proverb in the ancient schools that bears with some pungency upon this subject? It is in Latin, and I cannot borrow it at the moment. But I am certain there is a saying somewhere about a great experiment and a great exhibition being made on an insignificant and a worthless subject.

I am old enough to remember the time when the universal London press, led by *Punch* and the *Saturday Review*, week after week, mocked, trampled on, cried madman at, and tried to silence, young Spurgeon, very much as Festus tried to trample on and silence Paul. But *Punch* lived to lay a fine tribute on Spurgeon's grave. It was true of Paul, and it was true of Spurgeon, and it will be true, in its measure, of every like-minded minister, as well as of all truly Christian men, what old Matthew Mead says in his *Almost Christian*. "If," says old Matthew, "the preaching of Christ is to the world foolishness, then it is no wonder that the disciples of Christ are to the world fools. For, according to the Gospel, a man must die in order to live; he must be empty, who would be full; he must be lost, who would be found; he must have nothing, who would have all things; he must be blind, who would see; he must be condemned, who would be redeemed. He is no true Christian," adds Mead, "who is not the world's fool." And, yet, no! I am not mad, most noble Festus; but speak forth the words of truth and soberness.

KING AGRIPPA was the grandson of Herod the Great, and he had succeeded to the shattered throne of his fathers; or rather, he had succeeded to such splinters of that throne as Caesar had permitted him to set up. Agrippa was a king, but he was a king only in name. The Jews, as they themselves once said, had no king but Caesar. At the same time, Caesar sometimes, for reasons of state, set up sham kings over certain portions of his great empire. And Agrippa was one of those simulacrum sovereigns. Bernice, who here sits beside Agrippa, was his sadly-spotted sister. If you wade deep enough into the sixth satire of Juvenal, you will find Bernice more fully set forth in that pungent piece. As for ourselves, we will look in silence at Bernice, as Holy Scripture does, and will then pass her by. But take a good look at her brother Agrippa. Look well at King Agrippa, for he is the last king of the Jews you will ever see. There has been a long line of Jewish kings since Saul and David and Solomon, but this is the last of them now. The Jews are not to have even a shadow of a king any more. They are to have Caesar only, till they cease to be. What a scene! Festus, Agrippa, Bernice, and the whole place full of Roman soldiers and civilians, with Paul standing in his chains, as a sort of holiday show and sport to them all. What a company! What a providence! What an irony of providence! Thou art permitted to speak for thyself, said the king to the prisoner. And the prisoner, after having spoken for himself, was led back to his cell, there to await the issue of his appeal to Caesar. Great pomp and all, the ancient throne of David and Solomon is seen crumbling to its very last dust before our very eyes. While, bonds and all, Paul stands before Agrippa holding out, not his own hand only, but the very Hand of the God of Israel Himself, both to King Agrippa, to his sister Bernice, and to the whole decayed, dispersed, and enslaved house of Israel. So much so, that when Paul was led back to his prison that day Israel's doom was for ever sealed. We are now looking on one of the most solemnizing scenes that is to be seen in the whole of human history.

It was the wonderful story of Paul's conversion, and that story as told by himself, that so deeply impressed King Agrippa and his sister Bernice in Caesarea that day. Again, and again, and again, we have Paul's wonderful story fresh from his own heart. The story was new, and it was full of new wonderfulness to Paul himself, every time he told it. And it never failed to make an immense impression on all manner of people; as, indeed, it does down to this day. And no wonder. For, just look at him, and listen to him. "My manner of life," said Paul, stretching forth his hand with the chain on it, "know all the Jews. For I verily thought with myself that I ought to do many things contrary to the name of Jesus of Nazareth." And then, how he did those things, and how he was still doing them, when a voice from heaven struck him down, and said, Saul, Saul, I am Jesus whom thou persecutest. And so on, with his wonderful story, till Festus could only shake off the spell of it by shouting out that Paul was mad. And till Agrippa, who knew all these matters far better than Festus knew them, confessed openly that, for his part, he believed every word of Paul's conversion; and, indeed, felt almost at that moment as if he were about to be converted himself. "Almost thou persuadest me to be a Christian like thyself!" confessed King Agrippa. And to this day nothing is so persuasive to our hearts as just the story of a personal experience in religion. So much so, that without this so persuasive element, somehow or somewhere in his preaching, all any preacher says will fall short of its surest power. Even if his testimony is not always conveyed in that autobiographic and dramatic form in which Paul always tells his story; yet, unless there is something both of the conviction and the passion of a personal experience, both the pulpit and the pen will come far short of their fullest and their most persuasive power. Unless in every sermon and in every prayer the preacher as good as says with the Psalmist, "Come, and hear, all ye that fear God, and I will declare what He hath done for my soul;" unless there is some such heartbeat heard as that, both our sermons and our prayers will be but lukewarm, and neither cold nor hot. "I preached sin with great sense," says John Bunyan. Which is just his fine old English for great experience, great feeling, and, indeed, great passion. And down to this very day we feel the still unspent surges of Bunyan's pulpit passion beating like thunder on the rocky coasts of his *Grace Abounding* and his *Holy War*. And, just as this narration of Paul's personal experience was almost Agrippa's conversion; and just as this and other like narrations of Paul's experience were not only almost but altogether Luther's conversion; and then just as Luther's experience was Bunyan's conversion and Bunyan's experience; and his incomparable narration of it your conversion and mine; so will it always be. "The judicious are fond of originals," says an anonymous author. So they are. And we are all among the judicious in that respect. And thus it is that original autobiographies, and diaries, and dramatic narrations: David's Psalms, Augustine's Confessions, Luther's Sermons, Andrewes's Private Devotions, Bunyan's Grace Abounding, Fraser, Halyburton, Boston, Spurgeon, and such like, are always so interesting, so perennially popular, and so fruitful both in conversion at the time, and in edification and in sanctification for long after. Let all our preachers then stretch forth their own hands, and not another man's; and let them answer for themselves in their own pulpits, and to their own people; and, whether their hands are bound or free—"I often went to the pulpit in chains," says John Bunyan—Felix, and Festus, and Agrippa, and Bernice among their hearers will be compelled, each in their own way, to confess both the truth, and the authority, and the power, of all such preachers of an original, and a passionately undergone, experience.

"The ears of our audiences must first be propitiated," says Quintilian, that great teacher of ancient oratory. And Dante but borrows from that old master when he warns all public speakers that they must always begin by endeavoring to carry captive the goodwill of their hearers. Now, we can never enter a Jewish synagogue, nor stand beside him in a judgment-hall, nor pass by him as he preaches at a street corner, without both seeing and hearing Paul practicing the *captatio benevolentiae* of the ancient oratorical schools. And that, not because he had ever gone to those schools to learn their great art, but simply because of his own oratorical instinct, inborn courtesy, and exquisite refinement of feeling. No such urbanity, and no such good breeding, is to be met with anywhere in all the eloquence of Greece and Rome. It was his perfect Christian courtesy to all men, taken along with his massiveness of mind, his overmastering message, and his incomparable experiences—it was all that taken together, that lifted up Paul to the shining top of universal eloquence. Festus, fresh from the most polished circles of the metropolis of the world, behaved like a boor beside his prisoner. The only perfect gentleman in all that house that day stood in chains, and all the bad manners, and all the insolence, sat in Caesar's seat. Let us all, and ministers especially, aim to be gentlemen like Paul. In the pulpit, in the Presbytery, and in the General Assembly; ay, and even if we are at the bar of the General Assembly, as Paul so often was; let us behave there also like Paul, as far as our natural temperament, and supernatural refinement of temperament, will support us in doing so. Let us learn to say in effect, I think myself happy, King Agrippa, because I shall answer for myself this day before thee. Especially because I know thee to be expert in all customs and questions among the Jews. And when Festus assails us with his coarse-minded abuse, let us learn to say with all self-command, No, Most noble Festus. Or, far better still, let us hold our peace. Let us turn in silence from Festus and his brutality to Agrippa and Bernice, and say to them—I would to God, that not you only, but also all that hear me this day, were both almost, and altogether such as I am, except these bonds. Holding out his hands, "except these bonds." Beautiful and noble, beyond all Greek and Latin art. Is there a touch like that again in all the world? What a heart! What tenderness! What fineness of feeling! What gold would we not give for one single link of those iron bonds that day!

But Paul, with all his fascination, must not be permitted to draw our attention away from Agrippa. And that, because Agrippa has lessons to teach us tonight that Paul himself, with all his eloquence, and even with his wonderful conversion itself, is not able to teach us. For Agrippa, you must know, to begin with, was half a Jew. By blood he was half a Jew; whilst by education, and by interest, and by sympathy, he was wholly a Jew; if it had only been possible for Agrippa to be outwardly, and openly, and honestly, what, all the time, he really was in his heart. And thus it was that Paul so fastened upon Agrippa and would not let him go. Thus it was that Paul so addressed himself to Agrippa: so passed by Festus and all the rest of his audience, and spoke home to Agrippa, and that with such directness and such power. And Agrippa felt Paul's full power, till he openly confessed that he felt it. So much so, that when Festus forgot himself, and broke out upon Paul in such an indecent manner, Agrippa interposed, and said, "Not only is Paul speaking the words of truth and soberness, but he has all but persuaded me and my sister to take his side, and to be baptized." But, before I come to that, what do you think about this scene yourselves? Applying your own common sense, and your own imagination, to this whole scene, what do you say about it yourselves? About Agrippa's speech, that is. Was Agrippa speaking ironically and mockingly when he said that Paul had almost persuaded him to be a Christian? Or did he honestly and sincerely mean what he said? There is a division of opinion about that. Did he mean that, King

Agrippa as he was, and Festus's guest as he was, and Bernice's brother as he was, he was within a hairsbreadth of casting in his lot with Paul, and with Paul's Lord and Savior? I, for one, believe that Agrippa was entirely honest and true and without any guile in what he said. And that Paul and Agrippa were so near shaking hands before Festus and all the court at that moment; so near, that their not altogether doing so on the spot makes that one of the most tragical moments in all the world. A tragical moment only second to that you will perpetrate tonight, if you feel what Agrippa felt, and say what Agrippa said, and then go away and do what Agrippa did. "Almost," is surely the most tragic word that is ever heard uttered on earth or in hell. And yet, both earth and hell are full of it. Almost! Almost! Almost! An athlete runs for the prize, and he almost touches the winning-post. A marksman shoots at the target, and he almost hits it. A runner leaps for his life over a roaring flood, and he almost clears the chasm. A ship is almost within the harbor, when the fatal storm suddenly strikes her till she goes down. The five foolish virgins were almost in time. And Agrippa and Bernice were almost baptized, and thus their names almost entered into the Church of Christ. And so it is tonight with some of yourselves. Some of yourselves who were not, were almost, at the Lord's table today. You intended to be at it at one time. You were almost persuaded at the last Communion season. Now, just go down and ask Agrippa and Bernice what they would do if they were back in your place tonight. They have had experience of what you are now passing through, and of how it ends. But if you find that between you and them there is a great gulf fixed; so that they which would pass to inquire of them cannot, neither can they come back with their experience to you. In that case, I myself have had an experience not much short of theirs, and I will tell you with all plainness, and earnestness, and anxiousness, and love, what I think you ought to do tonight. Do not sleep; nay, do not so much as go home, till your name has been taken down altogether for the next Lord's table.

104
Luke, the Beloved Physician

WE have in our New Testament two most important books from the practiced pen of Paul's beloved physician. And if the style is the man in Holy Scripture also, then, what with Paul's great affection for his faithful physician, and what with his own sacred writings, we feel a very great liking for Luke, and we owe him a very deep debt. To begin with, Luke was what we would describe in our day as a very laborious and conscientious student, as well as a very careful and skillful writer. Luke takes us at once into his confidence and confides to us that what made him think of putting pen to paper at all, was his deep dissatisfaction with all that had hitherto been written about the birth, the boyhood, the public life, the teaching, the preaching, the death, and the resurrection and ascension of our Lord. And then in a right workmanlike way this evangelist sets about the great task he has with such a noble ambition undertaken. Luke has not given us what cost him nothing. He did not sit down to his desk till he had made innumerable journeys in search of all the materials possible. He spared neither time nor trouble nor expense in the collection of his golden contributions to our New Testament. Luke had never himself seen Jesus Christ in the flesh, so far as we know, and the men and the women who had both seen Him and heard Him when He was on earth were becoming fewer and fewer every day. Invidious death was fast thinning the ranks of those who had both seen and handled the Word of Life, till Luke had not a moment to spare if he was to talk with and to interrogate those who had actually seen their Lord with their own eyes. Joseph, and Mary, and James, and Joses, and Simon, and Judas, and His sisters, and His kinsfolk, and His twelve disciples—so many of them as were still in life—Luke set forth and sought them all out before he sat down to write his Gospel. Mary especially. And Mary opened her heart to Luke in a way she had never opened her heart to any one else. What was it, I wonder, that so opened Mary's so-long-sealed-up heart to this Evangelist? Was it that old age was fast coming on the most favored among women? Was it that she was afraid that she might suddenly die any day with all these things still hidden in her heart? Was it that she was weary with forbearing and could not stay? Were His words in her heart as a burning fire shut up in her bones? His words that were known only to God, and to His Son, and to Gabriel, and to Joseph, and to herself. Or was it Paul's great name, taken together with some of his great Epistles about her Son, that at last unlocked the treasure-house of Mary's heart and laid it open, full and free, to Paul's beloved physician and deputed secretary? Whatever it was, or however he got it, we have in Luke's Gospel as nowhere else, the whole hitherto hidden history of Mary's espousal, and Gabriel's annunciation, and the Virgin's visit to Zacharias and Elizabeth, as also Mary's Magnificat. And all up and down his great Gospel, and its so invaluable supplement, we have, on every page of his, fresh and abundant proofs both of Luke's industry and skill, as well as of his absorbing love, first for our Lord, and then for Paul. His characteristic Prefaces already prepare his readers both for his new and invaluable materials, as well as for an order and a finish in his books of an outstanding kind. There is an authority, and a presence of power, and, indeed, a sense of exhilaration, in Luke's two Prefaces, that only a discoverer of new and most important truth, and a writer of first-rate skill, is ever able to convey. Exhaustive inquiry, scrupulous accuracy, the most skillful and careful work, the most exalted instruction, and the most assured and fruitful edification—yes; the style is the man.

Such is Luke's literary skill, so to call it, that he makes us see for ourselves just the very verse in the Acts where his materials cease to be so many collections and digests of other men's memoranda and remembrances. With the sixth verse of the twentieth chapter this remarkable book all at once becomes autobiographical of Luke as well as biographical of Paul. Could anything be more reassuring or more interesting than to be able to lay one's finger on the very verse where the third person singular ends, and the first person plural begins? We feel as if we were looking over Luke's shoulder as he writes. We feel as if we saw the same divine boldness that moment take possession of his pen that marks with such peculiar power and authority the opening of his gospel. Paul was like Caesar, and like our own Richard Baxter, in this respect, that he went on performing the most Herculean labors, if not in actual and continual sickness, then with the most overpowering sickness every moment threatening him, and, not seldom, suddenly prostrating him. And since his was, out of sight, the most valuable life then being spent on the face of the earth, no wonder that the churches insisted that the Apostle must not any more make his journeys alone. And accordingly, first one deacon accompanied him and then another, till it was found indispensable that he should have a physician also always with him. And in all the Church of Christ that day a better deacon for Paul and a better doctor could not have been selected than just the Luke on whom we are now engaged. "Only remember," Paul would expostulate with the young scholar and student of medicine, "remember well what our Master said about Himself on a like occasion—the foxes have holes and the birds of the air have nests, but the Son of Man hath not where to lay His head." But Luke was equal to the occasion. Luke was already a well-read man, and he had his answer ready, and that out of Holy Scripture too. "Entreat me not to leave thee, or to return from following after thee; for whither thou goest, I will go; and where thou lodgest I will lodge; where thou diest will I die, and there will I be buried; the Lord do so to me, and more also, if aught but death part thee and me." Till, when waiting for his martyrdom in Rome, Paul is able to write like this to Timothy, "I am now ready to be offered up, and the time of my departure is at hand. Demas hath forsaken me, having loved this present world, and is departed into Thessalonica. But Luke, and Luke only, is with me." "Honor a physician," says the Son of Sirach, "with all the honor due to him. Of the Most High cometh healing, for the Lord hath created him. And the healer shall receive honor of the King. The skill of the physician shall exalt his head, and in the presence of great men shall he be held in admiration." Luke had by heart the whole chapter, till, by the grace of God, he had it all fulfilled in himself, as Paul's beloved physician and our beloved third Evangelist.

Lessons, both literary and religious, offer themselves to us before we bring our short study of Paul's physician to a close. But chiefly religious. I do not know that there is any class of men in our day, scarcely the ministers of religion themselves, who have so much in their power, in some ways, as our medical men. Take a young medical man just settling down in a provincial town, or in a country district, and what an event that is in interest and in opportunity. It is scarcely second to the settlement there of a good minister. What sort of a man, I wonder, is he? And what place will he take among us? it will be anxiously asked. And if he at once attaches himself to the Church; if he at once becomes a Sabbath-school teacher, a deacon, an elder, an abstainer, and so on; then, as Jesus the son of Sirach, says, that physician will be honored with all the honor due to him, and in the presence of all good men will he be held in estimation. And over and above his study and imitation of Paul's beloved physician, let every young doctor have always beside him the Autobiography, the *Religio Medici*, of that great writer and great honor to the medical profession, Sir Thomas Browne. And not his inimitable masterpiece only, but all his fascinating books, will make a rare shelf in any young doctor's library. If Sir Thomas Browne is such a ceaseless delight to such men of letters as Johnson, and Coleridge, and Carlyle, and Hazlitt, and Pater, what a life-long delight and advantage would he be to those who are of his own so beloved profession, if they are only of his still more beloved faith and hope. It is delightful to read of the towns of England competing and contesting as to which of them should have young Browne to settle down and practice among them: such were his attainments, and such was his character, in his student days, and in his early professional life, and such was the largeness and richness of his mind, taken together with the purity and the piety of his heart and his character. All of which purity and piety and true popularity is open to every young doctor everywhere. "Of the Most High cometh healing, for the Lord hath created the healer. The skill of the physician shall exalt his head, and in the presence of all men shall he be held in admiration," says the wise son of Sirach.

ONESIPHORUS was an elder in the Church of Ephesus, and a better elder there never was. Paul is but taking Onesiphorus's portrait when he says that an elder must be blameless, vigilant, sober, humble-minded, given to hospitality, one that ruleth his own house well, having his children in subjection with all gravity; moreover, he must have a good report of them that are without. Altogether, a striking likeness of a rare and a remarkable man. Paul had been Onesiphorus's minister for three years, and they had been three years of great labors and great sufferings on Paul's part, and you come to know your elders pretty well in three years like Paul's three years in Ephesus. The sacred writer has supplied his readers with Paul's farewell address to the elders of Ephesus, and a right noble address it is. "You know," he said, "from the first day I came into Asia, after what manner I have been with you at all seasons. Therefore, watch, and remember, that by the space of three years I ceased not to warn every one of you night and day with tears. And now, brethren, I commend you to God, and to the word of His grace, which is able to build you up, and to give you an inheritance among all them that are sanctified." And from that he goes on to give us the great scene on the seashore, when Onesiphorus fell on Paul's neck, and could not be torn off Paul's neck till the ship had almost sailed away without Paul. Onesiphorus sorrowing most of all at the words which Paul spake that he should see his face no more. And, no wonder at Onesiphorus's inconsolable sorrow, since it is a universal and an absolute law that you love a man, and cannot part from him, just in the measure that you have long loved him, and done him good, and suffered for his sake in time past. All the elders in Ephesus loved Paul, and had good reason to love him, but all taken together they did not love Paul as Onesiphorus did. For it was Onesiphorus, more than all his colleagues in the eldership of Ephesus, who had kept the apostle alive during those three years of such temptations and so many tears. Many and many a time Paul would have fainted altogether had it not been for Onesiphorus. It was of those heartbreaking years of his in Ephesus that Paul was thinking when he said to Timothy that an elder must be vigilant, and hospitable, and not a novice. That is to say, Onesiphorus never let Paul out of his sight, day nor night, all those three trying years to Paul. "Night and day with tears," is Paul's own summing up of his three years' ministry in Ephesus. But, then, Onesiphorus always wiped away Paul's tears faster than Paul shed them, such was his extraordinary vigilance and hospitality towards Paul. Many were the nights when after a trying day and then a refreshing supper Onesiphorus would give out this well-selected psalm at family worship—

> Who sow in tears, a reaping time
> Of joy enjoy they shall.

> That man who, bearing precious seed,
>   In going forth doth mourn,
> He doubtless, bringing back his sheaves,
>   Rejoicing shall return.

It was of those many Sabbath evening supper-parties that Paul remembered and wrote to Timothy in his Second Epistle to him: "How oft Onesiphorus refreshed me, and in how many things he ministered to me at Ephesus, thou knowest very well."

Now before we leave Ephesus and go to Rome with Onesiphorus, there is a lesson and an example here both for ministers who would fain imitate Paul, and for elders who would fain imitate Onesiphorus. Our ministers all have their own tears and temptations like the apostle. All men, indeed, have their own temptations and tears, but it is ministers we have now in hand. Our ministers, over and above the tears and the temptations which they share with all other men, have their own peculiar tears and temptations which it takes all Onesiphorus's vigilance to find out, and all his hospitality to alleviate. But, with all that, none of these things must move our ministers. They must only all the more bury themselves in their work. They must let none of these things move them but to more and to better work. They must not let the praise of men, nor anything that man can do for them, be dear to them. Nothing must really be dear to our ministers but to finish their course with joy, and their ministry, which they have received of the Lord Jesus. At the same time, there is always plenty of scope for Onesiphorus, and for all his vigilance, alongside of every such ministry. I do not remember that it is in as many words in our elders' ordination oath, that they are always to refresh their minister's heart when he would otherwise faint. But Onesiphorus did it out of his own vigilance of love, never thinking whether it was in his ordination oath or no. And I myself have been as well looked after as ever Paul was, and far better. I have always had elders myself, who, with all their own occupations and preoccupations, never let me out of their vigilant minds and hospitable hearts. I could give you their names, and I am tempted to do so in order to give point and authority to what I am now saying. But I daresay you all know the names of those elders yourselves. For such elders as Onesiphorus was do not content themselves with refreshing their minister's heart only; they carry out their holy office to all the flock over the which the Holy Ghost hath made them overseers. The whole world knows Onesiphorus's name now; and even in our own so unapostolic day, the house of Onesiphorus still holds on its vigilant and hospitable way.

But all that is years and years ago. And things have by this time come to this pass with Paul that he is now ready to be offered up, and the time of his departure is at hand. In other words, the apostle is just about to be brought before Nero for the second time, and everybody knows what that means. Now it is out of these circumstances that Paul pens these beautiful words to Timothy: "When Onesiphorus arrived in Rome, and was there, he sought me out with all the greater diligence that he knew I was in chains, till at last he found me." Now there are two interpretations of these words, and you are free to take either of those two interpretations that best commends itself to you. What do you think? How are you led to read this passage about Onesiphorus and his visit to Rome? Do you think it would be this?

That Onesiphorus, being a business man, had some mercantile errand to Rome; and then, after his hands were free of that matter he bethought himself that he would like to see his old minister before he returned home to Ephesus? Or does your heart revolt from that poor and mean and contemptible interpretation? And do you stand up for it, that it was something far better than the very best business-errand that brought Onesiphorus all the stormy way from Asia to Italy? Was it not once more to see his dearest friend on earth with whom he had so often transacted the great business of the soul, till he had by this time a great treasure laid up in heaven? If any of you owe your own soul, or your children's souls, to any minister, that entitles you to interpret this passage to us, and to say whether it was business or religion, money or love, that brought Onesiphorus to Rome toward the close of Paul's second imprisonment. Like all other interpreters, you will understand Onesiphorus just according to what you would have done yourself had you been in his place. Whatever it was that brought Onesiphorus from Ephesus to Rome, we are left in no doubt at all as to what he did before he left Rome and returned to Ephesus. Paul might be the greatest of the apostles to Onesiphorus, and he may be all that and far more than all that to you and to me, but he was only "Number So and so" to the soldier who was chained night and day to Paul's right hand. You would not have known Paul from any incognizable convict in our own penal settlements. Paul was simply "Number 5," or "Number 50," or "Number 500," or some such number. From one barrack-prison therefore to another Onesiphorus went about seeking for Paul day after day, week after week, often insulted, often threatened, often ill-used, often arrested and detained, till he was set free again only after great suffering and great expense. Till, at last, his arms were round Paul's neck, and the two old men were kissing one another and weeping to the amazement of all the prisoners who saw the scene. Noble-hearted Onesiphorus! We bow down before thee. What a coal of holy love must have burned in thy saintly bosom! Thou hast taught us all a much-needed lesson tonight. For we also have friends, and especially in the ministry, whose backs are often at the wall, whose names are often under a cloud, and who are forsaken of all men who should have stood by them. May we all come to be of thy vigilant and hospitable household! May we all have thy life-long and unquenchable loyalty to all those who suffer for righteousness' sake!

But now, my brethren, with all that, let us take very good care that the warmth of our present feelings over Onesiphorus does not all evaporate with this apostrophe to Onesiphorus. Let us not only admire and exalt Onesiphorus, let us forthwith imitate him. Let us, like him, seek out, and that too with all diligence, those who need, and especially those who deserve, our sympathy and our support. Ministers especially. Let us write them a letter of sympathy, let us make them a visit of sympathy, let us send them a gift of sympathy. Let us, in such ways as these, refresh them under their chains. Let us make them to feel that they are not so forgotten or so forsaken as they think they are. And this also. Like Onesiphorus also let us bring up our children to the same life of love. Let us take them with us sometimes when we go about doing good. Let them taste early the sweetness of doing good. And especially the sweetness and the reward of doing good to the suffering and the fainting in the household of faith. Let us set them to visit some godly and lonely old soul who will pray down present-day and last-day blessings on our head and on their heads, as Paul here does on the head of Onesiphorus and on the heads of his household. Send your children to the Sick Children's Hospital on the Sabbath afternoons with books and flowers. Send the older ones to the Infirmary and to the Incurable Hospital with the same and other gifts. And go to the prison yourself like Onesiphorus in Rome. And do it at once, before all this about Paul and Onesiphorus evaporates off your heart and leaves it harder than it was before. For if it all evaporates off your heart it had been better you had never heard Onesiphorus's noble name. We have all seen tonight Onesiphorus in Ephesus and in Rome, and we shall all see him at least once again; only, not in this world. We shall all see him again, but not till "that day," as Paul has it in the text. We have had too short time to give to him and to ourselves tonight, but there will be no such hurry on "that day." For that will be a long day. An immense amount of divine business will have to be taken up and gone through on that day. Do you think that the accounts of the whole world could be got through in a day such as we have hitherto counted days? Almighty God Himself will not be able to do it in a day of twelve hours. No, nor in twenty-four hours. And you may depend upon it He will not once rise off His great white throne till He is justified in all His judgments. There will be plenty of time that day. There will be all eternity to draw upon to make up that day. The sun will stand still as soon as he is well up, and he will not set till the last deed of mercy done on the earth has been sought out, and its reward made to run over. In spite of itself your left hand will be made to know on that day all that your right hand has hidden from it in this world: in Ephesus, and in Rome, and in Edinburgh. I was led a few moments ago to speak by way of illustration of some of our own Onesiphorus-elders. And one of them, who often refreshed his ministers, used to sit up there in the front gallery. I see him still as I now speak. It was dear Donald Beith. He will get a surprise on that day. He also will be found out on that day. Nay, I have found him out myself before that day. And since he is not here to deny it, I will tell you what you will hear about him from better lips than mine on that day. This will be told in your hearing, and you will say that you once heard it before in your accepted time, and in your day of salvation. More than one dark night my great friend sent his servant out to Fountainbridge, and up a dark stair, where a godly old soul lived without food or clothes or coals. The servant had strict injunctions to lay the heavy parcels up against the door, and then to knock and knock till he heard the deaf old cripple crawling toward the door, when he was to escape down the stair and out into the dark night like a thief from a detective. Donald Beith was a wily old Edinburgh lawyer, but I found him out sometimes, and you will see him with your own eyes found out again, to his consternation, on that day. What a day of surprises that day will be! What a day of leaping of all kinds of secrets to everlasting light will that day be! No wonder Paul so often calls it "that day," and the "day of Christ," and many suchlike great names. What a surprise, surprise after surprise, will Paul and Onesiphorus get on that day, and all stealthy and backstair men like Donald Beith. I think I see Paul, and Onesiphorus, and Donald Beith, and his Fountainbridge friend, all on one another's necks on that day, with their Savior smiling over them as He sees of the travail of His soul in them, and proclaims that He is satisfied. O my God, may I be among them and one of them on that day; both I and all those whom Thou hast given me! The Lord grant unto me also that both I and they may find mercy of the Lord in that day!

106
Alexander the Coppersmith

THERE are some most interesting and most important questions of New Testament scholarship, and New Testament sanctification, connected with Alexander the coppersmith of Ephesus. And the first of those questions is this: Have we got in our present text the very and identical words that Paul penned in his parchment to Timothy? Have we got the literal and exact expressions, and discriminations of expressions, that Paul so studiously employed? Have we got the very moods and tenses, both in grammar and in morals, that were in Paul's mind and heart at the moment when he wrote these two so difficult verses about Alexander? That is a very interesting, important, and indeed indispensable, question. Only, the settlement of that question must be left in their hands who alone are able to grapple with such questions. But, meantime, a question and a lesson of the very foremost importance faces us and forces itself on the most unlearned and ignorant of us. And that question and that lesson is this. Suppose that Paul both thought and felt and wrote about Alexander as our version literally reads, what are we to do? Are we free to follow Paul, and to do what he here does? Are we free to execrate and denounce bad men, and hand them over to be rewarded according to their works? Are we free, and is it our duty, to imprecate God's judgments on those who do us much evil, and who withstand the work of God which has been committed to our hands? A whole controversy of New Testament scholarship, and another whole controversy of New Testament morals and religion, have arisen around this text concerning Alexander the coppersmith. But, taking the text just as it has been put into our hands tonight, what are we able to make of it? What shall we succeed in taking out of it tonight for our own guidance tomorrow, and for every day we live on the earth?

The first time we come on Alexander he is a Jew of Ephesus, and a clever speaker to an excitable crowd. By the next time we meet with Alexander he has thought it to be for his interest to be baptized and to be seen openly on Paul's side. But Paul's side did not turn out to be so serviceable to the coppersmith as he had expected, and thus it is that he is next discovered to us as having made complete shipwreck of faith and a good conscience. And, then, as no man is so implacable at you as a complete renegade from you, so there was no man, among Paul's many enemies, who so hated Paul, and so hunted him down, as just this Alexander the coppersmith.

To go back to his beginning. Alexander had this temptation, that he was fitted by nature to be much more than a mere coppersmith, he was so clever and so captivating with his tongue. Unless you are a man of a very single heart and a very sound conscience, it is a great temptation to you to be able in a time of public commotion to speak so as to sway the swaying multitude and to command their applause and their support. You rise on a wave of popularity at such a season, and

498

you make use of your popularity for your own chief end in life. Many were the clever speeches the coppersmith made during his baptized days also; the Christians putting him forward to speak, just as the Jews were wont to put him forward when he was one of themselves. But, the wind working round and setting strongly in another direction, the coppersmith himself also instantly obeyed the law of the weather-cock he had fashioned with his own hands and had fastened on the roof of his workshop; for, as his copper creature did, so did he before the variable skies of those unsettled days. And thus it is, that when Paul is so soon to depart from all his false friends and all his implacable enemies alike, the Apostle writes this much-needed warning to his young and inexperienced successor, and says, "Alexander the coppersmith did me much evil, the Lord reward him according to his works, of whom be thou ware also, for he hath greatly withstood my words." Alexander did Paul and his apostolic work much evil, and that not out of ignorance and fanaticism, but out of sheer unmitigated malice. Sometimes malice is bought and sold in the open market, till everybody sees it and understands it. Sometimes a man is to be had for money, and he will write letters or make speeches for you as long as you pay him best. But genuine malice is a different article from that. There is no getting to the bottom of real and original and priceless malice. Its bottom is not here. Its bottom is in the bottomless pit. Unless Alexander sets himself, nay, unless God sets Alexander, to search in his own heart for the roots of his malice against Paul, no other man can come near understanding or believing the depth and the strength and the malignity of Alexander's ill-will. At the same time, Paul and the other apostles could not but see as clear as day, and every day, Alexander's ill-will and the malignity of it, so much was it thrust upon their painful experience continually. Alexander followed Paul about wherever he went, poisoning the minds and the hearts of all men to whom his tongue or his pen had access. One of our latest and best authorities thinks that Alexander even followed Paul to Rome, and did his best to poison Nero and his court still more against Paul. But, whether he made that malicious and superfluous journey or no, Alexander certainly did Paul and his good name and his divine work all the evil that his great gifts of speech and pen could do. It was no wonder that the constant presence of Alexander, and his implacable and sleepless malice, was almost too great a trial for Paul to bear. So studied, so systematic, and so persistent, were Alexander's evil words and evil deeds.

Now, surely there can be no question as to Paul's duty to Timothy in that case. Paul would have been sinning both against Timothy and against the Gospel had he not taken Timothy and warned him against the malignity of Alexander. True, Timothy had not yet suffered as Paul had suffered from the coppersmith. Alexander had not yet followed Timothy about poisoning the wells everywhere against him. But to prepare Timothy for what he might expect, and would be sure to meet with, Paul told Timothy, with all plainness and all pain, what his experience of Alexander and his malice had been. Now, what do you say? What do you do? Suppose such a man as Alexander the coppersmith has arisen in your community and is doing Alexander's very same work over again under your eyes every day, what do you do in that case? Do you content yourself with despising and detesting the mischief-making man in your heart? Should you not rather take some of his more wicked letters and speeches and point out to the simple and inexperienced the great lessons that lie on the face of such things? Is malice and misrepresentation less important to point out to a young man entering on life, than bad grammar and slovenly composition? There are studies in sheer malignity set us every day, as well as studies in style; and a teacher of morals should treat the one kind just as a teacher of letters always treats the other. Why should we be so careful to point out solecisms and careless composition to our young people, and pass by studied malice, misrepresentation, perversion, and suppression of the truth? And malice, too, that is not limited and localized in its scope as Alexander's malice was in his day, but which has all the resources of civilization in our day to spread it abroad. And resources also such that Alexander and his seed can do their wicked work in our day out of sight, and nobody know who they are till the day of judgment.

But by far and away our most important lesson out of Paul and Alexander is yet to come. Only, that lesson throws us back again on the previous question. Did Paul feel in his heart, and did he entertain and express to Timothy, all the anger and resentment that is expressed in the text? Did Paul actually say, "The Lord reward Alexander the coppersmith according to his evil works?" Whether he did or no, that makes no difference to us. Even if he did, we must never do so. Were another Alexander to rise in our day, ay, and were he to do all the evil to us and to our work that Alexander did to Paul and to his work, we must never say what Paul is here made to say. Paul was put by Alexander to the last trial and sorest temptation of an apostolic and a sanctified heart. And it is the last two-edged sword that pierces to the dividing of soul and spirit in ourselves, not to forgive insult and injury done to ourselves, but to forgive Alexander all that when he does it to the Church of Christ. Only, Christ Himself will have to be formed in you, and will have to live in you, and will have to think and feel and write in you, before you will be able to love that bad man, and to do him good, all the time he is doing, not you, but Jesus Christ Himself, evil. But when Jesus Christ truly dwells in you, then no malediction, and no revenge; nothing but good wishes and good words, will ever escape your lips or your pen. It is for this that bad men like Alexander are let live among us. It is first for their own repentance and reformation, and then it is that they may be the daily sanctification of men like Paul. Of men, that is, who would not be tempted by any less spiritual trial than anger and resentment at the enemies, not of themselves, but of the Church of Christ. And such men among us are sent to school, not to David on his deathbed, nor to Paul in his prison, but to Jesus Christ on His Cross; Who, when He was reviled, reviled not again; when He suffered, He threatened not; leaving us an example, that we should follow His steps. I once asked a friend of mine who had been subjected to more reviling than any other man of his land and day, how he thought such and such another man who had suffered still more reviling could go on with his public work under such diabolical ill-usage. "Oh," said he, "So-and-so always lives *in facie eternitatis.*" And nothing but the nearness of eternity and the nothingness of time, and the still more nothingness of either the praise or the blame of such men as Alexander; nothing but the constant presence of such things as these could support Paul and could keep his heart quiet and sweet under the malice and maltreatment of such a wicked man as the coppersmith. The face of eternity and the nearness of eternity will do it. The face of eternity and the nearness of eternity, and the face and the nearness of the Lord of eternity, that will do it.

Whether, then, this is some corruption in the text, as the scholars call corruption; or some of the remaining corruption in Paul's heart, as he would have called it himself, I do not know. But this I know, that it is the essence, and the concentration, and the core, of all corruption in my heart, when I again detect myself hating this man and that man for the love of God. Long after I am able to forgive this man and that man for what he has said or done against myself, I am compelled to cry out, O wretched man that I am! as often as I despise, or detest, or desire to hear of hurt to Alexander or to any of his widespread seed. I must not even let myself say, Vengeance is mine, I will repay, saith the Lord. No, I must rather say, "Let thy vengeance fall on me rather. For I have been a disappointment to Alexander's ambition. I have been a provocation to him and an offence to him in many ways. He has stumbled and has been broken on me. I am not without blame in his shipwreck of faith and a good conscience." Instead of cursing Alexander to God, William Law would the more have prayed for him late every night, according to that great man's life-long practice—"if you pray for a man sufficiently often, and sufficiently fervently, and sufficiently in secret, you cannot but love that man, even were he Alexander the coppersmith." That ye may be the children of your Father which is in heaven; for He maketh His sun to rise on the evil and on the good, and sendeth rain on the just and on the unjust.

But all questions of corruptions in the text, and in Paul's heart, apart, let us part with Paul when he is indisputably at his very highest and his very best. And he is at his very highest and his very best in the very next verse to his two unhappy verses about Alexander. "At my first answer no man stood with me, but all men forsook me: I pray God that it may not be laid to their charge." Paul is at his very best in that; for it is not Paul at all who says that, but it is He speaking in Paul who, when He also was forsaken, said, "Father, forgive them." "I am crucified with Christ," says Paul when he is at his best. "Nevertheless I live: yet not I, but Christ liveth in me: liveth in me and forgiveth Alexander the coppersmith in me: and the life I now live in the flesh I live by the faith of the Son of God, who loved me, and gave Himself for me."

107
Paul as a Student

PAUL was not born in the Holy Land like Jesus Christ, and like Peter and James and John. But Paul was proud of his birthplace, as he might very well be. For Tarsus was a great city in a day of great cities. Athens was a great city, Corinth was a great city, and Ephesus was a great city. But Tarsus in some respects was a greater city than any of them. Jerusalem stood alone, and Rome stood alone; but Tarsus engraved herself on her coins as the Metropolis of the East, and her proud claim was not disputed. An immense industry was carried on in the workshops of Tarsus, and an immense import and export trade was carried on in her docks. Nor were the eminent men of Tarsus mere manufacturers and merchants; they were men of education and refinement of manners also. But Saul's father was not one of the eminent men of Tarsus. He was one of the Hebrew dispersion, and he was making his living by the sweat of his brow in that industrious Greek city. And thus it was that Saul his son was far better acquainted with the workshops of Tarsus than with its schools or its colleges. Saul of Tarsus was not born with the silver spoon in his mouth any more than was Jesus of Nazareth, his future Master. It was one of the remarkable laws of that remarkable people that every father was expected, was compelled indeed, to send his son first to a school and then to a workshop. Rich and poor sat on the same school-seat; and rich and poor alike went from school to learn an honest trade. Rabbi Joseph turned the mill. Rabbi Juda was a baker. Rabbi Ada and Rabbi Jose were fishermen; and, may we not add, Rabbi Peter and Rabbi John? And so on: woodcutters, leatherdressers, blacksmiths, carpenters. And thus it was that Paul, again and again, held up his hands in the pulpit, and at the prisoner's bar, and said, "These hands, as you see, are full of callosities and scars, because they have all along ministered to mine own necessities, and to the necessities of those who have been dependent on me."

Saul of Tarsus, like Timothy of Lystra, from a child knew the Holy Scriptures. And thus, no doubt, there was found among his old parchments after his death a Table of Rules and Regulations for his college conduct in Jerusalem, as good as William Law's Rules for his college conduct in Cambridge; better Rules they could not be. But there is one possibility in Saul's student days in Jerusalem that makes our hearts beat fast in our bosoms to think of it. "And the Child grew," we read in a contemporary biography, "and waxed strong in spirit, filled with wisdom; and the grace of God was upon Him. Now His parents went up to Jerusalem every year at the feast of the passover. And when He was twelve years old, they went up to Jerusalem after the custom of the feast. And it came to pass after three days they found Him in the temple, sitting in the midst of the doctors, both hearing them and asking them questions." Now Gamaliel would be almost sure to be one of those astonished doctors; and what more likely than that he had taken his best scholar up to the temple to explain the passover to him that day? And did not the young carpenter from Nazareth, and the young weaver from Tarsus, exchange glances of sympathy and shake hands of love that day at the gate of the temple? I, for one, will believe that they did. Are there sports of providence like that in the Divine Mind? asked one of his like-minded students at Rabbi Duncan one day. Yes, and No, was the wise old doctor's answer.

Now the first instruction, as I think, intended to us out of Saul's student days is this—that the finest minds in every generation should study for the Christian ministry. Perhaps the very finest mind that had been born among men since the beginning of the world entered on the study of Old Testament theology when Saul of Tarsus sat down at Gamaliel's feet. And all Saul's fine and fast maturing mind will soon be needed now. For a work lay before that weaver boy of Tarsus second only to the work that lay before that carpenter boy of Nazareth, though second to that by an infinite interval. At the same time, there has been no other work predestinated to mere mortal man to do for God and man to be spoken of in the same day with this weaver boy's fore-ordained work. For even after the Lamb of God had said of His work—it is finished! how unfinished and incomplete our New Testament would have been without the life and the work of the Apostle Paul. There was a deep harmony pre-established from all eternity between the work of Jesus Christ, and the mind and heart of Paul His apostle. No other subject in all the world but the Divine Person and the redeeming work of Jesus Christ could have afforded an outlet and an opportunity and an adequate scope for Paul's magnificent mind. While, on the other hand, the law of God and the cross of Christ would have remained to this day but half-revealed mysteries, had it not been for God's revelation of His Son in Paul; and had it not been for Paul's intellectual and spiritual capacity to receive that revelation, and to expound it and preach it. Every man who has read Paul's Epistles with the eyes of his understanding in light, and with his heart on fire, must have continually exclaimed, What a gift to a man is a fine mind, and that mind wholly given up to Jesus Christ! Let our finest minds, then, devote themselves to the study of Christology. Other subjects may, or may not, be exhausted; other callings may, or may not, be overcrowded; but there is plenty of room in the topmost calling of all, and there is an ever-opening and an ever-deepening interest there. No wonder, then, that it has been a University tradition in Scotland that our finest minds have all along entered the Divinity Hall. The other walks and callings of human life both need, and will reward, the best minds that can be spared to them, but let the service of our Lord and Savior Jesus Christ first be filled. To annotate the Iliad, or the Symposium, or the Commedia; to build up and administer an empire; to command in a battle for freedom by sea or by land; to create and bequeath a great and enriching business; to conduct an influential newspaper; to be the rector of a great school, and so on—these are all great services done to our generation when we have the talent, and the character, and the opportunity, to do them. But to master Paul, as Paul mastered Moses and Christ; to annotate, and illustrate, and bring freshly home to ten thousand readers, the Galatians, or the Romans, or the Colossians; to have eyes to see what Israel ought to do, and to have the patience, and the courage, to lead a church to do it; to feed, and to feed better and better for a lifetime, the mind and the heart of a congregation of God's people, and then to depart to be with Christ—let the finest minds and the deepest and richest hearts in every new generation fall down while they are yet young and say, Lord Jesus, what wilt Thou have me to do with my life, and with whatsoever talents Thou hast entrusted to me?

And, then, the best of all callings being chosen, the better his mind and the better his heart are, the more profit, to employ Paul's own word about himself, will be made by the true student. For one thing, the better his mind, the more industrious, as a rule, the student of divinity will be. And the absolutely utmost industry in this supreme department of study is simply imperative and indispensable. An unindustrious divinity student should be drummed out of the Hall as soon as he is discovered intruding himself into it. With what a hunger for his books, and with what heavenward vows and oaths of work, young Saul would set out from Tarsus to Jerusalem! Our own best students come up to our divinity seats with thrilling and thanksgiving hearts, and it is only they who have such hearts who can at all enter into Saul's mind and heart and imagination as he descended Olivet and entered Jerusalem and saw his name set down at last on Gamaliel's roll of the sons of the prophets. Gamaliel would have no trouble with Saul, unless it was to supply him with books, and to answer his questions. "In all my experience I never had a scholar like Saul of Tarsus," Gamaliel would often afterwards say. And Saul's class-fellows would tell all their days what a help and what a protection it was to be beside Saul. "We entered the regent's class that year," writes James Melville in his delightful Diary, "and he took up Aristotle's *Logic* with us. He had a little boy that served him in his chambers, called David Elistone, who, among thirty-six scholars, so many were we in the class, was by far the best. This boy he caused to wait on me and confer with me, and well it was for me, for his genius and his judgment passed mine as far as the eagle the owlet. In the multiplication of propositions, in the conversion of syllogisms, in the *pons asinorum*, etc., he was as well read as I was in counting my fingers. This, I mark as a special cause of thankfulness." And young Saul of Tarsus would be just another David Elistone in Gamaliel's school. And you Edinburgh students of divinity must be as industrious and as successful as ever Saul was in Jerusalem, or little Elistone in St. Andrews. And you have far more reason. For you have far better teachers, and a far better subject, and a far better prospect, than ever Saul had. You are not eternally fore-ordained, indeed, to write the Epistle to the Romans, or the Epistle to the Ephesians. But you are chosen, and called, and matriculated, to do the next best thing to that. You are called to master those masterpieces of Paul, so as to live experimentally upon them all your student life, and then you are to teach and preach them to your people better and better all your pulpit and pastoral life. You are to work with your hands, if need be; you are to sell your bed, if need be, as Coleridge commands you, in order to buy Calvin on the Romans, and Luther on the Galatians, and Goodwin on the Ephesians, and Davenant on the Colossians, and Hooker on Justification, and "that last word on the subject," Marshall's *Gospel Mystery of Sanctification*; and you are to husband-up your priceless and irrecoverable hours to such studies, as you shall give account at the day of a divinity student's judgment. You are to feed your people, when you have got them committed of Christ to your charge, with the finest of the wheat, and with honey out of the rock. And that, better and better all your life, till your proud people shall make their boast in God about you, as the proud people of Anwoth made their boast about that great genius, and great scholar, and great theologian, and great preacher, and great pastor, Master Samuel Rutherford.

"Give attendance to reading," was Paul's old-age reminiscence of his student days, in the form of a counsel to young Timothy. "Paul has not lost his delight in books, even when he is near his death," says Calvin. And I myself owe so much to good books that I cannot stop myself on this subject as long as I see a single student sitting before me. I have a thousand times had Thomas Boston's experience of good books. "I plied my books. After earnestly plying my books, I felt my heart begin to grow better. I always find that my health and my heart are the better according as I ply my books." But you will correct me that Paul could not ply the great books that Thomas Boston plied to his own salvation, and to the salvation of his people in Simprin and Ettrick. Well, then, all the more, ply your pure Bible as Paul and Timothy did, and your profiting, like Paul's profiting and Timothy's, will soon appear unto all. Plying your English Bible even, your profiting will soon appear in your English style, both spoken and written. It will appear in the scriptural stateliness and the holy order of your pulpit prayers also. Your profiting will appear also in the strength, and the depth, and the spirituality, and the experimentalness, and the perennial freshness, of your teaching and your preaching. "Paul knew his Old Testament so well," says Dean Farrar in his splendid *Life of St. Paul*, "that his sentences are constantly molded by its rhythm, and his thoughts are incessantly colored by its expressions."

But, all the time—and it startles and staggers us to hear it—Saul was living in ignorance and in unbelief. They are his own remorseful words, written by his own pen long afterwards—ignorance and unbelief. The finest of minds, the best of educations, sleepless industry, blameless life, and all: with all that, the aged apostle shudders to look back on his student-days of ignorance and unbelief. What in the world does he mean? Strange to say, and it is something for us all to think well about, he declares to us on every autobiographic page of his, that all the time he sat at Gamaliel's feet, and for many disastrous years after that, he was in the most absolute and woe-working ignorance of the law of God. But that only increases our utter amazement. For, was it not the law of God that Gamaliel had opened his school to teach? What in the world, I ask again, can Paul mean? Have you any idea what the apostle means when he says, with such life-long shame, and such life-long remorse, that all his Jerusalem and Gamaliel days he was blind and dead in his ignorance of the law of God? It may, perhaps, help us to an understanding of what he means, if we try to mount up and to stand beside him on the far-shining heights of his exalted apostleship, and then look back from thence on his student and Pharisee days in Jerusalem. For it was just in the law of God that Paul afterwards became such a master. It was just the complete abolition of his ignorance of the law of God that set him so high above even the pillar-apostles in their remaining ignorance of it. It was just the law of God that he so reasoned out, and debated with them, as well as taught and preached it with such matchless success in every synagogue from Damascus to Rome. It was his incomparable handling of the law of God that first discovered to himself, and to the enraptured Church of Christ, the apostle's unique theological and philosophical genius, and the whole originality, and depth, and sweep, and grasp, of his matchless mind. An absolutely new world of things was opened up to the Apostolic Church when Paul came back from Arabia with the full revelation of the law and the gospel in his mind, and in his heart, and in his imagination. It was of Paul, and of the law of God in Paul's preaching, that our Lord spake when He said, "I have yet many things to say unto you, but ye cannot bear them now. Howbeit when He, the Spirit of truth, is come, He will guide you into all truth,"—which He did when He led Paul into Arabia. And then, after those three reading, meditating, praying, law-discovering, self-discovering, Christ-discovering, years, Paul came back to Damascus, carrying in his mind and in his heart the copestone of New Testament doctrine, with shoutings of grace! grace! unto it. It was Paul's imperial mind, winged as it was with his wonderful imagination, that first swept, full of eyes, over the whole Old Testament history, and saw, down to the bottom and up to the top, the whole hidden mystery of the Old Testament economies, from the creation of the first Adam on to the sitting down of the second Adam at the right hand of God. From the creation of Adam to the call of Abraham; and from the call of Abraham to the giving of the law four hundred and thirty years after; and from the giving of the law till the law was magnified in the life and death of Paul's Master. "I first of all mortal men have thought the Creator's thoughts after Him," exclaimed the great astronomical discoverer as he fell on his knees in his observatory. And the great discoverer of the whole mystery of God, in the law and in the gospel, must often have fallen down and uttered the very same exclamation. And his great revelations, and discoveries, and attainments, and experiences, are preserved to us in such profound, axiomatic, and far-enlightening New Testament propositions and illustrations and autobiographic ejaculations as these—"The law entered that the offence might abound. By the law is the knowledge of sin. The law worketh wrath. Without the law sin was dead. I was alive without the law once. I am so sold under sin. The law is our schoolmaster to lead us to Christ. By the works of the law shall no flesh be justified. But now we are no more under the law, but under grace. I am dead to the law, that being dead wherein I was held,"—and so on, through the whole of the Galatians and the Romans, and indeed throughout every Epistle of his. Yes, gentlemen, you may tonight be in as absolute ignorance of all that as the apostle once was; but, I tell you, there still lies scope and opportunity in all that for your most scholarly, most logical, and most philosophical, minds, and for your most eloquent, impressive, and prevailing preaching. Till you ascend for yourselves, and then lead your people up to this golden climax of the apostle concerning the law, and concerning Christ, and concerning himself in Christ—this golden climax—"For I through the law am dead to the law, that I might live unto God. I am crucified with Christ: nevertheless I live; yet not I, but Christ liveth in me: and the life I now live in the flesh I live by the faith of the Son of God, who loved me, and gave Himself for me."

108

Paul as Apprehended of Christ Jesus

THE first time we see Saul of Tarsus he is silently consenting to Stephen's death. Why the fierce young Pharisee did not take a far more active part in the martyrdom of Stephen we do not know; we can only guess. That a young zealot of Saul's temperament should be content to sit still that day, and merely keep the clothes of the witnesses who stoned Stephen, makes us wonder what it meant. But, beginning with his silent consent to the death of Stephen, Saul soon went on to plan and to perpetrate the most dreadful deeds on his own account. "As for Saul, he made havoc of the Church, entering into every house, and haling men and women, committed them to prison. Which thing I also did in Jerusalem; and many of the saints did I shut up in prison, and punished them oft in every synagogue, and compelled them to blaspheme. Beyond measure I persecuted the Church of God, and wasted it; I was a blasphemer, and a persecutor, and injurious." And thus it was that Saul actually went to the high priest in Jerusalem, and desired of him letters to Damascus, to the synagogues, that if he found any of this way, whether they were men or women, he might bring them bound to Jerusalem. And, accordingly, on that errand, out at the Damascus-gate of Jerusalem, he rode with his band of temple police behind him: out past Gethsemane: out past Calvary, where he shook his spear in the face of the Crucified, and cried, Aha, aha! Thou deceiver! and posted on breathing out threatenings and slaughter against the disciples of the Lord.

Gird Thy sword upon Thy thigh, O Most Mighty, with Thy glory and Thy majesty. Thine arrows are sharp in the hearts of the King's enemies, whereby the people fall under Thee!

And thus it was that, as Saul journeyed, and came near Damascus, suddenly there shone down upon him a great light from heaven. And he fell to the earth, and heard a voice saying to him, Saul, Saul, why persecutest thou Me? His eyes were as a flame of fire, and His voice as the sound of many waters. And out of His mouth went a sharp two-edged sword, and His countenance was as the sun shineth in his strength. Arise, go into the city, and it shall be told thee what thou shalt do. And Saul arose from the earth, and they led him by the hand, and brought him into Damascus. And he was three days without sight, and did neither eat nor drink. And Ananias entered the house where Saul lay, and putting his hands on him, he said, Brother Saul, the Lord, even Jesus, that appeared unto thee on the way as thou camest, hath sent me, that thou mightest receive thy sight, and be filled with the Holy Ghost. And immediately there fell from his eyes, as if it had been scales, and he received sight forthwith, and arose, and was baptized. Saul of Tarsus, I baptize thee in the name of the Father, and of the Son, and of the Holy Ghost. And there was great joy in the presence of the angels of God over the conversion and the baptism of Saul of Tarsus.

Now it is the suddenness of Saul's conversion that is the first thing arresting about it to us. It was literally, and in his own words, an "apprehension." "Suddenly," is his own word about it, as often as he tells us again and again the ever-fresh story of his conversion. The whole subject of conversion is a great study to those who are personally interested in the supremest of all human experiences. There is such a Divine Hand in every conversion; there is such a Sovereignty in it; taking place within a man, there is, at the same time, such a mysteriousness about it; and, withal, such a transcendent importance, that there is nothing else that ever takes place on the face of the earth for one moment to be compared with a conversion. And, then, there are so many kinds of conversion. So many ways of it, and such different occasions and circumstances of it. Some conversions are as sudden, and as unexpected, and as complete, as Saul's conversion was; and some are slowness itself. Some are such that the very moment, and the very spot, can ever afterwards be pointed out; while some other men are all their days subject to doubt, just because the change came so easy to them as to be without observation. They were born of the Spirit before they could distinguish good from evil, or could discern between their right hand and their left hand. A good sermon will be the occasion of one conversion, a good book of another, and a wise word spoken in due season of another. Hearing a hymn sung, as was the case one Sabbath evening in this very house; hearing a verse read, as was the case with St. Augustine. Just looking for a little at a dry tree will do it sometimes, as was the case with Brother Laurence. Hopeful saw Faithful burned to ashes; Christiana remembered all her surly carriages to her husband; and Mercy came just in time to see Christiana packing up. Their conversions came to Dr. Donne and to Dr. Chalmers long after they were ministers; and, after their almost too late conversion, those two great men became the greatest preachers of their day. A man of business will be on his way to his office on a Monday morning, and he could let you see to this day the very shop window, passing which, in Princes Street, he was apprehended. I was engaged to be married and she died, said a young communicant to me on one occasion. It was the unkindness of my mistress, said a servant-girl. Just as I am writing these lines this letter reaches me: "When the Lord opened my eyes the sight I saw broke me down completely. I tried to work myself right, till it turned out to be the hardest task I ever tried. But I would not give in till He took me by the coat-neck and held me over hell. Oh, sir, it was a terrible time! My sense of sin drove me half mad. But I kept pouring out my heart in prayer!" And then my correspondent goes on to tell me the name of the book that was made such a blessing to him. And then he asks that his mistakes in spelling be pardoned, and signs himself an office-bearer in the Church of one of my friends. But you will go over for yourselves all the cases of conversion you have ever heard about, or read about, and you will see for yourselves how full of all kinds of individuality, and variety, and intensity of interest, the work of conversion is, till like Mercy in *The Pilgrim's Progress*, you will fall in love with your own.

Some men put off their conversion because they have no sense of sin. But look at Saul. What sense of sin had he? Not one atom. He was an old and a heaven-ripe apostle before his full sense of sin came home to him. He was not groaning out the seventh of the Romans when he was galloping at the top of his speed on his way to Damascus. A sensibility to sin so exquisite and so spiritual as that of the apostle never yet came to any man but after long long years of the holiest of lives. To ninety-nine out of a hundred, even of truly converted men, it never comes at all. How could it? At the same time, who knows? your conversion, both in its present insensibility, and in its subsequent spirituality, may be to be of the same kind as Paul's was, if you will only on the spot submit to it. Accept your offered conversion, and go home and act at once and ever after upon it, and trust the Holy Ghost for your sense of sin. And if you belong to the same mental and moral and spiritual seed of Israel as Paul, your sense of sin will yet come to you with a vengeance. And, once it begins to come, it will never cease coming more and more, till you will almost be driven beside yourself with it. On the other hand, your conversion may not be to be of the heart-breaking kind. You may not be to be held over open hell by the coat-neck like my ill-spelling friend; your experience may be to be like that of Lydia. Like hers, your conversion may be to steal in upon your heart some night at a prayer-meeting—be it of whatever kind it is to be, take it when and where it is offered to you. And if your conversion is of the right kind at all, and holds, you will in due time and in your due order, get your fit and proper share of that saving grace, of which you say you are so utterly empty tonight.

But not only had Saul no sense of sin to prepare him for his conversion: he had no preparation and no fitness for his conversion, of any kind whatsoever. He brought nothing in his hands. He came just as he was. He was without one plea. Poor, wretched, blind; sight, riches, healing of the mind. Read his thrice-told story, and see if there is any lesson plainer, or more pointed to you in it all, than just the unexpectedness, the unpreparedness, and the completeness on the spot, of Saul's conversion. With, on the other hand, his instantaneous and full faith, his childlike trust, his full assurance, and his prompt and unquestioning obedience. Yes, it is just the absolute sovereignty, startling suddenness, total unpreparedness, entire undeservingness, and glorious completeness, of Saul's conversion that, all taken together, make it such a study, and, in some respects, such a model conversion, to you and to me.

There is another lesson told us three times, as if to make sure that we shall not miss nor mistake it. Saul got his conversion out of that overthrow on the way to Damascus, while all his companions only got some bodily bruises from their fall, and the complete upsetting of their errand out of it. The temple officers had each his own story to tell when they returned without any prisoners to Jerusalem: only, none of them needed to be led by the hand into Damascus, and none of them were baptized by Ananias, but Saul only. All of which is written for our learning. For the very same thing will take place here tonight. One will be Saul over again, and those who are sitting beside him will be Saul's companions over again. One will go straight home after this service, and will never all his days have Saul's sudden and unexpected conversion out of his mind, such a divine pattern is it to be of his own conversion. While his companions will be able to tell when they go home who preached, and on what, the fullness of the Church, the excellence of the music, and the state of the weather on the way home—and that will be all. "And they that were with me saw indeed the light, and were afraid; but they heard not the voice of Him that spake with me. And I said, What shall I do, Lord? And He said to me, Arise, and go into the city, and there it shall be told thee of all things which are appointed for thee to do."

"It is a trap set for us," said Ananias. "Lord," he said, "I have heard by many of this man, how much evil he hath done to Thy saints in Jerusalem. And how he has come here with authority to bind all that call upon Thy name. It is a trap set for our destruction," said Ananias. "Go to the street called Straight," said the Lord, "and if thou dost not find him in prayer, then it is a trap as thou fearest it is." The mark of Saul's conversion that silenced Ananias was this, that Saul had been three days and three nights in fasting and in prayer without ceasing. Behold he prayeth, said Christ, proud of the completeness and the success of His conversion of Saul. Has Jesus Christ, with His eyes like a flame of fire, set that secret mark on your conversion and on mine? Does He point you out to His ministering angels and sympathizing saints in heaven tonight, as He pointed out Saul to Ananias? How does your conversion stand the test of secret prayer? Behold, he prayeth! said Christ. And unceasing prayer, both for himself and for all his converts, remained to be Paul's mark, and token, and seal, down to the end of his days.

The best expositor by far that ever took Paul's epistles up into a pulpit, has said that the apostle never fell into a single inconsistency after his conversion. Now, with all submission, I cannot receive that even about Paul, any more than I can receive it about any other man that ever was converted on the face of this earth. That he never fell into a single inconsistency could only be said about One Man; and we never speak about His conversion. But the very fact that the profoundest preacher that I possess on Paul, and the profoundest preacher of conversion-consistency, has said such a thing as that, shows us what a splendid, what a complete, and what a consistent, conversion Paul's conversion must have been. How thoroughgoing it must have been at the time; and how holy in all manner of walk and conversation must Paul ever after have lived. Speaking here for myself, and not venturing to speak for any of you, when I read a thing like that, and a thing said by such a master in Israel as he was who said that, and then look at my own life in the searching light of that, I feel as if I can never up till now have been converted myself at all. Unless this also is a sure mark of a true conversion, which I have seen set down with incomparable power by this very same master in Israel, this—that it is a sure and certain mark of a true conversion that no man ever understands what inconsistency really is till he is truly converted. To be all but entirely void of offence, as Paul said of himself; to be all but completely consistent in everything, was one of the sure and certain marks of Paul's conversion. But, then, to feel myself to be full to the lips of offence: to see and to feel myself to be the most inconsistent man in all the world, is, by this same high authority, offered to me as a mark of my conversion, as good to me as Paul's magnificent marks were to him. "The disproportion of man" is one of Pascal's most prostrating passages; and the offensiveness, the inconsistency, and the disproportion, of my heart and my life, are the most prostrating of all my experiences. Indeed, nothing ever prostrates me, to be called prostration, but these experiences. At the same time, the whole and entire truth at its deepest bottom is this. That both things are true of Paul and of his conversion. Paul was at one and the same moment, and in one and the same matter, both the most consistent, and the most inconsistent, of all Christ's converts. He was both the most blameless, and the most blameable; the best proportioned, and the most disproportioned, of all Christian men. Such was the holiness of his life, and such was the spirituality of his mind and heart. And both experiences, taken together, combine to constitute the most complete and all-round mark of a perfect conversion. Now, all that, and far more than all that, combine to make Paul's conversion the most momentous, and the most wonderful, conversion in all the world. And yet, no. There is one other conversion long since Paul's, that will, to you and to me to all eternity, quite eclipse Paul's conversion, and will for ever completely cast, even it, quite into the shade.

109
Paul in Arabia

NO sooner was Paul baptized by Ananias, than, instead of returning home to Jerusalem, he immediately set out for Arabia. He had come down to Damascus with horses and servants like a prince, but he set out alone for Arabia like Jacob with his staff. For, all that he took with him was his parchments, and some purchases he had made in the street called Straight. A few of those simple instruments that tentmakers use when they have to minister to their own necessities, was all that Paul encumbered himself with as he started from Ananias's door on his long and solitary journey to Arabia.

What it was that took Paul so immediately and so far away as Arabia, we can only guess. If it was simply a complete seclusion that he was in search of, he might surely have secured that seclusion much nearer home. But, somehow, Sinai seems to have drawn Paul to her awful solitudes with an irresistible attraction and strength. It may have been an old desire of his formed at Gamaliel's feet, some day to see the Mount of God with his own eyes. He may have said to himself that he must hide himself for once in that cleft-rock before he sat down to his life-work in Moses' seat. I must see Rome, he said towards the end of his life. I must see Sinai, he also said at the beginning of his life. And thus it was that as soon as he was baptized in Ananias's house in Damascus, Paul immediately set out for Arabia.

Look at that weak bodily presence. But, at the same time, judge him not by his outward appearance. For he carries Augustine, and Luther, and Calvin, and Knox, in his fruitful loins. In that lonely stranger you are now looking at, and in his seed, shall all the families of the earth be blessed. Look at the eyes of his understanding as they begin to be enlightened. Look at him with his heart all on fire. See him as he unrolls his parchments at every roadside well, and drinks of the brook by the way. Thy word is more to me than my necessary food, and thy love is better than wine!

What a three years were those three years that Paul spent in Arabia! Never did any other lord receive his own again with such usury as when Paul went into Arabia with Moses and the Prophets and the Psalms in his knapsack, and returned to Damascus with the Romans and the Ephesians and the Colossians in his mouth and in his heart. What an incomparable book waits to be written about those three immortal years in Arabia! After those thirty preparation-years at Nazareth, there is no other opportunity left for any sanctified pen, like those three revelation-years in Arabia. Only, it will demand all that is within the most Paul-like writer, to fit him out for his splendid enterprise. It will demand, and it will repay, all his learning, and all his intellect, and all his imagination, and all his sinfulness, and all his salvation. Just to give us a single Sabbath out of Paul's hundred and fifty Sabbaths at Sinai—what a revelation to us that would be! It would be something like this, only a thousand times better. When first you fell in love: when first your captivated heart made you like the chariots of Ammi-nadib; the whole world was full of one name to you. There was no other name to you in all the world. Every bird sang that name. Every rock echoed with that name. You wrote that name everywhere. You read that name everywhere. You loved everybody and everything for the sake of that name. Now, it was something like that between Paul and Jesus Christ. Only, it was far better than that between Paul and Jesus Christ at the time, and it was far more lasting with them than it has been with you. Luther, who was almost as great a lover of Jesus Christ as Paul was, has this over and over again about Paul and Jesus Christ. "Jesus Christ is never out of Paul's mouth. Indeed, there is nobody and nothing now and always in Paul's mouth but Jesus Christ and His Cross." Now that is literally true. For, as often as Paul opens his Moses in Arabia, and finds the place he is seeking for, he cannot see the place when he has found it for Jesus Christ. Jesus Christ comes between Paul and everything. To Paul to read, and to meditate, and to pray, is Jesus Christ. So much so, that as soon as he finds the place at the very first verse of Genesis, he immediately goes off at the word, and exclaims, till the Arabs all around listen to his rapture—the mystery! he exclaims, which from the beginning of the world hath been hid in God, who created all things by Jesus Christ. And at this—Let there be light! For God, he exclaims again, who commanded the light to shine out of darkness, hath shined in our hearts in the face of Jesus Christ. And, does Adam burst out into his bridegroom doxology—This is now bone of my bone, and flesh of my flesh!—than Paul instantly adds, Amen! But I speak concerning Christ and His Church. And before he leaves the first Adam he gets such a revelation of the second Adam made in him that the Corinthians had many a glorious Sabbath morning on the two Adams, all the way from Arabia, long afterwards. And, again, no sooner does God speak in covenant to Abraham about his seed, than Paul immediately annotates that He saith not to seeds as of many, but as of One, which is Christ. But, on all that Moses ever wrote, there was nothing that Paul spent so much time and strength, as just on this concerning the father of the faithful—that Abraham believed in the Lord, and it was counted to him for righteousness. Now, said Paul, reasoning to himself over that revelation, and then reasoning to us—Now it was not written for Abraham's sake only, that it was imputed to him, but for our sakes also, to whom it shall be imputed, if we believe on Him who raised up Jesus our Lord from the dead; who was delivered for our offences, and was raised again for our justification. And so on, till to have spent a single Sabbath-day with Paul at Sinai would have been almost as good as to have walked that evening hour to Emmaus. So did Paul discover the Son of God in Arabia: so did Paul have the Son of God revealed to him in Adam, and in Abraham, and in Moses, and in David, and in Isaiah, but, best of all, in Paul himself.

And, then, Paul's first fast-day in Arabia. Paul was never out of the Psalms on those days that he observed so solemnly at Sinai. Till his David was like John Bunyan's Luther, so old that it was ready to fall piece from piece if he did but turn it over. But he always turned it over at such sacramental seasons till he came again to that great self-examination Psalm, where he found it written concerning himself: These things hast thou done, and I kept silence. Thou thoughtest that I was altogether such an one as thyself. But I will reprove thee, and set them in order before thee. And it was so. For, there they stood, set in order before him, and passed in order before him and before God. The souls of all the men and women and children he had haled to prison, and had compelled to blaspheme, and had slain with the sword. And, then, as he hid himself in the cleft rock—how the Name of the Lord would come up into his mind: and how, like Moses also, he would make haste and bow his head to the earth and say: Take me for one of Thy people. And, till God would again reveal His Son in Paul in a way, and to a degree, that it is not possible for Paul to tell to such impenitent and unprostrated readers of his as we are. And, then, far over and above those terrible sins of his youth, there was the absolutely unparalleled and absolutely indescribable agony that came upon Paul out of the remaining covetousness and consequent malice of his heart, and more and more so as his heart was more and more brought down under the ever-increasing and all-piercing spirituality of God's holy law. An agony that sometimes threatened to drive Paul beside himself altogether. And till, on the rocks of Sinai the shepherds would sometimes come on somewhat the same sweat of blood that the gardeners came on in the Garden of Gethsemane. For it was in Arabia, and it was under the Mount of God, that Paul's apostolic ink-horn was first filled with that ink of God with which he long afterwards wrote that so little understood writing of his, which we call the Seventh of the Romans. A little understood writing; and no wonder!

The Apostle came back from Arabia to Damascus, after three years' absence, absolutely ladened down with all manner of doctrines, and directions, and examples, for us and for our salvation, if we would only attend to them and receive them. Directions and examples of which this is one of the first. That solitude, the most complete and not short solitude, was the one thing that Paul determined to secure for himself immediately after his conversion and his baptism. And we have a still better Example of all that than even Paul. For, over and above His thirty uninvaded years, no sooner was that "Glorious Eremite" baptized, than He went away and took forty days to Himself before He began His public life. "One day"—sings concerning Him one of His servants who loved seclusion also, and put it to some purpose—

> One day forth walked alone, the Spirit leading,
> And His deep thoughts, the better to converse
> With solitude; till far from track of man,
> Thought following thought, and step on step led on,
> He entered now the bordering desert-wild,
> And, with dark shades and rocks environ'd round,
> His holy meditations thus pursued.

And thus it is that Holy Scripture is everywhere so full of apartness and aloneness and solitude: of lodges in the wilderness, and of shut doors in the city: of early mornings, and late nights, and lonely night-watches: of Sabbath-days and holidays, and all such asylums of spiritual retreat.

> Down to Gehenna, and up to the throne,
> He travels the fastest who travels alone.

But the Apostle's chief reason for telling us about Arabia at all is this, to prove to us, and to impress upon us, that it was not cities and colleges and books that

made him what by that time he was made. It was God Himself who made Paul
the Apostle he was made. I conferred not with flesh and blood, he protests. He
had books, indeed, as we have seen: he always had. He had the best of books: he
always had. But even Moses and David and Isaiah themselves are but flesh and
blood compared with God. Even grace itself is but flesh and blood compared with
Christ, says Thomas Shepard. And Paul is careful and exact, above everything,
to make it clear to us, that not only was it God Himself who immediately and
conclusively revealed His Son in Paul; but, also, that it was His Son that God so
revealed. It was not Jesus Christ, so much, distinguishes Paul, that God revealed
in him. Jesus Christ had revealed Himself to Paul already at the gate of Damascus,
but God's revelation of His Son in Arabia was a revelation of far more than of
Jesus Christ whom Paul was persecuting. For, this in Arabia is God's Eternal and
Co-Equal Son. And that, not merely as made flesh, and made sin: not merely as
crucified, and risen, and exalted, and glorified; but as He had been before all that,
and during all that, and after all that. It was God's Essential and Eternal Son: it
was God's very deepest, completest, and most crowning revelation possible of His
only-begotten Son; that God, in such grace and truth, made in Paul in Arabia.

In me, says Paul. In my deepest mind and in my deepest heart: in my very
innermost soul and strength. And thus it was that Paul underwent two grand revelations, over and above a multitude of lesser revelations which arose out of those
two epoch-making revelations, and which both perfected and applied them. The
one, that grand and epoch-making revelation made on the way to Damascus, and
made immediately by Jesus Christ, whom Paul was at that moment persecuting.
A revelation divinely suited to all the circumstances. A revelation outward, arresting, overpowering: taking possession of all the persecutor's bodily senses, and thus
surrounding and seizing all the passes into his soul. The other, made within and
upon Paul's pure and naked soul, and apart altogether from the employment of
his senses upon his soul. A revelation impossible adequately to describe. A revelation made by God of His Son, most inward, most profound, most penetrat-
ing, most soul-possessing: most-enlarging to the soul, most uplifting, and most
upholding: most assuring, most satisfying, most sanctifying: intellectual, spiritual,
experimental, evangelical: all-renewing and all-transforming: full of truth, full of
love, full of assurance, full of holiness, full of the peace of God, which passeth
all understanding. Jesus of Nazareth appeared to Saul the persecutor, as He had
already appeared to Mary Magdalene, and to the ten disciples, and to Thomas.
But God the Father revealed His Son in Paul the Apostle, as He had never revealed
Him before, and as He has never revealed Him since in mortal man. That is to say,
with a fullness, and with a finalness, that has made all God's subsequent revelations of His Son, at their best, to be but superficial and partial, occasional and
intermittent. Not that it need be so. Not that it ought to be so. For if we but gave
ourselves up to God and to His Son, as Paul gave himself up, we also, no doubt,
would soon reap our reward. But, as it is, Paul's apprehension of God's Son, Paul's
comprehension of God's Son, and Paul's service of God's Son, have remained to
this day, by far the first, by far the best, by far the most complete, by far the most
final, and by far the most fruitful, revelation of His Son, that Almighty God has
ever made in any of the sons of men.

110

Paul's Visit to Jerusalem to See Peter

PUT yourself back into Paul's place. Suppose yourself born in Tarsus, brought up at Gamaliel's feet in Jerusalem, and keeping the clothes of Stephen's executioners. Think of yourself as a blasphemer, and a persecutor, and injurious. And—then imagine yourself apprehended of Christ Jesus, driven of the Spirit into the wilderness of Arabia, and coming back with all your bones burning within you to preach Jesus Christ and Him crucified. But, all the time, you have never once seen your Master in the flesh, as His twelve disciples had seen Him. He had been for thirty years with His mother and His sisters and His brethren in Galilee. And then He had been for three years with the twelve and the seventy. But Paul had been born out of due time. And thus it was that Paul went up to Jerusalem to see Peter about all that. Paul had a great desire to see Peter about all that before he began his ministry. And you would have had that same great desire, and so would I.

At the same time, even with the prospect of seeing Peter, it must have taken no little courage on Paul's part to face Judea and Jerusalem again. To face the widows and the orphans of the men he had put to death in the days of his ignorance and unbelief. To Paul the very streets of Jerusalem were still wet with that innocent blood. Led in by Peter, Paul sat at the same Lord's table, and ate the same bread, and drank the same wine, with both old and young communicants, who had not yet put off their garments of mourning because of Paul. Deliver me from blood-guiltiness, O God, Thou God of my salvation. Then will I teach transgressors Thy ways. Do good in Thy good pleasure unto Zion; build Thou the walls of Jerusalem. And thus it was that, to the end of his days, Paul was always making collections for those same poor saints that were in Jerusalem. Paul would have pensioned every one of them out of his own pocket, had he been able. But how could he do that off a needle and a pair of shears? And thus it was that he begged so incessantly for the fatherless families that he had made fatherless in Judea and in Jerusalem. Now, if any of you have ever made any woman a widow, or any child an orphan, or done anything of that remorseful kind, do not flee the country. You cannot do it, and you need not try. Remain where you are. Go back to the place. Go back often in imagination, if not in your bodily presence. Do the very utmost that in you lies, to repair the irreparable wrong that you did long ago. And, when you cannot redeem that dreadful damage, commit it to Him who can redeem both it and you. And say to Him continually:—Count me a partner with Thee. And put that also down to my account.

"To see Peter," our Authorized Version is made to say. "To visit Peter," the Revised Version is made to say. And, still, to help out all that acknowledged lameness, the revised margin is made to say, "to become acquainted with Peter." But Paul would not have gone so far, at that time at any rate, to see Peter or any one else. Any one else, but Peter's Master. But to see Him even once, as He was in the flesh, Paul would have gone from Damascus to Jerusalem on his hands and his knees. "I went up to Jerusalem to *history* Peter," is what Paul really says. Only, that is not good English. But far better bad English, than an utterly meaningless translation of such a text. "To interview Peter," is not good English either, but it conveys Paul's meaning exactly. The great Greek historians employ Paul's very identical word when they tell their readers the pains they took to get first-hand information before they began to write their books. "I went up to interrogate and to cross-question Peter all about our Lord," that would be rough English indeed, but it would be far better than so feebly to say, "to see Peter," which positively hides from his readers what was Paul's real errand to Jerusalem, and to Peter.

Had Landor been led to turn his fine dramatic genius and his ripe scholarship to Scriptural subjects, he would, to a certainty, have given us the conversations that took place for fifteen days between Peter and Paul. Landor's Epictetus and Seneca, his Diogenes and Plato, his Melanchthon and Calvin, his Galileo and Milton and a Dominican, and his Dante and Beatrice, are all among his masterpieces. But his Paul and Peter, and his Paul and James the brother of our Lord, and especially his Paul and the mother of our Lord, would have eclipsed clean out of sight his most classical compositions. For, on no possible subject, was Peter so ready always to speak, to all comers, as just about his Master. And never before nor since had Peter such a hungry hearer as just his present visitor and interrogator from Arabia and Damascus. Peter began by telling Paul all about that day when his brother Andrew so burst in upon him about the Messiah. And then that day only second to it, on the Lake of Gennesaret. And then Matthew the publican's feast, and so on, till Peter soon saw what it was that Paul had come so far to hear. And then he went on with the good Samaritan, and the lost piece of silver, and the lost sheep, and the lost son. For fifteen days and fifteen nights this went on till the two prostrate men took their shoes off their feet when they entered the Garden of Gethsemane. And both at the cock-crowing, and at Calvary, Peter and Paul wept so sore that Mary herself, and Mary Magdalene, did not weep like it. Now, just trust me and tell me what you would have asked at Peter about his Master. Would you have asked anything? How far would you go tonight to have an interview with Peter? Honestly, have you any curiosity at all about Jesus Christ, either as He is in heaven now, or as He was on earth then? Really and truly, do you ever think about Him, and imagine Him, and what He is saying and doing? Or are you like John Bunyan, who never thought whether there was a Christ or no? If you would tell me two or three of the questions you would have put to Peter, I would tell you in return just who and what you are; just how you stand tonight to Jesus Christ, and how He stands to you: and what He thinks and says about you, and intends toward you.

And then if Mary, the mother of our Lord, was still in this world, it is certain to me that Paul both saw her in James's house, and kissed her hand, and called her Blessed. You may depend upon it that Mary did not remain very long away from James's house after his conversion. It was all very good to have a lodging with the disciple whom Jesus loved, till her own slow-hearted son believed. But I put it to you who are mothers in Israel, to put yourselves in Mary's place in those days, and to say if you would have been to be found anywhere, by that time, but in the house of your own believing son. And what more sure and certain than that God, here again, revealed His Son to Paul out of Mary's long hidden heart. "I have the most perfect, and at first-hand, assurance of all these things from them that were eye-witnesses and ministers of the Word," says Paul's physician and private secretary. Nowhere, at any rate, in the whole world, could that miraculous and mystery-laden woman have found such another heart as Paul's into which to pour out all that had been for so long sealed up in her hidden heart. "Whether we were in the body, or out of the body, as she told me about Nazareth, and as I told her about Damascus and Arabia, I cannot tell: God knoweth."

"From the Old Testament point of view," says Bengel in his own striking and suggestive way, "the progress is made from the knowledge of Christ to the knowledge of Jesus. From the New Testament point of view, the progress is made from the knowledge of Jesus to the knowledge of Christ." And have we not ourselves already seen how Paul's progress was made? Paul's progress was made from the knowledge of Jesus of Nazareth risen from the dead, to the knowledge of the Son of God; and then from the knowledge of both back to the knowledge of the Holy Child Jesus, and the Holy Man Jesus, as He was known to His mother, to James His brother, and to Peter His so intimate disciple. Paul went "back to Jesus," as the saying sometimes is; but when he went back he took back with him all the knowledge of the Son of God that he has put into his Epistles, ay, and much more than the readers of his Epistles were able to receive. And God's way with Paul is His best way with us also. You will never read the four Gospels with true intel-lectual understanding, and with true spiritual appreciation, till you have first read and understood and appreciated Paul's Epistles. But after you have had God's Son revealed in you by means of Paul's Epistles, you will then be prepared for all that Matthew and Mark and Luke and John have to tell you about the Word made flesh in their day. Paul's hand holds the true key to all the mysteries that are hid in the Prophets and in the Psalms and in the Gospels. Take back Paul with you, and all the prophecies and all the types of the Old Testament, and all the wonderful works of God in the New Testament—His Son's sinless conception, His miracles, His teaching and preaching, His agony in the garden, His death on the Cross, and His resurrection and ascension—will all fall into their natural and necessary places. It is in the very same order in which the great things of God were revealed to Paul, and apprehended by Paul, that they will best be revealed to us, and best appre-hended by us. First our conversion; and then the Pauline, Patristic, and Puritan doctrine of the Son of God; and then all that taken back by us to the earthly life of our Blessed Lord as it is told to us by the four Evangelists. Damascus, Arabia, Jerusalem—this, in our day also, is the God-guided progress, in which the true successors of the Apostle Paul are still travelling, in their spiritual experience, and in their evangelical scholarship.

111
Paul as a Preacher

WHEN it pleased God to reveal the cross of Christ in Paul, from that day the cross of Christ was Paul's special, peculiar, and exclusive Gospel. The cross of Christ is "my gospel," Paul proudly and constantly claims, in the face of all comers. The cross of Christ, he declares, is the one and the only Gospel that he preaches, that he always preaches, and that he alone preaches. The cross of Christ was profitable to Paul for doctrine, for reproof, for correction, and for instruction in righteousness: and nothing else was of any real interest or any real profit to Paul. The cross of Christ was the alpha and the omega, the beginning, and the middle, and the end, of all Paul's preaching. Paul drew all his doctrines, and all his instructions, and all his reproofs, out of the cross of Christ. He drew his profound and poignant doctrines of the sinfulness of sin, and the consequent misery of man, out of the cross of Christ. He saw and he felt all that in himself, and in the whole world; but the cross of Christ gave a new profundity, and a new poignancy, to all that to him. He drew his incomparably magnificent doctrines of the grace of God and the love of Christ out of the cross of Christ: those doctrines of his in the preaching of which he bursts out into such rapturous doxologies. The whole of the life of faith also, in all its manifoldness, and in all its universalness, and his own full assurance of everlasting life—all that, and much more than all that, Paul, by his splendid genius, and it all so splendidly sanctified and inspired, drew out of the cross of Christ. Take away the cross of Christ from Paul, and he is as weak as any other man. Paul has nothing left to preach if you take away from him the cross of Christ. His mouth is shut. His pulpit is in ruins. His arm is broken. He is of all men most miserable. But let God reveal the cross of Christ in Paul, and, straightway, he can both do, and endure, all things. Paul is henceforth debtor both to the Greeks and to the Barbarians; both to the wise, and to the unwise. Once reveal the cross of Christ in Paul, and you thereby lay a life-long necessity upon him. Yea, woe is unto him, ever after, if he preaches not the Gospel of the cross of Christ.

We preach not ourselves, Paul asserts with a good conscience in another sermon of his. And yet, at the same time, he introduces himself into almost every sermon he preaches. Paul simply cannot preach the cross of Christ as he must preach it, without boldly bringing himself in, as both the best pattern and the best proof of what the cross of Christ can do. Paul's salvation—the absolute graciousness of Paul's salvation, and his absolute assurance of it—these things are the infallible marks of their authenticity that Paul prints upon every Epistle of his. The cross of Christ, and Paul's salvation by that cross, are the two constant, and complementary, topics of Paul's pulpit; they are but the two sides of Paul's shield of salvation. The most beautiful English preacher of the past generation has told us that his conversion was so absorbing and so abiding that it made him rest ever after in the thought of two, and two only absolute and luminously self-evident beings, himself and his Creator. And so it was with Paul's conversion also. Only, in Paul's case it was not so much his Creator who was so luminously self-evident to Paul, it was much more his Redeemer. And thus it was that in Paul's preaching there were always present those two luminously self-evident subjects, Paul's sin and Christ's cross: Paul the chief of sinners, and Jesus Christ and Him crucified. And thus it is that Paul's so profound, and so experimental, preaching so satisfies us. And thus it is also that it alone satisfies us. When we are pining away under some secret disease if our physician comes and mocks at all our misery; if he treats our mortal wound as all imagination; if he rebukes and abuses us as if it were all so much melancholy—our hearts know their own bitterness. But if we fall into the hands of a wise man and a sound and skillful physician, he at once takes in the whole seriousness of our case. Before we have opened our mouth about ourselves, he has already laid his hand on our hurt, and has said to us—Thou art ill to death indeed. Thy whole head is sick and thy whole heart faint. And already we feel that there is hope. At any rate, we are not to die under the folly of a charlatan. And Paul is the furthest of all our physicians from a charlatan. Paul rips open all the dark secrets of our consciences, and all the hidden rottennesses of our hearts, till he is the one preacher of all preachers for us. And his the Gospel of all Gospels. At any rate, speaking for myself, as often as my own sin and misery, impossible to be told, again close in upon me till my broken heart cries out, Oh, wretchedest of men that I am! Paul is instantly at my bedside with the cross of Christ, and with his own case told to me to fetch back my life to me. Paul's prescription, as the physicians call it, never fails me. Never. As often as seventy times seven, every mortal day of mine, the amazement and the misery of my sinfulness overwhelms me, Paul no sooner sets forth to me Jesus Christ and Him crucified, than a great light falls on my amazement, and a great alleviation on my misery. It is a dark light. It is a dreadful light. It is a light like a drawn sword. But it *is* light, where no other light from heaven, or from earth, could give a ray of light to me. At the cross, before the cross, under the cross, upon the cross, I am reconciled to God, and God is reconciled to me. I am reconciled to you also, and you to me. All the hand-writings in heaven and earth and hell, that were so bitter against me, are all blotted out by His blood. All my injustices to you, all my injuries, all my animosities, antipathies, alienations, retaliations, distastes, and dislikes, all are rooted up out of my heart by the cross of Christ. For I am slain to myself because of the cross of Christ. The one and only cause of all my unspeakable sinfulness and misery—myself; I, myself, am slain to death for ever by the cross of Christ. My self-love, my self-will, my self-seeking, my self-pleasing; they are all slain; or what is as good they have got their sure deathblow by the cross of Christ. I am crucified with Christ: nevertheless I live; yet not I, but Christ liveth in me: and the life which I now live in the flesh, I live by the faith of the Son of God, who loved me, and gave Himself for me.

He alone is a "right divine" who can preach this faith of the Son of God properly, says Luther. He is a "right preacher" who can distinguish, first to himself, and then to his people, faith from the law, and grace from works, says the Reformer. Now Paul was a right divine and he was the first father and forerunner of all such. And never more so than when he is putting forth all his stupendous power to preach that divinest doctrine of his, that our best obedience, if offered in the very

least measure for our salvation, is a complete abandonment, and a fatal denial of
the cross of Christ. Some men will start up at that, and will protest at it, and debate
against it. So did Paul as long as he was still alive, and kept the clothes of them
that stoned Stephen. And so did I for a long time. But now that greatest and best
of all Paul's doctrines of grace, as often as I come on it in its bud in Abraham, and
in its full flower and fruit in Paul and in Luther, it makes my heart to sing and dance
within me. And it comes to me from the God of my salvation a thousand times every
day. Why was that blessed doctrine so long in being preached by some right divine
to me? Why was I, myself, so long in learning and in preaching this first principle of
the doctrine of Christ? And why do I go back so often, to this day, to Moses and to
myself? I have a desire to depart and to be with Christ, says Paul to the Philippians.
And so have I. But, before God, I lie not. He is my witness, that I beseech Him every
day about this very matter, and about little besides. I beseech Him every hour of
the day, that I may be spared for some more years yet, in order that I may grow, as I
have never yet grown, into this selfsame faith of the Son of God. Into the faith that
justifies the ungodly, and sanctifies the sinful, and brings love, and peace, and joy,
and hope, and full assurance of everlasting life, to my soul. And to preach all that
as I have never yet preached it: and, then, you would perhaps take my epitaph out
of Luther on the Galatians, and would write this sentence over me—"Come, and
see, all ye that pass by, for here lies a right divine." Why is it that this epitaph is so
seldom to be read in any of our churchyards over our ministers? Why are there so
few divines so right in Scotland as to satisfy Paul and Luther? Why are there so few
of our young preachers who make Paul's determination, and stand to it? As often
as I think of this great determination of his, I always remember Hooker's immortal
sermon on Justification. Hooker, in this matter at any rate, was a right Pauline and
Lutheran divine. And what does that master in Israel, and that equal master of an
English style, say to us on this point? Every preacher of Christ, and of faith in the
cross of Christ, should have this passage printed indelibly on his heart.

> Christ hath merited righteousness for as many as are found in Him. And in
> Him God findeth us, if we be faithful; for by faith we are incorporated into
> Him. Then, although we be in ourselves altogether sinful and unrighteous,
> yet even the man who is in himself impious, full of iniquity, full of sin; him
> being found in Christ through faith, and having his sin in hatred through
> repentance, him God beholdeth with a gracious eye; putteth away his sin by
> not imputing it; taketh quite away the punishment due thereunto, by par-
> doning it; and accepteth him in Christ Jesus, as perfectly righteous, as if he
> had fulfilled all that is commanded him in the law; shall I say more perfectly
> righteous than if himself had fulfilled the whole law? I must take heed what I
> say, but the apostle saith, "God made Him to be sin for us, who knew no sin,
> that we might be made the righteousness of God in Him." Such we are in the
> sight of God the Father, as is the very Son of God Himself. Let it be counted
> folly, or phrensy, or fury, or whatsoever. It is our wisdom, and our comfort:
> we care for no knowledge in the world but this, that man hath sinned, and
> God hath suffered: that God hath made Himself the sin of men, and that
> men are made the righteousness of God.

112

Paul as a Pastor

IN his painstaking industry for Theophilus and for us, Luke has provided us with an extract-minute, so to call it, copied out of the session-books of Ephesus. Paul had been the minister and the moderator of the kirk-session of Ephesus for three never-to-be-forgotten years. But he has now for some time past been away preaching the Gospel and planting Churches elsewhere, and another elder of experience and of authority has all that time sat in the Ephesian chair that the Apostle used to occupy with such authority and acceptance. But Paul is now coming near the end of his life. He knows that, and he has a great longing, and a most natural longing it is, to see his old colleagues in Ephesus once more before he goes to be with Christ. And thus it is that at his special request an *in hunc effectum* meeting of kirk-session has been called, an extract-minute of which is to be read by the curious to this day in the twentieth chapter of the Acts of the Apostles. Now from this priceless little paper of Luke's we learn that, the session being constituted, Paul immediately took occasion to review those long past three years that he had spent in their city, and had sat at the head of their court. Paul had given three of the best years of his life to Ephesus, and it was only natural that he should take occasion to go over those three years and look at some of the lessons that those three years had left behind them, both for himself and for his successors in the eldership of Ephesus. And it is just those fine lessons that this first of Church-historians, with such an admirable literary instinct, and with such sanctified industry, has here supplied us with. Paul never spoke better. Paul simply excels himself. There is all that stateliness that never forsakes Paul. There is all that majesty that Paul bears about with him at all times and into all places. All united to a humility, and an intimacy, and a confidingness, that always carry captive to Paul the hearts of all men who have hearts. Paul is simply unapproachable in a scene like this. Paul has no equal and no second in the matters and the manners of the heart. Paul is almost his Master over again in these matters and manners of the heart, so much so, that when it was all over, we do not wonder that they all wept sore, and fell on Paul's neck, and kissed him, sorrowing most of all for the words which he spake, that they should see his face no more. In no other single passage in all Paul's Life by Luke, or in all his own Epistles even, do we see the finished friend and the perfect pastor as in this sederunt, so to call it, of the kirk-session of Ephesus. This sederunt, and this extract-minute of it, is a very glass in which every minister and every elder may to this day see themselves, and what manner of minister and what manner of elder they are, and are not.

"Serving the Lord," says Paul about those three years. And Paul always begins with that same thing. He begins every sermon of his, and every Epistle of his, with serving the Lord. I, Paul, the servant of the Lord, is his salutation and seal in every Epistle of his. And hence his stateliness, and hence his high seriousness, and hence his unparalleled humility, and hence his overpowering authority, and hence his whole, otherwise unaccountable, life, pastoral and all. No: the elders of Ephesus did not need to be reminded that Paul had not spent those three years serving and satisfying them. They got splendid service out of Paul, both for themselves and for their families, but all that was because Paul did not think of them at all, but only of his Master. There was a colossal pride in Paul, and at the same time a prostrate humility, such that they had never seen anything like it in any other man; a submissiveness and a self-surrender to all men, such that, as those three years went on, taught to all the teachable men among them far more for their own character and conduct than all his inspired preaching. If Paul had both forgiven and forgotten those unfortunate misunderstandings and self-assertions that will come up among the very best ministers and elders, they had not forgiven or forgotten themselves for those days, or for their part in them. And thus it was that when Paul said these words:—"Serving the Lord," those who had known Paul best were the first to say that it was all true. Now that it was all long past, they all saw and admitted to themselves, and to one another, how in this disputed matter and in that, Paul had neither served himself, nor them, but the Lord only.

We do not at first sight see exactly why Paul should be so sore, and so sensitive, and so full of such scrupulosity, about money matters. But he had only too good cause to say all he said, and do all he did, in that root-of-all-evil matter. It was one of the many most abominable slanders that his sordid-hearted enemies circulated against Paul, that, all the time, he was feathering his own nest. He is collecting money, they said, from all his so-called Churches, and is stealthily laying up a fortune for himself and for his family in Tarsus and Jerusalem. You all know how certain scandals follow eminent and successful men as its shadow follows a solid substance. We are ashamed, down to this day, to see Paul compelled to defend his apostleship and himself from such tongues and such pens; from such whisperers and such backbiters. And yet, no. We would not have lost such outbursts as this for anything, or we would never have known Paul, or have loved him, or have believed in him and in his gospel, as we do, had we not been present at that table beside those men who had seen Paul with all their eyes day and night for three years. I defy you! he exclaimed, as he stood up in indignation and held out his callid hands—I defy you to deny it. I have coveted no man's silver, or gold, or apparel. Yea, ye yourselves know that these hands—and as he held them up, the assembled elders saw a tongue of truth in every seam and scar that covered them—these hands have ministered to all my own necessities, and to them that were with me. Noble hands of a noble heart!

Had his apostolic stipend been in their power to reduce it or to increase it; had a fund for his old age, or a legacy for his sister and her son been at all in Paul's mind; then, in that case, he might have been tempted to keep back some things in his preaching, and to put some other things forward. At the same time, though considerations of money had nothing at all to do with it, some other matters undoubtedly had to do with it. To me it is as clear as anything can be, that the apostle had been tempted, and even commanded, by those very men sitting there, to keep back some things out of his preaching that he was wont to bring forward into it.

Paul would never have said what he did say at that heart-melting moment, and he would never have said it with the heart-melting emphasis he did say it, unless be had been speaking straight to the point. It was all long past now. He would never again either please or displease any of those elders, or any of their wives or children any more. And thus it is that he so returns upon his past temptations, and with a good conscience toward the truth, tells them that they may safely take all he had ever taught them and build upon it; for he had neither kept back anything that had been committed to his ministry among them, nor, on the other hand, had he added anything of his own to it. I kept back nothing that was profitable to you. I shunned not to declare to you the whole counsel of God. In that also there is a glass held up for all ministers and all congregations in which to see and to examine both themselves, and all their past and fast-passing relations to one another, both in the pulpit and in the pew.

"And with all humility of mind." Evangelical humility, as Jonathan Edwards so splendidly treats it, lay deep down like a foundation-stone under all Paul's attainments as a saint of God and as an apostle of Jesus Christ. Paul's Master had taken the proper precautions at the beginning of Paul's apostleship that he should be all through it, and down to the end of it, the humblest man in all the world. By that terrible thorn in his flesh; by a conscience full of the most remorseful memories; as well as by incessant trials and persecutions and sufferings of all conceivable kinds, Paul was made and was kept the humblest of all humble men. As all our preachers and pastors still are, or ought to be. For they too have each their own thorn in their own flesh, their own crook in their own lot, their own sword of God in their own heart and conscience. If it were nothing else, their daily work is the most humiliating and heart-breaking work in all the world. All other callings may be accomplished and laid down; may reward and may bring pride to those who follow them with all their might; but never in this world the Christian ministry. And not his defeats and disappointments among his people only; but still more, the things in a minister himself that account for and justify all those defeats and disappointments—all that makes his whole ministry to collapse, and to fall in on his heart continually, like a house that has been built on the sand. Till, whatever other gifts and graces a minister may be lacking in, it is impossible for him to lack humility. With all humility of mind, says Paul to the assembled elders of Ephesus. Humility of all kinds, he means; and drawn out of all experiences; and shown to all sorts of people. Till, both for a garment of office, and for a grace of character, a minister is clothed from head to foot with spiritual and evangelical humility.

"And from house to house warning every one night and day with tears." The whole of Ephesus was Paul's parish. And, not once in a whole year, like the most diligent of us, but every day, and back again every night, Paul was in every house. Paul was never in his bed. He did not take time so much as to eat. As his people in Anwoth said about Samuel Rutherford, Paul was always working with his hands, always working with his mind, always preaching, always visiting. "At all seasons" are Paul's own enviable words. At marriages, at baptisms, at feasts, at funerals, at the baths, and in the marketplaces. Now down in an old woman's cellar, and now up in a poor student's garret. Some men find time for everything. They seem to be able to manufacture time just as they need it. The sun and the moon and the stars all stand still in order that some men may get sufficient time to finish their work. It is for such men that sun and moon are created, and are kept in their places; they take their ordinances from such men, and from the Taskmaster of such men. Paul, I suppose, is the only minister that ever lived who could have read Richard Baxter's *Reformed Pastor* without going mad with remorse, and with a fearful looking for of judgment. "Another part is to have a special care of each member of our flock. We must labor to be acquainted with all our people. To know all their inclinations and conversation: for if we know not the temperament or the disease, we are likely to prove but unsuccessful physicians. A minister is not only for public preaching. One word of seasonable and prudent advice will do that good that many sermons will not do. See that they have some profitable moving book besides the Bible in each family; and if they have not, persuade them to buy some small piece of great use. If they be not able to buy them, give them some. If you cannot, get some gentleman, or other rich man that are willing to do good, to do it. Another part lieth in visiting the sick, and in helping them to prepare either for a more fruitful life, or for a happy death." There are few things in ministerial history that make my heart bleed like the tragedy of Jonathan Edwards' breach with his congregation, and then his banishment from his congregation. And I never can get over it that, in spite of all else, had Edwards been a pastor like Paul, that terrible shipwreck could never have taken place. And, yet, I must frankly confess, that explanation does not satisfy every case, even in my own experience. For some of the best pastors I have ever known, have been the victims of the cruellest and most heartless treachery and ingratitude, and that from some of their most pampered people.

Even the Apostle Peter makes the confession that he had found some things in Paul's Epistles hard to be understood. And so have I. And not in the Romans and the Colossians only, but almost more in this kirk-session speech of his. I can understand him, even if I cannot compete with him, in his incomparable pulpit and pastoral work. I myself go about, in a way, preaching repentance toward God, and faith toward our Lord Jesus Christ. But after I am like to drop with my work; and most of all with the arrears of it; Paul absolutely prostrates me, and tramples me to death, when he stands up among his elders and deacons and says: "I take you to record this day that I am pure from the blood of all men!" I do not find his rapture into the third heavens hard to be understood, nor his revelations and inspirations, nor his thorn in the flesh, nor any of his doctrines of Adam, or of Christ, or of election, or of justification, or of sanctification, or of the final perseverance of the saints. It is none of all these things that I am tempted to wrest. But it absolutely passes my imagination how a horny-handed tentmaker, with twelve hours in his day, or make it eighteen, and with seven days in his week; a mortal man, and as yet an unglorified, and indeed, far from sanctified man, could look all his elders, and all their wives, and all their sons and daughters in the face, and could say those terrible words about their blood. Jesus Christ, who finished the work given Him to do, never said more than that. The only thing that ever I heard to come near that was when a Highland minister was leaving his parish, and said from the pulpit in his farewell sermon, that he took all his people to witness that he had spoken, not only from the pulpit, but personally, and in private, to every single one of his people about the state of their souls. Altogether, Paul was such a preacher, and such a pastor, and such a saint, that I cannot blame them for thinking in those days that he must be nothing less than the Holy Ghost Himself, who had been promised by Christ for to come. Such was Paul's character, and such was his work, and such was his success, both as a preacher and a pastor.

With all that, and after all that is said, I am still dazzled and absolutely fascinated with Paul's pastoral work. I cannot get Paul's pastoral work out of my mind. I cannot get it out of my imagination. I cannot get it out of my conscience. I cannot get it out of my heart. Above all his discoveries, when Professor Ramsay goes east to dig for Paul in Ephesus, I would like him to be able to disinter Paul's pastoral-visitation book. And with it the key to those cipher and shorthand entries about what he said and what he did in this house and in that, and day and night with tears. The hours he gave to it, his division of the day and of the night, the Psalms he read and opened up from house to house, the houses that made him weep, and the houses that sent him back to his tent-making singing. Did Paul make it a rule to read, and expound, and pray, in every house, and on every visit? Did he send word by the deacon of the district that he was coming? Or did he just, in our disorderly way, start off and drop in here and there as this case and that came up into his overcrowded mind? Till the learned Professor comes upon Paul's private note-book, for myself I will continue to interpret Paul's farewell address to the kirk-session of Ephesus with some liberality. Paul does not really mean me to understand that he was always weeping, and always catechizing, and always expounding, and always on his knees in the houses of Ephesus. No; Paul was Paul in all parts of his pastoral work, as well as in everything else. Paul is the last speaker to interpret in a wooden way, far less in a cast-iron way. Paul, you may depend upon it, was quite content some days just to have waved his hand in at that window, and to have saluted this and that man in the street, and to have been saluted in return by this and that gentlemanly little school-boy with his satchel on his back. Paul would often drop in, as we say, not indeed to curse the weather, and to canvass the approaching marriages, like William Law's minister, but, all the same, to rejoice with the bridegroom and the bride, and to set down their exact date in his diary, so as to be sure to be on the spot in good time, and in his best attire. If you are a pastor, and if your visits up and down among your people help to keep your and their friendships in repair; to re-kindle and to fan the smoking flax of brotherly love; if your visits operate to the cementing and the stability of the congregation; then, that is already more than one-half of the whole end of your ministry, both pulpit and pastoral, accomplished. And, with all your preaching, and with all your pastoral work performed like Paul's, in intention and in industry at least, you also will surely be able, with great humility as well as with great assurance of faith, to bid your people goodbye, and your kirk-session, saying—And now, brethren, I commend you to God, and to the word of His grace, which is able to build you up, and to give you an inheritance among all them which are sanctified.

113
Paul as a Controversialist

"WOE is me, my mother, that thou hast borne me a man of strife and contention to the whole earth," complained the sorrowful prophet. And the Apostle now before us might have made that very same complaint, and with much more cause. For Paul, from the beginning to the end of his apostleship, was simply plunged into a perfect whirlpool of all kinds of contention and controversy. Wherever Paul was sent to preach, north, south, east, and west, thither his persecutors pursued him. Till, what Jeremiah exclaimed somewhat passionately and somewhat hyperbolically concerning himself, became literally true in the case of Paul. For Paul, without any exaggeration, was made nothing less than a man of strife and of contention to the whole earth.

But, then, this is always to be kept in mind, that Paul had a splendid equipment, both by nature and by grace, for his unparalleled life of apostolic controversy. Paul started out to face that life of temptation, as nearly crucified and completely stone-dead to himself, as any man can ever hope to be in this mortal life. It is our incurable self-love that is the bitter root of all our controversies, whether those controversies are carried on by the tongue, or by the pen, or by the sword. Once slay our incurable self-love, and once plant in its place the love of God and the love of our neighbor, and you have already as good as beaten our swords into plowshares and our spears into pruning-hooks. It is our self-idolatry and our self-aggrandizement; it is our greed, and our pride, and our intolerance, and our contempt and scorn of all other men, that is the one and only cause of all our contentions and controversies. Now, look at Paul. You cannot read Paul's Epistles without being constantly captivated with the extraordinary geniality, courtesy, humility, simplicity, and loving-kindness, of Paul. The Apostle Paul, it has been said at the cost of a certain anachronism and anomaly of speech, was the finest gentleman that ever lived. And if we take both the etymology, and the old English usage of that term, then it may quite well be let stand as a most succinct and a most expressive description of the Apostle's character. Coleridge says that while Luther was by no means so perfect a gentleman as Paul, yet the Reformer was almost as great a man of genius. And Luther gives us a taste both of his own genius and of his own gentlemanliness also, in what he says so often about Paul. Luther is always saying such things as these about Paul. "Paul was gentle, and tractable, and makeable, in his whole life. Paul was sweet, and mild, and courteous, and soft-spoken. Paul could wink at other men's faults and failings, or else expound them to the best. Paul could be well contented to yield up his own way, and to give place and honor to all other men; even to the froward and the intractable. In short, Paul's unfailing gentlemanliness is his constant character in all the emergencies of his extraordinary life." So speaks of Paul one of the most Paul-like men of the modern world. And an English gentleman, if ever there was one, has said of Paul in more than one inimitable sermon: "There is not one of any of those refinements and delicacies of feeling, that are the result of advanced civilization, nor any one of those proprieties and embellishments of conduct in which the cultivated intellect delights, but Paul is a pattern of it. And that in the midst of an assemblage of other supernatural excellences which is the characteristic endowment of apostles and saints."

Now, all that arose, to begin with, out of Paul's finely compounded character by birth. After Mary, Paul's mother must surely have been the most blessed of women. And then after his birth in Tarsus there was his better birth from above. And then, with all that, there was the lifelong schooling that Paul put himself through, amid the endless trials and temptations, contentions and controversies, of his apostolic life. By all these remarkable, and indeed unparalleled, means, Paul came more and more to be of that unequalled grace of fellow-feeling with all other men, and that noble temper of accommodation and adaptation to all other men, in which he stands out and unrivalled at the head of all the saints of God. Unrivalled. For no sooner has Paul come into the same room with you, than, that moment, you feel a spell come over you. You do not know what it is exactly that has come over you, but you feel sweetened, and strengthened, and happy. It is Paul. You have never been in Paul's presence before, and therefore your present feelings are so new to you. For all the time you are together: all the time that he talks with you, and writes to you, and even debates and contends with you, Paul sees everything with your eyes, and hears everything with your ears, and feels everything with your feelings. It was this that so carried all men off their feet with Paul. It was this that made Paul such a preacher, and such a pastor, and such a friend, ay, and such an enemy. You could not have resisted Paul. You could not have shut Paul out of your heart, with all your prejudices at him, and with all your determination never to like him, and never to give in to him. Something like what Jesus Christ was to Paul, that Paul was to all men. You could not but give yourself up to Paul, he so gave himself up to you. Origen tells us that there were some men in the early church so carried captive by the Apostle that they actually believed Paul to be the indwelling Comforter Himself come in the flesh, and come into their hearts. And Origen confesses to having had a certain fellow-feeling with those heretics.

Now, my brethren, to come in all this to ourselves. For, here also, it is the old story, let a man examine himself. Well, Paul was born a gentleman already. Now, if you have not been so born, yet I have heard it said that grace will make the most unlikely of men a gentleman. I do not deny that; only, I must say I have never known a case of it. Tertullian has a saying to the effect that some men are as good as Christian men already, just by their birth of their mother. Now Paul was one of those happy men. Paul was born with a big and a tender heart, and divine grace had all that done to her hand beforehand in Paul. Persecutor and all, there was, all the time, the making of the most perfect Christian gentleman in all Christendom in Paul. Now, you will sometimes meet with men of Paul's noble begetting and noble breeding among ourselves. Not very often indeed, but sometimes. God has not left Himself wholly without a witness, even among ourselves. Men you cannot pick a quarrel with even when you try. Men you always get your own way with them. Men you always get a soft look and a soft answer from them. Men who, when you are a churl to them, are all the more gentlemanly to you. Men to whom you may be as self-opinioned and self-willed as you like, but it takes two to make a quarrel; and, after all, you are only one. Now, if any of you have any of that rare original in you, bless God for it every day, and bless all men round about you with it every day. For there is no greater blessing to men and glory to God in all this self-enclosed and alienated life. But, on the other hand, if you are not naturally a Christian gentleman, and yet truly wish to be such, then, know this, that God has surpassed Himself in fitting up and fitting out this present life for your trans-formation from what you are to what you wish to be. I did not say that the Holy Ghost could not make you, and make you behave like, a Christian gentleman, both at home and abroad. I took care what I said. I only said that I had not yet made your acquaintance.

Have you ever read that completely overlaid English classic, Paley's *Horae Pau-linae?* In that incomparable specimen of reasoning the Archdeacon has a fine expression and a fine passage on Paul's "accommodating conduct." And that mas-ter of the pen has given us in that epithet a characteristically happy description of the apostle. For everybody who has read about Paul at all, knows this about him, that some of the greatest sufferings of his life sprang to him just out of his far too nobly accommodating conduct. Paul cast his pearls before swine. Paul's sweet and beautiful yieldingness in every matter that touched his own opinions or his own practices, taken along with his iron will in what was not his own; these two things must be taken together to know Paul. Luther, that evangelical genius almost equal to Paul himself, hits the whole matter here in a way that would have delighted Paul. "If two goats meet each other in a narrow path above a piece of water, what do they do?" asks Luther. "They cannot turn back, and they cannot pass each other; there is not an inch of spare room. If they were to butt at each other, both would fall into the water below and would be drowned. What then will they do, do you suppose? What would you do? Well, Nature has taught the one goat to lie down and let the other pass over it, and then they both get to the end of the day safe and sound." Now, Paul was always meeting goats on narrow ledges of rock with the sea below. And so are you, and so am I. And God ordains to you and to me our meeting one another in this strait gate and on that narrow way, and right below us is the bottomless pit. Will you lie down and let me pass over your prostrate body, and then we shall both be saved?

"Above all things the servant of the Lord must not strive." So said the aged Apostle to Timothy, doing his best to put an old head on young shoulders. And I suppose every old minister who has learned anything in the school of life would say the same thing, to every young minister especially. Do not debate, said the greatest debater of his day, and one of the most masterly debaters in all literature. On no account, he said, enter into any dispute with any one, and especially about the truths of salvation. Give to all men every help to their salvation, but that of debating with them about it. And, according to my experience, William Law is wholly right. Far better let a man be demonstrably wrong in this and that opinion of his, than attempt to contradict and debate him out of it. You cannot do it. Far better a man be demonstrably ignorant in this and that even not unimportant matter, than that he be angry at you, and resentful at you, all his days, as nine out of every ten corrected and contradicted men will certainly be. You will never set a man's opinion right if you begin by hurting his pride and crossing his temper. Cross a sinner and you will have a devil, said Thomas Shepard. That may be a little too strong, but few men are angels exactly for some time after they are crossed, and contradicted, and corrected. They are joined to their idol, let them alone. Oh, but you say, So-and-so will not leave you alone. Well, my argument is not that, but this. Let you him alone. "They say. What do they say? Let them say." Do not you even say so much as Paul said. Do not say that their judgment is just. Santa Teresa is not one of the ladies of our Scottish covenant, but this is what she says on the matter in hand: "The not excusing of ourselves is a perfect quality, and of great merit. It is a mark of the deepest and truest humility to see ourselves condemned without cause, and to be silent under it. It is a very noble imitation of our Lord. What about being blamed by all men, if only we stand at the last blameless before Thee!"

"Doing nothing by prejudice or by partiality," says the apostle, still insisting on this same matter. Now, to be absolutely free of prejudice and partiality is, I fear, not possible to any one of us in this life. But we must both learn, and labor, and pray, to be delivered from the dominion of those wicked tempers, as much as may be. This passage is five-and-twenty centuries old, but it might have been written in London or Edinburgh yesterday. "No assurances, no pledges of either party, could gain credit with the other. The most reasonable proposals, coming from an opponent were received, not with candor, but with suspicion. No artifice was reckoned dishonorable by which a point could be carried. Every recommendation of moderate measures was reckoned either a mark of cowardice or of insincerity. He only was considered a completely safe man whose violence was blind and boundless; and those who endeavored to steer a middle course were spared by neither side." We could all set the names of living men, ay, and of Christian men too, over against every line of that terrible indictment. But the design of the great historian in publishing that passage, as well as my design in preaching it, is to set before you and before myself, in every possible way, the mischief and the shame of such a state of things. And to determine, God helping us, to purge our hearts of all prejudice and partiality. The best political and literary journal ever published in this country, for many years held up a statesman of the last generation as a paragon of every public virtue and every personal grace. All that was noble, all that was grand and stately, all that was truly Christian, met in that minister of the Crown. But a crisis came when that hitherto peerless statesman saw it to be his duty to take a certain step in public life. And from that fatal day, nothing he ever said or did was right. Everything in him, and everything in his party, was as bad as bad could be. All who spoke against him in Parliament, or on the platform, or in the press, were so many Burkes come back to life. Eloquent, statesmanlike, unanswerable, were but three of the eulogistic epithets we read in every article. While, if any writer or speaker had a single word to say for that fallen idol and for his policy, they were either rogues or fools. It was a weekly lesson. And not a few of us learned the lesson. Indeed it was written so large that no one could miss learning it. It was as if it had been printed at the head of every page—All you who would see prejudice and partiality, read what is written below. Speaking on this whole matter for myself, I owe a great debt to the conductors of that journal, and to Butler, and to Bengel. To Butler every day for that great saying of his—"Let us remember that we differ as much from other men as they differ from us." And to Bengel for this—*non sine scientia, necessitate, amore*: enter upon no controversy without knowledge, nor without necessity, nor without love.

114
Paul as a Man of Prayer

INTELLECTUALLY as well as spiritually, as a theologian as well as a saint, Paul is at his very best in his prayers. The full majesty of the Apostle's magnificent mind is revealed to us nowhere as in his prayers. After Paul has carried his most believing and his most adoring readers as high as they are able to rise, Paul himself still rises higher and higher in his prayers. Paul leaves the most seraphic of saints far below him as he soars away up into the third heaven of rapture, and revelation, and adoration. Paul is caught up so high into paradise in his prayers, that when he returns back into the body, he is not able to tell the half of the things that he has seen and heard in the presence of God. A great theologian, who is also a great devotional writer, has warned his readers against the dangers of an untheological devotion. Now, Paul's great prayers and great praises are the best examples possible of a devotion that is theological and Christological to the core. In the Ephesians and the Colossians especially, Paul's adoration flames up to heaven like the ascending incense of a great altar-fire. Paul's adorations in those two superb epistles especially reveal to us, as nothing else of Paul's composition reveals to us, the full intellectual strength, and the full spiritual splendor, of Paul's sanctified understanding. And then those unapproached adorations of his prove this also, that the Apostle's wonderful mind has found its predestined sphere and its sufficient scope in New Testament Theology, and especially in New Testament Christology. There may have been one or two as great intellects as Paul's in some of the surrounding dispensations of Paganism; but then those greatly gifted men had not Paul's privileges, opportunities, and outlets. God did not reveal His Son in those men. And thus it was that their fine minds never had full justice done to them in this life. But in Jesus Christ, and in Him ascended and glorified, Paul's profound mind had a boundless scope and a boundless satisfaction. The truth is, beyond the best adorations and doxologies of the Apostle Paul, the soul of man will never rise on this side the adorations and doxologies of the Beatific Vision itself.

Now my brethren, there is a lesson here of the very first importance and the very first fruitfulness to you and to me. And that lesson is this. Let us put our very profoundest Christology into our prayers. One reason why so many of our prayers, both in public and in private, are so dry, and so cold, and so full of repetition, is just because there is so little Christology in them; so little New Testament Scripture, that is. I do not mean that there is too little New Testament language in our prayers; but there is too little both Old and New Testament language meditated on, understood, believed, realized, and felt. There is too little Scripture substance, Scripture strength, Scripture depth, and Scripture height, in our prayers. It was this that led Dr. Thomas Goodwin, by far the princeliest preacher of the Puritan pulpit, to counsel the divinity students of Oxford to "thicken" both their devotions to God, and their exhortations to their people, with apostolic doctrine.

532

Now, even if you possess no students' books of apostolic doctrine, you possess the very Apostle himself in his Epistles, and I defy you to read his Epistles with the understanding and the heart, and not to be swept away, like their writer, into the most ecstatic and rapturous adoration. You will never be able to read in that way the doctrinal parts of the Romans, and the Ephesians, and the Colossians, or, indeed, any of Paul's Epistles, without being, now completely melted and broken, and now completely caught up into paradise, till you are a second Paul yourself. If your prayers hitherto have been a weariness to yourself, and to all men who have had to do with you, and to the Hearer of prayer Himself, get Paul's great Epistles well down into your understanding, and into your imagination, and into your heart henceforth, and out of your heart, and out of your mouth, there will flame up doxologies and adorations as seraphic and as acceptable as Paul's own doxologies and adorations in his greatest Epistles.

The absolute unceasingness also of Paul's prayers immensely impresses us. In his own well-known words about himself Paul was "praying always with all prayer and supplication in the spirit." Now that, read literally, may well look to us like the language of a man gone into absolute exaggeration and extravagance about prayer. But it is not so. All that was literally true of Paul. Paul confessed sin for himself, and he interceded for other men; he adored also and broke out into doxologies, literally without ceasing. Do you ever employ an horology in your devotional life? You will find an excellent specimen of that apparatus and assistance to unceasing prayer on page 155 of Oliphant's edition of Andrewes's *Private Devotions*. Now just as if he had an horological tablet like that page hung up, now on his workshop-wall, and now on his prison-wall, Paul prayed night and day, and all the hours of every night and of every day, without ceasing. Like the genuine horologist he was, Paul introduced every day of his life with praise and prayer. When I awake I am still with thee! he exclaimed as he awoke. He had fallen asleep last night full of praise and prayer, and in the morning he just began again where he had left off last night. As Augustine says, Paul brought the word to the water-bason every morning and every night and made it a sacrament. Wash me, he said, and I shall be whiter than snow. I put on His righteousness, he went on, and it clothed me, it was to me for a robe and for a diadem. Thy Word—he remembered this also out of Job as he broke his morning fast—is more to me than my necessary food. And then as the day went on, every instrument he took into his hands, and every product he put out of his hands, was oratorical to Paul. Like his divine Master, everything was to Paul another speaking parable of the Kingdom of Heaven. Everything to Paul was another call to prayer and praise. Till literally, and without any exaggeration or hyperbole whatsoever, Paul prayed and sang praises unceasingly. Until you are as old as Paul you will have no idea what a large liberty, what a rich variety, what an inexhaustible resource, and what a full range and reward, there is in prayer. What an outlet for your largest mind, and for your deepest heart, and for your richest and ripest individuality. Instead of the life of prayer being a monotony and a weariness, as we think it, there is simply no exercise of the body, and no operation of the mind, and no affection of the heart, for one moment to compare with prayer, for interest, and for variety, and for freshness, and for elasticity, and for all manner of intellectual and spiritual outlet and reward. I sometimes speak to you about Bishop Andrewes, and I do so because his *Private Devotions* is by far the best book of that kind in all the world. As also because it is never out of my own hand; and, naturally, I would like it never to be out of your hand either. And all that because Andrewes is a man after Paul's own heart, for the freshness, and for the fullness, and for the richness of his prayers. Andrewes has a Meditation for every day of the week, and an Adoration, and a Confession of faith, and a Confession of sin, and a Supplication, and an Intercession, and a Thanksgiving, with no end of Acts of Commendation, Acts of Deprecation, Acts of Pleading, and such like. And then he has an Horology, composed exclusively out of Holy Scripture, for every hour of the day and the night. And much more of the same kind besides. What a rich, fruitful, nobly intellectual, and nobly spiritual, life Paul secured to himself, just by his habits and his hours of meditation and prayer. As Andrewes also secured in his measure. And many more who have given themselves to prayer as Paul and Andrewes gave themselves. And just because, with all that, we will not learn to pray, what a wilderness we all make this life to be to ourselves, till we lie down weary of it, and die and are buried in it. Lord, teach us to pray!

Now, just as Paul prayed always and without ceasing, so will we, if we take Paul for our master in divinity and in devotion; and if, like Paul, we go on, in all that, to make Jesus Christ our continual atonement for our sins, and our continual sanctification from our sinfulness. If we know sin at all aright, and Christ at all aright, then this will be the proof that we do so—we will pray for pardon and for a holy heart, literally, without ceasing. How can any man cease, for a single moment, from repentance and prayer who has a heart full of sin in his bosom, and that heart beating out its sinfulness into his body and into his mind every moment of the day and the night? That man will never cease from prayer till he has ceased from sin, any more than Paul ceased. For, with that unceasingly sinful heart within him, there are so many men, and so many things, all around him, constantly exasperating his heart. You must all know that about yourselves. You are so beset with men whom you cannot meet in the street, or hear or see their very names, but you must surely, on the spot, flee to Christ to forgive, and heal, and hide you. Those men may never have hurt a hair of your head; they will never suspect what a temptation they are to you; but such is the rooted and ineradicable malice of your heart towards them, that, as long as you and they live in this world, you will have to pray for yourself and for them without ceasing. When you cease to pray for those men, you, that moment, begin again to sin against them; and that continually drives you back to the blood of Christ both for yourselves and for them. You will never acquit Paul of having gone extravagant, and of being beside himself about prayer, till you equal and exceed him in unceasing prayer, both for yourselves and for all men. And you will so exceed him when you take your exceedingly sinful heart in your hand, and hold it in your hand, watching its motions of sin, and its need of redemption, all the day. If it were possible, and, why, in the name of God, and of your immortal soul, should you not make it possible? If it were possible, I say, to take your private diary tomorrow, and to make a cross on the page for every time you have to flee from your own heart to the blood of Christ; and then to count up the number of the crosses at the end of the day—if you did that, "always," and "unceasing," would be the weakest words you could use about your sin and your repentance tomorrow night. On the midday street tomorrow you would stop to make those sad marks in your book, at your meals you would make them, at business, at calls, and in conversation with your wisest, and best, and least sin-provoking, friends. At your work, at your family worship, in your pew on Sabbath, at the Lord's table itself; and, if you were a minister, in your very pulpit. "Always" and "unceasing." Paul made no exception, and found no discharge from that war. And neither will you, till you see Paul, and share his place with him, so close to his and your Master's feet, that sin will not reach you. An horology for one day like that would make you at night read both Paul's doctrines and his doxologies as you never read them before.

And I will be bold, and particular, and personal, at this point, and will say one thing of the foremost importance to you and to myself—we must imitate Paul in this, and take far more *time* to prayer than we have ever yet taken. I am as certain as I am standing here, that the secret of much mischief to our own souls, and to the souls of others, lies in the way that we stint, and starve, and scamp our prayers, by hurrying over them. Prayer worth calling prayer: prayer that God will call true prayer and will treat as true prayer, takes far more time, by the clock, than one man in a thousand thinks. After all that the Holy Ghost has done to make true prayer independent of times, and of places, and of all kinds of instruments and assistances—as long as we remain in this unspiritual and undevotional world, we shall not succeed, to be called success, in prayer, without time, and times, and places, and other assistances in prayer. Take good care that you are not spiritual overmuch in the matter of prayer. Take good care lest you take your salvation far too softly, and far too cheaply. If you find your life of prayer to be always so short, and so easy, and so spiritual, as to be without cost and strain and sweat to you, you may depend upon it, you are not yet begun to pray. As sure as you sit there, and I stand here, it is just in this matter of *time* in prayer that so many of us are making shipwreck of our own souls, and of the souls of others. Were some of us shut up in prison like Paul, I believe we have grace enough to become in that sequestered life men of great and prevailing prayer. And, perhaps, when we are sufficiently old and set free from business, and are sick tired of spending our late nights eating and drinking and talking: when both the church and the world are sick tired of us and leave us alone and forget us, we, yet, short of Blackness or the Bass-rock, may find time for prayer, and may get back the years of prayer those canker-worms have eaten.

And now to come to the last and the best kind of all prayer and the crown and the finish of all Paul's prayer, intercessory prayer, namely. We have little else indeed of the prayer-kind drawn out into any length from Paul's pen but prayer for other people. If you were to collect together and tabulate by themselves all Paul's prayers of all kinds, as Dr. Pope has done in his golden book, you would find that they all come in under the head of salutations, or invocations, or benedictions: intercession, in short, of one kind or other; with, now and then, such a burst of doxology as cannot be classified except by itself. What a quiet conscience Paul must have had, and what a happy heart, in this matter of intercessory prayer, compared with the most of us. For, how many people, first and last, have asked us to pray to God for them, whom we have clean forgot. How many children, sick people, heart-broken people, has God laid on our hands, and we have never once brought them to His mercy-seat. How happy was Paul, and how happy were those churches who had Paul for their pastor. How happy to have been his fellow-elder in Ephesus, his physician, his son in the Gospel. Speaking of Paul's physician, I shall close with a few lines on this subject, out of the private papers of Sir Thomas Browne, a man of prayer, not unworthy to be named with the Apostle himself: "To pray in all places where quietness inviteth; in any house, highway, or street; and to know no street in this city that may not witness that I have not forgotten God and my Savior in it: and that no parish or town where I have been may not say the like. To take occasion of praying upon the sight of any church which I see, or pass by, as I ride about. To pray daily and particularly for my sick patients, and for all sick people under whose care soever. And, at the entrance into the house of the sick to say—the peace and the mercy of God be on this house. After a sermon to make a prayer and desire a blessing, and to pray for the minister. Upon the sight of beautiful persons to bless God for His creatures; to pray for the beauty of their souls, and that He would enrich them with inward grace to be answerable to the outward. Upon sight of deformed persons, to pray Him to send them inward graces, and to enrich their souls, and give them the beauty of the resurrection." Had Sir Thomas Browne lived in Paul's day the praying Apostle would have ranked him with Luke and would have called them his two beloved physicians.

Brethren, pray for me, said Paul. Pray for my soul, said Arthur also—

> Pray for my soul. More things are wrought by prayer
> Than this world dreams of. Wherefore let thy voice
> Rise like a fountain for me night and day.
> For what are men better than sheep or goats
> That nourish a blind life within the brain,
> If, knowing God, they lift not hands of prayer
> Both for themselves and those who call them friend?
> For so the whole round earth is, every way,
> Bound by gold chains, about the feet of God.

But that all-important matter of *time* comes back upon me, and will not let me go. Take *more time* to prayer, my brethren. Take one *hour* out of every twenty-four. Or, if you cannot spare an hour, take *half* an hour; or, if you would not know what to do or say for *half an hour*, take a *quarter of an hour*. Take from 8 to 9 every night, or from 9 to 10, or from 10 to 11, or *some part of that*. And, if you cannot fill up the time out of your own heart, take David, or Paul, or Andrewes, to assist you, and to show you how to pray in secret; for it is a rare, and a difficult, but an absolutely indispensable, art.

115
Paul as a Believing Man

THE extraordinary concentration of Paul's faith upon the Cross of Christ is by far the most arresting and impressive thing about Paul. It is in the way that Paul lets go everything else in order that he may rivet his faith upon the Cross of Christ alone—it is this that makes Paul our model and our master in this whole matter of the Cross of Christ. For the sake of the Cross of Christ Paul denies himself daily in many other of the great things of Christ. What splendid visions of Christ there are in Paul's magnificent Christology! What captivating and enthralling glimpses he gives us sometimes into the third heavens! But we are immediately summoned back from all that to be crucified with Christ. There is a time and there is a season for everything, says Paul. And I am determined, he says, that so far as I am concerned you shall know nothing in this life, at any rate, save Jesus Christ, and Him crucified. A great Pauline divine, the greatest indeed that I know, was wont to say that there are many things in our Lord far more wonderful and far more glorious than even His Cross. But Paul never says that. Or if he is ever carried away to say that, he instantly takes it back and says, God forbid that I should glory save in the Cross of Christ. Like the dove to its window, like the bird to its mountain, even after he has been caught up into the third heavens, Paul hastens back to the Cross of Christ. Once Paul is for ever with the Lord; once he is sat down finally with Christ in His kingdom; once he is at home in heaven, and not merely there on a short visit; once he is completely habituated to, and for ever secure in, glory, Paul will then, no doubt, have time and detachment to give to other things in Christ besides His Cross. And yet, I am not sure. At any rate, so long as Paul is in the flesh; so long as he is still carnal and sold under sin; so long as that messenger of Satan is still buffeting him, the Cross of Christ with its sin-atoning blood is the glory that excels all else in Christ to Paul. What grapples my own heart to Paul above all else is just the unparalleled concentration of Paul's experience, and of Paul's faith, and of Paul's preaching, upon the Cross of Christ.

Another thing in Paul's faith is the extraordinary way in which he identifies himself with Christ when Christ is upon His Cross. Christ and Paul become one sacrifice for sin on the Cross. Christ and Paul combine and coalesce and are united into one dying sinner on the accursed tree. It takes both Paul and Christ taken together to make up Christ crucified. Christ is apprehended, is accused, is condemned, and is crucified before God for Paul; and, then, Paul is crucified before God in, and along with, Christ. It is this transcendent identification of Christ with Paul and of Paul with Christ that the Apostle so labors, in the strength and in the style of the Holy Ghost, to set forth to us in his glorious doctrines of the suretyship and substitution of Christ, the imputation of Paul's guilt and pollution to Christ, and then the imputation of Christ's righteousness and the impartation of Christ's spirit to Paul. These great evangelical doctrines of Paul may be so divine and so deep that your heart does not yet respond to them. Paul's tremendously strong words about Christ and His Cross may stagger you, but that is because the law of God has not yet entered your heart. When it does, and when, after that, God reveals His Son in you, you will then become as Pauline in your theology and in its great language as Luther became himself. I can very well believe that Paul's so original, so powerful, and so cross-concentrated faith, staggers and angers some of you. It does not stagger and anger any of you half so much as at one time it both staggered and positively exasperated Paul himself. But now, he says, I am crucified with Christ: with Christ who loved me, and gave Himself for me. And once Paul's faith is in this way concentrated on the Cross of Christ: and once Paul is so identified with Christ crucified: everything in Paul's experience—past, present, and yet to come—all that only roots the deeper and the stronger Paul's faith in the Cross of Christ. I often recall the evidence that Admiral Dougall gave at the Tay Bridge inquiry as to the direction and the force of the winds that blow down the valley of the Tay. "Trees are not so well prepared to resist pressure from unusual quarters," said that observant witness. "A tree spreads out its roots in the direction of the prevailing wind." Now Paul's faith was like one of the Admiral's wind-facing trees. For Paul's faith continually spread out its roots in the direction of the coming storm. Only, the wind that compelled Paul's faith to spread out its roots around the Cross of Christ blew down from no range of earthly mountains. It was the overwhelming wind of God's wrath that rose with such fury upon Paul's conscience out of Paul's past life. The blasts of divine wrath that blew off the bleak sides of Sinai struck with such shocks against Paul's faith in Christ, that, like the trees on the wind-swept sides of the Tay, it became just by reason of that wind so rooted and grounded in Christ crucified, that however the rain might descend, and the floods come, and the winds blow and beat upon Paul's faith, it fell not, for it had struck its roots, with every new storm, deeper and deeper into the Cross of Christ.

Down suddenly out of the dark mountains of Paul's past life of sin, the most terrible tempests would, to the very end of his days, burst upon Paul. You must not idolise Paul. You must not totally misread and persistently misunderstand Paul, as if Paul had not been a man of like passions with yourselves. Paul was a far better believer than you or I are. But as to sin there is no difference. And the very greatness of Paul's faith; the very unparalleled concentration and identifying power of his faith; all that only made the sudden blasts that struck at his faith all the more terrible to bear. Oh, yes! you may depend upon it Paul had a thousand things behind him that swept down guilt and shame and sorrow upon his head to the day of his death. The men and the women and the children he had haled to prison; the holy homes he had desolated with his temple hordes; the martyrdoms he had instigated, the blood of which would never in this world be washed off his hands; in these, and in a thousand other things, Paul was a child of wrath even as others. And that wrath of God would awaken in his conscience, and would assault his faith, just as that same wrath of God assaults your faith and mine every day we live: if, that is to say, we live at all. No, there is no difference. The only difference is that Paul always met that rising wrath with a faith in Christ crucified that has never been equalled. "I, through the law," he said, or tried to say, every time the law clutched at him as its prisoner—"I through the law am dead to the law. For I am crucified with Christ." When the two thieves died on their two crosses on Calvary, ay and even after their dead bodies were burned to ashes in Gehenna, there would still come up to the courts of justice in Jerusalem, complaints and accusations against those two malefactors from all parts of the land. "He stole my ox." "He robbed my house." "He burned down my barn." "He murdered my son." But the judge would say to all such too-late accusations that the murderer was dead already. "He has been crucified already. He is beyond your accusations and my jurisdiction both. He has paid already with his life for all his deeds of robbery and of blood. His death has for ever blotted out all that can ever be spoken or written against him." And so it was with Paul. All his persecutions, and all his blasphemies, with all else of every evil kind that could come up out of his past life—it would all find Paul already a dead man. Paul is crucified. Paul has given up the ghost. Paul is for ever done with accusers and judges both: come up what will, leap into the light what will, it is all too late. A dead man is not easily put to shame, and no jailor carries a corpse to prison. Nay, Paul's case is far better than even that of the death-justified thieves. For, in Paul's case, two men are dead for one man's trangressions. And not two mere men, but one of them the very Son of God Himself. Truly the law is magnified and made honorable in Paul's case! Ten thousand times more honorable than if it had never been broken, since the Divine Lawgiver Himself has satisfied the broken law, and has Himself been crucified for Paul's transgressions.

And as it was with the thieves' past, and with Paul's past, so it is with your past and mine. With mine at any rate. "Let a man examine himself!" Paul kept saying to me all the week before last, and himself showed me the way. But indeed I did not need to examine myself, nor to be shown the way. My past, *of itself*, came down upon me like the thieves' past, and like Paul's past, and like that Sabbath night's storm on the Tay train. From every city and village and house I had ever lived in, the wind blew and beat upon my conscience. Out of every relationship of life that God had ever set me in. Out of my pulpit, out of my pastorate, out of my family life, out of my closest and best friendships. Sins of omission and sins of commission. What I should have done, and did not. What I hated, and yet did. The temptation and the trial I had been to other men. The sin and the sorrow I had caused. The provocation and the offence I had been. The blame I had brought on the ministry—and a thousand suchlike things. I could give you the names of the people and the places, only you would not know them. I leave the spaces blank for this reason also, that you may fill them in with the people, and the places, and the things, that sent you to the same Table in tears. What kind of a communion had you last Sabbath? I have no doubt many of you had both a better preparation and a better Communion Table than I had, though mine were by far the best I have ever had heretofore.

But Paul's peculiar and arresting form of speech in the text carries in it the secret of a great victory and a great peace. For mark well, what exactly Paul says. Paul does not say that he once was, or that he had been, crucified with Christ, but that he *is, at present,* so crucified. That is as much as to say that as long as Paul has any sin left so long will Christ be crucified. Not only is Paul's past sin all collected up and laid on Christ crucified; but almost more all Paul's present sinfulness comes up upon his conscience only to find Paul dead to his conscience, and to his sinfulness too, so truly and so completely is he crucified with Christ. It is impossible properly, or even with safety, to describe to a whole congregation Paul's experience. But those who have this blessed experience in themselves do not need it to be described to them, and their own tender hearts and holy lives are the best proof of its safety. I will attempt to describe to some of you what your life is, and the description will somewhat comfort and assure you concerning it. Your heart beats up its secret sinfulness with every pulse, so much so, that you would choke and consume and die with the guilt and the pollution of your heart, unless you were dead already. As it is, though nobody will believe it, or make sense of how it can so be, your unspeakable sinfulness never gets the length even of darkening your mind or imprisoning your conscience. And that is because your mind and your conscience are both in the keeping of Christ crucified. As Luther's conscience was. "The law is not the lord of my conscience," protested that Paul-like, that lion-like, believer. "Jesus Christ is Almighty God, and He is the Lord of my conscience. He is the Lord of the law also, both unbroken, broken, and repaired, and He keeps the law out of my conscience by keeping my conscience continually sprinkled with His own peace-speaking blood." In Paul's words again, the true believer is "dead," both to the law, and to the sin and the guilt of his own corruption. A true believer's corruption of heart comes up into his consciousness not in order to produce there a bad conscience, but in order to find the believer crucified already for all that corruption with Christ. For myself, I could not live a day, nor any part of a day, were I not crucified with Christ. I would sicken, I would swoon, I would fall down on the street, I would die. Come up beside me, my brethren! There is room in Christ crucified for us all. I am sure you live a miserable life down there, and out of Christ. It is not a dog's life down there. Come up hither to peace and rest. Learn to say, and then say it continually till you say it in your very dreams—I am crucified with Christ! And then you will be able to work in peace, and to eat and drink in peace, and to go out and in in peace, and to lie down in peace, and rise up. Then you will be able to die in peace, and to awake for ever to Christ and His never-to-be-broken peace. "I am crucified with Christ, nevertheless I live, yet not I, but Christ liveth in me, and the life which I now live in the flesh I live by the faith of the Son of God, who loved me, and gave Himself for me."

"HIMSELF for *me*, HIMSELF for *me!*" There is a faith that for once surely, if never again, will satisfy even Jesus Christ, and will set Him free to do some of His mightiest works. If He went about all Jewry, and all Galilee, and even crossed over into Syrophoenicia, seeking for faith, surely here it is to please Him at last. The SON OF GOD *for me!* Surely that must go to Christ's heart, and carry His heart captive. And we also will say it; I, at any rate, will say it with Paul. For as God is my witness I feel with Paul that nothing and no one but God the Son, and God the Son crucified, could atone for my sin. The Son of God on Calvary, with all heaven and all hell let loose upon Him—He, and He alone: He and His blood alone, can meet and make answer to the guilt and the pollution of my sin. But His blood, THE BLOOD OF GOD—It is surely able to speak peace in my conscience and comfort in my heart:

in my curse-filled conscience, and in my hell-filled heart. "HIMSELF for *me!* HIM-SELF for *me!*" For the shame, the spitting, the scourging, the staggering through the hooting streets, the bitter nails, the heart-gashing spear, the darkness of death and hell, all crowned by His Father forsaking Him—Yes, *that* is the desert of *my* sin. *That* answers to *my* sin. *My* sin explains *all that*, and needs *all that*, and will be satisfied with nothing short of *all that*. *My sin* alone, in heaven, or earth, or hell, is the full justification of *all that*. *All that*, borne for me by my Maker, my Lawgiver, and my Redeemer. But it is best just as Paul has left it—"HE loved *me*, and gave HIMSELF for *me*."

116
Paul as the Chief of Sinners

EVERYBODY knows what the most eminent saints of Holy Scripture think and say of their sinfulness. And here is what some of the most eminent saints who have lived since the days of Holy Scripture have felt and said about their own exceeding sinfulness also. And to begin with one of the very saintliest of them all—Samuel Rutherford. "When I look at my sinfulness," says Rutherford, "my salvation is to me my Savior's greatest miracle. He has done nothing in heaven or on earth like my salvation." And the title-page of John Bunyan's incomparable autobiography runs thus: "Grace abounding to John Bunyan, the chief of sinners. Come and hear, all ye that fear God, and I will declare what He hath done for my soul." "Is there but one spider in all this room?" asked the Interpreter. Then the water stood in Christiana's eyes, for she was a woman quick of apprehension, and she said, "Yes, Lord, there is more here than one; yea, and spiders whose venom is far more destructive than that which is in her." "My daughters," said Santa Teresa on her deathbed, "do not follow my example; for I have been the most sinful woman in all the world." But what she most dwelt on as she died was that half verse, "*Cor contritum*—a broken and a contrite heart, O God, Thou wilt not despise." "Do not mistake me," said Jacob Behmen, "for my heart is as full as it can hold of all malice at you and all ill-will. My heart is the very dunghill of the devil, and it is no easy work to wrestle with him on his own chosen ground. But wrestle with him on that ground of his I must, and that the whole of my life to the end." "Begone! all ye self-ignorant and false flatterers," shouted Philip Neri at them; "I am good for nothing but to do evil." "When a man like me," says Luther, "comes to know the plague of his own heart, he is not miserable only—he is absolute misery itself; he is not sinful only— he is absolute sin itself." "I am made of sin," sobbed Bishop Andrewes, till his private prayer-book was all but unreadable to his heirs because of its author's sweat and tears. "It has often appeared to me," says Jonathan Edwards, "what if God were to mark my heart-iniquity my bed would be in hell." "I sat down on the side of a stank," says Lord Brodie, "and was disgusted at the toads and esks and many other unclean creatures I saw sweltering there. But all the time my own heart was far worse earth to me, and filthier far than the filthy earth I sat upon." "This is a faithful saying," says Paul, "and worthy of all acceptation, that Christ Jesus came into the world to save sinners, of whom I am chief." Well may our Savior stop us and ask us whether or no we have counted the cost of being one of His out-and-out disciples!

I can very well believe that there are some new beginners here who are terribly staggered with all that. They were brought up positively to worship the Apostle Paul, and Luther, and Rutherford, and Bunyan. And how such saints of God can write such bitter things against themselves, you cannot understand. You would like to acquiesce in all that these men say about all such matters as sin and sinfulness;

542

but you do not see how they can honestly and truly say such things as the above about themselves.

> Fool! said my muse to me,
> Look in thy heart and write.

Remember these two lines of the true poet. Though they were not written about sin they never come to their fullest truth and their most fruitful application till they are taken home by the sinner who is seeking sanctification. Yes; look well into your own heart and you will find there the true explanation of your perplexity about Paul, and Luther, and Rutherford, and Bunyan, and all the rest. For your own heart holds the secret to you of this whole matter. If you have any real knowledge of your own heart at all, this cannot possibly have escaped you, that there are things in your own heart that are most shocking and prostrating for you to find there. There are thoughts in your heart, and feelings, and wishes, and likes and dislikes; things you have to hide, and things you cannot hide; things that if you have any religion at all you must take on your knees to Jesus Christ every day, and things you cannot take to anything even in Him short of His sin atoning blood. Well, you have in all that the true key to Paul's heart, and to the hearts of all the rest. So much so that if you advance as you have begun you will soon be staggering new beginners yourself with the Scriptures you read, and with the psalms and hymns you select, and with the petitions you offer ere ever you are aware; and, it may yet be, with the autobiography you will yet write to tell to all that fear God what He hath done for your soul. Just go on in the lessons of that inward school, and you will soon stagger us all by the passion that you, as well as David and Asaph, will put into the most penitential psalm.

"The highest flames are the most tremulous," says Jeremy Taylor. That is to say, the holiest men are the most full of holy fear, holy penitence, holy humility, and holy love. And all that is so because the more true spirituality of mind any man has, the more exquisite will be that man's sensibility to sin and to the exceeding sinfulness of sin. "The saints of God are far too sharp-sighted for their own self-satisfaction," says William Guthrie in his golden little book. So they are. For, by so much the holier men they become in the sight and estimation both of God and man, the more hideous and the more hopeless do they become to themselves. Such is their more and more sharpened insight into their own remaining sinfulness. Even when God is on the point of translating them to Himself because they so please Him, at that very moment they feel that they were never so near being absolute castaways. When all other men are worshipping them for their saintliness, and rightly so, those right saints of God are gnashing their teeth at the devilries that are still rampant in their own heart. They hate themselves the more you love them. They curse themselves the more you bless them. The more you exalt and enthrone them the more they lie with their faces on the earth. When you load them with honors, and banquet them with praises, they make ashes their bread and tears their drink. Their whole head will be waters, and their eyes one fountain of tears just at that moment when God is rising up in compassion, and in recompense, to wipe all tears from their eyes for ever.

And it is the sight of God that does it. It is the sight of Jesus Christ that does it. It is God's holy law of love entering our hearts ever deeper and deeper that does it. It is when I take my own heart, with all its wickedness-working self-love, and with all its self-seeking in everything, and self-serving out of everything and every one: with all its deceitfulness, and disingenuousness, and envy, and jealousy, and grudging, and malevolence, and lay it alongside of the holy heart of my Lord—it is that that does it. It is then that I sit down at a stank-side with poor Lord Brodie. It is then that my midnight Bible begins to open at unwonted places, and I begin to make bosom friends of unwonted people. It is then that I search the Book of Job, say, not any more for its incomparable dialectic and its noble literature. All these things, as Halyburton has it, have now become comparatively distasteful to me. Or if not distasteful, then without taste and insipid, as Job himself says about the white of an egg. No: my soul turns in its agony of pain and shame and seeks an utterance for itself in such consummating passages as these. "I have heard of Thee by the hearing of the ear: but now mine eye seeth Thee. Wherefore I abhor myself, and repent in dust and ashes. Behold, I am vile: what shall I answer Thee? I will lay my hand upon my mouth." And from that my Bible begins to open at the right places for me in David, and in Asaph, and in Ezra, and in Daniel, and in Peter, and in Paul: and so on to all Paul-like men down to my own day. And thus it comes about that the authors who are classical to me now are not the ephemerids in religion or in literature that I used to waste my time and my money upon when I was a neophyte: my true classics now are those masterly men who look into their own hearts and then write for my heart. It is the sight of God that has made them the writers they are, and it is the same sight that is at last making me the reader that I, too late, am beginning to be. It is the sight of God that does it, till my sinfulness takes such a deep spiritualness, and such a high exclusiveness, and such a hidden secretness, that I can find fit utterance for all that is within me in David, and in David's greatest psalms, alone. As thus:—"Against Thee, Thee only, have I sinned, and done this evil in Thy sight. The sacrifices of God are a broken spirit: a broken and a contrite heart, O God, Thou wilt not despise. Create in me a clean heart, O God, and renew a right spirit within me."

It was their own sin; or to speak much more exactly, it was their own sinfulness, that so humbled Rutherford and Bunyan and Christiana and Teresa, and broke their hearts. Nothing at all humiliates; nothing really touches the hearts of people like them; but the inward sinfulness of their own hearts. We shallow-hearted fools would think and would say that it was some great crime or open scandal that those saintly men and women had fallen into. Oh, no! there were no men nor women in their day of so blameless a name as they. One of themselves used to say that it was not "so humiliating and heart-breaking to be sometimes like a beast, as to be always like a devil. But, to be both!" he cried out in his twofold agony. The things of this world also that so humiliate all other men do not any more bring so much as a momentary blush to men like Rutherford, and women like Teresa. Just go over the things that humiliate and shame you in your earthly life and its circumstances; and then pass over into the ranks of God's saints, and you will there enter on a career of humiliation that will quite drink up the things that make you so ashamed now, till you will completely forget their very existence. What I am at this moment contending for is this, that sin alone truly humiliates a saint, even as holiness alone truly exalts him. It was sin, and especially sinfulness, that made those great saints cry out as they did.

A Greek fortune-teller was once reading Socrates's hands and face to discern his true character and to advertise the people of Athens of his real deserts. And as he went on he startled the whole assembly by pronouncing Socrates the most incontinent and libidinous man in all the city; the greatest extortioner and thief; and even worse things than all that. And when the enraged crowd were about to fall upon the soothsayer and tear him to pieces for saying such things about their greatest saint, Socrates himself came forward and restrained their anger and confessed openly and said, "Ye men of Athens, let this truth-speaking man alone, and do him no harm. He has said nothing amiss about me. For there is no man among you all who is by nature more predisposed to all these evil things than I am." And with that he quieted and taught and solemnized the whole city. Now in that again Socrates was God's dispensational apostle and preacher to the Greek people. For he was teaching them that there is, to begin with, no difference. That our hearts by nature are all equally evil. But that, as the Stoics taught, though all vice is equally in us all, it is not equally extant in us all. As also that he who knows his own heart will measure his own worth by his own heart and not by the valuation of the street and the market-place. As also that the noblest and best men in all lands, and in all dispensations, are those who know themselves, and who out of that knowledge keep themselves under, and wait upon God, till they attain in His good time to both a blameless heart, a blameless conscience, and a for ever blameless life.

Yet another use of this solemn subject is for the comfort of the true people of God. It is to let them see that they are not alone, and that no strange thing is befalling them, in all they are passing through. For myself, when I hear Paul saying this that is in the text, and Luther, and Rutherford, and Bunyan, and Andrewes, and Edwards, and Brodie, it is with me as it was with John Bunyan's pilgrim in the valley of the shadow of death. "About the midst of the valley I perceived the mouth of hell to be, and it stood hard by the wayside, and ever and anon the flame and smoke, with sparks and noises, would come out in such abundance that Christian said, What shall I do? One thing I would not that you let slip. Just when he was come over against the mouth of the burning pit, one of the wicked ones got behind him, and stepped up softly to him, and whisperingly, suggested many grievous blasphemies to him, which he verily thought had proceeded from his own mind. This put Christian to it more than anything he had met with before, yet could he have helped it, he would not have done it, but he had not the discretion, neither to stop his ears, nor to know from whence these blasphemies came." And here comes our point. "When Christian had travelled in this disconsolate condition some considerable time, he thought he heard the voice of a man, as going before him, saying, Though I walk through the valley of the shadow of death, I will fear none ill, for Thou art with me. Then was Christian glad, and that for these reasons. First, because he gathered from them that some one who feared God was in the valley as well as himself. Second, for that he perceived God was with them, though in that dark and dismal state; and why not, thought he, with me? though by reason of the impediment that attends this place, I cannot perceive it. Thirdly, for that he hoped to have company by and by. So he went on, and called to him that was before, but that he knew not what to answer, for that he also thought himself to be alone. But by and by the day broke. Then said Christian, He hath turned the shadow of death into the morning."

117
The Thorn in Paul's Flesh

THE circumstances with Paul were these. To prepare Paul for his great Apostolic work he had been endowed with the most extraordinary gifts of mind. Paul was a man of genius of the very foremost rank. To my mind no man that I know, sacred or profane, is worthy for one moment to stand in the same intellectual and spiritual rank with Paul. And then nothing exalts a man, sacred or profane, in his own esteem like a great intellect. A towering intellect is perhaps the greatest temptation that can be put upon any mortal man. And then the unparalleled privileges and promotions that were added to all that in Paul's case, combined to make Paul's temptation to vainglory the most terrible temptation that ever was put upon any human being—unless we call Jesus Christ a human being. But to keep to Paul. His election out of all living men for the greatest service and the greatest reward after the service and the reward of Jesus Christ Himself; his miraculous conversion; his unparalleled honors and privileges after his conversion far above all the greatest Apostles taken together; his labors more abundant than they all, and his transcending successes—all that was enough, according to Paul's own admission and confession afterwards, to exalt him above measure. Rightly received and rightly employed all these things ought only to have made Paul the humblest and the lowliest-minded of all men. But the very fact that He who knew His servant through and through saw it to be absolutely necessary to balance His servant's talents and prerogatives with such thorns and such buffetings, is a sure lesson to us that the humblest of saints is not safe from pride, nor the most heavenly-minded of men above dangerously delighting in the glory of this earth. In short, by far the best saint then living on the face of the earth was but half sanctified, and his Divine Master saw that to be the case, and took steps accordingly.

Now just what that thorn in Paul's flesh really was nobody knows. No end of guesses and speculations have been ventured about it, but with no real result. The Fathers and the Middle-age men for the most part took Paul's thorn to be something sensual, while the great body of Protestant and evangelical commentators hold that it must have been something wholly spiritual and experimental. Chrysostom thought he saw Hymenaeus and Alexander in it. Whereas Calvin took it to be the lifelong impalement of Paul's inner man upon all kinds of trouble and trial. Mosheim again felt sure it was the ranklings of lifelong remorse out of Paul's early days; and so on. In our own day interpretation has taken a line of its own on this matter. Lightfoot holds strongly that it was epilepsy. And while Dean Farrar admits that there is something to be said for epilepsy, he decides on the whole for ophthalmia. And then Professor Ramsay, Paul's latest, and in his own field one of Paul's very best commentators, has no doubt at all but that it was one of the burning-up fevers so frequent to this day in Asia Minor. Whatever his thorn really was, we are left in no doubt as to what Paul did with it. And we are left in just as little doubt as to what his Master's mind and will were about it. And then all that leads us up to this magnificent resolve of the Apostle—"Most gladly, therefore, will I rather glory in my infirmities, that the power of Christ may rest upon me." A splendid parenthesis, in a splendid argument. An autobiographic chapter of the foremost instructiveness and impressiveness, and of all kinds of profit and delight, to read and to remember.

Now while it will be the most fruitless of all our studies to seek to find out what exactly Paul's secret thorn was; on the other hand it will be one of the most fruitful and rewarding of all our very best studies, both of ourselves and of Holy Scripture also, if we can find out what our own thorn is, and can then go on to make the right use of our own thorn. To be told even by himself just what Paul's thorn actually was would not bring to us one atom of real benefit. But if I have a thorn in my own flesh, and if I know what it is, and why it is there, and what I am to do with it—that will be one of the divinest discoveries in this world to me; that will be the salvation of my own soul to me. Never mind the commentators on Paul's thorn; no not the very best of them, lest they draw your attention away from your own. Be you your own commentator on all such subjects. Be you your own thorn-student, especially. What is it then that so tortures you, and rankles in you, till your life is absolutely intolerable to you? What is it that gnaws and saps and undermines all your joy in this life? What is it that makes you beseech the Lord thrice, and without ceasing, that it may depart from you? Tell me that, and then I will tell you Paul's thorn.

Oh, no! you exclaim to me, it was not his sore eyes. It was not his bad head-aches. It was not even his frequent falling-sicknesses. Oh dear no, you say again. A thousand years of the most splitting headaches would not have laid you so low and so helpless; they would not have so taken the blood out of your cheeks, and so broken off all your interest and stake in life, and so cast you on your knees continually, as this thing has done that you point at so mysteriously, but with such evident assurance that you yourself have fallen into the same hedge of thorns with Paul. You cannot be absolutely and demonstrably sure, you admit, that it was not epilepsy, or ophthalmia, or a consuming fever in Paul. But you protest at us, as if we had been stealing Paul from you, that if it was either sore eyes, or a sick head-ache, or anything of that kind, then Paul was not the man that up till now you have taken him to be. But you will not let all the world, learned or ignorant, take away Paul from you. Almost as well take away his Master! No! you break out with Bunyan, Paul was that nightingale that sang his song from God to you because his breast was all the time pressed upon the thorn. You cannot sing like Paul, but you have not met with any man who follows Paul's song with more knowledge and with more enjoyment than you do; and therefore you reason that you have Paul's same thorn of God against your breast. And you speak so convincingly, and with such a note of assurance about it, that you almost persuade us that you have actually found out the riddle. Only, you are almost as mysterious about this whole matter as Paul was himself. There are some things, you say, that must remain mys-teries, till each man discovers them for himself. No man ever discovered and laid bare Paul's thorn to you, and you will never open your thorn to any man who has not already suffered from, and so discovered, his own. You only wait till our breast is at our thorn also; and then by our singing you will know what has happened to us also. When we so sing, or so listen to such singing, you will enroll us with Paul and with yourself among those who have come to visions and revelations of the Lord. Oh, no! you smile at our innocence, and say to us: Don't you see that the grace and the strength of Christ are not prescribed anywhere else in Holy Scripture for epilepsy or ophthalmia? Luke was there with his balsams, and with his changes of air, and with his rests in a desert place, for all these ailments of the Apostle. Don't you see, you demand of us, that this very prescription proclaims the malady; the very medicine more than half discovers the disease. Iron: a little wine: sound sleep: nourishing food: a month at the baths up among the mountains; these things would cure the commentators. But the grace and the strength of Christ are reserved for far other thorns than Luke could extract, or even alleviate.

It is no wonder that the most learned men have been at their wits' end about Paul's thorn. No blame to them since the very Apostle himself made such a profound mistake about his own thorn. With all his clearness of intellect, and with all his spiritual insight, Paul was as much at sea about his own thorn as if he had been a commentator of the dark ages. If I may say so, with my unsurpassed respect for so great an Apostle, he behaved like one of his own neophytes when his own thorn first came to him from Christ. By that time he ought to have been a teacher, but he had still need himself to be taught which be the first principles of personal religion, and had need of milk, and not of strong meat. For no sooner did the inward bleeding begin in Paul; no sooner did he begin to lose his night's rest because of the pain; no sooner did his heart begin to sink within him, than he fell to praying with all his well-known importunity that this whole thorn of his might be immediately taken away. Greatest of the apostles as he was; councillor almost of God Himself as he was; Paul's insight and faith and patience wholly failed him when his own thorn began its sanctifying work within him. You never made a greater mistake yourself than Paul made. With all his boasted knowledge of the mind of Christ, there was not a catechumen in Corinth or in Philippi with more of a fretful child in him than the so-called great Apostle was when his thorn came into his own flesh. For just hear his own ashamed confession long afterwards as to what he did. Without ever once asking either his Master or himself why that thorn had been sent to him; without ever looking once into his own heart for the sure explanation and the clear justification of the thorn, he instantly demanded that it should be removed. He acted as if his Master had paid no attention as to what befell His servant. He behaved himself as if his thorn had come to him out of nothing better than Christ's sheer caprice. "This," he said thrice, "is so much pure and purposeless pain. This is so much quite gratuitous suffering that Thou hast let come upon me. Let this thorn only depart from me," he cried, "and I will return to my faith, and to my love, and to my service of Thee and Thy people; but not otherwise. As long as this thorn lasts and thus lacerates me, how shall I serve Thee or finish Thy work?" But his Lord compassionately overlooked and freely forgave Paul all his unbelief and all his impatience and all his foolish charges, and condescended and said to him: My grace is sufficient for thee; for My strength is made perfect in weakness. Lord, exclaimed Peter in his precipitancy, not my feet only, but also my hands and my head. And Paul, a much stronger and a much less excitable man, said after he got his answer, and said it more and more all his days: "Lord, not in one part of my flesh only, but plant those soul-saving thorns of Thine in all the still sinful parts of my body and my mind, in order that the power of Christ may rest upon me. For now as often as I am weak then am I strong. I am become a fool in my complaining. I still mistake my own salvation even when it lies at my door."

But to come back to our riddle, and to set it over again to ourselves, so as to carry it home and work at it till we find out its true answer. What then is that thorn in the flesh of all God's best saints and of all Christ's best servants—that thorn which still humbles, and humbles, and humbles them down, past all possible glorying in anything they are, or have ever been, or can ever be? Humbles the most heavenly-minded men in all the world down to death and hell, and so humbles such men only? What is it that Christ sends to stab His best servants deeper and deeper every day, and to impale them and buffet them till they are so many dead corpses rather than living and breathing and Christian men? And then on the other hand, what is that same thorn and stake and devil's fist that at every stab and stound and blow draws down the whole grace of Jesus Christ on the sufferer, till the sanctified saint kisses his thorn, and blesses his Lord, and would not part with the one or the other for all the world? Samson offered so many sheets and so many changes of raiment to any Philistine who within seven days would declare his riddle. And after John Bunyan had reset Samson's riddle to the readers of his *Grace Abounding* he felt sure that his sheets and his changes of raiment were all quite safe, for, after his offer to them, he said: "The Philistines will not understand me. But, all the same, it is written in the Scriptures, the father to the children shall make known in holy riddles the deep things of God." I give you therefore the next seven days and seven nights, Philistines and all, to find out Paul's great riddle. And as many of the children of light as shall have found out the only possible answer by this night se'ennight shall here receive, along with the grace and strength of Christ, a change of raiment. Now Joshua was clothed with filthy garments, and stood before the angel. And He answered and said to those that stood before him, saying: Take away the filthy garments from him. And unto him He said: Behold, I have caused thine iniquity to pass from thee, and I will clothe thee with change of raiment. And I said, Let them set a fair miter upon his head. So they set a fair miter upon his head. And the angel of the Lord stood by. Such a reward still awaits all those who so plow with Paul's heifer as to find out his riddle. Yes; such a beautiful change of raiment awaits them, and such a fair miter upon their head.

118
Paul as Sold Under Sin

AS often as my attentive bookseller sends me "on approval" another new commentary on the Romans I immediately turn to the seventh chapter. And if the commentator sets up a man of straw in the seventh chapter, I immediately shut the book. I at once send back the book and say, No, thank you. That is not the man for my hard-earned money. Just as Paul himself would have scornfully sent back the same book with this message to its author—If I have told you earthly things, and you have so misunderstood me, how shall I trust you to interpret my heavenly things? No, thank you, I say, as I send back the soon-sampled book. But send me for my students as many Luthers on the Galatians as you can lay your hands on, and as many Marshalls on Sanctification, in order that they may one day be preachers after Paul's own heart. But no, not that blind leader of the blind.

It is an old canon of interpretation that Paul alone is his own true interpreter. And the true student will take the canon down. *Non, nisi ex ipso Paulo, Paulum potes interpretari.* That is to say—There is no other possible interpreter of Paul, in all the world of interpretation, but only Paul himself. And I have come upon two other exegetical rules that have had the most profound results out of this present text; "the right context is half the interpretation." And this out of the same incomparable interpreter of Paul—"If a man would open up Paul, let him do it rationally. Let him consider well the Apostle's own words both before the text and after it." Now when we take Paul in this present text as speaking seriously and not in a sacred jest; and then when we take the whole context, we get an interpretation altogether worthy of Paul; altogether worthy of the depth and strength and majesty of the Epistle to the Romans; altogether worthy of the grace of God, and of the blood of Jesus Christ, as, also, altogether worthy of the Holy Ghost. Then the seventh of the Romans becomes henceforth to us, what it most certainly is, the most terrible tragedy in all literature, ancient or modern, sacred or profane. Set beside the seventh of the Romans all your so-called great tragedies—your Macbeths, your Hamlets, your Lears, your Othellos, are all but so many stage-plays: so much sound and fury, signifying next to nothing when set alongside this awful tragedy of sin in a soul under a supreme sanctification. The seventh of the Romans should always be printed in letters of blood. Here are passions. Here are terror and pity. Here heaven and hell meet, as nowhere else in heaven or hell; and that too for their last grapple together for the everlasting possession of that immortal soul, till you have a tragedy indeed; and, beside which, there is no other tragedy. Only, as Luther says, give not such strong wine to a sucking child.

"Did I see," says Dr. Newman, "a boy of good make and mind, with the tokens on him of a refined nature, cast upon the world without provision, unable to say whence he came, unable to tell us his birthplace, or his family connections, I should conclude that there was some sad secret connected with his history." And did I hear or read of a man of refined mind, and of great nobility of nature that nothing could obliterate, and, withal, a truly Christian man; did I read or hear of such a man held in captivity by some vile, cruel, cannibal tribe in South America, or Central Africa, I would feel sure that he had a tale to tell that would harrow my heart. I would not need to be told by pen and ink the inconsolable agony of that man's heart. I could picture to myself that poor captive's utter wretchedness. I could see him making desperate attempts to escape his horrible captivity, only to be overtaken and dragged back to a still more cruel bondage. And were that captive able by some secret and extraordinary providence to send home to this country so much as a single page out of his dreadful life, it would scarcely be believed, so far past all imagination of free men at home would be his incoherent outcries. But all that would be but a school-boy's story-book beside this agonized outcry of a great saint of God sold under sin. Yes, a great saint of God. For no soul of man is sold under sin to such an agony as this who is not, all the time, a heaven-born and a holy man: holy almost as God is holy. This is the slavery of the spirit in a supremely spiritual man: a slavery past all imagination of the commonplace Christian mind. You see that in the incredulous, uncomprehending, and utterly misunderstanding way, in which Paul's agonized outbursts are sometimes stumbled at, even by some of our masters in Israel.

And no wonder, for the most complete and cruel captivity, the most utter and hopeless slavery you ever heard of, falls far short of being sold under sin. There is a depth of misery in being so sold; there is a bleak and blank hopelessness in being so sold: nay, there is a certain self-revenging admission of justice in being so sold, that all goes to make up this uttermost agony of the self-sold slave. For he was not taken in honorable battle. He was not suddenly surprised and swept away into all this terrible captivity against his own will, and against all that he could do to resist and to escape. No. The gnashing agony of his heart all his days will be because he so sold himself. This will be the deepest bitterness of his bitterest cup. This will be the cruellest rivet of his most galling chain. And then to be sold under sin! The vilest and cruellest savage chief who makes God's earth the devil's hell to himself and others, is not sin. Sin has made him what he is, and it has made his slaves and his victims what they are; but both his cruelty and their misery fall far short of the full cruelty and the full misery of sin. Sin could bring forth ten thousand hells like that, and it could still go on bringing forth as many more. Sin is sin. And the true saint of God feels that in his heart of hearts, till he scarce feels anything else. Till what all the whole life of a true saint sold under sin can be made in its agony, you may read in the seventh of the Romans; unless you have such an agony in your own bosom that the seventh of the Romans sounds flat and tame beside it. "What I hate, that do I!" Oh, no! That is no man of straw. That is no studied artifice of Pauline rhetoric. That is no young Pharisee. Oh, no, that is Paul the aged himself. That is the holy Apostle himself in all his unapproached holiness. Tragedies! Tragedies of hatred and of revenge! If you would see hatred and revenge red-hot, and poured, not on the head of a hated enemy, but, what I have never read in any of your stage-tragedies, poured in all its red-hotness in upon a man's own heart; if you would see the true hatred and the true revenge, come to this New Testament

theater. Come to Paul for a right tragic author. Or far better, come to holiness and
heavenly-mindedness yourself, and then you will have this whole agony enacted in
your own heart; and that with more and more passion in your heart, all the days
of your life on this hateful earth. My brethren, if you will believe me, there is nothing in heaven or on earth, there is nothing in God or in man, that from my youth
up I have read more about, or thought more about, than just this text and its two
contexts. And if the above interpretation is not the true interpretation of this text,
then I must just admit to you in the very words of St. Augustine—"I confess that I
am entirely in the dark as to what the Apostle meant when he wrote this chapter."
Only, I will add this. Unless Paul contradicts me himself, not all his commentators
on the face of the earth will ever convince me that this seventh of the Romans is
not to be taken seriously, but is to be taken as filled with the spiritual experiences
of a man of straw.

Now this is another sure rule of interpretation that whatsoever things were
written aforetime were written for our learning, that we through patience and
comfort of the Scriptures might have hope. And eminently to my mind the seventh of the Romans was written that those who need the very greatest patience
and the very strongest comfort and consolation, may have all that here. And in
this way. If even Paul was sold under sin: if even Paul when writing the Romans
was still carnal: if he that very day had said and done and thought and felt what he
would not if he could have helped it: if he hated himself for what came up upon
him out of his heart even with his inspired pen in his hand: if sin still dwelt in him,
till in his flesh there dwelt no good thing and, then, if we delight in the law of God
after the inward man, as he did: even if we find another law, as we every moment
do find it, warring against the law of our mind, and bringing us into captivity to
the law of sin, till we cry without ceasing, O wretched man that I am! and if all the
time we thank God through Jesus Christ our Lord, and walk not after the flesh,
but after the Spirit till there is therefore no condemnation to us—if all that is so, I
would like you to tell me where I can find another chapter so full of the profoundest, surest, most spiritual, and most experimental, comfort. I have not found it. I
do not know it, much as I need it. No. In its own wonderful way there is not a more
comfortable and hopeful Scripture in all the Book of God than this. And for my
part, I will not let any commentator of any school; no, not even of my own school,
steal from me this most noble, and most divinely suited, cordial for my broken
heart. As long as I am sold under sin I will continue to read continually this chapter, and all its context-chapters to myself, as all sent not to a man made of straw,
but to a man made of sin, till he is every day sold under sin. "It was the saying of
a good man, lately gone to his rest, whose extended pilgrimage was ninety-three
years, that he must often have been swallowed up by despair, had it not been for
the seventh chapter of Paul's Epistle to the Romans."

But if for the comfort and consolation of some men, this very same Scripture is written for the warning and admonition of other men. And I accordingly
admonish you, as many as need this admonition, and will take it at my hands, not
to praise yourselves because you are not yet sold under sin. "Don't speak to me,"
said Duncan Matheson on the market-square of Huntly to David Elgin-brod, "I

am a rotten hypocrite." "Ah, Duncan man," said old David, laying his hand on his friend's shoulder, "they never say Fauch! i' the grave." And Holy Writ itself says that where no oxen are, the crib is clean. My brother, do not boast that you do not know what it is to be sold under sin, and that you do not believe it about Paul either. A born slave, with a slave's heart, and a slave's habits, never complains that he is a slave. He knows nothing else. He knows nothing better. He wishes nothing more than that his ear be bored for ever to his master's door. Only a free-born, and a nobly-born, man, and a man who has been carried away captive, ever cries continually, O wretched man that I am! The Talmud-men denied the sinfulness of their sinful hearts as indignantly as any of you can deny yours. And they interpreted the sixty-sixth Psalm to their scholars in the same way that some commentators interpret the seventh of the Romans. "If I regard iniquity in my heart only, then the Lord will pass it by, and will not regard it," so they taught their scholars.

But to return once more to the inexhaustible comfort of this text, and then close. There is no shame and no pain in all this world of shame and pain for one moment to compare with the shame and the pain of the seventh of the Romans, as you do not need me to tell you, if you have that pain and shame in your own heart. But lift up your head, for it is to you and not to any other man, that God speaks in His holy prophet and says "For your shame you shall have double. And for your confusion of face you shall yet rejoice in your portion. Therefore in your land you shall possess the double, and everlasting joy shall be unto you." Agrippa was shut up in a cruel and shameful prison for Gaius's sake; but no sooner did Gaius ascend the throne than he had his friend instantly released and conferred upon him an office both of riches and renown. Moreover Gaius presented Agrippa with a chain of gold of double the weight with the chain of iron that he had worn in the prison for Gaius's sake. And so has Paul's Emperor done long ago to Paul. And so will He do before very long to you. To you, that is, who are now sold under sin for His sake. You will soon hear His voice speaking in anger to your jailors at your prison door and saying how displeased He is over all your affliction. And He will bring you forth with His own hand like Gaius; and for all your shame and pain He will bestow upon you double, with a chain of salvation round your neck that will make you forget all the sad years of your sold captivity.

> He comes the prisoners to release
>> In Satan's bondage held,
> The gates of brass before him burst,
>> The iron fetters yield.

119
Paul's Blamelessness as a Minister

MOMUS himself could have found no fault with Paul. Momus found fault with everybody, with one exception. But had he lived in Paul's day Paul would surely have been a second exception to the universal fault-finding. For Paul so magnified his ministry; he so gave himself up to his ministry; he so labored in season and out of season in his ministry; and above all he so pleased all men in all things for their good to edification; he so went about doing good and giving none offence that he lifted both his ministry and himself clear up above all the fault-finding of all fair-minded men. So much so that Paul stands next to our Divine Master Himself as a blameless model for all ministers, as well as for all other men of God. And both his own ministry and that of all his successors were so much on Paul's mind, that in every new Epistle of his he has given us something fresh and forcible as to how all ministers are to attain to a blameless ministry, till they shall be able to give a good account of their ministry, first to their people, and then to their Master.

Now immediately following the text and intended to illustrate and to enforce the text, Paul lays down a remarkable map; it is a whole atlas indeed of all his past ministry. A moral and spiritual atlas that is. It is not a chartographer's atlas of all the parishes and presbyteries and synods in which Paul has lived and labored. It is far more interesting and far more profitable to us than that. For it is nothing less than a faithful and feeling panorama of all the outstanding states of mind and pas-sions of heart that he and his successive congregations had come through while he lived and labored among them. Mr. Ferrier has lately given us an excellently-scaled and a most eloquent map of the parish of Ettrick. On that impressive sheet we are shown the situation of the church and the manse; the farm-towns where all Thomas Boston's elders lived who had a brow for a good cause; the hamlets also where he held his district prayer-meetings, and so on. And every inch of that minute map is a study of the foremost importance and impressiveness for all the parish ministers of Scotland. But Paul's pastoral map bites far deeper, and with far sharper teeth, into every minister's conscience than even Boston's mordant map will bite, though it is warranted to draw ordained blood also. Paul does not engrave topographically indeed all the cities, and all the synagogues, and all the workships, in which he had lived and labored. But he lays down with the greatest art the latitudes and the longitudes of all his trials, and temptations, and tumults as a minister. Instead of saying to us, Here is Philippi, and here is Ephesus, and here is Corinth, and so on: Paul says to us, Here were afflictions, and here were necessities, and here were troubles on every side. And just as in Thomas Boston's parish there are pillars and crosses set up to mark and to record to all time in Scotland his great victories won over himself, and his corresponding victories won over his people; so does Paul set up this and that great stone of ministerial remem-brance and has had these instructive things engraved upon it: "by pureness, by knowledge, by long-suffering, by kindness, by the Holy Ghost, by love unfeigned, by the word of truth, by the power of God, by the armor of righteousness on the right hand and on the left." There are able and devoted divinity-students here tonight who look forward before very long to have a church and a manse and a pulpit and a people of their own. What would you say for a relaxation some day soon after the session is over to make a real geographical map of all the places where Paul was a preacher and a pastor; and then to distribute beside those sacred sites all the afflictions, the necessities, the distresses, the imprisonments, the tumults, and the labors of the text. And then on the other side of the sacred site, the pureness, the knowledge, the patience, and suchlike, by all of which your great forerunner and example-minister came out of it all having given offence in nothing, but with an everlastingly honored name. Such an exercise, taken in time, and laid to heart in time, would surely help you to take in hand some hitherto unheard-of parish in Scotland, so as to make it an Anwoth, or an Ettrick, or suchlike. There are hundreds of parishes in Scotland up to this day absolutely nameless, but to some one of which some one of you may yet marry your name for ever, till your parish and you shall shine together for generations to come, like the brightness of the firmament, and as the stars for ever and ever. You still have it in your own hands tonight to do that. But in a short time it will be too late for you also. Go, my sons, in God's name and in God's strength, determined, as much as in you lies, to give your happy people disappointment in nothing, and offence in nothing, till their children shall bury your dust in your own churchyard, amid the lamentations of the whole country-side, and shall write it over your dust that you were absolutely another Apostle Paul to them, both in your preaching of Christ crucified, and in your adorning of that doctrine.

"In tumults," is Paul's own specially inserted expression; it is his own most feeling and most expressive description, for long periods and for wide spaces of his apostolic life. "In tumults," he says with special emphasis. Now we all know in what New Testament books, and in what painful chapters of those books, all those tumults are written. But it would be no profit to us to go back tonight on Paul's tumults, unless it were in order that we might the better lay our own tumults alongside of his, and lay ourselves in our tumults, alongside of Paul in his tumults. Well, then, come away, and let us do that. Come away, and let us speak plainly. What, then, have some of our tumults been, yours and mine, as minister and people, since we first knew one another? Was it Disestablishment? Was it Home Rule? Was it some heresy case? Was it the Declaratory Act? Was it the Union? Was it hymns, or organs, or standing at singing? or was it something else so utterly parochial, and petty, and paltry, that nobody, but you and I, could possibly have made a tumult out of it? Now whatever our tumult was, how did we behave ourselves in it? What are our calm thoughts about it, and about ourselves in it, now that it is all over? However it may be with you and me, it is certain that some men have gone to judgment, out of those very same tumults, with everlasting shame on their heads. How then do we stand in this matter of blame and shame? And blame and shame or no, are we any wiser men, and any better men today because of those tumults? Or after all our lessons are we just as ready for another tumult, and as ill-prepared for it as ever we were? Are we just as ill-read, and as ill-natured, and as prejudiced, and as hot-headed, and as full of pride and self-importance, as ever we were? What do you think? What do you feel? What do you say? You must surely see now, as you look back, what a splendid school for Christian character, and for Christian conduct, all those tumults were fitted, and intended of God, to be to you. Well then, how do you think you have come out of those great years in those great and costly schools? Has your temper and your character come out of those terrible furnaces like gold tried in the fire? For all those tumults, whatever you may have made of them, and they of you, they were all intended to be but means to a far greater end than their own end. That is to say, they were all intended to test and try and prove you and me as both ministers and men of God, and that by the only proof we can give to God or man. The proof, that is, of patience, and purity of motive, and sufficient knowledge, and long-suffering, and love unfeigned, and the word of truth, and the power of God. And to show to all men, as Paul did, that we have not received the grace of God in vain; because, amid our greatest tumults, we have given offence in nothing, and in nothing has our ministry been to be blamed.

My brethren, you are not ministers, thank God for that. But you will let your ministers tell you what is in their hearts concerning you, and concerning themselves, as they read this too-proud chapter of Paul's. If you were all ministers I would go on to say in your name, and you would agree with me, as to what a cruel chapter this is. For once—what a heartless chapter! Was it not enough for Paul that he should enjoy his own good conscience as a minister, but he must make my conscience even more miserable than it was before? What delight can it give him to pour all this condemnation and contempt upon me and my ministry? And, did he not know, did he not take time to consider, that he was trampling upon multitudes of broken hearts? I wonder at Paul. In so scourging the proud-hearted and uplifted Corinthians he must have forgotten all us poor ministers, who, to all time, would read his blameless and boasted ministry, only to be utterly crushed by it. It was not like Paul to glory over us in that way. But let us recollect ourselves, and say that it is all right. It is not for such as we are to be puffed-up, or even to be easy-minded, or to be anything else but bruised, and broken, and full of the severest self-blame. And, therefore, we will go back upon the ruins of our ministry with this self-condemning chapter in our hands, and will recall the tumults that so wounded the Church of Christ, and so many hearts in her, and all the unpardonable part we took in those tumults, that would never have been what they were had we not been in them. Our offences without number also in our very pulpits. Oh, my brethren, the never-to-be-redeemed opportunities of our pulpits; and the lasting blame of God and our people, and our own consciences, for our misuse and neglect of our pulpits! Rock of Ages, cleft for ministers! The "unedifying converse" of our pastorate, and so on: till we take up this terrible chapter, and read it continually, deploring before God and man, to our dying day, all that Paul was, and that we were not: and all that he was not, and that we were. But, with all that is for ever lost, there is one thing left that we shall every day do; and a thing that Paul did not do, on that day at any rate, when he wrote this proud chapter. We shall every day walk about amid the ruins of our past ministry, and shall say over it—Out of the depths have I cried unto Thee, O Lord. If Thou, O Lord, shouldest mark iniquity, O Lord, who shall stand! Deliver me from blood-guiltiness, O God, Thou God of my salvation; then will I teach transgressors Thy ways; and sinners shall be converted unto Thee. There is always that left to us, and that is better for us, and far more becoming in us, than the most blameless ministry.

Thomas Goodwin, that great minister, tells us that always when he was tempted to be high-minded and to forget to fear, he was wont to go back and take a turn up and down in his unre-generate state. Now, your ministers do not need to go so far back as that. All that we need to do is to open a few pages of our Communion-rolls and visiting books, and a short turn up and down those painful pages, with some conscience, and some heart, and some imagination, will always make high-mindedness, and fearlessness, for ever impossible to us. You do not need to keep up our faults and failures and offences against us, for we never forget them for a single day. You may safely forgive us, for we shall never in this world forgive ourselves. How could we? No other man can possibly have such a retrospect of faults and failures and offences as a minister. It is impossible. The seventh of the Romans has been called the greatest tragedy that ever was written in Greek or in English. If that is so, some of our Communion-rolls and pastoral-visitation books are not far behind it. For the supreme tragedy of his own sad ministry is all written there by each remorseful minister's own hand. And such tragic things are written, or, rather, are secretly ciphered there, as to raise both pity, and fear, and terror, to all ministers, enough to suffice them for all their days on earth.

Now, you may well think that Paul has left nothing at all for you tonight, but for ministers only. Well, take this, as if Paul himself had said it. Find as little fault with your ministers as is possible. Blame them as little as you can, even when they are not wholly blameless. It is not good for yourself to do it, and it is not good for your children to hear you doing it. Be like Bacon's uncle with his family; reprehend them in private and praise them in public. That is to say, if you have a minister who will take reprehension, either in public or in private, at your hands. But, even when it must be done, do it with regret and with reverence. Be careful not to humiliate your minister overmuch. I am sure you will never intentionally insult him, however much you may have to remonstrate with him. I admit that this lesson is not literally within the four corners of the text, but it is not very far away from it.

And there is this also about offences, and fault-findings, and in a far wider field than the ministry merely. It is very humbling, when once we begin to discover it, that our very existence is an offence to so many men. We are like a stumbling-stone in their way: they fall on us and are broken, even when they could not explain or justify why that should be so; sometimes, again, our offensiveness will only be too easily explained both to them and to ourselves. But, at other times, they will need to go down into their own hearts for the real root of all this bitterness. And, then, when they do that, you will not be much more troubled with your offensiveness to them, or with their hostility to you. At the same time, walk you softly, as long as you are in this life. It is a dreadful thing to be the cause, guilty or innocent, of another man's stumbles and falls. "Love to be well out of sight," was the motto of more than one of the great saints. And, though that does not sound at first sight like great saintliness, yet it is. There are few better evidences of great and sure saintship, than just to "seek obscurity" for such reasons as the above. Keep out of people's eyes, and ears, and feet, and tongues then, as much as you can, and as long as you continue to cause so many men to stumble, and to fall, and to be broken over you.

And, then, both ministers, and all manner of men, never allow yourselves to answer again, when you are blamed. Never defend yourself. Let them reprehend you, in private or in public, as much as they please. Let the righteous smite you: it shall be a kindness: and let him reprove you: it shall be an excellent oil, which shall not break your head. Never so much as explain your meaning, under any invitation or demand whatsoever. They just wish to pick a quarrel with you, and you have something else to do. Now, I always like to seal down such a great lesson as this by some great name. A great name impresses the most hardened hearer. And I will seal down this great lesson by this out of a truly great name. "It is a mark of the deepest and truest humility," says a great saint, "to see ourselves condemned without cause, and to be silent under it. To be silent under insult and wrong is a very noble imitation of our Lord. O my Lord, when I remember in how many ways Thou didst suffer detraction and misrepresentation, who in no way deserved it, I know not where my senses are when I am in such a haste to defend and excuse myself. Is it possible I should desire any one to speak any good of me, or to think it, when so many ill things were thought and spoken of Thee! What is this, Lord—what do we imagine to get by pleasing worms, or by being praised by creeping things! What about being blamed by all men, if only we stand at last blameless before Thee!"

120
Paul as an Evangelical Mystic

THE two words "mystical" and "mysterious" mean, very much, the same thing. Not only so, but at bottom "mystical" and "mysterious" are very much the very same words. Like two sister stems, these two expressions spring up out of one and the same seminal root. Now, as to mysticism. There are more kinds of mysticism than one in the world. There is speculative mysticism, and there is theosophical mysticism, and there is devotional mysticism, and so on. But to us there is only one real mysticism. And that is the evangelical mysticism of the Apostle Paul. And that mysticism is just the profound mysteriousness of the spiritual life, as that life was first created by the Holy Ghost in Jesus Christ, and will for ever be possessed by Jesus Christ as His own original life; and then as it will for ever be conveyed from Him down to all His mystical members.

Now, to begin with, Christ Himself is the great mystery of godliness. Almighty God never designed nor decreed nor executed anything in eternity or in time, to compare, for one moment, for mysteriousness, with Christ. All the mysteries of creation—and creation is as full as it can hold of all kinds of mysteries: all the mysteries of grace—and grace is full of its own proper mysteries also: yet, all are plain and easy to be understood, compared with the all-surpassing mystery of Christ. Ever since Christ was set forth among men the best intellects in the world have all been working on the mystery of Christ. And, though they have found out enough of that mystery for their own salvation, yet they all agree to tell us that there are heights and depths of mystery in Christ past all finding out. Christ, then, that so mysterious Person who fills the Gospels and the Epistles with His wonderful words and works—What think ye of Christ? Paul tells us in every epistle of his what he thinks of Christ, and it is this deep, spiritual, experimental, and only soul-saving, knowledge that Paul has of Christ, it is this that justifies us in calling him the first and the best of all mystics; the evangelical and true mystic: the only mystic indeed, worthy, for one moment, to bear that deep and noble name.

When you take to reading the best books you will be sure to come continually on such strange descriptions and expressions as these: Christ mystical; Christ our mystical Head; Christ our mystical Root; the mystical Union of Christ with all true believers; the mystical identity of Christ with all true believers—and suchlike strange expressions. But, already, all these deep doctrines and strange expressions of evangelical mysticism are to be found in the deep places of Paul: and, in his measure, in the deep places of John also; and that because those two apostles, first of all spiritually-minded men, discovered all these mysterious and mystical matters in their Master. Ere ever we are aware we ourselves are mystics already as soon as we begin to read in John about the Living Bread, and the True Vine; and in Paul about the Head of the Church and His indwelling in us. But Paul, after his great manner, goes on to show us that Christ is not the only mystical Head that this so mystically-constituted world of ours has seen. First and last, as that great evangelical and speculative mystic has had it revealed to him, there have been two mystical Heads set over the human race. Our first mystical Head was Adam, and our second mystical Head is Christ. Speaking mystically, says the most mystical of the Puritans, there are only two Men who stand before God; the first and the second Adam; and these two public Men have all us private men hanging at their great girdles. But, all the time, above Adam, and before Adam, and only waiting till Adam had shipwrecked his headship and all who were in it with him, stood the second Adam ready to restore that He had not taken away. And Paul so sets all that forth in doctrine, and in doxology, and in gospel invitation and assurance, that the Church of Christ in her gratitude to Paul has given him this great name of her first and most evangelical mystic. "And hath put all things under his feet," proclaims the great mystic, "and gave Him to be the Head over all things to the Church, which is His body." And again, "Him which is the Head, even Christ, in whom the whole body maketh increase unto the edifying of itself in love." And again, "And He is the Head of the body: for it pleased the Father that in Him should all fullness dwell."

But while Paul has many magnificent things to teach us about the mystical Headship of Christ over His Church, at the same time, it is the mystical union of Christ with each individual believer, and each individual believer's mystical union with Christ—it is this that completes and crowns Paul's evangelical doctrine and kindles his most rapturous adoration. And all that is so, because all Paul's preaching is so profoundly experimental. Paul has come through all that he preaches. Goodwin, that so mystical and so evangelical Puritan, says that all the "apostolical and primitive language was at once mystical and experimental." But there is a more primitive and a more experimental and a more mystical language than even the apostolical. "I am the bread of life: he that cometh to Me shall never hunger; and he that believeth in Me shall never thirst. This is the bread that cometh down from heaven, that a man may eat thereof and not die. Verily, verily, I say unto you, except ye eat the flesh of the Son of Man and drink His blood, ye have no life in you." As also in our Lord's so mystical and so beautiful parable of the true vine and its true branches. And then in the next generation, Paul comes forward with his own so profound experience of all that, and with his own so first-hand witness to all that, in such sealing and crowning testimonies and attestations as these:—"I live, yet not I, but Christ liveth in me: and the life I now live in the flesh, I live by the faith of the Son of God." And, again, "To me to live is Christ, and to die is gain," and so on in all his epistles. Paul has so eaten the flesh and has so drunk the blood of Christ: he has been of the Father so engrafted into Christ, that he possesses within himself the very same life that is possessed by the risen Christ. The very identical life that is in Christ glorified is already in Paul, amid all his corruptions, temptations, and tribulations. There are very different degrees of that life, to be sure, in Christ and in Paul; but it is the very same kind of life. There is not one kind of spiritual life in Christ, and an altogether different kind of spiritual life in Paul. The same sap that is in the vine is in the branch. The same life that is in the head is in the member. But that is not all. Amazing as all that is, that is far from being all. The riches that are treasured up in Christ are absolutely unsearchable. For Paul is not content to say that he has in his own heart the identical and very same life that is in Christ's heart: Paul is bold enough to go on to say that he actually has Christ Himself dwelling in his very heart. I—you and I—have in our hearts the very same life that was in Adam, with all its deadly infection and dreadful pollution; but, identified with Adam as we are, Adam does not really and actually dwell in our hearts. We still inherit the "fair patrimony" that he left us; but, I for one, both hope and believe, that Adam has escaped that patrimony himself. At any rate, wherever Adam dwells, he does not dwell in our hearts. But the second Adam is so constituted for us, and we are so constituted for Him, that He, in the most real and actual manner, and without any figure of speech whatever, dwells in us. Indeed, with all reverence, and with all spiritual understanding, let it be said, Christ has no choice; He has nowhere else to dwell. If Christ is really to dwell, to be called dwelling, anywhere, it must be in Paul's heart, and in your heart, and in my heart. Christ is so mystical and mysterious: He is so unlike any one else in heaven or earth: He is such an unheard-of mystery, that He has *three* dwelling-places. To begin with, He is the Son of God; and as the Son of God He dwells in the Father, and the Father in Him. And, then, ever since His Incarnation, He has been the Son of Man also. And as the Son of Man, and ever since His ascension and reception, He has dwelt in heaven as one of God's glorified saints, and at the head of them. But, over and above being both Son of God and Son of Man: from the mystical union of the Godhead and the Manhood in His Divine Person, He is the Christ also. And as He is the Christ, He dwells in His people, and can dwell nowhere else, in heaven or in earth, but in His people. Christ mystical is made up not of the Head only, but of the Head and the members taken together. And, as apart from the Head the members have no life; so, neither apart from His members has the Head anywhere to dwell. Nay, apart from His members, the Head has no real and proper existence. At any rate, as Paul insists, they are His fullness, and He is complete in and by them; just as they again are complete in and by Him. Paul, and you, and I, hung, originally, and in the beginning, at Adam's mystical girdle, and we have all had to take the consequences of that mystical suspension. But now we have all been loosened off from Adam, and have been united close and inseparably to Christ. Before God, we all hang now at Christ's mystical girdle. Ay, far better, and far more blessed than even that, Christ now dwells under our girdle, and dwells, and can dwell, nowhere else. That is to say, in simple and plain language, He dwells in our hearts by faith and love on our part, and by mystical incorporation on His part. I am crucified with Christ, nevertheless I live; yet not I, but Christ liveth in me. And, for this cause, I bow my knees unto the Father of our Lord Jesus Christ, that Christ may dwell in your hearts by faith.

Now, as might be looked for, a thousand things, mystical and other, follow from all that, and will, to all eternity, follow from all that. But take one or two things that immediately and at once follow from all that, and so close this meditation. And first, the mystical union between Christ and the soul is so mysterious that it is a great mystery even to those who are in it, and share it. As Walter Marshall, one of the greatest doctors in this mystery, has it: "Yea," says Marshall in his *Gospel*

Mystery, "though it be revealed clearly in the Holy Scriptures, yet the natural man has not eyes to see it there. And if God expresses it never so plainly and properly, he will still think that God is speaking in riddles and parables. And I doubt not but it is still a riddle, even to many truly godly men, who have received a holy nature from God in this way. For the apostles themselves had the saving benefit of this mystery long before the Comforter had discovered it clearly to them. They walked in Christ as the way to the Father, before they clearly knew Him to be the way. And the best of us know this mystery but in part, and must wait for the perfect knowledge of it in another world." So mysterious is this mystery of godliness.

But how, asks some one honestly and anxiously—how shall I ever become such a miracle of Divine grace as to be actually, myself, a member of Christ's mystical body? Just begin at once to be one of His members, and the thing is done. Your hands do not hang idle and say—How shall we ever do any work? Your feet do not stand still and say—How shall we ever walk or run? Nor your eyes, nor your ears. They just begin to do, each, their proper work, and the moment they so begin, your head and your heart immediately send down their virtue into your hands and your feet. And so is it with the mystical Head and His mystical members. Just begin to be one of His members, and already you are one of them. Believe that you are one of them, and you shall be one of them. Just think about Christ. Just speak to Christ. Just lean upon, and look to Christ. Just go home tonight and do that deed of love, and truth, and humility, and brotherly-kindness, and self-denial, in His name, and, already, Christ is dwelling in you, and working in you as well as in Paul. Saul of Tarsus just said as he lay among his horse's feet—Lord, what wilt Thou have me to do? and from that moment the thing was done.

Now, my brethren, if I have had any success tonight in setting forth Paul as an evangelical mystic, this also will follow as one of the many fruits of my argument. This fine word "mystical" will henceforth be redeemed in all your minds from all that dreaminess, and cloudiness, and unreality, and unpracticalness, with which it has hitherto been associated in your minds. "Vigor and efficacy" may not have been associated in many minds with the great mystical saints, and yet that is the very language that is used concerning them by no less an authority than Dr. Johnson. But just look at two or three of the greatest evangelical and saintly mystics for yourselves, and see if the great critic and lexicographer is not literally correct. Where is there vigor and efficacy in all the world like the vigor and efficacy of the Apostle Paul? Where is there less dreaminess or less cloudiness than in Paul? What a leader of men he was! What a founder and ruler of churches! What a man of business he was, and that just because of his mystical oneness with Christ. What an incomparably laborious, efficient, and fruitful life Paul lived! What a mystical conversation with heaven he kept up, combined with what stupendous services on earth! Take Luther also. There is not a more evangelically-mystical book in all New Testament literature than Luther's Galatians. And yet, or I should rather say, and therefore, what truly Pauline vigor and efficacy in everything! And take Teresa and her mystical deacon always at her side, John of the Cross. I would need to be a genius at coining right words before I could describe aright to you that amazing woman's statesmanship and emperorship in life and in character. Founding schools, selecting sites, negotiating finances, superintending architects and builders and gardeners; always in the kitchen, always in the schoolroom, always in the oratory, always on horseback. A mother in Israel. A queen among the most queenly women in all the world. And, unjust as Dr. Duncan is to William Law our greatest English mystic, Duncan is compelled to allow about Law that "he spoke upon the practical as with the sound of a trumpet. In practical appeals Law is a very Luther. Luther and Law were Boanerges." And, as Dr. Somerville, our west-end neighbor says, from whose fine book on Paul I have borrowed the title of this lecture:— "The intensity that characterized the religious life and experience of the late General Gordon, was all due to his evangelical mysticism. All associated in his case also with extraordinary efficiency in the practical affairs of life and in the management of men." But why argue out such remote and historical instances when we have it all within ourselves? Let any man among ourselves carry about Christ in his own heart; let any man abide in Christ as the branch abides in the vine: let any man cleave as close to Christ as a member of our body cleaves close to its head: let any man say unceasingly every day, and in every cross and temptation of every day, "I am crucified with Christ: nevertheless I live: yet not I, but Christ liveth in me;" and you will be absolutely sure to find that man the most willing, the most active, the most practical, and the most efficient man in every kind of Christian work. In one word, the more evangelically mystical any man is, the more full of all vigor and all efficacy will that man be sure to be.

121
Paul's Great Heaviness and Continual Sorrow of Heart

PAUL'S all-but complete blindness to the beauties of nature and to the attractions of art, as well as his all-but absolute indifference to the classic sites and scenes of Greece and Rome, has been often remarked on, and has been often lamented over. Paul's utter insensibility has been often set in severe contrast to our Lord's much-applauded love of nature. Calvin also has suffered no little vituperation for sitting all day over his Institutes, and never once lifting up his eyes to give us a description of the Alps overhead. The prince of Scripture commentators will never be forgiven for never having once stood up in rapture over the sun-risings and the sun-settings on the eternal snows. Pascal also has come under the same condemnation because he could see no scenery anywhere much worth wondering at outside the immortal soul of man. And we are all at one in despising and spurning St. Bernard because he rode a whole day along the shores of the lake of Geneva with his monk's cowl so drawn down over his eyes that he had to ask his host at sunset where that famous water was which he had heard so many people talking so much about. Now, I am not going to put forward any defence or excuse of mine for Paul's limitations and insensibilities. The very most I shall attempt to do is to offer you some possible explanation of that great heaviness of mind, and that great sorrow of heart, which has lost Paul the full approval of so many of his best friends. How was it possible for Paul to travel through those so famous scenes, how was it possible for him to live in those so classic cities, and never to give us a single sentence about persons and places, the very names of which make our modern hearts to beat fast in our bosoms to this day?

> In vain to me the smiling mornings shine,
>   And reddening Phoebus lifts his golden fire;
> The birds in vain their amorous descant join,
>   Or cheerful fields resume their green attire.
> These ears, alas! for other notes repine;
>   A different object do these eyes require;
> My lonely anguish meets no heart but mine,
>   And in my breast the imperfect joys expire.

Right or wrong; praise Paul or blame him; try to understand him, and to feel with him and for him, or no; the thing is as clear as day, that some iron or other has so entered Paul's soul, and an iron such, that it will never depart from his soul in this world. And, till that rankling spear-head, so to call it, is removed for ever out of Paul's mind and heart in another world than this, say what you will to blame Paul, he has no ear left for the singing of your amorous birds, and no eye left but for that holy whiteness that so stains to his eyes both Mount Salmon and Mont Blanc. Master, said the holiday-minded disciples, see what manner of stones, and what buildings are here. But He turned and said to the twelve, I have a baptism to be baptized with, and how am I straitened till it be accomplished. The immense size of those stones, and the exquisite carving of their capitals, would have interested Him at another time, but His own time was now at hand: and so much so that He could see nothing else, all that terrible week, but Gethsemane and its cup, and Calvary and its cross. And, to come down to His great servant: when Mont Blanc was so full to him of the glory of snow and sunshine on many a Sabbath morning, Calvin was wont to boast it all back into its own place with this out of the Psalms—"The hill of God is as the hill of Bashan; an high hill as the hill of Bashan. Why leap ye, ye high hills? This is the hill that God desireth to dwell in: yea, the Lord will dwell in it for ever"; and, so singing, Calvin went up again to Mount Zion. Cicero says somewhere that Plato and Demosthenes, Aristotle and Socrates, might have respectively excelled in each other's province, had it not been that each one of those great men was so absorbed in his own province. And Paul might have been a Christian Herodotus, and a New Testament Pausanias, had it not been for his own absolutely absorbing province of sin and salvation from sin.

> All thoughts, all passions, all delights:
>   Whatever stirs this mortal frame;
> All are but ministers of Love,
>   And feed His sacred flame.

Among all the heathenish doxologies of her voluminous devotees, nature has never had half such a noble tribute paid to her true greatness, as Paul pays to her, in three verses of his immortal eighth chapter. All the true lovers of nature: that is to say, all the true worshippers, not of nature, but of Jesus Christ; have by heart, and have deep down in their heart, the famous but wholly unfathomable tribute. Listen to nature's truest prophet, and truest priest, and truest poet, the Apostle Paul. "For the earnest expectation of the creature waiteth for the manifestation of the sons of God. For the creature was made subject to vanity, not willingly, but by reason of Him who hath subjected the same in hope. Because the creature itself shall be delivered from the bondage of corruption into the glorious liberty of the sons of God. For we know that the whole creation groaneth and travaileth in pain together until now. And not only they, but ourselves also, which have the first-fruits of the Spirit, even we ourselves, groan within ourselves, waiting for the adoption." Match that, if you can, for a tribute to nature's true greatness. Match that, if you can, out of all your sentimental stuff. You cannot do it. I defy you to do it. Pascal is constantly saying this of man, that man's great misery is the true measure of his greatness. Give me, therefore, Paul's profound lamentation over the bondage, and the vanity, and the groaning, and the travailing of nature; and over the shame, and the sin, and the misery of man her master. And, then, give me his magnificent prophecy over her evangelical future. To all of which profound pathos on the one hand, and to all of which magnificent hope on the other hand, your nature-worshipper's unbroken heart is utterly stupid and dead. Paul was such a great man, and such a great apostle of the Creator and Redeemer both of man and of nature, that, in their present state of sin and misery, and on that account, like his Master, he was a man of inconsolable sorrows. And yet babes at the breast will wail out against the insensibility of that mighty mind and mighty heart; will wail out at his insensibility and indifference to those toys and trifles that so sanctify and satisfy them, as they so often assure us. Whatever may be the true explanation of your entire satisfaction with nature, and with art, and with travel, and with yourself, this is undoubtedly the true explanation of Paul's great heaviness and continual sorrow of heart. The tremendous catastrophe of the fall of man, and the fall of all nature around man—that, to Paul, was so ever-present and so all-possessing, that there is no alleviation of his awful pain of heart on account of all that. At any rate, there is no alleviation or relief for him in the color of the morning or evening sky, or in the shape of the hills, or in the music of the woods and the waters. Miserable comforters are all these things to Paul's broken heart; but, most miserable of all, your mountebank comforters among men, who would thrust things like these upon Paul's profound and inappeasable sorrow. "A man in distress," says John Foster, "has peculiarly a right not to be trifled with by the application of unadapted expedients: since insufficient consolations but mock him, and deceptive consolations betray him." The whole truth about Paul, above all other mortal men, is this. Paul is so intensely religious in his whole mind, and heart, and imagination, and temperament, and taste: he is so utterly and absolutely godly: he is such an out-and-out Christian man and Christian apostle: he is so consumed continually with his hunger and his thirst after righteousness: he is so captivated, enthralled, and enraptured with the beauty of holiness, that nothing will ever satisfy Paul, either for nature, or for art, or for travel, or for man, or for himself, short of the new heavens and the new earth. And until that day dawns, and that day-star arises in Paul's heart, whatever you and I may do, he will continue to look, not at the things that are seen, but at the things that are not seen; for the things which are seen are temporal, but the things which are not seen are eternal. Renan sometimes hits the mark in a manner that both surprises and rebukes us. "Paul," says that truly wonderful writer, "belongs wholly to another world than this present world. Paul's Parnassus and Olympus; his sunrises and his sunsets; his whole Greece, and Rome, and Holy Land itself, are all elsewhere, and not here."

But not amidst nature and art and travel only, but amidst far better things than these, men like Paul are often made men of sorrow and of a heavy heart. "How, now, good friend, whither away after this burdened manner? A burdened manner indeed, as ever I think poor creature had. Hast thou a wife and children? Yes; but I am so laden with this burden, that I cannot take that pleasure in them as I once thought I would. Methinks, I am as if I had them not." A bold passage, but a right noble passage. A Paul-like passage. Paul had neither wife nor child, but he could not have written a better passage than John Bunyan's above passage, even if he had had as many children as John Bunyan had, and had loved them, and had wept over them, as only John Bunyan could love and weep. At the same time, it would have been an additional relief, and a real and a peculiar support to us, to have had a passage immediately from Paul's own pen on the heaviness of heart that cannot but accompany family life, when a man of Paul's sensibility, and of John Bunyan's sensibility, is at the head of that family. For Paul's most noble lamentation over the out-of-door creation is cold and remote, and is wholly without those bowels and mercies, that would have been stirred in Paul had he walked with a perfect heart before his house at home. But in the absence of Paul on the profoundest aspects of family life, I know nothing better anywhere than the Pilgrim's reply to Mr. Worldly Wiseman; and, some time after, to Charity. To Charity, who, though like the Apostle she has no children of her own body, yet like him, her love, and her imagination, and her genius for the things of the heart, all make her speak to us like a mother in Israel, and all make John Bunyan to speak in reply to her like a father in the same. As Thomas Boston also has it in one of his Shakespearian passages: "Man is born crying, lives complaining, and dies disappointed from that quarter. All is vanity and vexation of spirit. But I have waited for Thy salvation, O Lord."

Why are the ungodly generally so jocund? asks Thomas Shepard. Partly, he answers, their want of understanding. They may be very eloquent on scenery, and on travel, and on art, and yet the scales may be on their eyes and the shell on their heads all the time as to anything deeper than the surface of things. Most men, he asserts, remain total strangers to themselves, and to their true spiritual state, all their days. And a little after that, this pungentest of preachers goes on to ask why the truly godly are ofttimes so much more sad and melancholy than other people? And among other deep answers he supplies himself and us with this deep answer—It is not because they are too godly that they are so sad, but because they are not far more godly. They have grace enough to bring them off from casual and worldly delights, but not enough to enable them to live upon the spiritual and eternal world, and to fetch all their comforts from thence. Grace has for ever spoiled their joy in the creature, but they are not yet grown so spiritual as to live upon God, and hence it is that they are found so often hovering in sadness and dissatisfaction between earth and heaven. Thomas Shepard's *Ten Virgins*, and his *Zaccharus*, are perfect mines of the profoundest and most experimental truth. Lord Brodie also will give us his testimony on this same subject out of his heavy-hearted diary. Brodie was not Paul, nor Pascal, nor Bunyan, nor even Thomas Shepard, but he had sufficient heaviness of mind and sorrow of heart to purchase him a right and a title to be listened to on this matter now in hand. "I never could allow myself," he says, "much exuberant joy in any created thing. But I have always exercised myself to hold every such thing soberly and ready to be surrendered up." And a far better man, our own dear Halyburton, has much the same thing to tell us. "The strong power of sin that I found still remaining in me, and the disturbances thence arising, made life not desirable; and a prospect of final and complete riddance by death, made death appear much more eligible."

But to come back before we close to what we began with, that is to say, the true place of nature in the religious, and especially in the Christian, life. And instead of offering you my own weak words on such a high subject, take this classical passage out of the diary of Thomas Shepard's great pupil in the things of the soul, the greatest man, Dr. Duncan is inclined to think, since Aristotle. We all know the use that our Lord makes of nature in His preaching. Well, here are some examples of the uses that Jonathan Edwards makes of nature also. "Immediately after my conversion, God's excellency began to appear to me in everything—in the sun, in the moon, in the stars, in the waters, and in all nature. The Son of God created this world for this very end, to communicate to us through it a certain image of His own excellency, so that when we are delighted with flowery meadows and gentle breezes of wind we may see in all that only the sweet benevolence of Jesus Christ. When we behold the fragrant rose and the snow-white lily, we are to see His love and His purity. Even so the green trees, and the songs of birds, what are they but the emanations of His infinite joy and benignity? The crystal rivers and murmuring streams, what are they but the footsteps of His favor and grace and beauty? When we behold the brightness of the sun, the golden edges of the evening cloud, or the beauteous rainbow spanning the whole heaven, we but behold some adumbration of His glory and His goodness. And, without any doubt, this is the reason that Christ is called the Sun of Righteousness, the Morning Star, the Rose of Sharon, and the Lily of the Valley, the appletree among the trees of the wood, a bundle of myrrh, a roe, and a young hart. But we see the most proper image of the beauty of Christ when we see the beauty of the soul of man." So far the greatest mind since Aristotle.

But, now that I have come to an end, I see now that I might have spared both you and myself also all this time and trouble. For our Lord's great words, "they began to be merry"; and the elder's great words that "God would wipe away all tears from their eyes"; those two Holy Scriptures, rightly understood, rightly imagined, and rightly taken to heart, would, of themselves, alone, have saved both you and me this long and superfluous discourse tonight.

122
Paul the Aged

IT is calculated that the Apostle must have been somewhere between fifty-eight and sixty-four when he wrote of himself to Philemon as Paul the aged. Certain difficulties have sometimes been raised over the text. It has sometimes been asked whether Paul would have spoken of himself as an old man, say, at sixty, or sixty-three. But a thousand things may come in to make a man feel either old or young at that, or at any other age. The kind of life a man has lived; virtuous or vicious, religious or irreligious, idle or industrious, for himself, or for God and his generation, the state of his health, the state of his fortune, his family life, his disappointed or fulfilled hopes in life, and so on. Cicero wrote his *Cato* at sixty-three, and the great orator's design in that famous dialogue was to brace up those men around him whose knees were beginning to tremble, and their hands to hang down about that time of life. And Cicero goes on to fortify first himself and then his readers, with such examples as those of Plato, who died at his desk at eighty-one; and Isocrates, who wrote one of his best books at ninety-four, and who lived another five years on the fame of it; and Gorgias the Leontine, who completed a hundred and seven years, and never to the end loitered in his love of work, but died leaving this testimony on his deathbed, "I have had no cause for blaming old age," he said. "I, myself," adds Cato, "supported the Voconian law at sixty-five with an unimpaired voice and powerful lungs." And, best of all, at the age of seventy, Ennius lived in such a heart as to bear nobly those two burdens, which are by most men deemed the greatest—poverty and old age. Ennius bore those two burdens with what seemed to all men around him the greatest goodwill. On the other hand, in annotating the text Bishop Lightfoot reminds us that Roger Bacon complained of himself at fifty-three as already an old man. And so too Sir Walter Scott lamented of himself at fifty-five as "a gray old man." Now it must be admitted that those two Christians do not come out at all well when set beside the brave-hearted heathens. Only, Dr. Samuel Johnson's shout must not be forgotten—Drink water, Sir, and go in for a hundred! And who himself drank water and went in for reading the best and writing the best, till he published his masterpiece after he was threescore and ten. Dante's old age in the Banquet begins at forty-five. But, on the other hand, Tacitus declares that if he had one foot in the grave, it would not matter, he would still be reading and writing the best.

Now, with all his love and loyalty to Paul, and with all his perfect understanding of everything connected with Paul, for some reason or other, Luke all but completely fails us as Paul's old age approaches. "And Paul dwelt two whole years in his own hired house in Rome, and received all that came in unto him, preaching the kingdom of God, and teaching those things which concern the Lord Jesus Christ, with all confidence, no man forbidding him." These are Luke's very last words to us about Paul. I wish I could believe that these beautiful words described Paul's very last days down to the end. But when Luke, for some reason or other, drops into absolute silence, Paul's own Epistles of the Imprisonment come in to supply us with such affecting glimpses into the Apostle's last days as these. "I, Paul, the prisoner of Jesus Christ. For whom I am an ambassador in bonds. Be not ashamed of me His prisoner. For my bonds are manifest. This also thou knowest that all those that are in Asia be turned away from me. But the Lord have mercy on the house of Onesiphorus, for he oft refreshed me, and was not ashamed of my chain. For I am now ready to be offered up, and the time of my departure is at hand. Demas hath forsaken me, having loved this present world. Only Luke is with me. The cloak that I left at Troas, when thou comest, bring with thee, and the books, but especially the parchments." With one foot in the grave, like Tacitus, Paul is still reading books and writing parchments. "At my first answer no man stood by me, but all men forsook me. Do thy diligence to come to me before winter." You see Paul forsaken, lonely, cold and without his cloak, chained to a soldier, and waiting on one of Nero's mad fits for his martyrdom. Well may Paul say, if in this life only we have hope in Christ, we are of all men most miserable. But Paul has such an anchor within the veil that, amid all these sad calamities, old age and all, he is able to send out such Epistles of faith and hope and love as the Ephesians and the Colossians and the Philippians and the Pastorals and Philemon. Comparing the *Odyssey* with the *Iliad*, Longinus says, "If I speak of old age, it is nevertheless the old age of Homer."

I really wish I could prevail with you who are no longer young to put aside, as Butler beseeches you, your books and papers of mere amusement, and to read Cicero's *Cato*, and some of the other old age classics, if only to make those fine books to serve for so many foils in a fresh perusal of the Epistles of the Imprisonment. It is our bounden duty to read a Greek or a Roman masterpiece now and then, such as the *Phaedo* or the *Cato*, if only to awaken ourselves again to the immensity of the change that came into this world with the Incarnation and the Resurrection of our Lord. What a contrast between philosophy at its very best in Socrates and Cicero, and the Gospel of our salvation unto everlasting life in Paul's old age Epistles! The whole truth and beauty and nobility of such books as the best of Plato and Cicero is all needed the better to bring out the inconceivable contrast between this world at its very best before Christ, and the new heavens and the new earth that our Lord brought to this world with Him and left in this world behind Him. How such glorious passages as these shine out afresh upon us after we have just laid down the *Cato* and even the *Phaedo*. Such well-known, but so little realized, passages as these: "Christ shall be magnified in my body, whether it be by life or by death. For to me to live is Christ, and to die is gain. For I am in a strait betwixt two, having a desire to depart, and to be with Christ, which is far better. For our conversation is in heaven; from whence also we look for the Savior, the Lord Jesus Christ, who shall change our vile body, that it may be fashioned like unto His glorious body, according to the working whereby He is able even to subdue all things unto Himself. For I am now ready to be offered, and the time of my departure is at hand. I have fought a good fight, I have finished my course, I have kept the faith. Henceforth there is laid up for me a crown of righteousness, which the Lord, the righteous Judge, shall give me at that day; and not to me only, but unto all them also that love His appearing." What a man was Paul! If we did not know that this was Paul, we would certainly think that it was a Greater than even Paul. Really and truly, my brethren, it would be well worth your putting yourselves to some expense and some trouble in order to read, say, the Consolations of Cato to your old age, and then to turn to Paul's consolations and comforts. Unless, indeed, you already read your Paul with such understanding, and with such imagination, and with such heart, that you do not need the assistance that Plato and Cicero were raised up and preserved to this day to give you.

Well; after repeated readings lately of the Cato, and the Epistles of the Imprisonment, and the Art of Dying Well, and Jeremy Taylor, and suchlike authors for old age, I will now tell you some of the reflections, impressions, and resolutions, that have been left in my own mind. And take first Paul's so touching message to Timothy about his cloak, and his books, and his parchments. For all that comes in most harmoniously after we have just been reading *Cato* about our keeping on reading and writing our best to the end. Lest you might not be able to lay your hands on what Calvin says about Paul's books, I will copy out the passage for you. "It is evident from this," says the prince of commentators, "that the Apostle has not given over study even when he is preparing himself for death. Where are those men then, who think that they have made so great progress that they do not need any more to persevere? Which of you will have the courage to compare yourself with the Apostle? Still more surely does this passage refute the folly of those fools who, despising books, and neglecting all study, boast of their spiritual inspiration." And if I might be bold enough to add one word after Calvin. I am not now, alas! a neophyte in these matters, and I will therefore take boldness to say this to you. Read the very best books, and only the very best, and ever better and better the older you grow. Be more and more select, and fastidious, and refined, in your books and in your companions, as old age draws on, and death with old age. I wonder just what books they were that Paul missed so much in his imprisoned and apostolic old age at Rome. It might have been the *Apology*. It might have been the *Phaedo*. It might have been the *Cato Major*. It could not possibly have been Moses, or David, or Isaiah, or Micah. You may depend upon it, Paul did not forget his Bible when he was packing his trunk at Troas. You are far better off in the matter of books for your old age than Paul was with his Bible and all. Never, then, be out of your Old, and especially, never be out of your New Testament. As Paul says about prayer, read in your New Testament without ceasing. Never lay it down, unless it is to take up another letter of Samuel Rutherford, or another pilgrim's crossing of the river; or, if you have head enough left for it, another great chapter of the *Saint's Rest*. Nothing else. At least, nothing less pertinent and appropriate to your years and to your immediate prospects. Nothing less noble. Nothing less worthy of yourself. Nothing at all but just those true classics of the eternal world over and over again, till your whole soul is in a flame with them, and till your rapture into heaven seizes upon you with one of them in your hand.

You may remember how a great divine as he grew old was wont, for that and for some other reasons, to go back now and then and take a turn up and down in his unregenerate state. As Paul also was wont to do. For as Paul grew older and saintlier, he the oftener would go back upon the sins of his youth. Paul was like William Taylor, who when asked of God what He would choose for a gift in his old age, answered, repentance unto life. And thus it is that if you are well read in Paul's old-age Epistles you will find far more repentance unto life in his last years, than even in his years of immediate conversion and remorse. You meet with an ever deeper bitterness at sin, and at himself, as time goes on with Paul: and, then, a corresponding amazement at God's mercy. And you will do well to be followers of the Apostle, and the Puritan, and the Presbyterian, in this sinner-becoming practice. Go back, then, deliberately and at length, and take many a good look at the hole of the pit you had dug for yourself, and in which you had made your bed in hell. And come up from the mouth of that horrible pit, and up to that rock on which you now stand, and see if the result will not be the same in you that it was in Paul and in those two most Pauline of preachers and writers; see if it will not make you hate sin with a more and more perfect hatred, as also to make you long again, and as never before, to be for ever with the Lord.

And, not only read your very best, but pray your very best also, and that literally without ceasing. Yes, without one atom of exaggeration or hyperbole, always and without ceasing. If for no other reason than just to make up a little before you die for ever, for your long life, now for ever past, and in which you have found time for everything but prayer, and for every one but God. Or, have you no children or grandchildren to make up to them also for your neglect of their immortal souls? And have you in this matter ever considered God's acknowledged and accepted servant Job? How with him it always was so, that when the days of his children's feastings again came round, he sent and sanctified them, and rose up early in the morning and offered up burnt-offerings according to the number of them all. When do you offer up for your children, early in the morning, or late at night? Different fathers have different habits. Or, when you go back with Paul and take a turn up and down in your un-regenerate state, do you ever come upon slain souls who are now under the altar, and who cry continually concerning you— How long, O Lord, holy and true, dost Thou not judge and avenge our blood on them that dwell on the earth! Pray, O unforgiven old man! Pray without ceasing, all the time that is now left you. And who can tell, if God will turn and repent, and turn away from His fierce anger against you, that you perish not.

And every day and every night over your Paul and your Bunyan and your Rutherford and your Baxter, and suchlike, practice, as they all did, your imagination and your heart upon Jesus Christ. Practice upon Him till He is far more real to you, and far more present with you, than the best of those people are who have lived all your days in the same house with you. Jesus Christ either is, or He is not. If He is not, then there is nothing more to be said. But if He is, then set aside every one else, and practice His presence with you, and your presence with Him. Imagine Christ. Make pictures by that splendid talent that God has given you for the very purpose of making pictures to yourself of Christ. Make pictures to yourself of your meeting with Christ immediately after death. Forefancy your deathbed, said Samuel Rutherford. Do you ever forefancy yours? It was the forefancying of his deathbed that was the conversion and salvation of that old man to whom Ruther-ford sent the letter. Do you ever forefancy your first meeting with Christ? How do you think He will look? How and where will you look? Rehearse the scene, and have your part ready. It is to the old alone, be it clearly understood, that these things are spoken. The young, and the middle-aged, and those who are busy with other things than preparing to meet with Christ, and with other books than the above —they have plenty of time. But neither you nor I. Let us, at any rate, be up and doing. Santa Teresa felt a thrill go through her every time the clock struck on the mantelpiece. The same thrill, as she had been told, that all our earthly brides feel each time their slow clock strikes. An hour nearer seeing Him! she exclaimed, and clapped her hands. Up, all you old people, and be like her. Up, and make your-selves ready. Up, and abolish death. Up, out of your bondage all your days through fear of death. Up, and practice dying in the Lord, till you take the prize. Up, and read Paul without ceasing, and pray without ceasing, till you also shall stand on tiptoe with expectation and with full assurance of faith. Yes; up, till you also shall salute His sudden coming, and shall exclaim, Even so, come quickly, Lord Jesus!

123
Apollos

THE founding and the naming of Alexandria, its matchless situation, its architectural beauty, the rare wisdom of its statesmanship, and the splendid catholicity of its sacred scholarship—all these things greatly interest us and greatly impress us. And all these things tell at once upon the text and serve richly to illustrate the text. For Apollos, though a Jew, was born in Alexandria, and received his education in Alexandria. The repeated dispersions of the Jewish people had filled the Jewish quarter of Alexandria with tens of thousands of that expatriated people, but everywhere an industrious, enterprising, and successful, people. By that time the Jews of Alexandria had almost the half of the whole city given up to themselves, and the Jewish merchants, and bankers, and scholars of Alexandria were, in all their several walks of life, in the very foremost rank. And, without in any way forsaking or forgetting the faith of their fathers, the Jews of Alexandria had opened their own minds, and the minds of their children, to the best learning of that eminently learned city. Apollos, when an inquiring boy, would be taken up by his father to the famous synagogue every Sabbath day, where he would see the seventy elders sitting on their seventy thrones of gold, and where he would watch for the waving of the far-off flag that summoned the immense congregation to fall down at the same moment on their knees to say their Amen. On the weekdays, and in spite of the fierce anathemas of the fanatical scribes of Jerusalem, young Apollos would be sent to school where he would learn to read Homer and Plato, as well as Moses and Isaiah. And in his holidays he would be taken out of the city to walk along the seven-furlong mole to the famous lighthouse island, on which the Sacred Septuagint had received its finishing touches. And as the talented boy became a student he would often find his way to the world-renowned library of Alexandria, into which had been collected the whole literature of the ancient world, sacred and profane; all the best books of Israel, as well as all the best books of Greece and Rome and Egypt and India.

It is not in our power to fix down the exact date of Apollos's birth, but we are quite sure of this, that he was a contemporary, and almost certainly a schoolfellow, of Philo the famous Hellenistic Hebrew of Alexandria. We possess no book of Apollos's authorship, unless Luther's bold guess is also a correct guess that Apollos wrote the Epistle to the Hebrews in his mature years. And unless that other guess is also correct that he wrote the Book of Wisdom in his Alexandrian years. These, to be sure, are only guesses at his authorship, but the guesses of men of learning and genius have often far more truth in them than the proofs and certainties that satisfy less learned and less imaginative men. At the same time, if it is but an illuminating guess that we possess anything at all from Apollos's pen, we are quite sure about the many extant works of Philo. And so much alike were those two great contemporaneous men, that we can almost transfer to the one what we are told about the other. For, just as of Philo it may with absolute certainty be said that "he was a Jew, born in Alexandria, an eloquent man, and mighty in the Scriptures," so, on the other hand, it is no great stretch of the imagination to picture Apollos to ourselves as the author of *The Allegories of the Sacred Laws, The Theology of Moses,* and *The Indictment of Flaccus.*

Paul was not what we would call an eloquent preacher. The Apostle's detractors were wont to set Paul aside with this contemptuous sentence, that his bodily presence was weak, and his speech contemptible. But his greatest enemies could not say that about Apollos. Depth of mind and fluency of speech do not always go together. They did not go together in Moses and Paul, the two greatest men of the Hebrew race. But Apollos was both a man of a deep mind and of great oratorical genius. Quintilian, another contemporary of Apollos, has a fine chapter on this theme, that a great orator is just a good man well skilled in speaking. Now, Apollos satisfied both parts of that excellent definition also. For Apollos was first a good man, and then he was a skillful speaker. No man in the Apostolic Church was nearly such a skillful speaker as Apollos was. And the sacred writer is careful to add concerning Apollos that he was "mighty in the Scriptures" also. In saying that the sacred writer intends what he says to be all but the very highest praise that can possibly be given to Apollos. A great mind alone will not make a man mighty in the Scriptures. A great gift of oratory alone will not do it. It is the moral and spiritual qualities of the sacred orator, when they are added to his intellectual qualities, that make men confess his might when he handles the Holy Scriptures. The acknowledged might of Apollos in the pulpit was the might of conviction and of character; it was the might that has its seat in the conscience and the heart of a good man, taken together with that other might of a great intellect and real eloquence. The great might of Aristotle and Quintilian combined would still have left Apollos weak as other men in the things of God, unless there had been united with all that the might of a conscience on fire against all unrighteousness, and of a heart on fire with the love of all truth and all goodness. Apollos has much still to learn, but this is a right noble foundation on which to build up a great preacher of the Gospel: "a Jew, born in Alexandria, an eloquent man, and mighty in the Scriptures"; so far, that is, as he as yet understands the Scriptures.

This then was the Alexandrian scholar and orator who came to Ephesus on an Old Testament mission immediately after Paul had left that city. Paul and Apollos had no acquaintance as yet with one another. They had never met, and though they were both great preachers, they did not at all preach the same Gospel. With all his Alexandrian learning, and with all his finished eloquence, and with all his knowledge of Moses and Isaiah and John the Baptist, Apollos knew nothing, or next to nothing, of Jesus Christ. How Apollos had come to know so much as he did know, we are not told; but we are told distinctly that his knowledge came to an end with the preaching and the baptism of John, the son of Zacharias and Elizabeth. It perplexes us to be told that about such a man as Apollos was. That such a universal student, and such a lover of all kinds of truth, and especially of revealed truth, should have lived so long in the very metropolis of all intelligence, and not have got beyond the school of John—that quite staggers us about Apollos. At the same time, we must remember that with all his marvellous activity and success, Paul had never been so far as Alexandria. If Paul had preached Christ even once in that magnificent synagogue, what a chapter we would have had in the Acts of the Apostles about Paul's conversations with Apollos. But as it was, Apollos was still preaching just as John had both preached and baptized twenty years before at Bethabara beyond Jordan. John's doctrines and exhortations were preached by Apollos with tremendous passion and impressiveness; with all John's own tremendous passion and impressiveness; and with a polish of manner and a perfection of style to which John was an utter stranger. But that was all the preaching that Aquila and Priscilla listened to Sabbath after Sabbath, as Apollos stood up in the pulpit of Ephesus. Sabbath day after Sabbath day, Aquila and Priscilla came up to the synagogue and listened to Apollos preaching John; and every returning Sabbath day they listened to him with increasing regret that he had not come to Ephesus in time to have heard Paul preaching Christ. With a weekly increasing distress they listened to what they heard, or rather, did not hear, till, at last, they took Apollos and expounded unto him the way of God more perfectly.

Such then is this so beautiful passage, and so full of all manner of lessons for students, for young preachers, and for old people. And first, for old people, and for people far on in the spiritual life. I can overhear Aquila and Priscilla on their way home from the synagogue Sabbath after Sabbath; or, rather, I can overhear them after their children are asleep. For you may depend upon it, Aquila and Priscilla did not discuss Apollos's sermons at the church door or at the dinner table. Was that a good sermon today, father? asked young Keble. All sermons are good, my son, answered his wise father. And Aquila was like old Keble. All the way home from church Aquila talked to his sons and daughters about Alexandria and her schools; about the Septuagint; about Apollos's great learning and great eloquence; about the work that he had laid out on that sermon; about his noble style; about his commanding manner, and about the great lessons to be learned from every sermon of his. And then, when the Sabbath was over, and they were alone, Aquila and Priscilla would open their minds quite freely to one another about the young preacher. Now how would we have done had we been in Aquila's and Priscilla's place? This is what we would have done. We would have let the whole congregation see what we thought of Apollos. We would have shifted about in our seat. We would have looked at the clock. We would have held down our head. We would have covered our eyes with our hands. We would have glanced at our neighbors to see how they were taking it all. We would have smiled sadly, so that all might see us. And then, at the door—"How did you like him? Poor boy! he does not know the very A B C of the Gospel!" And so on, till it would all have been told to Apollos, and till we had ruined our influence with him, and his influence with us and with our children for ever. How Aquila and Priscilla managed it I cannot imagine. But manage it they did, for "they took Apollos unto them," says the sacred writer, "and expounded unto him the way of God more perfectly." "An old and simple woman, if she loves Jesus, may be greater than our brother Bonaventure."

I admire all the three so much, that I really do not know which to admire the most; Aquila and Priscilla in their quite extraordinary wisdom and tact and courage, and especially love; or Apollos in his still more extraordinary humility, modesty, and mind of Christ. A shining student of Alexandria, a popular and successful preacher, not standing-room when he preached in the synagogue, followed about by admiring crowds, and with many seals to his ministry among them; such a famous man to be taken to task about his pulpit work by two old workers in sail-cloth and carpets, and to be instructed by them how to preach, and how not to preach—"the whole thing is laughable, if it were not for its impudence." So I would have said had I been in Apollos's place. But like the true Alexandrian he was, and the true preacher, and the true coming colleague and successor of Paul, Apollos instantly saw who and what he had in Aquila and Priscilla. In a moment he felt they were by far his superiors in the things of the pulpit at any rate, and he at once made it both easy and successful for them to say to him all that was in their minds and hearts. I would far rather have Apollos's humble mind and quiet heart at that supreme moment of his life than all his gold medals, first-class certificates, and all his crowds to boot; the noble young Christian gentleman that Apollos at that moment proved himself to be.

It was their own experience of the way of God that enabled and authorized Aquila and Priscilla to take Apollos and teach him that way more perfectly. It was not Paul's preaching that did it. Their own experience, in their case, went before Paul's preaching, accompanied it, and came after it. They knew the doctrine of Christ perfectly because they had lived the life of Christ perfectly. Tent-makers as they were, and wholly unlettered as they were, they received it as soon as it was written, and read and quite well understood the Epistle to the Ephesians, because they had all its deep mysteries already in their own hearts. Paul in his best preaching had only told Aquila and Priscilla, with all his authority, what they knew to a certainty before. Every true preacher comes on the same thing continually among his people. And every wide reader of such literature knows where to find illustrations of the same thing. Brother Lawrence, the humble cook, instructing the theologians of his day about the practice of the presence of God; Jacob Behmen enlightening William Law; Thomas Boston's old soldier giving his minister a loan of "The Marrow"; and Cowper's poor Cottager. But the classical passage is in *Grace Abounding*. "Upon a day the good providence of God did cast me to Bedford to work on my calling; and in one of the streets of that town I came where there were three or four poor women sitting at a door in the sun, and talking about the things of God; and being now willing to hear their discourse, I drew near to hear what they said, for I was now a brisk talker myself in the matters of religion. But I may say, I heard, but I understood not; for they were far above, out of my reach. Their talk was about a new birth, the work of God in their hearts, also how they were convinced of their miserable state by nature. They talked how God had visited their souls with His love in the Lord Jesus, and with what words and promises they had been refreshed, comforted, and supported against the temptations of the devil. And, methought, they spoke as if joy did make them speak; they spoke with such pleasantness of Scripture language, and with such an appearance of grace in all they said, that they were to me, as if they had found a new world, as if they were people that dwelt alone, and were not to be reckoned among their neighbors.

Therefore I should often make it my business to be going again and again into the company of these poor people, for I could not stay away. And presently I found two things within me at which I did sometimes marvel; the one was a very great softness and tenderness of heart; and the other was a great bending of my mind to a continual meditating on them, and on all other good things which at any time I had read or heard of." All that might have been found in the best Alexandrian Greek among Apollos's papers after his death. Better Greek he could not have written, nor a better description of his experiences as he came and went to Aquila's and Priscilla's house in Ephesus. "By these things," adds Bunyan, "my mind was now so turned that it lay like a horse-leech at the vein, still crying out, give, give."

They complain that there threatens to be a dearth of candidates for the Christian ministry. But that can never be. For where can the flower of our youth find a field for their scholarship and for their eloquence like the evangelical pulpit? What other calling open to a talented young man can compete with spiritual preaching? What other occupation can possess and satisfy a pure mind and a noble heart, and that more and more, to the end of life? Where will our intellectual youth find a literature for one moment to compare with the literature of Jerusalem and Alexandria? And a sphere of work like a congregation full of such people as Aquila and Priscilla? How long halt the flower of our Scottish youth between two opinions? If the Lord be God, follow Him. But if Baal, then follow him. Choose ye this day whom ye will serve. Will ye also go away? Lord, to whom shall we go? Thou hast the words of eternal life.

124
Lois and Eunice

THIS Lois was a God-fearing woman herself, and a woman of a strong and an unfeigned faith. But with all that she made the tremendous mistake of giving her only daughter in marriage to a man who was still an absolute heathen. How such a good woman, how two such good women, could have fallen into this tremendous trap, we can only guess. But, then, we can guess; ay, and that only too well. For Eunice's lover, like so many of our own lovers, would begin to attend the synagogue-services for her sweet sake, till he was almost persuaded to become a proselyte of the gate for her sweet sake. And, but for some pagan and overpowering influences holding him back, under the transforming influences of Lois's noble character and Eunice's holy beauty he would surely have become all that Lois and Eunice prayed for so unceasingly that he might become before the marriage. But let Lois only give her consent; let Lois only give her dear daughter to him in marriage; and she will never have to repent putting her great trust in his hands. And the young Greek lover was not a false-hearted and a designing cheat in so saying. He really and honestly intended, after he was married, to live a godly husband's life. He said so, and Lois and Eunice believed him, and I believe him. We have all come through it ourselves. We have all had our own experiences of this self-deceivingness of a young man's heart. We have all ourselves seen and come through enough to convince us that Eunice's lover was entirely honest and honorable, as we ourselves were, when he said what he intended to be and to do as soon as he was a married man. Yes, we have all seen all that a thousand times, till we can sympathize, with all our heart, with all the three. That is to say, with the ardent and almost sanctified Greek lover, and with the two still-hesitating, but fast-yielding, Hebrew women. Till at last when she could hold out no longer, Lois gave her long-withheld consent to the mixed marriage. And in this way Eunice, a daughter of Abraham, became the married wife of this still heathen man; his wife, and in due time the mother of his uncircumcised sons. And he became her husband and her lord and the father of her children, still remaining all the time the same heathen man he had always been. And, alas! not only the same heathen man he had always been, but as time went on, and as his married life became a familiar possession and a disenchanted experience to him, he went further away from God and from family religion than ever he had been before. Nor did Peter's beautiful promise ever come true so as to mend matters in that so mixed and so unequally-yoked marriage. Peter's so beautiful promise to all good women when they waken up to see how they have sold themselves, and where they have landed themselves. "Likewise, ye wives, be in subjection to your own husbands, that if any obey not the Word, they also may without the Word, be won by the conversation of the wives, while they behold your chaste conversation coupled with fear." For some reason or other, that so apposite promise was never fulfilled to that so mismanaged marriage. Whether it was that Lois failed in her part as a mother-in-law, as she had so conspicuously failed as a mother; or whether it was that Eunice failed in fulfilling her part of the Apostle's promise; or whether it was owing to the pride and the obstinacy of the heathen heart of her husband; whatever was the cause, the father of Eunice's goodly child never came to walk with a perfect heart before his house at home. He was never won, as at one time he so solemnly promised that he would be won, and at that warm-hearted time actually was almost won, to his believing wife's Holy Scriptures and to her God and Savior.

Now nine women out of ten would simply have accepted Eunice's fate, and would gradually have sunk down to their husband's unbelieving level. But neither Lois nor Eunice were such weak women as that. Instead of that, and especially after the birth of little Timothy, the two God-fearing women set themselves all the more to a far more Scriptural, a far more prayerful, and a far more obedient, life than ever before. They did not cast up the days of their husband's love-making to his accusing conscience. Neither did they thrust their own repentance and remorse too much in his face. But neither did they hide out of his sight that divine faith and that domestic piety which had been the mainstay of their hearts before ever they had seen his face, and which was more than ever their only mainstay now that he had so fatally misled them. And the daily growth of the uncircumcised child only made the broken law of God against all such mixed marriages as theirs had been the more poignant to their broken hearts: as also, the same law of God as to the proper nurture and admonition of such unhappy children as their child was. The confirmed, and now hopeless, heathenism of the child's father, and the everpresent remorse of their own hearts, only made both Lois and Eunice determine to work with all their might in order to make up somewhat to their innocent child for the great wrong they had all three done to him. And that the two sorely chastened women succeeded in all but completely compensating their spiritually fatherless child, we have Paul's own testimony to that, and a testimony that Timothy must all his days have read with tears and thanksgivings. "Thou Timothy from a child hast known the Holy Scriptures, and that because of the unfeigned faith that dwelt first in thy grandmother Lois, and then in thy mother Eunice, and I am persuaded in thee also." And thus it came about that Timothy, unhappy enough in his birth, and handicapped enough in starting on the race of life, was more than compensated for all that through the labors and the prayers of his mother and his grandmother, and through the beneficial operation of that noble New Testament law—"He is not a Jew who is one outwardly: neither is that circumcision which is outward in the flesh. But he is a Jew who is one inwardly: and circumcision is that of the heart, in the spirit, and not in the letter, whose praise is not of men but of God."

That noble passage also in which the Apostle describes to Timothy his own upbringing is a classical passage to all Christian households. "But continue thou in the things which thou hast learned, and hast been assured of, knowing of whom thou hast learned them. And that from a child thou hast known the Holy Scriptures, which are able to make thee wise unto salvation, through faith which is in Christ Jesus. All Scripture is given by inspiration of God, and is profitable for doctrine, for reproof, for correction, for instruction in righteousness. That the man of God may be perfect, thoroughly furnished unto all good works." "Wise unto salvation." There is a whole volume of the inner history of that Greek-Hebrew household in those four verses, and in those three words that shine like an apple of gold in a picture of silver, at the heart of those four verses. The Greek father's bad conscience because he had never even tried to fulfill to those two over-trustful women what he had so often so solemnly promised them; his bad conscience would often exasperate his temper at them, and at the Scriptures they were always reading. He had his own Scriptures; and he was not wholly without excuse for exalting them as he did. Only, all his Greek and Roman Scriptures taken together could not give him peace of mind for the wrong he had done those two women. Nor could Lois and Eunice get the comfort and support they so sorely needed, out of any other Scriptures but the Psalms of David, and the promises of the Hebrew prophets. It was with Lois and Eunice's son as it was with the son of another self-deceived wife and mother long afterwards. The handwriting which was against us, which was contrary to us, is blotted out. This assurance the Platonic writings contain not. Plato's pages, with all their beauty, and all their wisdom, present not the image of this piety—Thy sacrifice, O Lord, is a broken heart. No man sings in Cicero or Plato—From Thee cometh my salvation. No one hears this call out of those books—Come unto Me all ye that labor. Not that it was young Timothy's time as yet to understand such deep and such spiritual Scriptures as these. But his time is coming when all Plato, and all Cicero, and all else, will no more satisfy his soul than they satisfied the soul of Monica's son. But that is still in the far and the unknown future. Timothy is still at that early stage of soul of which John Bunyan writes: "Wherefore falling into some love and liking for those things, I betook myself to my Bible, and began to take great pleasure in reading it; but especially with the historical part thereof. For, as for Paul's Epistles, and such like Scriptures, I could not away with them." Paul's Epistles were not written as yet in Timothy's youth, and he had no temptation to condemn them. But many were the delightful Sabbath hours that Lois his grandmother spent with Timothy her dawning grandson, over Bunyan's favorite Scriptures; over Abraham, and Isaac, and Jacob, and Joseph, and David, and Solomon. When, as he grew in wisdom, she would show him how all those great men of his mother's and his grandmother's Scriptures became wise unto salvation. As also, where they became foolish, and risked their salvation. Especially Solomon, who was in everything, except his salvation, the wisest of them all. Little did Lois dream as she went on with her pious occupation that she was thereby writing her name so impressively on the immortal pages of our New Testament. Little did she dream that we would actually be reading about her, and about her daughter Eunice, and about her grandson Timothy, in this far-off island of the sea. Little did that devout and chastened saint think that many of us in this congregation tonight would carry home lessons of salvation from her house to our own house at home. Great and marvellous are Thy works, Lord God Almighty: just and true are Thy ways, Thou King of Saints.

There is a piercing cry in this connection that often comes to my own heart out of one of Lois's Hebrew Psalms. And that heart-piercing and heart-uttering cry is this, "O, when wilt Thou come unto me? I will walk within my house with a perfect heart." I know the man who first uttered that cry to God. I see his house at home, as well as I see my own. And, more than that, I see him before he had a house. I see, and hear, and share in all his holy dreams, and high hopes, and solemn vows, and in all his protestations and resolutions. I made them all myself, and far more. But no sooner did that Hebrew bridegroom get the desire of his heart than he soon became a still worse husband than Eunice's Greek husband, and a still worse father than Timothy's father. And now so beset is he behind and before with his badly performed part as a husband and a father, that, O wretched man that he is, he is every day doing and saying things he ought not to do and say; doing and saying things that drive him to downright despair. No reformation prospers that he attempts. Everything seems to be bent against him in his life at home. And nowhere else so much as in his life at home. Till we come on this heart-breaking cry of his in our hundred-and-first psalm. Just as Eunice's husband and Timothy's father would have cried all his days, had he begun to look at himself as a husband and as a father in the glass of his wife's Holy Scriptures. For those Scriptures, while holy in everything, are in nothing more holy than just in the incessant and the inexorable demands they make on every husband, and father, and master, who reads them. How hard it is, but how heavenly good it is, to look continually at ourselves as householders in this glass of God that stands at this moment shining before us and searching us! How wise unto salvation it will yet make both ourselves and our households, if we will lay up in our hearts and practice in our lives the lessons even of this one Scripture we have had from the God of families tonight. And this great good will begin tonight with all those of us who are honestly asking ourselves before God, just what things they are, naming them, in which we have so sorely disappointed those who once so trusted us. Just in what things, and naming them, we have come so shamefully short of our marriage-vows, and of our honest, and at one time, warm-hearted, intentions. To accustom ourselves to make such an inquisition as that, will do this at any rate—it will teach us humility at home, and that is the beginning of all true reformation there. It will teach us patience also, which is so much needed at home. And it will give us a sore heart all our days for those whose unhappy lot it is to live all the rest of their days under our roof, and to have us for all the husband, and all the father, they are ever to have in this world.

And O you who are still full of promises, and vows, and fond intentions! You who cannot listen to God's severe truth tonight with patience, you are so full of ardent dreams about what a house of love, and honor, and religion, your house is to be! Begin, I beseech you, tonight, to make yourself what you are one day to make your happy house. It is far easier, believe me, to begin all these good things before your marriage than after it. I can tell you that; nobody better. But if you will not believe me, believe Lois and Eunice. For they are come here tonight to warn you against a mixed marriage like theirs. Be ye not unequally yoked! Both the grandmother and the mother are come here tonight to plead with you, with all their experience, and with all their authority.

But whatever other men and women, young and old, may do, this is what I, the present preacher, will do even if I do it alone—I will sing of mercy and judgment. Unto Thee, O Lord, will I sing. I will behave myself wisely in a perfect way. O when wilt Thou come unto me? I will walk within my house with a perfect heart. I will often return to the days of my youth. I will often return to the days of my warmth of heart, and of my many prayers in this matter, and my many vows. I will tell to my own heart all the steps in which Thou hast led me up to this present time. I will say, As for me and my house, we will henceforth serve the Lord. And one thing will I do; I will keep my heart well broken before Thee, and before my house all my days. I will clothe myself with humility as I go in and out before my house. I will put a bridle in my mouth. I will keep the door of my lips. I will not provoke my children to anger. I will reprehend them in private, and praise them in public. I will look on all their faults as what they have inherited from their father; and on all that is good in them as having come to them from their mother, and from their Father in heaven. The sins of my children shall always be their father's sorest chastisement at the hand of God, and their gifts and their graces shall always be his highest ornament and his greatest renown. O when wilt Thou come unto me?

125
Timothy as a Child

IT was something like this. It was something not unlike one of our own Scottish households where the father is not a church member, and where the minister is so strict that he will not baptize the child to the mother. In which case the grandmother and the mother would say to one another—"Very well. At any rate we shall all the more see to it that if our child wants the outward ceremony he shall have that want more than made up to him in the inward substance. What he has not received in the mere sprinkling with water, he shall, if we can help it, have it more than made up to him by the Holy Spirit. For we shall give God no rest till he has had far more mercy on our innocent child than our cruel-hearted minister has had." And it was so. Till the very heathenism of Timothy's father was far better for his uncircumcised child than if that Greek father had been such a Christian father as the most of our fathers are. For just because of the father's unbelief, the faith of the grandmother and the mother became all the more unfeigned, and prayerful, and importunate. The blot they had all three had such a hand in bringing upon their innocent child, lay so heavy on the heart of his mother and his grandmother that they could take no rest till they had seen that blot more than removed by the washing of regeneration, and the renewing of the Holy Ghost.

With such an unfeigned faith as that the two lonely women set themselves to bring up their little fatherless son in the nurture and admonition of the Lord. And they succeeded, if ever unfeigned women succeeded. And such unfeigned women as they were have always succeeded, and will always succeed, till the last of such women shall be called up to get her full wages from God. Such women, such mothers in Israel, as Hannah, and Elizabeth, and Mary, and Monica, and Halyburton's mother, and Wesley's mother, and the mother of Jonathan Edwards's children, and the mother of Thomas Boston's children, and many more. And in all those mothers it was their unfeigned faith that did it. Their unfeigned faith laid hold, first on God, and then on their children. For, not to speak of God, this kind of faith, and this kind of faith alone, takes hold of a child's heart. You cannot feign faith before your children. Even while they are still children they will find you out to their great pain and shame on account of their feigning mother. You may go on feigning faith with some success before every one else, but not before your children. You must walk with an unfeigned faith, and with a perfect heart at home, if you have such a child's eyes set on you as were set on both Lois and Eunice. Whatever the husbands and the fathers in our households may do, let all wives and mothers live a life like the lives of Lois and Eunice, and they will have their reward. At this point, and in a spare moment, I was led to take down an old favorite of mine who has always something pertinent to say on this matter now in hand. "Before all things, let the talk of the child's nurse not be ungrammatical." He is discussing the best education for an orator. "Chrysippus wished that every such nurse should be, if possible,

585

a woman of some liberality of education. For it is his nurse the future orator first hears speaking, and it is her words and her accents he will first imitate. We are by nature tenacious of what we have imbibed in our infant years, just as the flavor with which we scent our casks when they are new, remains in them to the end." With a few changes and substitutions you have Lois and Eunice in Quintilian's First Book, and their early education of a future apostle.

It is not for nothing, you may depend upon it, that Paul gives Lois and Eunice such a first-class certificate for their first-rate methods, and for their signal success in teaching Timothy to read, and so far to understand, the Holy Scriptures. Paul always, and to everybody, both spoke and wrote like the true gentleman he was. But these are not so many mere courtesies and compliments that the aged Apostle pays to these two Bible-teaching women. There is a studied descriptiveness, as well as all his own warmth of heart, in what Paul here says to Timothy about the wise and painstaking methods that Lois and Eunice took with him over Holy Scripture. It is of his early readings of Holy Scripture at home that Paul reminds Timothy when he exhorts him to divide the word of truth rightly, both in his own family, and in his catechumen's classes, and in his expository pulpit. I see Lois putting on her spectacles an hour before she summons in Timothy from the playground. I watch her as she selects with such care the proper passage she is going to read with him. I admire her as she reads and re-reads the passage to herself, in order to make sure that she understands it herself. After which she prepares, and tries them over on her own knees, two or three petitions proper for the child to repeat after her, and to which he is to say his intelligent and hearty Amen. There is much that is full of rebuke and instruction to us all in the manse of Ettrick. But there is nothing more full of rebuke and instruction to us than the way that Thomas Boston prepared himself for family worship before he rang the bell. And as a consequence and a reward he records it again and again in his grateful diary, how, after such preparation he often got light, and comfort, and strength, and guidance for himself, as well as for his family, out of "the exercise." "Remember the wise methods of Lois and Eunice," said Paul to Timothy, "when you are at your own family worship at home, as well as when you are at the head of a congregation."

But with all these most excellent preparations for it, the great change had still to come to Timothy. "Towardly child as Timothy was," says Thomas Goodwin, "he was all the time unconverted." Timothy was kept for Paul to finish the work that Lois and Eunice had so well begun. There is a great instruction here, and a great comfort. A very great comfort. For there are a great many young men among ourselves exactly like Timothy. Like Timothy they are richly talented, well-educated, religiously educated, and every way well brought up, young men. Like Timothy also they have received all that two generations of mothers of an unfeigned faith can do for them. And yet all the time they have not themselves taken the great step. And this goes on till one day their day of grace at last comes to them, as Timothy's day of grace came to him. A new minister stands in the pulpit; a skillful and urgent evangelist like Moody, or Drummond, or Kelman, or M'Neill, or George Clarke, or Mackay, visits the city and specially addresses such young men; or they are lead to read the right book at the right moment; or some special and personal dispensation of Divine Providence is sent to them. Till, in a day, in an hour, in a moment, the fine fruit that has for so long been slowly ripening falls at a touch into the husbandman's basket. Paul comes round and preaches one day at Lystra, and Timothy is converted on the spot. Keep up your hearts, Lois and Eunice. Keep up your hearts. Though it tarry, wait for it; because it will surely come, it will not tarry. Behold, the husbandman waiteth for the precious fruit of the earth, and hath long patience for it, until he receive the early and the latter rain. Be ye also patient; stablish your hearts; for the coming of the Lord draweth nigh.

At the same time, while I rejoice with Paul that he had Timothy for his spiritual son, I cannot but feel tenderly for Lois and Eunice in this matter. I feel for Eunice especially, that she was not blessed of God to bear her son in his second birth as well as in his first birth. Speaking for myself, I would value above all else that God can give me in this world to see all my children truly converted like Timothy. And I would rejoice to receive their conversion through any instrumentality that it pleases God to employ. A new minister; a passing-by evangelist; a good book; a dispensation of family or personal providence; or what not. But O! if it pleases God let me have all my children's souls myself! Let them all say in after days—"it was my father that did it." That would make my cup to run over indeed. And I will not despair of it. Why should I for one moment doubt of it? For He is a God that delighteth to make a man's cup to run over, in that way and in every other way. At the same time, while I most feelingly sympathize with Lois and Eunice in their loss of Timothy's soul to Paul, I have a creeping doubt in my conscience that, with all their excellent Bible-reading with him, they cannot have dealt closely enough with Timothy's very mind and heart about himself. "The Holy Scriptures, which are able to make thee wise unto salvation," is the Apostle's deep, and, as I think, significantly-situated, expression. I do not altogether know why it is, but I cannot get this question put to sleep in my conscience; this question: Did Lois and Eunice, after all, do all they ought to have done, to make Timothy wise unto salvation? Did they do all they ought to have done to bring home his own salvation to the very conscience and mind and heart and imagination of their little charge? I admit much, as I must, about Lois and Eunice in their training of Timothy. But, somehow, their not getting the full seal of God set on their training of Timothy, makes me doubt if, after all, they had made their training of Timothy ready for such a seal, "Wise unto *salvation*." Now, tell me, did Eunice, do you think, take her son Timothy, and show him till she made it plain to him, what it would be for her and for him to be saved, and what it would be for her and for him to be lost? And did she do that with all her tenderness and with all her lovingness? Did she see it herself, and did she show it to him, how the very tones of his little voice sometimes up and down the house, and how his little looks and actions, were the very things that salvation had been sent for? Did she show him how the holy name "Jesus" came home to their house, and spake of salvation to old and young within its walls? I may be quite wrong, and I may be doing both Lois and Eunice a great injustice in all this. But I am not without some compunction that they would have had Timothy's full salvation for their own wages if they had made it completely and convincingly clear to the thoughtful child, just what wisdom unto salvation would be in their case and in his case. At any rate, even if I am quite wrong in my reading of their case, it matters nothing to them now. Only, this disconcerting reading of their case may be blessed to make some of ourselves look somewhat more closely and conscientiously at our own case at home than we have ever yet looked at it. That is to say, are we at once clear-headed enough, and plain-spoken enough, and attracting and winning enough, with our children? Leave no suspicion, leave no doubt, in that direction undealt with, my brethren. Leave no stone unturned in seeking the salvation of your children. Go to the very root of the matter with them. Go to the very root of the word with them. Make them thoroughly to understand both the word, and the thing, salvation. Make them to see it. Make them to feel it. Make them to admit, and to confess to you, that you have now made them both see it and feel it. To see and to feel what it would be to be lost; and what it would be to be saved. And then when you have done that to the best of your ability, and with much prayer both with them and for them, there will be the less likelihood that some passer-by like Paul will come and carry off with him what would be the sweetest jewel in all your heavenly crown. Come, my brethren, and let us be so wise unto our own salvation, and unto the salvation of our children, that we shall be able to say to our God on that day—Here am I, and all the children Thou didst give me!

126
Timothy as a Young Minister

WE are come tonight to Timothy as a young minister. And though you are not ministers yourselves it cannot but interest you to be told how such ministers as Paul and Timothy and their true successors are made; how they make themselves; and how that self-making of theirs goes on all the time they live and labor among you.

"Till I come, give attendance to reading." This is one of Paul's outstanding exhortations to Timothy. Now if these words were addressed by an experienced minister to a new beginner in our day, something like this would be universally understood. "Attend to your studies. Be always at your studies. Grudge every moment that is stolen from your studies. Never sit down without a book and a pen in your hand. And let it never be an ephemeral, or an impertinent, or an unproductive, book. You have not the time. You have not the money. Read nothing that is not the very best of its kind. Neither in religion, nor in letters, nor in anything else. Be like John Milton in his noble youth, be both select and industrious in your reading."

But there is another interpretation of these words, and that on high authority too. "Reading," in Timothy's day—so the text is sometimes interpreted—would mean to him very much what is nowadays called expository preaching or "lecturing," as we say in Scotland. Timothy is here exhorted to read Nehemiah's autobiography and then to imitate that great reformer and his great colleagues in their exegetic and homiletic way of dealing with the law of God. The preachers of Nehemiah's day, so he tells us in his Memoirs of himself, stood upon a pulpit of wood, and read the law of God distinctly, and gave the sense, and caused the people to understand the reading. And this, many eminent exegetes assure us, is the "reading" to which Timothy is here commanded to attend. Whether that is the true interpretation of this text or no, as a matter of fact Nehemiah's method of handling Holy Scripture has been followed by all his successors in the pulpit, both in Bible times and in Church-history times. To begin with, Nehemiah's method was our Lord's method also as often as the Book was delivered to Him by the minister in the synagogue on the Sabbath day. And from the Acts we learn that this was the universal method of the Apostles also. Both the Greek and the Latin fathers followed this same Scriptural method; the expository lectures of Chrysostom and Augustine are extant to us to this day. Calvin also stood upon his pulpit of wood, and read the Word of God distinctly, and caused the people of Geneva to understand the reading. Just as he still causes us to understand the reading as often as we consult his incomparable commentaries. And that same labor-loving and labor-rewarding method of pulpit work made the Puritans in England and the Presbyterians in Scotland the two greatest schools of preachers and people the Church of Christ has ever seen. At the same time, and while I wholly accept that official interpretation, so to call it, my heart leans to the more personal application of Chrysostom and Calvin. Those two very foremost authorities here understand Paul to counsel Timothy not so much concerning his pulpit work, as concerning his own private and personal and devotional attention to the Word of God. Calvin, above all men, had ears to hear. And that master in Israel overhears Paul saying to Timothy something like this: "Read distinctly, and exhort convincingly, in your pulpit. But above and before all else, let the Word of God dwell richly in yourself. Even after you have known the Holy Scriptures from a child, still continue to call them constantly to mind by your systematic and assiduous reading and meditation. And by so doing thou shalt both save thyself, and them that hear thee." "What I owe to these two Epistles to Timothy," confesses Calvin, "can never be told."

"Rightly dividing the word of truth"; this is another of Paul's master-strokes in these masterly Epistles. And that master-stroke of the Apostle serves to set forth another of the many advantages of the consecutive and comprehensive exposition of Holy Scripture. In true expository preaching the right dividing of the whole word of truth is largely left to the Spirit of truth Himself. On no other method is it possible for any preacher to divide aright the whole consecutive and cumulative body of doctrines and duties, as well as of privileges and comforts, contained in the Holy Scriptures. There are multitudes of doctrines, and reproofs, and corrections, and instructions in righteousness, that the minister who preaches from detached and unconnected texts will never be able to divide out to his people. And even when such a preacher does come upon some of those instructions and corrections that his people need, his inconsequent method of preaching will be sure to tempt certain of his hearers to set down his words less to the wonderful perfection, and particularness, and individualizingness, of Holy Scripture than to some idiosyncracy of the preacher; or, it may be, to some personal animus of his. The preposterous charge of a personal intention and animus will not always be avoided by the best methods of pulpit-work; but the preaching that consecutively overtakes all the perfection and point of the Word of God will best meet and silence that vanity of mind, and that rebellion of heart, among our hearers. Every humble-minded hearer must often have felt and confessed the divine power with which some reproof came home to him, when it suddenly and unexpectedly leapt out upon him from the depths of some hitherto overlooked and unexpected passage of the manifold Word of God.

Another way of rightly dividing the whole word of truth is most excellently set forth by Jeremy Taylor in one of his golden charges to his clergy: "Do not spend your sermons on general and undefined things. Do not spend your time and strength on exhortations to your people to get Christ, to be united to Christ, and things of a like unlimited and indefinite signification. But rightly divide the whole doctrine of Christ. Tell your people in every duty what are the measures, what are the circumstances, what are the instruments, and what are the particulars and minute bearings, of every general advice. For, generals not explicated, do but fill the people's heads with empty notions, and their mouths with perpetual unintelligible talk, while their hearts remain empty and themselves unedified." Yes; O wise-hearted and golden-mouthed overseer. But we would need all thy oceanic reading, and all thy capacious intellect, and all thy splendid eloquence, and all thy unceasing prayerfulness, in order to come within sight of thy great counsels. And, my brethren, with the very best of methods, how much is still left to the individual minister himself to do. What ability, what study, what courage, what wisdom, what love, is needed rightly to divide the word of truth, Sabbath after Sabbath, to all the ages, and to all the understandings, and to all the circumstances, and to all the experiences, of a listening congregation. What a sleepless, what a many-sided, what an all-talented, what an all-experienced race of men the preachers of the Word of God would need to be!

And then if the Apostle says it once, he says it fifty times: "Shun controversy, like the bottomless pit, in the pulpit." Richard Baxter will surely be listened to on this subject. "Another fatal hindrance to a heavenly walk and conversation is our too frequent disputes about lesser truths. A disputatious spirit is a sure sign of an unsanctified spirit. They are usually men least acquainted with the heavenly life who are the most violent disputers about the circumstantials of religion. Yea, though you were sure that your opinions were true, yet when the chiefest of your zeal is turned to these things, the life of grace soon decays within. Let every sure truth even have but its due proportion, and I am confident that the hundredth part of our time and contention would not be spent as it is spent. I could wish you were all men of understanding and ability to defend every truth of God; but still I would have the chiefest truth to be chiefly studied, and no truth to shoulder out the thought of eternity. The least controverted points are usually the most weighty, and of most necessary and frequent use to our souls."

But as we work our way through these trenchant and pungent Epistles, what can the Apostle possibly mean by commanding a young minister of such infirm health as Timothy was to work for his pulpit and in his pastoral duties "in season and out of season"? And so commanding him, under the most tremendous imprecations; till we begin to suspect that it was not so much Timothy's bad health, as something far worse, that Paul had in his eye all the time. Was it not because one of the besetting sins of the ministerial calling was already setting in upon the very Apostolic Church itself? It would almost seem so. "We seek apologies for our slothfulness," says one of the most unslothful of ministers. Be that as it may; let all ministers, both those who are slothfully inclined, and those who are really infirm in health, and all young ministers especially, give attendance to reading the autobiographies of two of the most infirm, but at the same time two of the most resolutely unslothful, of all our Puritan and Presbyterian ministers: the *Reliquiae Baxterianae*, and Thomas Boston's *Memoirs of himself*, the latter edited by a young minister of our own who is neither slothful nor infirm.

With all his ailments, and whatever they were, Timothy never touched wine, either for stimulus or for strength. Just what it was that had made Timothy such a stern total abstainer we are not told. Whether it was the self-denying example of some of the great saints of his mother's Scriptures, or the awful falls of some others of those saints, we are not told. Only, we find the aged Apostle interposing and recommending Timothy to relax his rule somewhat and to take a little wine now and then. Now I would not interfere if any old minister, or any able and devout doctor, were to say to some young minister of my acquaintance what Paul here says to Timothy about his health and his inability for his work unless he begins to take wine. But for my part, and in our day, I would make sure that any infirm young friend of mine had tried some other expedients before he betook himself to this last expedient of all. I would do my very best to make sure that he kept early and regular hours both night and morning. And if I could get the ear of his session I would plead with them to see that their young minister took a Sabbath off every five or six Sabbaths. As also that he got a generous holiday once every summer. But above all that I would charge himself before God not to leave off his Sabbath preparation till the Saturday night. For I have seen far more woe worked in the manse and in the congregation by that last evil habit than I have seen worked even by strong drink. A real love for our books, and a real love for our pulpits, and a real love for our people, all that is far better for us ministers, and for our infirm health, than the very best of wines.

"Let no man despise thy youth; but be thou an example in thy conversation." Pascal has made "the disproportion of man" a proverb in our highest literature. And Richard Baxter has made the same word a barbed arrow in the consciences of all his ministerial readers. "The disproportion," that is, between our office and our walk and conversation in our office. I suppose there is not a minister on the face of the earth who does not gnash his teeth at himself continually as he returns home again from a conversation in which he has displayed such a disproportion to his office, and has taken such a scandal-causing part. Our young ministers may neither have Taylor, nor Baxter, nor Boston, nor any such master of ministerial deportment; but, as Behmen says, they have themselves. And if they begin early to examine themselves in this matter, and to improve upon themselves every time they cross their own doorstep, they will soon, and without books, become themselves as great examples and as great authorities as any ministerial-deportment author of them all. Let no man despise the youth and far less the age of any minister because of his disproportionate character and his disedifying conversation.

And, "take heed unto thyself," is just all that over again in other words. Take heed to thy doctrine indeed, but, first and last, take most heed to thyself. Fix thy very best and thy very closest attention on thyself. This is thy main duty as a pastor. Do not set thyself forward as a pattern to thy people. Only, make thyself a perfect pattern to them. For that minister who constantly and increasingly takes heed to himself in his walk and conversation; in preaching better and better every returning Sabbath; in discharging all the endless duties of his pastorate in season and out of season; in holding his peace in controversy; and in a life of secret faith and secret prayer; God Himself will see to it that such an apostolic minister will be imitated and celebrated both as a pattern minister and a pattern man; both before his people, and before all his fellow-ministers. All that, by the grace of God, may be attained by any minister who sets himself to attain it, even though his book-press is as poorly furnished as Thomas Boston's book-press was so poorly furnished. At the same time, you well-to-do people, whose Christmas and New Year presses are so full of the best books, and the best of everything else, you should at this season go over all the young ministers and all the poor ministers you know, and should see to it that, with the Pastoral Epistles, they have also the best commentary, for a Scottish minister at any rate, that was ever written on those Epistles; better even than Chrysostom or Calvin; I mean Thomas Boston's *Memoirs* of himself as a parish minister. That golden book for Scottish ministers is full of things like this: "The untender carriage of some ministers in Nithsdale was very wounding to me. As also meeting with a neighboring minister his foolish talking afforded me heavy reflections on the unedifying conversation of ministers, and my own among others, as one great cause of the unsuccess of the Gospel in our hands."

Well might Timothy, and well may every living minister today, lay down these two terrible Epistles, and say over them—Who is sufficient for these things? For no mere man is sufficient for such high things as these. No mortal man is sufficient for such a holy ministry as that. But then no mere and mortal man is expected to be sufficient. You must not go away and suppose that the arch-Apostle himself was sufficient for the half of the charges he laid, almost with a curse, on Timothy. Paul, you may be sure, threw down his pen again and again in the composition of these two pastoral Epistles, and betook himself to his knees and to the blood of Christ before he could finish what he had begun to write. And these two Epistles, so full of matter for ministerial remorse, are to this day put into our hands, not to drive us to despair and self-destruction, but rather to summon us out of our beds every returning Monday morning to give better and ever better attendance to our reading of the best books, and to our writing in connection with them. To our sick-visiting in the afternoon, and to our whole walk and conversation all the day, and all the week, and every week, till a Greater than Paul comes. And, more than that, these pastoral Epistles are not written to us who are your ministers only. But all you people are to read these Epistles and are to ponder them and pray over them continually, in order that you may have it always before you at what a cost a true minister of the New Testament is made. As also to teach you to value aright such a minister when he is entrusted to you, till he shall finish his ministry among you, both by saving himself and those among you who have ears to hear him.

Our Lord's Characters

I

The Sower Who Went Forth to Sow

NOT only in Jerusalem, and at the passover, but in Nazareth, and on days of release from labor, we may well believe that something like this would sometimes take place. "Son, why hast thou thus dealt with us? Behold, thy father and I have sought Thee sorrowing." But He would answer to His mother—"How is it that ye sought Me? Wist ye not that I must be about My Father's business?" So would His mother say to Him, and so would He answer her, as often as she sought for Him among their kinsfolk and acquaintance; while, all the time, He was out in the fields; now with the plowman, and now with the sower, and now with the reaper, and now with the husbandman who had his fan in his hand with which he was thoroughly purging his floor. And as He walked and talked with the plowman, and with the sower, and with the reaper, the Spirit of all truth would descend into His heart and would say to Him that all that husbandry He had been observing so closely was in all its processes and operations, not unlike the Kingdom of Heaven in all its processes, and in all its operations, and in all its experiences. Till, as He walked about and meditated, He would draw out to Himself the manifold likenesses between nature and grace; between the husbandry of the farm and the husbandry of the pulpit; when He would lay up all His meditations in His mind and in His heart, till we see and hear it all coming out of His mind and out of His heart in the teaching and the preaching of the text.

And, accordingly, nothing is more likely than that He had led His disciples to the sea-side that day along a way that was well known to Him. A way He had often walked as He went to watch the operations of the husbandman to whom that field belonged. And it being now the seed-time of the year, as the sower that day sowed, some of the seed fell under the feet of the twelve disciples, while flocks of hungry birds swooped down and devoured whole basketfuls of the sower's best sowing. And thus it was that no sooner had our Lord sat down by the sea-side than He forthwith pointed His disciples back to the field they had just passed through. And not only did He recall to their thoughts what they themselves had just seen, but He told them also all that He Himself had seen going on in that same field, year in and year out, for many spring days and many harvest days, when His mother could not make out where He was, or what He was doing. But all those observations and meditations of His now bore their hundredfold fruit in this great sermon so full of all kinds of instruction and illustration, and all taken from the field they had just left behind them. And then, at the petition of His disciples, our Lord expounded His homely riddle about the sower and his seed, till we have both that riddle and its exposition in our hands tonight in this far-off island of the sea.

"The seed is the Word of God," says our Lord. That is to say, every true preacher sows the Word of God with both his hands, and he sows nothing else but the Word of God. The true preacher must put nothing else into his seed-basket every

596

Sabbath morning, but the pure and unadulterated Word of God. The Christian pulpit is not set up for any service but one: and that one and sovereign service is the sowing of the seed of God in the minds and in the hearts and in the lives of men. The platform and the press are set up in God's providence for the sowing broadcast of His mind and will also: but the evangelical pulpit has an exclusiveness and a sanctification about it altogether peculiar to itself. Six days shalt thou read and write history, and biography, and philosophy, and poetry, and newspapers, and novels, but this is the Day the Lord has made. And He has made this Day, and has specially sanctified and hedged round this Day, for the sowing of that intellectual and spiritual seed which springs up, and which alone springs up, to everlasting life.

"And as he sowed, some seeds fell by the wayside. This is he that heareth the Word of the Kingdom, and understandeth it not." Our Lord was a man of understanding Himself, and He labored continually to make His disciples to be men of understanding like Himself. And all His ministers, to this day, who are to be of any real and abiding benefit to their people, must labor first to make themselves men of understanding, and then to make their people the same. And if the people are void of understanding their ministers are largely to blame for that. There are people, indeed, in every congregation that our Lord Himself could not make men of understanding: at the same time, it is the ministers who are mostly at fault if their people remain stupid in their intellects and dark in their hearts. "Understandest thou what thou readest?" said Philip the once deacon, and now the evangelist, to the dark treasurer of Queen Candace. "How can I?" answered that wise man from the East. And Philip went up into the chariot and sowed the seed of the Kingdom of Heaven in the understanding and in the heart of that black but comely convert to the cross of Christ. And the first duty of every minister is to make his pulpit like that chariot of Ethiopia. The first duty of every occupant of a pulpit is to sow the Word of God and the Word of God only, and his second duty is to see that the people understand what they read and hear. "And Ezra the scribe stood upon a pulpit of wood, which they had made for the purpose. And Ezra opened the book in the sight of the people: for he was above the people: and when he opened it all the people stood up. And he read in the book in the law of God distinctly, and gave the sense, and caused the people to understand the reading,"—till his reading was so distinct, and so full of understanding, that it brought forth fruit in some of his hearers an hundredfold. One of the last things that Sir Thomas Grainger Stewart said to me on his death-bed was this:—"Sometimes make them understand the psalm before you invite them to sing it, for we have often sung it in my time not knowing what it meant." It was a wise counsel and given in a solemn hour. But, then, there is no pulpit duty more difficult than just to say the right word of understanding at the right moment, and not a word too much or too little. Dr. Davidson of Aberdeen was the best at that one single word of explanation and direction of any minister I ever sat under. He said just one weighty word, in his own weighty way, and then we all sang in the West Church, as Paul made them sing in the Corinthian Church, with the understanding, and with the spirit also.

"And understandeth it not. Then cometh the wicked one and catcheth away the seed that has just been sown." There is a house I am sometimes in at the hour of family worship. In that house, after the psalm and the scripture and the prayer, the head of the house remains on his knees for, say, five or six seconds after he utters the Amen. And then he rises off his knees, slowly and reverently, as if he were still in the King's presence, with his eyes and his whole appearance full of holy fear and holy love. And I notice that all his children have learned to do like their father. And I have repeatedly heard his guests remark on that reverential habit of his, and I have heard them confess that they went home rebuked, as I have often gone home rebuked and instructed myself. There is another house I am in sometimes, which is the very opposite of that. They have family worship also, but before he has said Amen the head of the house is up off his knees and has begun to give his orders about this and that to his servants. He has been meditating the order, evidently, all the time of the prayer. It must have been in such a house or in such a synagogue as that in which our Lord saw the wicked one coming and catching away the seed that was sown in the worshippers' hearts. I think I have told you before about a Sabbath night I once spent long ago in a farm-house up among the Grampians. Before family worship the old farmer had been reading to me out of a book of notes he had taken of Dr. John Duncan's sermons when they were both young men. After worship I got up and spoke first and said—"Let us have some more of those delightful notes." "Excuse me," said my friend, "but we all take our candles immediately after worship." The wicked one was prevented and outwitted every night in that house, and he has been prevented and outwitted in the houses of all the children who were brought up in that rare old farm-house up among the Grampians.

And, then, the stony places is he that heareth the word with joy, yet hath no root in himself. I do not know any congregation, anywhere, that hears the Word of God with such joy as this congregation. As for instance. All last summer, every Monday, I got letters full of joy over the preaching that had been provided in this pulpit. And then when I came home, in every house and on every street I was met with salutations of joy over Dr. George Adam Smith's last sermon. The Professor's text was this—"Lord, teach us to pray." Now, that is three weeks ago, and the seed has had plenty of time to take root. And I am sent here tonight to ask you whether that so joyful hearing that Sabbath night has come, in your case, to any fruit. Have you prayed more these last three weeks? Have you been oftener, and longer at a time, on your knees? Have you been like Halyburton's mother—have you prayed more, both with and for your son, these three weeks? I did not hear the sermon, and I could not get anybody to tell me very much about it, beyond—O the eloquence and the delight of it! But some of you heard it, and God's demand of you tonight is—with what result on your heart, on your temper, on your walk and conversation, on your character? Or, is it written in heaven about you since that Sabbath night—"This is he who hears sermons with such applause, but has never had any root in himself. This is he who thinks that sermons are provided by God and man for him to praise or blame as suits his fancy." And, then, to keep His ministers from being puffed up with such idle praise as yours, God says to them—"Thou son of man, the children of thy people are still talking of thee by the walls and in the doors of their houses. And they come to hear thy words, but they will not do them. Lo, thou art unto them as one that has a pleasant voice, and can play well on an instrument. For they hear thy words, and show much love, but they do them not. But the day will come when they shall give an account of all that they have heard, and then shall they know that a prophet of mine has been among them."

And then he that receiveth the seed among thorns is he in whom the Word of God is simply choked, till he becometh unfruitful. There is only so much room and sap and strength in any field; and unless the ground is cleared of all other things, the sap and the strength that should go to grow the corn will be all drunk up by thorns and briars. You understand, my brethren? You have only so much time, and strength, and mind, and heart, and feeling, and passion, and emotion, and if you expend all these, or the greater part of all these, on other things, you will have all that the less corn, even if you have any corn at all. The thorns in the fields of your hearts are such things as contentions, and controversies, and debates, and quarrels. All these are so many beds of thorns that not only starve your soul, but tear it to pieces as you wade about among them. And not thorns only, but even good things in their own places, if they are allowed in your corn-field, they will leave you little bread for yourself and for your children, and little seed corn for next spring. Rose-bushes even, and gooseberry-bushes, beds of all sweet-tasting, and sweet-smelling herbs, are all in their own place in your garden; but you must have corn in your field. Corn is the staff of your life. And after corn, then flowers and fruits; but not before. After your soul is well on the way to salvation, then other things; but salvation first. Lest the cares of this world, and the deceitfulness of riches, and the lust of other things, entering in, choke your soul, till it is starved and lost: your soul and you.

We are indebted to Luke for many things that we would not have had but for his peculiar care, and industry, and exactness, as a sacred writer. And he reports to us one otherwise unreported word of our Lord's about the good ground that has its own lessons for us all tonight. "That on the good ground are they, which is an honest and good heart, having heard the Word, keep it, and bring forth fruit with patience." An honest heart. Now, there are honest, and there are dishonest, hearts in every congregation. The honest heart is the heart of the hearer who has come up here tonight with a right intention. His motive in being here is an honest motive. This is God's house, and that honest hearer has come to hear what God will say to him tonight. His eye is single, and this whole house has been full of light to him tonight. Already, tonight, he has heard words that he intends to keep tomorrow: to lay them up in his heart and to practice them in his life. He is an honest man, and God will deal honestly by him. But there are others, it is to be feared, in every congregation. They were in our Lord's congregations, and they are in ours. Hearers of the Word, with hearts that are not honest. They are in God's house, but they are not here to meet with God, or to understand, and lay up, and keep, His Word. They are here to see and to be seen. They are here to meet with some one who is to be met with here. They love music, and they are here because the music is good. Or they have some still more material motive; their office or their shop brings them here. Now, when God's Spirit says, Thou art the man! Admit it. Confess it where you sit. Receive this word into a good and honest heart, and say, Surely the Lord is in this place; and I knew it not. Say, this is none other but the house of God, and this is the gate of heaven. Say that God has been found of one man, at any rate, who did not come here tonight to seek Him. And come up here henceforth with that same good and honest heart that you have had created within you tonight, and you also will yet live to bring forth fruit thirty-fold, perhaps sixty-fold, and even an hundred-fold.

II

The Man Which Sowed Good Seed in His Field, but His Enemy Came and Sowed Tares Among the Wheat

THE Son of Man lived in obscurity in Nazareth till He began to be about thirty years of age, growing in wisdom every day, and every day saying to Himself—

—What if Earth
Be but the shadow of Heaven, and things therein
Each to other like more than on Earth is thought?

And one day in His solitary and meditating walks He came on a field in which blades of tares were springing up among the blades of the wheat all over the field. When, meeting the husbandman, He said to him, "From whence hath thy field these tares?" "An enemy hath done it," said the heart-broken husbandman. "While men slept, mine enemy came and sowed tares among the wheat, and went his way." It was a most diabolical act. Diabolical malice, and dastardly cowardice, taken together, could have done no more. That enemy envied with all his wicked heart the husbandman's well-plowed, well-weeded, well-sowed, and well-harvested, field, till he said within himself, Surely the darkness shall cover me. And when the night fell he filled his seed-basket, and went out under cover of night and sowed the whole field over with his diabolical seed. And when our Lord looked on the wheat-field all destroyed with tares, He took that field, and that husbandman's faith and patience with his field, and put them both into this immortal sermon of His. And here are we tonight learning many much-needed lessons among our tare-sowed fields also: learning the very same faith and patience that so impressed and pleased our Lord in this sorely-tried husbandman. And at the end of the world, when he is told about us, as we have been told about him, that husbandman will say, It was well worth a thousand fields of wheat to be the means of teaching a little patience and a little long-suffering even to one over-anxious and impatient heart. For, what that husbandman knew not about his field when he bore himself so wisely beside it, he will know when the harvest is the end of the world, and when the reapers are the angels.

Then Jesus sent the multitude away, and went into the house; and His disciples came unto Him, saying, Declare unto us the parable of the tares of the field. And He gave them an interpretation of His parable, which was to be the authoritative and the all-comprehending interpretation from that time to the end of the world. At the same time, and in and under that interpretation of His, there are occasional, and provisional, and contemporaneous, interpretations and applications of this

601

parable, that are to be made by each reader of this parable, according to his own circumstances and experiences. I will not take up your time, therefore, with the Donatist controversy in the days of Augustine; nor with the great struggles for toleration and liberty of thought recorded for all time in the Areopagitica, and in such like noble arguments. Only, there will no doubt yet emerge and arise new Donatist debates, and new demands for toleration of opinion, even of erroneous opinion, and with that, new calls for the utmost caution, and faith, and patience, especially in church censures, and in church discipline. Occasions will arise, and may be at the door, when we must be prepared, both by knowledge and by temper, to play our part in them like this husbandman in his field. Occasions and opportunities when the discretion, and the patience, and the long-faith of this wise-hearted husbandman, will be memorable and will be set before us for our imitation and our repetition.

Occasions have often arisen in the past, and they will often arise in the future, when a great alarm will be taken at the new discoveries, the new opinions, and the new utterances, of men who are under our jurisdiction, as the tares were under the jurisdiction of the servants in the parable. Now, for what other purpose, do you think, was this parable spoken to us by our Master, but to impose upon us patience, and caution, and confidence in the truth, and to deliver us from all panic, and all precipitancy, and all sudden execution of our fears? This is a very wonderful parable. No parable of them all is more so. Very wonderful. Very startling, indeed. Very arresting to us. For, even when the wheat-field was all covered with real, and not doubtful, tares, the wise husbandman still held in the hands of his indignant and devoted servants. Even when, demonstrably, and admittedly, and scandalously, and diabolically, an enemy had done it—No! said this master of himself, as well as of his servants—No! Have patience. Let the tares alone. Lest while you gather up the tares, you root up also the wheat with them. Let both grow together till the harvest. And then I will give the reapers their instructions myself.

My friends, if any one but our Lord had said that, or anything like that, in the presence of any actual instances of real or supposed tares, what would we have said to him, and said about him? I will not, for reverence sake, repeat what we would have said. But if our Divine Lord actually uttered these great and wonderful words, full of such calmness, and such patience, and such toleration, and such endurance; such endurance even of evil—shall we not take His wonderful words to heart, and humbly and believingly apply them, where it is at all possible; even erring, if err we must, on the safe side; and leave it to Him, when we at all can, to give His own orders about His own field at the end of the world? And, if we leave it to Him, it will be a sight on that day to see how He will vindicate our patience and His own parable.

Look back for a moment at what He Himself here calls some of the "scandals" in His Kingdom, and you will be fortified in your toleration of many things of that kind in time to come. Everybody has heard of the scandal of Galileo, to the shame of the Church of his day. And we are not without our own scandals in our own day. The highest dignitary now in the Church of England was, not very long ago, all but rooted up, as all but tares, both he and his beautiful writings. Whereas now he is where he is by universal acclamation. In Fitzjames Stephen's brilliant four-days' speech before the Court of Arches, that learned and eloquent counsel said—"My Lord, such differences have always existed in the Church. I might quote in favor of the accused party, some of the highest names in the Church of England. Hooker was charged, in his day, with subverting the authority of Scripture. Cudworth was called an atheist. Tillotson's life was embittered by persecution. Bishop Burnet, whose work afterwards became a theological text-book, was actually twice censured by the Lower House of Convocation. . . . My Lord, the one party viewing history, and criticism, and science, accept these results with gladness, and with candor, and the other party tremble before them. The one party would say with Hooker that to detract from the dignity of these things is to do injury even to God Himself, who being that Light which no man can approach to, has sent us these lesser lights as sparkles, resembling, so far, the bright fountain from which they spring." I will not quote what Stephen said about the other party. But he went on to say, "That, my Lord, is the real scope, tendency, and design of this prosecution, and that, as I said before, is its explanation, but not its justification."

And a greater than Fitzjames Stephen, the Golden-mouth of the English Church himself, says in his Discourse of the Liberty of Prophesying—"Let all errors be as much and as zealously suppressed as may be: but let it be done by such means as are proper instruments for their suppression; by preaching and disputation, by charity and sweetness, by holiness of life, by assiduity of exhortation, by the Word of God and prayer. For these ways are the most natural, the most prudent, the most peaceable, and the most effectual, instrument for the suppression of error. Only, let not men be hasty in calling every disliked opinion by the name of heresy. And if men will say that in saying this I persuade to indifferency, there is no help for me; I must bear it as I can. And I am not without remedy, for my patience will help me, and I will take my course."

And on the same subject a greater than either Stephen or Taylor has said: has sung—

Let not the people be too swift to judge,
As one that reckons on the blades in field,
Or ere the corn be ripe. For I have seen
The thorn frown rudely all the winter long,
And after bear the rose upon its top:
And bark, that all the way across the sea
Ran straight and speedy, perish at the last,
E'en in the haven's mouth.

But all that will only the more provoke some of you to retort on me and to demand—Do you really mean to say, that so and so are to be tolerated, and tolerated where they are? Now, I will not answer that which you put so passionately; for I am not debating with you, but am teaching to the teachable among you, a little of what I have been taught myself. And, moreover, what I have acted on more than once as I had opportunity, and have proved it to be true and trustworthy teaching, and have never repented it. And if, instead of debating about it, you also will receive it, and will act upon it, you also will live to prove it true. Now, with all this, I have not gone out of my way one inch tonight to seek out this wonderful parable, and its so timeous interpretation. Not one inch. For it met me in the very middle of my way to you. And, all I could examine it, and excogitate it, and go round about it, and look at it in every light, and indeed try to escape it—I could make nothing else out of it than what I have now said. But the day will declare both the eternal truth, and the present truth, about this parable of the wheat and the tares. On that day, He who preached this parable will winnow out, and will burn up all false interpretations of it, and mine among the rest. Only, may you and I be judged more tenderly and forgivingly by Him on that day than we have many a time judged other erring men!

The whole field of letters, also, is more or less like this husbandman's tare-tangled field. You can get at the pure truth in print scarcely in anything. You can with difficulty get a book of the past, and much less a magazine, or a journal, or a newspaper of the passing day, that is not all sown over with the author's own seed-basket; all sown over, now with partiality, and now with antipathy. That field in Galilee was a study in malice to our Lord: and there are fields all around us today of the same sickening spectacle. You are a public writer; and so many are the collisions of interests, and ambitions, and pursuits, and competitions; and such is the pure malice, sometimes, of your own tare-filled heart, that we cannot get from you the naked and real truth about that cause or that man. You simply will not let us get at the real, unadulterated, unvarnished, untampered-with, truth. And, besides, such are the resources and appliances of civilization in our day, that you can sow your evil seed under cover of anonymity, and your best friend will never know whose hand it was that stabbed him in the dark. You are reviewing a book by tongue or by pen. The author is not liked by you, or by your party, or by your employer; or, you are an author yourself, and the writer of the book before you has run away with your popularity and your profits. You would need to be a saint to review his new book aright. You would need to be an angel to say in your paper about him and about his book, what you would like him to say in his paper about you and about your book. And, indeed, considering what this world is, and what the human heart is, there is far more of such angelic saintliness abroad in it than you would expect to see, unless you were actually on the out-look for it. But, fair writing, and true writing, and loving writing, or no, we have no choice. We must act like this wise husbandman; we must take our history, and our biography, and our politics, and our art, and our law, and our criticism, and our morning and evening and weekly newspapers, as they are—tares and all. Lest if we forbid the tares entering our house we shut out both truth and love with them. Let them grow together until the harvest; and, meantime, make them all so many means of this and that grace to you. In one of his noblest papers Dr. Newman vindicates the study of the great classics—Greek, Latin, and English—in spite of the basketfuls of impurity that are sown so broadcast in some of them. And the old scholar and saint argues that in the interest of the very purity of mind and heart that we fear sometimes are so early poisoned in those shining fields. And now, before leaving this point, I will add this—I am not an author, nor a journalist, but a preacher, and

I will therefore add this—that he is a happy preacher who has lived through many times and seasons of temptation, and has never sown some of the tares of his own temper, and of his own partial mind, in his preaching, and even in his prayers. And I, for one, am not that happy preacher. Thomas Boston used to say, that of all men who needed the imputation of Christ's all-round righteousness, preachers and pastors were those men.

And then to come still closer to ourselves than even that. Such is the versatility, and the spirituality, and the inwardness, of our Lord's words in this wonderful parable, that they apply with the very greatest support and comfort to the heart of every sinful man also under his own all-searching sanctification. The heart of a great sinner, under a great sanctification, is the field of all fields. All other fields are but parables to him of his own field. And in nothing more so than in Satan and his satanic seed-basket. And worst of all, and saddest of all, that satanic seed is here almost part and parcel of the very field itself. For, from the beginning, that poisonous seed was, somehow, insinuated, and was already buried deep in the very original ground and soil of the soul; and so insinuated, and so rooted, that with the best husbandry it is never got out of the soil of the soul in this world. It is like those poisonous weeds in his best fields that so vex the husbandman's heart. Let him plow and harrow, and plow and harrow again; let him change his seed, let him rotate his crops; with all he can do, there is the accursed thing always coming up, choking the wheat, drinking up the rain and the sunshine from the wheat, and mocking all that the husbandman and his servants can do; mortifying and indeed breaking his heart. But here also—and startling and staggering to read it—our Lord here again advises patience. *Why* he does not cleanse the honest and good ground with one word of His mouth, He knows Himself. But that He does not so speak the word, and so cleanse the ground, all His best saints have learned to their bitter suffering, and their heart-breaking cost. And among all the counsels and comforts He speaks to our tare-tortured hearts, this wonderful, this even staggering, counsel is heard in and over them all. "Be patient with thine own sanctification, as with some other things, till I come. Behold, the husbandman waiteth for the precious fruit of the earth. Be ye also patient; for the coming of the Lord draweth nigh. And then the Son of Man shall send forth His angels, and they shall gather out of His kingdom all things that offend. And then shall the righteous shine forth as the sun in the kingdom of their Father. Who hath ears to hear, let him hear."

III

The Man Who Took a Grain of Mustard Seed, and Sowed It In His Field

OUR LORD'S parables are all so many applications of what we sometimes call the Sacramental Principle. That is to say, in all His parables our Lord takes up something in nature and makes it a lesson in grace, and a means of grace. The kingdom of heaven is like that, He said, as often as He saw a field of wheat all sown over with tares; or a vineyard with a husbandman working in it; or a lost sheep; or a prodigal son; or a marriage procession; or a few little children playing at marriages and funerals in the market-place. Our Lord so lived in heaven: He had His whole conversation so completely in heaven: His whole mind and heart and life were so absolutely absorbed in heaven, that everything He saw on earth, in some way or other, spoke to Him about heaven, and thus supplied Him with His daily texts, and sermons, and parables, about heaven. There are some men who are full of eyes, as Scripture says. They are full of eyes within and without. Now, our Lord was one of those men, and the very foremost of them. He was full of eyes by nature, and, over and above nature, He had an extraordinary and unparalleled unction from the Holy One. And thus it was that He discovered the kingdom of heaven everywhere and in everything. Already as a child He had deep and clear eyes both in His mind, and in His imagination, and in His heart. As a child He had often sown the least of all seeds in Joseph's garden, and had watched that mustard seed springing up till it became a great tree. And with what delight would He see the birds of the air building their nests in the branches of His own high mustard tree. And how He would feed them, and their young ones, with the crumbs that fell from His mother's table. And as He grew in wisdom and in stature, He would come to read in that same mustard tree yet another parable about His Father's house and His Father's business. Or, as we sometimes say, in our book-learned way, He would see in that mustard tree another illustration of that Sacramental Principle which was ever present with Him.

Now it was not so much the great size of the mustard tree that took such a hold of our Lord's imagination. It was rather the extraordinary smallness of the mustard seed. And that was a very fruitful moment for us when that small seed first fell into our Lord's mind and heart. For there immediately sprang up out of that small seed this exquisite little parable. This little parable, so exquisitely beautiful in its literature, and so inexhaustibly rich in its applications and fulfillments in no end of directions.

To begin with, the kingdom of heaven in Old Testament times was like a grain of mustard seed in its original smallness, and then in the great tree that it ultimately became. Take the very first of all the mustard seeds of the kingdom of heaven on this earth—the call of Abraham. What could be a smaller seed, at the time, than the emigration of the son of Terah out of Ur of the Chaldees and into the land of the Canaanites? Again, what seed could well be smaller than that ark of bulrushes, daubed with slime and pitch, and hidden away among the flags by the river's brink? And, then, what less likely to spring up into all the psalms and hymns and spiritual songs of the Church of God than those little snatches of sacred psalmody that a shepherd boy sang to his few sheep on the plains of Bethlehem? And to come to Old Testament institutions and ordinances also. What more like a mustard seed than those few drops of midnight blood sprinkled so stealthily on the lintels and the door-posts of those slave-huts in the land of Egypt? And yet all the passover-days in Israel, and all our own communion days in the Church of Christ, and the marriage supper of the Lamb in His Father's house, have all sprung up, and will yet spring up, out of that small mustard seed. And in like manner, all our divinity halls had their first original in that small school which Samuel set up on his father's little property at Ramah. Our own Oxford, and Cambridge, and Edinburgh, and Aberdeen, and many more such like schools of the prophets, are all so many great trees that have their long roots struck away back into Samuel's little mustard seed. As also when the carpenters of Jerusalem made a pulpit of wood for Ezra and his colleagues, standing on which they read in the book of the law distinctly, and gave the sense, and caused the people to understand the reading. There you have the first small seed out of which ten thousand pulpits have sprung up, down to our own day, and will spring up, down to the end of all evangelical time. Our Lord Himself stood upon a pulpit of the same wood; and so did Paul, and so did Chrysostom, and so did Augustine, and so did Calvin, and so did Thomas Goodwin, and so did Matthew Henry, and a multitude of pulpit expositors of the Word of God which no man can number.

Our Lord, you may depend upon it, had all those Old Testament instances in the eyes of His mind when He spake to His disciples this so charming and so instructive little parable. But, always remembering His own mustard-seed beginning, and always forecasting what was yet before Him, and before the whole world through Him, our Lord must always have looked on Himself as by far the most wonderful mustard seed that ever was sown. Would you see with your own eyes the most wonderful mustard seed that ever was sown in all the world? Come and look at that Holy Thing that lies in the manger of Bethlehem, because there is no room in the inn. Which, surely, was the least-looking of all seeds, but is now the greatest among herbs. And, then, what a seed of the same kind was the call of the twelve disciples, and the conversion of Saul of Tarsus, and the conversion of Augustine, and the conversion of Luther, and Wesley, and Chalmers, and General Booth. Paul's first mission to the Gentiles also, and the first missionary that landed on our shores, and the first printing-press, and the first sailing of the *Mayflower*, and so on.

But it is time to come to ourselves. And among ourselves that small mustard seed is eminently a parable for all parents. For every little word that a parent speaks to his child: every little action of a parent in the sight of his child: every little attitude even, and movement of his: every glance of his eye, and every accent of his voice—are all so many mustard seeds sown in the little garden of his child's mind and heart. Every little Scripture lesson learned together: every little prayer offered together: and, especially, alone together: every little occasional word to explain, and to make interesting, his child's little lesson and little prayer: every wise little word spoken to his child about his own and his child's Savior—every such small seed dropped by a parent's hand will yet spring up to his everlasting surprise, and to his everlasting harvest. Let all parents, then, and all nurses, and all tutors, and all schoolmasters, and all who have little children in the same house with them, lay this little parable well home to their imagination and to their heart. Let them not despise the day of small things. Let them have a great faith, and a great assurance of faith, in such small things as these. Let them have a great faith in Him, and in His wisdom, and His love, and in His faithfulness, who is continually, both in nature and in grace, folding up the greatest trees in the smallest seeds. And never more so than in the way He folds up your child's whole future in your little acts of faith, and prayer, and love, and wisdom, and patience, and hopefulness, done at home. Despise it not, for a great tree is in it. A great, a fragrant, and a fruitful tree, under which you will one day sit rejoicing in the shelter of it, and in the sweet fruitfulness of it.

Long before your son is ready to read Butler for himself, he will be a daily illustration to you of Butler's great principle of acts, habits, character. A little wrong act, another little act of the same kind, and another, and another, and another, and another, and all of them so small, that not one parent's eye in a thousand can so much as see them, the thing is so infinitely small, and the child himself is still so small. But, oh! the tremendous and irreparable oversight for you and for him! Read Butler for yourself till you have that wisest of Englishmen by heart. And as soon as your son is able to read his father's best books, buy him a good Butler for himself; and, some day when you are taking a long holiday walk together, have a good talk with him about that great teacher, both hearing your son's mind, and giving him in return your own mind, on that great man.

Thomas à Kempis's genesis of a fatal temptation is another instance of a mustard seed. An evil thought; the smallest seed of an evil thought, is, somehow, sown in our minds. In a thousand unforeseen ways such small seeds are being continually insinuated into all our minds. And if they are let enter our minds; if they are for a single moment entertained in our minds; evil thoughts, especially if they are of certain kinds, will immediately spread themselves out in our imaginations, and will so color, and so inflame, and so intoxicate, our imaginations, that our wills, and even our consciences, are completely carried captive before we are aware, till another deadly work is finished in body and in soul. A thought, says the old saint, then an imagination, then a delight, then a consent, and then our soul is sold for naught. The kingdom of hell also is like a grain of mustard seed, which, when it is grown, all the obscene birds of the bottomless pit come up and breed in the branches thereof. As the children's hymn has it long before they understand it,

> So our little errors
> Lead the soul away,

From the path of virtue
 Far in sin to stray.

But, blessedly, there is another side to all that. There is a genesis and a genealogy of things far more joyful to dwell on than that. A little thought of goodness, and of truth, and of love, will be sown in the garden of the soul. A little thought, as it looks, of God, of Jesus Christ, of heaven, well watered and shone upon by the Spirit of God. And then that little thought will open and will spread out into visions of beauty that will sanctify and fortify the soul, till the young soldier of Jesus Christ will step forward and will say like the brave man in John Bunyan—Set down my name, sir! When the heavenly watchers, seeing all that, will raise their songs over him, and will sing—

Come in, come in,
 Eternal glory thou shalt win!

And all from a small mustard seed of one good thought sown in a good and honest heart.

And so on, in a thousand other regions of religion and life. But I will close, with what will come home to us all—how to make our own home happy. For, what is the real secret of a happy home: a lifelong happy home? What but little mustard seeds of love, and of loving-kindness? What but little acts, and little habits, and then a great herb of character? A little act of forethought. A little act of respect. A little act of reverence. A little act of honor. A smile. A glance of the eye, A word of tact. A word of recognition. A word of praise. A word of love. A little gift. A little flower in a little glass of water. And many more things too small to put into a sermon for grown-up men.

With smiles of peace and looks of love
 Light in our dwellings we may make,
Bid kind good-humor brighten there,
 And still do all for Jesus' sake.

Little deeds of kindness,
 Little acts of love,
Help to make home happy
 Like the heaven above.

IV
The Man Who Cast Seed Into the Ground and It Grew Up He Knew Not How

DR. BRUCE is by far the best expositor of this exquisite little parable. Dr. Bruce is always himself. That is to say, he is always autobiographical, always experimental, always scientific, always masculine, always full of bone and blood, always strength itself, always satisfying. "A man's capacity," he says, "to expound particular portions of Scripture depends largely on his religious experiences. For here it holds good, as in other spheres, that we only find what we ourselves bring. The case is the writer's own. And therefore the parable to be studied has been to him for many years a favorite subject of thought, and a fruitful source of comfort. Viewed as a repetition in parabolic form of the Psalmist's counsel—Wait, I say, on the Lord." Dr. Bruce's book on the Parables is, to my taste, his best book. And then the exquisite little parable now open before us, shows Dr. Bruce, as I think, at his very best. So much so, that if there is to be anything of the nature of harvest to you tonight, let it be well understood that Dr. Bruce was the man who first cast the seed into the ground, but who fell asleep before the seed had sprung up in you and in me.

At the same time, the originality, and the freshness, and the force, of Dr. Bruce's exposition, is all to be traced back to the originality, and the freshness, and the force, of the parable which he so excellently expounds. You sometimes say to me that you do not know what style is. You have never been taught, you complain, to recognize style when you see it. And you ask me never to pass a piece of what I would call real style without stopping and calling your attention to it. Well, learn this little parable by heart, and say it to yourselves, till you feel the full taste of it in your mouth, and till you instinctively spew out of your mouth everything of a written kind that is not natural, and fresh, and forceful: everything that is not noble, and beautiful, and full of grace and truth, like this parable. "For the earth bringeth fruit of herself: first the blade, then the ear, after that the full corn in the ear." A little child might have said it. And He who did say it makes us all to feel like little children, with the naturalness, and the simplicity, and the truth, both to nature and to grace, of His exquisite words. The style is the man.

If we only had the eyes to see it, there is not a little of our Lord's teaching and preaching that is autobiographical, and experimental, and is consequently of the nature of a personal testimony. For, in all He went through, He went through it all because He was ordained to be the Firstborn among many brethren. He was in all points put to school and taught, and trained, from less to more, like as we are. He was Himself so led as to be made in due time the Leader and the Forerunner of the whole body of believers. Till He is able at every new step in His heavenward way to turn round and say to us—"Follow Me. He that followeth Me shall not walk in darkness, but shall have the Light of life." I like to look for our Lord's own foot-prints in every sermon of His, and what I look for I almost always find. As here. For, as it is in so many of His sermons, and as it is in so many of His parables that illustrate His sermons, this fine parable has, as I think, its first fulfillment in our Lord Himself. The seed of the kingdom was cast into the good ground of His own mind and heart also, and that from a child. And the seed that Mary, and Joseph, and the doctors in the temple, and the elders in the synagogue, all cast into that good ground sprang up, they knew not how. Till, when the sickle was put in for the first time, there was already such a harvest of grace and truth that they knew not what to make of it. Yes. It was so in Himself also: there was first the blade. For did He not grow up before them as a tender plant? And was He not subject to them as a little Child in the Lord? And was it not so that the Spirit of the Lord rested upon Him, they knew not how, till He began to be about thirty years of age? Matthew Henry sees our Lord Himself in this parable, and I am glad to have that great com-mentator's countenance in dwelling, as I so much love to dwell, on this delightful side of this delightful scripture.

And what was true of the Holy Child Jesus, will be true, in their measure, of your children and of mine. And if God the Father submitted His Son to His own divine law of gradual growth, and slow increase, and an imperceptible ripening, then we must not grudge to submit both ourselves and our children to the same divine ordinance. We must not torment ourselves with too much solicitude and anxiety about our children. We must not look for old heads on young shoulders. We must not thrust in the sickle on the same day as we sow the seed. We must not expect our sons to come all at once to the stature of perfect men, any more than we did ourselves. We were not perfect patterns at their age any more than they are. We were not by any means so deep in the divine life when we were young men as we now are. With ourselves also it was first the blade, then the ear, and only a long time after that, the full corn in the ear. We really must not embitter our own lives, and our children's lives, because they are not as yet run into all our mold, and are not shaped as yet into all our form of doctrine and manner of life. We must not demand of them that they shall sit up at night to read our favorite authors. They are still young, and they have their own favorite authors. Enough, if, say thirty or forty years after this, they are come to their full intellectual and spiritual man-hood. Enough, if, when we are no longer here to enjoy such masterpieces with them, they are by that time discovering the hid treasure, say, of Rutherford's *Let-ters*, and Guthrie's *Saving Interest*, and Baxter's *Saint's Rest*, and Marshall's *Gospel Mystery*, and William Law's immortal treatises, and are winding up every night with Bishop Andrewes's *Private Devotions*. By the time that we are done with those great guide-books of ours, and are distributing our choicest treasures to our chil-dren, we will write their names under our own names in our favorite copies, and will leave it to God to see that they write their children's names one day on the same revered pages. It was only after He was more than thirty years of age that we come on the Son of God Himself giving up whole nights at a time to secret prayer. Be you patient, therefore, brethren. Behold the husbandman waiteth for the precious fruit of the earth, and hath long patience for it, until he receive the early and the latter rain. Be ye also patient, stablish your hearts: for the coming of the Lord draweth nigh. Be you very thankful for the smallest signs of grace in your children. Despise not the day of small things. Look at that green blade in the spring field stealing its way so timidly round the obstructing clods and stones, and lifting up its hands towards the sunshine and the rain. And look for the same thing in your own house, and be thankful. For, in your house also, there will be first the blade, then the ear, and after that the full corn in the ear. You may not live to see it. You will most likely have fallen asleep before you see it. But you will be awakened to see it. And you will see no sweeter sight that sweet morning than the seed you sowed on earth at last come to its full ear in heaven. Yes, so is the kingdom of God. For when the fruit is brought forth, immediately He putteth in the sickle, because the harvest is come.

And, then, what a heart-upholding parable this is for all over-anxious ministers. It should be called the parable for all impatient parents and pastors; pastors especially. Our Lord is so bent upon consoling and comforting His ministers that He almost staggers us with what He here says about the unbroken peace of mind that every minister of His ought to possess. At all hazards, our Lord will, once for all, pluck up all over-anxiety, and all impatience with their people, out of the hearts of His ministers. So much so, that He startles us with the state of security, and almost of absolute obliviousness in sleep, that He would have all His ministers to enjoy. What a courageous comforter of His over-anxious ministers is Jesus Christ! Cast in the seed, He says, and take no more trouble about it. Sow the seed, and be secure of the harvest. Look at this wise sower how he sleeps, says our Lord to us. Imitate him. For so is the kingdom of heaven. It is as if our Lord came into this house and said:—So is this congregation. It is as if the ministers should preach, and hold their prayer-meetings, and teach their classes, and visit their sick, and should then wait in confidence till the seed should spring up, they know not how. And so it is as a matter of fact. We cast the seed of God's word into the earth, and the earth takes it, that is to say, God takes it, and it springs up, no man knoweth how, and the sowers of the seed least of all. Comfort My ministers, saith your God. Speak ye comfortably to My ministers, and say to them that the earth bringeth forth her fruit of herself, first the blade, then the ear, after that the full corn in the ear. There is another side, of course, to supplement all that; but one side is enough for one sermon of His, in our Lord's manner of preaching the kingdom.

I chanced upon this in my reading only last night. "Nothing great," says Epictetus, "is produced suddenly, not even a grape or a fig. If you say to me that you want a grape or a fig *now*, I will answer you that you cannot have it; a grape takes time. Let it flower first, then it will put forth its fruit, and then ripen. And would you have the fruit of a man's life and character all in a moment? Do not expect it." And again, "Fruit grows in this way, and in this way only. If the seed produces the fruit before the jointed stem, it is a product of the garden of Adonis. That is to say, the thing is for show only; it has no root in itself. You have shot up too soon, my man. You have snatched at fame before your season. You think you are something, but you will come to nothing. Let the root grow, then the first joint, then the second, and then the third, and then the fruit will come forth of itself." So Epictetus taught the young men in his Greek lecture-room. God never leaving Himself without a witness.

When a sinner first sets out on his sanctification, he begins already to sharpen his sickle, and to bind and stack his sheaves. He confidently promises himself and other people both sweet and strengthening bread to eat immediately out of his harvest. But both he, and all who have to do with him, soon find out that that is not at all the way of the kingdom of heaven. Not at all. In the kingdom of heaven, and in the sanctification of its subjects, it is first the blade here also, then the ear, after that the full corn in the ear. And sometimes, indeed, it threatens as if it were to be all blade in this field and no ear at all. Ay, and far worse than that: the very blade, with all its promise in it, will sometimes seem wholly to wither and absolutely to die. Why is it that I am so slow in growing any better? Why is my heart as wicked as ever it was, and sometimes much more so? You pray, in a way. You watch unto prayer, now and then. You study all the great authorities on sanctification that you can hear about, or can lay your hands on. But as soon as your secretly besetting sin is again suddenly let loose upon you, that moment you are down again in all your old agony of guilt and shame. Ah, my brethren, the kingdom of heaven is a very different experience from what you had at one time supposed it was. In our Lord's experimental words about it, the sanctification of the soul is first in the blade, then in the ear, and it is never, in this world, any more: it is never in this world the full corn in the ear. Whereas, poor soul, you thought that it was going to be the full ear with you all at once.

A great and a genuine sanctification, you must know, is the slowest work in all the world. There is nothing in heaven or earth so slow. The thing is sure, indeed, but the time is long. It would need to be sure, for oh, yes, sirs, it is long, long. And it is as sore, and as sickening, as it is long. There is a true description of it in our great Catechism. It is described there as "dying daily." And so it is. That is your case, is it not? It is dying by inches, is it not? It is having the two-edged sword driven daily into your heart, and never in this life healed out of your heart. Death is a process of pain, and shame, and ignominy. All possible pain, and suffering, and all manner of humiliation to mortal man, is collected up into the idea of death. But our everyday death is not true death at all, compared with the pain, and shame, and ignominy of death unto sin. And it all seems such a stagnation of sin, sometimes, and to some men. As, for instance, to the man who expostulated thus—"O my God, the more I do, the worse I am!" And to the man who first sang thus—

> And they that fain would serve Thee best,
> Are conscious most of wrong within.

Till, you may depend upon it, our Lord had His eye and His heart on His saints who are undergoing a great spiritual sanctification when He spake this many-sided and most comforting parable. He spake it first of Himself, and of His own growth in strength of spirit, and in wisdom, as well as in all manner of Messianic perfection. And then He spake it of parents and their children, and then of ministers and their people. But above all, He spake it of all those elect souls who are being kept for all their days under a slow but sure sanctification. There is first the blade of true holiness, He said, after that the ear, and then the full corn in the ear. But when the fruit is brought forth, immediately He putteth in the sickle, because the harvest is come.

V

The Woman Who Took Leaven and Hid It in Three Measures of Meal

BEING the first-born son in His mother's house, it would fall to the Holy Child Jesus to perform the part laid down for the first-born son in the feast of unleavened bread. And thus it was that after Joseph had struck the lintel and the two doorposts with the blood that was in the basin, and after the whole family had hurriedly eaten each a portion of the pascal lamb, and a piece of the unleavened bread, at that appointed moment the eldest son of the house came forward and said, Father, what mean you by this service? What mean you by the blood, and the unleavened bread, and the bitter herbs? And Joseph would say, It is the LORD's passover, because He passed over the houses of the children of Israel in Egypt, when He smote the Egyptians and delivered our houses. And Joseph, and Mary, and Jesus, and James, and Joses, and Simon, and Judas, and their sisters, all bowed their heads and sang the Hundred and Thirteenth and the Hundred and Fourteenth Psalms. And once every year till the Holy Child came to the full stature of the Christ of God: every returning passover He entered deeper and deeper into this great ordinance, both hearing Joseph and asking him questions. Till He came to be of more understanding about the feast of unleavened bread than all His teachers: and understood both the blood, and the bread, and the bitter herbs, far better than all the ancients.

As long as He was still a child, He spake as a child, He understood as a child, He thought as a child. And the *great haste* that the unleavened bread signified, was enough for His imagination and His mind and His heart as long as He was a child. But then, as time went on, He would watch His mother at her housewife-work, and would observe how her leaven *spread* till her three measures of meal was all leavened. And as He meditated on the process going on under His eyes, He would again see in the leaven and in the meal another parable of the kingdom of God. And He would lay up the leaven and the meal in His mind and in His imagination and in His heart for some of His future sermons. And thus it was that on that great day of teaching and preaching when He sat by the sea-side, He had already given out parable after parable, till any other preacher but Himself would have been exhausted; but He still went on as fresh and as interesting and as instructive as when He began in the morning. "I am full of matter," said Elihu. "The spirit within me constraineth me. I will speak that I may be refreshed." And our Lord was like Elihu in that. For though He had already that day illustrated and applied the kingdom of God by a long and splendid series of parables, His mind was still as full of matter as ever. And the more He tried to put the kingdom of God into this and that parable, the more He saw other things in that inexhaustible kingdom for which no parable had as yet been provided. And thus it was that at this point, and as if to teach them to keep their eyes always open for their own future preaching, their Master suddenly turned to His disciples and asked them whether any of them had any light to cast upon the subject in hand. As if He were asking some of them to help Him out with His great subject, He said to them—"Whereunto shall I go on to liken the kingdom of God?" And when none of them had a word more to say concerning the inwardness, and the hiddenness, and the all-assimilating power, of that kingdom, He called to mind a former reflection of His own which came to Him one day beside His mother's kneading-trough. He remembered that day her three measures of meal, and the way that she took to turn that raw meal into wholesome and palatable bread. "And so is the kingdom of God in some respects," He said. "It is in some respects like leaven which a woman took and hid in three measures of meal till the whole was leavened." And here are we tonight, and in this church, suddenly transported back into Mary's little kitchen in Nazareth, in order to learn there yet another of her Son's parables about the kingdom of God.

Beware of the leaven of the Pharisees, He said to His disciples on one occasion. Now, what did He mean by that saying, do you suppose? What would you say was the leaven of the Pharisees? I do not know any more than you do, but I will tell you what I think. Leaven, to begin with, is something that is hidden and inward, and then it works inwardly and secretly, till it works its way through the whole surrounding measures of meal. Now, what was the leaven of the Pharisees? It must have been something inward and hidden, to begin with. And then it had by that time worked its way through their whole heart and character till they were the Pharisees who were bent on our Lord's death and destruction. Well, a little lump of leaven that a woman can hold in her hand does not look to be much, nor to have much power in it. But wait and see. And a little self-esteem in a young man's heart is not very much to be suspected or denounced, is it? But wait and see. Let that young man set out on his life with that little lump of self-esteem in his secret heart, and, as sure as he lives, this will be his experience, and the experience of all who have to do with him. So many and so unavoidable are the oppositions, and the contradictions, and the collisions of life, that if his self-esteem is not by means of all these things, and by means of the grace of God co-operating with all these things, chastened and subdued and cast out, then all these collisions, and corrections, and contradictions, will only the more increase and exasperate his self-esteem, till he will end his days as full of self-righteousness, and pride, and hardness of heart, as very Lucifer himself. On the other hand, humility, that is to say disesteem of a man's self, is so much good leaven hidden in a good man's heart. These are the words of well-known master in Israel—"Humility does not consist in having a worse opinion of ourselves than we deserve, or in abasing ourselves lower than we really are. But as all virtue is founded in truth, so humility is founded in a true and just sense of our weakness, misery, and sin. So much so, that he who rightly feels and lives in this sense of his condition lives in humility." That is to say, he who at all rightly knows himself is done for ever with all self-esteem. There is not left in all his inward parts so much as a single ounce of that leaven of the Pharisees. But that sect in Israel were so set against all introspection, as they called it: their doctors of the law so denounced that sanctifying habit of mind and heart, that their scholars ended with crucifying the Lord of Glory. To such a lump of villainy and wickedness will a little leaven of self-esteem grow under the fit conditions, and in the fit heart, and left fitly alone. Now our Lord saw, only far too well, that evil leaven already at work in His twelve disciples. I do not take it upon me to say how far it is at work in any of you. I will not insist that your self-esteem is eating through your whole heart and is destroying your whole life and character. I will not fall out with you about that. I will not insist on what you call introspection, but I for one both feel and confess the truth of His words when my Lord says to me—Preacher, Beware! lest having discoursed so beautifully on humility to others, you yourself, through your self-esteem, should be a castaway from the kingdom of God. Till it has to be my prayer, with the candle of the Lord in my hand continually—Search me, O God, and know my heart: try me, and know my thoughts: and see if there be any of this wicked way in me, and lead me in the way everlasting!

The Apostle Paul also has this on this same parable: "Purge out therefore the old leaven. Know ye not that a little leaven leaveneth the whole lump? Therefore let us keep the feast, not with old leaven, neither with the leaven of malice and wickedness, but with the unleavened bread of sincerity and truth." Now, what is malice and wickedness? We have seen what self-esteem is, and how it works till it leavens the whole lump. But what is the leaven of malice? You may be old enough to know without being told. You may have enough of it in yourself, and you may have suffered enough from it in others; but there are new beginners in self-esteem, and in malice, and the word must be rightly divided to meet their case as well as yours. Now, you who are new beginners in morals and in religion—what think you is malice? For you cannot purge it out, nor keep it purged out, if you do not know it when you see it. Well, malice also is like leaven in this. Its first beginning is so small as not to be worth speaking about in a dignified pulpit. You do not like some one. Nothing is so common, surely, as that. Already, at school, at college, in the office, in the workshop, in the house, you do not like some one. Well, that is your first half-ounce of the leaven of malice. And your feelings toward that man, and your thoughts about him, and your words about him, and your actions toward him, are like the three measures of meal with the little leaven at its heart. You just dislike that man—that is all as yet. But then full-grown men are so leavened with that same dislike that they actually come to hate one another. And— "hates any man the thing he would not kill?" You see then where you are. You see on what road you are travelling. You are travelling on the road of the Pharisees. You are travelling on the road to hell. And there is no surer, no shorter, and no more inevitable, road to hell than hatred, which is just dislike, and umbrage, and a secret grudge, come to their three measures of meal. Malice is bad blood, as we say. It is ill-will. It is resentment. It is revenge. Till it is in God's sight very murder itself; hidden, as yet, it may be from your introspection in its three measures of surrounding and smothering-up meal. And it is while this red-handed murder is still at its early stages of dislike, and antipathy, and animosity, that Paul beseeches you to purge it out. But in order to purge it out, you must take a candle like this to the work. A clear candle like this. You have a neighbor. He may at one time have been a friend. He may never suspect but that he is a friend still. He may be befriending you all the time. But at heart you are not his friend any more. Something has happened to you. Something that you must search out and admit about yourself. However humbling, however self-condemning, however self-hating, it may turn out to be, you cannot be a good and a true man any more till you have found yourself out. Your friend forgot you on some occasion. Or he preferred some one else to you. Or he took his own judgment and conscience for his guide in some matter in which you demanded to dictate to him. Or he got some promotion, or praise, or reward, that you had not humility and love enough to stomach. Track out your heart, sir! Heaven and hell hang on your tracking out your heart in that matter. No. Hell does not hang upon it, for hell has possession of your heart already. That wicked heat in your heart at the mention of his name, that is hell. That blackness which we all see in your very look, that is the smoke of your torment already begun. Purge it out, implores Paul. Ah! it is easy saying purge it out. Did Paul manage to purge it out himself, after all his most earnest preaching about it? No: he did not. No more than you and I. And it was when he had lighted all the candles he could lay his hands on; and when with them all he could not get down to all the malice that was still hiding in his heart, it was then that his Master had mercy on His miserable servant, and said to him, My grace is sufficient for thee: for My strength is made perfect in weakness.

And though Pharisaic self-esteem and diabolical malice are all the instances to which our Lord's parable is applied first by Himself and then by His best Apostle, yet the parable is equally true of all the other leavenings of the devil that are insinuated into our souls. A little of the leaven of pride—think it out, with home-coming illustrations, for yourself. A little of the leaven of anger—think it out, with home-coming illustrations, for yourself. A little of the leaven of suspicion, and of jealousy, and of envy—with illustrations and instances taken from yourself. A little of the leaven of sensuality—"the inconceivable evil of sensuality"—as Newman calls it—with a whole portfolio of illustrations taken from yourself. A foul thought, a foul hint, a foul innuendo, a foul word, a foul image; a foul-mouthed boy in the playground; a foul-mouthed man in the workshop, in the office, in the bothy; a foul-mouthed woman in the workroom, in the kitchen, in the field; a foul book, a foul picture, a foul photograph in a shop-window in passing—think it out, with a thousand illustrations taken from your own experience, and you will be wiser in this universal leaven of sensuality than all your teachers. You will yet be a master in Israel yourself in such sickening, but at the same time necessary, self-knowledge.

It is surely very striking to discover that while our Lord says so plainly that the kingdom of God is like leaven, yet both He, and His best Apostle, descend into the kingdom of Satan for all their best instances, and all their most pungent applications of the leaven. They would seem in this to leave it to ourselves to apply and to verify the parable in its application to the things of the kingdom of God. Whereunto shall I liken it? He said to His disciples. As much as to say—find out more and better instances, and illustrations, and verifications, for yourselves. And His example, and Paul's example, would seem to say to all preachers—give your people one or two illustrations taken from things they are only too well acquainted with already, and then leave them to prosecute the parable further for themselves. Would, said Moses, that all the Lord's people were prophets! And I will leave this parable where our Lord and His Apostle left it, only saying over it and over you, Would that all the Lord's people were expositors and preachers, and that out of their own observation and experience!

VI

The Man Who Found Treasure Hid in a Field

IT was good stories like this in His sermons that made the common people begin to hear Him so gladly. There was not a carpenter's shop, nor a village market-place, in all Galilee where such stories of treasure-trove were not continually told. Stories of the same kind are not altogether unknown in our own land. But in the East, and to this day, such great finds as this man made are not at all uncommon. In times of commotion timid men will hide their treasures sometimes in the walls or under the floors of their houses, and sometimes they will bury them in their gardens and in their fields. And it will sometimes happen that the owner will die and will leave his secret treasure wholly undisclosed. And then some lucky man will come on that buried treasure some day in the most unexpected and accidental way; like this lucky man. He was plowing one day in his master's field; or, was he digging deep with his spade and his mattock? When, suddenly, he reeled with joy at the sight of the glittering hoard that his plowshare had laid bare. In one moment his resolve was made. Carefully covering up the shining spot, before the sun had time to set, he had already sold all that he possessed, and had made such an offer for the field that it was handed over to him, with all that it contained, before he slept. All the old books of the ancient world are full of such intoxicating stories as this. Perhaps the most famous of all those stories is that which Tacitus tells us about Nero. How a bold imposter hoaxed the emperor about an immense mine, full of all kinds of precious treasure, that was to be found in a distant part of his dominions. And Nero believed the wild tale till he became the laughing-stock of the whole world. But this was no hoax, this true find in that field of Galilee. Our Lord would seem to have known the fortunate plowman, and to have had his happy story from his own delighted lips. But the barest outline of the rich story is all that Matthew's pen has here preserved to us. We would far rather have had the whole sermon that our Lord preached from that fortunate man's find than we would have had all his furrow full of gold and silver. For the word of our Lord's mouth is becoming more and better to us than thousands of gold and silver. But it has seemed good to the Holy Ghost to have this man's story told to us in the shortest possible way, and then to leave us to find out all its heavenly likenesses for ourselves.

Well, the first and foundation likeness between this parable and the kingdom of heaven is surely this. Just as our Lord is the Sower in another parable, and just as He is the Planter of the mustard seed in another, and the Good Shepherd in another, and the Good Samaritan in another, so He is the happy plowing Man in this parable. And as the field was the world in a former parable, so is it here. And the kingdom of heaven, says our Lord, is like treasure hid in the field of this world.

And the first man who found the treasure that lay hid in the field of this world was the Son of man. All the world knows that though He was rich, yet for our sakes He became poor. All the world knows how that being in the form of God, He humbled Himself, and made Himself of no reputation, and became obedient unto death, even the death of the cross. All of which, taken together, was the price He paid for this field, and for the treasure hid in this field. Our Lord bought this world, so to say, for the sake of the elect souls that lay hidden in it, till He was able to say—"As thou, Father, hast given thy Son power over all flesh, that He should give eternal life to as many as thou hast given Him."

Incomparable Thomas Goodwin—incomparable to me, at any rate—says that Paul will be the second man in heaven, the Man Christ Jesus being the first man. And every one here will already have thought of Paul as soon as this fine little parable was read out to him. For, if ever any man could be said to have had every letter of this fine little parable fulfilled both in him and by him, that man was Paul. If ever any man, after the Man Christ Jesus, sold all that he had that he might buy the field, that man was the Apostle. Which field, in his case, was nothing less than Jesus Christ Himself. Jesus Christ Himself, with His justifying righteousness, held in Himself like hid treasure. This so fortunate plowman in our Lord's sermon sold his little cottage in Capernaum, with its little garden full of fruits and flowers, and with all its vines and fig trees, under which he was used to sit after his hard day's work was done. He determined to sell all those dear possessions and delights of his for the sake of the treasure his eyes had once got sight of in that enriching and entrancing field. And Paul, in like manner, was plowing at his daily task, when, lo, his horse's foot suddenly sank out of sight into such a wealth of unsearchable riches, that he straightway counted all things but loss in order to buy that field. Yes, truly. If Jesus Christ was the first plowing man of this parable, then, surely, Paul was the second.

But the kingdom of heaven is such a rich and various kingdom that there are many other fields with hid treasure in them, lying all around the central field. And in some of those adjoining fields there is no little treasure still lying hid and waiting for the first fortunate plowman to lay it open and to make it his own. You are not ministers. But you cannot fail to see what a rich field, and full of what treasure, every evangelical pulpit is, with its pastorate of the same character spreading out all around it. Only, here again, that minister who would possess himself of the hid treasure of his pulpit and his pastorate must sell all he has in order to buy up those two gold-filled fields. "At his first coming to his little village, Ouranius felt it as disagreeable to him as a prison, and every day seemed too tedious to be endured in so retired a place. He thought his parish was too full of poor and mean people that were none of them fit for the conversation of a gentleman. This put him upon a close application to his studies. He consequently kept much at home, writ notes upon Homer and Plautus, and sometimes thought it hard to be called to pray by any poor body's bedside when he was just in the midst of one of Homer's battles." "Mr. Kinchin," says George Whitefield, "was minister of Dummer in Hampshire, and being likely to be chosen Dean of Corpus Christi College, he desired me to take his place and officiate for him till that affair should be decided. By the advice of friends I went, and he came to supply my place in Oxford. His parish consisting chiefly of poor and illiterate people, my proud heart at first could not well brook it. I would have given all the world to be back in my beloved Oxford. But upon giving up myself to prayer, and reading Mr. Law's excellent Character of Ouranius, my mind became reconciled to such conversation as the place afforded me. I prosecuted Mr. Kinchin's plan, and generally divided the day into three parts; eight hours for study and meditation, eight hours for sleep and meals, and eight hours for reading prayers, catechizing and visiting the parish. The profit I reaped by these exercises was unspeakable. I soon began to be as much delighted with their artless conversation as I had previously been with my Oxford friends, and I frequently learned as much by an afternoon's visit as in a week's study. I remained at Dummer till a letter came from Mr. John Wesley in which were these words: 'Do you ask what you shall have in Georgia? Food to eat, and raiment to put on, and a house to lay your head in, such as your Lord had not. And a crown of glory that fadeth not away.' Upon reading this, my heart leaped within me, and as it were echoed to the call."

As I was saying, a minister who would dig up the hidden treasure out of his pulpit and pastoral fields must sell all his time and all his tastes; all his thoughts by day and all his dreams by night. He must spend and be spent. He must be the servant of all men. He must become all things to all men. He must not strive. He must have no mind of his own, but the mind of Christ only. Both his books, and his table, and his bed, must all go to the hammer. But then, by that time, he will begin to have a people about him of whom he will be able to say—"What is my hope, or joy, or crown of rejoicing? Are not even ye in the presence of our Lord Jesus Christ at His coming?" And then that all-surrendered minister will be summoned forward at the coming of his Lord, not any more to shame and everlasting contempt, but his Lord will say to him on that day when He makes up His jewels— "That jewel is yours," his Lord will say: "for that soul and that would have been lost to Me, but for your self-denying ministry." And then, on that day, the poorest parish in all Scotland, and the meanest mission-field in all the world, will be seen to yield up treasures that will dazzle the eyes of men and angels to see them. Then they that be wise in time shall shine as the brightness of the firmament; and they that turn many to righteousness as the stars for ever and ever.

And on the other hand, such a minister's ministry is the all-enriching field of his understanding and discerning people. A scholarly, studious, able, evangelical, experimental, preacher every Sabbath day; and then all the week an assiduous, unwearied, ever-mindful, all-loving, pastor—what a field, and full of what treasure to his people, is such a minister and such a ministry! What treasures of grace and truth lie hid there for the proper people. Ay, and lie hid, sometimes, even from his very best people. For how can any one know, or even guess at, what God has done so as to enrich them and their children in His fitting up and furnishing of their minister's whole life and experience? Ten thousand personal and ministerial providences and experiences have all befallen him for their sake. As also his ever sleepless labors for their understanding and edification. The half of which could not be told, and would neither be believed nor understood, even if it were to be told. Only, sometimes you will hear of one man in a thousand; sometimes you will meet with one rare and remarkable man who has sold not a little, in order to become possessed of that minister and his ministry. The multitude in every congregation stumble about lucklessly and unprofitably even among the richest of fields. But, here and there, and now and then, another manner of man will sometimes be met with. One happy man in a thousand runs his plowshare down into the treasure-trove of that pulpit, and then takes action accordingly. An old office-bearer of this very congregation told me long ago, how he had lately summoned a conference of his whole household in order to make a great family choice and decision. He put it to his wife, and to his sons, and to his daughters, whether he would build a house for them away out of Edinburgh, with a park and a garden and stables, and all that. Or whether he would buy a house in a west-end Crescent so as to be still near this church, and so as to let him remain in the session, and so as to let his family continue to sit under Dr. Candlish's ministry. And the eyes of that happy plowman of Capernaum did not glisten with tears of greater joy than did that old elder's eyes when he told me that he had determined on a house within reach of the pulpit to which he owed his own soul, and his children's souls. And his wife had been in Dr. Candlish's ladies' class. Things like that do not happen every day. But that is, largely, because there are not pulpits every day like Dr. Candlish's pulpit of those days.

And, then, all the more because you are not ministers, you have the gold-filled field of your Bible always before you. If you had been ministers you would have had a constant temptation in connection with your Bible that, as it is, you have clean escaped. If you had been preachers you would have been tempted to read your Bible almost solely with an eye to good texts. And, better not read your Bible at all, than just to make sermons out of it. What a promise! you say as you read alone, and you read no more that night. What a consolation! you say. What a psalm! and you say and sing it all that week after, and at all times and in all places. What a name for you is the Name of your God! you say. And, like Moses on the Mount, you make haste and bow your head and worship, and say—Pardon our iniquity and our sin, and take us for thine inheritance. Moses did not say—What a text for next Sabbath! And you have no temptation to say that either. There is nothing of that kind to come in between you and your immediate application of the rich grace of God's word to the needs of your own soul. Yes. What a field of fields to the right reader is the word of God! What a grace-laden field is the Psalms. And again, the Gospels. And again, the Epistles. What solid gold lies hidden in all these several spots of this rich field. Happy plowmen! O, my brethren, search deep in the Scriptures. For they are they which testify to you both of yourselves and of your Savior.

And then the field of prayer. O, the milk and honey of which every rig and furrow of that field is full! He maketh me to lie down in the green pastures of it. He leadeth me beside the still waters of it. And then, the treasure hid in it. And then, the enterprise of prayer, the exploration of it, the ventures in it, the sure successes of it. Surely this is the field in which there is a vein for the silver, and a place for the fine gold. Iron is here taken out of the earth, and brass is molten out of the stone.

The very stones of it are the place of sapphires, and it hath its dust of gold. It cannot be gotten for gold, neither shall silver be weighed for the price of it. This is a field that cannot be valued with the gold of Ophir, with the precious onyx or the sapphire. The gold and the crystal cannot equal it; and the exchange of it cannot be for jewels of fine gold. No mention shall be made of coral or of pearls; for the price of prayer is above rubies. The topaz of Ethiopia shall not equal it. Neither shall it be valued with pure gold. Verily, verily, I say unto you, Whatsoever ye shall ask the Father in my name, He will give it you. Hitherto ye have asked nothing in my name. Ask, and ye shall receive, that your joy may be full.

VII

The Merchant Man Who Sold All That He Had and Bought the Pearl of Great Price

THIS is one of those travelling jewellers of the East who compass sea and land in their search for goodly pearls. He is never at home. He is always on the look-out for more and more precious pearls. Till one day his long search is signally rewarded. He is engaged in exploring a certain market of precious stones, when suddenly his eye falls on a pearl the like of which he had never supposed to exist. Its great size, its perfect form, its exquisite beauty, its dazzling light—he had never expected to see such a gem. Ascertaining from its owner the great price of the pearl, the merchant man forthwith sells all that he possesses, and buys up on the spot that pearl of great price. We get a well-known word from the honorable name that is here given to this enterprising merchant man. Our Lord calls him an *emporium* man. And so he is. For he has spent his whole life in the search for the very best pearls, till his emporium is famous for the size, and the beauty, and the value, of its pearls. And his famous emporium is now more famous than ever because of this splendid purchase he has made on his last enterprising journey.

Now, the world of books, to begin with, is not unlike a merchant man seeking goodly pearls. For every really good book that a really good judge of books discovers becomes a pearl of great price to him. Till as his reading life goes on, he as good as sells all his former books for the sake of this and that pearl of books which he has discovered in the course of his reading. A new beginner in books reads everything he comes across. All printed matter interests him, and a poor and passing book will for a time satisfy him, and even entrance him. But as time goes on, and as the real use of a good book, and the real rarity of a good book, become revealed to him, the true reader will be found giving up all his reading time, and all his reading outlay, to the really great and life-long books of the world, and to them alone. As, for instance, Dr. Chalmers.

During my Christmas holiday I have been renewing my acquaintance with that true pearl of a book, Dr. Hanna's *Memoirs of Dr. Chalmers*. And among a multitude of lessons I learned and laid up for myself and for my classes out of that treasure-house, Dr. Chalmers's ever-growing appreciation of the very best books was one of the best lessons I again learned. "Butler made me a Christian," said Chalmers, somewhat hyperbolically, to one of his early friends. "Pascal's," he wrote to another friend, "is more than all Greek and Roman fame." Before his eyes were opened, and before his taste was refined to distinguish pearl from paste, Chalmers actually denounced John Newton, and Richard Baxter, and Philip Doddridge, from the pulpit, and as good as forbade his people to read them. But the day was fast coming when this great merchant man of ours was to sell all that he had in order to buy the very pearls he had so scouted in the days of his disgraceful and guilty ignorance. For as I read on I came on such entries in his private journal as these: "Began Richard Baxter, which I mean to make my devotional reading in the evenings." "Sept. 13.—I have begun Baxter's *Call to the Unconverted*, and intend it for circulation." And writing the same year to a younger brother of his, he says, "I look upon Baxter and Doddridge as two most impressive writers, and from whom you are likely to carry away the impression that a preparation for eternity should be the main business and anxiety of time." "Nov. 11.—Finished this day the perusal of Foster's *Essays*, which I have read with great relish and excitement. His profoundly evangelical views are most congenial to me. O my God, give me of the fullness of Christ! May I never lose sight of Christ, that through Him I may pass from death unto life." "March 14.—I am much impressed with the reality and business-like style of Doddridge's intercourse with God. O Heavenly Father, convert my religion from a name to a principle!" You may remember that there is an old evangelical classic entitled *The Marrow*. Sell a whole shelf of your juvenile books and buy it, and you will be wise merchant men, if Dr. Chalmers is a good judge.— "Sunday, August 23.—I am reading *The Marrow*, and derive from it much light and satisfaction. It is a masterly performance. August the 24th.—Finished *The Marrow*. I feel a growing delight in the fullness and sufficiency of Christ. O my God, bring me nearer and nearer to Thy Son!" And of another masterpiece of another master mind, he writes—"Read Edwards on the *Religious Affections*. He is to me the most exciting and interesting of all theological writers." "Who taught you to preach in that way?" asked David Maclagan one day long ago at Dr. Rainy in the vestry behind me here. "John Owen," was all the answer. Now, writing to Dr. Wardlaw, Dr. Chalmers says, "I am reading Owen just now on *The Person of Christ*. May the Spirit more and more take of the things of Christ and show them to me." And again, "Have finished Owen on *Spiritual-Mindedness*. O my God, give me the life and the power of those who have made this high attainment!" And again, "Have you read Owen on the Hundred and Thirtieth Psalm? This is my last great book, and I would strongly recommend it as eminently conducive to a way of peace and holiness." And of the very Doddridge against whom he had at one time warned his parishioners, he now writes—"I have been reading more of Doddridge, and do indeed find myself to be a very alienated and undone creature. But let me cleave to Christ so as to receive all my completeness from Him." And of another goodly pearl, whose title at least you all know, he writes, "I am on the eve of finishing Guthrie, which, I think, is the best book I ever read." And at a later date—"I still think it the best human composition I ever read relating to a subject about which it is my earnest prayer that we may all be found on the right side of the question." Romaine also, was such a favorite with Chalmers as he grew in years and in grace that I cannot begin to quote his constant praise of that fine spiritual writer. And to sum up with an extract from his *Journal* that bears on this whole question—"I breathe with delight in the element of godly books, and do fondly hope that their savor, at one time wholly unfelt by me, argues well for my regeneration." And at the very end of his saintly and splendid life—"I am reading Ebenezer Erskine on *The Assurance of Faith*, and I specially like it. Its doctrine is very precious to me." Such are some samples of the kind of books that Dr. Chalmers sold all in order to buy a taste for them, and a life-long enjoyment of them. Let every divinity student read Chalmers's *Memoirs* just before he is ordained, and once again every three or four years all his ordained days.

You may not be much of a merchant man in the world of books, and yet this parable may be found entirely true of you in some other world of your own. "I have no books," said Jacob Behmen, "but I have myself." And Apollo did not say, Know many books. What he kept saying continually was this, "Know thyself." Now, you may be this kind of a merchant man that not some book, but some doctrine, of the kingdom of heaven may be to you your pearl of great price. The true and full doctrine of New Testament faith, for instance. What New Testament, and evangelical, and justifying, and sanctifying, faith really is. What its true object really is, and what its true acts and operations really are. The true nature of Gospel faith has been a perfect pearl of great price to some great men when at last they found it. It was so to John Wesley. "Preach faith till you find it," said Peter Bohler, Wesley's Moravian master, to him; "and then preach it because you have found it." And all the world knows how John Wesley sold, so to speak, every other doctrine in order to hold and to preach immediate and soul-saving faith, and with what immediate and soul-saving results. Another will find his pearl of great price in the spiritual doctrine of holy love, as was the case with John Wesley's English master, William Law. As Law did also in a whole world of doctrines, and habits, and practices, connected with secret prayer. And as George Whitefield, John Wesley's predecessor in field-preaching, discovered such unsearchable riches to him in the Pauline doctrines of election, and assurance, and perseverance to the end. And as so many men of the Owen, and Goodwin, and Edwards type have discovered in the deep, spiritual doctrines connected with the entrance into their hearts of the holy law of God, and connected with the consequent sinfulness of sin, and then connected with the work of the Holy Ghost continually carried on within their hearts. And so on. Till every genuine merchant man has his own special pearls of divine truth; not to the denying or the despising of other men's purchases; but because his own pearls of great price have so attracted him, and have so enriched him.

But after all that has been said about pearls of great price and their purchase, every merchant man's own soul is his most precious pearl. And our Lord counsels us all to sell all our other pearls, good and bad, great and small, and buy up our own soul unto everlasting life. "What is a man profited," our Lord demands of every man among us, "if he shall gain the whole world and lose his own soul? Or what shall a man give in exchange for his soul?" Our Lord was the last to undervalue the world which He had made, and of which He is the Heir, and yet He says that if any man should have this whole world in one hand, and his immortal soul in the other hand, he will be a fool of the first water if he holds to the whole world and lets go his immortal soul. Yes. The pearl of all pearls to you and to me is our own immortal soul. And we do not have to compass sea and land in search of this pearl of great price. We have it in our hand already, and all we have to do in order to be the richest of merchant men, is to keep a good hold of it. Unless, indeed, we have already lost hold of it. As we have. Alas, as we all have. Oh, what a fatal market is that which goes on all around every man who has a soul to sell to his everlasting loss, or to keep to his everlasting enriching. Oh, what a mad market that is in which men's souls, worth more than the whole world, are sold away every day for naught, and for far less than naught. And thus it was that our Lord was not content with warning us as to the value of our souls; but He entered the soul-market Himself, and bought back our souls at a price that has for ever put His immense estimate upon them. He who alone knows the exchangeless value of our immortal souls, He came and redeemed our souls at a price which was worth far more than the whole world, and all our souls to the bargain. For He redeemed our souls at the price of His own precious blood.

But then all that only ends, as every parable of His has ended, in making our Blessed Lord Himself THE PEARL of all pearls to us. All these partial, and, as it were, preliminary, pearls take their value to us entirely from Him. They all run up their values into Him. All good books are really good books to us, just in the measure that they speak to us about Jesus Christ. If they speak not to us about Him— take them away. Light the fire with them. They are not worth their house-room. All our doctrines also of whatever kind; doctrines of science, of politics, of letters, of art, of theology, of morals—all are sound and safe for a man to go by himself, and to teach his children to go by, only in the measure that Jesus Christ is in them. It was really, and all the time, the Preacher Himself who was the goodly Pearl of that sermon and that day. "To whom can we go," said Peter when he was under the illumination of the Father—"but unto Thee? Thou hast the words of eternal life." All of you, then, who are seeking for goodly pearls, whether in the world of books, or of doctrines, or of any other kind of good things; here, under your very eye; here, to your very hand, is the greatest and the best Pearl in all the world. For Jesus Christ gathers up into Himself all the truth, and all the beauty, and all the satisfaction, that your heart has for so long been seeking in vain. He is the Father's Pearl of great price. He is the one perfect Chrysolite of heaven on sale on earth. Who, then, on the spot will sell all that he has, and will be for ever after the wisest of merchant men? Nay, who will take away with him tonight God's greatest Pearl as God's free gift, without money and without price? For the gift of God is eternal life, through Jesus Christ our Lord.

VIII
The Man Who Went Out to Borrow Three Loaves at Midnight

FOR thirty years and more our Lord had been laying up materials for His future sermons. And He had started to collect His materials with something like this as one of His guiding principles:—

> What surmounts the reach
> Of human sense, I shall delineate so,
> By likening spiritual to corporal forms,
> As may express them best; though what if Earth
> Be but the shadow of Heaven, and things therein
> Each to other like, more than on Earth is thought?

Our Lord knowing that to be the case, and taking that for one of His guiding principles in His preaching, it came about that what we call His parables, were, in reality, not so much parables of His at all, as they were His observations of human life, and His experiences of human life, with His divine intuitions of grace and truth irradiating and illuminating them all. In our artificial and superficial way we think of our Lord as making up His parables as He went on with His sermons, and throwing them in just as they occurred to Him at the moment. But that was not His way of preaching at all. His way of preaching, and of preparing for His preaching, was a far better way than that. For, not seldom His parables were His own personal experiences, and His own immediate observations, collected and laid up in His mind and in His memory and in His heart, and to be afterwards worked up into His sermons. As we find them worked up with all the freshness and impressiveness and authority that personal experience always gives to preaching, whether that preaching is our Lord's own incomparable preaching, or such poor preaching as our own.

Our Lord, says the evangelist, was praying in a certain place. Our Lord was always praying, and in every place, and the evangelist knew that quite well. But he is a practiced and a skillful writer, and what he here writes is written, every word of it, with an intended purpose. The evangelist here gives his readers this report of that day just as he had received it from an eye and ear witness of the occurrences of that day, and he introduces this most important narrative with a certain studied circumstantiality of style. There had been something quite out of the ordinary in our Lord's private devotions that day. He had been much longer absent from His disciples that day than was His wont. And, besides, when He joined them again there was something about Him that specially arrested the attention of one of His disciples. Whoever he was, that disciple went up to his Master and said to

628

Him, Lord, teach us to pray, as Thou Thyself so often prayest. And thus it was that that happy disciple, whoever he was, got on the spot, "Our Father, which art in heaven," as his Master's answer to his request. A great reward to him and to us for his holy boldness, and for his timeous petition that day. And not the Lord's Prayer only; but that richly-favored disciple got for himself and for his fellow-disciples and for us also, what we call the parable of the friend at midnight. Our Lord not only taught His disciples that prayer of prayers that day but—to enforce the lesson, He told them a story out of His rich treasure-house of such stories; a story that has all the freshness, and all the lifelikeness, and all the pointedness, of a personal experience. "Which of you," He said, turning to the twelve, "shall have a friend, and shall go to him at midnight, and shall say unto him, Friend, lend me three loaves. For a friend of mine on his journey has come to me, and I have nothing to set before him?" Now there is only too good ground for believing that the carpenter's house was one of the poorest houses in all Nazareth and Capernaum. Sickness, death, suretyship, losses in business, and trouble upon trouble of every kind, had overtaken Joseph's house-hold, till, with all their industry, and all their frugality, his household would seem to have been poor beyond any of their kindred or any of their acquaintances. So much so, that nothing is more likely than that Joseph had oftener than once undergone the very indignity that is here so feelingly described. And not Joseph only, but He who here tells this touching story was found under Joseph's roof as one of his sons, and all His days on earth He was one of the poorest of men. No. Depend upon it, He did not make up the parable of the importunate poor man at midnight. He did not need to make it up. He was Himself in all points made like that poor and importunate man. Poor and importunate, not for Himself, but for men poorer than Himself who had thrown themselves upon Him. Our Lord was an experimental preacher. Just as He was and is an experimental priest.

It is a most pathetic, but at the same time a most amusing, story. It has been said sometimes that our Lord never laughed. Perhaps not. But we both laugh and weep at once over this scene as He here sets it before us. The well-supped churl is folded up in his warm bed and is just falling asleep, when a knock comes to his door so loud that it wakens the very dogs in the street. And then his angry denial is only answered with louder and louder knocking. Till we see that the well-fed and warmly laid down householder is completely at the mercy of that dreadful neighbor of his at the door. His very love for his bed lays him open to every knock that resounds through his well-supped and well-bedded house. I tell you I cannot rise! he shouts. Ay, but he will have to rise if the man at the door only holds on. Let him only hold on knocking loud enough and long enough, and as sure as that householder loves his warm bed, so sure will the traveller in the other house get his supper. And not three loaves only. But once he is out of bed the sleepy man thrusts more loaves on the knocking man than he wants. His love for his bed makes him afraid that this noisy neighbor of his may come back again before the night is over. How many travellers did you say had come to you? And how many loaves will they need? Three? Take four. Take six. Oh, no, says the petitioner, three will do. Take four, at any rate, says the half-naked and generous-hearted householder. Take as many as you can carry, lest you should have to come back again. And he loads the man at the door with an armful of his best bread. Good-night! And he shuts his door and returns to his bed, glad at any cost to get rid of such an untimeous and unceremonious neighbor.

"Importunity" cannot be called a bad rendering exactly. Only it is not by any means the best rendering of the original writing. Nor does it by any means bring out to us the whole intended instructiveness of the scene. We must not water down our Lord's words, even when they are too strong for our feeble digestion. What our Lord actually said was not importunity but "shamelessness." "I say unto you because of his shamelessness he will rise and give him as many as he needeth." Think shame, man! the passers-by exclaimed as they heard him making that so disgraceful noise in the midnight street. The neighbors also looked out of their windows and shouted "Think shame!" at him. And they were right. For it was nothing short of a shameless knocking that the determined man made. Indeed, it was the very shamelessness, that is to say, the lateness and the loudness, of the knocking, that was the success of it. To be shameless in that way and to that degree was the man's wisdom, and hence his utter shamelessness is our Lord's very point with His disciples and with us. Never mind who cries shame, says our Lord to us. Keep you on knocking, shame or no shame. Think shame, woman! the devil said to Santa Teresa. A woman at your time of life having to make such a confession. And presumptuously hoping for pardon for such shameless sins. Think shame! Or if you will still presume to pray for forgiveness, at any rate, wait a little. Do not go to God and you still reeking with such uncleanness. Wash in the holy water first. Perform a time of penance first. "The devil never so nearly had my soul for ever, as just after another fall of mine, and when he cried, For shame, O woman, for shame." These are her very identical words to us in this matter: "Never let any one leave off prayer on any pretence whatsoever; great sins committed, or any pretence whatsoever. I tell you again that the leaving off of prayer after sin was the most devilish temptation I was ever met with."

Importunity, then, and shameless importunity, and that in midnight prayer, is the great lesson of this scripture. Indeed, the whole point of the story here told by our Lord turns upon the untimeousness of the hour when the knocking took place. The thing could never have taken place in the daytime. It is a story of midnight importunity, and it is told to teach us the great lesson of midnight and importunate prayer. Travelling, with all its accompanying incidents such as this, takes place mostly at night in the East, and importunate prayer in the West. And this lesson that our Lord gives us is quite as much to teach us to pray at night as it is to pray with importunity, and for excellent reasons. The Psalms, when we begin to attend to what we read and sing, are full of night, and midnight, and early morning, prayer. I was greatly struck, no longer ago than last night, with what I had never felt with such force before. I was reading the fifth and sixth verses of the sixty-third Psalm at family worship. I find that reading a single verse sometimes will impress our hearts at home more than a whole Psalm. Well, I was reading to them those two verses, and it occurred to me to turn them round and read the sixth verse first and then the fifth, in this way: "When I remember thee upon my bed, and meditate on Thee in the night watches; my soul, as often as I do that, is always satisfied again as with marrow and fatness." As much as to say—"When my soul thirsteth for Thee; when my flesh longeth for Thee; when my soul is like the man in the parable who had a hungry traveller in his house, and had nothing to set before him; then I remember the Lord. I remember His name and all that His name contains. I remember His merciful and gracious name, and I call like that loud-calling man upon His merciful and gracious name. I meditate and remember, and remember and meditate, and that in the night watches, till my soul is again satisfied as with marrow and fatness." The sixty-third Psalm is just the eleventh of Luke before the time. The eleventh of Luke is all in the Psalms. As soon as we get all the best teaching of the New Testament about prayer, we return and find it all already in the Psalms. We would not have found it in the Psalms but for the New Testament; only, once we have the whole doctrine of New Testament prayer taught to us, we come to our full astonishment at David and his companions in prayer. With David, then, and with David's Son, both teaching us to pray, we ourselves should surely come to some success and proficiency in prayer. With these, and with such a wealth of other experiences and testimonies and examples of praying men as we possess, and of praying men at night, we should surely learn to pray. Take this home with you from Father John of the Greek Church. "When praying at night," he says to his people, "do not forget to confess with all importunity, and sincerity, and contrition, those sins into which you have fallen during the past day. A few moments of importunate repentance, before you sleep, and you will be cleansed from all your iniquity. You will be made whiter than the snow. You will be covered with the robe of Christ's righteousness, and again united to Him. Often during the day I myself have been a great sinner, and at night, after importunate prayer, I have gone to rest washed and restored, and with the deepest joy and the most perfect peace filling my heart. How needful it will be for our Lord to come and save us in the evening of our life, and at the decline of our days! O save me, save me, save me, most gracious Lord, and receive me at the end of my days into Thy heavenly kingdom."

IX

The Importunate Widow

WITH all his ungodliness and with all his inhumanity, there was a widow in that city who brought the unjust judge to his senses. His boast within himself was that he neither feared God nor regarded man, but there was a widow in that city who made him both fear her and regard her. There were many widows who had adversaries in our Lord's land and day, and He must have known more than one of them. His own mother Mary may very well have been one of them. Who knows but that she herself was this very widow with an adversary? Nothing is more likely. At any rate, whoever this widow was, by this time she was driven all but beside herself with adversity and oppression and robbery. She had spent all her living on daysmen and mediators, but the unjust judge was a companion of thieves and he would not hear her advocates. And, had it not been for her fatherless and fast-starving children, she would soon have been laid out of sight and out of hearing in her dead husband's forgotten grave. It was her orphaned and starving children that made their mother to be like a she-bear robbed of her whelps. Avenge me of mine adversary! She stood in the way of the unjust judge's chariot all day and cried out, Avenge me of mine adversary! She burst in upon the business of his court and cried, Avenge me of mine adversary! She stood under his window all night and cried out, Avenge me of mine adversary! And he would not for a while. But after that day when this wild woman suddenly sprang in upon him with a knife hidden away among her rags—after that day he said, Because this widow troubleth me, I will avenge her, lest by her continual coming she weary me. There is a tinge of blood in the original ink that is lost in the tame translation, because there was a gleam of blood in the widow's wild eye on that last day of her warning and appeal to the unjust judge. And the Lord said, Hear what the unjust judge saith. And shall not God avenge His own elect which cry day and night to Him, though He bear long with them? I tell you that He will avenge them speedily.

Now it is not by any means every woman who has the making of a "widow indeed" in her. And it is not by any means every soul under sanctification who cries for victory over sin day and night. There are many—even gracious souls among us—to whose case this Scripture does not by any means answer. But there are some other souls who say unto their Lord as soon as He has spoken this about the widow and her adversary to them: Lo, now speakest Thou plainly, and speak-est no parable. Now we are sure that Thou knowest all things, and needest not that any man should ask Thee: for by this we believe that Thou camest forth from God. Such souls are sure that He knows all things about them, at any rate; and by His knowledge of them and of their adversary they believe that He has come forth to them from God. And, like one who has come forth from God and who knows the secret things of God, He here announces to us who are God's elect among us, and who are not. Every elect soul, He says, is like that widow in that city. For every elect soul is poor, and downtrodden, and dispossessed, and desolate. Is, or ought to be. As that widow had an adversary who had done all that to her, even so, every soul, elect to a great salvation, has an adversary who has done all that to it, and far more than all that. I do not know, and I cannot tell you, the name of that widow's adversary in that city. But if you do not know I will tell you the name of the universal adversary of all God's elect in this city. It is sin. This widow had only one adversary, and so it is with the elect. You never hear from their lips a demand for vengeance against any adversary of theirs but one. And all elect souls have one and the same adversary. And this is as good to them all as the seal of their election, this, that their only and real adversary is sin. Now you would all like to be assured, would you not, that you are among God's elect? You would all like to get a glimpse, for a moment, into the book of God's decrees, so as to read your name there. But you do not need to climb up to heaven in order to make your election sure. Who is your adversary? Who makes your life a burden to you? Who persecutes and oppresses and impoverishes your soul day and night continually? Against whom is it that you, almost demented, cry without ceasing, Avenge you of your adversary? Sin is the spot of God's children. Sin, and the woe it works in the soul, is the seal of God's elect. Have you that spot? Have you that seal? Has your sin dispossessed you, and beggared you, and driven you beside yourself? Nevertheless, the foundation of God standeth sure, having this seal. Now, are you such? Look well into yourself and see. Among all your adversaries, who is it that drives you day and night to God, like this woman to the judge? Do you think that our Lord counts you up among His Father's elect? I think He does. I am sure He does, if your adversary that you cry to be revenged upon is sin.

Avenge me! the widow cries. Her heart is full of her great wrongs. Her heart is full of a great rage. Her heart is full of fire. And she here puts her hot words into our mouth. She teaches our sin-tortured souls how to pray. She says to us, Remember me. Imitate me. I got vengeance done at last on mine adversary. Take no rest until you have got vengeance done on yours. She being dead, yet speaketh. Let us imitate her. Let us call on God as she called on the judge. Let us dwell day and night before God on our great wrongs. Let us keep ever repeating before Him what we have suffered at our adversary's hands. Tell Him that it is past telling. Tell Him that you are beside yourself. Tell Him that all He can do to your adversary will not satisfy your fierce feelings. O sin! O sin! How thou hast persecuted my soul down to the ground! How thou hast robbed and desolated my soul! How thou hast made my life a burden to me! How thou hast driven me sometimes beside myself with thy cruel and bitter bondage! How my soul sometimes seeks death to escape from thee! O thou foul and cruel tyrant, I will surely be revenged upon thee yet!

And He spake this parable unto them to this end, that men ought always to pray. Not once; not twice; not seven times; not a thousand times. But always till we are avenged of our adversary. We are not to pray against a besetting sin for a time, and then to despair and let it have its own way with us. We are to pray always. We are to pray on till we need to pray no longer. No sooner is one such prayer offered than we are to begin another. No sooner have we said, Amen! than we must say with our very next breath, O Thou that hearest prayer; to Thee shall all flesh come. No sooner have we risen off our knees than we must return to our knees. No sooner have we opened the door to come out of our closet than we must shut the door again, and return to our Father who seeth in secret. To whom else can we go? To whom else can we tell it all out, how our iniquities still continue to prevail against us?

Always, or as it is rendered in the seventh verse, day and night. All day and all night; the first thing in the morning and the last thing at night. The first thing in the morning and then all the day. When you open your eyes, and before that, always say this, When I awake, I am still with Thee. When you rise off your bed always say, Awake, my soul, and with the sun thy daily stage of duty run. When you wash your hands and your face say, Wash Thou me, and I shall be clean. When you bathe your whole body say, There is a fountain filled with blood, and sinners plunged beneath that flood, lose all their guilty stains. When you dress yourself say, He hath clothed me with the garments of salvation, He hath covered me with the robe of righteousness. And then when you go forth to your day's work say with David when he went forth to his day's work, On Thee do I wait all the day. What is your occupation? Whatever it is say as you again enter on it, The kingdom of heaven is like this, and that, more than on earth is thought. Are you a carpenter? say So was He. Are you a mason? say Other foundation can no man lay than that is laid. Are you a laundress? say His raiment was shining, exceeding white as snow; so as no fuller on earth can white them. Are you a cook? When you burn yourself, then say with Brother Lawrence, Who among us shall dwell with the devouring fire? Who among us shall dwell with everlasting burnings? And say with him also, Even the dogs eat of the crumbs. Are you a preacher? say Lest that by any means, when I have preached to others, I myself should be a castaway. Are you a physician? say Physician, heal thyself. And say Esculapius healed many, but at last he succumbed himself. And say at every patient's door with Sir Thomas Browne, Peace be to this house, and health from the God of their salvation. Are you a banker? say to yourself, Thou wicked and slothful servant, thou oughtest to have put my money to the exchangers, and then at my coming I should have received mine own with usury. And cast ye the unprofitable servant into outer darkness. Are you an aurist? say He that planted the ear, shall He not hear? Are you an oculist? say He that formed the eye, shall He not see? Do you own horses, or ride or drive, horses? say Be ye not as the horse, or as the mule, which have no understanding; whose mouth must be held in with bit and bridle. And are you not good at driving? Then say like the English clown: I have driven into the ditch, O Jesus Christ, take Thou the reins! When on the street you see a prisoner in the hands of his jailor, say There goes John Newton, but for the grace of God. No, it was when John Newton saw a scaffold that he said that. And, speaking of John Newton, if you are a shoe-black, say If only for the credit of Christ, I will be the best shoe-black in the parish. When you meet a funeral, take off your hat and say The sands of time are sinking. When you meet a marriage, say Behold, the bridegroom cometh! When the sun sets in the west, say There shall be no night in heaven. When you lay your head down on your pillow say, if only out of respect to your sainted mother, This night I lay me down to sleep, I pray the Lord my soul to keep. When you cannot sleep, say At midnight will I rise and praise Thee. And when you awake in the morning, say Nevertheless, I am still with Thee. And shall not God avenge His own elect, which cry day and night unto Him, though He bear long with them? I tell you that He will avenge them speedily.

There is a well-known system of medicine that, most paradoxically as one would think, for a cure prescribes a little more of that which caused the sickness. I do not know whether that is sound science, or whether it is what its enemies call it. That is not my field. But this is. And I am safe and certain to say that whether homeopathy is sound medicine or no, it holds in divinity, and especially in this department of divinity, unfainting prayer for sanctification. If you are fainting in prayer for sanctification I recommend and prescribe to you Samuel Hahnemann's dictum *similia similibus curantur.* Only not in small doses. The opposite of that. Small doses in prayer will be your death. The very thing that has caused your whole head to be sick, and your whole heart to be faint—hitherto unanswered prayer, answered or unanswered, pray you on. The answer is not your business. It is importunate and unfainting prayer that is your only business. And, always, more and more importunate and unfainting prayer. *Similia similibus.* Mix up your medicine with every meal. Make your whole meal upon your medicine. Have it standing ready at your bedside all night. Take it the last thing at night and the first thing in the morning. And if you hear the hours striking all night, betake yourself to your sure febrifuge and sleeping draught. In plain words, when you faint in prayer for a holy heart continue all the more instant in that prayer. Pray always for a holy heart, with all prayer and supplication in the Spirit, and watch thereunto with all perseverance. The next time you feel your heart ready to faint in that kind of prayer, call to mind Who says this to you, and where He says it. This, that men ought always to pray against this adversary, and not to faint.

Nevertheless, when the Son of Man cometh, shall He find such prayer on the earth? I do not know. I cannot tell. The earth is too large for me to speak for it, and too far away from me. My matter is, shall He find such prayer in me? Shall He find me in my bed, or on my knees? Shall I be reading this parable of His for the ten thousandth time to keep my heart from fainting? Shall, Avenge me of mine adversary, be on my lips at the moment when the judgment-angel puts the last trump to his lips? And shall I be found of him on my knees, and with my finger on this scripture, when the trumpet shall sound, and I shall be changed?

X
The Prodigal Son

A CERTAIN man had two sons. And the younger of them said to his father, Father, give me the portion of goods that falleth to me. And he divided unto them his living. And not many days after the younger son gathered all together, and took his journey into a far country, and there wasted his substance with riotous living. The country-bred boy had been told stealthy and seductive stories about the delights of city life. "A young man with a little money," he had been told, "can command anything he likes in the great city. A young man who has never been from home can have no idea of the pleasures that are provided in the city for young men whose fathers have money. The games, the shows, the theaters, the circuses, the feasts, the dances, the freedom of all kinds; there is absolutely nothing that a young man's heart can desire that is not open to him who brings a good purse of money to the city with him." All these intoxications were poured into this young man's imagination, and he was but too good a pupil to such instructions.

How long will my father live? he began to ask. How long will that old man continue to stand in my way? It is not reasonable that a young man should be kept so long out of what really belongs to him. It is not fair to treat a grown-up man as if he were still a child. "Father, give me the portion of goods that falleth to me." It was a heartless speech. But secret visions of sin will soon harden the tenderest heart in the world. *Cogitatio et imaginatio*, according to à Kempis, are the two first steps of a young man's heart on its way down to the pit. Keep a young man's thoughts and imaginations clean, and he is safe, and will be a good son. But once pollute, by bad books or bad companionships, a young man's mind and imagination, and nothing in this world will hold that young man back from perdition.

And not many days after the younger son gathered all together, and took his journey into a far country, and there wasted his substance with riotous living. Let one who lived for a long time in that far country describe it. "A darkened heart is the far country. For it is not by our feet, but by our affections, that we either leave Thee or return to Thee. Nor did that younger son look out for chariots, or ships, or fly with visible wings, that he might go to the far country. Unclean affections, and a God-abandoned heart, that is the far country. This was the world at whose gate I lay in imagination, while yet a boy. And this was the abyss of my vileness when I was cast away from before Thine eyes. Who was so vile before Thee as I was? I was vile even to myself."

And when he had spent all, there arose a mighty famine in that land; and he began to be in want. "A mighty famine" is perfect English. It is one of those great strokes of translation that sometimes surpass the original. "A mighty famine" puts a perfect picture of that far country before us. Now what chance, in the midst of a mighty famine, had a prodigal son who had already wasted all his substance with riotous living? What hope was there for him? What could a penniless spendthrift

636

do? Till, covered with rags, and with all his bones staring till they could be counted, he threw himself upon a citizen of that country, and said:—"Only give me one crust-of-bread and water, and I will do anything you like to command me. I have a father at home, but that is far away. Oh, for my father's sake, and he will repay you, give me something to eat." And he sent him into his fields to feed swine. "Did I see a boy of good make and mind, with the tokens on him of a refined nature, cast upon the world without provision, unable to say whence he came, or who were his family connections, I should conclude there was some secret connected with his history, and that he was one of whom, from one cause or another, his parents were ashamed." Such is Dr. Newman's picture of the human race, as it is fallen away from God, and gone into a far country.

"AND WHEN HE CAME TO HIMSELF."—Underline these words. Print these words in capitals. Engrave these words in letters of gold. For up till now sin has abounded, but henceforth grace is much more to abound. And already the abounding grace that the prodigal son is so soon to be met with, is beginning to drop from His lips Who here tells the prodigal's sad story. Look at the beautiful way in which the terrible truth is softened in the telling. Every word is so tenderly, and almost apologetically, chosen. You do not upbraid a son of yours when he is brought home to you safe and sound from the asylum. Whatever he may have said or done during his illness there, you refuse to listen to it. You say, My poor possessed child! You say, My son at that time was not responsible. And you shut your ears to all the heartless tales they tell about what he said and what he did when he was still beside himself. You rebuke his cruel accusers. You tell them that nobody reckons to a recovered man the things that would be reckoned and punished to an entirely sound-minded man. These grace-chosen words, "When he came to himself," already prepare us for the speedy return and complete restoration of this unhappy son, whose infirmity and affliction, rather than his sin and guilt, are the subject of his history as it is here told to us.

"But when he was yet a great way off, his father saw him." And we see him. Our Lord sees him, and He makes us see him. Look at him! Look how he runs! He runs like a man running for his life. He forgets his bleeding feet and his hungry belly. He outstrips everybody on the same road. He runs as he never ran before. But when he comes to the first sight of his father's house his strength suddenly fails him. He stands still, he sinks down, he beats his breast. He cries out as with an intolerable pain till the passers-by hasten on in fear. The man is possessed, one says to him. How long wilt thou be drunken? says another. But he sees them not. He hears them not. The only thing he sees is his father's house through his tears and his sobs. And all that any of the people in the fields or on the road could make out from him was always this: "Against thee, thee only, have I sinned, and done this evil in thy sight!"

And, then, all this long far-country time, his father's gray hairs were being brought down with sorrow to the grave. His father had never been the same man since that evil day when his son had left his father's door without kissing his father. He had ever since that day gone up and down his house a broken-hearted man. His very reapers had wept for him as they saw him walking up and down alone in his harvest fields. Every night also he sat and looked out of his window till the darkness fell again on all the land. And all through the darkness he listened all night for a footstep that never came. But, at last one day—That is none other than my long-lost son! And when he was yet a great way off, his father saw him, and had compassion, and ran, and fell on his neck, and kissed him.

And now, among many other things, our Lord, I feel sure, would have us learn from this family history such things as this—The unspeakable evil of a mind early stained with the images of sensual sin. This young man was at one time as innocent of this sin, and was as loyal to his father and mother, as are any of your sons or mine. But on a fatal day some bad man told him a bad story. Some one whispered to his heart some of the evil secrets of Satan's kingdom. And then, as the *Imitation* has it, there was first the sinful knowledge, and then there arose out of that a sinful imagination, a picture of the sin, and then the young sinner's heart took a secret delight in the knowledge and the vision, and then he sought for an opportunity, and the opportunity soon came. A bad companion will do it. A bad book will do it. A bad picture will do it. The very classics themselves will sometimes do it. It is being done every day in our bothies, and in our workshops, and in our schools, and in our colleges. A bad story will do it. A bad song will do it. A bad jest will do it. Indeed, it is in the very air that all our sons breathe. It is in the very bread they eat. It is in the very water they drink. They cannot be in this world and clean escape it. For myself, one of the saintliest men I ever knew once told me certain evil things, just out of the evil fullness of his heart, when I was not asking for them. Evil things that I would not have known to this day but for that conversation. Supply me with a knife deep enough and sharp enough to cut that corrupt spot out of my memory, and I will, from this moment, cast it out on the dunghill of the devil for ever—as we had, at last, to cut off and cast him. It was some one like my early friend who polluted that young man's imagination till nothing could keep him back from becoming the prodigal son of whom our Lord here tells us all these things for our warning and for our rebuke.

The very finest point in all this history full of fine points, is this—"When he was a great way off, his father saw him, and had compassion on him." And there is nothing more true in our own history than just this, and nothing more blessed for us to be told than just this, that our Father also sees us when we are yet a great way off from Him, and has compassion on us. When we are just beginning to remember that we have a Father; when we are just beginning to repent toward Him; when we are just beginning to pray to Him; when we are just beginning to believe on Him, and on His Son Jesus Christ our Savior; when we are still at the very first beginnings of a penitent, returning, obedient, pure, and godly, life; ay, when we are yet a great way off from all these things, our Father sees us, and has compassion on us, and comes to meet us. I do not know a sweeter or a more consoling scripture anywhere than just this—"When he was yet a great way off." For, what grace is in that! What encouragement, what hope, what comfort, what life from the dead is in that! Blessed be the lips that told this whole incomparable story, and added to it these words of gold—"a great way off."

And, then, to sum up. This whole story, in every syllable of it, has its exact and complete fulfillment in ourselves every day. A prince of Scripture exposition holds it to be doubtful whether our Lord intends under this family story to set forth the first conversion of a great sinner, or the repeated restorations of a great backslider. But the truth is, our Lord intends to set forth both; and much more than both. For not one, nor two, nor three, but all the steps and all the stages of sin and salvation in the soul of man, are most impressively and most unmistakably set before us in this masterpiece of our Master. From the temptation and fall of Adam, on to the marriage supper of the Lamb—all the history of the Church of God, and all the experiences of the individual sinner and saint, are to be found set forth in this most wonderful of all our Lord's histories. John Howe warns us that we must not think it strange if all the requisites to our salvation are not to be found together in any single passage of Holy Scripture. But, on the other hand, I will take it upon me to say that all the incidents and all the experiences of this evangelical history are to be found together in every soul of man who is under a full and perfect salvation. In a well-told story like this, all that the prodigal son came through, from first to last, must of necessity be set forth in so many successive steps and stages: the one step and stage following on the other. But that is not at all the case in the actual life of sin and grace in the soul. The soul is such that it is passing through *all* the steps and *all* the stages of sin and salvation at one and the same time. Some of the steps and stages of sin and salvation may be more present and more pressing at one time than at another time, but they are all somewhere or other within the soul, and are ready to spring up in it. We speak in our shallow way about the Apostle Paul being for ever out of the seventh of the Romans and for ever into the eighth. But Paul never spoke in that superficial fashion about himself. And he could not. For both chapters were fulfilling themselves within their profound author: sometimes at one and the same moment. Sometimes the old man was uppermost in Paul, and sometimes the new man; sometimes the flesh, and sometimes the spirit; sometimes the law and sin and death had Paul under their feet, and sometimes he was more than a conqueror over all the three. But, all the time, all the three were within Paul, and every page he writes, and every sermon he preaches, shows it. And so it is with ourselves, so far as this history, and so far as Paul's history, is our history. For, like the prodigal son, we are always having lewd stories told us about the far country. We are always dreaming of being at liberty to do as we like. We are always receiving our portion of goods, and we are always wasting our substance. We are always trying in vain to fill our belly with the husks that the swine do eat. And we are always arising and returning to our Father's house. In endless ways, impossible to be told, but by all God's true children every day to be experienced, every step and every stage of the prodigal's experience, both before he came to himself, and after it, is all to be found in the manifold, boundless, all-embracing, experience of every truly gracious heart. In His unsearchable wisdom, God has set both the whole world of sin, and the whole world of salvation, in every truly renewed heart. And that, not in successive and surmounting steps and stages, but at one and the same time. And that accumulating, complex, and exquisitely painful, state of things, will go on in every truly regenerate heart, till that day dawns when the greatest prodigal of us all, and the saddest saint of us all, shall begin to be merry.

XI
The Much Forgiven Debtor and His Much Love

WE will sometimes ourselves be like Simon the Pharisee. We will sometimes invite a man to come to take a meal with us when we do not really mean it. We were in a warm mood of mind at the moment when we asked him to dine or sup with us. We met him in circumstances such that we were led into giving him the invitation when we did not really intend it. So much so that when the man comes we had quite forgotten to expect him, and we can scarcely hide our vexation at the sight of him. Now it was something not unlike that with Simon the Pharisee that night.

We must put out of our mind all our modern ideas and all our sound doctrines about our Lord. It is not easy for us to do that, but we will never read a single page of the four Gospels aright, unless we go back in imagination to the exact circumstances of that extraordinary time. We must accustom ourselves to return to those early days when our Lord was still half a carpenter of Nazareth, and half a preacher at the street corner. Some men holding Him to be a prophet come from God, and some holding that He was just Joseph's son gone beside Himself. It was in these circumstances that our Lord was sometimes invited to dine or to sup, His hosts sometimes forgetting that they had invited Him, and sometimes heartily wishing that He would not come, and, when He did come, positively not knowing what to do with Him. Such exactly was Simon's case. He had undoubtedly invited this so-called prophet to sup at his house that night. But when He came at the hour appointed, Simon was wholly occupied with looking after much more important people. When we arrive at any man's door on his distinct invitation and see that we are not expected; when nobody knows us or pays any attention to us; when the head of the house sees us quite well, but has not so much as a moment or a nod or a smile to spare to us—it is all we can do not to put on our hat and go away home again. And if we do go in and sit down at his table, we are in a most sour and unsocial state of mind all the evening. But Simon's neglected Guest was quite accustomed to that kind of treatment. Every day He put up with incivility, and said nothing. No insult ever angered Him. No openly exhibited or plainly intended slight ever embittered Him. And thus it was that He went in and sat down at Simon's supper-table that night, with a quiet mind and an affable manner, and was the best of neighbors to all who sat near Him.

But who and what is this? For, behold a woman in the city, which was a sinner, when she saw that Jesus sat at meat in the Pharisee's house, brought an alabaster box of ointment, and stood at His feet behind Him weeping, and began to wash His feet with tears, and did wipe them with the hairs of her head, and kissed His feet, and anointed them with the ointment. Now, when the Pharisee which had bidden Him saw it, he spake within himself, saying, This man, if He were a prophet, would have known who and what manner of woman this is that toucheth Him: for she is a sinner. "I have made a great mistake," said Simon within himself. "I am always far too precipitate with my invitations. I might have known better. What a scene! I will never hear the end of it. I will never forgive myself for it. I should never have had him across my doorstep. I was warned against him and against his followers, and I see now that they who so warned me were right. Whatever he is, he is not a prophet. If he were a prophet he would at once have put a stop to this scandalous scene."

Simon, I have somewhat to say unto thee. And he saith, Master, say on. There was a certain creditor which had two debtors: the one owed five hundred pence, and the other fifty. And when they had nothing to pay, he frankly forgave them both. Tell Me, therefore, which of them will love him most? Simon answered, and said, I suppose that he to whom he forgave most. And He turned to the woman, and said unto Simon, Seest thou this woman? I entered into thine house, thou gavest me no water for My feet: but she hath washed My feet with tears, and wiped them with the hairs of her head. Thou gavest Me no kiss: but this woman, since the time I came in, hath not ceased to kiss My feet. My head with oil thou didst not anoint: but this woman hath anointed My feet with ointment. Wherefore I say unto thee, her sins, which are many, are forgiven; for she loved much: but to whom little is forgiven, the same loveth little.

From that scene, then, at Simon's supper-table, we are to learn this tonight. The less forgiveness, the less love: the more forgiveness, the more love: no forgiveness at all, no love at all: but, nothing but forgiveness, then nothing but love. And then love is always love. Love, in short, is always like that woman. If you would see love at its very best, just look at that woman. Simon, being neither a publican nor a sinner, had needed so little forgiveness that he had not love enough to provide his Savior with a bason and water wherewith to wash His feet. Simon had neither love enough, nor anything else enough, to teach him good manners. I am afraid for Simon. For, even a very little forgiveness, even fifty pence forgiven, even five pence, even five farthings, would surely have taught Simon at least ordinary civility. When I see any man among you hard and cruel to another man, discourteous and uncivil, not to say intentionally and studiously insolent, I say to myself, either that man has not yet been forgiven at all, or he has been forgiven so little that he does not feel it any more than a stone. The truth is, grant forgiveness enough and you will soon convert the greatest churl among you to be the most perfect gentleman among you. Nothing else will do it, but forgiveness enough will do it. Grant forgiveness enough, and love enough, and you will have all considerateness, all civility, all generosity, all gratitude, springing up in that man's heart. Would you have a true gentleman for a friend, or for a lover, or for a husband, or for a son? Then manage, somehow, to have him brought to Simon's Guest for a great forgiveness, and the thing is done.

This, then, was the whole of Simon's case. He called our Lord Master, in as many words. He had our Lord at his table that night; but, all the time, he loved our Lord very little, if any at all. In other words, Simon had been forgiven by our Lord very little, if any at all. Simon did not need much forgiveness, if any at all, and in that measure Simon's case was hopeless. Simon, in short, was a Pharisee, and that explains everything concerning Simon. I know nothing more about Simon than I read in this chapter. I know nothing of his past life. I suppose it was, touching the righteousness which is in the law, blameless. But, blameless or no, I am sure of this about Simon, that the holy law of God had never once entered Simon's heart. All Simon's shameful treatment of our Lord, and all his deep disgust at that woman, and all his speeches to himself within himself, all arose from the fact that the holy law of God against all kinds of sin and sinners, and especially against himself, had not yet begun to enter Simon's hard heart. My brethren, to make the holy law of God even to begin to enter your hard heart would be the greatest service to you that any man could do to you. Only, no man can do you that service. No mere man, as the Catechism says, but that Man only who sat that night at Simon's supper-table and said to him—"Simon, I have somewhat to say unto thee." Your minister may preach to you till he is old and gray-headed, but he will be to you as one that plays on an instrument; you will not take him seriously. You will pay no attention to him, till after the law enters. And just to the depth and to the poignancy with which the law of God enters your sinful heart, just in that measure will you possess in your broken heart a great or a small forgiveness, and will manifest before God and man a great or a small gratitude. Let no true preacher then be brow-beaten by all the Pharisees in the world from laboring to make the law enter the innermost hearts of his people: both the law legal, and the law evangelical.

Then they that sat at meat with Him began to say within themselves, Who is this that forgiveth sins also? He and they had up till now been talking in the most friendly way together as they ate and drank. They had been talking over the latest news from Rome and Jerusalem: over the gossip of the town: over the sudden deaths of last week, and over the foul and fair weather of last week: when, suddenly, their talk was cut short by the unaccountable conduct of that woman. Some of them who sat at meat with Him had for months past been much exercised in their minds about Him. At one time they had thought one thing about Him, and at another time they had thought another thing about Him. Some could scarcely eat their supper for watching Him, how He ate, and how He drank, and how He talked, and all what He said and did. Till, when He spoke out, and told the story of the creditor and his two debtors, and then wound up the story with such a home-thrust at Simon, they wished themselves seated at another table. They wished that they were well home again. And then when His voice rose to a tenderness and a solemnity they had never heard in any man's voice and manner before, it was no wonder that they said within themselves, Who is this that forgiveth sins also?

Now, listen to this, my brethren. Listen, and receive this. That same Man who forgiveth sins is here also. Here, at this moment, in this house. And He is here on the same errand. He is here seeking and saving sinners. Come to His feet then as that sinful woman came. Come if you are as unspeakably vile as she was, and with the same unspeakable vileness. Come if she is your sister in sin. Up till tonight a Pharisee like Simon; or up till tonight a harlot like this woman; equally come. And come all the more quickly. This woman was on her way to throw herself into the pond when she heard our Lord preaching one of His sermons of salvation: and before He had done with His sermon she was at His feet. Come even if you are intending to take your own life tonight. A woman once had the arsenic bought on a Saturday night, when she said to herself that she would go once more to the church before she took it. The text that morning was this: What profit is there in my blood? She told me her whole story long afterwards. Come if you have the arsenic in your pocket. Come and cast it at His feet.

And then He will have in you the wages for which He worked; for how you, for one, will love Him! Jesus Christ is not easily satisfied with love; but He will be satisfied, and to spare, with your love. And every day on earth will add coals of fire to your love to your Redeemer. And no wonder. For He will have to say to you ten thousand times this same thing: Thy sins, which are still many, are all forgiven thee. Again, and again, and again, He will have to say it, for, having begun to say it to you, He will say it to you to the end. Thy faith hath saved thee, go in peace, He will say.

Samuel Rutherford was wont to set this riddle of love to the old saints in Anwoth: Whether they would love their Savior more for their justification or for their sanctification? And some said one thing and some said another thing. And some wary old ones said both things. Oh yes! What a love, passing all earthly love, will He be loved with to all eternity! By some men and some women, that is. All His redeemed will love Him, but some will love Him more than these. To have been frankly forgiven such a fearful debt, and then, as if that were not enough, to have been washed whiter than the snow, and from such unspeakable pollution. Tell me, therefore, which of them will love Him most? I suppose that they to whom He forgave most. Yes; but what about those to whom He did both? Both frankly forgave them their fearful debt; and also, though their sins were as scarlet: though they were

> From scalp to sole one slough and crust of sin,

made them as white as snow; and though they were red like crimson, made them to be as wool. Let Rutherford take that woman for his answer. For no better answer will ever be given to his riddle of love in this world. Behold, a woman in the city, which was a sinner, brought an alabaster box of ointment, and stood at His feet behind Him weeping, and began to wash His feet with tears, and did wipe them with the hairs of her head, and kissed His feet, and anointed them with the ointment. Wherefore I say unto thee, her sins, which are many, are forgiven; for she loved much.

> When I stand before the throne
> Dressed in beauty not my own
> When I see Thee as Thou art,
> Love Thee with unsinning heart,
>   Then, Lord, shall I fully know,
>   Not till then how much I owe.
> Chosen not for good in me,

Wakened up from wrath to flee,
Hidden in the Savior's side,
By the Spirit sanctified,
   Teach me, Lord, on earth to show,
   By my love, how much I owe.

XII
The Ten Virgins

EVERYTHING that our Lord saw on the earth immediately made Him think of the kingdom of heaven. Our Lord was of that angel's mind who said to Adam— "What if earth be but the shadow of heaven, and things therein each to other like, more than on earth is thought." And thus it was that when our Lord and His disciples were called to that marriage where the original of this parable took place, as soon as He saw the five wise virgins admitted to the marriage, and the five foolish virgins shut out, He turned to the twelve and said—The kingdom of heaven is just like that. It would have been well, and we would have been deep in their debt, had some of the twelve said to their Master at that moment: Declare to us the parable of the ten virgins also. It would have been a great assistance to us if, over and above the parable itself, we had possessed our Lord's own exposition of it. For, who and what are the ten virgins, and why are they so called? Why are they exactly ten, and why are they so equally divided into five and five? What are their lamps also, and what are their vessels with their lamps, and what is the oil that the wise had, and that the foolish had not? What does the tarrying of the bridegroom mean, and what the slumbering and sleeping of the whole ten? And then who are they that make the midnight cry, Behold the bridegroom cometh? And then the hurried trimming of the lamps, with the going out of the lamps of the foolish—what is the meaning of all that? The request of the foolish for a share of the oil of the wise, with the refusal of the wise to part with any of their oil—what are the spiritual meanings hidden under all that? And specially, who sell the oil, and where do they sell it, and at what price? And then the shutting of the door? And then what it is to be ready? as well as what it is to watch, and when we are to watch, and where? It would have been an immense service done to us all had the disciples petitioned their Master for His own authoritative answer to all these questions. As it is, we are left to our own insight into the things of the kingdom of heaven, and to our own experience of its mysteries, to find out for ourselves and for others the true key to this parable.

The wisdom, whatever it was, of the five wise virgins is, plainly, the main lesson set to be learned out of this whole parable. All the rest of its lessons, however good and however true, are subordinate to that. All the rest is, more or less, the framework and the setting of that. Other lessons, more or less essential, more or less interesting, and more or less instructive, may be extracted out of this remarkable parable, but its supreme and commanding lesson is the richly rewarded wisdom of the five wise virgins. They that were foolish took their lamps, and took no oil with them. But the wise took oil in their vessels with their lamps.

Now if you would fain know what, exactly, this oil is of which so much is made in this parable, this oil the possession of which made the five virgins so wise, just look into your own heart for the answer to that. What is it that makes your heart to be so dark, and so sad, and so unready, sometimes? Why is there so little life and light and joy in your heart? Why is your religious experience so flat and so stale, when it should be as full of gladness as if your whole life were one continual making ready for your marriage? What is really the matter with you and with your heart? In plain English, and in few words, it is the absence from your heart of the Spirit of God. It is God's Holy Spirit Who makes God Himself to be so full of Life and Light and Blessedness. It is God's Holy Spirit Who makes our Lord Himself what He always is, and what He always says and does. The fruit of the Holy Spirit in God and in man, on earth and in heaven, is love, joy, peace, longsuffering, gentleness, goodness. Now, that is the whole of the matter with us all. It is the lack of the Spirit of God that makes all of us to be the lump of darkness and death that we are. If we had God's Holy Spirit shed abroad in our heart we would make every house in which we live, and every company into which we enter, like a continual marriage supper. Our very face would shine with heavenly light, and we would shed abroad life and love and beauty everywhere we go. No question, then, what this oil is, nor why we are such children of the day when we have it, and are such children of the night when we have it not. Fix this firmly in your mind, that the Holy Ghost is this light-giving and life-giving oil, and you will have in that, not only the true key to this whole parable, but at the same time the true key to all your own light and darkness also.

"Not so: lest there be not enough for us and you: but go ye rather to them that sell, and buy for yourselves." You go to the oil-sellers when your oil is done, and when the long and dark nights are coming on. And, in the very same way, you must go to God for the Holy Spirit. God the Father is the real seller of this Holy Oil. The Holy Ghost proceeds from the Father. The Son Himself had the Holy Ghost, not of Himself, but of the Father. When the night fell the wise virgins had the oil already in their vessels. They had been at the oil-sellers in good time, and before the darkness fell. Go you in good time also. Be beforehand with the darkness. Have the Holy Ghost already in your heart, and then you will not walk in darkness, nor be shut out into the darkness, however suddenly the Bridegroom may come.

And then this is the remarkable law of this oil-market. "What things soever ye desire, when ye pray, believe that ye receive them, and ye shall have them." That is to say, as soon as in prayer you ask the Father for the Holy Spirit, immediately believe that your prayer is answered. Immediately begin to live in the Spirit. Immediately begin to walk in the light. Do not put off walking in the light till you feel your heart full of light and love and joy and peace and all such holy illumination. But begin at once to live in the Spirit, and He will begin to live in you. As soon as you begin to ask for the Spirit of love and joy and peace to be shed abroad in your heart, begin yourself to shed that Spirit abroad in all your life. Let all your words and deeds, let all your moods of mind, and all your affections of heart, be full of love and joy and peace, and He will not fail to work in you to will and to do of His good pleasure. This is a most wonderful oil, and a most wonderful oil-market, and a most wonderful oil-merchant! Go all of you to Him who sells, and buy for yourselves, and you will soon be wiser in this divine marketry than all your teachers. Were I to enter on all the times, and all the places, when and where, this holy oil is bought and sold, I would have to say of it that there is no time and no place when and where you may not buy this oil. At the same time there are special seasons, and special spots, when and where, as a matter of experience, that oil is specially dispensed to all buyers. Olive oil, and all other kinds of oil, are to be bought in the oil-shops. And the Holy Ghost is best to be bought, is only to be bought, in secret prayer. Oil merchants advertise their oil; its qualities and its prices and where their place of business exactly is. And here is a copy of the heavenly advertisement: "Ask, and it shall be given you; seek, and ye shall find; knock, and it shall be opened to you. For how much more shall your Heavenly Father give the Holy Spirit to them that ask Him." And again: "But thou, when thou prayest, enter into thy closet, and when thou hast shut thy door, pray to thy Father which is in secret, and thy Father which seeth in secret shall reward thee openly." Could anything be clearer? Could anything be plainer? A wayfaring man, though a fool, could not miss where this oil is to be had. "What," demanded his Master, in shame and pain at Peter's sloth and indifference in this very same matter, "What, could ye not watch with Me one hour?" Watch and pray for the Holy Spirit, He means. For it was just this heavenly oil that Peter needed above all things that dark and sudden midnight. And had Peter but spent that one hour with Him who hears prayer and thus sells His oil, he would have played a far better part all through the thick darkness of that dark night, and all through the still thicker darkness of tomorrow and tomorrow night. It is still the old story, my brethren. There is no getting past the old story. You had better yield and surrender at once. That "hour" of prayer, which is now so haunting you, will never all your days let you alone. It will follow you wherever you go and whatever you are doing. Not till the door is shut will that secret "hour" of prayer give over pursuing you. Not till it ceases pursuing you and says, Sleep on now, and take your rest!

Though it is literally true that this holy oil is to be had for the asking, at the same time, and as a matter of fact, what amounts to a tremendous price has to be paid down for it. As Seneca says, "Nothing is so dear as that which is bought by prayer." A man may buy oil for his household lamps to last him for a whole winter, and yet may not be sensibly the poorer for his purchase. He may pay his oil bill, and yet have plenty of money left wherewith to buy wine and milk for himself and for his family. But not in this oil-market. To buy the Holy Spirit is as costly to a sinner as buying Christ Himself and all His righteousness. And you know how penniless that purchase left Paul. Indeed, ever since Paul's day the price of Christ and His righteousness has been a proverb of impoverishment in the Church of Christ. And had the apostle been led to tell us how much he had to lay down to win the Holy Spirit, it would just have been the same all-impoverishing story over again. Not one penny had Paul left. Not one farthing. And so is it with every man who once really enters this same oil-market. If you do not follow my argument, just take an hour tonight in that market for yourself, and tell me tomorrow morning how you get on in it. Tell me how much you have left to call your own after you have once bought this priceless oil. See what it will cost you so much as to enter this oil emporium. There are some places of sale, bazaars and such like, where a great income is made just by the entry-money. Tell me how much is demanded of you before you are able to shut your door upon God and yourself alone tonight, not to speak of what He will charge you for the oil after you are in. You will see how everything you have hitherto valued will have to go. No wonder that only the half of the ten virgins had the heart to make the impoverishing purchase. For my part, I often wonder there were so many.

Our Lord does not explicate, point by point, all this parable to us, but He is most emphatic, and even alarming, in His application of it. Watch, therefore, He warns us, for ye know neither the day nor the hour wherein the Son of Man cometh. He may be here, and your time may be at an end any moment. And then, it takes far more time than you would think to buy this oil and to have it always ready. Even to get well into the place where this oil is sold takes time. To get your money ready takes time. To get your vessel well filled takes time. And to make due allowance for all the obstacles and accidents by the way, and for all the unforeseen interruptions and delays in the market—all that, taken together, takes up more time than any one would believe beforehand; immensely more time and trouble than any one would believe who has not gone through it all. And thus it is that our Lord is always pleading with us to give an hour to it every night. Better too much time, He argues with us, than too little. You may get through the transaction quicker than some others, He admits. But then there is this also, that it may turn out to take much more time in your case than you have left to give it.

And, once more, watch, for the wisest are sometimes to be found playing the fool, like the foolish, in this tremendously precarious matter. The five wise virgins slumbered and slept when they should have been employing their spare time in trimming their lamps, and in keeping both themselves and their fellows awake and ready. And had it not been that they were, all the time, much wiser than they seemed to be, they would have been shut out with the rest. But as it turned out they had oil, all the time, in their vessels with their lamps. And that made all the difference when the bridegroom came so suddenly. Now, where, and how, will the same difference come in among ourselves? It will come in, and you will see it, this very night, and in this very way. Tonight some here will hasten home as soon as the blessing is pronounced. They will try to escape their talkative neighbors at the door. All the time of supper and prayers at home they will be hiding this terrible parable in their hearts. And then when the house is quiet, the true business of this whole day will begin with those wise men. I have told you before, but not once too often, of a Sabbath night I once spent long ago in the Alrick with old John Mackenzie. After supper and prayers I petitioned for another half-hour's reading of the notes he had preserved of Dr. John Duncan's Persie sermons. "Pardon me," said the old saint, "but we always take our candles immediately after prayers." The difference will be that the foolish among us will sit tonight and talk and talk till they extinguish this parable and all its impressions clean off their minds and their hearts, while the wise among us will take their candles.

XIII
The Wedding Guest Who Sat Down in The Lowest Room

IT is my deliberate opinion that this wedding guest who sat down in the lowest room was none other than our Lord Himself. I think I see enough to justify me in believing that this parable was no parable but was an actual experience of our Lord Himself. I feel as sure as if I had seen Him do it, that He sat down in the lowest room when He entered that supper chamber. The two sons of Zebedee chose out the chief rooms for themselves, their mother encouraging them to do it. Go up yonder, she said. There are two seats at the head of the table, go up at once and take them. And they went up, their mother pushing them up. But Mary and her Son sat down at the foot of the table. The more I imagine myself present at that marriage, the more convinced I become that our Lord was that humble-minded man Himself. At any rate, whether our Lord only invented and composed this parable, or actually Himself experienced it, at any rate, it has all been performed by Him and fulfilled to Him by this time, in every jot and tittle of it, first in His earthly life, and then in His heavenly life. For did He not sit down in the lowest room in the over-crowded inn? And as His birth was so was His whole life on earth down to the end of His life in the lowest of all this earth's low rooms. Till a Voice came from the head of the table, which said to Him, Friend, come up higher. And now, as this parable says, He has worship in the presence of them that sit at meat with Him. Yes; I for one am to delight myself, and impress myself, and instruct and rebuke myself, with believing that our Lord's whole earthly life, and now His whole heavenly life, was all enacted, in small, at that wedding supper to which He was called and with Him His twelve disciples.

"A new commandment give I unto you," said their Master to His disciples at the last supper of all. But at this present supper now spread before us He gives both His disciples and us this new commandment of His also. "When thou art bidden of any man to a wedding, go and sit down in the lowest room." And then, like the Shorter Catechism, He annexes His reasons, which, when drawn out, are such as these. No man can ever say to you, Give this man place; no man can ever say to you, Sit lower down, if you have already chosen for yourself the lowest seat. No man can humiliate you and clothe you with shame if you are always clothed with humility. But on the other hand, if you are always and everywhere exalting yourself: if you are always scheming for yourself, and are always choosing out the best seats for yourself, depend upon it you are laying up shame and humiliation for yourself. If you are constantly pluming yourself on your own performances, and on your high deservings of praise and what not at all men's hands, depend you upon it, your humiliation will not tarry. You will be disappointed, superseded, over-looked, over-stepped, and over-ridden, absolutely every day. It will seem to you, and not without good grounds, as if all men were in one plot against you, for so they are. If they can help it, you shall with shame begin to take the lowest room. But if I were you, I would outwit them. I would lay this wise commandment of our Lord's to my heart if I were you, till I had completely outwitted them. When you are next bidden to anything, begin to sit down in the lowest room; yes, in the very lowest room you can get. Begin at once to humble yourself everywhere, and in everything. Put on the sackcloth of humility immediately and always. Set less and less store by your own talents, attainments, performances, and deserts; and set more and more store by all other men's talents, deserts, and performances. Pooh-pooh your own heart when it says to you—What a grand man you are! When it says to you—What a grand sermon that is you have just preached! What a grand book that is you have just published! What a grand run in the race-course that was with all men's eyes upon you! And what a grand leap that was, leaving all your rivals far behind you! Turn upon your puffed-up heart and tell it that nobody is thinking about your grand sermons, or your grand books or your grand runs, or your grand leaps; nobody but yourself. Only, all your competitors in preaching and in leaping, *they*, indeed, are thinking almost as much, and almost as often, about you as you are about yourself. Only, in a very different way. And in a way that, if you knew it, would make you take down your top-sail, as Samuel Rutherford says. My friends, expect nothing for yourselves and you will not be disappointed; demand nothing for yourselves and you will be continually surprised how praise and promotion will pour in upon you, and that at the most unexpected times and from the most unexpected people. How does Jupiter occupy himself on Olympus? asked Chilo at Aesop. In humbling the high, was Aesop's answer, and in lifting up the low. Just as Peter has it, who was present at that supper-table. "Yea, all of you be clothed with humility; for God resisteth the proud, and giveth grace to the humble."

Only, there is humility and humility. And the best kind of humility is that kind which Thomas Shepard, so far as I know, was the first to call "evangelical humility." Jonathan Edwards has now made this borrowed phrase famous in some of the golden pages of his *Religious Affections*. Hear then, what this master in Israel says:—"Evangelical humility is the sense that a Christian man has of his own utter insufficiency, utter despicableness, and utter odiousness: with an always answerable frame of heart. This humility is peculiar to the true saints. It arises from the spirit of God implanting and exercising supernatural and divine principles: and it is accompanied with a sense of the transcendent beauty of divine things. And then, God's true saints all more or less see their own odiousness on account of sin, and the exceedingly hateful nature of all sin. The very essence of evangelical humility consists in such humility as becomes a man in himself exceeding sinful but now under a dispensation of grace. It consists in a mean esteem of himself, as in himself nothing, and altogether contemptible and odious. This indeed is the greatest and the most essential thing in true religion." My brethren, you will not be long troubled with *that* guest choosing out the chief rooms for himself. If you would have all the chief rooms to yourselves, and to your children, frequent those feasts, and engineer to get your children invited to those feasts, to which none but Thomas Shepard's disciples are invited.

Parents are terribly perplexed at present as to what is the proper education for their children; and for their sons especially. Shall they take the ancient or the modern side of the University? Shall it be the classics, and almost nothing else, as was the old way? Or shall it be a commercial education almost exclusively? And one adviser advises the one way, and another adviser advises the other way, till many anxious parents are driven distracted. Whichever side you determine on, be sure that your sons take Moral Philosophy in the curriculum. If it is Latin and Greek, and the old culture, that you decide on, be sure they take Aesop with it as above. Or if it is a military or a commercial education, still take Aesop as above, even if it is only in translation. Whether they are to be men of all literature, or men of one book only, and that the ledger, see to it that they mix all their books with humility. That will make your sons true gentlemen, whichever side they take in education. And that will make your daughters true ladies, whatever school and college, whatever course you decide on for them. Housewifery, like their mothers and their grandmothers, or a degree, like their fathers and their brothers. I will not quarrel with your choice for them if only you mix it well with humility. If your sons have the head and the heart to read Shepard and Edwards—and it will need all the head and all the heart you can give them to read those two masters— then I will prophesy your sons' prosperity from either culture; the ancient or the modern. And if you bring up your daughters to respect the servants and to share their work; to rise early in the morning, to make their own beds, to decorate their own rooms, and to brush their own boots, then they can add a University degree to that with the applause of all men, both young and old. If they are but popular downstairs, I will read their names in the *Scotsman* and the *Times* with a pride almost as much as your own. Only begin their education while they are yet infants; or, at any rate, little children. It so happens that just as I am composing these lines for you I have come in our morning worship on this children's hymn for your children and mine:—

> Day by day the little daisy
>   Looks up with its yellow eye,
> Never murmurs, never wishes
>   It were hanging up on high.
>
> And the air is just as pleasant,
>   And as bright the sunny sky,
> To the daisy on the footpath
>   As to flowers that bloom on high.
>
> God has given to each his station;
>   Some have riches and high place,
> Some have lowly homes and labors;
>   All may have His precious grace.

"All our humility on earth will come to its head in heaven," says Samuel Rutherford. Till the only difficulty at the Marriage Supper of the Lamb will be to get the chief rooms at that Supper to be filled with their proper guests. It will be somewhat like that Highland Communion at which I was present. Friends, come up higher! the minister pled with his people. But with all his authority, and with all his promises and pleas, he could not overcome his people's shame and pain of heart that day. And all the assisting minister could do, with all his fresh promises and pleas and encouragements, it was long before the Lord's Table was even half filled that day. And so, somewhat, will it be with ourselves at the Lord's Table above. Our eyes will seek for them, and, as soon as we enter the supper-room, we will see men and women already seated there, the sight of whom will so awaken and inflame our old sin and shame, that we will turn to flee: only, by that time, escape will be impossible, for the door will be shut. The sight of the Table and of Him who sits at the head of the Table, and of some of the guests already in their seats there, and a thousand other things, will all rush in upon us till we shall fall down as dead. "And he laid His right hand upon me, saying unto me, Fear not: I am the first and the last. I am He that liveth and was dead, and, behold, I am alive for evermore, Amen: and have the keys of hell and of death." Friend! He will say to us, as He lifts us up in glory as He used to do in grace. Friend! and this word of His will at once revive us. And we will sit down humbly just where He seats us. No one else will have taken our place. Wherever at His Table our place is it will be ours alone, and no stranger will intermeddle with it. And, to borrow a word from this night's scripture, it will be with shame that we will sit down in the place prepared for us. Only, it will be with a sweet, holy, heavenly, blessed and beatific shame. Friend! He will say, go up higher. Then shalt thou have worship in the presence of them that sit at meat with thee. For whosoever exalteth himself shall be abased; and he that humbleth himself shall be exalted.

XIV

The Bidden to the Great Marriage Supper and Some of Their Excuses

YOU are all bidden to this great marriage supper. The invitations sent out to our marriage suppers have to be limited to the more intimate friends of the bride and the bridegroom. Our largest houses would not hold the half of the friends we would like to see with us on such happy occasions. But there is no such limitation here. You are all bidden to this marriage. And the only limitation tonight lies entirely with yourselves. What, then, is your answer to be tonight?

This is a most extraordinary marriage and marriage supper. And therefore you must not measure what is now to be said about this marriage by what you have seen or heard of the marriages of this world. For there are far better worlds than this world, and there are far better marriages than this world has ever seen. Indeed, this marriage that is in your offer tonight is the only real and true and perfect marriage that has ever been made in this or in any other world, or that ever will be made. You have been dreaming about marriages all your days, but a marriage like this has never entered your most extravagant imaginations. For this is nothing less than the marriage of the Eternal Son of God with your own immortal soul. You, sitting there, are the bride, and Jesus Christ is the Bridegroom. And the Father of the Bridegroom has His heart so much set upon this marriage that he has sent His servant tonight to say to you that all things are now ready. Some of our marriages take a long time to get all things ready. And this great marriage has not by any means been made ready in a day. This marriage was actually proposed and planned for and the preparations began to be made for it before the foundations of this world were laid. You like to read and hear about marriages, and the arranging of marriages, and how the course of true love did, or did not, run smooth. Well, I, like you, have read many love romances in my day, and have delighted in them in my day; but this great love, and the sometimes smooth, and sometimes stormy, course it has had to run, quite out of sight eclipses all other romances to me now. So much so, that I have for long wholly given up reading anything else except about this everlasting love. But this is the immediate and the main point that all things are ready now. All things that the bride needs to make herself ready are ready now. And all things that the Bridegroom needs are ready now. The Father is ready to receive you. The Son stands ready to be for ever united to you, and to have you united to Him. And the Holy Ghost stands beside the Son ready, and book in hand like the minister, to pronounce you the Lamb's wife. And it only remains for you to say yes, or no. It only remains for you to say that your heart within you is as the chariots of Amminadib in the Song of Solomon, and your marriage is consummated, or will be consummated immediately.

This very same message and invitation was once sent to a congregation of people just like yourselves; and they all, with one consent, began to make excuse. We can scarcely believe it about them, but it must be true, else it would not be recorded against them to all time, as it is here recorded. Come, said the servant to those that were bidden: Come, for all things are now ready. But they all, with one consent, began to make excuse. The first said unto the servant, I have bought a piece of ground, and I must needs go to see it; I pray thee have me excused. And another said, I have bought five yoke of oxen, and I go to prove them; I pray thee have me excused. And another said, I have married a wife, and therefore I cannot come. You are sometimes like that yourselves among the dinner and supper invitations of our own city. You hear with apprehension sometimes of certain dinners and suppers that are soon to come on. Your hearts are not in those intended entertainments, and you would give anything not to be invited to them. And when you are invited you are at your wits' end how to answer so as not to give an unpardonable offence. You sit at your desk and you bite your pen over your excessively difficult answer. You try one form of answer and you tear it up; the lie is too transparent. "Thank you," you at last answer, "but I have an engagement already on my hands for that very evening. I have done my best to get out of it, but it is impossible." Or you try this—A friend of yours, that you have not seen for many years, has offered you a visit on that evening on his way through the city and you cannot put him off; or, you have a most important meeting down for that evening and for that hour, at which, indeed, you are already advertised to take the chair. "Accept my most sincere apology," you add, "and convey my best respects to your honored guest." The dinner belongs to another political, or ecclesiastical, or civic, party than that to which you belong. There are old sores in your mind against your proposed host as well as against some of the guests who are sure to be there. In short, you cannot and you will not go. Even at the risk of your absence being misunderstood, and taken in ill part, you will not go. "We will not trouble him again," say the host and the hostess to one another over your transparent subterfuge; "he will come the next time he is asked to any dinner of ours."

Those were clever enough excuses that your predecessors in Israel made. Indeed, they were entirely true excuses, rather than merely clever. For the real truth was they had no heart for that invitation. All their treasure, and consequently all their heart, was elsewhere. The first man's treasure was his newly-bought piece of ground. The second man's treasure was his five yoke of oxen. While the third man had the best treasure and the best excuse of all. For he had a young wife at home, and the dinner was never dressed that would draw him away from her side so soon. Now what is your excuse tonight? You have an excuse that you have sent up as your answer before now; often before now. Is it to be the same excuse and answer tonight again? It is as if an angel had come straight from heaven to you with an invitation addressed to you in his hand. There he is, standing in the passage at the end of your pew. Yes, there he is. It is not the first time I have seen him standing impatiently there. But tonight it may be the last time. When he goes home tonight empty again his Master may well be so angry this time that He may swear that your invitations shall be no longer. "He is joined to his ground, and to his oxen, and to his wife—let him alone." And, then, what will all these things do for you against the anger of Almighty God, and against the wrath of the Lamb? Whereas, say Yes! and all things are yours, and you are His, and He is God's. Wait one moment, then, O impatient angel: wait, just wait one moment! And then speed up with your answer to your Lord.

But even that sufficient danger and disaster is not all. There are more men involved in your salvation or damnation than yourselves. Your ministers are almost as much involved as you are. O light-hearted students, go and make your piece of bread in some much safer calling. For God lays this same awful order on all His ministers—Go, He says, and compel them to come in. Compel is His very word. That is your minister's ordination oath, and if you are lost: if you go on to the end making excuses and refusals, your lost eternity will be at your minister's door, as well as at your own. Your minister must compel you therefore, if he is not to be involved in your ruin. "Did you do all that it was commanded you to do?"— it will be demanded of him on that day! "You knew quite well that that man there, and that woman there, were no more saved than were the seats they sat on, and what did you do? Did you let them fall asleep while you delivered my message to them? Did you tell them plainly how it would end with them? Or were you afraid to offend them, and lose their approval and their patronage? Did you demand of them every Sabbath day what provision they had made against death and judg- ment? Did you preach every sermon of yours as if it were your last and their last? And as if you and they might be summoned before the great white throne at the end of your sermon? Did you compel them to see that there were only two things possible before them—the right hand or the left: heaven or hell: the wrath of the Lamb, or His everlasting love? If you did all that, then you are clear of their blood. But if you did not do all that, and that continually, you are no minister of mine." O men and women! Be not so inhuman as to drag down your minister with yourselves. Say, at any rate, to God's angel that your minister is not to blame. Say to him that your minister did all that mortal man could do. Say to him that your minister's hands are pure of your blood, and that you alone are without excuse.

This parable, it is much to be feared, will have a very visible fulfillment in this house during the next fortnight. For this day fortnight the marriage supper of the Lamb is to be made ready here. And from tonight onward this call will go forth to all this congregation—The Lord's Supper is again made ready. Come and partake of it. Prepare yourselves in the ways appointed you, and then come to the Lord's Table. But when the two days of special preparation are come, what will we see here? We will see the church on the Thursday evening, and on the Saturday after- noon, not one-fourth full: till your ministers will be ashamed to have brought two of God's servants to preach to your empty pews. So many intending com- municants will, with one consent, begin to make excuse. One will say, The hour is so late. Another will say, The weather is still so unsettled. Another will say, Those services are getting antiquated and out of date and so few people attend them. Another will say, To tell the truth I had wholly forgotten about the communion, and my wife and I have a dinner-party in our house that evening. Another will say, The young people are at their lessons on Thursday night, and they need fresh air on Saturday afternoon, and are away out of the town on their bicycles. And then the ministers and the elders will get such a refreshment and such a preparation from those two services that they will look round and will say to themselves:—Oh, why were so and so not here? What a blessing they have lost. What can they have got elsewhere to make up to them for the loss of such a preparation-service as this has been? And then those who so excused themselves on the Thursday and the Saturday will come up so unprepared on the Sabbath that when the King comes in to see the guests it will be impossible for Him to wink at the state of matters between Him and many who will intrude themselves that day. Till in very faithfulness He will say to them, Friend, how camest thou in hither not having a wedding garment? But be not speechless tonight. Come tonight. Say yes tonight. For all things are now ready, wedding garment and all.

XV
The Man Who Had Not
on a Wedding Garment

SUPPOSE this. Suppose you were commanded to sup with King Edward the Seventh on this day week. Then what else than that command would you think about all the intervening six days and six nights? I feel sure you would think about nothing else. The great invitation, and the coming supper in the king's palace, would never be out of your thoughts for a moment. You would discourse about your high honor all day, and you would dream about it all night. But at the same time, you would rejoice at the prospect with trembling. And you would do this. You would seek out those in this city who had sometimes been at court. You would apply to those ministers, or other highly honored men, who had dined or supped with the late Queen, his Majesty's mother, and you would beseech them to tell you all about the palace and its royal rules and regulations. You would interrogate them about a thousand things, from the way in which you should reply to such a command, down till you were safely back again in your own house. You would be in such mortal terror lest in your inexperience and ignorance you should fall into some awful mistake. You have never been much in good society, not to say in such society as a crowned head keeps, and it would not be to be wondered at if you scarcely slept with anxiety till it was all over and you were safely home again. And if there was any book of palace etiquette and court ceremonial to be had for love or money, you would sit up all night over it; you would set your very Bible aside night after night in order to give all your mind to the Court Guide. Your Bible could wait, but not your preparation for the great event of your life. And if in studying its directions you came on any expressions and descriptions you did not understand, you would go back again to the king's chaplain rather than risk the smallest misunderstanding or mistake. And if you could accuse yourself of neglecting the very utmost precaution, and thus fell into some disgraceful blunder at court, you would never forget it, and you would never forgive yourself, to your dying day. And who would blame you for all that solicitude? Who would say that you were anxious over much? We would all envy you for your high honor, but we would all be thankful that we had not to go through your ordeal. And as often as we thought of your certainty to make some terrible mistake, we would say to ourselves—Better him than me.

Intending communicants! Your own hearts have already interpreted to you what I have been driving at all this time. For this day seven-night you are all commanded to be ready to present yourselves before your Lord in His Father's house. Now what are you intending to do all this week with a view to the Lord's Supper? With whom do you intend to take counsel? Do you know, in all your circle of acquaintances, any one you feel sure is at home in such matters? What books will you read this week, and what books will you judge it impertinent, and unseasonable, and unbecoming, to read this week? How do you intend to lay out your nights especially? In short, what steps do you intend to take to secure and guard yourself against some awful slip or oversight when you are ushered into the King's presence? Have you any plan? Have you any programme? Six days and six nights look a long time in which to prepare. But they will all be past and gone before you know where you are. For one thing, I have a great faith myself in the proper books. I shall owe my own soul, if it is saved at last, to the proper books. And if your soul is lost at last that catastrophe will be accounted for largely by your persistent reading of unseasonable and unbecoming books, and especially in the night-watches of the communion week. Some intending communicants will do something like this. Tomorrow night they will take time and will read again all about the institution of the Passover in Israel, and they will apply all the lessons of the Passover to their own hearts, and to their own lintels and side-posts. On Tuesday night if you went in on them late you would find them deep in the Fifty-first Psalm. And on Wednesday night deep in the Fifty-third of Isaiah. On Thursday we used to have all the shops shut, and all the churches open; and we still have our communion books, if we choose, that no one can shut as they have shut the churches. And all Thursday night they will be still deeper in the arrest and the trial and the cross of their Redeemer. What else, in the name of sin and salvation, would you expect to find them reading on such a night and in such a week! And all the week they will have among their choicest books some classic on the communion, say like Robert Bruce, and they will work their soul-saving way through that great book again. Robert Bruce's book is not in the circulating library, and it is too dear for you who are laymen to be expected to buy it. But if there is any divinity student here who hopes one day to be a good minister of Jesus Christ, let him get his hands somehow or other on Bruce before tomorrow night, and master one of "that stately Presbyterian divine's" sermons on the Sacrament every night all the week. I have not read Bruce so often, I am ashamed to say, as Jowett had read Boswell. But I read him for the first time forty years ago, and I read him again last week. And in the strength of many readings of that great Edinburgh preacher I will venture this prophecy that if you begin Bruce at this communion, you will still be reading him forty years after this, and you will be liking him better and better at every returning communion in your ministry—a sure mark of a masterpiece.

But with all that, you must not sit at home and read your Bible and Bruce on the Sacraments all the week, and do nothing else. "Therefore we must," says Jeremy Taylor, "before every communion especially, remember what differences or jealousies are between us and any one else, and recompose all such disunions, and cause right understandings between each other. Offering to satisfy whom we have injured, and to forgive those who have injured us." And so on, in his heart-searching and eloquent treatise. As for instance. One of our own elders on the Sabbath before one communion heard a sermon on the text, "Leave there thy gift before the altar, and go thy way: first be reconciled to thy brother, and then come and offer thy gift." Now that elder had long ago had a miserable quarrel with a

2__

man in the same profession as his own, and whose office was in the same street as his own. And on the Monday before the communion, as if it were tomorrow, he left his own office-door and crossed the street and rang his enemy's bell. He felt, as he told me himself, that he would almost as soon have faced a lighted cannon as rung that bell. But he did it. And when he stood before his old foe he did not speak. He only held out his hand. The two estranged men looked at one another. They shook hands and parted without words. But a load of anger and hatred and wickedness that had lain like a mill-stone on both their hearts was from that moment removed. And the two men came to the table next Sabbath reconciled to God and to one another. Will you do that same preparatory act tomorrow forenoon? Or still better, will you do it tonight on your way home from the House of God?

And then when the communion day dawns this day week, rise early. Be like Moses that morning when he was hidden in the cleft rock, and when he first heard the Name of the Lord. And have something suitable in your mind the last thing on Saturday night that you are to say the first thing on Sabbath morning. Have this: When I awake I am still with Thee. Or this: I shall be satisfied when I awake with Thy likeness. Or this: This is the day the Lord hath made. Or this: He was delivered for our offences, and was raised again for our justification. Or this: Bless the Lord, O my soul, and forget not all His benefits. And then finish up with this: I will take the cup of salvation, and call upon the name of the Lord. And, all the morning hours, let your mind go back to that first Lord's day morning. Think you see Mary Magdalene while it is yet dark. Think you hear what she says to her Risen Lord, and what He says to her. Go through their dialogue with them. And open and read the journey to Emmaus, and think you are one of them, till your heart burns within you. And be up here in good time. We will have the doors open in good time. Come so as to have a quiet half-hour to yourself. Do not come late and agitated with getting ready. Have a good half-hour to read and think and pray. And enter at once into the stream of psalms and hymns and spiritual songs, and make melody in your heart to the Lord. Follow the action-sermon with your whole attention. Miss nothing that is said. I think it will suit you next Sabbath. And then at the table rise to your best faith, and to your best love. And if your heart has resisted all the preparations of the week and you are ready to sink into the earth when the elders bring forward the elements, then give vent to your heavy heart in such ejaculations as this: I am not worthy, Holy Lord. And this: Then will I to thine altar go. And this: Just as I am. And this: Cleft for me. And then when the King comes to see the guests He will find you singing in your heart to Him and to yourself this acceptable song:—

O let the dead now hear thy voice:
Now bid thy banished ones rejoice—
Their beauty this, their glorious dress,
Jesus, Thy blood and righteousness.

And then take a moment or two at the Table to pray for those who are as dear to you as your own soul. For those you love as Christ has loved you. And, after your own flesh and blood, then for those you love almost as much, your choicest and most select friends. And wind up with the man you were reconciled to last week. For that is the best friendship, and that is the surest reconciliation, that is sanctified and sealed at the Lord's Table.

And then, when your Savior says to you after supper, Know you what I have done to you? you will have your answer ready. My blessed Lord, you will say, I know only too well what Thou hast done for me. I doubt, in all Thy great doings for sinners, if ever Thou hast done for mortal man what Thou hast done for me. Many men call themselves the chief of sinners; but I know, and Thou knowest, better than that. If I do not know all Thou hast done for me, keep the full knowledge of it back till I am able to bear it. For I am not able to bear any more today. Oh! the past, the past! you will cry in your agony of remorse mingled with faith and love. For you see your past sins and your present sinfulness at every returning communion blacker and blacker. Yea, Lord, Thou hast redeemed me. Thou hast substituted Thyself for me. Thou hast borne my sins in Thine own body on the tree. Thou hast come after me, and Thou hast been full of unparalleled long-suffering with me. Thou hast endured me far past all other men. No man has provoked Thee to the uttermost as I have done. And yet, you will say—I am not in hell, but at the Lord's Table!

And then, with all that possessing your heart, you will go home from the Lord's Table a new creature. You will go home at peace with God and with your own conscience through the sin-atoning death of the Son of God. At peace also with all men, and full of love and prayer for all men. And you will henceforth walk with a far more perfect heart before your house at home. And you will henceforth possess your heart with a holy patience among all the crooks in your lot, and under all the crosses that God sees good to lay upon you. And amid all these things you will henceforth be one of the most watchful, and prayerful, and humble-minded, and easy to live with, of men. A miracle to yourself, and a wonder to many. From one day to another living for nothing else so much as to perfect holiness in the fear of God. And God every day more and more perfecting in you what He has begun in you, till the day of Christ. Till that day, that is, when He shall come in to see the guests, and to go no more out.

XVI
The Pharisee

DR. PUSEY has said somewhere that a Pharisee was just a Jew with divine light but without divine love. And that saying of Dr. Pusey's is just the thirteenth chapter of 1st Corinthians put into an epigram. Paul was once a Pharisee himself, and in the beginning of that famous chapter to the Corinthians he describes himself as a Pharisee to perfection. Every finished Pharisee, he tells us, had not the tongue of a man only, but the tongue of an angel. In some instances the Pharisee had the gift of prophecy also, and could understand all mysteries, and all knowledge. There had been Pharisees known to Paul who had a faith that could actually remove mountains. While others again had been known not to give a tenth only of all that they possessed, but who positively bestowed all their goods to feed the poor. While some went the awful length of giving their very bodies to be burnt. Our hearts bleed for the Pharisees. Our hearts bleed within us for men who could do and endure all that, and yet after all that were complete castaways from the kingdom of heaven. Who then, my brethren, can be saved?

In answer to that staggered exclamation of ours, the Apostle, who was one of them and one of the very best of them, goes on to accuse the Pharisees with such unanswerable accusations as these. With all that, says the Apostle, the finished Pharisee was wholly without love in his heart. To come to particulars and instances of that, says the Apostle. The true Pharisee entirely lacked large-heartedness and brotherly-kindness, he entirely lacked appreciation and admiration for other men. He vaunted about himself in everything, he was puffed up with himself in everything. He took no pleasure in hearing other men praised for their talents, or for their performances, or for their conduct, or for their character. The true Pharisee took no pleasure in the pure truth about other men. Nay, he had no better pleasure than in all unjust judgments and in all harsh censures concerning all other men. When he heard a backbiter he delighted in him, and he was a partaker with busybodies. He wholly lacked liberality of mind and hospitality of heart. He wholly lacked trust and hope and love. In Dr. Pusey's short and sharp way of it the true Pharisee of our Lord's day had plenty of divine light in his head, only he was wholly lacking in divine love in his heart.

But let us go back again upon some of the Pharisee's good points. And that not only for his sake but for our own sakes. For the better a man the Pharisee was the more solemnizing will his history and his character and his condemnation be to us. If the Pharisees had been out and out bad men, their condemnation would not have been so startling and so solemnizing to us as it is. Now when you study your New Testament well you will see how much there is to be said in behalf of the Pharisees. Compared with the Sadducees, for instance, the Pharisees were men of a high religious character. They loved the Bible. They knew the Bible by heart. They sanctified the Sabbath day. None of you better. They observed the Fast days.

and all the other church ordinances, with what we would call a Puritan scrupulosity and self-denial. In short, all the best people in Israel in our Lord's day belonged to the party of the Pharisees.

But, with all that, the Pharisee was all wrong in his heart. The true Pharisee's heart was not a broken heart; and thus it was that nothing was right that the Pharisee ever said or did. This sounds a hard saying that nothing was right he ever said or did, but it is the simple truth. In one of the most powerful of his Roman Catholic sermons, entitled "The Religion of the Pharisee," Dr. Newman brings out this about a Pharisee's unbroken heart in his own incomparably powerful and impressive way. I will not water down the passage, but will give you the enjoyment and the profit of it just as it stands. "The characteristic mark of the religion of Christ," he says, "is a continual confession of sin, and a continual prayer for mercy. What is peculiar to our divine faith, as to Judaism before it, is this, that confession of sin enters into the idea of its highest saintliness, and that its pattern worshippers, and the very heroes of its history, are only, and can only be, and cherish in their hearts, the everlasting memory that they are, and carry with them into heaven the rapturous avowal of their being, restored transgressors. Such an avowal is not simply wrung from the lips of the neophyte, or of the lapsed; it is not the cry of the common run of men alone, who are buffeting with the surge of temptation in the wide world; it is the hymn of saints, it is the triumphant ode sounding from the heavenly harps of the Blessed before His throne, who sing to their Divine Redeemer, Thou wast slain, and hast redeemed us to God in Thy blood, out of every tribe, and tongue, and people, and nation. And what is to the saints above a theme of never-ending thankfulness is, while they are yet on earth, the matter of their perpetual humiliation. Whatever be their advance in the spiritual life, they never rise from their knees, they never cease to beat their breasts. So it was with St. Aloysius, so it was with St. Ignatius, so it was with St. Philip Neri who, when some one praised him, cried out, Begone! I am a devil, and not a saint! And who, when going to communicate, would protest before his Lord that he was good for nothing but to do evil. Such utter self-prostration, I say, is the very badge and token of the servant of Christ; and this indeed is conveyed in His own words when He says, I am not come to call the righteous, but sinners to repentance. And it is solemnly recognized and inculcated by Him in these words: Every one that exalteth himself shall be abased, and every one that abaseth himself shall be exalted. Could contrast be greater than between that and this? God I thank Thee that I am not as other men are, or even as this publican. I fast twice in the week, I give tithes of all that I possess. No; contrast could not further go than that between the true penitent, and the true Pharisee."

The very name that the Pharisee took to himself condemned him to his face. To be a "Pharisee" was to be a self-selected and a separated man. Now while all good and true men must sometimes, at whatever cost, separate themselves from all bad men, and from all bad causes among bad men, at the same time, all good and true men will make the separation with great humility, and will make it as short as possible. They will not flaunt abroad their separation like a flag. They will not lay their separation like a foundation stone, and they will not build their church upon it. Now that is just what this true Pharisee was doing in the temple all that day when our Lord discovered him and denounced him. He was flaunting his flag of superiority and separation in the face of God and man. He was taking up his stance on this standing-ground before God and man, that he was so much better than all other men. He must be correctly reported, and if he is, he here puts all other men on one side, and separates himself from them all, and thanks God for it. "Stand by," he says to every other worshipper in the temple. "Come not near to me; for I am holier than thou." You have the true Pharisee in all ages, and out of his own mouth, in that speech of his. You have here that detestable spirit of sectarianism and schism that tore to pieces the Church of God in Israel, and that is tearing to pieces the Church of Christ to this day. Wherever you see any man, high or low, great or small, dwelling continually on his superiority over all other men, and on the superiority of his church over all other churches, there speaks the true Pharisee. Especially when you see him laboring by tongue or pen or purse to keep open the running sores in the Body of Christ, to dwell upon those sores, to exasperate them, to spread them, and to perpetuate them.

Now, to apply all that to the topic of this day—Christian Unity—and to our own part in the topic of this day.

To begin with, if we are ever to take any true part in healing the grievous wounds in the Body of Christ, we must first of all have clean hands ourselves; that is to say, we must have clean hearts; that is to say, we must have broken, humble, contrite hearts. What kind of a healer would he be who came to you to bind up your wounds with his hands all dropping with all manner of taint or infection? You would say to him, Physician, heal thyself. And we must all look to ourselves before we begin to bind up the Body of Christ. It is our universal and incurable self-love and self-righteousness that is the real root of all our sectarianisms and schisms and controversies, whether those controversies are carried on by the tongue or by the pen or by the sword. It is our pride and our self-idolatry; it is our contempt and scorn of all other men; it is not our love of truth, so much as our love of ourselves, that is the real cause of all our contentions and controversies. Paul was a tremendous Churchman and a tremendous sectarian controversialist as long as he was a Pharisee: that is to say, as long as his heart was unbroken. But look at him after he was born again and had become a new creature. What a contrast to his former self! What humility, what condescension, what geniality, what courtesy, what catholicity, what universal loving-kindness; in short, and in modern language, what a Christian gentleman! Coleridge says that while Luther was not perhaps such a perfect gentleman as Paul, he was almost as great a genius. And Luther gives us a taste both of his genius and of his gentlemanliness also in what he says about Paul after Paul had ceased to be a Pharisee. "Paul was gentle, and tractable, and peaceable, in his whole Christian life. Paul was meek, and courteous, and soft-spoken. Paul could wink at other men's faults and failings, or else he would expound them to the best. Paul could be well contented to yield up his own way, and to give place and honor to all other men, even to the froward and the intractable." So speaks of Paul the most Paul-like man of the modern world. And an English gentleman, if ever there was one, has said of Paul in more than one inimitable sermon: "There is not one of those refinements and delicacies of feeling that are the result of advanced civilization, nor any one of those proprieties and embellishments of conduct in which the cultivated intellect delights, but Paul is a pattern of it. And that in the midst of an assemblage of other supernatural excellences which is the characteristic endowment of apostles and saints." But then every fiber of that, if you search down deep enough for it, you will find it all rooted in such a soil as this: "Putting me into the ministry: who was before a blasphemer, and a persecutor, and injurious." And still more in this: "O wretched man that I am! who shall deliver me from the body of this death?" That is the true temper of Church unity, even as the Pharisee's prayer is the true temper of all separation and sectarianism and laceration of the Body of Christ. Only set the chief of sinners, and with broken enough hearts, as the earthly heads and leaders of all your churches, and the days of debate and division and separation are from that day doomed.

As you are my witnesses I am always beseeching you to work together with God in driving out of your hearts the seven devils of prepossession, and prejudice, and partyspirit, and narrowmindedness, and narrowheartedness. And that by reading the very best books, and especially by reading the very best of your enemy's books. I will repeat to you what I took it upon me to say on this subject last May in the General Assembly of the Church of Scotland. I had the honor, I told them, and the happiness, to be one of Dr. John Duncan's students, that so catholic genius and true saint, and among the many lessons of truth, and grace, and genius, and rare Christian wisdom, he taught his students I always remember this. "If," he said, "I met a man from New England, I would say to him, Read the Marrow Men; and if I met a Marrow Man, I would say, Read the New Englanders." And, though I almost owe my soul to the great Puritans, yet acting on Dr. Duncan's advice, I have read Hooker, the great opponent of the Puritans, till I have come to see that in many of their contentions Hooker was in the right, and Travers in the wrong. And this very morning, I told them, I counted seven very different authors all standing most amicably on my desk. There was Hooker at their head with his *Polity*, there was John Donne with his *Sermons*, there was Edwards with his *Affections*, there was Newman with his *Grammar*, and there was Dante with his *Banquet*. I had been making a banquet for my classes out of them all, and there they stood, not excommunicating one another any more, but rather supplementing, and supporting, and assisting, one another, and me. And not only do all those authors agree on my desk today, but they all agree themselves now where they now are. They are all reading one another's books now with an open mind and with an open heart. They are all blaming their own past prejudices now, they are all ashamed of all their past party spirit now. They are all rejoicing in their neighbor's truth now, and in his prosperity, and in his fame. In the pulpit of the Heavenly Temple the forenoon no longer speaks Canterbury, and the afternoon Geneva. And not only the great masterpieces of the past, but to read the periodicals and the newspapers of other churches than your own will reward you, and that not only with information that you will not get elsewhere, but with a wider sympathy, a more catholic, and a more liberal and generous, temper. And that will be Christian unity accomplished already, as far as you are concerned. That will be heaven already, with its love and its peace, descended into you.

And on the other hand shun controversial literature of all kinds, unless you are very far advanced in all knowledge and in all love. If controversial literature must be written and read, I doubt if you are the man either to write it or to read it. You are not, unless your heart is far more full of love and its fruits than most men's hearts are. Richard Baxter, you must admit, has purchased a right and a title to speak to us all on this matter now in hand. "Another fatal hindrance to a heavenly walk and conversation," he says, "is our too frequent disputes. A disputatious spirit is a sure sign of an unsanctified spirit. They are usually men least acquainted with the heavenly life who are the most violent disputers about the circumstantiality of religion. Yea, though you were sure that your opinions were true, yet when the chiefest of your zeal is turned to these things, the life of grace soon decays within. I could wish you were all men of understanding and ability to defend every truth of God; but, still, I would have the chiefest truth to be chiefly studied, and no truth to shoulder out the thought of eternity. The least controverted truths are usually the most weighty and of most necessary and frequent use to our souls." So testifies to us the seraphic author of the *Saint's Rest*. And, to wind up with, listen to a very different voice from that of Richard Baxter. Listen to what Homer says, who though dead yet speaketh through the mouth of Aeneas to Achilles:—

> Long in the field of words we may contend,
> Reproach is infinite, and knows no end,
> Arm'd, or with truth or falsehood, right a wrong:
> So voluble a weapon is the tongue,
> Wounded we wound; and neither side can fail,
> For every man has equal strength to rail.

The God of peace did not leave Himself without a witness wherever even a Homer sang his immortal *Iliad*.

XVII
The Publican

OUR Lord was teaching and healing daily in the temple. And among the multitudes who came and went while He was so employed He paid special attention to a Pharisee and a publican. The Pharisee came up to the temple not caring who saw him or who heard him when he was at his prayers. He had nothing to say in his prayers of which he had any reason to be ashamed. Whereas the publican stood afar off, and would not lift up so much as his eyes to heaven. But all the same, there was One teaching and healing in the temple that day who not only saw both the Pharisee and the publican, but who, without listening, heard them both pray, and read all that was in both their hearts. He needed not to leave His seat where He was teaching and healing, because at all that distance, and notwithstanding all that surging multitude, He knew in Himself what those two men were thinking and what they were saying. For—I am He that searcheth the reins and the hearts. And I will give to every one of you according to your works.

The Pharisee need not detain us long. He is no deep study to us. He is familiar to us. We have him among ourselves. There are multitudes like him among ourselves. At the same time, would that there were more men like him among ourselves. For he was a blameless man. He was man of a spotless life. He was an upright man in all his dealings with other men. He was a cornerstone of the city. He was a pillar of the temple. There was no one in the temple that day who did not do him obeisance as he passed by. He was admired, and honored, and praised, of all men. Yes. Would that there were more men like him in all our cities and in all our temples also.

It is the publican who is here brought forward by our Lord for our special learning. The publican is discovered to us for our very closest study. His name is familiar to us, but not his state of mind. There were few men of his state of mind in his day, and they are not many in our day. God be merciful to me a sinner! was what the publican beat his breast and said. *The* sinner! that was, in exact terms, what he felt and what he said. *The* sinner—as if there was no other sinner in existence but himself. The publican was as possessed with his sinfulness as the Pharisee was possessed with his righteousness. The Pharisee thought that no other man in all the world was at all his equal in his righteousness, and that was exactly what the publican thought about himself in his sinfulness. The publican felt utterly alone in the temple that day. He felt utterly alone in the whole world every day. And the definiteness of the word that he instinctively used about himself—*the* sinner, is to this day the best possible test of the state of mind of all who either read this parable or speak about it. Coleridge, when he is writing in one place about Santa Teresa, lapses for once into a stupidity that is unaccountable in a man of such spiritual insight and such spiritual sympathy. The saint had been speaking to herself about herself in her Journal, and that in the very same terms in which the publican spoke about himself in the temple, and in the very same terms in which Paul speaks about himself in his first Epistle to Timothy, when the great critic breaks out upon her for her insincerity and her extravagant language in a way very distressing to his admirers to read, and very unlike himself. Were it not such an exception to his usual insight and sympathy, I would be tempted to say that such a censure of such a saint is, to my mind, and I think I have the mind of Christ, a far worse sign of Coleridge than all the opium he ever ate, and all the procrastinated work he died and left unfinished. It was not that the publican was, speaking coarsely, the absolutely most immoral man in all the city. It was not that Paul was, stupidly speaking, actually the chiefest of all the actual sinners of his day. It was not that Santa Teresa was the very worst and wickedest woman in all Spain in her day. But to put this truth about them all in a somewhat homely way, it was something not unlike this. I have good reason to believe that other men than myself have suffered from toothache and rheumatism. Only, I have never had the actual and personal experience of any man's excruciating pain but my own. And indwelling and secret sinfulness is the toothache, and the neuralgia, and the cancer, and the accumulated and exasperated agony, of each spiritual man's own soul. It was not what the publican had actually and openly done that festered like hell-fire in his heart and conscience, it was what he himself inwardly was, and inwardly was to himself alone. The heart knoweth its own bitterness, he would have said to Coleridge writing far too flippantly about Teresa. It was because Solomon's prayer, offered long ago at the dedication of the temple, was fulfilled in the publican. Which, said Solomon, shall know every man the plague of his own heart, and shall spread forth his hands toward this house. The whole of the publican's case is explained beforehand in that one profound petition of Solomon's prayer. O poor publican! O publican to be pitied both of God and man! God be merciful to all men everywhere and in every day who know the plague of their own heart!

Why did our Lord not say sanctified? Or, still better, why did He not say both justified and sanctified? Why did He confine Himself to justified? It was sanctification that the publican needed even more than justification, and our Lord knew that quite well. Whereas, He only said that this man went down to his house justified. Justification was but the half of the publican's prayer, and it was not the most poignant and most pressing half. For, if he is only justified today he will be back to the temple tomorrow nothing better of having been justified but rather worse. If our Lord in His great mercy to the publican's misery had only said sanctified what a happy worshipper the publican would have been from that day! And what a happy house he would have had at home from that day! Now, why did our Lord not say the word? Why did He not both say it and do it to this poor wretch on the spot? He would need to have a good reason to show why He did not say sanctified. And no doubt He will have a good reason to show when He is judged. Though it is not always easy for us to see what His reason can be. Perhaps He tried to say sanctified that day in the temple and could not. Who can tell but that He was so carried away with pity for the poor publican that He said Father, if it be possible, let us send this miserable man to his house sanctified? And perhaps He had to submit and say, Thy will be done. For justification is an immediate act of the Father's free and sovereign grace. An act, on the spot, of God's own mind and heart and holy will. And therefore the publican went down to his house only justified. Whereas, sanctification is "an exceedingly complex work," as John Wesley used to call it. God is sending sinful men down to their own houses justified every day, but not sanctified. It takes a long lifetime, in most cases, to sanctify a sinner; and at the end it is the miracle of all miracles to the old sinner himself that he is ever sanctified. Both are miracles. Both justification and sanctification. Samuel Rutherford used to pose the saints of his day with this dilemma, which of the two miracles they will wonder most at to all eternity, their justification or their sanctification? For what is justification? Justification is an act of God's free grace, wherein He pardoneth all our sins, and accepteth us as righteous in His sight, only for the righteousness of Christ imputed to us, and received by faith alone. And what is sanctification? Sanctification is the work of God's free grace, whereby we are renewed in the whole man after the image of God, and are enabled more and more to die unto sin, and live unto righteousness. And, as many of yourselves know, it takes many a visit to the temple, and many a far-off stand in the temple, and many a penitent prayer both in the temple and in your own house, and many a beat of the breast everywhere, before the exceedingly complex work of sanctification can be safely said to be begun in you, not to say finished in you.

Now, on this whole scene I will make this one more observation, and so close. You are not to suppose that this was the first time, much less the one and the only time, those two men had come up in that way to the temple to pray. You may depend upon it the Pharisee never neglected public worship, and by this time neither did the publican. And the oftener the Pharisee went up to the temple the more he went down to his house despising others. Whereas, on the other hand, the oftener the publican went up the more poignant was the pain in his breast. For if he went down every Sabbath day justified, as he did, the more all the next week he loathed himself in his own sight for his iniquities and for his abominations. And that went on till at last God was merciful to him, and took him up to the heavenly temple where he was at last both sanctified and glorified as well as justified. He had often fallen back in the agony of his heart on such Scriptures as this: "As for me, I will behold Thy face in righteousness; I shall be satisfied when I awake with Thy likeness." But with that, and with many more Scriptures like that, to alleviate his agony, he had often charged God foolishly for the length and the depth of his misery. But when the shore was won at last, no more he grudged the billows past. For by that time he was like the prisoner in Plutarch who received a chain of gold with as many links in it, and each link as heavy, as had been that chain of iron, bound with which he had lain so long in prison for his exiled sovereign's sake. And you must learn not to grudge or repine at your lifelong visits to this temple in search or sanctification. The thing you so unceasingly seek is not here. At the same time, this is the way to it. And, meantime, you will every Sabbath day go down to your house at any rate justified. And while falling infinitely far short of a finished sanctification, you will find here many incidental blessings that will help to keep your heart from wholly fainting, till to you also it will be said, O thou sinner of all sinners, be it unto thee in this matter of sanctification also, even as thou wilt. And then for all your shame you shall have double, and for confusion you shall rejoice in your portion, therefore in that land you shall possess the double, everlasting joy shall be unto you.

XVIII
The Blind Leaders of the Blind

ALL the same, the Scribes and Pharisees were quite right, as they often are. And our Lord's disciples were wholly in the wrong, as they often are. The disciples had no business to sit down to eat with unwashen hands, and the Scribes and Pharisees were only doing their bounden duty in entering their protest against such disorderly conduct. Moses never sat down to eat till he had washed both his hands and his feet. And the Scribes and Pharisees sat in Moses' seat for the very purpose of seeing to it that the great lawgiver was obeyed and imitated in all things great and small that he had ever said and done. But, indeed, Nature herself should have taught the disciples to observe ordinary decency in all their habits at table, as well as everywhere else. And, though the complainers could not know it, they had our own John Wesley with them also. For Wesley was wont to preach this high doctrine of Moses, and of Nature herself, to the people called Methodists, this high doctrine of his, that cleanliness is next to Godliness. And, more than all that, the Scribes and Pharisees had the Master of the disciples so far with them. If the beam had not been in their own eye He would have been wholly with them in pulling this mote out of the eyes of His disciples. You are quite right, He as good as said to the complainers. You are only doing your duty in what you say to My disciples. At the same time, why do you get yourselves into such a wicked temper about it? And why is it that you come down all the way from Jerusalem to do nothing else but to find fault about such matters as the washing of hands, and feet, and cups, and pots, and tables? Have you no washing to do yourselves at home? Wash your own hearts, you hypocrites. And with that He turned on them in a way that made Peter interpose and reprove Him. "It is not safe; it is not wise," said Peter, "to speak to the authorities in that way. Such language will be sure to bring sharp reprisals on us all one day." But instead of the timidity and the restraint the disciples would have had their Master observe to those men of such power, He all the more went on with some of the most plain-spoken words He ever uttered. "They be blind leaders of the blind. And if the blind lead the blind, both shall fall into the ditch." Till Peter's prophecy at last came true. And till His enemies took the most terrible reprisals on Peter's Master for His heart-searching eye and for the fearlessness of His speech.

Now, the great value of this passage to us lies in this, that we have two classes of preachers here set before us for our learning. We have those teachers and preachers who are wholly taken up with the outside of things; with cups, and pots, and pans, and tables, and beds, as this passage has it. And on the other hand, we have our Lord who passes by all these things in order that He may get at once at the hearts of men. And it is a most fearful picture that our Lord here gives us of the hearts of men, and of the work that He and His successors in the Christian ministry have to do in the hearts of men. "For from within, out of the hearts of men, proceed evil thoughts, adulteries, fornication, murders, thefts, covetousness, an evil eye, blasphemy, pride, foolishness." No wonder young Newman said that amid all his wine-parties, and all his musical evenings, and all his readiness and eagerness to join in any merriment, he was shuddering at himself all the time.

Generalia non pungunt. No. But there are no pointless generalities in our Lord's preaching. His preaching is quick and powerful, and sharper than any two-edged sword, piercing even to the dividing asunder of soul and spirit, and is a discerner of the thoughts and intents of the heart. Neither is there any creature that is not manifest in His sight; but all things are naked and opened to the eyes or Him with whom we have to do. "In the department of Christian morality," says John Foster, "many of our most evangelical preachers are greatly and culpably deficient. They rarely, if ever, take up some one topic of moral duty, such as honesty, veracity, impartiality, good temper, forgiveness of injuries, improvement of time, and such like, and investigate the principles, and the rules, and the discriminations, and the adaptations, of such things. There is little, nowadays, of the Christian casuistry found in many of our old divines. Such discussions would cost labor and thought, but they would be eminently useful in setting people's judgments and consciences to rights." And Robert Hall, in an ordination charge addressed to a young minister, says, "Be not afraid of devoting whole sermons to particular parts of moral conduct and religious duty. Sometimes dissect characters, and describe particular virtues and vices. Point out to your people, and with unmistakable distinctness, both the works of the flesh and the fruits of the Spirit." John Jamieson of Forfar, for one, would have satisfied both John Foster and Robert Hall. For, long before their day, he had preached and published fifty most powerful sermons on our Lord's present text, treating the text as our Lord returned to it and treated it continually in His sermons, and as Foster and Hall demanded that it should be treated in every pulpit worth the name. And even after those two clear-eyed volumes of heart-searching sermons, Jamieson is bold to assert that every hearer and reader of his, who knows the plague of his own heart, will admit that the half of the shame and the pain and the wretchedness and the downright misery of his heart has not yet been told him. And those fifty Gennesaret sermons delivered in Forfar dug the deep foundations on which more than a hundred years of great preaching has been laid in Forfar, and is being laid in that privileged town down to this day. Would that every pulpit in Scotland had such Christian casuistry in it, and such unmistakable distinctness! But, then, that would not only cost the preacher labor and thought, as Foster admits, but, like the poet, such preachers would have to cease biting their pens for arguments and eloquence, and would have to look into their own hearts for all the arguments and all the eloquence of their sermons. It is the Spirit that quickeneth both you and your preaching, our Master is always saying to us preachers. And it is when our hearts are quickened to see in our own hearts all that He sees in them, it is then, and only then, that we shall be able to deal as He would have us deal, and as John Foster and Robert Hall would have us deal, and as John Jamieson actually did deal, with the hearts of his hearers. The Scribes and the Pharisees had eyes enough to preach against adultery and murder when these things once came out of the hearts of the people; but they were as blind as moles to the real roots of these things, as well as to the kindred roots of pride, and covetousness, and envy, and deceit, of which their own hearts, and the hearts of all their blinded hearers, were full. And these are the things that truly defile a man—evil thoughts, covetousness, deceit, an evil eye, and such like.

Are ye so without understanding also? demanded their Master of His still ignorant disciples. Without understanding, that is, of what it is that really defiles a man, and where it comes from. It is bad enough to have some secret and deadly disease about you. But to have your physician stark ignorant of what is the matter with you, and how to treat you, that is simply despair and death to you. I was once summoned to a deathbed around which stood three of the most eminent doctors in the city. Surely it is not come to that, I said, as the dying man sent for me to bid me good-bye. It need not come to that said the three doctors, if he would only rouse himself and determine not to die. You will see! said the dying man, smiling to me. He felt the hand of death on him, but his doctors were stark blind to what he felt, and why he felt it. They were without understanding, and so he was in his grave before the week was at an end. Tragedies like that will occur sometimes even with the best physicians, but such tragical cases are of every day occurrence with us ministers. The diseases of our patients are so deep down in their hearts, and we are so blind to our own hearts, and to the diseases of our own hearts, that such blood-guilty deaths take place with us every day. In the plain-spoken words of this very Scripture, we attend too much to the outside of things; to pots, and pans, and tables, and beds, and too little to our own hearts and the hearts of our hearers.

When the Pilgrim was making his progress through the valley of the shadow of death, his rare biographer tells us some things about the pilgrim's experiences that always speak home to my heart. About the middle of the valley was the mouth of hell, and it stood also hard by the wayside. Also he heard doleful voices, and rushings to and fro, so that sometimes he thought he should be torn to pieces, or trodden down like the mire in the streets. Just when he was come over against the mouth of the burning pit, one of the wicked ones got behind him, and stept up closely to him, and whisperingly suggested many grievous blasphemies to him, which he verily thought had proceeded from his own heart. When Christian had travelled in this disconsolate condition for some considerable time, he thought he heard a voice of a man, as going before him, saying, Though I walk through the valley of the shadow of death, I will fear no evil, for Thou art with me. Now, this Scripture at present open before us has much the same effect on me as that voice in the valley of the shadow of death had upon Christian. For, as from that voice he gathered that some one who feared God was in that valley as well as himself; so, from this scripture I gather that He who here searches the hearts of men, knows my heart down to the bottom, with all its wickedness, and all its wretchedness, and all its possession of the devil. Speaking only for myself in all these matters, but speaking honestly for myself, I confess to you that I find far more comfort just in this dreadful discovery of the hearts of men, and of my own heart, than I find in far more ostensibly evangelical scriptures. To me this awful scripture is as cheering sometimes as was the voice of that as yet unseen man in the valley of the shadow of death. And for much the same reason. I told you about the three doctors and their fast-dying patient. Now, he died of sheer despair because his disease was so much deeper than his doctors' diagnosis. Had those three doctors put their finger on the deadly spot and said, thou ailest here and here; and thou ailest with this kind of agony and that—then that dead man would have been back at his work within a week. But as it was he was in his grave before the next Sabbath day dawned. And it is just because my great Doctor, Jesus Christ, puts His Divine finger straight on this agony of mine and that: it is this that makes me turn away from every other practitioner of the heart, and say to Him, To whom can I go but to Thee! And it is this same thing that makes me always go away back to John Bunyan, and to the other great specialists of his deep and true school. Almost all the doctors who stand round my bed in these days seem to me to be far too much taken up with the outside of things; while, all the time, I am dying of a heart like the pilgrim's heart, and like this same heart that Christ here lays bare to His apostles and to the people. And thus it is that my Master's so perfect diagnosis of me, even before He has begun to prescribe to me, is already such a message of hope to me. The seventh of Mark, as well as the seventh of Romans, and the *Pilgrim's Progress*, and John Owen, and all the rest of that great heart-searching kind, all make me glad, and for these reasons: First, because I gather from them that some who feared God were in this valley as well as myself. Second, for that I see that God was with them, though in that dark and dismal state, and why not with me? And, third, that I shall have them for my company all the rest of my way.

And when He had called all the people unto Him He said unto them, Hearken unto Me, every one of you, and understand. And, every one of you people here tonight, hearken and understand all that He here says to you about your own hearts, every one of you. And then understand this also, that they that be whole need not a physician, but they that are sick. And, every one of you, understand with me also, and act with me. And act with me in this way. His discovery to me of the state of my own heart only the more entitles me and encourages me to take my heart to Him, and to claim at His hands all His skill in such hearts as mine, and all His instruments for them and all His remedies for them. It is my part to hear and to understand what He here says to me about myself, and then it is His part to heal me. And I warn Him, and I take all you people for witnesses, that I will give Him no rest till my heart is as clean and as whole as His own.

XIX
The Rich Man and Lazarus

AT table one day Dr. Luther was asked whether he took the story of the rich man and Lazarus for a parable, or for an actual fact. The Reformer replied that to his mind the opening passage at any rate is evidently historical. The description of the rich man is so life-like. There is his dress, and his table, and his five brothers all following in his footsteps. And then the painful picture, as if it also had been taken from the life, of a certain well-known beggar with his sores, named Lazarus. Yes, said Luther, I do think our Lord must have known the rich man and Lazarus in Galilee, or in Samaria, or in Judea.

Now, whether it is pure history, or pure parable, or founded on fact, this tremendous Scripture is equally true and is equally solemnizing to us, since it comes straight to us from our Lord's own lips. And our main errand here this evening is to enquire in His temple just what lessons our Lord would have us all to learn and to put in practice out of this terrible story.

The very first thing, as I think, that we are to see clearly in this scripture is this, that the rich man is not in hell simply and wholly because he had starved Lazarus to death. I used to read this parable so superficially as to think that the rich man is where he is altogether because of his starvation of Lazarus. But I see now that our Lord nowhere says so. No. Let the full truth be told even about a man in hell. Let him get all the advocacy, and all the exculpation, and all the palliation, possible. No; it is nowhere said that Lazarus died of this rich man's neglect. Not at all. On the other hand, the crumbs that were sent out to Lazarus must, as I think, have been much more than mere crumbs. They must have been both many and large and savory crumbs, as I think, else Lazarus would not have been laid so regularly and so long at that gate. Those who carried Lazarus to that rich man's gate every morning did so, as I think, because they had found out by experience that this was the best gate in all the city at which to lay Lazarus down. They had tried all the other gates in the city, but they always came back to this gate.

It is quite true, the rich man might have done much more for Lazarus than he did. For instance, he might have fitted up one of his many out-houses for Lazarus to live in; or he might have arranged for a weekly pension to be paid to the incurable pauper in his own hovel; he might even have sent his own physician to report to him as to the symptoms and the progress of Lazarus's sores. But he did not do any of these gracious actions to Lazarus. At the same time he did not issue an angry order that that putrifying corpse, called Lazarus, must no more pollute the air before the door of his mansion. He might have given orders to his servants that that disgusting carcass was to be carted away for ever from out of his sight. But it is not said that he was so hard-hearted as that. He is in hell, indeed, but he is not in hell for that; his hell would have been both deeper and hotter than it is, if he had said and done all that against Lazarus. For you must know that there are degrees in hell as there are in heaven; there are depths and deeper depths there; and there are hot and hotter beds there; and with less and less water to cool tormented tongues. And that being so, this rich man might have been even worse than he is, as He here tells us, who has the key of hell and of death in His hands.

Both our Bible and our daily life are full of the real lesson of this scripture—the great danger of great riches to the rich man's immortal soul. Every day we see great riches simply ruining their possessors' souls both for time and eternity. Rich men are so tempted to become high-minded, proud-spirited, arrogant, imperious, selfish, forgetful, and cruel. Rich men get their own way from everybody, and there is nothing in this world so bad for a man as just to get his own way in everything and from everybody. All men yield to a rich man. All men prostrate themselves before a rich man. He speaks when he pleases, and he is silent when he pleases. All are silent when he speaks and wait till he has finished what he has to say. He will not bear to be contradicted or corrected, and all men learn to leave him alone. A rich man would need to be a very good man before his riches come to him, and then he would both know the temptations that lie in his riches and would strive successfully against those temptations. And if he is not a truly good man before he is a rich man; if he is not a meek, modest, humble-minded, considerate Christian gentleman before he is a rich man, a thousand to one he never will become such a gentleman after he has become rich. At the same time, while all that is true, great riches are sometimes great stepping-stones to a high place in heaven; that is to say, when they are in the possession of a man whose treasure does not lie in his riches. To go no further than Abraham in the history now open before us. Abraham was a very rich man. One of the finest chapters in all the Old Testament turns upon Abraham and his great riches. So rich was Abraham that his mere overflow was quite enough to make Lot his nephew a rich man also. Only, though Abraham in his generosity could make Lot a rich man, he could not make him a gentleman. Abraham might have turned upon Lot and might have said to him that every horn and hoof that Lot possessed he possessed through his uncle's liberality. But what did Abraham as a matter of fact say? He said these immortal words to Lot. "Let there be no strife, I pray thee, between me and thee, and between my herdmen and thy herdmen; for we be brethren. Is not the whole land before thee? Separate thyself, I pray thee, from me: if thou wilt take the left hand, then I will take the right: or if thou depart to the right hand, I will go to the left." What a Christian gentleman was Abraham, and that too such a long time before the day of Christ! And what an abominable mind his nephew in his greed exhibited! And the root of the whole contrast lay in this. Abraham had begun life believing God. He had sought first the kingdom of God and His righteousness, and all those flocks and herds were added to him. And with them there was also added an ever humbler, an ever nobler, and an ever-heavenlier, mind. Once get Abraham's humble, noble, heavenly, mind, and then set your heart upon making riches as much as you like. For the good that you will then be able to do all your days, both to yourself and to all other men, will be simply incalculable.

But it is time to pass the great gulf, our Lord leading us across it, in order to learn from Him some of the great lessons that He here sets us to learn, both in heaven and in hell. And first in heaven. Well, Lazarus who now lies in Abraham's bosom, had his own temptations as he lay at the rich man's gate. And had he yielded to those temptations he would not have been where he now is. He would have been where the rich man now is. Lazarus's temptations were to be embittered, and to repine, and to complain, and to find fault with God and man. Lazarus had Asaph's temptations over again and the Seventy-third Psalm may have helped Lazarus to overcome his temptations.

"As for me," said Asaph, "my feet were almost gone: my steps had well-nigh slipped. For I was envious at the foolish, when I saw the prosperity of the wicked. For their eyes stand out with fatness: they have more than heart could wish. Therefore his people return thither: and waters of a full cup are wrung out to them. For all the day have I been plagued, and chastened every morning." And like Jeremiah also, Lazarus would remember the sins of his youth, and then he would lament in this manner—"Wherefore doth a living man complain, a man for the punishment of his sins? He sitteth alone and keepeth silence. He putteth his mouth in the dust if so be there may be hope." And then, since he had been brought up to read and remember his Bible, he would call this out of Micah to mind. "I will bear the indignation of the Lord, until He plead my cause, and execute judgment for me." Which He did one day. For one day when the rich man's servant took out his morning crumbs to Lazarus he was nowhere to be found. For just when the previous night was at its darkest, and just before the dawn, the angels came down and carried Lazarus up into Abraham's bosom.

Perhaps the most terrible piece of pulpit rhetoric that ever fell from any preacher's lips is to be found in one of Newman's Catholic sermons. I had intended to quote it at this point but I feel now that I dare not. It is too terrible. It is literally true, but you would turn sick under it. For it describes what every lost sinner will say and do when he comes to himself too late before the judgment-seat of Christ. Just think for yourself what you will say and do if you come to yourself for the first time there. Well, that is Newman's terrible sermon. And then he goes on with his fearful satire to give us the conversations about this and that lost soul that go on in every mourning coach on the way home from every such rich man's funeral. But, terrible as Newman's pulpit can be, there is no pulpit anywhere with the concentrated terror of our Lord's pulpit when as here He takes us and lays our ears against the door of hell. The rich man also died, and was buried. And in hell he lift up his eyes, being in torments, and seeth Abraham afar off, and Lazarus in his bosom. And he cried, and all hell heard him, Father Abraham, have mercy on me, for I am tormented in this flame. And all hell listened till it heard Abraham's answer. And Abraham said, Son, remember! And the smoke of their torment went up, as never before, when they all began again to remember.

It is hell on earth already when any sinner begins to remember. Myself am hell! cried Satan when he began to remember. And we are all Satan's seed in that. We simply could not continue to live if we did not manage, one way or other, to forget. When God comes and compels us to remember, what a tornado of despair overwhelms our hearts till we manage again to forget. Now, as you would not lie down in hell, Son, remember! Relieve God of His strange work, and remember.

Set your past sins in order before yourself from time to time. Take the remorseful work out of God's hand and take it up into your own hand. Go back and remember. Go back to that day. Go back to that night. Go back to that hour and power of darkness. Remember those who are now in hell and who were once your companions in sin. Remember that man. Remember that woman. Remember all that they remember about you. We sometimes speak of the book of memory. Read often in it, especially in the blackest pages of it. "I have no books, but I have myself," said a great genius and a great saint. Well, you may not have many books, but you all have one book. It is a great book. It is a tragic book. It is such a book that there is no other book like it to you for terror and for horror. And then it is all true. It is no romance. It is no invention. For it is the literal record of your own past life. Return often to that book. Hold daily readings in that book.

There are many more lessons in this terrible scripture. But there is one lesson specially intended, as I think, for us who are ministers. This lost soul seems to have had no hope for his five brothers if they were left alone with the minister he had been wont to meet with at his father's table, and had been wont to hear preaching on Sabbath. In hell he seems to have come to be of the mind of our forefathers who magnified the reading, but "especially the preaching, of the word." That is to say, he became a Puritan in his appreciation of earnest preaching, when it was too late. He admitted that his five brothers had the Prayerbook and the Bible. "But so had I," he said. "Only, I never opened them. I did not understand them. And none of the young fellows who dined and danced in our house ever once opened their Bible any more than I did. Among my father's servants we had a man in black who read prayers morning and night: but I seldom was present, and when I was present, I always fell asleep. Nobody paid any attention to his dronings. He never spoke to me alone. Nor did my father nor did my mother. Nobody ever took me and told me that the wages of a life like mine would be paid me in this place of torment. Else, if they had, do you think I would have been where I now am! O Father Abraham: pity my poor brothers, and send and deliver them from those dumb dogs that eat and drink till they cannot bark."

A lesson from hell—as it seems to me—how to read, and how to teach, and how to preach; especially how to preach. "Put a *testimony* into it," he says to us toothless preachers. "Testify" is his very word to us from hell. "Show your people that you believe it, if no one else does. Especially, speak straight out to your young men; they are open and honest. They will believe you, and will honor you, and will through you escape this place of torment." "Testify!" and again he says—"Testify!"

Son, remember, testified Abraham, that thou in thy lifetime receivedst thy good things, and likewise Lazarus evil things. Now, my sons and my daughters, what are your good things? And what are your evil things? What is your treasure? And where is it? On what is your heart set day and night? When you pray to your Father in secret, for what do you most importunately and unceasingly ask? Child of God, I will answer for you. I know what your evil things are, and what are your good things. Just go on in that mind. Just go forward in that pursuit. And some day soon—the day is at the door—the same angels that carried up Lazarus to Abraham's bosom will come and carry you up to be for ever with the Lord, and to be for ever like Him. And, till they come, make this your song every morning and every night and the whole of every day and every night—

> God is the treasure of my soul,
>   The source of lasting joy;
> A joy which want shall not impair,
>   Nor death itself destroy.

XX
The Slothful Servant Who Hid His Lord's Money

HAD we been with our Lord on the Mount of Olives that day, this parable would have ended far differently from the way we would have expected it to end. As we heard the servant with the five talents introduced, and then the servant with the two talents, and then the servant with the one talent, we would have felt sure that some very severe things were soon to be said about the greatly gifted among men, and the continually prosperous. All our sympathies would have been with that under-estimated and overlooked servant who had only one talent entrusted to him. And at the beginning of this parable we would have felt sure that before it closed the Divine Preacher would take the side of the despised and untalented servant, and would say some of His severest things about the rich, and about the great, and about those who were full of all manner of prosperity. But we would have been disappointed in our expectations. We would soon have seen that our Lord's thoughts are not our thoughts about such men and such matters. The talented and the privileged and the prosperous in life are always the few and not the many. It is the untalented and the unsuccessful and the obscure and the overlooked who are always the multitude. And it is to the multitude, and to the peculiar temptations of the multitude in the matter now in hand, that our Lord here speaks.

The servant with the one talent started on his stewardship with a great grudge at his master. He is a hard master, said that sullen servant in his heart. At any rate, he has been a hard master to me. He felt himself to be as good a man and as deserving as any of his fellow-servants, and he may very well have been in the right in so thinking and in so saying. And here was he treated in this hard and cruel manner. No wonder he was soured at his heart with the treatment he had got. No wonder that he took up his one talent with a scowl, and cast it into a hole of the earth with disgust, saying as he did so that a harder or a more unjust master no honest servant ever had. Those five talents, and those two talents, and then that one talent, all rankled in his heart, till he was the most embittered and resentful and rebellious of men.

When Ouranius first entered holy orders he had a great haughtiness in his temper. The rudeness, ill-nature, or perverse behavior, of any of his flock used at first to betray Ouranius into impatience. At his first coming to his little village, it was as disagreeable to him as a prison, and every day seemed too tedious to be endured in so retired a place. He thought his parish was too full of poor and mean people, that were none of them fit for the conversation of a gentleman. This put him upon a close application to his studies. He kept much at home, writ notes upon Homer and Plautus, and sometimes thought it hard to be called to pray by any poor body's bedside when he was just in the midst of one of Homer's battles. The slothful servant was the father of Ouranius.

This servant who hid his talent in the earth was the father of that young Highland minister also who hid his sermon in the snow. His history was this. A city congregation was looking out for a colleague and successor to their old minister. They had heard of a preacher of great promise in a remote locality, but before they would commit themselves to him they sent four of their number to hear him in his own pulpit. It was mid-winter and a great snowstorm came on that Saturday night. The ambitious and not unfaithful young minister had his sermon all ready, but as there would be a small congregation that snowy morning he would not throw away his whole week's work on such a handful, and so he left his sermon at home. When he entered the pulpit it was too late now when he saw a seatful of city-looking men in the far end of the empty church. And the explanation he stammered out to them did not mend matters. Till it is to be feared that his Master's prophecy at the end of this parable was, some of it, fulfilled in that manse that Sabbath night. He had for long been ambitious of the city, and he had a sharp punishment that day for despising his small congregation; for hiding his talent at home because there would not be enough people to appreciate it.

This servant who hid his lord's money was the father also of all those ministers among us who will not do their ordained work because they have so little to do. Their field is so small that it is not worth their pains taking off their coat to gather out the stones, and to weed out the thorns, and to plow up the fallow ground, and to sow in their too small pulpit and pastorate the seed of the kingdom of heaven. If they had as large a field as that five-talented fellow-servant of theirs; if they had a city pulpit; if they had a people of education and intelligence, they would prepare for the Sabbath in a very different fashion from what they do. But as it is, what is the use? He was the father of all those probationers also who stand idle till they are settled. Once they are settled and married they will lay out their days, and read the best, and rise in the morning, and preach every Sabbath to the top of their ability. You will see if they will not. But a probationer with an unsettled mind cannot work in that way. He is here today and there tomorrow, and he has no heart to tackle a serious task of any kind. Indeed what can he do but wait on and on for a call? With all those drawbacks, two probationers rise up before me who had another father than this wicked and slothful servant. The one of them did this among other things all his probationer time. When he preached in a vacancy, or for a friend, as he was preaching it, for the first time he found out the faults of his sermon. He found out the loose links that were in it; the want of a beginning and a middle and an end there was in it; the want of order and proportion there was in it; the want of march, and of progress, and of coming to a head there was in it; and the many other faults of all kinds there were in it. And on Monday morning the first thing he did, while the shame and the pain of his bad work were still in his heart, he rose and took his sermon to pieces, re-arranged it in the light of yesterday, re-wrote it from beginning to end, and preached it again next Sabbath, a completely new creation, and a conscientious, a living, and a life-giving, message. Newman re-wrote all his sermons three times over, and one of his best-written books he re-wrote five times. And that probationer did that again and again and again till he not only made his first sermons perfect, but, better than that, by that fidelity and by that labor he worked his whole mind into a methodicalness, and into an order, and into a clearness, and into a consecutiveness, and into other high qualities, that have all combined to make him one of the foremost preachers of our day. The other probationer who rises up before me executed editorial and other work during that same period of his life: work which stands on all our shelves a quarry of resource to us, and a monument of honor to him. And at the same time he began to lay up those immense stores of reading and writing that make his every sentence today a model of fullness, and clearness, and finish.

The unprofitable servant was the father of Clemens, and Fervidus, and Eugenia also. For Clemens is always proposing to himself what he would do if he had a great estate. He would outdo all the charitable men that have gone before him; he would retire from the world; he would have no equipage; he would allow himself only necessaries, in order that widows and orphans, the sick and the distressed, might find relief out of his estate. Come to thy senses, Clemens. Do not talk what thou wouldst do if thou wert an angel, but consider what thou canst do as thou art a man. Make the best use of thy present state. Remember the poor widow's mite, Clemens. You will find Clemens in the Law gallery also. Fervidus, again, is only sorry that he is not in holy orders. He is often thinking what reformation he would make in the world if he was a priest or a bishop. He would then have devoted himself wholly to God and religion, and have had no other care but how to save souls. But do not believe yourself, Fervidus. For why do you neglect as you do those whose priest and bishop you already are? You hire a coachman to carry you to church, and to sit in the street with his horses whilst you are attending divine service. You never ask him how he supplies the loss of divine service, or what means he takes to preserve himself in a state of piety. And so on, Fervidus, through all your un-Christian life. Eugenia, again, is a good young woman, full of pious dispositions. She is intending if ever she has a family to be the best mistress of it that ever was. Her house shall be a school of religion, and her children and servants shall be brought up in the strictest practice of piety. She will spend her time in a very different manner from the rest of the world. It may be so, Eugenia. The piety of your mind makes one think that you intend all this with sincerity. But you are not yet the head of a family, and perhaps never may be. But, Eugenia, you have now one maid. She dresses you for church, you ask her for what you want, and then you leave her to have as little religion as she pleases. You turn her away, you hire another, she also comes, and after a time goes. You need not stay, Eugenia, to be so extraordinary a person. The opportunity is now in your own hands. Your lady's maid is your family at present. She is under your care. Be now that religious governess that you intend to be. Teach her the catechism, hear her read and exhort her to pray. Take her with you to church, and spare no pains to make her as holy and devout as yourself. When you do this much good in your present state, then you are already that extraordinary person you intend to be. And, till you thus live up to your present state, there is but little hope that the altering of your state will alter your way of life. Eugenia also, you will all see, is one of his daughters who said: If I had had five talents committed to me, or even two, I would have traded with the same and made them other five talents and other two.

But let Eugenia be done at once and for ever with such a father. Let Eugenia be born again till she has her Father in heaven, not in name only, but in deed and in truth. Come out this week to Fountainbridge, Eugenia. In our mission district in Fountainbridge you will find a prepared scope for all your talents of every number and of every kind. There are hundreds of girls out there who sorely need just such a friend as you could be to them. They need above everything else an elder sister and a more talented sister just like you. Solitary girls in lodgings have a hard fight of it to keep their heads above water. Poor girls starved to death for want of some one to love them, and befriend them, and counsel them, and encourage them in virtue and godliness. You may not have many talents, you may not be rich, you may not be very clever, or very far on yourself in the best things, but you are better off, a thousand times, than those poor sisters of yours out there. And you can speak to them, and know their names, and tell them your name, and go sometimes to see them. At your very poorest and very least talented you can teach two or three neglected children for an hour every Sabbath day. You can take them down to the water-side on a Saturday. You can take them home to a little tea-party every week or two. You can give them little books to read, and make them tell you what they have read, and better and better books as they grow up. Good books for children are so cheap nowadays that you do not need to be rich in order to have a delightful little library provided for every poor girl's lodgings, and for every Sabbath-school child's mother's house. Come out and make a beginning with your one talent this very week. We are all making a beginning again this very week in that famous old field so well known to your forefathers and foremothers in such noble work. Let Clemens, and Fervidus, and Eugenia all come. Let the five-talented, and the two-talented, and the one-talented, and the no-talented at all, come. For there is a field for all in Fountainbridge, and many a Well done, good and faithful servant! will before long be purchased there again, as in days gone by. Come away then, O servant of God with the one talent! Come and light a lamp, like Samuel. Come and keep a door, like David. Come and give two mites, like the poor widow. Come and give a cup of cold water in the name of a disciple. For,

> Little drops of water,
>   Little grains of sand,
> Make the mighty ocean
>   And the pleasant land.

> Little deeds of kindness,
>   Little words of love,
> Help to make earth happy,
>   Like the heaven above.

XXI
The Unmerciful Servant

IF you had been destined by your parents to be a minister, and if at twelve years old you had come to the same decision yourself, from that day you would have begun to think continually about your future office, and you would every day have done something to prepare yourself for your future office. You would have made it your custom every Sabbath day to go up to the sanctuary both to hear and to ask questions about the Word of God, in the reading and preaching of which your whole life was to be spent. Even if your teachers had not shown you the way you would have found out your own way of reading the Word of God, and meditating upon it, and employing, not your memory only, but your pen and ink also, in order to store up your observations and your readings and your meditations against the time to come. You would have been like Apelles the painter who never passed a day without drawing at least one line and filling it in. *Nulla dies sine linea*, was all that artist's secret, and it was all his advice to his privileged apprentices. And all your days you would have attributed any success of yours to that teacher who first printed that proverb on your young conscience, and at the same time showed you how to perform it. Now, *mutatis mutandis*, that is to say, after making all the necessary changes, that was our Lord's exact case till He began to be about thirty years of age. And thus it was that, having been made in all things like unto His brethren, He both observed, and read, and meditated, and laid up, the greatest treasures of grace and truth against the day of His showing to Israel. And thus it was that, in all His ministry, He was never once taken unawares or unprepared. Give Him suddenly any Old Testament text to open up and He was ready on the spot to do it. Set Him any intricate question, whatever your motive might be, and immediately you got your answer. As for instance in the case now before us. When Peter came to Him and said, Lord, how oft shall my brother sin against me, and I forgive him? His Master that moment recalled that Roman procurator to mind whose case had been the conversation and congratulation of all Galilee in years now long past. And how well that case fitted into the kingdom of heaven for one parable of that kingdom, all the world has seen ever since that day on which our Lord gave that procurator's case as His answer to Peter's complaint.

Peter, for a long time, was a most interfering and offensive disciple. Peter was continually running up against all other men. He was always both giving offence and taking offence. He was always inflicting wounds and receiving the same. When Peter was converted from all that he splendidly strengthened his brethren. But during the process of his conversion, and till it was perfected, he both caused himself many stumbles and many falls, and was the cause of many such things to his fellow-disciples. What the exact matter was at that moment we are not told. Only, we have Peter coming with this remonstrance to his Master—How oft shall my brother sin against me, and I forgive him? till seven times? Jesus saith unto him, I say not unto thee until seven times: but, until seventy times seven. And then He told Peter the story of that Roman officer who is now known to all time as the Unmerciful Servant. And in this so apposite story, our Lord was like a scribe, as He says Himself, which is instructed unto the kingdom of heaven, which bringeth forth out of his treasure things new and old. And then after telling Peter and all the Twelve this story of Caesar and his degraded and imprisoned procurator, our Lord added this application to the story—So likewise shall My Heavenly Father do also unto you, if ye from your heart forgive not every one his brother their trespasses.

Now, we are all to learn from this scripture, as we have all learned it already from our own experience, that Almighty God has His reckoning times with all His servants, even in this life. He is to have a great, a universal, and an irrevocable, reckoning time with all men at the end of this life; but the first point in this parable is this, that He has preliminary and preparatory reckoning times in which He begins to take account of His servants even in this world. Caesar would take account of his servants, says our Lord. Now the best way to understand this is to look back at our past lives. Unless, indeed, we have all along been let alone of God, as is sometimes the case. But, no doubt, those reckoning times have, by God's special grace to us, come already to some of us. When Dr. Chalmers's reckoning time first came to him he was a greatly gifted, but as yet an utterly unprofitable, servant. It came to him in his brother George's illness and death; and then it came back again to him in his own long, and all but fatal, illness. It came to that young communicant I told you about, when her mother died. And it came to that other young communicant when—"I was engaged to be married, sir, and she died." I have one time, especially, ever before me, when my own reckoning time once came to me. And ever since that time I see myself in this chapter as in a glass. This chapter always reads to me like a literal prophecy of myself. How did your reckoning time come to you? What was it that brought your debt to a head? What was it that brought you up to God's judgment seat before the time? What great trespass was it of yours? What great accumulation of debt was it of yours? And did you do like this Galilean procurator? Did you fall down and worship God and appeal to His patience? Did you promise to pay all the debt if only He would let you have sufficient time in which to pay it? Did you swear to Him that you would never commit that great trespass again? Did you engage also that you would watch, and pray, and would crucify your flesh, with its affections and lusts, if only He would not deliver you to the tormentors. And how did it all end? Or, is it all ended yet?

But the same servant went out, and found one of his fellow-servants which owed him an hundred pence; and he laid his hands on him and took him by the throat, saying, Pay me that thou owest. Now we are such, and our fellow-servants are such, that they are continually running into all kinds of debt to us, and to all depths of debt. Our brother is like Peter's brother, in that he is sinning against us seven times every day. Partly through his offensiveness and injuriousness, and partly through our imagining all kinds of offences and injuries at his hand, the most immense debts are being run up between us. Seven things in a single day, sometimes, will come between us and our brother. He forgot us. He overlooked us. He preferred some one else to us. He acted on his own intelligence, and judgment, and conscience, in some matter in which we had the insolence and effrontery to dictate to him. He got some promotion, or some praise, that we had not friendship enough to him to stomach. He was more talked about than we were. He carried his custom to another shop than ours. We wrote a book, we preached a sermon, we made a speech, we sang a song, and he did not praise us to the top of our bent. Say, how often shall my brother sin against me in such ways as these, and I forgive him? No, I cannot do it. I have tried it, and I cannot do it. From the heart to forgive debts like these no, never, I cannot do it. And dost Thou actually expect it of me? Or, is this only another economy of Thine? At any rate, it cannot be done. It has never been done, and it never will be done, so as to justify my Heavenly Father in forgiving me my trespasses. If He suspends my forgiveness on my forgiving such trespasses as these—who shall be saved? Not one. No, not one. Not I, at any rate. "Do you think it will ever be possible to construct an instrument to discover and to exhibit our thoughts against our neighbor?" asked a *Pall Mall* interviewer at Mr. Edison, the great American inventor. "Such an instrument is possible," returned Edison. "But what then? Every man would flee from the face of his neighbor, and would flee to any shelter." So he would. And so he does seventy times every day. As Peter afterwards said, Lord to whom shall I flee but unto Thee? Who shall shelter me and my unforgiving heart but Thee! Who can justify a man like me, both now and at the last account, but Thee and Thy Heavenly Father in Thee! Likewise also say all His disciples. As well ask us to cast Arthur's Seat into the sea.

I feel sure you all say the Lord's Prayer every night before you sleep. Well, how do you do when you come to the fifth petition, which is this—And forgive us our debts, as we forgive our debtors? Dr. Chalmers confesses in one place that he did not feel that dreadful sense of sin and guilt which so overwhelmed Halyburton every night. There are some advantages, you see, in not having such an overwhelming sense of sin as Halyburton had. For one thing, you get sooner to sleep every night, and you get your sleep more unbroken with dreams of the coming day of account. Amen! stuck in my throat, says Macbeth. And Amen stuck many a night in Halyburton's throat over the fifth petition. His brother in St. Andrews had trespassed against him that day. He had outrun him in some race. He had outbidden him in some market. He had damned Halyburton's sermon with faint praise. He had just hinted a fault, and had hesitated dislike. He had been reported to Halyburton as having sneered at the scholarship and the style of Halyburton's first publication. He had trespassed against Halyburton that day in a way that Halyburton has not the courage to set down in black and white in his diary that night, and therefore he could neither say Amen, nor get to sleep. But Chalmers got his fill of Halyburton's sense both of the guilt and the pollution of sin, long before he went so suddenly to his last account, as we see in this mathematical illustration of it:—"The wider the diameter of light, the larger the circumference of darkness." And in this "far ben" entry of it:—"What would I do if God did not justify the ungodly!"

There is a fine touch in this ancient history that must not be neglected. When the fellow-servants of this unmerciful servant saw him so forget his own ten thousand talents as to take his hundred-pence debtor by the throat and cast him into prison, they were both sorry and angry, and went and told their Lord what had taken place. It was an excellent saying of one of the seven wise men of Greece, who, when he was asked what would rid the world of injuries, answered:—"When the bystanders shall resent an injury as keenly as he does who suffers the injury." Now those fellow-servants did that, and their resentment is told us in order that we may imitate them in their resentment. That would largely banish all injury from among ourselves, if we would all do what that wise man of Greece advised, and what those fellow-servants actually did. If we would put ourselves in the places of the men who are injured unjustly by their wicked neighbor. When we read or hear of any man being wickedly attacked by tongue or by pen, ten to one all the offender's fault has been that he has disappointed, or offended, or crossed the self-love, and the self-interest, of that revengeful and implacable man. And that, often in the utmost innocence, and even in the most absolute righteousness. Ten to one the root of the wicked treatment is nowhere else but in the wicked heart of that mortally offended, unforgiving, and revengeful, man. Keep well in mind, my brethren, what the wise man said, when you see any man or any cause truculently attacked by tongue or by pen. Resent the injury as if it were done to yourself, and that will somewhat help to rid the world of all such injuries, and of all such injurious men. At any rate, be you not such injurious men yourselves. Forgive, and you shall be forgiven. For with the same measure that you mete withal, it shall be measured to you again.

XXII
The Unprofitable Servant

ACCORDING to some ancient authorities Bartholomew was a nobleman of Galilee before he was a disciple of Christ. Not many mighty, not many noble, were called; but Bartholomew was called as if to show that no class of men is shut out from the discipleship and the apostleship of Christ and His church. Bartholomew was a sort of gentleman-farmer, and, like Matthew the publican, he made a supper to his neighbors before he finally parted with his patrimonial estate. And it was while they were all sitting at supper that this incident, so it is supposed, took place, and this conversation that completed the incident. One of Bartholomew's men-servants came in from the field, put off his everyday clothes, girded himself with a waiting garment, and then served the table till his master and all his master's guests had risen from their supper. Are you not much too tired? said Peter sympathetically to the servant. Are you not doing two men's work? And besides, you must be faint by this time with hunger. O no! said Bartholomew's serving-man smiling, I am only doing my bounden and delightful duty in waiting on my good master, and on his honored guests. And then I will sit down to my own excellent supper immediately. "Hear ye what this so exemplary servant saith," said their Master to the twelve, "Verily, I say unto you, Wheresoever this gospel shall be preached in the whole world, there shall also this, that this man has said and done, be told for a memorial of him."

Our Lord applied that incident in its first intention to the twelve. Their Master was teaching and training the twelve by everything that happened every day to Him and to them. In order to teach and to train the twelve for their fast-coming work, their Master found tongues in trees, books in the running brooks, sermons in stones, and this great lesson in Bartholomew's plowman-waiter. The twelve had this lesson taught them first, and, after them, all their successors are taught the same lesson, down to this day. That willing-minded, many-handed, plowing-man is a pattern to all preachers and pastors to the end of time. For he worked for Bartholomew in season, out of season. He made more work for himself when all his proper work was done. One day, so Hermas tells us in his ancient history, when this servant was commanded by his master to run a paling round a vineyard, he not only ran the paling round the vineyard, but he dug a ditch also round the same vineyard, and then he gathered the stones and the thorns out of it; and such things he did always, till, when Bartholomew became a disciple, he left one whole farm, with its full plenishing on it, as a bequest to this plowman as if he had been his own son and his true heir. He is a fine pattern for all plowmen and for all feeders of their masters' cattle; but he is a perfect prototype to all preachers and pastors especially. Every single syllable of this scripture is a study for us who are ministers. Whatever other men may make or may not make of this fine scripture, no minister can possibly miss or mistake its meaning for him, or get away from

686

Christ's all-seeing eye as he reads it. Christ sets every minister before this ministerial looking-glass, in order that in it he may see what manner of minister he now
is, and may forecast what his place is likely to be when his Master sets His supper,
and Himself serves it, for all His plowmen and for all His vine-dressers. Only, far
better have ten plowmen's work to do than one minister's work. A plowman may
finish his tale of furrows, and may then give his fellow-servant a hand in feeding
his master's cattle, and may then take another and a willing hand in the work of
the house, after which he will sit down to his supper with a sense of satisfaction
over his hard day's work. But I defy any apostle of Jesus Christ ever to have that
plowman's good conscience. And much less any successor of an apostle. If you
have been bold enough to be numbered among the true successors of the apostles
you have taken up a task that makes self-satisfaction for ever impossible to you.
You may write your sermon over and over again as often as Dr. Newman wrote his
masterpieces; but as long as you have not torn it up "fiercely," and written it yet
again, you will preach it on Sabbath with such jolts and jars in it as will make you
blush and stagger before your people. And you may visit your dying parishioners
every afternoon, and your sick, and aged, and infirm, every ten days, but you will
never be able to say this plowman's grace over your supper all the days and nights
of your pulpit and pastoral life. For, "the wider the diameter of light," as Dr. Chalmers demonstrated to Dr. Hanna's parishioners on a blackboard at Skirling—"the
larger the circumference of darkness."

Our Lord tells all His true ministers to say every night that they are unprofitable servants, and they all say it. But at the same time He solemnly warns all His
so-called ministers that He will irrevocably pronounce this very sentence at the
last day against some of them. "Cast ye that slothful and unprofitable servant into
outer darkness: there shall be weeping and gnashing of teeth." I was told about
such a threatened minister of Christ and of His Church in Scotland only last night.
He got a good congregation committed to his charge when he was ordained. But
at the present moment he has neither Sabbath School, nor Prayer Meeting, nor
Bible Class, nor Endeavor Society, nor Band of Hope, and as for his pastoral work,
an old man died the other day, not many stonecasts from the manse, who had not
seen his minister for two years. Would any institution set up among men but the
Church of Christ endure a scandal like that? Would the army endure it? Or a bank?
Or a railway? But let us not despair of any man. Even John Mark once ran away
from his work. And yet, long after Paul had denounced and deposed him, we have
the Apostle actually saying, Take Mark and bring him with thee, for he is profitable
to me for the ministry. John Mark's whole story is told first in the Acts, and then
in the Epistles, just to guide and encourage the Church in all her dealings with all
such unprofitable ministers as Mark once was. And by far the best way of dealing
with all our unprofitable ministers would be to induce and enable them to visit
Bridge-of-Allan, or Dunblane, or Perth, or Keswick, or Mildmay. "We've gotten a
minister noo!" said an old elder to me after his hitherto unprofitable minister had
been induced and enabled to make such a visit. Or send him a Life of Wesley, or of
Whitefield, or of Boston, or of Chalmers, or of Spurgeon. Or perhaps better than
all that, get an evangelist on fire to spend a week with him in his parish. "Demas

apostatizes," says Bengel, "but Mark recovers himself." If you have the means and the opportunity, help your Mark in these ways to recover himself, and he may live to write a gospel for you before all is done.

But all the time, though this character-sketch is intended by our Lord for us ministers in the first place, it is not intended for us only. Our Lord's true people are all ministers in their own measure, as Moses prayed they might all be. You are all true and direct successors of the disciples and the apostles. And, minister or people, a plowman or a feeder of cattle, putting up pailings, digging ditches, gathering out stones, or hewing up thorns, when you have done all, end all, as Bartholomew's plowman ended his long and arduous day's work. End it all with his proverb in your mouth, and in your heart. For be sure of this, that he of God's servants who thinks that he has fully finished and done what he was commanded to do, that man neither knows his Master, nor his Master's commands, nor does he know the a, b, c, of true knowledge about himself. Well may Paul ask, Where is boasting then? And well may he answer himself, It is excluded. And there can be no better mark of the mind and heart of a true and an accepted servant of God than just that he says in his mind and in his heart, after every new and better service of his, that he is the most unprofitable of all God's servants. "The more," says Newman in one of his thrice-written sermons, "any man succeeds in regulating his own heart, the more he will discern its original bitterness and guilt." And all who are engaged in regulating their own heart—which is our Master's whole commandment—will subscribe to what the great preacher says about that. We are fresh in the classes from Chalmers, and Spurgeon, and Foster, and the Wesleys, and Whitefield, and we found them all subscribing to Newman and to Bartholomew's plowman. But not one of them all is so much to my own remorseful taste in this matter, as is Thomas Shepard, the Pilgrim Father. Not one of them—passionate as some of them are—is passionate enough for me, till I come to the author of *The Ten Virgins*. Shepard is the most heart-broken, and the most heart-searching, and the most pungently profitable of all God's heart-plowing servants to me.

At the same time, while all that is true, and not even Shepard has told the half of the truth, there is another side to all that. And I have never seen that other side so well put as in Marcus Dods of Belford's *Incarnation of the Eternal Word*. "A Book," says the noble-minded and generous-hearted Chalmers, "of great mental wealth and great mental vigor, rich in scholarship, and of a massive and an original power." John Foster demands more case-preaching in our evangelical pulpits, and Marcus Dods's case-page is exactly what Foster wants. And I refer to that page because it so restores the true balance of evangelical and experimental truth in this matter now in hand. It sometimes happens, says Dods, that the true Christian is so far from boasting of himself that he goes much too far in the opposite direction. He dwells far too much upon the defects of his services, or upon some impropriety of motive that had mingled with them. He feels the very acutest anguish over his best and his holiest performances. But there is often a certain taint of self-righteousness in all that. For such a sufferer not seldom forgets to give the atonement, and the intercession of his great High Priest for him, their true and their full place. He will not take rest nor peace of mind short of the most absolute perfection in his services, leaving no room for the rest and the peace that Christ offers, and Himself is, to all His true-hearted servants. You admit and believe that your services are accepted of God in and through the merit of Christ alone. And yet you are inconsolably distressed because you still detect imperfections in them, and you fear that both you and your services will be for ever cast out of God's presence. Now what is that but making Christ of none effect as your High Priest? What is that but making Him die, and rise again, and intercede for you, in vain? "I have found," says this eminent theologian and evangelical preacher, "this mode of reasoning successful in enabling the mourner to detect the source of his cause-less sorrows, and to recover that peace of mind which results from a simple and unhesitating reliance upon our great High Priest, for the pardon of all our sins, and for the acceptance of all our services."

Now, it is all this that explains Paul, and justifies Paul, and makes Paul our greatest evangelical example, where he says with such assurance of heart—"I have fought a good fight, I have finished my course, I have kept the faith." The best fight Paul ever fought was not with wild beasts at Ephesus, but it was with his own self-righteous heart. It was fought that he might be found in Christ, with all his ever-increasing self-discovery and self-condemnation. And it is his profound grasp of the evangelical faith, that enables Paul so to assure us also that if we only look to Christ alone as our righteousness, and "love His appearing," we shall have our crown of righteousness given to us also at that great day. To be the most unprofit-able of servants in our own eyes; to sink into the dust every night speechless with shame and pain over another all but lost day; and at the same time to lie down to sleep accepted in the Beloved—that is truly to fight the good fight of faith, and to fight it with the whole armor of God: that is really and truly to keep the faith of the gospel till we shall hear our Master's voice saying over us also—Well done, thou good and faithful servant! Enter thou into the joy of thy Lord.

XXIII
The Labourer with the Evil Eye

AESOP'S dog in the manger, and our Lord's laborer with the evil eye, are two companion portraits. Aesop's famous fable taught the very same lesson in ancient Greece that our Lord's present parable taught to Israel in His own day, and still teaches to Christendom in our day.

But before we come to that, there are one or two preliminary lessons that we are intended to learn from the very framework, so to call it, of this parable. And to begin with, let us look well at this unheard-of husbandman. For the like of this husbandman has never been seen before nor since in Galilee, nor in Jewry, nor in Samaria, nor anywhere else. This singular husbandman plants and reaps his vineyard less for the sake of his vines, than for the sake of his vinedressers. This so altruistic husbandman, as we would call him, occupies his vineyard not at all for his own advantage, but for the sole advantage of his laborers. Their well-being is better to him than all the wine they will ever produce. Indeed, and to let out the whole truth at once, this husbandman is a perfect portrait of God the Father, drawn by the skillful and loving hand of God the Son. My Father is the husbandman, says our Lord in another parable. And it must be so here also. For no other husbandman in all the world ever went out at all hours of the day to hire his laborers, and at the same wages. No other husbandman could afford to pay for one hour's work in the evening of the day as much as he pays for the burden and heat of the whole day. No; this husbandman's portrait is no pure invention of our Lord's sanctified genius, as some of His other portraits are. This is no original stroke of our Lord's holy and fruitful imagination. This is as real and as genuine a likeness as is the likeness of the snarling laborer himself. Only, the snarling and snapping laborer is a likeness taken from this envious and spiteful earth. Whereas this husbandman is the speaking likeness of Heavenly Love. My Father is the husbandman.

"Which went out early in the morning to hire laborers into his vineyard." Ah, me! With what a sharp stroke does that incidental-looking statement come home to those of us the morning of whose days is now long past! For we remember well how God came to us early in our life, and before we had as yet hired ourselves out to other masters. O young people, if you would only believe it! If we could only put our old hearts into your young bosoms! How fast you would fall in with the husbandman's earliest offer! And what a life of blows, and starvation, and all kinds of cruel usage, would you thus escape! Satisfy our children, O Lord, early with Thy mercy, that they may rejoice and be glad in Thee all their days.

But of all the hours of this husbandman's laborer-hiring days it is His eleventh hour that comes most home to my own heart. It is His eleventh hour that makes all us old men to exclaim—Who is a God like unto Thee! Whether any young people will be won to God through this scripture tonight, I do not know. But I will answer for some of the old. For He came to us also at the first hour of the day, and at the third hour of the day, and at the sixth hour, and at the ninth hour. But if He will still take us at the eleventh hour, we are His on the spot. The holy child Samuel, and many more early-called, and early-employed, children of God have had their own long and happy lives of highly rewarded labor. But the thought of all such holy and happy laborers is a positive hindrance and stumbling-block to us. All such wise and good men are a rebuke to us rather than an encouragement. It is the thief on the cross who, of all saved men, is our especial example. The thief on the cross was the great eleventh-hour laborer of our Lord's day, and we come into the vineyard with him. At the end of our evil life we come with him. When the sins of our youth, and all our sins, have found us out we come with him. When the wages of our life-long service of sin has become death to us also we come with him. When this mocking taunt is thrown in our teeth—What fruit have ye now of those things of which ye are now ashamed? we come with him. Those who are still in the early morning of their days have never heard of the thief on the cross. They have never once read his so heart-encouraging history. It is not yet written for their learning. Not till they are as old as we are will they be able to read the thief's so heartening history as we read it. But it is now the eleventh hour with us as it was with him, and we come with him. Since God takes the bitterest dregs of our sinful lives, and, like this husbandman, pays so altruistically for them, we come. Take us, O God; O do Thou take us. And where our sin has abounded, let Thy grace much more abound.

Is thine eye evil? said the good husbandman to the murmuring laborer. Now, an "evil eye" is just our old Bible English for the Latin word "invidia." Is thine heart so selfish and so envious as that? was what our Lord said to this man who could not enjoy his own wages for grudging and growling at his neighbor's wages. Aesop's dog in the manger had his own bone, and he did not deny that it was both a big and a sweet bone. But he was such a hound at heart that he could not see his master's ox beginning to munch his bottle of straw in his manger without snarling and snapping at him. And no more did this dog of a laborer complain that his wages were not quite enough for all the work he had done. All his unhappiness lay in this that his neighbor had so much wages to take home with him that night to his happy wife and children. He did not complain that he was underpaid himself. All his misery came from this, that his fellow-servant was so much overpaid. Both Aesop's dog, and our Lord's dog-like laborer, were sick of that strange disease—their neighbor's health. This wretched creature was so full of an evil eye that every one must have seen it. Even if he had held his peace every one must have seen his evil heart running out of his eye. Even if you were a perfect stranger to me; even if I had never seen you before, I would undertake to tell to all men the name of the man you both envy and hate, if I were near enough to see your eye when your rival is being praised and rewarded in your presence. Nay, I would know it from the very tone of your voice; aye, from the very cough in your throat. For envy, like love, will out. And, as our Lord is always saying to us, it will out at the eye. "As to the motive of those attacks on Goethe," says Heine, "I know at least what it was in my own case. It was my evil eye." Now, who is your Goethe? Who is your fellow-laborer in your special line of life? "Potter envies potter," says Aristotle.

Who is your companion-potter? And do you have the self-knowledge that even poor Heine had, to say to yourself every day—"As for these dislikes, and aversions, and antipathies, that I feel in my heart; as well as for these depreciations and contempts that pass continually through my tongue and my pen; I know what their motive is in my own case at least, it is in my own evil eye."

> Envy so parched my blood, that had I seen,
> A fellow man made joyous, thou hadst mark'd
> A livid paleness overspread my cheek.
> Such harvest reap I of the seed I sow'd.
> O man, why place thy heart where there doth need
> Exclusion of participants in good?

If he is rightly reported, a Greek commentator who bears a great name makes a very shallow remark at this point. He says that it is difficult for him to believe that any man who is really within the kingdom of heaven himself, and is in its service and is receiving its rewards, could have an evil eye at another man for his work and for his wages in that kingdom. A more stupid remark never fell from an able man's pen. A more senseless and self-exposing annotation was never made. A young friend of Mr. George Meredith's once came to him in an agony of pain and shame. "This is too bad of you!" he cried. "Willoughby is me!" "No, my dear fellow," said the great writer, "Willoughby is all of us." And in like manner, instead of it being difficult to believe that there was ever such a dog in the manger as this murmuring laborer, we are all such dogs, and he who does not know and confess it—the shell is yet on his head. Yes, Willoughby is all of us. The truth is, an evil eye, like this laborer's evil eye, is not only in all our hearts, but it is the agony of every truly good man's heart that it is so: it is very hell itself to every truly good man's heart that it is so: to every man's heart who is so much as even beginning to know what true goodness really is. Instead of there being no envy among the disciples of Jesus Christ, and among those who labor in His Father's vineyard, as this stupid old annotator would have us believe; instead of that, the true hellishness of envy is never tasted by any man till he is far up in the kingdom of heaven, and is full of its mind and spirit. Dante was far up on his way to Paradise when the fine dialogue on envy and on love took place. Dante sounds his deepest depths in his heart-searching cantos on envy, even as his most seraphic flights are taken in his cantos on love.

"Behold we have forsaken all, and followed Thee; what shall we have therefore?" That miserable speech of Peter's, which gave occasion to this parable, utterly vitiated all Peter's previous work for his Master, however hard he had worked, and however much he had forsaken for his Master's cause. For it is yet another of the absolute principles of this noble vineyard that it is *motive* in its laborers that counts with its Master. It is motive alone that counts with Him, far more than strength, or skill, or early morning promptitude and punctuality, in His laborers. Unless all these admirable qualities are informed and animated by the right motives, they all go for next to nothing in this so singular and so spiritual vineyard. "An unexamined life is no true life at all," Socrates kept saying continually, as he both examined his own motives every day and set all other men on the daily examination of their own motives. We know from Peter's own mouth what his motives had been in his discipleship up till now. And Peter's shame is told us here that we may see our own shame in our own motives also and up till now. Why, then, do I do this and that work in the vineyard? Why do I study? Why do I preach? Why do I visit the sick and dying? Why am I an elder? Why am I a deacon? Why do I subscribe to this fund and that? Why am I a Sabbath-school teacher? And why am I a member of this church rather than of that? It is our mean and self-seeking motives that lurk so unexamined in our hearts that make us all so many dogs in the manger, and so many envious and murmuring laborers in the vineyard. And as it was at Peter and his miserable motives that his Master levelled this parable, so it is at us and at our miserable motives, and at the miserable envies and jealousies that spring out of our miserable motives, that He levels this same parable in this house tonight.

And now in summing up our Lord adds this noble lesson to all His other noble lessons in this noble and ennobling scripture. Many are called, He adds, but few are chosen. Take them all together, He says; take those called at the first hour of the day, and those called at the third hour, and those called at the sixth hour, and those called at the ninth hour, and those called at the eleventh hour—when they are all counted up—many are called. But, with all that, the chosen men; the truly choice spirits even among the men who are called; the men who are sincere and single in their motives; the men who are full of humility about themselves, and about their work, and about their wages; the men who are so full of brotherly love that they have no evil eye left at their brother's good work or good wages, but who rather rejoice in all the good things that fall to their brother-laborer's lot—such men are not many even in the vineyard of heaven itself. There are many in that vineyard who say with Peter—What shall we have, therefore? But they are few who work at all hours of the day, and still receive their wages at night with pain and shame, and say to themselves that they are the most unprofitable of all their fellow-servants. They are the few, even among God's true servants, who continually look on all they receive and possess as so many proofs of His singular and unparalleled grace and goodness to themselves. They are the few who so think and so feel and so speak; but, then, they are the very finest and the very choicest of all His saints. They are the elect of His elect. Their true place on earth is in such a noble vineyard as this, and they are the true servants of such a noble Master as this. My brethren, at whatever hour you enter this vineyard, early or late, work all your days in this fine and noble spirit. So work for your Master, and so love your neighbor as yourself, that you may be found at last, not only among the many called, but among the few chosen.

XXIV

The Children of Capernaum Playing at Marriages and Funerals in the Market-Place

IT is the market-place of Capernaum and it is the cool of the day. The workmen and the workwomen of the town are sitting in the shade after the work of the day is over, and the children, having been released from school, are boisterously engaged in their evening games. "Come," cries a leading boy, "Come and let us have a marriage. This here will be the bride's house, and I will be the bridegroom, and we will all get our lamps lighted, and we will go to the bride's house to bring her home to my house." "No," shouts another. "No. We had a marriage yesterday, when you were the bridegroom. Let us have a funeral today. And I will be the dead man, and you and you and you will take me up and carry me out of the gate, and all the rest will come out after us lamenting and mourning and weeping." But the bridegroom would not have a funeral, and the dead man would not have a marriage, till a quarrel arose, and till fathers and mothers had to separate their children and take them home. And till One who had sat in the market-place and had seen it all, arose and went out into the hill-country and was all that night alone and in prayer. And as He looked on Capernaum He wept and said, "And thou, Capernaum, whereunto shall I liken thee, but to thine own children playing in the market-place, and calling to their fellows, and saying—We have piped unto you, and ye have not danced: we have mourned unto you, and ye have not lamented."

> The childhood shows the man,
> As morning shows the day—

sings Milton about the childhood of our Lord. And that childhood scene in the market-place of Capernaum already shows the coming manhood and womanhood of those contending children. And it shows, not their childhood and manhood and womanhood alone, but our own childhood and manhood and womanhood also. The self-will and the bad humor and the obstinacy and the fault-finding of those Capernaum children in the marketplace, and of their parents in the synagogue, are all held up before us in this glass of God, looking into which we are instructed to see, not our own children only, but our grown-up selves also. Just because a marriage was proposed by one playfellow his neighbor would not have a marriage. He would have a funeral. His little willful heart at once rose up within him to resist his neighbor's proposal. He would have a funeral that day and in nothing but a funeral would he take any part. The marriage game was surely a far more delightful game than the funeral game. But it was not delight that he

694

was now set upon; it was his own will and his own way. "The cause is in my will," said Caesar. "I will not come. Let that be enough to satisfy the senate." And it was enough that this little Caesar of Capernaum said that he would not have a marriage but a funeral. Immense libraries have been written, first and last, on the will: and that by our very ablest and very best men. But behind Caesar's will in Rome, and behind this little tyrant's will in Capernaum, no philosopher or theologian of them all has ever been able to go. We see self-will every day and we taste the bitter fruits of it every day. But why the human will should be so incurably evil, that is past the wit of our wisest men to find out. An evil will is the true mystery of iniquity, till the whole world is one huge marketplace of Capernaum, and all owing to your evil will and mine. I will not play with you unless I get my own will and way in everything. And you will not play with me unless you get your own will and way in everything. "He is a very nice man when he gets his own way," said one of yourselves the other day when he was praising one of yourselves. And Elizabeth, as we are told, was a very nice queen when her bishops tuned their pulpits to keep time to her dancing. But when they tuned their pulpits to the truth she showed herself a very virago. She would play at churches with them every day, and all day, if they would but play to please her. But if they did not, they would know the consequences. To how many things, both in church and in state, and both at home and at play, has Caesar given us the one true and complete key—"The cause is in my will. Let that satisfy the senate."

It was the mother of the dead man of last night who came with her son in her hand to our Lord as He was preparing to preach in the market-place next morning. "Master," she said, "I saw all Thy sorrow and shame over my son last night. I watched Thee all the time and I knew all that was in Thy thoughts about him. But they were not such sad thoughts as mine were. And now I have brought my little son that Thou mayest lay Thy hand upon him and make him a new heart. And if not, I would rather he had never been born; I would rather see him a dead man indeed, and carried out of the city on his dead bier, than live to see him grow up as he began last night." And Jesus had pity on her. And He laid His hand on her little son's head, and said, "Blessed be the son of such a mother. For of such mothers, and of the sons of such mothers, is the kingdom of heaven.

> They that have my Spirit,
> These, said He, are mine."

Now my brethren, if you and I have grown up, and are growing old, without having been blessed of God with a new heart: that is to say with a gentle, humble, meek, affable, and complying heart: if we are come to manhood and womanhood with a hard and stony heart: a proud, self-willed, obstinate, despotic, and tyrannical heart still within us—how is it all to end? and when? and where? We cannot be content, surely, to go on and on with such an evil heart within us, making ourselves miserable, and making all who have to do with us miserable also. And if the New Testament is true; if we suddenly die with such a heart still in us it will be to be devils for ever ourselves, and the playfellows of devils for ever. If we are hardening our hearts against God and man, and are set on having our own will in everything;

if we go about tyrannizing over everybody, and making everybody suffer from our insolent temper, what is there in death, or after death, to give such as we are a new heart? There are abundance of promises in death and after death to the meek, and to the sweet, and to the submissive, and to the self-surrendering, and to the self-sacrificing. But I have not found any such promises and consolations to the high-minded, and the sour-tempered, and the quarrelsome, and the self-asserting—have you? I have met with not a few warnings and threatenings and divine denunciations against such, both in this world and in the world to come. And you must have met with the same. And to all such among you, amid scenes of misery caused by your wicked temper and your tyranny, your own conscience must have told you to your face that you are the man. Now what are you doing to alter that? Or are you doing anything? And are you content to go on as you are, with such a heart as yours and you taking no step to mend it? Yes what step are you taking to mend it? For even if you came to Him to whom that Capernaum mother came, He would only say to you what He said to her, and what He said to her far-off fathers and mothers through His servant Ezekiel. "Repent," He will say to you, "and turn yourselves from all your transgressions; so your iniquity will not be your ruin. Cast away from you all your transgressions, whereby ye have transgressed, and make you a new heart, and a new spirit, for why will you die? For I have no pleasure in the death of him that dieth, saith the Lord God; wherefore turn yourselves, and live ye." Come away then, and let us look at some of the times and the places when and where you must set about making yourselves a new heart; that is to say, a broken, contrite, chastened, tender, yielding, companionable, heart.

"How shall a man like me ever become of an affectionate and companionable temper?" asks Epictetus, the Stoic professor, at his students in his lecture-room in Nicopolis. And this is the answer he gives himself in their hearing. I take his answer out of the notebook of one who was present. And I take Epictetus because our Lord said, "And thou, Capernaum; they shall come from the east and the west, and shall sit down in the kingdom of heaven, while many of the children of the kingdom, such as thou and thy children are, shall in nowise enter into it." "How," asks the old Stoic, "shall a man like me ever become of a truly noble and divine disposition?" And he answers himself in this way. "Every man is improved by the corresponding acts. The carpenter is improved by the acts of carpentry. And the orator is improved by the acts of oratory. But if a carpenter slovens over his work he will never become a good carpenter. And if an orator does not speak better and better every time he rises to his feet he will soon be hissed out of the pulpit. And in religion and morals it is the very same thing. Thus, modest actions preserve and improve the already modest man, and immodest actions destroy him. Shamelessness strengthens the shameless man, faithlessness the faithless man, abusive words the abusive man, angry words and angry acts make the man more and more a man of anger, and avaricious acts end in making a man a miser." And the great Stoic has line upon line, and precept upon precept to his scholars in this all-important matter. For in another page of Arrian's notebook I come upon this—"Every habit and faculty is maintained and increased by the corresponding actions. The habit of walking by walking, and the habit of running by running. If you would be a good reader, read; if a good writer, write. Lie down ten days and then attempt a long walk, and you will see how your power of walking has gone from you. Generally, then, if you would make anything a part of your character, practice it. When you have been again angry today, you have not only been again angry today, but you are all that the more open to anger tomorrow. Till today's anger, and tomorrow's anger, and the next day's anger, will all unite to make you an absolute savage to all who live near you. But if you wish not to be such a savage, do not do the acts of a savage, but the acts of a gentleman. Do not feed your savage temper by savage words and savage actions. Keep your bad temper in hand, till you can count the days on which you have not been angry. I used to be in a passion every day at something or somebody, now every second day, then every third, then every fourth day. But if you have intermitted thirty days without an explosion of anger, make a thanksgiving sacrifice to God. If you escape for two or three months, be assured that you are in a very good way. Great is the combat, divine is the work; it is for freedom, it is for happiness, it is for holiness. Remember God, and go on." So far Epictetus.

Are you then a self-willed, proud-hearted, intolerant, and tyrannical, man? Or are you a virago of a woman? And would you be a gentleman and a gentlewoman? Epictetus has told you the way tonight. Butler has told you the same way in your own tongue, but Epictetus was beforehand by two thousand years. Gentlemanly acts will end in making you a gentleman, and nothing else will. No man was ever born a gentleman; no mere man. But multitudes have made themselves gentlemen and gentlewomen. And that on the Epictetus-principle of acts, habits, character. The next time, then, that opinions and proposals differ where you are concerned, seize you this assurance, that God Himself has brought about that difference of opinion, and those conflicting proposals, with His eye set on you. Opinions and proposals are nothing to Him: but you, and your moral character, and your Christian conduct are everything to Him. Tonight yet, and before you have slept this scripture of His off your mind, and tomorrow, to a certainty, two opinions and two proposals will be tabled before you, and that in order to put it to the proof if you have paid any attention tonight. In order to see if your visit to the playground of Capernaum, and to the mountain of prayer above Capernaum, has done you any good. Be you ready. Be you prepared. Play you the man that moment. If it is a marriage that is proposed, put yourself at their disposal. Say that you will undertake to see the registrar and the minister. Do not mention the other engagements you had made for that week and that day. But put them all off till you have seen this marriage carried smoothly and sweetly through. And after you have seen them away to their honeymoon, you will be far happier in your lonely lodging than if you had been the bridegroom himself. Do it and see! At any rate, there will be better than bridegroom-joy in heaven over you because this playground of Capernaum has not been lost upon you tonight.

XXV
The Samaritan Who Showed Mercy

A CERTAIN man went down from Jerusalem to Jericho, and fell among thieves, which stripped him of his raiment, and wounded him, and departed, leaving him half dead. And by chance there came down a certain priest that way; and when he saw him, he passed by on the other side. And likewise a Levite, when he was at the place, came and looked on him, and passed by on the other side. But a certain Samaritan, as he journeyed, came where he was: and when he saw him, he had compassion on him, and went to him, and bound up his wounds, pouring in oil and wine, and set him on his own beast, and brought him to an inn, and took care of him. And on the morrow, when he departed, he took out two pence, and gave them to the host, and said unto him, Take care of him: and whatsoever thou spendest more, when I come again, I will repay thee.

"And, by chance, there came down a certain priest that way," says our Lord, telling the story after the manner of men. He knew better than any one that there is nothing left to "chance" in this world; not even the fall of a sparrow; not even a hair of our head. "It will be obvious to the intelligent reader," says Thomas Boston's son in editing his father's priceless *Autobiography*, "that the radical principle upon which this narration is founded, is that *God hath preordained whatsoever comes to pass*. This principle the author believed with all his heart, it was often an anchor to his soul, and every minister of the Church of Scotland is bound, by his subscription and ordination vows, to maintain it. This, kept in view, will account for the author's ascribing to an overruling Providence many incidents, which some may think might be resolved into natural causes." I do not know what, all, this priest's ordination vows may have been. But I am quite sure that if any one had asked him in the temple yesterday saying, Master, what shall I do to inherit eternal life? He would have answered him, Thou shalt love the Lord thy God, with all thy heart, and with all thy soul, and with all thy strength, and with all thy mind; and thy neighbor as thyself. But the pity with this priest was, that as soon as he got his temple duties over yesterday, he forgot all that about his neighbor till he put on his gown again next Sabbath morning in Jericho. And thus it was that he was on his way down to Jericho that day when, by chance, he came on a half-dead man on the way-side. Being a temple priest, he should have said to himself as he set out on his journey—

> The Lord shall keep thy soul: He shall
> Preserve thee from all ill.
> Henceforth thy going out and in
> God keep for ever will.

And then he should have been making the "bloody pass" safe to himself and to others by singing to himself—

698

Show me thy ways, O Lord:
    Thy paths O teach thou me:
And do thou lead me in thy truth,
    Therein my teacher be.

For thou art God that dost
    To me salvation send,
And I upon thee all the day
    Expecting do attend.

But not setting out in that way, and not singing to himself in that way, the priest missed his chance of salvation and of eternal life—for that day at any rate.

The Levite who followed him would seem, for one thing, to have had somewhat more curiosity than the priest, and to have come all that the nearer that day to eternal life. The priest saw enough at the first glance to suffice and satisfy him: but the Levite stopped and went to the side of the road and looked at the half-murdered man, but that one look was enough for him also, for he also passed by on the other side. If the half-dead man's eyes were not entirely torn out by the thieves, and if he was able to open his eyes for a moment as he heard the coming footsteps, how his heart must have beat back to life again at the sight of the priest and the Levite. When a beggar at one of our road-sides sees a minister coming along with his black clothes and his white neckcloth, the poor wretch feels sure that he will not be passed by this time without a kind word at any rate. But his disappointment is all the more when the man of God looks the other way and passes by in silence on the other side.

Now, nobody who knew what the Samaritans were would have wondered at one of them setting out on a journey any morning and every morning without a Psalm, and then coming "by chance" on this man and that, all the day, and passing them by without a thought. But however he set out, psalm or no psalm, and however this Samaritan was occupied as he rode down the Jericho-pass, as God would have it, Behold, there is a half-dead Jew lying in the ditch at the roadside. Were ever any of you as full as you could hold of mortal hatred at any enemy of yours? At any enemy of your church or your country? Were you ever in such a diabolical state of mind at any man, or at any race of men, that it would have made you glad to see him lying wounded and half dead? Well, that was the very way that the Jews and the Samaritans felt to one another in our Lord's day. They had nothing short of your mortal hatred at one another. And, had that been a half-dead man of Samaria, it would have been nothing wonderful to see the Samaritan traveller doing all that to his fellow-countryman. But to do it to a Jew—that is why this Samaritan's name is so celebrated in heaven. What do you think would be the thoughts of the half-dead Jew as he saw his own temple-kinsmen passing by on the other side, and then saw this dog of a Samaritan leaping off his mule? What would he think and say all night as he saw this excommunicated Samaritan lighting the candle to pour oil and wine into his wounds and watching all night at his bedside? That Samaritan mule hobbling down the Jericho-pass with that half-dead burden on its back always reminds me of Samuel Johnson hobbling along to Bolt Court with the half-dead streetwalker on his back and laying her down on old Mrs. Williams's bed to nurse her back to life. The *English Dictionary* has long been superseded, and it is only one enterprising student of the best English literature here and there who goes back to *The Lives of the Poets*. But that immortal picture of that midnight street in London, and that immortal picture of that bloody pass of Adummim, will be sister portraits for ever among the art-treasures of the new Jerusalem. And if you love your neighbor as yourself in this city, as this Samaritan and Dr. Johnson did in Jericho and in London, you will yet see those two portraits and the originals of them with your own eyes, in the art-galleries of the heavenly country.

Then said Jesus to the lawyer, Go, and do thou likewise. But he, willing to justify himself, began, lawyer-like, to raise speculative and casuistical questions, instead of immediately setting about to do his duty. "Thou shalt love thy neighbor as thyself." "Yes," said the man of law, "but who is my neighbor? Distinguish, and clear up to me who, exactly, my neighbor is," said this subtle casuist. My brethren, all men are your neighbors. Absolutely all men. Absolutely every man. But more immediately every stripped, and wounded and half-dead, man. And still more, every enemy of yours. Yes, absolutely every man. For, who is so unrobbed, and so unwounded, and so full of life and love, as not to stand in need of your brotherly love, and of every kind of life-giving office at your hands? Who is there on the face of this earth who does not need, and will not welcome, the oil and the wine of your loving kindness poured into his many wounds? No man. No woman. It is not only in the bloody pass of Adummim and on the midnight street of London that your neighbors are to be come on wounded and half-dead: they are to be found everywhere. Many who have their own beasts to ride upon, and who are quite able to pay their own bill to the inn-keeper and your bill also: many such stand in as much need of your love and your services of love as did that half-dead Jew on the road to Jericho. A kind thought, a kind look, a kind word, a kind deed; carry about that oil and that wine with you, and you will not lack wounded and half-dead men and women to bless the day on which they first saw your face and heard your voice.

But some lawyer here, willing to justify himself, will stand up to tempt me, and will demand of me whether I mean to deny all my late sermons on the Romans? And to teach tonight that this Samaritan was justified before God simply because of this good deed of his? I quite admit that both our Lord, and His Apostle, some-times teach economically, and paradoxically, and one-sidedly even, on occasion. All the same—go you and do you as this good Samaritan did. And if death and judgment overtake you walking beside your mule on the way to the inn at Jericho: or if your Lord summons you to give in your account when you are up smoothing the pillow of a half-dead enemy of yours; I would far rather take your chance of eternal life than if death and judgment overtook you still debating, however Cal-vinistically, about your evangelical duty. Yes: Go at once tonight and do likewise.

Spurgeon says somewhere that wherever his text is, and whatever his text is, he will find his way, somehow, to Jesus Christ before he leaves his text. Now it is not to go far from this text to go to Him who is The Good Samaritan indeed. It has been said of Goethe that, like this priest and this Levite, he kept well out of sight of stripped, and wounded, and half-dead, men. I hope it is not true of that great intellectual man. At any rate it is not true of Jesus Christ. For He comes and He goes up and down all the bloody passes of human life, actually looking for wounded and half-dead men, and for none else. Till He may well bear the name of The one and only entirely Good and True Samaritan. They are here to whom He has said it and done it. "When I passed by thee, and saw thee wounded and half dead, I said unto thee when thou wast in thy blood, Live; yea, I said unto thee when thou wast in thy blood, Live. Now when I passed by thee, and looked upon thee, behold, thy time was a time of love. Then washed I thee with water, and I anointed thee with oil." And we ourselves are the proof of it. That we are here tonight, in the land of the living and in the place of hope, is the sufficient proof of it. We are as it were in the inn of Jericho tonight. But tomorrow He will come back and will repay whatever they are tonight spending here upon us. And as soon as we are able to be removed He will come and take us home with Him, for a greater and a better and a bigger-hearted than the best Samaritan is here. He will take us to that land with Him where no man falls among thieves and where they rob not nor wound nor leave a man half-dead. Go, said His Father to Him, and love Thy neighbor and Thine enemy as Thyself. And instead of wishing to justify Himself; instead of saying, But who is My neighbor—you know what He said, and what He did, and to whom He said it and did it. And we who were in the bloody pass, and were stripped, and wounded, and half-dead, we are the proof of it, and will for ever be the proof and the praise of it.

And now, my brethren, is it not a cause of the profoundest praise and thanksgiving to Almighty God that peace has come, and that there is not a man on the face of the whole earth that we any more wish to see wounded and half-dead? And must it not be a sweet thing to our King to think about on his bed, and to all his Royal House, that he has no enemy now to his throne and scepter and crown in all the wide world. And that is so, because He, The Good Samaritan, is our peace, Who hath made both one, and hath broken down the middle wall of partition between us: having abolished in His flesh the enmity; for to make in Himself of twain one new man, so making peace. And that He might reconcile both unto God in one body by the Cross, having slain the enmity thereby. For through Him we both have access by one spirit unto the Father; through Jesus Christ, in whom all the building fitly framed together groweth unto an holy temple in the Lord, in whom ye also are builded together for an habitation of God through the Spirit.

XXVI
Moses on the New Testament Mount

THE Sermon on the Mount is the last sermon of Moses that has come down to us. It is the last sermon and it is the best of that great lawgiver. In this last sermon of his we have Moses rising above himself and stretching himself beyond himself. But all the time, and with all that, this is still Moses. The mouth, indeed, is the mouth of a far greater than Moses, but the hands and the heart are still the hands and the heart of the old lawgiver. For as we sit under this sermon we soon find that we are still in the hands and the heart of the law. The law is at its most spiritual indeed; the law is at its most holy, and just, and good indeed, in the Sermon on the Mount. But the very spirituality of its holiness only serves to make our condemnation under it all the more hopeless, and our death at its hands all the more certain and inexorable. Till we cry out under this sermon, as the murderers of his Master cried out under Peter's sermon—Men and brethren, what shall we do? The eight beatitudes with which this sermon begins are undoubtedly very beautiful. There is no denying that. That is to say they are very beautiful to him who finds himself in a position to claim them as his due, and to possess them and to expatiate upon them. But let him who has tried with all his might to purchase them and to claim them, let him tell us what he thinks of their beauty and what effect their beauty always has upon his heart and upon his conscience. Orion and the Pleiades are very beautiful, he will tell you. But he will tell you also that he will sooner hope to build his house up among their sweet influences, than he will hope to possess the beatitudes of the Sermon on the Mount by anything he can ever suffer or perform or attain. The pole-star is not so far out of his reach, he will tell you, as is the nearest to him of those beautiful, but heart-breaking, beatitudes of the Sermon on the Mount. I do not know how it is in this matter with you. But I will tell you frankly how it is with me. Ever since I first saw something of their terrible spirituality, I cannot bear to read so much as one single beatitude, or indeed any other sentence in this sermon, till I have again strengthened my heart with the Epistle to the Romans. To me the Epistle to the Romans is the true foundation-stone, corner-stone, and cope-stone, of the whole New Testament. Nay, its bold-hearted author is bold enough to take his Epistle to the Romans, and his Epistle to the Galatians, and to lay them away up before and underneath even the Book of Genesis itself. And as often as I read again his so ancient and so unanswerable argument, I forthwith feel that I hold in my hand, not only the true key to all the promises and prophecies and types and emblems of the Old Testament; but what is far better to me, I hold in my hand the true and only key to let me out of that dungeon of despair into which Moses again shuts me, as often as I read any of his sermons, and forget my Romans and my Galatians. I can walk at liberty around Mount Sinai itself; I can climb to the very top of its most threatening precipices, and can look down over them to their very bottom, if I have Paul as my mountain guide to lean upon, and his Romans to direct me and to encourage me.

Luther—"not such a perfect gentleman as Paul, perhaps, but almost as great an evangelical genius,"—Luther labors with all his might, and it is not little, to keep Moses in his right place and not to let him move out of his right place, no, not by so much as one single inch, or, rather, out of his three right places. The first of Moses' right places is what the Reformer calls his political place. That is to say, the place from which the great lawgiver issues his laws for the good government of states and cities and households. Moses' second place is that of a universal prosecutor and accuser of all men; for out of his second place he convicts all men of sin and death and shuts all men's mouths. And his third right place, according to Luther, is to be an overseer and task-master of all wise and safe housebuilding, as in the text. Now come and let us take this approved housebuilder tonight, and let us address ourselves to learn some communion-evening lessons from him, and from Moses, and from Paul.

Well then, let it be remarked and remembered that the first praise that is given to this wise house-builder is this, that he digged deep down for a foundation before he began to build his house. And this sermon which leads up to him, digs deep down also, if ever sermon did. As you will see if you will but walk over the ground it covers and with your eyes open. Take, to begin with, that hunger and thirst after righteousness to which the fourth beatitude is attached, and you will see what a deep and central shaft that sinks into your own soul. Then take all kinds of purity of heart, and that is, as you must confess, another very deep and very secret shaft. And take your demanded reconciliation to your offended brother, before you need seek for your reconciliation to your offended God, and that, you must allow, is not surface work. Neither is the command to do good to the men who hate you and despitefully use you. Now all that is what this sermon describes as digging deep. And one of our very first lessons from all that should surely be that as this sermon digs so deep, so should all sermons do. The true worth to us of every sermon is not its learning, or its eloquence, but its depth: the depth of him who preaches it, and the depth of them who hear it. Thomas Goodwin, whose depth has drawn me to him all my days, has this passage on this subject. "By this digging deep I do not mean deep terrors, for it is not necessary that all kinds of earth should be digged out with iron pickaxes. God uses such tools to none but hard earth only. Very small spades and shovels suffice to dig up and empty out some men. Only, all men must be dug up and emptied out somehow. All men must be emptied out by a spiritual insight into their true estate, and made to see down to the bottom of their own hopelessly evil hearts. And must be made to confess their utter inability to build a single stone of a safe house for themselves, except out of and then upon that Rock which is Christ."

There is no saying of His in all this sermon of His that is more deep-digging and fundamental than what our Lord here says to us about much secret prayer. For there is nothing that we scamp and skim over more than just much secret prayer. The Preacher of this sermon had all His own days dug deep, and had laid the foundations of His own house deep, in continual and unceasing secret prayer.

And He went on doing that till the time came when He Himself was to be likened to a wise man. For all that night in the garden of Gethsemane He was still digging deep, and was making absolutely sure that His house was founded on God His Father, and on Him alone. And it was so, that when the rain descended, and the floods came, and the winds blew and beat upon that house all that night, it fell not: for it was founded on a Rock. And had Peter taken his Master's advice and example all his days, and even that one night, his house would not have fallen with such a sad fall, all that night and all next day. Do this deep saying of Christ yourselves, O all you communicants of today! For there are clouds rising that will soon burst on your house also, and if it is not dug deep with much secret prayer, you may depend upon it, great will be the fall of it.

And now as you go over all this deep-dug ground, what do you say to all these sayings of His about meekness, and about hunger after righteousness, and about purity of heart, and about peacemaking, and reconciliation to your offended brother, and about cutting off your right hand, and plucking out your right eye, and about loving your neighbor as yourself, and about closet prayer, and about laying up treasure in heaven, and about seeking first the kingdom of God and His righteousness, and about judging not, that you be not judged, and about entering in at the strait gate—what do you say to all these sayings of His who came not to destroy the law but to fulfill it, and to have it fulfilled in you? What do you really think and feel about the whole of this Sermon of His on the Mount? Babes at the breast; preachers and writers with the shell on their heads, chatter their praises of the Sermon on the Mount, and incessantly advertise us that all their New Testament, and all their creed, and all their catechism, are summed up in the Sermon on the Mount. My brethren, you know better. You have dug deeper. The law of God has been dug deeper than that into your understanding and your heart and your conscience. Yes, this is very Moses to you, and Moses with his two-edged sword in his hand, as never before. "By the law is the knowledge of sin." And by this deep law of wise house-building all your foolish building is discovered and denounced to you. Just try your hand at a truly spiritual house, and see. Take— "Blessed are the meek; for they shall inherit the earth." And begin at once to found deep, and to build up, your spiritual house. Begin to live a life of meekness. Study humility. Keep ever before your eyes the many and deep reasons there are why you should be the meekest and the humblest-minded of men. Set yourself with all your might to put up with all injustice, and all ill-usage, and all contempt, and all neglect on all hands. Suffer long and be kind. And your house will rise, for a time, on that foundation, till one day a storm will come. One dark day the rain will descend and the floods will come, and the winds will blow and beat upon your house of meekness, till it will fall, and will bury you under it. Another will attempt his house on this foundation, "Judge not, that you be not judged. For with what judgment you judge, you shall be judged; and with what measure you mete, it shall be measured to you again." Begin to lay judgment to the line, and righteousness to the plummet, and tell me how long your refuge lasts you. And so on, through all the foundations laid on Sinai.

Yes. This whole sermon is still Moses and his two tables of stone, rather than Jesus Christ and His Cross and Righteousness. Literally, no doubt, Jesus Christ did preach this sermon. Nobody disputes that. But then, the real truth is, that it is not Christ's preaching that proves Him to be the true Christ to you at all; it is not His sermons but His Cross that is the sure proof of that to you: and His Cross is still a far way off. We have far greater preachers of Christ in the New Testament Church than Christ was Himself. It was not yet the time for any one fully to preach Christ. As He said Himself to His mother at the marriage of Cana—My time is not yet come. The truth is—I will say it for myself, if you will not let me say it for you— unless far other sermons than the Sermon on the Mount had been preached in the New Testament Church it had been better for me I had not been born. But for Paul's preaching of Christ, I, for one, would be of all men the most miserable. "Far greater and far better sermons than mine shall be preached," He said, "because I go to the Father. I have yet many things to say unto you, but you cannot bear them now. Howbeit, when He, the Spirit of truth, is come, He will guide you into all truth. He shall glorify me; for He shall receive of mine, and shall show it unto you."

Wherefore then serveth the Sermon on the Mount? you will demand of me; to which demand of yours Paul will answer you. "It was added because of transgressions, till the seed should come to whom the promise was made. Is the law then against the promises of God? God forbid; for if there had been a law given which could have given life, verily righteousness should have been by the law. But the Scripture hath concluded all under sin, that the promise by faith of Jesus Christ might be given to all them that believe." In other words—The Sermon on the Mount sets forth, as never before nor since, a splendid exhibition of the majestic and noble righteousness, as well as the exquisitely inward spirituality, of God's holy law. And this sermon commands all men, and more especially all men of a spiritual mind, to keep looking at themselves continually in this glass that Christ Himself here holds up before them. Holds up with His own hands before them in order that they may see, and never for a moment forget, what manner of men they still are. And then His redeeming death being accomplished, and Paul being raised up to preach the true, and full, and complete, and final, Gospel; and after we have heard and believed that Jesus Christ is made of God to us wisdom, and righteousness, and sanctification, and redemption, we now return to the Sermon on the Mount to see in all its beatitudes and in all its commandments what manner of persons we ought to be in all holy conversation and godliness.

XXVII

The Angel of the Church of Ephesus

YOU are not to think of an angel with six wings. This is neither a Michael nor a Gabriel. I cannot give you this man's name, but you may safely take it that he was simply one of the oldest of the office-bearers of Ephesus. No, he was no angel. He was just a chosen and faithful elder who had begun by being a deacon and who had purchased to himself a good degree, like any one of yourselves. Only, by reason of his great age and his spotless character and his outstanding services, he had by this time risen till he was now at the head of what we would call the kirk-session of Ephesus. By universal acclamation he was now the "president of their company, and the moderator of their actions," as Dr. John Rainoldes has it. This angel, so to call him, had grown gray in his eldership and he was beginning to feel that the day could not now be very far distant when he would be able to lay down his office for ever. At the same time, it looked to him but like yesterday when he had heard the prince of the apostles saying to him those never-to-be-forgotten words—"Take heed to thyself, and to all the flock over which the Holy Ghost hath made thee an overseer, to feed the flock of God, which He hath purchased with His own blood." And, with many mistakes, and with many shortcomings, this ruling and teaching elder of Ephesus has not been wholly unmindful of his ordination vows. In short, this so-called angel of the Church of Ephesus was no more an actual angel than I am. A real angel is an angel. And we cannot attain to a real angel's nature, or to his office, so as to describe such an angel aright. But we understand this Ephesus elder's nature and office quite well. We see his very same office every day among ourselves. For his office was just to feed the flock of God, as Paul has it. And again, as James has it, his office was just to visit the widows and orphans of Ephesus in their affliction, and to keep himself unspotted from the world of Ephesus. And he who has been elected of God to such an office as that in Ephesus, or in Edinburgh, or anywhere else, has no need to envy the most shining angel in all the seven heavens. For the most far-shining angel in the seventh heaven itself desires to look down into the pulpit and the pastorate of the humblest and obscurest minister in the Church of Christ. And that because he knows quite well that there is nothing for him to do in the whole of heaven for one moment to be compared with the daily round on this earth of a minister, or an elder, or a deacon, or a collector, or a Sabbath-school teacher.

Now, there is nothing so sweet, either among angels or among men, as to be appreciated and praised. To be appreciated and praised is the wine that maketh glad the heart of God and man. And the heart of the old minister of Ephesus was made so glad when he began to read this Epistle that he almost died with delight. And then as His all-seeing and all-rewarding way always is, His Lord descended to instances and particulars in His appreciation and praise of His servant. "I know thy works. I chose thee. I gave thee all thy talents. I elected thee to thy charge in

Ephesus. I ordained thee to that charge, and my right hand hath held thee up in it. Thou hast never been out of my mind or out of my eye or out of my hand for a moment. I have seen all thy work as thou wentest about doing it for me. It is all written before me in my book. All thy tears also are in my bottle."

We have an old-fashioned English word that exactly sets forth what our Lord says next to the angel of Ephesus. "I know all thy painfulness also," He says. It is a most excellent expression for our Master's purpose. No other language has produced so many painful ministers as the English language, and no other language can so well describe them. For just what does this painfulness mean? It means all that is left behind for us to fill up of His own painful sufferings. It means all that tribulation through which every true minister of His goes up. It means cutting off now a right hand and plucking out now a right eye. It means taking up some ministerial cross every day. It means drinking every day the cup of the sinfulness of sin. It means to me old Thomas Shepard more than any other minister that I know. "Labor," as our bloodless version has it is a far too dry, a far too wooden, and a far too tearless, word for our Lord to employ toward such servants of His. Depend upon it He will not content Himself with saying "labor" only. He will select and will distinguish His words on that day. And to all who among ourselves have preached and prayed and have examined themselves in and after their preaching and praying, as it would seem that this angel at one time did, and as Thomas Shepard always did, their Master will signalize and appreciate and praise their "painfulness" in their own so expressive old English, and they will appreciate and appropriate His so suitable word and will appreciate and praise Him back again for it.

His patience is another of the praises that his Master gives to this once happy minister. I do not suppose that the angel of Ephesus counted himself a specially happy man when, all unthought of to himself, he was laying up in heaven all this eulogium upon himself and upon his patience. But all the more, with such a suffering servant, his Master held Himself bound to take special knowledge of all that went on in the Church of Ephesus. And to this day and among all our so altered circumstances, patience continues to take a foremost place in the heart and in all the ministry of every successor of the true apostleship. Nay, patience was not only an apostolic grace, it was much more a Messianic grace. Patience was one of the most outstanding and far-shining graces of our Lord Himself as long as He was by far the most sorely tried of all His ministers. And He has all men and all things in His hands to this day that He may so order all men and all things as that all His ministers shall be put to this school all their days, as He was put all His days by His Father. The whole of every minister's lot and life is divinely ordained him so as to win for him his crown of patience, if he will only listen and believe it. "I know all thy patience," said our Lord to the angel of Ephesus.

I do not the least know who or what the Nicolaitans of Ephesus were, and no one that I have consulted is any wiser than I am, unless it is Pascal. And Pascal says that their name is equivocal. When that great genius and great saint comes upon the Nicolaitans in these Epistles, he has an original way of interpretation all his own. He always interprets this name, so he tells us, of his own bad passions. And not the Nicolaitans of Ephesus only; but the Egyptians, and the Babylonians, and as often as the name of any "enemy" occurs in the Old Testament, and it occurs in the Psalms continually, that so great and so original man interprets and translates them all into his own sinful thoughts and sinful feelings and sinful words and sinful actions. That is I fear a far too mystical and equivocal interpretation for the most of us as yet. To call the Nicolaitans of Ephesus our own wicked hearts, is far too Port-Royal and puritan for such literalists as we are. Only, as one can see, the minister of Ephesus would be swept into the deepest places, and into the most spiritual experiences, both of mysticism and of puritanism before their time, as often as he set himself, as he must surely have henceforth set himself every day of his life, to hate the deeds of the Nicolaitans, whoever they were, and at the same time to love the Nicolaitans themselves. To a neighbor minister in the same Synod our Lord sends a special message about the sharp sword with the two edges. And it would need all the sharpness of that sword and all its edges to divide asunder the deeds of the Nicolaitans from the Nicolaitans themselves in their minister's heart. To divide them, that is, so as to hate their evil deeds with a perfect hatred, and at the same time to love the doers of those deeds with a perfect love. The name Nicolaitan is equivocal, says Pascal.

A *litotes* is a rhetorical device by means of which far less is said than is intended to be understood. A true *litotes* has this intention and this result that while, in words, it diminishes what is actually said, in reality, it greatly increases the effect of what is said. What could be a more condemning charge against any minister of Christ than to tell him in plain words that he had left his first love to his Master and to his Master's work? And yet, just by the peculiar way in which that charge is here worded, a far more sudden blow is dealt to this minister's heart than if the charge had been made in the plainest and sternest terms. To say "nevertheless I have somewhat against thee"—to say "somewhat," as if it were some very small matter, and scarcely worth mentioning, and then suddenly to say what it is, that, you may depend upon it, gave a shock of horror to that minister's heart that he did not soon get over. You would have thought such a minister impossible. Had you heard his praise so generously spread abroad at first both by God and man you would have felt absolutely sure of that minister's spiritual prosperity and praise to the very end. You would have felt as sure as sure could be that behind all that so immense activity and popularity there must lie hidden a heart as full as it could hold of the deepest and solidest peace with God; a peace, you would have felt sure, without a speck upon it, and with no controversy on Christ's part within a thousand miles of it. But the ministerial heart is deceitful above all other men's hearts. And these shocking revelations about this much-lauded minister have been recorded and preserved in order that all ministers may see themselves in them as in a glass. Now, there is not one moment's doubt about when and where all this terrible declension and decay began to set in. His Master does not say in as many words just when and where matters began to go wrong between them two. But that silence of His is just another of His rhetorical devices. He does not tell it from the housetops of Ephesus, as yet. But the minister of Ephesus knew quite well, both when and where his first love began to fail and he to fall away. He knew quite well without his Master's message about it, that all this declension and collapse began in the time and at the place of secret prayer. For, not this Ephesus minister only, but every minister everywhere continues to love his Master and his Master's work, ay, and his Master's enemies, exactly in the measure of his secret reading of Holy Scripture and his secret prayerfulness. Yes, without being told it in as many words I am as sure of it as if I had been that metropolitan minister myself. You may depend upon it; nay, you know it yourselves quite well, that it was his habitual and long-continued neglect of secret prayer. It was from that declension and decay that his ministry became so undermined and had come now so near a great catastrophe. "With all my past praise of thee, I give thee this warning," said that Voice which is as the sound of many waters, "that unless thou returnest to thy first life of closet communion with Me, I will come to thee quickly and will remove thy candlestick out of its place. I gave thee that congregation when I might have given it to another. And I have upheld thee in it, and have delivered thee out of a thousand distresses of thine. But thou hast wearied of me. Thou hast given thy night watches to other things than a true minister's meditation and prayer for himself and for his people. And I will suffer it at thy hands no longer. Remember from whence thou hast fallen, and repent, and do the first works."

And now with all that in closing take this as the secret prayer of the angel of Ephesus the very first night after this severe message was delivered to him. "O Thou that holdest the stars in Thy right hand, and walkest in the midst of the seven golden candlesticks. Thou hast spoken in Thy mercy to me. And thou hast given me an ear to hear Thy merciful words toward me. Lord, I repent. At Thy call I repent. I repent of many things in my ministry in Ephesus. But of nothing so much as of my restraint of secret prayer. This has been my besetting sin. This has been the worm at the root of all my mistakes and misfortunes in my ministry. This has been my blame. O spare me according to Thy word. O suffer me a little longer that I may yet serve Thee. What profit is there in my blood? Shall the dead hold communion with Thee? Shall the grave of a castaway minister redound honor to Thee? Restore Thou my soul. Restore once more to me the joy of Thy salvation, then will I teach transgressors Thy ways, and sinners shall be converted to Thee. The sacrifices of God are a broken spirit; a broken and a contrite heart, O God, Thou wilt not despise. Do good in Thy good pleasure unto Zion; build Thou the walls of Jerusalem."

XXVIII

The Angel of the Church in Smyrna

IF Polycarp was indeed the angel of the Church of Smyrna, then we know some most interesting things about this angel over and above what we read in this Epistle addressed to him. All John Bunyan's readers have heard about Polycarp. "Then said Gaius, is this Christian's wife and are these his children? I knew your husband's father, yea, also, and his father's father. Many have been good of this stock. Stephen was the first of them who stood all trials for the sake of the truth. James was another of the same generation. To say nothing of Peter and Paul, there was Ignatius, who was cast to the lions. Romanus, also, whose flesh was cut by pieces from his bones. And Polycarp, that played the man in the fire." You possess Polycarp's whole history in a nutshell in that single sentence of John Bunyan about him. And if you but add that one sentence to this Epistle you will have a full-length and a perfect portrait of the angel of the Church of Smyrna.

Polycarp was born well on in the first century. And it must have been a matter of constant regret to Polycarp that he had not been born just a little earlier in that century so as to have seen his Lord with his own eyes and so as to have heard Him with his own ears. But as it was, Polycarp was happy enough to have been born, and born again, quite in time to enjoy the next best thing to seeing and hearing his Savior for himself. For Polycarp was a disciple of the Apostle John, and he must have often heard the Fourth Gospel from John's lips long before it had as yet come from John's pen. And that was surely a high compensation to Polycarp for not having seen and heard the Divine Word Himself. And then we are very thankful to possess a circular-letter which the elders of the Church of Smyrna sent round to the Seven Churches telling the brethren everywhere how well their old minister had played the man in the fire. After narrating some remarkable incidents connected with Polycarp's apprehension the circular-epistle proceeds:—

"When Polycarp was brought to the tribunal the pro-consul asked him if he was Polycarp. Have pity on thy great age, said the humane Roman officer. Swear but once by the fortunes of Caesar. Reproach this Christ of thine with but one word, and I will set you free. 'Eighty-and-six years,' answered Polycarp, 'I have served Jesus Christ, and He has never once wronged or deceived me, how then can I reproach Him!' And then as some of the executioners were binding the aged saint, and others were lighting the fire, certain who stood by took down this prayer from his lips: 'O Father of Thy well-beloved Son Jesus Christ. I bless Thee that Thou hast counted me worthy of this day and this hour. I thank Thee that I am permitted to put my lips to the cup of Christ. And I thank Thee for the sure hope of the resurrection and for the incorruptible life of heaven. I praise Thee, O Father, for all Thy soul-saving benefits. And I glorify Thee through our eternal High-Priest, Jesus Christ, through whom, and in the Holy Ghost, be glory to Thee, both now and ever, Amen.' Eleven brethren from the Church of Philadelphia suffered with

Polycarp, but he is famous above them all; the very heathen venerate his name. He was not only an eminent teacher and an illustrious martyr, but in all he did he did it out of a truly apostolical and evangelical spirit. Polycarp suffered his martyrdom on the great Sabbath, at the eighth hour of the day. I, Pionius, have transcribed and posted this letter to all the Churches round about. So may our Lord gather my soul among His elect, Amen."

Apostolical, evangelical, and most illustrious, martyr, as Polycarp proved himself to be at the last, yet, when he began his ministry in Smyrna he was a man of like fears and flinchings of heart as we are ourselves. You may depend upon it, Polycarp was for a long time in as great bondage through fear of death as any of yourselves. And every syllable of this Epistle is the proof of that. His Master dictated every syllable of this Epistle with the most direct and the most pointed bearing on Polycarp and on his ministry in Smyrna. Every iota of this Epistle shows us that it was addressed to a minister who was at that time of a timid heart and one whose continual temptation it was to flinch and flee. The very name that Polycarp's Master here selects for Himself in writing to Polycarp spoke straight home to Polycarp's trembling heart. "These things saith He which was dead and is alive." Polycarp was in constant danger of death and in constant fear of death. But after this Epistle, and especially after that opening Name of His Master, Polycarp became another man and another minister. Till this was Polycarp's song every day till the day when he played the man in the fire—

> Death! thou wast once an uncouth, hideous thing!
> But since my Master's death
>   Has put some blood into thy face,
> Thou hast grown sure a thing to be desired
>   And full of grace!

We found the *litotes* device in the first of these Seven Epistles, and we find here the *parenthesis* device in the second of the Seven. When the Spirit speaks to the Seven Churches He does not despise to make use of the rhetorician's art. He recognizes and sanctifies that ancient accomplishment by His repeated employment of it, and in His repeated employment of it He gives us so many lessons in our employment of it. "The parenthesis is the delight of all full minds and quick wits." Now though these exact words have never before been applied to Him whose Epistle to Polycarp we are now engaged upon; at any rate, we may surely go on to apply these so expressive words to His so-talented amanuensis. And this fullminded and quick-witted parenthesis comes in here in this way. Polycarp's poverty was one of his many trials and temptations as the minister of Smyrna. And just as the ever-present image of his Divine Master's death and resurrection nerved Polycarp to overcome all fear of his own death, so in like manner his poverty is here put to silence for ever by this parenthesis, ("but thou art rich"). And not only have we a parenthesis here, but a paradox as well. And both of these rhetorical devices are demanded here in order to give utterance to the fullness of the mind and the quickness of the wit both of the true Author of this Epistle and of the highly privileged amanuensis of it. So he was. Polycarp was both poor and at the same time rich. As many of his best successors in the ministry still are. They are almost as poor as he was as far as gold and silver go. But they are even richer than he was in many things that gold and silver cannot command. For one thing, they are far richer than Polycarp could possibly be in the riches of the mind. They are surpassingly rich in so far as they possess the talents and the trainings and the tastes of cultivated and refined Christian scholars. Money is greatly coveted because it gives its possessor the entrance into the best society of the day. But a well-educated and a well-read minister has entrance not only into the very best society of his own day, but of every day, and he will deign to enter no society of any day but the very best. He keeps company with the aristocracy only. Again, riches are to be desired for what they enable their possessor to be and to do and to enjoy. Riches enable their possessor to the true enjoyment of life, to the true use of life, to true power in life, and to the opportunity and the ability of attaining to the true end of life. Unchallengeably, riches in the right owner's hand immensely assist in the attainment of all these high ambitions. But sure I am, there is no class of men among us who are so rich in all these respects as just our well-educated, well-read, hard-working, absolutely-devoted, ministers. No doubt the parenthesist had in his eye Polycarp's riches toward God exclusively. But had he written in our day he would certainly have extended his arms to embrace a poor minister's few but fit books, and his select friendships, as well as many other things that go to alleviate and even to make affluent his remote and arduous life. Money brings troops of friends also, so long as it lasts. But when Polycarp was robing for presentation at Court, so Pionius tells us, his young men would not let him so much as touch his own shoe-latchet. Now you may have your shoes put on and taken off for money, but you cannot have them tied with heart-strings, as Polycarp's shoes were tied that day.

Malicious and abusive language was another of Polycarp's tribulations. I have not enough ancient Church History to be able to inform you just what outlets they had for their malice in that subapostolic day. We have Letters to the Editor among the resources of our civilization. And neither do I know beyond a guess just what Polycarp did when he was again ill-used by the tongues and pens of his day. But if you will hear it I will tell you what Santa Teresa did. And it is because she did what I am to invite you to do, that I for one entirely and with acclamation, acquiesce in her canonization. "After my vow of perfection I spoke not ill of any creature, how little soever it might be. I scrupulously avoided all approaches to detraction. I had this rule ever present with me, that I was not to wish, nor assent to, nor say such things of any person whatsoever, that I would not have them say of me. Still, the devil sometimes fills me with such a harsh and cruel temper; such a spirit of anger and hostility at some people, that I could eat them up and annihilate them. At the same time, concerning things said of myself in detraction, and they are many, and are very prejudicial to me, I find myself much improved. It is a mark of the deepest and truest humility to see ourselves condemned without cause, and to be silent under it. Indeed, I never heard of any one speaking evil of me, but I immediately saw how far short he came of the full truth. For, if he was wrong or exaggerated in his particulars, I had offended God much more in other matters that my detractor knew nothing about. O my Lord, when I remember in how many ways Thou didst suffer detraction and misrepresentation, I know not where my senses are when I am in such haste to defend and excuse myself. What is it, O Lord? what do we imagine to get by pleasing worms like ourselves, or by being praised by them! What about being blamed by all men, if only we stand at last blameless before Thee." The slander of the synagogue of Satan in Smyrna was not met, I am sure, with a mind more acceptable to the First and the Last than that.

The last thing that He which was dead and is alive said to Polycarp was this mysterious utterance of His, "Thou shalt not be hurt of the second death." Did Polycarp fully understand that assurance, I wonder? Do you fully understand it? At any rate, you understand what the first death is. In our first death our souls will leave our bodies, and then corruption will so set in upon our dead bodies that those who loved us best will be the first to bury us out of their sight. Now, whatever else and whatever beyond that the second death is, it begins with God leaving our souls. God is the soul of our souls. He is the life, the strength, the support, the light, the peace, the fountain, of all kinds of life in soul and body. And when He leaves our souls that is the beginning of the second death. Only, God does not, properly speaking, leave the soul. He is driven out of the soul. In spite of all that God could do, in spite of all that love and grace and truth could do, the lost soul has banished God for ever out of itself. It has insulted and despised God in every way. It has trampled upon Him in every way. It has shut its door in His face ten thousand times, and has taken in and has held revels with His worst enemies. Had Polycarp feared death more than he feared Him who was now alive; had he feared the fires in the market-place of Smyrna more than the fires that are not quenched; had he deserted his post in Smyrna because of its difficulties; had his soul soured at God and man because of his poverty; when he was reviled, had he reviled back again; when he suffered, had he threatened; and had he reproached Christ when he was bribed with his life so to do—Polycarp is here told plainly that he would have died the second death with all that it involves. But as it was, he died neither the first death nor the second. Polycarp was changed, rather than died. Polycarp had such a Master that He died both deaths for His servant. It was not for nothing that He said to Polycarp that He was once dead but is now alive. For He was dead with both deaths for Polycarp. It was when He was hurt of the second death for Polycarp that, under the soreness of the hurt, He cried out first in the garden, and then on the Cross. Have we not seen that in the second death the soul is forsaken of God? And was He not forsaken till Golgotha for the time was like Gehenna itself to Him? He that hath an ear, let him hear what the Spirit saith to the Churches: He that overcometh shall not be hurt of the second death. I will ransom them from the power of the grave. I will redeem them from the fear of death. O death, I will be thy plague. O grave, I will be thy destruction.

XXIX

The Angel of the Church in Pergamos

IN his beautifully-written but somewhat superficial commentary, Archbishop Trench says that there is a strong attraction in these seven Epistles for those scholars who occupy themselves with pure exegesis. And that strong attraction arises, so the Archbishop says, from the fact that there are so many unsolved problems of interpretation in these seven Epistles. Now, I am no pure exegete and those unsolved problems of pure exegesis have little or no attraction for me. My irresistible attraction to these seven Epistles lies in this that they are so many looking-glasses, as James the Lord's brother would say, in which all ministers of churches everywhere to the end of time may see themselves, and may judge themselves, as their Master sees them and judges them. Another thing that greatly attracts our commentators to Pergamos is the intensely interesting and extraordinarily productive field of pagan antiquities that Pergamos has proved itself to be. Pergamos was the most illustrious city in all Asia. It was a perfect city of temples. Zeus, Athene, Apollo, Dionysus, Aphrodite, Aesculapius, were all among the gods of Pergamos, and all had magnificent shrines erected and administered to their honor. Here also Galen the famous physician was born. Pergamos possessed a library also that rivalled in size and in value the world-renowned library of Alexandria itself. Two hundred thousand volumes stood entered on the catalogue of the public library of Pergamos. Our well-known word "parchment" is derived to us from the stationers' shops of Pergamos, and so on. Whether the minister of Pergamos found all that heathen environment as full of delight and edification to himself, and to his proselyte people, in his day as it is to us in our day, is another matter. But of the deep interest and the great delight that all these things have to us there can be no doubt. For the most of our expositors spend both their time and our time in little else but in telling and hearing about the antiquities of Pergamos. But with all those intellectual and artistic attractions filling every part of his parish, after the minister of Pergamos had this Epistle sent to him, all the rest of his days in Pergamos he would have neither time nor thought nor taste for anything else but for this, that Satan had his seat in Pergamos.

It was to bring home the discovery of this fearful fact to the minister of Pergamos that was the sole object of this startling Epistle to him; just as his receiving of this Epistle was the supreme epoch and the decisive crisis of his whole ministerial life. And no wonder. For to be told, and that on such absolute authority, that while Satan had his colonies and his dependencies and his outposts in Ephesus, and in Smyrna, and in Thyatira, yet that his very citadel and stronghold was in Pergamos—that must have been an awful revelation to the responsible pastor of Pergamos. Pergamos is Satan's very capital, said this Epistle to the overwhelmed minister of Pergamos. It is the very metropolis of his infernal empire. All his power for evil, both against God and man, is concentrated and entrenched in

Pergamos. "London is a dangerous and an ensnaring place," writes John Newton in his *Cardiphonia*. "I account myself happy that my lot is cast at a distance from it. London appears to me like a sea, wherein most are tossed by storms, and many suffer shipwreck. Political disputes, winds of doctrine, scandals of false professors, parties for and against particular ministers, fashionable amusements, and so on. I often think of the difference between London grace and country grace. By London grace, when genuine, I understand grace in a very advanced degree. The favored few who are kept alive to God, simple-hearted and spiritually-minded, in the midst of such deep snares and temptations, appear to me to be the first-rate Christians of the land. Not that we are without our trials here. The evil of our own hearts and the devices of Satan cut us out work enough. My own soul is kept alive, as it were, by miracle. The enemy thrusts sore at me that I may fall. In London I am in a crowd of temptations, but in the country there is a crowd of temptations in me. To what purpose do I boast of retirement, when I am myself possessed of Satan's legions in every place? My mind, even at Olney, is a perfect puppet-show, a Vanity Fair, an absolute Newgate itself."

John Newton is one of the three best commentators I have met with on this Epistle. John Newton, and James Durham, and Miss Rossetti. And what so greatly interests those three commentators in Pergamos is this, that they see from this Epistle to the minister of Pergamos that Satan really had his seat in that minister's own heart, just as that same seat is in their own heart. No other antiquity in Pergamos has any interest to James Durham at any rate, but that antique minister's heart in Pergamos. For Satan, if he is anything, is a spirit. And if he has a seat anywhere in this world it is in the spirits of men. Satan dwells not in temples made with hands, either in Pergamos, or in Olney, or in Edinburgh, but only in the spirits of men; and, most of all, in the spirits of ministers, as this Epistle teaches us, and as all the best commentators tell us it teaches us. And the reason of that so perilous pre-eminence of ministers is plain. Ministers, if they are real ministers, hold a kind of vicarious and representative position both before heaven and hell, and the swordsmen and archers of both heaven and hell specially strike at and sorely wound and grieve all such ministers. Satan is like the King of Syria at the battle of Ramoth-Gilead. For before that battle the King of Syria commanded his thirty-and-two captains that had rule over his chariots, saying, "Fight neither with small nor great save only with the King of Israel." And Satan is right. For let a minister but succeed in his own battle against Satan, let a minister but "overcome," as our Lord's word is in every one of these ministerial Epistles, and his whole congregation will soon begin to share in the spoils of their minister's victory.

> Thus Satan trembles when he sees
> A minister upon his knees.

O poor and much-to-be-pitied ministers! With Satan concentrating all his fiery darts upon you, with the deep-sunken pillars of his seat not yet dug out of your hearts, with all his thirty-two captains fighting day and night for the remnants of their master's power within you, and all the time, a far greater than Satan running you through and through with that terrible sword of His till there is not a sound spot in you—O most forlorn and afflicted of all men! O most bruised in your mind, and most broken in your heart, of all men! Pity your ministers, my brethren, and put up with much that you cannot as yet understand or sympathize with in them. And never for a day forget to pray for them in secret, and by name, and by the name of their inward battle-field. Do that, for your ministers have a far harder-beset life than you have any idea of; with both heaven and hell setting on them continually and to the last drop of their blood. May my tongue cleave to the roof of my mouth before I say a single word to turn any young man away from the ministry, who is called of God to that awful work. At the same time, let all intending ministers count well the cost lest, haply, after they have laid the foundation and are not able to finish, both men and devils shall point at them and say, this minister began to build for himself and for his congregation, for eternity, but come and see the ruin he has left! Count well, I say again, whether or no you are able to finish.

A single word about "Antipas my faithful martyr" in Pergamos. "It is difficult," complains the commentator mentioned in opening, "to understand the silence of all ecclesiastical history respecting so famous a martyr as Antipas." But faithful martyrs are not surely such a rarity, either in ancient or in modern ecclesiastical history, that we need spend much regret that we are not told more about one out of such a multitude. At any rate, we have a pretty long roll of well-known names in our own evangelical martyrology, and the cloud of such witnesses is by no means closed in Scotland. Whether this Antipas was a martyred minister or no, I cannot tell. Only there are many martyred ministers in our own land and Church whose names are as little known as the bare name of Antipas. Only, the silence and the ignorance and the indifference of earth does not extend to heaven. The silence and the ignorance and the indifference of earth will only make the surprise, both of those ministers and of their persecutors, all the greater when the day of their recognition and reward comes. "Then shall the righteous man stand before the face of such as have afflicted him, and have made no account of his labors. When they see it they shall be troubled with terrible fear, and shall be amazed at the strangeness of his salvation, so far beyond all they had looked for. And they, repenting and groaning for anguish of spirit, shall say within themselves—This was he whom we had sometimes in derision, and made a proverb of reproach. We fools counted his life madness, and his end to be without honor. But now he is numbered among the children of God, and his lot is among the saints!" For then shall be fulfilled that which is written, To him that overcometh will I give to eat of the hidden manna. And I will give him a white stone, and in the stone a new name written, which no man knoweth saving he that receiveth it.

This new name which no man knoweth saving he that receiveth it is plain. This is no unsolved problem of interpretation. For, a name in Scripture is always just another word for a nature. That is to say, for the very innermost heart and soul of any person or any thing.

> I named them as they passed, and understood
> Their nature; with such knowledge God endued
> My sudden apprehension,

says Adam to the angel. And a new name is always given in Scripture when a new nature is imparted to any person or to any thing. And so will it be beyond Scripture when that day comes to which every scripture points and promises, and for which every holy heart yearns and pants and breaks. That day when He which hath the sharp sword with two edges shall make all His redeemed to be partakers of His own nature; whose nature and whose name is Love. And just as no man knoweth the misery of that heart in which Satan still has his seat but the miserable owner of that heart, so only God Himself will know with them the new name that He will give to His holy ones on that day. As every sin-possessed heart here knows its own bitterness, so will every such heart alone know its own unshared sweetness in heaven, and no neighbor saint nor serving angel will intermeddle with things that are beyond their depth. And ministers especially. When they have overcome by the blood of the Lamb; when their long campaign of sanctification for themselves and for their people has been fought out and won; a new name will be given to every such minister that he alone will know and understand, and that, as Adam said, by a sudden apprehension. When we are under our so specially severe sanctification here—

> Not even the tenderest heart, and next our own,
> Knows half the reasons why we smile or sigh,

and much more will it be so in the uninvaded inwardness and uniqueness of our glorification. No man knows the hardness and the blackness of a sinful heart but the unspeakably miserable owner of it, and no man knows the names he calls himself continually before God, but God who seeth and heareth in secret. And, as a consequence and for a recompense, no man shall see the whiteness of the stone, or hear the newness of the name written in that stone, saving he that receiveth it. For your shame ye shall have double; and for confusion they shall rejoice in their portion; therefore in their land they shall possess the double; everlasting joy shall be unto them. He that hath an ear, let him hear what the Spirit saith unto the churches, and unto the ministers of the churches.

XXX

The Angel of the Church in Thyatira

READ the first three chapters of Hosea and this Epistle to the angel of the Church in Thyatira together, and substitute the *dura lectio*, the hard reading, "thy wife," for the easy reading, "that woman" in the twentieth verse, and it will be seen at once that the angel of the Church in Thyatira is just the prophet Hosea over again. Very much the same scandal and portent that Hosea and his house were in Israel; nay, almost more of a scandal, has the house of the angel of the Church in Thyatira been in Christendom. Our classical scholars have a recognized canon of their own when they are engaged on their editorial work among old and disputed manuscripts; a canon of criticism to this effect that the more difficult to receive any offered reading is the more likely it is to be the true reading. Nay, the more impossible to receive the offered reading is the more certain it is to have stood in the original text. And this so paradoxical-sounding, but truly scientific, principle of our great scholars, has been taken up by some of our greatest expositors and preachers, and has been applied by them to the exegetical and homiletical treatment both of Hosea's household history in the Old Testament, and of this so similar household history in the New Testament. And, indeed, as if it were to forewarn us, and to prepare us for some impossible-to-be-believed disclosures in Thyatira, our Lord introduces Himself to the minister of Thyatira and to us under a name that He has not taken to Himself in the case of any of the other seven ministers of the Seven Churches. Only the very greatest and very grandest of the classical tragedies ever dared to introduce and endure the descent and the intervention of a god. Now Thyatira at this crisis in her history is a great and a grand tragedy like that. For our glorified Lord puts on His whole Godhead when He comes down to deal with this tragical minister in Thyatira and with his tragical wife and children. These things saith the Son of God, and He armed with all the power and clothed with all the grace of the Godhead. The Son of God who has His eyes like unto a flame of fire wherewith to search to the bottom all the depths of Satan that are in Thyatira. That is to say, to search to the bottom the reins and the heart of the minister of Thyatira, and the reins and the hearts of all his household, and of all his people. And then His feet are like fine brass wherewith to walk up and down in Thyatira, till He has given to the minister of Thyatira and to his house and to all the rest in Thyatira according to their works. Neither let a god interfere, unless a difficulty should happen worthy of a god descending to unravel; nor let a fourth person be forward to speak, is the advice of Horace to all his young dramatists.

It was not the schools of the prophets in Israel that made Hosea the great and original and evangelical prophet that he was. It was his life at home that did it. It was his married life that did it. It was his wife and her children that did it. We would never have heard so much as Hosea's name had it not been for his wife and her children. At any rate, his name would not have been worked down into our hearts as it is but for his awful heart-break at home. And so it was with the minister of Thyatira. We might have heard that there was a certain minister in that ancient city in the days of the Revelation, but this so terrible Epistle would never have been written to him or transmitted to us but for his household catastrophe—a catastrophe so awful that it cannot be so much as once named among us. His Divine Master would have known all the good works of His servant in Thyatira, but He would not have been able to say that the last of those good works of his were so much better than his first works, had it not been for that terrible overthrow in his house at home. The minister of Ephesus had left his first love to God and to God's work because he was so happy in the love of his wife and children. But his co-presbyter in Thyatira had never known what the love of God really was till all his household love had decayed, and had died, and had been buried, and had all turned to corruption and pollution. Both the prophet Hosea in the Old Testament and this apostolical minister in the New Testament had come to see that when any man is called of God to this work of God, all he is and all he has, all his talents, all his affections, all his possessions, all his enjoyments, his very wife and children, must all be held by him under this great covenant with God, that they are all to be possessed and enjoyed and used by him, in the most absolute subordination to his ministry. And all the true successors of those two typical men have at one time or other, and in one way or other, to make this same great discovery and have to submit themselves to this same sovereign necessity.

Marriage or celibacy, an helpmeet or an hindrance, children or childlessness, good children or bad, health or sickness, congregational prosperity or congregational adversity, and all else; absolutely and without any reserve *everything* must come under that great law for all men, but a thousand times more for all ministers; that great law which the greatest of ministers has thus enunciated:—"For we know that all things work together for good to them that love God, to them who are the called according to His purpose." Hosea learned at home, and all the week, that new sensibility to sin, that incomparable tenderness to sinners, and that holy passion as a preacher, with all of which he carried all Israel captive Sabbath after Sabbath, and so did his antitype in Thyatira. His antitype, the minister of Thyatira, was a fairly good preacher before he had a household, but he became an immeasurably better preacher as his household life went on and went down to such depths as it did. As many as had ears to hear in Thyatira they could measure quite well by the increasing depth of his preaching and his prayers the increasing depths of Satan through which their minister was wading all the week. We have never had deeper-wading preachers than Jonathan Edwards and Thomas Boston, and never since the garden of Eden has there been two ministers happier at home than they were. And it is very happy for those of us who are ministers to see also that the two happiest homes in all New England and in all old Scotland were also the homes of two such deep and holy and heavenly-minded and soul-winning preachers. But they were not without this same universal and indispensable training in sin and sorrow. Only they got their training in those things in other ways than in shipwrecked homes. With all their happiness in their wives and children, the author of the *Religious Affections*, and the author of the *Crook in the Lot* and

the *Autobiography*, had not their sorrows to seek. Some of the sorrows that sanctified them and taught them to preach so masterfully all their readers see and know,
while some of his most constant and most fruitful sorrows the closest students
of Boston have been absolutely beat to find out. But it is enough for us to be
sure that such noble sorrows were there though the deepest secrets of the manse
of Ettrick then were, and still are, with the Lord. And thus it is that with two
such enviable households as were the households of Edwards and Boston, those
two ministers also in their own ways are another two outstanding illustrations of
Luther's great pulpit principle—"Who are these so incomparable preachers, and
from what divinity hall did they come up? These are they who climbed the Gospel
pulpit out of great tribulation, and have washed their robes and made them white
in the blood of the Lamb."

Though you are not ministers you must know quite well how the same thing
works out in yourselves. You are not ministers, and therefore it is not necessary
that you should be plunged into such depths of experience as your ministers are
plunged into continually if they are to be of any real use to you. But you are hearers, and good hearing is almost as scarce, and almost as costly to the hearer, as
good preaching is to the preacher. To hear a really good sermon, as it ought to be
heard, needs almost as much head and heart, and almost as much blood and tears,
as it needs to preach a really good sermon.

> A jest's prosperity lies in the ear
> Of him that hears it, never in the tongue
> Of him who makes it.

Yes; but a sermon's prosperity lies in both the tongue of the preacher and the ear
of the hearer. And a sermon's true prosperity is purchased by both preacher and
hearer at more or less of the same price.

There is still left one more of those cruxes of interpretation that had almost
turned me away from this Epistle to the minister of Thyatira altogether. And it
is this: "He that overcometh, and keepeth my works to the end, to him will I give
power over the nations. And he shall rule them with a rod of iron; as the vessels of
a potter shall they be broken to shivers; even as I received of my Father. And I will
give him the morning star." What a strange promise to make to a minister—a rod
of iron! Yes, this is just one more of those scripture-passages of which Paul once
said that the letter killeth, but the spirit giveth life. For the letter here had almost
killed out all my hope in this passage till a gleam of the Spirit came to light me
into it and to light me through it. "He that overcometh" is just that minister who
meets all the temptations and trials of life, at home and abroad, with more and
more charity, and with more and more faith, and with more and more patience,
as long as there is a hard heart in his house at home or in his congregation abroad.
It is just to the minister who so overcomes his own passions in his own heart first,
that his Master will give power to break in shivers the same passions in all other
men's hearts, as with a rod of iron. By his charity and by his patience, by these two
rods of iron, especially, any minister will overcome as the angel of the Church in
Thyatira at last overcame. All the iron rods in the world would not have broken

men's hard hearts as that reed broke them, that our Lord took so meekly into His hand when the soldiers were mocking and maltreating Him. And if you just strike with all your might, and with that same rod, all the hard hearts that come near you, you will soon see how they will all go to shivers under it. Till for your reward your Master will give to you also the morning star. That is to say, when many other ministers that sleep in the dust of the earth shall awake, some to everlasting life, and some to shame and everlasting contempt, they that be wise shall shine as the brightness of the firmament; and they that turn many to righteousness as the stars for ever and ever.

XXXI
The Angel of the Church in Sardis

THEMISTOCLES, Plutarch tells us, could not get to sleep at night so loud was all Athens in the praises of Miltiades. And the ministers of the other six churches in Asia were like Themistocles in the matter of their sleep, so full were all their people's mouths of the name and the renown of the minister of Sardis. When he went to the communion-seasons at Ephesus and Smyrna and Pergamos and Thyatira, for years after the captivated people could tell you his texts and at every mention of his name they would break out about his preaching. His appearance, his voice, his delivery, his earnestness and impressiveness, and his memorable sayings, all contributed to make the name of the minister of Sardis absolutely a household word up and down the whole presbytery. Now it was after some great success of that pulpit kind; it was immediately on the back of some extravagant outburst of his popularity as a preacher, that his Master could keep silence no longer toward the minister of Sardis. In anger at him, as also at those who so puffed him up; both in anger and in love and in pity, his Master sent to His inflated servant this plain-spoken message and most solemn warning. "Thou hast a great name among short-sighted men. Thou hast much praise before men, but not before God. All men think well of thee, but not God. All thy great sermons are so much sounding brass before God. And what is not already spiritually dead in thee is ready to die, and will soon be for ever dead, unless thou dost become a new manner of minister, not before men, but before God."

"Of all men in the world," says James Durham, "ministers are most obnoxious to this tentation of vanity. And that because most of their appearances are before men, and that in the exercise of some gift of the mind which is supposed to hold forth the inward worth of a man more than any other gift. Now when this meeteth with applause, that applause has a great subtility in its pleasing and tickling of them, and is so ready to incline them to rest satisfied with that applause." Durham is right in that. For praise and popularity is the most dangerous of all drugs to a minister. Dose a minister sufficiently with praise, and you will soon drown his soul in perdition, if God does not interpose to save him. He is as happy as a king all that day after a sufficient draught of your soul-intoxicating praise. He is actually a sanctified and a holy man all the rest of that day. His face shines on all the men he meets all that day. He loves all the men he meets. He even walks with God all that day. But you must give him his dram again on his awaking tomorrow morning, else as soon as he has slept off his debauch he will be a worse man and more ill to live with than he was before. To him who lives on praise all the world is as dark as midnight and as cold as mid-winter to him when he cannot get his praise. The wings of an angel sprout in his soul as long as he gets enough praise, but he is as good as in his grave when he opens his mouth wide and you do not fill it. It is true that is a very weak mind which values itself according to the opinion and the applause of other men. But then it is well known that God chooses the weakest of men to make them His ministers. For many reasons He does that, some of which reasons of His all His ministers know, and some of which reasons the wisest of them have not yet found out. "It were vain," says one of the wisest of ministers, "to pretend that I do not feel in me that mean passion that can be elated by applause, and mortified by the contrary; but there is nothing under heaven that I more sincerely and totally despise, and nothing which ever makes me so emphatically despise myself. I feel it infinitely despicable at the very moment the passion for praise is excited, and I hope by degrees, as time goes on, to be substantially delivered from it. I have a thousand times been astonished that this mean passion of mine should not have been completely extirpated by the sincere and deliberate contempt I have long entertained for human opinion. Opinion, I do not mean, as regarding myself, but as regarding any other person, or any other book. To seek the praise that comes from God only, is the true nobleness of character; and if a due solicitude to obtain this praise were thoroughly established in the soul, all human notice would sink into insignificance, and would vanish from our regard." By the end of his ministry the angel of Sardis will subscribe to every syllable of John Foster. But he is a long way from that as yet, and he will need to have some plain words told him about himself, and about his ministry, before he comes to that.

For one thing, admitting and allowing for all the good work His servant did, I have found it far from perfect, his Lord says. But perfection in the work of the ministry at Sardis or anywhere else is quite impossible; and thus it is that when we look closer into our Lord's words we find that it was not so much absolute perfection that his Master demanded, as ordinary honesty, integrity, and fidelity. What He really said was this, "I have not found thy work at all filled up on its secret and spiritual and God-ward side. On its intellectual and man-ward side I have nothing to complain about—but not before God." You see the state of the case yourselves. No man can long command pulpit popularity without hard work. And it is not denied that this minister paid for his popularity with very hard work. He was a student. He took off his coat to his sermons. He wrote them over and over again till he got them polished to perfection. And his crowds of polished people were his reward. But while doing so much of that kind, and no man in all Asia doing it half so well, at the same time he left a whole world of other things not done. Milton did all his work from his youth up under his great Taskmaster's eye. And so did the minister of Sardis. Only his taskmaster was the great crowds that hung on his elaborated orations. Take away the eyes and the ears of those captivated crowds and this thrilling preacher was as good as dead. "Dead," indeed, is the very word that his Master here so bitterly charges home upon him. "Thou hast a name that thou livest, and art dead." His preaching was all right. None of his neighbor ministers, not the most accepted of God and the most praised of God of them all, could preach half so well. His preaching was perfect; but his motives in it, his aims and his ends in it, the sources from which he drew his pulpit inspiration, his secret prayers both before his sermons were begun, and all the time they were under his hand, and while they were being delivered, and still more after they were delivered—in all these things—"thou hast a name that thou livest, and art dead."

"Be watchful, and strengthen these things," said his Master to him. "It is good to study, only strengthen it with much faith and with much prayer before God. It is good to give thyself to reading, only read and write in the presence of God. It is good to bring up thy very choicest work to these great congregations of thine, only seek their salvation in every sentence of thy great sermons. It is good to take captive with thy wonderful eloquence the attention and the admiration of these crowds, only do so in order to take their hearts captive, not to thyself as heretofore, but to Me henceforth. Strengthen, I say unto thee, the things that remain and are ready to die. And above all else, and with a view to all else, and as a means to all else, strengthen thy closet-prayer before God. Strengthen it in the length of it, and in the breadth of it, and in the depth of it, and in the height of it. Strengthen it in the time you take to it, in the intensity you put into it, and in the way you work it up into your sermons, both in their composition, and in their delivery, and in the way you continue to wait and to pray after your sermons; to wait, that is, not for the applause of the hearers, but for their profit and My praise."

And his heart-searching Master still proceeds with His pastoral counsels to this minister of His, very unwilling to give him over to the decay of soul into which he has fallen. "Remember how thou hast received, and heard, and hold fast, and repent." As if He were to say to some such minister among ourselves—"Remember thy conversion, and the spirit of truth and love that was instilled into thee, and that made thee turn into this ministry of Mine. Remember thy college days, and the high hopes and generous vows made to Me in those days. Remember also how I delivered thee when in thy deep distresses thou didst call on Me, and what communings and confidences used to go on between us. Remember thy ordination day, and the laying on of the hands of the presbytery, and the way thy heart swelled within thee as they pronounced and enrolled thee a minister of Mine." Yes, even to call such things to remembrance, my brethren, will work together with the seven Spirits that are in Christ's right hand, and with many other things, to set a fallen-down minister on his feet again, and to give him a new start even after he is as good as dead and deposed in the sight of God. Ay, such remembering and such repenting will yet save this all but lost minister of Sardis, and it will save some ministers among ourselves who are quite as far gone as he was. And as he was saved through this Epistle, so will they; and like him they will yet receive the heavenly reward that is here held out to us all by Him who has the seven Spirits of God and the seven stars.

The last thing of the nature of a threat that is addressed to the minister of Sardis is this, "If therefore thou shalt not watch, I will come on thee as a thief, and thou shalt not know what hour I will come upon thee." There is a certain note of terror in that warning which is here addressed to all ministers, the most watchful, the most prayerful before God, and the best. And yet, no; for perfect love casteth out all such terror; perfect love to Christ, and to His work, and to His coming, delivers them who through fear of His coming have all their days been subject to terror. If I love you, you cannot come too soon to me. And the more unexpected your coming is to my door the more welcome will you be to me. If I am watching and counting and keeping the hours till you come, you cannot come on me as a thief.

Christ could not come on Teresa as a thief as long as she clapped her hands for His coming every time her clock struck. He cannot come too soon for me if I am always saying to myself—why tarry the wheels of His chariot? If my last thought before I sleep is about you I will be glad to see your face and hear your voice the first thing in the morning. When I awake I am still with Thee. The name of that chamber was Peace, and its window opened to the east. And every night after he received and read this Epistle, the minister of Sardis always slept in that chamber till the sun-rising.

And now that the tide is beginning to turn in this Epistle, and in this minister's heart and life, this so unexpected word of encouragement and comfort is spoken to him, "Thou hast a few names even in Sardis which have not defiled their garments: and they shall walk with Me in white: for they are worthy." It was with the minister of Sardis somewhat as it was with Thomas Scott when he was first awaking to his proper work. Scott in his youth had been ambitious to be an author, but he was now beginning to see that preaching was second to nothing on the face of God's earth; and that it had praise of God as nothing else had when it was well done. Scott's preaching was not yet well done by a long way, but it was far better than it once was. And one of the best proofs of its improvement was this, that his parishioners began to come to ask guidance from him in the things of their souls. But at that stage Scott had put all he knew into his sermons and he had little to add as pastoral counsel to his inquiring parishioners. And it would be something like that in Sardis. Some of his people had somehow been kept in life all through their minister's declension and death. There is nothing more surprising and touching than to see how a tree will sometimes cling round a rock and will suck sap and strength out of a cairn of stones. "How do you manage to keep yourself alive, then?" I asked an old saint who is in a case not unlike those few names in Sardis. "O," she said, "I have an odd volume of Spurgeon's Sermons, and I have a son at the front." I did not ask her, but I suppose she meant that the thought of her son in his constant danger made her life of intercessory prayer in his behalf perfect before God, and all Spurgeon's readers will bear her out about his sermons. Even in Sardis, their sons in constant peril, and a volume of some first-century Spurgeon, kept alive those few names all those years that their minister was dead.

And then to put the copestone on this farshining case of a minister's recovery, and to send him back to his work till, like his much-tried neighbor in Thyatira, his last years should be far better than his first, this splendid seal was set on his second conversion—"to him that overcometh, the same shall be clothed in white raiment: and I will not blot his name out of the book of life, but I will confess his name before my Father and before His angels." It will be on that day to the minister of Sardis like that great day when Joshua stood before the angel of the Lord and Satan stood at his right hand to resist him. Satan will resist him and will tell to his face how he sought his own things in the early days of his ministry and not the things of his people or of his Master. How he swelled with vanity in the day of his vanity. How his own name was in every thought of his and nothing else but his own name. Only let his name be blazoned abroad, Satan will say, and he was happy and all about him were happy. And so on, till Christ will stop the accuser's mouth, and will confess His servant's name. The Lord rebuke thee, O Satan; even the Lord that hath chosen Jerusalem rebuke thee; is not this a brand plucked out of the fire? And he answered and spake unto those that stood before him, saying, Take away the filthy garments from him. And unto him he said, Behold, I have caused thine iniquity to pass from thee, and I will clothe thee with change of raiment. And I said, Let them set a fair miter upon his head. So they set a fair miter upon his head, and clothed him with garments. And the angel of the Lord stood by.

XXXII
The Angel of the Church in Philadelphia

IF James Durham had lived in Kirriemuir in Disruption days he would to a certainty have said that very much what Daniel Cormick was in the presbytery of Forfar, that the angel of Philadelphia was among the seven churches in Asia. No minister all round about had less strength of some kinds than Daniel Cormick: but, then, like the angel of Philadelphia, by universal consent, he was by far the holiest man of them all and by far the most successful minister of them all. Mr. Cormick used to say in his humility that had it not been for the liberality of Lady Fowlis he would never have got to College at all, and that had it not been for the leniency of some of his professors he would never have got the length of being a minister. Be that as it may, it will be to the everlasting salvation of many that Daniel Cormick was ever sent to College, was carried through his studies, and was ordained a minister. When I was a lad in Kirriemuir our minister's name was widespread and dear to multitudes, not so much for his pulpit gifts, as for his personal and pastoral graces. The delightful stories of Mr. Cormick's unworldliness of mind, simplicity of heart, and beauty of character, crowd in upon me at this moment till I can scarcely set them aside. And it was such things as these in Daniel Cormick that far more than made up for the fewness of the talents his Sovereign Master had seen good to commit to the stewardship of His servant. I see myself standing in the passage all through the forenoon and afternoon services, the church was so full. I see Dr. Mill in his crowded pew, a much-honored man, who largely shared in his minister's saintliness. And there sits Mr. Brand, the banker and writer, whose walk and conversation, like the same things in Dr. Mill, influenced and edified the whole town and country round about. Mr. Brand's copy of Halyburton's *Memoirs*, with his name and my mother's name on it in his own handwriting, is always within reach of my chair, and I am sure I have read it at least as often as Dr. Jowett said to Lady Airlie he had read Boswell. And dear old heavenly-minded, if somewhat sad-hearted, Duncan Macpherson, the draper. A saint if ever I knew one; if, perhaps, a little too much after the type of Mr. Fearing and Mr. Weteyes. There never was a kirk-session in Kirriemuir or anywhere else like Daniel Cormick's kirk-session, and the pillars of it were almost all and almost wholly of their minister's own quarrying and hewing and polishing and setting up. When David White of Airlie became awakened to see what he was, and what a minister ought to be, he sought out Daniel Cormick for his counsellor. As Walter Marshall sought out Thomas Goodwin, and as Thomas Scott sought out John Newton, so did David White sit at Daniel Cormick's feet. The two ministers used to tryst to meet in the woods of Lindertis, where they strolled and knelt and spent hours and days together, till Mr. Cormick was honored of God to lead one of the ablest men I ever knew into that grace in which he himself stood with such peace and such assurance of faith. To Mr. Cormick's kind and winning ways with children I can myself testify.

Is *James Laing: A Lily Gathered*, still in circulation in Dundee? I well remember that red-letter day to me when Mr. Cormick took me to his lodgings with him and gave me that little book to take home with me. But I am wandering away from my proper subject before I have even begun it. I am taking up too much time with Daniel Cormick, deserving of it all as he is. The angel of the church in Philadelphia could not be more deserving. It was James Durham, in the way he speaks about "the little strength" of the angel of Philadelphia, that led me back to speak of Daniel Cormick with all this love and reverence and thankfulness.

If his Sovereign Master allowed to the minister of Philadelphia but little strength of intellect, as James Durham in his profound commentary holds it was, and but little learning; then, what he lacked on the mere mental side was more than made up to him on the moral and spiritual side. And that wisest by far of all the seven ministers in Asia soon found out where his true strength lay and threw himself with all his weakness upon his true strength. William Law complains with all his incomparable scorn that so many of the ministers of his day spent so much of their time and strength in the pulpit on such subjects as the seasons and the directions of the wind called Euroclydon, and on the times when the Gospels were writ. Now Daniel Cormick had not that temptation, for he possessed none of its literature, and even had he lived in our so-learned day and possessed all the learned apparatus of our day, he would not have given way to our temptations in his pulpit. "You, brethren," said Andrew Bonar in Daniel Cormick's funeral sermon, "are witnesses that in all his ministry your pastor ceased not to preach in public, and from house to house, repentance towards God, and faith towards our Lord Jesus Christ. His first sermon after his ordination was on this great text: 'Be ye reconciled to God.' And was not that commencement truly characteristic of Mr. Cormick's whole ministry among you? For, whatever subject he handled he failed not to arrive at sin and salvation before he left it. And such was the unction of his words that even when he was not exhibiting very intellectual views of the text, still his personal affection in setting forth the subject was always felt to be refreshing and quickening."—And this Epistle pays the same praise to the minister of Philadelphia for the way he preached his Master's name, and his Master's name only, in every sermon of his. I have myself, to my confusion of face I confess it, wasted many a precious hour in this pulpit on Euroclydon, and on the times when the Prophets, and the Psalms, and the Gospels, were writ. But I am beginning now to number my days, and I am, as you must witness, turning my own attention and yours far more to the name of Jesus Christ, in imitation of the minister of Philadelphia. Now, what is His name? and what is His Father's name? if you have begun to learn those great names from me and with me? For we ministers should preach the name of the Father and the name of the Son far more than we do. And you, our people, should read far more than you do read, both in your Bible and in other books, on those so foundation and so fruitful subjects. Just what a name is, what its root is, and when and where this and that name of the Father, and the Son, and the Holy Ghost were first heard; these inquiries, as Clement says, breed great light in the souls both of preachers and hearers. To turn up and read continually the very chapter where God first gave His full and true name to Moses, and then to trace that name and see that once it was given to Israel there is little or nothing else in the whole of the Old Testament but that name. And then to see how the Father's name gives place to the Son's name in the New Testament—all that breeds great light in the soul, as Clement says. Even with as little strength as there was in Philadelphia and Kirriemuir, a minister will win great praise, both from God and from God's people, if he keeps close to God's word and more and more holds up God's name.

Tentatio, meditatio, oratio, were Luther's three indispensable qualifications for a minister. Now we gather that the minister of Philadelphia had quite a special training in the school of temptation. We hold far too coarse ideas about temptation. We think of temptation as if it were for the most part to whoredom and wine. But the temptations that make a minister after Luther's own heart are as far as the poles asunder from such temptations as these. The holier and the more heavenly-minded a minister is, the more he lays himself open to a life of unspeakable temptation. With every new advance in holiness, with every new progress in the knowledge of God and of himself, with every deeper and deeper entrance of the exquisitely holy law and spirit of God into his heart and conscience, a minister's temptations multiply upon him, till he feels himself to be the most beset, behind and before, of all beset men that dwell upon the earth. And there is good reason for that. For if a minister is to be a real minister; if he is to know, as by the best and the latest science, all the diseases and all the pains in the souls of the saints who are in his ward, of necessity he must have been taken through all those spiritual experiences himself; of necessity they have all been made to meet in him. O, wretched man that he is! before he is fit to feel for and to prescribe to like wretched men with himself. And that is the reason why He who was Himself made perfect through temptation has specially promised that He will keep His ministers in the hour and power and crisis of their temptations, as He was kept in the hour and power and crisis of his own. Tentatio, meditatio, oratio. Oratio especially. Now, there was one special kind of prayer that Daniel Cormick was greatly noted for among those who were intimate with him. All ministers pray much and earnestly before preaching. And the reason is, they are so afraid that they may not do so well today. The minister of Sardis, who never prayed at any other time in all the week, to be called prayer, was always in real anxiety and earnestness before he entered the pulpit, because he had such a name for preaching to keep up. And so it is still with all who are like him. They are so afraid that they may forget or displace things, or in other ways disappoint your expectations, that they pray with all their heart till God, according to His promise, hears them and carries them through again without a stumble. The difference with Daniel Cormick was that he would get, now Robert M'Cheyne, and now Andrew Bonar, and now John Baxter, to pray both with him and for him *after* his preaching. As I remember Thomas Shepard also always did: and as, I feel sure, the angel of Philadelphia also did. The "honest weak ministers," that they all three were, as James Durham, that honest but not weak minister, in his incomparable commentary calls them.

"Behold, I come quickly: hold fast that thou hast, that no man take thy crown," said He that is holy, He that is true, to this minister of His. As if He had said, "Hold fast by thy temptations, and thy meditations, and thy prayers both before and after preaching. And hold fast also by My name, and by all that is due to My name in thine office, as well as in thine own soul. Let no man take thy crown in that matter. Be suspicious, be jealous, of all men. Let no man invade on thy work. Give up not an atom of thy work thou canst by any possibility perform thyself. Never weary for one moment in thy well-doing. Let not thy hand for one moment become slack. Do not let thyself lie down to die till all thy work is fulfilled and finished. For if thou dost so die, then thy successor in Philadelphia will take thy crown which I had intended for thee." As John Newton took Thomas Scott's crown as long as Scott neglected his dying parishioners till they sent for Newton. And as ministers' crowns are dropping off their heads in every parish all round about for any ambitious man to pick them up and put them on. Any one, that is, who will visit such and such a sick-bed, and read a Psalm there, and after it one of the Pilgrims' crossings of the Jordan. Hold fast, O all you ministers and elders and nurses and doctors! Hold fast as Dr. Mill held fast at so many deathbeds in and around Kirriemuir, till he stole some shining gems even out of Mr. Cormick's crown. Hold fast lest some aspiring man run off altogether with the crown your Master had at one time intended for you. If it took a man like Daniel Cormick all his might to keep his crown from being all stolen from him, what chance, think you, have the most of us ministers?

But look up! Who is that glorified saint shining as the brightness of the firmament, and as the stars for ever and ever? That is the angel of the Church that once was in Philadelphia. That is he, built in for ever as a "pillar" in the heavenly temple to go no more out. He was such a true pillar on earth that the whole of the seven Churches in Asia were strengthened and upheld by means of him. And now he is set in the very midst of the city of God which is new Jerusalem. And, behold, with the name of his God also written upon him, so that all men can read that name on him, as they pass by. Had the name of his God been strength of understanding, or depth and power of mind, or stores of learning, or an eloquent tongue; had it pleased God to save His people by dialectics, then that pillar had not borne as he now bears the name of his God. But God's nature is not like to ours. For we read in letters of gold God's glorious nature and name, and it is this—the Lord; the Lord God, merciful and gracious, long-suffering, and abundant in goodness and truth, keeping mercy for thousands, forgiving iniquity and transgressions and sins. And that name was taken up with such Paul-like determination, and was so preached in Philadelphia and nothing else was preached, till both the preacher and the people knew none other name. Like preacher, like people. That preacher of Philadelphia fed his people on the finest of the wheat till it became bone of their bone and flesh of their flesh, and till God's great name came out in letters of light all over their foreheads, and was written in works of love all over their lives. What a comfort to the most of us ministers! For the most of us ministers must always be far more like the minister of Philadelphia with his little strength than like the minister of Sardis with his great name. For ye see your calling, brethren, how that not many wise men after the flesh, not many mighty, not many noble are called. But God hath chosen the foolish things of the world to confound the wise; and God hath chosen the weak things of the world to confound the things that are mighty. That, according as it is written, He that glorieth, let him glory in the Lord.

XXXIII
The Angel of the Church of the Laodiceans

THE Archippus who is so remonstrated with in the Epistle to the Colossians concerning his neglected ministry, may very well have lived on to be the lukewarm angel of the Church in Laodicea. As a matter of fact, there is both internal and external evidence that the angel of the Church in Laodicea was none other than this same inculpated Archippus now grown old in his unfulfilled ministry. And if the external evidence had only been half as strong as the internal the identity of those two unhappy men would have been proved to demonstration. It is much more than a working hypothesis then, the assumption that this angel now open before us is none other than young Archippus at last grown gray in neglect of his work and in ignorance of himself. Archippus was still to all intents and purposes a young minister when this message was sent to him from the aged Apostle, "Say to Archippus, take heed to the ministry which thou hast received in the Lord, that thou fulfill it." But instead of taking that timeous reproof to heart, Archippus had gone steadily down in his declension and decay till he had this last reproof addressed to him, and which has been a last reproof to so many ministers and their people since his day and down to our own day.

The English language has inherited one of its most contemptuous and denunciatory epithets from this Epistle to this lukewarm minister and his lukewarm church. We call a man a Laodicean. We have no other single word that so graphically describes a certain detestable type of human character. "I know thy works, that thou art neither cold nor hot. I would thou wert cold or hot. So then because thou art neither cold nor hot, I will spew thee out of my mouth." That is plainspoken enough and in few words. But ever since this so scornful Epistle was written, all that, and more than all that, has been collected up into this one supremely scornful word—thou art a Laodicean! And thus it is that to all time the angel of the Church in Laodicea will stand forth as the spiritual father of all such spiritual sons. Archippus will stand at the head of a long apostolic succession that has descended from his ancient diocese into all the churches: Episcopal, Presbyterian, and Independent. And this Epistle now open before us is a divinely fashioned looking-glass, as James the Lord's brother would have called it, in which all Laodicean ministers and people are intended to see themselves.

"Because thou sayest, I am rich and increased with goods, and have need of nothing." But Archippus with all his stark stupidity could never by any possibility have said that. He was not such an absolute idiot as actually to say that. No, not in so many words. No minister ever, out of Bedlam, said that in so many words. No. But at the same time by the very Scriptures he read and expounded

731

to his people, as well as by the Scriptures he did not read; by the very psalms and hymns and spiritual songs he sang, and did not sing; but especially by his prayers, Archippus all his days sealed down his people in the same deadly ignorance in which he lay sealed down himself. And indeed it is just of this deadly ignorance of himself that his Master here so scornfully speaks. "Thou knowest not that thou art wretched, and miserable, and poor, and blind, and naked." On the margin of a copy of Thomas Adams' *Private Thoughts* now preserved among the treasures of the British Museum, Coleridge has written these pencilled lines: "For a great part of my life I did not know that I was poor, and naked, and blind, and miserable. And even after I did know that, I did not feel it aright. But I thank God I feel it now somewhat as it ought to be felt. Stand aside, my pride, and let me see that ugly sight, myself. I have been deceived all my life by sayings of philosophers, by scraps of poetry, but most of all by the pride of my own heart, into an opinion of self-power, which the Scriptures plainly tell me, and my repeated failures tell me, that I possess not. It is the design of the religion of Jesus Christ to change men's views, to change their lives, and to change their very tempers. Yes. But how? By the superior excellence of its precepts? By the weight of its exhortations, or by the promise of its rewards? No. But by convincing men of their wretchedness, and guilt, and blindness, and helplessness. By inculcating the necessity of the remission of sin, and the necessity of supernatural light and assistance, and by promising to the penitent sinner, and by actually conveying to him, these evangelical blessings." Well might Charles Lamb say, "Reader! lend thy books to S. T. C., for he will return them to thee with usury. He will enrich them with his annotations, and thus tripling their value. I have had experience, and I counsel thee. Shut not thy heart, nor thy library, against S. T. C."

Among all the terrible things here threatened against this miserable minister of Laodicea, his "nakedness," and "the shame of his nakedness," is surely the most terrible. There is nothing that is more terrible to the heart of man than shame. Shame and contempt, as a parallel passage in the Old Testament has it. Shame and contempt are far worse to face than death itself. When we speak of shame, in our shallow and superficial way we usually think of the shame of a naked body. But there is no real shame in that. When the Bible speaks of shame it is always of the infinitely more terrible shame of a naked soul. Take away the terrible shame of a naked soul and there is no shame at all in the nakedness of the body. But once strip a soul naked, and death is its only refuge and hell its only hiding-place. Take it home to yourselves and see. Suppose your innermost soul laid absolutely bare to us who are your friends and neighbors. Suppose your most secret thoughts about us told to us from the housetops. Suppose all your malicious thoughts about us told, and all your secret hatred of us, and all your envy of this man and that man, naming him, and for what. Suppose it, if you dare for one moment to suppose it, the whole bottomless pit of your evil heart laid bare. Now all that is the threatened case of this miserable creature here called an angel. Indeed his case is far worse than yours; unless, indeed, like him you are a minister. For he will have all the shame that you will have, and, over and above all that, being a minister he will have the special shame and the special contempt and the special revenge both of

God and man to bear, and that, if the prophet is right, to everlasting. It is the awful forecast of all this to Archippus that makes his Master's heart to relent once more and to address to him this last-trumpet Epistle. "I counsel thee to buy of Me gold tried in the fire, that thou mayest be rich; and white raiment, that thou mayest be clothed, and that the shame of thy nakedness do not appear; and anoint thine eyes with eyesalve, that thou mayest see." It was this same salvation offered to all such ministers as Archippus in the Old Testament, that made Micah exclaim at the end of his ministry, Who is a God like unto Thee!

And then there is this evangelical invitation to crown all. "Behold, I stand at the door and knock. If any man hear My voice, and open the door, I will come into him, and will sup with him, and he with Me." This, I feel quite sure, is a reminiscence of what had often happened to Him who here speaks. For He was often that He had not where to lay His head. He was often that He had to stand at the door and knock. The parable of the friend at midnight was not so much a parable after all. He must often have been that poor and importunate man Himself. For if He hungered on His way to the city, much more must He have hungered and thirsted and been nigh unto fainting, on His way out of the city. And at such times of temptation, Satan would say to Him—"If thou be the Son of God, command these stones to become bread, and command the wayside streams to run with wine and milk." But He would say to Satan—"Neither have I gone back from the commandment of His lips: I have esteemed the words of His mouth more than my necessary food." And so saying He entered a certain village, and knocked at the door. And the man from within answered, "Trouble me not; the door is now shut, and my children are with me in bed, I cannot rise and let thee in." But in the next street there was a lamp still burning, and a voice from within answered, "Come in, Thou Blessed of the Lord." And they supped together that night. When you next think you hear His knock, rise off your seat, rise off your bed even, and open the door. Yes: go and actually open the door. Think to yourself that He is actually in the street, and is actually, and in the body, standing at your door. This is the sacrament night. And it will be a sacramental action to go and actually open your room door or your street door late and alone tonight. Imagine to yourself that you see Him dim in the darkness of the night. Put out your hand into the darkness. Lead Him in. Set a seat for Him. Ask Him when and where He broke His fast this morning. Ask Him where He has been all day, and going about and doing what good. Tell Him that you are sure He has not had time so much as to eat. And set the best in your house before Him, and He will come in and will sup with you, and you with Him. Believe and be sure that He is in this city tonight. Believe that and it will make you to be on the watch. Do not put off your coat, do not wash your feet, till you have opened the door to Him. Sit up for Him. Expect Him. Set your candle in your window. Have your door standing already ajar. And even if you should again and again be deceived and disappointed: even if again and again you should mistake some other sound in the street for His footstep, do not despair of His coming. Do not shut the door whatever you do. Far better a thousand such mistakes through overwatchfulness than to be dead asleep when at last He comes. And besides, who can tell, He may not have eaten a morsel or drunk a drop in all the city this day—all these communion-tables notwithstanding. And would it not be wonderful if all the entertainment He is to get in this city this whole day still awaits Him in your house this night. And then there is this; whosoever or what-soever you are, let nothing debar you from supping with Christ tonight. You may not have been at our table today. We lay down rules and restrictions as to who shall, and who shall not, sup with Him in this house. But, all the time, He is the Master, and He can lift off all our restrictions, even when they are quite right in us to lay them down, and He can and He will sup when and where and with whom He pleases. And these are His own undoubted words about this night that is yet before Him and before you and before us all. These words: "If *any* man hear My voice, and open the door,"—communicants, He means, or non-communicants; members or adherents; young or old; minister or elder; especially any minister. For as He stood that night at Archippus's door in Laodicea, so will He stand at all ministers' doors in Edinburgh this night. And, all the more, if they are all asleep, have you your lamp still burning on your window-sill for Him. And you will be able to tell us tomorrow how your heart burned as He supped with you and you with Him. For it was a proverb in Athens that they were always well in health, and full of all sweet affability all next day, who had supped last night with Plato.